POLITICAL SOCIOLOGY

POLITICAL SOCIOLOGY

A READER

Edited and with Introductions by

S. N. EISENSTADT

BASIC BOOKS, INC., PUBLISHERS | *New York, London*

© 1971 by Basic Books, Inc.

Library of Congress Catalog Card Number: 75–103091

SBN 465–05941–4

Manufactured in the United States of America

FOR EDWARD SHILS

PREFACE

In this anthology an attempt has been made to present a comprehensive view of political sociology that emphasizes the combination of the analytical and the comparative approaches. According to this view—more fully exposed in the General Introduction and in the Concluding Remarks—the combination of these approaches constitutes the crux of the development of political sociology.

This combination has been developing through the convergence of various trends: the more speculative classical approaches, the more recent analytical and theoretical ones, and the comparative one. This latter approach by itself developed from diverse disciplines —anthropology, history, sociology—and from sociological, political, or economic analyses of contemporary societies throughout the world. Although each of these disciplines tended to deal with different types of societies—the primitive, the historical, contemporary European and American societies on the one hand, and the so-called New Nations on the other—in their analytical approaches and concepts, more and more of a convergence can be discerned.

This upsurge of comparative studies found one of its major expressions in the publication of special journals, of which *Comparative Studies in Society and History,* edited by Professor S. Thrupp and from which many articles presented in this book are taken, has perhaps been the most outstanding although certainly not the only one. But this development of comparative approach was not limited to such special journals; it can also be found in the "traditional" media of each of the various disciplines, whether anthropology, sociology, political science, or history.

In this anthology we have attempted to draw on all these as well as a great variety of other sources and to show, with the help of these varied materials as well as in the General Introduction and the introductions to the various sections, how these varied approaches tend now to converge into a comprehensive and systematic view of political sociology as well as how they indicate possible new lines of inquiry which the field now faces.

From the point of view of my own interests, this anthology, with its introductions, and other comments, can be seen both as an extension of my earlier work on political sociology—especially *The Political Systems of Empires* (New York: The Free Press, 1963) and *Modernization, Protest and Change* (Englewood Cliffs, N.J.: Prentice-Hall, 1966)—and also as an attempt to go beyond several of the analytical assumptions of these works.

In the preparation of this reader, undertaken more than five years ago, I have been helped by many people. Several friends have assisted greatly in going over the contents: Professors A. Diamant, W. Delany, Edward Shils, and especially S. M. Lipset. Professor A. Fuks and Professor Ch. Wirschubski have helped in the selections on city-states. Mrs. Y. Atzmon has commented in great detail on the introductions.

Most of the introductions to the selections were prepared during my stay in 1967 at the Villa Serbelloni as a guest of the Rockefeller Foundation, whose support of my research has also greatly facilitated other parts of this work. I would like to express my gratitude to the foundation for its support and to Mr. and Mrs. John Marshall for their wonderful hospitality at the Villa.

Mrs. R. Chaco has aided in the preparation of

the materials and with the correspondence with authors and publishers. Miss J. Rainer has also helped with regard to the preparation of the materials, while Mrs. P. Gurevich has made a great contribution in the final preparation of the manuscript.

Last, but not least, I am grateful to all the authors and publishers who have given me permission to reprint the various articles presented here.

Jerusalem   S. N. EISENSTADT
The Hebrew University
November, 1970

CONTENTS

PART ONE

THE SCOPE AND PROBLEMS OF
POLITICAL SOCIOLOGY:
THE SOCIOLOGICAL STUDY OF
POLITICAL PROCESSES AND
POLITICAL SYSTEMS

CHAPTER I

General Introduction: The Scope and Development of Political Sociology

Part One

I

The concern with political power, organization, and authority has been of paramount importance in the history of the reflection on the nature of the cosmos and of society alike.[1] This reflection tended to focus on political organization and institutions, on power and authority, and on the behavior of rulers and subjects as the major forces of organized social human activity. Traditions of folk- and ritual-symbolic thought and imagery dealt with the nature of human destiny as manifest in the cosmic and social orders. These traditions have already shown a tendency in their magical and ritual expressions to focus on political authority and the community as crucial aspects of social life and of human existence.

Both the general orientations and the concrete particulars of such reflection differed, as we shall see in greater detail later, especially in the extent to which they emphasized the political sphere as the most important dimension of human existence in relation to other types of human associations, particularly family and kin groups, with the interpersonal relations and primordial ties.[2] Yet they all had in common the vision of the political community as a focal point of *organized* social life and of political relations—relations between rulers and subjects, or relations among co-citizens—as the focus at least of earthly social relations. Within this common tradition of viewing the political as the focus of earthly social life or as encompassing it, three major substreams of reflections can be discerned.

One such substream—that of Greek philosophy and of the Hebrew prophets—is that of the quest for the best political order in terms of moral values, or, in other words, in the evaluation of political systems according to moral criteria. This is best known and most fully evident in "Western" tradition.[3]

A second such substream, to be found in almost all civilizations and especially elaborated and most fully articulated in the great empires, is one which is best illustrated by various "mirrors for princes"—compendiums which were composed to guide the rulers in the conduct of affairs of state. Some, probably most, of these compendiums were but manuals for the manipulation of court intrigues or of administration. But others, fewer probably in number but most outstanding in their impact on subsequent political thought, focused on what today we would call some central aspects of political sociology—the problem of the bases of cohesion of different political systems, the bases of obedience and compliance of subjects, the proper political behavior of rulers, and above all, proper administrative organization and behavior as one of the central aims or mainstays of any polity.[4] Even the most outstanding among these more sophisticated treatises—as, for instance, the Arthashastra of Kautilya—never attempted a systematic analysis of the bases of political-social life or of its great variety, as can be found in Aristotle. But in many ways, by being less bound to the tradition of a city-state and less limited by viewing the political and ethical systems as almost closed systems, we find in these treatises more insight into the focal points of cohesion and continuity of great political (usual imperial) systems in which the relations between the ruler and the subject, and not between co-citizens, were the most crucial ones. But for them also—perhaps even more than in the philosophical or the purely religious traditions—the political sphere constituted the focus for reflection on the secular social order.

The same was true of the third substream of reflection on political life which developed and which is probably best represented by Ibn-Khaldun. This is the consideration of the *variety* of political regimes and their destinies: their use and demise. This tradition stems to some extent from the historical—and historiosophical—reflections on antiquity from Herodotus and Polybius (and to a smaller extent from Thucydides) and from Aristotle's comparative works which attempted to analyze systematically the great variety of different types of regime known to him. Ibn-Khaldun and some of his contemporaries and later followers, like Vico, had, however, a greater and more varied experience of range of interests than Aristotle. They could draw on some of the experiences of later Greek and Roman history and on more contemporary experience in the destiny of various Islamic empires which occurred later. With Ibn-Khaldun, the element that became predominant in this approach was that of the fascination with the fall of great (imperial) political structures.[5]

These different trends all contributed in various degrees to the development of modern political sociology. In the initial stages of this development, two substreams concerned with political matters were of special importance: the moral philosophical and the comparative-historical traditions. The tradition concerned with the political matters embodied in the mirrors of princes was of much less importance. The moral-philosophical traditions were transferred from the Greek to all medieval philosophy—Christian, Jewish, and Moslem alike—and passed, together with other elements such as Roman legal traditions, into the first trends of modern political philosophy up until the eighteenth century, encompassing the first great modern political thinkers such as Machiavelli, Hobbes, Locke, and Rousseau.[6] Comparative historical analysis, although not so prolific through the late medieval and early modern period, was revived especially in the eighteenth century in the works of historians such as Gibbon, of histo-philosophers such as Vico, and above all in the works of the early comparativists such as Montesquieu and the Scottish moralists, such as Adam Smith, Ferguson, and others.[7]

Here the concern with the variety of institutions and societies, although still focused on those of politics and the state, already evinced greater concern with nonpolitical institutions—whether with the family or with economic institutions—and greater

sensitivity to problems of interrelations among these spheres of social life, as well as between them and various environmental factors. But this recognition was as yet intermittent and not fully systematic. It had certainly not developed to an extent where it could be compared with the recognition of the autonomy of economic behavior and systems, as seen in the *Wealth of Nations*. Nor could it be compared with the recognition of the reevaluation of the moral nature and social commitments, as seen in the work of the Scottish moralists, particularly Adam Smith.

II

It is only with the transformation of these varied forms of social-philosophical thought into modern social thought and analysis that this comparative stream, together with the moral-philosophical one and to a smaller degree the technical-political one, united in the more general trend of modern political sociology. The most central and basic change in this transformation was, of course, the shift from the philosophical emphasis to the more sociological one; and the most salient characteristic of modern political sociology is, from this point of view, its development as part of general sociology. The political is seen as only one social institution, even if often crucial and central. This relatively simple change entails several basic transformations and changes of the whole *Problemstellung* about the nature of social and political order. These changes and transformations constitute the crux of the development of modern sociology.

One such change was the growing emphasis in social and political thought on the differentiation between the civil and political orders, the growing perception of civil society as a distinct, autonomous entity. This entity was not submerged under the political or "natural" order but was an autonomous force, or congeries of forces, tending, in later theoretical formulations, to subsume the political order itself as only one of its several basic constituent institutional spheres. Rousseau, in his definition of the problematics of the general will, may perhaps be seen as the main point of transition to this point of view. The names of Lorenz von Stein, de Tocqueville, and, in a different way, Marx are most closely related to the first phase of this trend. The trend was further developed in a more systematic and detailed way, in conjunction with other developments, by all the great figures of sociological thought in the latter part of the nineteenth and in the early twentieth centuries: Spencer, Pareto, Durkheim, Max Weber, and later Karl Mannheim.[8]

The second major starting point of modern sociological inquiry was rooted in what may be called the dialectical dissociation of patterns of individual behavior and orientations among the transcendental and moral order, the sociopolitical order, and the order of individual life. Here first was the growing recognition of the great variety of possible orientations and commitments of individuals to the transcendental and moral realm, the awareness that these orientations and commitments are only one constituent of individual behavior and that they—as other components of such behavior—develop to a large extent in social settings, and that the variations of these components cannot therefore be explained in terms of purely individual differences. Second was the growing awareness of the improbability that any single institutional arrangement can fully epitomize the best moral order or represent in the fullest way any transcendental order and, as a result, the improbability that different types of social or political regimes can be scaled according to the degree of conformity to such ideal types. The major figures which represented the initial development of these orientations were, of course, those of Hobbes and Rousseau and to a smaller extent Locke.[9] It was they who, by posing the question of the very possibility of social order and by not assuming some "natural" givenness of such order, opened up this question in modern terms, even if their specific answers were closely tied to the older conceptions and perceptions. Still more crucial were the later contributions of the Scottish moralists Ferguson and, above all, Adam Smith.[10]

The third starting point of modern sociological thought was the growing recognition of the great variety of different types of social order, of their changeability, and of the recognition of the temporal (historical) dimension as at least one, if not the only, determinant of such variety and changeability. The recognition of the variety of types of social, or rather political, order goes back, as we have already noted, at least to Aristotle, as does the search for the relation between such variety and different types of civic attitudes and moral postures of individuals. In these two respects modern sociological thought is very much in the Aristotelian tradition. It goes, however, in its *Problemstellung* beyond this tradition because of its incorporation of the two preceding standpoints. Thus it goes beyond Aristotle, first, by refusing to identify the social with the political order and thence by stressing the greater variety of their possible interrelations; second, by stressing the variety of the interrelations among moral commitments and transcendental orientations and types of social

order. In this respect, as Shils has pointed out, "Sociology has partially closed the gap left by Aristotle between the *Ethics* and the *Politics*."[11] Third, and probably most important, it goes beyond Aristotle by attempting to incorporate or account for temporal developments as one major mechanism of the variety and changeability of types of social order.

The fourth starting point of modern sociological theory was the growing recognition of the importance of environmental factors as influencing, or even determining, social order in general and the variety of the types of such order in particular. Here the first major modern figures are again Montesquieu and some of the Scottish moralists, especially Ferguson and Millar,[12] the various ethnologists and anthropologists such as Tylor,[13] and later the various evolutionary schools of the nineteenth century to be followed, in different ways, by the great upsurge of comparative studies in the social sciences in the forties of the twentieth century.

III

Out of these orientations, in the perception of the problems of social order, there emerged a great many new trends and orientations of thought—ideological, social-philosophical, and historiosophic—as well as the more specific sociological orientations. This last, while very closely related to the others, developed, even if intermittently and haltingly, its own specific *Problemstellung* or *Problemstellungen,* which can perhaps be formulated broadly as the search for the conditions and mechanisms of the continuity, disruption, and change of social order, particularly the variety of different types of such order.

The sociological *Problemstellung* was characterized by not asking about the "natural" conditions or characteristics of the social order or for the single "best type" of such order, but by shifting the major focus of inquiry to the analysis of the *conditions* and *mechanisms* of social order and of its constituent component, its continuity and change in general and of such order in particular. The importance, in the development of sociological thought, of this search for the conditions and mechanisms of social order, instead of the search for the general characteristics of society as a "natural" or purely moral fact or order, can be seen best, first, in the ways in which problems of social disorder, disorganization, and change have become the central focal points of sociological theory, and second, in the crucial importance of the development of some general laws about the conditions of social order in different societies.

The existence of social disorder, the ubiquity of internal conflicts, and the demise of sociopolitical systems have, of course, been long recognized (at least since Plato and Aristotle) as constituting a basic facet of any society (or polity), or, as in Hobbes, as a basic starting point for the analysis of the possibility of social order. The specific sociological concerns become manifest by making the analysis of these phenomena into starting points for the understanding of the mechanisms of social order, of the conditions of functioning and change of such order in general and of its varying types in particular. This implies that social disorder is not prior to, and, hence, different from social order, but constitutes a special type of constellation of elements which, in a different combination, constitutes the core of continuity of social order itself. Therefore social disorganization may become a starting point for the analysis of change of the social order. Moreover, it focuses sociological analysis on the transformative propensities, not of some "external" or "random" events, but of the major aspects of the phenomena of social order.

The search for an explanation of the conditions and mechanisms of social order and its various forms could take off from each of the "natural" starting points or components of ordered social life: first, the individual, his personality, goals, aspirations, and orientations; second, the various "autonomous" characteristics of social structure (groups, institutions, "total" societies); third, the nature and organization of the basic products of cultural activity—the various realms of symbolic creativity; and last, the various environmental (such as geographical, ecological) or biological factors.

IV

Each of these components did indeed constitute a starting point for sociological analysis and for continuous recrystallization of problems of research. These various starting points of sociological thought were very closely related to some of the major philosophical traditions from the eighteenth century onward, especially to the utilitarian and idealistic schools.[14] But with the passage of time they loosened their connection to these traditions and acquired some autonomy of their own in terms of their own specific approaches, problems, and concepts. These trends of thought and analyses have necessarily greatly shaped the development of the various trends of political sociology proper, which also developed

their own specific problems in the broad context of the general sociological *Problemstellungen*.

In order to be able to understand these specific problems it might be worth while to analyze very briefly the setting of modern sociology, particularly political sociology.

The general social conditions that gave rise to modern sociology have been often closely related to, or concomitant with, the general development of modernity, of modern society, and of polity which we shall analyze in greater detail later on. (See the introduction to Part Three.) At this stage of our discussion, perhaps the most important aspect of these broad conditions leading to the development of modern sociology, particularly political sociology, is the development—in the symbolic perception of social order of leading intellectual groups in Europe —of a growing dichotomy between "state" and "society" as two distinct, relatively autonomous, and yet closely interrelated entities. This dichotomy was especially stressed in German and to some extent French sociopolitical thought. From there it permeated much of the general social thought and analyses since the early nineteenth century.

This conceptualization of the dichotomy between state and society tended to oscillate between extreme poles in the history of political sociology, often, but not always, connected with different ideological stances. One pole tended to belittle the specificity or autonomy of the political sphere institutions and processes and to see in them but a reflection of "deeper social forces," whether—as in Marxism—of economic or class structure, the general "spirit" of a nation, or of various environmental or technological forces. The other pole, best seen in some of the elitist trends (Mosca, Pareto, or to some degree Schumpeter),[15] tended to view political institutions as primary or dominant spheres, reducing the other social spheres to a secondary status. The extent to which either of these poles became ideologically predominant was greatly influenced by changes and fashions both in general ideological trends and in the development of sociological analysis and research.

The varied ideological trends and problems that were focused around the dichotomy between state and society tended to become diversified and changed throughout the decades in different countries. The perception of this dichotomy was, as we have seen, from the very beginning much stronger and more fully articulated in Germany and eastern Europe than in the Western Hemisphere or the United States. For quite long periods it was not the focus of sociopolitical thought even in the former countries. But it re-emerged very sharply and in new, highly articulated ways with the rise of totalitarianism, especially of right-wing totalitarianism (Fascism and Nazism). Perhaps the most important exponents of this new emphasis on this problem, in this phase, were Karl Mannheim, Eduard Heimann,[16] and the group of religious socialists, on the one hand, and the ideologies of the different totalitarian camps, Carl Schmitt[17] of the right and Lenin and Stalin[18] of the left, on the other.

V

Most of the specific *Problemstellungen* derived from this basic dichotomous conception of state and society were largely concerned in one way or another with the quest for the understanding of the specific qualities and problems of modern society and of modern social and political order. This quest focused around several basic poles or dichotomies.

One such pole was that of *liberty versus authority,* which focused around the examination of the possibility of combining liberty with the maintenance of order or authority. Here the central problem was the search for the bases of consensus through which some stability and order could be maintained together with the growth of the areas of liberty. The conception of such order, and also the conception of the relation between state and society, differed widely in various ideological camps. This will be dealt with in greater detail when we discuss the modern political order.

Several major orientations developed: the "conservative," which tended to give priority to the maintenance of order and authority as against any libertarian orientation; the libertarian or liberal, which tended to stress the priority of liberty; and another two, the "liberal-political" and the "revolutionary," which, each in its own way, refuted dichotomy as such. The "liberal political" tradition,[19] emphasized, in direct link with some aspects of the Greek tradition, that liberty is meaningless beyond the political order. The extreme revolutionary orientations, whether Jacobite or Communist, tended to assume that this dichotomy becomes resolved in the great revolutionary act which establishes a political order without conflict. Closely related to such revolutionary orientations, and yet very often sharply opposed to them in their concrete political or social orientations, were the utopian trends, which attempted to conceive a social order in which the whole problem of authority disappeared because of the ability to establish a true, voluntary basis for consensus.

The second major problem or concern about the quality of modern society was that of *stability and continuity versus change.* This concern was rooted in the perception of the possibility of change ("progress" or "development") as an inherent structural tendency in modern society, as a positive value, and therefore as posing before the modern polity and society the problem of the possibility of combining change in some degree with institutional stability or continuity. Here again the relations between state and society were often envisaged in different ways or, rather, in different combinations of some basic "structural" elements by the followers of different ideological camps. Some tended "naturally" to equate liberty with change and authority with stability, but in various philosophical or ideological traditions these elements tended to combine (as we shall yet see in greater detail in the chapter on the modern political order) with more diversity. But whatever the details and variances of their standpoints, they all accepted the dichotomy of state versus society as a basic starting point for all their reflections.

VI

The persistence of this dichotomy could be also discerned, with the further development of sociological analyses proper, when other analytical concepts, or, for example, those of class and class relation, bureaucracy, and mass society, were merged in the definition of the basic problems concerning the nature of the modern social order.

Through a brief survey of the basic attitudes toward bureaucracy as they developed in modern sociopolitical thought,[20] it is possible to illustrate the variety of these developments and the persistence of the dichotomy of state versus society.

This concern with bureaucracy can be traced, on the one hand, to Ferguson's theories of oriental despotism, which stressed the special character of officialdom as an instrument of oppression in oriental states. On the other hand, this concern can be found in the writings of Marx and de Tocqueville, both of whom discerned the trend toward "bureaucratization," toward the growing regimentation of social life in the modern world. Both tried to interpret it according to their major analyses of the trends in the development of modern society. In all these writings, however, the discussion of bureaucracy was embedded in, and constituted only a part of, analyses that were focused mainly on other problems. It was only with Max Weber, Robert Michels, and Gaetano Mosca[21] that the structure of bureaucracy and processes of bureaucratization became a focus of independent major analysis. In their works, analysis of bureaucracy and bureaucratization processes became closely interwoven, on the one hand, with the examination of problems of power and its control and legitimation in modern society and, on the other hand, with the analysis of processes of rationalization, in terms of growing efficiency and specialization. It has been rightly said that "roughly" for Max Weber, bureaucracy plays the same part that the class struggle played for Marx and competition for Sombart.[22] Mosca was the first to treat the bureaucratic state as a distinct type of political system and organization of the ruling class. He contrasted it with the feudal regime (and to some extent with city-states) and attempted to analyze what may be called its internal dialectics of stability and disorganization.[23]

Bureaucracy and bureaucratization were interpreted from a different viewpoint in the works of political scientists like Friedrich and Finer[24] and, in the last attempt at a major "total" sociological interpretation of modern society, in the work of Karl Mannheim.[25] In their writings, these problems are thrown into sharp relief as major trends in the development of modern society. Here, bureaucracy and bureaucratization are related to, and closely interwoven with, problems of democracy, totalitarianism, and mass society.

Almost all the classical works dealing with bureaucracy are preoccupied with one basic dilemma: namely, whether the bureaucracy is master or servant, an independent body or a tool—and if a tool, whose interests it can be made to serve. This dilemma is posed in different ways. Max Weber[26] considers bureaucracy to be the epitome of rationality and efficiency, the most rational means of implementing a given goal. From his standpoint it follows that bureaucracy is directed by those who can set the goals, although he did not systematically examine the problem of the relation of bureaucracy's structure to the nature of the policy's goals. On the other hand, however, he frequently alludes to and analyzes bureaucracy as a powerful, independent body which advances and conquers new areas of life in modern society, monopolizes power, and tends to rule over and regulate the life of the individual. It is this second standpoint that underlies Weber's critique of socialism and his partial resignation to its inevitability in some countries, at least.

An ambivalent attitude toward bureaucracy characterizes much of the social thought of the latter half of the nineteenth century and the first decade of the twentieth, and it is especially prominent in liberal-socialist polemics. It is significant that no side—neither the liberals, the conservatives, nor the socialists—took an unequivocal and clear stand in relation to bureaucracy. The liberals and the conservatives often strongly objected to bureaucracy and depicted it as a colossus which would engulf the various areas of life, cancel the traditional liberties of the people, and engender a mechanized and oppressive civilization, choking the individual and regimenting his every activity. While this view in its extreme form, as expressed, for instance, by L. von Mises, is no longer taken seriously, the problem itself remains and looms large in contemporary social thought. On the other hand, many liberals and conservatives stressed the importance of bureaucracy as a means of implementing social reforms and upheld the ideal of a neutral civil service. While many of the naïve assumptions about the clear, unadulterated benefits that would accrue from social reforms implemented by bureaucracy are long forgotten, the main problem remains and is accentuated by the growing awareness of the problem of power.

An ambivalent attitude toward bureaucracy is also featured by the socialist and the Communist camps. On the one hand, there is the realization of its importance as a means of implementing social goals and reforms. On the other, there is the suspicion of it as a tool in the hands of the capitalist ruling classes. From a different vantage point, the socialists have often depicted bureaucracy as a mere appendage of capitalist society and oppression which will become obsolete and unnecessary under socialism and its rational "management of things," not of men. Paradoxically, the tables have recently been turned on the socialists and especially on the Communists by the liberal or social-democratic camp, with the growing realization that bureaucracy may easily become a tool of oppression, especially under conditions of great concentration of power—the very fear expressed by socialists regarding capitalistic bureaucracy. This camp has come to realize that one of the major problems facing modern regimes is the effective political and democratic control of the bureaucracy on the one hand and the planning for possible debureaucratization in different spheres of life on the other.

VII

Similar ambivalent attitudes also developed, as has been noted above, toward other basic components of the modern social order, or around other analytical concepts of modern sociology, such as "class." Here, on the one hand, a classless society was envisaged as the epitome of liberty and as the dialectical synthesis and "overcoming" of the distinction between class and society. On the other hand, liberty was seen as contingent on the existence of a variety of different hierarchies in class and status.[27] Similar attitudes also developed with regard to other concepts, such as "mass" and "elite," which we shall encounter in our discussion of modern political order.[28] Thus it can be seen that these various approaches—whatever concept they were focused around—were derived to a large extent from the dichotomous conception of state and society. Only gradually has sociology, particularly political sociology, been able to free itself from these extreme approaches. Together with this, new analytical conceptual approaches developed in sociological analysis which placed more emphasis on systematic research and its basic problems and became less interwoven with ideological perceptions.

With the development of more analytical sociological thought, this perception of state and society gradually gave way, in totally dichotomous ways, to a more differentiated view in which "society" itself was greatly modified into various institutions—economic, social organization, and family—while the political itself came more and more to be seen as one of these institutions. And yet the dichotomous perception of "state or society" did bequeath to political sociology, as we shall see later, a very large part of the *Problemstellungen* with its basic analytical assumptions. It may appear paradoxical that this became evident once the various traditions of research and analysis in political sociology converged around common basic analytical concerns.

VIII

Within the general framework of sociological thought and analysis in general and of modern political sociology in particular, there developed several more specific trends of analysis. These trends of research set out from different starting points, often each separated from the others and creating its own separate tradition. But gradually these separate trends tended to converge into a common basic analytical focus. It would be out of place to attempt to survey all these trends here, but many of them will be represented in the materials presented in this reader. We might briefly mention here several basic trends that focus around the analysis of internal components of political system and activities and other trends that focus mainly around comparative analysis.

One aspect of the internal structure of the political system around which an important tradition of research developed was the study of the recruitment, composition, and changes of the various political elites, of their relations with various nonelite groups, and of the pattern of political organization and mobilization used by them. The works of Pareto, Mosca,[29] and Weber[30] and later of Schumpeter, K. Mannheim, Lasswell, and Raymond Aron,[31] are perhaps the most important illustrations of this concern with the recruitment and circulation of elites.

Another closely connected aspect of the political systems, around which an important tradition of research developed, was the study of different types of political organization. This trend, as exemplified in the works by Ostrogorski, Michels, and later Duverger,[32] studied the interaction between elites and the broader strata, including, especially, the political parties. In this context come also the various studies of the rules of the political game as practiced by those who participate in it. Many such studies, like treatises on constitutional law, were of purely formal-legal type, but many others had already gone beyond this and attempted more systematic analysis of the rules.[33]

A relatively recent addition to this systemic approach came from a theory of games. This proved to be very illuminating in the analysis of the growth of both internal and international political systems.[34] Another recent aspect of the internal working of political systems was the study of political participation of different groups and strata. Here two substreams can be discerned: first, the study of voting; second, the study of the pattern of influence, of informal political processes, and of private political ideologies.[35] In this context there developed studies of political socialization: of the ways in which different societies "socialize" their members into becoming subjects or citizens.

Gradually these various trends of research tended to converge around some of the more perennial central problems of political sociology. Thus studies of patterns of political struggle and of the recruitment and circulation of elites became, through the emphasis on their relation to conflicts on the one hand, and through attempts to study social cleavages and conflicts in their consensual or dissensual effects on the political system on the other, closely related to the study of continuity of political systems.

The major analytical breakthroughs have been made in those studies which combined the study of patterns of political behavior with that of elite selection and of structural cleavages and patterns. The various studies which addressed themselves to these problems have gradually progressed from a mostly descriptive stage—as, for instance, the general distribution of voting—to more sophisticated levels, such as the study of regional, occupational, and class bases of voting, to the relations between the patterns of political participation and political ideology, and to types of political socialization. Here the works of Parsons, Lipset, Bendix, Rokkan, and Dahl[36] are the most important ever developed, incorporating as they did the earlier tradition of Mosca, Mannheim, and Schumpeter with the recent analytical and methodological developments in social science.

IX

A similar growing convergence can be found in the development of comparative studies in political sociology. Such interest in the comparative study of political systems initially went its own way, as we have seen, and was not very closely connected with the other traditions of research mentioned above.

Anthropology, history, some tradition of comparative constitutions, and legal history have been concerned, each in its own way, with comparative analysis—refining and systematizing in various ways the great tradition of Aristotle, Ibn-Khaldun, and Vico. This was taken up in the eighteenth century by Montesquieu, Ferguson, and Millar and combined in various ways the systematic and the comparative perspectives. These different trends of comparative research, by stemming from various sources—social anthropology and comparative history,[37] as well as the great new upsurge of studies of developing societies and of New Nations—also slowly came to converge around several common focal points.

A crucial link between them has been, of course, the attempt to compare them in terms of variation of the basic categories of the political system on the one hand and of the major analytical problems of continuity and change on the other. Here, too, there emerged, as an especially important crucial aspect, the analysis of the specific conditions for the continuity and change of different types of political system and the extent to which they can be subsumed under the general hypotheses or laws of continuity of political systems.

Of special importance in this context were the growing studies of modern societies. Much of the more recent works in political sociology have been focused around the investigation of the social conditions of emergence and especially of stability and continuity of various types of modern regimes—particularly the democratic, autocratic, and totalitarian ones—and of the transition from one such type to another, especially from the democratic to the autocratic or totalitarian, and to a smaller degree

also in the reverse direction.[38] The conditions of their stability, continuity, and breakdowns were studied here in terms of internal political struggle and participation, of patterns of voting in relation to more specific structural characteristics of these regimes, and of their broader social conditions, in this way combining the behavioral and the systematic comparative approach.[39]

It has been the unique opportunity of modern societies to study, within their settings, some of the repercussions of actual patterns of political behavior and attitudes on the stability and continuity of different types of political system.

Part Two

X

Out of the general modern sociological *Problemstellung,* out of the many varied ideological problems and questions on the one hand, and varied traditions of sociological research on the other hand, there developed more specific, basic problems of modern political sociology, around which the problems of research began to converge in the last two or three decades. The first such general problem has been that of the *sociological nature of political power,* relations, organizations, and institutions as a distinct aspect, part, or sphere of the social order. Here there developed three major focuses of interest. One was the description of the formal, "static" characteristics or attributes of the political system; second, the nature of its relations, of its "inputs and outputs" with other spheres of the social order; and last, the conditions of the stability, continuity, and change of a political system in general and of various specific types of political systems in particular.

Despite a wide variety of definitions and a great amount of controversy about the "basic" nature of the "political," a relatively broad range of consensus can now be discerned with regard to some of the minimal definitions of the systematic nature of the political institutions in any society or part thereof. The following definition of the attributes of the political system and its relation to other parts of social system would probably be generally accepted.[40]

1. The political system is the organization of a territorial society having the legitimate monopoly over the authorized use and regulation of force in the society.

2. It has defined responsibilities for maintaining the system of which it is a part.

3. Therefore, its organization imposes severe secular sanctions in order to implement the society's

main collective goals, maintain its internal order, and regulate its foreign relations. All social roles or groups fulfilling these distinct functions in a society, regardless of what other tasks they may perform, constitute the society's political system.

This definition presupposes that every society necessarily features a political system; that is, that no society exists that implements its collective goals and maintains internal and external order without having a legitimate pattern of interaction by means of which these goals are implemented or this order is maintained. Specific political roles, as such, may not be clearly distinguishable in some societies. But to deny their existence would be to argue that the fulfillment of political functions is random. Accordingly,

> . . . intermittent action on the part of the oldest male of a band, in response to specific situations, or informally formulated consensus on the part of a group dealing with some serious threat to internal order, or some problem of foreign relations, implies a special type of political structure, not its absence.
>
> In other words, it is now usually accepted that the traditional distinction between primitive societies constituting a state (the so-called "segmentary" tribes) should be reformulated as a distinction based on the extent to which the several political activities and organizations in these societies can be discerned and differentiated.[41]

The analysis of the major characteristics of all political systems enables us to understand the basic types of activity within them. It indicates that the major types of political activities existing in every political system are as follows:

1. The "legislative decision-making" or the "ultimate ruling" activity; that is, the determination of the society's primary goals and formulation of general rules for maintaining (or changing) the existing order in the society.

2. The administrative activity, dealing with the execution of these basic rules in different social spheres and with the organization of technical activities necessary for their efficient execution. The main purpose of the administrative activity is to provide various services to various groups in the society and to regulate and assure the provision of resources to the political system (such as revenue) by different strata and groups.

3. "Party-political" activity; that is, activity mobilizing support for different political measures and rules and for the holders of different political positions.

4. The juridical activity, concerned with testing and authorizing the validity of applying the basic rules to particular, concrete cases arising in the society.

In discussing the main types of political activity, we must distinguish between the parts played by the "rulers" and the "ruled." The rulers are those who play the active part in the political process: those who define the goals, formulate and execute the rules, adjudicate, and contend for political support. The ruled are those who are subject to the rules, who demand adjudications, and who wish to influence the legislators. In many societies, the same person may be a "ruler" at one time or in one respect and "ruled" at another time and in another respect; and the rulers may be also subject to the different rules promulgated by themselves. However, the broad distinction between rulers and ruled is inherent in the very nature of political activity.

These different types of political activity are analytically distinct, but they necessarily supplement each other. The continuous interaction between them constitutes the political process in a society. True, the degree to which each of these types of political activity is differentiated varies greatly from one society to another and constitutes, as we shall see, an important problem for comparative study. But all are inherent in any political system, and they indicate and specify the nature of the interrelations between the political institutions and other parts of the institutional structure of a given society. They point out both the kinds of input (that is, the types of support and resources) the political system needs in order to fulfill its functions and the nature of the system's major contributions, or outputs, to the society as a whole.

What, briefly, are these interrelations between the political and other institutions in the society? The polity's specific output to other institutional spheres consists of various authoritative decisions concerning the following: (1) definition of the major collective goals that can be implemented and determination of their order of priority; (2) allocation of prestige, influence, and authorized use of power and facilities to various groups in the society; (3) distribution of various facilities, benefits, and rights to such groups and individuals. Through these decisions, the political institutions can perform their major functions in the society: to articulate their specific characteristics in relation to other parts of the society. However, these activities cannot be performed, of course, without help from other social spheres and institutions— from those very spheres toward which its decisions are oriented.

The polity is dependent on other institutional

spheres for the continuous inflow of resources, services, and support needed for implementation of the collective goals, for maintenance of the polity's position in the society, and for fulfillment of its regulative and integrative functions. From the economic sphere, the polity must receive various manpower, labor, material, and monetary resources. It depends on the cultural institutions for basic support of the regime, identification with its symbols, the legitimation of the rulers, and motivation for the performance of political roles. The sphere of social stratification and organization provides the polity with the necessary support of different policies and with the ability and willingness of different groups and people to engage in various political activities.

However, the interactions between the polity and other institutional systems of the society are not limited to the mutual contributions just outlined. These contributions are articulated through the demands that the political institutions make on different groups and strata in the society and through the transmission of political decisions from the rulers to the ruled. The amount or extent of the resources and support available to the polity is never given or fixed; those in political roles must always make continuous demands on other institutional spheres for them. These demands are, of course, closely connected with and largely contingent on the demands made by these different groups on the polity to implement various types of decisions. Like the resources accruing to the polity, the decisions of the polity are neither given nor fixed. The demands of the various groups are neither directly transmitted to the polity nor fixed. The demands of the various groups are transmitted through the political orientations and activities of the groups—mainly through the articulation of their interests in political terms and the aggregation of these interests in frameworks of some political organizations. The continuous interaction between the polity and other institutional spheres, in terms of their specific contributions and demands, constitutes the dynamics of political processes in any society.

XI

This definition brings out the fact that the central problems of the political system are seen as focused around two basic concepts. One is the legitimate use of power, or of the conversion of power in authority. The other is the implementation of some common goals and of the relation between the two. Here, the central problem is that of legitimacy and legitimation of political power and authority, of their efficacy,

and of the interrelation between the two and of the conditions—both internal to the political system (given in the internal organization of the political institution) and external (given in the broad societal setting, in other social spheres, or in other societies, as, for example, in the international system of any given society)—under which these tend to develop.

XII

Some more or less accepted primary criteria for differentiating between political systems developed here, just as they had with regard to the basic systemic properties of political systems and to the basic dimension of comparative analysis. They are focused mainly around the following dimensions:[42]

1. The extent to which the political roles and institutions constitute a fully organized subsystem in the society; or, in other words, the degree to which this subsystem is organizationally differentiated from other subsystems in the society.

2. The extent of emphasis in each political system on the main types of political activities and orientations—the administrative, executive, "party-political," and juridical-cultural.

3. The scope of political activity in the society. By this is meant, first, the areas of social life and the social groups which are affected by the activities of central political organs and are dependent on those activities for the maintenance of their own solidarity and organization; and, second, the extent of participation by these groups in political activities.

4. The type of legitimacy that a given system enjoys, the ways in which this legitimacy directs and limits the system's activities, and the extent of its means of mobilization of political support.

5. The extent and nature of changes possible in a given political system.

Different aspects of the internal workings of political systems can also be differentiated accordingly. Thus different types of political organization may be classified according to the following general criteria:

1. The distinctness in the organization of political activities from other social activities and groupings.

2. The perpetuation and continuity of such political organizations.

3. The extent, type, and homogeneity or heterogeneity of the social groups which participate in the organization and its consequent ability to channel "free-floating" political power (not committed to any ascriptive group).

4. The extent of legitimation of such activities in the society.

5. The main channels of political struggle that exist in these societies.

The issues or main aims of the political struggle can be classified according to the following criteria:

1. The scope and breadth of the issue in terms of the groups to which it refers, and the extent to which it cuts across various groups.

2. The extent and specific articulation of the issue as a political issue.

3. The generality of the principle of the criterion involved in the issue.

4. The political institutions toward which it is oriented.

5. The attitude of these institutions toward the basic premises of the given political order.

XIII

Not only was there to be found a growing convergence and consensus *within* the areas of the systematic analysis of political systems and of comparative studies, but side by side with these there was also a growing convergence between these two areas, focusing around the problems of conditions, patterns, and directions of change and transformation of political systems; of the conditions of stability or change in different types of system; and of their ability to accommodate different types of change. The most important aspects of this problem are:

1. The extent of change that is engendered by the social conditions and group structure of these societies.

2. The extent of change that can be accommodated in the system, and the role of the political process and levels of political consensus in the development of such various accommodative mechanisms.

3. The conditions under which change cannot be accommodated and developed, and the role of various aspects of the political process—various intergroup relations and conflicts, the policies of the rulers, etc.—in the diffusion and restriction of these types of change.

The great emphasis on processes of change and transformation and of their relation to patterns of political struggle emphasizes the importance of the study of patterns of protest, rebellions, and revolutionary movements and of the comparative analysis of such movements, especially from the point of view of the extent to which they may serve as starting points for structural and symbolic transformation. These may also help, perhaps, in a re-evaluation of the evolutionary problem or perspective in sociology in general and in political sociology

in particular—a perspective the importance of which has been recently recognized more and more—although there is as yet but little consensus about the answers to the problem it poses.[43]

The great importance of the study of patterns of change and transformation of political systems, particularly of their comparative analysis, brings us to the next stage in our analysis of the development and problems of political sociology.

Part Three

XIV

The growing conceptual analytical and theoretical convergence in political sociology is becoming more and more evident in the various streams of research, be they anthropological, historical, macrosociological, microsociological, or psychosocial studies. Yet each of these tends obviously to go in its own direction. It can be seen in the growing similarity of problems and concepts and in the continuous mutual interrelationships between these various streams of research.

As often happens in such cases, this convergence tends to bring out not only the basic common assumptions that are by now accepted by these various approaches but also their limitations. These assumptions and limitations alike are evident on two levels: on the level of the basic *Problemstellungen* of political sociology and on the level of its conceptual and analytical assumptions, and in the relations between the two.

However great the concrete diversity of the varied researches and approaches of political sociology, their broad, largely implicit *Problemstellungen* were still rooted in the basic dichotomy of state versus society and in the concomitant assumptions about the existence of two strong, viable, and relatively autonomous units or spheres of social life designated as "state" and "society"—in whatever concrete way they may be actually defined—and in the consequent concentration of interest on the varied forms of confrontation between them. The limits of these assumptions were to be put to the test, even if only haltingly and intermittently, with the new upsurge of interest in comparative political and sociological analysis which was connected with the growing interest in so-called underdeveloped areas, developing societies, or "New Nations."

In the beginning the approaches to the study of these societies were also mostly couched in terms of the conception of dichotomy of state and society, as, for instance, in the search for existence of the social (nonpolitical) conditions for development of different types of regimes or in the importance of the one-party state for the creation of general social-national cohesion. With the development of these studies it became clear that most of these formulations were not adequate to cope fully with the problems of these societies. This was due to two closely interrelated, relatively simple reasons. One was that in many of these societies—especially in those which developed from tribal societies—the very existence of "state" or "society," as conceived in terms of the European tradition as strong, autonomous units, could not be taken for granted. In many of these societies, as in the African ones, there did not exist a strong political center. Most of them exhibited the relative centerlessness of primitive societies (see Part Two-A, on primitive systems), while most of the centers that developed with them or were imposed on them came from alien, external sources. Similarly, in these cases the existence of states of relatively homogeneous national communities and political units could not be taken for granted.

Seemingly, this could have brought these states back to the roots of modern European political thought—to the political thought of Hobbes, Rousseau, or Burke,[44] with their emphasis on the problem of consensus and of the development of the "common will." But, in fact, the confrontation with the problems of the bases of a modern social and political order was of a different kind here. All these classical European thinkers took the existence of a "state" or society for granted. Even when they were afraid of anarchy or civil war, the civil war they envisaged was within the traditions of a relatively strong, centralized, political framework. In many of the New States it was, however, the existence both of any viable center and of a wider transtribal community that was highly problematic; and the conditions under which it could develop at all had to be more fully investigated.[45]

The revision of the basic conceptions of political order was also necessitated by the encounter with many Asian societies which had strong imperial traditions. Although here there could be no doubt about the existence of a strong state, the very interrelations of the state with the social order have been envisaged in ways different from those of Western tradition. This political tradition did not envisage the same type of split or dichotomy between state and society as did the European tradition. Instead, it tended more to stress the congruent relations between the cosmic order on the one hand and the sociopolitical order on the other. Unlike

the Western tradition, the interrelation between the political and the social was not envisaged in terms of an antithesis between two powers. Rather it was more often stated in terms of coalescence of these different functions in the same group or organization, centered around a common focus in the cosmic order.

Lastly, these new developments in political life brought out another aspect of political sociology which has been greatly neglected in modern sociology in general and in political sociology in particular—namely, the importance of the international setting or the international system as a basic determinant or aspect of any given "internal" political system. The reason for this neglect, by modern sociology, to examine more fully the international aspect of political societies is to no small degree to be found in the fact that the major focus of modern sociology was on the autonomous, self-sustaining national or political community which began to emerge in Europe in the nineteenth century and tended to constitute relatively central societies which were not colonies or peripheries of other cultural centers.

XV

Similar problems and limitations, developing side by side, but not to the same degree, could be found not only with regard to the *Problemstellung* of political sociology but also with regard to some of its *analytical* or conceptual assumptions about the place or roots of the political order in the broader social order.

The exercise of political power—that is, of the "necessity" for a political order—was derived, as we have seen, from two systemic or prerequisite needs of any social system in general and of a total society in particular. These are the maintenance of order and the regulation of force on the one hand, and on the other, the implementation of some common goals perceived as representing the collectivity.

But in most works of political sociology one can discern a feeling that there exists some basic contradiction between these two: that the exercise of power and the representation or implementation of the goals or values of a society are basically incompatible with each other. This feeling of contradiction can be seen best in the great ambivalence toward power that is found in most discourses and researches and through the attempts to overcome this ambivalence by the strong emphasis on political consensus as the basis for maintaining the legitimation of a given political system. This political system is mostly conceived in terms of the agreement of the ruled with the goals represented and implemented by the rulers. A very large part of the most intensive controversies of political sociology tended to focus around the problem of whether any such legitimation —that is, any acceptance of the goals of a polity and of its alleged needs by its members—is more than a contrivance by those who succeed in monopolizing power in any given society—a sort of "opium for the people." Here, frequent claim is made that the so-called "needs" of any society for the maintenance of any given political order are not actually given in the real nature or problems of any given society but were set up and represented as basic values by those who wanted to monopolize power. It has been claimed further that they are the ones who impose certain goals on the society, attempting to define the goals as basic needs. Hence, the consensus that might seemingly be engendered by the apparent allegiance to these goals was really only a "sham," imposed by the rulers and not derived from any real or genuine, independent convictions of the ruled. It was also claimed that the best proof of this was the fact that the "ruled" could not develop or use power for their own goals and that any such use would deplete the power of the rulers. In more general terms, this implied a view of the social order which was perceived as something external to the individual's own wishes or goals, as something basically imposed on them.

XVI

There seems indeed to be some parallelism between the limitations inherent in the *Problemstellungen* and in the hitherto generally accepted analytical assumptions of political sociology. These parallelisms seem to focus around two common focuses; namely, the relation among power and systemic or organizational needs of varied social systems on one hand and broader (nonpolitical) value orientations, goals, or conceptions of sociopolitical order on the other hand. In both cases, power and other nonpolitical aspects of the social or cultural orders are conceived as somewhat separate, distinct, and yet self-contained entities. They may, indeed, be interrelated, but the relations between them are conceived as dichotomous, tenuous, antithetic, and fixed. Analytically this was closely connected with the existence of a given, limited amount of power in a society and with the alleged difficulties of explaining, through the use of this concept of power in systemic analysis, the potentialities to social change and political change.

But, as has been pointed out above, this state of the discipline gave rise to some dissatisfactions, which were rooted, as we have seen, in various ideological

stances in the Western society to a growing encounter with societies in which either the existence of strong centers could not be taken for granted or the interrelation between the political and nonpolitical aspects of the society seemed to be of a rather different kind.[46] It is only lately that sociology, especially political sociology, has found some ways to overcome these limitations.

From an analytical point of view, the crucial step was the refutation of the conception of political power as a "zero sum" game.[47] This is very closely related to a general theoretical reorientation in sociology in general and political sociology in particular. This new orientation has two major focuses. One is a reformulation of the nature of the individual's orientation to the social order. The other is the redefinition of the nature of the institutional loci of this orientation and of the relation of these loci to the political sphere.

With regard to the first focus of this reorientation, the most important breakthrough in recent sociological thinking was the re-emphasis of the fact that not only is social order given by some external forces and imposed in some way on individuals and their desires (or else it is only an outcome of their rational premeditated selfish evaluation of their interests or of the exigencies of social economic division of labor engendered by these interests) but also that a quest for some such order, in organizational and symbolic terms, is among the basic wishes or orientations of people.[48] In other words, this implies that among the "egotistical" wishes of people, a very important part is played by their quest for a conception of symbolic order, of the "good society," and of the quest for participation in such an order. This quest constitutes a basic, although differential, component in the whole panorama of social and cultural activities, orientations, and goals. It calls for a rather special type of response, and this response tends to be located in specific, distinct parts or aspects of the social structure.

This quest for an adequate symbolic or social order and for participation in it is very closely related to the quest for some relation or attachment to the charismatic, "with the 'vital,' serious, ultimately serious event of which divinity is one of many forms."[49]

The crucial role of the charismatic dimension and symbols in social order was first fully explored by Weber, and only recently has it been taken up again by Shils, who stressed also that the charismatic not only is something extraordinary (as has been often interpreted in sociological literature) but also has a specific continuous, institutional location in any social order in general and macrosocietal order in particular. He attempted also to specify at least one of the institutional loci of the charismatic; namely, in what he designated as the center of the society. Here we might quote briefly from his definition of the center.

Society has a centre. There is a central zone in the structure of society. This central zone impinges in various ways on those who live within the ecological domain in which the society exists. Membership in the society, in more than the ecological sense of being located in a bounded territory and of adapting to an environment affected or made up by other persons located in the same territory, is constituted by relationship to this central zone.

. . . The central zone is not, *as such,* a spatially located phenomenon. It almost has a more or less definite location within the bounded territory in which the society lives. Its centrality has, however, nothing to do with geometry and little with geography.

The centre, or the central zone, is a phenomenon of the realm of values and beliefs. It is the centre of the order of symbols, of values and beliefs, which govern the society. It is the centre because it is the ultimate and irreducible, and it is felt to be such by many who cannot give explicit articulation to its irreducibility. The central zone partakes of the nature of the sacred. In this sense, every society has an "official" religion, even when that society or its exponents and interpreters conceive of it, more or less correctly, as a secular, pluralistic, and tolerant society. The principle of the Counter-Reformation: *Cuius regio, eius religio,* although its rigor has been loosened and its harshness mollified, retains a core of permanent truth.

The centre is also a phenomenon of the realm of action. It is a structure of activities, of roles and persons, within the network of institutions. It is in these roles that the values and beliefs which are central are embodied and propounded.[50]

Thus, it can be seen that the tendency toward the institutional convergence of the charismatic in the center or centers of society is rooted in the fact that both the charismatic and the center are concerned with the provision and maintenance in a society of some meaningful, symbolic, and institutional order. But this close relationship between the two does not imply their total identity. Rather, it raises many new questions and problems. What is the structure of such centers, and what are their structural relations to the periphery? How many centers which embody such a charismatic orientation are there in a society; that is, the political, cultural, religious or ideological, and other centers? What is the relation between the "ordering" and "meaning" (that is, charismatic) functions of such centers on the one hand and of their more organizational and administrative activities on the other?

This especially brings us to the problem of the ways in which both the symbolic and the organizational aspects of routinization of charisma vary among the major institutional spheres of a social order. Given that the quest for order is evident throughout the major spheres of a society and that it is not something purely "abstract" or symbolic, but closely related to the organizational "needs" and problems of these spheres, it necessarily follows that the process of routinization of charisma and the charismatic qualities may differ greatly among different institutional spheres.

This necessarily raises the problem of the special place of the political field in relation to the center. Truly enough, at first sight, it seems that in any society the central political organization, whatever its exact form or composition, constitutes its "natural" center. But this does not necessarily denote that the political center or institution in any society is the only focus or locus of centrality or of charisma. As we have already seen above, by their very nature such charismatic orientations tend to be diffused, although probably in different degrees, in almost all institutional spheres.[51] And yet there can be no doubt that the political sphere has a special, although not exclusive, relation to such centrality. The political field, the field of authority, constitutes a special locus of the "ordering" qualities of the charismatic; it constitutes at least one major referent of every societal center. This special place of the polity as a locus of centrality, the great affinity between centrality and the political sphere, is rooted in the nature of authority. In a sense, as we have seen, the essence of the political is the conversion of power into authority, and this conversion is rooted in the affinity of the political to the charismatic qualities and symbols to the center.

Hence, the polity evinces a double relation to the quest for order. First of all, the polity is the organizational center through which the exigencies and needs of such order and of concomitant institutional locus of the regulation of power are focused. Second, the polity plays a central role in the setting up of the center or centers of the social order.

XVII

It is the recognition of these facts—of the existence of institutional localization of the charismatic in the centers of society, of the special and yet not exclusive relation of the political institutions to such centers—that entails a reformulation of many of the basic questions and problems of political sociology which have been analyzed above. It does not negate or invalidate the various questions and answers about the systemic qualities of political organization and about the basis of cohesion, political consensus, and legitimation which we have seen above as having been central to political sociology; but it does enable us to put them in a more differentiated way and in a wider analytical conceptual setting.

First of all, it entails the reformulation of the problem concerning the nature of the relations between what may be called the "functional prerequisites" or "organizational exigencies" of any social system with which any political system has to deal and the goals or values of this system. The preceding analysis indicates that this relation is a twofold, or two-way, one. In any given macrosocial situation and at a certain level of social differentiation or specialization, some minimal needs or integrative problems exist without which the survival of these entities may be in doubt. These organizational needs or exigencies pose a range of problems with which each social or political system has to deal. But they do not in themselves contain the nature of the answers which can be given to these problems. The range of such answers—even the possibility that in any given situation no such institutional answer will be given—is, in any given situation, rather wide.

In these varied, concrete, institutional answers, the contours and goals of any polity are not given by the nature of its organizational needs or by the organizational necessities of order or exigencies of power; but they develop as a special aspect of the general process of institution building of which the orientation to some charismatic order is an important component. It is only when such "answers" and goals are institutionalized—even if, as is usually the case, only to a very limited extent—that they engender various systemic types of need which, if they are not taken care of by the development of some specific types of social organization, make the implementation of such goals impossible.

The focus of the crystallization of the basic institutional answers to problems facing any social order lies in the process of center building: the formation of centers in general and the political center in particular. The special place of the centers, especially the political center, is rooted, of course, in the center's affinity to the charismatic dimension of the social order and to the quest for participation in the respective social and cultural orders in which this dimension becomes embodied.

But just as the political center is not the only locus of the charismatic, so also the orientation to the purely charismatic is not the only component of center formation and of the formation of political centers. Therefore, in order to be able to understand the processes and conditions of center formation and the different structures of the centers, it is necessary to specify in greater detail the other components of center formation.

The first such component is the institutionalization, in both symbolic and organizational terms, of the quest for the ordering of social and cultural experience and for some participation in such charismatic orders. Closely related to this quest, but not identical with it, is another component of center formation; namely, the crystallization of the common societal and cultural collective identity based on common attributes or on participation in common symbolic events. It is this element which contributes the basis for the "precontractual" elements of a social order so strongly stressed by Durkheim himself[52] and also designated by him as an important aspect of mechanical solidarity.

What is of crucial importance from the point of view of our analysis is that (and here it is put in a somewhat different way than by Durkheim) this element is not just embedded in the nondifferentiated units of a "simple" ("primitive") society but tends also in more developed societies to become localized in special institutional frameworks in the various centers. At the same time it is very important to indicate that in no society are such attributes of common collective identity simply given. Rather, they constitute a focus and a part of the continuous process of institution building in general and of center formation in particular.

A third component of center building, which may indeed be closely related to both the formation of attributes of common identity and the institutionalization of some broader order, but which is analytically distinct from them, is that of the crystallization and articulation of collective goals—of "organizational" goals which are conceived of as the goals of the collectivity or polity.

A fourth component of center formation, very often stressed in sociological literature and often seen as closely related to the degree of social differentiation and specialization, is that of the regulation of intrasocietal and intergroup relations, of dealing with so-called integrative problems which tend to rise out of a growing complexity of the social division of labor.

A fifth component of center building or center formation is that of the regulation of internal and external force, or power relations. Paradoxically enough, the importance of sheer force or power in its coercive aspects in the internal, and especially in the systemic external, relations of a system has not been dealt with in political sociology in a manner that is systematic or sufficiently differentiated.[53] They have been either neglected or overexaggerated. Truly enough, the regulation of force has always been envisaged as a basic component of any political system; but in most cases this element has been either treated as the basic, predominant component of any political system or conceived as a problem with which each system has to deal, as an "obstacle" to be overcome, or at most as a means for the implementation of the basic goals of the polity.

To be sure, all these elements or components of the center have been recognized, of course, as a basic constituent of political activity or as closely related to it; but as we have already noted above, their systematic interrelations, in general analytical and in comparative terms alike, have not been fully explored. This has been due in no small degree to the ambivalent attitude in sociological thought toward the concept of force and power, which we have noted above, as well as to the strong emphasis on the dichotomy between state and society which has dominated so much of this thought, as we have also seen.

By viewing, in the preceding analysis, each of these elements as basic components of center building or center formation engendering a special type of relation to the broader social and cultural order and dealing with specific organizational problems, we may advance our understanding of the dynamics of social and political systems.

We find, then, that each of these elements or components of the center is related first to various institutional problems and second to the orientations to the charismatic with which a center has to deal—but to different degrees and in different ways. Further, this analysis also indicates that while each of these components may exist in every center, they may vary in their relative importance in the constitution of the different centers. But at least some of these components exist in every center and are activated by the center in order to establish the basic, exclusive framework of the social, cultural, or political order which the center represents and molds.

This analysis may also throw some additional light on the nature of the tension inherent in the political, social, and cultural centers and orders. It shows that this tension is due not only to the antithesis, often stressed in Western thought, between organization and exercise of power and participation in the maintenance of broad sociocultural order—although this antithesis may, indeed, constitute an important basis of the tension. Beyond this, tension is also inherent, first, in the fact that the charismatic qualities of social order and the quest for participation in them are not, as we have seen above, focused or centered in only one institutional sphere but are dispersed, albeit differentially, in all institutional spheres.

This in itself tends to explain to some extent the existence of a plurality of authorities in any society, with the "natural" predilection of the holders of political power to attempt to monopolize centrality and to regulate it, and also their ultimate inability to do so.

Second, this tension is also due to the fact that each center—political, cultural, or societal—is composed, albeit in different degrees, of the different components enumerated above, each of which may have different relations to the charismatic dimension of social order and may have to deal with different institutional or organizational problems.

The recognition of the multiple roots of such tensions also brings out the importance of another distinction which has been largely neglected in modern political sociology; namely, that between "strong" and "weak" centers. A weak center is one which, while performing its own technical tasks (such as, external political and administrative activities of the political center or the ritual and theological activities of a religious center), has but little autonomous interrelationships with other centers or symbolic orders of social life and has little access to or control over them. Such a center cannot derive strength and legitimation from the other centers or orders of social and cultural life, nor does it perform very adequately some of its potential charismatic ordering and legitimizing functions. Hence, it commands only a minimal commitment beyond its own limited sphere, and sometimes not even within it. Its relations with other centers or with broader social groups and strata are mostly purely adaptive (as, for instance, in the case of many nomad conquerors in relation to the religious organizations of the conquered people); and such a center may symbolically and perhaps even organizationally become totally submerged in them, as was, for instance, the case of some of the Southeast Asian religious centers which were almost entirely submerged in the political ones.

In contrast to this, a "strong" center is one which enjoys access to other centers and can derive its legitimation from them—either by monopolizing and controlling them or by some more autonomous interdependence with them—and can accordingly command some commitment both within, but also beyond, its own specific spheres.

XVIII

The emphasis on the existence of a great variety of components of centers and the ensuing great variety of relations between the political and the charismatic and on the distinction between strong and weak centers enables us to go, to some degree, at least, beyond the specific Western tradition of political sociology. This tradition has tended to take the existence of strong centers for granted and to assume that within all centers all components of center formation exist in a certain given order or fixed co-operative or antithetic relations among them. It has tended especially to emphasize the importance in any center of the regulation both of intergroup relations and of force on the one hand and of a close relation to the charismatic symbols of the social and cultural orders on the other.

However, the preceding analysis indicates that in many political systems the affinity of the political institutions to charismatic "centrality" may be rather small, and, instead, either some other components of the center may be predominant or the combinations among such components may be rather weak or tenuous. Moreover, the preceding reformulation of the problems of political sociology poses very sharply the problem of how centers may emerge— what are the conditions under which viable centers, and especially different types of centers in terms of the relative importance of their components, may emerge. As we have seen, this problem is of special relevance with regard to the development of the New States, where indeed one central problem is that of the new viable centers and of their very development, while another is that centers may develop in which only some components in the centers may develop. But, as we shall see in greater detail later, the same problems are also relevant for the analysis of many historical settings.

XIX

The exploration of the relations among the political and the varieties of centrality and authority, which has been presented above, enables a reformulation of many of the central questions of political sociology, especially on the problems of legitimation of political systems, of the quest for participation in the political sphere, and on the process for selection of political elites.

First, the preceding analysis, paradoxically enough, both broadens and narrows the nature and scope of the importance of such legitimation for the functioning of political systems. On the other hand, it broadens the scope of legitimation and makes it encompass a much wider realm of components. It makes it less dependent, as it was often formulated in Western thought, either on the efficiency of a political system in terms of the regulation of intergroup relations or

on its affinity to some conceptions of broader social and cultural orders; and it broadens the scope of the criteria of legitimation to any of the components of center building outlined above. But at the same time it also potentially limits the importance of legitimation in terms of any of these components of center formation for the continuity of political orders. Or rather, instead of treating the relation between legitimation in terms of any such component and the affinity of a system as a postulate, and the continuity of a political system as a postulate, it makes these relations into a variable.

As the problem of the legitimation of political systems has been very closely related to the assumption that the stability or continuity of a political system is dependent on the consensus about its legitimation, the preceding analysis also indicates some necessary steps in the reformulation of the place of consensus in the functioning of political systems.

First, it indicates that it is necessary to see what is the scope and basis of consensus; that is, to what extent any given political system is indeed viewed by those who participate in it as "acceptable" in terms either of organizational "efficiency" of some broader charismatic orientations and of its centrality for them, or in terms of any other component of center building. Second is the problem of the differential acceptance or evaluation of any polity by the different participants in the system. And last is the problem of the different levels of consensus on the stability, continuity, and potentialities for change in any given political system.

A similar reformulation is necessitated with regard to several additional central problems of political sociology; namely, with regard to the nature of political participation and struggle and the selection of elites. The preceding analysis indicates that the usual exposition of the quest for participation in the political sphere, and hence also for political struggle, as a quest for participation in the distribution of power and in "authoritative" decisions about the distribution of values and facilities in society, is only partially true. Given the close relation between authority and centrality and its different components, the quest for participation in the political can be seen not only as a quest for the enjoyment of power in the narrow organizational sense of this term, but also as participation, either in the central spheres of the society and the broader meaningful order, which this centrality and its charisma represent, or in some of the organizational or institutional derivatives of other components of the center.

Hence, the selection of political elites is to be viewed not only in terms of pure efficiency or of power struggle but also in terms of other components, be they the ability of the elites to reorder and reorganize both the symbolic and cognitive order which is potentially inherent in such broader orientations and in the institutional order in which these orientations become embodied, or any other of the components of the centers.

Different elites tend to stress or to combine in different ways some of the basic elements or components of center formation. And the investigation of the conditions under which different types of elites may indeed arise constitutes one of the most difficult problems of political sociology.

XX

Perhaps the most important reorientation that can be derived from the preceding reformulation of the relation between the various aspects of consensus and the sources of legitimation of the political systems relates to the changeability and transformability of political systems.

Probably none of the components of center formation constitutes a necessary focus of stability or of continuity of the system. While this has been amply illustrated or taken for granted for such elements as force and power, we can find also in sociology the assumption that common values or symbols of common identity necessarily constitute a focus or condition of such continuity. But the preceding analysis indicates that this need not be the case and that the quest for participation in a meaningful order does not always constitute a focus of consensus. It may easily become a focus of dissension, conflict, and change.

As is well known, many initial assumptions of many sociological analyses of charisma have stressed its disruptive effects, its contribution to the destruction of existing institutions and to social change. The recognition that charismatic activities or symbols also constitute a part or aspect of the ordinary institutional framework does not negate this basic insight: it only enables us to approach the relation between charisma and social change and transformation in a much more differentiated and systematic way. It enables us to see that the very quest for participation in a meaningful order may be related to processes of change and transformation, that it may indeed constitute, at least in certain circumstances, the very focus of processes of social transformation.

Whatever the success of the attempt of any political entrepreneurs to establish and legitimize common norms in terms of common values and symbols, these norms are probably never fully accepted by the entire society. Most groups tend to exhibit some autonomy in terms of their attitudes toward these norms and in terms of their willingness or ability to provide the resources demanded by the given institutionalized system. For very long periods of time, a great majority of the members of a given society or parts thereof may be identified to some degree with the values and norms of the given system and may be willing to provide it with the resources it needs. However, other tendencies also develop.

Some groups may be greatly opposed to the very premises of the institutionalization of a given system, may share its values and symbols only to a very small extent and may accept these norms only as the least among evils and as binding on them only in a very limited sense. Others may share these values and symbols and accept the norms to a greater degree but may look on themselves as the more truthful depositories of these same values. They may oppose the concrete levels at which the symbols are institutionalized by the elite in power and may attempt to interpret them in different ways. Others may develop new interpretations of existing symbols and norms and strive for a change in the very bases of the institutional order. Hence, any institutional system is never fully "homogeneous" in the sense of being fully accepted or accepted to the same degree by all those participating in it, and these different orientations to the central symbolic spheres may all become focuses of conflict and of potential institutional change.

XXI

The reformation of the relations among charisma, center formation, political institutions, and processes may also help us in a re-examination of some of the major attributes of political symbolism, reflection, and philosophy and possibly also of their relations with political sociology. In all cultural traditions the focus of political symbols and thought is on the concern with the relations between the political order and the other types of "charismatic"—cosmic, moral, and social—order and especially with those orders which are conceived, in the tradition of a given society or culture, as the most central and important delineators of its basic cultural and collective identity and as the most important parameters of human existence.

The basic poles of this relation are usually conceived in terms of the mutual symbolic and organizational relevance of these orders, of their legitimation, autonomy, and responsibility. Are the other ("nonpolitical") orders highly relevant to the political one?

And, whatever the degree of their relevance, how are they conceived; and how are these relations perceived and organized?

Is the political order an embodiment of the cosmic, or is it just its appendant subjugated to it, secondary to it? Where is the central symbolic locus of the broader over-all order? Is it in the political or in the cosmic, in the moral or in the religious sphere? What is the relevance of the political dimension for human existence in the cosmos? What is the extent of possible or actual symbolic and organizational autonomy of the various centers in which these different orders are located, and what is the consequent locus of legitimation and accountability of the political order? How are these related to the specific organizational problems of the political organization and roles, to the different components of center formation, and to the organizational exigencies of other social spheres?

A second focus of political symbolism and thought, necessarily connected with the former, is the conception of the relation between the center or centers and the periphery—and of the pattern of participation and access of the "periphery," of the broader groups and strata in the various centers in general and in the political center in particular. This is necessarily very strongly connected with the basic conception and imagery of the political center and of its relation to the other centers, of the political order in its relation to other orders.

Here of especial interest is the relative importance attributed, in any given society, to the different components of centers and the degree to which participation in them, as distinct from participation in other aspects of components of the center, is stressed as important.

The third major focus of any political symbolism and imagery is that of what may be called the pattern of behavior appropriate to rulers and to the ruled—of the good ruler and of the good subject, or citizen. Here two basic problems seem to be outstanding. One is the definition of these reciprocal relations in terms of the basic contents of the predominant order, of the basic nature of the central charismatic symbols of any tradition, and of the ability or willingness of the rulers and ruled alike to abide, in the political sphere, by the precepts of this order.

The second major problem here is the relation between the ideal patterns of behavior of rulers and of the ruled, of their mutual obligations and reciprocal relations as derived from these basic conceptions of the "charismatic" and of its relations to political organizational exigencies and to administrative effi-

ciency. In almost all political philosophies and imageries, the requirements of any of the structural components of a center—whether those of the political game, that is, of the necessity of a ruler to keep a balance between different factions in the society at large or in his private entourage, or of relatively efficient administration—are fully recognized and commented on. But the nature of their relations to the "deeper" levels of good or proper order and political behavior is conceived in different terms in different cultural traditions.

The differences relate to the extent to which any of the components of the center—the technical administrative and the political ("power"), the regulation of intergroup relations, and so on—are seen as important dimensions of human existence and to the extent to which one of them is seen as symbolically more predominant and central. In most premodern (and noncity-state) regimes the conception of the relative autonomy of the political order was related to the extent of development of partial secularism, often paradoxically combined, as in India, with the "ritual" or ideological, but not with the organizational, of the "sacred" and with the belittling of the importance of the political dimension of human existence.

But whatever these differences, three areas or problems constitute in most traditions the major focuses around which the interrelations between the "technical" or "organizational" and the more "ideological" or symbolic aspects of the political sphere tend to become crystallized in most political symbols, rituals, and philosophies. First is the conception of the nature of the rules and the norms of political struggle. Second is the conception of the nature and importance of the extent to which the political systems should provide some satisfaction for the broader groups in the society, whether on a material or security level or on a wider "charismatic" one. Third is the problem of the extent to which participation in the political sphere, in any of the components of center, constitutes an important goal in the universe of individuals' goals and desiderata.

In somewhat different paraphrase—to take up Rousseau's terminology—one of the central focuses of political imagery is the conception of the relations between common will and "will of all," of the extent and ways in which there is in the "private" will of different people also a conception of the common good and of the extent to which this common good is conceived in political terms—in terms of participation in the political order.

These problems seem to be common to all cultures, whatever their level of articulation in abstract or "rational" form. Moreover, the most central focus of all these problems usually has been the quest after the "good" political order and the "good" ruler, citizen, or subject. But such goodness has not always, in all the cultures and civilizations of mankind, been conceived in the same manner.

The answers given to these problems, as well as the extent to which these are articulated in highly elaborated and philosophical terms, have greatly varied in different traditions. In this great panorama of different traditions of reflection on political matters, the Western way of posing these problems, and especially answering them, is only one among many.

In this tradition, the philosophical concern with the polity was to no small degree equated with the search for the moral good, defined mostly in what may be called "secular," moral, private, or civic terms. According to this, political good is equated with the moral goodness of individuals, and political behavior is equated with good moral behavior.

However, this formulation of the problem of the relation between the political, cultural, and moral spheres—and especially of the specific answers to this problem—is unique to Western civilization. In many other civilizations private goodness or private morality has been very secondary in the evaluation of the social and political order and of the relations between the two. At most it has been conceived of as the manifestation of some deeper conception of "goodness" or as a goodness of a different kind.

In general the types of answers given to these problems or questions are necessarily very great, and the number of combinations and permutations that are possible is also great, although certainly not limitless.

Among the most important variables that tend to influence the way in which these answers are crystallized were several of the aspects of political institutions and center formation that have been pointed out above: the scope of differentiation and specifically of political organization, the relative predominance of different components of the center, and, of course, the number and nature of the centers or types of order as conceived symbolically in any given society. These are probably the major determinants of the specific answers given to these problems—answers which are to be found in the religious texts on the one hand and in the imagery of the center, be it architectural or pictorial, on the other.

In the following sections we shall attempt to present in a systematic way some of the answers and problems of this relation as it pertains to the actual organization of the political institutions and

activities and to broader social and cultural conditions and traditions.

NOTES

1. For general surveys, see Charles H. McIllwain, *The Growth of Political Thought in the West* (New York: Macmillan, 1932); George H. Sabine, *A History of Political Theory* (3rd ed.; New York: Holt, Rinehart, and Winston, 1961). For further materials, see the bibliography.

2. Ernst Barker, *Greek Political Theory: Plato and His Predecessors* (4th ed.; New York: Barnes and Noble, 1951); Plato, *The Republic of Plato* (New York: Oxford University Press, 1953); Aristotle, *The Politics of Aristotle* (Oxford: Clarendon Press, 1952). For further materials, see the bibliography.

3. On some of the most important differences between these two traditions, see Leo Strauss, "Jerusalem and Athens, Some Introductory Reflections," *Commentary*, XLIII, No. 6 (June 1967), 45–58.

4. R. Levy, *A Mirror for Princes* (London: Cresset, 1951); Rudrapatna Shammasastry, ed., *Kautilya's Arthashastra* (5th ed.; Mysore: Mysore Printing and Publishing House, 1960).

5. Ibn-Khaldun, *The Muqaddimah* (London: Routledge and Kegan Paul, 1958), II, Ch. 3, p. 45, "How disintegration befalls dynasties."

6. John Locke, *Two Treatises of Government* (Cambridge: University Press, 1960); Machiavelli, *The Prince and the Discourses* (New York: Modern Library, 1950); Thomas Hobbes, *Leviathan, or the Matter Form and Power of a Commonwealth, Ecclesiastical and Civil* (Oxford: Blackwell, 1956); Jean J. Rousseau, *The Social Contract* (London: Sonnenschein, 1895); Rousseau, *Political Writings* (New York: Thomas Nelson and Sons, 1953).

7. Edward Gibbon, *The Decline and Fall of the Roman Empire* (New York: Harcourt, Brace, 1960); Giambattista Vico, *Principe d'une science nouvelle relative à la nature commune des nations* (Paris: Nagel, 1953); Charles Montesquieu, *The Spirit of the Laws* (New York: Hafner, 1949); Adam Ferguson, *An Essay on the History of Civil Society* (8th ed.; Philadelphia: A. Finley, 1819). For a new concise presentation of the Scottish moralists, see Louis Schneider, ed., *The Scottish Moralists on Human Nature and Society*, The Heritage of Sociology (Chicago: University of Chicago Press, 1967).

8. Lorenz von Stein, *Staat und Gesellschaft* (Zurich: Rascher, 1934); Alexis de Tocqueville, *Democracy in America* (New York: Knopf, 1954); De Tocqueville, *L'ancien régime et la Révolution*, trans. N. W. Patterson (Oxford: Basil Blackwell, 1937); Karl Marx, *The Communist Manifesto*, English translation (Chicago: C. H. Kerr, 1888); Marx, *Capital* (New York: Modern Library, 1936); Herbert Spencer, *Essays: Moral, Political and Aesthetic* (New York: Appleton, 1871); Vilfredo Pareto, *The Mind and Society* (London: J. Cape, 1935); Émile Durkheim, *Professional Ethics and Civic Morals* (London: Routledge and Kegan Paul, 1957); Max Weber, *The Theory of Social and Economic Organization* (New York: Oxford University Press, 1947); Karl Mannheim, *Ideology and Utopia* (London: Routledge and Kegan Paul, 1936); Mannheim, *Man and Society in an Age of Reconstruction* (London: Kegan Paul, 1940).

9. Hobbes, *op. cit.*; Rousseau, *The Social Contract*; Rousseau, *Political Writings*; Locke, *Two Treatises of Government*, notes 1 and 6.

10. Ferguson, *op. cit.*; Adam Smith, *The Works of Adam Smith* (Aalen, Netherlands: Zeller, 1963); and Schneider, *The Scottish Moralists*.

11. Edward Shils, "The Calling of Sociology," in Talcott Parsons *et al.*, eds., *Theories of Society* (New York: The Free Press, 1965), II, 1419.

12. Ferguson, *op. cit.*

13. Edward B. Tylor, *Anthropology—An Introduction to the Study of Man and Civilization* (London: Watts, 1946); and for a general history of anthropology as related to these problems, see R. Lowie, *History of Ethnological Theory* (New York: Holt, Rinehart and Winston, 1937).

14. See on this in greater detail Talcott Parsons, "Unity and Diversity in a Modern Intellectual Discipline. The Role of the Social Science," *Daedalus*, XCIV, No. 1 (Winter 1965).

15. Gaetano Mosca, *The Ruling Class* (New York: McGraw-Hill, 1939).

16. Karl Mannheim, *Man and Society in an Age of Reconstruction* (London: Routledge and Kegan Paul, 1940); Eduard Heimann, *Communism, Fascism or Democracy?* (New York: Norton, 1938); Heimann, *Freedom and Order: Lessons from the War* (New York: Scribner, 1947).

17. Carl Schmitt, "The Concept of 'The Political,'" *Archiv für Sozialpolitik*, Vol. LVIII (September 1927).

18. V. I. Lenin, *The State and Revolution* (New York: International Publishers, 1932); Joseph Stalin, *Foundations of Leninism* (New York: International Publishers, 1932).

19. See B. Crick, *Freedom as Politics* (Sheffield: Sheffield University Press, 1966).

20. See S. N. Eisenstadt, "Bureaucracy, Bureaucratization and Debureaucratization," *Administrative Science Quarterly*, IV, No. 3 (December 1959), 302–320.

21. M. Weber, "Bureaucracy," in H. H. Gerth and C. Wright Mills, eds., *Essays in Sociology* (London: Kegan Paul, Trench, Trubner and Co., 1947), pp. 196–266; R. Michels, *Political Parties* (Glencoe: The Free Press, 1949); Mosca, *op. cit.* For further indications, see the bibliography.

22. Weber, "Bureaucracy"; Marx, *Capital;* Werner Sombart, *Der Moderne Kapitalismus* (Munich: Duncker, 1926–1928; Sombart, *Socialism and the Social Movement in the 19th Century* (New York: Putnam, 1898).

23. Mosca, *op. cit.*

24. Carl J. Friedrich, *Man and His Government: An Empirical Theory of Politics* (New York: McGraw-Hill, 1963); Herman Finer, *The Theory and Practice of Modern Government* (London: Methuen, 1958).

25. Karl Mannheim, *Freedom, Power and Democratic Planning* (London: Routledge and Kegan Paul, 1951).

26. Weber, "Bureaucracy."

27. Seymour M. Lipset, "Social Class," *International Encyclopaedia of the Social Sciences*, David Sills, ed., V (New York: The Free Press and The Macmillan Co., 1968), pp. 296–316.

28. William Kornhauser, *The Politics of Mass Society* (Glencoe: The Free Press, 1959); Emil Lederer, *State of the Masses* (New York: Norton, 1940); Edward A. Shils, "The Theory of Mass Society," *Diogenes*, Vol. XXXIX.

29. Pareto, *The Mind and Society;* Mosca, *The Ruling Class.*

30. Weber, *The Theory of Social and Economic Organization;* Weber, *The Protestant Ethic and the Spirit of Capitalism*, trans. T. Parsons (New York: Oxford University Press, 1930); Weber, *The Sociology of Religion*, trans. Ephraim Fischoff (Boston: Beacon Press, 1964); Weber, *The Religion of China*, trans. and ed. by H. H. Gerth (Glencoe: The Free Press, 1951); Weber, *Ancient Judaism*, trans. and ed. by H. H. Gerth and Don Martindale (Glencoe: The Free Press, 1952); Weber, *The Religion of India*, trans. and ed. by H. H. Gerth and Don Martindale (Glencoe: The Free Press, 1958).

31. Joseph A. Schumpeter, *Capitalism, Socialism and Democracy* (New York: Harper, 1947); Mannheim, *Freedom, Power and Democratic Planning;* Mannheim, *Man and Society in an Age of Reconstruction;* Harold D. Lasswell, *Politics: Who Gets What, When, How* (New York: Meridian, 1958); Raymond Aron, "Social Structure and the Ruling Class," *British Journal of Sociology*, I, No. 1 (March 1950), 1–16; I, No. 2 (June 1950), 124–143; Aron, *L'Age des empires et l'avenir de la France* (Paris: Editions Défense de la France, 1946); Aron, *Industrial Society* (New York: Basic Books, 1967).

32. M. Ostrogorski, *Democracy and the Party System in the United States* (New York: Macmillan, 1910); R. Michels, *Political Parties, a Sociological Study of the Oligarchical Tendencies of Modern Democracy* (Glencoe: The Free Press, 1958); Maurice Duverger, *Political Parties, Their Organization and Activity in the Modern State* (London: Methuen, 1964).

33. Carl Friedrich, *Constitutional Government and Democracy Theory and Practice in Europe and America* (Boston: Ginn, 1950); Friedrich, *Constitutional Government and Politics: Nature and Development* (New York: Harper, 1937).

34. James G. March and Herbert A. Simon, *Organizations* (New York: Wiley, 1958); Morton A. Kaplan, *System and Process in International Politics* (New York: Wiley, 1957).

35. Robert R. Alford, *Party and Society* (Chicago: Rand McNally, 1963); Bernard Berelson and M. Janowitz, eds., *Reader in Public Opinion and Communication* (Glencoe: The Free Press, 1953); Bernard Berelson *et al., Voting* (Chicago: University of Chicago Press, 1954); Angus Campbell and H. Cooper, *Group Difference in Attitudes and Votes* (Ann Arbor: Survey Research Center, 1956); Heinz Eulau, "Identification with Class and Political Perspectives," *Journal of Politics*, XVIII (May 1956), 232–253; Robert E. Lane, *Political Ideology* (New York: The Free Press, 1962); Paul Lazarsfeld *et al., The People's Choice* (New York: Columbia University Press, 1948); Clinton Rossiter, *Parties and Politics in America* (Ithaca: Cornell University Press, 1960); and also, especially for the relation between political behavior and ideology, see Robert E. Lane, "The Decline of Politics and Ideology in a Knowledgeable Society," *American Sociological Review*, XXXI, No. 5 (October 1966), 649–662; and H. McClosky, "Consensus and Ideology in American Politics," *American Political Science Review*, LVIII, No. 2 (June 1964).

36. Talcott Parsons, *Sociological Theory and Modern Society* (New York: The Free Press, 1967); Seymour M. Lipset, "Some Requisites of Democracy: Economic Development and Political Legitimacy," *American Political Science Review*, LIII, No. 1 (March 1959), 86–100, Lipset, *Political Man* (New York: Doubleday, 1963); R. Bendix, *Nation Building and Citizenship* (New York: Wiley, 1964); Stein Rokkan, "The Structure of Mass Politics in the Smaller European Democracies—A Developmental Typology," paper presented at the Seventh World Congress of Political Science, September 1967; S. M. Lipset and S. Rokkan, "Cleavage Structures, Party Systems and Voter Alignments," in Lipset and Rokkan, eds., *Party Systems and Voter Alignments* (New York: The Free Press, 1967); Robert Dahl, *Political Opposition in Western Democracies* (New Haven: Yale University Press, 1966).

37. In the anthropologic framework, the classic study is M. Fortes and E. E. Evans-Pritchard, eds., *African Political Systems* (London: Oxford University Press, 1961). See also Ronald Cohen, ed., *Comparative Political Systems* (Garden City, N.Y.: Natural History Press, 1967). For best approaches in comparative history, see Marc Bloch, *Feudal Society* (Chicago: University of Chicago Press, 1961). For illustrations of developments in these fields, see especially the following periodicals: *Annales, économies, sociétés, civilizationes, Comparative Studies in Society and Past and Present.*

38. See Lipset, *Political Man*, and Juan Linz, "An Authoritarian Régime: Spain," in E. Allardt and Y. Littunen, eds., *Cleavages, Ideologies and Party Systems*, Transactions of the Westermark Society (Helsinki: Academic Bookstore, 1964), X, 293–341.

39. Stein Rokkan, "Electoral Systems," *International Encyclopaedia of the Social Sciences*, V, 6–21.

40. Taken from S. N. Eisenstadt, *The Political Systems of Empires* (Glencoe: The Free Press, 1963), Ch. I.

41. J. M. Roberts and G. Almond, "The Political Process in Primitive Societies," mimeographed (Stanford, California).

42. See, in greater detail, Eisenstadt, *The Political System of Empires.*

43. Talcott Parsons, "Evolutionary Universals in Society," *American Sociological Review,* XXIX, No. 3 (June 1964), 339–357; Robert N. Bellah, "Religious Evolution," *ibid.,* pp. 358–374; S. N. Eisenstadt, "Social Change, Differentiation and Evolution," *ibid.,* pp. 375–385. See also Talcott Parsons, *Societies in Comparative and Evolutionary Perspectives* (Englewood Cliffs: Prentice-Hall, 1966).

44. Ali A. Mazrui, "Edmund Burke and Reflections on the Revolution in the Congo," in S. Thrupp, ed., *Comparative Studies in Society and History,* V (1962–1963), 121–133.

45. Carl G. Rosberg and William H. Friedland, eds., *African Socialism* (Stanford: Stanford University Press, 1964).

46. See Bendix, *op. cit.,* as well as some of the recent discussions of the social aspects of Marx's work, such as those of George Lichtheim, Marx and the Asiatic Mode of Production, St. Anthony's Papers No. 14 (1963); Daniel Thorner, "Marx on India and the Asiatic Mode of Production," *Contributions to Indian Sociology,* No. 9 (December 1966), pp. 3–66, which contains a full bibliography of this controversy; F. Tokei, *Sur le Mode de Production Asiatique,*

Studia Historica Academiae Scientiarum Hungaricae (Budapest; Akadémiai Kiadó, 1966).

47. See Talcott Parsons, "On the Concept of Political Power," *Proceedings of the American Philosophical Society* (1963), pp. 236–258.

48. Talcott Parsons, "Culture and the Social System: Introduction," in Parsons *et al., Theories of Society,* II (New York: The Free Press, 1965), 963–993; S. N. Eisenstadt, "Development of Sociological Thought," *International Encyclopaedia of the Social Sciences,* XV, 23–36.

49. From Edward A. Shils, "Charisma, Order and Status," *American Sociological Review,* XXX (April 1965), 199–213.

50. Edward Shils, "Centre and Periphery," in *The Logic of Personal Knowledge,* essays presented to Michael Polanyi (London: Routledge and Kegan Paul, 1961), pp. 117–131.

51. See on this, in greater detail, S. N. Eisenstadt, ed., "On Charisma and Institution-building," introduction to the Heritage of Sociology Series (Chicago: University of Chicago Press, 1968).

52. Émile Durkheim, *On the Division of Labour in Society* (Glencoe: The Free Press, 1947), pp. 174–190.

53. For one of the few important exceptions, see Talcott Parsons, "Some Reflections on the Place of Force in Social Process," in his *Sociological Theory and Modern Society* (New York: The Free Press, 1967) pp. 266–297.

INTRODUCTION TO THE READINGS

The following selections have been chosen to represent the development of political sociology. The selections range from classical forerunners through the first modern examples and up to the most recent developments.

1

The Politics

Aristotle

In common use they define a citizen to be one who is sprung from citizens on both sides, not on the father's or the mother's only. Others carry the matter still further, and inquire how many of his ancestors have been citizens, as his grandfather, great-grandfather, etc., but some persons have questioned how the first of the family could prove themselves citizens, according to this popular and careless definition. Gorgias of Leontium, partly entertaining the same doubt, and partly in jest, says, that as a mortar

is made by a mortar-maker, so a citizen is made by a citizen-maker, and a Larissæan by a Larissæan-maker. This is indeed a very simple account of the matter; for if citizens are so, according to this definition, it will be impossible to apply it to the first founders or first inhabitants of states, who cannot possibly claim in right either of their father or mother. It is probably a matter of still more difficulty to determine their rights as citizens who are admitted to their freedom after any revolution in the state. As, for instance, at Athens, after the expulsion of the tyrants, when Clisthenes enrolled many foreigners and city-slaves amongst the tribes; and the

From *The Politics of Aristotle,* trans. William Allis (Oxford: Clarendon Press, 1952), pp. 14–15. Reprinted by permission of the Clarendon Press.

doubt with respect to them was, not whether they were citizens or no, but whether they were legally so or not. Though indeed some persons may have this further doubt, whether a citizen can be a citizen when he is illegally made; as if an illegal citizen, and one who is no citizen at all, were in the same predicament: but since we see some persons govern unjustly, whom yet we admit to govern, though not justly, and the definition of a citizen is one who exercises certain offices, for such a one we have defined a citizen to be, it is evident, that a citizen illegally created yet continues to be a citizen, but whether justly or unjustly so belongs to the former inquiry.

We ought not to define a democracy as some do, who say simply, that it is a government where the supreme power is lodged in the people; for even in oligarchies the supreme power is in the majority. Nor should they define an oligarchy a government where the supreme power is in the hands of a few: for let us suppose the number of a people to be thirteen hundred, and that of these one thousand were rich, who would not permit the three hundred poor to have any share in the government, although they were free, and their equal in everything else; no one would say, that this government was a democracy. In like manner, if the poor, when few in number, should acquire the power over the rich, though more than themselves, no one would say, that this was an oligarchy; nor this, when the rest who are rich have no share in the administration. We should rather say, that a democracy is when the supreme power is in the hands of the freemen; an oligarchy, when it is in the hands of the rich: it happens indeed that in the one case the many will possess it, in the other the few; because there are many poor and few rich. And if the power of the state was to be distributed according to the size of the citizens, as they say it is in Æthiopia, or according to their beauty, it would be an oligarchy: for the number of those who are large and beautiful is small.

Nor are those things which we have already mentioned alone sufficient to describe these states; for since there are many species both of a democracy and an oligarchy, the matter requires further consideration; as we cannot admit, that if a few persons who are free possess the supreme power over the many who are not free, that this government is a democracy: as in Apollonia, in Ionia, and in Thera: for in each of these cities the honours of the state belong to some few particular families, who first founded the colonies. Nor would the rich, because they are superior in numbers, form a democracy, as formerly at Colophon; for there the majority had

large possessions before the Lydian war: but a democracy is a state where the freemen and the poor, being the majority, are invested with the power of the state. An oligarchy is a state where the rich and those of noble families, being few, possess it.

We have now proved that there are various forms of government and have assigned a reason for it; and shall proceed to show that there are even more than these, and what they are, and why; setting out with the principle we have already laid down. We admit that every city consists not of one, but many parts: thus, if we should endeavour to comprehend the different species of animals we should first of all note those parts which every animal must have, as a certain sensorium, and also what is necessary to acquire and retain food, as a mouth and a belly; besides certain parts to enable it to move from place to place. If, then, these are the only parts of an animal and there are differences between them; namely, in their various sorts of stomachs, bellies, and sensoriums: to which we must add their motive powers; the number of the combinations of all these must necessarily make up the different species of animals. For it is not possible that the same kind of animal should have any very great difference in its mouth or ears; so that when all these are collected, who happen to have these things similar in all, they make up a species of animals of which there are as many as there are of these general combinations of necessary parts.

The same thing is true of what are called states; for a city is not made of one but many parts, as has already been often said; one of which is those who supply it with provisions, called husbandmen, another called mechanics, whose employment is in the manual arts, without which the city could not be inhabited; of these some are busied about what is absolutely necessary, others in what contribute to the elegancies and pleasures of life; the third sort are your exchange-men, I mean by these your buyers, sellers, merchants, and victuallers; the fourth are your hired labourers or workmen; the fifth are the men-at-arms, a rank not less useful than the other, without [whom] you would have the community slaves to every invader; but what cannot defend itself is unworthy of the name of a city; for a city is self-sufficient, a slave not. So that when Socrates, in Plato's *Republic*, says that a city is necessarily composed of four sorts of people, he speaks elegantly but not correctly, and these are, according to him, weavers, husbandmen, shoe-makers, and builders; he then adds, as if these were not sufficient, smiths, herdsmen for what cattle are necessary, and also merchants and victuallers, and these are by way of appendix to his first list; as if a city was established for necessity, and not happiness, or as if a shoemaker and a husbandman were equally useful. He reckons not the military a part before the increase of territory and joining to the borders of the neighbouring powers will make war necessary: and even amongst them who compose his four divisions, or whoever have any connection with each other, it will be necessary to have some one to distribute justice, and determine between man and man. If, then, the mind is a more valuable part of man than the body, every one would wish to have those things more regarded in his city which tend to the advantage of these than common matters, such are war and justice; to which may be added council, which is the business of civil wisdom (nor is it of any consequence whether these different employments are filled by different persons or one, as the same man is oftentimes both a soldier and a husbandman) : so that if both the judge and the senator are parts of the city, it necessarily follows that the soldier must be so also. The seventh sort are those who serve the public in expensive employments at their own charge: these are called the rich. The eighth are those who execute the different offices of the state, and without these it could not possibly subsist: it is therefore necessary that there should be some persons capable of governing and filling the places in the city; and this either for life or in rotation: the office of senator, and judge, of which we have already sufficiently treated, are the only ones remaining. If, then, these things are necessary for a state, that it may be happy and just, it follows that the citizens who engage in public affairs should be men of abilities therein. Several persons think, that different employments may be allotted to the same person; as a soldier's, a husbandman's, and an artificer's; as also that others may be both senators and judges.

Besides, every one supposes himself a man of political abilities, and that he is qualified for almost every department in the state. But the same person cannot at once be poor and rich: for which reason the most obvious division of the city is into two parts, the poor and rich; moreover, since for the generality the one are few, the other many, they seem of all the parts of a city most contrary to each other; so that as the one or the other prevail they form different states; and these are the democracy and the oligarchy.

But that there are many different states, and from what causes they arise, has been already mentioned: and that there are also different species both of democracies and oligarchies we will now show. Though this indeed is evident from what we have already

said: there are also many different sorts of common people, and also of those who are called gentlemen. Of the different sorts of the first are husbandmen, artificers, exchange-men, who are employed in buying and selling, seamen, of which some are engaged in war, some in traffic, some in carrying goods and passengers from place to place, others in fishing, and of each of these there are often many, as fishermen at Tarentum and Byzantium, masters of galleys at Athens, merchants at Ægina and Chios, those who let ships on freight at Tenedos; we may add to these those who live by their manual labour and have but little property; so that they cannot live without some employ: and also those who are not free-born on both sides, and whatever other sort of common people there may be. As for gentlemen, they are such as are distinguished either by their fortune, their birth, their abilities, or their education, or any such-like excellence which is attributed to them.

The most pure democracy is that which is so called principally from that equality which prevails in it: for this is what the law in that state directs; that the poor shall be in no greater subjection than the rich; nor that the supreme power shall be lodged with either of these, but that both shall share it. For if liberty and equality, as some persons suppose, are chiefly to be found in a democracy, it must be most so by every department of government being alike open to all; but as the people are the majority, and what they vote is law, it follows that such a state must be a democracy. This, then, is one species thereof. Another is, when the magistrates are elected by a certain census; but this should be but small, and every one who was included in it should be eligible, but as soon as he was below it should lose that right. Another sort is, in which every citizen who is not infamous has a share in the government, but where the government is in the laws. Another, where every citizen without exception has this right. Another is like these in other particulars, but there the people govern, and not the law: and this takes place when everything is determined by a majority of votes, and not by a law; which happens when the people are influenced by the demagogues: for where a democracy is governed by stated laws there is no room for them, but men of worth fill the first offices in the state: but where the power is not vested in the laws, there demagogues abound: for there the people rule with kingly power: the whole composing one body; for they are supreme, not as individuals but in their collective capacity.

Homer also discommends the government of many; but whether he means this we are speaking of, or where each person exercises his power separately, is uncertain. When the people possess this power they desire to be altogether absolute, that they may not be under the control of the law, and this is the time when flatterers are held in repute. Nor is there any difference between such a people and monarchs in a tyranny: for their manners are the same, and they both hold a despotic power over better persons than themselves. For their decrees are like the others' edicts; their demagogues like the others' flatterers: but their greatest resemblance consists in the mutual support they give to each other, the flatterer to the tyrant, the demagogue to the people: and to them it is owing that the supreme power is lodged in the votes of the people, and not in the laws; for they bring everything before them, as their influence is owing to their being supreme whose opinions they entirely direct; for these are they whom the multitude obey. Besides, those who accuse the magistrates in-

sist upon it, that the right of determining on their conduct lies in the people, who gladly receive their complaints as the means of destroying all their offices.

Any one, therefore, may with great justice blame such a government as being a democracy, and not a free state; for where the government is not in the laws, then there is no free state, for the law ought to be supreme over all things; and particular incidents which arise should be determined by the magistrates or the state. If, therefore, a democracy is to be reckoned a free state, it is evident that any such establishment which centres all power in the votes of the people cannot, properly speaking, be a democracy: for their decrees cannot be general in their extent. Thus, then, we may describe the several species of democracies.

2

The Muqaddimah

Ibn-Khaldun

How Disintegration Befalls Dynasties

It should be known that any royal authority must be built upon two foundations. The first is might and group feeling, which finds its expression in soldiers. The second is money, which supports the soldiers and provides the whole structure needed by royal authority. Disintegration befalls the dynasty at these two foundations.

We shall mention first the disintegration that comes about through might and group feeling, and then, we shall come back and discuss the one that comes about through money and taxation.

It should be known that, as we have stated, the dynasty can be founded and established only with the help of group feeling. There must be a major group feeling uniting all the group feelings subordi-

From Ibn-Khaldun, *The Muqaddimah,* trans. Franz Rosenthal (London: Routledge and Kegan Paul, 1958), Volume 2, Chapter 3, §45, pp. 118–124; §47, pp. 128–130. Bollingen Series XLIII, Pantheon Books. Copyright 1958 by Bollingen Foundation, New York. Reprinted by permission of the publishers and the Bollingen Foundation.

nate to it. This (major group feeling) is the family and tribal group feeling peculiar to the ruler.

When the natural luxury of royal authority makes its appearance in the dynasty, and when the people who share in the group feeling of the dynasty are humiliated, the first to be humiliated are the members of the ruler's family and his relatives who share with him in the royal name. They are much more humiliated than anyone else. Moreover, luxury has a greater hold on them than on anyone else, because they have a share in royal authority, power, and superiority. Thus, two agents of destruction surround them, luxury and force. (The use of) force eventually leads to their being killed. They become sick at heart[1] when they see the ruler firmly established in royal authority. His envy of them then changes to fear for his royal authority. Therefore, he starts to kill and humiliate them and to deprive them of the prosperity and luxury to which they had become in large measure accustomed. They perish, and become few in number. The group feeling that the ruler had through them is destroyed.

(That group feeling) was the major group feeling, which united all the other groups and subordinated them to itself. It dissolves and its grip weakens. Its place is taken by the inner circle of clients and followers who enjoy the favors and benefactions of the ruler. A (new) group feeling is derived from them. However, (this new group feeling) does not have anything like the powerful grip (of the other group feeling), because it lacks direct and close blood relationships. We have mentioned before that the importance and strength of a group feeling results from close and direct blood relationships, because God made it that way.

The ruler thus isolates himself from his family and helpers, those who have natural affection (for him). This (in turn) is sensed by the people of other groups. Very naturally, they become audacious vis-à-vis the ruler and his inner circle. Therefore, the ruler destroys them and persecutes and kills them, one after the other. The later people of the dynasty follow the tradition of the former in that respect. In addition, they are exposed to the detrimental effect of luxury that we have mentioned before. Thus, destruction comes upon them through luxury and through being killed. Eventually, they no longer have the coloring of (their) group feeling. They forget the affection and strength that (used to) go with it. They become hirelings for the military protection (of the dynasty). They thus become few in number. As a consequence, the militia settled in the remote and frontier regions becomes numerically weak. This, then, emboldens the subjects in the remote regions to abandon the cause (of the dynasty) there. Rebels who are members of the ruling family and other (types of rebels) go out to these remote regions. They hope that under these circumstances, they will be able to reach their goal by obtaining a following among the inhabitants of the remote regions of the realm. (They hope that) they will be secure from capture by the (government) militia. This (process) keeps on and the authority of the ruling dynasty continues gradually to shrink until the rebels reach places extremely close to the center of the dynasty. The dynasty then often splits into two or three dynasties, depending on its original strength, as we have stated. People who do not share in the group feeling of (the dynasty) take charge of its affairs, though they obey the people who do share in the group feeling of (the dynasty) and accept their acknowledged superiority.

This may be exemplified by the Arab Muslim dynasty. At the beginning it reached as far as Spain, India, and China. The Umayyads had complete control of all the Arabs through the group feeling of

'Abd-Manâf. It was even possible for Sulaymân b. 'Abd-al-Malik in Damascus to order the killing of 'Abd-al-'Azîz b. Mûsâ b. Nuṣayr in Córdoba. He was killed, and (Sulaymân's) order was not disobeyed. Then, luxury came to the Umayyads, and their group feeling was wiped out. (The Umayyads) were destroyed, and the 'Abbâsids made their appearance. They curbed[2] the Hâshimites. They killed all the 'Alids (descendants of Abû Tâlib) and exiled them. In consequence, the group feeling of 'Abd-Manâf dissolved and was wiped out. The Arabs grew audacious vis-à-vis (the 'Abbâsids). People in the remote regions of the realm, such as the Aghlabids in Ifrîqiyah and the inhabitants of Spain and others, gained control over them, and the dynasty split. Then, the Idrîsids seceded in the Maghrib. The Berbers supported them, in obedience to their group feeling. Also, they were secure from capture by the soldiers or militiamen of the dynasty.

Men with a cause, for which they make propaganda, eventually secede. They gain control over border areas and remote regions. There, they are able to make propaganda for their cause and achieve royal authority. As a result, the dynasty splits. As the dynasty shrinks more and more, this process often continues until the center is reached. The inner circle, thereafter, weakens, because luxury undermines it. It perishes and dissolves. The whole divided dynasty weakens. Occasionally, it lingers on long after that. (The dynasty) can dispense with group feeling now, because it has colored the souls of its subject people with the habit of subservience and submission for so many long years that no one alive can think back to its beginning and origin. They cannot think of anything except being submissive to the ruler. Therefore, he can dispense with group strength. In order to establish his power, hired soldiers and mercenaries are sufficient. The submissiveness generally found in the human soul helps in this respect. Should anyone think of disobedience or secession—which hardly ever happens—the great mass would disapprove of him and oppose him. Thus, he would not be able to attempt such a thing, even if he should try very hard. In this situation, the dynasty is often more secure (than ever), as far as rebels and rivals are concerned, because the coloring of submissiveness and subservience is firmly established. Individuals would scarcely admit to themselves the least thought of opposition, and the idea of straying from obedience would not enter anybody's mind. (The dynasty), therefore, is safer (than ever) so far as the trouble and destruction that come from groups and tribes are concerned. The dynasty may continue in this condition, but its substance dwindles, like natural heat in a body that lacks nourishment. Eventually, (the dynasty) reaches its destined time. "Each term has a book," and each dynasty has an end. God determines night and day.

As for the disintegration that comes through money, it should be known that at the beginning the dynasty has a desert attitude, as was mentioned before. It has the qualities of kindness to subjects, planned moderation in expenditures, and respect for other people's property. It avoids onerous taxation and the display of cunning or shrewdness in the collection of money and the accounting (required) from officials. Nothing at this time calls for extravagant expenditures. Therefore, the dynasty does not need much money.

Later comes domination and expansion. Royal authority flourishes. This calls for luxury. (Luxury) causes increased spending. The expenditures of the ruler, and of the people of the dynasty in general, grow. This (tendency) spreads to the urban population. It calls for increases in soldiers' allowances and in the salaries of the people of the dynasty. Extravagant expenditures mount. It spreads to the subjects, because people follow the religion (ways) and customs of the dynasty.

The ruler, then, must impose duties on articles sold in the markets, in order to improve his revenues. (He does so,) because he sees the luxury of the urban population testifying to their prosperity, and because he needs the money for the expenditures of his government and the salaries of his soldiers. Habits of luxury, then, further increase. The customs duties no longer pay for them. The dynasty, by this time, is flourishing in its power and its forceful hold over the subjects under its control. Its hand reaches out to seize some of the property of the subjects, either through customs duties, or through commercial transactions, or, in some cases, merely by hostile acts directed against (property holdings), on some pretext or even with none.

At this stage, the soldiers have already grown bold against the dynasty, because it has become weak and senile as far as its group feeling is concerned. (The dynasty) expects that from them, and attempts to remedy and smooth over the situation through generous allowances and much spending for (the soldiers). It cannot get around that.

At this stage, the tax collectors in the dynasty have acquired much wealth, because vast revenues are in their hands and their position has widened in importance for this reason. Suspicions of having appropriated tax money, therefore, attach to them. It becomes common for one tax collector to denounce another, because of their mutual jealousy and envy. One after another is deprived of his money by confiscation and torture. Eventually, their wealth is gone, and they are ruined. The dynasty loses the pomp and magnificence it had possessed through them.

After their prosperity is destroyed, the dynasty goes farther afield and approaches its other wealthy subjects. At this stage, feebleness has already afflicted its (former) might. (The dynasty) has become too weak to retain its power and forceful hold. The policy of the ruler, at this time, is to handle matters diplomatically by spending money. He considers this more advantageous than the sword, which is of little use. His need for money grows beyond what is needed for expenditures and soldiers' salaries. He never gets enough. Senility affects the dynasty more and more. The people of (other) regions grow bold against it.

At each of these stages, the strength of the dynasty crumbles. Eventually, it reaches complete ruin. It is open to domination by (any) aggressor. Anyone who wants to attack it can take it away from those who support it. If this does not occur, it will continue to dwindle and finally disappear—like the wick of a lamp when the oil is exhausted, and it goes out.

God owns all things and governs the whole creation. There is no God but Him. . . .

How a New Dynasty Originates

It should be known that when the ruling dynasty starts on the road to senility and destruction, the rise and beginning of the new dynasty takes place in two ways:

(The one way is) for provincial governors in the dynasty to gain control over remote regions when (the dynasty) loses its influence there. Each one of them founds a new dynasty for his people and a realm to be perpetuated in his family. His children or clients inherit it from him. Gradually, they have a flourishing realm. They often compete bitterly with each other and aspire to gain sole possession of it. The one who is stronger than his rival will gain the upper hand and take away what the other had.

This happened in the 'Abbâsid dynasty when it started on the road to senility and its shadow receded from the remote regions. The Sâmânids gained control over Transoxania, the Ḥamdânids over Mosul and Syria, and the Tûlûnids over Egypt. The same thing happened in the Umayyad dynasty in Spain. Their realm was divided among the *reyes de taïfas* who had been their provincial governors. It was divided into several dynasties with several rulers, who passed their realms on after their death to their relatives or clients. This way of forming a new dynasty avoids the possibility of war between the (new rulers) and the ruling dynasty. (These new rulers) are already firmly established in their leadership and do not want to gain domination over the ruling dynasty. The latter is affected by senility, and its shadow recedes from the remote regions of the realm and can no (longer) reach them.

The other way is for some rebel from among the neighboring nations and tribes to revolt against the dynasty. He either makes propaganda for some particular cause to which he intends to win the people, . . . or he possesses great power and a great group feeling among his people. His power is already flourishing among them, and now he aspires with the help of (his people) to gain royal authority. (His people) are convinced that they will obtain it, because they feel that they are superior to the ruling dynasty, which is affected by senility. Thus, to (the rebel) and his people, it is a fact that they will gain domination over it. They constantly attack it, until they defeat it and inherit its power.

This was the case with the Saljûqs in relation to the descendants of Sebuktigîn, and with the Merinids in the Maghrib in relation to the Almohads.

"God has the power to execute His commands."

NOTES

1. That is, they become unreliable and rebellious [trans.].
2. Literally, "lowered the reins," a phrase which is explained to mean gentling a horse. . . . Here Ibn-Khaldûn was apparently thinking of his theory that a dynasty tends to repress the members of its own family [trans.].

3

The Spirit of the Laws

C. Montesquieu

Book II: Of Laws Directly Derived from the Nature of Government

1. Of the Nature of Three Different Governments

There are three species of government: republican, monarchical, and despotic. In order to discover their nature, it is sufficient to recollect the common notion, which supposes three definitions, or rather three facts: that a republican government is that in which the body, or only a part of the people, is possessed of the supreme power; monarchy, that in which a single person governs by fixed and established laws; a despotic government, that in which a single person directs everything by his own will and caprice.

This is what I call the nature of each government; we must now inquire into those laws which directly conform to this nature, and consequently are the fundamental institutions.

From Charles Montesquieu, *The Spirit of the Laws*, trans. I. Nugent (New York: Hafner Publishing Co., 1949), pp. 8–18. Reprinted by permission of the publisher.

2. Of the Republican Government, and the Laws in Relation to Democracy[1]

When the body of the people is possessed of the supreme power, it is called a democracy. When the supreme power is lodged in the hands of a part of the people, it is then an aristocracy.

In a democracy the people are in some respects the sovereign, and in others the subject.

There can be no exercise of sovereignty but by their suffrages, which are their own will; now, the sovereign's will is the sovereign himself. The laws, therefore, which establish the right of suffrage are fundamental to this government. And indeed it is as important to regulate in a republic, in what manner, by whom, to whom, and concerning what suffrages are to be given, as it is in a monarchy to know who is the prince, and after what manner he ought to govern.

Libanius says that at "Athens a stranger who intermeddled in the assemblies of the people was punished with death." This is because such a man usurped the rights of sovereignty.[2]

It is an essential point to fix the number of citizens

who are to form the public assemblies; otherwise it would be uncertain whether the whole or only a part of the people had given their votes. At Sparta the number was fixed at ten thousand. But Rome, designed by Providence to rise from the weakest beginnings to the highest pitch of grandeur; Rome, doomed to experience all the vicissitudes of fortune; Rome, who had sometimes all her inhabitants without her walls, and sometimes all Italy and a considerable part of the world within them; Rome, I say, never fixed the number; and this was one of the principal causes of her ruin.

The people, in whom the supreme power resides, ought to have the management of everything within their reach: that which exceeds their abilities must be conducted by their ministers.

But they cannot properly be said to have their ministers, without the power of nominating them: it is, therefore, a fundamental maxim in this government, that the people should choose their ministers —that is, their magistrates.

They have occasion, as well as monarchs, and even more so, to be directed by a council or senate. But to have a proper confidence in these, they should have the choosing of the members; whether the election be made by themselves, as at Athens, or by some magistrate deputed for that purpose, as on certain occasions was customary at Rome.[3]

The people are extremely well qualified for choosing those whom they are to intrust with part of their authority. They have only to be determined by things to which they cannot be strangers, and by facts that are obvious to sense. They can tell when a person has fought many battles, and been crowned with success; they are, therefore, capable of electing a general. They can tell when a judge is assiduous in his office, gives general satisfaction, and has never been charged with bribery: this is sufficient for choosing a prætor. They are struck with the magnificence or riches of a fellow-citizen; no more is requisite for electing an edile. These are facts of which they can have better information in a public forum than a monarch in his palace. But are they capable of conducting an intricate affair, of seizing and improving the opportunity and critical moment of action? No; this surpasses their abilities.

Should we doubt the people's natural capacity, in respect to the discernment of merit, we need only cast an eye on the series of surprising elections made by the Athenians and Romans; which no one surely will attribute to hazard.

We know that though the people of Rome assumed the right of raising plebeians to public offices, yet they never would exert this power; and though at Athens the magistrates were allowed, by the law of Aristides, to be elected from all the different classes of inhabitants, there never was a case, says Xenophon,[4] when the common people petitioned for employments which could endanger either their security or their glory.

As most citizens have sufficient ability to choose, though unqualified to be chosen, so the people, though capable of calling others to an account for their administration, are incapable of conducting the administration themselves.

The public business must be carried on with a certain motion, neither too quick nor too slow. But the motion of the people is always either too remiss or too violent. Sometimes with a hundred thousand arms they overturn all before them; and sometimes with a hundred thousand feet they creep like insects.

In a popular state the inhabitants are divided into certain classes. It is in the manner of making this division that great legislators have signalized themselves; and it is on this the duration and prosperity of democracy have ever depended.

The law which determines the manner of giving suffrage is likewise fundamental in a democracy. It is a question of some importance whether the suffrages ought to be public or secret. Cicero observes that the laws[5] which rendered them secret towards the close of the republic were the cause of its decline. But as this is differently practised in different republics, I shall offer here my thoughts concerning this subject.

The people's suffrages ought doubtless to be public;[6] and this should be considered as a fundamental law of democracy. The lower class ought to be directed by those of higher rank, and restrained within bounds by the gravity of eminent personages. Hence, by rendering the suffrages secret in the Roman republic, all was lost; it was no longer possible to direct a populace that sought its own destruction. But when the body of the nobles are to vote in an aristocracy,[7] or in a democracy the senate,[8] as the business is then only to prevent intrigues, the suffrages cannot be too secret.

Intriguing in a senate is dangerous; it is dangerous also in a body of nobles; but not so among the people, whose nature is to act through passion. In countries where they have no share in the government, we often see them as much inflamed on account of an actor as ever they could be for the welfare of the state. The misfortune of a republic is when intrigues are at an end; which happens when the people are gained by bribery and corruption: in this case they grow indifferent to public affairs, and avarice becomes their predominant passion. Unconcerned about the government and everything belonging to it, they quietly wait for their hire.

It is likewise a fundamental law in democracies, that the people should have the sole power to enact laws. And yet there are a thousand occasions on which it is necessary the senate should have the power of decreeing; nay, it is frequently proper to make some trial of a law before it is established. The constitutions of Rome and Athens were excellent—the decrees of the senate had the force of laws for the space of a year, but did not become perpetual till they were ratified by the consent of the people.

3. Of the Laws in Relation to the Nature of Aristocracy

In an aristocracy the supreme power is lodged in the hands of a certain number of persons. These are invested both with the legislative and executive authority; and the rest of the people are, in respect to them, the same as the subjects of a monarchy in regard to the sovereign.

They do not vote here by lot, for this would be productive of inconveniences only. And indeed, in a government where the most mortifying distinctions are already established, though they were to be chosen by lot, still they would not cease to be odious; it is the nobleman they envy, and not the magistrate.

When the nobility are numerous, there must be a senate to regulate the affairs which the body of the nobles are incapable of deciding, and to prepare others for their decision. In this case it may be said that the aristocracy is in some measure in the senate, the democracy in the body of the nobles, and the people are a cipher.

It would be a very happy thing in an aristocracy if the people, in some measure, could be raised from their state of annihilation. Thus at Genoa, the bank of St. George being administered by the people gives them a certain influence in the government, whence their whole prosperity is derived.

The senators ought by no means to have the right of naming their own members; for this would be the only way to perpetuate abuses. At Rome, which in its early years was a kind of aristocracy, the senate did not fill up the vacant places in their own body; the new members were nominated by the censors.[9]

In a republic, the sudden rise of a private citizen to exorbitant power produces monarchy, or something more than monarchy. In the latter the laws have provided for, or in some measure adapted themselves to, the constitution; and the principle of government checks the monarch: but in a republic, where a private citizen has obtained an exorbitant

power,[10] the abuse of this power is much greater, because the laws foresaw it not, and consequently made no provision against it.

There is an exception to this rule, when the constitution is such as to have immediate need of a magistrate invested with extraordinary power. Such was Rome with her dictators, such is Venice with her state inquisitors; these are formidable magistrates, who restore, as it were by violence, the state to its liberty. . . . The best aristocracy is that in which those who have no share in the legislature are so few and inconsiderable that the governing party have no interest in oppressing them. Thus when Antipater made a law at Athens, that whosoever was not worth two thousand drachms should have no power to vote, he formed by this method the best aristocracy possible; because this was so small a sum as to exclude very few, and not one of any rank or consideration in the city.

Aristocratic families ought, therefore, as much as possible, to level themselves in appearance with the people. The more an aristocracy borders on democracy, the nearer it approaches perfection: and, in proportion as it draws towards monarchy, the more is it imperfect.

But the most imperfect of all is that in which the part of the people that obeys is in a state of civil servitude to those who command, as the aristocracy of Poland, where the peasants are slaves to the nobility.

4. Of the Relation of Laws to the Nature of Monarchical Government

The intermediate, subordinate, and dependent powers constitute the nature of monarchical government; I mean of that in which a single person governs by fundamental laws. I said the intermediate, subordinate, and dependent powers. And, indeed, in monarchies the prince is the source of all power, political and civil. These fundamental laws necessarily suppose the intermediate channels through which the power flows: for if there be only the momentary and capricious will of a single person to govern the state, nothing can be fixed, and, of course, there is no fundamental law.

The most natural, intermediate, and subordinate power is that of the nobility. This in some measure seems to be essential to a monarchy, whose fundamental maxim is, no monarch, no nobility; no nobility, no monarch; but there may be a despotic prince.[11]

There are men who have endeavored in some

countries in Europe to suppress the jurisdiction of the nobility, not perceiving that they were driving at the very thing that was done by the Parliament of England. Abolish the privileges of the lords, the clergy and cities in a monarchy, and you will soon have a popular state, or else a despotic government.

The courts of a considerable kingdom in Europe have, for many ages, been striking at the patrimonial jurisdiction of the lords and clergy. We do not pretend to censure these sage magistrates; but we leave it to the public to judge how far this may alter the constitution.

Far am I from being prejudiced in favor of the privileges of the clergy; however, I should be glad if their jurisdiction were once fixed. The question is not, whether their jurisdiction was justly established; but whether it be really established; whether it constitutes a part of the laws of the country, and is in every respect in relation to those two laws: whether between two powers acknowledged independent, the conditions ought not to be reciprocal; and whether it be not equally the duty of a good subject to defend the prerogative of the prince, and to maintain the limits which from time immemorial have been prescribed to his authority.

Though the ecclesiastic power be so dangerous in a republic, yet it is extremely proper in a monarchy, especially of the absolute kind. What would become of Spain and Portugal, since the subversion of their laws, were it not for this only barrier against the incursions of arbitrary power? a barrier ever useful when there is no other: for since a despotic government is productive of the most dreadful calamities to human nature, the very evil that restrains it is beneficial to the subject.

In the same manner as the ocean, threatening to overflow the whole earth, is stopped by weeds and pebbles that lie scattered along the shore,[12] so monarchs, whose power seems unbounded, are restrained by the smallest obstacles, and suffer their natural pride to be subdued by supplication and prayer.

The English, to favor their liberty, have abolished all the intermediate powers of which their monarchy was composed.[13] They have a great deal of reason to be jealous of this liberty; were they ever to be so unhappy as to lose it, they would be one of the most servile nations upon earth.

Mr. Law, through ignorance both of a republican and monarchical constitution, was one of the greatest promoters of absolute power ever known in Europe. Besides the violent and extraordinary changes owing to his direction, he would fain suppress all the intermediate ranks, and abolish the political communities. He was dissolving[14] the monarchy by his chimerical reimbursements, and seemed as if he even wanted to redeem the constitution.

It is not enough to have intermediate powers in a monarchy; there must be also a depositary of the laws. This depositary can only be the judges of the supreme courts of justice, who promulgate the new laws, and revive the obsolete. The natural ignorance of the nobility, their indolence and contempt of civil government, require that there should be a body invested with the power of reviving and executing the laws, which would be otherwise buried in oblivion. The prince's council are not a proper depositary. They are naturally the depositary of the momentary will of the prince, and not of the fundamental laws. Besides, the prince's council is continually changing; it is neither permanent nor numerous; neither has it a sufficient share of the confidence of the people; consequently it is incapable of setting them right in difficult conjunctures, or of reducing them to proper obedience.

Despotic governments, where there are no fundamental laws, have no such kind of depositary. Hence it is that religion has generally so much influence in those countries, because it forms a kind of permanent depositary; and if this cannot be said of religion, it may of the customs that are respected instead of laws.

5. *Of the Laws in Relation to the Nature of a Despotic Government*

From the nature of despotic power it follows that the single person, invested with this power, commits the execution of it also to a single person. A man whom his senses continually inform that he himself is everything and that his subjects are nothing, is naturally lazy, voluptuous, and ignorant. In consequence of this, he neglects the management of public affairs. But were he to commit the administration to many, there would be continual disputes among them; each would form intrigues to be his first slave; and he would be obliged to take the reins into his own hands. It is, therefore, more natural for him to resign it to a vizier,[15] and to invest him with the same power as himself. The creation of a vizier is a fundamental law of this government.

It is related of a pope, that he had started an infinite number of difficulties against his election, from a thorough conviction of his incapacity. At length he was prevailed on to accept of the pontificate, and resigned the administration entirely to his nephew. He was soon struck with surprise, and said, "I should never have thought that these things were so easy." The same may be said of the princes of the East, who, being educated in a prison where eunuchs corrupt their hearts and debase their understandings, and where they are frequently kept ignorant even of their high rank, when drawn forth in order to be placed on the throne, are at first confounded: but as soon as they have chosen a vizier, and abandoned themselves in their seraglio to the most brutal passions, pursuing, in the midst of a prostituted court, every capricious extravagance, they would never have dreamed that they could find matters so easy.

The more extensive the empire, the larger the seraglio; and consequently the more voluptuous the prince. Hence the more nations such a sovereign has to rule, the less he attends to the cares of government; the more important his affairs, the less he makes them the subject of his deliberations.

NOTES

1. Compare Aristotle's "Polit." Book VI. cap. ii., wherein are exposed the fundamental laws of democratic constitutions.—Franz Newman.

2. Libanius himself gives the reason for this law. "It was,"

he avers, "in order to prevent the secrets of the republic from being divulged."—Franz Newman.

3. The Roman senators were invariably chosen by magistrates in whom the people had vested the power.—Crévier.

4. Edit. Wechel, Ann. 1596, pp. 691–692.

5. They were called Leges Tabulares; two tablets were presented to each citizen, the first marked with an A, for "Antiquo," or "I forbid it"; and the other with a U and an R for "Uti Rogas," or "Be it as you desire."

6. At Athens the people used to lift up their hands.

7. As at Venice.

8. The thirty tyrants at Athens ordered the suffrages of the Areopagites to be public, in order to manage them as they pleased.—Lysias, "Orat. contra Agorat.," cap. viii.

9. They were named at first by the consuls.

10. This is what ruined the republic of Rome. See "Considerations on the Causes of the Grandeur and Decline of the Romans."

11. This maxim brings to mind the unfortunate Charles I, who said, "No bishop, no monarchy"; while Henry IV of France declared to the Seize, "No nobility, no monarch!"—Voltaire.

12. Voltaire is inclined to doubt the justice of this comparison.—Franz Newman.

13. On the contrary, the English have tendered the power of their spiritual and temporal lords more legal, and have augmented that of the Commons.—Voltaire.

14. Ferdinand, King of Aragon, made himself grand-master of the orders, and that alone changed the constitution.

15. The Eastern kings are never without viziers, says Sir John Chardin.

4

The Social Contract

J. J. Rousseau

We saw in the last chapter what causes the various kinds or forms of government to be distinguished according to the number of the members composing them: it remains in this to discover how the division is made.

In the first place, the Sovereign may commit the charge of the government to the whole people or to the majority of the people, so that more citizens are magistrates than are mere private individuals. This form of government is called *democracy*.

Or it may restrict the government to a small number, so that there are more private citizens than magistrates; and this is named *aristocracy*.

Lastly, it may concentrate the whole government in the hands of a single magistrate from whom all

others hold their power. This third form is the most usual, and is called *monarchy,* or royal government.

It should be remarked that all these forms, or at least the first two, admit of degree, and even of very wide differences; for democracy may include the whole people, or may be restricted to half. Aristocracy, in its turn, may be restricted indefinitely from half the people down to the smallest possible number. Even royalty is susceptible of a measure of distribution. Sparta always had two kings, as its constitution provided; and the Roman Empire saw as many as eight emperors at once, without its being possible to say that the Empire was split up. Thus there is a point at which each form of government passes into the next, and it becomes clear that, under three comprehensive denominations, government is really susceptible of as many diverse forms as the State has citizens.

Reprinted from J. J. Rousseau, *The Social Contract, Discourses* (London: Sonnenschein, 1895), Book III, Ch. III, pp. 53–54, and Chs. X–XIV, pp. 70–77.

There are even more: for, as the government may also, in certain aspects, be subdivided into other parts, one administered in one fashion and one in another, the combination of the three forms may result in a multitude of mixed forms, each of which admits of multiplication by all the simple forms.

There has been at all times much dispute concerning the best form of government, without consideration of the fact that each is in some cases the best, and in others the worst.

If, in the different States, the number of supreme magistrates should be in inverse ratio to the number of citizens, it follows that, generally, democratic government suits small States, aristocratic government those of middle size, and monarchy great ones. This rule is immediately deducible from the principle laid down. But it is impossible to count the innumerable circumstances which may furnish exceptions. . . .

The Abuse of Government and Its Tendency to Degenerate

As the particular will acts constantly in opposition to the general will, the government continually exerts itself against the Sovereignty. The greater this exertion becomes, the more the constitution changes; and, as there is in this case no other corporate will to create an equilibrium by resisting the will of the prince, sooner or later the prince must inevitably suppress the Sovereign and break the social treaty. This is the unavoidable and inherent defect which, from the very birth of the body politic, tends ceaselessly to destroy it, as age and death end by destroying the human body.

There are two general courses by which government degenerates: i.e. when it undergoes contraction, or when the State is dissolved.

Government undergoes contraction when it passes from the many to the few, that is, from democracy to aristocracy, and from aristocracy to royalty. To do so is its natural propensity.[1] If it took the backward course from the few to the many, it could be said that it was relaxed; but this inverse sequence is impossible.

Indeed, governments never change their form except when their energy is exhausted and leaves them too weak to keep what they have. If a government at once extended its sphere and relaxed its stringency, its force would become absolutely nil, and it would persist still less. It is therefore necessary to wind up the spring and tighten the hold as it gives way: or else the State it sustains will come to grief.

The dissolution of the State may come about in either of two ways.

First, when the prince ceases to administer the State in accordance with the laws, and usurps the Sovereign power. A remarkable change then occurs: not the government, but the State, undergoes contraction; I mean that the great State is dissolved, and another is formed within it, composed solely of the members of the government, which becomes for the rest of the people merely master and tyrant. So that the moment the government usurps the Sovereignty, the social compact is broken, and all private citizens recover by right their natural liberty, and are forced, but not bound, to obey.

The same thing happens when the members of the government severally usurp the power they should exercise only as a body; this is as great an infraction of the laws, and results in even greater disorders. There are then, so to speak, as many princes as there are magistrates, and the State, no less divided than the government, either perishes or changes its form.

When the State is dissolved, the abuse of government, whatever it is, bears the common name of *anarchy*. To distinguish, democracy degenerates into *ochlocracy,* and aristocracy into *oligarchy;* and I would add that royalty degenerates into *tyranny;* but this last word is ambiguous and needs explanation.

In vulgar usage, a tyrant is a king who governs violently and without regard for justice and law. In the exact sense, a tyrant is an individual who arrogates to himself the royal authority without having a right to it. This is how the Greeks understood the word 'tyrant': they applied it indifferently to good and bad princes whose authority was not legitimate.[2] *Tyrant* and *usurper* are thus perfectly synonymous terms.

In order that I may give different things different names, I call him who usurps the royal authority a *tyrant,* and him who usurps the sovereign power a *despot*. The tyrant is he who thrusts himself in contrary to the laws to govern in accordance with the laws; the despot is he who sets himself above the laws themselves. Thus the tyrant cannot be a despot, but the despot is always a tyrant.

The Death of the Body Politic

Such is the natural and inevitable tendency of the best constituted governments. If Sparta and Rome perished, what State can hope to endure for ever? If we would set up a long-lived form of government, let us not even dream of making it eternal. If we are to succeed, we must not attempt the impossible, or flatter ourselves that we are endowing the work of man with a stability of which human conditions do not permit.

The body politic, as well as the human body, begins to die as soon as it is born, and carries in itself the causes of its destruction. But both may have a constitution that is more or less robust and suited to preserve them a longer or a shorter time. The constitution of man is the work of nature; that of the State the work of art. It is not in men's power to prolong their own lives; but it is for them to prolong as much as possible the life of the State, by giving it the best possible constitution. The best constituted State will have an end; but it will end later than any other, unless some unforeseen accident brings about its untimely destruction.

The life-principle of the body politic lies in the sovereign authority. The legislative power is the heart of the State; the executive power is its brain, which causes the movement of all the parts. The brain may become paralysed and the individual still live. A man may remain an imbecile and live; but as soon as the heart ceases to perform its functions, the animal is dead.

The State subsists by means not of the laws, but of the legislative power. Yesterday's law is not binding to-day; but silence is taken for tacit consent, and the Sovereign is held to confirm incessantly the laws it does not abrogate as it might. All that it has once declared itself to will it wills always, unless it revokes its declaration.

Why then is so much respect paid to old laws? For this very reason. We must believe that nothing but the excellence of old acts of will can have preserved them so long: if the Sovereign had not recognized them as throughout salutary, it would have revoked them a thousand times. This is why, so far from growing weak, the laws continually gain new strength in any well-constituted State; the precedent of antiquity makes them daily more venerable: while wherever the laws grow weak as they become old, this proves that there is no longer a legislative power, and that the State is dead.

How the Sovereign Authority Maintains Itself

The Sovereign, having no force other than the legislative power, acts only by means of the laws; and the laws being solely the authentic acts of the general will, the Sovereign cannot act save when the people is assembled. The people in assembly, I shall be told, is a mere chimera. It is so to-day, but two thousand years ago it was not so. Has man's nature changed?

The bounds of possibility, in moral matters, are less narrow than we imagine: it is our weakness, our vices, and our prejudices that confine them. Base souls have no belief in great men; vile slaves smile in mockery at the name of liberty.

Let us judge of what can be done by what has been done. I shall say nothing of the Republics of ancient Greece; but the Roman Republic was, to my mind, a great State, and the town of Rome a great town. The last census showed that there were in Rome four hundred thousand citizens capable of bearing arms, and the last computation of the population of the Empire showed over four million citizens, excluding subjects, foreigners, women, children, and slaves.

What difficulties might not be supposed to stand in the way of the frequent assemblage of the vast population of this capital and its neighbourhood. Yet few weeks passed without the Roman people being in assembly, and even being so several times. It exercised not only the rights of Sovereignty, but also a part of those of government. It dealt with certain matters, and judged certain cases, and this whole people was found in the public meeting-place hardly less often as magistrates than as citizens.

If we went back to the earliest history of nations, we should find that most ancient governments, even those of monarchical form, such as the Macedonian and the Frankish, had similar councils. In any case, the one incontestable fact I have given is an answer to all difficulties; it is good logic to reason from the actual to the possible.

It is not enough for the assembled people to have once fixed the constitution of the State by giving its sanction to a body of law; it is not enough for it to have set up a perpetual government, or provided once for all for the election of magistrates. Besides the extraordinary assemblies unforeseen circumstances may demand, there must be fixed periodical assemblies which cannot be abrogated or prorogued, so that on the proper day the people is legitimately called together by law, without need of any formal summoning.

But, apart from these assemblies authorized by their date alone, every assembly of the people not summoned by the magistrates appointed for that purpose, and in accordance with the prescribed forms, should be regarded as unlawful, and all its acts as null and void, because the command to assemble should itself proceed from the law.

The greater or less frequency with which lawful assemblies should occur depends on so many considerations that no exact rules about them can be given. It can only be said generally that the stronger the government the more often should the Sovereign show itself.

This, I shall be told, may do for a single town; but what is to be done when the State includes several? Is the sovereign authority to be divided? Or is it to be concentrated in a single town to which all the rest are made subject?

Neither the one nor the other, I reply. First, the sovereign authority is one and simple, and cannot be divided without being destroyed. In the second place, one town cannot, any more than one nation, legitimately be made subject to another, because the essence of the body politic lies in the reconciliation of obedience and liberty, and the words subject and Sovereign are identical correlatives the idea of which meets in the single word 'citizen.'

I answer further that the union of several towns in a single city is always bad, and that, if we wish to make such a union, we should not expect to avoid its natural disadvantages. It is useless to bring up abuses that belong to great States against one who desires to see only small ones; but how can small States be given the strength to resist great ones, as formerly the Greek towns resisted the Great King, and more recently Holland and Switzerland have resisted the House of Austria?

Nevertheless, if the State cannot be reduced to the right limits, there remains still one resource; this is, to allow no capital, to make the seat of government move from town to town, and to assemble by turn in each the Provincial Estates of the country.

People the territory evenly, extend everywhere the same rights, bear to every place in it abundance and life: by these means will the State become at once as strong and as well governed as possible. Remember that the walls of towns are built of the ruins of the houses of the countryside. For every palace I see raised in the capital, my mind's eye sees a whole country made desolate.

The moment the people is legitimately assembled as a sovereign body, the jurisdiction of the government wholly lapses, the executive power is suspended, and the person of the meanest citizen is as sacred and inviolable as that of the first magistrate; for in the presence of the person represented, representatives no longer exist. Most of the tumults that arose in the comitia at Rome were due to ignorance or neglect of this rule. The consuls were in them merely the presidents of the people; the tribunes were mere speakers;[3] the senate was nothing at all.

These intervals of suspension, during which the prince recognizes or ought to recognize an actual superior, have always been viewed by him with alarm; and these assemblies of the people, which

are the aegis of the body politic and the curb on the government, have at all times been the horror of rulers: who therefore never spare pains, objections, difficulties, and promises, to stop the citizens from having them. When the citizens are greedy, cowardly, and pusillanimous, and love ease more than liberty, they do not long hold out against the redoubled efforts of the government; and thus, as the resisting force incessantly grows, the sovereign authority ends by disappearing, and most cities fall and perish before their time.

But between the sovereign authority and arbitrary government there sometimes intervenes a mean power of which something must be said.

NOTES

1. The slow formation and the progress of the Republic of Venice in its lagoons are a notable instance of this sequence; and it is most astonishing that, after more than twelve hundred years' existence, the Venetians seem to be still at the second stage, which they reached with the *Serrar di Consiglio* in 1198. As for the ancient Dukes who are brought up against them, it is proved, whatever the *Squittinio della liber tà veneta* may say of them, that they were in no sense Sovereigns.

A case certain to be cited against my view is that of the Roman Republic, which, it will be said, followed exactly the opposite course, and passed from monarchy to aristocracy and from aristocracy to democracy. I by no means take this view of it.

What Romulus first set up was a mixed government, which soon deteriorated into despotism. From special causes, the State died an untimely death, as newborn children sometimes perish without reaching manhood. The expulsion of the Tarquins was the real period of the birth of the Republic. But at first it took on no constant form, because, by not abolishing the patriciate, it left half its work undone. For, by this means, hereditary aristocracy, the worst of all legitimate forms of administration, remained in conflict with democracy, and the form of the government, as Machiavelli has proved, was only fixed on the establishment of the tribunate: only then was there a true government and a veritable democracy. In fact, the people was then not only Sovereign, but also magistrate and judge; the senate was only a subordinate tribunal, to temper and concentrate the government, and the consuls themselves, though they were patricians, first magistrates, and absolute generals in war, were in Rome itself no more than presidents of the people.

From that point, the government followed its natural tendency, and inclined strongly to aristocracy. The patriciate, we may say, abolished itself, and the aristocracy was found no longer in the body of patricians as at Venice and Genoa, but in the body of the senate, which was composed of patricians and plebeians, and even in the body of tribunes when they began to usurp an active function: for names do not affect facts, and, when the people has rulers who govern for it, whatever name they bear, the government is an aristocracy.

The abuse of aristocracy led to the civil wars and the triumvirate. Sulla, Julius Caesar, and Augustus became in fact real monarchs; and finally, under the despotism of Tiberius, the State was dissolved. Roman history then confirms, instead of invalidating, the principle I have laid down.

2. 'Omnes enim et habentur et dicuntur tyranni, qui potestate utuntur perpetua in ea civitate quae libertate usa est' (Cornelius Nepos, *Life of Miltiades*). ['For all those are

called and considered tyrants, who hold perpetual power in a State that has known liberty.'] It is true that Aristotle (*Nicomachean Ethics*, Bk. viii, ch. x) distinguishes the tyrant from the king by the fact that the former governs in his own interest, and the latter only for the good of his subjects; but not only did all Greek authors in general use the word 'tyrant' in a different sense, as appears most clearly in Xenophon's *Hiero*, but also it would follow from Aristotle's distinction that, from the very beginning of the world, there has not yet been a single king.

3. In nearly the same sense as this word has in the English Parliament. The similarity of these functions would have brought the consuls and the tribunes into conflict, even had all jurisdiction been suspended.

5

The Ruling Class

Gaetano Mosca

Among the constant facts and tendencies that are to be found in all political organisms, one is so obvious that it is apparent to the most casual eye. In all societies—from societies that are very meagerly developed and have barely attained the dawnings of civilization, down to the most advanced and powerful societies—two classes of people appear—a class that rules and a class that is ruled. The first class, always the less numerous, performs all political functions, monopolizes power and enjoys the advantages that power brings, whereas the second, the more numerous class, is directed and controlled by the first, in a manner that is now more or less legal, now more or less arbitrary and violent, and supplies the first, in appearance at least, with material means of subsistence and with the instrumentalities that are essential to the vitality of the political organism.

In practical life we all recognize the existence of this ruling class (or political class, as we have elsewhere chosen to define it). We all know that, in our own country, whichever it may be, the management of public affairs is in the hands of a minority of influential persons, to which management, willingly or unwillingly, the majority defer. We know that the same thing goes on in neighboring countries, and in fact we should be put to it to conceive of a real world otherwise organized—a world in which all men would be directly subject to a single person without relationships of superiority or subordination, or in which all men would share equally in the direction of political affairs. If we reason otherwise in theory, that is due partly to inveterate habits that we follow in our thinking and partly to the exag-

gerated importance that we attach to two political facts that loom far larger in appearance than they are in reality.

The first of these facts—and one has only to open one's eyes to see it—is that in every political organism there is one individual who is chief among the leaders of the ruling class as a whole and stands, as we say, at the helm of the state. That person is not always the person who holds supreme power according to law. At times, alongside of the hereditary king or emperor there is a prime minister or a major-domo who wields an actual power that is greater than the sovereign's. At other times, in place of the elected president the influential politician who has procured the president's election will govern. Under special circumstances there may be, instead of a single person, two or three who discharge the functions of supreme control.

The second fact, too, is readily discernible. Whatever the type of political organization, pressures arising from the discontent of the masses who are governed, from the passions by which they are swayed, exert a certain amount of influence on the policies of the ruling, the political, class.

But the man who is at the head of the state would certainly not be able to govern without the support of a numerous class to enforce respect for his orders and to have them carried out; and granting that he can make one individual, or indeed many individuals, in the ruling class feel the weight of his power, he certainly cannot be at odds with the class as a whole or do away with it. Even if that were possible, he would at once be forced to create another class, without the support of which action on his part would be completely paralyzed. On the other hand, granting that the discontent of the masses might succeed in deposing a ruling class, inevitably, as we shall later show, there would have to be another organized minority within the masses themselves to discharge the functions of a ruling class. Otherwise all organization, and the whole social structure, would be destroyed. . . .

Finally, if we were to keep to the idea of those who maintain the exclusive influence of the hereditary principle in the formation of ruling classes, we should be carried to a conclusion somewhat like the one to which we were carried by the evolutionary principles. The political history of mankind ought to be much simpler than it is. If the ruling class really belonged to a different race, or if the qualities that fit it for dominion were transmitted primarily by organic heredity, it is difficult to see how, once the class was formed, it could decline and lose its power. The peculiar qualities of a race are exceedingly tenacious. Keeping to the evolutionary theory, acquired capacities in the parents are inborn in their children and, as generation succeeds generation, are progressively accentuated. The descendants of rulers, therefore, ought to become better and better fitted to rule, and the other classes ought to see their chances of challenging or supplanting them become more and more remote. Now the most commonplace experience suffices to assure one that things do not go in that way at all.

What we see is that as soon as there is a shift in the balance of political forces—when, that is, a need is felt that capacities different from the old should assert themselves in the management of the state, when the old capacities, therefore, lose some of their importance or changes in their distribution occur— then the manner in which the ruling class is constituted changes also. If a new source of wealth develops in a society, if the practical importance of knowledge grows, if an old religion declines or a new one is born, if a new current of ideas spreads, then, simultaneously, far-reaching dislocations occur in the ruling class. One might say, indeed, that the whole history of civilized mankind comes down to a conflict between the tendency of dominant elements to monopolize political power and transmit possession of it by inheritance, and the tendency toward a dislocation of old forces and an insurgence of new forces; and this conflict produces an unending ferment of endosmosis and exosmosis between the upper classes and certain portions of the lower. Ruling classes decline inevitably when they cease to find scope for the capacities through which they rose to power, when they can no longer render the social services which they once rendered, or when their talents and the services they render lose in importance in the social environment in which they live. So the Roman aristocracy declined when it was no longer the exclusive source of higher officers for the army, of administrators for the commonwealth, of governors for the provinces. So the Venetian aristocracy declined when its nobles ceased to command the galleys and no longer passed the greater part of their lives in sailing the seas and in trading and fighting.

In inorganic nature we have the example of our air, in which a tendency to immobility produced by the force of inertia is continuously in conflict with a tendency to shift about as the result of inequalities in the distribution of heat. The two tendencies, prevailing by turn in various regions on our planet, produce now calm, now wind and storm. In much the same way in human societies there prevails now the tendency that produces closed, stationary, crystallized ruling classes, now the tendency that results in a more or less rapid renovation of ruling classes.

The Oriental societies which we consider stationary have in reality not always been so, for otherwise, as we have already pointed out, they could not have made the advances in civilization of which they have left irrefutable evidence. It is much more accurate to say that we came to know them at a time when their political forces and their political classes were in a period of crystallization. The same thing occurs in what we commonly call "aging" societies, where religious beliefs, scientific knowledge, methods of producing and distributing wealth have for centuries undergone no radical alteration and have not been disturbed in their everyday course by infiltrations of foreign elements, material or intellectual. In such societies political forces are always the same, and the class that holds possession of them holds a power that is undisputed. Power is therefore perpetuated in certain families, and the inclination to immobility becomes general through all the various strata in that society.

So in India we see the caste system become thoroughly entrenched after the suppression of Buddhism. The Greeks found hereditary castes in ancient Egypt, but we know that in the periods of greatness and renaissance in Egyptian civilization political office and social status were not hereditary. We possess an Egyptian document that summarizes the life of a high army officer who lived during the period of the expulsion of the Hyksos. He had begun his career as a simple soldier. Other documents show cases in which the same individual served successively in army, civil administration and priesthood.

The best-known and perhaps the most important

example of a society tending toward crystallization is the period in Roman history that used to be called the Low Empire. There, after several centuries of almost complete social immobility, a division between two classes grew sharper and sharper, the one made up of great landowners and high officials, the other made up of slaves, farmers and urban plebeians. What is even more striking, public office and social position became hereditary by custom before they became hereditary by law, and the trend was rapidly generalized during the period mentioned.

On the other hand it may happen in the history of a nation that commerce with foreign peoples, forced emigrations, discoveries, wars, create new poverty and new wealth, disseminate knowledge of things that were previously unknown or cause infiltrations of new moral, intellectual and religious currents. Or again—as a result of such infiltrations or through a slow process of inner growth, or from both causes—it may happen that a new learning arises, or that certain elements of an old, long-forgotten learning return to favor so that new ideas and new beliefs come to the fore and upset the intellectual habits on which the obedience of the masses has been founded. The ruling class may also be vanquished and destroyed in whole or in part by foreign invasions, or, when the circumstances just mentioned arise, it may be driven from power by the advent of new social elements who are strong in fresh political forces. Then, naturally, there comes a period of renovation, or, if one prefer, of revolution, during which individual energies have free play and certain individuals, more passionate, more energetic, more intrepid or merely shrewder than others, force their way from the bottom of the social ladder to the topmost rungs.

Once such a movement has set in, it cannot be stopped immediately. The example of individuals who have started from nowhere and reached prominent positions fires new ambitions, new greeds, new energies, and this molecular rejuvenation of the ruling class continues vigorously until a long period of social stability slows it down again. We need hardly mention examples of nations in such periods of renovation. In our age that would be superfluous. Rapid restocking of ruling classes is a frequent and very striking phenomenon in countries that have been recently colonized. When social life begins in such environments, there is no ready-made ruling class, and while such a class is in process of formation, admittance to it is gained very easily. Monopolization of land and other agencies of production is, if not quite impossible, at any rate more difficult than elsewhere. That is why, at least during a certain period, the Greek colonies offered a wide outlet for all Greek energy and enterprise. That is why, in the United States, where the colonizing of new lands continued through the whole nineteenth century and new industries were continually springing up, examples of men who started with nothing and have attained fame and wealth are still frequent—all of which helps to foster in the people of that country the illusion that democracy is a fact.

Suppose now that a society gradually passes from its feverish state to calm. Since the human being's psychological tendencies are always the same, those who belong to the ruling class will begin to acquire a group spirit. They will become more and more exclusive and learn better and better the art of monopolizing to their advantage the qualities and capacities that are essential to acquiring power and holding it. Then, at last, the force that is essentially conservative appears—the force of habit. Many people become resigned to a lowly station, while the members of certain privileged families or classes grow convinced that they have almost an absolute right to high station and command.

A philanthropist would certainly be tempted to inquire whether mankind is happier—or less unhappy—during periods of social stability and crystallization, when everyone is almost fated to remain in the social station to which he was born, or during the directly opposite periods of renovation and revolution, which permit all to aspire to the most exalted positions and some to attain them. Such an inquiry would be difficult. The answer would have to take account of many qualifications and exceptions, and might perhaps always be influenced by the personal preferences of the observer. We shall therefore be careful not to venture on any answer of our own. Besides, even if we could reach an undebatable conclusion, it would have a very slight practical utility; for the sad fact is that what the philosophers and theologians call free will—in other words, spontaneous choice by individuals—has so far had, and will perhaps always have, little influence, if any at all, in hastening either the ending or the beginning of one of the historical periods mentioned.

6

The Basis of Legitimacy

Max Weber

The Definition, Conditions, and Types of Imperative Control

"Imperative co-ordination" was defined above as the probability that certain specific commands (or all commands) from a given source will be obeyed by a given group of persons. It thus does not include every mode of exercising "power" or "influence" over other persons. The motives of obedience to commands in this sense can rest on considerations varying over a wide range from case to case; all the way from simple habituation to the most purely rational calculation of advantage. A criterion of every true relation of imperative control, however, is a certain minimum of voluntary submission; thus an interest (based on ulterior motives or genuine acceptance) in obedience.

Not every case of imperative co-ordination makes use of economic means; *still less* does it always have economic objectives. But normally (not always) the imperative co-ordination of the action of a considerable number of men requires control of a staff of persons. It is necessary, that is, that there should be a relatively high probability that the action of a definite, supposedly reliable group of persons will be primarily oriented to the execution of the supreme authority's general policy and specific commands.

The members of the administrative staff may be bound to obedience to their superior (or superiors) by custom, by affectual ties, by a purely material complex of interests, or by ideal (*wertrational*) motives. *Purely* material interests and calculations of advantage as the basis of solidarity between the chief and his administrative staff result, in this as in other connexions, in a relatively unstable situation. Normally other elements, affectual and ideal, supplement such interests. In certain exceptional, temporary cases the former may be alone decisive. In everyday routine life these relationships, like others, are governed by custom and in addition, material calculation of advantage. But these factors, custom and personal advantage, purely affectual or ideal motives of solidarity, do not, even taken together, form a sufficiently reliable basis for a system of imperative co-ordination. In addition there is normally a further element, the belief in legitimacy.

It is an induction from experience that no system of authority voluntarily limits itself to the appeal to material or affectual or ideal motives as a basis for guaranteeing its continuance. In addition every such system attempts to establish and to cultivate the belief in its "legitimacy." But according to the kind of legitimacy which is claimed, the type of obedience, the kind of administrative staff developed to guarantee it, and the mode of exercising authority, will all differ fundamentally. Equally fundamental is the variation in effect. Hence, it is useful to classify the types of authority according to the kind of claim to legitimacy typically made by each. In doing this it is best to start from modern and therefore more familiar examples.

1. The choice of this rather than some other basis of classification can only be justified by its results. The fact that certain other typical criteria of variation are thereby neglected for the time being and can only be introduced at a later stage is not a decisive difficulty. The "legitimacy" of a system of authority has far more than a merely "ideal" significance, if only because it has very definite relations to the legitimacy of property.

2. Not every "claim" which is protected by custom or by law should be spoken of as involving a relation of authority. Otherwise the worker, in his claim for fulfillment of the wage contract, would be exercising "authority" over his employer because his claim can, on occasion, be enforced by order of a court. Actually his formal status is that of party to a contractual relationship with his employer, in which he has certain "rights" to receive payments. At the same time the concept of a relation of authority naturally does not exclude the possibility that it has originated in a formally free contract.

From Max Weber, *The Theory of Social and Economic Organization,* ed. Talcott Parsons, trans. Talcott Parsons and A. M. Henderson (New York: Oxford University Press, 1947), pp. 324–329. Reprinted by permission of the editor.

This is true of the authority of the employer over the worker as manifested in the former's rules and instructions regarding the work process; and also of the authority of a feudal lord over a vassal who has freely entered into the relation of fealty. That subjection to military discipline is formally "involuntary" while that to the discipline of the factory is voluntary does not alter the fact that the latter is also a case of subjection to authority. The position of a bureaucratic official is also entered into by contract and can be freely resigned, and even the status of "subject" can often be freely entered into and (in certain circumstances) freely repudiated. Only in the limiting case of the slave is formal subjection to authority absolutely involuntary.

Another case, in some respects related, is that of economic "power" based on monopolistic position; that is, in this case, the possibility of "dictating" terms of exchange to contractual partners. This will not, taken by itself, be considered to constitute "authority" any more than any other kind of "influence" which is derived from some kind of superiority, as by virtue of erotic attractiveness, skill in sport or in discussion. Even if a big bank is in a position to force other banks into a cartel arrangement, this will not alone be sufficient to justify calling it a relation of imperative co-ordination. But if there is an immediate relation of command and obedience such that the management of the first bank can give orders to the others with the claim that they shall, and the probability that they will, be obeyed purely as such regardless of particular content, and if their carrying out is supervised, it is another matter. Naturally, here as everywhere the transitions are gradual; there are all sorts of intermediate steps between mere indebtedness and debt slavery. Even the position of a "salon" can come very close to the borderline of authoritarian domination and yet not necessarily constitute a system of authority. Sharp differentiation in concrete fact is often impossible, but this makes clarity in the analytical distinctions all the more important.

3. Naturally, the legitimacy of a system of authority may be treated sociologically only as the probability that to a relevant degree the appropriate attitudes will exist, and the corresponding practical conduct ensue. It is by no means true that every case of submissiveness to persons in positions of power is primarily (or even at all) oriented to this belief. Loyalty may be hypocritically simulated by individuals or by whole groups on purely opportunistic grounds, or carried out in practice for reasons of material self-interest. Or people may submit from individual weakness and helplessness because there is no acceptable alternative. But these considerations are not decisive for the classification of types of imperative co-ordination. What is important is the fact that in a given case the particular claim to legitimacy is to a significant degree and according to its type treated as "valid"; that this fact confirms the position of the persons claiming authority and that it helps to determine the choice of means of its exercise.

Furthermore, a system of imperative co-ordination may—as often occurs in practice—be so completely assured of dominance, on the one hand by the obvious community of interests between the chief and his administrative staff as opposed to the subjects (bodyguards, Pretorians, "red" or "white" guards), on the other hand by the helplessness of the latter, that it can afford to drop even the pretence of a claim to legitimacy. But even then the mode of legitimation of the relation between chief and his staff may vary widely according to the type of basis of the relation of authority between them, and, as will be shown, this variation is highly significant for the structure of imperative co-ordination.

4. "Obedience" will be taken to mean that the action of the person obeying follows in essentials such a course that the content of the command may be taken to have become the basis of action for its own sake. Furthermore, the fact that it is so taken is referable only to the formal obligation, without regard to the actor's own attitude to the value or lack of value of the content of the command as such.

5. Subjectively, the causal sequence may vary, especially as between "submission" and "sympathetic agreement." This distinction is not, however, significant for the present classification of types of authority.

6. The scope of determination of social relationships and cultural phenomena by authority and imperative co-ordination is considerably broader than appears at first sight. For instance, the authority exercised in the school has much to do with the determination of the forms of speech and of written language which are regarded as orthodox. The official languages of autonomous political units, hence of their ruling groups, have often become in this sense orthodox forms of speech and writing and have even led to the formation of separate "nations" (for instance, the separation of Holland from Germany). The authority of parents and of the school, however, extends far beyond the determination of such cultural patterns which are perhaps only apparently formal, to the formation of the character of the young, and hence of human beings generally.

7. The fact that the chief and his administrative staff often appear formally as servants or agents of those they rule, naturally does nothing whatever to disprove the authoritarian character of the relation-

ship. There will be occasion later to speak of the substantive features of so-called "democracy." But a certain minimum of assured power to issue commands, thus of "authority," must be provided for in nearly every conceivable case.

The Three Pure Types of Legitimate Authority

There are three pure types of legitimate authority. The validity of their claims to legitimacy may be based on:

1. Rational grounds—resting on a belief in the "legality" of patterns of normative rules and the right of those elevated to authority under such rules to issue commands (legal authority)

2. Traditional grounds—resting on an established belief in the sanctity of immemorial traditions and the legitimacy of the status of those exercising authority under them (traditional authority)

3. Charismatic grounds—resting on devotion to the specific and exceptional sanctity, heroism or exemplary character of an individual person, and of the normative patterns or order revealed or ordained by him (charismatic authority)

In the case of legal authority, obedience is owed to the legally established impersonal order. It extends to the persons exercising the authority of office under it only by virtue of the formal legality of their commands and only within the scope of authority of the office. In the case of traditional authority, obedience is owed to the *person* of the chief who occupies the traditionally sanctioned position of authority and who is (within its sphere) bound by tradition. But here the obligation of obedience is not based on the impersonal order, but is a matter of personal loyalty within the area of accustomed obligations. In the case of charismatic authority, it is the charismatically

qualified leader as such who is obeyed by virtue of personal trust in him and his revelation, his heroism or his exemplary qualities so far as they fall within the scope of the individual's belief in his charisma.

1. The usefulness of the above classification can only be judged by its results in promoting systematic analysis. The concept of "charisma" ("the gift of grace") is taken from the vocabulary of early Christianity. For the Christian religious organization Rudolf Sohm, in his *Kirchenrecht,* was the first to clarify the substance of the concept, even though he did not use the same terminology. Others (for instance, Hollin, *Enthusiasmus und Bussgewalt*) have clarified certain important consequences of it. It is thus nothing new.

2. The fact that none of these three ideal types . . . is usually to be found in historical cases in "pure" form, is naturally not a valid objection to attempting their conceptual formulation in the sharpest possible form. In this respect the present case is no different from many others. . . . It may be said of every empirically historical phenomenon of authority that is not likely to be "as an open book." Analysis in terms of sociological types has, after all, as compared with purely empirical historical investigation, certain advantages which should not be minimized. That is, it can in the particular case of a concrete form of authority determine what conforms to or approximates such types as "charisma," "hereditary charisma," . . . "the charisma of office," "patriarchy," . . . "bureaucracy," . . . the authority of status groups, and in doing so it can work with relatively unambiguous concepts. But the idea that the whole of concrete historical reality can be exhausted in the conceptual scheme about to be developed is as far from the author's thoughts as anything could be.

7

On the Concept of Political Power

Talcott Parsons

The above may seem a highly elaborate setting in which to place the formal introduction of the main

From Talcott Parsons, "On the Concept of Political Power," *Proceedings of the American Philosophical Society,* CVII, No. 3 (1963), 236–243, 257–258. Reprinted by permission of the author and the American Philosophical Society.

subject of the paper, namely the concept of power. Condensed and cryptic as the exposition may have been, however, understanding of its main structure is an essential basis for the special way in which it will be proposed to combine the elements which have played a crucial part in the main intellectual traditions dealing with the problems of power.

Power is here conceived as a circulating medium, analogous to money, within what is called the political system, but notably over its boundaries into all three of the other neighboring functional subsystems of a society (as I conceive them), the economic, integrative, and pattern-maintenance systems. Specification of the properties of power can best be approached through an attempt to delineate very briefly the relevant properties of money as such a medium in the economy.

Money is, as the classical economists said, both a medium of exchange and a "measure of value." It is symbolic in that, though measuring and thus "standing for" economic value or utility, it does not itself possess utility in the primary consumption sense—it has no "value in use" but only "in exchange," i.e. for possession of things having utility. The use of money is thus a mode of communication of offers, on the one hand to purchase, on the other to sell, things of utility, with and for money. It becomes an essential medium only when exchange is neither ascriptive, as exchange of gifts between assigned categories of kin, nor takes place on a basis of barter, one item of commodity or service directly for another.

In exchange for its lack of direct utility money gives the recipient four important degrees of freedom in his participation in the total exchange system. (1) He is free to spend his money for any item or combination of items available on the market which he can afford, (2) he is free to shop around among alternative sources of supply for desired items, (3) he can choose his own time to purchase, and (4) he is free to consider terms which, because of freedom of time and source, he can accept or reject or attempt to influence in the particular case. By contrast, in the case of barter, the negotiator is bound to what his particular partner has or wants in relation to what he has and will part with at the particular time. The other side of the gain in degrees of freedom is of course the risk involved in the probabilities of the acceptance of money by others and of the stability of its value.

Primitive money is a medium which is still very close to a commodity, the commonest case being precious metal, and many still feel that the value of money is "really" grounded in the commodity value of the metallic base. On this base, however, there is, in developed monetary systems, erected a complex structure of credit instruments, so that only a tiny fraction of actual transactions is conducted in terms of the metal—it becomes a "reserve" available for certain contingencies, and is actually used mainly in the settlement of international balances. I shall discuss the nature of credit further in another connection later. For the moment suffice it to say that, however important in certain contingencies, the availability of metallic reserves may be, no modern monetary system operates primarily with metal as the actual medium, but uses "valueless" money. Moreover, the acceptance of this "valueless" money rests on a certain institutionalized confidence in the monetary system. If the security of monetary commitments rested only on their convertibility into metal, then the overwhelming majority of them would be worthless, for the simple reason that the total quantity of metal is far too small to redeem more than a few.

One final point is that money is "good," i.e. works as a medium, only within a relatively defined network of market relationships which to be sure now has become world-wide, but the maintenance of which requires special measures to maintain mutual convertibility of national currencies. Such a system is on the one hand a range of exchange-potential within which money may be spent, but on the other hand, one within which certain conditions affecting the protection and management of the unit are maintained, both by law and by responsible agencies under the law.

The first focus of the concept of an institutionalized power system is, analogously, a relational system within which certain categories of commitments and obligations, ascriptive or voluntarily assumed—e.g. by contract—are treated as binding, i.e. under normatively defined conditions their fulfillment may be insisted upon by the appropriate role-reciprocal agencies. Furthermore, in case of actual or threatened resistance to "compliance," i.e. to fulfillment of such obligations when invoked, they will be "enforced" by the threat or actual imposition of situational negative sanctions, in the former case having the function of deterrence, in the latter of punishment. These are events in the situation of the actor of reference which intentionally alter his situation (or threaten to) to his disadvantage, whatever in specific content these alterations may be.

Power then is generalized capacity to secure the performance of binding obligations by units in a system of collective organization when the obligations are legitimized with reference to their bearing on collective goals and where in case of recalcitrance there is a presumption of enforcement by negative situational sanctions—whatever the actual agency of that enforcement.

It will be noted that I have used the conceptions

of generalization and of legitimation in defining power. Securing possession of an object of utility by bartering another object for it is not a monetary transaction. Similarly, by my definition, securing compliance with a wish, whether it be defined as an obligation of the object or not, simply by threat of superior force, is not an exercise of power. I am well aware that most political theorists would draw the line differently and classify this as power (e.g. Dahl's definition), but I wish to stick to my chosen line and explore its implications. The capacity to secure compliance must, if it is to be called power in my sense, be generalized and not solely a function of one particular sanctioning act which the user is in a position to impose,[1] and the medium used must be "symbolic."

Secondly, I have spoken of power as involving legitimation. This is, in the present context, the necessary consequence of conceiving power as "symbolic," which therefore, if it is exchanged for something intrinsically valuable for collective effectiveness, namely compliance with an obligation, leaves the recipient, the performer of the obligation, with "nothing of value." This is to say, that he has "nothing" but a set of expectations, namely that in other contexts and on other occasions he can invoke certain obligations of the part of other units. Legitimation is therefore, in power systems, the factor which is parallel to confidence in mutual acceptability and stability of the monetary unit in monetary systems.

The two criteria are connected in that questioning the legitimacy of the possession and use of power leads to resort to progressively more "secure" means of gaining compliance. These must be progressively more effective "intrinsically," hence more tailored to the particular situations of the objects and less general. Furthermore, in so far as they are intrinsically effective, legitimacy becomes a progressively less important factor of their effectiveness—at the end of this series lies resort, first to various types of coercion, eventually to the use of force as the most intrinsically effective of all means of coercion.[2]

I should like now to attempt to place both money and power in the context of a more general paradigm, which is an analytical classification of ways in which, in the processes of social interaction, the actions of one unit in a system can, intentionally, be oriented to bringing about a change in what the actions of one or more other units would otherwise have been—thus all fitting into the context of Dahl's conception of power. It is convenient to state this in terms of the convention of speaking of the acting

unit of reference—individual or collective—as *ego*, and the object on which he attempts to "operate" as *alter*. We may then classify the alternatives open to ego in terms of two dichotomous variables. On the one hand ego may attempt to gain his end from alter either by using some form of control over the situation in which alter is placed, actually or contingently to change it so as to increase the probability of alter acting in the way he wishes, or, alternatively, without attempting to change alter's situation, ego may attempt to change alter's intentions, i.e. he may manipulate symbols which are meaningful to alter in such a way that he tries to make alter "see" that what ego wants is a "good thing" for him (alter) to do.

The second variable then concerns the type of sanctions ego may employ in attempting to guarantee the attainment of his end from alter. The dichotomy here is between positive and negative sanctions. Thus through the situational channel a positive sanction is a change in alter's situation presumptively considered by alter as to his advantage, which is used as a means by ego of having an effect on alter's actions. A negative sanction then is an alteration in alter's situation to the latter's disadvantage. In the case of the intentional channel, the positive sanction is the expression of symbolic "reasons" why compliance with ego's wishes is "a good thing" independently of any further action on ego's part, from alter's point of view, i.e. would be felt by him to be "personally advantageous," whereas the negative sanction is presenting reasons why noncompliance with ego's wishes should be felt by alter to be harmful to interests in which he had a significant personal investment and should therefore be avoided. I should like to call the four types of "strategy" open to ego respectively (1) for the situational channel, positive sanction case, "inducement"; (2) situational channel, negative sanction, "coercion"; (3) intentional channel, positive sanction "persuasion," and (4) intentional channel negative sanction "activation of commitments" as shown in Table 7–1.

A further complication now needs to be introduced. We think of a sanction as an intentional act

Table 7–1

Sanction Type	Channel		
	Intentional		Situational
Positive	Persuasion	3	1
Negative	Activation of Commitments	4	Inducement
			2 Coercion

on ego's part, expected by him to change his relation to alter from what it would otherwise have been. As a means of bringing about a change in alter's action, it can operate most obviously where the actual imposition of the sanction is made contingent on a future decision by alter. Thus a process of inducement will operate in two stages, first contingent offer on ego's part that, if alter will "comply" with his wishes, ego will "reward" him by the contingently promised situational change. If then alter in fact does comply, ego will perform the sanctioning act. In the case of coercion the first stage is a contingent threat that, unless alter decides to comply, ego will impose the negative sanction. If, however, alter complies, then nothing further happens, but, if he decides on noncompliance, then ego must carry out his threat, or be in a position of "not meaning it." In the cases of the intentional channel ego's first-stage act is either to predict the occurrence, or to announce his own intention of doing something which affects alter's sentiments or interests. The element of contingency enters in in that ego "argues" to alter, that if this happens, on the one hand alter should be expected to "see" that it would be a good thing for him to do what ego wants—the positive case—or that if he fails to do it it would imply an important "subjective cost" to alter. In the positive case, beyond "pointing out" if alter complies, ego is obligated to deliver the positive attitudinal sanction of approval. In the negative case, the corresponding attitudinal sanction of disapproval is implemented only for noncompliance.

It is hence clear that there is a basic asymmetry between the positive and negative sides of the sanction aspect of the paradigm. This is that, in the cases of inducement and persuasion, alter's compliance obligates ego to "deliver" his promised positive sanction, in the former case the promised advantages, in the latter his approval of alter's "good sense" in recognizing that the decision wished for by ego and accepted as "good" by alter, in fact turns out to be good from alter's point of view. In the negative cases, on the other hand, compliance on alter's part obligates ego, in the situational case, not to carry out his threat, in the intentional case by withholding disapproval to confirm to alter that his compliance did in fact spare him what to him, without ego's intervention, would have been the undesirable subjective consequences of his previous intentions, namely guilt over violations of his commitments.

Finally, alter's freedom of action in his decisions of compliance versus noncompliance is also a variable. This range has a lower limit at which the element of contingency disappears. That is, from ego's point of view, he may not say, if you do so and so, I will intervene, either by situational manipulations or by "arguments" in such and such a way, but he may simply perform an overt act and face alter with a *fait accompli*. In the case of inducement a gift which is an object of value and with respect to the acceptance of which alter is given no option is the limiting case. With respect to coercion, compulsion, i.e. simply imposing a disadvantageous alteration on alter's situation and then leaving it to alter to decide whether to "do something about it" is the limiting case.

The asymmetry just referred to appears here as well. As contingent it may be said that the primary meaning of negative sanctions is as means of prevention. If they are effective, no further action is required. The case of compulsion is that in which it is rendered impossible for alter to avoid the undesired action on ego's part. In the case of positive sanctions of course ego, for example in making a gift to alter, cuts himself out from benefiting from alter's performance which is presumptively advantageous to him, in the particular exchange.

Both, however, may be oriented to their effect on alter's action in future sequences of interaction. The object of compulsion may have been "taught a lesson" and hence be less disposed to noncompliance with ego's wishes in the future, as well as prevented from performance of a particular undesired act and the recipient of a gift may feel a "sense of obligation" to reciprocate in some form in the future.

So far this discussion has dealt with sanctioning acts in terms of their "intrinsic" significance both to ego and to alter. An offered inducement may thus be possession of a particular object of utility, a coercive threat, that of a particular feared loss, or other noxious experience. But just as, in the initial phase of sequence, ego transmits his contingent intentions to alter symbolically through communication, so the sanction involved may also be symbolic, e.g. in place of possession of certain intrinsically valuable goods he may offer a sum of money. What we have called the generalized media of interaction then may be used as types of sanctions which may be analyzed in terms of the above paradigm. The factors of generalization and of legitimation of institutionalization, however, as discussed above, introduce certain complications which we must now take up with reference to power. There is a sense in which power may be regarded as the generalized medium of coercion in the above terms, but this formula at the very least requires very careful interpretation—indeed it will turn out by itself to be inadequate.

I spoke above of the "grounding" of the value of money in the commodity value of the monetary metal, and suggested that there is a corresponding relation of the "value," i.e. the effectiveness of power, to the intrinsic effectiveness of physical force as a means of coercion and, in the limiting case, compulsion.[3]

In interpreting this formula due account must be taken of the asymmetry just discussed. The special place of gold as a monetary base rests on such properties as its durability, high value in small bulk, etc., and high probability of acceptability in exchange, i.e. as means of inducement, in a very wide variety of conditions which are not dependent on an institutionalized order. Ego's primary aim in resorting to compulsion or coercion, however, is deterrence of unwanted action on alter's part.[4] Force, therefore, is in the first instance important as the "ultimate" deterrent. It is the means which, again independent of any institutionalized system of order, can be assumed to be "intrinsically" the most effective in the context of deterrence, when means of effectiveness which *are* dependent on institutionalized order are insecure or fail. Therefore, the unit of an action system which commands control of physical force adequate to cope with any potential counter threats of force is more secure than any other in a Hobbesian state of nature.[5]

But just as a monetary system resting entirely on gold as the actual medium of exchange is a very primitive one which simply cannot mediate a complex system of market exchange, so a power system in which the only negative sanction is the threat of force is a very primitive one which cannot function to mediate a complex system of organizational coordination—it is far too "blunt" an instrument. Money cannot be only an intrinsically valuable entity if it is to serve as a generalized medium of inducement, but it must, as we have said, be institutionalized as a symbol; it must be legitimized, and must inspire "confidence" within the system—and must also within limits be deliberately managed. Similarly power cannot be only an intrinsically effective deterrent; if it is to be the generalized medium of mobilizing resources for effective collective action, and for the fulfillment of commitments made by collectivities to what we have here called their constituents; it too must be both symbolically generalized, and legitimized.

There is a direct connection between the concept of bindingness, as introduced above, and deterrence. To treat a commitment or any other form of expectation as binding is to attribute a special importance to its fulfillment. Where it is not a matter simply of maintenance of an established routine, but of undertaking new actions in changed circumstances, where the commitment is thus to undertake types of action contingent on circumstances as they develop, then the risk to be minimized is that such contingent commitments will not be carried out when the circumstances

in question appear. Treating the expectation or obligation as binding is almost the same thing as saying that appropriate steps on the other side must be taken to prevent nonfulfillment, if possible. Willingness to impose negative sanctions is, seen in this light, simply the carrying out of the implications of treating commitments as binding, and the agent invoking them "meaning it" or being prepared to insist.

On the other hand there are areas in interaction systems where there is a range of alternatives, choice among which is optional, in the light of the promised advantageousness, situational or "intentional," of one as compared to other choices. Positive sanctions as here conceived constitute a contingent increment of relative advantageousness, situational or intentional, of the alternative ego desires alter to choose.

If, in these latter areas, a generalized, symbolic medium is to operate in place of intrinsic advantages, there must be an element of bindingness in the institutionalization of the medium itself—e.g. the fact that the money of a society is "legal tender" which must be accepted in the settlement of debts which have the status of contractual obligations under the law. In the case of money, I suggest that, for the typical acting unit in a market system, what specific undertakings he enters into is overwhelmingly optional in the above sense, but whether the money involved in the transactions is or is not "good" is not for him to judge, but his acceptance of it is binding. Essentially the same is true of the contractual obligations, typically linking monetary and intrinsic utilities, which he undertakes.

I would now like to suggest that what is in a certain sense the obverse holds true of power. Its "intrinsic" importance lies in its capacity to ensure that obligations are "really" binding, thus if necessary can be "enforced" by negative sanctions. But for power to function as a generalized medium in a complex system, i.e. to mobilize resources effectively for collective action, it must be "legitimized" which in the present context means that in certain respects compliance, which is the common factor among our media, is not binding, to say nothing of being coerced, but is optional. The range within which there exists a continuous system of interlocking binding obligations is essentially that of the internal relations of an organized collection in our sense, and of the contractual obligations undertaken on its behalf at its boundaries.

The points at which the optional factors come to bear are, in the boundary relations of the collectivity, where factors of importance for collective functioning other than binding obligations are exchanged for such binding commitments on the part of the collectivity and *vice versa,* nonbinding outputs of the collectivity for binding commitments to it. These "optional" inputs, I have suggested above, are control of productivity of the economy at one boundary, influence through the relations between leadership and the public demands on the other.[6]

This is a point at which the dissociation of the concept of polity from exclusive relation to government becomes particularly important. In a sufficiently differentiated society, the boundary-relations of the great majority of its important units of collective organization (including some boundaries of government) are boundaries where the overwhelming majority of decisions of commitment are optional in the above sense, though once made, their fulfillment is binding. This, however, is only possible effectively within the range of a sufficiently stable, institutionalized normative order so that the requisite degrees of freedom are protected, e.g. in the fields of employment and of the promotion of interest-demands and decisions about political support.

This feature of the boundary relations of a particular political unit holds even for cases of local government, in that decisions of residence, employment, or acquisition of property within a particular jurisdiction involve the optional element, since in all these respects there is a relatively free choice among local jurisdictions, even though, once having chosen, the citizen is, for example, subject to the tax policies applying within it—and of course he cannot escape being subject to any local jurisdiction, but must choose among those available.

In the case of a "national" political organization, however, its territorial boundaries ordinarily coincide with a relative break in the normative order regulating social interaction.[7] Hence across such boundaries an ambiguity becomes involved in the exercise of power in our sense. On the one hand the invoking of binding obligations operates normally without explicit use of coercion within certain ranges where the two territorial collectivity systems have institutionalized their relations. Thus travelers in friendly foreign countries can ordinarily enjoy personal security and the amenities of the principal public accommodations, exchange of their money at "going" rates, etc. Where, on the other hand, the more general relations between national collectivities are at issue, the power system is especially vulnerable to the kind of insecurity of expectations which tends to be met by the explicit resort to threats of coercive sanctions. Such threats in turn, operating on both sides of a reciprocal relationship, readily enter into a vicious circle of resort to more and more "intrinsically" effective or drastic measures of coercion, at the end of which road lies physical force. In other words, the danger

of war is endemic in uninstitutionalized relations between territorially organized collectivities.

There is thus an inherent relation between both the use and the control of force and the territorial basis of organization.[8] One central condition of the integration of a power system is that it should be effective within a territorial area, and a crucial condition of this effectiveness in turn is the monopoly of control of paramount force within the area. The critical point then, at which the institutional integration of power systems is most vulnerable to strain, and to degeneration into reciprocating threats of the use of force, is between territorially organized political systems. This, notoriously, is the weakest point in the normative order of human society today, as it has been almost from time immemorial.

In this connection it should be recognized that the possession, the mutual threat, and possible use of force is only in a most proximate sense the principal "cause" of war. The essential point is that the "bottleneck" of mutual regression to more and more primitive means of protecting or advancing collective interests is a "channel" into which all elements of tension between the collective units in question may flow. It is a question of the many levels at which such elements of tension may on the one hand build up, on the other be controlled, not of any simple and unequivocal conception of the "inherent" consequences of the possession and possible uses of organized force.

It should be clear that again there is a direct parallel with the economic case. A functioning market system requires integration of the monetary medium. It cannot be a system of N independent monetary units and agencies controlling them. This is the basis on which the main range of extension of a relatively integrated market system tends to coincide with the "politically organized society," as Roscoe Pound calls it, over a territorial area. International transactions require special provisions not required for domestic.

The basic "management" of the monetay system must then be integrated with the institutionalization of political power. Just as the latter depends on an effective monopoly of institutionally organized force, so monetary stability depends on an effective monopoly of basic reserves protecting the monetary unit and, as we shall see later, on centralization of control over the credit system.

The Hierarchical Aspect of Power Systems

A very critical question now arises, which may be stated in terms of a crucial difference between money and power. Money is a "measure of value," as the classical economists put it, in terms of a continuous linear variable. Objects of utility valued in money are more or less valuable than each other in numerically statable terms. Similarly, as medium of exchange, amounts of money differ in the same single dimension. One acting unit in a society has more money—or assets exchangeable for money—than another, less than, or the same.

Power involves a quite different dimension which may be formulated in terms of the conception that *A* may have power over *B*. Of course in competitive bidding the holder of superior financial assets has an advantage in that, as economists say, the "marginal utility of money" is less to him than to his competitor with smaller assets. But his "bid" is no more binding on the potential exchange partner than is that of the less affluent bidder, since in "purchasing power" all dollars are "created free and equal." There may be auxiliary reasons why the purveyor may think it advisable to accept the bid of the more affluent bidder; these, however, are not strictly economic, but concern the interrelations between money and other media, and other bases of status in the system.

The connection between the value of effectiveness —as distinguished from utility—and bindingness implies a conception in turn of the focussing of responsibility for decisions, and hence of authority for their implementation.[9] This implies a special form of inequality of power which in turn implies a priority system of commitments. The implications of having assumed binding commitments, on the fulfillment of which spokesmen for the collectivity are prepared to insist to the point of imposing serious negative sanctions for noncompliance, are of an order of seriousness such that matching the priority system in the commitments themselves there must be priorities in the matter of which decisions take precedence over others and, back of that, of which decision-making agencies have the right to make decisions at what levels. Throughout this discussion the crucial question concerns bindingness. The reference is to the collectivity, and hence the strategic significance of the various "contributions" on the performance of which the effectiveness of its action depends. Effectiveness for the collectivity as a whole is dependent on hierarchical ordering of the relative strategic importance of these contributions, and hence of the conditions governing the imposition of binding obligations on the contributors.

Hence the power of *A* over *B* is, in its legitimized form, the "right" of *A,* as a decision-making unit involved in collective process, to make decisions which take precedence over those of *B,* in the interest of the effectiveness of the collective operation as a whole.

The right to use power, or negative sanctions on a barter basis or even compulsion to assert priority of a decision over others, I shall, following Barnard, call authority. Precedence in this sense can take different forms. The most serious ambiguity here seems to derive from the assumption that authority and its attendant power may be understood as implying opposition to the wishes of "lower-order" echelons which hence includes the prerogative of coercing or compelling compliance. Though this is implicit, it may be that the higher-order authority and power may imply the prerogative is primarily significant as "defining the situation" for the performance of the lower-order echelons. The higher "authority" may then make a decision which defines terms within which other units in the collectivity will be expected to act, and this expectation is treated as binding. Thus a ruling by the Commissioner of Internal Revenue may exclude certain tax exemptions which units under his jurisdiction have thought taxpayers could claim. Such a decision need not activate an overt conflict between commissioner and taxpayer, but may rather "channel" the decisions of revenue agents and taxpayers with reference to performance of obligations.

There does not seem to be an essential theoretical difficulty involved in this "ambiguity." We can say that the primary function of superior authority is clearly to define the situation for the lower echelons of the collectivity. The problem of overcoming opposition in the form of dispositions to noncompliance then arises from the incomplete institutionalization of the power of the higher authority holder. Sources of this may well include overstepping of the bounds of his legitimate authority on the part of this agent. The concept of compliance should clearly not be limited to "obedience" by subordinates, but is just as importantly applicable to observance of the normative order by the high echelons of authority and power. The concept of constitutionalism is the critical one at this level, namely that even the highest authority is bound in the strict sense of the concept bindingness used here, by the terms of the normative order under which he operates, e.g. holds office. Hence binding obligations can clearly be "invoked" by lower-order against higher-order agencies as well as *vice versa.*

This of course implies the relatively firm institutionalization of the normative order itself. Within the framework of a highly differentiated polity it implies, in addition to constitutionalism itself, a procedural system for the granting of high political authority, even in private, to say nothing of public organizations, and a legal framework within which such authority is legitimized. This in turn includes another order of procedural institutions within which the question of the legality of actual uses of power can be tested. . . .

Conclusion

This paper has been designed as a general theoretical attack on the ancient problem of the nature of political power and its place, not only in political systems, narrowly conceived, but in the structure and processes of societies generally. The main point of reference for the attack has been the conception that the discussion of the problem in the main traditions of political thought has not been couched at a sufficiently rigorously analytical level, but has tended to treat the nation, the state, or the lower-level collectively organized "group," as the empirical object of reference, and to attempt to analyze its functioning without further basic analytical breakdown. The most conspicuous manifestation of this tendency has been the treatment of power.

The present paper takes a radically different position, cutting across the traditional lines. It takes its departure from the position of economic theory and, by inference, the asymmetry between it and the traditional political theory,[10] which has treated one as the theory of an analytically defined functional system of society—the economy—and the other as a concrete substructure, usually identified with government. Gradually the possibility has opened out both the extension of the analytical model of economic theory to the political field and the direct articulation of political with economic theory within the logical framework of the theory of the social system as a whole, so that the *polity* could be conceived as a functional subsystem of the society in all its theoretical fundamentals parallel to the economy.

This perspective necessarily concentrated attention on the place of money in the conception of the economy. More than that, it became increasingly clear that money was essentially a "symbolic" phenomenon and hence that its analysis required a frame of reference closer to that of linguistics than of technology, i.e. it is not the intrinsic properties of gold which account for the value of money under a gold standard any more than it is the intrinsic properties of the sounds symbolized as "book" which account for the valuation of physically fixed dissertations in linguistic form. This is the perspective from which the conception of power as a *generalized symbolic medium* operating in the processes of social interaction has been set forth.

This paper has not included a survey of the empirical evidence bearing on its ramified field of problems, but my strong conviction is not only that the line of analysis adopted is consistent with the broad lines of the available empirical evidence, but that it has already shown that it can illuminate a range of empirical problems which were not well understood in terms of the more conventional theoretical positions—e.g. the reasons for the general egalitarian pressure in the evolution of the political franchise, or the nature of McCarthyism as a process of political deflationary spiral.

It does not seem necessary here to recapitulate the main outline of the argument. I may conclude with the three main points with which I began. I submit, first, that the analytical path entered upon here makes it possible to treat power in conceptually specific and precise terms and thus gets away from the theoretical diffuseness called to attention, in terms of which it has been necessary to include such a very wide variety of problematical phenomena as "forms" of power. Secondly, I think it can advance a valid claim to present a resolution of the old dilemma as to whether (in the older terms) power is "essentially" a phenomenon of coercion or of consensus. It is both, precisely because it is a phenomenon which integrates a plurality of factors and outputs of political effectiveness and is not to be identified with any one of them. Finally, light has been thrown on the famous zero-sum problem, and a definite position taken that, though under certain specific assumptions the zero-sum condition holds, these are not constitutive of power systems in general, but under different conditions systematic "extension" of power spheres without sacrifice of the power of other units is just as important a case.

These claims are put forward in full awareness that on one level there is an inherent arbitrariness in them, namely that I have defined power and a number of related concepts in my own way, which is different from many if not most of the definitions current in political theory. If theory were a matter only of the arbitrary choice of definitions and assumptions and reasoning from there, it might be permissible to leave the question at that and say simply, this is only one more personal "point of view." Any claim that it is more than that rests on the conception that the scientific understanding of societies is arrived at through a gradually developing organon of theoretical analysis and empirical interpretation and verification. My most important contention is that the line of analysis presented here is a further development of a main line of theoretical analysis of the social system as a whole, and of verified interpretation of the empirical evidence presented to that body of theory. This body of theory must ultimately be judged by its outcomes both in theoretical generality and consistency, over the whole range of social system theory, and by its empirical validity, again on levels which include not only conventionally "political" references, but their empirical interrelations with all other aspects of the modern complex society looked at as a whole.

NOTES

1. There is a certain element of generality in physical force as a negative sanction, which gives it a special place in power systems. . . .
2. There are complications here deriving from the fact that power is associated with *negative* sanctions and hence that, in the face of severe resistance, their effectiveness is confined to deterrence.
3. I owe the insight into this parallel to Professor Karl W. Deutsch of Yale University (personal discussion).
4. "Sadistic" infliction of injury without instrumental significance to ego does not belong in this context.

5. I have attempted to develop this line of analysis of the significance of force somewhat more fully in "Some Reflections of the Role of Force in Social Relations," in Harry Eckstein, ed., *The Problem of Internal War* (Princeton: Princeton University Press, 1963).
6. Thus, if control of productivity operates through monetary funds, their possessor cannot "force" e.g. prospective employees to accept employment.
7. This, of course, is a relative difference. Some hazards increase the moment one steps outside his own home, police protection may be better in one local community than the next, and crossing a state boundary may mean a considerable difference in legal or actual rights.
8. *Cf.* my paper "The Principal Structures of Community," *Nomos 2* and *Structure and Process in Modern Societies* (Glencoe: The Free Press, 1959), Ch. 8. See also W. L. Hurst, *Law and Social Process in the United States* (Ann Arbor: University of Michigan Law School, 1960).
9. As already noted, in this area, I think the analysis of Chester I. Barnard, in *The Function of the Executive* (Cambridge: Harvard University Press, 1938), is so outstandingly clear and cogent that it deserves the status of a classic of political theory in my specific sense. See especially Ch. 10.
10. I myself once accepted this. *Cf. The Social System* (Glencoe: The Free Press, 1951), Ch. 5, pp. 161–163.

8

Representation and the Nature of Political Systems

Francis X. Sutton

Introduction

The study of comparative politics is currently invigorated by a world-wide perspective. There is now a lively concern with the politics of societies hitherto little regarded or left comfortably to specialists, and these societies often challenge familiar assumptions based on Western experience. Efforts to understand unfamiliar institutions or why formally similar political institutions perform differently in different societies inevitably force attention outward from the political focus into wider reaches of each society.

The present paper is sociological and it attempts to show how the political institutions of a society appear from this viewpoint. The discussion begins in generality, stressing the element of representation in any social system and coming to political science through the notion of representative agencies over territories. This approach displays political institu-

tions in a matrix of social institutions, particularly social stratification, that may be suggestive for research. The embedding of political institutions in society suggests that a classification of types of societies is a natural basis for a division of labor in comparative politics. In the concluding section of the paper, a scheme of comparative politics for "agricultural" and "industrial" societies is sketched.

Representation, Stratification, and Authority

Early in the development of modern sociology, Maine and Weber emphasized that social systems may possess structures and symbols that permit the whole system to be represented over against its individual members and sub-groups, or outside groups and individuals.[1] This feature of social systems has an obvious importance for political science.

Obviously, not all social structures are made up of corporate groups. All social structures can be viewed as *classifications, reticulations,* or *collectivities.*[2] There are some institutionalized classifications of individuals that carry no direct implications of soli-

From Francis X. Sutton, "Representation and the Nature of Political Systems," *Comparative Studies in Society and History*, II (1959), 1–10. Reprinted by permission of the author and the Editorial Committee of *Comparative Studies in Society and History.*

darity or common purposes: sex, age and education provide familiar examples. Kinship gives a major example of reticulations among roles that cut across solidary groupings. There are, of course, many social structures with definite boundaries and within which the members have a sense of solidarity, common values and purposes. These are the structures that have been called collectivities.[3]

The lines between these categories tend, of course, to be fluid. One important problem of social integration is found in the tendency of classifications to generate collectivities. We are familiar in the modern world with norms and ideologies directed at controlling these tendencies—e.g., the "Americanization" movement in our own society was a movement against emphasis on ethnic status and we also have universalistic restraints that inhibit organized expressions of class status.[4] In modern industrial societies there are persistent efforts to form representative agencies for social classifications that have some plausible common interests or solidary sentiments; the ease of building "associational" structures is no doubt responsible, and this process is one reason for the peculiarly dynamic character of modern industrial societies. Obviously, not all would-be representative agencies make classifications into corporate groups.

The need for some discrimination of *representative* and *autonomous* activities of individuals in a collectivity should be evident. In the "foreign relations" of any collectivity it is important that the actions and intentions of the collectivity as such be discriminated from the "private" actions and intentions of its component members. Thus if business firms are to incur obligations as firms there must be means of defining just how these are legitimately incurred. Similarly, in a great variety of internal matters it is often essential to know whether or not the shared values and goals of the collectivity are in question or whether matters are the autonomous concern of individuals or sub-systems. An appropriate set of symbols and role differentiations must thus exist to provide regularized channels and contexts of representation. In most societies these symbols and structures have a religious character, for reasons familiar since Durkheim's classic analysis in *The Elementary Forms of the Religious Life.*

The study of corporate groups and representation is a general topic in sociology, underlying such diverse fields as kinship, business organization, and government. I shall take the view here that our special concerns are with a particular kind of representative agency, viz., those arising from the fact that territorial relations have a special character and im-

portance in societies. Territorial claims are obviously a fundamental part of social structure, not only in the familiar legal forms of property but in a much broader sense. The claims associated with location must be recognized and maintained by the members of effectively interacting groups. But they are also intrinsically subject to invasion by outsiders who do not share the norms of the resident group. The potential use of force is of special importance in these matters and there is a familiar connection between territorial organizations and the control of the use of force. The fact that human beings have a territorial locus means that the diverse social systems in which they participate tend to have an intimate spatial juxtaposition; diverse social systems thus tend to share common location and integrative problems are intimately linked to the fact of territoriality.

The upshot of these remarks is that territorial classifications tend to fall into collectivities and to require representative agencies. I think it wise at this point to proceed illustratively and empirically, with two examples of territorial representation in primitive societies.

Example 1.

Leach's monograph on the Kachins, *Political Systems of Highland Burma,*[5] has given us an admirably analyzed picture of territorial groupings. The Kachins are a patrilineal people living in villages and village clusters. Each village contains members of several patrilineages, but there is one lineage that "owns" the village. Leach calls this the "principal lineage" and in the terminology I am using here it would be the "representative" lineage. Similarly there is a principal or representative lineage for each cluster of villages; one village is considered to be senior to others in the cluster and its principal lineage becomes the principal lineage for the whole cluster. A male from the principal lineage is in turn a representative figure for the village or village cluster. The heads of village clusters have a special honorific title, *duwa,* and Leach calls them "thigh-eating chiefs" from their prerogative of receiving a hind thigh from animals sacrificed within the village cluster. Village headmen sometimes claim the title *duwa* but lack other legitimate prerogatives of the thigh-eating chiefs.[6]

The representative or principal lineage "owns" the land of a village or village cluster in a special sense. Rights of usufruct in the land rest with individual households; they "eat it." Chiefly ownership implies little or no economic advantage but rather a bundle of rights (pp. 155–156), (1) to commit violence on the land, (2) to make offerings to the chief of the sky-spirits, *Madai nat,* (3) to dig ditches around the graves of members of the chiefly lineage, (4) to erect a special kind of house post, (5) to hold a certain kind of communal ceremony called a *manau,* (6) to perform certain annual rituals associated with the earth spirit, *ga nat* or *shadip.*[7]

In the analytical terms I am using here, items (3) and (4) in this list refer to modes of symbolizing a special representative status of the chief. There are normally no "public buildings" in a Kachin village, but the dwelling-place of the headman or chief is differentiated both by its house posts and by containing the setting (*madai-dap*) for the sacrifices to the sky-spirit. Both the chief sky-spirit (*Madai nat*) and the earth spirits, *ga nat,* rule over matters of general importance to the whole village collectivity. The sky-spirits control wealth and prosperity; the earth-spirits, fertility, both human and agricultural. The chief thus has exclusive right of ritual approach to these spirits (ideologically, his right is based on distant affinal kinship to Madai, and his ritual actions preserve prosperity and fertility). He thus becomes the representative figure for the collectivity's interests vis-à-vis supernatural powers in his capacities (2), (5) and (6). His rights of control over violence in his territory lack an intrinsically communal character, but conform to the universal tendency for these rights to be restricted to territorial representative figures.

A more extended territorial control is vested in certain chiefly lineages. The Kachins have the notion of a "domain" (*mung*) which may contain only a single village cluster, but may be much larger. Where such domains exist, there is a representative lineage. The domain chief (the *mung duwa*) and all subordinate chiefs within the domain are of the same lineage, the subordinate chiefs representing junior branches. (Actually, the Kachins observe ultimogeniture so that the senior lineage is a "youngest son lineage.") The status relations of the chiefly hierarchy are thus grounded in kinship rankings. This is carried further in a system of ranking lineages through their affinal connections (the *mayu-dama* system). Ideally, a chief of any territorial grouping is from a lineage senior to resident lineages with which it has affinal connections.

In general form, the characteristics of this society are very familiar. The use of a lineage as a representative agency over a territory is familiar in the monarchies of Western history, in China, and throughout the world. Before passing on to another example, I emphasize the following points:

1. The linkage of representation and high status
2. The inter-relations of representative figures at different levels through ideology, kinship, and stratification
3. The restriction of action for a collectivity to the representative figures

Example 2.

Because of the peculiarly "acephalous" and unpolitical character of their society, I venture to recall a few facts about the Nuer of the Southern Sudan, as described by Evans-Pritchard. The Nuer number some 300,000 and are spread out sparsely in villages over a large region around the upper Nile. They have a common language and culture but are not a collectivity in the sense used here. The largest solidary units are tribes which are economically self-sufficient and lay exclusive claim on definite territories. Within a tribe there are means for settling disputes and grievances but no such means exist between tribes. Tribes are internally segmented into sections, each with its territory and some degree of solidarity; sub-sections of these primary sections also exist. Villages are grouped into tribal sections; they also tend to fall into districts in a accordance with the ease of communication and these districts tend to coincide with tertiary tribal sections.[8] At no level in Nuer society is there a figure properly called a chief, i.e., one enjoying representative status and exercising authority and ritual powers accordingly. There is, however, a kind of representative status associated with kinship groups. The Nuer have clans which are segmented at various levels into systems of lineages. Neither clans nor lineages are localized, but members from a given clan or lineage may be found in different tribes, tribal sections, or villages. There is, nevertheless, a special association of kinship groups with territorial groupings. In each tribe there is a clan (usually in numerical minority) which enjoys a special status; its members are aristocrats, *diel,* in that tribe though not in others.[9] Similarly primary tribal sections are associated with maximal lineages as its "aristocrats." The "aristocrats" have special prestige in their territorial groupings, some claims to leadership, but no formal authority; they are not the judges of disputes nor the agencies for execution of justice.

The significance of kinship groups as territorially representative groups in this case must apparently be traced to the Nuer needs for conceptualizing social relationships in kinship terms. The relations of tribes and sub-sections are in any case fluid and easily disturbed. Evans-Pritchard treats their relations as hostile *opposition,* occasionally breaking out in feuds and undergoing processes of fission and fusion. These relations are, however, not wholly anarchic; there are restraints on the modes of fighting feuds and wars (e.g., the women and children are not killed or enslaved). A conceptualization of distinctiveness but also of relatedness and over-arching unity is provided by the kinship structure through the device of "aristocratic" or representative status for particular clans or lineages.

A close linkage between *representation* and *stratification* stands out in these examples. This is a general characteristic of corporate group structure. Representative symbols and agencies must evoke sentiments related to the common values of a corporate group. They must symbolize these values in a positive fashion. Insofar as individuals enter these representative contexts and agencies they must share in this high positive valuation. In any society, then, representative figures must either be drawn from those possessing a generalized high status in some form, or the roles they fill must have sufficient prestige to assure high status for their incumbents. It also follows that in any society territorially representative institutions must be shaped by the character of the stratification system.

Representation also has intimate links to *authority*. In a highly segmental and traditionalistic society, there is limited need for representative figures to mobilize a total group and commit it to a program of action. Hence the very weak authority of Kachin chiefs and the practical non-existence of territorial authority figures among the Nuer. But insofar as representation does imply the capacity to commit a group to action or to perform coordinated acts for its general welfare, it implies *authority*. The legitimate bases of this authority are the bases of legitimate representation. Weber's well-known stress on the problem of legitimacy for political systems is a stress which might be applied in any corporate group. As I see the matter, the prominence of legitimacy questions in political systems derives from the delicacy and difficulty of integrating social systems about legitimate representative agencies. All institutionalized structures are "legitimate" in some sense but representative agencies must have a peculiarly high and difficult kind of legitimacy.

The Nature of Political Systems

The territorial representative agencies I have been discussing would be called political institutions in familiar usages of the term "political." The question immediately arises whether or not they constitute the essential core of political systems. There is good reason to regard them in this way. The study of political systems then becomes the study in the first instance of representative agencies over territories. The same sort of fuzziness in the boundaries of political systems exists which exists for social systems in general. But on this showing, the study of political systems has a special focus and other features of a total society enter the study only insofar as they bear on the structure and functioning of territorial representative institutions.

I do not believe that this view of the nature of political systems is in any sense radical or original. I would, however, argue that it is a much more convenient and practical definition of the political than some others, in particular than the view that political systems are constituted by all the manifestations of power and authority in a society. The difficulty with this latter view is that any social structure contains patterns of power and authority. A political scientist who took seriously the view that his field is the comprehensive study of power and authority would have to busy himself with families and factories as well as with princes and parliaments. There might for some special purposes be advantages in such catholicity, but for most purposes I believe this would be a confusing and disheartening commission.

It is a familiar sociological argument that territorially representative institutions become ultimate agencies of social control. I thus conceive that I am not in conflict with Weber's definition of the "political" as exclusive control over the legitimate use of force in a territory but I see advantages in not putting the control of the use of force in the definitional center. Political institutions are representative agencies and the ultimate sanctions they can exercise are only one feature of their activity.

There is some sociological theory which can be applied directly to general discussion of the structure of territorially representative agencies (or "political institutions," as I shall now freely call them). For example, the kind of distinction Bagehot made when he talked of the "dignified" and "efficient" parts of the English constitution is observed clearly in many states. In extreme form, the principal symbolic figures may be quite cut off from the effective operation of political authority. Bagehot's queen kept a stubborn grip on affairs but others like the Japanese emperors under the Tokugawa Regime have lost it almost completely. The discrimination of functions here rests, of course, on an analytical distinction relevant in any political system. It is that between symbolic representation and executive control.

Comparative Politics in Different Types of Societies

A general scheme for the study of comparative politics is implied in the conception of political systems as focussed about territorial representative agencies. From the preceding discussion it appears that these agencies will reflect the social structures they represent and a classification of societies should provide some basis for dividing the vast field of comparative politics. This observation may seem only to throw back one problem on the solution of a more obscure and difficult one. But one need not have in hand a sophisticated and rigorous classification of societies for a rough charting of domains in comparative politics. The familiar distinction of industrial and pre-industrial societies is an important and useful distinction if one reduces the sprawl of the latter category. This may be done by neglecting a large range of so-called primitive societies and concentrating on those having intensive settled agriculture. In the following paragraphs I offer some evidence that it is possible to characterize in a general way the political systems that arise in *agricultural* and *modern industrial* societies.[10]

It would be very helpful at this point if there were a general political science of pre-industrial, agricultural societies. Weber's essay on Patrimonialism in *Wirtschaft und Gesellschaft* is an isolated monument reminding us of what is possible.

A unified state in these societies has commonly depended on a representative lineage. The structure of the political system has been basically particularistic in accordance with the character of the underlying society. There have consequently been great problems in maintaining unity over extended areas. Local particularism has meant a kind of federative structure.[11] Most of the members of a local community have not been direct members of the political system in the sense that a modern citizen is. They have entered into the political system through local representative figures who have normally held a diffuse high status. The integration of the state has then depended on the coherence of an aristocratic class and its relations to the royal lineage. The structure of political institutions reflects this general social structure. (Thus, in the Middle Ages in the West, kings were surrounded by aristocratic councils.) Various devices in different states have appeared to counterbalance the claims of local aristo-

crats to representative statuses. They have usually involved some measure of universalistic recruitment. Some, like the Chinese bureaucracy, were extraordinarily successful over long periods. Others like the slave households of the Ottomans have been more desperate measures and correspondingly more susceptible to rapid decay. The executive competence of these "patrimonial governments" looks extremely limited by comparison with modern bureaucratic states. They are often sufficient to the needs of a stable agricultural society but very ill adapted to the efficient direction of social change which is of such central importance in modern bureaucratic governments. They have been hampered in effective operation by fixed particularistic claims and Weber has shown a universal tendency for hard-won centralization to crumble into a loose feudalism.

Many special problems which are of minor or trivial significance in modern industrial societies assume central importance in these pre-industrial societies. One obvious example is the subject I like to call "kingship and kinship." Over the world a great many different arrangements have emerged to assure regular succession to royal status. The fact that kings have siblings, collateral and affinal relatives poses a whole series of integrative problems. The interest in the incest problem, for example, has led to considerable attention to the famous royal exception among the Ptolemies, the Azande and elsewhere. Royal incest invites comparisons with different devices having similar functional significance, for example, the Ottomans' elimination of their problems with in-laws by slave marriages and their problems with siblings by extermination. Other arrangements like those of the Banyankole or the Zulu invite comparative attention.

A general comparative politics for pre-industrial societies would doubtless be of primary interest to pure scholarship but it might also be a valuable base point for understanding the transitional societies which crowd the contemporary scene.

In the pure type of a modern industrial society we should expect the representative territorial agency to have the following characteristics: (1) It should be an *association* rather than a lineage or a patrimonial household. (2) In its symbolism and ideology it should reflect the universalistic values of the collectivity it represents. If for no other reason, one expects the government to be an association because it must provide rational direction in a continually changing and dynamic society. The universalism in the class structure probably also requires an associational form—there should be no diffusely qualified aristocracy to whom governmental functions might of right be allocated. As in the examples cited above, the symbolism of government must conform to the underlying social structure and its dominant values.

Actual and historical societies approximate to this model, but with characteristic modifications reflecting their history of transition from agricultural-type societies. In the Western world the urge toward equality which Tocqueville saw as the dominant passion in the 19th century has issued in the universalistic concept of citizenship and the ideology of popular government. The idea of a nation as the underlying collectivity has slowly lost its ambiguities. Montesquieu could still speak of "la nation, c'est-à-dire les seigneurs et les évêques," and later De Maistre answers his question: "Qu'est-ce qu'une nation? C'est le souverain et l'aristocratie." Such limitations of the "nation" to its high status groups seem to represent a natural confusion of collectivities with their representative figures, but the confusion has become progressively less likely. The norms of universalism and the facts of status mobility have fostered the conception of a nation as an undifferentiated mass of citizens. The break-up of local particularism and the decline of ascriptive statuses have produced problems of security for individuals that have given great emotional force to nationalism. Various forms of symbolic participation, through elections and otherwise, have reinforced ideologies of government as representative of all the people.

The form of political institutions as associations built on elective offices and bureaucratic hierarchies is basically compatible with universalistic values. A high seriousness deriving from the force of national sentiment provides a high status for representative authority without direct dependence on the class status of those who hold governmental offices. The status of persons in government is, of course, integrated more or less closely with status rankings in other categories. In no modern society are legislators and officials drawn indiscriminately from all class strata; the upper strata make disproportionately heavy contributions and this is no mere survival of older patterns.[12]

The anarchist (and Marxist) ideal of a government run by genuinely "common" people is incompatible with the extensive authority and technical difficulty of modern governments. A progressive extension of universalistic recruitment has, of course, been characteristic. We find gradual elimination of the disabilities which kept Jews and Social Democrats out of the old German imperial civil service or which kept the French civil service in the hands of the *haute bourgeoisie*.[13] The familiar high status of

representative figures is nevertheless maintained, although tempered by an ideology which makes them "servants of the people."

The problems of integration for political systems in modern industrial societies are distinctly different from those I have suggested for agricultural societies. The resistances of local particularism have been removed and questions of sheer territorial integration are displaced to the international level. In contrast to patrimonial governments, modern bureaucratic governments seem to have lesser problems of organizational stability. The stiff autonomy of aristocrats has given way to the dependable compliance of salaried officials. Recent history, nevertheless, shows no want of difficulties and instabilities in the structure of representative authority. These difficulties seem to rise in part from the strains of transition and in part from intrinsic problems of industrial societies.

From this general picture, I conclude that there is a legitimate *special* kind of comparative politics for modern industrial societies. The conclusion is in a sense very trite—no professional student of modern governments need be told that his study has its own personal complexities. It may not, however, be trivial to suggest that there are theoretical as well as pragmatic bases for specialization—the earnest student of comparative politics in its familiar Western scope need not then feel that his specialization is merely a practical consequence of limited energy and erudition. Actually, of course, the rapid diffusion of Western-model political institutions has produced many mixed and transitional situations that blur the lines of convenient division. But these should admit of study in precisely the fashion that their labels suggest, viz. as intermediate or mixed forms between generally understood types of societies and political systems.

NOTES

NOTE: This paper was first presented in considerably extended form at a conference under the auspices of the Committee on Comparative Politics of the Social Science Research Council, at Princeton University, June 2–4, 1955.

1. I have found Maine's discussion of primogeniture in his *Ancient Law* particularly instructive on the ideas developed here. Weber used the notion of a *Verband* extensively in his work. In their translation of the first part of Weber's systematic treatise, *Wirtschaft und Gesellschaft*, Parsons and Henderson have translated *Verband* as "corporate group." *Theory of Economic and Social Organization* (New York: Oxford University Press, 1947), pp. 145–148.

2. Radcliffe-Brown has used precisely this classification (with different terminology). *Structure and Function in Primitive Society* (Glencoe, Illinois, 1952), p. 191.

3. C. Parsons and Shils, *Toward a General Theory of Action* (Harvard University Press, 1952), pp. 192–195.

4. I shall assume some familiarity with the concepts of universalism and particularism, ascription and achievement,

as developed by Parsons and Linton respectively. I shall also make use of the idea of an "association" as a very general term for social structures like business firms, hospitals, governmental agencies, etc., which have delimited functions and are largely ruled by norm of universalism and achievement.

5. Harvard University Press (for London School of Economics), 1954.

6. I restrict myself here to *gumsa* organization. There is a different form (*gumlao*).

7. Leach omits this last point from his list but from other evidence in his monograph I conclude he did it through oversight.

8. M. Fortes and E. E. Evans-Pritchard (eds.), *African Political Systems* (New York, 1940), p. 275.

9. E. E. Evans-Pritchard, *The Nuer* (Oxford, 1954), pp. 211 ff.

10. The typology of societies was developed at some length in the SSRC conference presentation from which this paper derives.

11. S. F. Nadel's *A Black Byzantium* (Oxford, 1942) gives a good picture of this kind of structure in a Nigerian kingdom. I have also found instruction in Funck-Brentano's account of French villages before 1789, *The Old Regime in France* (London, 1929), Ch. VIII, and in Marian W. Smith's picture of the integration of Indian villages into wider political structures (*American Anthropologist*, LIV, 1952), pp. 41–56. "Federative" is perhaps too loose a term for what I have in mind; where there is a centralized "capital," the solidarity is radial and there is motivated opposition among the points (village committees) at the periphery.

12. Cf. the survey of the backgrounds of parliamentary representatives in various European countries (including the Soviet Union) by Mattei Dogan, *L'origine sociale du personnel parlementaire dans l'Est et l'Ouest de l'Europe* (*Transactions of 2nd World Congress of Sociology, 1954*, II, pp. 175–179).

13. On this latter see the paper by Bottomore, pp. 143–153 in the *Transactions* just cited.

9

A Developmental Approach to Political Systems

Gabriel A. Almond

The Capabilities of Political Systems

More than four decades ago when Max Weber delivered his lecture on "Politics as a Calling," he discouraged us from thinking of politics in terms of performance. He told us:

> . . . The state cannot be defined in terms of its ends. There is scarcely any task that some political association has not taken in hand, and there is no task that has always been exclusive and peculiar to political associations. . . . Ultimately, we can define the modern state only in terms of the specific means peculiar to it . . . namely, the use of physical force.[1]

Contemporary empirical political theory tends to follow Weber in its stress on power and process, the "who" and the "how" of politics. It emphasizes two questions: (1) Who makes decisions? (2) How are decisions made?[2] The performance of political systems tends to be inferred from structure and process or evaluated according to moral and ideological norms. When we introduce the concept of capabili-

ties, their development and transformation, we explicitly add two more questions to the "who?" and the "how?" The first of these is what impact does the political system have, what does it do, in its domestic and international environments? And the second question is, what impact does the society and the international environment have on the political system?

Parsons comes closer to meeting the needs of the contemporary political theorist when he speaks of the function of the polity as that of the ". . . mobilization of societal resources and their commitment for the attainment of collective goals, for the formation and implementation of 'public policy.' "[3] Francis Sutton similarly emphasizes the importance of the functions of political systems in their social and international environments, stressing integration for the internal environment and representation for the international.[4] The development of the concept of the capabilities of political systems represents a pursuit of these leads, but we have had to go farther in specifying types of relationships between the political system and its environments, for "goal attainment," "integration," and "representation" must be broken down into their components, and these elements treated as continua, if we are to be able to

From Gabriel A. Almond, "A Developmental Approach to Political Systems," *World Politics*, XVII (April 1965), 195–203. This excerpt from a longer article has been reprinted by permission of the publisher.

code the performance of political systems in the environment in a discriminating way.

The concept of capabilities, then, is a way of characterizing the performance of the political system and of changes in performance, and of comparing political systems according to their performance. Our particular classification of capabilities is a coding scheme, derived from a kind of informal pre-testing operation. We have to try it out to determine whether it helps us discriminate among political systems, or handle political development in a meaningful way.

We suggest five categories of capability derived from our classification of inputs and outputs proposed at an earlier point. These are: (1) extractive, (2) regulative, (3) distributive, (4) symbolic, and (5) responsive. These five categories of capability may be viewed as functional requisites; that is, any political system—simple or complex—must in some measure extract resources from, regulate behavior in, distribute values in, respond to demands from, and communicate with other systems in its environments. There are surely other ways of categorizing the functional requisites of political systems at the system-environment level;[5] but this particular classification is presented as a useful starting point. It is the product of an informal coding of historical and contemporary political systems. A rigorous test of their usefulness can be made only by formal and explicit employment of these categories in coding historical and contemporary data.

But to say that these are functional requisites of any political system is only the beginning, since we are not interested in defining the minimal political system. We are concerned with characterizing real political systems both historical and contemporary, comparing them with one another at the system-environment level, dividing them into meaningful classes, and discovering their developmental properties.

For these purposes, we need to treat capabilities as performance magnitudes, either actual performance or potential performance. We stress that capability refers to performance and has to be separated from the institutions and agencies involved in the performance. To relate the institutions and structures to performance is one of the central problems of political analysis, and we ought not to confuse rates of performance with the means or instruments of performance.

Perhaps capabilities may be best thought of as ranges of particular kinds of performance. An examination of a particular political system may show variation in its rate of resource extraction over time. In war situations, the rate may be high; in normal periods, the rate may be substantially lower. But the problem of ascertaining the range of capability is more complex than examining rates of performance in normal and crisis situations. We may need to specify the extractive *potential* of a political system. What rate of extraction is this system capable of and under what conditions? This is only partly inferable from past record of performance. To get at this aspect of the range of capability we need to look at the support aspects of capabilities.

It is also necessary to distinguish between capabilities and elite policies and goals. Elite policies and goals may and usually do involve more than one capability. For example, a policy of economic development will require increases in resource extraction, and regulation, perhaps holding the line on distribution, and coping with demand inputs by increasing the symbolic capability. From this point of view capabilities may be viewed as ends intermediate to the policy goals of the elites. Since policies are made up of different doses of the different classes of outputs, capabilities analysis is essential to rigorous comparative policy analysis. It may enable us to distinguish sharply and operationally among different kinds of economic development, welfare, and other kinds of public policies.

It may also be in order to point to the implications of capabilities analysis for normative political theory. The inclusion of the performance or capabilities aspect of political systems may help bridge the gap which has been developing between the scientific and normative study of political systems. Questions regarding the "proper ends" of the state need to be grounded on empirical evidence of the different ways different kinds of political systems interact with individuals and groups in their domestic societies, and with political and social systems in the international environment. Empirical studies of the *performance* of political systems, of the *what* of politics (in addition to the *who* and *how*), should enable us to grapple operationally with what we mean when we speak of good and evil, just and unjust, political systems.

We may turn now to definitions of the five categories of capability. By the *extractive* capability, we mean measures of the range of performance of the political system in drawing material and human resources from the domestic and international environment. We separate this capability out because there have been political systems like the Mongol Empire, the warlords in China, guerrilla chieftains in Mexico, which have had little more than an extractive capability. Thus it makes sense to treat it separately, since it is to be found in all political systems, and is the distinguishing mark of a particular class of political systems. The extractive capability may be estimated quantitatively as a proportion of the national product; and its variations may be estimated quantitatively over time.

The *regulative* capability refers to the flow of control over behavior and of individual and group relations stemming from the political system. It is even more difficult to express it in quantitative terms than is the extractive capability, though aspects of it are measurable, and in a general way its magnitude, its pattern, and changes in its magnitude and pattern can be estimated. Here we have to concern ourselves with the objects of regulation, the frequency and intensity of regulation, and the limits of tolerance of regulation. While formulating indices to measure changes in this capability is a complex problem, the utility of this concept as an approach to political classification and development is evident. With these two capability concepts we can distinguish between primarily extractive political systems such as those referred to above, and extractive-regulative ones such as the historic bureaucratic political systems described by Eisenstadt in his recent book.[6] Furthermore, we can chart the developmental process from the one to the other, as regulative outputs cease being primarily unintended consequences of or instrumental to extraction and acquire goals of their own, such as some conception of social justice, order, economic advantage, or religious conformity.

The *distributive* capability refers to the allocation of goods, services, honors, statuses, and opportunities of various kinds from the political system to individuals and groups in the society. It is the flow of activity of the political system as dispenser of values or as redistributor of values among individuals and groups. Some aspects of this capability are more readily measurable than others. The structure of taxation may be viewed in its distributive aspects. The magnitude of welfare and educational programs can be expressed quantitatively, as proportions, and in terms of the social strata affected. Thus, while the general impact of public policy on social stratification is difficult to express quantitatively, there are aspects of it which are measurable, and the total pattern may be characterized for comparative and developmental purposes.

What we have said about political capabilities suggests a logic of capability analysis. An extractive capability implies some regulation and distribution, though these consequences may be unintended. A regulative capability implies an extractive capability, if only to gain the resources essential to regulation; and it is difficult to conceive of a regulative capability which would not in some way affect the distribution of values and opportunities. They are not only logically related. They suggest an order of development. Thus political systems which are primarily extractive in character would appear to be the simplest ones of all. They do not require the degree of role differentiation and specialized orientations that extractive-regulative systems or extractive-regulative-distributive ones do. Regulative systems cannot develop without extractive capabilities; thus the development of the one implies the development of the other. Increasing the extractive capability implies an increase in the regulative capability, as when, for example, political systems move from intermittent collection of tribute or raids to some form of regularized taxation. Similarly, a distributive system implies an extractive capability, and obviously can reach a higher distributive level if it is associated with a regulative capability as well.

At an earlier point we spoke of *symbolic* inputs, referring to demands for symbolic behavior on the part of political elites—displays of the majesty and power of the state in periods of threat or on ceremonial occasions, affirmations of norms, or communication of policy intent from political elites. We referred to symbolic supports, meaning such behavior as showing respect for, pride in, or enthusiasm for political elites, physical symbols of the state such as flags and monuments, and political ceremonials. And we spoke of symbolic outputs, including affirmations of values by elites, displays of physical symbols, displays of incumbents of sacred or honored offices, or statements of policies and intents. Thus we need to deal with the *symbolic capability* of political systems and treat its relations to the other forms of capability. Surely we do not mean by symbolic capability simply the quantitative flow of symbolic events into and out of the political system. If capability is a profile of rates of performance—e.g., rates of extraction, regulation, and distribution—then symbolic capability is a rate of *effective symbol flow,* from the political system into the society and the international environment. The displays of flags, troops, and ships, the conduct of ceremonies on the occasion of anniversaries, or on the birth, marriage, coronation, and death of princes, kings, presidents, and the like, the construction of monuments, visits by royalty or high officials, are symbolic outputs either in response to demands or independently initiated by elites. The effectiveness of symbolic outputs of this kind are difficult to measure, but political elites (and journalists and scholars) often attempt to do so by counting crowds and audiences, recording the decibels and duration of applause, examining reports on the demeanor of audiences, or conducting surveys of attitudes. Similarly, affirmations of values by elites may be effective or ineffective. They may create or mobilize reserves of support, as did Churchill's speeches during World War II. Statements of policies may facilitate other kinds of system capability, increasing the rate of acquiescence in extraction, obedience to regulation, acceptance of distribution, and reducing the input of demands.

Symbolic output is not the same thing as symbolic capability. The output of symbols may cease to be edifying, menacing, stirring, credible, or even observed, listened to, or read. Royalty or high officials may be spat upon, pelted with rotten vegetables, statues thrown down from high places, pamphlets cast aside, television and radio sets turned off. Or, as in the case of new nations, the symbolism may have little if any resonance. Symbolic messages may be transmitted but not received. The symbols of local authority may be the only ones granted legitimacy, while the central symbolic output may have little, if any, meaning or effect.

While extractive, regulative, distributive, and symbolic capabilities are ways of describing the pattern of *outputs* of the political system into the internal and external environments, the *responsive* capability is a relationship between *inputs,* coming from the society or the international political system, and *outputs.* The responsive capability is an estimate of the degree to which outgoing activity is the consequence of demands arising in the environments of the political system. Again, the usefulness of this concept is suggested by the fact that it implies operational measures, i.e., a given quantity of responses to demands over the total of the demands. We are not minimizing the difficulties in translating this concept of responsiveness into specific measurable relationships. Obviously, in reality we shall have to settle for approximations, for measurement of aspects of the relationship between inputs and outputs.

The reader must forgive the crudeness of this provisional formulation of the concept of political capability. It is the logical next step from treating the political system in terms of interaction with its foreign and domestic environments, in input-conversion-output terms. The capabilities of a political system are a particular patterning of input and output, particular performance profiles of political systems. We are more interested in demonstrating the importance of this level of analysis than in making claims for the effectiveness of this particular schema, more concerned with focusing and directing theoretical speculation and research than in present-

ing what would be a prematurely formalized theory. The truth of the matter is that we shall only arrive at a good capabilities theory through historical and contemporary studies in which we test out these and other coding schemes.

Tentatively we suggest that we may use the same capabilities scheme for the international interaction of political systems. Just as a political system may have an extractive capability in regard to its own society, so also may it have an extractive capability in regard to the international environment. Thus it may draw spoils, booty of war, and tribute from the international environment, or it may conduct or protect trade and investment, receive subsidies or loans. In the same sense a political system may have an international regulative capability, as in the conquest and the assimilation of other territories and peoples, or in limiting the freedom of other political systems in their political, religious, or military arrangements, or through participation in international organizations which affect the conduct of nations. An international distributive capability may be expressed in tariff arrangements, the granting of subsidies, subventions, loans, and technical aid. The international symbolic capability is a set of measures of the impact of symbol output on political systems in the international environment. Revolutionary symbol output may have great impact on the performance and development of other political systems, and increase the impact of other capabilities in the international environment. Symbol output into the international environment in the form of appeals to common culture and tradition may similarly affect the performance and development of other political systems, and initiate feedbacks which benefit the initiating political system. Statements by political elites of foreign policies and intents may have important effects on the other capabilities of the initiating political system, as well as on the capabilities of other political systems. An international responsive or accommodative capability may be expressed as a relation between its extractive, regulative, and distributive capabilities, and demands from the international environment.

Again this concept of capabilities enables us to handle the relations between internal and international capabilities more systematically than has been the case in the past, just as it enables us to handle the relations among capabilities. Thus a political system which has developed only an internal extractive capability is unlikely to develop other forms of capability in the international environment. Only when a political system develops the institutions and orientations necessary for societal regulation is it likely to pursue regulative goals in the international environment. Similarly, a political system which has not developed an internal distributive capability is unlikely to pursue distributive goals in the international environment. Finally, a political system which has a high internal responsive capability will manifest a different kind of international responsiveness than a system in which internal responsiveness is less well developed. What we suggest here is that there are relations between domestic and international capabilities. But beyond this we can only say that the interrelation among domestic and international capabilities is a matter for deductive and empirical method used together, rather than for simple reliance on logical inference.

Thus the aims of research on political systems must be: (1) to discover and compare capabilities profiles summarizing the flows of inputs and outputs between these political systems and their domestic and international environments; (2) to discover and compare the structures and processes which convert these inputs into outputs; and (3) to discover and compare the recruitment and socialization processes which maintain these systems in equilibrium or enable them to adapt to environmental or self-initiated changes.

We have also to speak of the capabilities of other social systems. Just as the political system has a particular level and range of performance which we can summarize in terms of a capabilities profile, so also do other social systems in the society of which the political system is a part, and the international political system of which it is a member, have capabilities. Such social systems as the economy, the religious community, or family, kinship, and tribal structures also extract resources from the environment, regulate behavior, distribute values, display and transmit symbols, and respond to demands. Similarly, political systems in the international environment have capabilities, and the international political system may have some extractive, regulative, distributive, symbolic, and responsive capability. The flow of inputs into political systems, the kinds of problems they confront, and the pressure on them to develop capabilities will vary with the performance patterns or the capabilities of these other social systems. The distributive capability of an economy will affect the rate and intensity of demands for distribution, regulation, and the like entering into the political system. The need for developing the regulative capability of a political system will vary with the regulative capability of other social systems, including the international political system. When we think of the factors affecting the capabilities of a particular political system, we must see this problem in the context of interacting social systems, of which the political system is only one.

NOTES

1. Gerth and Mills, eds., *From Max Weber*, 77.
2. See, for example, Harold D. Lasswell, *Politics: Who Gets What, When and How* (Glencoe, 1959); Dahl, *Modern Political Analysis* (New Jersey: Prentice-Hall, 1963).
3. Talcott Parsons, *Structure and Process in Modern Societies* (Glencoe: The Free Press, 1959), 181.
4. "Social Theory and Comparative Politics," in Eckstein and Apter, eds., *Comparative Politics* (New York, 1963), 77.
5. See, for example, David Apter, "A Comparative Method for the Study of Politics," in *ibid.*, 82 ff.
6. S. N. Eisenstadt, *The Political Systems of Empires* (Glencoe: The Free Press, 1963).

10
Charisma, Order, and Status

Edward Shils

Here I will explore the ramifications of charismatic sensitivity, i.e., the propensity to impute charismatic qualities to actions, persons, institutions and cultural

From Edward Shils, "Charisma, Order, and Status," *American Sociological Review*, XXX, No. 2 (April 1965), 199–213. Reprinted by permission of the author and publisher.

objects. My analysis takes its point of departure in Max Weber's analysis of charismatic authority. In trying to analyze charismatic authority more systematically than Weber was able to do, I have concluded that he was dealing with one particular variant of the charismatic propensity, which has more far-reaching, more permeative manifestations than his analysis has hitherto led us to believe.

Charisma According to Max Weber

Max Weber repeatedly emphasized that none of the three types of legitimate authority he set forth was ever found in its pure form. In his analysis of the structure of religious, monarchical, and feudal institutions, he dealt repeatedly with the coexistence of the charismatic and the other types of authority. In his analysis of modern bureaucratic-political—and to a lesser extent administrative and economic—institutions, he also dealt with the recurrent appearance of charismatic personalities in the midst of bureaucratic organizations, in conflict with them or dominating them. His attention was given to the charismatic personality, i.e., to the charismatic quality imputed to a spectacular, extraordinary, disruptive exercise of authority by an individual.

Central to Weber's interpretation of society was the distinction between the "extraordinary," or the explosively novel, and the recurrent processes through which institutions reproduce themselves by virtue of the effective empirical validity of the traditional and legal rules or norms, and by the attachment of "significant" sectors of a society or its institutional sub-systems to the results of these norms or rules. He wished to distinguish innovators and creators from maintainers—in W. I. Thomas' old classification, "creative persons" from "philistines." It was in the pursuit of this central theme that he distinguished the "charismatically" legitimated authority of an individual innovator from the "traditionally" and "rational-legally" legitimated types of authority which keep a system moving in a stereotyped manner. The distinction between the extraordinary, the creative, the innovative, on the one side, and the ordinary, the routine, the recurrently reproduced, is not merely a distinction between infrequent and frequent actions, or between actions generated by "great" personalities and those which are the result of anonymous adherence to roles and rules. It is underlain implicitly in Weber's scheme of analysis by a distinction between an intense and immediate contact with what the actors involved believe to be ultimate values or events and a more attenuated, more mediated contact with such values or events through the functioning of established institutions. Weber regarded the former as the locus of the charismatic which he seems to have believed to be intrinsically alien to the latter. I do not think the matter is as clearcut as Weber apparently thought. It seems to me that an attenuated, mediated, institutionalized charismatic propensity is present in the routine functioning of society. There is, in society, a widespread disposition to attribute charismatic properties to ordinary secular roles, institutions, symbols, and strata or aggregates of persons. Charisma not only disrupts social order, it also maintains or conserves it.

Of course, Weber was not blind to particular instances of this conserving, institutionalized manifestation of the charismatic propensity. He certainly attended to the ways in which ecclesiastical institutions retained a considerable component of the charismatic authority with which they were endowed by their prophetic founders. Nonetheless it remains true that he saw the charismatic element as essentially alien to the other modes of authority by which churches are governed. Likewise, in his studies of bureaucratic, political, and administrative machines, he emphasized that charismatic personalities emerge and establish an ascendancy beyond that called for by a "rational-legal" definition of their roles. But these are only instances of coexistence; they testify to the irrepressibility of the need to attribute charismatic properties to individuals under certain conditions, and to the probability that certain kinds of personality—expansive and dominating, with strong and fundamental convictions—will emerge, under conditions of stress, in specific decision-making, power-exercising roles.

Weber's problem was to describe the mechanisms and to state the conditions of the emergence of charismatic leadership and its subsidence into a routine and occasionally dynamic coexistence with traditional and bureaucratic authority. My aim is to see the charismatic phenomenon in a more comprehensive perspective. I wish to examine the mechanisms of the charismatic phenomenon in secularized societies, to see it at work in the non-ecclesiastical institutions that have conventionally been considered entirely free of the charismatic, except for the occasional disruptive or transforming intrusion of charismatic personalities. The problem then becomes the elucidation not only of the conditions under which the propensity to impute charismatic qualities is concentrated on individuals but also of the conditions under which it finds a more dispersed focus on institutions and strata and on the properties of roles.

The Redefinition of Charisma: Awe-Arousing Centrality

In this section I wish to render more explicit what is already implicit in the current usage of the concept of charisma and in so doing I will disclose the unity of the religious and the secular conceptions of charisma.

Charisma in the narrower and original sense is the state or quality of being produced by receipt of the gifts of grace.[1] In Weber's usage, charisma is, in the first instance, a property of conduct and personality regarded by those who respond to it as a manifestation of endowment with, or possession by, some divine power. (Weber did not insist that the person really be "possessed" or "endowed"; only that he be thought to be possessed by or endowed with these qualities.) Weber did not restrict his usage of "charisma" to refer only to manifestations of divinity. He often used the term to refer to extraordinary individualities, i.e., powerful, ascendent, persistent, effectively expressive personalities who impose themselves on their environment by their exceptional courage, decisiveness, self-confidence, fluency, insight, energy, etc., and who do not necessarily believe that they are working under divine inspiration. He used the term to refer to politicians, artists, scientists, soldiers, and other occupations the incumbents of which nowadays think of themselves as having, or are thought to have, nothing to do with religion, in the conventional sense, in the performance of their roles. Sometimes, indeed, he made the content of charisma quite psychological, using it to refer to a particular constellation of personality qualities. (In this latter sense charisma has come to be widely used in current high- and middle-brow speech, in sociological and political analyses, and in the superior ladies' magazines.) The common feature of these different manifestations, religious and psychological, was extraordinariness—an extraordinariness constituted by the high intensity with which certain *vital, crucial* qualities are manifested, in contrast with the low intensity with which they appear in the ordinary round of life.

The charismatic quality of an individual as perceived by others, or himself, lies in what is thought to be his connection with (including possession by or embodiment of) some *very central* feature of man's existence and the cosmos in which he lives. The centrality, coupled with intensity, makes it extraordinary. (Infrequency is only an incidental feature, although of course the combination of intensity of presence and centrality of significance is infrequent.) The centrality is constituted by its formative power in initiating, creating, governing, transforming, maintaining, or destroying what is vital in man's life. That central power has often, in the course of man's existence, been conceived of as God, the ruling power or creator of the universe, or some divine or other transcendent power controlling or markedly influencing human life and the cosmos within which it exists. The central power might be a fundamental principle or principles, a law or laws governing the universe, the underlying and driving force of the universe. It might be thought to reside in the ultimate principles of law which should govern man's conduct, arising from or derived from the nature of the universe and essential to human existence, discerned or elucidated by the exercise of man's most fundamental rational and expressive powers. Scientific discovery, ethical promulgation, artistic creativity, political and organizational authority (*auctoritatem, auctor,* authorship), and in fact all forms of genius, in the original sense of the word as permeation by the "spirit," are as much instances of the category of charismatic things as is religious prophecy.[2]

This extended conception of a charismatic property (as perceived by one who is responsive to it, including the "charismatic person" himself) refers to a vital, "serious," ultimately symbolic event, of which divinity is one of many forms. Presumptive contact with the divine, possession by the divine, the possession of magical powers, are only modes of being charismatic. Contact with this class of vital, "serious" events may be attained through reflective wisdom or through disciplined scientific penetration, or artistic expression, or forceful and confident reality-transforming action. All these are also modes of contact with, or embodiment of, something very "serious" in Durkheim's sense, which is thought to be, and therewith becomes, central or fundamental to man's existence.

This contact through inspiration, embodiment or perception, with the vital force which underlies man's existence, his coming-to-be and passing-away, is manifested in demeanor, words and actions. The person who through sensitivity, cultivated or disciplined by practice and experience, by rationally controlled observation and analysis, by intuitive penetration, or by artistic disclosure, reaches or is believed to have attained contact with that "vital layer" of reality is, by virtue of that contact, a charismatic person.

Most human beings, because their endowment is inferior or because they lack opportunities to develop the relevant capacities, do not attain that intensity of contact. But most of those who are unable to attain it themselves are, at least intermittently, responsive to its manifestations in the words, actions and products of others who have done so. They are capable of such appreciation and occasionally feel a need for it. Through the culture they acquire and through their interaction with and perception of those more "closely connected" with the cosmically and socially central, their own weaker responsiveness is fortified and heightened.

All of these charismatic "connections" may be manifested intensely in the qualities, words, actions and products of individual personalities. This was emphasized by Weber and it has entered into contemporary sociology. But they may also become resident, in varying degrees of intensity, in institutions—in the qualities, norms, and beliefs to which members are expected to adhere or are expected to possess—and, in an attenuated form, in categories or strata of the members of a society.

Weber's chapter on the transformation of charisma touched on institutionalized forms of charismatic phenomena of lesser intensity, but he did not subject them to more elaborate consideration.[3] He discussed the transformation of genuine, i.e., intense, individually concentrated, charisma into such patterns as "kinship charisma"[4] (*Gentilcharisma*), "hereditary charisma" (*Erbscharisma*), and "charisma of office" (*Amtscharisma*).[5] In his treatment, the institutionalization of charisma was confined to ecclesiastical, monarchical, and familial institutions, where the sacred and the primordial are massively or tangibly present. Even there, he tended to think of such charismatic patterns as lacking the genuinely charismatic element, and as greatly supported by considerations of "interest" in guaranteeing stable succession and continuing legitimacy. For the most part, he dealt with the "segregation" of charisma in the course of institutional establishment through its concentration into specific action, roles, or occasions, while it evaporated from the rest of the system, which was constituted by elements of action wholly alien to "genuine charisma."

He did not consider the more widely dispersed, unintense operation of the charismatic element in corporate bodies governed by the rational-legal type of authority.[6]

In other words, Weber had a pronounced tendency to segregate the object of attributed charisma, to see it almost exclusively in its most concentrated and intense forms, and to disregard the possibility of its dispersed and attenuated existence. He tended indeed to deny the possibility that charisma can become an integral element in the process of secular institutionalization. (This might well be part of Weber's more general tendency to see the modern world as *entzaubert,* as devoid of any belief in the possibility of genuine charisma.)

Weber's intent was to characterize the modern social and political order as one in which belief in transcendent values and their embodiment in indi-

viduals and institutions was being driven into a more and more restricted domain, as a result of the processes of rationalization and bureaucratization, which he so rightly underscored as characteristic of modern society. This historicist concern to delineate the unique features of "modern society" hindered his perception of the deeper and more permanent features of all societies.

The Need for Order

No one can doubt the grandeur of the historical-philosophical vision in Weber's view of the uniqueness of modern society, or that it represented vast progress in sociological analysis. Yet it is too disjunctive in its conception of the uniqueness of modern societies, and in a way not differentiated enough. It is too historicist.

A great fundamental identity exists in all societies, and one of the elements of this identity is the presence of the charismatic element. Even if religious belief had died, which it has not, the condition of man in the universe and the exigencies of social life still remain, and the problems to which religious belief has been the solution in most cultures still remain, demanding solution by those who confront them. The solution lies in the construction or discovery of order. The need for order and the fascination of disorder persist, and the charismatic propensity is a function of the need for order.[7]

The generator or author of order arouses the charismatic responsiveness. Whether it be God's law or natural law or scientific law or positive law or the society as a whole, or even a particular corporate body or institution like an army, whatever embodies, expresses or symbolizes the essence of an ordered cosmos or any significant sector thereof awakens the disposition of awe and reverence, the charismatic disposition. Men need an order within which they can locate themselves, an order providing coherence, continuity and justice.

A Digression: Individual Variations in the Need for Order

The need for order is not equally great among all men. Many, of course, whose "antennae" are short, whose intelligence and imagination is either limited or has not been aroused by a cultural tradition which exhibits events of central significance, do not have the need to "know" the cosmos or society as a whole or to be in contact with its "vital" or "animating" principle. For such persons, who are many in the world, the need for affection, for self-maintenance, for justice, for self-transcendence, can be gratified largely in personal primary groups with spouse and offspring and kinsmen, or in working collectivities with colleagues and immediate subordinates. Much of the order they need, as well as the affection and rewards they desire, perhaps even most that is of value to them, is found in such circles of small radius. Their minds must be prodded by education and exhortation to seek the wider reaches of the cosmos and society, and in most instances, these do not have much impact. There is a constant falling away from attachment to the wider order. Only idiots (idiots in a sense halfway between the classical Greek usage and our present-day psychological usage) can, however, dispense entirely with cosmic and social order. Most people, occasionally, and intermittently, feel the need to see themselves in a deeper, wider frame of things. Birth, death, marriage, transitions from one ordered condition to another (even when they are orders of narrow radius) cause faint or dormant sensibilities to open. Their judgments of the justice of allocations within their narrow circles often invoke explicitly a standard connected with a more general rule, something more universal in scope and validity. Their judgments of worthy and unworthy tasks and accomplishments are judgments referring, however vaguely, to a scale of distance from or proximity to central things. Wars, national elections, large-scale disorders, bring men into confrontation with events of the larger world.

In no society can the problem of the larger order be avoided entirely. For one thing, some individuals, by virtue of high intelligence or moral sensitivity or preoccupation with power, need to locate themselves and connect themselves with a larger order that gives meaning to discrete and otherwise meaningless events. Then, too, the desire of men for power and for the expansion of the small orders they have created or generated leads to collisions that shake those who would dwell in peace within their narrow confines. The reverberations of the collisions of the larger orders shake the framework of the smaller. Even without natural catastrophes, the catastrophes of national markets, military vicissitudes, and the mismanagement of human affairs, indeed, the very existence of national economies alone would force those, who by their spontaneous and normal sensitivity, would not reach out far enough to become aware of the events of the larger frame or to locate themselves in relation to them.

The major religions recommend themselves by providing such ordering patterns. They "explain" by reference to divine intention how the world came into existence and why it exists. They assess society

in the light of this order and assert what it should be.

The fundamental discoveries of modern science in cosmology, astronomy, medicine, neurology, geology, genetics, are significant as disclosures of the basic order of the cosmos. Scientific order, like the order disclosed by theology, has its imperatives. Being in "regular relations" with the truths of science, doing things the "scientific way," having a "scientific attitude" are as much responses to the imperatives of the order disclosed by scientific research as pious godfearingness is a response to the imperatives of the theologically disclosed religious order.

Metaphysics, the philosophy of history, political and moral philosophy, even sociology, seek to discern an order that is coherent, continuous, and just. More secularly, the constitution and the legal system, effective governmental institutions and the moral opinion in which they are embedded, provide such meaningful orders. It is within the context of such orders that the life of the individual and that of his society become meaningful to him. Perception of and "belief" in such orders permit events and actions to be sorted out and discriminated by reference to the "forces" thought to lie at their root. They calm the mind, or they become the objects of criticism. They gratify by putting the individual into the "right relationship" to what is important, or they leave him discontented by forcing him to be out of the "right relationship."

This "perception of the central" and the "seriousness" of mind it arouses are accompanied by the "attribution of sacredness" to the powers, transcendent or earthly, which men perceive as ruling their lives. Those in contact with them by being possessed by them or by being in cognitive or expressive contact with them, or who are charged with their earthly objectivation, become the objects of the attribution of charisma.

The Charisma of Ordering Power

The disposition to attribute charisma is intimately related to the need for order. The attribution of charismatic qualities occurs in the presence of order-creating, order-disclosing, order-discovering power as such; it is a response to great ordering power.[8] The effectiveness or successful exercise of power on a large scale, on a macro-social scale, evokes a legitimating attitude. Every legitimation of effective large-scale power contains a charismatic element.

All effective rulers possess charismatic qualities, i.e., have charismatic qualities attributed to them, unless it is known that they are *fainéants,* who have abdicated their responsibilities out of moral weakness or are otherwise incompetent. Even then, it is not easy to divest failed incumbents of the charismatic qualities attributed to them during their sovereignty (e.g., kings in exile, abdicated monarchs, ex-presidents, retired generals, the Duke of Windsor, King Carol, King Peter, and even the Comte de Paris, Don Carlos, or the Archduke Otto of Habsburg). What was attributed to the person in the role adheres to him in attenuated form after he has ceased to occupy it, or even when by his own weakness he diminishes the expected effectiveness of the role itself.

Why does great power as such arouse man's propensity to attribute intense, concentrated charismatic qualities to persons or attenuated and dispersed charisma to collectivities, roles and classes of persons? Great power announces itself by its power over order; it discovers order, creates order, maintains it, or destroys it. Power is indeed the central, order-related event.

The highly imperative, the extremely powerful, in nature and in society, intervenes in man's life or is acknowledged to be capable of such intervention on a drastic, life-changing scale. Earthly power, as well as transcendent power, can protect or damage, it has the power to end life or to continue it, it has the power to create new forms of social life, to maintain and protect both the new and the old patterns. It is involved in processes, as vital as those at the disposal of priests and magicians.

The highest authorities of a society—presidents, kings, prime ministers, party secretaries, governors, judges, law-makers—are the rulers of the fullest, most inclusive order of existence here on earth. Great earthly power has a manifold, obscure affinity with the powers believed to inhere in the transcendent order. Those who believe in divinely transcendent orders also believe that earthly powers, to enjoy legitimacy, must have some connection with transcendent powers, that rulers are necessarily involved in the essential order of things. Rulers themselves have claimed that their rule and the rules issuing from it are continuous with (i.e., legitimated by) something even more ultimate than themselves—the will of divinity[9]—through primordial contact with a charismatic person (hereditary kingship), through a cumulative insight, engendered by continuous tradition, into the nature of existence, into the ethical imperatives and the prudential considerations disclosed by long-enduring, continuous existence, or through the will of all the adults who constitute the community (popular sovereignty). Today, almost all the rulers of state-bound societies claim legitimation from the charismatically endowed citizens who form the electorate—although they do so with different degrees of reluctance.

The most fundamental laws of a country, its constitution, its most unchallengeable traditions and the institutions embodying or enunciating them, call forth awe in the minds of those in contact with them; they arouse the sense of *tremendum mysteriosum* which Rudolf Otto designated as the central property of the "idea of the holy." The ritual surrounding the highest office, even in republics, the awe before the place where the ruler sits (as the Presidential Office in the White House, or the Kremlin, or the Élysée) testify to the ways in which high "secular" authority draws to itself from those who exercise it and from those who are its objects, the disposition to attribute charisma.

Of course, a liberal, democratic, secular republic is a far cry from an absolute, caesaropapistic monarchy or a theocracy. A secular bureaucracy is different from a religious sect or church. The scope of the charismatic element in a system of authority resting on rational-legal legitimation is different from its scope in a system of authority resting on preponderantly and permeatively charismatic legitimation. The difference between the former and the latter is a difference in the locus and intensity of charisma in the two systems. In the rational-legal system, the charisma is not concentratedly imputed to the person occupying the central role or to the role itself, but is dispersed in a diminished but unequal intensity throughout the hierarchy of roles and rules. The charisma is felt to inhere in the major order-affecting system of roles. In the democratic order, there is both a legitimacy conferred on rulers by the acknowledgment of the charisma-bearing populace, and the legitimacy drawn simply from the charisma of very powerful (and effective) authority as such.[10]

Rational-legal legitimation is, of course, unique in some respects. It is manifested in a property of a role which derives from its position in a more or less logical cosmos or system of rules. Legitimacy dwells in the substance of the rule realized by the role, in the procedure of establishing the role, and in the procedure of appointing its incumbent. The role of the civil servant issuing a command to a subordinate, or of a judge rendering a judgment—leaving aside the coercive power available to each for enforcing the command or judgment—is perceived as legitimate, as Weber said, because it has been created and filled in a manner procedurally subsumable under a valid general principle or by another higher legitimate authority possessing, in accordance with that valid principle, the right to act authoritatively. The command or the judgment uttered might also be perceived as itself subsumable under or derived from a more general rule or a particular judgment with generalizable validity. In that image of the right to create and fill the role and promulgate the law, of which civil servants' and judges' declarations are particular applications, and in the commands and judgments themselves, there is an element deriving from the ultimate charismatic legitimation of government resting on the "will" of the charismatic sovereign or, in a democracy, on the "will" of the charismatic populace.

But beyond this, the authority of the official and his rule has another charismatic source. That is the perception of a property derived from the "participation"[11] of the particular official role and its official incumbent in the inclusive corporate body, which is conceived of as being under a supreme authority. The particular command or judgment is conceived—very vaguely, perhaps ineffably—as a "part" or as an emanation of the cosmos of commands and judgments at the center of which is a supremely authoritative principle or a supremely authoritative role incorporating that principle. The particular incumbent of the role of civil servant, administrator, or judge is perceived as a manifestation of a larger center of *tremendous* power.

What the "subject" responds to is not just the specific declaration or order of the incumbent of the role—as the definition of rational-legal authority would have it—but the incumbent enveloped in the vague and powerful nimbus of the authority of the entire institution. It is a legitimacy constituted by sharing in the properties of the "organization as a whole" epitomized or symbolized in the powers concentrated (or thought to be concentrated) at the peak. This is "institutional" charisma; it is not a charisma deduced from the creativity of the charismatic individual. It is inherent in the massive organization of authority. The institutional charismatic legitimation of a command emanating from an incumbent of a role in a corporate body derives from *membership in the body as such, apart from any allocated, specific powers.*

The awareness of the grant of powers to the individual incumbent of the role, the knowledge that the rule or judgment he enunciates derives from a higher, more comprehensive rule, closer to the source of all rules—rational-legal legitimation in the narrow sense—fuses with the response to the official and his command or judgment as a participant in the *powerful* organization.

Institutional charisma permeates but does not by any means completely saturate the entire corporate structure. It is present in every act of obedience, even though it does not account for the whole act of obedience. To the individual "representative" of the organization "as a whole" (representative in the sense of being endowed with some of its properties), some of this charisma is attributed. (This is perhaps one of the reasons why contacts with the police and the courts are abhorrent to quite innocent persons who might seek their aid against infringements of the law—entirely apart from the residue of fear of dealing with wicked, arbitrary, exploitative, and immoral authorities.)

Thus, the mixture of the charismatically and the rational-legally legitimated types of authority involves not just the appearance of an occasional charismatic personality in the higher stratum of the corporate body, nor is it simply concentrated at the peak of a bureaucratic structure, which is as much as Weber seemed ready to acknowledge. The charisma of an institution or of a corporate body does not depend on its foundation by a charismatic person (although it might well be true that only charismatic persons can command the authority and resources to create a new and very powerful institution or corporate body). Corporate bodies—secular, economic, governmental, military, and political—come to possess charismatic qualities simply by virtue of the *tremendous* power concentrated in them.

Of course, earthly authority—political or governmental—has to contend with the attachments of various groups to their own patterns of life, their own desired ends, and their conceptions of what will affect those ends negatively or positively ("interests"). It has to contend with disobedience impelled by "interests," competing loyalties and sheer antinomianism. It has to contend with the fact that its charisma might not reach to all sectors of the population living within the boundaries over which it claims to be sovereign. Authority might be hated, partly because it is injurious to the realization of private or sectional aspirations. (Likewise, authority may be sustained not only by its own charismatic legitimacy but by its contribution to the realization of ends desired by the members of particular subsectors of the society.)

Charismatic Activities and the Allocation of Deference

But effective, massive power over the affairs of men is not sufficient in itself to satisfy the need for order, much as it contributes to its satisfaction and great though the charisma (i.e., the connection with vital things) which is attributed to it may be. Effective power, however great, does not automatically and completely legitimate itself simply by its effective existence. The social order it appears to create, maintain or control, must not only give the impression of being coherent and continuous; it must also appear to be integrated with a transcendent moral order. It must incorporate a standard of justice referring to an order beyond that already realized in existing institutions.

The "allocative problem," the problem of who is entitled to what, must be recurrently resolved. Here coercive power alone, even if it could be generated in sufficient magnitude, could not in and of itself provide a generally acceptable answer in any society. Even the mighty, whose power itself engenders a belief that those who possess it are entitled to do so, must reinforce that belief by invoking a standard that *justifies* their possession of power and reward by their qualities and their performances. The demand for justice, or for the alleviation of injustice, both in the system as a whole and in particular relationships within a limited sector of the distribution, derives from the demand for a social order consonant with a transcendent moral standard. If the effective exercise of earthly power alone were the only locus of presumptive charisma, the problem of injustice in the actions of the powerful would never arise. If men were willing to regard it as just that rewards should be exclusively proportionate to the exercise of a society-wide, order-creating and maintaining power, and to proximity to those who exercise it, the problem of a just order might not arise. That is, however, not the case; in too many instances the distribution of rewards proportionately to power arouses the criticism that it diverges from a distribution enjoined by an ultimate standard. "Accidents" of inheritance in societies in which primordial connections have lost their once self-evident charisma are illustrative of this divergence. Furthermore, there are other connections with the charismatic or transcendent order: scientific insight, theological reasoning, medical intervention, or physical heroism which faces and overcomes danger on behalf of order. The holders of the greatest power over the lives of others are not necessarily in harmony with the elites of the spheres in which these other order-connected activities are carried on. Each elite prizes and feels most immediately the particular sector or conception of the transcendent order to which it is attached and for which it claims responsibility.

Even though different sectors of the elite tend to be in consensus and to support each other, from the sense of affinity generated by their common centrality, their consensus cannot be complete. The very differences in their relations to the cosmic and social orders, the differences in the intensity of their contact with it, produce some degree of dissensus. This intra-elite dissensus spreads to other sectors of the society and finds particular reception among strata and groups already unwilling to acknowledge the claims of the powerful to supreme and exclusive embodiment of principles of cosmic and social order.

Still dissensus notwithstanding, the center of the society does impose itself. Its centrality is acknowledged widely. Evidence of this acknowledgment abounds. The acknowledgment takes form in spontaneous law-abidingness and in the deference system. The judgments constituting the deference system confirm the superiority of the center from which order is discerned, sustained and controlled, and represent an assent to the unequal distribution of rewards and facilities.

In the results of sample surveys regarding the prestige or status of various occupations in the United States,[12] Supreme Court Justices, State governors, physicians, Federal legislators, Cabinet members, nuclear physicists and other scientists, professors, and metropolitan mayors, receive the most deference. Somewhat further down but still very high are lawyers and directors of large corporations. Some of these occupations—those of State governors, for instance—involve the exercise of great authority through commands that affect many persons; others, like scientists and professors, can command very few people and in their central activity, the authority they exercise has no coercive power associated with it. The case of the Supreme Court Justice, who heads the list, is especially instructive, for he asserts the highest law, the Constitution, in the light of its most general principles. General conceptions of rational justice and the common good, transcendent principles by which individual articles of the Constitution are interpreted, are at the very center of transcendent order. (The recurrence of the terminology of natural law is itself expressive of this connection.) The Justice of the Supreme Court is the link between the transcendent order and the earthly order. Scientists and scholars, seeking the general pattern of the universe, of man's nature and the objectivations of his creative powers, participate in the same order. Creative and expressive persons, to the extent that their objectivations become known, are likewise regarded as connected with this ultimate normative and symbolic stratum. Legislators who create law, in accordance with the higher law of the Constitution, likewise participate in this connection between the higher, charismatic order and the earthly order, the maintenance of which is in their charge; they deeply affect the order of life of many people by their decisions. Lawyers who interpret this law and who enter into authoritative positions in government likewise receive high deference.

Below the peaks, the esteemed occupations entail, in some measure, an attenuated contact and collaboration with the central institutional and value systems, or they permit an attenuated measure of creativity in ordering things. School teachers, welfare workers, the skilled manual trades, and small business managers are instances of these.

The occupations enjoying least esteem are farthest from the center of society and from the central value system formed around the expressive, moral and cognitive activities directed toward the charismatic stratum of being. The unskilled, uncreative occupations whose incumbents order very little, handle brute matter as brute matter, express little that is vital, and do not penetrate intellectually into the nature of anything, rank very low. The occupations whose incumbents handle only the detritus of man's existence and do so only by manipulating it directly come lowest. Functionally, these occupations perform indispensable tasks, but they rank low because they do not approximate the charisma-affected orders.

To summarize, deference is an acknowledgment of, a response to the presumptive charismatic connections of roles at the center of society and at the center of life.[13] The main recipients of deference are those who exercise authority in the central institutional system and those who occupy the main positions in the central value system of the society. They are occupations which perceive and enunciate the most general principles (laws, rules, judgments) in their most immediate manifestation of or connection with the ultimate or charismatic, or which maintain or protect the earthly order enjoined by these principles. The most powerful roles, even where they do not occupy themselves directly with the norms deriving from ultimate cosmic or moral order, arouse by the generality and magnitude of their power, a sense of the charismatic. They thereby become the recipients of deference; so do the roles that directly protect vitality in consequence of their immediate connection with such central things as great physical power and cognitive penetration into and control over nature.

The wealthy and the highly remunerated are esteemed, not for the possession of great wealth or income as such, or the comfort they afford, but because wealth arises from—or permits—the exercise of authority, or is thought to be the reward for order-creating activities or the manifestation of creative, penetrative powers. Style of life is esteemed because it is a ritualized manifestation of what is the necessity and obligation of those at the charismatic center; it is part of a pattern appropriate to proximity to the center. Education is esteemed because it opens the way to contact with the norms and the cultural objectivations which constitute the central value system and because it facilitates entry to the central institutional roles in which authority is exercised, or contact with persons in such roles.

The properties that appear to be relevant to the assessment of the deference-worthiness of a role or an action are wealth, income, occupation, the power to order by command, prohibition and control over resources, style of life, standard of living, education, primordial connections, including kinship, with persons possessing these properties, and the power to protect or benefit the community or life itself. The distributions of these properties are distributions of primary or derivative distances from the charismatic. Those at the upper ends of the distributions are close to it; at the lower ends, they are remote from it. Personal and organismic qualities such as humor, generosity, gentleness, physical strength, and beauty are significant in the distribution of deference in face-to-face relationships, but they are not taken into account when the "objectively existent" status system, the "serious" status system, is considered. They are regarded as irrelevant, and given man's charismatic propensity, they are irrelevant because they are not closely involved in the charismatic order. They have scarcely any connection with the ultimate determinants of cosmic order or the ultimate grounds of power and justice.

Some of the macrosocially relevant deference or status qualifications are primary; they are authority, creativity, penetration and promulgation, as embodied in occupational role and education. These things are at the center of the institutional and cultural systems of any society. Income and style of life are derivative. Kinship connection too is derivative in highly differentiated societies, and so, in large measure, is ethnicity. The primary and the derivative properties are intertwined in very complicated ways and the latter often acquire a certain measure of autonomy as primary objects of judgment, striving and emulation.

The Plurality and Parodoxy of Charismatic Objects

In the foregoing, I have given instances of the working of an attenuated and dispersed charisma in corporate bodies and in the stratification system. In both instances I have contended that charismatic responses are evoked by the manifestations of powerful authority as such, without regard to concentration in individual personalities, or possession by divinity. I have implied that there is a widespread but not all-inclusive consensus throughout much of the society in the assessment of those affected with charismatic properties. I have suggested, also, that dissensus is apt to arise between persons whose occupational roles are concerned with perceiving and promulgating order and those whose roles are concerned with its conduct and management. This notwithstanding, a considerable degree of consensus exists among the various sectors of the elite.

An endemic dissensus, however, coexists with the society-wide consensus. (A great deal of "idiocy" is also fostered by isolation, ignorance, and insensitivity.) The sources of this dissensus are many and I cannot deal with all of them here. The most important arise from divergent conceptions of the locus and substance of charisma. I shall touch on a few of these.

Their immediate proximity to the sources of charisma, their awareness of the majesty, distorts the minds of those who live in such proximity. This distortion tends in the direction of an identification of the transcendent with the social orders, so that considerations of state and of individual and group advantage are made out to be in accord with the dictates of the transcendent order.

Then too, there is a differential sensibility to the respective orders. Some persons are by temperament, just as some are by their culture, more sensitive than others to the transcendent order or to particular transcendent orders, and more attached to the transcendent. For the transcendentally more sensitive, the claim of the managers and beneficiaries of the social order to be the exhaustive theophany of the transcendent order is not reasonable. The social order seems relatively unimportant in comparison with the transcendent order and unequal to it in dignity. The pretensions of the custodians of the social order to be the sole and proper agents of the transcendent order seem so obviously implausible that they scarcely would need refutation but for the pragmatic strength of the "earthly powers."

These two sources of dissensus recur in the internal relationships of various sectors of the elite, but another pattern of dissensus affects the modal and lower sections of the distribution. Those who suffer the burdens of distance from the center, who are the victims of the unequal distributions of dignity and more tangible rewards, are inevitably somewhat hostile toward those who dominate the earthly order. All charisma calls forth not only awe and deference but also a sacrilegious, "atheistic" hostility. In a firm and stable order where the earthly elites are patently effective, these antinomian dispositions are held in check. Nonetheless, the impulse exists and the critical attitude of the more transcendentally oriented sector of the elite strengthens it. It leads to some measure of refusing the pretensions and claims of the earthly elite.

Those near the lower ends of the distribution are, for example, impelled by their condition toward somewhat different criteria for esteeming occupational roles. They do not wholeheartedly acknowledge authority and creativity; they value wealth somewhat more as a criterion. Because their own occupational roles derogate them, they evaluate occupation less highly than some of the more accessible primary and derivative criteria such as education and style of life, which might be more easily acquired. And even with respect to a given deference-relevant property, they might seek to invert the prevailing standard of evaluation in ways that would enhance their own dignity.

There are, moreover, multiple interpretations of transcendent orders, flowing from different cultural traditions and different complexes of experience. There are divergent "interests," too, in the vulgar sense of the word—the desire to possess scarce things that are or might be possessed by others; the very desire is evidence of the weakness with which charisma is attributed to those who possess the desired things. These give rise to dissensus in opinion and conflicts among those who espouse the divergent interpretations.

The contents of the transcendent order can never be unequivocally specified; they are bound to be ambiguous and to give rise to and sustain divergent interpretations, especially among those who are very sensitive to transcendent things. Thus, out of considerations of the balance of ease and pain, from the desire for dignity as well as from more intellectual disagreements, the spread of consensus about the locus of the charismatic over an entire society encounters obstacles.

But in addition to these endemic sources of dissensus about the locus and content of the charismatic, two others merit special mention. The oldest carriers of earthly charisma are the primordial collectivities, kinship and local territorial groups and ethnic aggregates. Primordial qualities still function powerfully as charismatic qualities and their conflict with the charismatic claims of ordering authority is a constant feature of historical societies. The problems of the new states as well as the Negroes' civil rights problems in the United States testify to the tenacity of the belief in the ultimate validity of primordial qualities.[14]

The other variant form of the dispersion of charisma which restricts, and even sets up a counter-standard to the charismatic claims of earthly authority, is the charisma of the nation or of the populace. The two, though somewhat different, have much in common. The proponents and beneficiaries of this dispersion attribute charismatic qualities to the sectors of the society that are peripheral with respect to their share in the exercise of authority and the embodiment of culture and in the distribution of wealth, income, and education. Where charisma is attributed to these strata, the distance between center and periphery is diminished and their position in the hierarchy of deference is much elevated. The spread or range of the distribution of deference is narrowed as the periphery is brought closer to the peaks.

Through this dispersion of charisma into the periphery, the society moves toward a civil society. A widely dispersed charisma is an indispensable condition of civility, but it is not a sufficient ground for its existence. Civility entails not only the imputation of charisma to the mass of the population by itself; it also requires that the established and effective elite impute charisma to the mass as well, that the elite regard itself, despite all its differences as sharing some of the charisma that resides in it with the rest of its society. It requires, too, that the virtues implicit in this widespread and consensual dispersion of charisma should be practised in and with respect to the central institutional system—government and law, above all.

The Motives and Mechanisms of the Dispersion of Charisma

There is a strong tendency toward a consensual "acknowledgment" of the charismatic quality of those in positions of highest authority. So far as authority is visible—this is part of its effectiveness—it does have a self-legitimating consequence. It arouses the attribution of charisma and this is why an often uncomfortable alternation exists in references to the "upper classes," the speaker denying their superiority emphatically, while acknowledging it implicitly as an "objective" fact that has nothing to do with his explicit individual evaluation, which is negative. The denial is made because the affirmation is already there, and both are genuine.

The mechanism of simultaneous affirmation and denial comes into play where the distance from the charisma-generating center is so great that its effec-

tiveness is enfeebled, but not so enfeebled as to be without consequence. The consequence of distance from the charismatic center is a sense of inferiority. Those who are far from the locus of charisma experience that distance painfully.

The sense of being inferior is most painful for those who cannot divert their attention to their orders of narrow radius. The condition of inferiority is itself a strong impetus to deny the validity of the distribution in which they fare so badly. This usually entails a denial of the connection between the transcendent order and the moral standards it implies or asserts, and the social order in which they are relegated to a position so distant from the center. One of the major responses of the sensitive who are placed at the periphery is to invoke the charisma of the transcendent order and to insist on its disjunction from the prevailing social order and its authority—which, however, still compels a reluctant attribution of charisma, despite the intense and genuine efforts to deny it. This is the motive for disassociating the allegedly theophanous rulers from the transcendent order.

This account does not exhaust the subject. There are deeper causes. One is the capacity and impulsion of every human being toward individuality. Everyone has in some degree this capacity and impulse. It dies early in most human beings, partly because it is not strong itself and partly because it is crushed by primordial ties, and by primordial, corporate, cultural authority. It needs cultivation if it is to flower in any but the most forceful. (Weber's observations about charismatic education, the nurturing of the charismatic capacity, apply as well to this property of man's spirit and are capable of a broader application than he himself made.) Where individuality, the perception of the self and the appreciation of its value, comes into substantial existence, it is accompanied by an increased sympathy, a greater readiness to perceive the minds of others and to appreciate them emphatically as entities with inherent qualities (not just as instances of a category). The consequent perception of other individualities contributes to the process of attributing charisma to them.

Another positive factor implicit in what I have said, which has led in modern times to the widening dispersion of charisma over the whole society and hence to the belief in the charisma of the people, is the growth of the national state, entailing a visible, tangible, coherent and effective central authority. The sharing of this charisma which flows from the central authority, however small that share might be, with a multitude of others who live within a territory ruled by the central authority, has gradually and in conjunction with the factors already mentioned led to the direct attribution of charisma to all citizens of the national state.

Free, universal education works in the same direction. It brings the oncoming generation directly into contact with the central value system. It gives those who receive it a sense of sharing in what is central in the cosmos and in their own society. The mere acquisition of literacy has a similar impact. It changes a person's image of himself; he too gains, by virtue of education, contact with the transcendent and earthly orders, and with their central symbols.

The Permanent Tension Regarding the Locus of Charismatic Qualities

The dispersion of charisma can never go so far as to engender a completely equalitarian society. Quite apart from the differences in the creative powers of individuals, and the unequal distribution of rewards and motives which impel men unequally to contact with charismatic things, there remains the basic and irrefragible fact of authority. In a large-scale society which has many demands and which therefore generates many tasks, authority is bound to be unequally distributed. Indeed the very dispersion of charisma, by enhancing the individual's conception of his own rights and value, increases his demands for performance on the part of elites. These performances cannot be carried out without a very considerable allocation of authority.

Authority, when it is massive and continuous, calls forth, by its mere existence, the attribution of charisma. It calls it forth from those who are not in authoritative roles and who attribute it to themselves, and even in the elites who also impute charisma to the rest of their society. It cannot do otherwise. It is too important, too *serious* a matter to do otherwise, even in secular societies. Authority is too crucial to the creation and maintenance of order to be able to avoid the sentiments that need and are evoked by order.

The consequence is that large modern societies, even more than the large societies of the past, are enmeshed in a perpetual strain of competing conceptions about the ultimate locus of charisma. The discerners and interpreters of the transcendent order, the agents of earthly order, and the populace which wishes to share in these higher orders and already regards itself as sharing in them sufficiently, are bound to be engaged in a contest with each other. The earthly elite is under pressure from the charisma

of the transcendent order and from charisma embodied in the populace. It can never avoid its attribution of charisma to its own central position but neither can it avoid contention, pressure, and criticism from the other bearers of charismatic qualities. And any improvement in the position of any one of the three contestants is bound to arouse and strengthen the affirmation of their own charisma in the other two, while at the same time laying it open to criticism and refusal.

With these concluding but not definitive observations, we come again to Weber's famous proposition about the revolutionary character of charisma. As in so much else that he said, much truth resides. But the truth of the matter is more complicated, the phenomenon is more protean, and the distance to be traversed for its understanding is still very great.

NOTES

1. These are the gifts of grace conferred by the Spirit: "For to one is given by the Spirit the word of wisdom; to another the word of knowledge by the same Spirit; to another faith by the same Spirit; to another the gifts of healing by the same Spirit; to another the working of miracles; to another prophecy; to another discerning of spirits, to another divers kinds of tongues, to another the interpretation of tongues; but all these worketh that one and the self-same Spirit, dividing to every man severally as he will." I *Corinthians* 12:8–11. (See also *Romans* 12.)

2. The legitimacy of this extension of Weber's analysis and its affinity with his own insight are exhibited by the following lines (*Wirtschaft und Gesellschaft*, I. 758–759): "Der Charisma ruht in seiner Macht auf Offenbarungs- und Heroenglauben, auf der emotionellen Überzeugung von der Wichtigkeit und dem Wert einer Manifestation religiöser, ethischer, künstlerischer, wissenschaftlicher, politischer, oder welcher Art immer, auf Heldentum, sei es der Askese, oder des Krieges, der richtlerichen Weisheit, der magischen Begnadung oder welcher Art sonst"; . . . "die mathematische 'Phantasie' etwa eines Weyerstrauss ist 'Intuition' genau im gleichen Sinn wie die diejenigen irgend eines Künstlers, Propheten und—Demagogen . . . Sie alle auch die Künstlerische ihre Ralitat zu bewahren, in 'Ergreifen' oder, wenn mann will. Ergriffenwerden von Forderungen des 'Werks' bedeuten, und nicht ein subjektives 'Fühlen' oder 'Erleben' wie irgend ein anderes. Er liegt . . . überhaupt nicht in der Person oder in den seelischen in der Art, wie sie von den Beherrschten oder Geführten, innerlich angeeignet von ihnen 'erlebt' werden."

3. He came closest to it in his discussion of the influence of the Lutheran idea of authority on the German attitude toward the state (*Wirtschaft und Gesellschaft*, I, 775–776): "Die grundsätzlich ganz andere Stellung [the contrast is with the English Puritanical denial of charismatic quality to the state] etwas des normalen Deutschen zum Amt, zu der etwas Überpersönliches gedachtem Behörde und deren Nimbus ist allerdings zum Teil durch die ganz konkrete Eigenart der lutherischen Reliogiösität, bedingt, entspricht aber, in der Ausstattung der Gewalten mit dem Amtscharisma der 'gottgewollten Obrigkeit,' einem sehr allgemeinen Typus, und die rein empfindungsmässige Staatsmetaphysik, welche auf disem Boden wachst hat politisch weittragende Konsequenzen."

4. Charismatic qualities may be manifested in primordial things (in blood or in locality) and in the roles defined by

primordial properties (kinship roles or membership in a territorial community).

5. "Das Amtscharisma . . . der Glaube an die specifische Begnadung einer sozialen Institution als solcher ist keineswegs eine nur den Kirchen und noch wenigen eine nur primitiven Verhältnisse eigene Erscheinung. Es äussert sich auch unter modernen Beziehungen der Gewalte unterwürfenen zur staatlichen Gewalt." *Wirtschaft und Gesselschaft,* I, 775.

6. His identification of the charismatic and the extraordinary in the sense of the infrequent, and the disjunction he saw between the extraordinary and the charismatic, one on the one side, and the routine and the ordinary on the other, was paralleled by the disjunction he asserted between charismatically and rational-legally legitimated structures of authority.

7. I do not know why this need for order exists. It is not simply a need for an instrumentally manageable environment, though that is part of it. It is more like the need for a rationally intelligible cognitive map, but it obviously is more than cognitive. There is a need for moral order—for things to be fit into a pattern which is just as well as predictable.

8. Order-destroying power, great capacity for violence, attracts too, and arouses the charismatic propensity. It does so because it promises in some instances to provide a new and better order, one more harmonious with the more inclusive and deeper order of existence. Order-destroying power also arouses the charismatic propensity because of a profound ambivalence in men's relations to the central things. Order not only gives meaning; it also constricts and derogates.

9. Although much has been written about the divine right of kings, few efforts have been made to see this phenomenon as one instance of a general class. Alexander Ular's *Die Politik,* in *Die Gesellschaft: Sammlung sozialpsychologischer Monographien,* Frankfurt am Main, 1909, is one of the very few attempts to do so. The recent publications—*La régalité sacrée,* Leiden: E. J. Brill, and Luc de Heusch *et al.: Le Pouvoir et le Sacré,* Annales du Centre d'Etude des Religions 1, Université Libre de Bruxelles, Institut de Sociologie, 1962 —do not go beyond the conventional understanding of this phenomenon.

10. In modern societies where belief in both the charisma of the populace and the charisma of the highest authority is a common phenomenon, the tensions of populism and constitutionalism are not uncommon.

11. In the sense developed in the writings of Lévy-Bruhl and Przyluski.

12. The most important of these was conducted by the National Opinion Research Center and is reported in Albert Reiss *et al., Occupations and Social Status,* New York: Free Press of Glencoe, 1961.

13. Weber refers explicitly to charismatic proximity as a major criterion in his discussion of the status of various Japanese noble families. *Wirtschaft und Gesellschaft,* pp. 772–774, especially p. 772.

14. The case of the Southern Whites is instructive, since it discloses the relations between primordial charisma and national charisma, their conflicts and their interdependence. Except for their relations with the Negroes, the Southern Whites have become as integrated into the national (white) American society as an uneducated, ignorant, impoverished and, relatively recently, conquered people can be. Yet the strength of their attachment to particularistic, primordial qualities indicates that they have been unable to impute the charisma of national membership to their Negro fellow-Southerners. They do not believe that the charisma resident in themselves is shared by all inhabitants of the national territory, but belongs only to the white members. They have become populists, i.e., they attribute charisma to the ordinary people at the periphery of society, but they have not yet been able to attribute it to a primordially alien, in this instance, ethnically alien, group within their own society.

The destruction of the effectiveness of the Southern elite after the Civil War permanently deprived Southerners of a center for their society; and their dissenting and sectarian Protestantism made it easier for them to find the locus of charisma in themselves. They protected their own society when they did not have an elite to protect it for them; they became custodians of the local or regional charismatic order.

The South had formed a coherent regional society at a time when the national elite was not sufficiently ascendant in its powers and therewith in its charismatic properties. When the Southern elite faded, and the Northern elite was patently hostile and therefore patently unjust, Southern society became a centerless society in which charisma became concentrated in the strata that had previously formed its periphery.

A strong center, in touch with a transcendent order, is a necessity for the growth of a civil society. The national elite do not provide such a center for the South, and having lost the charisma of authority, the South deteriorated into an ethnically primordial community within a national state imposing an authority which has come in the course of decades to acquire a frail legitimacy. The civil rights movement is an attempt to disrupt this primordial community. In response to this threat of disorder, the sense of primordiality which has been almost the sole basis of whatever order has existed in the South, has become more intense.

PART TWO

MAJOR TYPES OF PREMODERN POLITICAL SYSTEMS AND THEIR SOCIAL CONDITIONS

CHAPTER **II**

The Embedment of the Political in Social Structure in Primitive Societies: Introduction

I

The fascination with primitive political systems is of long standing in the history of political and social thought and theory, and has its roots in the assumed equivalence between primitive and elementary. It was often believed, or tacitly assumed, that in a simple society, the simplest, most basic elements of social behavior and relations in general and of political behavior and relations in particular can be discerned and that it is there that the basic nature of pure politics has remained unadulterated by any additions derived from the accumulation of more complex superstructures. This assertion or assumption may seem rather paradoxical, as it has been quite obvious that primitive (or simple) societies are, by definition, the least differentiated or specialized. Hence, they lack also any highly developed and centralized political institution; or, to use a very widespread term, they are "stateless."[1]

But in some ways it was indeed this simplicity or statelessness of primitive societies that seemed to justify their special importance for political and sociological analysis. In older evolutionary theories, it was believed that it is in the transition from the stateless to the first states, in situations of so-called "origin of the state," that this pure essence of politics

could be found and fully analyzed. This view equated this pure essence of politics or of state with exploitation in general and with conquest in particular and with the possibility of accumulating some surplus which can then be exploited and monopolized by the rulers and used by them, in turn, to maintain their coercive powers. The fullest expression of this view could be found in Franz Oppenheimer's famous *The State*.[2] It was, however, also very widespread among many sociologists and anthropologists of the late nineteenth and early twentieth centuries.

This assumption tended to persist, even if in a modified way, among modern approaches, too, such as those of Sahlins, Diamond, and Krader,[3] who do not fully accept such simple evolutionary or historical views. Among other scholars it was the very lack of full-fledged political institutions in primitive societies that indeed seemed to make possible the analysis of the pure nature of the political struggle or process, disembedded, as it were, from the "external" paraphernalia of formal political institutions.

In order to be able to evaluate the extent to which these assumptions and approaches contain an element of truth, and hence to evaluate the importance of the analysis of primitive political systems for political sociology, it is necessary to examine them from the point of view of the major problems and criteria of analysis which have been presented above.

II

Before proceeding to a somewhat more concrete analysis of the political systems of primitive societies, it might be worth while to point out one methodological problem—namely, the lack of written traditions among these societies. Because we have little which can be considered as valid records of such societies in the past, for purposes of analysis we have to make assumptions. We must assume—and this assumption is not unproblematic in itself—that the contemporary primitive (illiterate, tribal, and the like) societies as studied by the ethnologists and anthropologists are to a considerable extent similar to those that existed in the early history of mankind.

Be that as it may, most of the analysis of these societies is necessarily based on the work of contemporary anthropologists, with only secondary help or support from records of such primitive conditions as have been transmitted in the tradition of the various literate societies.

III

The first step in our analysis is necessarily to specify the characteristics of primitive societies, especially of primitive political systems, from the point of view of the major criteria of comparative analysis given above.

The basic characteristics of primitive societies are those of simplicity—structural, technological, and cultural. Most existing, contemporary, primitive political systems as described and analyzed by anthropologists are indeed characterized by such simplicity or relatively low degree of social differentiation.

In the economic system of these societies, we do not find any far-reaching occupational and economic specialization, although some embryonic developments—such as the development of some craft specialization, that is, guilds and castes—can be found among many of the more "developed" or differentiated of these societies. And yet, such specialization in all primitive societies does not go beyond some minimal limits. These limits are perhaps most evident from the fact that the amount of surplus, or the possibility of accumulating a surplus, is very small, owing to the low level of technology in such societies. In the cultural systems, this lack of surplus and of accumulation of products can be seen in the noninvention of writing in any form and hence in the lack of the possibility of accumulating and transmitting tradition beyond what can be handed down through more or less direct intergenerational activities and encounters.

Within these broad structural, technological, and cultural limits there exists, of course, among what are usually called primitive societies, a great variety of types. In their structural composition, these primitive societies range from simple bands—societies organized in segmentary kinship units, clan federations, aristocratic lineage societies, or societies focused around voluntary associations—through more centralized chieftainships and kingdoms.

In economic terms, they range from simple food gatherers or hunters through agriculturists, cattle breeders, and so on. Similarly, in cultural terms, they may vary from societies with relatively simple, unelaborated world views of some of the Australian aborigines to much more complex cosmological and mythological systems with elaborate mythical and magical concepts.[4]

And yet beyond these differences there stand out those basic common characteristics or "limitations" of primitive societies which have been designated above. The common denominator of these limitations is the prevalence in most primitive societies of a relatively high degree of structural equivalence of the different units composing them, of a relatively high degree of mechanical as against "organic" solidarity in them, of a very high degree of embedment of the sociopolitical in the cultural order; in the "contents" side of the cultural tradition, the very strong emphasis on primordial relations and symbols, while these limitations are especially evident in those major social mechanisms which seem to be prevalent in most primitive societies and which tend, as it were, to maintain their continuity.[5]

The first such mechanism is the interaction of the same persons or groups in different situations—an interaction which makes their mutual commitments in one situation or group greatly influence their behavior in others. In the societies studied by anthropologists, the existence of such close relations between the same people in different groups and situations constitutes a very important mechanism regulating social behavior on the one hand and intergroup relations on the other. It has also been shown how such close interrelations among the same people in different situations create conflicts between them and how these conflicts, while seeming disruptive, in reality help to enhance the solidarity and functioning of the groups and the society through the crosscutting of interests among the same people participating in these varying situations.

The second such mechanism is the specific type of relation between what may be called "culture," or rather "values" and ritual symbols on the one hand, and social relations on the other. Anthropologists have emphasized both the autonomy and the distinctiveness of the sphere of values in the societies they study, as well as the direct relevance of primordial or sacred symbols and rituals for most types of social activity and the interlocking of these activities in a way which assures that they be given "meaning" in terms of these symbols and values.

The third such mechanism is the continuous interrelation in these societies of different types of social activity in most groups and situations. Ritual, jural, contractual, and political activities—clearly distinguishable from one another—are seen as interwoven in most situations and groups of these societies, so that each activity directly depends on, articulates with, and is upheld in terms of the others. Epstein has stated this point thus: "Most of the major social functions are fulfilled by the same small groups."[6]

All these mechanisms tend to uphold the predominance in most of these systems of the type of social division of labor and solidarity which has been designated by Durkheim as mechanic (as opposed to organic). Such mechanic solidarity is founded on a small extent of social differentiation, basically a differentiation of likeness; that is, on the existence of different social units, relatively self-contained in a similar social structure and bound mostly by symbols of common identity fully activated in common rituals.[7]

IV

This relative noncomplexity or simplicity of the primitive social systems does find its counterparts, of course, in their political organization, where we also find several limits to their complexity. These are of crucial importance from the point of view of our comparative analysis. In the political sphere—and in the cultural, as we shall yet see—these limits are mostly evident in the nature of the "centers" of these societies. Seemingly, almost by definition, these societies are almost centerless in the sense of not having any specific localized institutional, central political organization.

According to the older sociological or anthropological parlance, such societies would be defined as stateless, as we have mentioned above. Yet this centerlessness of the primitive societies would seem to be only a partial truth at the most. In some of these societies, such as the "centralized" or "federative" states like the kingdom of the Zulu,[8] the Bemba Federation,[9] or the Divine Kingship of the Shilluk,[10] the political system of the Annuak,[11] or in various "associational" states such as the Yako,[12] some emerging centralized organizational and symbolic

focuses of power and authority are to be found.[13] Here we may also find already a somewhat greater specialization of political or administrative roles and organizations.

Even in many other primitive societies in which there did not exist even such limited specific political organization and roles, there tended to develop specific types of receiving situations in which different types of political or centerlike activities—regulation of internal or external force or of intergroup relations—were activated as the need or exigency arose. But, from the point of view of our discussion, perhaps more important than these embryonic developments of specific political roles and social organizations and situations is the fact that throughout these societies one crucial component or aspect of a "center"—namely, the structural localization of the conceptions of a social and cosmic order—is very pronounced.

In all these societies there exist—even if not always articulated in abstract, rational philosophical forms and modes—full conceptions of cosmic and moral orders to which the social or sociopolitical order is closely related, perhaps in a much closer way than in many more differentiated societies. The representation of this order takes place in very different and varied structural locations of the social order—in the various offices, and in special ceremonies—such as various first-fruit ceremonies which seem to encompass all the social units of the society. The especial salience of these ceremonies in many spheres of social life in most primitive societies underlines this centrality to an even greater degree.

Thus, insofar as centrality is synonymous with some structural "localization" and manifestation of a wider order, it would be wrong to assert that these primitive societies are centerless. And yet there seems to be a very important grain of truth in the assertion that structurally, even in those primitive societies in which we can clearly discern the beginning of "state" —that is, in those societies in which some central loci of authority and administration and of other components of center formation exist—they are indeed centerless in that they do not have full-fledged, distinct structural and symbolic centers.

This is due to a basic structural fact common, it seems, to all or at least most of these societies; namely, that however much such central loci of power are developed, structurally they are not distinct or different from other basic units of the societies. This holds true for the various types of kinship groups (be they small bands, clans, or kin groups) and for the so-called voluntary associations, or a combination of kinship and territorial units, such as the wider tribal units. Thus, for instance, the royal household of the Zulu[14] or of Dahomey,[15] the aristocratic lineages of the Annuak,[16] or the "stools" of the Polynesian chiefs,[17] or the central association among the Yako[18] or the Plains Indians[19] do not differ structurally from other units of the society. They are only of higher standing, more powerful or more respected than the other units; but they do not differ from them in their basic principles of social organization, in the basic symbols of their collective identity, and in their mutual orientations to one another. This, of course, is one basic manifestation of the prevalence in most primitive societies of a very high mechanic solidarity and of a very low degree of organic solidarity. It is in this sense that these societies can be said to be centerless, because no structural difference between the center and the periphery exists in them. In this sense, however, it may also be said that these societies are composed only of centers; and, paradoxical as this may seem, there is an interesting element of truth in such an assertion.

This grain of truth is rooted in the basic imagery of the social and political order and of the reciprocal rights and duties between the basic structural units which compose these societies and especially between the more and the less powerful units.

As we have seen above, the basic imagery and symbolism of sociopolitical order in these societies is couched mostly in symbols of primordial, interpersonal, kinship and territorial relations and images. True, the basic orientations and the goals of the sociopolitical order that can be found in these societies seem to include almost all the possible permutations of variations which are also to be found in more developed societies. Here we can find great emphasis on power and political expansion, on maintenance of a given "static" ritual world order, or on economic activities and enrichment. But, whatever the concrete contents of these orientations and goals, their basic social referents as well as their basic imagery is always couched in symbols of primordial units and relations. The basic conception of the scope, validity, and meaning of order, cosmic and social alike, is couched in these terms. As this type of order can be most fully embodied in the basic primordial interpersonal and kinship units, it is these units that constitute the "natural" loci of centrality—a centrality which is, therefore, distributed—structurally, even if not in terms of actual power differentials among all such units.

Here we come to the second aspect of the paradox of a whole society being a center; namely, to the conception of the reciprocal duties among its various units. In most primitive societies, these duties and obligations tend to be couched in terms of what has been called by Karl Polanyi those of "reciprocity,"[20] in which the "need" and ability are fused, and in what may also be called basic communistic terms of "to each according to his need and from each according to his ability." In this sense, the myth "primitive communism" has in it a grain of truth. Not that it applies to all social relations in primitive societies. Quite obviously, as has been abundantly demonstrated in anthropological literature, many relations in these societies are purely instrumental or economic. But the more "communistic" relations do indeed apply to the specifically political or central relations, to the relation between chiefs and their tribes (or clans), between the more or less aristocratic lineages.

There are, however, a few other types of basic criteria according to which the suitability for political office is usually measured in these societies. The possession of various skills, such as military or administrative, which the very nature of the activity may determine as prerequisites are taken into consideration, and the lack of them may well lead to the demotion of a chief or hero. But they do not constitute the sole criteria according to which the performance of the role is judged.

The absence of these basic attributes or skills may indeed deny the holders of such offices the possibility of exercising their authority in the appropriate situations, and the possession of them may help in the attainment of some more temporary (military or economic) offices (especially in the more achievement-oriented primitive societies such as the Yako or the Plains Indians), but they are usually conceived as part and parcel of the "broader" social or cultural qualities of chiefdom, and not as the major criteria of such offices.

This is very evident in the symbolism of chiefdom or kingship found in most primitive societies, in the great emphasis of its representative and mediating functions between the social order and the cosmic order. The chief is responsible not only for the provision of the basic prerequisites of life, economic and political, but also for the very close relations between such provision and the maintenance of the proper, mediating relations with the cosmic order. And beyond all this, it is evident in the conception of the obligations of chiefs or of "aristocrats" with regard to other members (or units) of their tribes in terms of their over-all responsibility for their welfare, on their duty to give from their own wealth or reserves to secure the well-being of the community. It is this unconditional giving that constitutes one of the main tests of successful chieftainship. Through it the chiefs muster and maintain the unconditional support of their followers.

Such unconditional mutual obligations, which are characteristic of relations in the center of society, permeate the major political interrelations between the various units of the society. Hence, again the whole society may be envisaged as the center.

V

This great emphasis on the noninstrumental attributes of chieftainship—and of the cosmic and social orders which they represent—points to an interesting paradox in the relation in primitive societies between what has been designated as "needs" or exigencies of social systems and types of responses to them. On the one hand, primitive societies operate at the lowest level of technology, and hence they necessarily evince a very high dependence on their external "natural" (and to some extent "international") environment. Very large parts and aspects of their institutional arrangements, including camping agreements, distribution of property rights, relations between various such groups, are to a very large degree dependent on the expected or unexpected vagaries of this environment and can be explained at least partially as attempts to cope with them.

Hence, in many ways, it is in these societies that the purely "need"- or "exigency"-oriented activities seem to be most predominant. At the same time, however, in these societies there exists (perhaps again in a much more articulate way than in many more fully-developed societies) a very strong emphasis on the importance of symbolic qualities of the social, moral, and cosmic order, as the major guiding templates for all kinds of social activities, and a very strong emphasis on the direct relations between such varied concrete and specific social relations and the broader conceptions of cosmic and social order.

This is especially evident in these societies in the strong embeddedness of the various types of instrumental activities in the primordial—personal and kinship—relations, units, and symbols on which we have already touched.

VI

It is these characteristics of "primitive" societies analyzed above that explain the paradox of primitive society being centerless on the one hand, while on the other the whole society is compounded of centers. These basic characteristics are closely related to the nature of the political struggles that are found in them. Here again a rather paradoxical situation emerges.

On the one hand, due to the minimal specificity of the political spheres (as distinct from other social spheres and especially from the sphere of kinship relations), most political issues are necessarily couched in terms of the goals, symbols, and activities of such other spheres. There are but few explicitly political tasks (except for transient technical or administrative ones) or norms of political struggle as distinct from the more general norms of social, kinship, territorial, or interpersonal relations. Hence, most concrete issues and aims of political struggle—and of the consequent activities oriented to their maximization—are conceived in terms of the relative position or standing of the existing social or interpersonal units in their relation to one another and in the necessity to mobilize resources for them and to regulate their interpretations.

The relative complexity of this struggle in any given primitive society depends on the complexity of these units; it is, of course, much more complex in a tribal kingdom or aristocratic federation than in purely segmentary tribes. But even in the former the explicit rules of the political game articulated within specific political institutions are developed only to a minimal degree. Hence there exists in many primitive societies a strong emphasis on purely "moral" or "reasonable" behavior, not as disembodied from any actual social relations, but as embedded, in a way, in all of them and therefore not specific to any one of them.[21]

On the other hand, because of this relative lack of autonomy and distinctiveness of the political sphere and of the relatively full embedment of political activities in structurally given primordial, interpersonal, and kinship units, political struggle and process in primitive societies tend very much to exhibit (as has been demonstrated, for instance, among others, by Barth) the "purest" characteristics of "game theory" or game behavior.[22]

In more complicated, differentiated systems, in which the political sphere is more autonomous and has more distinct, specific norms, these very norms, whatever their origin, regulate and to some extent limit the articulation of such "pure" game behavior. In primitive societies, however, such norms are largely embodied in other primordial and territorial structural units. In the relations between these units there may indeed develop to a very large extent such pure game behavior which it is difficult to envisage in other more complex types of political systems.

VII

Yet, as we have seen above, it is true that there exist among the various primitive societies great differences with regard both to the degree of structural differentiation and to other basic goal orientations, and these have been found to be closely related also to the extent of development of special political roles, activities, and organizations as well as to the extent of the articulation of issues of political struggle.[23] But, whatever the degree of development of such more articulated political roles, organizations, and institutions, they do not, in primitive societies, come beyond the limitations analyzed above.

This necessarily brings us to the problem of the possibilities of change and transformation from within and of the relation of such possibilities to the pattern of internal political struggle. And here, we are greatly handicapped by the unsatisfactory nature of the available evidence (that is, by the lack of adequate historical documents) and by the difficulties in comparing the processes of change in "contemporary" primitive societies (usually in a colonial or semicolonial setting) and "historical" ones (either directly precolonial or those further back in the "dawn" of human history). We must add to the lack of documentation the fact that by the very nature of their setting, the contemporary primitive systems have evinced only a very small degree of changeability and transformability.

The most important patterns of political change recorded in contemporary primitive political systems have been very much in line with the nature of the basic characteristics of their political structures and political struggle as analyzed above. Thus, most anthropological studies have tended to emphasize mostly the following types of change:

First, changes in any given system of the relative position of the different units in it, be it a segmentary system, a tribal federation, or a primitive monarchy.[24]

Second, processes of segmentation; that is, of the establishment by some process of fission from the "mother" unit and the creation of similar units beyond the territorial scope of the mother unit.[25]

Third, processes of federative alliance between various units leading to the creation of clan or tribal federation.[26]

Last, processes of conquest, sometimes leading to the obliteration of former units and to the establishment (as in the case of the Zulu[27]) of new, more centralized and somewhat broader units or structures, yet with little transformation of the basic units of the society.

The common denominator of all these changes is the relatively small extent of transformability of these societies in the direction of a greater degree of organic solidarity and of the establishment of centers that are structurally different from other basic units of the society. This is closely related to the pattern of political struggle in these societies in the relatively low specificity and autonomy of either symbolical orientations or structural organizations and of concrete issues of political struggle and the very high degree of their embedment in other relations and contacts, especially those that are primordial and territorial, social, and interpersonal.

Hence, it is very difficult indeed to perceive how, out of the conflicts that developed among these units, there could emerge such new orientations or conditions. It is not mere chance that anthropologists like Gluckman,[28] who have stressed the importance of conflict in these societies, have also emphasized the "equilibrating" influence of these conflicts, and not their potential for change. This is indeed especially evident in the study of primitive rebellions; that is, of rebellions in primitive societies, that are not related to outside (such as European) influences. Perhaps the most important indication of such rebellions as reported by anthropologists is that there did not develop in them a conception either of different types of political order or of structural reservoirs of resources from which new, more differentiated types of organizations and institutions could be developed.

Only a few studies of such societies (for example, Sahlin's and Goldman's studies of chiefhood in Polynesian societies[29]) have indicated some mechanisms, the most important of these being the development of a discrepancy between political and "social" status. In societies where this development can be seen, perhaps together with demographic and ecological changes, it can indeed serve as central points for breakthroughs beyond the structural and cultural limits of primitive societies in relatively contemporary settings.

Similarly, we have only a few studies of the actual transition of one "type" of contemporary primitive society to another and of the actual conditions and mechanisms of such a transition.[30] In the contemporary settings it was only, or mostly, under the impact of external forces—in this case of European or American expansions—that some such new conceptions and possibilities of new types of activities have indeed developed in the contemporary primitive societies. In this, contemporary primitive societies may indeed differ from the earlier, preliterate historical primitive societies from which, presumably, other more advanced types of social and cultural order did develop.

But, whatever the limits of the validity of such

parallelism between the historical and contemporary primitive societies, there can be little doubt that the most contemporary societies, as depicted by anthropologists, do constitute an interesting model or a limiting case for the study of political sociology.

NOTES

1. Franz Oppenheimer, *The State, Its History and Development* (Indianapolis: Bobbs-Merrill, 1914); R. H. Lowie, *Primitive Society* (New York: Boni and Liveright, 1920); Lawrence Krader, *The Origins of the State,* Foundation Series of Anthropology (Englewood Cliffs: Prentice-Hall, 1968).

2. Oppenheimer, *op. cit.*

3. Marshall D. Sahlins, "Culture and Environment: The Study of Cultural Ecology,'" in Sol Tax, ed., *Horizons of Anthropology* (Chicago: Aldine, 1964), pp. 132–147; Stanley Diamond, "The Search for the Primitive," in I. Galdston, ed., *Man's Image in Medicine and Anthropology* (International University Press, 1963), pp. 62–115; Krader, *op. cit.*

4. W. E. H. Stanner, "On Aboriginal Religion, I," *Oceania,* XXX (December 1959); Stanner, "On Aboriginal Religion II," *ibid.* (June 1960); Stanner, "The Dreaming," in T. A. G. Hungerford, ed., *Australian Signpost* (Melbourne: Cheshire, 1956), reprinted in William Lessa and Evan Z. Vogt, eds., *Reader in Comparative Religion* (Evanston: Row, Peterson, 1958).

5. On this in greater detail, see S. N. Eisenstadt, "Anthropological Studies of Complex Societies," in *Eisenstadt, Essays in Comparative Institutions* (New York: Wiley, 1965), pp. 77–107.

6. See A. L. Epstein, *Politics in an Urban African Community* (Manchester: Manchester University Press, 1958), p. 234.

7. See Émile Durkheim, *On the Division of Labour in Society* (Glencoe: The Free Press, 1947).

8. Max Gluckman, "The Kingdom of the Zulu of South Africa," in M. Fortes and E. E. Evans-Pritchard, eds., *African Political Systems* (London: Oxford University Press, 1940).

9. Audrey I. Richards, "The Political System of the Bemba of Northern Rhodesia," in Fortes and Evans-Pritchard, *op. cit.*

10. E. E. Evans-Pritchard, *The Divine Kingship of the Shilluk of the Nilotic Sudan* (Cambridge: Cambridge University Press, 1948).

11. E. E. Evans-Pritchard, *The Political System of the Annuak of the Anglo-Egyptian Sudan* (London: London School of Economics, 1940).

12. Daryll Forde, "Ward Organization among the Yako," *Africa,* XX (1950), 267–289.

13. For a very representative collection of articles on primitive political systems, see Ronald Cohen and John Middleton, eds., *Comparative Political Systems—Studies in the Politics of Pre-industrial Societies* (New York: Natural History Press, 1957).

14. Gluckman, *op. cit.*

15. Melville J. Herskovits, *Dahomey: An Ancient West African Kingdom* (Illinois: Northwestern University Press, 1967).

16. Evans-Pritchard, *The Political System of the Annuak of the Anglo-Egyptian Sudan.*

17. Marshall D. Sahlins, *Social Stratification in Polynesia* (Seattle: American Ethnological Society, 1958); Sahlins, "Poor-Man, Rich-Man, Big-Man, Chief," *Comparative Studies in Society and History,* V (1963), 285–303.

18. Forde, *op. cit.*

19. E. Adamson Hoebel, "Associations and the State in the Plains," *American Anthropologist,* XXXVIII (1936), 433–438.

20. Karl Polanyi, Conrad M. Arensberg, and Harry W. Pearson, *Trade and Market in Early Empires* (Glencoe: The Free Press, 1957).

21. Max Gluckman, *Politics, Law and Religion in Tribal Society* (Chicago: Aldine, 1965); Gluckman, *The Ideas of Barotse Jurisprudence* (New Haven and London: Yale University Press, 1965).

22. Frederick Barth, *Political Leadership among Swat Pathana* (London: University of London Press, 1959).

23. See S. N. Eisenstadt, "Primitive Political Systems: A Preliminary Comparative Analysis," *American Anthropologist,* LXI, No. 2 (April 1959), 205–220.

24. Audrey I. Richards, "The Political System of the Bemba Tribe of Northern Rhodesia," in Fortes and Evans-Pritchard, *op. cit.*

25. Meyer Fortes, "The Political System of the Tallensi of the Northern Territories of the Gold Coast," in Fortes and Evans-Pritchard, *op. cit.*

26. See, for instance, Evans-Pritchard, *The Political System of the Annuak of the Anglo-Egyptian Sudan.*

27. Gluckman, "The Kingdom of the Zulu of South Africa."

28. Max Gluckman, *Custom and Conflict in Africa* (Oxford: Blackwell, 1955).

29. Sahlins, "Poor-Man, Rich-Man, Big-Man, Chief"; Sahlins, *Social Stratification in Polynesia* (Seattle: University Press, 1958); Irving Goldman, "The Evolution of Polynesian Societies," in Stanley Diamond, ed., *Culture in History* (New York: Columbia University Press, 1960), pp. 687–712; Goldman, "Status Rivalry and Cultural Evolution in Polynesia," *American Anthropologist,* LVII (1955), 680–697.

30. James A. Barnes, *Politics in a Changing Society* (Cape Town: Oxford University Press, 1954). See also, for more recent approaches, Victor Turner and Marc Swatz, eds., *Political Anthropology* (Chicago: Aldine, 1966).

INTRODUCTION TO THE READINGS

In the following section several selections dealing with primitive political systems are presented. Most of the essays attempt some type of comparative analysis. Lloyd Fallers' article compares different African political systems and attempts to suggest the different potentials for political modernization inherent in them. Fallers tends to emphasize the importance of center formation in the primitive society as a facilitating factor in the process of modernization. Morton H. Fried's contribution represents the evolutionary approach to the analysis of primitive political systems, with special emphasis on the ways in which the development of stratification determines the crystallization of differentiated political organizations. Max Gluckman indicates how partial differentiation of the political organization in a primitive kingdom like the Barotse, in which a political center developed that was symbolically but not structurally differentiated from the periphery, influences the perception of the nature of power and of the polity and the incidence of civil war. He then draws very interesting structural analogies to early feudal Europe. The excerpts that open this section, from the editor's "Primitive Political Systems," are an attempt to classify various primitive political systems and to present on the basis of this analysis some more general hypotheses about the conditions that influence the degree to which autonomous political organizations, activities, and roles develop.

11

Primitive Political Systems: A Preliminary Comparative Analysis

S. N. Eisenstadt

The starting point of this analysis is the extent of articulation of special political positions and organizations. The first broad group is composed of tribes which seemingly have no specially organized, central political authority or organization; political activity takes place within the subgroups of the society and through their interaction. Beyond this common denominator there are many differences between these tribes, particularly in the nature of the main subgroups among which interaction takes place, and the extent of and the main social spheres of this interaction (our sample does not include all variations, but those presented suffice for our preliminary analysis). This category includes: (*a*) tribes with but rudimentary political interaction between various loose bands, small family and territorial units (only cursorily mentioned); (*b*) segmentary tribes organized in corporate lineages between which there is extensive political and ritual interaction; (*c*) tribes in which, in addition to the organized kinship groups, other important groups and principles of social and political interaction exist, notably in those cases where various criteria of universalistic allocation of roles are manifested in age-groups and regiments; (*d*) those where association is based on particularistic criteria of membership and oriented either to ritual or collective (war) activities; (*e*) tribes in which the kinship and lineage groups interact on the basis of

a special hierarchical stratification into classes (mostly in the ritual field); and finally (*f*) the so-called "acephalous villages" in which the importance of family and kinship groups diminishes in favor of various specialized associations based on the universalistic criteria of achievement and interacting chiefly in the economic and social spheres.

The next category includes those tribes among which central political authority and organization undoubtedly exist, subdivided according to the types of groups which bear the political action and positions. The first are (*g*) tribes in which kinship and lineage groups are the most important units that bear political action; the second are (*h*) tribes in which some universalistic groups also exist, such as regiments or age-groups; and the last are (*i*) societies in which various types of associations perform such central tasks.

While we call each type by a descriptive name, usually the one most commonly found in the literature, it should be borne in mind that they are not a series of discrete, discontinuous categories, but derive from the analytical criteria enumerated above.*

I. Types of Segmentary Tribes

A. Band Organization

The simplest type of political and social organization can be found among "simple," noncentralized societies, such as Australian and Pygmy tribes, and

From S. N. Eisenstadt, "Primitive Political Systems: A Preliminary Comparative Analysis," *American Anthropologist,* LXI, No. 2 (April 1959), 205–220. Reprinted by permission of the American Anthropological Association.

* See Introduction to this chapter.

tribes such as Jicarilla Apache[1] and the Plateau Tonga.[2] They are composed of relatively undifferentiated, loose groups, families and territorial units. There is little division of labor, and the extent of interaction and interdependence is relatively small except for intermarriage. Roles are mainly allocated to members of the family and other small particularistic groups, and there is relatively little scope for individual initiative and achievement, except occasionally in the field of leadership. The main goal orientations are adaptive and ritual; i.e., adaptation to the physical environment, procurement of wellbeing for the tribe, and maintenance of its main patterns of life. These goals are attained through the internal activities of the main subgroups of the society and through their interaction. The system of stratification, insofar as it exists, is focused on these units, with status determined in terms of the common ritual values and to some extent in terms of the relative wealth between the various local and kinship groups. In these tribes, we find few fixed "political" positions and a high extent of self-regulation of the main component groups.

B. "Classical" Segmentary Tribes.

The "classical" segmentary societies are best exemplified by the Tallensi[3] and Bantu Kavirondo[4] and less well by the Nuer.[5] Among them, the basic lineage groups—the various maximal lineages—are the primary bearers of political roles and tasks. There is a high degree of organized interdependence and complementarity among the various component units. The main unit of social specialization is the lineage, i.e., a segment of the clan in which the members are genealogically related to one another. The lineages may be of various generation depths and may split off after some generations, but the common identification expressed in terms of common ancestry persists. The lineages and clans are usually localized groups with a strong corporate organization. Their interrelations are defined in corporate terms and the most important political, judicial, and ritual interaction of their members is carried on in the name of these corporate units, the individual members acting as their representatives. The mutual specialization and interdependence of corporate lineages and clans is manifest among the Tallensi in the two types of chiefdoms, the *na'am* and the ritual *tendaam* (Custodian of the Earth); the first is related to earth and the second endowed with rainmaking powers. Both of these offices are permanently vested in certain clans, and thus the main offices of leadership reside in corporate kinship groups. There exists some competition between the various lineages and their respective officers as to prestige and influence, although these relative positions are seemingly defined largely by tradition and the dominant ritual values of the society. The leaders of the society are concerned principally with ritual functions, and to a smaller degree with the settlement of disputes between the lineages. In most other respects, the single lineage is the unit of collective action. Most administrative-technical problems are settled and organized within the maximal lineages, and most collective action—such as the organization of fishing expeditions—is largely, if not entirely, within the province of the lineages. Most of the interaction between lineages—in addition to intermarriage and kinship ties—is concerned with ritual, and to a much smaller extent with economic activities. It is in the field of ritual that the main values of the society lie.

C. Universalistic (Age-Groups) Segmentary Tribes

The Nandi and Masai have usually been regarded as falling within the segmentary category, but nevertheless differ from the tribe just described.[6] There are no corporate lineages: the clans and subclans are not territorial organizations, and the territorial groups are not composed of homogeneous kin and family elements. The kin group does not constitute the basic unit of the social division of labor, and the main political roles are allocated according to universalistic criteria of membership. There is also some achievement orientation with respect to excellence in warfare and, to a lesser degree, accumulation of wealth. The main goal and value orientations are in the fields of ritual and warfare, where social differentiation is highest. Interaction between the various subunits of these tribes is regulated by a purely local and territorial hierarchy, beginning with the smallest units and extending upward toward the wider and more inclusive ones. The judicial system is similarly organized. Quarrels which cannot be settled within a small local unit, or in which several such units are involved, are settled by representatives of larger territorial units; nowhere are these judiciary offices vested in representatives of lineages, clans, or other kin groups. The same holds true of ritual offices. The extent of self-regulation of the various kinship and territorial groups is somewhat smaller than in the former types, and there are groups of elders or "village" councilmen which, while they do not have great formal power, are an important factor in molding public opinion and in mediating and resolving conflicts. There also appear semiformalized leaders and chiefs with rather special positions. Unlike positions of leadership among the segmentary tribes, these are not necessarily vested in any lineage or other group but are achieved through individual attainment. Such leaders are important in making decisions regarding wars or raids.

The specific organizations for the implementation of warfare are the military regiments and the age-groups, which need not be identical but usually have a strong interrelationship.[7] They cut across kinship and local ties, and perform important functions in warfare and other collective activities such as the juridical process. In connection with these collective activities, as well as with some of the disputes that may arise, we find a certain amount of what we have called party-political activities. Disputes may arise as to the wisdom of a certain policy, initiation of a war-party, allocation of available manpower for tribal tasks, and there also may be informal competition between individuals for positions in the tribal council or tribunals.

D. The "Associational" Tribes

A type of tribe which does not have centralized political organization can be found among some of the Plains and Pueblo groups, especially the Hopi, the Zuni,[8] the Kiowa and other Plains societies.[9] In most of these tribes with the partial exception of five Plains tribes which have a strong age-group organization and a larger extent of individual achievement orientation[10] the most important offices are vested either in members of hereditary kinship groups or in members of the various associations which are characteristic of these tribes. As a general rule, these associations perform important functions in integrating the various kinship and territorial groupings, and membership in them is largely determined on the particularistic grounds of kinship and personal relations. There are few full-fledged political offices and organizations which are distinct from other roles and groups. Some types of chiefs exist whose main functions are performance of rituals and mediation, and who usually have little coercive power or authority. On the whole, the various kinship, territorial, and associational groups are self-regulatory. These different types of groups tend to perform complementary functions in the integration of the tribe, although they may not always succeed in coping with all the tensions that exist and in regulating all the interrelationships between the component groups. The main goal and value orientations of these societies are similar to those of the tribes previously discussed, but some important differences exist between them. Among the Pueblos the main values are ritual-adaptive ones, while among

the Plains tribes there is a greater emphasis on achievements in war and on pursuit of collective goals, and these have repercussions on the structure and goals of the associations.

The principal exception to this relative lack of co-ordinated activity is found among the Plains tribes, during the periods when the bands gather and engage in common efforts—especially in hunting and war expeditions. On these occasions, a relatively distinct leadership emerges, various associations perform basic directive functions, and their chiefs become fully authorized leaders of the tribe.[11] One association is delegated the task of directing the expeditions; another has the full policing authority. The emergence of specific executive and juridical positions is here closely related to the need to perform common collective tasks and to regulate the available manpower resources for their execution. The extent of party-politics is relatively small, although competition exists among various associations for prestige, for the performance of different ritual functions, and for ownership of various "bundles."

E. The Ritually Stratified Tribes

The Annuak,[12] the Shilluk,[13] and the Ankole[14] display many differences, but share common characteristics in political organization. Among them we find some degree of differentiation and stratification in the ritual-symbolic field, but very little in any other major field of social life. The main goal-orientations are collective-ritual, i.e., are expressed in attempts to "wrest" ritual power in behalf of various collectivities. These goals constitute the common tribal framework of interaction and afford the main criteria of stratification, according to which the lineages and kinship groups are judged. These groups are relatively self-sufficient economically and administratively but interact in ritual matters. In most of these societies, there are two "classes"—nobles and commoners. The nobles are the active competitors for the main political positions, which entail little actual authority and power. Their political systems can best be described as centralized, stratified, focused on competition for ritual positions, and with minimal administrative and juridical organization. The chiefs and nobles may distribute any surplus to their followers. They have little juridical power, and most subunits of the society (lineages, villages) enjoy relative autonomy and regulate most of their own affairs. The main value of political positions is symbolic-ritual and, in the words of Evans-Pritchard,[15] "it is the acceptance of a common value, and not corporate action, which constitutes the policy." Around these ritual positions a continuous struggle is waged between nobles of different lineages, who try to mobilize support among the commoners. Thus, we find a rather intensive pattern of party-political activities which gives rise to a special type of political intermediary—a member of the class of commoners who is in the political service of a noble or chief, organizes his supporters, and comes to his aid in various quarrels. Beyond these activities, focused on the ritual-political field, there are few specialized, administrative, or executive activities or organizations.

F. Acephalous, Autonomous Villages

The so-called acephalous villages are best exemplified by the Yako,[16] Ibo, Ibibio,[17] and some Yoruba groups.[18] Their main specific characteristic is the presence of so-called associations that have an especially important place in their life. The graded titles and membership positions in these associations are not hereditarily vested in families, lineages, or other descent groups, but are acquired individually, although perhaps with the help of the families. Thus, the main principles of role allocation are here universalistic, achievement-oriented, and to some degree specialized. Most of the specialization is especially prominent in the activities related to the attainment of instrumental gratification and economic and social goals, which are also the main values of the society.

Among the Yako, the most fully described of these peoples, the village (or town) is divided into several wards which form the basic administrative units of the society. Within these wards several family groups and patri-clans live together, while other members of the same patri-clans may be found in other wards. Except on the lower, family-unit level, the organization of the ward is not based on the corporate interaction of the family and kin groups. The patri-clan has certain corporate functions and its heads perform both ritual and judiciary roles, but this is true only with respect to members of other patri-clans, members of a ward, or to the common economic enterprises and ritual observances which bind the village together. The common affairs of the ward are supervised by various officers, elected not on the basis of kin affiliation or membership but on the basis of wealth, age, wisdom, and various other personal qualities and attainments.

Among the Yako we also find a relatively more complicated governmental system than in the former types. The main centers of power are the ward and village councils, and the associations divide among themselves, as it were, many functions of government

and social control. Quite strong competition exists between individuals over the attainment of positions within the associations, semipolitical positions as ward heads or members of the village council, and between some of the associations as to their relative influence in village life. Here is high degree of group interaction, especially in the economic field. Each group is to a large extent dependent on the labor force of other groups, and many economic tasks are undertaken in common by a ward or village. The extent of economic activities also explains the great importance of various technical-administrative activities within the structure of governmental framework. Thus, we find that one of the main concerns of the "central authorities" is to arrange for common economic activities, maintenance of the water supply, or clearing of the bush. Most activities are performed by members of various age groups, and are directed by village and association officials.

As has already been implied, most of the higher "political" positions are closely related to positions in associations, but at the same time certain more specialized political, and especially administrative, positions also tend to develop. Here are special administrators of the various wards or of the village councils, who are usually in charge of the administrative works performed by the age groups.

II. Centralized Chiefdoms

The so-called centralized chiefdoms are best exemplified by the Zulu,[19] Ngoni,[20] Swazi,[21] Tswana,[22] Bemba,[23] Ashanti,[24] Pondo,[25] and Khoisa.[26] The most important characteristics shared by these chiefdoms is that within their kingdoms, the political sphere is distinct from that of lineage and kinship relations, and political positions acquire a certain degree of autonomy. The relative importance of corporate descent groups, lineages, clans and the like for the definition of the territorial units of society and for the general political life of the tribe is smaller than among the various segmentary tribes, with the possible exception of the Ashanti.

In most of these societies there is also less self-regulation of internal affairs and fewer mutual interrelations of the major subgroups of the society.

G,H. Centralized and Federative
Monarchies

But beyond this common characteristic there are certain important differences among them. The chiefdoms mentioned above can be roughly divided into two types: The first (to be called the centralized monarchy) is illustrated by Zulu, Ngoni, Swazi, and Tswana; the second (to be called the federative monarchy) is illustrated by Bemba, Ashanti, Pondo, and Khoisa.

The distinction between the two types of "primitive" kingdoms may be said to be broadly that of a difference in the degree to which (a) the major groups regulate their own affairs in various spheres, and (b) the extent to which the major political offices are vested in various ascriptive groups or, conversely, the extent to which the political sphere is organized on a level different from that of local kin and economic spheres.

If we compare the two groups of peoples according to these criteria, we find some broad and striking differences. First, we find that in general the extent of self-regulation of territorial and kin groups in economic, juridical, and ritual matters is much smaller in the centralized than in the federative monarchies. Second, among the centralized monarchies, the most distinguishing characteristic is universal membership in the widest political unit of the tribe through direct allegiance to the king. Although the king's relationship to his subjects is couched in kinship terms (manifest in the national royal ritual), from the standpoint of membership this relation is distinctly universalistic, i.e., open to anyone who will swear allegiance and attach himself to the chief. Moreover, allegiance to the chief and membership in the political community are not necessarily dependent upon membership in any intermediary group. The contrary is true of the federative monarchies, which are usually composed of amalgamations of lineages, clans, or local kin groups which have been incorporated as groups within the total social unit, with membership in the latter attainable only through these subunits.

In the centralized monarchies, the king may approach his subjects directly in judicial matters, and especially in exacting tribute and calling up the army for either military exigencies or "public works," and the king has ultimate authority over the various heads and local chiefs. In the federative monarchies, the king's ultimate dependence on the lesser chiefs and on the organized, corporate activities of the various kin and territorial groups is most clearly evident among the Ashanti and somewhat less so among the Khoisa, Bemba, and Pondo.

Differences in the composition of the king's council are also important. Truly enough in both types, the council is composed of certain members of the royal clan (family), heads of certain leading clans and families, and certain personal favorites of the king. However, the relative importance of these elements, especially the last two, varies considerably among the societies. Among the centralized monarchies, the commoner members of the council are not merely private advisers and favorites of the king, but full members of the council, holding central offices. Among the federative monarchies the advisers are usually more limited in number and act in a more private capacity. In these latter societies, the council is composed principally of heads of the various territorial units, clans, and lineages, who have an inherent membership right and without whom the council cannot properly act. Among the Swazi and Zulu such hereditary councillors, although important, are not as independent of the king's will in holding their offices as they are among the federative monarchies.

Differences also exist between the two groups in relation to the major goal emphases. Among the centralized monarchies there is a strong emphasis on collective goals (war, expansion), and many ritual activities are even geared to these goals. Among the federative monarchies there is a much stronger emphasis on adaptive-ritual goals.

There are corresponding differences between the two types in the organization and articulation of various governmental activities. First, as has been implied in the earlier discussion, in the centralized monarchies we generally find a greater articulation of specific political positions and organizations. As we have seen, the various positions on the king's council in the royal courts, and so forth, are more independent of membership in other groups (lineages, clans) than in the federative monarchies, and there are also more positions of this kind in the first type than in the second. Further, in the centralized monarchies there are many more organized collective activities, common to all the tribes and directed by the main chief. The two most important are military expeditions and various kinds of public works. These public works are usually performed for the benefit of the central authorities or for the maintenance of efficient networks of communication. While some such activities are also organized in the federative monarchies, they are usually more limited and confined to local enterprises and are directed by heads of lineages or clans. In the centralized monarchies, most such activities are performed by specific organizations, namely, the various age-groups or age-regiments. The age-regiments cut across the existing lineage and territorial units, and are directed by the king or his representatives. There are no age-regiments in the federative tribes, and most military and public works activities are performed by lineages and clan groups.

Another important characteristic of the centralized

monarchies is the relative intensity of party-politics, although some party-politics can also be found in the federative monarchies—most of it centering around the struggle of various lineage and kinship groups for positions of influence and prestige in the political framework. The Ashanti confederation perhaps shows the greatest amount of such conflict, but it can also be found among the Bemba, Pondo, and others. In these tribes, however, political conflict has been largely between corporate groups, with little room for individual or subgroup activities. In the centralized monarchies, there is much more intensive party-political activity; there is strong competition between the king and members of his own clan, between king and local chiefs, between various councillors and between kinship and local groups versus the central authorities. In certain respects this intensity of party-political activities resembles that of the segmentary tribes of the Nandi type. Here, as in the tribes of the latter type, we also find relatively little administrative activity directed toward the organization of economic activities and conditions.

I. Monarchies Based on Associations and Secret Societies

A distinct type of centralized chiefdom found among the Mende and other tribes of Sierra Leone and Liberia[27] resembles the Bemba and Ashanti, in that most political positions are vested in members of hereditary groups. But here an additional factor intervenes—namely, the existence of many associations, most of the "secret society" types. The best examples of this are the Poro and the Zande associations among the Mende. These perform important political and administrative functions, especially in economic and cultural fields and in the general maintenance of social control. Here is also a greater elaboration of special political and administrative apparatus, some of which is under the control of the king and some under the control of the associations. In addition to this wide range of administrative functions which deal with the organization of certain economic activities, some degree of party-politics also exists. The party-politics usually center in the upper echelons of the secret associations and in the relations between the associations and the kings, and are not as public and open as among the Zulu or Swazi. Here also, the extent of self-regulation by the various subgroups of the society—kinship and locality groups—is very small, and more of the regulatory functions are performed by the central organs. This can be seen especially in the relatively centralized juridical organization of these tribes.

Of the societies studied here, the highest degree of centralization and of development of special political and administrative organs can probably be found among the Dahomey.[28] This society shows a highly centralized hereditary monarchy, based on a hierarchical organization of various hereditary subunits—localities, groups of families, and the like. Most secondary political positions are vested in such groups, but the various officials are to a considerable extent dependent upon the king, and do not have the semiautonomous status that such officials have among the Bemba and Ashanti. There is a relatively marked economic differentiation between the king and his entourage and other groups in the society. The administrative and centralized juridical activity is focused largely on the provision of adequate economic and manpower facilities for the king. The various subunits have little autonomy, and can regulate directly only a few of their own affairs and their interactions with other groups. There seem to be few "secret" associations among the Dahomey, and those that do exist are of a much more private nature than those of the Mende. Moreover, they do not play an important part in the political life of the tribe. However, relatively strong cult-groups seem to exist, and the heads of these have some political influence. Because of the highly authoritarian and ascriptive character of the political institutions, there is little party-politics, but such activities go on among the heads of cult-groups, the king's councillors, and the people holding the higher administrative positions. The elaborate and well-knit central administrative staff deals with the organization of economic activities, keeping the peace, and the maintenance of discipline and obedience toward the king, performing these functions on behalf of the subgroups of the society.

Types of Social Structure and of Political Organization: Some Tentative Hypotheses

We have described some of the main characteristics of the political organization and social structure of selected types of primitive societies. We may now inquire as to how these aspects of the social structure are related to characteristics of the political structures.

Social Differentiation and Levels of Political Organization

We may first inquire what the material presented tells us about the conditions under which different levels of articulation of political positions and organizations are found. Generally speaking, this material bears out the hypothesis that the greater the differentiation and/or the inability of various subgroups of a society to regulate their interrelations, the greater would be the development of special political organizations, other conditions being equal. As we have seen earlier, such a hypothesis is implicit in some of the existing discussions about comparative primitive political systems. It is in line with that advanced lately by Schapera,[29] although it aims at a more inclusive definition of the nature of differentiation. Such a hypothesis may seem to be tautological, since it may be claimed that obviously the more differentiated a society is, the more specialized will be its constituent parts of which the political system is one. But it need not be tautological if it can be shown that greater articulation of political organization will take place no matter in what sphere (e.g., economic, ritual, and so on) there is greater differentiation and specialization. In other words, the level of differentiation need not be the same in all subsystems of a society, and political subsystems (unlike other subsystems) are most sensitive to problems arising out of differentiation in any other part of the society.

If we consider societies discussed above in the order of their differentiation, we find that in general this hypothesis is borne out. We have analyzed in each of the types the extent of differentiation and of self-regulation of the various groups of which the society is composed. We have seen in each category the number and type of groups found, the extent to which these groups manage their own affairs in the economic, ritual, and legal field, and their relations with other groups. We have also seen how many special political positions and organizations exist in each. These two variables—the extent of differentiation and self-regulation, and the extent of articulation of political positions—have been established by independent criteria. The less differentiated societies —the so-called segmentary tribes of different types —have minimal special political positions, but even among these there are significant differences. Tribes such as the Nandi and Masai, where some differentiation exists between spheres in which roles are allocated by universalistic or particularistic criteria, and where there is some stratification based on achievement, show a greater development of political roles than do such peoples as the Tellensi. Among the Annuak and Shilluk, where some differentiation of strata exists, we also find a few specific political offices, centered especially in the ritual field.

In the various autonomous villages, where we have seen much greater differentiation and where wide spheres of life are regulated by universalistic and achievement orientations, and where a correspondingly complex system of groups and stratification is formed, we have also seen the greater existence of political organization. The same principle applies if we analyze the centralized chiefdoms, all of which have relatively greater differentiation. Among these kingdoms we also find that the societies which have strong universalistic and achievement orientations (such as the Zulu and Swazi) have a more complex system of political organization than do those whose division of labor is based on particularistic and ascriptive criteria.

Organization of Different Types of Political Activities

In general, the first hypothesis is borne out by the data presented here. A closer examination of these data, in relation to this hypothesis, shows several interesting facts: First, the dichotomy between "segmentary" and "centralized" primitive societies is not a true dichotomy. Rather, there is a continuum in the articulation of political positions and of organization of political activities. In all societies at least some of the basic political functions are performed by some specific roles or units and it is not possible to distinguish entirely between stateless and "state" societies. What distinguishes one society from another is not so much the existence or nonexistence of central political organization, but the extent to which different types of political functions are performed by different specialized units and the extent to which the functions are organized in various types of roles and organizations.[30]

Second, this hypothesis is too general to account for many significant differences in the political organization of the tribes analyzed here. It treats the concept of "differentiation" in too homogeneous a way and consequently tends to treat diverse political activities as a homogeneous unit. Neither does it take into account the fact that emphasis may be placed on different aspects of political activity. The data show that societies may differ in the extent of articulation of political roles and moreover may emphasize different aspects of political activities (as, for instance, the strong emphasis on executive and party-political activities of the Zulu as against the emphasis on ritual and juridical activities of the Bemba). It is necessary to account for these differences.

We have seen that the main interrelations between the political and the other institutions of a society can be understood in terms of the functions which the political institutions perform, and in terms of the types of resources these institutions must mobilize in order to perform these functions. Thus, in any detailed consideration of the relation between the political structure and other aspects of the social structure, it is important to see what goals and needs the society emphasizes; what exigencies it faces; to what extent these goals and needs can be implemented and the exigencies dealt with by the various subgroups of a society without recourse to special political and administrative agencies, and where such agencies do develop, what kinds of resources are most important for them.

On the basis of these considerations and the material analyzed above, the following hypotheses can be proposed: That the relative emphasis on different types of political activities is dependent on the main goal and value-orientations of a society.

(*a*) An emphasis on collective goals, preoccupation with warfare, extension of collective power, or with other collective endeavors is closely related to executive activities which deal with the mobilization, manipulation, and organization of internal manpower resources. In such cases, the need arises to emphasize executive leadership and decision-making, and to enable such leadership to organize the available resources for the maximization of collective goals and for dealing with the exigencies which are created through the emphasis on them. Both the Nandi and Masai groups and the Zulu and Swazi are good illustrations of this correlation. Interesting support for this hypothesis can be found among many of the Plains societies. Here executive leadership is operative only when the tribe is engaged in a collective endeavor—e.g., war raid, hunting party—and is not operative when the tribe is dispersed and its component parts are dealing primarily with adaptive problems. Also, many embryonic types of leadership found in simple bands and tribes seem to be closely connected with the performance of collective tribal tasks.

(*b*) Special emphasis on instrumental goals and economic gratifications seems to be more closely related to development of administrative functions. The implementation of such goals usually necessitates the organization of many technical aspects of common activities and creates many exigencies in the technical cooperative fields. The best illustrations of this correlation can be found among the Yako and Ibo, and to some extent among the Mende.

(*c*) A strong emphasis on solidary values and integrative goals seems to be related to a special articulation of party-political activities. Insofar as the society emphasizes maintenance of the basic solidarity of the collectivity, with the consequent

regulation of all subgroups within its framework, it would also be necessary to manipulate those subgroups in such a way as to assure their allegiance to the common goal. As the maintenance of solidarity and integration is of some importance in all societies, some party politics can be found in all the societies studied. However, they are most evident in societies such as the Tallensi, Annuak, Shilluk, and Mende, which tend to emphasize the goal of solidarity.

Party-political activities also increase when the problems of maintaining solidarity become more complex and acute, especially insofar as many groups with differing principles of social organization participate in the political struggle.

(*d*) Also of interest is the special place of ritual activities, which must deal with the legitimation of the political system in terms of the society's values. Obviously such activities are closely related to an emphasis on cultural values. Some aspects of such values seem to be predominant in most of the primitive societies studied, and the maintenance of their given traditions and patterns of life is a common basic orientation of their values. In most of the societies discussed here, the performance of ritual functions which emphasize these orientations is therefore a basic part of the activities of holders of political positions, and there are few differences between them in this respect.

Social Differentiation, Societal Goals, and Political Organization

But the value orientations and goals predominant in a society are not the only determinants of the relative emphasis on different aspects of political activity. These goals tend to delineate the general orientation of the political activities of a society, but in themselves they do not determine the actual organization of these activities. It is entirely conceivable that a particular society may be able to implement its major goal and value orientation through the activities of its component groups, without recourse to any specific political organization, simply by special emphasis on this or that aspect of political activity. The hypothesis may be suggested that the full articulation of any aspect of political activity, in the form of special organizations, will be determined by: (*a*) the main goals and value orientations of a society; (*b*) the types of resources needed for their maximization; and (*c*) the extent to which these resources are not available through the internal work of various subgroups of the society.

In all the tribes discussed above, we saw examples

of societies which could maximize goals with little recourse to specialized positions and agencies. The Tonga, Tallensi, and Pueblos are good examples of this.

In other tribes, however, a relatively great differentiation and consequent lack of self-regulation of various subunits exist in areas of social life which are most closely related to the main goals of the society. Among the "universalistic" segmentary tribes (e.g., Nandi, Masai) and among the centralized monarchies (e.g., Zulu, Swazi) the existence of both universalistic and particularistic principles of role allocation has repercussions on the availability of resources which are necessary for the maximization of their collective goals. The most important of these is the fact that such resources—manpower, wealth, group loyalties—are not "given" by various ascriptive subgroups, but have to be mobilized through special political-executive and party-political activities.

Among the Pueblos, executive leadership arises on occasions when the goal-emphasis is shifted to collective tasks which cannot be performed by the self-regulated interaction of various subunits. Among the Annuak, the special articulation of political-ritualized positions is found in relation to the relatively great differentiation and stratification in the ritual-solidary field and to the high level of rather unregulated competition between the subgroups in this field.

Among the Yako and Ibo, the special organization of administrative activities is closely related to the strong interdependence (and the relative lack of self-sufficiency) between various local and family groups in the economic and instrumental fields. Significantly enough, in those areas of social life where such differentiation does not exist and/or which are not related to the main goals and value-orientations of the society, the articulation of special political positions is smaller. Thus, among the universalistic-segmentary tribes and centralized monarchies, there are few purely administrative positions which deal with organization of economic and instrumental activities; among the autonomous villages there are few special executive positions, and so on.

While many more illustrations could be given, those given above suffice to demonstrate the feasibility of the approach presented here. At this stage of analysis, this approach does not presume to say anything about the historical development of different political institutions or to deal with the problem of what mechanisms these institutions develop under certain social conditions. It aims only to establish meaningful correlations between different aspects of social structure and political organization.

NOTES

1. R. N. Bellah, *Apache Kinship Systems* (Cambridge: Harvard University Press, 1952), pp. 12–41.

2. E. Colson, "Social Control and Vengeance in Plateau Tonga Society," *Africa*, XXIII (1953), 199–212.

3. M. Fortes, "The Political System of the Tallensi of the Northern Territories of the Gold Coast," in M. Fortes and E. E. Evans-Pritchard, eds., *African Political Systems* (London: Oxford University Press, 1940); M. Fortes, *The Dynamics of Clanship among the Tallensi* (Oxford: Oxford University Press, 1945); M. Fortes, *The Web of Kinship among the Tallensi* (Oxford: Oxford University Press, 1949).

4. G. Wagner, *The Bantu of North Kavirondo* (Oxford: Oxford University Press, 1949), Vol. I.

5. E. E. Evans-Pritchard, *The Nuer* (Oxford: Oxford University Press, 1940).

6. S. N. Eisenstadt, "African Age Groups," *Africa*, XXIV (1954), 100–113; *From Generation to Generation—Age Groups and Social Structure* (Glencoe: The Free Press, 1956), Ch. 3 and Bibliography.

7. Eisenstadt, *From Generation to Generation—Age Groups and Social Structure.*

8. F. Eggan, *Social Organization of the Western Pueblos* (Chicago: University of Chicago Press, 1950); M. Titiev, "Old Oraibi," *Papers of the Peabody Museum,* Vol. XXII (1944).

9. R. Lowie, "Plains Indian Age Societies: Historical and Comparative Summary," *Anthropological Papers of the American Museum of Natural History,* Vol. XI (1916); A. Bowers, *Mandan Social and Ceremonial Organization* (Chicago: University of Chicago Press, 1950).

10. S. N. Eisenstadt, "Plains Indian Age Groups," *Man,* LIV (1954), 6–8.

11. D. Mandelbaum, "Social Groupings," in H. L. Shapiro, ed., *Man, Culture and Society* (New York: Oxford University Press, 1956).

12. E. E. Evans-Pritchard, *The Political System of the Annuak* (London: London School of Economics, Monograph in Anthropology, 1940).

13. A. Butt, *The Nilotes of the Anglo-Egyptian Sudan* (London: International African Institute, 1952).

14. K. Oberle, "The Kingdom of Ankole in Uganda," in Fortes and Evans-Pritchard, *op. cit.*

15. Evans-Pritchard, *The Political System of the Annuak,* p. 138.

16. C. D. Forde, "Government in Umor," *Africa,* XII (1939), 129–162; "Ward Organization among the Uakö," *ibid.,* XX (1950), 267–289.

17. M. M. Green, *Ibo Village Affairs* (London: Sidgwick and Jackson, 1948).

18. P. Lloyd, "The Traditional Political System of the Yoruba," *Southwestern Journal of Anthropology,* X (1954), 361–384.

19. M. Gluckman, "The Kingdom of Zulu," in Fortes and Evans-Pritchard, *op. cit.*

20. J. A. Barnes, *Politics in a Changing Society* (Oxford: Oxford University Press, 1955).

21. H. Kuper, *An African Aristocracy* (Oxford: Oxford University Press, 1947).

22. I. Schapera, *A Handbook of Tswana Law and Custom* (Oxford: Oxford University Press, 1955).

23. A. Richards, "The Political System of the Bemba Tribe, Northern Rhodesia," in Fortes and Evans-Pritchard, *op. cit.*

24. K. Busia, *The Position of the Chief among the Ashanti* (Oxford: Oxford University Press, 1951).

25. M. Hunter, *Reaction to Conquest* (Oxford: Oxford University Press, 1936).

26. G. P. Lestrade, "Some Notes on the Political Organization of the BeChwana," *South African Journal of Science,* XXV (1928), 427–432.

27. M. McCulloch, *The Peoples of Sierra Leone Pro-*

tectorate (London: International African Institute, 1950); D. W. Schwab, "Tribes of the Liberian Hinterland," *Papers of the Peabody Museum,* Vol. XXXI (1947).

28. M. Herskovits, *Dahomey* (New York: J. J. Augustin, 1938).

29. I. Schapera, *Government and Politics in Tribal Societies* (London: Watts, 1956), p. 219.

30. M. G. Smith, "Segmentary Lineage Systems," *Journal of the Royal Anthropological Institute,* LXXXVI, No. 2 (1956), 39–81.

12

Political Sociology and the Anthropological Study of African Politics

Lloyd Fallers

I

The most basic question to which this work draws our attention is, quite simply: what is "the political"? The problem is of more than definitional interest, for only by means of some generally applicable conception of the political field can systems of widely varying kinds be made commensurable—be brought within range of comparative analysis. Faced with an extraordinarily wide variety of polities, from the great kingdoms of the Western Sudan and the interlacustrine region to the tiny autonomous kinship groups of the Khalahari Bushmen, anthropologists working in Africa have sought to define a field of comparative political study which would encompass them all. Clearly the former have kinds of political apparatus that the latter have not—hence the common practice of terming the latter "stateless" or "acephalous." But this need not mean that the less differentiated societies lack politics or political systems of any sort.

The solution to which social anthropologists concerned with African polities have tended in their search for a universal conception of the political—and in this their thinking has converged with that of many sociologists and political scientists—involves considering the polity and its major constituent elements as analytical, functional concepts. As in the work of Parsons, Levy, Easton and others, the polity or political system is viewed, not as a concretely distinct part of the social system, but rather as a

functional aspect of the whole social system: that aspect concerned with making and carrying out decisions regarding public policy, by whatever institutional means.[1] Of course the political system operates through actual social groups and relations, but these need not be specialized "governmental" or "state" organizations. Just as political scientists have increasingly come to the view that in modern Western societies the political system cannot be adequately understood if attention is confined to the formal organization of government, so social anthropologists working in Africa have concluded that the absence of such organization is not most profitably interpreted as an absence of political institutions and processes as such. And just as political scientists and political sociologists have been led to examine the political functions of classes, occupational groups, religious communities and "non-political" associations, so social anthropologists have found polities, where none seemed to exist, by examining the activities of multifunctional social groups—particularly the unilineal descent groups, or lineages, which are so common in Africa. Even where over-arching state organization, consisting of rulers and their subordinates, does not exist, they have concluded, decisions regarding public policy are made and carried out through the activities of such groups.[2] Of course the fact that political organization in such societies is not clearly differentiated from, say, that of economics and religion—the fact that the people who are together concerned with the formation and execution of public policy are the same as those who work and worship together—has important consequences for the nature of the political process in

From "Political Sociology and the Anthropological Study of African Politics," *European Journal of Sociology,* IV (1963), 311–329. Reprinted in an abridged form by permission of the author and the publisher.

such societies. It restricts the degree to which the polity, as distinct from the religious and economic fields, can be elaborated and made the focus of continuous attention. It does not, however, mean that political systems and political processes cannot exist.

As both Easton and Mair have pointed out, a further common consequence of this "embedding" of the polity in multifunctional social groups (or, to describe the same phenomenon from the opposite point of view, the lack of specialized political organization) is to render problematical and situational the boundaries of the "public" on behalf of which policy decisions are made and carried out.[3] In situations where the village or the band encampment is fully autonomous politically and where, consequently, its relations with other such groups may be viewed as essentially "foreign relations," there may be little difficulty in defining the boundaries of the polity. In such situations, the boundaries of local community and polity are the same.[4] But in many parts of Africa one finds societies without specialized political organization in which, nevertheless, a wider, multicommunity political order is capable of operating in particular situations to produce decisions applying to a field wider than that of the local community. Such societies—too thoroughly knit together politically to be regarded as congeries of autonomous communities but yet too discontinuously united to be called "states"—have been objects of particular interest to social anthropologists.

The best-known examples are the so-called "segmentary societies," in which political relations are viewed as resting upon a widely ramifying unilineal (patrilineal or matrilineal) system of genealogical relations. In such societies, the local community is thought of, for political purposes, as forming a single corporate lineage, but the genealogical system stretches beyond the local community; increasingly more extensive territorial units are viewed as comprising an ever-widening series of more inclusive unilineal descent groups so that, in extreme cases, the whole society may appear to its members as a single lineage whose constituent units, down to the local community, are lineage segments of varying scale. In this way, the Nuer of the Sudan and the Tiv of central Nigeria, for example, are able, without rulers or officials, to order political relations among hundreds of local communities and tens of thousands of persons.[5]

It is important to stress here the point that the genealogical framework that unites the several local communities in such societies is a *cultural* system, a system of *ideas*—in fact a kind of *political theory* —which may have rather little to do with "biological reality." It is a way of thinking and talking about community and trans-community political relations in the idiom of kinship and in terms of this idiom persons of the most diverse biological origins may, by means of "legal fictions," be treated for political purposes as if they were members of a single unilineal descent group.[6] In most such societies persons ordinarily become members of their local communities through unilineal descent and the several local communities which form a wider territorial unit are often composed in the main of descendants of a common ancestor, but it is not the rigid following of rules of unilineal descent for affiliating individuals to groups that is essential to the political functioning of such societies. What is important for political purposes is rather the fact that community and trans-community territorial units are treated *as if* they were lineages. And this fictional, "as-if" character of the system is quite clearly recognized by the people themselves; they explicitly make use of the genealogical idiom to manipulate their political relations.

I have said, however, that the political order that results is of a problematical, situational character and it is when one examines the nature of decision-making processes within such an order that this becomes most clear. A problem requiring decision may arise, for example, in the form of a dispute between communities, or between individual members of different communities, concerning the possession of territory for grazing or agriculture. In such situations, since there is no chief or council to exercise continuous, society-wide authority, decisions must be arrived at by *ad hoc* gatherings of representatives of the groups concerned or through arbitration by neutral parties. Such conciliation or arbitration is usually successful, however, only when the groups concerned are roughly equivalent in size and when they are in a position of what Fortes has called "complementary opposition" in the genealogical scheme; since there is no superordinate authority able to impose a solution, an effective decision must represent a high degree of consensus and must be supported by a substantial balance of power.[7] Groups related to those immediately concerned tend to be drawn into the dispute until larger groups, of equivalent scale and complementary genealogical position, are engaged, at which point accommodation becomes possible.

Figure 12–1 will perhaps help the reader to visualize the way in which the genealogical scheme of political theory is used in making decisions.

In the diagram, A, B, C and D are local communities, each associated with a unilineal descent

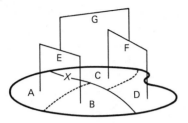

Figure 12–1

group. In the lineage political theory, A and B are thought of as fraternal segments within the larger lineage E; similarly, C and D are considered fraternal segments within lineage F. In turn, E and F are territorial units within the larger unit G and are thought of as fraternal segments within the total lineage associated with all of G. If, now, a dispute arises at point *X* along the border between E and F, which at this point is also the border between A and C, how can it be resolved? The initial dispute will likely involve only a few persons on either side of the border. All members of A and C, the local communities involved, will be obliged to go to the aid of their respective fellows. But, even if A and C are units of roughly equal size and power, it will not be possible for them to settle it by themselves, for A and C are not in "complementary opposition"— are not groups which, at the next level in the genealogical system of political theory, are fraternal segments within a larger lineage. They are incapable, by themselves, of forming a consensual community. Only after B comes to the aid of A and D to the aid of C is this condition fulfilled. When this happens, E and F, groups in complementary opposition within the still larger unit G, are engaged; in terms of the genealogical political theory, an institutional framework which "encloses" the disputing parties, enabling them to form a consensual community, comes into being and a settlement becomes possible. We may note that, had the dispute arisen on the border between A and B, the mobilization of a different, less extensive, part of the genealogical system would have sufficed. Since A and B are in complementary opposition within E, F and its constituent segments would have remained uninvolved.

It seems reasonable to describe what takes place here as "decision-making regarding public policy," despite the transitory character of the polity: a particular distribution of territory, with its accompanying resources, among the groups concerned, is defined and legitimated. To this extent there is in operation here a genuine political system. The proceedings are more than a matter of diplomatic negotiation among essentially sovereign powers, for

the trans-community genealogical scheme provides a wider institutional system into which the several local communities may fit as constituent parts. But most of the time this wider institutional system is merely potential; the decision-making machinery comes into being only with the appearance of the policy problem—the dispute. There are no chiefs or officials to represent its continued existence. When there are no problems, it is in abeyance. And the boundaries of the polity—the "public" on behalf of which policy is made—also vary with the policy problem. Only such groups as are necessary to resolve the particular problem at hand become involved. Thus the political system is, in Easton's useful phrase, a "contingent political system," as contrasted, we may say, with a continuous one.

The contingent political system would seem to be a necessary consequence of the absence of specialized, continuously functioning political roles and institutions in terms of whose jurisdiction fixed boundaries for the polity might be defined. As I have noted, the phenomenon has been discussed most frequently in connection with the "segmentary societies," in which the relations that obtain among territorial communities are thought of in a unilineal genealogical idiom. Indeed, as Easton has pointed out, the social anthropologists who have studied these matters in the field have tended to interest themselves primarily in the structures of unilineal descent which give form to polities in these societies rather than in the nature of the polities themselves; they have studied lineage politics more from the point of view of lineages than from the point of view of politics and it is perhaps for this reason that it was left to a political scientist, commenting upon the social anthropological literature, to formulate the concept "contingent" to conceptualize the phenomenon in a more general way. In fact, however, the contingent political system is probably a feature of "stateless" societies generally, wherever local communities are not entirely "sovereign," as they probably seldom are. We may therefore expect to find a variety of contingent polities, making use of kinds of political theory other than the genealogical one.

The Baamba of the middle Uganda-Congo border area lack the trans-community genealogical framework characteristic of the segmentary societies, though their villages are organized internally along lineage lines, each village consisting mainly of men of a single lineage, together with their wives and children.[8] Internally, the village and its dominant lineage are segmented in terms of a genealogical framework, but quite different principles are made use of in the field of inter-community relations. These the Baamba order by means of alliances between village-lineages. Just how these alliances are established is not entirely clear, but they are not, apparently, conceived of genealogically. Each lineage and its associated village are allied to a series of other lineages and villages and within the alliance group both marriage and warfare are prohibited. Each community's total group of alliances, however, is unique; each is allied with certain other communities with which its allies are not allied. Thus, when a dispute arises and allies come to the aid of the disputing communities, a point is ultimately reached at which some community is allied with both disputants. At this point accommodation becomes possible: a contingent polity capable of reaching a policy decision binding upon a unit which embraces the disputing communities comes into being, however fleetingly.

There are no doubt still other types of contingent polity with other kinds of political theory for manipulating relations among acephalous territorial units; but the usefulness of the concept of the contingent political system is not limited to the analysis of relations among semi-autonomous village communities. It may also shed a certain light upon the political systems of the larger, more differentiated and more clearly bounded polities. Perhaps the most general way of setting forth the concept is to say that it draws our attention to all those non-continuous polities that function wherever the political system is not characterized by absolute sovereignty, either on the community or some higher level. To the extent to which there is sovereignty, there is continuous authority within the unit and war and diplomacy without. But, despite the fascination with which Western political philosophers have regarded the concept of sovereignty, its more extreme manifestations are probably rare and its existence in pure form impossible. Jouvenel tells us that even in the West its prominence is quite recent.[9] Probably much more common are polities in which society-wide authority is limited, both within and without, leaving room for contingent political arrangements both among societies, in the form of institutions which go beyond diplomacy, and within societies, in the shape of the many processes of policy-making that take place in spheres lying beyond the authority of the state. These arrangements, like those we have seen at work in the segmentary societies, are no doubt similarly dependent upon consensus and balance for their successful operation. To the extent to which such phenomena do appear within and among the more differentiated polities, the more markedly contingent political systems of Africa are not some-thing exotic—something limited to traditional African and other non-literate societies—but rather represent a particularly marked development of an element common, in some degree, to all or most of the world's political systems.

II

As I have indicated, social anthropologists working in Africa have given a great deal of attention to the sociology of unilineal descent groups—in part, of course, simply because such groups are so extremely common and important in African societies. Lineages are to sub-Saharan Africa what caste is to South Asia: a pervasive structural theme tending to appear, with variations, throughout the area. In the "acephalous" or "stateless" segmentary societies, lineages, as we have seen, provide the framework for "contingent polities." But of course not all African societies are of this kind; many have specialized political roles and institutions which serve to define more continuously functioning polities and these societies, too, very often contain unilineal descent groups. Just as the detailed study of the structure and functioning of lineages of the segmentary societies has produced ideas relevant beyond the range of these particular societies, so analyses of the role of lineages in the more continuously functioning polities of Africa are also proving to have a wider relevance. In particular, they promise to contribute usefully to the discussion of the limits and determinants of the centralization of power and authority. Just as, that is to say, a study of lineages in segmentary societies has taught us something about the conditions for the functioning of any stateless, trans-community polity, so also a study of their role in African kingdoms teaches us something about the distribution of power and authority in any state.

As I noted when discussing the work on segmentary societies, social anthropologists have tended to approach these phenomena with a primary interest in institutional particularities, such as lineages and chiefship, rather than in their political functions in a wider comparative perspective, and this has sometimes delayed the recognition of the different functions that may be performed by similar institutions in polities of different types. In their famous introduction to *African Political Systems*—a statement which has been the point of departure for most anthropological studies of political systems since its publication—Fortes and Evans-Pritchard classified the societies described in the volume into two types: "centralized primitive states," with specialized administrative and judicial institutions; and lineage-based "stateless societies," which lacked such institutions.[10] It was immediately apparent that there were difficulties with this classification: it rather implied that politically important lineages and specialized political roles and institutions were mutually exclusive, though the authors cannot have meant this, for among the societies described in the book were some, like the Zulu, for example, in which both were obviously present. At any rate, the classification served to raise the question: if, in the segmentary societies, the function of the lineage system was to order trans-community political relations in the absence of specialized political institutions and roles —the functioning of what Easton was later to call the "contingent political system" was by this time quite well understood, for in addition to the brief accounts of such societies published in *African Political Systems,* Evans-Pritchard had at about the same time published his first full monograph on the Nuer[11]— what then were the functions of lineages in the states that possessed such specialized political institutions?

In the years following World War II there appeared, in answer to this question, a series of excellent monographs, among which perhaps the most important were Barnes's study of the Ngoni of Northern Rhodesia and Nyasaland, Southall's of the Alur of northwestern Uganda, and Busia's of the Ashanti of Ghana.[12] All were clearly what Southall termed "segmentary states": polities having specialized political institutions in the form of hereditary rulers, with at least rudimentary administrative staffs, as well as politically significant lineages.[13]

I should perhaps pause here to explain what "politically significant" means in this context. A unilineal descent group is, in its minimal sense, simply a group formed by the descendants, in either the male or the female line, of a common ancestor.[14] It may have many or few, important or trivial, functions. In the segmentary societies, lineages, or territorial units based upon lineages in terms of a political theory, are the sole political units, as we have seen. The complementary opposition of such lineage-based units provides the sole institutional framework for decision-making. "Citizenship" means membership by descent, actual or fictional, in such a unit, or series of progressively more inclusive units. In some African societies, on the other hand, such as Buganda and the other interlacustrine states, lineages hold property rights but are not the basic building-blocks of the polity at large: its territorial sub-units are not in any sense lineage-based and citizenship means primarily membership in the national state through loyalty to the king.

The segmentary states—clearly a common political form in Africa—illustrate an intermediate situation.

They are "states" in the sense that they have hereditary rulers, around whom gather councillors and retainers, forming a (more or less) continuously functioning body capable of taking decisions on behalf of a (more or less) clearly bounded polity. But they are also "segmentary" in the sense that (*a*) the sub-divisions of the polity, which are the primary units for citizenship, are formed around unilineal descent groups, and (*b*) each of these sub-divisions is part of a hierarchy of more or less inclusive units of the same segmentary type, ranging from the local community to the whole state. What makes it possible for them to be segmentary states instead of segmentary stateless societies is the presence within each unit in the hierarchy of some principle of seniority by which, at each level, a chiefly line is distinguished, making possible in turn hereditary rulership. But, as in the segmentary stateless society, the boundaries of the polity as a whole remain problematical to a degree (though to a lesser degree than in the former case). A local community's membership in the state as a whole, like that of an individual, is not direct but rather is mediated by that of the next most inclusive unit. As in the segmentary society, units can only be mobilized for policy decisions in order of inclusiveness. Each unit's primary loyalty is to the next most inclusive unit, not to the whole polity.

Thus, such polities tend to be loose and often rather fragile. They are, as Fortes has noted, essentially "federal" in nature.[15] The polity as a whole has a less shadowy existence than that of the segmentary society, for there is a hierarchy of chiefs to symbolize its continuity and mobilize it for decision-making. But the authority of the paramount ruler tends to be limited, since each subordinate unit exercises a good deal of autonomy, and problematical, since each, possessing its own hereditary ruler, is potentially autonomous. The authority of the paramount over the whole state depends upon his ability to maintain a balance of power among the subordinate units.

If we return to the diagram of the segmentary society above, we may, by visualizing within each lineage at each level a senior line, bearing an hereditary chief, use it to represent the segmentary state. The paramount, G, does not rule A, B, C and D directly, but only through and by virtue of his authority over E and F. Neither does the paramount appoint any of these subordinate chiefs; rather, they are chosen, according to some hereditary principle, through processes taking place within their respective segments.[16] G possesses little military force of his own; he is, in one sense, simply another lineage head, although the most senior. His authority over F depends, ultimately, upon the willingness of E to support him against F, thus maintaining a polity, capable of decision-making, which includes both E and F. If he proves incapable of maintaining this balance, the state may split. Thus, the principle of "complementary opposition," which in segmentary societies is necessary to bring a larger polity into occasional operation, is, in the segmentary state, necessary to maintain its existence. The segmentary state might perhaps be characterized as a contingent polity manipulated by chiefs.

Both the stateless segmentary society and the segmentary state are, of course, "ideal type" concepts and one finds, among the actual societies of Africa, a range of intermediate cases in which the chiefship element is present but relatively little developed.[17] Similarly, there are numerous cases in Africa in which segmentary states have moved in the direction of more unitary ones, producing a similar series of intermediate cases in the opposite direction. These latter seem typically to have resulted from the efforts of paramount chiefs to lessen their dependence upon the loyalty of lineage heads by building up central administrative staffs, particularly on the military side. The Asantehene, paramount chief of the Ashanti Confederacy, built up within his own chiefdom of Kumasi an appointive administrative staff with both civil and military functions. This organization to some extent superseded the lineage-based political structure and enabled the Asantehene to assert within the confederacy as a whole a position amounting to rather more than that of a *primus inter pares*.[18] Similarly, Shaka, the early nineteenth-century Zulu paramount, was able for a time to exert, through control over the military age-regiments which he organized, a strongly centralized authority over what had formerly been a much more segmentary polity.[19] Neither of these efforts was, ultimately, entirely successful, though both states were for a time capable of formidable military operations. Our interest in these cases, however, lies less in their particular histories than in the light they throw upon the political process in segmentary states.

As we have seen, the limited authority of the ruler in the ideal-typical segmentary state, like the rulerless political order of the segmentary society, depends for its existence upon the complementary opposition of subordinate units. It is the paramount's ability to confront a rebellious segment with the juxtaposed power of another, more loyal, segment that enables him to maintain such limited authority as he enjoys. But the same lineage solidarity that underlies this order-through-complementary-opposition also stands in the way of a ruler's attempts to increase the scope of his authority. Viewed from the vantage point of the segmentary society, the lineage structure in the hands of a segmentary state-type ruler supports a somewhat more "solid," less contingent, polity; from the point of view of a more unitary state, however, the same lineage structure appears divisive, productive of a more limited, more problematical, polity. From this latter point of view, lineages are the commonest sources of political pluralism in African kingdoms—the commonest sources of political sub-structure capable of limiting the authority of rulers and of providing media of political expression for social sub-groups.

Our understanding of the functional significance of this lineage-based pluralism in African society has recently been greatly enhanced by the writings of M. G. Smith, growing out of his studies of the political system of the Hausa-Fulani emirate of Zazzau (Zaria) in Northern Nigeria.[20] Within every political system, Smith suggests, it is useful to distinguish analytically between "politics" and "administration." (Smith uses the term "government" to mean what I have termed the "political system" or "polity"—the overall system of which politics and administration are analytical aspects. I prefer not to follow him in this, though I attach little importance to the choice of terms.) As in our everyday use of these words, "politics" is the exercise of power—the process of struggle or competition through which decisions regarding public policy are arrived at—while "administration" is the exercise of authority—the process through which such decisions are carried out. Of course our use of these terms in common speech is associated historically with the separation in modern Western polities of parliaments and parties on the one hand from administrative bureaucracies on the other; but Smith argues, convincingly, that, even where such separation does not exist, the analytical distinction is worth making because an analysis of the degrees and kinds of fusion and differentiation between administration and politics helps us to understand the ways in which different kinds of polities function.

The lineage-based polities, he suggests, represent situations in which administration and politics are most completely fused; both lodge in the same units—the lineage-based territorial segments. In the segmentary societies (to extrapolate from his rather brief remarks on such societies), the lineage-based units which, through complementary opposition, come to policy decisions, are also the units by which the decisions are carried out. More concretely: since there are no administrators or policemen, the person whose right to certain benefits is legitimated by a gathering of lineage representatives is left, with the support of public opinion, to take appropriate action

—a process which has been called "self-help justice." In the segmentary states, though their polities are more continuously functioning, politics and administration are also fused; the chiefs who are the heads of lineage-based segments are both politicians and administrators vis-à-vis their paramount. The latter can come to a policy decision only with their concurrence and through a process in which they are the political contenders on behalf of the territorial units of which they are heads; he then depends upon them, in their capacity as administrators, to carry out the policy decision. And of course if the system is multi-tiered the same processes are repeated at all levels. It is essentially the mixed administrative-political character of the chiefly hierarchy in such societies that makes the centralization of authority difficult. The paramount cannot exercise purely administrative authority through subordinates who are at the same time the legitimate political representatives of the major sub-units of the society.

It is only when administrative units are more differentiated from the political sub-units of the society that higher degrees of concentration of administrative authority become possible. Over the large parts of Africa where unilineal descent groups are the most prominent elements in the sub-structure of society and thus the commonest bases for the formation of political groups, this means separation of administration from the lineage system. Examples of societies in which this has occurred are the kingdom of Buganda in southern Uganda and the Nigerian emirate of Zazzau, studied by Smith.[21] In both cases the territory of the state proper was mainly administered by officials appointed by, and responsible to, the hereditary ruler. The central areas were administered much more closely and continuously than is possible in any segmentary state—a fact perhaps best exemplified by the regular systems of taxation that prevailed—though in each case, to be sure, there was a penumbra of tributary vassal states, under their own hereditary rulers, which was much more loosely controlled. Since within the state territory proper officials were not, at the same time, the political representatives of the groups they were responsible for administering, administration in the true sense of the handing down of orders supported by legitimate authority was possible to a degree to which it is not in segmentary states. Every administrative act was not, as it tends to be in segmentary states, simultaneously a process of political negotiation.

What then becomes of politics in such societies? Policy, Smith tells us, is formed by the competition of political groups; if it does not, as in the segmentary states, lodge in lineage-based territorial segments which are simultaneously administrative and

political groups, where then is it to be found? There is, of course, no electoral system of popular representation of the sort found in modern Western societies—no differentiated legislature where politicians, representing the interests of diverse groups, may contend over a policy which, when arrived at, may be handed to a set of civil servants who are insulated from politics. In such traditional bureaucratic (or, to use Max Weber's term, "patrimonial") states, politics tends to lodge in the hierarchy of administrative officials itself and their groups of supporters. It is one of Smith's most important insights which, if not original with him, has at any rate been stated by him with a new force and clarity, that political power cannot be monopolized by a ruler, however despotic.[22] However dependent his officials may be upon him, he is also dependent upon them and hence they are in a position to contend among themselves for influence upon his policy decisions, including decisions regarding appointments to office. When he dies they, being in possession of the administrative apparatus, may contend for the role of king-maker, with all its attendant rewards in the form of enhanced political weight in future policy struggles.

Thus it would be inaccurate to say that politics and administration are completely differentiated in such polities. (Nor, Smith suggests, can they ever be; the most purely bureaucratic administrative systems, as we know, always develop systems of internal politics. And the relatively high degrees of differentiation of administration and politics found in modern Western societies are probably limited to those societies.) But the two are differentiated in Buganda and Zazzau in a sense in which they are not in segmentary states, and this kind of differentiation makes possible higher degrees of centralization of authority. Administrators in these states are perhaps always also politicians, but the units over which they are administrators are not the units on behalf of which they act as politicians. The former are the territorial and functional divisions of the state; the latter are kinsmen, clients and colleagues distributed through the administrative hierarchy. Thus, as factions or rudimentary parties lineages and other kinship groups may play an important political role in such societies; indeed their role is now much more specifically political in Smith's sense, for they are no longer administrative units as well. It is this breaking of the direct link between administrators and administered—the loss by the administrator of his role as political representative of the administered—that makes possible both the centralization of authority and elite politics—the concentration of high politics within a relatively restricted social circle.

It is, of course, easy to over-emphasize the degree

of concentration of power and authority which may result from this. On the one hand, the dilution of authority by politics brought about by the ruler's dependence upon his subordinates is repeated at lower levels in the administrative hierarchy. On the other hand, widespread networks of political allegiance may draw large numbers of persons into the political process. Administrative centralization and political autocracy, furthermore, are distinct, and not always co-variant, phenomena. Nevertheless, there remains an important difference between a state each of whose servants is the legitimate political representative of the people he governs and one in which the official is chosen through processes distinct from his unit of administrative responsibility, however political these processes may be.

The possibilities for fruitful comparative study suggested by Smith's ideas concerning the relationship between administration and politics are obviously extensive. Their relevance for contemporary political scientists' and political sociologists' preoccupation with "pluralism" and "group theory" in the study of highly differentiated modern polities, as well as for historical studies of the development of Western political systems from decentralized "feudal" to centralized "patrimonial" ones, is apparent.[23] By restating in terms of a general conception of the polity and its analytic elements ideas which other social anthropologists have tended to express in terms of the structural peculiarities of African societies, Smith has, I believe, helped to make possible a fruitful dialogue between the rich corpus of research on African political systems and other bodies of thought concerning comparative politics.

NOTES

1. D. Easton, *The Political System: An Inquiry into the State of Political Science* (New York: Alfred A. Knopf, 1953); M. J. Levy, *The Structure of Society* (Princeton: Princeton University Press, 1952); T. Parsons, *The Social System* (Glencoe: The Free Press, 1951).

2. Perhaps the best analysis of this process is L. Bohannan's essay, "Political Aspects of Tiv Social Organization," in Middleton and Tait, *Tribes without Rulers* (London, 1958).

3. L. P. Mair, *Primitive Government* (Baltimore: Penguin Books, 1962).

4. This is essentially the situation among the !Kung Bushmen of the Khalahari, described by L. Marshall in "'!Kung Bushman Bands," *Africa*, Vol. XXX (1960).

5. P. J. Bohannan, *Justice and Judgement among the Tiv* (London, 1957); E. E. Evans-Pritchard, *The Nuer* (New York: Oxford University Press, 1940).

6. M. Fortes, "The Structure of Unilineal Descent Groups," *American Anthropologist*, Vol. LV (1953); L. Bohannan, *op. cit.*; G. Lienhardt, "The Western Dinka," in Middleton and Tait, *op. cit.*

7. L. Bohannan, *op. cit.*; Fortes, *op. cit.*

8. E. A. Winter, "The Aboriginal Political Structure of Bwamba," in Middleton and Tait, *op. cit.*

9. B. de Jouvenel, *Sovereignty: An Inquiry into the Political Good* (Cambridge, 1957), Ch. 10.

10. M. Fortes and E. E. Evans-Pritchard, eds., *African Political Systems* (London, 1940), pp. 5–7.

11. E. E. Evans-Pritchard, *The Nuer*.

12. J. A. Barnes, *Politics in a Changing Society* (London, 1955); K. Busia, *The Position of the Chief in the Modern Political Systems* (London, 1951); A. W. Southal, *Alur Society* (Cambridge, 1954).

13. *Ibid.*, Ch. 9.

14. Corporate bilateral descent groups also exist, but have not been reported from Africa.

15. Fortes, *op. cit.*, 1953.

16. These processes may vary from quite rigid rules of seniority to relatively open election from among the members of a lineage.

17. Several such intermediate cases are described in Middleton and Tait, *op. cit.*

18. Busia, *op. cit.*

19. M. Gluckman, "The Rise of a Zulu Empire," *Scientific American*, CCII (1960).

20. M. G. Smith, *Government in Zazzau* (London, 1960).

21. Smith, *op. cit.*; L. P. Mair, *An African People in the Twentieth Century* (London, 1934).

22. See also H. Goldhammer and E. A. Shils, "Types of Power and Status," *American Journal of Sociology*, Vol. XLV (1939).

23. T. F. Tout, *Chapters in the Administrative History of Medieval England* (Manchester, 1920–1933); M. Weber, *Wirtschaft und Gesellschaft* (Tübingen, 1947), pp. 679–752.

13

On the Evolution of Social Stratification
and the State

Morton H. Fried

The Non-Rank, Non-Stratified Society

Every human society differentiates among its members and assigns greater or less prestige to individuals according to certain of their attributes. The simplest and most universal criteria of differential status are those two potent axes of the basic division of labor, age and sex. Beyond are a host of others which are used singly or in combination to distinguish among the members of a category otherwise undifferentiated as to sex or age group. Most important of the characteristics used in this regard are those which have a visible relation to the maintenance of subsistence, such as strength, endurance, agility, and other factors which make one a good provider in a hunting and gathering setting. These characteristics are ephemeral; moreover, the systems of enculturation prevalent at this level, with their emphasis upon the development of subsistence skills, make it certain that such skills are well distributed among the members of society of the proper sex and age groups.

The major deviation from this system of subsistence-oriented statuses is associated with age. However, it makes no difference to the argument of this paper whether the status of the old is high or low since the basis of its ascription is universal. Anyone who is of the proper sex and manages to live long enough automatically enters into its benefits or disabilities.

Given the variation in individual endowment which makes a chimera of absolute equality, the primitive societies which we are considering are sufficiently undifferentiated in this respect to permit us to refer to them as "egalitarian societies." An egalitarian society can be defined more precisely: it is one in which there are as many positions of prestige in any given age-sex grade as there are persons capable of filling them. If within a certain kin group or territory there are four big men, strong, alert, keen hunters, then there will be four "strong men"; if there are six, or three, or one, so it is. Eskimo society fits this general picture. So do many others. Almost all of these societies are founded upon hunting and gathering and lack significant harvest periods when large reserves of food are stored.

There is one further point I wish to emphasize about egalitarian society. It accords quite remarkably with what Karl Polanyi has called a reciprocal economy.

Production in egalitarian society is characteristically a household matter. There is no specialization; each family group repeats essentially similar tasks. There may be individuals who make certain things better than do others, and these individuals are often given recognition for their skills, but no favored economic role is established, no regular division of labor emerges at this point, and no political power can reside in the status.[1] Exchange in such a society takes place between individuals who belong to different small-scale kin groups; it tends to be casual and is not bound by systems of monetary value based upon scarcity. Such exchanges predominate between individuals who recognize each other as relatives or friends, and may be cemented by such procedures as the provision of hospitality and the granting of sexual access to wives.

Within the local group or band the economy is also reciprocal, but less obviously so. Unlike the exchanges between members of different local groups which, over the period of several years, tend to balance, the exchanges within a group may be quite asymmetrical over time. The skilled and lucky hunter may be continually supplying others with meat; while his family also receives shares from the

From Morton H. Fried, "On the Evolution of Social Stratification and the State," in Stanley Diamond, ed., *Culture in History* (New York: Columbia University Press, 1960), pp. 713–731. Reprinted by permission of the publisher.

catch of others, income never catches up with the amounts dispensed. However, the difference between the two quantities is made up in the form of prestige, though, as previously mentioned, it conveys no privileged economic or political role. There frequently is a feeling of transience as it is understood that the greatest hunter can lose his luck or his life, thereby making his family dependent on the largesse of others.

In all egalitarian economies, however, there is also a germ of redistribution. It receives its simplest expression in the family but can grow no more complex than the pooling and redisbursing of stored food for an extended family. In such an embryonic redistributive system the key role is frequently played by the oldest female in the active generation, since it is she who commonly coordinates the household and runs the kitchen.

The Rank Society

Since a truly egalitarian human society does not exist, it is evident that we are using the word "rank" in a somewhat special sense. The crux of the matter, as far as we are concerned, is the structural way in which differential prestige is handled in the rank society as contrasted with the way in which egalitarian societies handle similar materials. If the latter have as many positions of valued status as they have individuals capable of handling them, the rank society places additional limitations on access to valued status. The limitations which are added have nothing to do with sex, age group, or personal attributes. Thus, the rank society is characterized by having fewer positions of valued status than individuals capable of handling them. Furthermore, most rank societies have a fixed number of such positions, neither expanding them nor diminishing them with fluctuations in the populations, save as totally new segmented units originate with fission or disappear as the result of catastrophe or sterility.

The simplest technique of limiting status, beyond those already discussed, is to make succession to status dependent upon birth order. This principle, which is found in kinship-organized societies, persists in many more complexly organized societies. At its simplest, it takes the form of primogeniture or ultimogeniture on the level of the family, extended family, or lineage. In more complex forms it may be projected through time so that only the first son of a first son of a first son enjoys the rights of succession, all others having been excluded by virtue of ultimate descent from a positionless ancestor. There are still other variants based on the theme: the accession to

high status may be by election, but the candidates may come only from certain lineages which already represent selection by birth order.

The effects of rules of selection based on birth can be set aside by conscious action. Incompetence can be the basis for a decision to by-pass the customary heir, though it would seem more usual for the nominal office to remain vested in the proper heir while a more energetic person performed the functions of the status. A strategic murder could also accomplish the temporary voiding of the rule, but such a solution is much too dangerous and extreme to be practical on the level which we are considering. It is only in rather advanced cultures that the rewards associated with such statuses are sufficient to motivate patricide and fratricide.

Whether accomplished by a rule of succession or some other narrowing device, the rank society as a framework of statuses resembles a triangle, the point of which represents the leading status hierarchically exalted above the others. The hierarchy thus represented has very definite economic significance, going hand in hand with the emergence of a superfamilial redistributive network. The key status is that of the central collector of allotments who also tends to the redistribution of these supplies either in the form of feasts or as emergency seed and provender in time of need. Depending on the extent and maturity of the redistributive system, there will be greater or lesser development of the hierarchy. Obviously, small-scale networks in which the members have a face-to-face relationship with the person in the central status will have less need of a bureaucracy.

In the typical ranked society there is neither exploitative economic power nor genuine political power. As a matter of fact, the central status closely resembles its counterpart in the embryonic redistributive network that may be found even in the simplest societies. This is not surprising, for the system in typical rank societies is actually based upon a physical expansion of the kin group and the continuation of previously known kinship rights and obligations. The kingpin of a redistributive network in an advanced hunting and gathering society or a simple agricultural one is as much the victim of his role as its manipulator. His special function is to collect, not to expropriate; to distribute, not to consume. In a conflict between personal accumulation and the demands of distribution it is the former which suffers. Anything else leads to accusations of hoarding and selfishness and undercuts the prestige of the central status; the whole network then stands in jeopardy, a situation which cannot be tolerated. This, by the way, helps to explain that "anomaly" that has so frequently puzzled students of societies of this grade: why are their "chiefs" so often poor, perhaps poorer than any of their neighbors? The preceding analysis makes such a question rhetorical.

It is a further characteristic of the persons filling these high status positions in typical rank societies that they must carry out their functions in the absence of political authority. Two kinds of authority they have: familial, in the extended sense, and sacred, as the redistributive feasts commonly are associated with the ritual life of the community. They do not, however, have access to the privileged use of force, and they can use only diffuse and supernatural sanctions to achieve their ends. Indeed, the two major methods by which they operate are by setting personal examples, as of industriousness, and by utilizing the principles of reciprocity to bolster the emergent redistributive economy.[2]

Despite strong egalitarian features in its economic and political sectors, the developing rank society has strong status differentials which are marked by sumptuary specialization and ceremonial function. While it is a fact that the literature abounds in references to "chiefs" who can issue no positive commands and "ruling classes" whose members are among the paupers of the realm, it must be stated in fairness that the central redistributive statuses *are* associated with fuss, feathers, and other trappings of office. These people sit on stools, have big houses, and are consulted by their neighbors. Their redistributive roles place them automatically to the fore in the religious life of the community, but they are also in that position because of their central kinship status as lineage, clan,[3] or kindred heads.

From Egalitarian to Rank Society

The move from egalitarian to rank society is essentially the shift from an economy dominated by reciprocity to one having redistribution as a major device. That being the case, one must look for the causes of ranking (the limitation of statuses such that they are fewer than the persons capable of handling them) in the conditions which enable the redistributive economy to emerge from its position of latency in the universal household economy, to dominate a network of kin groups which extend beyond the boundaries of anything known on the reciprocal level.

Though we shall make a few suggestions relating to this problem, it should be noted that the focus of this paper does not necessitate immediate disposition of this highly complicated question. In view of the history of our topic, certain negative conclusions are quite significant. Most important of all is the deduction that the roots of ranking do not lie in features of human personality. The structural approach obviates, in this case, psychological explanations. To be precise, we need assume no universal human drive for power[4] in comprehending the evolution of ranking.

It is unthinkable that we should lead a reader this far without indicating certain avenues whereby the pursuit of the problem may be continued. We ask, therefore, what are the circumstances under which fissioning kin or local groups retain active economic interdigitation, the method of interaction being participation in the redistributive network?

In a broad sense, the problem may be seen as an ecological one. Given the tendency of a population to breed up to the limit of its resources and given the probably universal budding of kin and local groups which have reached cultural maxima of unit size, we look into different techno-geographical situations for clues as to whether more recently formed units will continue to interact significantly with their parent units, thereby extending the physical and institutional range of the economy. Such a situation clearly arises when the newer group moves into a somewhat different environment while remaining close enough to the parent group to permit relatively frequent interaction among the members of the two groups. Given such a condition, the maintenance of a redistributive network would have the effect of diversifying subsistence in both units and also providing insurance against food failures in one or the other. This is clearly something of a special case; one of its attractions is the amount of work that has been done upon it by another student of the problem.[5]

It is possible to bring to bear upon this problem an argument similar to that employed by Tylor in the question of the incest taboo,[6] to wit: the redistributive network might appear as a kind of random social mutation arising out of nonspecific factors difficult to generalize, such as a great personal dependence of the members of the offspring unit upon those they have left behind. Whatever the immediate reason for its appearance, it would quickly show a superiority over simple reciprocal systems in (*a*) productivity, (*b*) timeliness of distribution, (*c*) diversity of diet, and (*d*) coordination of mundane and ceremonial calendars (in a loose cyclical sense). It is not suggested that the success of the institution depends upon the rational cognition of these virtues by the culture carriers; rather the advantages of these institutions would have positive survival value over a long period of time.

We should not overlook one other possibility that seems less special than the first one given above. Wittfogel has drawn our attention on numerous occasions to the social effects of irrigation.[7] The emergence of the superfamilial redistributive network and the rank society seem to go well with the developments he has discussed under the rubric "hydroagriculture," in which some supervision is needed in order to control simple irrigation and drainage projects yet these projects are not large enough to call into existence a truly professional bureaucracy.

It may be wondered that one of the prime explanations for the emergence of ranking, one much favored by notable sociologists of the past, has not appeared in this argument. Reference is to the effects of war upon a society. I would like in this article to take a deliberately extreme stand and assert that military considerations serve to institutionalize rank differences only when these are already implicit or manifest in the economy. I do not believe that pristine developments in the formalization of rank can be attributed to even grave military necessity.

The Stratified Society

The differences between rank society and stratified society are very great; yet it is rare that the two are distinguished in descriptive accounts or even in the theoretical literature. Briefly put, the essential difference is this: the rank society operates on the principle of differential status for members with similar abilities, but these statuses are devoid of privileged economic or political power, the former point being the essential one for the present analysis. Meanwhile, the stratified society is distinguished by the differential relationships between the members of the society and its subsistence means—some of the members of the society have unimpeded access to its strategic resources while others have various impediments in their access to the same fundamental resources.

With the passage to stratified society man enters a completely new area of social life. Whereas the related systems of redistribution and ranking rest upon embryonic institutions that are as universal as family organization (*any* family, elementary or extended, conjugal or consanguineal, will do equally well), the principles of stratification have no real foreshadowing on the lower level.

Furthermore, the movement to stratification precipitated many things which were destined to change society even further, and at an increasingly accelerated pace. Former systems of social control which rested heavily on enculturation, internalized sanctions, and ridicule now required formal statement of their legal principles, a machinery of adjudication, and a formally constituted police authority. The emergence of these and other control institutions was associated with the final shift of prime authority from kinship means to territorial means and describes the evolution of complex forms of government associated with the state. It was the passage to stratified society which laid the basis for the complex division of labor which underlies modern society. It also gave rise to various arrangements of socioeconomic classes and led directly to both classical and modern forms of colonialism and imperialism.

NOTES

1. Eleanor Leacock, "Status among the Montagnais-Naskapi of Labrador," *Ethnohistory*, V, Part 3, 200–209.
2. For an ethnographic illustration of this point, see Douglas Oliver, *A Solomon Island Society* (Cambridge: Harvard University Press, 1955), pp. 422 ff.
3. These, of course, would be ranked lineages or ranked clans. Cf. Morton H. Fried, "The Classification of Corporate Unilineal Descent Groups," *Journal of the Royal Anthropological Institute*, LXXXVII (1957), 23–26.
4. As does Leach. Cf. E. R. Leach, *Political Systems of Highland Burma* (Cambridge: Harvard University Press, 1954), p. 10.
5. Marshall Sahlins, "Differentiation by Adaptation in Polynesian Societies," *Journal of the Polynesian Society*, LXVI (1957), 231–300; and his *Social Stratification in Polynesia* (Seattle: American Ethnological Society, 1958).
6. Edward B. Tylor, "On a Method of Investigating the Development of Institutions; Applied to Laws of Marriage and Descent," *Journal of the Royal Anthropological Institute*, XVIII (1888), 267; Leslie White, "The Definition and Prohibition of Incest," *American Anthropologist*, L (1948), 416–435.
7. For a summation of his latest thinking, see Karl A. Wittfogel, *Oriental Despotism* (New Haven: Yale University Press, 1957).

14

Civil War and Theories of Power in Barotseland: African and Medieval Analogies

Max Gluckman

It is appropriate to start this description of the Barotse political structure with a myth, since myths reputedly are the stock-in-trade of anthropologists. According to Lozi mythology, the royal family is descended from a daughter of God Nyambe, whom he took as his wife. One of their sons, a member of the Lozi tribe, was out hunting on the plain, which was then inhabited by many tribes, and members of a foreign tribe decided it would be polite to present him with part of their catch of fish. The Lozi were impressed by this propriety, when compared with their own practice of keeping all catches for themselves. So they chose this son of God Nyambe and his daughter to be king and agreed to give him part of their produce. Although God and the wife he created to bear the mother of the first king lie only ten generations back from the present-day king, the Barotse do not think of this as a limited number of generations. I doubt if any of them has ever counted the generations: for the Barotse they cover almost the whole of time. They believe the events narrated in the myth occurred only slightly later than the beginning of creation.

This myth emphasizes that the kingship was established by the people, who themselves undertook the obligation to render tribute. Thus, there inheres an idea of a contract between king and people. The myth also hallows the kingship because the family which claims the kingship is descended from God, mated with his own daughter. All eighteen of the Barotse kings have come from that ancestral origin, by virtue of agnatic descent.[1] It is inconceivable that someone not thus descended from the line of kings should gain the throne. During revolts by pow-

From the *Yale Law Journal*, LXXII, No. 2 (July 1963), 1515–1546. Reprinted by permission of the Yale Law Journal Company and Fred B. Rothman and Company. This article is a shortened version of Chapter II, *The Ideas in Barotse Jurisprudence* (New Haven: Yale University Press, 1965), and permission has also been granted by Yale University Press.

erful councillors against a king and his favorites, the rebels have had to find an ambitious prince, or even cajole a reluctant prince, into leading them. Hence revolts attacked particular kings, but not the kingship or the rights of the royal family to it. They were clearly rebellions and not revolutions.[2]

The princes are very numerous for kings had many wives, though princeliness is lost when a man's tie to a reigning king is more than three or four generations away. Descent through a princess within this range still transmits princeliness, but this female link bars a man from the kingship. Among the agnatic descendants of kings, anyone is eligible to be selected by the national council, but ideally candidates should be the product of a union between a reigning king and a woman on whom one of a number of queenly titles has been conferred. This is the Barotse definition of being born in the purple.

Barotse who can speak English define the kingship as "a constitutional monarchy." The king is supposed to legislate and judge only with the consent of his councils, and to take action only through their members. A simplified explanation of these councils will help demonstrate Barotse ideas about their government. When the king sits in full court, his magnates are seated in three divisions about his throne. On his right sit the most powerful councillors, as well as a number of junior councillors. These councillors-of-the-right are said by the Barotse to represent the common people and the commoners' interests in the kingship, which are seen as distinct from the interests of the royal family and the reigning king in that kingship. The reigning king's interests are represented by councillors who sit on his left. I shall refer to these men as the king's stewards, because besides acting as judges and national administrators they, rather more than councillors-of-the-right, have the duty of looking after the king's property, his queens, and princes and princesses. The Barotse refer to them as "wives" or "boys" of the king because, theoretically at least, they look mainly to the reigning king's own interests.

A third group is constituted by the princes and the husbands of princesses. This group represents the interests of the royal family in the kingship, as against the reigning king; in council, this group, symbolically, sits facing the king.

The full court is thus seen as a balance around kingship of the interests of nation, reigning king, and royal family, somewhat in the way in which we in Britain think of our Sovereign in Parliament, if we equate Lords with royal descent. And, like the British Parliament, the Barotse councils can only act constitutionally if all three elements are represented. In making up a delegation to report or discuss matters with the British Government, or at another capital, the Barotse always take care to see that the delegation contains members of each set in the council. Similarly, the senior councillor-of-the-right will always stop a trial if he sees that there are too few members of each set present at that moment.

Like the British, too, the Barotse think that membership in one part of the council is inimical to membership in another part; however, many councillors-of-the-right and stewards are married to princesses and are entitled to sit in the royal division in their capacity as royal consort, as well as with their commoner fellows. But, normally, princes by descent in any line from a recent king should not be appointed to councillorships-on-the-right, or to stewardships. Such an appointment would vest more power in those princes to intrigue against the king. Moreover, the Barotse believe that they should not be appointed as councillors-of-the-right because their interests as princes might conflict with their duty to represent the common people.

This latter reason applies particularly to the chief councillor-of-the-right, who holds the title "Ngambela." The king is closely identified with this chief councillor, who is appointed by the king and acts as his principal adviser and executive. However, the Ngambela, by his appointment, moves into a titled position which is independent of the king. Although the king can secure the deposition of a particular incumbent, the Barotse do not consider it possible for a king to abolish the Ngambelaship. Therefore, Barotse speak of the Ngambela, in relation to the king, as "another chief or king." The Ngambela is thus seen by Barotse both as servant to the king and as independent of and opposed to the king. It would, of course, be foolish of a king to appoint a prince, thus granting great power to a potential rival for the throne. The people would be equally concerned by such an appointment. They ask: How can a prince

represent us against the king? Even when a prince who was barred from kingship by descent through a princess was appointed Ngambela in 1921, the common people predicted disaster. And their predictions were fulfilled when, eight years later, he was deposed after being charged with murder and sedition.

Theoretically the king is a member of all courts and he confirms all verdicts reached in the capital. Even in the district courts, which he does not visit, he is held to confirm the verdict if the losing party does not say he will appeal, and the successful litigant gives the royal salute to the court building. Hence the king cannot be tried by a court or bring suit in court: for, in addition to such immunity as he possesses from his august status, Barotse hold that no man can be judge in his own cause. For this reason, treason cases were not tried in court; rather, the king acted outside the courts. It is interesting to note the similarity on this point of Barotse law and the English medieval law of treason. According to Pollock and Maitland[3] when there was "a charge of treason [in England], the king himself [was] the accuser, and life, limb and inheritance [were] at stake; therefore it [was] not seemly that the king, either in person or by his justices, who represent [ed] his person, should be judge; so Bracton throws out the suggestion that the cause should come before the 'peers.' " Thus in England, as well as Barotseland, there evolved a special rule for all cases of high treason based on the maxim that "no one should be judge in his own cause."

Another Barotse rule states that "the king does nothing." By this they mean that the king should not personally try to implement any of his wishes or orders, because if in so doing he trespasses on the rights of a subject, it is impossible for that subject to seek redress in court. Here again note the parallel to English medieval concepts.

Vinogradoff, from his analysis of the Year Books, reports the following: ". . . Sir John Markham, Chief Justice of the King's Bench in the time of Edward IV, had told this king that he could not personally arrest a subject on suspicion of treason, while one of his lieges could, and this for the reason that if the king did wrong, nobody could have an action against him."[4]

The Barotse take very seriously the constitutional doctrine that the king must not act himself lest he bar a subject from suit in court. One of their kings, who ruled after the British protectorate was established, disapproved strongly of beer-drinking and passed laws to control it. He once discovered and broke the beer-pots of some subjects in his capital. His councillors made him vacate his chair on the dais in court, and sit on the ground, where they harangued him severely, and told him that if he wanted to be a policeman, instead of a king, they would dress him in uniform and send him around the country looking for malefactors. I was told that had it not been for the pleas of white officials and missionaries, the king would have been deposed. The theory is that the king should only act through his officials, since they can be sued by aggrieved persons. Although the king can do no wrong for which he can be tried, if he continuously commits or orders actions which affect a subject, he is liable to deposition. But it is difficult to criticize the king in connection with such actions. Where litigants accuse an official of acting under the king's explicit directions, they may open themselves to a charge of slander. And though everyone knows that in many of these cases a trespassing official has done wrong under the instructions of the king, he cannot plead those instructions in his defense. If he does, he is accused of an offense, "working or spoiling the king's name," for which he can be severely punished. Therefore, an official ordered by a king to carry out an arbitrary action should refuse to obey orders and seek the support of the council for his refusal.

I did not check carefully enough the various versions of the king's threatened depositions, but my notes indicate that he was not tried as ordinary malefactors are, since no case was made against him nor did he put forward a defence. He only pleaded for forgiveness. The offence was here public and obvious. An analogous instance, although more properly a plot than a trial, involved the "removal" of an early Barotse king who was a cannibal. The Council, in secret, discussed his villainous habit and decided to kill him. Since he could not swim, it was relatively simple to dispose of him. Holes were bored in his barge and he was taken out in the river and left to drown, since the blood of a king should not be shed. His escorting councillors swam ashore. . . .

We now have the background in which we can interpret the basis of the Barotse's theory of power. In many African states, such as the Zulu kingdom, great councillors of the king had armies to support them; they were princes and rulers of counties. Against these potentially hostile leaders with their independent powers the king had to rely on his own private advisers, the stewards who ran the capital, and the commanders of regiments composed of men recruited in age-sets from the whole nation. The Barotse were at approximately the same stage of technological and economic development as the Zulu, but the organization of their council was very different. No great men with independent armies sat

in the Barotse tribunal. Their nation was not divided for administrative purposes into territorial divisions. All the men of the nation were attached for purposes of jurisdiction, war and some state labour works, to different great councillors-of-the-right. Nor did the men thus attached to a particular councillor reside in adjacent villages, and this was especially true in the flood-plain itself. Men of neighboring villages, and sometimes even members of the same village, might be attached to different councillors. The members of an administrative unit attached to a senior councillor, which I term a "political sector," were thus widely dispersed in the nation. In result, then, a councillor or a prince did not have a localized group of men, who could develop strong loyalty to him. Moreover, since councillors were deposed, or promoted fairly regularly to higher titles, or moved to other tasks, there was even less chance of any substantial loyalty developing. In addition, all the men thus attached to councillors-of-the-right were also attached to stewards and to royals, but in such a way that not all the men who shared attachment to a leader on the right were associated together in attachment to a steward, or to a prince. Three major sets of attachments thus cut the nation into diverse groups—groups in which men did not constantly associate together. The Barotse took seriously their loyalties to their lords in the capital but those loyalties were divided.

When I studied the Barotse they were working with a territorial system of administration created for and to some extent by the British Administration.[5] I was able to work out the structure of their old system from earlier writings on the Barotse and from what they themselves told me. But it is difficult to assess precisely how the old system worked, though it still operated within the new system. Jurisdiction for the settlement of disputes was established by allegiance to councillors-of-the-right. If a dispute could not be settled in consultation with important persons, two litigants of the same political sector went to the capital where their case was heard at the courtyard in the capital of their senior councillor, supported by other councillors of that sector. If men of different political sectors had a dispute, the case was tried by a combined court of councillors of both sectors, sitting in the courtyard of the senior—i.e., the one who sat nearer to the king. Appeal lay to the full council, which heard the case anew. The Ngambela was also owner of a sector, but as he was head of the full council, cases involving members of his sector were heard under the presidency of his own deputy, the "Ngambela" to the Ngambela; otherwise the Ngambela himself would have had to listen on appeal to the case he had already judged as head of a court, and then it would not have been an appeal. "How can the same man judge an appeal against himself?" ask the Barotse. This applied only to the Ngambela, the titular head of the council. Other councillors who had heard their sector's cases at lower levels still sat as judges in full council.

It is worth noting, however, that in practice an aggrieved person could take his complaints through his stewards to a royal or a queen, to plead on his behalf; and I have recorded one case where a man feeling violently aggrieved by his immediate lords, and prevented by his wife from committing suicide in protest, brought his complaint directly to the king by going through a steward other than his regular one.

The political sectors were also the units in which men assembled for war or purposes of state labour. But to work for the king and his queens, the nation was mobilized through the stewards; these stewards also mobilized the Barotse for work on behalf of the prince or princess to whom they were attached.

Lest you wonder whether this complex system of political sectors is typically African, there are reports of similarly intricate African systems of political administration. Even among the Zulu, while commoner chiefs ruled territorial areas, the men of these countries were attached to the king's queens, and hence to the sons of these queens, in a system by which adjacent areas held allegiance to different princes—so that in revolts involving royalty, the country did not side with a particular prince in a solid block liable to secede from the nation.[6]

In an analysis of a Northern Nigerian kingdom,[7] M. G. Smith has distinguished administrative action from political action. Political action may be regarded as a system of competition for power to control resources and men, and matters of public policy. This involves competition, coalition, compromise, and so forth. Political action thus aims at securing control over the means of managing the public affairs of the group and its component sections. One of these means is the system of administrative action, through which the business of government is carried on. Here the organization is hierarchial and authoritative, for it typically deals with problems of order and with the associated protection of rights and enforcement of obligations. It is a powerful political tool. The distinction between administrative and political action is analytic, of course, because in all polities the administrative apparatus acquires power, and political action involves use of that apparatus. Through the history of Europe, the political and administrative systems became segregated from one another. However, in African states competitive struggles for power tend to occur between the very persons who occupy a series of organized positions in relation to one another in the hierarchy of administration. As stated, the chief of a Zulu county was an officer of the king ruling his county for the king and a contender for power backed by the army of his county. The Barotse do not distinguish between political and administrative systems; indeed, they describe them both with one word. In Barotseland, except for a short period, the councillors organized for administration in the hierarchy were also the main contenders for power around the king, and, save for small groups of their own followers, they did not have private armies. When the men assembled in their armies for military or state-labour service, they did so in public, to serve the king. As allegiance and authority were concentrated in the administrative system at the capital, where the powerful councillors spent most of their time, struggles for power were concentrated there. Because of the relatively undeveloped economy, and the other factors I have listed, the political system still contained strong tendencies to segmentation, which appeared on the surface in dynastic rivalry and rebellion, actual or potential—potential in the sense that the threat of a rebellion hung all the time over the king, and deposition over a councillor (as an election theoretically hangs over the British Prime Minister). The various kinds of councillors, and shifting alliances of councillors, did not represent groups differentiated from one another by varied roles in a complex economic system, and bound to one another in that mutual interdependence which Durkheim called organic solidarity.[8] In the end, each councillor or steward in the capital represented neither the interests of a territorial group nor a functional group, but only himself. This probably explains why relations among the councillors were marked by incessant personal intrigues. Groups of councillors still move about, whispering to one another about important and unimportant affairs and passing information around in limited circuits, in a way I never observed among the Zulu. The Barotse called this whispering *kusebela,* a verb whose root also describes slandering and culminating. Other councillors always fear that vital information is being kept from them and that the whispers they do not hear must be to their disadvantage. Everyone tries to join the series of inner circles which they believe to exist. Of course, the administration of justice is palpably carried on in public, and so is the administration of affairs. For example, the head of a court periodically stops a trial to announce some matter and seek the opinion of his fellows, or to tell them what has been decided. But there is a feeling that intrigues go on behind the scenes and the circles of information are being closed. And these intrigues focus, through factions of councillors, on selected princes, since each prince is a potential king.

In Barotseland, contentions for power were in fact rarely marked by the direct threat of the spear. Instead, they were pursued in these secretive negotiations. I suggest that this is one of the main sources of the highly elaborated Barotse theory of power. King and Ngambela, the Ngambela and his deputy, the councillors-of-the-right and the stewards and the princes—all of these are seen as involved in constant intrigues for power and they thus come to represent the different categories of persons who comprise the nation. And these intrigues for power are absorbed into their discharge of administrative duties for the state and the manner in which they represent the interests of dependents in the administrative hierarchy. Hence each administrative position, which is also a position of power, is seen as posed in ceremonial opposition to a series of other administrative positions; and the interests of the subordinates of each position have to be represented against it. The result is an elaborate network of administrative offices and councils to which the people of the nation are linked in a number of sets of cross-cutting ties of allegiance and opposition. Out of this situation, in practice there does seem to emerge considerable stability for the state as a whole.

The dominant position of the capital in Barotse polity appears to have an ecological basis, and therefore some economic support. The river-routes of Barotseland center in the plain. The products of the great flood plain differ markedly from the products of all the surrounding woodland regions. Trade lies between the plain and the woodland regions as a whole, and between various parts of the plain, but not between the various woodland regions. Thus every surrounding woodland region is linked by profitable exchange with the plain, while the different woodland regions are not interlinked with one another. The plain dominates the economy of the region by controlling what differentiation there is in the general economy; and this may explain why the tribe which inhabits the plain dominates the region politically.[9]

Within the plain itself, the effect of the flood on people's lives probably accounted for the concentration of power, as well as administration, in the capital. As people move between their dry-season and flood-season villages, many of the inhabitants of villages disperse, going to different villages along the margin where they seek accommodation with various relatives or friends. Some members of a village may go to the western margin, while others go to the eastern margin. Young men may escort the cattle to graze at small plains in the woodlands, either camping or staying with relatives or blood-brothers or friends. Some villages move as a unit, and accordingly many plain villages have their margin counterparts. But even then, neighbouring villages may relocate at widely separated places on the margins. Some people remain permanently in the plain through the flood, despite its discomforts; others may move within the plain to temporary camps on uninhabited patches of higher land, or go in various years to temporary camps at different points on the margins. A village in mid-plain may move to a village nearer the margin, whose inhabitants have moved to the margin itself. The total effect is that through the course of a year, the same people are not associated in territorial units. I believe that this fact accounts for the absence of a highly organized territorial administrative system among the Lozi of the plain, even though small territorial areas have names and the inhabitants profess allegiance to some prominent royal in the neighbourhood. In the absence of a territorial administrative system, we have the intricate system of political sectors leading to the council in the capital. The result is that the capital dominates political life. Even the outer provinces, although organized along territorial lines, were not tightly administered as territories. The capital only sent representatives to live among them in order to oversee the forwarding of tribute. Just like other Barotse people, the provincial people were attached to councillors in the capital.

Since the powerful Barotse administrators, who were also rulers of the nation, did not have their own regimented and localized bodies of followers, there was a general tendency to establish an intricate marking of status to differentiate these individuals. I have explained that in states like that of the Zulu the court is filled with great magnates who attend in their own right because they rule over counties. They come as authorities with private armies. This was not true of the Barotse leaders, which may explain why, in the capital, councillors entered into an established hierarchy of titles. It is a general rule that the less are the real bases of differentiation between the roles of persons in a society, the more social conventions will exist to mark slight differences of roles. I have developed this argument elsewhere to explain why tribal societies have more elaborate ceremonies to mark changes of status than modern industrial societies have.[10] In kinship groups which act to achieve a multiplicity of purposes, the entry of persons on each role directed to a different purpose tends to be marked by the multitude of conventions and taboos which are characteristic of tribal society. These indicate what role a person is playing at a particular moment. Roles, so to speak, are segregated by customs and conventions, and by elaborate mystical theories. Thus, since there is relatively little actual difference between officials in the Barotse council, conventions, taboos, and an elaborate theory of power, attach to the titles within the council and segregate them from one another.

I have already suggested, in discussing the laws of treason, that the less the king is separated from his people by material circumstances, the more elaborate will be his insignia and special conventions, and the more heinous trespass on his privileges. The similar tendency in this direction within the king's palace and the Barotse council is strengthened because in this type of society they are the aim of most ambitious men. In the palace household there is, as seemingly in all royal households in relatively undifferentiated states, a multiplication of offices and officials, and of servants, each with his special duties, secular and ritual. There are royal priests, fishermen and hunters, royal attendants in the bedchamber, caretakers for dugouts and dogs, praise-singers and jesters. In the council many more titles exist than are necessary for actual administration in order to provide for all the ambitious. There are no barriers to upward mobility, and the brave and able secure appointments of some kind, while marriage to a princess is a short cut to appointment. The conventions of the titles include ideas of their being linked to one another in terms of their association with Barotse history, for various titles represent ancestral kings, princes and princesses, and great councillors. The titles, conciliar and royal, are thus distinguished from one another since each represents an episode in the past which has contributed to the cumulative build-up of the Barotse nation. In this legendary hallowing of titles a dual measure of authority is involved: those near to the reigning king and recent kings are in practice most powerful, those representing the early kings are most sanctified. Thus varied measures of power and control of power are embodied in the conventional separation of titles, complicating further the elaborate, and seemingly unusual, theory of power I am attempting to explain.

I have now, after my excursion through the laws of rebellion, treason, and royal succession, indicated the lines along which I would seek an answer to the ultimate problem posed in this lecture. That problem is, can we relate the elaborate Barotse theory of power to the Barotse mode of production, standards of living, and political organization? Barotse ideas of power state a thesis, found in all states as far as I know, that power corrupts; but they seem to me to have an exaggerated terror of this corruption. Certainly the manner in which this theory is worked out through their several sets of hierarchies of office, through their chambers, through the relation of superior office-holders and their deputies, and through royal and conciliar authorities as sanctuaries from one another, does not appear to be entirely justified by the facts of their life. The limited technological equipment and the egalitarian standards of living do not lead to that clear cleavage of interests between king and royal family, and commoners, from which the whole theory stems. Cleavages of interest run vertically through society, rather than horizontally across it; and actual power relations are manifested in tendencies to recurrent, legitimate rebellion, with the associated laws of treason and succession which I have discussed. I have, therefore, suggested that the doctrines of power which attach to each type of office and the several offices within each type, are conventionalized means of elaborating differences between the powerful men of the nation. These men do not come to their positions of power as representatives of either territorial sections with their own armies, or as representatives of functional groups. Yet through them operate the divisive vertical tendencies which I have described as attributes of this type of tribal economy and polity. The statement of the power of each office in relation to other offices is thus part of its insignia, just as the office's role in incapsulating Barotse history, as well as its special praise-songs, and in some cases its special dress, salutes, and other privileges, are part of its insignia. The elaborated theory of power helps to distinguish positions where there are, in reality, few differences.

In general terms, I suggest that the less the material bases which underlie struggles for power within a system where those who compete for this power are also the personnel of administration, the more elaborate is likely to be the doctrine of power. I have not been able to check this suggestion, since no other student of a tribal state has discussed its theory of power in detail, and it is difficult to extract facts of critical importance for such an analysis. My colleagues who have studied African states were not interested in these problems, and they do not outline clearly who in a rebellion sided with which party, or what was the law of treason under which losing parties were punished. What does seem certain is that the more the divisions of a state are vertical, rather than horizontal, the more is native theorising about authority and power concentrated on the mystical attributes of office. The mediaeval European concern with the relation between king and God seems to fit here. Through the centuries emphasis came to be placed increasingly on analysis of real bases of power. This would fit with Durkheim's view of the development of types of religion. I see the Barotse theory as an efflorescence out of this general structure of "early philosophy."

In Africa, the answer to these problems may arise from arranging states in a morphological series,[11] ranging from the symbolic ritual kingship of the Shilluk, which lacks administrative powers, but represents the unity of the nation, to the great states of West Africa, with their large capitals and slave plantations—states well characterized by Nadel's description of Nupe as a black Byzantium.[12] A step beyond the Shilluk are the small chiefdoms of South Africa, which were subject to constant segmentation. Then came states like the Zulu and Bemba, where princes and chiefs administer for the king territorial counties but mobilize armies of their followers in support of their attempts at power. Next I would place the Barotse-type system, dominated by what I call "politics of the capital." Buganda also may fall within this category. In these systems the council of the king does not consist of landed magnates, but of a number of title-holders appointed to their positions by the king in council. They are not specialized bureaucrats, since the kingdoms still have the limited technology and economy which I take as a master explanatory principle. The king moves people between offices to which are attached estates and followers, and no great man establishes permanent ties with a loyal body of followers. Social mobility of the brave and able is still possible. The next type may be the "caste" states of the cattle-keeping conquerors of peasants, like Ruanda. Here there are caste-like categories specializing in different subsistence activities—still subsistence only—but there is a radical restriction of the rights of the peasants to positions of high power. Significantly, we find here, in addition to dynastic struggle and rebellion, reports of a religious revolutionary movement of protest among the peasants, such as is not reported

from the other states, and which offers parallels with the millenarian movements of the early Middle Ages.[13] The West African states, like Dahomey, Nupe and Zazzau, have a more differentiated economy with slave labour and external trade on a large scale. There exist great landed magnates, with town and country houses, and factions of aristocrats who vie, according to one bare statement, for the support of a city mob in a capital of 50,000 people. Mercenaries and mercenary generals enter the arena of politics. Dynastic struggles still exist, but one account reports a large-scale peasants' revolt. Perhaps consideration of the African states in such categories will deepen our understanding of the interrelations between revolts and how people adhered to rebellious leaders in these states, and the associated laws of treason and succession, as well as indigenous theories of power.

NOTES

1. The third king in modern versions was a son of God, own mother's brother to the first king and a son of God. The first European records gave him as younger brother. See Gluckman, *The Lozi of Barotseland in North-Western Rhodesia* (1951), pp. 2–3, and Colson and Gluckman, eds., *Seven Tribes of British Central Africa* (1951).

2. The implications of this situation are examined in Gluckman, *Order and Rebellion in Tribal Africa* (1963), and more fully developed and differentiated in Gluckman, *Rule, Law and Ritual in Tribal Society* (in press).

3. Pollock and Maitland, *The History of English Law* (2nd ed., 1905), p. 400.

4. Vinogradoff, *Collected Papers* (1928), p. 196.

5. See Gluckman, *Essays on Lozi Land and Royal Property* (1943).

6. Maquet, *The Premise of Inequality in Ruanda* (1961), brings out brilliantly how this cross-cutting of allegiances in Ruanda gave stability to their system.

7. M. G. Smith, *Government in Zazzau, 1800–1950* (1960). I follow Smith, but amend his analysis somewhat, and necessarily for lack of space I simplify it substantially.

8. Durkheim, *De la Division du Travail Social* (1893).

9. I have summarized these differences in Gluckman, *The Lozi of Barotseland in North-Western Rhodesia* (1951), from a fuller account of the situation, with detailed evidence, in Gluckman, *The Economy of the Central Barotse Plain* (1941).

10. For the full exposition of, and the supporting evidence for, this thesis see Gluckman, "Les Rites de Passage," in Gluckman, ed., *Essays on the Ritual of Social Relations* (1962).

11. I have attempted such an analysis in Chapter IV of Gluckman, *Rule, Law and Ritual in Tribal Society*.

12. Nadel, *A Black Byzantium* (1942).

13. Cohn, *The Pursuit of the Millennium* (1957).

B. PATTERNS OF INITIAL DEVELOPMENT OF POLITICAL CENTERS

CHAPTER **III**

Major Types of Breakthrough from Preliterate Societies: Introduction

I

As we have pointed out in the introduction to the section on Primitive Political Systems, it has been a common assumption in historical and ethnological research that in the earliest history of the human race—a beginning or prehistory, which, timewise, was certainly much longer than its written record—all societies were "primitive" according to the criteria specified above and therefore very similar to contemporary primitive societies. It has also been often assumed that it was out of these primeval, primitive societies that the various types of archaic and historical societies developed. In a very broad sense, this is unquestionably true. There can be no doubt that the first human societies were indeed preliterate and had a low level of technological development. Literacy and even minimal technological development are of relatively recent invention. They appeared quite late in the history of human societies and only in parts of the human race. They were usually connected at first with the evolution of more complex social structures with a greater degree of structural specialization and differentiation.

There can also be no doubt that a crucial aspect of such development and a necessary, if not sufficient, condition for it have been a degree of technological or organizational advance which facilitated the crea-

tion and accumulation of some surpluses, together with the invention of literacy, which enabled and facilitated the transmission of accumulated tradition.[1] But it is also true that we know little about the exact conjunction through which such different "advances" have developed, whether of the nature of social differentiation, literacy, or more highly specialized technology.

There exists some archaeological and historical evidence through which some of the more general trends of such developments can indeed be identified. More and more recent archaeological research is in fact moving in the direction of providing us with somewhat more detailed analyses of how such development and breakthroughs to the more "advanced" stages of social life took place.[2]

It is to be hoped that with the advance of research, we may arrive at some more specific indications of the nature of these processes, even if—by the very nature of the available and nonavailable evidence (that is, the lack of adequate literary evidence, beyond what is *given about* these earlier periods of their history in the historical records of societies which have passed into the more advanced stage)—it is doubtful whether we shall ever have such full and detailed accounts of these transitions as we have about contemporary primitive societies.

112

II

Still, however little we know in detail about the ways in which such breakthroughs from the primitive to the more advanced historical societies have taken place, there can be little doubt that in all known cases of historical societies some such transitions did occur. To this, the traditions and records of all civilizations—Greek, Roman, German, or the various Asian societies—attest.

As such breakthroughs were always connected with the development of literacy and of a literary tradition, we know much more about what may be called the different "end results" of such breakthroughs—that is, about the new types of social and political orders that developed and emerged in such breakthroughs—than about the processes of transition. Probably, however, even many of these types are still unknown to us or have not yet been fully analyzed.

But, whatever the limitations of our data, we can also point out some of the general, common characteristics of those varied types of "archaic" or "historical" societies which developed in the dawn of recorded human history.

These societies were characterized by (*a*) technological innovations and concomitant "ecological" adaptation resulting in the production of surplus and of the possibility of accumulating such surplus; (*b*) ecological and demographic trends resulting in the development of some centers, be they economic (urban), ritual (temples), or political ones; (*c*) a growing differentiation between the prevalent structure of the broader social units of the society, the periphery and the structures of these centers; (*d*) a growing internal social-economical differentiation within the centers and periphery alike and a concomitant development of some wider strata or classes; (*e*) a growing, *symbolic* differentiation between prevalent, existing units and the symbolic expression of the centers; (*f*) a general disembedment of symbolic spheres and its anchorage in primordial symbols, and the growing development of varied autonomous symbolic systems, and the growing development of varied autonomous symbolic spheres in religion, philosophy, and so on, and a potentially growing rationalization of these symbolic spheres in terms of the formulation of their problems in a more general abstract way and even of the answers to them—although this, in a much more limited way; (*g*) growing differentiation and *specialization* between societies.

Thus, in general, these archaic and historical societies are characterized, by comparison with the ideal type of primitive society, by a growing intra- and intersocietal differentiation. Within these broad common characteristics, there developed various types of new, more differentiated and complex systems and conceptions of political order.

In terms of our basic criteria of comparative analysis, all these systems of the early history of mankind were characterized by a certain limited extent of development of the specialization of political activities and roles and, to a smaller extent, of political organizations also.

Second, they were characterized by the development of some different types of center: of expressedly political as well as religious or societal centers and frameworks which were, to some extent at least, structurally and symbolically differentiated from the broader strata and prevalent social orders and of their internal political and cultural activities in particular. The activities of these broader strata of the periphery continued to be very much in the pattern of closed primitive communities, except that now they had also to add the special "representative" activities toward the new center. This meant, of course, that there developed a growing difference in the nature of the political and cultural activities of the center and the periphery.

Thus, in general, there developed some autonomy of the political sphere, embodied in the centers and involving a transformation of the relations between the center and the periphery. The more specialized organizational and symbolical political activities became, as well as the different components of center-formation, no longer dispersed in intermittent situations but more and more institutionally crystallized in different centers, and there also developed a growing differentiation of levels of political activities and organization. Among the most important activities of such centers in their relations to the periphery were those of lawmaking and of formalization and codification of laws.[3] It is the combination of these developments that has been designated usually as the emergence of the state.[4]

Closely related to this was the first development of what may be called a political class, or of a political elite, structurally differentiated not only from the lower classes of the periphery but, at least in embryonic form, also from the upper strata, whether tribal chiefs and aristocrats or leaders of local territorial families.

In close association with the structural differentiation of the political center, there took place as well a parallel development in the relation of the symbolic sphere of the political order. Here also several dimensions of differentiation in the symbolic sphere and dissociation between center and periphery can be discerned. One is the growing disembedment of the symbolic sphere from wider, more diffuse primordial symbols, attached to narrow kinship and territorial units, and the concomitant transformation of such primordial symbolic images into parts of a more "rational" order, disembedded from concrete primordial (family, kinship, and, to some extent also, territorial units) and focused around the symbolism of the center and the ruler.[5]

Second has been the growing differentiation of the various dimensions of the several spheres of the symbolic order in general and within it of the symbols of political order in particular. Thus, the cosmic, the sociopolitical, and the religious spheres—as well as other symbolic spheres—tend more and more to become differentiated from one another and organized in somewhat separate, autonomous ways from the point of view of both the symbolic "contents" and the organizational and institutional one.

Third, there took place also a growing variability and changeability in the contents of these symbolic spheres.

In conjunction with all these characteristics there developed in most of these societies, with the partial exception of some city-states, what has often been designated as traditionality—but a traditionality different from that of the primitive, "centerless" societies, with somewhat different premises.

Among these premises the most important in the political field are the continuing symbolic and cultural differentiation between the center and periphery; the concomitant limitation on the access of members of broader groups to the political center or centers and on participation in them. These premises, in turn, were closely connected in traditional regimes to the fact that the legitimation of the rulers is couched in basically traditional religious terms and to the further fact that there was a lack of distinction in the basic political role of the subject societal roles, such as membership in local communities; that it was often embedded in such groups, but the citizens or subjects did not exercise any actual direct or symbolic political rights through a system of voting or franchise.

In the cultural sphere the basic premises of traditionality, common to all "traditional" societies, however great the differences between them, seem to be the acceptance of tradition, of the givenness of some past event, order, or figure (whether real or symbolic) as the major focus of their collective identity, as the scope and nature of their social and cultural order, as the ultimate legitimizer of change, and as the delineator of the limits of innovation. In traditional societies tradition serves not only as a symbol of continuity but as the delineator of the legitimate limits of creativity and innovation and as the major criterion of their legitimacy, even if in fact any such symbol of tradition might have been forged as a great innovative creation which destroyed what till then was perceived as the major symbol of the legitimate past.

These cultural connotations of traditionality had definite structural implications. The most important of these was that parts of the social structure and of some groups were, or attempted to become, designed as the legitimate upholder, guardian, and manifestation of those collective symbols, as their legitimate bearers and interpreters, and, hence, also as the legitimizers of any innovation or change. In the more differentiated among the traditional societies these functions became crystallized into the symbolic and institutional distinctiveness of the central focuses of the political and cultural orders from the periphery. Here this symbolic and institutional distinctiveness of the center in traditional societies was manifest in a threefold symbolic institutional limitation. The three aspects of this limitation were: limitation in terms of reference to some past event of the scope, contents, and degree of changes and innovations; limitation of access to positions the incumbents of which are the legitimate interpreters of such scope of the contents of the traditions; and limitation of the right to participate in these centers and to forge the legitimate contents and symbols of the social and cultural orders.

III

The preceding characteristics of the sociopolitical and cultural spheres and of traditionality in general and of the political sphere in particular have been common, insofar as we have records of them, to what may be called the "archaic" historical societies. But within this broad common framework there developed on different parts of the earth a great variety of concrete types of social and cultural organization in general and of political regimes in particular. The most important among these are city-temples, tribal federations of different kinds, city-states, patrimonial and feudal regimes. The number and variability of such concrete types, however, are much greater than can be briefly catalogued. As can be seen from the list we have given, most of the types included have thus far only been described, although with some analytical assumptions which have not yet been fully explicated and systematized. In the following pages we shall attempt some further explication and systematization of these assumptions. At this point of our discussion, it may be worthwhile only to point out some very general and preliminary indications of the direction our analysis will take.

One such indication is that the different characteristics of the "archaic" social and political systems that have been enumerated above—that is, the extent of differentiations of roles and organizations, the development of structural differentiation between center and periphery, and the emergence of different symbolic spheres and of different types of international systems—did not necessarily develop everywhere to the same degree. These societies varied also among themselves with regard to the number, structure, and strength of centers that developed in each of them and with regard to the relative predominance of the different components of center formation in their respective centers. The different concrete types of these societies can be seen as different concrete constellations of these characteristics, each of which created its own systematic qualities, problems, courses, and possibilities of transformation and change.

The second such indication is that the development of these different types of archaic societies was related not only to the developments of various processes of internal differentiation but also to processes of differentiation in their intersocietal, international relations—to changing international settings. This could take on a great variety of forms: population increase and immigration, greater concentration of population in certain areas, processes of conquest, or different combinations of all these. Such processes of differentiation in the intersocietal relations were primarily manifest in the growth of relatively continuous semistable international units composed of structurally different types of societies —that is, great patrimonial or semi-imperial units together with tribal federations, temple-cities, or city-states as in the Middle East or in Southeast Asia; and second, the growth and continuity in such international systems, of special types of enclaves, such as city-temples or city-states or religious communities with some special characteristics of centrality.

It is important to stress that from the very beginning of these breakthroughs no single political type developed in isolation. Structurally similar—more often structurally different—political systems, city-states, tribal federations, patrimonial chiefdoms and kingdoms, and in later stages feudal and imperial systems tended not only to coexist side by side but also to impinge on one another. In addition, they tended very often to merge into one another, and the process of change and framework of these systems often constituted changes of one to another. There

can be no doubt that it was some convergence between the various internal conditions enumerated above and their international settings that facilitated and created these breakthroughs from the prehistorical, primitive societies to the more advanced stages of civilization. It is probably through such constellations of internal and external circumstances that these societies developed the specific transformative capacities in which they differ greatly from contemporary primitive tribes.

However, we do not always know exactly how these varied conditions and constellations developed in concrete cases, and there is much systematic research work that has yet to be done on this subject before a full analytical comparison can be attempted.

Hence, our major aim will be to analyze the specific constellation of such characteristics in each of these types, the types of political process that developed in each of them, and, insofar as possible, the conditions of their development, continuity, and change. We shall attempt as best we can to identify also both intra- and inter-societal conditions related to the development of some of these major types of political systems.

In the following sections we shall deal first with three types of such political regimes: first, the archaic stage of human history, the tribal federation, the temples and city-states, and the patrimonial chiefdoms and kingdoms. Then we shall attempt to analyze two of the more developed traditional systems, the imperial and the feudal ones.

NOTES

1. Jack Goody and Ian Watt, "The Consequences of Literacy," *Comparative Studies in Society and History*, V, No. 3 (April 1963), 304–346.

2. Robert M. Adams, *The Evolution of Urban Society* (Chicago: Aldine, 1966); Friedrich Katz, "Die sozialökonomischen Verhältnisse bei den Azteken im 15 and 16, Jahrhundert," *Ethnographische Forschungen*, III, Part 2 (Berlin: VEB Deutscher Verlag der Wissenschaften, 1956); Katz, "The Evolution of Aztec Society," *Past and Present*, No. 13 (1958), pp. 14–25.

3. Max Weber, *On Law in Economy and Society*, trans. Edward A. Shils and Max Rheinstein (Cambridge: Harvard University Press, 1954).

4. See F. Oppenheimer, *The State: Its History and Development* (Indiana: Bobbs-Merrill, 1914); R. Lowie, *The Origins of the State* (New York: Russell and Russell, 1962); and more recently, L. Krader, *Formation of the State*, Foundation of Modern Anthropology Series (New York: Prentice-Hall, 1968).

5. Of relevance in this context, and especially in the study of traditional societies, are the concepts of Great and Little traditions as developed by Redfield and Singer. R. Redfield, *Peasant Society and Culture* (Chicago: University of Chicago Press, 1956); Redfield, "The Social Organization of Tradition," *Far Eastern Quarterly*, Vol. XV (1965); R. Redfield and Milton Singer, "The Cultural Role of Cities," *Economic Development and Cultural Change*, III (1954), 53–73.

INTRODUCTION TO THE READING

The passages from Max Weber's *Theory of Social and Economic Organization* provide a basic analytic framework for a comparative sociological study of archaic polities. In his analysis of tribal federations and various patrimonial empires he defines some general social criteria which indicate the characteristics of this last type of political organization. According to Weber, the transformation of any tribal federation into a patrimonial political system is marked by the transition of the status of the individual person from that of active member in the community to passive subject in the political organization. This process is accompanied by the formation of an administrative staff—military and civil—that is personally committed to the chief or king of the territory. Also, Weber indicates how the transformation of the tribal association into a patrimonial political system implies a process of symbolic and structural differentiation between the political center and the periphery.

15

Gerontocracy, Patriarchalism, and Patrimonialism—and Types of Patrimonial Authority

Max Weber

Gerontocracy, Patriarchalism, and Patrimonialism

1. The most primitive types of traditional authority are the cases where a personal administrative staff of the chief is absent. These are "gerontocracy" and "patriarchalism."

The term "gerontocracy" is applied to a situation where so far as imperative control is exercised in the group at all it is in the hands of "elders"—which originally was understood literally as the eldest in actual years, who are the most familiar with the sacred traditions of a group. This is common in groups which are not primarily of an economic or kinship character. "Patriarchalism" is the situation where, within a group, which is usually organized on both an economic and a kinship basis, as a household, authority is exercised by a particular individual who is designated by a definite rule of inheritance. It is not uncommon for gerontocracy and patriarchalism to be found side by side. The decisive characteristic of both is the conception which is held by those subject to the authority of either type that this authority, though its exercise is a private prerogative of the person or persons involved, is in fact pre-eminently an authority on behalf of the group as a whole. It must, therefore, be exercised in the interests of the members and is thus not freely appropriated by the incumbent. In order that this shall be maintained, it is crucial that in both these cases there is a complete absence of an administrative staff over which the individual in authority has personal control. He is hence still to a large extent dependent on the willingness of the group members to respect his authority, since he has no machinery to enforce it. Those subject to authority are hence still members[1] of the group and not "subjects." But their membership exists by tradition and not by virtue of legislation or a deliberate act of adherence. Obedience is owed to the person of the chief, not to any established rule. But it is owed to the chief only by virtue of his traditional status. He is thus on his part strictly bound by tradition.

The different types of gerontocracy will be dis-

From Max Weber, *The Theory of Social and Economic Organization,* ed. Talcott Parsons, trans. Talcott Parsons and A. M. Henderson (New York: Oxford University Press, 1947), pp. 346–365. Reprinted by permission of the editor.

cussed later. Primary patriarchalism is related to it in that the authority of the patriarch carries strict obligations to obedience only within his own household. Apart from this, as in the case of the Arabian Sheik, it has only an exemplary character, similar to charismatic authority. He is able to influence people only by example, by advice, or by other non-compulsory means.

2. With the development of a purely personal administrative staff, especially a military force under the control of the chief, traditional authority tends to develop into "patrimonialism." Where absolute authority is maximized, it may be called "Sultanism."

The "members" are now treated as "subjects." An authority of the chief which was previously treated principally as exercised on behalf of the members, now becomes his personal authority, which he appropriates in the same way as he would any ordinary object of possession. He is also entitled to exploit it, in principle, like any economic advantage—to sell it, to pledge it as security, or to divide it by inheritance. The primary external support of patrimonial authority is a staff of slaves, coloni, or conscripted subjects, or, in order to enlist its members' self-interest in opposition to the subjects as far as possible, of mercenary bodyguards and armies· By the use of these instruments of force the chief tends to broaden the range of his arbitrary power which is free of traditional restrictions and to put himself in a position to grant grace and favours at the expense of the traditional limitations typical of patriarchal and gerontocratic structures. Where authority is primarily oriented to tradition but in its exercise makes the claim of full personal powers, it will be called "patrimonial" authority. Where patrimonial authority lays primary stress on the sphere of arbitrary will free of traditional limitations, it will be called "Sultanism." The transition is definitely continuous. Both are distinguished from primary patriarchalism by the presence of a personal administrative staff.

Sometimes even Sultanism appears superficially to be completely bound by tradition, but this is never in fact the case. The non-traditional element is not, however, rationalized in impersonal terms, but consists only in an extreme development of the sphere of arbitrary will and grace. It is this which distinguishes it from every form of rational authority.

3. When, in a system of patrimonial authority, particular powers and the corresponding economic advantages have become appropriated, this will be called "decentralized"[2] authority· As in all similar cases appropriation may take the following forms:

Appropriation may be carried out by an organized group or by a category of persons distinguished by particular characteristics. It may, on the other hand, be carried out by individuals, for life, on a hereditary basis, or as free property.

Decentralized authority thus involves, on the one hand, limitations on the chief's power of free selection of his administrative staff because positions or governing powers have been appropriated. Thus they may be limited to the members of a corporate group or of a group occupying a particular social status.

In addition, on the other hand, there may be appropriation by the individual members of the administrative staff. This may involve appropriation of positions, which will generally include that of the economic advantages associated with them, appropriation of the non-human means of administration, and appropriation of governing powers.

Those holding an appropriated status may have originated historically from the members of an administrative staff which was not previously an independent class. Or, before the appropriation, they may not have belonged to the staff.

Where governing powers are appropriated by members of an independent group, the costs of administration are met from the incumbent's own means, which are not distinguishable from his personal property. Persons exercising military command or members of this type of army provide their own equipment and may even recruit units of the army on their own responsibility. It is also possible that the provision of means of administration and of the administrative staff can be made the object of a profit-making enterprise which exploits access to payments from the stores or the treasury of the chief. This was the principal mode of organization of the mercenary armies in the sixteenth and seventeenth centuries in Europe. Where appropriation by independent groups is complete, all the powers of government are divided between the chief and the different branches of the administrative staff, each on the basis of his own personal rights. It is also, however, possible for these rights to be regulated by special degrees of the chief or special compromises with the holders of appropriated rights. The first type is illustrated by the court offices of a realm when they have become appropriated as fiefs; the second, by landlords who, by virtue of their privileged position or by usurpation, have appropriated powers of government. The former is apt to be merely a legalization of the latter.

Appropriation by an individual may rest on leasing, on pledging as security, on sale, or on privileges —which may in turn be personal, hereditary, or freely appropriated—may be unconditional, or may be subject to performance of certain functions. Such a privilege may be purchased in return for services or granted for compliance with the chief's authority, or it may constitute merely the formal recognition of actual usurpation of powers.

Appropriation by an organized group or by those occupying a particular social status is usually a consequence of a compromise between the chief and his administrative staff or between him and an organized social group. It may leave the chief relatively free in his selection of individuals, or it may lay down rigid rules for the selection of incumbents.

Appropriation, finally, may rest on a process of education or apprenticeships. It will be necessary to devote a special discussion to this case.

1. In the case of gerontocracy and patriarchalism, so far as there are clear ideas on the subject at all, the means of administration are generally appropriated by the corporate group as a whole or by the household of the individual who carries out the governing functions. The administrative functions are performed "on behalf" of the group as a whole. Appropriation by the chief personally is a phenomenon of patrimonialism. It may vary enormously in degree to the extreme cases of a claim to full proprietorship of the land[3] and to the status of master over subjects treated as slaves. Appropriation by particular social groups generally means the appropriation of at least a part of the means of administration by the members of the administrative staff. In the case of pure patrimonialism, there is complete separation of the functionary from the means of carrying out his function. But exactly the opposite is true of decentralized patrimonialism. The person exercising governing powers has personal control of the means of administration—if not all, at least of an important part of them. This was true of the feudal knight, who provided his own equipment, and of the count, who by virtue of holding his fief took the court fees and other perquisites for himself and met his obligations to his superior lord from his own means, in which these appropriated sources of income over which he had full control were included. Similarly, the Indian *jagirdar,* who provided and equipped a military unit from the proceeds of his tax benefices, was in complete possession of the means of administration. On the other hand, a colonel who recruited a mercenary regiment on his own account, but received certain payments from the royal exchequer and paid his deficit either by curtailing the service or from booty or requisitions, was only partly in possession of the means of administration and was subject to certain regulations. On the other hand, the Pharaoh, who organized armies of slaves or coloni, put his clients in command of them, and clothed, fed, and equipped

them from his own storehouse, was acting as a patrimonial chief in full personal control of the means of administration. It is not always the formal mode of organization which is most decisive. The Mamelukes were formally slaves recruited by the purchases of their owner. In fact, however, they monopolized the powers of government as completely as any feudal class has ever monopolized fiefs.

There are examples of land appropriated in fief by a closed corporate group without any individual appropriation. This occurs where the land is granted to individuals quite freely by chiefs so long as they are members of the group, as well as subject to regulations specifying qualifications. Thus, military or possibly ritual qualifications have been required of the candidates, whereas, on the other hand, once these are given, close blood relations have had priority. The situation is similar in the case of artisans attached to a court or to guilds or of peasants whose services have been attached for military or administrative purposes.

2. Appropriation by lease, especially tax farming, by pledging as security, or by sale, have been found in the Western World, but also in the Orient and in India. In Antiquity, it was not uncommon for priesthoods to be sold at auction. In the case of leasing, the aim has been partly a practical financial one to meet stringencies caused especially by the costs of war. It has partly, also, been a matter of the technique of financing, to insure a stable money income available for budgetary uses. Pledging as security and sale have generally arisen from financial necessities. This is true of the Papal States as well as others. Appropriation by pledging played a significant role in France as late as the eighteenth century in filling judicial posts in the *Parlements.* The appropriation of officers' commissions by regulated purchase continued in the British army well into the nineteenth century. Privileges, as a sanction of usurpation, as a reward, or as an incentive for political services, were common in the European Middle Ages, as well as elsewhere.

Modes of Support of the Patrimonial Retainer

The patrimonial retainer may receive his support in any of the following ways: (*a*) By maintenance at the table and in the household of his chief; (*b*) by allowances from the stores of goods or money of his chief, usually primarily allowances in kind; (*c*) by rights of use of land in return for services; (*d*) by the appropriation of property income, fees, or taxes; (*e*) by fiefs.

So far as in an amount or within a scope which is

traditionally stereotyped, they are granted to individuals and thereby appropriated, but not made hereditary, the forms (*b*) to (*d*), inclusive, will be called "benefices." When an administrative staff, according to its fundamental principle of organization, is supported in this form, it will be said to be based on "praebends." In such a situation it is possible to maintain a system of promotion on a basis of seniority or of particular objectively determined achievements. And it is also possible to require a certain social status as a criterion of eligibility and to make use of the corresponding sense of honour of a distinctive social group.

A set of appropriated governing powers will be called a "fief" if it is granted primarily to particular qualified individuals by a contract and if the reciprocal rights and duties involved are primarily oriented to conventional standards of the honour, particularly in a military connexion, of a distinctive social group. The situation where an administrative staff exists which is primarily supported by fiefs, will be called "feudalism."

The transition between fiefs and military benefices is so gradual that at times they are almost indistinguishable.

In cases (*d*) and (*e*), sometimes also in (*c*), the individual who has appropriated governing powers pays the cost of his administrative function, and possibly also of equipment, from the proceeds of his benefice or fief. In that case his own position of authority over the subject may take on a patrimonial character and thus become hereditary, and capable of division by inheritance.

1. The earliest form of support for royal retainers, household officials, priests and other types of patrimonial followers has been their participation at the table and in the household of the chief or their support by allowances arbitrarily paid out from the stores. The "men's house," which is the oldest form of professional military organization . . . very often has the character of communistic consumption. Separation from the table of the chief or of the temple or cathedral and the substitution of allowances or the use of land for this direct mode of support has by no means always been regarded with approval. It has, however, been the usual consequence of the establishment of independent families. Allowances in kind granted to temple priests and officials who have left the chief's household constituted the original form of support of officials throughout the Near East and have also existed in China, India, and to a large extent in the Western World. The use of land in return for military services is found throughout the Orient from very ancient times and also in Medieval Germany as a means of providing for household officials, officers

of the court and other functionaries. The sources of income of the Turkish *spahis,* of the Japanese *samurai,* and of various other types of Oriental retainers and knights are, in the present terminology, "benefices" and not "fiefs." . . . In some cases they have been derived from the rents of certain land; in others, from the tax income of certain districts. In the latter case, they have not necessarily been combined with appropriation of governmental powers in the same district; but this has, however, been the general tendency. The concept of the fief can be further developed only in relation to that of the state. Its object may be land under a patrimonial system, or it may be any one of various kinds of claims to property income and fees.

2. The appropriation of property income and rights to fees and the proceeds of taxes in the form of benefices and fiefs of all sorts is widely distributed. It became an independent form of organization in a highly developed fashion in India in particular. The usual arrangement was the granting of rights to these sources of income in return for the provision of military contingents and the payment of administrative costs.

Decentralized Patrimonial Authority

In patrimonial systems generally, and particularly in those of the decentralized type, all governmental authority and the corresponding economic rights tend to be treated as privately appropriated economic advantages. This does not, of course, mean that they cannot be qualitatively differentiated. This is true particularly in that some of them are appropriated in a form subject to special regulations. Furthermore, the appropriation of judicial and military powers tends to be treated as a legal basis for a privileged class position of those appropriating them, as compared to the appropriation of purely economic advantages having to do with the income from domains, from taxes, or other sources. Within the latter category, again, there tends to be a differentiation of those which are primarily patrimonial from those which are primarily extrapatrimonial or fiscal in the mode of appropriation. For the present terminological purposes the decisive fact is that, regardless of content, governing powers and the associated advantages are treated as private rights.

Von Below[4] is quite right in emphasizing strongly that it was especially the appropriation of judicial authority which was made the basis of special treatment and a source of privileged class status. Indeed it is not possible to prove that the medieval political organization had either a purely patrimonial or a purely feudal character. Nevertheless, so far as judicial authority and other rights of a purely political origin are treated as private rights, it is for present purposes terminologically correct to speak of patrimonial authority. This concept itself, as is well known, has been most consistently developed by Haller in his *Restauration der Staatswissenschaften*. Historically there has never been a purely patrimonial state in the sense of one corresponding perfectly to the ideal type.

Where traditional authority is decentralized through the appropriation of governing powers by privileged social groups, this may become a formal case of the separation of powers when organized groups of the members of such a privileged class participate in political or administrative decisions by a process of compromise with their chief.

The subjects of such compromises may be rules or concrete administrative decisions or measures regulating the administrative process. The members of such groups may possibly exercise imperative control on their own authority and by means of their own administrative staff.

1. Under certain circumstances groups, such as peasants, which do not enjoy a privileged social position, may be included. This does not, however, alter the concept. For the decisive point is the fact that the members of the privileged group exercise independent rights. If all kinds of socially privileged groups were absent, the case would obviously belong under another type.

2. This type has been fully developed only in the Western World. . . .

3. The possession of his own administrative staff by a member of such a privileged group has been unusual. The exercise of independent governing authority on his part is still more exceptional.

NOTES

1. *Genossen.*
2. *Ständische Herrschaft.* The term *Stand* with its derivatives is perhaps the most troublesome single term in Weber's text. It refers to a social group the members of which occupy a relatively well-defined common status, particularly with reference to social stratification, though this reference is not always important. In addition to common status, there is the further criterion that the members of a *Stand* have a common mode of life and usually more or less well-defined code of behaviour. There is no English term which even approaches adequacy in rendering this concept. Hence it has been necessary to attempt to describe what Weber meant in whatever terms the particular context has indicated. In the present case it is the appropriation of authority on the part of the members of the administrative staff, in such a way that their position becomes independent of the arbitrary will of their chief, which is decisive. This particular aspect is brought out by describing it as "decentralized authority." It should not, however, be forgotten that in describing it as he does, Weber implies that this group not only has a distinctive status in the organization of authority, but also in other respects.—Talcott Parsons.
3. *Bodenregal.*
4. *Der Deutsche Staat des Mittelalters.*

CHAPTER IV

The Tribal Federations:
Confrontation between the Ruler,
the Ruled, and the Cosmic Order

I

Out of the great variety of different types of political systems which presumably developed from the primeval primitive communities, we shall deal here first with what may be called the "tribal federation": federations or congeries of tribes converging into, but not fully amalgamated in, some new types of center.

The most important historical illustrations of such tribal federations can be found in the ancient Middle East, especially in the regions of biblical history, in the broad international setting between the great patrimonial and imperial systems of Egypt, Assyria, Babylonia (some of which might indeed have developed from such federations, although we have direct evidence to this effect in only a few cases), of some of the city-states that developed regions—like the Phoenician and Summerian; and as part of the great Euro-Asia tribal immigrations in the second and first centuries B.C. Of these federations the most important can be found in the confines of Canaanite—Phoenician, Philistine[1]—civilization, the various political units of the Semite tribes, among whom the tribes of Israel made the greatest impact on further history.

Various types of tribal federation could also be found in most of the great nomad settlements in Asia and Europe. Similar types of tribal federation probably developed in other places, such as in Mesoamerica, but much less is known about them. Among "contemporary" primitive societies, the closest to this type seems to be some of the Annuak[2] and Shilluk[3] as well as, to some extent, the Bembas.[4]

The very term "tribal federation," descriptive as it is, denotes already some of the basic structural characteristics of these political systems. They constitute a congregation of different "tribal" units based largely on kinship and territorial units not dissimilar from those of large primitive societies. Usually, they have been brought, by some combination of internal and external forces, to cooperate or converge into units wider than their "original" ones, without, however, giving rise—at least in the first stages of the process of their development—to great changes in their basic structural characteristics. And yet, the very coming together of such units tended to develop pressures for the creation of some intertribal centers.

In these types of center there could develop several different types of activity: "political" or "administrative" on the one hand, and "ritual" and "symbolic" on the other. The political-administrative were mostly oriented toward such external problems as common defensive or offensive military organization or to such internal problems as the regulation of intertribal organization of common economic or trade relations. The more symbolic and ritual activities were oriented toward the development and maintenance of some new, relatively elaborate cults or sanctuaries which could be common to several different tribes or tribal units, stemming probably from some common origins.

II

Thus, in these centers there tended to develop a strong emphasis on certain components of center formation: the development and crystallization of new symbols of common collective and sociocultural identity; regulation of external force; and, to a smaller extent, regulation of intergroup relations. But usually it was only one such component—which may have varied, of course, from case to case—that tended to develop in such tribal centers, and in these systems it did not tend to merge with others to any great extent.

Hence, most of these centers, whatever the variety of their composition, evinced several basic structural characteristics. In almost all cases these centers constituted, in their broader setting, structural enclaves which were often transient and intermittent in their existence and mostly did not develop into permanent distinct, ecological settings with continuous population and identity of their own. It is exactly because of this that in these centers there could sometimes develop nucleuses of new, more differentiated social and cultural orientations and organizations. But whatever the extent of development of such different organizations and roles, these centers were always composed of several different structural elements which rarely coexisted peacefully or merged into relatively homogeneous groups or strata.

The first such element was composed of the representatives, in the more central organization or units, of the various original tribal or kinship units, whose main point of reference was these units.

The second such element is that of some special, distinct groups of elites, somewhat separate from the existing social units and with a different structural composition.

Such special groups may be of several different kinds. They may be groups of the same basic structural types as the major constituent elements of the federation (such as basically kinship or kinship/territorial groups) which tend to specialize in some administrative or economic (especially crafts and trade) and especially ritual function. The Levites of Israel[5] or some of the semicastes of traders and ironmongers in Arabia seem to be the best illustration of this kind of element.[6] The second type of such groups consisted already of more specialized elements, mobilized according to new principles and criteria, transcending the existing units, and tending accordingly to develop some wider identity of their own.

It was the combination of these various elements that may explain the very weak development in these centers of what may be called a specific ruling class of elites. No cohesive ruling class or elite tended to develop in most of these centers. Rather, we find here some embryonic elements of such an elite which on the whole did not as yet crystallize into a fullfledged cohesive group.

One element in the composition of such embryonic elites is the person of a king, or kingly, or princely, family, with its secondary administrative and military appendage very often consisting of mercenaries. Another such element—sometimes in partial alliance with the former, but usually structurally different from it—consists of the older, aristocratic families, who, while being structurally rooted in the tribal units, may yet attempt to use the new, broader frameworks for furthering their own interests and may accordingly attempt to establish themselves as the predominant element in the new federation. Last may be the varied, specialized ritual groups, especially, as we have seen above, insofar as they were not structurally identical with the basic kinship or territorial units, but were composed of groups of transient priests or prophets and tended to be constituted according to new criteria and develop a separate, distinct identity of their own.

Between those different groups and social elements there existed within these centers continuous tensions and conflicts, and there developed concomitant tensions between different conceptions of the nature and function of these centers in relation to the other groups in the society. On the one hand there was the conception of the center which encouraged it only as performing some "given," mostly ritual, or, at most, intermittent political functions for the various constituent parts of the federation and as governed entirely by the interests of these parts, and constituting merely an extension of the conceptions of centrality that existed in these units and of their concomitant ritual and political activities. On the other hand, there could develop in these centers conceptions of sociopolitical and cosmic order transcending such units.

It was the combination of the different elements specified above that greatly influenced the extent to which special elite groups with orientations transcending the tribal order tended to develop in these centers.

The minimal development of structural units and symbolical orientations transcending the existing units was connected with the development of small differentiation in each of the constituent units of such federations, with a high level of homogeneity of the various units which converged into these centers, and with rather marginal and intermittent interaction among them and between them and external forces.

But insofar as their different constituent elements were more varied and heterogeneous, and insofar as their interaction with the different internal and international settings was more continuous, there could indeed develop in them new, broader, organizational, and especially symbolic orientations. The best illustration of these are again to be found in the Israelite tribes in the periods of Judges and to some extent throughout the history of the kingdom of Judah and Israel.[7]

Thus, it can be summed up that the division of labor which developed in these societies can be characterized by the widening of the scope of units among which there develops a "mechanical" division of labor and their growing convergence into some center.

In contrast to the city-states, there did not develop here a relatively unified, highly diversified community with a very high level of internal, organic division of labor. In contrast to patrimonial systems, there did not develop here a unified administrative and political framework which performed common tasks for a variety of structural units when there was relatively little organic division of labor. Here the scope of dependence of these units on the common center was much smaller. This center tended to emphasize—and even here rather intermittently—their common symbolic and external relations, and only to a smaller extent to perform also internal integrative functions in the interrelations of these groups. Moreover, as we have pointed out above, usually it was only one such element or component of center formation that tended to develop in any one of these centers. It is because of this that these centers as specific units were not very stable and continuous. They could easily become submerged into some of the existing tribal units or could develop a very high degree of independence, which, however, was usually coupled with relatively smaller continuity.

At the same time, however, in the more heterogeneous centers there could often develop new types of charismatic orientations which were usually the result of some redefinition of the nature of cosmic and social orders and the relation between the two and were usually developed by various ritual, religious, and political elites.

III

These developments in the symbolic field were usually most clearly manifest in the redefinition of the nature of the cosmic order, of its relation to the socio-political order and to patterns of participation

in it. Such redefinition could develop in several directions.

One such direction was the redefinition of the nature of the cosmic order in terms of greater dissociation between the natural and the supernatural orders and in growing emphasis on the transcendence of the latter and in growing rationalization of the conception of the cosmic order.[8] Here also the old mythical order tended to become transformed into a more historical dimension with regard to both the cosmic and the social orders.

The second such direction was the redefinition of the nature of the relations between this new type of cosmic order and the socio-political one. Here also there developed growing rationalization of this conception, closely related to the conception of the distinctiveness of these orders.

Here it is interesting to observe the two different tendencies which could develop. One, usually weaker, was that of the attempts of the new emerging political elite to monopolize or at least to control the symbolization of the new cosmic order and of its representation, thus in a sense moving into a patrimonial or an imperial direction. But even here the pattern of political responsibility of the rulers was conceived in terms different from most patrimonial regimes. The second, and much stronger, tendency was the transposition and transformation of the older tribal pattern of political participation into the new cosmic order, to a large degree as against the claims of the political elite. By this very process the symbols of political participation became transformed and transposed into a more universal direction. In this case some groups, other than the political elite, conceived themselves the potential bearers of the new cosmic order in its socio-political implication. But the right to represent them became a bone of contention between several such groups: the representatives of the older true "tribal" orders, such as tribal elders or heads of tribal subunits, and the bearers of the new symbolic order, usually priests and especially prophets. Both such groups claimed a sort of symbolic and even structural political primacy over each other and especially over whatever new political elite may have developed in these new centers.

In this way a new definition of political responsibility and participation "evolved." This definition tended to stress greatly the relativity of political power in relation to religious and cosmic orders, the ultimate primacy of the latter, and consequently the accountability of the rulers to the representatives of the true "cosmic" order—be it conceived in tribal-communal or prophetic universal terms or in some combination of these two. This accountability was to no small degree couched here in terms of equivalence between private and public-political morality, with the legalization of the legitimacy of any distinct, specific *raison d'état*.

The possibility of development of such new broader orientations could develop in many such cases of tribal federations. But it was only in very few cases that there also developed in these centers the possibility of evolving the organizational prerequisite for the institutionalization of such orientations.

The very coexistence in their centers of these various structural elements analyzed above, which facilitated the development of such broader orientations, also made very difficult the matching of the structural political orientation to these broader orientations. Thus, these orientations could only in very rare cases become closely related to actual politics. True enough, different participants in the actual political struggle tended to become closely related to such orientations. But only very rarely were they able to redefine the actual scope and activity of the political community and of the concrete issue of political struggle.

This can be relatively clearly seen in the nature of legal activities that were developed in such centers. There were either activities and arbitration between different constituent units of the federation, or attempts to develop new types of sacral law which would encompass the legal traditions of such units. As against these, there were few developments of a new autonomous, communal order or of civil law.

IV

These basic structural characteristics of these tribal federations, the different levels of social differentiation within the relatively intermittent centers and in the periphery, define also the relations between center and periphery and the levels or types and issues of political struggle which tended to develop in them.

The focus of these relations here was the struggle over the very nature and legitimacy of this new intertribal center. As we have seen, within each part of the periphery their own centers and center-(charismatic)-oriented activities naturally persisted. Hence the major focus of center-periphery relations was indeed the extent to which the new, intermittent center could establish its claim to the symbolic order, as well as to be able to mobilize the resources necessary for its activities. This, in turn, was closely related to the scope of political struggle that tended to develop here and beyond the "internal" struggle

which was going on continuously in the various groups of the periphery according to their own established procedures.

The first type is the struggle over the extent of relative benefits accruing from participation in the given centers—whatever their concrete contours might be—and over domination by different tribal, city, or ritual groups over these centers. Here of special importance were such issues as the extent to which different tribal or family groups could participate in the organs of the center and in its decisions.

A second type of issue was the scope of access of such different groups to the center on the one hand and their ability to limit any possible infringements of their autonomy by the center on the other.

This last issue or problem—that of the autonomy of the various tribal or city groups—brings us to the next level of political struggle in these federations, which was focused around the redefinition and setting up of the nature and limits of the new centers. It was probably here that the tensions and conflicts between the various structural elements which converged in the center tended to become most acute and articulated.

Here there tended also to develop those few types of specifically political organization, such as special court or aristocratic cliques, or religious sects, or some sort of "religious-political" parties, which attempted to mobilize free political groups or individuals not wholly attached to the various kinship groups. But even these groups tended to be on the whole embedded in various existing, kinship, territorial, or at most the specialized religious or cult groups.

V

The preceding analysis brings us to the problem of the conditions of development, continuity, and change of these systems.

As in all the other types of archaic societies, it is not very easy to point out the exact condition of development, continuity, and change of tribal federations and of the relation of these conditions to the political process in them. Much comparative research still needs to be done in order to allow for a full systematic treatment of this problem. Some preliminary indications, however, may be attempted with regard to the conditions of their continuity and change. These were very closely related to the continual composition of different types of such federations.

In each of these types there developed a certain kind of "equilibrium" among the varied elements of which such federations and their centers were composed. By definition, the type of level of such equilibrium—and the concomitant pattern of political struggle—was least complicated among the "simplest," most homogeneous federations and much more complex among the more heterogeneous ones. It was, of course, in each of them closely related to the nature and complexity of the different levels of political struggle.

These, in their turn, could affect the process and direction of change of these systems. In the federation with the lower levels of equilibrium, the disturbances and demises of any given regime tended to be connected mostly with the impact of various external forces and from the disrupture of the ties of mechanical solidarity between the different subunits, giving rise to their possible secession or to the transference of their allegiances to some new federations. In such cases the existing tribal federation tended usually to develop in the direction of decomposition into smaller tribal units or of submergence into larger patrimonial or imperial units.

In the more complex types of these federations, the equilibrium of the different levels of political struggle was much more precarious and the whole system much more sensitive to various internal developments in the direction of more organic division of labor, as well as to the impact of international political and economic forces, the two being here, as in the city-states, very closely interconnected. Moreover, it was in these systems that the broader orientation, transcending the given sociopolitical units, tended mostly to develop, and they themselves could serve as a starting point for some transformative orientations. These could develop either in the direction of new forms of broader political (such as imperial) systems or in the direction of self-enclosed enclaves in which some of these orientations could be perpetuated.

Here, as in various city-states, even the institutionalization of any of these broader possibilities was to no small degree contingent on the fusion or incorporation of such federations, and especially of their centers with some other types of political units, particularly with smaller patrimonial units. It was usually such fusion which could provide, through the patrimonial units, the resources necessary for the institutionalization of such new order, while the centers of tribal federation could provide the nucleuses of new, broader charismatic orientations.

NOTES

1. R. H. Hall, "The Keftians, Philistines, and Other Peoples of the Levant," *The Cambridge Ancient History* (Cambridge: Cambridge University Press, 1940), II, 275–295; C. J. Gadd, "The Cities of Babylonia," *ibid.*, Rev. ed. (1962), Vol. I, Ch. 13; Hugh Tinker, "The City in the Asian Polity" (London: School of Oriental and Asian Studies, 1966); Georges Contenau, René Grousset *et al., Les Premières Civilisations* (3rd ed. revisée et augmentée, 1935); Georges Contenau, *La Vie Quotidienne à Babylone et en Assyrie* (Paris: Hachette, 1950); Contenau, *La Civilisation d'Assur et de Babylone* (Paris: Payot, 1937). For a general review of the ancient Near Eastern setting, see S. Moscati, *The Face of the Ancient Orient* (New York: Doubleday, 1962), especially Chs. 2, 3, 5.

2. E. E. Evans-Pritchard, *The Political System of the Annuak of the Anglo-Egyptian Sudan* (London: London School of Economics, 1940).

3. E. E. Evans-Pritchard, *The Divine Kingship of the Shilluk of the Nilotic Sudan* (Cambridge: Cambridge University Press, 1948).

4. Audrey I. Richards, "The Political System of the Bemba of Northern Rhodesia," in M. Fortes and E. E. Evans-Pritchard, eds., *African Political Systems* (London: Oxford University Press, 1940).

5. Th. J. Meek, "Moses and the Levites," *American Journal of Semitic Languages and Literature*, LVI (1939), 113–120; H. H. Rowley, "Early Levite History and the Question of the Exodus," *Journal of Near Eastern Studies*, III (1944), 73–78; M. Greenberg, "A New Approach to the History of the Israelite Priesthood," *Journal of the American Oriental Society*, LXX (1950), 41–46; R. De Vaux, *Ancient Israel* (London: Downton, Longman, and Todd, 1961), p. iv.

6. Henri Rosenfeld, "The Social Composition of the Military in the Process of State Development in the Arabian Desert," *Journal of the Royal Anthropological Institute*, Vol. XLV, Parts I, II (1965).

7. See Albrecht Alt, *Essays in Old Testament History and Religion* (Oxford: Basil Blackwell, 1966); and De Vaux, *Ancient Israel, passim.*

8. C. Geertz, "Ideology as a Cultural System," in D. Apter, ed., *Ideology and Discontent* (New York: The Free Press, 1964); Robert N. Bellah, "Religious Evolution," *American Sociological Review*, XXIX, No. 3 (June 1964), 358–374; Eric Voegelin, *Order in History* (Baton Rouge: Louisiana State University Press, 1956–1957).

INTRODUCTION TO THE READINGS

Within the framework of the section on tribal federations, we have presented analyses of some of the aspects and problems of kingship among the ancient Semitic monarchies, monarchies that developed from within such federations and that often continued to function within such federative frameworks.

J. Gray analyzes the place of the Cana'anite kingship in the cosmological and social order. He bases his argument mainly on texts found in the Ugarit and Amarna excavations but also uses some Hebrew texts. His article tries to differentiate between the theoretical premises of the functions and structure of the political center as embodied in Cana'anite kingship and their modifications in reality.

In "Organs of Statecraft in the Israelite Monarchy," Abraham Malamat analyzes the tribal structure's impingement on the monarchical center. He shows how, throughout the period of Hebrew monarchy in Judah and Israel, the representative body of the people played an important role in the coronation of kings and in decision making about crucial political issues. He suggests that according to the Old Testament the Hebrew kingship was never fully legitimized as an independent and autonomous body and that the elders of the tribes could accept or reject the authority of certain kings. The rule of the monarch was based on his charismatic qualities rather than on traditional legitimation. Hence the political center was not fully differentiated and independent.

16

Cana'anite Kingship in Theory and Practice

J. Gray

The principle of hereditary kingship and the stability of the royal line may well have had a religious sanction in ancient Canaan until the Amarna Age, when as yet the cultural and political equilibrium of the ancient Near East was not upset by the irruptions of barbarians and tribesmen of the Iron Age. It was an accepted fact in Mesopotamia that "kingship came down from the gods." The king, then, stood in a special relation to god, which is expressed in the *Krt* saga by the father-son relationship of El and the king. El, the senior god of the pantheon of Ugarit, asks:

Who is *Krt* that he weepeth? . . . . . .
Does he desire the kingship of the Bull his father?
Or sovereignty as the Father of men?[1]

Here kingship, *mlk,* is the peculiar property of El. This in itself constitutes an essential link between the god and the earthly king. Much has been written in support of the theory of divine kingship among the Western Semites to demonstrate that the king was the earthly representative of god, particularly of the dying and rising god, in the seasonal festivals.[2] Here, however, it should be noted that El, with whom *Krt* is so closely related, is not a dying and rising deity whose cult is associated with the alternation of the seasons, but is a god concerned with moral issues.

The corner-stone of the theory that the king in ancient Canaan was the incarnation of the dying and rising god is the role that the king played in the Horus-Osiris ritual in Egypt and in the Babylonian *Akitu* festival, which is attested in its most complete form in a text from the time of Nebuchadrezzar.[3] This view assumes that Canaan, lying as it did, between the two great seats of civilization and empire in Egypt and Mesopotamia, was bound to reflect the culture of both. This view does not strictly accord with facts determined by archaeology in Canaan. We do not deny certain cultural influences in the ma-

From J. Gray, "Cana'anite Kingship in Theory and Practice," *Vetus Testamentum* (Leiden: E. J. Brill, Ltd., 1952), II, 198–200, 203, 216–220. Reprinted by permission of E. J. Brill, Ltd.

terial life and literature of Canaan, but at all stages of their history Palestine and Syria manifested a stubborn and wholesome independence of one or the other. This is admirably manifested at Ras Shamra, where, in spite of the political influence of Egypt and the cultural influence of Mesopotamia, a native literature grew and flourished in a dialect which has comparatively little affinity with Accadian. The pantheon too, in the mythological texts, shows similar independence of Egypt and Mesopotamia. To emphasize the influence of Egypt or Mesopotamia in Canaan is to neglect certain vital factors in the history of the land. Of those we should particularly emphasize infiltration and irruption of desert tribesmen, especially at the beginning of the Middle Bronze Age at the end of the 3rd millennium and at the beginning of the Iron Age (c. 1200 B.C.), with the latter of which the Hebrews were associated. It was this factor which gave the culture of Canaan its own idiomatic turn, as distinct from the cultures of Mesopotamia or Egypt. Laying emphasis on this element, we venture to propose a somewhat new approach to the question of the special relationship in which the ancient Canaanite being stood to god, as expressed in the *Krt* saga at Ugarit. . . .

As the embodiment of the community the king represents the people before god. He does so preeminently in the capacity of priest. In the *Krt* saga and in the *'Aqht* or *Dn'el* text the king mourns in cultic seclusion. In both cases the occasion is childlessness and it may be thought that this was a purely private discipline. We believe, however, that nothing that the king did was purely private but had always a communal significance. So we propose to treat all the rites which the kings *Krt* and *Dn'el* perform as public functions. . . .

In our investigation of the various aspects of Canaanite kingship we have already anticipated most of what can be said regarding the royal *entourage*. In the *Krt* saga, which, as apart from the administrative texts, we have taken as setting forth the ideal rather than the actuality of the royal office, we find that close to the king stood his heir-apparent and his family. They do not seem, however, to have participated in government and, indeed, the claim of *Krt*'s heir *Yṣb* is indignantly rejected. In the *Krt* text the queen-mother enjoys great respect, and in later times, the deferential way in which the king addresses his mother in a letter[4] suggests the position which Bathsheba enjoyed at the court of her son Solomon.[5] In the *Krt* text there are certain intimates admitted to a feast in the palace called variously the "bulls" and "gazelles" of the king and the "bulls" and "gazelles" of *Hbr,* which was the name of *Krt*'s city.[6]

Apparently the "bulls" were seventy in number and the "gazelles" eighty. The identity of these is still uncertain. It is possible that they are clansmen named after the animals in question as, for instance, the Arab tribe Beni Sokr. On the other hand, two priestly orders may be indicated, that of Ba'al, whose cult animal was the bull and who was represented with bull's horns on his helmet, and that of Reshef, who was represented with gazelle's horns on his head-dress. Since Reshef was the deity of plague, death, and the under-world, it is appropriate that his priests and those of the vital god Ba'al should be entertained in the crisis of the king's health. Another possibility is that the "bulls" may be chiefs representing the sedentary population of the kingdom and the "gazelles" those representing the nomad element or those who still cherished memories of their nomad antecedents. The consciousness of this double element was felt in other West-Semitic states, notably in Israel and Judah, where the latter element asserted itself in the Rechabites, and in the Northern Aramaean state of Sam'al, where the king *Klmw* mentions משכבם and בעררם,[7] distinguishing probably the settled element and those who had not yet accepted the restraints of sedentary civilization. The situation finds a parallel in Syria and Palestine after the Moslem Conquest when the Arab conquerors maintained themselves as a race apart living in the desert or in military camps in the conquered provinces, as at Homs on the Orontes, Jabiyah in the Hauran, and Amwas, Tiberias and Ramleh in Palestine. Whatever the identity of the "bulls" and "gazelles" in the *Krt* text, they do stand obviously in close association with the king, though they are, equally obviously, subservient to him.

Others who stand probably in the same relation to the king in a sacral capacity are, we think, the *rp'um,* whom we have already mentioned. They are seven in number and are obviously human persons, since they perform their journeys by horse and chariot, a means of conveyance not associated with gods in the Ras Shamra texts. We have already suggested that the *rp'um* or "healers" were the attendants of the king in his capacity of dispenser of fertility.

We have noted, further, the association of the king with the notables, *'adrm* in the *Dn'el* or *'Aqht* text in his role as judge. Alt notes that in the Hebrew narratives of the conquest the monarchic system in the Canaanite towns, insofar as it had ever functioned, was breaking down and the duties originally proper to the king had largely devolved upon oligarchies of elders or local notables.[8] Rib-Addi of Byblos in the Amarna Tablets mentions the "city-lords"[9] which Pedersen assumes to be a kind of elders.[10] In this connection it should be noted that the expulsion of Rib-Addi and Abimilki of Tyre recorded in the Amarna Tablets[11] indicates the rising force of popular opinion as a counterpoise to royal authority.

The administrative texts of Ugarit, which we emphasize as exemplifying the actuality rather than the ideal of kingship in Canaan in the Amarna Age, show that the royal authority in its various aspects was no longer concentrated in the hands of the king but had devolved upon several classes. The priestly authority we have seen still to have been exercised to a degree by the king himself and to have been vested in the priestly caste of the royal clan of $\underline{T}'$ and the clan of *Dtn,* which represents, we think, an older royal house, probably affiliated with $\underline{T}'$ by marriage. Those, however, are but two of twelve such priestly families, though none of the rest, according to the state payment recorded, is nearly so significant except *bn mglb,*[12] which is assessed at the same amount as *bn t'y* and *bn dtn.* The military office of the king in the field, too, had devolved upon a professional class, often non-Semitic, which was a prominent feature of Syria and Palestine in the Late Bronze Age. This process is particularly well exemplified in the state of Israel where in the lifetime of Saul the professional army, including non-Israelites, became the dominant factor in the foundation of the dynasty of David, himself a professional soldier, first under Saul and then under the Philistine ruler Achish of Gath.[13]

From our study it emerges that the institution of the kingship in Canaan had undergone various vicissitudes in the eventful phases of the Middle and Late Bronze Ages. The ancient powers of the king, so manifold and highly concentrated, were much modified. In Palestine particularly we have expressed the view that the various chiefs mentioned in the Amarna Tablets were not, as is usually held, local dynasts, but mercenary commandants, with the probable exception of the king of Hazor in the East of Upper Galilee, the comparative remoteness of which invited the development of a territorial state under the direction of a ruler of ambition. All this must, of course, be taken into serious consideration when we investigate the problem of the Hebrew monarchy. It has been, we think, too freely assumed that the Hebrew kingship was modelled on a Canaanite prototype. Certain elements, no doubt, do indicate such influence and we trust that we have made this sufficiently clear. Two factors, however, must regulate our further thought on the problem. First, the Canaanite prototype is much modified, not to say mutilated. Second, historical circumstances had done much to bring this about. Since the period visualized in the *Krt* text, the feudal system had been introduced, giving rise to a permanent class of professional soldiers and tactical specialists. Palestine and Syria, moreover, had been reduced by repeated Egyptian expeditions to the status of provinces with local garrisons and commandants. The Hittites from Anatolia had pursued a similar policy in North Syria. Just how seriously this affected this political and social situation in Palestine may be gathered from the Memphis stele of Amenhotep II (1448–1420 B.C.) who mentions among persons deported from *Rtnw,* or Southern Syria, 144 princes and 139 brothers of princes taken in his seventh campaign and 217 princes and 189 brothers of princes taken in his ninth expedition in Asia.[14] A similar policy was pursued by Thothmes III, Seti I, and Ramses II. Finally we must reckon with the Philistine and the Aramaean invasions and settlements at the end of the Late Bronze Age and the beginning of the Iron Age. In the case of the Aramaean invasions, with which we associate the Hebrew settlement in Palestine, we have confederacies of tribes, whose polity was, of course, radically different from any monarchic system. In the foundation and development of the Aramaean states in Transjordan, Syria, and Palestine the institution of kingship was seen established. Unfortunately only the records of Israel are full enough to permit a full study of this process. Here we may trace most conveniently, as Alt has done so admirably,[15] the evolution of the kingship from a more primitive stage than is attested even in the myths and sagas of Ras Shamra to the absolutism of Solomon. In this respect the Hebrew records have a peculiar value in that this development—and we should insist that it is a development, though an extraordinarily rapid one—may be studied over a period of little more than two generations.

NOTES

1. Gordon, *Ugaritic Handbook,* Krt, 38 ff.
2. The corner-stone of this theory is the myth and liturgy of the Babylonian *Akitu,* or New Year Festival. This is attested in its most complete form in a text from the time of Nebuchadrezzar. Gadd, "Babylonian Myth and Ritual," in S. H. Hooke, ed., *Myth and Ritual* (1933), p. 47. See also Snaith, *The Jewish New Year Festival* (1946), pp. 212 ff.
3. This may be a late recension of a much earlier original.
4. Gordon, *op. cit.,* p. 117.
5. 1 Kings 2:19.
6. Gordon, *op. cit.,* p. 128, col. iv, 6–7, 8–9.
7. Lidzbarski, *Ephemeris für semitische Epigraphik,* III, 109–115, pp. 218–238, b. 14. Here Nöldeke is cited as attesting the meaning in Syriac as "wild, barbarian," p. 235.
8. Alt, *Die Staatenbildung . . . ,* p. 32.

9. *amelutu bel ali,* Knudtzon, *op. cit.,* pp. 49, 138.
10. Pedersen, *Israel* (1926), I, 499, note.
11. Knudtzon, *op. cit.,* pp. 137, 152.
12. Gordon, *op. cit.,* p. 400, col. vi, 32.

13. Alt, *op. cit.,* pp. 44 ff.
14. Badawi, "Die neue historische Stele Amenophis II," *ASAE,* XLII (1942), 1 ff.
15. Alt, *op. cit.*

17

Organs of Statecraft in the Israelite Monarchy

Abraham Malamat

Rehoboam and the Schism within the Kingdom

The main burden of my remarks will concern the specific aspects of the political apparatus and organs of statecraft as they emerge from the first half of I Kings 12.[1] This section deals with King Rehoboam and the circumstances surrounding the split within the United Monarchy, i.e. the kingdoms of David and Solomon.

The reference here is twofold: (1) the demand of the northern tribes to alleviate the burden of taxes and corvée imposed upon them by Solomon, Rehoboam's father, this being a prior condition to their acquiescence in Rehoboam's election; (2) Rehoboam's consultation with the "elders" and "young men" before replying to the tribes' ultimatum. The uncompromising attitude adopted by Rehoboam on this matter brought about the end of the United Kingdom of Israel and determined the course of Jewish history for generations to come.

As a starting point, I should like to dwell upon the question of Rehoboam's enthronement or rather lack of enthronement, at Shechem which, in fact, serves as the framework for the events described in the chapter under discussion. The opening phrase refers to Rehoboam's arrival in Shechem, "For all Israel were come to Shechem to make him king." I accept the assumption of some scholars that we are

From Abraham Malamat, "Organs of Statecraft in the Israelite Monarchy," *El-Ha-Ayin Series,* reprinted in the *Biblical Archaeologist,* XXVIII, No. 2 (May 1965), 34–50. The article was first delivered as a lecture before the Bible Study Group on August 22, 1963, at the home of David Ben Gurion. The Study Group now meets regularly at the home of the State President, Zalman Shazar. The lectures are followed by a lively discussion among the noted scholars who attend these meetings. Reprinted by permission of the author, the World Jewish Bible Society, and the Israel Society for Biblical Research.

confronted here with a second enthronement or, put somewhat differently, that Rehoboam had been automatically acclaimed previously as king in Judah, where the Davidide House had taken root. This was not the case, however, as regards the northern Israelite tribes, where it was by no means taken for granted that Solomon's offspring ought to rule over them. For it must be borne in mind that those tribes had attached themselves to the House of David by a covenantal act (II Sam. 5:1–3).

Covenant between King and People[2]

As prelude to the covenant we read in II Samuel 3 of the negotiations between David and Abner, intended to bring the northern tribes under David's sway. In verse 12, it is stated: "Make thy league with me and my hand shall be with thee to bring over all Israel unto thee." Verse 17 then relates that Abner has urged the elders (*sic!*) of Israel to enter into a treaty with David. Note how the institution of the elders is still playing an authoritative role in covenant-making and the election of kings. Abner then goes to meet David in Hebron, taking along twenty men to conduct the negotiations. David greets them with a feast, a ceremony which has, at times, been associated with the covenantal act, according to the Bible and ancient Near Eastern sources.

Further on in the same chapter (v. 21) we hear Abner saying to David: "I will arise and will gather all Israel unto my lord the king, that they may make a covenant with thee, and that thou mayest reign over all that thy soul desireth." In other words, preparations are afoot to conclude a treaty in Hebron with the northern tribes. Typologically speaking, we are confronted with an exact parallel to the Rehoboam incident. Rehoboam has come to Shechem where the northern tribes have convened for the coronation ceremony. We are justified in inferring that here, too, preparations are being laid for a covenant betwixt king and populace.

As it turned out Abner was murdered, but the Bible is most explicit in stating that all of Israel came under David's rule as a result of the pact between him and the elders (again!) of the north: "So all the elders of Israel came to the king to Hebron; and King David did make a covenant with them in Hebron before the Lord and they anointed David king over Israel" (II Sam. 5:3).

The Shechem Event in the Light of David's Enthronement over Israel

The enthronement of David may offer some concept as to what might have transpired at Shechem. True, there are important circumstantial differences, pointing to Rehoboam's weakness as against David's position of strength at the time of the coronation. The delegation from the north came to David at *his* capital in Hebron for the conclusion of the treaty. Rehoboam, on the other hand, goes, or is compelled to go, to Shechem, center of the northern tribal confederation, in order to have them make their pact with him. Yet both incidents are basically one: the rule of the Judaean kings over the northern tribes is conditioned upon a covenantal agreement between the king and his future subjects.

David Ben Gurion: Why by-pass Solomon when discussing the covenant?

Lecturer: I shall come back to this intriguing question in my reply. In any event, it is not feasible to include in our discussion this evening the broader problem as to whether, in the course of time, a new covenant was required with each royal accession. It seems reasonable, however, to assume that such a covenant renewal was required procedure only with the advent of a new dynasty or when the royal succession was interrupted. In Israel there were ten such change-overs during a period of two hundred years, and one is justified in assuming that a royalty-pact was customary in such cases, even though the Bible makes no specific mention of such a detail.

As for Judah, there is one definite instance of covenant-making within the context of the coronation-ritual. A crisis had been brought about by the rule of Queen Athalia, regarded in Judah as an alien from the North whose rule had, in fact, severed the Davidic line. Consequently, at her dethronement and assassination, the need was felt for a covenant-renewal between the new king, Jehoash, one of the progeny of the House of David, and his subjects. Thus we read in II Kings 11:17: "And Jehoiada made a covenant between the Lord and the king and

the people . . . and between the king also and the people." The verse seems a bit cumbersome and has led Bible critics to propose alternate emendations:

1. The latter part of the verse "between the king also and the people" is to be deleted. In other words, a covenant was concluded only between the Lord and the people, whose representative was the king.

2. In contrast with this Martin Noth, in a recent study, does away with the first part of the verse. Yet there is no real difficulty in accepting the complete phrase which presents us with a two-fold covenant: between God and the king on the one hand, betwixt king and people on the other.[3] Since the Davidic line had been sundered it was necessary to renew the treaty between the people of Judah and the lineal descendant of the House of David. Incidentally, we have here a most interesting type of covenant between two parties effected by an intermediary, in this case Jehoiada, the High Priest.[4]

Dr. Haim Gevaryahu: Perhaps Jehoiada was acting as guardian of the under-age king (Jehoash was only seven when he was officially acclaimed).

Lecturer: He was certainly acting both as High Priest and as the supreme authority in Judah during the period of royal crisis.

The People's Representative Body

The covenantal act, in the cases of David and Rehoboam, is preceded by negotiations with the representative body of the people. It is essentially this body which participates in the covenant ceremony in the event of a successful conclusion to the negotiations. In David's case, it was the elders who served in this capacity whereas, regarding Rehoboam, it is related in I Kings 12:3: "and Jeroboam and all the congregation (*qāhāl*) of Israel came and spoke unto Rehoboam saying. . . ." A problem of no immediate moment to us is whether Jeroboam actually participated in the delegation or whether he was still in Egyptian exile and appeared only later when called to the northern assemblage (*ibid.*, v. 20). If so, the mention of Jeroboam in verse 3 (as well as in v. 12) would be a later addition, as maintained by some authorities.

The Hebrew term for the aforementioned representative body is *qāhāl* (usually translated "congregation" but more precisely referring to an assembly). It is noteworthy that the same term is employed in a case where covenant-making with royalty is specifically mentioned, namely, in the previously referred to coronation ritual of Jehoash: "And all the congregation (*qāhāl*) made a covenant with the king in the house of God" (II Chron. 23:3; the parallel account in II Kings is completely lacking in these details).

The word *qāhāl* is virtually synonymous with the term *'ēdā* ("assembly"), also frequently used, both terms at times serving interchangeably or even in combination. It would appear that the biblical source known as the Priestly Code tends toward the usage *'ēdā,* in contrast to the other sources which employ *qāhāl* overwhelmingly.[5]

The question of terminology is especially apropos here, as in a later passage of our chapter (I Kings 12:20) it is this very *'ēdā* (referred to only once in the book of Kings) which elects Jeroboam, following the unsuccessful negotiations with Rehoboam. True, no covenant is explicitly mentioned but it is certainly implied in this instance of the founding of the first Israelite dynasty. It is not entirely impossible, however, that one may assume a slight difference in connotation here, with *qāhāl* referring to the group (in vs. 12–16 called simply *'am,* "people") conducting the negotiations with Rehoboam and, in effect, acting as the representative of the broader gathering, the *'ēdā.*

The assembly, comprised of the people's representatives, was the supreme authoritative body especially during the pre-monarchic period. It was empowered both to elect kings (as in the case of Jeroboam) and to reject would-be rulers (as was done with Rehoboam). To cite yet another example from Shechem some 200 years earlier, there is the enthronement of Abimelech by the gathering of the leading people of that town (*ba'alê šekæm*) as stated in Judges 9:6. Most enlightening in this respect is the reference in Deut. 33:5: "And there was a king in Jeshurun, when the heads of the people were gathered, all the tribes of Israel together." Here is additional testimony that the accession ceremony required an assembly of the leaders of the populace, regardless whether the interpretation of our verse refers to the enthronement of the Lord or of a king of flesh and blood.[6]

Dissolution of Covenant and Assembly

The comparison between the Shechem event and David's coronation over Israel may tend to clarify the closing episode in the Rehoboam affair. On the one hand, we have the case of David, whose negotiations with the northern representatives are brought to a successful close with the conclusion of the treaty. In accordance with the theological orientation of the redactor of the book of Samuel, the depiction of the covenantal act is preceded by the following insertion: "And the Lord said to thee: thou shalt feed my people Israel, and thou shalt be prince over Israel" (II Sam. 5:2).

The very antithesis of this is the Rehoboam affair,

what with the latter's failure in the negotiations on economic concessions to the northern tribes. Thus we hear of Rehoboam in I Kings 12:15: "So the king hearkened not unto the people," followed by the redactor's parenthetical remark: "For it was a thing brought about of the Lord, that He might establish His word which the Lord spoke by the hand of Ahijah the Shilonite." The biblical historiographer attributes Rehoboam's adamant refusal, in the last analysis, to divine causality. The net result is that instead of a covenant we have the people's negative reaction (v. 16): "What portion have we in David? neither have we inheritance in the son of Jesse; to your tents, O Israel; now see to thine own house, David."

This last verse has been the subject of a great deal of debate. The usual surmise has been that the actual slogan of rebellion is intimated therein. Yet the immediate reaction to this call shows the reverse situation to be the case, namely, the people dispersed and returning to their homes. It seems to me that this matter should be viewed within the context I have tried to delineate: the convening of the Shechem assembly aiming at the conclusion of a covenant as a prerequisite to Rehoboam's coronation. The striking slogan "To your tents, O Israel" then becomes no more than a formula signifying assembly disbandment with the emphatic addition "what portion have we in David," etc., an outright nullification of the treaty with the Davidide House.[7] This general formula, employing the characteristic terms "tents" and "portion and inheritance" may well date back to the days of Israelite settlement, the formula having its roots in the tribal organization and assembly.

The very same connotation of covenant nullification would appear to be intended in the second instance where the formula is mentioned, namely, in Sheba, the son of Bichri's stand against David. We note, in passing, that here "Every man to his tents, O Israel" (II Sam. 20:1) is a secondary formulation to the direct and perhaps original exclamation, "To your tents, O Israel" in the Rehoboam affair. Understandably, the dissolution of the covenant tends to act as precursor of the revolt. The fact of revolt is specially indicated in II Samuel 20:2: "So all the men of Israel went up from following David and followed Sheba, the son of Bichri," as well as in I Kings 12:19: "So Israel rebelled against the House of David unto this day" (referring to the Rehoboam incident). The actual slogan for military alignment, on the other hand, must be in reverse form: "We will not any of us go to his tent, neither will we any of us turn unto his house" (Judges 20:8). This, in fact, is the well-versed outcry of the confederation of

Israelite tribes, as they prepare for war against Benjamin to avenge the disgrace of Gibeah. It is noteworthy that here, too, it is the assembly (*'ēdā*), convening at Mizpah (Judges 20:1) which serves as the organ for major policy decisions, in this case the matter of joint military action. In conclusion, therefore, we find that the negative usage "We will not any of us go to his tent" etc., indicates that a common decision has been reached by the assembly, as against the opposing slogan signifying a severing of mutual ties and dissolution of assembly and covenant.

In this connection, one may revert for one further moment to David's enthronement. There we find a positive conclusion to the royal covenant expressed in the remark: "We are of thy bone and thy flesh" (II Sam. 5:11), which is antithetical to our formula "What portion have we in David, neither have we inheritance in the son of Jesse." Similar phraseology (although in this instance based primarily on genealogical ties) is employed by Abimelech in his attempt to induce the people of Shechem to crown him king: "Remember also that I am your bone and your flesh" (Judges 9:2).

As regards the covenant, we revert to our original contention that the northern tribes were bound to the Davidide monarchy by virtue of this selfsame act of treaty. Consequently they felt it their prerogative to stipulate the conditions for renewal of the covenant leading to the enthronement itself. Should their conditions then be rejected, they would have no hesitation in undoing the bond of union. We note in the coronation ceremony two basic elements that have already been pointed out by various scholars, especially by Alt in his penetrating analysis of kingship in Israel: the anointing, or divine aspect of the covenant, and the acclamation, expressing approval of the king by the populace.[8] This approval was indicated by the joyous shout (*tᵉrū'ā*) of the assemblage, as in the case of Saul and Jehoash: "and all the people shouted and said: 'Long live the king!'" (I Sam. 10:24); "And they clapped their hands and said: 'Long live the king!'" (II Kings 11:12). This ancient procedure of public acknowledgment of a legal act contrasts with the written signature in modern pact-making.

"Elders" and "Young Men"—In Advisory or Decisive Capacity?[9]

It is significant that during the negotiation with Rehoboam on the matter of alleviating the tax burden of the northern tribes, the king did not exercise his prerogative of immediate decision. Instead, he asked for a three-day delay in order to take

counsel with both the elders (*zᵉqēnīm*) and "young men" (*yᵉlādīm*) whom the Bible describes as advisory bodies to royalty.

Here we are confronted with several hypothetical questions the solution of which may help clarify both the political situation and machinery upon which Rehoboam depended in the hour of his decision.

1. What in fact motivated Rehoboam to have recourse to these two bodies? Was he empowered to take an independent course of action? Would David or Solomon have reacted in the same fashion under similar circumstances?

2. Was it incumbent upon him to turn to the "young men" after having consulted with the elders? Or did he rather consult them because the elders' conciliatory counsel did not suit his disposition?

3. What actual competence did these two bodies possess? Were they acting in advisory capacity, their word not being binding on the king? Or was it possibly the counsel of the "young men" that was solely binding?

Before we pursue these questions further, we shall endeavor to establish the elders and "young men" as actual bodies or institutions that participated in policy making and not as mere biological groupings, as commonly held.

As for the elders, it would be superfluous to go into any lengthy discussion.[10] It is common knowledge that they served as a central institution in the patriarchal-tribal society throughout the Near East, including premonarchic Israel. As is well known, this institution persisted far into the days of the monarchy, especially in the more conservative northern kingdom, where we find the elders far more active than in Judah. Their powers, nevertheless, waned with the passing years. We will confine ourselves here to the appearance of this institution in decisions of state under royalty.

Ahab, too, like Rehoboam stood in need of the elders' counsel. To be more precise, he may have been virtually dependent upon the very decision of the elders in his fateful dilemma, namely, the Aramean siege of his capital Samaria and his response to the degrading terms of surrender imposed on the Israelite king by Ben-Hadad (I Kings 20:1 ff.). Two Aramean delegations present an ultimatum to Ahab. While accepting the terms of the first, Ahab is defiant to the harsher demands of the second and decides to convene an emergency council. In vs. 7–8 of chapter 20 we read: "Then the king of Israel called all the elders of the land and said, 'Mark, I pray you, and see how this man seeketh mischief; for he sent unto me for my wives, and for my children, and for my silver, and for my gold and

I denied him not,' and all the elders and all the people said unto him: 'Hearken thou not, neither consent.' " Whereupon Ahab accepts the elders' advice and rejects the surrender terms.

Yet another instance of political counselling is that of Amaziah, king of Judah, faced with the decision of launching a war against Jehoash of the sister-kingdom of Israel. In the Chronicler's version (II Chron. 25:17) we read: "Then Amaziah . . . took advice and sent to Joash, the son of Jehoahaz, the son of Jehu, king of Israel, saying: 'Come, let us look one another in the face!' " (The parallel passage in II Kings 14:8 omits the phrase "took advice"). There can be no doubt that the reference is to a political body which the king was wont to consult in an emergency, as did Rehoboam and Ahab. It is not inconceivable that here, too, it is the elders that are implied. In any event the words "took advice," when appearing in the context of a peace-or-war decision, are ones to ponder.

During the days of David, the elders were equally well known as a body wielding great political influence. We have already noted their decisive role in concluding the treaty with David by which he assumed the crown over the North, as well as during his preliminary negotiations with Abner. The institution of the elders of both North and South is remembered particularly for its activity during Absalom's revolt. When Ahithophel offered his counsel, it was directed to Absalom and the elders of Israel (II Sam. 17:4). This is the forum accredited to act upon his advice. On liquidation of the revolt, David turns to Zadok and Abiathar saying (II Sam. 19:12) ". . . 'Speak unto the elders of Judah saying: Why are ye the last to bring the king back to his house?' " Once again, we note the importance of this body—here the "elders of Judah."

The Various Branches of Government

As far as the Solomonic kingdom is concerned, no real mention is made of the elders, save for one passage, product of a late redactor (I Kings 8:1–3), on the installation of the Ark in Solomon's temple. But the existence of the elders as a special council during this period clearly emerges from the chapter under review (I Kings 12:6), reading: "And King Rehoboam took counsel with the elders, that had stood before Solomon his father while he yet lived." Various commentators here identify the elders with the ministers (*śārīm*) of Solomon in precisely the same way that "the young men" are identified with the ministers of Rehoboam. There is no valid founda-

tion in this case, either, for such a hypothesis. On the contrary, several passages offer proof that ministers and elders are distinctly separate entities of government, on the town as well as on the national level. In fact the two appellations appear side by side, as in Judges 8:14, portraying the city government of Succoth in the Gideon story, or in I Kings 21:8, which depicts the royal administration in the time of Ahab and Jezebel.

Of special interest is a third passage where the elders are mentioned separately from the ministers of the northern kingdom. This concerns the negotiations between Jehu and the leadership in Samaria, with the aim of transferring rule into his hands (II Kings 10:5). Here the capital authorities are comprised of two ministers, the royal chamberlain (*ªśær 'al habbayit*) and the city governor (*ªśær 'al hā'īr*), the elders, and the guardians (*ōmᶜnīm*). The same leaders are mentioned in verse 1 of this chapter although in comparison with the Masoretic text greater clarity is evinced by the Greek and Latin versions (Septuagint and Vulgate), which read: "Jehu wrote a letter and sent it to Samaria (!): to the governors of the city and to the elders and to the guardians."

Despite the lack of sufficient grounds for a clear distinction between the various divisions of government (today's executive, legislative, and judiciary), it may nevertheless be assumed that the ministers, as under David and Solomon, are the equivalent of today's executive authority, while the elders might conceivably be regarded as serving in an advisory capacity.

Among all the lists of officialdom during the reigns of David and Solomon, as recorded in II Samuel and I Kings, there is no mention of the title "counsellor." Ahithophel, even though acting as "David's counsellor," is not included in the list of ministers since these comprise the executive branch which alone is recorded therein.

On the other hand, Adoram, who is "over the levy," is included as befits a member of the executive arm, having been sent to mobilize the corvée in Ephraim (I Kings 12:18). Only in I Chronicles 27:32–33, do we read: "also Jonathan, David's uncle, was a counsellor and Ahithophel was the king's counsellor." This verse, however, is not to be taken as evidence of an official ministerial listing, but rather as a record of the king's personal entourage. True, Adoram was considerably advanced in years during the time of Rehoboam, having served under David (II Sam. 20:24) and Solomon (I Kings 4:6), i.e., over a period of forty years. This would place him at least in his sixties at the outset of Rehoboam's reign. All this notwithstanding, he is still not entitled "elder," but comes under the category of ministers or senior officials.

J. Braslavi: In other words, not the Latin "senex" but "senator." In Arabic, too, the word "sheikh" denotes both an old man and one holding an important position, young though he be.

Lecturer: These are illustrative parallels. Various other languages also distinguish between the two concepts of the biological and the functional embodied within the one term. The Mari documents of the early second millennium B.C., with their striking portrayals of tribal society, serve as a fine example of this.[11] In conclusion one must nevertheless be mindful of the fact that the elders in their capacity as patriarchal notables were frequently elderly individuals.

"Elders" and "Young Men"—Two Political Outlooks

Whereas the general topic of the "elders" has been sufficiently dealt with in the past, this is not the case with the "young men," whose clarification is the task to which we shall now address ourselves.

In contrast with the elders, the "young men" whom Rehoboam consulted are unknown as a distinct entity or institution elsewhere in the Bible. Consequently, it is difficult to determine the nature of this group. This very designation "young men" (*yᵉlādīm*—actually, "boys," "children"), is inappropriate to a political institution of any sort. Nevertheless, the term is not to be taken in its literal sense. The Bible explicitly states that they *grew up together* with Rehoboam, who was forty-one years of age when he ascended the throne (I Kings 14:21). This is a rather high accession age when compared with Solomon, who may well have been under twenty when he assumed the crown, and with other rulers who were still in their teens.[12] As a matter of fact it is the highest accession age of any Judean king. The *yᵉlādīm,* consequently, must have been middle-aged, and as such could easily constitute a political body.

It is more likely that the informal usage "young men" is one of the flowery epic embellishments, not without its pejorative note, to which the narrator resorted in order to emphasize the psychological and biological differentiations between both groups. The elders, wise in the ways of the world and in statecraft (Job 12:12), preach a policy of moderacy. As for the "young men," force is their refuge and impatience their lot; and if results are to be the measuring rod, their political vision, too, was on the short side. Yet above and beyond the disparity in maturity and temperament, still another factor is at

work here: the elders are the "old guard" brought up in David's generation on the ideal of the twelve-tribe confederation. The "young men," on the other hand, represent the "new wave," to use a current expression, rising to eminent position along with Rehoboam and growing up in the later, oppressive years of Solomon's administration. We have here a decisive gap of one generation between the time of David, visionary of the greater Israelite empire, and the generation of Solomon which witnessed the firm establishment of a powerful, heavy-handed regime especially as it affected the northern tribes.

It is difficult to ascertain what grouping the "young men" comprised. Nor should it be assumed that they were Rehoboam's newly appointed ministers. There is no evidence for the opinion expressed at times that Rehoboam, upon his accession, embarked on an administrative reform of sorts, replacing his father's ministers by people from amongst his own circle. On the contrary, the example of the sole minister, Adoram, chief of the corvée, mentioned during his reign, testifies to a continuity of royal administration. Certainly the veteran Adoram could not conceivably have been one of the "young men" who grew up together with Rehoboam.

The "Young Men"—Princes of the Court

I am of the opinion that the "young men" were primarily princes, the offspring of Solomon, reared together with their half-brother, Rehoboam. While the 1,000 wives of Solomon appear exaggerated in number, what emerges clearly is that the sovereign had embarked on ramified marriage alliances, with the international aspect of his manifold ties of wedlock actually becoming a mainstay of his foreign policy. I have discussed this subject elsewhere.[13] But what seems most apparent is that these royal scions must perforce have attained to high status at the court and most probably also held high rank in the military. Conceivably, their opinions carried great weight, upon the death of Solomon, in domestic and foreign affairs.

One should draw attention in this respect to a noteworthy passage previously referred to concerning Jehu's negotiations with the Samaria leadership, upon the deaths of Ahab and Jehoram. Listed among the central authorities we find, in addition to ministers and elders, the guardians who brought up Ahab's seventy sons (II Kings 10:1–6). It would appear that these three bodies had been functioning during Rehoboam's reign, with the exception that at the time, the "young men" or princes appear as such in their own right.

Concerning the identification of the "young men" with the king's offspring, one should note the especially instructive Rehoboam family chronicle as preserved in II Chronicles 11:18–23. Here Rehoboam, continuing in his father's footsteps, is described as having a considerable harem and fathering 28 sons and 60 daughters. Abijah, moreover, who was crown-prince and heir-apparent, was appointed at the head of his brothers and made ruler (*nāgīd*) over them. This portrayal bears eloquent testimony to the internal organization of the royal household, the princes serving as a political entity under the heir-apparent, Abijah. It is a fair assumption that the crown-prince Rehoboam was himself appointed over his brothers during his father's lifetime and that they acted as a kind of "young men's" council. Abijah has been similarly credited with a considerable progeny—22 sons and 16 daughters (II Chron. 13:21) and one may anticipate court-organization of a nature comparable with that of Rehoboam. Abijah's shortlived reign of three years, however, may have precluded the routine functioning of just such a princely council.

As a further example we may refer to the various sons of King Jehoshaphat, mentioned in the Bible by their very names and the noteworthy remark of the Chronicler: "And their father gave them great gifts of silver, and of gold, and of precious things, with fortified cities in Judah (!); but the kingdom gave he to Jehoram, because he was the first-born" (II Chron. 21:3).

Participation and Voting in the Assembly

It is evident from the foregoing that the assemblages of elders and "young men" of Rehoboam's reign were not mere spontaneous gatherings but rather official bodies within the framework of the kingdom. This is implied further in the very terminology of the chapter describing each grouping: "that had stood before Solomon" and "that stood before him," that is, before Rehoboam (I Kings 12:6, 8).

The expression "to stand (*'ōmed*) before" denotes, as is well known, attendance upon a high-ranking personage. More significantly, however, it may bear the occasional reference of membership or participation in assembly or council. Several instances of this usage are to be found throughout the Bible, depicting a heavenly assembly or "council of the Lord," which, in effect, is a reflection of its earthly counterpart. It would be impossible to render a full enumeration of these passages within the framework of this lecture.[14]

An intriguing problem posed by the assemblies of the elders and "young men" is the manner in which decisions were reached at these gatherings, which were convened from time to time to advise and even decide on matters of vital importance. Owing to the regrettable lack of evidence on the overall procedure at such meetings, this question remains unresolved. Even the more abundant material on the ancient Near Eastern assemblies provides but scattered hints on this score. Ephraim A. Speiser has pointed out that there were times when the assembly did not succeed in reaching a final decision.[15] This attests the fact that discussions must have ensued among the different members of the assembly with the possibility of divergent views among them. However, the vote, as such, as a means of reaching a decision, is not to be accepted with assurance. Thorkild Jacobsen, in his fundamental work on ancient Mesopotamian institutions, found no evidence for the voting technique as being in use there, this system apparently first coming into common practice in post-Homeric Greece. Basing himself on Sumerian myths, Jacobsen could demonstrate that the assembly's assent was voiced by the shouts of individual members, "let it be!"[16] The foregoing surmises open possible avenues of approach for a fuller comprehension of the workings of Israelite assemblies. In any event, the voting technique hardly enters the historical picture.

The Rehoboam Event in Light of the Sumerian Epic

It might be highly revealing to produce external parallels to our subject matter, which treat historical situations wherein the ruler is compelled to turn to various political bodies for vital decisions. I will restrict myself here to citing but one example which, from the typological point of view, bears a unique resemblance to the Rehoboam episode. I refer to the Sumerian epic known as "Gilgamesh and Agga" which reflects political conduct in the city-states of Sumer during the first half of the third millennium B.C. For the publication and detailed treatment of this epic, thanks are due to Samuel Noah Kramer, as well as to other Sumerologists such as Jacobsen, Evans and Falkenstein, who have devoted special studies to the subjects.[17]

Briefly put, the plot is as follows: Gilgamesh, lord of Uruk, Biblical Erech, listed in the "table of nations" (Gen. 10:10) and Agga, ruler of Kish, are engaged in a power struggle for hegemony in Sumer. The king of Kish issues an ultimatum to Gilgamesh that he and his subjects submit themselves as corvée to Kish, or else Agga will wage war against them. Gilgamesh, like Rehoboam, does not reply to the emissaries on his own. Instead, he approaches two bodies in his kingdom for their resolution on the matter. Like Rehoboam he first appeals to the "assembly of the elders" or, more precisely, to the "town fathers." These pursue a path of moderacy and suggest that Gilgamesh submit to the enemy, that he avoid war at all costs. Gilgamesh rejects this proposal and turns to the council of "men," that is, the young armsbearers of the realm who are in favor of rejecting the terms even at the price of war. Gilgamesh, like Rehoboam, acquiesces in their urging but, unlike Rehoboam, goes off to war.

In addition to the "bicameral" nature of the institutions and their respective policies regarding peace and war, one may even find parallel terminology employed in the Biblical account and the Sumerian epic where these institutions are dealt with. The "council of men" in the Sumerian city-state is composed of various sectors: "those who stand," "those who sit," "those who were raised with the sons of the king," etc., with the first group immediately calling to mind "those who stood" before Solomon and Rehoboam. Aside from this, the Biblical and Sumerian narratives present a striking similarity in literary features, such as in the recurring use of metaphor describing the onerous corvée.

The focal point as already stated, however, is that notwithstanding all differences in historical circumstances and literary character of the two accounts, the similarity lies in the ruler's lack of freedom in independently exercising his prerogative of decision. It would appear that as far as the two councils are concerned, it is their advice and, perhaps even more, their backing and consent which ought to be underlined. It is interesting that in both instances, the elders' counsel is rejected (thereby placing them, *ipso facto*, in an advisory capacity), reflecting as it does the philosophy of the older generation. Preference is given to the stand of the "young men," these being representative of the social strata and political forces to which Gilgamesh and Rehoboam belong.

The issue we have raised on the degree of competence of the two bodies in the Rehoboam affair has been debated by scholars in connection with the Sumerian epic: were these merely advisory entities, or was the council of "men" at least sovereign and possessor of ultimate authority?[18] On this latter point, there is no clue in the sources themselves and any inference to be drawn must remain hypothetical. Considering, however, the relatively primitive character of the societies in question, it would seem that

concrete forces rather than abstract legalities determined the course of events. Put somewhat differently, the king was obliged to rely on the active support of those bodies which, in fact, or at least in his opinion, had the power to aid him in implementing his decisions and without whose assistance no decision could be of any real consequence. One may conclude, then, that these bodies consisted of the council of "men" under Gilgamesh and the assembly of "young men" during Rehoboam's reign.

In any event, the very fact of reliance in crucial matters of state on these councils which represented various social levels of the populace is symptomatic of the relative weakness of the crown and testifies to a severe political crisis. It is not entirely unexpected, therefore, to find that in grave moments such as these, both Gilgamesh and Rehoboam had recourse to such bodies for moral and physical support. In the last analysis, conduct of this sort on the part of the ruler points up the restriction of his absolute powers and the democratization of the political process.

It has been my main purpose . . . to present various ideas in connection with Rehoboam's kingship and I trust that my discourse may serve as a contribution toward some clarification of the political apparatus and organs of statecraft during the Biblical period.

NOTES

1. See commentaries: A. Sanda, *Die Bücher der Könige* (1911), I, 334 ff.; J. A. Montgomery, *The Books of Kings* (1951), pp. 248 ff.; J. Gray, *I and II Kings* (1964), pp. 278 ff.; also E. Nielsen, *Shechem* (1955), pp. 171 ff., for the discussion of textual problems which are not dealt with here.

2. For the problem in general see the recent studies by G. Widengren, *Journal of Semitic Studies*, II (1957), 1–32, and by G. Fohrer, *Zeitschrift für die alttestamentliche Wissenschaft*, LXXI (1959), 1–22. Important extrabiblical material on the general problem of covenant between king and people is to be found in the recent work of D. J. McCarthy, *Treaty and Covenant* (1963).

3. M. Noth, *Gesammelte Studien zum Alten Testament* (1957), pp. 151 f., and K. Baltzer, *Das Bundesformular* (1960), pp. 85 ff.; Gray, *op. cit.*, pp. 523 f., even sees here a threefold covenant.

4. For this type of treaty see for the present H. W. Wolff, *Vetus Testamentum*, VI (1956), 316–320.

5. On the significance of these two terms see L. Rost, *Die Vorstufen von Kirche und Synagoge im Alten Testament* (1938); R. Gordis in *Alexander Marx Jubilee Volume* (1950), pp. 171 ff. For the term *ʿēdā* and *mōʿed*, "assembly," see also C. U. Wolf, *Journal of Near Eastern Studies*, VI (1947), 100 ff. A parallel institution designated by the same team is attested for the kingdom of Byblos in the eleventh century B.C.; see J. A. Wilson, *Journal of Near Eastern Studies*, IV (1945), 245.

6. On this problem see now I. L. Seeligmann, *Vetus Testamentum*, XIV (1964), 75 ff. For a similar function of the assembly (Sumerian: *unkin*; Akkadian: *pukhrum*) in Mesopotamia, see the bibliographical references in notes

16, 17. For the assembly (*pankus*) in the Hittite kingdom which, according to some authorities, was originally an elective monarchy, see O. R. Gurney, *The Hittites* (1952), pp. 63 ff.; A. Goetze, *Kleinasien²-II* (1957), pp. 86 ff.

7. See Fohrer, *op. cit.*, p. 8.

8. A. Alt, *Vetus Testamentum* I (1951), 2–22, reprinted in *Kleine Schriften,* II (1953), 116–134. For the coronation rites see R. de Vaux, *Ancient Israel* (1961), pp. 102–107. There see also pp. 70–72 and 524 on the institution of the "people of the land," whose investigation lies outside the scope of this lecture.

9. For a somewhat fuller treatment of several points in the following part of the lecture, see my recent paper, *Journal of Near Eastern Studies,* XXII (1963), 247 ff.

10. For the institution of the "elders" in the biblical sources, see especially the latest treatments by J. L. McKenzie, *Analecta Biblica,* X (vol. I, 1959), 388–406, and J. Van der Ploeg, *Festschrift Hubert Junker* (1961), pp. 175 ff.

11. See H. Klengel, *Orientalia,* XXIX (1960), 357 ff.

12. S. Gevirtz, *Patterns in the Early Poetry of Israel* (1963), pp. 30 ff., stressed the point that persons of an extremely young age became kings and military leaders in the ancient Near East.

13. *Journal of Near Eastern Studies,* XXII (1963), p. 8.

14. *Journal of Near Eastern Studies,* XXII (1963), 250, n. 11, and there further bibliographical references. In addition see now H. P. Müller, *Zeitschrift für die neutestamentliche Wissenschaft,* LIV (1963), 254 ff.

15. E. A. Speiser, *The Ideal of History in the Ancient Near East* (1955), p. 53.

16. See Th. Jacobsen's basic study, *Journal of Near Eastern Studies,* II (1943), 159–172, and, on the point in question, p. 171, n. 68; *Zeitschrift für Assyriologie,* XVIII (1957), 101 and n. 12. For the introduction of voting as a parliamentary device in Greece, see J. A. O. Larsen, *Classical Philology,* XLIV (1949), 164 ff.

17. For the scientific edition see S. N. Kramer, *American Journal of Archaeology,* LIII (1949), 1–8; translated also in *Ancient Near Eastern Texts,* pp. 45 f., and with slight improvements in Kramer, *The Sumerians* (1963), pp. 187 ff. For a discussion of the epic, see the articles of Jacobsen cited in the preceding note, as well as G. Evans, *Journal of the American Oriental Society,* LXXVIII (1958), 1 ff.

18. For the former opinion, see A. Falkenstein, *Cahiers d'histoire mondiale,* I (1954), 801; for the latter, Jacobsen's articles cited in note 16.

CHAPTER V

Patrimonial Systems: Introduction

I

In the first historical stage of breakthrough from primitive systems—in what may be called the pre-imperial and prefeudal stage—the great majority of political systems consisted of patrimonial regimes. Yet they have probably been less studied and more often treated as a sort of "residual category," as "predecessors" of imperial symbolic systems, or as "underdeveloped," "embryonic" types of such systems.

Even Weber, in whose writings the fullest exposition of the basic characteristics of patrimonial systems can be found, does not distinguish on the whole between patrimonial and imperial systems, although just because of this he succeeds in pointing out the persistency of many important patrimonial elements in the more developed of differentiated imperial systems.[1]

Let us first list briefly some of the most important historical examples of patrimonial systems. They would include many of the earlier kingdoms in the Near and Middle East, such as the Ancient Egyptian Empire,[2] Assyrian[3] and Babylonian[4] kingdoms, and smaller empires like ancient Akkad;[5] the many nomad kingdoms or "empires," ranging from relatively loose tribal conquerors such as those of the Hyksos[6] and the Hittites[7] up to the more fully organized ones of the Mongols;[8] most of the first Germanic[9] and Slavic[10] tribes that settled in Europe; many of the Indian and Southeast Asian[11] and also, to some extent, the Middle American kingdoms,[12] as well as, probably, many of the medieval Balkan and Slavic states mentioned above. Possibly also several embryonic types of such political systems could be found in Polynesia.[13]

The greatly varied historical and cultural settings of these regimes also indicate the broad variety of their origins. They developed from tribal systems or federations of different kinds, from city-states, from different congeries or convergences of these systems, or from the breakdowns of feudal and imperial systems. They could develop through processes of immigration and conquest by nomad tribes, or through processes of amalgamation and settlement of primitive or semiliterate groups, as well as through some combination of these various processes. Within this great variety, two basic ecological types of such regimes can be discerned: the sedentary and the nomadic.[14] Each of them necessarily developed some specific problems and characteristics.

As in the case of the other major types of systems which developed at this stage—that is, tribal federation with states—these various systems existed, in almost all known cases, in very close geopolitical proximity to one another and could very often merge into one another.

II

Despite this great historical, cultural, and geographical spread of such patrimonial systems, whenever they arose they developed some characteristics that were common from the point of view of dynamics of political regimes and systems. What are these common characteristics?[15] We may perhaps start with Weber's definition.

With the development of a purely personal administrative staff especially a military force under the control of the Chief, traditional authority tends to develop into "Patrimonialism," where absolute authority is maximized, it may be called "Sultanism."

The "members" are now treated as "subjects." An authority of the Chief which was previously treated principally as exercised on behalf of the members, now becomes his personal authority, which he appropriates in the same way as he could any ordinary object of possession. He is also entitled to exploit, in principle, like any economic advantage—to sell it, to pledge it as Security, or to divide it by inheritance.[16]

This definition points to what seems to be the most important "positive" and "negative" characteristics of these systems. The major positive characteristic of patrimonial regimes is the development of a relatively separate administrative, political, and sometimes also religious center, which is both ecologically and to some extent also structurally and symbolically distinct from the periphery, from the broader strata of the society, and of a concomitant element of a new distinct ruling class.

The centers which developed in most (especially, but not only, sedentary) patrimonial systems were ecologically markedly different from the periphery. The major nucleus of such a center was the household of the prince or ruler, or in some cases of a priestly group. While structurally this household was not dissimilar from other aristocratic households, it did tend, insofar as it was successful in establishing itself in the centers, to become greatly transformed. These centers were inclined to be located in cities, mostly administrative cities or temple-cities. It was here that the great monuments of centrality, in the form of temples and palaces, were erected.

These cities were characterized by a much higher degree of concentration of population, by a much higher degree of internal division of labor than the periphery. They were characterized by the weakening of many of the relatively undifferentiated kinship units, by the growth of more specialized units: craft and merchant organizations, some groups of laborers and especially of new administrative and ritual organizations. The basic social units in these cities—administrative and religious units—as well as the various guilds of craftsmen, of laborers, were internally more differentiated and encompassed a wider set of specialized activities than any of the ecological units in the periphery.

In all these spheres—the administrative and the religious centers, and the craft and merchant organizations—there took place developments of specialization, of embryonic bureaucratic, and/or of specialized craft units. But it was not only that somewhat more specialized units and roles tended to develop here. The very composition of the ruling elite tended to change somewhat the base of recruitment to these roles in a more flexible direction than in the periphery. Thus, the recruitment to these roles was not entirely limited to memberships in specific kinships or territorial units; it was not necessarily conceived as representative of such units, and it opened up some new, wider channels of mobility.

Moreover, even the nature of the predominant social units tended to change. The more extensive territorial kinship units which were predominant in the periphery tended in the centers to give place to restricted family units which became more differentiated from the broader kinship-territorial units. Above all, the strong connection between kinship groups and a given restricted territorial base was much weakened. Similarly, more specialized cult groups organized themselves in special frameworks. These could be temples, temple-states, cult associations, or groups of prophets, and they could become very powerful and influential. Such groups were often structurally more specialized than those of the periphery, although not entirely dissimilar from the administrative and political units. But at the same time this specialization was rather limited, especially as compared with other types of urban concentration.

In many such capitals of patrimonial regimes, the commercial or manufacturing activities were either secondary or nonexistent; they sometimes undermined the possibilities of maintaining any stable administrative—political—center. In some patrimonial regimes these functions were performed outside the capital cities in some sort of international enclaves: caravan cities, temple centers, some city-states, or by some secondary centers.[17]

Therefore, in these centers the urban community did not develop fully its own collective identity in a differentiated or autonomous way, as was the case in most of the city-states. The most active and formative elements in these cities, in contrast to the city-states, were the various political groups (the king, his entourage, and his administration), on the one hand, and the various cult groups and the various religious elites, priestly congregations and the like, on the other. Through the activities of these groups, which aspired to forge these centers, the specific new central activities developed and erected the movements of centrality. They also constituted the components of the new embryonic ruling class.

III

Although the urban community did not develop in these centers its own full identity, the centers were distinct from the broader group of the society not only in ecological, but also in structural and symbolic, terms, even though this distinction was not as great—and more in degree than in kinship—as in the imperial systems. These broader strata of the society were, in most of these systems, especially in the nomad regimes, organized either in kinship and tribal units or (as in most of the sedentary regimes) in village communities based on kinship and territorial bases—in a way typical "peasant" communities, as described by Redfield and by Wolf.[18]

In these peasant communities there already tended to develop, as compared with most primitive countries, a much greater degree of economic and social differentiation, some degree of internal class divisions, and some degree of private ownership of land. Moreover, within many of these regimes there also developed some local urban centers of their own; in some cases such patrimonial regimes attempted also to engulf more developed city-states or commercial cities.

As against these broader groups of the periphery the center was here already conceived as something much wider, which both symbolically and organizationally encompassed the periphery in a way entirely different from most primitive regimes. It was not merely an extension of the conception of the special position of the royal lineage or clan in respect to other structurally equivalent clans or lineages.

In most patrimonial regimes there developed a conception which was to be found only in embryonic forms in primitive monarchies. According to this conception, the whole society became symbolically and to some extent actually organized as part of the royal household. The concrete household of the king constituted a special central unit of this society and had special functions and a distinct position with regard to other social units and to the social order in general.

Two such functions, which did not always develop in all these regimes to the same degree, were here of especial importance. One was the monopolization of the mediation between the cosmic and the social order and the concentration of all the major magical and protective functions with regard to the cosmic order in the hands of the kings, and the concomitant development of new symbols and structural dimension, although not always of the contents of this mediation. Although this function of the center could be very weak and intermittent, on the whole it was already based on the conception of a smaller degree of embedment of the social order in the cosmic order. It was based on a growing differentiation between them and on the concomitant assumption that the center was either much closer to or most fully representative of the major cosmic order. The center had the monopoly of symbolizing the direct, central fundamental function of mediation between these orders, especially insofar as they related to political organization.

Second, this center attempted to concentrate in its hands all the "external" relations with other political units or at least to control such relations of the other

units. It was a center which, unlike that of the tribal federation and in a way more like the city-states, attempted to maintain a political administrative unity with regard to "external" political affairs, to minimize or control any attempts of various peripheral groups (patrimonial subunits)—tribal groups, city-states—and to develop autonomous external relations. It attempted to enfold such units in one framework either through the creation of a gradation of subcentral patrimonial units or through the total encompassing of them in the control of the center, but without at the same time allowing them any great degree of impingement on the center.

Thus, in most patrimonial systems two components of center formation were especially prominent: the maintenance of symbols of cosmic order and the regulation of internal and external force. Other components—such as the development of symbols of common identity, the crystallization of collective goals, and the regulation of intergroup relations—were of secondary importance, often absent or left in the scope of activities of various subcenter or external centers.

Therefore, from the basic nucleus of this center—the royal or princely household—there developed new special administrative organs whose major aims were to supervise the periphery with its tributes or taxes, to maintain the royal peace internally, and to defend the realm from outside attacks. These administrative organs were usually personal organs of the king, staffed either by members of his own family, personal relatives, mercenaries, or some active elements from the periphery especially mobilized by the king. These constituted the power base of this new center and distinguished it from the more limited bases of primitive chiefs, sometimes making it look like an imperial center. However—and this is the meaning of the connotation of these regimes as patrimonial—the basic conception of the center was still couched in terms of kinship and household units, even if these units were internally much more specialized and encompassed a much wider and more diversified scope of different roles and activities.

The very extension of scope of the political framework broadened the potential scope of different political and administrative activities, especially of the higher groups and strata, such as the higher aristocratic priesthood. But, significantly, while taking advantage of such opportunities, most used them according to "older" (such as family and kinship) structural orientations in order to enable themselves or their lineages to gain stronger positions in the royal household or to get a greater share of wealth or power over the periphery, rather than to create new types of political and social organizations, although by their very convergence into the center, the higher local groups tended to become transformed into country-wide strata.

A similar picture emerges with regard to the religious-ritual sphere. Here again one of the major connotations of patrimonialism stands out. The symbolic or cosmic order which it represented was not necessarily entirely different from those of the periphery. It was the same type of order, but more so—and perhaps more general, more encompassing, and more articulate.

Insofar as some separateness and structural diversity between the ritual-religious and the political centers emerged, there also developed tensions between these religious groups and the rulers who wanted to monopolize for themselves the representation of the central symbols and of the society. But all such struggles were waged basically in the confines of a symbolic system which, while denoting the distinctiveness and separateness of the center, on the whole did not yet conceive an entirely distinct, new content of the major political referents of this symbolic order or a new conception of political center.

Truly enough, there took place here, as compared with primitive order, changes in the concrete contents of the symbolic order. This transformation of symbolic tradition from its primitive origins could indeed have very great significance, especially in terms of articulation and rationalization of the symbolic sphere.[19] But, however great these changes might have been from the point of view of the perception of some distinction between the social and the cosmic order, they were all bound within the basic premises of homology or parallelism between them and of the center as forming the focus of the relations between them.

It was only in these cases, as in many of the Western Asian and early medieval European cases, in which the religious centers were outside the political centers or constituted parts of "international" enclaves or of autonomous city-states or tribal federations, that some new types of "sectarian" conceptions of the cosmic order which envisaged the possibility of lack of congruence between the cosmic and the social orders and different new possibilities of political participation did develop. On the whole, they had little direct influence or impact on the confines of the given patrimonial system.

This limited difference in kind between center and periphery was manifest in most of such societies—again with the exception of the various enclaves in supranational religious units—in the few, relatively small distinctions that developed in them between "little" and "great" traditions. Many local subcenters and units tended naturally to maintain their own autonomy without impinging too much on the center. But as this center was also very often conceived as basically a local center, even if of greater scope and splendor, the differences between this center and the different subcenters were more of degree than of kind.

Thus, it may be said that the basic characteristics of the center-periphery relations in these types of regime were, first, that this center was seen as almost completely different from the periphery, distant from it, and barely accessible to it; second, that there were, at the same time, few differences of kind between the center and the periphery; and, third, that the center was perceived as totally encompassing the structurally similar but politically passive periphery.

IV

This relatively limited extent of structural and symbolic difference between the center and broader peripheral strata of society, connected as it was with great structural and symbolic distance, can be seen to an even clearer degree in the nature of the links between the center and the periphery that tended to develop in these patrimonial regimes. Perhaps the most important characteristic of these links was that they created little basic structural change in either the groups and strata of the periphery or in the center itself.

The center impinged on the local (rural and urban) or tribal communities mainly in the form of some administration of law, the maintenance of peace, the exaction of taxation, and maintenance of some cultural and/or religious links to the centers. But most of these links, with very few exceptions, were effected through the existing local kinship (territorial and ritual) units, taking the form of rather "external" and adaptive relations. They did not tend to interpenetrate structurally and to create new types of interlinking structural or symbolic mechanisms. At most the developments here, especially among the higher (aristocratic) tribal or urban groups, tended toward the formation of country-wide strata, focused around the center.

The nature of these links between center and periphery in these regimes was perhaps most clearly seen in the fact that the channels of mobility that developed in these societies between the center and the periphery, although important in comparison with some primitive regimes, were really relatively restricted. Great parts of mobility toward the higher political positions seem to have been either of relatively random individual characters or confined to the circulation of personnel with the center.

It was probably mostly within the periphery, in the various subcenters or in the various enclaves, that such mobility could be found to some extent—a mobility which created new structural units (such as embryonic city-states or, even ephemerous local centers) and which also transformed some of the existing family and kinship patterns.

Thus, on the whole, there tended to develop here but few contacts, orientations, or structural mechanisms through which the center permeated the periphery or the center impinged on the periphery. There were few structural criteria or channels which would undermine the existing social and cultural patterns of either the center or the periphery or at least inject into them new common orientations, as was the case in imperial systems.

This can perhaps be most clearly seen in the nature and scope of the specific legal activities developed by such patrimonial centers. These were usually confined to criminal and administrative (tax) law, to special religious law, but only to a very limited degree to the development of civil and contractual law. At most, such centers tended to uphold whatever arrangements were developed, in these spheres, by the various local groups or subcenters.

The major new basic structural elements that were often introduced into these centers stemmed, as we shall yet see, not so much from the conception of a broader political or social order, or of entirely new patterns of political participation in the center, but from the more personal attempts of the kings and rulers to break through the limits imposed on them by their own "aristocratic" and kinship units. However, in contrast to the imperial systems, these personal attempts were rarely connected with the development of a broader conception of the political order which would break through. In no case did they really attempt to establish new types of structural linkages between the center and the periphery.

There were few exceptions to this, of which the attempts of Charlemagne[20] or Genghis Khan[21] to establish new imperial systems have been among the most notable. But these exceptions prove the case that such new conceptions could not subsist in the limits of patrimonial regimes.

The best illustrations of these limitations on the efforts of patrimonial rulers to extend and to create a somewhat new type of political regime can be found in the nomad conquest empires, such as, for instance, those of the Mongols. In these, the duality between the conquered people, the sedentary periphery, and the conquering nomads who established the new centers was probably the greatest. Both retained their original structural characteristics and cultural orientations while emphasizing the common bond of creation of a center which would indeed be able to rule effectively in the purely administrative or protective sense.

Here there was also, of course, a much greater degree of cultural alienation and possibly also some lack of structural homology between the more sedentary people organized in territorial units and the nomads who were organized in much wider kinship units. The common political bond that developed between them was patrimonial in the purest administrative or external political sense, with few new common symbolic overtones or orientations. Here sometimes—even more than in other ("sedentary") types of patrimonial kingdoms—it was the kings who often attempted to change and broaden the nature of the political order, but they were very often defeated by their own mighty aristocratic families.

It is very significant that the transformation of these dual-nomad regimes into more centralized, stable, homogeneous, nondualistic political systems could take place mainly in situations where some religious or cultural groups—such as the church in the settlement of the German,[22] Slavic,[23] and Hungarian[24] tribes in Europe, or Islam[25] in many Central Asian cases—did come in from the outside and create some new common bonds of identity between the two segments. Here they could also build on some internal or international commercial enclaves.

V

We have thus briefly summed up some of the basic structural characteristics of these systems. As we have seen above, from the point of view of the differentiation of roles and collectiveness, we find in the political field a relatively high degree of development of special political units and frameworks, a smaller degree of political roles at the center, and only minimal development at the periphery. The most important feature of these societies is the tendency toward a relatively continuous maintenance of united and homogeneous over-all political and administrative frameworks with attempts to maintain relatively fixed boundaries, within which, however, the various local units retained their own systems and activities.

Thus, it can be said that from the point of view of the nature of the social division of labor these systems were characterized by what, in Durkheim's terms, may be called a quantitative extension of the units of "mechanical" solidarity, with relatively little push toward a higher level of organic solidarity.

The centers that developed in these societies did not perform many internal regulative tasks for the units of the periphery but mostly served as focuses of common symbols and of some common external or adaptive activities. But there could develop important differences between different types of patrimonial regimes. Of especial importance here is the relation between the political and the religious centers in these societies, first, according to the extent of segregation of these centers, whatever the contents of their ideologies or symbols; second, according to their relative strength or weakness; and, third, according to their relative dominance.

Thus, on the one hand, in many cases (as in many of the nomad empires), there developed central political and administrative frameworks which had a tendency to maintain the external contents of various traditional symbols without simultaneously maintaining any strong commitments to them, and at the same time display almost exclusive concern for the preservation of the existing weak frameworks of power. This gave rise to a continuous succession of weak centers.

On the other hand, there could also develop, as in several Southeast Asian societies, strong political centers which pre-empted the monopoly or control of the religious symbolism and made the religious centers very weak. As we shall yet see in greater detail, these differences are of especial importance from the point of view of the processes of change and transformation of these systems.

VI

The basic structural characteristics of patrimonial systems outlined above also explain the basic pattern of political struggle in them. The basic issue of political struggle developed on several levels; first, the level of the relation between the various aristocratic groups and the patrimonial center. Here one major issue was the extent of the autonomy of the center vis-à-vis such various units, or vice versa, that is, the scope of the ability of the center to exact from them allegiance and resources on its own terms; or conversely the extent of the ability of such units to limit the effectiveness and autonomy of political action of the center. (In extreme cases this could lead to secession from the center.) The second issue here was that of struggle for greater shares of benefits that the center could allocate among such various aristocratic or distinct territorial groups.

Both kinds, or levels, of issues could also develop in the relation between the center and the "lower" (nonaristocratic) "peripheral" groups, except that these groups had, on the whole, a much lesser degree of access to the center. Here there were also the attempts of the center to supervise, and if possible to limit, the internal political struggles and processes in the major groups of the periphery and to minimize the possible impingement of such struggles on the center.

The main participants in the different levels of the political struggle were the representatives of the basic constituent groups (kinship, territorial, religious, or purely personal or family cliques). There developed few specific types of politiacl organization beyond the cliques of royal households and of the administration. It was only in the latter and in the religious embryonic forms that some beginnings of somewhat more differentiated and specific types of political organization could be discerned. Accordingly there developed few special types of political organization based on the mobilization of nonascriptive, freefloating economic resources and political or cultural orientations.

Hence there tended to develop in these centers relatively few types of new political orientations or demands for new types of political participation. The only partial exception to this, as we have seen, was sometimes the rulers themselves and some of the religious groups or commercial-urban groups, especially those which constituted parts of other systems or in some international religious or economic systems.

Given these basic characteristics of the political struggle and structure of patrimonial societies, it can be easily understood that, in sharp contrast to citystates and tribal federation orientation, there was no strong tendency for the development in them of new concepts of political symbolism distinct from the political implications or derivation of the new, more articulated cultural or religious symbolism. Within this symbolism the political tended to be either seen as the very focus of the cosmic center or submerged under it in some secondary capacity. It was rarely an autonomous symbolic dimension.

This perhaps may also explain the related fact that on the whole there did not develop in them more than a very few great works of "historiography" in the strict sense of this word.*

---

* Most of the historiographies that developed in these systems were rather akin to semiritual chronicles (like the Javanese chronicles) and dealt only to a limited extent with depicting the unfolding of the political or religious order as an autonomous order.

Hence, unlike the great architectural movements which symbolized the convergence of the cosmic and the social order, they had small impact on posterity in terms of trans-

VII

These basic structural characteristics of the patrimonial systems are closely related to the conditions of their development. As in other types of development of archaic societies, the most important conditions here were a combination of internal and international circumstances. In this case, as with regard to the other types of political systems discussed in this section, it is not easy to specify the exact combinations of these forces which gave rise to them, as distinct from other types of political systems. Some indications may not be out of place. Among the most important internal conditions of their development have probably been the growth of contacts between various units of relatively low levels of differentiation and the possibility of their becoming dependent on some cooperation for defense or for the maintenance of some common technological prerequisites (like common works of irrigation).

The push to such contacts usually tended to come either from some external events or forces, such as movements of population, or from changes in technology which facilitated the development of technique of agricultural cultivation and made more extensive trade relations possible. It was these changes which enabled the growing accumulation of various resources and the new developments in the symbolic or initial fields.

The units which could be engulfed into any patrimonial system could be either relatively homogeneous (constituting different, smaller tribal-patrimonial units) or more heterogeneous (comprising different types of elites as well as both the nomad and sedentary populations).

It was such a combination of internal and external forces which gave rise to the major structural characteristics of the patrimonial systems and to the scope of specialization and of division of labor that developed in them. Hence, also, the possibility of maintenance and continuity of such political order was predicated on the existence of the combination of a strong structural distinctiveness, in terms of political participation, between the peripheral and the more central spheres, with structural similarity between the center and the periphery and with the need and possibility of maintaining bonds of common

cultural identity and common caretaking of various changing adaptive internal and external problems and needs.

The continuity of these regimes was predicated to no small degree on the maintenance of balance between the different structural and territorial forces of which they were composed. Any strong change in one such direction—a possibility given in the very nature of both the external environment and the internal process of political struggle—could easily disturb the balance. The extent to which such conditions could subsist was, as in all other types of political regimes, largely dependent on the scope of political struggle that developed in them.

Here many differences developed between the various types of patrimonial regimes. Some of these differences are related mainly to disparities in the relative strength of the major participants in the political struggle: the king with his potentially wider political group; the traditional aristocratic groups or other more "flexible" religious or urban groups. Other differences relate to the strength of the impingement of external forces on the center and of their sensitivity to such forces. In some cases some external forces could easily reinforce the "local" forces of aristocratic groups at the expense of the more central orientations, or vice versa. Similarly, the internal dynamics of such regimes, in terms of the demands on resources for maintenance of the royal center and the continuous performance of its functions, could give rise to depletion of resources and easily undermine the internal balance of forces in any patrimonial system.

The preceding analysis also points out the directions of possible changes and transformation of these systems. Three major possibilities of such change or transformation stand out.

First is the possibility of personal, dynastic, or territorial changes without any great changes in the basic nature of the regimes. This possibility was probably most frequent when there were relatively strong political centers which were able to maintain their own continuity and served as focuses of attractiveness for various—especially aristocratic—groups.

Second, and especially in the case of weak centers, is the dismemberment of any given patrimonial system into another patrimonial unit, which was the very frequent case in the eastern European and Southeast Asian cases.

Third is the possibility, sometimes connected with the first, of the transformation of patrimonial systems into more differentiated types of polities: first of all into imperial or feudal systems, or, given a certain type of a given regime, also into other subunits

<hr>

mission of the images of their own collective identity. This lack of weakness of such historiography probably explains why, despite the fact that these types of regimes constituted the greater majority of types of regimes in the "archaic" and even postarchaic stages of development of human polities, they left few permanent written monuments of themselves in subsequent history. Here they were entirely overshadowed by the subsequent chronicles of the great empires.

or enclaves, like city-states or new focuses of tribal federation. This possibility was most frequent in cases of great heterogeneity in the composition of the constituent units of such federations and especially insofar as among such heterogeneous elements there were also relatively strong, independent political or religious groups and elites which could serve as focuses of new charismatic orientations and center, on the one hand, and/or commercial or manufacturing forces which could also serve as bases of more differentiated resources, on the other hand.

NOTES

1. Guenther Roth, Book Review on S. N. Eisenstadt, *The Political Systems of Empires: The Rise and Fall of the Historical Bureaucratic Societies,* in *American Journal of Society,* LXXI (1966), 722–723.
In the following footnotes only general bibliographical indications are given; further details are presented in the bibliography.
2. J. A. Wilson, *The Burden of Egypt* (Chicago: Chicago University Press, 1951); W. F. Edgerton, "The Government and the Governed in the Egyptian Empire," *Journal of Near Eastern Studies,* VI (1947), 152–160.
3. Campbell Thompson, "Assyria," *The Cambridge Ancient History,* II (Cambridge: Cambridge University Press, 1940), 227–251; Sidney Smith, "The Age of Ashurbanipal," *ibid.* (1928), III, 39–112; Smith, "The Foundation of the Assyrian Empire," *ibid.* (1929), III, 1–31; Smith, "The Supremacy of Assyria," *ibid.,* pp. 32–60; Smith, "Ashurbanipal and the Fall of Assyria," *ibid.,* pp. 113–131.
4. Campbell Thompson, "The New Babylonian Empire," *ibid.* (1929), III, 206–225; Thompson, "The Influence of Babylonia," *ibid.,* pp. 226–250.
5. Stephen H. Langdon, "The Dynasties of Akkad and Lagush," *ibid.* (1928), I, 402–434.
6. H. R. Hall, "The Middle Kingdom and the Hyksos Conquest," *ibid.* (1928), I, 299–325.
7. D. G. Hogarth, "The Hittites of Syria," *ibid.* (1929), III, 132–148; Hogarth, "Hittite Civilization," *ibid.,* pp. 148–168; Hogarth, "The Hittites of Asia Minor," *ibid.* (1940), II, 252–274.
8. H. H. Vreeland, *Mongol Community and Kinship Structure* (New Haven: Yale University Press, 1954).
9. Martin Bang, "Expansion of the Teutons," *The Cambridge Medieval History,* I (Cambridge: Cambridge University Press, 1936, 183–217; M. Manitius, "The Teutonic Migrations 378–412," *ibid.,* pp. 250–276; Ludwig Schmidt, "Teutonic Kingdoms in Gaul," *ibid.,* pp. 277–291.
10. Kamil Krofta, "Bohemia to the Extinction of the Premyslids," *ibid.* (1936), VI, 422–447; Alexander Bruce-Boswell, "Poland, 1050–1303," *ibid.,* pp. 447–462.
11. For India and Southeast Asia, see Milton Singer, ed., *Traditional India: Structure and Change* (Philadelphia: American Folklore Society, 1959); H. N. Sinha, *Sovereignty in Ancient Indian Polity* (London: Luzac, 1938); Romila Thapar, *A History of India* (London: Pelican, 1966), Vol. I; Michael D. Coe, "Social Typology and the Tropical Forest Civilizations," *Comparative Studies in Society and History,* II (1955), 67–92.
12. For the Middle American empires, see *ibid.;* Sylvanus G. Morley, *The Ancient Maya,* 3rd ed., rev. by George W. Brainard (Stanford: Stanford University Press, 1956); John V. Murra, "On Inca Political Structure," *Proceedings of American Ethnological Society* (1958), pp. 30–41; and Robert M. Adams, *The Evolution of Urban Society* (Chicago: Aldine, 1966).
13. Marshall D. Sahlins, *Social Stratification in Polynesia* (Seattle: University of Washington Press, 1958).
14. Franz Oppenheimer, *The State—Its History and Development* (Indianapolis: Bobbs-Merrill, 1914); Lawrence Krader, "Principles and Structures in the Organization of the Asiatic Steppe Pastoralists," *Southwestern Journal of Anthropology,* XI (1955), 67–92.
15. William Delany, "The Development and Decline of Patrimonial and Bureaucratic Administration," *Administrative Science Quarterly,* VII, 458–501.
16. Max Weber, *The Theory of Social and Economic Organization* (New York: Oxford University Press, 1947), p. 347.
17. See on this R. Redfield, *Peasant Society and Culture* (Chicago: University of Chicago Press, 1956); R. Redfield and Milton Singer, "The Cultural Role of Cities," *Economic Development and Cultural Change,* III (1954), 53–73.
18. Redfield, *op. cit.;* E. Wolf, *The Peasants* (Englewood Cliffs: Prentice-Hall, 1967).
19. See R. N. Bellah, "Religious Evolution," *American Sociological Review,* XXIX (June 1964), 358–375; C. Geertz, "Ideology as a Cultural System," in D. Apter, ed., *Ideology and Discontent* (New York: The Free Press, 1964).
20. L. Halphen, *Charlemagne et l'empire Carolingien* (Paris: Albin Michel, 1947).
21. G. Vernadsky, "The Scope and Contents of Genghis Khan's Yasa," *Harvard Journal of Asiatic Studies,* III (1938), 337–380; Vreeland, *op. cit.*
22. Rev. J. P. Whitney, "Conversion of the Teutons," *The Cambridge Medieval History,* II (Cambridge: Cambridge University Press, 1936), 515–532; Austin L. Poole, "Germany: Henry I and Otto The Great," *ibid.,* III, 179–203; Poole, "Germany, 1125–1152," *ibid.,* V, 334–359.
23. V. Jagic, "Conversion of the Slavs," *ibid.* (1936), IV, The Eastern Roman Empire, 215–229; Kamil Krofta, "Bohemia in the Fourteenth Century," *ibid.,* VII, 155–182.
24. Louis Legner, "Hungary, 1000–1301," *ibid.* (1936), VI, 463–472.
25. See Bertold Spuler, *The Muslim World,* trans. F. R. C. Bagley (Leiden: E. J. Brill, 1960).

INTRODUCTION TO THE READINGS

In the excerpts presented here, several aspects or types of patrimonial systems are analyzed. These systems are characterized by the development of a relatively strong political center, which combines institutional differentiation from the periphery with structural similarity in terms of consanguinity ties. One type of such center is analyzed in Krader's "Principles and Structures in the Organization of the Asiatic Steppe-Pastoralists."

Krader sums up the nature of the system by saying, "The society of the steppes is a consanguinal unity with which a politico-territorial unity was combined and interwoven. . . . [Yet] the Mongol or Turkic princes had a clear distinction between the public fiscus and their private wealth."

Coe's article, which compares the Classic Khmer in Cambodia with Classic Maya civilization, illustrates that patrimonial political systems developed independently in various parts of the world and shows how in all these cases there existed a close connection between social differentiation and the production of surplus. He also indicates the existence in such systems of a relatively high differentiation within the cities (the center) with a relatively undifferentiated periphery.

Heine-Geldern explores the relations of the conceptions of kingship in Southern Asia with the basic cosmological picture found in many such systems and points to the broad possibilities of dynastic change in the framework of the basic traditional legitimation. He analyzes also the nature of the political center in these empires and the congruence between the political autonomous center and the structure of the central religious ideas. In this context he shows the importance of the differentiated capital as a structural and symbolic center in these empires.

18

Principles and Structures in the Organization of the Asiatic Steppe-Pastoralists

Lawrence Krader

The social organization of these peoples is a complex one, in which the social structure has a double facet, the consanguineal and the political. The consanguineal is exclusively patrilineal-agnatic; the political is identical with it both in general and in detail.

We distinguish in our thought between a given form or structure and a principle which underlies it, which is exemplified embodied in it; e.g., the principle of democracy is embodied in a given parliamentary institution.[1] In like manner, the Altaic pastoralists differentiate in their thought between a principle of social organization, e.g., the principle of patrilineal descent, and a particular social structure, e.g., the clan. The specific, concrete social units are labelled as such by these peoples, in addition to being named groups. That is, these peoples have words for structures which we identify as the extended family, the kin-village, the clan, etc., and each one of these in turn has a proper name. The existence of native terms for these units is usual and not surprising. Less usual and more surprising is the fact that the natives also have a concept and a term for a principle of social organization, such as patrilineal descent. A principle is on a "higher" level of abstraction than a social unit. The clan as a social structure can be observed to function; a family has a visible life; not so

From Lawrence Krader, "Principles and Structures in the Organization of the Asiatic Steppe Pastoralists," *Southwestern Journal of Anthropology*, XI (1955), 68–85. Reprinted by permission of the publisher.

a principle, which involves a different order of thought from that which—at times—may be perceived.

Again, we must distinguish between specific structures and sets of relationships which are conceptualized by the members of the society in collective kinship terms, but which are nevertheless without intrinsic form or structure. Thus, the pastoralists of the Asiatic steppe have separate terms for an individual's consanguinei, for his spousal kin, for his paternal kin (agnates), for his maternal kin; they have also conceptualized the unit of exogamy, which is a shifting unit from sibling group to sibling group. But none of these relationships have a social substance; that is, the body of any man's relatives by marriage, or maternal kin, or that group within which he is forbidden to marry, may differ from any other man's; it is without inner organization. Suppose that the rule of exogamy forbids marriage within the fifth degree of agnatic relationship (this has been reported on the steppes). I cannot marry, therefore, a girl whose Fa Fa Fa Fa is the same as mine. It may be that all the direct descendants of that patrilineal ancestor live together in one village, under the same village elder, and pasture their herds and flocks together. But this would be a matter of chance; generally it is not so. They may form a clan, but this too would be a matter of chance. Moreover, it is a rare coincidence that the body of maternal kin or the body of affinal relatives form a discrete social unit, identifiable by other means than the range of application of the collective kinship term by a given individual.

The Mongols of Outer and Inner Mongolia and the Kalmuks of the Volga have had a highly developed and intricately organized religious hierarchy. Likewise, the Buryat shamans are more like an organized priesthood than shamans as such. The religious organization falls outside the scope of this paper, however, for the principles of the ecclesiastic structure are different from those of the politico-consanguineal. It may be noted in passing that the ecclesiastic hierarchy appears to rise, and at times even form a theocracy, when the lay polity of the steppe is in decline. The Mongol and Kalmuk priests are lamas, that is, celibates under vows of chastity, usually living in monasteries. One of the theses of the present paper will be to show how the entire sense of the consanguineal organization is directed to the perpetuation of the male descent line. This is contrary to the sense of the celibate lamasery. If the monks are not always true to their vows, they are to that extent outside both the lay and ecclesiastic systems. It is as though the lamaseries are an escape vent from the rigorous patrilineality of the social system on the steppe where such escape vents are few.

Principles of Steppe Organization

The conjoint political and consanguineal dimensions in the social organization of these peoples have been mentioned, i.e. every political enterprise of theirs has been defined by the agnatic bond. The subjects of a principality were in theory descended from the same ancestors in the direct male line as the prince. Therefore, recognizing the given structure as political, we may say that, notwithstanding, the society was—and is—agnatically defined. The social structure is founded on the principle of patrilineal descent. In the past there were slaves. For a slave to achieve membership in the society he had to be given a fictional kinship relation to his manumittor and a genealogy to bear out the fiction. The patrilineal genealogies may be described as the founding charter, the membership roll, and the rule for admission to membership of these societies. The genealogies make explicit the constitutive elements of the society. Within the genealogies, descent lines are traced and ranked according to the order of birth of the founder. Since the genealogies show the relative collateral rank of a descent line, they define a man's social status.[2] Therefore, they are to this day assiduously kept, and youths of ten or twelve are able to recount their ancestries through many generations, together with those of closely related collateral lines. Some of these genealogies are twenty, thirty, fifty or more generations long. The ancestry of Chingis Khan as recounted in the *Secret History of the Mongols,* a 13th century epic, is 24 generations long.[3]

Consistent with the principle of patrilineal descent, the unit of exogamy is a patrilineal unit; the rule of residence is patrilocality; authority is patriarchal or generally vested in the senior male.

There is little relief to this structure of patrilineality in the society. The mother is a distaff father, ruling with stern authority the females of the household including her unmarried daughters, her sons' wives, her grandchildren, her husband's junior wives and concubines if the family is polygynous, and other females of the extended family household. She is no warm lap or bosom offering comfort to the child, and the poetry does not conceive of her as such. Mothers are not figures celebrated for their softness. Thus another extension of the same principle—authority by virtue of her seniority of birth for males— gives authority to women by virtue of order of marriage and of order of birth of the woman's husband or father, depending on her status as married or unmarried.

The escape from this stark pattern of authority by generation and by order of birth is the warmth of relationships among people of the same generation. The poetry tells of love between friends, betrothed couples, and sometimes siblings.

The relationship both to the maternal and affinal kin is one of respect. In addition, there is an avuncular relationship, but it is a varying one. Among the Monguor of Kansu, a Mongol people under heavy Chinese acculturation, the Mo Br tells of a girl who is about to marry that she may always draw support from him.[4] On the other hand, the avuncular relationship among the Kazakhs and the Kalmuks is a rivalrous one. When a Kazakh or a Kalmuk boy comes of age, he is entitled to collect part of his patrimony from his Mo Br, and this is usually resented, for the youth comes from afar under the rule of patrilocal residence, and may disrupt plans for division of his estate among his own sons by the Mo Br, i.e., the Mo Br Sos. The Si So must therefore be ready to drive off his share of the estate of the Mo Br as livestock by night, secretly. This practice, *baranta,* or legal cattle rustling, frequently disrupted the civil peace.[5] Rules had to be devised whereby only three sisters' sons could practice the *baranta,* and then had to divide their spoils among their brothers and cousins who came of age later. On a world scale this form of the avunculate is rare.

The basic form of the cousin system on the steppe, i.e., that of the ancient Turks and Mongols, and of the modern Ordos Mongols, has no term for paternal cross-cousin. (There is a term for Fa Si, but not for her child.) She marries away, and her offspring are not reckoned as kin by her brother's children. However, among the Kazakhs and Kalmuks, Fa Si Ch is regarded as kin, and is given a kinship term which is the same as Si Ch, a feature of the Omaha kinship system. This term is *zē* (Kalmuk) or *džien* (Kazakh), both etymologically derived from classical Mongol *džige(n)*. This breach in the patrilineal system among the Kazakhs and Kalmuks is expressed in fact by the rules of inheritance of both these peoples. I have rights in a share of my Mo Fa estate, which in fact is a claim on the Mo Br estate, said of his Si So.[6] This statement simply means that the sister in moving off has not completely cut her natal family ties, that she has rights in her father's estate not in her own person, but in the person of her sons. This relationship is only of limited significance in terms of the over-all social picture, but presents an interesting problem. It is closely identified with the shift in cousin terminology which has introduced

certain Omaha features onto the steppe, at least among the Kazakhs and Kalmuks. It is a clear-cut instance of the social dynamism in the behavioral correlates of kinship terminology, to use Murdock's fine phrase.

In the inheritance pattern, a distinction is made between practices regarding the corporeal property and the incorporeal. The family is an extended family, and sons remain by the father even after marriage, as a rule. But when they come of age, usually in their middle teens, they are given their portion. Part of this portion is made over in the son's name by the father to the family of the son's bride, because coming of age is associated not only with receiving of one's share of the patrimony but marriage as well. The bride-wealth (or bride-service for a poor nomad) is the basis for marriage. The son's share of the estate is effectually not his, but remains under the common control of the father; but it is reckoned as the son's. All sons in theory inherit equal shares of the paternal estate. If the son is not yet of age when the father dies, the mother holds his share of the estate in trust until he comes of age.

As to incorporeal property, the ranks, titles, honors of the father go to the eldest son, in whom the authority is vested over the entire extended family. If he is not of age, a younger brother of the father may succeed to the position of head of the family. Here there may be conflict when the eldest son does achieve his majority. Second and third sons might be given a lesser title if the father is a man of high rank; the youngest son usually receives a minor title just as the other younger sons; but in addition, he receives a special title with religious significance. The family hearth is a center of religious rites; the youngest son is residuary legatee of all that part of the estate which the father does not divide among his sons during his lifetime, the residuary estate including the paternal tent and hearth. He receives with the hearth the title of *galīn edzin,* master of the hearth. It is not the case that the youngest son inherits according to the principle of ultimogeniture; ultimogeniture is a principle which assigns the place of principle inheritor to the youngest son. Here in respect to the incorporeal property as well as the authority, the eldest son is the principal inheritor.

The marriage pattern may best be described as a contract by one line for the services of a female of another line in bearing a son. The principle involved is that of lineage exogamy. Contract is used in an extended sense, but in view of the possibility of reckoning fairly exactly the movement of property and other social goods between the two lines, we may use the term. Child betrothal, even pre-natal betrothal, is practiced; the prospective marriage pair is in no case consulted, for marriage is an arrangement between descent lines as corporate units. The family of the bride receives a gift as bride-wealth, which is relatively large. The bride takes with her to her husband's home her own portion as dowry, which is materially smaller than the bride-wealth, despite the fact that it includes expensive sumptuary wear, such as silver headpieces, silver-ornamented garments, etc. In addition, both families feast each other in relatively equal degrees. Both groom and to a lesser extent his family pay great respect to the family of the bride; and finally, the bride moves from her natal to her marital family. Payment of respect is figurative payment. However, it has economic consequences in associated gifts and services rendered. This total pattern of exchange is sometimes reciprocated over the generations, whereby a girl moves from line A to line B in marriage, while her daughter moves back, as marriage with Fa Si Da and Mo Br So. This practice is found among the Monguor. Much more common, indeed preferred, is Mo Br Da[7] marriage involving a constant flow of women from line A to line B without payment of bride-wealth, i.e. without reciprocity, as Lévi-Strauss has analyzed it. There are arrangements reported of the Kazakhs where families agree to exchange daughters in marriage, and even a type of Kazakh marriage, rare on the steppes, where three families reach an accord, a daughter of line A marrying in B, a daughter of B marrying in C, and a daughter of C marrying in A.[8]

While polygyny is practiced, it is largely limited to the rich and influential. However, the levirate is the rule, creating a family structure similar to polygyny, but different insofar as it involves no exchange of wealth. A widow without sons passes, on the death of her husband, to her husband's younger brother, and exceptionally, to any brother. But this is the case only if she is without sons. If she has a son, she maintains a household apart, inheriting her deceased husband's estate, and holding it in trust until her son or sons come of age. If she has no sons on being widowed, her part in the marriage contract is not fulfilled. She has to remarry within her husband's line, in order to assure the continuity through the bearing of sons. Only if she has already borne a son is she exempt from this practice. The bearing of daughters was not a condition fulfilling the marriage contract, and did not exempt her from the levirate. The levirate is not loved by the women, for they move from a chief place in their own households to a subordinate place in a household with a wife senior to them.[9]

The emphasis of the entire marriage pattern on the bearing of sons is a reflection of the general principle of patrilineal descent and its corollary, the perpetuation of the given patrilineal structure through the birth of sons. The levirate is but one more reflex of that principle, as is the nature of the marriage contract per se. Part and parcel of the entire scheme in regard to the descent practices are the adoption procedures. The most common adoption is that of Br So or Fa Br So. The primary reason for adoption is lack of sons of one's own. In the kinship terminology, both Br So and So So are called *aci* in Mongol generally. In Kazakh and Kirgiz they are both called *nemere*. If my own line is in danger of dying out, there is a practice ready to hand, with its terminological correlate to assure its perpetuation.

Since descent lines are collaterally ranked, it is important to keep their members distinct. The terms for parents' siblings are of the bifurcate collateral types, that is uncles are terminologically differentiated from the father, and are in turn differentiated from each other. Moreover, grand-uncles in the fifth generation are distinguished terminologically from the direct ancestor in the fifth generation, and the direct line is traced in the kinship terminology to the grandson in the fifth descending generation. Paternal uncles are differentiated as senior and junior to the father. This will be discussed below.

Further insights into these various principles may be gained by tracing the changing statuses of women in their life cycles. From birth to marriage, the female on the steppes is relatively without rights, she has little socio-legal status. In ancient days she could be sold into slavery in payment of a fine levied on her father for a crime.[10] On marriage she receives her dowry, and over this she has rights which are in general inalienable, but only in general. Under certain circumstances, e.g., if her husband commits a crime, the dowry can be seized and made over in part payment of the fine if he cannot pay it with his own wealth and that of his close kin. Her person could never be seized; she could never be sold. Among the Buryats and Kazakhs the wife achieves even further rights when she has borne a son. If her husband is well-to-do, she receives her own tent to rear her son, and in this tent she is mistress. She now has the right of refusing to marry her husband's brother under the rule of the levirate should she be widowed. She has further right to hold her husband's estate in trust for her son if he was not yet of age on the death of the father. And she can remarry at her pleasure among a wider group of kin.[11] Divorce is easy while she is childless or has only daughters. Once she has borne a son, her husband can divorce her only if he wishes to defy his own kinsmen, for they have a stake in the marriage now; the grandson or nephew is the general concern of the extended family. If a woman has no son, she can be sent back to her father, and the bride-wealth reclaimed. The bride-wealth is lost if she bears a son and then is divorced.

In sum, the steppe pastoral society is a hyper-rigid structure based on the agnatic bond and patrilineal descent. Genealogies are the sole bases for delineation of membership and relative position in the societies. Social differentiation is based on primogeniture; here common descent leads to differentiation rather than equality.

Structures of Steppe Organization

During the 19th century, a number of investigators gradually came to a commonly accepted picture of the social structure of these pastoralists. The first of these was A. Shchapov, working among the Buryats of Lake Baikal in the 1870s; the second was Radloff who worked among the Kazakhs and Kirgiz of the southern Altai through the last part of the century; the third was A. Pozdneev, among the Khalkhas of Outer Mongolia in the 1890s. The classical statement of this general picture is that given by W. Radloff.[12]

Radloff describes the core of pastoral society as the family with its common property. Related families and individual poor families as hangers-on form the smallest social group-unit, the *aul*. The Kazakh and Kirgiz *aul* is the nomadic village composed of kinsmen. It corresponds to the Khalkha Mongol *ail*, with which the Turkic term is etymologically cognate. The sedentary village of the Mongour, farmers of northwest China, who speak an archaic Mongol dialect, is *ayir*. In Radloff's account, the leader of each *aul* is the senior member, and that family achieves predominance whose influence is greatest, measured by wealth or physical numbers. The *auls* group into lineages, the lineages into clans, each bearing the name of the founding ancestor. Clan confederations further combine as hordes. But these larger politico-consanguineal units had great fluidity, fluidity of the state-entity being a necessity for the nomads of old. To Radloff, political leadership, whether on the small scale as a grouping of several kin-villages under a mediator *bii*, or on the large scale as a grouping of several clans or hordes under a khan or prince, is always a usurpation.

The theory of usurpation of power by a powerful political personality has been criticized recently by Harmatta.[13] Harmatta argues that merely because a structure is fluid or evanescent it is not without form; that instead of attributing the birth of the state to the momentary impact of some great personal organizing genius, the state on the steppe arose through the disintegration of the tribal organization, in the course of which the tribal society was transformed into a class society. The two viewpoints are not necessarily incompatible. For example, after the establishment of states and empires, the consanguineal bonds of the societies continued to form the basis of citizenship; and even after the state system disappeared the consanguineal structures which remained continued to maintain political functions, including tax-collection, troop levies, mediation of disputes among smaller kin units. The usurpation is not a normal procedure on the steppe, although there may have been individual cases of usurpations. The norm was rather ascribed status in the ruling stratum by right of birth, i.e. descent from a past leader, such as Chingis Khan. For example, among the oldest records that give details of the pattern of rule among the nomads are the Chinese documents of the 6th and 7th centuries A.D. bearing on the eastern Turks. According to these documents, the usual pattern was succession of the son to the throne of the father.[14] In 611 A.D. there was an instance in which the Fa Br succeeded to the throne of the son who had inherited it from his father. However, we infer that the son had died without issue, and that the throne then passed to the next collateral line. Yet succession in the senior paternal line was not always carried out. There was one instance in the year 573 A.D. when a prince cut off his own son and gave the succession to his younger brother. This younger brother later cut off his own son and gave the throne back to his older brother's son, thus restoring the senior line. In this case, however, the people said that the mother of this son was of low estate, and gave the throne back to the younger brother's son.[15] Succession was governed by the rule of primogeniture among the 19th century Kazakhs (see above), Khalkhas, and Kalmuks.[16]

Among the Buryats, Shchapov found a similar hierarchy of structures.[17] The Mongol *ail* corresponded to the Buryat *ulus*, composed of a series of enclosures in circular or elliptical form. Each enclosure is an extended family, together with adherents. Collaterally descended families occupy neighboring enclosures, and in more distant enclosures live more distant agnatic kin. Yet further related kinsmen live in other *uluses* with similar inner organization. The entire group of related *uluses* form a single clan divided into genealogical branches as *ulus* communities, just as the *ulus* communities are divided into smaller family communities.

An identical structure is attributed to the Khalkha

Mongols by Pozdneev. Here the social unit is again the extended family composed of persons descended from the same ancestor over three or four generations. The head is the eldest member of the family. Neighboring families are more distant relatives; groups of related families occupying a common territory form a kin-village.[18]

So powerful was this idea of the organization of the steppe nomads that it was taken as a model for the description of the Kalmuks by Leontovich who, however, had no first-hand knowledge of this people such as Shchapov, Pozdneev, and Radloff had of theirs. On the other hand, Pallas in the 18th century has a parallel description of the concentric Kalmuk organization but this time in political terms.[19] As a point of departure, this general picture of the social structure is a useful one. Ideally, the extended family does group into kin-villages, although by the end of the 19th century, when acculturation had proceeded rather far, such a rule must have been honored more in the breach than in the observance. Radloff's village was no longer bound together by close ties of blood.[20] In areas of the steppe where acculturation had not proceeded so fast, as among the Buryats, Petri[21] still found early in the 20th century a close correlation between kinship and common territory; this was axiomatic for Bogdanov, a contemporary native Buryat.[22]

The unilineal kin unit as a corporative structure has been well analyzed by Fortes. Its primary attribute is perpetuity, that is, its capacity to survive the individuals who form its membership at any point in time.[23] This corresponds to Maine's analysis of the corporation as a perpetual structure. To Maine's criterion Fortes then adds Weber's, and above we have shown how the genealogy supplies functions which meet Weber's criteria of the corporation, as a unit with a locus of authority and rules of membership. These we may call the constitutive elements of the corporations. Fortes, bearing the African social structures chiefly in mind, restricts his attention largely to the lineage.

If we agree that a lineage is a structure intermediate between a kin-village and a clan on the range of unilineal social structures, then the lineage on the Asiatic steppe conforms least to the theory of the corporative consanguineal entity, for it definitely lacks an internal structure, a locus of authority, a clear territorial delineation. It is a perpetuating structure of weak constitutive elements.

The extended family has its collective property under the rule of the patriarch, its own territory for grazing, its common religious functions. The personality of the patriarch as the locus of family authority is sharp and unmistakable. Unlike the conjugal or simple family, the extended family is defined as one in which the man's natal family is identical with the family he procreates. The extended family is a unit of perpetuity, for it survives the life of any individual member.

The ideal village is similarly constructed, with a seat of authority, a common territory, a common set of agnatic bonds, etc. The collective property is weak or non-existent, but grazing lands are jointly administered, and the annual nomadic grazing cycle is followed together. The clan likewise has a common locus of authority, a common territory wherein grazing lands are jointly administered under the direction of the clan chief whose main function in this regard is the settling of disputes over pastures among the clansmen. The lineage alone has no morphological features.

The unit of exogamy is the lineage. That is, a youth is forbidden to marry anyone who shares a common patriline in a given number of generations. As a rule the number of generations within which marriage is proscribed, i.e. the prohibited degree of agnatic relationship, is seven. At times it has been reported as high as ten; and latterly under conditions of severe acculturation it has shrunk to five and even three generations. But the central tendency has been seven. Whatever the specified number of prohibited degrees may be, however, the fact remains that my father's exogamic unit is not my own; I may marry a girl whose mother my father could not have married. This shifting unit cannot have a morphology of its own, that is, it has no seat of authority, no territory, etc. It is a unit abstractly existent to be evoked at will, that is, when it is required to affirm or reject the possibility of a proposed marriage.

The steppe lineage, despite its amorphous nature, is a named group. It is defined by the number of generations comprised in the lineage out of the total number of direct male ancestors in the genealogy. Its name is the eponymous name of the ancestor who stands at the head of the lineage. However, lineages vary in length according to the purpose for which the segment of the total genealogy is demarcated. To this extent it is an operational concept. It may be seven generations long and given the name of the ancestor in the seventh generation in determining the exogamic unit. The lineage may be five, seven, nine, or any other magic number of generations in length in a ceremony of ancestor worship; or it may go as far back as a famous ancestor to be evoked in a battle-cry in time of war. In these battle-cries (*uran* in Turkic, related to English "Hurrah") an ancestor who had fame as a warrior is acclaimed by a group of his descendants who assert their unity with him and with each other and the courage of that unity in his name.

Among the steppe-pastoralists, Turks and Mongols both, the clan is generally *omok* or *obok* (-*m*- and -*b*- in intervocalic position are allophones of the same phoneme). The clan is sometimes known as *otok* in Kalmuk and *uruk* in Turkic. It is always a named group of common patrilineal descent from an eponymous ancestor, real or mythical. Descent from that ancestor is traced in reality or by a fiction through genealogies. The clan is composed of a series of ranked collateral lines. It occupies a common territory, maintains religious rites in common, and is ruled by a clan chief. By way of example, there is a list of clan chiefs of the Kazakh hordes by name, together with their rank, the names of their respective clans, the number of people in each clan, and the towns with which they habitually traded. This list was compiled in the year 1803 by a Tatar merchant, Shakhmuratov, serving as an agent for the Russian government.[24]

The veritable corporative structures had until recent decades a number of political functions: the clan was a unit of tax-collection, both in labor and in kind, and it was a unit of military levies, supplying a company or troop to the army of the prince. It distributed these various burdens among its component villages, and these in turn made exactions upon the extended families. The clan leader adjudicated disputes between villages or between families. Further than this the law did not go. The regulation of life within the family was left to the family itself; that is, settling of intra-family disputes was left to the patriarch; theft or adultery among family members was left to the family for punishment. Thus the smallest socio-legal unit, the smallest legal personality, was the extended family.

Systematic concepts of criminal law have not been fully worked out on the steppe, but to the extent that they were, the unit of responsibility for the crime of an individual was the family collectivity. Moreover, if an outsider suffered an injury within the domain of a given village and guilt could not be fixed, the village might collectively be liable for damages in any action. And a clan similarly could be held responsible if guilt could not be more precisely fixed. Punishment usually took the form of fines levied on the smallest unit accordingly determinable. In the case of murder or physical injury, a wergeld or blood-money was paid. The member of the family directly responsible paid the largest share, but close kin contributed also, and more distant kin as well, on a decreasing basis. The closest kin of the victim received the largest share, and more distant kin proportionally less.[25] Such a distribution of wergeld is described in early Irish law.

The units of legal responsibility—and, be it added, legal interest—correspond to the units of corporative structure. These are also the basic economic units and the political units. They are the extended family, the kin-village, and the clan. In contrast to these social structures, the unit of exogamy is an entity of an entirely different order. The unit determined by Fortes to be the embodiment of the corporative principle in Africa, the lineage, is in fact not the ideal embodiment of this principle on the Asiatic steppe. The corporative principle is somewhat different in details of its application between Africa and Asia. Nevertheless, the general theory of corporative kin groups of unilineal descent is equally well exemplified in the pastoral societies of Central and Inner Asia.

The interrelationship of political and consanguineal organization of the peoples of the steppe was alluded to in the controversy between Harmatta and Radloff. And again, the political and consanguineal elements are both to be found in Kalmuk society in Pallas's 18th century description.[26] The chief of the entire society was a supreme ruler or Khan. His domain was divided into four major divisions, and these in turn into a number of *uluses* or provinces at the head of each of which ruled a prince (*noyon*), over whom the Khan had little authority. The four major divisions (*oirat*) were actually the largest units where common descent was genealogically demonstrable. Each *ulus* was in turn divided into a number of *aimaks* over each of which ruled a *zaisang*. The Khan and the *noyons* and their immediate families comprised the higher nobility, the *zaisangs* the lower nobility. "Each *aimak* is divided according to pasture again into communities of ten to twelve tents which comprise a *khoton*. . . . There are officials over each *khoton* who owe obedience to the highest *zaisang* of their *aimak,* just as these obey the *noyon*. The *noyon* receives from his subjects a tithe of all stock annually." The *noyon* has the right of corporal punishment over his subjects, but not the right of death sentence. Each of the communities or *khotons* was composed of a number of closely related families; neighboring *khotons* in an *aimak* were more distantly related. In addition to the tax and adjudicative functions each of the units was subject to a troop levy.

Bergmann has corroborated Pallas's description. Between Pallas's day (1760s) and Bergmann's (1802–1803) a number of radical changes had taken place in Kalmuk life. For one thing, as many as half the Kalmuks had left their pasturage on the lower Volga to return to China early in 1771. Again, some of the Kalmuks had joined in the revolt of the Russian Pugachev against the Russian crown and some had allied with Russia to suppress the revolt. The Russians had deprived the remaining Kalmuks of the rank of Supreme Khan, and permitted retention only of the title of Vice-Khan. This title was now permanently lodged in one of the four major divisions, the Dörbet. After the Vice-Khan were the *taishi,* the highest nobility under the crown. The four major divisions were now divided into fourteen *uluses,* each with a prince (*noyon*) at the head. The *uluses* ranged in size from 6,000 to 10 to 15 tents or families. The entire system was more firmly tied to the authority of the Vice-Khan than it had been in Pallas's time; from each of the major divisions a fixed number of eight councillors (*zargachi*) were supplied who regulated the affairs of all Kalmukdom as well as the relations between the Khan and the *uluses.* In addition to the council of state the Khan had an indeterminate number of privy councillors (*tüshimel*). Taxes (*alba*) were levied in kind on two bases—according to the number of tents in a community, and according to the herds of the individual owners. As in Pallas, Bergmann has the *ulus* divided into *aimaks,* each *aimak* ruled by a *zaisang.* These *aimaks* were composed as a rule of 200 to 300 tents. Succession passed to the eldest son among all levels, low and high.[27]

Russian contact had reinforced briefly during the period of Bergmann's stay a political system which had been disintegrating during the 18th century. With intensification of Russian influence through agriculture, trade, and closer political surveillance, native political institutions collapsed, and the consanguineal system gradually transformed itself, so that by the 20th century it had changed into a system which Borisov and Aberle have noted. The unit of exogamy is now the village or neighborhood rather than the lineage; the tracing of descent lines was discontinued; a system of patronymics is now the basis for clan identification rather than genealogical trees. Collateral ranking of descent lines has likewise disappeared, for this system is incompatible with exclusive use of patronymics in clan identification. On the other hand, the Omaha cousin terminology continues in force (Aberle), and primogeniture governs the succession to leadership both in the family and in the clan. (Aberle has found that the first-born succession is no longer practiced by Kalmuks today.) The transition which the Kalmuks underwent during the 19th and early 20th centuries parallels the transition which the Monguor of Kansu, the Uzbeks, the Bashkirs, and many other erstwhile pastoralists have undergone in the process of sedentarization.

The problem of acculturation aside, the conjoint politico-agnatic categories used by Pallas and Bergmann to describe the Kalmuks are found among the Buryats, the Kazakhs, and, with important variations imposed by the Manchu political system, among the Mongols of Inner and Outer Mongolia during the same period, the 17th to 19th centuries. Each kinship structure—the extended family, the kin-village, the clan—was composed of a group of agnatic kin and their wives, concubines, and other adherents. Each kin unit was simultaneously part of a political system, performing political functions including the payment of taxes, judging and policing, raising an army, fighting wars; the territory of each state was defined and defended as well as possible. The Khan was surrounded by a court and courtiers, both lay and ecclesiastic.

The lowest of the nobility or the highest of the commoners were a group of men who had a special social position—those freed of tax—and who formed a separate descent group. While each individual descent line had a proper name of its own, this entire class of people was known as *darkhan* (plural *darkhat*), a term possibly of Persian origin which has the literal meaning of smith in Mongol. The *darkhat* are above the commoners (*albatu,* the tax-burdened, from *alban* tax), but are below the nobility in rank. Among the Buryats the *darkhat* form a separate descent line and a group of specialized religious function, in rank below the regular shaman-priest class, outside the lay social hierarchy. They propitiate a group of smith-spirits also known as *darkhat* from whom they are descended.

The manifest political structure of the various steppe societies may be now integrated with the theory of the corporative kin group. The corporative structure does not necessarily have a political form as we know it in Western society. Nevertheless there is an implicit political organization in the corporative kin group. It is defined as a group having a locus of authority, rules of membership, an internal structure, and a perpetual life. It is conceivable that such a group may be a flat structure, that is, that it does not form part of a hierarchy. Such a situation would be realized if the corporative groups in question were a number of extended unilineal families or kin-villages, each forming an exogamous unit, joined with other such units in a common territory and recognizing a common tribal name for all. This system is found among some of the Tien-Shan Kirgiz and the Turks of the Altai Mountains. Among the Kazakhs and the Mongols, however, the various named groups form part of a hierarchy extending from the corporative family to the confederation of clans, a horde, a principality. The hierarchized nature of the various kin groups among these latter of itself requires and calls forth a political being, in which the subordinated elements pay allegiance and owe obedience to the super-ordinated in the person of the head of the principality. Subordination and super-ordination, in turn, require a supreme locus of authority as the center of a system in which all other loci of authority take their places.

When Harmatta seeks for the conditions of the birth of the state in the dissolution of the tribal system he is pursuing an argument with the concept of unilinear evolution as the suppressed premise. The fact that on the steppes of Asia a system of states arose in a matrix formed by the continuing existence of a web of agnatic relationships is a special condition of the history of the societies of the steppes. In the ancient Near East, in the societies of classical antiquity, and feudal Europe, on the contrary, the fact of a primal consanguineous (unilineal) bond is of interest only genetically. The social structures of these societies during their florescence had no significant consanguineous structure. They were by then politico-territorial unities, not consanguineal.

Comparisons with Western institutions may bring out significant features of steppe society. In seeking to make meaningful to Western readers the polity of the Asiatic steppe, many writers have shown parallels between the European feudal regime and the nomadic. The retinue of the feudal lord has its parallel in that of the steppe prince; the division of society into nobility and commonalty is among the traits of social organization shared by both cultural worlds. Moreover, the feudal lords maintained a line of descent separate from the commoners: purity of birth is a basic feature of the European nobility. We have seen how the steppe nobility maintained itself as a separate lineage system, albeit within the framework of common descent of the entire society. However, feudal analogies may be stretched too far. First, the feudal lord had no distinction between his public and his private person: he was the private landowner and the public seigneur of his domain. Servile payments, both in kind and in corvée or labor service, were rent and tax combined. In the masterly summation of Maitland,[28] feudalism had no distinction between public and private law. The Mongol or Turkic princes on the other hand had a clear distinction between the public fiscus and their private wealth. They had their own herds and lands, and their own commoners to tend them. The commoners in direct service of the prince were known as *čaxar* in Classical Mongol according to Kotwicz.[29] These crown commoners lived on the herds of the prince or noble.

In exchange, they paid a private due or rent, both in kind and in labor-service, to the prince as a private person. There were other commoners, the ordinary *albatu,* who were not in the direct and permanent service of the prince. They paid taxes (*alban*) to the state under the authority of the prince, supplying a portion of their herds to the state herds, and performing corvée and military service. Both crown and public commoners were required to perform corvée in the post and communication system of the state, maintaining the horses in the communication system, and to serve as soldiers. The two categories of commoners and the two kinds of herds in the public and private treasuries were kept separate.

Second, the social bonds, the sources of social unity, are different in feudal Europe and on the Asiatic steppe. The feudal unit was an agnatic unit by origin but during the period of florescence, as we have noted, it was territorial. On the contrary, the Mongols traced a common male ancestry with their supreme Khan. The Kazakhs likewise, from the humblest to the highest, were all united by the common agnatic bond, that is, by descent from a common ancestor, *Alash*. Both these relations obtained at the beginning and during the flowering of the culture. The importance of the genealogies, their very length for the tracing of the bond, can thus be readily understood. The state system on the steppes is thus an anomaly insofar as it was founded among a series of peoples whose political structure was at the same time consanguineal. The anomaly is only a seeming one, however, because the corporative unilineal structure itself called forth the state system; that structure found its expression in the state. The society of the steppes is a consanguineal unity with which a politico-territorial unity was combined and interwoven. This consanguineal unity is missing in feudalism, or perhaps is not so important.

There are a number of other differences between feudalism and the nomad polity. The vassal idea, whereby the lord and his vassal were bound by a set of mutual obligations of fealty and support, is not found on the steppe. The pastoral Khan was an absolute ruler when he could find the military force to support him. And such ancillary feudal doctrines, such as "The vassal of my vassal is not my vassal" is missing on the steppes, for the Khan had in theory universal control. The theoretically absolute control by the Khan empowered him to raise a commoner to the nobility for valor in war or simply because he could write. On the other hand, the wergeld or blood-money for injury was practiced in both feudal Europe and the Asiatic steppe, and from time to time a theocracy has arisen in both areas. In sum, the feudal analogies are often suggestive and have a definite heuristic value. But the basic structural features of European feudalism and those of the steppe polities are different.

The collateral ranking of descent lines created the possibility for the division of the societies into social classes, nobles and commoners. On the one side, all men were brothers and cousins. On the other side, no man was his brother's equal. The first-born outranked his junior brothers; his line outranked the lines of his juniors. Out of this system of collateral ranking emerged the social cleavage within the common agnatic matrix. The kinship terminology is a sensitive expression of the social division. In all these societies, there is a term for older brother, *axa,* a term for older sister, *egeci,* and a term for younger sibling, *degü,* optionally further distinguished as to sex. Children of the Fa Br, the paternal parallel cousins, are similarly differentiated: Fa Br So senior to me is *üye axa;* Fa Br So junior to me is *üye degü,* etc. Fa Ol Br is *abaga;* Fa Yo Br is *axa,* the same term as Ol Br; thus there is generation up-grading. Wives similarly differentiate the husbands' brothers and husbands' paternal uncles according to seniority at the concomitant up-grading. Fathers so differentiate their sons and grandsons. Thus in the extended family, as well as in the society at large, no man has his social equal. Women marrying in are ranked according to the status of the husband and his line. The system thus delineated is the Classical Mongol system (13th to 17th centuries), which is found in one etymologically related variant or another everywhere on the steppes.[30]

The system of ranking by seniority of birth and up-grading by a generation those who are senior is found among the Finno-Ugrian peoples, who occupy the Eurasiatic forests north of the steppe. Among the Votyak, Cheremis, Mordvin, Lapps, etc., it is a characteristic that the siblings are differentiated by sex and seniority, and at the same time, the Fa Yo Br is called by the same term as the Ol Br, and the Fa Yo Si by the same term as the Ol Si.[31] One of the most interesting traits of the Finno-Ugrian system of kinship terminology is the strong emphasis on age-difference (*starke Betonung des Altersunterschieds*).[32]

The Altaic system of collateral ranking is not a timeless one, however. Unless there were an infinite number of gradations of the *aristoi,* eventually the cadet branches of the first-born line would lose their patent of nobility. But there was neither an infinite number of gradations nor did the lesser nobility lose their status. History enters into the picture. The line of primogeniture and those lines close to it formerly

had flowed imperceptibly into the lesser lines. As the result of an event at a given point in time they ceased to do so. The cleavage between the upper and the lower and the resulting division into the social classes took place on the occasion of a migration, a fusion of lineages, or a war. These recurring phenomena are part of the culture and history of the steppe; they are documented in the *Secret History of the Mongols,* in the history by Rashid-ed-Din, and by incipient developments in the 18th and 19th centuries among the Turks of the Altai Mountains and Kirgiz of the Tien-Shan range. These two latter groups were despised by their neighbors, the Kazakhs, because they lacked a hereditary nobility. The Kirgiz communities were ruled by a number of elective, non-hereditary *manaps.*[33] A *manap* would seek to bequeath his position to his son when he had gained a greater following through lineage fusion or through a successful raid, etc. To this limited extent, and only to this extent, is Radloff's view on usurpation justified. His view fails because it does not take cognizance of the total consanguineal matrix within which such a usurpation could take place, a matrix which developed among all the steppe peoples into a system of ranked collateral lines. The authority in the senior of these lines was as ephemeral among the Altai Mountain Turks and the Tien-Shan Kirgiz as it was in the empires of their neighbors.

The political state of the Asiatic steppes contained as a part of its structure the concept of social inequality, based on a consanguineal principle of ranking lines of descent. The corporative hierarchically ranked structure of the patrilines achieved political expression in the state.

NOTES

1. The existence of a vigorous discussion on the nature of a social structure in which Radcliffe-Brown, Murdock, Fortes, Evans-Pritchard, Lévi-Strauss and others have participated is a matter of which I am keenly aware. The discussion of basic conceptual schemes is beyond the scope of this paper; the terms and distinctions here proposed are offered as convenient *axiomata media* rather than as basic systematic thoughts.

2. Chokan Chingisovic, Valikhanov, *Sochineniia* [Works] (Zapiski, Imperatorskoe Russkoe Geograficheskoe Obschestvo, po otdeleniiu Etnografii, 1904), XXIX, 161–163, 286. Valikhanov, a Kazakh prince of mid-19th century, has expressed himself on the subject of principles of Kazakh organization as follows: "The very pattern of division upon which the rule of seniority and the power of a tribe rest and which in the mind of the Kirgiz [read Kazakh] is expressed by the law of physical primogeniture, has great significance in their law of descent and has a completely genealogical meaning; for which reason the form of relationship from horde to horde, and within the lineages of a horde among themselves, correspond to the law of blood [agnatic] kinship, and the relation of a lineage to its horde is the relation of a son to

a father in the case of the eldest line of the senior horde; and is the relation of nephew to [paternal] uncle above all in the case of the other line, characterizing this patriarchal clan life. . . ."

3. Korbe, 1951, pp. 71–72; *Secret History*, par. 1–60. Cf. the 54 generation genealogy given in Aristov, 1894; also Bogdanov, 1926, pp. 90–92.

4. P. Louis Schram, *Le mariage chez les T'ou-Jen de Kan-Sou (Chine)* (Variétés Sinologiques 1932), LVIII, 49.

5. Other circumstances under which the *baranta* was legal were: to collect a debt, a bride-wealth, and a wergeld or blood-money. Valikhanov, *op. cit.*, pp. 173–174; P. I. Nebol'sin, *Ocherki byta Kalmykov Khoshoutskago Ulusa* [Sketches of Kalmuk Life of the Khoshut Ulus] (Biblioteka dlia Chteniia, 1852, No. 113, Parts 5 and 6; No. 114, Part 1), Part 6, p. 129.

6. L. F. Balliuzek, *Narodnye obychai imevshie, a otchasti nyne imeiuschie, v Maloi Kirgizskoi Orde silu zakona* [Popular Customs which have had and in part still have the Force of Law among the Little Horde Kirgiz] (Zapiski Orenburgskago Otdela, Imperatorskoe Russkoe Geograficheskoe Obshchestvo, No. 2 [1871], pp. 45–167), p. 109.

7. N. P. Dyrenkova, *Brak, terminy rodstva i psikhicheskie zaprety u Kyrgyzov* [Marriage, Kinship Terms and Psychic Taboos among the Kirgiz] (Sbornik Etnograficheskikh Materialov, 1927, No. 2, pp. 7–25), II, 23.

8. N. Izraztsov, *Obychnoe Pravo ("Adat") Kirgizov Semirechinskoi Oblasti* [Customary Law ("Adat" of the Semirechinsk Kirgiz] (Etnograficheskoe Obozrenie, 1847, vol. IX, No. 3, pp. 67–99; No. 4, pp. 1–36), pp. 73–74.

9. N. I. Grodekov, *Kirgizy i Karakirgizy Syr-Dar'inskoi Oblasti* [Kirgiz and Karakirgiz of the Syr-Darya District] (Tashkent, 1889) p. 42.

10. Iakinf Bichurin, *Sobranie Svedenii o narodakh obitavshikh v Srednei Azii v drevnie Vremena* [Collections of Accounts of the Peoples Inhabiting Central Asia in Ancient Times] (Moscow-Leningrad, 2 vols., 1950 [first published 1851]), I, 230 (270).

11. B. E. Petri, *Territorial'noe Rodstvo u Severnykh Buriat* [Territorial Kinship among the Northern Buriat] (Irkutsk, 1924), p. 139; M. N. Khangalov, *Iuridicheskie Obychai u Buriat* [Juridical Customs of the Buryat] (Etnograficheskoe Obozrenie, 1894, VI, No. 2, pp. 100–142), p. 139; Izraztsov, *op. cit.*, pp. 68, 93.

12. Radloff, 1891, pp. lii–lv. For others, see below.

13. J. Harmatta, *The Dissolution of the Hun Empire* (Acta Archaeologica, Academia Scientarum Hungaricae, 1952, II, No. 4, pp. 277–304), pp. 283–284.

14. Chavannes, ed., *Documents sur les Tou-Kiue (Tures) Orientaux* (St. Petersburg, 1900), p. 26.

15. *Ibid.*, pp. 23, 48.

16. George Timkowski, *Travels of the Russian Mission through Mongolia to China in the Years 1820–1821*, translated with notes by Julius von Klaproth. 2 vols. (London, 1827), pp. 305–306.

17. A. P. Shchapov, *Buriatskaia ulusnaia rodovaia obshchina* [Uryat Ulus Kin Community] (Izvestiia Vostochno-Sibirskago Otdela, Imperatorskoe Russkoe Geograficheskoe Obshchestvo, 1874, V, Nos. 3–4, pp. 128–146).

18. Pozdneev, quoted in Riasanovsky, 137, pp. 212–213.

19. P. S. Pallas, *Reise durch Verschiedene Provinzen des Russichen Reiches*, 6 vols. (St. Petersburg, 1771).

20. Radloff, *op. cit.*, I, 513.

21. Petri, *op. cit.*, pp. 5–6, 11.

22. M. N. Bogdanov, *Ocherki Istorii Buriat-Mongol'skogo Naroda* [Historical Studies of the Buryat Mongol People] (Verkhneudinsk, 1926), pp. 90–97.

23. M. Fortes, "The Structure of Unilineal Descent Groups," *American Anthropologist*, LV (1953), 25 ff.

24. Antoine Mostaert, *Dictionnaire Ordos* (Monumenta Serica Monographs, no. 5, 1941–1944).

25. Izraztsov, *op. cit.*, pp. 12–14.

26. Pallas, *loc. cit.*

27. Benjamin Bergmann *Nomadische Streifereien unter den Kalmüken in den Jahren 1802 und 1803* (4 parts, Riga, 1804–1805), pp. 30–37.

28. F. W. Maitland, *The Constitutional History of England* (London, 1908), pp. 23–39.

29. Wiad Kotwicz, *Contributions à l'histoire de l'Asie Centrale* (Rocznik Orientalisticzny, 1949, XV, pp. 159–195), p. 168.

30. J. E. Kowalewski, *Dictionnaire Mongol-Russe-Français*, 3 vols. (Kasan, 1844–1849).

31. F. Ahlqvist, *Die Kulturwörter der Westfinnischen Sprachen* (see Harva, 1939), p. 211. Originally published 1875.

32. Uno Harva, *Der Bau des Verwandtschaftsnamensystems bei den Finnougriern* (Finnisch-Ugrische Forschungen, 1939, XXVI, Nos. 2–3, pp. 91–120).

33. Radloff, *op. cit.*, I, 533. For considerations on election of chiefs among the Altai Turks, cf. Potapov, p. 296. Potapov states that election there was, but from among a limited group of "aristocratic" lineages. Unfortunately, he has not documented his case. These "aristocratic" lineages are not true noble lines, rather descent groups of identical form, but of greater prestige than the others.

19

Social Typology and the Tropical Forest Civilizations[1]

Michael D. Coe

Introduction

Types of Solidarity and the Theory of Exchange

Probably the single most influential concept in the study of human society is the theory of solidarity proposed by Durkheim in his book *The Division of Labor*.[2] There are essentially two types of solidarity, and two kinds of society which correspond to these. Societies based on what he calls mechanical solidarity are relatively undifferentiated; if they are divided into segments (i.e., clans, etc.), these tend to be alike. The solidarity is one of likeness, and all the individuals within it are bound up under a single moral system which Durkheim terms the "collective conscience"; it is clear that he means by this the religion of the people. This unitary moral organization is expressed through laws which tend to be penal and repressive; that is, the religion is the all-pervading source of sanctions. Opposed to this are societies which are organized on the basis of organic solidarity. Here, what were formerly undifferentiated segments have now become organs: the division of labor has resulted in the differentiation of the constituent parts of the society, so that each is functionally dependent on the other. Religious sanctions have diminished, and law is generally restitutive rather than repressive.

Durkheim emphasized that these were polar social types and not likely to be found in extreme form anywhere in the world (although in our own time Nazi Germany would be the ideal mechanical society). Nevertheless, he maintained that there has been throughout history a definite evolutionary trend from the one to the other, beginning with the primitive, almost completely undifferentiated horde, through segmental societies which are nevertheless still mechanical, into truly organic societies based upon the division of labor.

The great contribution of his pupil Mauss was to demonstrate exactly how organic cohesion was brought about. In his cross-cultural study of prestation,[3] he demonstrated that the seemingly useless exchanges of gifts or competitive banquets in native societies (such as the *kula* of the Trobrianders or potlatch of the Northwest Coast tribes) actually play an overwhelmingly important role in these societies. That is, organic solidarity is brought about by the exchange of goods which often seem to us purely ceremonial rather than practical, but which serve to bind even distant peoples into a single system of reciprocity. Thus, exchange is the social glue itself, and is ultimately based on the division of labor; in its highest and most effective form it consists of large-scale trade.

> Societies have progressed in the measure in which they, their sub-groups and their members, have been able to stabilize their contracts and to give, receive and repay. In order to trade, man must first lay down his spear. When that is done he can succeed in exchanging goods and persons not only between clan and clan but between tribe and tribe and nation and nation, and above all between individuals.[4]

As Mauss above points out, this exchange can be in persons, and it is this kind of analysis which has been further carried out by Lévi-Strauss[5] who views society as ultimately based on the exchange of women between its constituent parts by a system of rules which is embodied in the kinship terminology.

The Typology of Early Civilizations

This argument can be extended in an attempt to throw light on problems in the typology of early civilizations. There is no satisfactory definition of

From Michael D. Coe, "Social Typology and the Tropical Forest Civilizations," *Comparative Studies in Society and History*, IV, No. 1 (1961), 65–85. Reprinted by permission of the publisher.

the word "civilization"; dictionary definitions tend to be completely value-loaded and ethnocentric (i.e., from "civilize . . . Bring out of barbarism, enlighten, refine," *Concise Oxford Dictionary*) and therefore are useless. Most scholars offer lists of criteria which can be used to distinguish such a kind of culture. Among these are usually writing, advanced political states, technologically sophisticated architecture and art styles, and cities.[6] In fact, the word has been largely associated with city-dwelling and is derived from it. A major problem is that there is now excellent evidence that many early cultures which possessed all of the other criteria of civilization (especially the one that seemed to Childe of outstanding importance, writing) seem to have been non-urban. Among these are the Maya, Khmer, Mycenaean, and pre-18th Dynasty Egyptian civilizations; more could perhaps be added. This immediately suggests that other factors may be involved in the rise of civilization than cheek-by-jowl contiguity with its accompanying intellectual stimulation. Among the causes of civilization no one would deny the outstanding importance of economic surplus, for otherwise the body of specialists who manufacture the goods and the administrators who direct the state would not be able to exist. The surplus cannot be everything, however, for Malinowski has given to us the instructive example of the uncivilized Trobrianders, with their heaps of surplus food left rotting in the fields.

It is suggested here that there are basically two kinds of early civilizations: *unilateral* (corresponding to Durkheim's mechanical, but using an alternate term proposed by him) and *organic*. These are polar types of social and economic organization, and are derived from the concepts of Durkheim and Mauss presented above.

This typology rests on a geographical base; that is, areas which are environmentally undifferentiated will tend to lack an early growth of urbanism, as opposed to regions which are divided into more or less strongly contrasted sub-areas. Large towns and cities almost always consist of dense populations of non-food producers, and, in particular, of persons engaged directly or indirectly in commerce or trade regulation (an exception might be made for the very atypical farming towns of some Mediterranean countries). These cannot exist unless the gross profits of urban activities are more than the cost of food; therefore, food must be raised and brought into the cities from the countryside cheaply, as exchange for the craft products sold there. Here there are two basic preconditions, of which the first is the most important: (1) a highly productive agricultural system *which is regionally differentiated,* and (2) adequate transportation. Poor transportation, such as one might find in excessively forested or hilly areas, would raise to a prohibitive level the price of food imported into the city, no matter how much was produced. However, unless the products of one sub-area are different from those of another, and this especially applies to kinds of basic food crops and to differences in harvest times, no trade at all will be found, or only minor commercial transactions in luxury products; this is the case with the unilateral civilizations.

Ultimately, both the degree of variation in food crops and the availability of easy transport are dependent upon ecological conditions such as climate, soils, topography, natural flora, etc. An area highly differentiated with good and cheap transportation available will favor interregional exchange and the growth of markets into true urban centers of full-time mercantile specialists. It is this kind of development which Sanders,[7] in a discussion of the Mexican Highlands, has labeled "symbiotic," and which Durkheim would have called organic. When a number of specialized regions are bound up in a symbiotic interdependence, within which are found mercantile urban centers, the seeds are present for the growth of higher forms of the state. In fact, in combination with other factors as control systems arising from the irrigation or drainage of agricultural land, the foundations may be laid for imperial expansion. Thus, organic civilizations are characterized by true cities and by advanced political hierarchies.

In contrast, undifferentiated areas, which are usually in the inner lowland regions of the world, tend to produce the same crops throughout. An area which produces maize and beans in one part and the same in another, with no spacing of growing season or harvest time, is unlikely to develop much interest in trade. If such an area also has a poorly developed communication system, lacking good roads or waterways, there would be neither the incentive nor the opportunity for the concentration of commercial specialists into cities. This system would be self-maintaining, for peoples with nothing to exchange have little interest in perfecting roads or using waterways, as will be shown later. Civilizations without cities are here classified together as unilateral, and are confined to such areas.

These social types are accompanied by significant variation in socio-political organization. The unilateral civilizations are not unorganized; in fact, Durkheim[8] pointed out that a high degree of political centralization may accompany mechanical solidarity, for while there is a division of labor in one sense, the ruler's or chief's relations with his subjects are *unilateral*. It is a simple step from the segmented society exercising communal rights over property to the transferral of these rights to the person who directs the society and remains above it; the religious sanctions of mechanical solidarity are unchanged. In a unilateral civilization, each respective area was organized directly (unilaterally) into the support by tribute or corvée labor of a royal and/or religious cult as represented by the growth of non-urban ceremonial centers. In contrast, the organic civilizations were characterized by urban concentrations of merchants and administrators, surrounded by peasant farmers, and organized into a state in which the most rich and powerful of a number of crystallizing social classes selected or controlled the ruler. Of these classes, the merchant group was often the most influential because of its economic position. Tribute and corvée labor were exacted only from subject peoples.

Tropical Forest Civilizations

For many years the puzzling resemblances between the two great tropical forest civilizations known to history, the Classic Khmer of the Angkor Period (802–1431 A.D.) and the Classic Maya (ca. 300–900 A.D., according to the Thompson correlation), have stimulated both professionals and amateurs to postulate direct trans-Pacific connections between them. Most recently, Heine-Geldern and Ekholm[9] have collaborated in a new attempt to account for these resemblances by arguing for a long-term diffusion of cultural elements out of Southeast Asia and across the Pacific to the New World. As it is well established that aboriginal American navigation, with the exception of that of coastal Peru and Ecuador, was too poorly developed for long voyages across oceans, this traffic has been pictured as one-way, from west to east. If one accepts this hypothesis, Maya architecture of the Classic Period would be at least in part a derivative of the Khmer temple and "palace." The theory is intriguing, but contains one flaw which demolishes the whole structure: that is, under either of the two Maya-Christian calendar correlations accepted today (that of Spinden or that of Thompson), the Classic Maya development reached its peak at least two centuries *before* the construction of any of the Khmer buildings supposedly antecedent to it. For instance, the little pyramid-temple of Baksei Chamrong at Angkor, which so resembles the gigantic pyramid-temples of Tikal in the Maya area, was dedicated in 947 A.D., *after* the collapse of Classic Maya civilization. One

would be forced to argue for east to west diffusion, which we know would have been extremely unlikely due to the simplicity of Maya navigation.

The continued and so far fruitless insistence on actual connections between the Cambodian and Mesoamerican civilizations has obscured what is of greater scientific interest in this subject, namely, the important analogy that may be investigated here. Regardless of their ultimate origins (for we know that much of Khmer culture was imported from India, and many Classic Maya traits from the Olmec region), unquestionably the Khmer Empire and the Classic Maya civilization were the highest cultures ever developed in the tropics. They both arose under natural conditions which were almost the same: relatively flat, low, inland plains, heavily forested, with high temperatures and an annual monsoon cycle. With the environment held constant, within approximately the same span of elapsed time both Khmer and Maya evolved remarkably similar cultural forms and ultimately completed this span by abandoning what they had created and withdrawing to a small portion of their once great lands.

With such regularities in cultural form and natural environment, the foundations are laid for a comparative study of tropical forest civilizations (one that might be extended to the lesser civilizations of early West Africa, when these are better known). It is impossible at the present time to account satisfactorily for the remarkable similarity of Khmer and Maya art and architecture; while it is undoubtedly the result of convergence, even this must be explained. However, as will be shown here, both had identical settlement patterns, being without true cities, and apparently both had the same form of socio-political organization. Both were unilateral civilizations. It is the purpose of this paper to examine the evidence for the factors behind such similarities, and to contrast this social type with known organic civilizations.

Settlement Patterns

Cambodia and the Classic Khmer

In treating the mode of settlement of ancient Cambodia, one must distinguish between the early kingdom of the Funan Period (1st century A.D. to the middle of the 6th century), which was centered on the coast of Indo-China, and the subsequent states of the Chenla (middle of the 6th century to 802 A.D.) and Angkor Periods, which were located in inland Cambodia. Funan, as described by the Chinese sources, was a maritime kingdom situated on the main trade route between India and China. Apparently sizable urban clusters of pile houses grew up along the coast; at one dependency of Funan, strategically located at the trans-shipment point of the Malay Peninsula, the *Liang-shu* describes a city of 10,000 persons daily engaged in commerce.[10]

The inland Chenla kingdom, from what we know of the Angkor Period which followed it, was probably non-urban in character. We find in this period a custom which becomes characteristic of Cambodia in later centuries, namely, the creation of a new capital by a king on his accession to the throne, with the frequent abandonment of the earlier capital. Such high-handed transferals could never have involved long-established mercantile urban centers, which necessarily would have been located, as were those of early Funan, on strategic trade routes. Ma Tuan-lin describes the 7th century capital of Isanapura as a city with more than 20,000 families, with more than 30 other cities, each with its own governor. However, Briggs states: "The 'cities' and their surrounding territories were doubtless the provinces into which the kingdom was divided."[11]

The process of the creation of new capitals and abandonment of the old ones can best be seen in the Angkor, or Classic, Period. The great capital of Yasodharapura was laid out by Yasovarman I at Angkor and dedicated in 893 A.D. The levees of earth which surround it enclose no less than 16 square kilometers. Notwithstanding the huge size and apparent importance of this "city," an inscription of Rajendravarman II, who came to the throne in 944 A.D., states: "He restored the holy city of Yasodharapura, long deserted, and rendered it superb and charming by erecting there houses ornamented with shining gold, palaces glittering with precious stones."[12] In an interval of what cannot have been much more than sixty years, a capital was built and dedicated, then deserted when a new royal center was constructed at Chok Gargyar, 100 miles north and east of Angkor, by Jayavarman IV, and finally the latter was in turn abandoned when the original capital was rebuilt and rededicated. How could a capital be abandoned so rapidly and set up elsewhere unless it was not truly a city? When the capital of the early United States was shifted from New York to Philadelphia and then to Washington, the two former were not deserted, because they were also urban mercantile centers. Only a ruler and his court could move with such impunity, and that is exactly what seems to have happened, since the Khmer capital was solely the cult center of the Khmer Empire, wherein resided the king, his court and retinue, and all the other persons necessary to maintain the royal cult and administer the country.[13]

The priest-king of the Khmer Empire was the intermediary between his royal ancestors and his realm. The royal cult centered on his *devaraja,* a stone lingam housed in a great temple-mausoleum which on his death became a temple dedicated to the worship of one who was now God-King. Some of the most important Khmer monuments were thus not palaces or even temples in the ordinary sense of the word, but rather what Coedès[14] calls "funerary temples." Such great complexes as Angkor Wat and the Bayon of Angkor Thom would have been constructed for such purposes. In fact, the bulk of the stone architecture at a site like Angkor consisted not of civil but religious architecture, constructed by corvée labor, and dedicated to the royal cult. These cult centers were commissioned by each king on his accession to power to house his own *devaraja,* and his ashes at death.[15] These sacred "cities" were microcosms of the divine world: the central structure, with its characteristic five towers on a central pyramid, represented the holy Mount Meru, the center of the universe; the surrounding walls were the rock wall which enclosed the universe; and the water-filled ditch bounding all was the great ocean.[16]

Like the rulers of Cambodia today, the king and his court did not reside in any of these stone edifices, but in a palace of wood roofed with tiles. Our best source on Cambodia, Chou Ta-kuan,[17] who was commercial attaché in a Chinese embassy which arrived in Angkor in 1296 A.D., relates that the king had 1,000 to 2,000 servants and 3,000 to 5,000 girls and concubines. The nobility lived within the city and were entitled to tile roofs. There was a group of merchants, probably (from other evidence) largely foreigners. Moreover, each of the great temples had its own priests, retainers, and dancers.

From such a description of Angkor in the late 13th century, it can be inferred that this was essentially a royal cult center from which the country was administered. This does not mean that there were not several thousand people within its walls, for as we have seen, cult and administration demanded many officials and retainers. However, compared to truly urban centers of similar area, its actual population density was probably pitifully low. The original cult center of Angkor, the Yasodharapura of Yasovarman I, enclosed a very large area, with the temple housing the *devaraja* on the summit of the natural hill known as the Phnom Bakheng at its center. While axial avenues radiate to the four points of the compass, the "city" was probably, as Briggs suggests, "largely an agglomeration of villages and markets, interspersed with rice fields."[18] Around the base of the central hill and along both sides of the avenues are heaps of pottery and tile, indicating former houses, but probably of the several thousand persons engaged in the maintenance of the royal establishment. With the royal cult centers of such a nature, it hardly seems surprising that Khmer kings could shift their capitals with such ease. Similar transferals may have been more difficult in the earlier and urban Funan Period.

Chou Ta-kuan states that there were ninety provincial capitals, each with its surrounding wooden palisade and each with its own "mandarin." It would appear that these capitals were smaller editions of the great cult and administrative centers. The mass of the Khmer population were rice farmers and lived in thousands of small villages throughout the Cambodian countryside. From certain Khmer inscriptions, especially those dedicating temples, it is apparent that many, if not most, villages were grouped together administratively as ecclesiastical properties belonging by spiritual tenure (or frank-almoign) to the great temples of the central and provincial capitals. The temple of the Ta Prohm group at Angkor was granted by its charter 3,140 villages for its support; the total number in its service was 79,365 persons. Prah Khan, another group at Angkor, was inaugurated in 1191 A.D. and had 5,324 villages and a total of 97,840 persons available as food producers and corvée labor. By 1191, there were 306,372 persons living in 13,500 villages devoted to the support of the Khmer temples and their cults.[19] This figure surely must have represented a large part of the adult Khmer population at that time.

How so much land came to be ecclesiastical is a problem. The king seems to have been originally sole land owner. By the Angkor Period, some estates were in the hands of nobles who had received grants from the king. It appears to have been the king himself who gave lands to temples and monasteries. However, nobles might and did give in their turn some of their royal grant lands to the same beneficiary.[20] The process was so accelerated that almost all lands seem to have been tied up in spiritual tenure.

The Khmer center of the Angkor Period was, then, not a city with a dense mercantile population, but the locus of royal administration and royal cult. Through a strong bureaucratic system operating from the provincial capitals, all of Cambodia was organized into a kind of machine for the support by rice and corvée labor of the cult centers. With the king and the royal family at the summit, then the nobles and priests, with the mass of the village people

below, it may have been that rare phenomenon, a truly pyramidal society. At any rate, this is what is meant by the phrase "unilateral civilization."

The Classic Maya

Lacking either eye-witness reports or decipherable inscriptions, we are forced to rely solely upon archaeological field reports for our knowledge of the settlement pattern of the Classic Maya. By the time that the first reliable accounts of the Maya were written, by the Spaniards and Hispanicized Maya after the Conquest, the natives of the Yucatan peninsula had obviously passed through a long period in which they had been heavily influenced by invaders and immigrants from the Mexican Highlands. This influence is particularly shown by the late urbanization known to have taken place in Yucatan.

In the Classic Period, we know of well over a hundred important architectural clusters (noncommittally termed "sites" by the archaeologists) scattered through the Maya Lowlands; Morley[21] lists 116, but there must be many more awaiting discovery. If even smaller sites were included, the list would undoubtedly run into several thousand. The larger and more impressive of these sites, such as Tikal, Copan, or Uxmal, have a considerable amount of standing stone architecture, which includes tall temple-pyramids, multi-chambered structures called "palaces," long buildings with rows of rooms resembling cloisters, courts for the ceremonial ball game, and sweat baths. These structures, especially the temple-pyramids, are usually arranged around courts or plazas; the so-called "palaces" often have interior courts.

What were all these buildings used for? With a few exceptions, such as the ball-court and the sweat bath, we are still ignorant of this point. The "palaces," as has often been pointed out, would make particularly cramped, dark, and damp quarters for a king, prince, noble, priest, or whoever ruled the Classic Maya. Moreover, it is a reasonable assumption from the many palace and temple substructures which enclose elaborate tombs, that many or most of the great structures found at any one Maya site were built, like those of Angkor, to house the remains of a ruler on his death. This has been demonstrated by the exciting discovery by Alberto Ruz L. at Palenque that the Temple of the Inscriptions at that site was actually a cenotaph constructed, like the pyramids of Egypt, by a king or prince so that he might lie in funeral luxury within it on his decease. Many other similar findings in the Maya area point to the same practice.[22] From this, one can infer the existence of more powerful political authority at the head of the Maya social order than has yet been assumed by writers on this question—perhaps even absolute kings. The initial function of such temples as tombs does not necessarily mean that all ceremonies after the dedication were solely for the royal cult; these and other buildings were surely used for all the highly elaborate rituals of which we have hints from the Bonampak murals and occasional graffiti found on the inner walls of temple rooms. Some of the more complex "palaces" may have housed religious orders or served as temporary retreats; they were certainly not built for comfort, however. The ruler, himself, as in Cambodia, may have lived in a wooden palace.

Morley[23] always referred to sites as "cities," but were they? The Maya of the Classic Period built their houses on low mounds, to raise them above the ground during the heavy tropical rains of the summer. A count of the house mounds within, near, and away from a site should give a clear picture of the settlement pattern: whether this was or was not an urban center with a concentrated domestic population. Yet, it is surprising, considering the intensive nature of Maya exploration and excavation in the last fifty years, how seldom this has been done. There are published reports of only two such investigations so far, that undertaken by the Carnegie Institution at Uaxactun in the Peten,[24] and the recent Peabody Museum field program at Barton Ramie, on the Belize River in British Honduras.[25]

At Uaxactun, two strips each 400 yards wide and one mile long, meeting in the form of a great cross with one of its arms penetrating part of the ceremonial center, were carefully surveyed. While some of the land, being low-lying and therefore swampy in the rainy season, is uninhabitable, only 78 house ruins were found in an area which, Brainerd[26] points out, is known to have been inhabited for over a thousand years. No house mounds were discovered among the ceremonial sections of Uaxactun proper.[27] As one would suspect, much of the debate over the urban or non-urban character of Maya settlement arises from different ideas about what is and what is not a city. Under no definition could Uaxactun, given the above evidence, have been a true city. Excluding the areas taken up by the ceremonial precincts and by uninhabitable land, Ricketson made calculations of the density of population at Uaxactun. Assuming 5 persons for each house mound and that all the mounds were simultaneously occupied, he reaches a density figure of 1,083.35 persons per square mile; if, as seems more likely, only a fourth of the house mounds were in use at the same time,

then the density was 270.83 persons per square mile. Ricketson then compares this latter figure with population densities of the *states* of New York and Rhode Island, instead of cities within them. The 1958 population density of a city for which I have the figures at hand, Knoxville, Tennessee, is 4,696 persons per square mile, and that is not excluding business centers, parks, playgrounds, bodies of water, and other "uninhabitable" land, the subtraction of which from the area would bring the figure much higher. Furthermore, while domestic refuse is found at Uaxactun, the excavators, in spite of long search, could find but one midden of any size at the site, a sure indication of a very low population.

The Barton Ramie evidence[28] shows a greater density of population in what was a village region away from any large centers than does Uaxactun itself. House mounds are clustered into hamlets and villages, spread out "ribbon-wise" along the river. In a mile square area were found 264 house mounds, but as some such crop as cacao may have stimulated a higher population density, the situation is somewhat atypical for the Maya Lowlands. The nearest center of any size is Baking Pot, which is of the most minor size compared to Uaxactun.

Generally, house mounds in the Maya Lowlands are grouped together, often three around a tiny court, like the house and outbuildings (kitchens, etc.) of the modern Yucatan Maya. William Bullard, who has recently completed a survey of settlement patterns of the Classic Period sites of the eastern Peten, reports that clusters of these house mound groups are found distributed almost continuously throughout the entire area, especially where *bajos* (low areas which fill with water during the rainy season) are nearby.[29] Similar conclusions were drawn by P. W. Schufeldt,[30] after years of Peten exploration.

Available evidence, then, indicates a scattered rural population throughout the Maya Lowlands in Classic times, with larger agglomerations in more favorable areas such as alluvial bottomlands. Cities were lacking, but large ceremonial centers, perhaps in part royal cult centers, were undoubtedly supported by maize and corvée labor supplied by these hamlets and villages. The hierarchy of ceremonial centers descended down to the smallest settlement, as shown by the Barton Ramie expedition and other research in British Honduras, so that even villages had their own local centers to which they owed allegiance; these villages surely were beholden to pay tribute in the form of food and work to one of the larger centers, also, possibly even to Uaxactun or Tikal. Tikal itself may have been the capital, where ruled a powerful king, with lesser sites like Uaxactun, Copan, and Palenque as provincial centers, each with its own governor. This is largely inference, but seems supported by the admittedly meager archaeological data available. What is certain is that the settlement pattern of the Classic Maya was analogous to that of the Khmer of the Angkor Period in that it was non-urban, with cult centers drawing on the support of a large rural population. In this sense, Maya civilization can also be said to have been organized on a unilateral basis.

Environment and Economy

Cambodia

The Khmer civilization arose in the area of the lower Mekong River, one of the great Asian fluvial systems, in the present state of Cambodia (the ancient Kambuja). Although in its upper reaches the Mekong is a deep-valley torrent, in Cambodia it flows gently over a fairly low plain, annually covering large parts of it with rich silts. An important part of this drainage system is the Tonle Sap, or Great Lake, a huge inland body of water which floods over in the rainy season, a phenomenon due in part to the backing up of its outlet to the Mekong. The Tonle Sap is a vital part of the country's economy. At the mouth of the Mekong there has been built up in relatively recent times a large delta which has only been of economic importance since the introduction of drainage and reclamation techniques. Malaria is fortunately rare in the Cambodian lowlands but is virulent in the highlands to the west, north, and east.

Cambodia, which has an annual temperature of about 80 degrees Fahrenheit, lies in the monsoon belt and therefore has strongly marked seasonal changes. While most of the area receives 40 to 60 inches of rain annually, a large part of this falls in the wet season, from June to October; this, by the way, is not a particularly high amount of precipitation for the tropics. The natural vegetation reflects these factors of soil and precipitation, and while the tree cover is both dense and high, this is not a true tropical rain forest but a monsoon forest, in which many of the trees lose their leaves in the dry season. Throughout the region are scattered fairly large savannahs. In general, the Cambodian lowlands present an environment highly suitable for the raising of tropical cereal crops, especially (with water available for irrigation) rice.

Since ancient times rice cultivation has been the principal form of livelihood for the inhabitants of Cambodia. Just as today, irrigation was carried on by somewhat primitive methods during the Angkor Period, although some large reservoirs like those of Chok Gargyar[31] were probably available. Throughout Cambodia, excluding the Delta, there is but one rice harvest, in autumn at the end of the rainy season, although a dry season crop may be produced in poor years.[32] In the actual area occupied by the Khmer during the Angkor Period, then, there was but one main crop which was grown wherever feasible (that is, with the exclusion of savannahs). This had a single uniform harvest time.

The importance of the Tonle Sap in the modern economy of Cambodia cannot be overrated. The lake is not deeper than 6 feet in the dry season and has an area of about 1,000 square miles; during the high waters of June to October, the area may be as much as 4,000 square miles.[33] Low water during the dry season concentrates an incredible number of fish in the lake, and in the winter and spring fishing season today about 30,000 people gather on the banks of the Tonle Sap. The intensity of fish production in the Tonle Sap is the highest in the world, the volume for a given surface area being ten times that of the North Atlantic or North Sea.[34] That these natural sources of protein were taken advantage of by the ancient Khmer is a certainty from the representations in the Bayon reliefs of lakes filled with fish and market scenes of fishmongers.

At all times, even in this century, Cambodia has had great transportation difficulties. The country has been effectively blocked until recently from intensive communication with the lands to the west, north, and east by the rough terrain of the highlands and the malaria which is endemic in those regions. Moreover, land transport in the Cambodian lowlands is obstructed by a difficult climate and thick forests. It is no wonder, then, that before the arrival of the French, waterways were the principal means of transportation. However, on many rivers, like the waterway between the Tonle Sap and the Mekong, which is choked with sediments, navigation is only feasible in high water.

The basic reason why Cambodia has had such poor communications is not the difficulty of the environment, but the almost total lack of incentive to trade. As a recent handbook for Indo-China perceptively states: "The greatest obstacle to interregional traffic has been the existence of rice culture in nearly all parts of the country, so that exchange of goods on a large scale has not developed."[35] Groslier[36] notes that the Khmer disinterest in trade goes back to the beginning of their history. Even in early times, what trade there was seems to have been entirely in Chinese hands; for instance, the merchants sent in the 5th century by Jayavarman Kaundinya to Canton were probably themselves Chinese.

The Khmer were in quest of needed products not found on their soil, and these were brought by the Chinese. The list given by Chou Ta-kuan for 13th century Angkor shows that these were all luxury products, including such items as lacquer dishes from Wenchou, umbrellas, blue Ch'uanchou porcelain, mercury, iris roots; Chinese gold and mottled silk were also sought by the Khmer.[37] Chou states that they really desired above all else wheat and broad-beans, but China had prohibited export of these. It is interesting to speculate what changes might have been made in the Khmer settlement pattern if such large-scale trade in agricultural products had been permitted. In their turn, the Khmer exported for the Chinese trade fisher-martin feathers, which were the most precious of all their products, rhinoceros horn, beeswax, and other luxuries of the Cambodian tropics. Notwithstanding the influence of Chinese merchants, money was not of great importance in internal trade, for, according to Chou, the Khmer for most transactions paid in rice, Chinese objects, other cereals, and cloth, in that order of importance. Only for large transactions did they pay in gold and silver. An 11th century text enumerates even she-goats, cattle, and buffalo as "money."[38]

The final disposition of these imported products is of interest. Groslier[39] cites a stela of Ta Prohm (late 12th century) which lists the following offerings to the divinities: 45 cloth veils from China, 967 more Chinese veils, 20 Chinese beds, 25 Chinese textiles of unspecified nature. Although much may have been taken up by the king, and ruling classes, some of this luxury was consumed in the ecclesiastical system.

Perhaps the fish crop, in dried form, of the Tonle Sap qualified as a major item in inter-regional trade of the Angkor Period. Today, however, all this trade is under Chinese control. The market fish depicted in the Bayon reliefs is clearly fresh; the trade in the dried variety is apparently a development by Chinese merchants which has remained in Chinese hands. It seems likely that the Tonle Sap fishing industry during the Angkor Period was for the benefit of only settlements and cult centers near the lake.

Ancient Cambodia was a broad lowland with essentially a single food crop which was harvested everywhere at the same time. Transportation is and was difficult. The combination of poor communication possibilities with a single crop which was growing throughout the area and so did not need to be transported anywhere (excepting, of course, temple rice which came in from the hinterlands) ruled out the possibilities of any widespread interregional trade.

The Maya Lowlands

The lowlands of the Department of Peten, in northern Guatemala, and the Yucatan peninsula were the region in which developed the Classic Maya civilization. The area presents, in spite of radically different drainage patterns, a rather similar environmental picture to that of Cambodia. It is an immense limestone formation of generally low and usually even flat relief. Tropical conditions have produced in some places a very rough karst topography, particularly in the south at the base of the Guatemalan Highlands (which forms a very effective barrier, even today, to penetration of the Peten from the Highlands). To the north, in Yucatan, rainfall and the water table have developed underground caverns and cenotes (natural wells), which are often the only source of water there. The only true drainage in the area consists of the river systems to the west and east of the Peten; these have in some cases formed flood plains, and in other instances deep ravines. The soils of the Peten and Yucatan are tropical, somewhat leached, of extraordinary thinness in some parts, but relatively fertile for a slash-and-burn farmer.

Temperature and rainfall are quite similar to those of Cambodia. The thermometer in the Peten remains around 80 degrees Fahrenheit the year round. Precipitation is monsoonal, most of it in the rainy season from May to November; actually the rains have two peaks within this season, one in May and the other in September. At the Paso Caballo station in the Peten, an average annual rainfall of about 70 inches was recorded over a ten-year period.[40] However, there are serious fluctuations in the precipitation pattern, and severe droughts have been known, with lasting effects upon the livelihood of the inhabitants. Like that of Cambodia, the forest cover of the Maya Lowlands is of the monsoon type, with many deciduous species which drop their leaves in the winter dry season. As one travels north toward the Yucatan peninsula, the rainfall gradually lessens, and the forest height decreases accordingly; in the northern part of the State of Yucatan there is only a dense scrub thicket for cover. Nevertheless, rainfall seasons are essentially the same for all parts of the Maya Lowlands, an important factor in the synchronization of harvest time.

As in all of Mesoamerica, the great food crop was maize, with various kinds of beans, cucurbits, and peppers also supplementing the diet. The importance of maize is reflected in both the art and the religion of the Classic Maya. It was and still is grown in all places where there are people, even in the back yards of modern cities. The agricultural technique was slash-and-burn: cutting down a patch of forest, letting it dry, burning it, then planting the seed with a digging stick. While the present-day Maya of Yucatan must shift to a new clearing after two years, farmers farther south in the Peten have the advantage of up to 8 or 10 years or even longer of soil fertility in any one field. It is important here to emphasize that the Classic Maya had a basic food crop which could be grown where it was needed; and also that because of the synchronization of the seasons throughout the area, the time of maturation of this crop is always the same—September and October.[41]

We have little information on ancient Maya transportation routes. Nevertheless, there is one outstanding factor which made pre-Spanish land traffic difficult: the total lack of beasts of burden. Either one transported goods via bodies of water in canoes, or else put the load on one's back. We do know from the Aztec tribute list (Codex Mendocino) that considerable quantities of material were carried into Mexico City from all over the Empire via human beasts of burden. Similar information is available for the latest period in Yucatan. The topography and forest cover of the Maya Lowlands (the country looks flat only to those who have never traveled through it) would not have been easy for foot transport. With a few exceptions, the waterways of the area would not have been promising, as most of the so-called rivers of the Peten dry up in the winter. Only the Usumacinta drainage to the west and the Belize River to the east would have eased the transportation problem.

Most important of all would have been the universal prevalence of the same economically important commodities, such as maize and beans. By the time of the Conquest, cacao had considerable importance as a commercial product, from Mexico to Honduras. This could be grown only in places that had a good supply of ground water, in particular alluvial valleys and plains. It is obvious from this that some regions could grow it, like the Usumacinta plain, and others could not. The question is, can the cacao trade be pushed back as far as the Classic Period? There is little evidence in Maya art of the time of any preoccupation with cacao or its production. We cannot say that there was no cacao trade, but there are really no data on one side or the other. In late times, there is also information available on a fairly intense coast-wise trade (but probably of less

economic significance than the "secondary" trade carried on by a primitive people like the Trobrianders) around the Yucatan peninsula by boat, as shown by the boatload of Maya traders met by Columbus off Honduras, with their cargo of cotton mantles, cacao, copper objects, and flint-edged wooden swords.[42] In spite of this and what Landa says about the love of the Maya for trading, commerce in this area does not seem to have ever progressed beyond the level of peddling and may really have no roots at all in the Classic Maya Period. After all, these people had been under Mexican influence for perhaps as long as 600 years before the arrival of the Spaniards.

Archaeologically, one can say very little on the subject. The environment has destroyed all but imperishable objects. What has struck all investigators, however, is the rarity in Classic Maya offerings, caches, tombs, and refuse of anything known to have come from outside the Maya Lowlands. Furthermore, lowland Maya manufactures are practically unknown at other sites: a few bowls in the Guatemalan Highlands, a mother-of-pearl plaque from Tula in the Mexican Highlands, and a few other instances. This is in strong contrast to the far-flung dispersal of highland Mexican products over the entire Mexican realm in Classic and Post-Classic times (for instance, the very widespread occurrence of Teotihuacan pottery in the Early Classic Period). One can only interpret this as a lack of interest in trade on the part of the Classic Maya.

In summary, the Maya Lowlands were, like Cambodia, characterized by a single, universally distributed crop of importance which matured everywhere at the same time. The incentive was lacking for large-scale trade, and the archaeology suggests that such trade was not practiced.

Discussion

Strikingly different from the two unilateral civilizations above described are early organic civilizations. In Mesoamerica, several areas, usually in the uplands, had strongly developed city life based on a foundation of highly varied ecological sub-areas; these organic civilizations were characterized by advanced political administrations which were made even more complex through systematic conquest.

Palerm[43] shows that Totonacapan in central Vera Cruz had four large population clusters which were true cities; one of these, Cempoala, had 80,000 to 120,000 inhabitants. The neighboring zone of Papantla had only scattered rural settlements under the control of a ceremonial center in which lived the king and his court. Totonacapan is hot and dry, forming a sharp contrast to the neighboring tropical forests. While Papantla is more mountainous, it is an area characterized by an undifferentiated, hot, and humid rain forest. Even though Palerm interprets the urbanization of Totonacapan as the result of irrigation (which is largely hypothetical anywhere in Mesoamerica in pre-Spanish times), he states: "Urban development may also have been stimulated through trade with the very distinct natural regions nearby, the proximity of the sea and the availability of water transport."[44] Here lies the crux of the matter. This zone was itself part of a larger area which was differentiated into strongly contrasting regions; between these arose a heavy trade in commodities, for instance maize, which would have had staggered growing seasons. With the availability in Totonacapan of good transportation, large urban conglomerations of persons were enabled to form; these were engaged in manufacture and commerce, and could rely on adequate and cheap food for their support.

The Valley of Mexico presents one of the best documented cases of urbanization resulting from organic interdependence of strongly contrasted natural regions. Central Mexico is a "region of complex internal microgeography and intricate zoning of natural products,"[45] in which "all communities were interlocked into a tight trading system based on periodic markets and formalized exchange. . . . It is safe to say that no community was truly self-sufficient."[46] Such exchange included the truck-garden crops of Chalco-Xochimilco, maize from areas differentiated by non-synchronic harvests, and so forth; that is, it was truly a heavy trade. Transportation was greatly facilitated by the water route of the great lake (unlike the Tonle Sap of Cambodia which, because of its huge annual fluctuations, was unsuitable for water traffic). With such opportunities for trade and the cheap transport of food, it is no surprise that urbanization in the Valley goes back to the Classic Period, as shown at the site of Teotihuacan which shows evidence of having been a center of commerce in the Early Classic Period.[47] The capital of the Aztec Empire, Tenochtitlan, was urban in every sense of the word. It was a large city of priests, politicians, artisans, and traders. Irrigation may have contributed to urbanism in the Valley of Mexico, but the evidence indicates that such concentrations of full-time merchant specialists were a function of large-scale trade resulting from regional differentiation of products and ease of transportation. In the Durkheimian sense, the urban civilizations of the Mexican Highlands were organic.

The simple one-to-one correlation of large agricultural surplus with urbanization has been overplayed. Production figures available for Cambodia and the Maya Lowlands imply that those regions also had more than subsistence economies during the Classic civilizations. Every year Cambodia exports large quantities of rice, in contrast to many other countries of East and Southeast Asia. This is possible not because of high land productivity (in fact, it is low for wet rice culture), but because the density of population is sufficiently low. In the Cambodian rice lands, the number of persons per square mile varies from 50 to 400; the figure is over 1,000 per square mile in some parts of the Tonkin delta, which has little or no surplus in spite of better and more intensive cultivation.[48] Modern Yucatan produces a maize surplus which in part is taken up by the requirements of the modern system of sisal production and the urban development stimulated by it. Some of this surplus is available for export, however. This is a result of the high annual yield of the average Maya cornfield, in combination with a low population density. The modern Maya household, including livestock, consumes on the average a total of 64 bushels of shelled maize per year, but produces 168 bushels, leaving a surplus of 104 bushels per year, which is turned into cash to buy outside necessities.[49] Similar surpluses, which may have been even larger in the ancient Peten, must have been available for the support of the Classic Maya civilization.

Yet, neither Cambodia nor the Maya Lowlands in the Classic Period had cities. A surplus is surely the precondition of civilization, for lacking it, a society cannot support the non-food producing specialists (like priests and artisans) who are the creators of civilization. As already mentioned, what matters is what becomes of this surplus. In the urban, organic civilizations it is consumed by the cities; in the non-urban, unilateral civilizations it is taken up as tribute for the support of cult centers. These are two possible modes of civilized life.

The "mechanical" nature of the Classic Khmer and Classic Maya societies and settlement patterns may be reflected in the suddenness of their downfall. As Durkheim[50] pointed out, the relative force of mechanical solidarity is quite weak and powers based on it are subject to rapid overthrow. A social order founded on the sanctions necessary to enforce tribute and corvée labor is extraordinarily brittle to social change, whether internal or external. The double threat presented to the Angkor rulers by the democratic and anti-authoritarian Hinayana Buddhism, on the one hand, and by Siamese invasion on the other, was enough to finish Classic Khmer civilization.[51] The Classic Period in the Maya Lowlands ended with the mass abandonment of the entire Peten and adjoining regions and the desertion of all ceremonial centers even in Yucatan, where the Maya population continued to survive. In the case of the Maya one can only speculate on immediate causes, but what certainly must have underlain such a disaster was the rigidity of the social organization. In contrast, such organic civilizations as China have maintained themselves in spite of millennia of wars, foreign invasions, famine, and the like. The civilization of the Valley of Mexico likewise has managed to survive in peasant form even the total cataclysm of the Spanish Conquest. The unwritten charters of urban, organic civilizations, being based on inter-regional dependence and therefore on interests which are mutual and universal within each society, are by their nature more resilient and adaptable to outside pressure.

The polar opposition which has been drawn in this paper between organic and unilateral civilizations is capable of being applied to parts of the world other than Cambodia and the Maya Lowlands. In medieval Indonesia, great trading cities such as those at the Kingdom of Srivijaya arose on the coasts, where interregional trade was intense, in contrast to the capitals of the interior, like Borobudur, which were cult centers and royal seats. An opposition of Mesopotamia to Egypt suggests itself, the former being regionally specialized into micro-geographical units and exhibiting an early growth of urbanism, the latter being one of the most undifferentiated regions (within the "Nile Tube") on earth. Egypt really had no development of true cities until the 18th Dynasty, when imperial conquest had brought within its sway the trading nations of the eastern Mediterranean. Mesopotamia was clearly organic, and Egypt was unilateral. Furthermore, these poles might also represent different points of origin for the state: one based on the necessity for trade regulation,[52] the other on the authoritarian control of tribute and corvée.

Civilization, as a concept, has been so tied to the rise of cities that it is difficult to conceive of non-urban civilizations. While this paper does not pretend to account for all cases where cities are lacking (for example the Mycenaean civilization of Greece), the best explanation for the very similar settlement patterns of two non-urban civilizations of the tropical forest, the Maya and the Khmer, is that the natural environment denied them the opportunity for the development of trade.

Summary

1. The Classic Khmer and the Classic Maya civilizations had cult centers but not true centers. They both arose in areas which were regionally undifferentiated.

2. Easy transportation and heavy trade were lacking because of the area-wide uniformity of crops and the difficult terrain. Consequently, urban centers were not and could not be supported.

3. Both areas did produce a surplus and therefore could support civilized life. The social orders of each were so set up that through religious sanctions this surplus, which included labor, could be utilized for the creation and support of huge cult centers. Such a kind of organization might be considered as unilateral (mechanical) in the Durkheimian sense.[53]

4. In contrast, true cities arose in productive agricultural areas which were regionally specialized, with symbiotic interdependence of a Maussian nature. Trade and trade routes were highly developed so that commodity prices were sufficiently low to enable large groups of persons engaged in commerce to live together and yet make a profit on their activities. Internally specialized civilizations of this sort have been termed organic.

5. It is suggested that among the organic civilizations, the state may have had its origin in the regulation of trade; among the unilateral civilizations, in the compulsion of tribute and corvée labor.

NOTES

1. This manuscript has been read by Gordon R. Willey and Sophie D. Coe. The author is indebted for their advice and emendations.

2. Émile Durkheim, *The Division of Labor in Society* (Glencoe, Ill., 1949), An English translation.

3. Marcel Mauss, *The Gift; Forms and Functions of Exchange in Archaic Societies* (Glencoe, Ill., 1954).

4. *Ibid.*, p. 80.

5. Lévi-Strauss, "The Family," *Men, Culture, and Society*, ed. Harry L. Shapiro (New York, 1956).

6. See discussion in Gordon C. Childe, *Social Evolution* (New York, 1951), pp. 23–29.

7. William T. Sanders, "The Central Mexican Symbiotic Region, a Study in Prehistoric Settlement Patterns," *Prehistoric Settlement Patterns in the New World*, ed. Gordon R. Willey (= *Viking Fund Publications in Anthropology* No. 23) (New York, 1956), pp. 115–127.

8. Durkheim, *op. cit.*, p. 180.

9. Gordon F. Ekholm, "A Possible Focus of Asiatic Influence in the Late Classic Cultures of Mesoamerica," *Asia and North America, Transpacific Contacts*, ed. Marian W. Smith (= *Society for American Archaeology Memoir*, 9) (Salt Lake City, 1953).

10. Lawrence P. Briggs, "The Ancient Khmer Empire," *Transactions of the American Philosophical Society*, Vol. XLI, Pt. 1 (Philadelphia, 1951).

11. *Ibid.*, p. 49.

12. *Ibid.*, p. 124.

13. I am indebted to Robert M. Adams for calling my

attention to the peculiar exception of Samarra. In 836 A.D. the Caliph Mu'tasim began construction of a vast royal city, apparently urban in every sense of the word, moving the capital to this location from Baghdad, 60 miles away. After an occupation of only 45 years, the city was abandoned and the court returned once more to Baghdad. The whole history of Samarra sounds very much like a noble experiment in town planning which could have gone astray because of the poor mercantile possibilities of this site as compared with Baghdad; *ex post facto* one might say that the Caliph had tried to impose unilateral, mechanical structure on a population of traders and shopkeepers, and failed. The wonder is that he was able to move them in such a manner.

14. George Coedès, *Pour mieux comprendre Angkor* (Paris, 1947), p. 84.

15. Briggs, *op. cit.*, p. 125.

16. Coedès, *op. cit.*

17. Paul Pelliot, *Mémoires sur les coutumes du Cambodge de Tcheou Ta-kouan* (Paris, 1951).

18. Briggs, *op. cit.*, p. 109.

19. Coedès, *op. cit.*

20. Briggs, *op. cit.*, pp. 163, 166.

21. Sylvanus G. Morley, *The Ancient Maya*, 3rd ed., rev. by George W. Brainerd (Stanford, 1956), Table VII.

22. Michael D. Coe, "The Funerary Temple among the Classic Maya," *Southwestern Journal of Anthropology*, XII, No. 4 (1956), 387–394.

23. Morley, *The Ancient Maya*, 1st ed. (Stanford, 1946).

24. O. G. Ricketson, Jr., and E. B. Ricketson, *Uaxactun, Guatemala, Group E–1926–31* (=Carnegie Institution of Washington Publication, No. 477) (Washington, D.C., 1937).

25. Gordon R. Willey, "Problems Concerning Prehistoric Settlement Patterns in the Maya Lowlands," *Prehistoric Settlement Patterns in the New World*, ed. Gordon R. Willey (= *Viking Fund Publications in Anthropology*, No. 23) (New York, 1956), pp. 107–114.

26. George W. Brainerd, "Changing Living Patterns of the Yucatan Maya," *American Antiquity*, XXII, No. 2, Pt. I (1956), 162.

27. Ricketson and Ricketson, *op. cit.*, p. 162.

28. Willey, *op. cit.*, p. 110.

29. William R. Bullard, "Maya Settlement Pattern in Northeastern Peten, Guatemala," *American Antiquity*, XXV, No. 3 (1960), 355–372.

30. P. W. Schufeldt, "Reminiscences of a Chiclero," *Morleyana* (Sante Fe, 1950), pp. 224h–229.

31. Briggs, *op. cit.*, p. 117.

32. Canada, Department of Mines and Technical Surveys, Geographical Branch, "Indo-China, a Geographical Apprecia-tion," *Foreign Geographical Information Series*, No. 6 (Ottawa, 1953).

33. E. H. C. Dobby, *Southeast Asia* (London, 1951).

34. Canada, Department of Mines, *op. cit.*, p. 49.

35. *Ibid.*, p. 59.

36. George Groslier, *Recherches sur les Cambodgiens* (Paris, 1921), pp. 21–23.

37. *Ibid.*, p. 23.

38. *Ibid.*

39. *Ibid.*

40. Sylvanus G. Moriey, *The Inscription of Peten* (= Carnegie Institution of Washington Publication, No. 437), 5 vols. (Washington, D.C., 1937–1938), I, 7.

41. Morley, *The Ancient Maya*, 3rd ed., revised by Brainerd, p. 129.

42. Ralph L. Roys, *The Indian Background of Colonial Yucatan* (= Carnegie Institution of Washington Publication, No. 548) (Washington, D.C., 1943), p. 3.

43. Angel Palerm, "The Agricultural Basis of Urban Civilization in Mesoamerica," *Irrigation Civilizations, a Comparative Survey* (= Pan American Union Social Science Monographs, No. 1) (Washington, D.C., 1955), pp. 32–34.

44. *Ibid.*, p. 34.

45. Sanders, *op. cit.*, p. 126.

46. *Ibid.*, pp. 120–121.

47. *Ibid.*, p. 125. René Millon feels that Teotihuacan may have been urban as early as the Late Formative (ca. 300 B.C.–300 A.D.). (Information from G. R. Willey.)

48. Canada, Department of Mines, *op. cit.*, fig. 19.

49. Morley, *The Ancient Maya*, 3rd ed., revised by Brainerd p. 140.

50. Durkheim, *op. cit.*, pp. 148–152.

51. Briggs, *op. cit.*, pp. 258–261.

52. Julian H. Steward, "Some Implications of the Symposium," *Irrigation Civilizations, a Comparative Survey* (= Pan American Union Social Science Monographs, No. 1) (Washington, D.C., 1955), p. 70.

53. Milton Altschuler, in his article "On the Environmental Limitations of Mayan Cultural Development," *Southwestern Journal of Anthropology*, XIV, No. 2. 189–198, has proposed a dichotomy of societies based upon *economic* and *political* means of livelihood, following Oppenheimer. The first is based on the division of labor and the exchange of goods, and therefore would correspond to my "organic" category; the second is clearly the same as my "unilateral." However, Altschuler's assignment of the Classic Maya to the former runs counter to my argument and is certainly not in accordance with the known facts about this admittedly little known society.

20

Conceptions of State and Kingship
in Southeast Asia

Robert Heine-Geldern

At a time when the whole political system of South-east Asia seems to be in a new cycle of development, dominated by native forces, an inquiry into the ideological foundations of native government will not be out of place and, perhaps, will even be of more than purely theoretical interest. What were the religious and philosophical conceptions which underlay and shaped the states of Southeast Asia? Are they still living forces with which we have to count or are they dead and gone? Is it possible to inoculate new ideas into old traditions, thereby avoiding a complete break with the past, a dangerous uprooting of oriental thought and culture?

In view of the limited space I shall confine myself to a discussion of some fundamental conceptions of state and kingship in those parts of Southeast Asia where Hindu-Buddhist civilization prevailed.

Macrocosmos and Microcosmos

The primary notion with which we shall have to deal is the belief in the parallelism between Macro-cosmos and Microcosmos, between the universe and the world of men. According to this belief humanity is constantly under the influence of forces emanating from the directions of the compass and from stars and planets. These forces may produce welfare and prosperity or work havoc, according to whether or not individuals and social groups, above all the state, succeed in bringing their lives and activities in harmony with the universe. Individuals may attain such harmony by following the indications offered by astrology, the lore of lucky and unlucky days and many other minor rules. Harmony between the empire and the universe is achieved by organizing the former as an image of the latter, as a universe on a smaller scale.

From Robert Heine-Geldern, *Conceptions of State and Kingship in Southeast Asia*, Southeast Asia Program Data Paper No. 18 (Ithaca: Cornell University, April 1956), pp. 1–13. Reprinted by permission of the author.

It is well known that this astrological or cosmo-magic principle, as we may call it, originated some-where in the Near East. It was well established in Babylonia in the 3rd millennium B.C. and there are indications that it may go back there at least as far as the middle of the 4th millennium, and possibly farther. Again, we have indications that it existed in Northwest India in the second half of the 3rd millennium. It influenced Europe in various ways and at various times, especially during the periods of Hellenism and of the Roman empire and in the Middle Ages. It is difficult to tell when it first reached China. Anyway it had developed there into a highly specialized system during the Chou and Han periods. It came to Southeast Asia by way of India as well as of China, and this double influence may account for its prominence there and for the strong hold it had on the minds of the peoples of Farther India and Indonesia. Its long life-span and its spread over vast regions with divergent cultures, and even more so the fact that it had to adapt itself to the locally dominant religions, to various forms of paganism as well as Hinduism, Buddhism and Confucianism, and occasionally even to Christianity and to Islam, natu-rally resulted in the development of numerous variants with often widely differing traits. It is with the special aspect of the cosmo-magic principle as expressed in the organization of Hindu and Buddhist kingdoms in Southeast Asia (and to some extent in their Mohammedan successors in Malaya and Indo-nesia), that we are here concerned.

Relation between State and Universe

Whereas speculation pertaining to the relation be-tween state and universe formed an important subject of ancient Chinese literature, we would look in vain for a theoretical treatise on this topic in the various literatures of Southeast Asia.[1] Yet, there is over-whelming evidence of the cosmological basis of state and kingship in this area. This evidence is found in numerous passages in literature and inscriptions, in the titles of kings, queens and officials, in the "cosmic" numbers of queens, ministers, court priests, provinces, etc., in rites and customs, in works of art, in the lay-out and structure of capital cities, palaces, and temples. One need only put these various items together to obtain a relatively clear picture. This picture will be more complete in continental Southeast Asia, where the old forms of Buddhist state and kingship survived into very recent times. It will be hazier in the Archipelago as a result of Mohammedan and European influences.

According to Brahmanic doctrine the world consists of a circular central continent, Jambūdvīpa, surrounded by seven annular oceans and seven annular continents. Beyond the last of the seven oceans the world is closed by an enormous mountain range. In the center of Jambūdvīpa, and thus in the center of the world, rises Mount Meru, the cosmic mountain around which sun, moon and stars revolve. On its summit lies the city of the gods surrounded by the abodes of the eight Lokapalas or guardian gods of the world.

In the Buddhist system, too, Mount Meru forms the center of the universe. It is surrounded by seven mountain ranges separated from each other by seven annular seas. Beyond the last of these mountain chains extends the ocean and in it lie four continents, one in each of the cardinal directions. The continent south of Mount Meru is Jambūdvīpa, the abode of men. Here, too, the universe is surrounded by an enormous wall of rocks, the Chakravala Range. On the slopes of Mount Meru lies the lowest of the paradises, that of the four Great Kings or guardians of the world, on its summit the second paradise, that of the thirty-three gods with Sudarsana, the city of the gods, where Indra reigns as king. Above Mount Meru lower one above the other the rest of the heavenly abodes.[2]

It will be seen that the Brahman and the Buddhist systems, in spite of differences in detail, agree in fundamental traits: their circular form and the arrangement in concentric zones around Mount Meru. An abbreviated image of either of them thus has the same symbolic meaning for devotees of both faiths.

The Capital as the Magic Center of Empire

In Southeast Asia, even more than in Europe, the capital stood for the whole country. It was more than the nation's political and cultural center: it was the magic center of the empire. The circumambulation of the capital formed, and in Siam and Cambodia still forms, one of the most essential parts of the coronation ritual. By this circumambulation the king takes possession not only of the capital city but of the whole empire. Whereas the cosmological structure of the country at large could be expressed only by the number and location of provinces and by the functions and emblems of their governors, the capital city could be shaped architecturally as a much more "realistic" image of the universe, a smaller microcosmos within that macrocosmos, the empire. The remains of some of the ancient cities clearly testify to the cosmological ideas which pervaded the whole system of government. Fortunately, a number of inscriptions and some passages in native chronicles may help us in interpreting archaeological evidence.

As the universe, according to Brahman and Buddhist ideas, centers around Mount Meru, so that smaller universe, the empire, was bound to have a Mount Meru in the center of its capital which would be if not in the country's geographical, at least in its magic, center. It seems that at an early period natural hillocks were by preference selected as representative of the celestial mountain. This was still the case in Cambodia in the 9th century A.D. Yeśodharapura, the first city of Angkor, founded toward 900 A.D., formed an enormous square of about two and a half miles on a side, with its sides facing the cardinal points and with the Phnom Bakheng, a small rocky hill, as center. An inscription tells us that this mountain in the center of the capital with the temple on its summit was "equal in beauty to the king of mountains," i.e. to Mount Meru.[3] The temple on Phnom Bakheng contained a Lingam, the phallic symbol of Śiva, representing the Devarāja, the "God King," i.e. the divine essence of kingship which embodied itself in the actual king. More frequently the central mountain was purely artificial, being represented by a temple only. This was quite in accordance with prevailing ideas, practically every temple in Southeast Asia, whether Hindu or Buddhist, whether built of stone, brick or wood, being considered as the image of a mountain, usually, though not invariably, of Mount Meru. In ancient Cambodia a temple was quite ordinarily referred to as "giri," mountain, and the many-tiered temples of Bali are still called Meru. The Cambodian inscriptions are very explicit with regard to such identifications. Thus, to give an example, one of them says that King Udayádityavarman II (11th century) "seeing that the Jambūdvīpa had in its center a mountain of gold, provided for his capital city, too, to have a golden mountain in its interior. On the summit of this golden mountain, in a celestial palace resplendent with gold, he erected a lingam of Śiva."

The Lay-Out of Angkor Thom

The actual ruins of Angkor Thom are the remains of the latest city on this site, built by King Jayavarman VII in the second half of the 12th century A.D. As Jayavarman was an adherent of Mahāyāna Buddhism, the central "mountain" in this case was a Buddhist sanctuary, which contained a large image of the Buddha Amitabha, while the four faces of Bodhisatva Lokeśvara, the "Lord of the World," adorned its numerous towers. The city was surrounded with a wall and moat forming a square almost two miles on each side, its sides being directed toward the four cardinal points. There are gates in the middle of each side and a fifth one on the East leading to the entrance of the royal palace. The towers above the gates are crowned with the same four-fold faces of Lokeśvara as those of the central temple. Thus, that smaller world, the city of Angkor, and through its means the whole Khmer empire were both put under the protection of the "Lord of the Universe." The cosmic meaning of the city was further emphasized by a curious device. The balustrades of the causeways leading over the moat to the city gates were formed by rows of giant stone figures, partly gods, partly demons, holding an enormous seven-headed serpent. The whole city thus became a representation of the churning of the primeval milk ocean by gods and demons, when they used the serpent king Vāsuki as a rope and Mount Meru as churning stick.[4] This implies that the moat was meant to symbolize the ocean, and the Bayon, the temple in the center of the city, on which all the lines of churning gods and demons converged, Mount Meru itself.

The Capital of Burma

Burmese chronicles say that Śrīkshetra (Old Prome) on the lower Irrawaddy, the capital city of the ancient kingdom of the Pyu, was built by the gods themselves with Indra at their head, built as an image of Indra's city Sudarśana on the summit of Mount Meru, with thirty-two main gates and a golden palace in its center. The remains of the city show in fact a decided attempt at a circular lay-out though complete regularity has not been achieved. It seems to have been an old custom in Burma that each of the capital's gates corresponded to one of the empire's provinces or vassal states. Thirty-two vassals or heads of provinces with the king as thirty-third in the center would of course correspond to the thirty-three gods who reside on the summit of Meru and among whom Indra is king. Thus not only the cap-

ital city but the whole empire of the Pyu must have been organized as an image of the heavenly realm of Indra.

In later capitals of Burma the square form was substituted for the circular one though the cosmological principle as such was retained. It will suffice to say a few words about Mandalay, the last capital of independent Burma, built by King Mindon in 1857 A.D. The inner city was surrounded by a wall and moat forming a square of more than a mile on each side, its sides facing the cardinal points. The royal palace, which occupied the center of the city, and more specifically the seven-tiered tower over the throne in the great audience hall, was identified with Mount Meru. There were three gates on each side of the city, twelve in all, and they were marked with the signs of the zodiac, thereby indicating that the city was meant to be an image of heaven with its stars spread out around the celestial mountain in its center.

Cosmic Roles of King, Court and Government

Thus the stage was set for the enacting of the cosmic roles of king, court and government. We may choose Burma as an example. There, the king was supposed to have four provincial queens and four queens of secondary rank whose titles, "Northern Queen of the Palace," "Queen of the West," "Queen of the Southern Apartments," etc., show that they originally corresponded to the four cardinal points and the four intermediary directions. There are indications that at an earlier period their chambers actually formed a circle around the hall of the king, thereby emphasizing the latter's role as center of the universe and as representative of Indra, the king of the gods in the paradise on the summit of Mount Meru. Sir James George Scott's observation that King Thibaw's (the last Burmese king) failure to provide himself with the constitutional number of queens caused more concern to decorous, law-abiding people than the massacre of his blood relations, shows how important this cosmic setting was considered to be.[5] There were four chief ministers each of whom, in addition to their functions as ministers of state, originally had charge of one quarter of the capital and of the empire. They obviously corresponded to the four Great Kings or Lokapālas, the guardian deities of the four cardinal points in the Buddhist system. However, the task of representing the four Lokapālas had been delegated to four special officers, each of whom had to guard one side of the palace and of the capital. They had flags in the colors attributed to the corresponding sides of Mount Meru, the one representing Dhattarattha, the

Lokapāla of the East, a white one, the officer representing Kubera, the Lokapāla of the North, a yellow flag, etc. The cosmological principle was carried far down through the hierarchy of officialdom, as revealed by the numbers of office bearers. Thus, there were four under-secretaries of state, eight assistant secretaries, four heralds, four royal messengers, etc.

Very much the same kind of organization existed in Siam, Cambodia and Java. Again and again we find the orthodox number of four principal queens and of four chief ministers, the "four pillars" as they were called in Cambodia. In Siam, as in Burma, they originally governed four parts of the kingdom lying toward the four cardinal points.

There are indications that in ancient times the cosmological structure of the state was carried even farther. I have already mentioned the probability that the old kingdom of the Pyu in Burma had thirty-two provinces or vassal states, their governors together with the king having corresponded to the thirty-three gods of the paradise on the summit of Mount Meru. Similarly the kingdom of Pegu in the 14th century had thirty-two provinces. The principality of Keng Tung, one of the largest Shan States, significantly is called "The Thirty-two Towns of the Khün," the Khün being the ruling tribe in that state. A passage in the *New History of the T'ang Dynasty* indicates that the kingdom of Java in the 9th century was divided into twenty-eight provinces, their governors together with the four ministers again having numbered thirty-two high officials. This may have been a somewhat older form of the same system, in which the provinces corresponded to constellations, the twenty-eight "Houses of the Moon," and the four ministers to the guardian gods of the cardinal points. It is clear that in all these cases the empire was conceived as an image of the heavenly world of stars and gods.

Throughout the kingdoms of Farther India the system based on the compass was largely supplemented and modified by the division into offices of the right and left hand, right and left in this case referring to the place on the side of the king due to the respective office bearer on ceremonial occasions. As the king, when sitting on the throne, always faced the East, right corresponded to the South and left to the North. In Siam, for instance, there were a major and a lesser queen each of the right and of the left. Civilian officers had their places on the left of the king, officers of the army on his right, i.e., "in the South," because the planet Mars, connected with war, was considered to be the planet of the South. Indeed, the population of Siam was divided into the two classes of the right (South) and of the left

(North). The former had to render military and the latter civilian services.

Influence on Coronation Ritual

The cosmic and divine role of the king was and still is specially emphasized in the coronation ritual. In Burma, the structure erected for this purpose was significantly called Thagya-nan, "Indra's Palace."[6] Even in the Buddhist kingdoms of Farther India the ritual is conducted by Brahmans. One of its principal features consists in the king sitting on a throne representing Mount Meru and being surrounded by eight Brahmans as representatives of the eight Lokapalas, the guardian gods of the eight directions in the Brahman world system. Moreover, four maids of honor, representing the four cardinal points, render homage to the king.

An official document published on the occasion of the coronation of King Sisowath of Cambodia in 1906 gives a slightly different explanation of the cosmic role of the king. According to this document the king is identified with Mount Meru itself, his right eye representing the sun, his left eye the moon, his arms and legs the four cardinal points, the six-tiered umbrella above his head the six lower heavens, his pointed crown the spire of Indra's palace on the summit of the Meru and his slippers the earth. This means that the king is identified with the axis of the universe. The same idea seems to be expressed by the title Paku Buwono, "Nail of the World," of the Susuhunan of Solo in Java. However, the identification of the king with the Meru is in no way incompatible with that with Indra. Plural symbolism is very frequent in Buddhist Farther India. Thus in Burma, where the king has all the attributes of Indra, he was also identified with Viśvakarma, the divine architect and shaper of the world. Moreover, there is strong evidence of his having been identified also with the sun.

The Cosmic State and the Divine King

The cosmic state, as it existed in Southeast Asia, was intimately bound up with the idea of divine kingship. The divinity of kings was conceived in various ways according to the prevailing religion. Where Hinduism prevailed the king was considered to be either an incarnation of a god or a descendant from a god or both. Mostly it was Śiva who was thought to incarnate himself in kings or to engender dynasties. Thus in a Cham inscription of the 9th century Uroja, the founder of the royal dynasty, is said to have been a son of Śiva. The Javanese poem

Nāgarakrtāgama (14th century) says bluntly that all kings are incarnations of Śiva. The same poem tells us more specially that King Rājasanagara of Majapahit (1350–1389 A.D.), as proved by various portents which occurred about the time of his birth, among others a volcanic eruption, was an incarnation of Bhatāra Girinātha, i.e. Śiva as "Lord of the Mountain." In the Javanese chronicle Pararaton King Krtajaya of Kadiri (13th century) on one occasion even shows himself in the superhuman form of Śiva with four arms and a third eye in the middle of the forehead and floating in the air. In ancient Cambodia and Champa the monarchy was intimately bound up with the cult of a lingam which was considered the seat of the divine essence of kingship. As we have seen, in Cambodia this lingam, representing the Devarāja, the "God King," was adored in the temple in the center of the capital. The actual king was considered to be a manifestation of the divine power of the Devarāja and therefore, as the latter's visible form, the lingam, implies, obviously of Śiva himself.

However, Śiva was not the only god to incarnate himself in kings. King Airlangga of Java (11th century) considered himself an incarnation of Vishnu. His memorial monument shows him in the form of Vishnu riding on the latter's man-eagle Garuda. Another noteworthy example of an incarnation of Vishnu was King Sūryavarman II of Cambodia (12th century) who erected his own memorial monument as a gigantic temple of Vishnu: the famous Angkor Wat. We find further the idea of plural incarnation, also known from ancient India. Thus the Pararaton tells us that Angrok (13th century), the founder of the dynasty of Singasari and ancestor of the kings of Majapahit, was an incarnation of Vishnu, begotten by Brahmā from a mortal woman, and at the same time a son of Śiva. King Krtarājasa (died 1316 A.D.), the founder of the empire of Majapahit, is immortalized by a statue representing him as Harihara, a compound of Vishnu and Śiva. Even the simultaneous incarnation of Hindu and Mahāyāna Buddhist deities occurs. Thus, to quote only one example, the Javanese King Krtanagara (killed 1292 A.D.) was considered as an incarnation of Śiva as well as of the Dhyāni Buddha Akshobhya. Accordingly, he became known in Javanese tradition under the name of Śiva-Buddha.

It may be added that the theory of divine incarnation could be used not only as a means to exalt the position of the legitimate king, but equally well as a justification for usurpation of the throne. Thus the above-mentioned Angrok, the founder of the kingdom of Singasari, was a usurper with a long criminal career as embezzler, robber and murderer.

Yet, in spite of his criminal past, he became king, according to the Pararaton, because he was an incarnation of the gods.

The theory of divine incarnation as found in Hinduism and Mahāyāna Buddhism is incompatible with the doctrine of the Buddhism of the Hīnayāna. This difference in tenets is clearly expressed even in the lay-out of capital cities. In ancient Cambodia a temple formed the center of the capital and thus the Mount Meru of city and empire. In Burma the center of the capital is invariably occupied by the royal palace, and it is this latter which is identified with Mount Meru. In ancient Cambodia either Śiva in his form as Devarāja, the eternal essence of kingship, or the Bodhisatva Lokeśvara, the "Lord of the Universe," inhabited the "central mountain" and from there pervaded the empire. Hīnayānist Buddhism does not recognize an eternal deity. Indra is but the king of one of the lowest heavens, the second one from the earth. He is as little exempt from death and rebirth as any human being, except that his life lasts longer. The same may be said of the inhabitants of the higher heavens. All these "gods" of Hīnayāna Buddhism should more appropriately be called angels. They have no temples and no cults. Thus it is easy to understand why in Burma no temple could be set in the center of the capital city. The adaptation to cosmological principles and the deification of the king here had to be attempted by other means. By erecting the palace in the center of the city and by identifying it with Mount Meru, the lord of the palace, i.e. the king, became automatically the representative of Indra. We might even say that he was "the Indra" of this smaller universe, the Burmese empire, but he held his place only by the magic of parallelism and he was no incarnation of the real Indra as the ancient Javanese and Cambodian kings had been incarnated of Śiva and Vishnu.[7] This scheme explains the great sanctity in which the royal palace was held in the Buddhist empires of Farther India. The palace was the symbol of the celestial mountain, nay, more than a mere symbol: it was "the Mount Meru" of the microcosmos Burma, or Siam, or Cambodia. Anybody nearing the palace had to show his reverence by dismounting from his horse, by shutting his parasol, by bowing to the palace spire or even kneeling down. Attempts to exact the same expressions of reverence from British envoys led to endless negotiations and frictions as the latter refused to comply with a demand which they considered humiliating. "King of the Golden Palace" was one of the most important titles of Burmese monarchs. Yet, the fact that the king "was Indra" and therefore ruler of the country only as possessor of the empire's Meru, the palace, involved great dangers. It worked as a constant temptation for would-be usurpers, be it from the ranks of the royal family or outsiders, as the occupation of the palace might be achieved by a coup-de-main with relatively small forces and usually meant the conquest of the whole empire. Many Burmese and Siamese kings therefore were virtual prisoners in their palace which they did not dare to leave for fear it might be seized by a usurper. The last king of Burma, Thibaw, preferred even to forego the important coronation ritual of the circumambulation of the capital to offering one of his relatives a chance to make himself master of the palace while he was away.

In Hīnayāna Buddhism the idea of divine incarnation as justification of kingship is replaced by that of rebirth and of religious merit. It is his good karma, his religious merit acquired in previous lives, which makes a man be born a king or makes him acquire kingship during his lifetime, be it even by rebellion and murder. A typical instance is that of King Nyaung-u Sawrahan (10th century) as told in the *Glass Palace Chronicle of the Kings of Burma*. Nyaung-u Sawrahan, a farmer, kills the king who has trespassed on his garden and whom he had not recognized. Thereupon he is himself made king against his wish. So strong is his karma that, when one of the ministers objects to his installation, the stone statue of a guardian deity at the palace door becomes alive and kills the minister. The chronicle's comment is significant: "Although in verity King Sawrahan should have utterly perished, having killed a king when he was yet a farmer, he attained even to kingship simply by strong karma of his good acts done in the past." But the moment the karma of his past good acts is exhausted, that same stone statue which formerly had killed his adversary becomes alive again and hurls him from the palace terrace.

No merit could exceed that of a service rendered to the Buddha himself. Thus the *Glass Palace Chronicle* tells us that the ogre-guardian of a mountain, who had shielded the Buddha from the sun with three leaves, had received from the latter a prophecy that he would thrice become king of Burma. In the 10th century he is reborn in lowly surroundings as Saleh Ngahkwe, who later becomes king by murdering his predecessor and, "being reborn from the state of an ogre, was exceeding wrathful and haughty," indulging in gluttony and sadistic murder, till he is at last killed by his own ministers. One should think that the merit of having shaded the Buddha would have been exhausted by a life full of crimes. However, according to the Burmese chronicle, this is not so. The former mountain spirit is reborn in the 12th

century as Prince Narathu who becomes king by murdering his father and brother and throughout his reign excels by bloody deeds, and in the 13th century as King Narathihapate. This leads us to a very characteristic conception of historical events as based on the enormous importance attributed to prophecies and portents. Indeed, one could say that, especially as far as alleged prophecies of the Buddha are concerned, in the view of Burmese historians events are not prophesied because they will happen, but they happen because they have been prophesied. The "discovery" of ancient prophecies and the "observation" of contemporary portents was a generally used expedient in Burmese politics and still forms a potent factor in what we may call political folk-lore.

The whole idea and outward form of kingship in Southeast Asia, and especially in the Buddhist kingdoms of Farther India, was of course based on the conception of the Chakravartin, the Universal Monarch. Now it is known that a Chakravartin is the worldly alternative to a Bodhisatva, a future Buddha. Under these circumstances the theory of rebirth and of karma was bound to induce monarchs with a very high idea of their religious merits to consider themselves as Bodhisatvas. Thus, Oung Zaya, the founder of the last dynasty of Burma, took as king the name Alaungpaya which designated him as an Embryo Buddha. His son, King Bodawpaya (1782–1819), claimed outright to be the Bodhisatva Maitreya. However, his claim was rejected by the clergy and he dropped it. A similar claim was put forth by King Taksin of Siam (1767–1782).

The theory of vocation to kingship either on the basis of divine incarnation, as in Java and ancient Cambodia, or by karma acquired in former lives, as in Burma, Siam and modern Cambodia, did not deprive that of the heredity of the right to the crown of its importance. Again and again usurpers have striven for a semblance of legitimacy by construing genealogies linking themselves either to the dynasty they had overthrown or to a dynasty which at an earlier period had governed the country. Occasionally, fantastic genealogies were constructed deriving native Southeast Asiatic dynasties from some famous dynasty of ancient India. The best-known case is that of the recent kings of Cambodia who claim descent from the ancient kings of Indraprastha (Delhi). The last Burmese dynasty, founded by a village headman in the 18th century, claimed descent from the Sakya kings of Kapilavatthu, a claim which would have made them blood relatives of the Buddha himself. One type of such fictitious genealogies deserves special attention as it has a deeper meaning than merely to serve the glorification of the dynasty. The kings of Funan (3rd to 7th centuries A.D.) and those of ancient Cambodia were said to descend from a Brahman who had come from India and from the daughter of the serpent king of the country. The legend is still alive in Cambodia, the Brahman being replaced in the modern version by a prince of Southeast Asia. The meaning is clear. The Nāgas, the serpent demons, are the original masters of the soil. By his descent from the daughter of the Nāga king the monarch had a legitimate claim to the soil of his kingdom which, in theory at least, thereby became his personal property. A Chinese report tells us that in the 13th century the people of Cambodia believed that the king nightly cohabited with the serpent goddess of the soil who visited him in his palace in human form. Obviously he was thought thereby to renew the connection between himself and the soil of his kingdom. Thus the king in ancient Cambodia, as an incarnation of the Devarāja and as a descendant and at the same time spouse of the goddess of the soil, formed a real magic circle linking the empire to the divine sources of the heavens as well as of the earth.

Any account of the conceptions of state and kingship in Southeast Asia would be incomplete without at least mentioning the great importance of the regalia. Some of these, as the umbrella and the crown, have cosmological meaning as noted above. Moreover, the umbrella was thought to be the seat of a protective genius who favored the king with his advice and who in critical moments might even actively intervene on behalf of the dynasty. Other regalia are thought to be possessed of magic forces, such as the royal sword of Cambodia which, it is believed, if drawn from its scabbard without the prescribed ritual, would bring disaster upon the country. This magical character of the regalia is even more stressed in the Malay Peninsula and in Indonesia. It culminates in the curious conception prevalent among the Bugis and Makassarese of Celebes, according to which it is really the regalia which reign, the prince governing the state only in their name.

The deification of the king, while raising him to an almost unbelievably exalted position with regard to his subjects, has in no way succeeded in stabilizing government; rather the contrary. As explained above, the theory of divine incarnation, and even more so that of rebirth and of karma, provided an easy subterfuge for usurpers. The fact that the relatively easy task of seizing the palace, as in Burma and Siam, or of seizing the regalia, as in certain parts of Indonesia, often sufficed to be accepted as king by the whole nation, was bound to act as an additional incitement to rebellion. Moreover, the immense power and the lack of restrictions which the king enjoyed invited abuses which in the end made the

monarch obnoxious to his subjects and hastened his downfall. To this came the vagueness of the rules of succession. Sometimes the king himself chose his successor. Sometimes the ministers appointed a prince as king. Then again the queens unofficially but efficiently exercised their influence in favor of a prince of their choice. Often the crown simply fell to the prince who was the quickest to seize the palace and to execute his brothers. Under these circumstances it is no wonder that the empires of Southeast Asia from the very beginning were torn by frequent rebellion, often resulting in the overthrow of kings or even dynasties. The earliest reports we have, those from Chinese sources on the kingdom of Funan, reveal such conditions to have existed as early as the 3rd century A.D. If there was a long period of oppression and unrest, rebellion and its concomitant, dacoity, could become practically a popular tradition which it was difficult to eradicate. Such was the case, for instance, in Burma during the 18th and 19th centuries, and it is in the light of such a past that recent events in that country ought to be seen.

Survival of Traditions

In order to realize how deeply the populations of Farther India were affected by the cosmological structure of the state one need only think of the division of the Siamese people into the classes of the right and of the left which, not long ago, determined the services each person was obliged to render to the state. Moreover, it must not be forgotten that the cosmo-magic principle as applied to the state really forms only part of a much wider complex and resulted from a conception of the universe and of human existence which regulated, and to a large extent still regulates, also the private lives of individuals. When in Siam and Cambodia people wore cloths of different color on different days of the week according to the color ascribed to the planet for whom the day is named, or when in Burma before any important undertaking they examine their horoscope and the lore of lucky and unlucky days, or when they kneel down for prayer on that side of the pagoda which in the cosmological system corresponds to the planet of the weekday on which they were born, they act on the same principle which governed the structure of their empires, their ideas of kingship and the ritual of their royal courts. It is clear then that the cosmo-magic ideas, until a very recent past, had an extremely strong hold on the minds of the people.

Is all this a crumbling structure, giving way under the impact of modern civilization or may it still influence the political activities of the peoples concerned? The question is not easily answered. Information on this point is scarce. There are, however, a few indications.

We have it on the authority of H. G. Quaritch Wales that the people of Siam, around 1930, still held the ancient state ceremonies in high esteem, those ceremonies which to a large extent are governed by cosmological ideas. One may ask oneself, how much of this old tradition may have been at the bottom of the royalist rebellion of 1933.

In Burma the following cases may be considered as significant. In 1897, twelve years after the annexation of Upper Burma by the British, a Buddhist monk, U Kelatha, fell in love with a princess of the dethroned dynasty who promised to marry him if he became king of Burma. There followed the usual dreams or visions which revealed to him that in a former life he had been a Burmese prince and, moreover, that he would be king the moment he sat on the throne of the palace in Mandalay. With eighteen followers, all armed with swords only, he rushed through the city gates and tried to reach the royal palace, at that time seat of the English club. A few English officers armed with hunting rifles made an end to his attempt. The incident proves the extreme vividness of cosmo-magic ideas at the close of the 19th century. As we have seen, whoever held the palace, the Mount Meru of the Burmese empire, thereby became the representative of Indra and the king. It is completely in accord with the cosmo-magic way of thinking that U Kelatha and his followers believed the mere occupation of the throne would make him automatically lord of the whole empire.

Unfortunately, very little authentic information is available on the Burmese rebellion of 1930–1931. However, the following detail, as revealed at the time by newspaper dispatches, is significant. One of the first actions of Saya San, the leader of the rebellion, was to build a "palace," in reality a bamboo hut somewhere in the jungle, with an inscription designating it as the "Palace of the Buddhist King." It is, of course, very easy to ridicule such pretensions, but it is more important to understand them. We have seen how inseparable king and palace were according to Burmese ideas. No kingdom could exist without a palace representing Mount Meru and forming its magic center, and the king, the "Lord of the Golden Palace," was king in the first line by his possession of the palace. Saya San's action in building a palace, a magic center for his embryonic empire, therefore corresponds closely to that of U Kelatha when he wanted to seat himself on the throne of the palace in Mandalay.

The story of the Myinmu rebellion of 1910, as told by Paul Edmonds in his book *Peacocks and Pagodas,* if it does not directly contribute to our knowledge of cosmo-magic ideas, at least gives a significant instance of the power of the belief in rebirth, prophecies and portents. A young man of eighteen years, Maung Than, was returning from work in the fields smoking a cigar. Some people who passed him thought they saw smoke issuing from his arms. They talked about it in the village and the rumor reached some elders who were familiar with an old tradition according to which a former king of Burma, Chanyeiktha, would be reborn in the shape of a youth who had the power of making smoke issue from his arms. "Other signs and portents were looked for. Needless to say, they were forthcoming. The griffins at the foot of an old pagoda were seen to shake; gold showers fell on another pagoda; and everywhere omens multiplied which pointed to young Maung Than as the long-foretold reincarnation of King Chanyeiktha." Maung Than entered into the spirit of the game and put forth the usual claims of being invulnerable and of possessing the power to make himself invisible. With a crowd of a thousand followers armed with swords and spears he attacked the police station at Myinmu but was repulsed and eventually captured.

One may ask whether there is any possibility of this same conception becoming the basis of future constructive developments. The question is difficult to answer. Orientals with western education, and above all the leaders of nationalist movements, tend to disregard and to despise the "superstitions" which governed their nations in the past. Yet, there is the vast mass of the common people, grown up in the old traditions, people to whom the modern ideas of democracy and representative government mean little or nothing and who cannot be educated overnight. A sudden complete break of cultural traditions has almost always proved disastrous to national and individual ethics and to the whole spirit of the peoples affected. A compromise between old and new conceptions therefore would seem desirable. Many, at least, of the outward expressions of the old ideas could easily be kept intact and gradually filled with new meaning, without in the least impairing educational and material progress. After all, the case of Japan shows that an idea decidedly more primitive than that of the cosmic state and less adaptable to ethical reinterpretation than the latter, the belief in the descent of the Mikado from the Sun Goddess (or at least the fiction of such belief) may very well survive and coexist with all the refinements of modern science and technique. The current problems of Southeast Asia hitherto have been discussed almost exclusively from the point of view of economics and of political science. It would be a grave mistake to disregard the importance of native culture and tradition for a future satisfactory reorganization of that region.

NOTES

1. However, it must be taken into account that Burmese, Mon and Thai literatures are still very imperfectly known.

2. There usually are twenty-six heavens in all, including those on Mount Meru, but the number occasionally varies.

3. Although Brahman and Buddhist cosmologies usually ascribe to the world a circular shape, the "cosmic" cities of Southeast Asia, with rare exceptions, affect the square form. It would take too long to explain this apparent, but not very important, discrepancy.

4. In the original myth Mount Mandara is used as churning stick. In Southeast Asiatic variants of the myth Mount Meru usually takes its place.

5. Similarly, H. G. Quaritch Wales comments on the bad impression created among the people by the abolition of the harem system by King Rama VI of Siam.

6. Thagya is the Burmese form of Sanskrit Sakra, the Buddhist designation for Indra.

7. However, strong traces of the belief that Siva and Vishnu incarnate themselves in the king survive in the coronation rituals of Siam and Cambodia.

CHAPTER VI

The City-States. The Breakthrough to the Conception of Autonomous Citizenship and Legal Order: Introduction

I

One of the most important types of political system that developed in many different places in human history is the city-state, which may be called the first, "archaic" stage of breakthrough from the primitive order, and it tended to persist in the imperial and feudal systems. The most famous in the Western tradition are the city-states of Greece and Rome,[1] but they certainly were not the only ones. In the Near East and Mediterranean regions there also developed many different types of city-states, such as the Sumerian, Assyrian, Babylonian, Phoenician, and Philistine.[2] In other parts of the world—Southeast Asia, India,[3] Mexico, and Peru[4]—similar types of city-states developed and flourished for long periods. They were also prominent in parts of Europe, especially in the Low Countries, Switzerland, and Italy,[5] from the beginning of medieval times up to the first breakthroughs into the age of absolutism.

City-states developed from different origins: directly from different types of tribal settlement, from temples that existed in tribal federations, or from patrimonial regimes. Some of them, such as certain of the Philistine and Phoenician city-states, were very quickly absorbed into other types of political systems, such as tribal federations or more especially into patrimonial and imperial systems. Others continued in a sort of marginal existence in the interstices of such systems, as enclaves with little political autonomy, and without exerting any special influence of their own. Perhaps the best example of such cities are the "caravan cities."[6]

Others might have persisted as enclaves with wider, autonomous, supranational orientations and influence. In only rather exceptional cases, of which Greece, Rome, and to some extent the city-states of medieval Italy are the most important illustrations, did the city-states (or especially groups of city-states) develop into relatively full-fledged, self-contained, autonomous political entities.

II

As in the case of tribal federations or patrimonial regimes, the development of city-states was contingent on the convergence of internal conditions—certain types of differentiation and settlement of the various primitive or nomad tribal groups—together with some broader "international" relations. While the initial impetus to the development of many of the city-states probably came from within the internal patterns of tribal settlement and differentiation, their persistence and development were very much contingent on constellations of external factors. Such international settings were especially important in determining whether the newly developing city-states would remain in positions of marginality in more encompassing systems or whether they would develop into relatively full-fledged, autonomous polities.

Thus, the Greek and Phoenician city-states have to be understood in the context of the Eastern Mediterranean political systems and imperial contexts, and the Italian in terms of the late medieval and early Renaissance political systems. Moreover, the patterns of continuity and discontinuity of these polities greatly depended on the constellation of such international forces or on their ability to maneuver special places for themselves in these systems.[7]

III

What, then, are the basic structural characteristics of the city-states, especially from the point of view of the development of political institutions? The very term "city-state" is, as Finley has put it, something of a misnomer. As he says:

The Greek word *Polis* (from which we derive such words as "political") in its classical sense meant "a self-governing state."

However, because the *polis* was always small in area and population the long-standing convention has been to render it "city-state," a practice not without misleading implications. The biggest of the *Polis,* Athens, was a very small state indeed by modern standards— about 1,000 square miles, roughly equivalent to the Duchy of Luxemburg or the state of Rhode-Island— to call it a city-state gives a doubly wrong stress; it overlooks the rural population, who were the majority of the citizen body, and it suggests that the city ruled the country, which is inaccurate. And Athens, in the extent and quality of its urbanization, stood at one end of the Greek spectrum, together with a relatively small number of other states. At the other end were many which were not civic centers. When Sparta, for example, in 385 defeated Mantinea, then the leading *Polis* in Arcadia, her terms were that the "city" be razed and the people return to the villages in which they had once lived.[8]

And yet there is, of course, a kernel of truth in this connotation of city-state, based on the fact that almost all city-states have been characterized by a certain type of social transformation of the tribal communities—a transformation characterized first of all by growing ecological concentration.

As Finley has rightly pointed out, such concentration could have been both relative and limited, but in terms of the realities of that time it was quite real and distinct. Moreover, whatever the internal differences among city-states, this concentration encompassed all the major segments of the community, even though in varying degrees and even though the lower groups participated to a lesser extent in such concentration. Only those who "did not belong"— the slaves or serfs or some of the alien groups— could be excluded from participating in the new concentrated community. But even they, on the whole, had a part in some of its ecological and institutional arrangements.

However, it was not the mere fact of concentration of population in what can be called urban enclaves that was important but rather the combination of two important consequences of such concentration— the growing internal social and economic differentiation of the population together with the emergence, in the confines of the same ecological and social communities, of new types of center.

Unlike the tribal federation or patrimonial systems, there developed a pattern unique in the archaic world, in which the impetus to the formation of centers originated from the same sources that created the forces of internal differentiation of the community.

The processes of internal differentiation in the city-states were probably among the most intensive as compared with similar urban concentrations of population in archaic societies. In the economic field, we find a growing occupational differentiation between the economic ties to the land and the urban vocations, be they in trade, craft, industry, or the ritual and educational fields. This phenomenon was also very closely connected with the development of the availability of many free economic resources —partially even land and manpower resources— not bound to ascriptive social units, the concomitant development of widespread internal and external, relatively free, market activities, and the accumulation of relatively mobile capital.

Similarly, in the social field, we witness the growth of some universalistic and achievement criteria in the composition of strata which emerged from within the older community and which, in their turn, gave rise to new social divisions. The major criteria of such division are a combination of family and kinship traditions, ownership of land, and economic, occupational, and ritual status.

In political spheres, a growing differentiation of special central political roles and activities (which we shall analyze in somewhat greater detail later) also took place.

In the cultural sphere the most important aspects of this development and differentiation were the breakdown of the primordial and kinship symbols as the focuses of social, political, and cultural identity of the community, the development of a conception of the differentiation and distinctiveness of the sociopolitical and the cultural cosmic orders, and the concomitant decline of the sanctity of traditionality.

These processes of differentiation developed in most city-states to more or less similar degrees in all social spheres. Although the degree of such differentiation differed greatly among the city-states, they cut across all groups almost equally and were all concentrated in the scope of relatively limited, autonomous political communities.

At the same time, the high level of differentiation and specialization that tended to develop in most city-states was of a rather peculiar nature in that most of its products were oriented toward external and not internal markets. The economic production that developed outstripped by far the internal demands. Similarly, the cultural, and sometimes also the political, orientations that developed in at least some of these city-states extended far beyond the boundaries of any given local community. Hence, by their very nature these communities were geared to some international system and were naturally very sensitive to various changes in it.

Although the degree of such differentiation necessarily varied greatly among the different city-states, the tendency to such differentiation and concomitant concentration was common to most of them.

IV

This growing concentration and differentiation created new problems of organization and integration. First, there developed in both internal and external relations "concrete" administrative, political, or economic problems. Internally the growing differentiation, cleavages, and division of strata and wealth, together with new types of economic activity, created new administrative, economic, and legal problems, which necessitated the development of new regulative rules and institutions that were certainly beyond the scope of any of the older tribal arrangements. Externally, many new problems tended to develop, such as intertribal, intercity-state, and international problems on the political, economic, and "purely" military levels.

The second level on which new problems tended to arise was that of the definition of the new common identity of the new community, of forging a new symbolic definition of cosmic and sociopolitical orders beyond the relatively narrow primordial, particularistic, and traditional terms of the primitive order.

These problems differed from those that developed in other cases of breakthrough from primitive patterns in that they appeared together in a relatively intensive way in small, concentrated, and highly differentiated communities. But the unique aspect of the city-states was probably not so much the problem itself as the nature of their solutions to the problems, which were all focused in a rather particular type of center. It was the formation of this center that constituted the main characteristic

(specific to city-states) of the transformation of the tribal community.

Although this type of center was almost entirely identical with the periphery (that is, with the whole collectivity in terms of membership) both structurally and symbolically, it was almost entirely distinct from it. Structurally and organizationally the center was distinguished from the periphery in the central symbols, temples, and offices. The holders of the various central offices dealt with the internal external, and international problems specified above.

Ecologically the center was largely identical with the more concentrated parts of the resettled tribal community and was localized usually in central places around special places of public meetings, of temples, central treasures, and courts.

Most members (citizens) of the community could also participate in the center, even though many groups could do so to a much more limited degree, as was the case especially in the more oligarchic types of city-state. But in most cases the limitations of participation in the center were not dissimilar from the social distinction made in the periphery. Most of the more active members of the community participated both in older or peripheral structures (kinship, land and family cults) and in the center. In a sense, one could talk about a continuous phase-movement of the population between these two poles. These movements created, as we shall see, a very high degree of potential social and political tensions in the new political systems.

The reason for the development of this type of center-periphery relation was largely rooted in the fact that in one sense the "real" periphery or "hinterland" of many city-states lay beyond their own frontiers, in the broader economic and political international system in which they were able to perform their specialized functions.

The preceding factors also tended greatly to influence the structure of the centers in terms of their components. Most—especially the more developed—city-states tended to combine several such components, especially those that crystallized attributes of common identity, regulated intergroup relations, and, to a lesser degree, upheld collective goals and regulated internal and external forces.

The relatively small degree of development of a special ruling class, as distinct from the leaders of different social groups and divisions, was perhaps the most important structural outcome or derivative of the combination of a relatively high level of structural differentiation, of a structurally and symbolically distinct center, and of the overlapping of membership between the center and the periphery.

At the same time in most city-states there developed many embryonic nucleuses of elite groups with a very high degree of potential for social, cultural, and political creativity. Of especial importance from this point of view, of course, was the system of rotation and temporary incumbence of most public offices, which was characteristic of many city-states. This system was closely related to the organizational structure of these centers, which was characterized by the development—in response to rising needs and problems—of various specialized tasks performed by relatively fluid nucleuses of elites or by representatives of various social groups and not by a high degree of structural specialization of roles and organizations.

V

The lack of distinction between membership in the community and in the center and the fact that participation in the center was very often perceived as the performance of the political roles or task of the major social divisions of the community also account for some of the major dimensions of political symbolism that tended to develop in the city-states.

The main background of the development of this symbolism was the potential universalization of the pattern of participation in the political and cultural orders that were concomitant with the transpositions of the older arrangements of the tribal or semi-patrimonial communities and their arrangements into the new setting. Indeed, many such arrangements were often transposed into the new settings. The new structurally and symbolically differentiated centers were often seemingly built up on the model of the older semiequalitarian and semicommunal arrangements of the tribal communities. This was the case, for instance, in the system of the rotation of offices and the obligation of the wealthy to perform public duties, which developed in several Greek city-states.[9] It can also be seen in the pattern of public office in the more oligarchic city-states, such as Carthage,[10] which evinced many similarities with the more hierarchical and chiefly distinctions that were to be found in many primitive communities.

Beyond this, there developed in the city-states the attempt to transpose, on a much more differentiated and culturally sophisticated symbolic and institutional level, the basic identity between the social and the political order and the lack of distinction between center and periphery that had probably been characteristic of the older tribal communities. Paradoxically, this tendency was especially discernible in the socially and politically more developed and emancipated city-states.

The special combination of the levels of differentiation, the relations between center and periphery that developed in city-states, and the simultaneous growing differentiation of the community obviated all attempts to maintain effectively any organizational and structural similarities between the city-states and the primitive communities. But such tendencies to "return" to the "purity" and simplicity of the tribal community could easily become rallying political slogans of revolutionary forces.

It is out of this background that there developed several trends of political symbolism specific to the city-states, the full potentialities of which burgeoned only in the more developed city-states, especially in the Greek and some of the European ones, and in Rome.

While it would be out of place here to attempt even a superficial exposition of either of these varied trends of development, it might be worth while from the point of view of our general comparative analysis to point out some of their basic characteristics.

Political symbolism in the city-states was based on several important assumptions. The first, and perhaps most important, was the recognition of the autonomy of the moral order as distinct from the tribal or social order. This perception was coupled with a quest for a reintegration of these orders through the autonomy of the individual. It also brought with it the recognition of the possibility of tensions and conflict between them, as in the "moral protest" of the autonomous individual that was depicted in some of the Greek tragedies. At the same time, the quest for reintegration was based on the conception of complete identity of the social and political order and on the assumption of "totalistic" participation of citizens in the body politic. This was extended to include the capacity of all citizens to represent the essence and center of the community.

It was in all these respects that we witness, in the more socially and culturally diversified city-states, the breakdown of some of the structural and symbolic limitations of traditionality. This can be seen in the fact that the periphery was able to participate in the formation of the center and that the very contents of the sociocultural order were no longer taken for granted but became subject to the possibilities of change. Although this breakdown took place in only a few of the city-states, it was the first and only one before the onset of modernity. But because of the institutional limitations of city-states, with which we shall deal later, an institutional order oriented toward the absorption of continuous change could not develop, as it did in modern societies.

The most important common denominator of the political symbolism of city-states was that of citizenship,[11] which was adopted afterward in various places in Europe and later, in a largely transformed way, in the modern state. Particular importance was attached first to the potentially full and equal participation of individuals as individuals, freed of particularistic-primordial ties, in the body politic and second to their individual political or legal responsibility and the concomitant responsibility of the (almost always temporary) rulers before the ruled.

The conceptions of universal participation in the political or cultural order and of citizenship developed in different directions in Rome and Greece. In Rome it was focused around law and legal institutions and around the possibility of extension of the idea of citizenship beyond the original confines of the local city-state. In the Greek city-states, and especially in Athens, this tendency focused in general on the sphere of cultural creativity and in particular on philosophy, which has remained the guide for political thought in the West. But, unlike the Roman, the Greek conception did not prove capable of transcending in either legal or institutional terms the confines of the local city-state community. As a result, there was continuous tension between the universalizing tendencies of political and cultural symbolism and the institutional realities of the city-community.

VI

The special structural characteristics of the center and of center-periphery relations account for most of the specific characteristics of political struggle and processes in the city-states. The basic poles of such a struggle were given in the structural tension between center and periphery, in the great extent of overlapping of membership between them, in the growing structural and symbolic differentiation in the community, in the tendencies toward equation of center and periphery on the central institutional and symbolic levels, and in the consequent possible tendencies to universalism.

Several different levels of such struggle can be discerned in the city-states. The first such level was the rather simple "traditional" level of representing different specific interests of various groups (for example, family, social strata), of attempting to influence policy in terms of the distribution of benefits from the public domain or the allocation of various public offices to these groups. In many city-states, such as the Phoenician, Sumerian, Mesoamerican, the political struggle probably did not develop very much beyond this level. But there are many other city-states that made a special impact on the history of political institutions and served as models for modern civil societies. In them the political struggle developed several additional dimensions.

One was aimed at a relatively far-reaching redistribution of economic resources (especially of land and debts) among different social groups in the community. Demands of this sort could be and often were connected with demands for legislation to deal both with economic relations and with political rights. This dimension of political struggle very often merged into another one: the struggle over the basic social-economic contours of the whole community and over the contents and patterns of participation in its center. It was a struggle that could be waged both in socioeconomic terms and in terms of their political constitution. The most important and well-known illustrations of this level are, of course, to be found in the Roman and Greek regimes. Here we see very clearly the struggles over the distribution of property, for changes in the pattern of stratification, and about the promulgation of laws that would regulate property relations between different groups and strata.

This dimension of political struggle often developed together with struggles over the scope of participation of different social groups in the political life of the community, or what in more modern political parlance would be called the scope of political equality.

The merging of various more general socioeconomic demands, along with the demands for the reconstitution of the body politic, was rooted in the almost total identity between polity and society, the social differentiation in the community, and the structural distinction of the center from the periphery. It was because of this that these struggles over the change of regime—from autocracy to aristocracy, from aristocracy to democracy or to tyranny, or vice versa—were not only described as such by historians or philosophers but even perceived as the possible goal by the actual participants in the political struggle.

In its close relationship between social and political crises and in its "secular" definition of politics and of participation in the political order, the political process in the city-states resembled that of modern societies. However, in contrast to modern societies, the city-state did not allow distinction and separateness between the social and the political spheres, and it had few institutional arrangements for maintaining the differentiation between them. The lack of any separation of the social from the political sphere had many repercussions on the contours of political organization in the city-states in general and on their relations to processes of change in particular.

From the point of view of political organization, we find here the simpler, less differentiated types of political cliques and direct or indirect representation of existing social groups in the central political organs. On the other hand, we also find, especially in the more developed city-state, the more differentiated types of political organization which seem to be the most extreme autonomous types of political organization—cliques and semiorganized political parties similar to modern ones. But these organizations were not as distinct from other structural units, such as social strata and kinship units, as modern parties tend to be. The extent both of their organizational continuity and of their separateness and autonomy from other social spheres was much smaller than that of modern parties. On the other hand, the populist element in them, continuously converging on the center, was much stronger.

For the reasons specified above and because these political demands were almost entirely identified with social problems and questions, their sociopolitical impact could be very pervasive, and, thus, they tended to create total divisiveness and cleavages. As we have seen, they were frequently consciously oriented to the change of the regime. Hence they were very directly related to the processes of change in these systems.

VII

The extent to which these different patterns of political struggle developed varied greatly among different city-states. The more extreme and articulated types of political struggle and the concomitant predisposition to change developed in Greece, Rome, and many medieval and postmedieval Italian city-states. Less intensive struggles developed in other city-states, such as the Phoenician and Mesopotamian ones. There are records of some attempts at change in the social structure through an open political process and struggle. In most of them, however, such an attempt probably never progressed beyond the more restricted levels of the additional patterns of representing the interests of the various existing groups.

Such limited types of political struggle were closely related to the predominance of ascriptive and hierarchical social systems, a small degree of dissociation from primordial and kinship-oriented symbols, differentiation between the cosmic and the social order, and the relative isolation or continuous stability in their respective international setting.[12]

Insofar as the breakup of the ascriptive social order and the predominance of the various primordial-kinship symbols of collective identity and the level of internal differentiation and international involvement increased, as was indeed the case in Greece and Rome, more "extreme" symbolic and actual patterns of political orientation and struggle tended to develop.

VIII

As in all other types of political system, and also in many of the city-states, the patterns of political struggle were very closely related to the processes of change in them and to the possible demise or transformation of these systems, which in turn were rooted in the discrepancy between the scope of internal and international problems and the exigencies they faced and the very limited scope of their executive and administrative organization. Because of the delicate balance between these forces, most city-states evinced a very high level of susceptibility to the impingement of changes in international settings. This sensitivity tended to be more in evidence where there was a possibility of very close interrelation between external and internal changes.

The crucial test of almost all city-states was the degree of their ability to respond to the social demands and to absorb the various social revolutions that could be engendered in them. At the same time, they were expected to maintain and even increase their political, executive, and administrative abilities to deal with both such internal problems and their international involvements.

The different constellations of internal and international conditions greatly influenced the extent of stability in different city-states and the directions of their transformation. Insofar as it was impossible to absorb all these changes within the confines of the city-state, there developed several different types of demise or, in very rare cases, of transformation of their systems.

The first such tendency was some sort of segmentation of the given polity in the form of colonization and immigration. This was a very frequent pattern in many city-states—not totally dissimilar from the pattern of segmentation in primitive tribes, tribal federations, and patrimonial kingdoms.

Another pattern or type of change, already much more radical, is that of a tendency to total civil war, of "stasis" and of the consequent possible demise of the given system of the city-state—very often connected with and facilitating foreign conquest—and submergence in various patrimonial or imperial units.

The less differentiated and politically articulated types of city-state evinced, on the whole, a smaller extent of ability to absorb far-reaching changes; accordingly, they tended to develop only the simpler, less radical types of political struggle and secession. Among the differentiated city-states, the tendency to segment the city-states or to incorporate them through conquest was greater. At most, they could continue either in a marginal existence as separate enclaves within the intensified differentiation, resulting in their total disappearance, or as separate distinct units.

Insofar as they became fused with other types of political regime, such as tribal federations, they could also facilitate the development of new—mostly patrimonial—political units, in which some of the external symbolisms of city-states could be perpetuated by the new rulers as sort of symbolic appendages to their own centers.

IX

The more developed and politically articulated city-states were usually able, almost by definition, to absorb a much greater degree of change; but in most of them this ability was relatively limited. Moreover, these city-states were more sensitive to a wider range of internal and external forces, which tended to give rise, within them, to the more radical types of political cleavage and demise.

The potentialities for more radical types of change were often rooted in the tendency to universalize the political or cultural community. Insofar as this tendency was strong, there necessarily developed in these communities potentially transformative orientations; that is, orientation to development from within their own premises. But these tendencies could rarely become fully realized and institutionalized from within the political confines of the city-states.

This was due mostly to the fact that most of these universalistic orientations tended to develop in the symbolic rather than in the actual political sphere. One might say that the relations of these orientations to concrete politics were rather unrealistic in the sense that they could not be easily institutionalized in the confines of the existing political communities.

The inability to institutionalize such transformative universalistic orientations was rooted first in the small scale of the actual political community and in the fact that the conception of the totality of participation necessarily imposed great limitations on the organizational development and scope of the ex-

ecutive. It was also rooted in the concomitant weakness and lack of cohesion of a special political elite or ruling class capable of transcending the limits of the local community and its parts vis-à-vis the populist impingements on the center.

Given the greater dependence of these types of city-states on international settings and exigencies, these limitations could indeed become catastrophic, stemming from the inability to deal with the external pressures and intensifying the propensities for civil war.

In some cases (to a limited degree in Greece and in medieval Italy, for example) some attempts at federative arrangements between different city-states were made. But these were not very fruitful or of long duration because basically they did not transcend the structural limitation pointed out above. They usually gave rise only to very intermittent and unstable intercity coalitions. Only in Rome did there develop from within the city-states a new, broader imperial system that maintained a relatively high degree of cultural and political continuity with the city-state, while attempting to uphold many of the political symbols of the city-state.

Rome's development was due to several factors. The first was that the peculiar structure of the Roman constitution and legal institution enabled the development of a more cohesive and widely oriented ruling class and facilitated its possible institutional isolation from the populist impingement. Second, it was due to the special universalistic tendencies of Roman legal institutions. Last, it was due to the fact that at a crucial point in the history of the Roman republic the decision was taken—after much dispute and civil strife—not only to extend the Roman citizenship to citizens of other Italian cities but also to distribute it throughout the different tribes, thus broadening the scope of the Roman political community. But all these instances are peculiar to Rome, and, from a comparative point of view, they only tend to emphasize the limitations of other city-states.

In all other city-states in which there existed such a high level of symbolic transformative orientations with little executive or institutional ability, their demise was usually more dramatic than in the case of the politically less developed city-states. Even when such demise took on the form of incorporation into larger imperial or patrimonial units or continuous existence on the margins of such units, it was also connected with some continuity of the city-state tradition—a tradition that could become a center of autonomous, independent political orientations and symbolism.

Moreover, in such cases the city-states could provide very important ingredients or bases for the constitution of new, more differentiated political regimes, whether feudal or imperial. In them the specific symbolism of the city-states not only was a sort of appendage to that of the patrimonial or tribal ruler but could also constitute the basis of new, wider political orientation and symbolism.

NOTES

1. For Greece, see Victor Ehrenberg, *The Greek City-State* (Oxford: Basil Blackwell, 1960); M. I. Finley, *The Ancient Greeks* (New York: Viking, 1963); A. Gouldner, *Enter Plato* (New York: Basic Books, 1965). For Rome, see A. R. E. Boak, *History of Rome to 565 A.D.* (New York: Macmillan, 1955); L. Homo, *Roman Political Institutions* (London: Routledge and Kegan Paul, 1962); R. Syme, *The Roman Revolution* (Oxford: Basil Blackwell, 1939). For Sumer, see Anton Deimel, "Sumerische Tempelwirtschaft zur Zeit Urukaginas und Seiner Vorgänger," *Analecta Orientalia*, No. 2 (Rome: Pontifical Biblical Institute, 1931); Samuel N. Kramer, *The Sumerians: Their History, Culture and Character* (Chicago: University of Chicago Press, 1963); Anna Schneide, *Die sumerische Tempelstadt* (Essen: G. D. Bädiker, 1920). For Babylonia, see C. J. Gadd, "The Cities of Babylonia," *The Cambridge Ancient History*, 2nd ed., Vol. I (Cambridge: Cambridge University Press, 1962), Ch. 13; Stephen H. Langdon, "Early Babylonia and Its Cities," *ibid.* (1928), I, 356–402. For Assyria, see Robert M. Adams, *The Evolution of Urban Society* (Chicago: Aldine, 1966); J. J. Finkelstein, "Mesopotamian Historiography," *Proceedings of the American Philosophical Society*, CVII, 461–472, 1963.

2. Robert J. Braidwood and Gorden R. Willey, eds., *Courses Towards Urban Life: Archeological Considerations of Some Cultural Alternates*, Viking Fund Publications in Anthropology (New York, 1962), No. 32; Dietz O. Edzard, *Die Fruhdynastiche Zeit. In die altorientalischen Reiche, I:*

Fischer Weltgeschichte, Bd. 2, ed. Elena Cassin, Jean Bottéro and Jean Vercoutter (Frankfurt am Main: Fischer Bucherei, 1965); Adam Falkenstein, "La cité-temple sumérienne," Cahiers d'Historie Mondiale (1954) I, 784–814.

3. For India and Southeast Asia, see Milton Singer, ed., *Traditional India: Structure and Change* (Philadelphia: American Folklore Society, 1959); Michael D. Coe, "Social Typology and the Tropical Forest Civilizations," *Comparative Studies in Society and History*, II (1955), 67–92; Hugh Tinker, *The City in the Asian Polity* (London: School of Oriental and African Studies, 1966); Lawrence P. Briggs, "The Ancient Khmer Empire," *Proceedings of the American Philosophical Society*, Vol. XLI, Part I (Philadelphia: 1951).

4. For Mexico, see Adams, *op. cit.*; Angel Palerm and Eric R. Wolf, "Ecological Potential and Culture Development in Mesoamerica," *Studies in Human Ecology* (Washington, D.C.: Panamerican Union, Social Science Monographs, No. 3, 1957); Sylvanus G. Morley, *The Ancient Maya*, 3rd ed., rev. by George W. Brainard (Stanford: Stanford University Press, 1956). For Peru, see John V. Murra, "On Inca Political Structure," *Proceedings of American Ethnological Society* (1958), pp. 30–41.

5. See the classical exposition of Henri Pirenne, *Early Democracies in the Low Countries*, trans. J. V. Saunders (New York: Harper and Row, 1963), and the bibliography.

6. Mikhail Rostovtsev, *Caravan Cities*, trans. D. and T. Talbot Rice (Oxford: Clarendon Press, 1932).

7. For greater detail on this, see A. Bozeman, *Politics and Culture in International History* (Princeton: Princeton University Press, 1960), Chs. 2 and 3.

8. Finley, *op. cit.*, p. 37.

9. A. W. Gomme, "The Working of the Athenian Democracy," *History*, XXXVI (1951), 12–28; A. H. M. Jones, "The Social Structure of Athens in the Fourth Century B.C.," *Economic History Review*, Second Series, VIII, No. 2 (1955), 141–155.

10. Charles C. Picard, *La Vie Quotidienne à Carthage au Temps d'Hannibal* (Paris: Hachette, 1958).

11. Max Weber, "Citizenship," in *General Economic History*, trans. Frank H. Knight (New York: Collier, 1961), pp. 233–248.

12. J. B. Bary, *A History of Greece to the Death of Alexander the Great*, 2nd ed. (London: Macmillan, 1924), Chs. II–III; Bozeman, *op. cit.*

INTRODUCTION TO THE READINGS

The material on the city-states is divided into two sections. In the first we present three excerpts from the works of some of the classical historians and philosophers that (as does also the excerpt from Aristotle in the first section) represent some of their reflections on the nature of political order in general and that of the city-state in particular.

The passages taken from *The Histories* by Polybius discuss the advantages and disadvantages of different forms of government—monarchy, oligarchy, and democracy, the latter of which he

calls "mob-rule." He also gives a historical-sociological analysis of the conditions for the development of the different types of government, points out the differences between Sparta and Rome, and weaves into this analysis his appreciation of the constitution of Lycurgus. Polybius analyzes also the process of change through revolution in the city-states.

"The Funeral Oration of Pericles," which is taken from Thucydides' *Peloponnesian War*, represents Athenian political and social order at the peak of its development. In our terms it can be said that Pericles epitomized the need for high institutional differentiation in a situation in which there was but little difference in the membership of the center and periphery.

The selections from *The Annals* by Tacitus throw

light on the importance of external exigencies in shaping the political order of the city-state. Caesar's oration, as cited by Tacitus, deals also with internal relations, which are clearly marked by the growing participation of the periphery in the political center, and with the crucial development of the Roman political system which facilitated its transformation into an imperial one.

In the second section, several modern historical and sociological analyses of various political systems of different city-states and of processes of change in them are presented. Schachermeyr, in "The Genesis of the Greek Polis," describes the development of Greek society from its early beginnings as a tribal association to its formation of the polis. He shows how ecological concentration enhanced the tendencies of social equality in the social and political spheres. The whole process is analyzed in relation to external events during the formative centuries.

The selections from Aymard give a brief description of the major institutional spheres in the classical Greek city. Gomme's essay on "The Working of the Athenian Democracy" analyzes in detail the structure of the Greek political system and compares it to the Roman one. His article indicates that in Athens there developed relatively differentiated political institutions (the assembly, the archons, and others) with but little differentiation between center and periphery. For a long time the assembly had broad influences on the political decision making. In Athens, therefore, the development of specialized political roles was limited. Truly enough, the reforms of Solon and Keistenes tried to establish an effective representative council which would maintain the political rights of the citizens. But this council never developed into a full-fledged professional political executive. The frequent circulation of the incumbents' political roles prevented such a development and contributed to the weakness of Athenian democracy.

Becker's article on Florence covering the years 1282–1382 represents an analysis of the medieval city-state which formed an autonomous political system. In these cities there was a clear differentiation between the ruling oligarchy and the periphery. Yet, there was a constant impingement of the periphery on the center in the form of petitions. Becker shows also how the centralistic orientations were enhanced by external exigencies.

The selections from Vernadsky's *History of Russia* analyze the developments in early medieval Russia.

a. THE CITY-STATES AS SEEN BY THEIR OWN HISTORIANS

21

From *The Histories*

Polybius

On the Forms of States

3. In the case of those Greek states which have often risen to greatness and have often experienced a complete change of fortune, it is an easy matter

Reprinted from Polybius, *The Histories,* trans. W. R. Paton (Cambridge: Harvard University Press, n.d.), Book VI, Part II, pp. 271–293. Reprinted by permission of the publishers and the Loeb Classical Library.

both to describe their past and to pronounce as to their future. For there is no difficulty in reporting the known facts, and it is not hard to foretell the future by inference from the past. But about the Roman state it is neither at all easy to explain the present situation owing to the complicated character of the constitution, nor to foretell the future owing to our ignorance of the peculiar features of public and private life at Rome in the past. Particular attention and study are therefore required if one wishes to attain a clear general view of the distinctive qualities of their constitution.

Most of those whose object it has been to instruct us methodically concerning such matters distinguish three kinds of constitutions, which they call kingship, aristocracy, and democracy. Now we should, I think, be quite justified in asking them to enlighten us as to whether they represent these three to be the sole varieties or rather to be the best; for in either case my opinion is that they are wrong. For it is evident that we must regard as the best constitution a combination of all these three varieties, since we have had proof of this not only theoretically but by actual experience, Lycurgus having been the first to draw up a constitution—that of Sparta—on this principle. Nor on the other hand can we admit that these are the only three varieties; for we have witnessed monarchical and tyrannical governments, which while they differ very widely from kingship, yet bear a certain resemblance to it, this being the reason why monarchs in general falsely assume and use, as far as they can, the regal title. There have also been several oligarchical constitutions which seem to bear some likeness to aristocratic ones, though the divergence is, generally, as wide as possible. The same holds good about democracies. 4. The truth of what I say is evident from the following considerations.

It is by no means every monarchy which we can call straight off a kingship, but only that which is voluntarily accepted by the subjects and where they are governed rather by an appeal to their reason than by fear and force. Nor again can we style every oligarchy an aristocracy, but only that where the government is in the hands of a selected body of the justest and wisest men. Similarly that is no true democracy in which the whole crowd of citizens is free to do whatever they wish or purpose, but when, in a community where it is traditional and customary to reverence the gods, to honour our parents, to respect our elders, and to obey the laws, the will of the greater number prevails, this is to be called a democracy. We should therefore assert that there are six kinds of governments, the three above mentioned which are in everyone's mouth and the three which are naturally allied to them, I mean monarchy, oligarchy, and mob-rule. Now the first of these to come into being is monarchy, its growth being natural and unaided; and next arises kingship derived from monarchy by the aid of art and by the correction of defects. Monarchy first changes into its vicious allied form, tyranny; and next, the abolishment of both gives birth to aristocracy. Aristocracy by its very nature degenerates into oligarchy; and

when the commons inflamed by anger take vengeance on this government for its unjust rule, democracy comes into being; and in due course the license and lawlessness of this form of government produces mob-rule to complete the series. The truth of what I have just said will be quite clear to anyone who pays due attention to such beginnings, origins, and changes as are in each case natural. For he alone who has seen how each form naturally arises and develops, will be able to see when, how, and where the growth, perfection, change, and end of each are likely to occur again. And it is to the Roman constitution above all that this method, I think, may be successfully applied, since from the outset its formation and growth have been due to natural causes.

5. Perhaps this theory of the natural transformations into each other of the different forms of government is more elaborately set forth by Plato and certain other philosophers; but as the arguments are subtle and are stated at great length, they are beyond the reach of all but a few. I therefore will attempt to give a short summary of the theory, as far as I consider it to apply to the actual history of facts and to appeal to the common intelligence of mankind. For if there appear to be certain omissions in my general exposition of it, the detailed discussion which follows will afford the reader ample compensation for any difficulties now left unsolved.

What then are the beginnings I speak of and what is the first origin of political societies? When owing to floods, famines, failure of crops or other such causes there occurs such a destruction of the human race as tradition tells us has more than once happened, and as we must believe will often happen again, all arts and crafts perishing at the same time, then in the course of time, when springing from the survivors as from seeds men have again increased in numbers and just like other animals form herds—it being a matter of course that they too should herd together with those of their kind owing to their natural weakness—it is a necessary consequence that the man who excels in bodily strength and in courage will lead and rule over the rest. We observe and should regard as a most genuine work of nature this very phenomenon in the case of the other animals which act purely by instinct and among whom the strongest are always indisputably the masters—I speak of bulls, boars, cocks, and the like. It is probable then that at the beginning men lived thus, herding together like animals and following the lead of the strongest and bravest, the ruler's strength being here the sole limit to this power and the name we should give his rule being monarchy.

But when in time feelings of sociability and companionship begin to grow in such gatherings of men, then kingship has struck root; and the notions of goodness, justice, and their opposites begin to arise in men. 6. The manner in which these notions come into being is as follows. Men being all naturally inclined to sexual intercourse, and the consequence of this being the birth of children, whenever one of those who have been reared does not on growing up show gratitude to those who reared him or defend them, but on the contrary takes to speaking ill of them or ill treating them, it is evident that he will displease and offend those who have been familiar with his parents and have witnessed the care and pains they spent on attending to and feeding their children. For seeing that men are distinguished from the other animals by possessing the faculty of reason, it is obviously improbable that such a difference of conduct should escape them, as it escapes the other animals: they will notice the thing and be displeased at what is going on, looking to the future and reflecting that they may all meet with the same treatment. Again when a man who has been helped or succoured when in danger by another does not show gratitude to his preserver, but even goes to the length of attempting to do him injury, it is clear that those who become aware of it will naturally be displeased and offended by such conduct, sharing the resentment of their injured neighbour and imagining themselves in the same situation. From all this there arises in everyone a notion of the meaning and theory of duty, which is the beginning and end of justice. Similarly, again, when any man is foremost in defending his fellows from danger, and braves and awaits the onslaught of the most powerful beasts, it is natural that he should receive marks of favour and honour from the people, while the man who acts in the opposite manner will meet with reprobation and dislike. From this again some idea of what is base and what is noble and of what constitutes the difference is likely to arise among the people; and noble conduct will be admired and imitated because it is advantageous, while base conduct will be avoided. Now when the leading and most powerful man among the people always throws the weight of his authority on the side of the notions on such matters which generally prevail, and when in the opinion of his subjects he apportions rewards and penalties according to desert, they yield obedience to him no longer because they fear his force, but rather because their judgment approves him; and they join in maintaining his rule even if he is quite enfeebled by age, defending him with one consent and battling against those who conspire to overthrow his rule. Thus by insensible degrees the monarch becomes a king, ferocity and force having yielded the supremacy to reason.

7. Thus is formed naturally among men the first notion of goodness and justice, and their opposites; this is the beginning and birth of true kingship. For the people maintain the supreme power not only in the hands of these men themselves, but in those of their descendants, from the conviction that those born from and reared by such men will also have principles like to theirs. And if they ever are displeased with the descendants, they now choose their kings and rulers no longer for their bodily strength and brute courage, but for the excellency of their judgment and reasoning powers, as they have gained experience from actual facts of the difference between the one class of qualities and the other. In old times, then, those who had once been chosen to the royal office continued to hold it until they grew old, fortifying and enclosing fine strongholds with walls and acquiring lands, in the one case for the sake of the security of their subjects and in the other to provide them with abundance of the necessities of life. And while pursuing these aims, they were exempt from all vituperation or jealousy, as neither in their dress nor in their food and drink did they make any great distinction, but lived very much like everyone else, not keeping apart from the people. But when they received the office by hereditary succession and found their safety now provided for, and more than sufficient provision of food, they gave way to their appetites owing to this superabundance, and came to think that the rulers must be distinguished from their subjects by a peculiar dress, that there should be a peculiar luxury and variety in the dressing and serving of their viands, and that they should meet with no denial in the pursuit of their amours, however lawless. These habits having given rise in the one case to envy and offence and in the other to an outburst of hatred and passionate resentment, the kingship changed into a tyranny; the first steps toward its overthrow were taken by the subjects, and conspiracies began to be formed. These conspiracies were not the work of the worst men, but of the noblest, most high-spirited, and most courageous, because such men are least able to brook the insolence of princes. 8. The people now having got leaders, would combine with them against the ruling powers for the reasons I stated above; kingship and monarchy would be utterly abolished, and in their place aristocracy would begin to grow. For the commons, as if bound to pay at once their debt of gratitude to the abolishers of monarchy, would make them their leaders and entrust their destinies to them. At first these chiefs gladly assumed this charge and

regarded nothing as of greater importance than the common interest, administering the private and public affairs of the people with paternal solicitude. But here again when children inherited this position of authority from their fathers, having no experience of misfortune and none at all of civil equality and liberty of speech, and having been brought up from the cradle amid the evidences of the power and high position of their fathers, they abandoned themselves some to greed of gain and unscrupulous moneymaking, others to indulgence in wine and the convivial excess which accompanies it, and others again to the violation of women and the rape of boys; and thus converting the aristocracy into an oligarchy aroused in the people feelings similar to those of which I just spoke, and in consequence met with the same disastrous end as the tyrant. 9. For whenever anyone who has noticed the jealousy and hatred with which they are regarded by the citizens, has the courage to speak or act against the chiefs of the state he has the whole mass of the people ready to back him. Next, when they have either killed or banished the oligarchs, they no longer venture to set a king over them, as they still remember with terror the injustice they suffered from the former ones, nor can they entrust the government with confidence to a select few, with the evidence before them of their recent error in doing so. Thus the only hope still surviving unimpaired is in themselves, and to this they resort, making the state a democracy instead of an oligarchy and assuming the responsibility for the conduct of affairs. Then as long as some of those survive who experienced the evils of oligarchical dominion, they are well pleased with the present form of government, and set a high value on equality and freedom of speech. But when a new generation arises and the democracy falls into the hands of the grandchildren of its founders, they have become so accustomed to freedom and equality that they no longer value them, and begin to aim at pre-eminence; and it is chiefly those of ample fortune who fall into this error. So when they begin to lust for power and cannot attain it through themselves or their own good qualities, they ruin their estates, tempting and corrupting the people in every possible way. And hence when by their foolish thirst for reputation they have created among the masses an appetite for gifts and the habit of receiving them, democracy in its turn is abolished and changes into a rule of force and violence. For the people, having grown accustomed to feed at the expense of others and to depend for their livelihood on the property of others, as soon as they find a leader who is enterprising but is excluded from the honours of office by his penury, institute the rule of violence; and now uniting their forces massacre, banish, and plunder, until they degenerate again into perfect savages and find once more a master and monarch.

Such is the cycle of political revolution, the course appointed by nature in which constitutions change, disappear, and finally return to the point from which they started. Anyone who clearly perceives this may indeed in speaking of the future of any state be wrong in his estimate of the time the process will take, but if his judgment is not tainted by animosity or jealousy, he will very seldom be mistaken as to the stage of growth or decline it has reached, and as to the form into which it will change. And especially in the case of the Roman state will this method enable us to arrive at a knowledge of its formation, growth, and greatest perfection, and likewise of the change for the worse which is sure to follow some day. For, as I said, this state, more than any other, has been formed and has grown naturally, and will undergo a natural decline and change to its contrary. The reader will be able to judge of the truth of this from the subsequent parts of this work.

10. At present I will give a brief account of the legislation of Lycurgus, a matter not alien to my present purpose. Lycurgus had perfectly well understood that all the above changes take place necessarily and naturally, and had taken into consideration that every variety of constitution which is simple and formed on one principle is precarious, as it is soon perverted into the corrupt form which is proper to it and naturally follows on it. For just as rust in the case of iron and wood-worms and ship-worms in the case of timber are inbred pests, and these substances, even though they escape all external injury, fall a prey to the evils engendered in them, so each constitution has a vice engendered in it and inseparable from it. In kingship it is despotism, in aristocracy oligarchy, and in democracy the savage rule of violence; and it is impossible, as I said above, that each of these should not in course of time change into this vicious form. Lycurgus, then, foreseeing this, did not make his constitution simple and uniform, but united in it all the good and distinctive features of the best governments, so that none of the principles should grow unduly and be perverted into its allied evil, but that, the force of each being neutralized by that of the others, neither of them should prevail and outbalance another, but that the constitution should remain for long in a state of equilibrium like a well-trimmed boat, kingship being guarded from arrogance by the fear of the commons, who were given a sufficient share in the government, and the commons on the other hand not venturing to

treat the kings with contempt from fear of the elders, who being selected from the best citizens would be sure all of them to be always on the side of justice; so that that part of the state which was weakest owing to its subservience to traditional custom, acquired power and weight by the support and influence of the elders. The consequence was that by drawing up his constitution thus he preserved liberty at Sparta for a longer period than is recorded elsewhere.

Lycurgus then, foreseeing, by a process of reason-ing, whence and how events naturally happen, con-structed his constitution untaught by adversity, but the Romans while they have arrived at the same final result as regards their form of government, have not reached it by any process of reasoning, but by the discipline of many struggles and troubles, and always choosing the best by the light of the experience gained in disaster have thus reached the same result as Lycurgus, that is to say, the best of all existing constitutions.

22

The Funeral Oration

Thucydides

34. In the course of this winter the Athenians, in accordance with the custom of their forefathers, buried at the public expense those who had first fallen in the war, after the following manner. Having erected a tent, they lay out the bones of the dead three days before, and each one brings to his own relative whatever [funeral offering] he pleases. When the funeral procession takes place, cars convey coffins of cypress wood, one for each tribe, in which are laid the bones of every man, according to the tribe to which he belonged; and one empty bier is carried, spread in honor of the missing, whose bodies could not be found to be taken up. Whoever wishes, both of citizens and strangers, joins in the procession; and their female relatives attend at the burial to make the wailings. They lay them then in the public sepulcher, which is in the fairest suburb of the city, and in which they always bury those who have fallen in the wars (except, at least, those who fell at Marathon; but to them, as they con-sidered their valor distinguished above that of all others, they gave a burial on the very spot). After they had laid them in the ground, a man chosen by the state—one who in point of intellect is considered talented, and in dignity is pre-eminent—speaks over them such a panegyric as may be appropriate; after which they all retire. In this way they bury them:

and through the whole of the war, whenever they had occasion, they observed the established custom. Over these who were first buried,[1] at any rate, Pericles son of Xanthippus was chosen to speak. And when the time for doing so came, advancing from the sepulcher on to a platform, which had been raised to some height, that he might be heard over as great a part of the crowd as possible, he spoke to the following effect:

35. "The greater part of those who ere now have spoken in this place, have been accustomed to praise the man who introduced this oration into the law; considering it a right thing that it should be delivered over those who are buried after falling in battle. To me, however, it would have appeared sufficient, that when men had shown themselves brave by deeds, their honors also should be displayed by deeds—as you now see in the case of this burial, prepared at the public expense—and not that the virtues of many should be periled in one individual, for credit to be given him according as he expresses himself well or ill. For it is difficult to speak with propriety on a subject on which even the impression of one's truth-fulness is with difficulty established. For the hearer who is acquainted [with the facts], and kindly disposed [toward those who performed them], might perhaps think them somewhat imperfectly set forth, compared with what he both wishes and knows; while he who is unacquainted with them might think that some points were even exaggerated, being led to

From Thucydides, *History of the Peloponnesian War,* trans. Rev. Henry Dale (New York: Harper & Brothers, 1893), pp. 110–118.

this conclusion by envy, should he hear anything surpassing his own natural powers. For praises spoken of others are only endured so far as each one thinks that he is himself also capable of doing any of the things he hears; but that which exceeds their own capacity men at once envy and disbelieve. Since, however, our ancestors judged this to be a right custom, I too, in obedience to the law, must endeavor to meet the wishes and views of every one, as far as possible.

36. "I will begin then with our ancestors first: for it is just, and becoming too at the same time, that on such an occasion the honor of being thus mentioned should be paid them. For always inhabiting the country without change, through a long succession of posterity, by their valor they transmitted it free to this very time. Justly then may they claim to be commended; and more justly still may our own fathers. For in addition to what they inherited, they acquired the great empire which we possess, and by painful exertions bequeathed it to us of the present day: though to most part of it have additions been made by ourselves here, who are still, generally speaking, in the vigor of life; and we have furnished our city with every thing, so as to be most self-sufficient both for peace and for war. Now with regard to our military achievements, by which each possession was gained, whether in any case it were ourselves, or our fathers, that repelled with spirit hostilities brought against us by barbarian or Greek; as I do not wish to enlarge on the subject before you who are well acquainted with it, I will pass them over. But by what mode of life we attained to our power, and by what form of government and owing to what habits it became so great, I will explain these points first, and then proceed to the eulogy of these men; as I consider that on the present occasion they will not be inappropriately mentioned, and that it is profitable for the whole assembly, both citizens and strangers, to listen to them.

37. "For we enjoy a form of government which does not copy the laws of our neighbors; but we are ourselves rather a pattern to others than imitators of them. In name, from its not being administered for the benefit of the few but of the many, it is called a democracy; but with regard to its laws, all enjoy equality, as concerns their private differences; while with regard to public rank, according as each man has reputation for any thing, he is preferred for public honors, not so much from consideration of party, as of merit; nor, again, on the ground of poverty, while he is able to do the state any good service, is he prevented by the obscurity of his position. We are liberal then in our public administra-tion; and with regard to mutual jealousy of our daily pursuits, we are not angry with our neighbor, if he does any thing to please himself; nor wear on our countenance offensive looks, which though harm-less, are yet unpleasant. While, however, in private matters we live together agreeably, in public matters, under the influence of fear, we most carefully abstain from transgression, through our obedience to those who are from time to time in office, and to the laws; especially such of them as are enacted for the benefit of the injured, and such as, though unwritten, bring acknowledged disgrace [on those who break them].

38. "Moreover, we have provided for our spirits the most numerous recreations from labors, by cele-brating games and sacrifices through the whole year, and by maintaining elegant private establishments, of which the daily gratification drives away sadness. Owing to the greatness too of our city, every thing from every land is imported into it; and it is our lot to reap with no more peculiar enjoyment the good things which are produced here, than those of the rest of the world likewise.

39. "In the studies of war also we differ from our enemies in the following respects. We throw our city open to all, and never, by the expulsion of strangers, exclude any one from either learning or observing things, by seeing which unconcealed any of our enemies might gain an advantage; for we trust not so much to preparations and stratagems, as to our own valor for daring deeds. Again, as to our modes of education, *they* aim at the acquisition of a manly character, by laborious training from their very youth; while *we,* though living at our ease, no less boldly advance to meet equal dangers. As a proof of this, the Lacedæmonians never march against our country singly, but with all [their confederates] to-gether: while we, generally speaking, have no diffi-culty in conquering in battle upon hostile ground those who are standing up in defense of their own. And no enemy ever yet encountered our whole united force, through our attending at the same time to our navy, and sending our troops by land on so many different services: but wherever they have engaged with any part of it, if they conquer only some of us, they boast that we were all routed by them; and if they are conquered, they say it was by all that they were beaten. And yet if with careless ease rather than with laborious practice, and with a courage which is the result not so much of laws as of natural disposition, we are willing to face danger, we have the advantage of not suffering beforehand from coming troubles, and of proving ourselves, when we are involved in them, no less bold than those who are always toiling; so that our country

is worthy of admiration in these respects, and in others besides.

40. "For we study taste with economy, and philosophy without effeminacy; and employ wealth rather for opportunity of action than for boastfulness of talking; while poverty is nothing disgraceful for a man to confess, but not to escape it by exertion is more disgraceful. Again, the same men can attend at the same time to domestic as well as to public affairs; and others, who are engaged with business, can still form a sufficient judgment on political questions. For we are the only people that consider the man who takes no part in these things, not as unofficious, but as useless; and we ourselves judge rightly of measures, at any rate, if we do not originate them; while we do not regard words as any hinderance to deeds, but rather [consider it a hindrance] not to have been previously instructed by word, before undertaking in deed what we have to do. For we have this characteristic also in a remarkable degree, that we are at the same time most daring and most calculating in what we take in hand; whereas to other men it is ignorance that brings daring, while calculation brings fear. These, however, would deservedly be deemed most courageous, who know most fully what is terrible and what is pleasant, and yet do not on this account shrink from dangers. As regards beneficence also we differ from the generality of men; for we make friends, not by receiving, but by conferring kindness. Now he who has conferred the favor is the firmer friend, in order that he may keep alive the obligation by good will toward the man on whom he has conferred it; whereas he who owes it in return feels less keenly, knowing that it is not as a favor, but as a debt, that he will repay the kindness. Nay, we are the only men who fearlessly benefit any one, not so much from calculations of expediency, as with the confidence of liberality.

41. "In short, I say that both the whole ctiy is a school for Greece, and that, in my opinion, the same individual would among us prove himself qualified for the most varied kinds of action, and with the most graceful versatility. And that this is not mere vaunting language for the occasion, so much as actual truth, the very power of the state, which we have won by such habits, affords a proof. For it is the only country at the present time that, when brought to the test, proves superior to its fame; and the only one that neither gives to the enemy who has attacked us any cause of indignation as being worsted by such opponents, nor to him who is subject to us room for finding fault, as not being ruled by men who are worthy of empire. But we shall be admired both by present and future generations as

having exhibited our power with great proofs, and by no means without evidence; and as having no further need, either of Homer to praise us, or any one else who might charm for the moment by his verses, while the truth of the facts would mar the idea formed of them; but as having compelled every sea and land to become accessible to our daring, and every where established everlasting records, whether of evil or of good. It was for such a country then that these men, nobly resolving not to have it taken from them, fell fighting; and every one of their survivors may well be willing to suffer in its behalf.

42. "For this reason, indeed, it is that I have enlarged on the characteristics of the state; both to prove that the struggle is not for the same object in our case as in that of men who have none of these advantages in an equal degree; and at the same time clearly to establish by proofs [the truth of] the eulogy of those men over whom I am now speaking. And now the chief points of it have been mentioned; for with regard to the things for which I have commended the city, it was the virtues of these men, and such as these, that adorned her with them; and few of the Greeks are there whose fame, like these men's, would appear but the just counterpoise of their deeds. Again, the closing scene of these men appears to me to supply an illustration of human worth, whether as affording us the first information respecting it, or its final confirmation. For even in the case of men who have been in other respects of an inferior character, it is but fair for them to hold forth as a screen their military courage in their country's behalf; for, having wiped out their evil by their good, they did more service collectively, than harm by their individual offenses. But of these men there was none that either was made a coward by his wealth, from preferring the continued enjoyment of it; or shrank from danger through a hope suggested by poverty, namely, that he might yet escape it, and grow rich; but conceiving that vengeance on their foes was more to be desired than those objects, and at the same time regarding this as the most glorious of hazards, they wished by risking it to be avenged on their enemies, and so to aim at procuring those advantages; committing to hope the uncertainty of success, but resolving to trust to action, with regard to what was visible to themselves; and in that action, being minded rather to resist and die, than by surrendering to escape, they fled from the shame of [a discreditable] report, while they endured the brunt of the battle with their bodies; and after the shortest crisis, when at the very height of their fortune, were taken away from their glory rather than their fear.

43. "Such did these men prove themselves, as became the character of their country. For you that

remain, you must pray that you may have a more successful resolution, but must determine not to have one less bold against your enemies; not in word alone considering the benefit [of such a spirit] (on which one might descant to you at great length —though you know it yourselves quite as well— telling you how many advantages are contained in repelling your foes); but rather day by day beholding the power of the city as it appears in fact, and growing enamored of it, and reflecting, when you think it great, that it was by being bold, and knowing their duty, and being alive to shame in action, that men acquired these things; and because, if they ever failed in their attempt at any thing, they did not on that account think it right to deprive their country also of their valor, but conferred upon her a most glorious joint-offering. For while collectively they gave her their lives, individually they received that renown which never grows old, and the most distinguished tomb they could have; not so much that in which they are laid, as that in which their glory is left behind them, to be everlastingly re-corded on[2] every occasion for doing so, either by word or deed, that may from time to time present itself. For of illustrious men the whole earth is the sepulcher; and not only does the inscription upon columns in their own land point it out, but in that also which is not their own there dwells with every one an unwritten memorial of the heart, rather than of a material monument. Vieing then with these men in your turn, and deeming happiness to consist in freedom, and freedom in valor, do not think lightly of the hazards of war. For it is not the unfortunate [and those] who have not hope of any good, that would with most reason be unsparing of their lives; but those who, while they live, still incur the risk of a change to the opposite condition, and to whom the difference would be the greatest, should they meet with any reverse. For more grievous, to a man of high spirit at least, is the misery which ac-companies cowardice, than the unfelt death which comes upon him at once, in the time of his strength and of his hope for the common welfare.

44. "Wherefore to the parents of the dead—as many of them as are here among you—I will not offer condolence, so much as consolation. For they know that they have been brought up subject to manifold misfortunes; but that happy is *their* lot who have gained the most glorious—death, as these have,—sorrow, as you have; and to whom life has been so exactly measured, that they were both happy in it, and died in [that happiness]. Difficult, indeed, I know it is to persuade you of this, with regard to those of whom you will often be reminded by the good fortune of others, in which you yourselves also

once rejoiced; and sorrow is felt, not for the blessings of which one is bereft without full experience of them, but of that which one loses after becoming accustomed to it. But you must bear up in the hope of other children, those of you whose age yet allows you to have them. For to yourselves individually those who are subsequently born will be a reason for your forgetting those who are no more; and to the state it will be beneficial in two ways, by its not being depopulated, and by the enjoyment of security; for it is not possible that those should offer any fair and just advice, who do not incur equal risk with their neighbors by having children at stake. Those of you, however, who are past that age, must consider that the longer period of your life during which you have been prosperous is so much gain, and that what remains will be but a short one; and you must cheer yourselves with the fair fame of these [your lost ones]. For the love of honor is the only feeling that never grows old; and in the helplessness of age it is not the acquisition of gain, as some assert, that gives greatest pleasure, but the enjoyment of honor.

45. "For those of you, on the other hand, who are sons or brothers of the dead, great, I see, will be the struggle of competition. For every one is accustomed to praise the man who is no more; and scarcely, though even for an excess of worth, would you be esteemed, I do not say equal to them, but only slightly inferior. For the living are exposed to envy in their rivalry; but those who are in no one's way are honored with a good will free from all opposi-tion. If, again, I must say anything on the subject of woman's excellence also, with reference to those of you who will now be in widowhood, I will express it all in a brief exhortation. Great will be your glory in not falling short of the natural character that belongs to you; and great is hers, who is least talked of among the men, either for good or evil.

46. "I have now expressed *in word,* as the law required, what I had to say befitting the occasion; and, *in deed,* those who are here interred, have already received part of their honors; while, for the remaining part, the state will bring up their sons at the public expense, from this time to their man-hood; thus offering both to these and to their posterity a beneficial reward for such contests; for where the greatest prizes for virtue are given, there also the most virtuous men are found among the citizens. And now, having finished your lamentations for your several relatives, depart."

NOTES

1. Or, "accordingly over these," etc.
2. Literally, "on every occasion, either of word or deed, that may from time to time present itself."

23

From *The Annals*

Tacitus

XXIII. In the consulate of Aulus Vitellius[1] and Lucius Vipstanus, the question of completing the numbers of the senate was under consideration, and the leading citizens of Gallia Comata,[2] as it is termed, who had long before obtained federate rights and Roman citizenship,[3] were claiming the privilege of holding magistracies in the capital. Comments on the subject were numerous and diverse; and in the imperial council the debate was conducted with animation on both sides:—"Italy," it was asserted, "was not yet so moribund that she was unable to supply a deliberative body to her own capital. The time had been when a Roman-born senate was enough for nations[4] whose blood was akin to their own; and they were not ashamed of the old republic. Why, even to-day men quoted the patterns of virtue and of glory which, under the old system, the Roman character had given to the world! Was it too little that Venetians and Insubrians[5] had taken the curia by storm, unless they brought in an army of aliens to give it the look of a taken town? What honours would be left to the relics of their nobility or the poor senator who came from Latium? All would be submerged by those opulent persons whose grandfathers and great-grandfathers, in command of hostile tribes, had smitten our armies by steel and the strong hand, and had besieged the deified Julius at Alesia.[6] But those were recent events! What if there should arise the memory of the men who essayed to pluck down the spoils, sanctified to Heaven, from the Capitol and citadel of Rome?[7] Leave them by all means to enjoy the title of citizens: but the insignia of the Fathers, the glories of the magistracies,—these they must not vulgarize!"

XXIV. Unconvinced by these and similar arguments, the emperor not only stated his objections there and then, but, after convening the senate, addressed it as follows:[8]—"In my own ancestors, the eldest of whom, Clausus, a Sabine by extraction, was made simultaneously a citizen and the head of a patrician house, I find encouragement to employ the same policy in my administration, by transferring hither all true excellence, let it be found where it will. For I am not unaware that the Julii came to us from Alba, the Coruncanii from Camerium,[9] the Porcii from Tusculum; that—not to scrutinize antiquity—members were drafted into the senate from Etruria, from Lucania, from the whole of Italy;[10] and that finally Italy itself was extended to the Alps,[11] in order that not individuals merely but countries and nationalities should form one body under the name of Romans. The day of stable peace at home and victory abroad came when the districts beyond the Po were admitted to citizenship, and, availing ourselves of the fact that our legions were settled throughout the globe, we added to them the stoutest of the provincials, and succoured a weary empire. Is it regretted that the Balbi crossed over from Spain and families equally distinguished from Narbonese Gaul? Their descendants remain; nor do they yield to ourselves in love for this native land of theirs. What else proved fatal to Lacedaemon and Athens, in spite of their power in arms, but their policy of holding the conquered aloof as alien-born? But the sagacity of our own founder Romulus was such that several times he fought and naturalized a people in the course of the same day! Strangers have been kings over us: the conferment of magistracies on the sons of freedmen is not the novelty which it is commonly and mistakenly thought, but a frequent practice of the old commonwealth.—"But we fought with the Senones."—Then, presumably, the Volscians and Aequians[12] never drew up a line of battle against us.—"We were taken by the Gauls."—But we also gave hostages to the Tuscans[13] and underwent the yoke of the Samnites.[14]—And yet, if you survey the whole of our wars, not one was finished within a shorter period[15] than that against the Gauls: thenceforward there has been a continuous and loyal peace. Now that customs, culture, and the ties of marriage have blended them with ourselves, let them bring among us their gold and their riches instead of

Reprinted from Tacitus, *The Annals*, trans. John Jackson (Cambridge: Harvard University Press, n.d.), Book XI, Chs. XXIII–XXIV, pp. 285–291. Reprinted by permission of the publishers and The Loeb Classical Library.

retaining them beyond the pale! All, Conscript Fathers, that is now believed supremely old has been new: plebeian magistrates followed the patrician; Latin, the plebeian; magistrates from the other races of Italy, the Latin. Our innovation, too, will be parcel of the past, and what to-day we defend by precedents will rank among precedents."

NOTES

1. The future emperor.
2. "Long-haired Gaul" (the three imperial provinces of Aquitania, Lugdunensis, and Belgica), as opposed to "trousered Gaul" (the senatorial and completely romanized Gallia Narbonensis).
3. Their clans were *foederati;* they themselves, full Roman citizens, but without senatorial rank, and therefore ineligible for the official career.
4. The Latin and Italian communities.
5. Types of the Gallic population north of the Po, enfranchised by Caesar at the outbreak of the Civil War (49 B.C.).
6. The scene of the siege, in 52 B.C., of Vercingetorix by Caesar and of Caesar by the relieving Gaulish army (Caes. *B.G.* VII. 68 etc.); now Alise-Sainte-Reine, a village of some 600 inhabitants, between Semur and Dijon.
7. The text is desperate, but refers to the capture of Rome and siege of the Capitol by the Senonian Gauls after Allia (390 B.C.).
8. Large fragments of the actual speech, here re-written, rearranged, and condensed by Tacitus, were discovered at Lyons in 1524, and printed by Lipsius in an excursus to his famous edition fifty years later. They may be conveniently consulted in Orelli, Nipperdey, or Furneaux.
9. In Latium, like Alba and Tusculum; but the site is uncertain.
10. In virtue of the extension of the franchise to all Italy south of the Po, at the end of the Social War.
11. The reference is to Caesar's grant of the *civitas* to the Gallic communities north of the Po, in 49 B.C., a date which makes the following *tunc solia domi quies* curious.
12. Southern and eastern neighbors respectively of ancient Rome; associated with the legends of Coriolanus and Cincinnatus.
13. After the surrender of Rome to Porsenna.
14. At the Caudine Forks in 321 B.C.
15. In ten years (59–50 B.C.). There were many shorter conquests; and, in his actual speech, Claudius emphasizes the obstinacy of their resistance.

b. MAJOR TYPES OF CITY-STATES AND THE CONDITIONS OF THEIR DEVELOPMENT AND CHANGE

24

The Genesis of the Greek Polis

Fritz Schachermeyr

For the scholar of ancient history, the "polis" is the most important and most worthy subject of study. By "polis" we mean that well-known type of Greek city which with its territory constituted an autonomous state and, in this respect, was quite similar to the centres of the Italian Renaissance. Ancient Hellas was made up of a great number of such "polis" cities. Each of them had its own freedom, its individual pride as an independent republic. But in the over-all picture we recognise in the institution of the polis the ground that nourished the dynamic and in a sense revolutionary spirit of the

From Fritz Schachermeyr, "The Genesis of the Greek Polis," *Diogenes,* No. 4 (1953), pp. 17–30. Reprinted by permission of the publisher.

ancient Greeks. Aeschylus, Sophocles, and Euripides, Cleisthenes and Themistocles, Pericles and Alcibiades, Protagoras and Democritus, Plato and Aristotle were the sons of polis cities. We may even assert that these men could be what they were only in the emancipated and inspired atmosphere of the polis. No other ancient culture could have given them birth. If we consider the Greek polis from the point of view of universal history we come to a rather astonishing conclusion: the polis differs from all other comparable cultural institutions in Asia, Egypt, and Europe by a very fundamental and special trait: Europe knew only a primitive, barbarian, rustic way of life. People were either roving nomads or tillers of the soil who lived in simple villages. The Celtic *oppida* and the Adriatic *castella* were both rustic in character. Urban specialisation, the kind of industriousness that goes with it, a dynamic and independent rise of culture—these were lacking everywhere.

In the Orient, on the other hand, we find at that same time an old, venerable and highly developed urban culture, based on a hierarchical order. These Oriental cultures, however, remained conservative in their religious ideas, and in so far as internal politics were concerned, they were not able to develop genuine democracies. Jerusalem alone shows a revolutionary and creative spirit akin to that of the polis, though tending in a different direction. To some (though a less) extent this is true also of the Phoenecian cities. For the rest the cities of the Near East and of Egypt clung to their old traditions. In the Mediterranean, only Etruria and Carthage developed a somewhat dynamic form, but in many respects this development took place only under Greek influence. Rome, in the beginning, tended towards a more conservative and rustic type of life and did not show any of the characteristics of the Greek polis. It began to draw closer to the Greek model only in the times of the Scipios.

The Greek polis, then, with its dynamic and revolutionary spirit—by nature *novarum rerum cupidus* —as a type of political life stood very much alone in early antiquity. Only gradually did it spread all over the ancient world. This happened mainly in the Hellenistic and in the Roman periods. We should not like to assert, however, that the dynamic spirit of the polis was transmitted in the same way as its outward forms.

The peculiar ways of the Greek polis prompt us to look into the origins of this strange phenomenon. Until recently one would hardly have dared to raise this question at all, since indeed there was little hope for an answer. The material provided by recent excavations and a great deal of information furnished by sociologists, ethnologists, and related palaeological fields open up new approaches to the problem.

The following remarks are meant as an attempt in this direction. We are concerned mainly with two aspects of the problem: 1. How did it happen at all that the urban principle became the determining cultural factor in the Aegean? 2. Why did those Aegean cities take on that peculiar nature so characteristic of and indispensable to the Greek polis?

Recently[1] it has become possible to give a satisfactory account of the early beginnings of the Greek city. The polis did not rise by any means from local origins: There are no traces that would lead us from the Epipalaeolithic caves of the early hunters and food-gatherers to the first urban settlements. British and American excavations have proven beyond any doubt that the decisive step to agricultural, permanent, and city-like settlement was taken in Cilicia, northern Syria, and Upper Mesopotamia as early as the fifth and fourth millennia B.C. As early as about 3500 B.C. the people of those countries had risen to a high level of city culture known as the "Tell Halaf." Here we have the cradle of the city culture of the whole Eastern Mediterranean. It was at the same time the homeland of ceramics, a refined art of weaving, miniature sculpture, and advanced architecture. Also the techniques of fortification had reached a high standard in those days with the Cilicians.[3]

This cultural movement spread from Cilicia—and perhaps also from the area about Malatia[4]—and reached Greece partly via Asia Minor, partly by sea, and created the so-called "Sesclo culture"[5] in that region. Agriculture, permanent settlement, and stone construction, specialisation of the various crafts, among which weaving, ceramics, and the plastic arts were prevalent, were thus introduced in the Aegean from the East. The fertile plains of Thessaly show an astonishing density of population. Indeed, it seems that during the so-called "Neolithic period" about twice as many villages existed in that region as today.[6] That some settlements had even developed into real small towns is demonstrated by Sesclo itself. Remarkably enough the most extensive settlement was found on the sites of Athens. It is true that the Neolithic remains, except for very few specimens, have fallen victim to late building periods, with the result that often only the shafts of wells of that time, containing some casual potsherds, testify to the former existence of houses. A map indicating the various locations where such remains have been found, shows that the regions south, north, and north-west of the Acropolis were inhabited. This makes for quite an extensive area, especially since the citadel itself was most likely a part of the settlement. In all probability Athens was one of the largest places in Greece even in Neolithic times, and it may be that the name of the city goddess Athena spread all over the Aegean at that time with the generic meaning of "protectress of the city." Another rather large Neolithic settlement was located at Cnossos on Crete, probably even larger than the well-known later Great Palace. On the other hand it is true that this island is indebted to the Near Eastern civilisations only for a part of its high cultural attainments. The other part is due to an influx of cultural elements from Egypt. On the whole we may say that the city culture, imported as it was from the

Orient, had taken roots in the Aegean area as early as the first half of the third millennium. Further expansion of this urban civilisation to the Balkans and the valley of the Danube or to Italy did not take place.

A new wave of this city culture reached Greece about the beginning of the Early Bronze Period, or about 2600.[7] At about that time innumerable small towns were founded in the western part of Asia Minor. Some of them retained their importance even in later times, as, for instance, Troy and Gordion and the Anatolian predecessor of what later became Smyrna. Troy was distinguished by its superb fortifications and the beautiful palaces with their spacious courts surrounded by colonnades in the style of the Greek megaron.[8] This urban civilisation, together with the use of copper (or bronze) which became increasingly important, spread from Western Anatolia to the other countries of the Aegean. Poliochni on the island of Lemnos speaks eloquently of this movement. The place was surrounded by a city wall reinforced by strong towers: it had a paved main street, public wells, and gathering or market places. A large hall was found with stone steps to sit on, a tiled bathroom and a cistern.[9] The art of fortification spread from there to the Cyclades and to Aegina. Such Anatolian devices as the fishbone pattern in masonry, the use of the stone hinge, the storage rooms called *bothroi,* and perhaps also the type of megaron with apsidal end[10] have spread as far as the Greek mainland. An unusually extensive settlement was formed at Tiryns, where powerful princes seem to have had their residence as the circular constructions of that place indicate. The urban characteristics of the Anatolian settlement—one should almost say, those characteristics of the small, provincial town—became even more pronounced on the islands and on the Greek mainland, much more so even than in the Neolithic period; and they grew constantly in importance with the now dominating trade and industrialisation.

Greece and Asia Minor now form a cultural unit. On the other hand, the urban civilisation has not advanced, even at this time, to the North and the West. Thus in Europe city culture is limited to Hellas and the Aegean islands.

This seems to take care of our first question concerning the origins of the Aegean city culture; for from then on the urban character of the settlements was preserved for all times, together with the old Aegean names in *-nthos* and *-ssos.*[11]

The Aegean area was thus more than 2,000 years ahead of the rest of Europe in the development of a city culture. The importance of this fact will be obvious if we consider that only the urban forms of life have been able to overcome certain obstacles and thus could lead to more differentiated and higher forms of civilisation.

We now come to our second question: How did this form of city culture, indigenous in the Orient, acquire the characteristics peculiar to the Greek mentality?

This problem is much harder to tackle since a great variety of rather heterogeneous factors have come into play. Quite certainly the very topography of the country—so different from the continental Orient—played an important role. At the risk of repeating well-known facts we must again point to the consequences of the insular and peninsular conformation of the Aegean area of settlement. Its scattered components could not create a united empire. This fact divided Greece into small restricted territories and states. Greece, as it were, breathed from the sea-side, both economically and politically. It is a matter of fact that "the air of the sea makes for freedom." In the Orient we thus find, for the same reason, a more liberal and adventurous way of life among the Phoenicians or the Cyprians than among the peoples of the other large territories in the centre of Asia Minor, Egypt, or for that matter of the whole Near East, these countries being cut off from the sea.

The geographical situation is responsible not only for the particular open-mindedness of the Aegean populations; it has also provided them with a special receptivity for visual experience. The great variety of the scenery, the wealth of ever new beauty, forming the natural surrounding of these people, made them into "eye-men" (visual types). This is not to say that such possibilities were missing elsewhere. But the accents seem to lie differently with the Greeks, and this is the reason why art had such a special meaning for them, why it was so much more an independent, autonomous thing, why the artist and his genius were so greatly honoured.

That the Aegean civilisation experienced a certain enlargement and enfranchisement due to geographic conditions can best be shown by a reference to Minoan art. It is true, on Crete as in the Orient we are faced with the great palaces of the rulers, rulers "by the grace of God," or of princes with the sanctity of priests. And art was determined entirely by the tastes and directions of the court. Yet both in form and in contents there is a significant difference: in the Orient, art served above all the glorification of the ruler, as, e.g., in the oversize representations of the Egyptian Pharaohs. In that country the higher officials as well liked to be represented at the head of all their subordinates. In Minoan art we look in vain for such hierarchical tendencies. The rests of one single fresco painting seem to represent a ruler or prince, the so-called "Prince with the feather crown"; but he is not seated on a throne nor is he arrayed in marked dignity. Rather, he is seen strolling in his garden among butterflies and flowers.[12] It does not happen either, in Cretan art, that a person is represented larger than others merely on account of his higher rank. On one fresco the audience at a dance in a sacred olive grove form just an ordinary assemblage of people, and only a number of fashionable ladies enjoy the privilege of special seats.[13] The harvest procession on a vase of steatite[14] takes its motif from the ways of the ordinary people, and when occasionally a group of gift-bearers or an officer with his soldiers[15] are represented, there is always much more of a lyrical, or simply human, than of a hierarchic-imperial inspiration. Minoan art, indeed, tends towards the idyllic scene or the *genre*. We guess at a friendly and natural relation between the ruler and his subjects, a horizontal relation, so to speak, in contrast to the more solemn, vertical one, from higher to lower, usual in Egypt, Assyria, and Babylon. I think it is safe to say that the geographical nature of the respective countries is responsible for this state of things.

And yet it cannot be said by any means that in the case of the Minoan residences we are already dealing with the "polis." True, Cnossos was a big city. Evans has estimated its population at well over 80,000.[16] But it had a palace at its centre just as Mallia, Gurnia and others.[17] Polis and palace, however, are mutually exclusive, politically as well as in terms of the general intellectual climate.

I am thus inclined to think that we have missed another factor so far, a factor which is not linked with the local, the geographic conditions, and which did not come from the Orient (as did city culture itself), but which was imported by the invading Greeks.

The earliest Greeks moved into Hellas about 2000 B.C.[18] At that time, however, they occupied only the mainland, while simultaneously the indigenous Minoan palace culture, which had nothing to do with Greek culture, reached its fullest bloom on Crete. The invaders mixed with the older population on the mainland; they took over their city culture; they came under the influence of the geography of the Aegean; but they brought along with them an entirely new element, an element which was to be of the greatest importance for the development of the polis: the principle of the political community on the basis of personal association. In order to explain this we must go further back.

The invading Greeks belonged to the family of the so-called Indo-European peoples.[19] The particular traits of these peoples are not known to us in their original form; but we can draw certain inferences from the similarities among their numerous descendants. Above all, we are able to gather from such a comparison that while they also tilled the soil they were predominantly cattle breeders. It seems further that they were generally rather unsettled. The soil was used for pasture and for the most primitive kind of agriculture, using the hoe rather than the plough. When the soil was exhausted, they simply moved on, into the territory of the neighbours or over larger distances.

As a consequence of this unsettled way of life no concept of the state as bound to a fixed territory could arise among the Indo-European peoples. Indeed, one gets the impression that there was no such thing at all as the "state," but that instead they lived in personal "associations." These, of course, were not confined to the Indo-Europeans. This kind of association of individuals, these corporations, are found among all migrant peoples, as e.g., the Bedouins of the Near East—in this case conditioned by the economic necessities of their nomad life.[20] The essential point of all these groups is their system of joint living, of joint shepherding, of joint fighting. The members of such associations are usually related to one another by family ties. Foreigners may be incorporated while unworthy members may be expelled. The main thing, however, is that the association considers itself as a sovereign body and that its members are not "subjects." They are guided by only one thing: the *public opinion* of the whole association. The chieftain or the sheik or his like has to yield to this public opinion; he is but the bearer of the will of the whole, a *primus inter pares*.

All this is in direct opposition to what we find in the civilisations with a developed agriculture, civilisations which demand permanent settlement; which have experienced the fertility of the soil in all its sanctity and mystery; whence they form the concept of the territorial state. Here the protection of a king is requisite, with a centralised military system; here people are prepared to bow as "subjects," if this will guarantee them the possession of their soil. And this is in fact the mentality of the soil-tilling cultures of the Orient. Similar conditions, though perhaps somewhat laxer as we saw above, may have prevailed in the Aegean area before the Indo-European invasion.

And now a rather important point: True, the principle of *personal* association of the Oriental Bedouins is in contrast with the *territorial* principle of the agricultural imperial Orient. But as soon as the Bedouins settle down, change to agriculture, and form city communities, they almost entirely abandon the *personal* principle of their social order and adopt the territorial one. The Indo-European reaction was quite different. Even when they penetrated into agricultural regions and subjugated the indigenous populations while adopting their economic system, they retained the personal structure of their society, in some cases with astonishing tenacity. This explains why in Rome the *populus Romanus,* together with the *quirites,* is the carrier of the authority of the state. This explains the *civitas civium* in Italy, the Aurunci, the Volsci, etc. It explains, likewise, the prevalence of ethnic designations like "Athenians," "Corinthians," etc., in Greece. By indicating the personal bearers of the state these names symbolise the state itself while "Attica," "Corinthia," etc., designate merely territories and never entered into the concept of the state. It should be noted, on the other hand, that the invaders took over not only the pattern of city settlement but in most cases even the very cities themselves, Corinth, Mycenae, Tiryns, Athens, among others. But they filled these places so much with their own conceptions of the state as a *personal association* that down to the latest times the Athenian state was always represented by "the Athenians" and never by "Athens" or "Attica." The state itself is always called *politeia* by the Greeks, which means simply the body of the citizens or the institution of the citizens, in other words, the same as *civitas.* The word "polis" was used occasionally but only in a secondary way and, as it were, for brevity's sake.

In the Orient, with its sedentary way of life, this was different. There the ethnic name was never used for the state. Only such nomad people as, e.g., the Churri or the Achlame and Chabiri, who had no fixed territory, formed an exception. As a rule the city itself (the Assyrian word is *alu*) with its territory (*matu*) stood in the foreground. If one wanted to express the concept "the Babylonians" one had to say: "the people (*ameluti*) of the territory (*matu*) of the city (*alu*) of Babylon." The state also was embodied in "the territory of the city of Babylon, Assur," etc., or their kings respectively ("king of the territory of the city of Babylon, Assur' etc.).

It is this tendency towards personal association which I think to be the third component in the formation of the Greek polis; for this principle added to the city culture and the Mediterranean breadth and liberality that self-assertion and autonomy which were to play such an outstanding role in the forthcoming developments. But it took more than a millennium to bring these three elements into complete harmony.

The period which followed the invasion of about 2000 B.C. and lasted till about 1600 did not achieve this harmony. Of course, we know little about that period. On the one hand the small cities of the pre-Hellenic time were maintained. But the rulers or lords seem to have had no palaces that could be distinguished from the private buildings,[21] and in general the excavations have revealed a much more rustic and simple cultural niveau. The splendour of the close-by Minoan palaces may have had a rather paralysing effect on the development of those early Hellenes. Moreover, the Cretans still controlled the sea.

It was as late as 1580 that the introduction of the chariot and of chivalric warfare brought about a complete change in social and cultural conditions. This was the beginning of the Mycenaean period. The same era witnessed the rise of an aristocratic-chivalric class from the common people, a class which entered into close relations with Crete and at times with the Orient.[22] From there they took over the palace-like houses, and, in keeping with the new aristocratic style, they fortified these residences or even made them into real citadels.

This change, indeed, led in a direction quite different from the one the polis was actually to follow. For all over Greece two separate social strata, a higher and a lower one, were now formed, which were no longer dependent on the individual cities. The upper stratum was embodied in a chivalric class, which applied the principle of association on an entirely different and rather supranational plane. Still in the Iliad we recognise how the lords, from Thessaly to Ithaca and to the Peloponnesus, form a unified social stratum, with its own public opinion and with the king of Mycenae as "the most kingly," *primus inter pares,* at the helm. It is characteristic of that development that the position of this hegemon was rather shaky. According to the Iliad, there was so much criticism and opposition on the part of the other noble lords that an overlord such as Agamemnon had a hard time saving his prestige and the prerogatives of his position. But the point which concerns us most is that the local factors lost importance and interest in favour of the feudal cross-relations, arising from friendships among "hosts" and "guests" and family ties cutting across all territorial boundaries. A cultural expression of this supranational nobility is found—as Nilsson has taught us—in the evolution of a master religion of the Olympic gods with Zeus as the hegemon and with the *étiquette* of that nobility.[23]

Between 1200 and 1000 B.C. other invasions of the Eastern Mediterranean took place, to which the Mycenaean culture largely succumbed. The castles, palaces, and most of the settlements were destroyed. Many of the Mycenaean Greeks emigrated to the islands and to the west coast of Anatolia. The coarse, uncivilised Dorians and north-western Greeks pushed in from the mountain ranges of the Balkans.

When at about 1000 B.C. this movement came to a stop at last, it became evident that the nobility had survived the turmoil. We now find them also in the new Greek settlements on the islands and in Ionia. Even the Dorians produced an analogous ruling class, which inserted itself adroitly into the indigenous nobility. And yet we recognise a decisive turn: the nobility had manifestly become impoverished, and the old castles and palaces were not rebuilt. They were replaced mostly by sanctuaries. In Ionia, likewise, we find no separate residences for the lords who now live in the city among the other citizens—as for instance Ulysses in the Odyssey—unless they preferred an estate in the countryside.

At this point the city life began to exercise its strongly equalising force in Hellas. The noble dynasties were the first victim. One by one the various families were deprived of their princely prerogatives. They were levelled down, as it were, into the stratum of nobles, a process for which the Odyssey gives a revealing illustration in the events on Ithaca. Thus we may fix the change from monarchy to aristocratic republic at about the eighth century. City and state had always been identical in Greece with its naturally small territories. Now the city-state became a *republic* for the first time. This was a major step toward the polis.

However, the supra-national connexion within the caste of nobles was still the more powerful factor. Friendship and hospitality were not barred by national boundaries, and the Lelantian feud, e.g., divided the Hellenic nobility according to such friendships. But everywhere we can observe how, gradually, this ruling class loses cohesion and finally disintegrates. Ever since the kings had been eliminated, the nobility had wielded absolute power and had given themselves to a shameless exploitation of the common people. The ensuing unbearable conditions made for disunity among the nobility itself; individual families quarrelled with one another; and now emerged the drawing power of what was to become the "polis."

The aristocratic-supranational interpretation of the principle of association was now opposed by a new interpretation of this same principle, in the *territorial* sense, applied to the inhabitants representing the individual *state,* and thus to the "people of the state" (*Staatsvolk*). The "citizenship" suddenly moved into the foreground. It is true that there were as yet many gradations in so far as rights were concerned; but the citizen body was already felt as a whole and as something that exceeded the distinctions of class. There was thus a *politeia* in the sense of *civitas,* defined as "the Athenians," "the Corinthians," etc. The assembly of the people, too, clearly demarcated this *politeia,* regardless of the fact that the poor enjoyed no active civic rights beyond that of participating in this assembly. But they were "Athenians," or "Corinthians," they had the basic privileges and the protection of their home-state and, in all probability, a vote in the assembly of the people.[24]

For the first time patriotism became the highest virtue in this *politeia.* For the first time the Greeks were filled with ambition and pride *as citizens;* and polis began to compete with polis. We seem to be witnessing the labour pains of the polis—a process which took place athwart the seventh and sixth centuries.

It is worth noting that the idea of the polis was first promoted by two rather different historical factors: by lawgivers like Solon and Pittacus on the one hand, and by tyrants and autocrats like Kypselos and Peisistratus on the other. In both cases the purpose was to break the hybris and injustice of the aristocratic regime and to free the people from lawlessness and economic distress.[25] Solon and Pittacus, who themselves belonged to the noble class, tried to find a compromise solution which would be bearable for both parties. Again and again we find the word *patris* in the poems of Solon; it is the polis of Athens, according to his words, over which the goddess Athena holds her protecting hands; on behalf of this polis he implores the gods to grant them *Eunomia,*[26] the boon of adulthood.

The polis idea of the tyrants was conceived differently. They too rejected the one-sided demands of the nobility, to which they incidentally belonged, and tried to reconcile the people with the upper classes on the basis of a common patriotism.[27] But they did not credit the people, the citizenship, which they thus created, with political maturity and the capacity for self-government. They claimed supreme authority, based on their personal and hereditary power. Here lay the inconsistency which eventually was to lead to their overthrow. The merit of the tyrants, however, was that they introduced and upheld the idea of *representative government* in the polis which was to take over the functions exercised so far by the courts of the nobility: the protection of the arts. Solemn festivals, competitive sports, and magnificent buildings were now in the service of this supreme cause; poets and poetry were promoted and supported.

When the Peisistratides fell and Solon's ideas finally triumphed over those of the tyrants, his young, and as yet very moderate, democracy took over from the tyrannis the supreme ideal of a representative polis, dedicated to the protection and promotion of the arts. This finally signified the *kairos* of optimal harmony among the three components of the polis, each of which had existed separately for a long time. The genesis of the polis was completed.

How the polis fulfilled its great mission in the fifth and fourth centuries cannot be developed in detail in these pages. We shall restrict ourselves to a summary enumeration of its most important innovations and creations.

In literature we owe to the polis tragedy and comedy; in the plastic and graphic arts the polis inaugurated the style we call "classical," with its own ideal of beauty which has remained the ideal down to modern times. The revolutionary spirit of the polis manifested itself in a constant fight against the monarchical, dictatorial, or oligarchical forms of government and in the promotion of the democratic ideal and the autonomy of the citizen body. This achievement was paralleled by another revolutionary act: the emancipation of intellectual life from Greek mythology and the attempt to create a new concept of the universe with the help of philosophy, ethics, and science. The polis, in fact, succeeded in bringing philosophy to a bloom, in laying the foundations for science, and pointing the way to a new ethics. Plato and Aristotle failed, on the other hand, in their efforts to erect a new faith in the gods in place of the old religion which the age of enlightenment had undermined. At this point we see the limits that were set to the creative possibilities of the polis. Its revolutionary spirit had been able to destroy the old religion; but in its anthropocentric attitude it was unable to create a new one.

In conclusion let me mention one more important fact: the principle of autonomy in personal association remained valid throughout the bloom and maturity of the polis. Indeed, one gets the impression that the "personal" character of association was even intensified. The sovereignty of the citizenry tolerated less and less restrictions, not even the smallest. It became more and more impatient of its own officials and functionaries and sought to free the assembly of the people (as the sole carrier of public opinion) of any restrictions whatever. For this purpose "ostracism" was introduced already under Cleisthenes, and it became thus possible to exile every year one citizen for a period of ten years, often for no other reason than for having attracted public displeasure or suspicion. A short time later the election of the higher officials was replaced by appointment by lot: whereby, of course, these offices lost their significance. It is true that the individual citizen now enjoyed absolute freedom. He was allowed to write and teach, to act and create as freely as nowhere else in the world, for he was a co-sovereign and nobody's subject. But he who excelled in true creativeness found himself watched more suspiciously than ever by public opinion, which wielded supreme power. This public opinion threatened him with ostracism and lawsuits. Thus Anaxagoras was exiled; Pheidias died in prison; Aspasia was threatened with prosecution; Pericles was deprived of his office. Blind passion issued death sentence after death sentence in the lawsuit against the Hermocopidae; and capital punishment was meted out to the victorious generals of the battle of the Arinnusae. Finally public suspicion hit even the greatest and most innocent, Socrates. Freedom and creativity, passion and blind arbitrariness thus are close neighbours in this polis. Here again we become aware—as so often in history—of the ineluctable connexion between light and shadow in the same picture.

This brings us to the conclusion of these pages, in which we tried to show what a long and painstaking way history often has to go to arrive at the optimal result. The coincidence of Oriental, Aegean, and Indo-European factors, and an experimentation of well over a thousand years with all these components eventually brought about the polis.

NOTES

1. Cf. my demonstration in *La Nouvelle Clio*, I, 1950, pp. 567 *et seq.* Further investigations of this problem will appear i.a. in my treatment s.v. "Praehistorische Kulturen in Griechenland" in the *Realencyklopædie der klassischen Altertumswissenschaften* and in my new book about the oldest civilisations of Greece.

2. For a basic investigation cf. Braidwood in *Archiv fuer Orientforschung*, XVI, 1952, pp. 137 *et seq.*, and Garstang, *Prehistoric Mersin*, 1953.

3. Garstang, Fig. 79.

4. *Archiv fuer Orientforschung*, XVI, 1952, pp. 151 *et seq.*

5. Cf. my treatment in *La Nouvelle Clio, loc. cit.*

6. Cf. Grundmann's map, *Athenische Mitteilungen*, LXII, 1937, plate 37.

7. Further detail will be given in my "Praehistorische Kulturen." My treatment in *Klio*, XXXII, 1939, pp. 251 *et seq.* has to be modified accordingly, since recent investigations have led me to the conclusion that at the beginning of the Early Bronze period (i.e., the beginning of the Early Helladic I) the Greeks were under Anatolian influence only through their metallurgy. Somewhat later such influence seems to have been exercised also through migrations from Asia Minor into Greece (at the beginning of Early Helladic II).

8. Blegan-Caskey-Rawson-Sperling, Troy I, 1950; cf. Fig. 417 with Fig. 451.

9. So far we have only preliminary reports, e.g., in

Archaeologischer Anzeiger, 1932, pp. 166 *et seq.; ibid.,* 1933, pp. 245 *et seq.; ibid.,* 1934, pp. 181 *et seq.;* 1935, pp. 234 *et seq.; ibid.,* 1936, pp. 154 *et seq.; ibid.,* 1937 pp. 167 *et seq.*

10. A more detailed account will be found in my treatment in "Praehistorische Kulturen" and in my forthcoming book.

11. In my opinion these names of places reached Greece from Cilicia and the Mesopotamian and Anatolian border region, partly along with the oldest cultural exchange, partly with the expansion during the Early Bronze period. More will be said on this point in my "Praehistorische Kulturen."

12. Bossert, *Altkreta,* 3rd ed.; but it remains quite uncertain whether the fragments collected at this place actually belong together at all.

13. Evans, *The Palace of Minos,* III, plate 18.

14. Bossert, *op. cit.*

15. *Ibid.*

16. Evans, *op. cit.,* II, pp. 563 *et seq.*

17. Boull, *Correspondence Hellenique;* cf. also Bossert, *op. cit.*

18. Cf. to this point my treatment in *Klio,* XXXII, 1939, pp. 261 *et seq.;* more detail in my forthcoming article "Praehistorische Kulturen."

19. The German, Austrian, and Swiss scholars use the expression "Indo-Germanic" with the same meaning, but for objective reasons the expression "Indo-European" is to be preferred.

20. On my stay in the Orient from 1917 to 1919 I had an opportunity to observe directly how the principle of personal (tribal) association works among the Mesopotamian Bedouins.

21. In my opinion the house Nr. D of Asine has rightly been claimed as the residence of a lord (cf. Froedin-Persson, *Asine,* 1938, Figs. 42, 49, 47); the same is true for the central establishment of Malthi (Valmin, *Swedish Messenia Expedition,* 1938, pp. 77 *et seq.,* figs. 19 *et seq.*).

22. Cf. especially my treatment in *Hethiter und Achaeer,* 1935, pp. 158 *et seq.*

23. Nilsson, *Geschichte der Griechischen Religion,* I, 1941, pp. 327 *et seq.;* some further information also in my book on *Poseidon und die Entstehung des griechischen Goetterglaubens,* 1950, p. 153.

24. In Aristotle this aspect of the *politeia* has been rather distorted, in as much as he neglects the fact that, basically, membership in the citizenry was assured by the right of domicile, a right which was never contested, not even by the oligarchs, as is well known. Compared to this basic right of belonging to the citizenry, even the right to participate in the assembly of the people must appear as secondary.

25. Pittacus belonged to the nobility at least through his marriage with a woman of the Eupatridae family.

26. Diehl, *Anthologia Lyrica Graeca,* 1949, Pallas Athena, Figs. 3, 4; patris, Figs. 2; 23, 9; 24, 8; eunomia, Figs. 3, 32.

27. How closely Peisistratos was related to the noble caste is revealed by the assistance which the nobility of Eretria, Thebes, and Argos gave him at his second return to Athens. Further, the Archon lists by Meritt, *Hesperia,* VIII, 1939, pp. 59 *et seq.* show that the Alcmaeonids lived unharmed and unmolested in Athens up to the assassination of Hipparchus and that they even held the highest positions.

25

Greek Cities during the Classical Epoch. Their Political and Judicial Institutions; Social and Economic Institutions

André Aymard

For a Greek of the 5th and 4th centuries B.C., the city represented the ideal form of organization: he associated it closely with his ideal of civilization. It can be defined as an entirely independent community of citizens, sovereign over all its members, cemented together by cults, and governed by laws. Between aristocracies and democracies one may note differ-

From André Aymard, "Greek Cities during the Classical Epoch: Their Political and Judicial Institutions" (English summary), *Recueils de la Société Jean Bodin, La Ville,* VI (1955), 67–68, and "Greek Cities during the Classical Epoch: Social and Economic Institutions" (English summary), *Recueils de la Société Jean Bodin, La Ville,* VII, (1955), 86–87. Reprinted by permission of the publisher.

ences of degree, but not of kind: their institutions were built on common principles and the same general features can be easily perceived in the one as in the other.

No Greek city, at this period, was "open." None created many citizens who did not possess that status by birth. All of them maintained in an inferior legal status a large number of men who lived within their territory.

The ideal of the city would certainly imply legal equality between the citizens. But while aristocracies distinguished between active and passive citizens, no democracy, however advanced, ever realized, either in law or in fact, an absolute equality of political rights.

The body of fully qualified citizens being sovereign, there was no division of powers in the Greek city; it gave to its most important organs at least an all-embracing authority. But it strove to suppress all intermediary organs between the citizens and the State.

The primary assembly of citizens was, then, necessarily sovereign in theory. The magistrates and the council were only delegates charged with executing its decisions: though variable, and sometimes even extensive, the powers they exercised had no independent basis.

The examination of legal institutions leads to the same conclusions: there was no separation between political or administrative and legal organs; consequently theoretical, and sometimes effective, sovereignty resided in the mass of the citizens acting in assembly or in huge popular juries.

No city of the classical Greek world, of which there are a great number, is exactly the mirror of any other. The institutions and customs of each always preserved original features. To give a general account is tantamount to creating a composite and, therefore, non-existent city.

Social institutions always distinguished several juridical categories. Slavery, in the full sense of the word, was known everywhere. Bondage existed in several cities. The Spartan *hilots* furnished the best-known example, but a very special one since they were bondsmen of the state. Among freemen, a widespread distinction corresponding to the fundamental notion of the citizen's commonwealth recognized the category of resident foreigners or *metoikos,*

well known in Athens. For citizens, indeed, the Greek city was hostile to naturalization and, in a fully democratic period, the Periclean law (451/0) clearly expressed this hostility.

For military purposes and taxation, citizens were divided into tax-paying classes. But the true structure of the civic body was different. The original organization had filiation or family ties as its principle; a later organization that of residence. Conceived as a means of destroying the nobility's influence, this system had not yet taken root everywhere at the end of the classical period. Even where it existed, it had not supplanted the other (filiation) in all spheres. The classical Greek city still preserved many archaic characteristics.

It was the same in economic matters. The majority of the Greek world lived by the soil, not by industry or commerce. The state tried to intrude as little as possible in economic affairs. Rent was used to exploit wealth. The state had to take care of the provisioning of the population and to assure for its treasury the highest possible return—but nothing more. However much it practised a political and financial imperialism, it is impossible to speak of a true economic imperialism. Further, it did not attempt to utilize taxation as a social instrument. The constant program of Greek revolutionaries put forward the abolition of debts, and consequently of mortgages, and the redistribution of land. It was a program which arose in the conditions of rural life and remained there. The Greek ideal always remained that of the small proprietor making the most of his property. It never adapted to an economy founded on exchange, the production of manufactured objects in great quantity, and maritime trade.

26

The Working of the Athenian Democracy[1]

A. W. Gomme

The French historian Gustave Glotz said of the Athenians that they turned what should have been

From A. W. Gomme, "The Working of the Athenian Democracy," *History,* XXXVI (1951), 12–28. Reprinted by permission of Mrs. A. W. Gomme and Basil Blackwell & Mott Ltd., London.

an organ of control into an organ of administrative action. The criticism explicit in this statement may well be just; but let us forget it, and substitute for "should have" the words "has been normally in other democracies"; the Athenians turned what elsewhere has been an organ of control—the popular assembly, plebiscites or general elections in larger states—into an organ of administration, that is, of legislative and, more important, of executive action. How did they manage it? Not "Was this wise or foolish?" but "How did it work at all?" How can mass meetings—meetings which were not even given an experienced chairman—deal with legislative and executive problems?

Let us first make it quite clear that they were mass meetings, and that they did deal with these problems. Thousands attended them; and we know, from the keen-sighted and sympathetic wit of Aristophanes, from the equally keen-sighted but less sympathetic criticism of Plato, as well as from the testimony of Thucydides, that these thousands were drawn from all classes of men, artisans, peasants and shop-keepers, merchants and manufacturers, aristocrats and plebeians, rich and poor, the humble and the ambitious—all of them also at some time or other in their lives soldiers or sailors, a matter of moment in a democratic state that was often at war. Thucydides indeed, in a well-known passage,[2] says that the oligarchs of 411 B.C. argued that not more than 5,000 citizens (out of 30,000 or more) ever attended the assembly; but note the reasons they gave: διὰ τὰς στρατείας καὶ τὴν ὑπερόριον ἀσχολίαν, service in the army and activity overseas—in other words, they were thinking of the war conditions just of that time. In peace, or during the Archidamian war, conditions were different. (In passing, if I may digress, we may note that, by this argument, which is so lovingly followed by those historians who do not like the Athenian democracy, it was the younger men, the soldiers and sailors, the latter especially, who could not attend many of the meetings; why did not the older generation, whom the more simple-minded among us, the willing victims alike of the comedy of Aristophanes and the commonplaces of Isokrates, believe to have been wisely and consistently opposed to the war, why did they not take the opportunity to end it? But to return.) I do not deny that the use of much slave labour made political activity for all classes easier than it would otherwise have been; nor that those who lived in or near Athens itself attended more often than distant countrymen, and may have from time to time, though not during the Peloponnesian war, dominated it. But I do not believe in the picture of Athenian citizens as a leisured class supported by the tribute of subject cities. For one thing, the same type of democratic government was at work in the fourth century when there were no subject cities and no tribute; and for another, if all citizens were leisured, what becomes of Plato's criticism that men cannot do two things well—attend both to their

own and to public affairs—and of Perikles' assertion that at Athens they could? Mass meetings therefore they were (even 5,000 would make a mass meeting), and of all sorts of people, the majority of them workers and comparatively poor men.

Secondly, did this assembly really rule? or were its meetings only an empty show, and all decisions made elsewhere? We can make a simple test: when government is by discussion, as it certainly was in Athens, where did the discussion take place, where were the great speeches made? In this country, in the eighteenth and early nineteenth centuries, they were made in parliament, in the lords or the commons, with a growing preponderance of the commons; in the later nineteenth century in the commons and on the hustings; now over the radio as well; the house of commons, with some control by the people, rules. In Rome, in the great days of the Republic, the speeches were made in the senate; for the senate ruled. In Athens they were made only in the assembly. (I believe that we have only one mention of speeches in the *boulê* or council, in Aristophanes, in that brilliant parody of a debate in *The Knights*.) Government, then, was by the people.

The assembly, that is, ruled in fact: if we make a very rough comparison with modern practice we might say that, as the Athenian assembly chose the principal officers of state, so does the modern electorate choose, though in most countries indirectly, the government (*i.e.* the electorate in this country not only choose the party to govern, but know who will form the government—in 1945, Mr. Attlee and his prominent colleagues, or Mr. Churchill and his); secondly, that the assembly also controlled finance and legislation, that is, voted moneys and passed laws, which with us is the concern of parliament, and decided questions of foreign and domestic policy—war and peace, alliances (when ambassadors of foreign powers would appear before it), the nature and size of the armed forces—which now are decided by parliament and government combined; and thirdly, that this assembly had functions, for example in war-time the decision to send an army or a fleet on a particular campaign, its size and composition and its commanders, which are now the exclusive concern of the executive. Government *by* the people with a vengeance; and Thucydides is full witness to this. Contrast what can be said now— one of the difficulties of democratic government for us is the relation of the people, whose will *ex hypothesi* must prevail, to a parliament; and the more stable the form of government, the more powerful will be the parliament, and the greater its moral authority: *The Times*[3] said not long ago in a leading article—"the problem which recurs in every age is that of the relation of delegate to principal. The people are the source of political authority, but cannot govern. They must commit the function to representatives; in Mr. Amery's succinct phrase, we have 'government of the people, for the people, with but not by the people.' "

It is not sufficient to say that it was possible in a small community like the ancient Greek states, the largest of which had no more than 35,000 to 40,000 citizens, who all lived within 25 miles or so of the political centre and most very much nearer: and for two reasons. Firstly, even in these conditions the majority, busy with their own affairs, cannot meet very often—the very politically minded Athenians restricted themselves to forty meetings of the *ekklesia* a year, at least in the fourth century, and many of these must have been formal; and public business is a day-by-day affair. Secondly, a mass meeting of thousands, even if no more than 5,000, is not by itself a suitable organ—one might say, *by itself* not a possible organ—for the conduct of public affairs; and in fact not many Greek states whose affairs were as important as those of Athens did conduct them in this way. A small state, that is to say a Greek small state, was not necessarily a democracy of the Athenian type, with effective government by the people. And, in order that this Athenian type may work at all, two other things are essential: somebody—one or two words—somebody or some body —there must be to deal with affairs from day to day; and somebody to prepare business for the mass meeting, the *ekklesia*, or the meeting will accomplish nothing; it will go astray. Of these two activities the latter was, for the working of the democracy, the more important; to whom could it be entrusted? The Athenian solution of this problem, which was the institution of a council or *boulê* to perform both functions—day-to-day affairs and the preparation of business for the *ekklesia*—is really the theme of this paper.

Every state must have an executive of some kind —magistrates in the widest sense of the word—to which more or less wide powers are granted, on whom more or less effective checks can be imposed. Among the powers granted to the executive in some ancient states was that of preparing business for, and presiding over, meetings of the assembly of citizens; notably this was the case in Rome—the consuls for the important *comitia*, the tribunes for the *concilia plebis*—in the days, that is, when the assemblies counted for something. Now everyone knows how important these duties are, in any society, from a national parliament to a learned academy or private club. Give those duties, as Rome did, to men who are already powerful—powerful because they are popular in some way, popularly elected, because they are magistrates with specific executive authority, and above all because they are in the know—they know what is going on far better than the majority of their fellow-citizens—and it is seen at once what influence they will have at the assembly, the mass meeting, when in effect they decide what questions are to be put. The assembly will be, at best, an organ of control only.

Athens was not going to allow any such powers to her executive officers. None of them presided over or prepared business for her *ekklesia*, nor had any special functions in it, except that the most important, the *stratêgoi*, could demand a special meeting of the *ekklesia* to deal with some urgent matter. Naturally the executive often had matters to report to the *ekklesia*, and therefore was given first hearing; naturally also, if they had been elected to office because they were well known and popular, they would at any time be listened to and applauded; they would sway the meeting; but as citizens like any other, not by right as magistrates. And it is highly characteristic of Athens that many of her most influential politicians for long years held no office at all, and fought shy of it; they were content with their influence as talkers, and wanted no further responsibility. It is equally characteristic that the Athenians would have no permanent president of the *ekklesia*, only a chairman and a sort of chairman's committee for each meeting: a man chosen to preside at every meeting, even for a limited period, would have much too much power.

So these indispensable duties were given to a council, the *boulê* of 400 members instituted by Solon, changed to that of 500 by Kleisthenes, a sort of general purposes committee of the assembly. But Athens already had a council, the *Areiopagos*, a body much respected, even revered, which Solon certainly did not wish to push on one side, nor apparently Kleisthenes: yet it was not given the duty of preparing business for the assembly, as it might have been. The *Areiopagos* was, like the senate at Rome, recruited from the higher magistracy: a man who had been elected one of the nine annual *archons* became a member of it after his year of service, and, in the ordinary way, a member for life. Had Solon's constitution survived it might have become the all-important council of the city, for it would contain within it, as did the Roman senate, all the most important executive experience and would develop its own methods of influence because its members did not change. Give it the function of preparing the business of the assembly as well, and there would be scarcely any limit to its power. It was in Solon's day also an oligarchic body, because the *archons* were chosen from the richer classes; Solon wished to preserve this feature, but wanted a democratic check on them too. For this he must free the assembly from the influence both of the magistrates and of the *Areiopagos;* and the only way this could be done was by giving it its own council as general purposes committee. Without any committee, it would be ineffective, because it could not function in any orderly way; with a powerful external body as its committee, it would have been weak because it would have been controlled. Solon was truly regarded as the father of the Athenian democracy: he had rescued the assembly, saved it for democracy, so to speak. An assembly of some kind was age-old and found in every Greek state, as in Rome: Solon saw to it that in Athens it should be politically important, effective —firstly, by freeing so many of its proper members from economic slavery, so that the assembly was properly constituted, open to all citizens; and secondly, by making it independent of all other powers in the state by giving it its own general purposes committee. Aristotle, who noted so clearly the former as the essential preliminary to democracy in Solon's reforms, did not notice the importance of the latter; and modern scholars have sometimes continued his neglect.

How important it was can be seen in the history of the century or so after the overthrow of the tyrants in 510 B.C. One of Kleisthenes' first actions then, in establishing a democratic form of government, was the restoration of this council in a new form as the *boulê* of 500—not the restoration of the *ekklesia,* for that, in theory at least, and however enfeebled, had always been there; but he must make its authority effective. The first action of the oligarchs in their revolution of 411 B.C. is to turn out the *boulê,* and set up one of, practically, their own choice; they do indeed try to introduce some modification in the membership of the assembly as well, but it is the overthrow of the *boulê* which is the necessary first step in establishing an oligarchy. And this procedure is exactly followed by the Thirty and the Spartan garrison in 404: in form not the assembly, but the *boulê,* is suppressed. It is the essential cog-wheel of the machine: without it the machine will not work.

But what was to prevent this council itself from obtaining power, if only gradually and unnoticed, at the expense of the assembly? It was fully representative of the people—it had that sort of authority—and it had important duties. As a body or

through a committee it met daily and did the day-to-day work of the state; it received ambassadors of foreign states; it worked with the *stratêgoi* and other executive officers; it had some executive powers of its own; and above all it prepared all the business of the assembly and gave a provisional opinion on all matters to come before it—the assembly put this restriction on itself, and on the whole faithfully observed it, that it should consider nothing that had not previously been considered by the council. Large enough powers: why did no big debate take place in the council on the question of what should be brought before the assembly?, or what should be the council's own "provisional" recommendation?; or why did it not, in practice if not in theory, make decisions, and leave the assembly to be at most but an ultimate organ of control? This danger was met in a characteristically logical way.

The power of a modern parliament rests largely on that corporate feeling which is created when a number of people work together for a considerable number of years in the same place and on the same matters. No matter what genuine differences of opinion and outlook may exist within it or what the personal rivalries, all are at the same time, in relation to all other citizens, privileged members of parliament. (Think of the touchiness of our own parliament with regard to its privileges—not any longer those *vis-à-vis* the crown, but those *vis-à-vis* the public which has elected it. Think of the late James Maxton, so lonely in his convictions, but liked for his character: how good a parliamentarian he was.) The members form one body; they have power; they are the people in the know; they are in fact rulers. Robert de Jouvenel, in his book *La République des Camerades,* said: "Il y a moins de différence entre deux députés dont l'un est révolutionnaire et l'autre ne l'est pas, qu'entre deux révolutionnaires dont l'un est député et l'autre ne l'est pas": an acute and penetrating observation which has perhaps in recent years lost a little of its truth by the adoption of a new technique of revolution by the Communists, but which was certainly true up to ten years ago. It applies of course not only to parliament, but to other politically important bodies—central committees of parties, executives of the T.U.C. or C.G.T., and many others. The Roman senate was the best example of such a council in ancient history: consisting as it did in practice of ex-consuls, ex-praetors, etc., members for life, it contained within itself all the influence that comes from executive command, political experience, and from popularity itself whenever the people had exerted itself in the election of magistrates; its members all knew each other, they all had certain privileges, they were all in the know. Even without that conservative tendency of the Romans which led them continually to elect to office members of the senatorial families (so that the newly elected and perhaps ambitious young consul and senator found himself met by the frowns and the equally formidable smiles of his father, his uncles and his cousins—his own set), such a council was bound to have real power, more power than any assembly of the ignorant, especially an assembly presided over and led by magistrates—no matter how clearly the constitution laid it down that only the assemblies could pass laws, make war and peace, and elect those magistrates who will later become members of the senate. The assembly at Athens also passed laws, made war and peace, and elected the magistrates; but there laws were debated, foreign ambassadors came before it to discuss war and peace or alliance, and there was no council that ruled. The *Areiopagos* had lost its influence when the lot was introduced in the election of the *archons* from which it was recruited; henceforth the politically able and ambitious did not become *archons,* and the *Areiopagos* lost all that authority which comes from being the home of experience, like the senate at Rome. The council of 500, the assembly's own council, never acquired such influence, because from the first, as though consciously to avoid such danger, the Athenians decided that election to the council was to be for a year only, that no one could be elected more than twice, and that (how they did think of everything!) not in successive years. (The lot was used in the election: but this I think was not in this case of primary importance; for when such a large proportion of the citizens were to serve on the council once at least in a lifetime, the lot was used rather to determine the order in which they should serve than to keep out the ambitious and dominating. It was also of importance in bringing on to the council citizens of small and outlying *demoi* who might otherwise never have appeared in Athens.) This simple device—not more than two years on the council for anyone and those years not consecutive —prevented the growth of anything like that *corporate* feeling which comes when men work side by side for many years together, and which is so powerful a factor in the creation of privilege; the councillors were strangers to each other, at least as much as any other men in a small community, and we must remember that Thucydides, contrasting Athens with much smaller states, notes[4] that the conspirators of 411 B.C. had an easier task because in a large city men did not know one another. It prevented also the concentration of political experience in a small body

of men, and at the same time, spread political experience among as large a number of citizens as possible; and in this way worked both positively and negatively towards the predominance of the assembly. For with service as councillor for never more than two separated years, a citizen did not get so much more experience, nor influence, than his fellows, important and indispensable as his work was; and with at least 250 becoming councillors for the first time every year and the same number retiring into the citizen body for good (probably many more than 250 on the average, for there is no reason to suppose that the majority of councillors did serve their two years), from a quarter to a third or more of citizens over thirty at any one time had had such political experience as membership of the council gave; the difference, that is, in experience and knowledge, between the average councillor and the average citizen in the assembly at any time was not great. Most of the citizens had had, as councillors and in one of the many minor administrative offices, some close experience of the day-to-day conduct of state affairs; none had had much. Doubtless the ambitious and the intriguers got their names put down as candidates for the council, and the humble and retiring did not: Kleon and Demosthenes, typical πολυπράγμονες, busybodies, were councillors, though perhaps not more than once; but Socrates, the least ambitious of men, served too when the lot fell to him. So that Athens avoided the difficulty inherent in the large modern state, which was so well put in the maxim of de Jouvenel: she knew no long-lived body like a parliament or a party executive, or a permanent council like the Roman senate. She also had no skilled bureaucracy; but this I think is less important; it illustrates the much greater simplicity of public affairs in the small city state rather than anything else. It is the absence of a parliament which is important: both knowledge and experience of affairs were shared by a majority of the population. There was very little difference in Athens between two men of the same party one of whom was, for the moment, a deputy and the other was not.

We have therefore this apparent paradox: the council is so important that it is indispensable; it is the lynch-pin of the democracy; it is the first object of attack by the enemies of the democracy; but it is not powerful. By its activity, its effective execution of its many duties, it secured the predominance of the assembly and so its own subordination: government of the people, for the people, *and* by the people.

I should perhaps add that when I say "Athens avoided this difficulty" or "knowledge and experience were shared," I am speaking comparatively, not absolutely: this was much more nearly true of Athens than of any other important state—any other state, that is, that has been large in its own world, that fought wars against even larger states, that for a time ruled an empire, that had a large commerce and an imposing financial structure, that entered into alliances and was a member of a league of nations, that knew great victories in war and crushing defeat and survived both, that above all knew what orderly and free government meant and, by and large, did not abuse its powers. There were of course in Athens many simple, ignorant men (ignorant of politics, I mean), just as there were clever knowing ones, with sharp little eyes: men like the chorus in *Oedipus*[5] (a strangely unaristocratic chorus, though they are addressed as chiefs of Thebes), who answer an awkward question of Kreon with the words "I do not know: I do not see what the rulers do," or the conventional farmer of Euripides' *Orestes,*[6] rough in appearance but brave, who seldom came to the city for public meetings, for he had his own work to attend to, "but intelligent"—and the poor peasant of *The Suppliants*[7] who, though no fool, yet was too busy to be able to have an eye on public affairs; Demosthenes' "innocent and quiet people," ἄκακοι καὶ 'απράγμονες[8]; best shown in that excellent scene in Aristophanes' *Peace,*[9] where, when Hermes has explained the origin of the war in the misfortunes of Pheidias and Perikles' fear of being implicated, first Trygaios says that he had never heard *that* tale before, then the chorus add "Nor I, till now. A lot of things happen above our heads"—πολλά γ' ἡμᾶς λανθάνει. And these were not innocents, but waspish *dicasts* whose temper Perikles had been afraid of. We must bear all this in mind, especially when we read in the funeral speech in Thucydides the proud claim that Athenians were not prevented by private business from attending to the city's affairs. But we are, as I said, speaking comparatively: compared with any other people who have played so important a part in politics, it is true that de Jouvenel's maxim does not apply to the Athenians, that they did enjoy, or suffer from, government by the people.

And it was consciously intended; let us look at one detail. The council of 500 was itself rather large for meeting *every* day: it was divided into 10 "presiding committees" consisting each of them of the 50 members of a *phylê,* and each of these groups of 50 served in turn for a tenth of the year, actually sitting every day of its turn, for the day-to-day business. The order in which they were to serve was determined by lot; but, fearful lest undue influence might be exerted or something "wangled" if it were known

beforehand in what order all the groups would serve in the course of the year, lots were drawn at the end of each period to decide which group should preside next, so that, except for the last period, it was never known beforehand which group would form the next committee. Further, neither the assembly, as I said above, nor the council and its committees had a permanent chairman, for that would give far too much power to the individual because he would know the ropes: instead, the presiding committee of the council elected by lot a new president every day (so that 36 or 37 of its 50 members would be chosen);[10] if a full meeting of the council was to be held the president of the committee for the day would preside; if the assembly was to meet, the same man would preside there with some others in support. (In the fourth century, as a refinement on this, because, I suppose, the choice was a little too narrow, another elected by lot from the councillors who did *not* form the presiding committee presided at the assembly.) No one was in the chair at these multitudinous and sometimes tumultuous assemblies more than once in his life. At these assemblies debate was free: the president announced the business, the "motion before the house," and the provisional vote of the council; and then asked, 'τίς ἀγορεύειν βούλεται;' "who wishes to speak?"

I need not say much about popular control of the executive, of the officers of state, at Athens, because it is familiar. The "specialists"—so far as Athens listened to specialists at all—generals, engineers, architects, doctors—were elected by vote; the others by lot; all for a year only. (Election of specialists by popular vote would seem to us as absurd a method as the lot; but it must be admitted that the men who elected Pheidias and Iktinos, and gave so many prizes to Sophocles, did not choose so badly.[11]) By a fine stroke of logic the specialists could be re-elected any number of times, the rest only once in a life-time, so that again the chief purpose of the lot was to decide the order of service and to secure a fair distribution. All were subjected to an audit at the end of their year, or in the middle of it if the assembly so wished, before auditors themselves elected by lot and subjected to the same rules. When I said at the beginning of this paper that the great political speeches in Athens were made in the assembly, I was of course inaccurate, but not, I think, misleading: many of them were made in the law-courts when public men were on trial. So also in Rome; but in what very different law-courts! For the *dicasteries* at Athens were also mass-meetings, especially in political trials, with 1,000 or more jurors and no skilled judge to guide them—they were judicial committees, as it were, of the assembly. I would like to mention two points. As I have already said, no elected, and therefore influential, because popular, magistrate held any office in the assembly itself; but besides this, note a particular contrast with early Rome. There a special office, the tribunate of the *plebs,* had been instituted for the protection of the individual citizens against oppression by the magistrates, especially the magistrates invested with *imperium.* If I understand the matter rightly, Augustus in 30 B.C. was offered and accepted the tribunician power *ad tuendam plebem,* in order to revive the memory of this ancient democratic institution: to "protect the people," he must hold an office. No such thing in Athens; no such office was necessary—instead "anyone might prosecute" a magistrate. Aristotle noted as the second of the specially democratic elements in Solon's constitution, this law that anyone might prosecute. And just as a meeting of the assembly began, after prayer and other formalities, with the president's question, "who wishes to speak?", so at the annual audit of magistrates the question was put 'τίς κατηγορεῖν βούλεται;' "who wishes to prosecute?"

The second point is this: in modern parliamentary states (I mean those in which the executive is dependent on a majority in parliament) if a government's policy is defeated in parliament, on a major issue, the government resigns, even though in other respects, as an administration, it may be approved. Necessarily so, because it is responsible for policy; it has the initiative (especially in this country if expenditure of money is involved, as it usually is); if it cannot command assent, its authority is so weakened that it could not carry on. But at Athens even so influential a man as Perikles, in so vital a question as war and peace, could find his advice ignored by the assembly, yet did not resign; for policy was not the business of the executive, but of the assembly, and any citizen in it could initiate it: Perikles often did, but because he was a persuasive speaker and a popular man, not because he held office as *stratêgos.* In the U.S.A. also Congress can ignore the president's policy and reject his advice, and he does not resign; but neither can Congress dismiss him from office nor diminish his powers, as a parliament can (in effect) dismiss a government which is part of it. The Athenian assembly could do both: dismiss him at any time, or ignore his advice and retain his services.

This remarkable constitution worked: it did not break down. It had many weaknesses, all of which were pointed out by Athenians themselves. But it is surprising how little we hear of packed meetings or snap votes, or of meetings postponed or broken up by an abuse of "bad omens."[12] The constitution lasted 200 years, longer, by the way, than any modern democracy has lasted so far. Its peace was only once interrupted by attempted revolution within, in the dark days of a long war; at other times, after military defeat so decisive that an enemy garrison was installed and imposed the change. When the garrison was got rid of, with remarkable steadfastness and decision, the Athenians would restore their beloved democracy, practically unchanged— they did not despair and waver because the world was not perfect, nor cry out that the fourth republic must by all means be different from the third and then give up hope because it turned out to be so very like. They had an almost unique genius for democratic politics, which must have been widespread amongst all classes of the population, but which is perhaps illustrated best by the fact that the rich, both the old rich and the new, were prepared to take their share in it, and not only to play their part in the assembly and in high executive office, to obtain by demagogic arts the power which previously they had claimed by right of wealth and birth, but as holders, for brief periods, of one or other of the many dignified offices, to which men were appointed by lot. We are not accustomed to associate σωφροσύνη, sobriety of conduct, with the Athenians, especially in their politics; we prefer to quote the assembly which voted that Kleon should go to Pylos, which laughed at his idle boasting and light-heartedly risked the safety of the state: an example surely of reckless folly, ἀφροσύνη, and not a unique one. We do right; for the Athenians did the same. But think of the self-discipline required to carry through that meeting at all, to vote the resolution, however foolish, in a constitutional manner, so that it was effective, and that without an experienced chairman. And think of the more normal meetings that passed elaborate financial measures like those of Kallias in the fifth century, or such decrees as the alliance with Chios in 384 B.C. which seems so strangely up-to-date—the preliminaries of an Aegean Pact carefully phrased to show that it is no infringement of that covenant of United Nations which we call the Peace of Antalkidas; that Aegean Pact itself, five years later, which was openly stated to be a defensive measure against the encroachments of Sparta, though the "covenant" still stands, and carefully guarded, in words, against any encroachments by Athens; the ticklish negotiations with the autocratic, aggressive and vain dictator, Dionysios of Syracuse, ending with a treaty for all time, or with the more distant and more reasonable kings of Sidon or the Kimmerian Bosporos; the detailed treaty—two and a half closely printed pages in a modern text—with the small island of Keos, after some fighting there between two parties who became, inevitably, pro-Athenian and anti-Athenian and who are proclaimed as loyal democrats and treaty-breakers respectively; or with the same island on the export of ruddle.[13]

But I would rather leave this day-to-day politics, and remember two longer-lasting enactments of this democracy, because they imposed some limitation on the assembly and in a most interesting way. The Athenians were aware—none more so—of the dangers of hasty legislation, not only because the new law might be a foolish one, but because it might, unnoticed, conflict with an existing law not expressly abrogated, and confusion would result. In the fourth century, therefore, a legislative commission was set up, the *nomothetai,* which, after the assembly had given a general assent, examined a proposed new law principally with a view to seeing if the way was clear for it. But what sort of a commission was this, and what sort of examination? A body of 500 or 1,000, in fact a *legislative* committee of the *ekklesia,* and the examination was conducted like a trial, with counsel for and against the new law, and no skilled man to preside. The other institution I had in mind is the *graphê paranomon,* whereby a decree of the sovereign assembly could be indicted, by anyone, as unconstitutional (in that, *e.g.* it had not come before the council first). This has been compared by Goodwin with the power of the Supreme Court in U.S.A. to declare unconstitutional, and so invalid, an act of Congress, on the initiative of some citizen. The comparison is a useful one; but what a contrast between the courts: the half-dozen eminent judges of America, the *dicastery* of 1,000 or more in Athens! One of the best moments in Athenian history was in just such a case: after the foreign occupation and undemocratic rule of 317 to 307 B.C. had been ended by the "liberation" in 307 by the Macedonian commander, Demetrios, and the democracy restored, certain persons were in danger, notably Theophrastos, Aristotle's successor at the Lyceum, no friend of the people, a foreigner, and certainly friendly with the enemy just driven out; to get rid of him the democrats got a decree passed by the assembly that there were to be no schools of philosophy, that is corporate bodies owning property, set up in the city without previous consent of the people in the assembly. This was indicted by a *graphê paranomon;* and was declared by the jury of 1,000 to be unconstitutional because it conflicted with a law of Solon which guaranteed freedom of association; so Theophrastos, the foreigner, the "col-

laborator," remained. Another good moment was that a hundred years earlier, in 403, when another foreign garrison left, an oligarchy had been overthrown and the city liberated—genuinely liberated this time: the decrees of amnesty for past actions were so wisely framed:—

All legal decisions in civil cases and all arbitration rulings made before the overthrow of the democracy shall stand,

to avoid an intolerable reopening of old disputes, and to preserve contracts,

but all pending criminal charges from the same time to be dropped, and a complete amnesty proclaimed, and no one shall refer to them. A new code of laws is to be considered and, once approved by the assembly, published; no one is to be tried except by a law thus published, none by an unwritten law; no decree, whether of council or of the people, is to have force against this published law, and no law is valid against an individual, but only against one and all.

I mention these two actions with some emphasis, because they show the Athenian respect for law, their *sophrosyne,* and, what is perhaps more important, their understanding of the quality of law—surprising in a people who never developed a science of jurisprudence—as well as their courage in maintaining freedom of thought. This is what I meant when I said earlier that the *demos* on the whole did not abuse its powers—I was thinking of internal administration only. Yet, so weak is human nature, so utterly fallible, that at the same time as that assertion of law and freedom in 306, men indulged in the most fulsome and servile flattery of the prince who had "liberated" them, and the great act of amnesty in 403 was soon followed by the worst crime in Athenian history, the execution of Socrates.

A last point: one thing that is fascinating about the Athenians is their complete awareness of the weakness of their democracy: not only the almost inevitable weakness of any democracy, or any form of government by discussion, in external affairs, as in dealings with a formidable enemy like Philip of Macedon, but the special weaknesses as well of their own—as we see in Aristophanes and Demosthenes. But they would not give it up, nor reform it out of all recognition in the interests of efficiency. They liked it; it was their life, or their political life. It is not really sensible to take a good poet from a hungry garret and set him in a fine house, if at the same time you destroy his poetry; nor should a scientific mission to Central Africa spend so much time, money and energy in perfecting its means of self-defence against possible attacks by man and beast that it has none left for its scientific purpose. One must risk something: Plato would have sacrificed all freedom and variety on the altar of wisdom and virtue; the Athenians deliberately risked security for the sake of the freedom and variety of life and thought which they prized so highly. They succumbed to the attacks of Philip because he was a better statesman and a better general than anyone they could produce. True: but at least it was Athens which succumbed, not an altered city which, in a vain attempt at efficiency for the sake of security, had tried to imitate a system which was her mortal enemy.

NOTES

1. A paper read before the Hellenic Society in May, 1949.
2. viii, 72, 1.
3. 20 Sept., 1948.
4. viii, 66, 3.
5. Sophocles, *Oedipus Tyrannus*, 530.
6. *Orestes*, 918–921.
7. *Suppliants*, 420–442.
8. Demosthenes, xviii, 82.
9. *Peace*, 615–618.
10. There were ten of these "presiding committees"; so in a year of 365 days, half would serve for 36, half for 37 days. (At other times a lunar calendar was in use, with many resulting complexities.)
11. See on this Plato, *Gorgias*, 455 B-C, 514 A-E.
12. The assembly met in the open, on a somewhat exposed hillside. "Bad omens" might be rain or a gale.
13. For these see Tod, *Greek Historical Inscriptions*, ii, Nos. 118, 123, 135, 136, 142, 162.

27

Some Aspects of Oligarchical, Dictatorial, and Popular *Signorie* in Florence, 1282–1382[1]

Marvin B. Becker

This paper attempts to differentiate the forms of political regime that held sway in the city of Florence over the century following the formation of the Florentine constitution in 1282. It aims to establish certain pragmatic criteria for distinguishing between these *Signorie,* and to incorporate these into a framework that may be of some value in subsequent comparative study of the politics of the Italian city state in the later Middle Ages. The method employed is inductive. The more conventional deductive approach is rejected because the setting up of definitions at the outset is likely to create the illusion that political forms existed in a pure state. Dictatorship, oligarchy and popular government did not exist in the form of "ideal types" but rather were characterized by frequent changes of form and function. During periods of challenge and struggle their true nature became more clearly discernible than in eras of relative quiescence and this fact in part explains the conflicting interpretations that have arisen.[2] . . .

From Marvin B. Becker, "Some Aspects of Oligarchical, Dictatorial and Popular *Signorie* in Florence, 1282–1382," *Comparative Studies in Society and History,* II (1960), 421, 427–437. Reprinted by permission of the publisher.

One of the most pronounced tendencies of popular government was its penchant for legal reforms and the impartial administration of justice. *Gente nuova* and public-spirited patricians joined forces to mitigate certain of the inequities of the prevailing legal system in the interest of protecting "the poor and the weak." These enactments read like a page from the chronicle of the gentle Dino Compagni and one is not surprised to discover that this good burgher and his friend, Giano della Bella, were in the vanguard of those who sponsored these humanitarian reforms.[3] Programs of this type have been variously interpreted and those who served in the *Signoria* during these intervals have been credited with altruistic and democratic proclivities for which there is little evidence. Modern historians have attempted to demonstrate that these acts were calculated to better the lot of the Florentine working class.[4] While it is unquestionably true that the masses stood to benefit from these measures, their lot, as workers, was actually worsened, at times, under the hegemony of popular *Signorie.* Not only were important concessions annulled, but the authority of the guild consuls was increased to the detriment of *il popolo minuto* and to the impairment of their economic freedom.[5] The *gente nuova* who were themselves capitalists had no enthusiasm for policies calculated to bestow privileges upon their employees. In fact, they joined forces with the patrician entrepreneurs in order to crush any rebellious movements that might arise among *il popolo minuto*. Compassion for the plight of the poor and the weak did not imply that the *nouveaux riches* desired to improve the general position of *il popolo minuto*. Legislation passed under the aegis of this type of regime was never favorable to the aspirations of the working class but rather was sympathetic to their employers who, except for the brief hour of the Ciompi, held a complete monopoly of political power.[6]

The ultimate failure of popular government in Florence can in part be explained in terms of its inability to gain the unqualified support of the polar extremes of communal society—*il popolo minuto* and the urban patriciate. While it was not deliberately hostile to the interests of the aristocratic families, this type of *Signoria* tended to encourage the development of impersonal forces that would act to limit the authority of their membership. In periods of patrician hegemony, rewards, honors and offices tended to be at the disposal of the great families who headed the contending factions. When the franchise was broadened, however, the bestowal of these symbols of esteem was in the hands of those elected officials whose power was legitimatized by the constitution.[7] The significance of popular regimes at this level is to be found in a shift of the center of political gravity from the orbit of the personal influence of the great clans to the more impersonal organism of the state. This resulted in a clarification of the zone between public law and private rights which had, hitherto, been somewhat obscure. There is no evidence to suggest that this movement was fundamentally ideological. Rather, it appears to have emanated from the historical exigencies of the times and the socio-economic background of the *gente nuova*. These newcomers who had neither the cohesion of a closely knit aristocracy nor the support of venerable institutions such as the church and the *Parte Guelfa*, could defend their political tenure only through the impartial rule of law. Although the *novi cives* were wealthy men in their own right, they had little status in the eyes of their contemporaries; it was, therefore, necessary to effectuate a wide distribution of public offices in order to diminish the influence of the great and powerful families.[8] This policy was repeatedly favored by a propitious turn of events. Each time that popular government was initiated it had emerged as an indirect consequence of serious reversals that had befallen the patricians on the battlefield or in the counting-house.[9] The new *Signoria* could not afford to permit the discredited *ottimati* to continue to dominate public life. In particular, those patricians who had abused public trust and had escaped punishment would now incur the animus of *il populo minuto*.[10] The lower classes, however, were not permitted to hold political office or gain direct representation. At this point it is possible to suggest that the material interests of the *minuti* were better served under the rule of the patriciate.[11]

The *gente nuova* who entered the *Signoria* for the first time in large numbers as a result of popular revolutions (1293, 1343, and 1378), were obviously ambitious to rise socially. Many of them soon gravitated into the orbit of the urban patriciate through marriage, political alliance or business affiliation.[12] Popular regimes tended therefore to be episodic in nature, since their members came to regard them as a vehicle for their own advancement rather than as an end in themselves. This lack of class cohesiveness among the parvenus does not preclude the fact that during these intervals important changes were inaugurated. But it does suggest that men who entered popular *Signorie* as opponents of special privilege and extra-legal authority tended to become reconciled to its existence after only a brief tenure in office.[13]

Oligarchical Government

Constitutions and legislation give one little insight into the nature of the oligarchical form of *Signoria*. At these times, political power was concentrated in the hands of the members of the great banking and industrial families of the City of the Red Lily.[14] These *popolani grassi* and *grandi*, matriculated for the most part in the greater guilds, did not feel that they were necessarily bound by legalistic considerations; therefore, disregard for the dictates of communal law is more pervasive under oligarchical hegemony than under popular rule.[15] The wealthy and the well-born were frequently able to evade the rigors of communal justice—especially in the decisions of the courts. Judicial dispensation was the most common means sought.[16] Private petitions and political pressure were also used.[17] In a society where wealth and status were so closely linked, patricians did not consider the legislative enactments and judicial decisions of their social inferiors as irrevocable. Immediately following the downfall of popular *Signorie*, the powerful oligarchs would grant certain members of their class dispensation from court verdicts and permit important legislation to fall into abeyance.[18] During periods of patrician rule the priorate would accept numerous private petitions, mostly from the ranks of the *magnati* and *popolani grassi*. Such petitions encompassed a variety of demands calculated to annul or mitigate obligations and responsibilities or penalties that had been imposed against the *ottimati*. Men who had made fraudulent use of communal funds or who had plotted revolution against the state, would request absolution from the verdicts of the judiciary.[19]

In times when the great oligarchs held undisputed hegemony, concerted attacks were directed against those institutions that had been established for the purpose of compelling the *potentes* to live under the rule of communal law. For example, during the reign of popular *Signorie,* special officials were frequently authorized to enforce the collection of taxes and to compel the holders of communal property to fulfill their contractual obligations. When the patricians acquired power they tended to curtail the authority of these men.[20] This laxity was most evident in the *contado* where much of the landed wealth of the great families was concentrated; flagrant abuses were chronic.[21] Oligarchical rule was also characterized by the creation of special *balie,* or commissions, which were granted extraordinary powers and were not accountable either to the courts or the councils. Through these bodies, which they packed almost exclusively with their own men, the *magnati* and *popolani grassi* were able to punish their enemies and reward their friends with impunity and thus to perpetuate themselves in office. During the decade of the 1330's, when oligarchical power was at its apogee, the members of the *balie* tended to conduct the government as if it were their own private business preserve.[22] They granted members of their own class immunity from direct taxation and imposed indirect taxes upon the masses that were subsequently used as security for loans made to the Republic by the oligarchs at the rate of approximately fifteen per cent a year.[23] They also acted to negate the force of communal law as it pertained to the greater guilds. In the 1320's they had granted the *arti maggiori* to which their members belonged, corporate exemption from taxation.[24] They now took further action to protect the autonomy of these guilds.

The fourteen minor *arti* were less well treated. During eras of patrician domination, their petitions were regularly rejected, in the 1330's not a single one being approved by the communal councils.[25] The greater guildsmen did more than simply turn a deaf ear to these pleas; they actively sought to weaken the corporate strength of the lesser guilds. The jurisdiction and authority of their consuls were severely limited and appeals were permitted from their verdicts to the Court of the Mercanzia—a tribunal staffed exclusively by members of the greater guilds.[26] Fragmentation of minor guilds was encouraged and many small producers of goods and services were incorporated into the juridical orbit of the greater *arti*.[27] Control of all crafts auxiliary to Florence's great wool industry was vested in the hands of an official who was elected by the *maggiori* and whose actions were not subject to review by communal authorities.[28] Finally, a commission of seven men, elected by the major guilds, was authorized by the *Signoria* to examine the corporate constitutions of the lesser *arti* periodically and to cancel any enactments that they deemed adverse to the interest of the *maggiori*.[29]

One may indeed not unfairly suggest that during epochs of oligarchical domination, the boundary line between the authority of the state and the influence of the patrician families was at best a twilight zone. While one might define the nature of the state juridically, any such definition would be an abstraction that would fail to reflect certain historical realities of the era. Not only did the great families and the major guilds (two aspects of a single entity) tend to exist outside the legal environment of the commune but they also sought to institutionalize this preferential status. Nowhere is this tendency more evident than in the history of that patrician organization the *Parte Guelfa*. The oligarchs resisted any attempt to bring this bastion of upper-class interests under the control of the rectors of the Republic. It became the rallying point for those who sought to curtail popular tendencies in Florentine political life.[30] The authority of the *Parte* was strengthened as a result of the Republic's dependence upon it for loans. It is difficult to trace its fiscal relations with the *Signoria,* just as it is arduous to untangle the nexus between the patrimonies of the great families and the funds of the Florentine treasury.[31] In fact, at times they become virtually inseparable. Control over election procedures, diplomatic missions, administration in the *contado* and extensive representation in the communal councils was also frequently vested in the hands of the Captains of the *Parte*.[32] These *Capitani* were eager to champion institutions and groups of comparable status and compatible interests—the most important of these being the church and the *magnati*.[33] The politics that were generated out of this tentative alliance of interests further accelerated the shift of power from the hands of elected communal officials to those classes and institutions over which the Republic could hope to exercise little control.

Despite this apparent unanimity, there were sharp cleavages within the framework of oligarchical government. In part, these were due to the inability of the urban patriciate to achieve a complete monopoly of social prestige and economic power. They consequently fell short of complete domination of the state. Repeated disasters in the field of foreign policy raised doubts as to their political fitness to govern.[34] Bankruptcies and economic crises raised further doubts about their economic fitness and prudence.[35] Their economic failings eventually led to disaffection among the lower classes culminating in the revolution of 1378–1382. A prime motive in this revolution was the desire of the more successful segments of the artisan and shopkeeper class for a political status commensurate with the improved social status that they were able to attain.[36]

The fact that the urban patriciate were themselves divided into factions meant that each faction was eventually compelled to bid for the adherence of socio-economic inferiors and to offer them important concessions.[37] The net result of this competition was to modify the character of oligarchical government through the introduction of *minori* and *gente nuova* into offices that had formerly been the exclusive preserve of the most aristocratic elements of communal society.[38]

The process of the withering away of the state during eras of oligarchical *Signorie* was further checked by other characteristics of Florentine political factionalism. Since the contending parties were not divided on grounds of ideology, it was possible for them to exchange political roles with impunity. If one faction gained control of the *Parte Guelfa,* the other could immediately champion the cause of popular government against this bastion of the Florentine aristocracy, despite explicit prior commitments to the contrary.[39] Another area in which similar political tendencies were manifested was in the realm of communal relationships with the church.[40] The total effect of these partisan maneuvers was to prevent the great families from completely assimilating the machinery of the state within the orbit of their personal power and influence, since the ever-present opposition was compelled, inadvertently, to support the cause of impersonal government. This was the only alternative available to them, short of revolution. The tension generated as a result of this struggle helped to precipitate the downfall of the oligarchy in the year 1378.[41]

Dictatorship

Analysis of the nature of dictatorial *Signorie* is more difficult. In the first place their tenure in *Trecento* Florence was brief. The bias of the chroniclers, our principal literary source for this type of regime, and inveterate foes of despotism in any form, is another difficulty.[42] Their distaste for Charles of Calabria (1325–1328) and Walter of Brienne (1342–1343) is also shared by the liberal historians of the nineteenth century.[43] Therefore, this form of government, so significant for future communal history, has been dimly understood and its influence upon the evolution of Florentine culture has not been assessed. Finally, there are certain fundamental ambiguities in the character of this type of *Signoria* that make it necessary to qualify any pragmatic definition of its nature.[44] Analysis has first to consider the conflicting policies that generated these ambiguities in order to frame a definition that takes cognizance of them.

Dictatorship, like popular government, with which it had much in common, was established as a result of economic crises and military disaster. It was precipitated by the excesses and failures of oligarchical rule. To some extent, therefore, despotism acquired certain of its characteristics from the pressing need for the institutionalization of reforms. Nowhere is this more in evidence than during the brief tenure of Walter of Brienne. At his insistence and with popular support, officials who had served in the preceding oligarchical *Signoria* were brought to justice on the charge of peculation of communal funds.[45] Other important patricians who had escaped the rigors of the law in former times were now condemned for malfeasance in office.[46] Members of aristocratic families were compelled to disgorge ill-got gains.[47] *Popoli* and rural communes were also penalized for their repeated failure to fulfill their obligations in money and services to the Republic.[48] This movement culminated in sweeping fiscal reforms that were instituted in the city as well as in the *contado*.[49] Arriving on the scene at the moment of impending financial disaster, the dictator could ill afford to neglect any potential source of revenue.

During past eras of patrician hegemony, the oligarchs had shunned the use of the *estimo* as a means of raising revenue. As has been previously mentioned, they bitterly opposed the imposition of direct taxes of any kind—especially those that might fall on property. Both Walter of Brienne and Charles of Calabria levied this form of taxation, much to the chagrin of the *ottimati*.[50] This type of measure was an important facet of the fiscal policies inaugurated by these two despots. The effect of their innovations was to lessen the regressive character of Florentine taxation.[51] They even went so far as to suspend many of the traditional fiscal immunities and privileges that had been granted by former oligarchical *Signorie*.[52] Particularly disturbing to the upper bourgeoisie were the taxes that were imposed upon the *arti*. The greater guilds had grown accustomed to the idea of maintaining their corporate existence outside of the purview of communal law and were, therefore, antagonized by this turn of events.[53]

The despot attempted much more than fiscal reform. His policies had the effect of destroying the delicate social and economic equilibrium that had evolved as a result of generations of patrician domination. The *Signoria* had been the exclusive preserve of the greater guildsmen who had used it to reinforce their social and economic dominance in Florentine life. Nowhere is this better illustrated than in their treatment of the wool dyers. These men, mostly small artisans, had been denied any representation in the government and had been compelled to submit to the jurisdiction of the consuls of the greater guilds in matters concerning their trade. But with the advent of the dictator Walter of Brienne the situation was radically altered. The dyers, along with other highly skilled artisans, were granted representation in communal affairs and freedom from the domination of the *ottimati* in guild matters.[54] The dictator made many other concessions to the lower orders which appear to have stimulated their latent desires for political preferment and socio-economic mobility.[55] The *minuti* were further encouraged by receiving more equitable treatment in the courts than had been customary. They were also accorded occasional dispensations from condemnations and fines to which they were liable.[56] This improvement in their status appears to have made the lower orders unwilling to accept the restoration of the absolute hegemony of the urban patriciate. Contemporary chroniclers are unanimous in the opinion that revolutionary ardor among *il popolo minuto* was intensified by the despotism of Brienne and that the proletarian revolutionaries of 1378 paid tribute to this fact when they took the name of "Ciompi" and their coat-of-arms in memory of the events that occurred during his tenure.[57]

By advancing the status of the lower orders, the despot threatened the interests of the upper classes. He further contributed to their insecurity by restoring the rights of citizenship to many of their political enemies who had formerly been banished. By pursuing this policy, he placed himself in the position of subverting the authority of that organization which had been responsible for the original condemnations —the *Parte Guelfa*. Most of the men who had been exiled had been accused, by the Guelph Captains, of harboring Ghibelline sentiments or of materially assisting this seditious movement.[58] By granting these "traitors" dispensation from their former sentences, the dictator demonstrated a singular lack of respect for that most esteemed organ of patrician power—

the *Parte Guelfa*. The same attitude was reflected in his treatment of both *magnati* and *popolani grassi*. The accrued status and affluence of the Bardi, Medici, Rucellai, Rossi, Altoviti, Ricci and others did not deter the despot from attempting to compel these patricians to live under the rule of communal law. There is no doubt that the severe justice meted out to members of the great families was one of the major factors precipitating the revolution by which Brienne was ousted.[59]

In opposition to the foregoing policies were certain tendencies that lend the despotic regime an ambiguous quality. The early months of the despot's rule were characterized by a tone of impersonality; however, as fiscal pressures mounted, this quality was somewhat modified because of practical exigencies. The need for revenue compelled relaxation of the rigor of communal law in certain areas. Absolutions were granted and judicial dispensations were sold to members of all classes.[60] Ultimately, as a last resort, loans were sought from the great families.[61] With popular opinion turning against him and revolution imminent, the tyrant was obliged to compromise his position in this way in order to be able to hire troops.[62]

NOTES

1. Research for this article was done while the author was a recipient of a Guggenheim Fellowship.
2. This is particularly true of the period between the overthrow of the dictatorship of Walter of Brienne (1343) and the fall of the regime established after the Ciompi Revolution (1382). For contrasting judgments concerning this era of Florentine history, see N. Rodolico, *I Ciompi* (Florence, 1946); G. Scaramella, *Firenze allo scoppio del tumulto dei Ciompi* (Pisa, 1914); F. Perrens, *Historie de Florence* (Paris, 1877–1883), IV, 343 *ff*.; A. Doren, *Die Florentiner Wollentuch-industrie von vierzehnten bis zum sechszehnten Jahrhundert* (Stuttgart, 1901), pp. 239 *ff*.; F. Schevill, *History of Florence from the Founding of the City through the Renaissance* (New York, 1936), pp. 260 *ff*.
3. These men were among the fourteen who were elected to institute reforms in the court system "maxime pauperibus et impotentibus."
4. *Il popolo minuto* made no gains except during periods of dictatorship. For bibliography and a discussion of this question, see G. Brucker and M. Becker, "The Arti Minori in Florentine Politics, 1342–1378" *Mediaeval Studies*, XVIII (1956), 98–99.
5. In practice, those *minuti* who desired to ply a trade over which one of the minor guilds held jurisdiction were required to pay matriculation fees and other assessments that were levied by the consuls. Cf. *Atti Esecutore*, 29, fols. 196r–197; *ibid.*, 40, 112.
6. *Atti Capitano*, 17, f. 72. All concessions that were made to the wool workers by Walter of Brienne in 1342–1343 were annulled by the popular government in 1344.
7. This tendency is reflected in the Popular government's policy of using syndics extensively to review the actions of communal officials. This had the effect of placing definite limits upon the authority of the Republic's office-holders. Cf. G. Masi, "Il sindacato delle magistrature comunali nei secoli XIV–XVI," *Rivista Italiana per le Scienze Giuridiche* (1930), V, 20 *ff*.; *Statutum Bladi Reipublicae Fiorentinae* (1348), ed.

G. Masi (Milan, 1934), pp. 34 ff. For the strict controls that were initiated over the *magnati* who held office at this time, see *P.*, 32, f. 73 (14 November 1343); *L. F.*, 24, fols. 5–6, 7r–8, 10.

8. The greater the political influence of the *novi cives*, the more elaborate were the laws that aimed at effecting a wide distribution of public offices. Cf. *P.*, f. 4r (21 July 1378).

9. The first two regimes of this type followed the failure of the despotisms of Charles of Calabria in 1328 and Walter of Brienne in 1343. The last popular *Signoria* was inaugurated in 1378, immediately after the disastrous war with the papacy.

10. Paolino Pieri, *Chronica delle cose d'Italia*, ed. A. Adami (Rome, 1755), p. 58.

11. For example, during eras of oligarchical hegemony, the authority of the consuls of minor guilds over small artisans and tradespeople was severely limited. Cf. *P.*, 6, f. 24; *ibid.*, 10, f. 181r.

12. The records of the minutes of the advisory councils suggest that these men were among that segment of the population which gave the patricians unqualified support. The twenty-five *minori* who most frequently held the office of Prior between the years 1348 and 1378 did not often voice opinions antithetical to those expressed by the oligarchs. Cf. *C. P.*, 1, 4, 8, 12.

13. Cf. especially the documents pertaining to the career of the butcher, Andreas Benis, in *L. F.*, 13, I, fols. 51, 58r; *ibid.*, II, fols. 5, 86; *P.*, 23, 89r; *P.*, 24, fols. 60, 76.

14. For example, at the height of patrician power (1328–1342), 71 per cent of the individuals who sat in the *Signoria* were matriculated in only three of the 21 *arti; the Lana, Cambio* and *Calimala*. Their holdings in the funded communal debt averaged 636 florins. Cf. *Monte*, vols. 1–4.

15. This statement is based upon analysis of the *Camera del Comune* for the *Trecento*. This source reveals that during periods of patrician domination the law was not enforced with the vigor that characterized popular governments. Cf. especially vols. 28–29; *Appelli*, 121.

16. The history of virtually every Florentine family is replete with instances in which judicial dispensation played a decisive role in salvaging the patrimony or the person of one of its members. Note the cases involving members of the Strozzi, Bardi, Medici, della Tosa, Gherardini, Nerli Adimari, Infangati, etc. Cf. *ibid.*, 122–123.

17. Cf. M. Villani, III, 58; Stefani, rub. 660, 739. See also petitions presented requesting absolution by the Pazzi (*P.*, 37, f. 76), Ricasoli (*P.*, 39, f. 170r), Tornaquinci (*P.*, 39, 185), Castiglionchi (*P.*, 42, f. 133r) and Medici (*C. C.*, 57, f. 128).

18. Cf. *C. C.*, 33–34 (June–July, 1349). For other aspects of oligarchical policy at this time, see A. Doren, *Entwicklung und Organisation der Florentiner Zünfte im 13. und 14. Jahrhundert* (Leipzig, 1897), p. 31.

19. *P.*, 51, f. 171r. One of the Donatis was pardoned for the crime of treason. *Ibid.*, 54, f. 48r. A member of the Antella family was pardoned after having been convicted on a charge of peculation of communal funds. See a similar case involving a member of the Bardi clan. *P.*, 53, f. 65.

20. Cf. *L. F.*, 14, f. 51; *ibid.*, 17, 15; Stefani, rub. 738.

21. Cf. *C. C.*, 1 *bis;* N. Ottokar, *Il Comune di Firenze alla fine del dugento* (Florence, 1926), pp. 278 ff.

22. A. Sapori, *La crisi delle compagnie mercantili dei Bardi a dei Peruzzi* (Florence, 1926), pp. 107 ff.; *L. F.* 17, f. 52; *Capitoli Protocoli*, 12, fols. 219, 227.

23. *L. F.*, 17, f. 154; *ibid.*, 19, fols. 29–36; *P.*, 36, f. 132r. For opposition to these practices, see B. Barbadoro, *op cit.*, p. 600; *Balie*, 17, f. 75r; *P.*, 67, fols., 1–13; *L. F.*, 40, f. 301.

24. *P.*, 25, f. 70r. They lost this immunity during the despotism of Charles of Calabria (1325–1328).

25. Cf. *L. F.*, vols. 17–21.

26. *P.*, 6, f. 24; *ibid.*, 9, f. 74r; *ibid.*, fols. 100, 181r. For a further consideration of this question at the end of the *Trecento*, see A. Doren, *Le arti fiorentine*, trans. G. B. Klein (Florence, 1940), II, 280.

27. *Seta*, I, f. 66r; *Lana*, 5, bk., rub. 16. For a general consideration of the political implications of this problem, see Scaramella, *op. cit.*, pp. 29–30.

28. One of the first steps that the woolcarders took when they were admitted to the *Signoria* in the year 1378 was to abolish this office. Cf. *P.*, 67, fols. 2 ff.; *L. F.*, 40, f. 302.

29. The *statuti* of the fourteen lesser guilds were subject to the authority of this *Balia*. Cf. for example, *Vinattieri*, 1, fols. 39–39r (10 March 1344).

30. In 1350 the fee required for the admission of those whose fathers had not been members of the *Parte* was raised from 50 to 100 florins. This represented approximately 25 years' rent on the average shop and it can be assumed that this sum was an effective deterrent against the democratization of the *Parte Guelfa*. Cf. U. Dorini, *Notizie storiche sull' Universita' die Parte Guelfa in Firenze* (Florence, 1902), p. 24. *Parte Guelfa, numeri rossi*, 1, f. 31.

31. Cf. B. Barbadoro, "Parte Guelfa," *Marzocco*, XXVIII (1923), n. 14; G. Salvemini, *Magnati e popolani in Firenze del 1280 al 1295* (Florence, 1899), pp. 64 ff.; *P.*, 19, f. 1r; *P.*, 21, f. 70r; *P.*, 22, f. 4; *C. C.*, 22, f. 57.

32. *Tratte*, 138. They were accorded representation at the sessions of the advisory councils. Cf. especially *C. P.*, 3, fols. 5r–15r; *ibid.*, 13, fols. 48r–49, 64r. In May of 1359, the *Capitani* were granted permission by the *Signoria* to hold communal office while serving as Guelph functionaries. Cf. *P.*, 46, f. 144. They were also granted immunity from prosecution for debts contracted during the tenure of their office. Cf. *Statuti*, 15, bk. 2, rub. 100 (1355).

33. Between 1323 and 1358 the nobles held half of the major offices of the Parte. Cf. Stefani, rub. 748; *C. P.*, 14, f. 54, *ibid.*, 15, fols. 66–66r.

34. Cf. footnote 9; G. Villani, IX, 214; XI, 130; A. Sapori, *Le marchand Italien au moyen âge* (Paris, 1952), pp. 141 ff.

35. Cf. *Atti Capitano*, 42, f. 11. This source contains the records of a case that involved the planning of a riot to be launched against the bankrupts. Cf. also *Tratte*, 1105; A. Sapori, *op. cit.*, pp. 163–164.

36. In the vanguard of those who led the proletariat were the butchers and dyers. These men were among the most affluent segment of the artisan-shopkeeper class. Cf. *Monte*, vols. 1–4.

37. D. Velluti, p. 242.

38. Stefani, rub. 734.

39. M. Villani, X, 24–25; Stefani, rub. 685. The Ricci, who had formerly been supporters of the *Parte*, championed a measure to give representation to the *minori* in the office of the *Capitani*. Cf. *P.*, 54, f. 67; *L. F.*, 38, fols. 54–54r; *Parte Guelfa, numeri rossi*, 5, f. 21 (3 November 1366).

40. Cf. Stefani, rub. 720, 726.

41. Members of the Medici, Strozzi, Covoni, Ricci, Guadagni families, and others, not only served in the popular government (1378–1382), but also resisted the attempts of the Albizzi faction to exercise complete domination over Florentine politics. Cf. *C. C.*, 184–204; *Manoscritte varii*, 222, f. 182. See a discussion of the advisory council in which measures were taken to check factionalism and to conserve the city "in sua libertate." *C. P.*, 12, f. 14 (31 March 1372).

42. For a reiteration of the opinions of the chroniclers, see C. Paoli, *Della Signoria di Gualtieri Duca D'Atene in Firenze* (Firenze, 1862), pp. 7 ff.

43. K. Hopf, "Walter VI von Brienne, Herzog von Athens, und Graf von Lecce," in *Raumer's Historisches Taschenbuch* (Leipzig, 1854), pp. 301–401. F. Sassenay, *Les Brienne de Lece et d'Athenes* (Paris, 1869).

44. Bernardino Barbadoro has noted that contradictions in policy stemmed from the despot's attempt to gain popular support while, at the same time, seeking to placate the

"discredited oligarchy." Cf. *Le finanze Repubblica fiorentina* (Florence, 1929), p. 620.

45. *Balie,* 2, 143–152; Paoli, *op. cit.,* pp. 103–104.

46. *C. C.,* 1 *bis,* fols. 19r, 32, 80r; G. Villani, XII, 2.

47. On November 30, 1342, Brienne appointed special officials for the purpose of recovering communal property. They were authorized to keep "unum registrum" in which they were to inscribe all the property and rights ("bona et iura") of the commune. Cf. *Balie,* 2, fols. 110–112. For condemnations by these officials of individuals who had usurped the property of the state, see *ibid.,* 2, f. 165 (30 March 1343). For fines levied against the powerful Adimari and Rossi families by these officials on the same charge, see *C. C.,* 1 *bis,* fols. 249, 276 (18 April, 14 May 1343).

48. *Ibid.,* fols, 130, 209–221.

49. *Balie,* 2, fols. 58–63; Paoli, *op. cit.,* pp. 25–30.

50. *P.* 25, f. 45 (3 December 1326); *C. C.,* 1 *bis,* f. 357. See also B. Barbadoro, *op. cit.,* pp. 161–189, 207–211. When the priorate invited Brienne to become *Signore* of the city, the Bardi Company reduced their capital by half in order to escape direct taxation which they knew he would establish on the model of his predecessor, Charles of Calabria. Cf. A. Sapori, *Compagnie e mercanti di Firenze antica* (Florence, 1955), p. XXIII.

51. Complaints to the despot were frequently concerned with the regressive nature of Florentine taxation. Cf. Paoli, *op. cit.,* p. 114, doc. 260; *Balie,* 2, f. 66. Revision of the tax system was a commonplace under the rule of the despots. Cf. P. Silva, *Il governo di Pietro Gambacorta in Pisa* (Pisa, 1912), pp. 116–117.

52. The *Signoria,* with the permission of the Duke of Calabria, was granted the authority to suspend immunities and privileges that formerly had been conferred upon certain inhabitants of the *contado.* Cf. *P.,* 23, f. 67 (9 February 1327). Brienne also appointed a special official to perform this same function. Cf. Paoli, *op. cit.,* p. 75. Severe fines, ranging from 500 florins to 3,932 florins, were exacted from members of the Ricci and Ricciardi families who did not comply with this edict. Cf. *C. C.,* 1, fols. 9r, 27 (October–November, 1342).

53. Cf. footnote 24: *P.,* 25, f. 70r. For a further analysis of the effects of the policies of a despot upon the *arti,* see N. Rodolico, *Del Comune alla Signoria. Saggio sul governo di Taddeo Pepoli in Bologna* (Bologna, 1898), pp. 84 *ff.* In 1373, attempts were made to reintroduce this form of taxation. The advisors to the *Signoria,* however, were successful in thwarting the passage of this measure. Cf. *C. P.,* 12, f. 56r.

54. Cf. N. Rodolico, *Il popolo minuto* (Bologna, 1899), p. 141; Paoli, *op. cit.,* pp. 82–83; *Balie,* 2, fols. 92–93.

55. For the first time since the end of the preceding century, large numbers of *novi cives* were admitted to office. Cf. *P.,* 32, f. 145.

56. See especially the document that records the pardon of Jacabo, a wool-beater, who had been condemned to death in 1318 by the "official foreigner of the Lana" for conspiring with other workers against the masters of the guild. *C. C.,* 1 *bis,* fols. 46–47 (19 December 1342). A certain Cione was also granted dispensation by Brienne from the sentence of death. He had been condemned by the Executor for instigating a conspiracy against the rule of the guilds. *Ibid.,* f. 187r (16 February 1343). Two years earlier, the Councils of the Commune had refused to take this action on his behalf. *Appelli,* 122, III, f. 25 (26 May 1341).

57. Stefani, rub. 566.

58. Upon payment of fines to the ducal treasury, certain members of the Falconery, Pulci, Amadori and Corbizzi families were pardoned. They had formerly been convicted for having fought against their native city on the side of the Emperor Henry VII in the year 1312. *C. C.,* 1 *bis,* fols. 70–92.

59. A scion of the house of the Bardi was fined 500 florins for attacking a *popolano. C. C.,* 1 *bis,* f. 5r (19 October 1342). Two other members of the same family were condemned to pay a fine of 5,813 florins, along with a member of the Rucellai clan, for peculation of communal funds. *Ibid.,* f. 132r (18 January 1343). See also *ibid.,* fols. 204r–205, 209–211. Members of the Adimari, Bordoni, Tornaquinci and Spini families who had posted bonds for fellow members of the patriciate, were required to make payment into the communal treasury when those for whom they were responsible, defaulted. *Ibid.,* fols. 175r, 211r.

60. M. Becker, "Gualtieri di Brienne e l'uso delle dispense giudiziarie," *Archivio Storico Italiano,* CXIII (1955), pp. 245–251. These arbitrary and capricious actions of the despot also served to intensify opposition to his rule.

61. Shortly after the overthrow of Brienne, the Republic obligated itself to pay five per cent interest a year to those who had loaned money to the despot. The total of these loans was 41,480 florins. Cf. *Provvisioni Duplicati,* 7, 52r. During the last month of the Duke's tenure, loans from the Bardi family alone accounted for approximately one-fourth of the monies paid into the treasury. *C. C.,* 1 *bis,* f. 336 (22 July 1343). Less than a week before the outbreak of the revolution against Brienne, a new *estimo* was imposed upon the citizenry and a new *prestanza* was levied. *Ibid.,* fols. 335–357 (20 July 1343).

62. Many of the leaders of the conspiracy against the despot were members of the same families who had been compelled to pay heavy fines and to make forced loans to the ducal treasury. Cf. G. Villani, XII, 16 and footnote 59.

28

Russian City-State

George Vernadsky

Every Russian principality of the Kievan period was, in its political essence, a combination of a city-state and of the princely system of administration. In most cases the princely authority, superimposed upon the city, gradually took the lead. In Novgorod, however, the historical process went in the opposite direction, with the prince's role eventually reduced

From George Vernadsky, *A History of Russia,* Vol. II: *Kievan Russia* (New Haven: Yale University Press, 1948), pp. 196–201. Reprinted by permission of the publisher.

to that of a mediator or magistrate engaged by the city.[1] If the story of the "calling of the Varangians" is to be credited, the role originally assigned by the Novgorodians to Riurik was exactly of this kind. However, both he and his immediate successors obviously overstepped their bounds. For some time Novgorod became subject to princely power.

With the shifting of the princely throne to Kiev the position of Novgorod deteriorated even more. The Novgorodians obviously objected to the predominance of Kiev; hence their eagerness to help Iaroslav wage war against his brother Sviatopolk. The Novgorodian assistance proved invaluable to Iaroslav and after his victory he had to recompense the Novgorodians by granting them certain charters, one of which seems to have been the original version of the *Russian Law*. It is significant that in the very first article of this code the equality of the wergeld of a Slav (i.e., Novgorodian) with that of a Russian (i.e., Kievan) is proclaimed.

Following Iaroslav's death it became customary for the prince of Kiev, as head of the Russian state, to appoint his eldest son as his lieutenant in Novgorod. Since the latter was apparently bound by Iaroslav's charter, the Novgorodians did not at first object to such an arrangement. Later on, however, with the decline of the authority of the prince of Kiev and the growing rivalry between the different branches of the house of Riurik, the Novgorodians found themselves in a position to make their choice among several princely candidates and they knew how to use their opportunity.

In 1095 a disagreement arose between the Novgorodians and their prince David, son of Sviatoslav, as a result of which David temporarily left the city. The Novgorodians bade him never return and themselves invited another prince from Rostov to take his place. Seven years later, when Prince Sviatopolk II of Kiev proclaimed his intention of appointing his son to the Novgorodian throne, the Novgorodian emissaries appeared before him with the following blunt message: "We were sent to you, oh Prince, with positive instructions that our city does not want either you or your son. If your son has two heads, let him come."[2] In 1136, as we know, the Novgorod veche took a decisive step toward asserting the sovereign rights of the city: both the prince and his non-Novgorodian retainers were deprived of the right to own landed estates within the boundaries of the Novgorodian state.

By the middle of the twelfth century the office of the prince of Novgorod became in fact an elective one and in 1196 the privilege of the Novgorodians to elect their prince of their own will was formally recognized by a congress of Russian princes, with the understanding that they would choose their candidates from among members of the house of Riurik only.

Four years later, however, being severely defeated by Prince Vsevolod III of Suzdal, the Novgorodians, addressing him as the "Lord Grand Duke" (*Gospodin Velikii Kniaz'*), asked him to send his son as their prince and, if the statement of the Suzdalian chronicler is to be credited, even agreed to recognize Novgorod as his patrimony (*otchina i dedina*). At any rate, from this time on most of the Novgorodian princes were chosen among Vsevolod's descendants. This fact, however, did not impair the Novgorodian independent rights, which by this time were firmly secured, and in 1211 Vsevolod himself confirmed their old liberties.

Each new incumbent, upon assuming the principate, had to sign a special contract with the City of Novgorod. Unfortunately no copy of such a contract for the Kievan period has been preserved; the earliest known text is that of 1265. From the evidence of the chronicles of the Kievan period at least four important clauses of a typical contract may be reconstructed, however. One was the prohibition (from 1136 on) of the owning of landed estates in the Novgorodian state by the prince or his retainers. The second important point was the freedom of the Novgorodians to elect city officials without interference on the part of the prince (confirmed by Vsevolod III in 1211). With this the third provision was connected: the prince had no right to dismiss city officials without a veche decision or a court trial. According to the chronicles, in 1218 Prince Sviatoslav announced at a meeting of the veche that he had decided to dismiss the mayor, Tverdislav. He was immediately asked what his accusation was against the mayor. The prince could only say that he did not like him. The veche accordingly resolved that if no fault could be laid to the mayor he should not be removed. He stayed. Fourth, the supreme judicial authority of the veche was guaranteed; in the words of Vsevolod III, the Novgorodians were free to punish criminals.

The state sovereignty of Novgorod rested with the city and not with the prince. The city was spoken of as the Lord Novgorod the Great (*Gospodin Velikii Novgorod*). The supreme organ through which the sovereignty materialized was the city assembly (veche). It had its own chancellery, housed in the city hall (*izba*), and its own seal.

As in Kiev, the Novgorod city assembly usually met either in the square before the prince's palace ("Iaroslav's Courtyard") or in that before the St.

Sophia Cathedral. The meeting was called by the pealing of the city bell, which thus became the symbol of Novgorodian liberties. After the conquest of the city by the grand duke of Moscow in the late fifteenth century, the latter's first order was to remove the veche bell.

The city assembly combined the supreme executive, legislative, and judiciary power. Actually only major problems of the executive were submitted to the consideration of the veche, current administration being dealt with by the prince and the mayor. Similarly, the courts were given sufficient latitude for their current work and the veche acted as the supreme court in major cases only, such as the trial of the prince or of a high city official. Broadly speaking, then, the city assembly was chiefly a legislature.

As in other Russian cities of the period every Novgorodian citizen had the right to vote at meetings of the city assembly and—as elsewhere—unanimous approval was required for all decisions of the veche. To prevent the recurrence of violent conflicts between two parties when there was no overwhelming majority, a special council came to being in Novgorod, whose chief concern was to prepare bills for the consideration of the veche. This council met under the chairmanship of the archbishop and consisted of three hundred members, to wit: the prince's lieutenant, the senior city officials, and the boyars. The German merchants called this council *Herrenrath* ("Council of Lords"). In Russian it was known as *Gospoda* ("the Lords").[3]

From the strictly legal point of view this institution was not an upper chamber, since the veche's authority was indivisible, but a committee of the city assembly. For practical purposes the Gospoda exerted the moderating influence of an upper chamber but its advice could always be overruled by the veche.

The constitution of the Novgorodian state may be characterized as a democracy limited to a certain extent by the interests of the upper classes—*de facto,* if not *de jure.* Furthermore, it should not be forgotten that certain categories of the population, such as the smerdy and, of course, the slaves, were disfranchised altogether.

The two major city officials were the mayor (*posadnik*) and the chiliarch (*tysiatsky*). Both were elected by the city assembly for a brief term, not precisely specified, and could be reëlected. It is noteworthy that any former posadnik, even if not reëlected, was considered a notable and continued to have some part in directing Novgorodian affairs. All were members of the Gospoda. It has been observed that from the early twelfth to the middle

of the thirteenth century, five generations of the same family held the office of posadnik in Novgorod, with some intervals. It was a certain Giuriata who occupied the post in the early twelfth century. From 1126 to 1134 the position was held by his son Miroslav; from 1137 to around 1175, by the latter's son Iakun; from 1211 to 1219, by Iakun's son Dimitri; and for several years after 1220, by Dimitri's son Ivanko.[4]

The duties of the posadnik consisted mainly in the general supervision of the city administration. He was also the chief justice for litigation about land. As to the tysiatsky, he was the commander of the city militia and the chief justice for commercial litigation.

The City of Novgorod may be called a commonwealth consisting of five autonomous communes, each in one of the five boroughs (*konets,* literally "end") into which the city was divided. These boroughs were called as follows: Slavensky (Slovenian), Plotnitsky (the "Carpenters' Borough"), Zagorodsky ("Beyond the City Walls"), Goncharsky (the "Potters' Borough"), and Nerevsky. Each borough commune elected its own mayor, known as the *starosta* (elder); each consisted, in turn, of "street" guilds (*ulitsa*), and each of the latter, of "rows" (*riad*).

Novgorod was, however, not merely a city; it was the metropolis of a state commanding a vast territory stretching from the Gulf of Finland to the Urals and from Lake Ilmen to the White Sea and the Arctic Ocean. This was a territory rich in natural resources, except grain, and able to provide the metropolitan merchants with many an item for their export trade.

The metropolis itself was favorably located from the commercial point of view. A junior partner in the Novgorodian commerce was the city of Pskov, which attained independence in the Mongol period. In the Kievan period Pskov was considered only a dependent town (*prigorod*). Like every other Novgorodian by-town, Pskov enjoyed local self-government under the supervision of a mayor appointed by the Novgorod veche. Pskov residents were entitled to Novgorodian citizenship. Actually, as usual in the period, it was hard for them to attend the meetings of the chief city assembly of their land and few were able to do so.

The population of other by-towns of Novgorod was in the same position. In the rural districts there were few people holding Novgorodian citizenship and even those who did—especially those living in remote provinces—usually failed to exercise their right to vote. The majority of the provincial population were not granted citizenship. For practical reasons, then, the people of the city of Novgorod ruled not only the city but the whole Novgorodian empire as well. In Novgorod, as in Rome of the republican period, the city *was* the state.

In regard to administration the territory of the Novgorodian state was divided into two distinct parts. Its western section, closest to the capital, consisted of five provinces (*volost'*), which in a later period became known as "fifths" (*piatiny,* from *piat',* "five"). The northern and eastern area of the state, consisting of vast and thinly populated territories with many native tribes of Lapp and Finno-Ugrian extraction living on them, was the Novgorodian colony.

The pentamerous organization of the Novgorodian provinces was not accidental. Each of the five provinces was ascribed to one of the boroughs, to wit: Bezhetskaia to Slavensky, Obonezhskaia to Plotnitsky, Shelonskaia to Zagorodsky, Derevskaia to Goncharsky, and Vodskaia to Nerevsky. Among the duties of the population of each province was that of repairing the street paving in the borough to which the province belonged. For this task either workers were drafted (which seems to have been the original method) or money collected.

The northern and eastern area subject to Novgorod consisted of several colonies of which the richest and the most important was the Dvina land north of the city of Vologda; it was also known as Zavolochie ("Beyond the Portage"—i.e., the area beyond the portage by which the Northern Dvina River could be reached). This colonial part of the Novgorodian empire was ruled not by the boroughs but by the City of Novgorod as a whole, through governors and other agents appointed by the prince

in concurrence with the mayor. These officials were assisted in their task by hundreders representing the local Russian population and the tribal chiefs of the native peoples.

At times the population of the colonies would be aroused by the ruthless exploitation of their wealth by the metropolis as well as by the arbitrary behavior of the Novgorodian agents. In the second half of the twelfth century the colonial city of Khlynov (later known as Viatka; now Kirov) seceded from Novgorod. The opposition in the Dvina land was kept in check until the late fourteenth century.

Novgorod was not the only Russian city-state of the period. Polotsk seems to have been another. According to Narbutt the sons of Prince Vseslav of Polotsk (reigned 1044–1101) willed their authority to the city, which after their death became a republic ruled by the veche and the council of boyars. Unfortunately, Narbutt fails to refer to the source of his information.[5] In the case of Khlynov it is positively known that after seceding from Novgorod it became a city-state in its own right. It was organized as a democratic republic.[6]

NOTES

1. For a general outline of Novgorodian government and history, see N. I. Kostomarov, *Severnorusskie narodopravstva* (St. Petersburg, 1863), 2 vols.; V. S. Ikonnikov, *Opyt Russkoi istoriografii* (Kiev, 1891–1908), 2 vols., each in 2 parts, II, Pt. 1, Ch. 7; see also Bibliography.

2. Cross, p. 291.

3. A. I. Nikitsky, "Ocherki iz zhizni Velikogo Novgoroda, I, Pravitelstvennyi Soviet," *ZMNP, 145* (1869), 294–309.

4. Vladimirsky-Budanov, *Obzor istorii Russkogo prava* (7th ed. Petrograd and Kiev, 1915), p. 67.

5. See *idem,* pp. 64–65.

6. Kostomarov; *op. cit.,* I, 241–251.

C. PATTERNS OF CENTERS IN DEVELOPED TRADITIONAL SOCIETIES

CHAPTER **VII**

Patterns of Multiple Centers. Feudal Systems: Introduction

I

Feudal regimes constitute one of the most fascinating types of social and political system in the history of mankind.[1] The term "feudalism" has been conventionally applied to the type of society and the political system originating and dominant in western and central Europe during the greater part of the Middle Ages. The term has also been applied to types of society and systems of government featuring similar characteristics in antiquity and in medieval times in other parts of the world and, by the Marxist school, to a type of society and economy characterized by serfdom, usually succeeding the economic systems based on slavery and preceding capitalism.

Although a great variety of definitions of feudalism exist, some minimal common characteristics of a fully developed feudal system are accepted by most scholars. Such characteristics include lord-vassal relationships, a personalized government most effective on the local level and with relatively little separation of political functions, a system of land-holding consisting of fiefs given in return for service and assuring future services, private armies, a code of honor in which military obligations are stressed, and specification of seignorial and manorial rights of the lord over the peasant.[2]

The basic features of feudalism imply traits in each of the major institutional spheres of a society: in economics, polity, law, and in social stratification and organization. It may be worth while to spell out these characteristics in each sphere in greater detail.

Perhaps the fullest definition of feudalism in the political sphere is given by Weber, who characterizes it as one type of patriarchal "authority." According to this definition, political feudalism is marked by:

1. The authority of the chief which is reduced to the likelihood that the vassals will voluntarily remain faithful to their oaths of fealty.

2. The political corporate group is completely replaced by a system of relations of purely personal loyalty between the lord and his vassals and between the vassals and their own subvassals (subinfeudation) etc. Only a lord's own vassals are bound by fealty to him; whereas they in turn can claim the fealty of their own vassals, etc.

3. Only in the case of a "felony" does the lord have a right to deprive his vassal of his fief. . . .

4. There is a hierarchy of social rank corresponding to the hierarchy of fiefs through the process of subinfeudation. . . . This is not, however, a hierarchy of authority in the bureaucratic sense. . . .

5. The elements in the population who do not hold fiefs involving some element of patrimonial or other political authority are "subjects," that is they are patrimonial dependents. . . .

6. Powers over the individual budgetary unit, including domains, slaves, and serfs, the fiscal rights of

the *political group* to the receipt of taxes and contributions, and specifically political powers of jurisdiction and compulsion to military service—thus powers over free men—are all objects of feudal grants. . . .[3]

In the sphere of social organization and stratification an important element of feudalism is that arms-bearing is a class-defining profession. In the economic sector, feudal government and society appear to rest on a landed or locally self-sufficient economic base as distinguished from a pastoral, commercial, or industrial one. The merchant community, though it may play a significant role in the economy, is essentially outside the feudal nexus. The appearance of certain technological features of government and economy, notably centralized communications and means of large-scale political organization, undermine these feudal institutions.

Within each of these spheres—economic, social, and political—there may also exist many differences in the details of various institutional arrangements, such as the relative strength of serfdom or tenancy or of the contractual element in the lord-vassal relationship. But whatever these variations, some of which we shall subsequently analyze, perhaps the most important problem in the analysis of feudal systems is the extent to which the feudal characteristics develop and converge in all the major institutional spheres and the conditions of different degrees of such convergence.

II

It was mainly in the west European classical age of feudalism that the basic characteristics of the feudal system developed in most institutional spheres of the social system. The closest resemblance to this over-all development is probably that of Japan in the Kamakura (1185–1333) and Ashikaga as well as somewhat later periods (sixteenth to eighteenth century).[4]

In most other cases we find only a partial development of feudal institutions. Thus, for instance, in the late Byzantine Empire, in many Moslem states, and in many Indian states a constellation of feudal traits developed which were characterized by the relative predominance of economic independence of the small estates combined with a growing political decentralization—without, however, the concomitant development of an over-all system of vassalage, feudal-chivalrous military class, or special feudal political institutions.

This type of feudal institution is found in many other societies, especially in the periods of decline of the great empires, such as the end of the Roman Empire, the later Sassanid period in Iran, and the aftermath of Asoka's kingdom in India.[5] In many cases this type of feudal institution developed when many of the local officials usurped the right to collect taxes and turned their offices into hereditary fiefs. In other cases the political aspects of feudalism—in the form of the existence of many self-sufficient patrimonial units with some political interrelations and orientation toward one budding center—were more highly developed than the economic ones. Such cases can be found in the so-called feudal period in China under the Shang and especially under the Chou,[6] in ancient Mesopotamia under the Kassites, in Mittani, in the Parthian regime in Iran, and possibly also in ancient Egypt.[7]

In none of these cases, with all their variations, do we find the development of a full-fledged institution of vassal-lord relations on the one hand or a full-fledged social organization of a military-political class on the other. At most we find only rudiments of each.

III

In many such cases these partial feudal institutions, especially in the political field, tended to converge into some type of patrimonial system or into a weakened imperial one. But there is a great difference between the cases of dismemberment or weakening of imperial or patrimonial settings and of what may be called genuine feudalism, although in many cases there may, of course, be a great deal of overlapping between them. This difference is mainly due to the fact that in many instances of such dismemberment, however great the tendency might have been to some weakening of the central framework, on the whole, all efforts of the aristocracy were oriented toward one existing order. In many ways they might have aimed not so much at changing the structure of the center as at the establishment of a more powerful subcenter with greater autonomy vis-à-vis the center. In genuine feudal systems the relations between the center and the periphery tended to be of a different order, although, as we have already pointed out, there might have been strong overlapping.

The outstanding characteristic of the structure of the centers in most feudal societies was that there existed in them many centers and subcenters, each of which tended to have multiple orientations—political, cultural, and economic. These centers and subcenters tended to become arranged in a rather complicated, rigid, but never unified, hierarchy in which none of the centers was clearly predominant.

Each of the central and local centers tended to emphasize different components of center formation. Thus, for instance, the development and maintenance of some of the symbols of common identity tended to be located in the more central political and cultural centers, while the regulation of intergroup relations and of force tended to be in the various local subcenters. At the same time, no single center had the total monopoly on any of these components of center formation.

Naturally enough, the activities of the more central ("higher") centers were of a wider scope than those of the local ones, but they did not have a total monopoly over any one of the components of central activities. Each of the local centers had some degree of independent dominance over some of its resources, over some central activities, as well as over its access to the higher centers.

Moreover, the various centers were not completely separated from one another. There existed continuous mutual orientations, as well as structural interrelations among them. The most important fact is that any group that had control over some resources necessary for the development of any of the political or cultural orientations of the centers had some legitimate and autonomous, even if differentiated, access to any of the centers. Not only the church but also many local or status groups were to some degree autonomous in their ability to convert their resources from one institutional sphere to another and from the periphery to the centers.

Among the components of the identity and styles of life of these last groups and strata, primordial territorial ties played an important role. But these frameworks were not closed in themselves or entirely ascriptively fixed in their relations to other groups and to the centers. They were open toward the various centers—both toward the political centers (national or "state") and to the various cultural supranational ones—and none of them had full access to positions in or control over any institutional market. The autonomy of a group was never total, and the regulation of access to the center was rarely left by the center itself to any single group. Moreover, neither the central nor the local centers were entirely homogeneous. Both on the central and on the more local levels, several special *types* of center existed.

Of especial importance on the more local level were the various urban centers, which often contained within themselves some of the ingredients of city-states, including a relatively high level of politi-

cal participation, although they rarely existed as fully autonomous and self-sufficient units.

On the more central level, the major autonomous types of centers were various translocal or transnational cultural organizations, such as the Church in Christendom or some parallel organization with wide, universal types of orientation.

The special characteristics of the center and of subcenter-periphery relations in feudal systems—as distinct, for instance, from those in city-states or in patrimonial regimes—can best be seen in the nature and composition of the various social strata and especially of the upper strata; that is, of the feudal (usually military) aristocracy.

Even though the basic resources of most of the higher and middle strata were necessarily based on local territorial units over which they ruled, from the point of view of composition and strata consciousness and interrelations these strata were not locally bound but were forged by their relations and orientations to the center.

The various social groupings (especially, but not only, the upper ones) tended to converge into a much wider—very often international—stratum, the scope of which was always broader than that of any of the local subcenters. The development of such strata was based not only on a common background but also on a common orientation to some center or centers. These orientations involved the acceptance of some predominance of the various centers and the undertaking of obligation toward them, and they were based also, in contrast to patrimonial regimes, on relatively independent access of these strata to the center.

Thus it can be said that in most feudal regimes the distinction between center and periphery was—with the exception of the purely servile strata—of degree rather than of kind. This was closely related to the nature of the social division of labor that developed in these regimes. We find here different degrees of the development of mechanical as compared with organic solidarity and of societal differentiation on different levels—on local as against central levels, as well as among different institutional spheres. Thus the local levels were composed mainly of small units with a relatively high degree of mechanical solidarity, which was especially evident in the economic and administrative spheres. On the other hand, on the more central levels, and especially in the political and cultural spheres, we find a higher degree of differentiation as well as a higher degree of organic division of labor than in the local and economic spheres.

IV

These characteristics of social division of labor are, of course, closely related to the conditions for the development of feudal systems. We can find some common elements in and also great differences between different systems. However great the differences in their concrete historical setting, feudal institutions tended to develop in conjunction with specific sets of conditions, although the extent to which these conditions existed varied greatly from one case to another.

One such set of conditions is the partial dismemberment of relatively comprehensive sociopolitical systems—often an imperial system or a system that upheld some ideals of empire.[8] The reasons for such a dismemberment vary greatly; it might be due to a clash of cultures, the invasions of nomads, or the development of some of the internal contradictions ushered in by such empires as a result of which the imperial system loses its effectiveness and the resources it needs for the maintenance of its basic maneuvers. It is not the mere dismemberment that is of crucial importance for the development of feudalism, but the combination of the dismemberment with the persistence, or development, among some of those active elite groups who have taken over many of the governmental and economic functions (such as the church, or the new military class itself) of the ideals of great empires and of orientations to broader frameworks.

In some cases, such as that of Chinese feudalism, these orientations had been developed by active groups that had not been able to establish any viable broader system but had developed some vision of such a system.

Thus, in most feudal systems, ideological orientations to such broader frameworks are of great importance even if they are only partially institutionalized. Therefore, any feudal system is characterized by some inherent imbalances in its structure because it contains both more and less differentiated centripetal and centrifugal structures and orientations. The exact location of such institutional imbalances—whether they are in the economic, political, or cultural spheres—varies greatly in different feudal systems.

The fullest development of feudalism tends to take place in those rather unusual circumstances in which imbalances exist at least to some degree in all the institutional spheres. Partial development of feudal institutions exists in those cases where imbalances develop in only a few institutional spheres.

V

The preceding analysis also throws some light on the nature of issues and the channels of political struggle that tended to develop in feudal systems. As in all other types of traditional systems, a very large part of such struggle was limited of course to a relatively simple level of political issues of organization, such as the distribution of various benefits from the rulers to the ruled, struggles among family or territorial groups about their relative political or economic standing, and so on. In this respect the process of political struggle here was similar to that of patrimonial systems and to the simpler levels of political struggle in the imperial systems or in the city-states.

But beyond this level, an additional important dimension of political struggle developed especially in the more fully developed feudal societies—a struggle that was concerned with the very formation, symbols, and scope of the center and with access to it. This type of political struggle was not, as in some patrimonial or imperial systems, oriented only toward the minimization of the power of the center over the periphery. In some cases, at least, it was also much more closely oriented to the reformation and restructuring of the center itself in terms of its basic symbols, patterns of political participation, and rules of access.

The struggle for reformation of the center was not so all-encompassing here as it was in the more fully developed city-states. A much smaller extent of identity in membership between center and periphery existed; hence there was a much greater distinction between the different levels of social and political activity, which minimized the direct impingement of the periphery on the center.

Of especial importance from this point of view has been the development of some special types of political organization. We do not find in feudal centers the equivalent of modern parties. We do find, however, the development of a new type of political organization, which existed, to some degree, in imperial systems—representative institutions, that were, of course, especially important in European societies.

It is here that a new type of political relation between the center and the periphery, differing from the ones prevalent in imperial regimes and city-states alike, is found. The most important characteristic of this relation is the potential spread of the right of access to the centers to large parts of the periphery, but without, as in city-states, the total obliteration of symbolic and organizational distinctiveness of center and periphery.

In close connection with this, as well as with the multiplicity of centers characteristic of feudal societies, we can understand the special place that kings or emperors had in the political process of feudal societies. On the one hand, they were the holders of the most central (political) positions and therefore were interested in enlarging the scope and strength of their domain, power, and organization. As such they waged an incessant political struggle with the representatives of the various other centers (such as the church), subcenters, and localities over their relative standing, power, and scope of their respective domains. Moreover, they constituted the focal point of the simpler levels of political struggle mentioned above.

But beyond all this the kings or emperors constituted very important focuses of the possible restructuring and reformation of the center. They also constituted important focuses of possible tendencies for bringing the pluralistic feudal centers together not only into an administratively more centralized regime but also into a more homogeneous and unified center that would combine to a much larger degree the various components of center formation and create a more homogeneous political framework.

At the same time, however, they served as the focuses for the crystallization of the various autonomous strata that claimed autonomous access to the centers. Because of this, the homogeneous political units that could germinate from within the feudal ones also had a large potential for developing into a flexible, differentiated, and pluralistic regime.

VI

The preceding analysis of the political struggle in feudal systems necessarily brings us to the problem of the conditions for continuous change and transformation in such systems. By their very nature— that is, by virtue of the different levels of differentiation in the center, in the periphery, and above all in different institutional spheres, and by virtue of their multiple interweaving centers—these regimes were institutionally unbalanced ones.

Insofar as any of the structural elements tended to become dominant or the conditions for the autonomy of some of these elements tended to become weakened through the heterogeneous political process that developed in them, there could easily arise

processes through which the whole system could become undermined. In more concrete terms, the demise of the feudal system was predicated on changes in those conditions—technological, political and economic—that could restore the effectiveness of the wider frameworks and enable the reestablishment of a more unitary center and homogeneous sociopolitical framework.

The transformation of the feudal centers could take place in several different directions. Under conditions of smaller differentiation and of relative weakness of the respective subcenters of the feudal regime, the processes of change of the concomitant political struggle could give rise to the restoration of patrimonial or small urban communities or, at most, to the development of new imperial systems. Significantly enough, the latter development was very rare.

In the more differentiated societies these processes of change could facilitate the development of more flexible modern regimes. This could happen, as it did in Japan, in the form of a direct transition into centralized regimes or, as in most parts of Europe, through the stage of the *Standestaat*. Such development could take place especially when the feudal regimes evinced a combination of relatively strong but autonomous centers.

We can thus see that, in general, the feudal regimes were among the most transformative of the various political regimes we have analyzed, in the sense that they could develop forces from within themselves that facilitated transformation and, at the same time, maintained some continuity of cultural and political identity.

NOTES

1. This introduction is based in part on the article by J. Prawer and S. N. Eisenstadt, "Feudalism" in the *International Encyclopedia of the Social Sciences*, vol. 5, ed. David L. Sills (New York: The Macmillan Co. and The Free Press, 1968), pp. 393–403.

2. See R. Coulborn ed., *Feudalism in History* (Princeton: Princeton University Press, 1956), and the various case studies included there. On Europe, see the classic study by Marc Bloch, *Feudal Society* (Chicago and London: University of Chicago Press, 1961).

3. Max Weber, *The Theory of Social and Economic Organization* (New York: Oxford University Press, 1947), pp. 344–345.

4. See E. Reischauer, in Coulborn, *op. cit.*, pp. 26–48.

5. See the various case studies in Coulborn, *op. cit.*

6. Derk Bodde, "Feudalism in China," in *Feudalism in History*, pp. 49–93.

7. See the cases in Coulborn, *op. cit.*

8. See D. Hintze, *Wesen und Herbreitung des Feudalismus Sitzungsberichte der Preussischen Akademie der Wissenschaften* (Berlin: Phil. Hist. Klasse, 1929), pp. 321–347; and Coulborn, *op. cit.*, Part III.

INTRODUCTION TO THE READINGS

In the following excerpts we have attempted to present materials dealing with several aspects of different feudal systems. The article by Chroust analyzes the political symbolism and ideals that developed in medieval feudal Europe. The articles by Vernadsky and Asakawa analyze three non-European feudal systems and point out both the similarities and differences among them. Asakawa's article is of especial importance because it deals with the only feudal system beyond Europe which ultimately gave rise to a modern political system. The article by Cam brings us back to the processes of change and decline of the European feudal system.

29

The Corporate Idea and the Body Politics in the Middle Ages

Anton-Hermann Chroust

To the mediaeval mind in general the destiny and preordained end of Christendom was always identical with that of mankind at large.[1] All of mankind, or to be more exact, the whole of Christendom is but a single universal community founded and directed by God Himself. Hence "we should desire to be subjected to Him," Origen exhorts us, "even as the Apostles are, and all the Saints who have followed Christ."[2] Thus freedom in its profoundest meaning was subjection to God and oneness with Him. Christendom, therefore, was primarily one single "*corpus mysticum*," a single indivisible and indissoluble *universitas,* a spiritual as well as temporal kingdom under the rule of God. This *universitas* found its most sublime and adequate expression in the idea of an *ecclesia universalis*[3] governed by one law and guided by one government.[4] Thus, in fact, an ideal constitution was immediately derived from the concept of one single *lex aeterna* or *ius divinum,* a constitution, that is, which by virtue of the universal sovereignty of the spiritual oneness of all men applied to the whole of mankind.

These ideas which identified the whole of mankind with the *ecclesia universalis* and, at the same time, proclaimed that mankind itself and with it every form of society or association is a living organism, already became manifest in the theological teachings and religious life of early Christianity, and above all, in the Christian conception of one *Ecumenical Church.* As a matter of fact, they were first voiced by St. Paul in his *First Epistle to the Corinthians* (12:4–27; 14:26; 10:16–17) as well as in his *Epistle to the Ephesians* (1:23, 3:6; 4:4; 4:14–16; 5:23; 5:30) and to the *Romans* (12:4–5). From such basic and authoritative pronouncements the social and political philosophers of the Middle Ages drew their main inspirations as to the true nature, function, and end of society and social institutions. Thus Remigio de Girolami, for instance, in complete dependence on St. Paul, insists that all Christians constitute a single body without blemish or defect, governed by a single head.[5] As a matter of fact, as early as the ninth century the terms "world," "empire," "mankind," "Church," and "Christendom" were often used as synonymous expressions.[6] By putting the whole before the part, mediaeval thought, on the one hand, plainly restated a classical principle of antiquity; while emphasizing the intrinsic value and, implicitly, the basic or original

From Anton-Hermann Chroust, "The Corporate Idea and the Body Politics in the Middle Ages," *Review of Politics,* IX (1947), 430–433, 445–452. Reprinted by permission of the author and publisher.

226

rights of the individual, it definitely laid, on the other hand, the foundation of a type of lego-political and social philosophy which is essentially alien to the Ancient mind.[7] For this is perhaps one of the most characteristic hallmarks of the mediaeval mind: that it conceives the universe as being a single articulated and organic whole. Yet it was able to see in every single being within this total universe not only a part of the whole, but at the same time a whole in itself. As a mere part of the universal whole every individual being was strictly determined by the whole and the laws governing the whole, and yet, as an individual, it had laws of its own as well as a final cause of its own.[8] Hence every social order and every form of ordering human society had to be understood as a partial aspect of the universal order of things and of the whole; and, again, as a whole in itself with its own final cause as well as with its own object and own end or ends. This social order, like the cosmic order, existed because God existed, and was good because God in His infinite charity had decreed it to be. . . .

The social body, like the animal body, stood in need of a manifold and graded organic articulation without which there could be no lasting peace and order.[9] These articulations were found not only in the *regimen ecclesiasticum,* but also in the *regimen civile.*[10] But the very concept of a *regimen* or *regimen universale* demanded a single order under the guidance of a single head. For the good rule of the whole required the rule of one who is at the head of the whole of mankind.[11] And, as Jonas of Orleans pointed out, "the prince is the head of the *corpus politicum.*"[12] Thus all *regimina singularia* corresponded to members of and were, therefore, related to the *regimen universale* either directly or indirectly. Prompted by the idea of a *regimen universale* Guido Vernani, the eloquent antagonist of Dante's political views, insisted that the last monarchy would be one which embraced the whole of mankind under the laws of the New Gospel. For only then everything could be really one and all men would be united into this grandiose *ordinatio ad unum.*[13] This *regimen universale,* this universal order or "constitution," which swept any and every member of the social actuality into an organic and strictly articulate whole, called for an organization which would order, adjust, and balance each individual part in such a manner that every part itself might act upon every other part without being itself either dislocated or destroyed or without dislocating or destroying these other parts.[14] Jonas of Orleans, for instance, appealed directly to Pepin to do his duty as a Christian prince by keeping the Empire

together thus avoiding a repetition of the previous disastrous territorial division of western Europe.[15] At the same time the postulate of an effective and harmonious articulation and integration of many into a single whole required that the "lower" parts or forces should be set into motion, controlled, and guided by the "higher" forces;[16] and that all these forces should be directed in unison by the highest force.[17] For "that which is more perfect is superior to the less perfect."[18] In the social body as "in the human body there are certain functions and activities which pertain exclusively to the higher members; and there are also such functions which belong to the head alone."[19] For in the well-ordered and properly functioning social organism "everything and every one must have the proper estate and exercise the proper activity to which he is entitled according to his standing."[20]

From this was derived the notion of a single and uniform social *function* of the single and uniform, although strictly articulated, social whole. This idea conceived, in the final analysis, of every member as performing some socially significant function and as being therefore, a mere *organ* or agent of the whole.[21] But since every function or activity performed by any one organ of the whole was but part or a partial manifestation of the single and uniform over-all function of the whole; and since every such uniform over-all function was considered as permeating the whole as well as its parts, a single "centralized" moving force, a *summum movens* had to be presupposed which enlivens, regulates, and directs in unison the whole organism in all its stratified functions and activities.[22] For no prosperous social life could exist among a multitude of essentially different individuals unless it were under the direction of one "who looks after the common good."[23] But we are also reminded that the soul, the *pars principans,* in its relation to the complete body, could only move in a physical sense through the medium of the body and its many members.[24] Hence every social organism or body required a single and unified governing part or *pars principans,* because "many seek many things, whereas one—the single *pars principans*—attends only one."[25] In other words, there had always to be a single *summum movens* which was at the same time the *pars principans,* and which controlled all the manifold motions of the various limbs or members.[26] The body politic, like the body animal, always needed a *primum principium et movens,* for otherwise the organism would either fall apart or become completely paralyzed.[27] Only by virtue of the right interrelation with and proper adjustment to *principium movens* of the whole social organism could there be purposive motion and fruitful life not only for the whole but also for every part of the whole.[28]

Inasmuch as the very essence of the social organism consisted of the principle of unity, and inasmuch as it was also held that this very unity had to be represented and become effective in what might be called a single governing part or *pars principans,* the Middle Ages insisted that this organic unity could best be achieved if the governing part be itself a single unity of wills (*unitas in voluntatibus*).[29] The governing part in its manifold yet unified functional aspects was always identified with the concept of office.[30] Thus Jonas of Orleans claimed that "*nemo regum a progenitoribus regnum sibi administrari, sed a Deo . . . credere debet dari.*"[31] At the same time the relationship between this office and the community, that is to say, between the governing and the governed part of the whole was emphatically declared as a *sui generis* relationship which involves reciprocal or correlative rights and duties. For both the governing and the governed part had their distinct rights and clearly defined duties.[32] And only through the reciprocity and correlativity of these rights and duties could the articulated social organism function effectively. Within the social union all individuals without exception stood in certain clearly defined legal relationships to the ruling part.[33] These relationships, which were definitely of a bilateral nature, precluded from the very beginning the possibility that the *pars principans* could ever be thought of in terms of absolute right and privilege. On the contrary, in view of the absolute spiritual and moral worth of every individual any form of rulership was conceived as a most onerous and serious duty, a calling, that is, which primarily consists in rendering service to and ministering unto the whole.[34] For "whosoever will be great among you, let him be your minister; and whosoever will be chief among you, let him be your servant." (*Matthew* 20:26–27; *Mark* 10:43:44). The ruler, at least the rightful ruler, was, to be sure, instituted by God.[35] "*Possunt tamen principes dici vicarii Dei implicite . . .*"[36] But these *principes* were instituted, not for their own sake but for the sake of the people.[37] This alone should indicate that the office of rulership was always defined and delimited by the terms and the spirit of divine appointment which puts the whole above the part, or to be more exact, the whole people above the *pars principans.*[38] The proper and, as a matter of fact, sole task of the *pars principans,* in other words, of the office, was to promote, under the laws of God, the welfare of the whole as well as the utmost freedom of every individual.[39] In this fashion

the Middle Ages laid the foundation of two eminently important social tenets, first, that every duty of obedience on the part of the subject rested upon the rightfulness of the command and, secondly, that there was no such thing as an unconditional and morally blind duty of obedience and submission[40] —two truly heartening principles in days of ruthless tyrants or public lawlessness.

The restriction of the *pars principans* to the spirit and terms of divine appointment under the laws of God endowed the *universitas civium,* the whole organic body of the people with certain inalienable rights consonant with the spiritual and moral dignity of man. These rights of man were, in the final analysis, of divine origin.[41] Hence within the social organism it was always the people in its divine and divinely ordained rights which constituted what might be called the remote cause, the *causa secunda* of all social institutions and public offices. "*Ubi rex, ubi curia, ubi ministri, ubi plebs invenitur, civitas est: neque enim talia essent in malis civitatibus, nisi prius essent in singulis hominibus, qui sunt tamquam elementa et semina civitatum.*"[42] By giving actual and effective expression to these rights the people themselves endowed the whole body politic with an articulate form. They also created, at least indirectly, as well as distributed offices and by doing this bound these various offices into an organic whole.[43] Viewed from these rights of the people and of every individual the office of rulership was thus limited to the discharge of such business as the *universitas civium* could not effectively perform by itself.[44] But the office of rulership nevertheless always remained a mere part of the whole—the *pars principans*—or the organ of the always superior whole and as such was always subservient to the whole.[45] It was, in other words, the *instrumentalis sive executiva pars* of the organic social whole. And since it was also an organ or agency, namely that part of the whole through which the latter, as the principal, acts in purposive unison, it had always to conform to the will of the people, the organic whole, and to be in agreement with the common welfare of the people.[46] For although all earthly power, including that of the rightful ruler, primarily stemmed from God, it was the divinely inspired will of the people in which the divine resolve became most apparent. Durandus de S. Porciano went even so far as to insist that "*magis esse secundum naturam, quod totus populus haberet rationem principis . . . Ergo potestas et dominum ad regendum populum est in hominibus secundum debitum rationis et divinae ordinationis.*"[47] And Patricius of Siena suggested outright that a commonwealth which embraced the whole of mankind might

:ery well be a republic, the more so, since unity was one of the foremost elements of republican government.[48] Hence any rightful government displayed its divine origin and mandate above all in the voluntary consent of the governed.[49] Gerhoh of Reichersperg carried the idea of popular sovereignty so far as to suggest a popular election of all secular princes.[50] For all God-pleasing rulership was, in the final analysis, founded on the *voluntas subjecti et consensus populi*. Only as the creature of the always supreme whole—creature in so far as he enjoys the consent of the people—could the ruler be called the rightful head of the whole and of its many and diversified parts or members. For all rulership was merely a popular mandate or office and as such always restricted by the very terms of this mandate.[51]

It was the mediaeval conception of the body politic as an organic and articulated whole which brought about not only a morally sound and socially adequate distinction and relation between the rights and duties of governments and those of the governed, but also evolved into the eminently satisfactory idea that all public offices are mere mandates and as such representative institutions declarative of and, hence, subservient to the will of the whole. Moreover, the very principle of an integrated organism demanded a clearly defined and strictly delimited apportionment as well as division of powers and functions. For it was held that each of these offices, mandates, or institutions constituted merely a part of the whole and thus only represented in an articulate form the supreme organic whole in some of its many vital functions and activities.

NOTES

1. Compare, in general, *Episcoporum ad Hludowicum Imperatorem Relatio*, in: *Monumenta Germ. Hist. Capit.* II, 29, (Now: *Mon. Germ. Hist., Leg.* sect. 3, vol. II, 2, p. 610).
2. Origen, *Peri Archon* (in the translation of Rufinus), I, 6, 1.
3. The theologians of the Middle Ages very frequently use the term *ecclesia universalis* in order to define or describe the whole of mankind as being one single order or unity. Compare, for instance, Engelbert of Volkersdorf (1250–1311), *De Ortu, Progressu et Fine Romani Imperii* 15; 17; 18; Augustinus Triumphus de Ancona (1243–1328), *Summa de Potestate Ecclesiastica* I, quaest. 1, art. 6; Alvarus Pelagius, *De Planctu Ecclesiae* I, 13; William of Occam, *Octo Quaestiones*, quaest. 3, Chap. 1; *Dialogus* III, tact. 2, lib. 1, chap. 1.
4. At the councils (synods) of Worms and Paris (829) as well as in the *Capitulary of Worms* (see: *Monumenta Germaniae, Leges* 1, 333) it was stated that the "*universalis sancta ecclesia Dei unum corpus manifeste esse credatur eiusque caput Christus.*" Similar ideas which express the notion that mankind is but a single body with a divinely ordained spiritual as well as temporal constitution of its own, we find in Jonas of Paris (died 843), *De Institutione Regia;* See also Pope Gregory VII, *Registrum* I, *Epistola* 19, anno 1073 (in: *Monumenta Gregoriana*); Ivo of Chartres (died 1115), *Epistola* 106 (in: Migne, *Patrol. Lat.* vol. 162, 217 ff.); St. Bernard (1091–1153), *Epistola ad Conradum Regem, anno* 1146 (in: *Patrol. Lat.*, vol. 182, 440 ff.); Gerhohus Reicherspergensis, *De Corruptione Statu Ecclesiae*, praef. p. 11 (in: *Monumenta Germaniae, Libelli de Lite* III, p. 131 ff.); Hugo Floriacensis, *Tractatus de Regia et Sacerdotali Dignitate I* 1; St. Thomas Cantuarensis (St. Thomas Becket, 1116–1170), *Epistola* 179 (in: *Patrol. Lat.*, vol. 190, 652); Pope Innocent III (1198–1216), *Registrum super Negotiis Romani Imperii* (in: *Patrol. Lat.*, vol. 216, 997; 1012; 1162; St. Thomas Aquinas, *Summa Theologica* III, quaest. 8, art. 1; art. 2; Vincent of Beauvois, *Speculum Doctrinale* VII, 31.
5. *Contra Falsos Ecclesiae Professores*, eighth and ninth argument.
6. See, for instance, *Episcoporum ad Hludowicum Imperatorem Relatio* (829) in: *Monumenta Germaniae Histor., Capit.* II, 29 (now: *Mon. Germ. Hist., Leg.* III, vol. II, 2, p. 610).
7. The Roman legal genius, to be sure, already had conceived the legal order as an effective institution for delimiting and securing the various interests and powers of action which in their aggregate make up what is commonly called the *legal personality* of every Roman citizen. This concept of the *legal personality* as it was devised by the Roman jurists is the first tangible and practical expression of the idea of the irreplaceable and irreducible worth and dignity of the human personality and individuality. The declaration that within a politically organized society established by law men in their relations to one another are endowed with certain clearly defined and rigorously delimited rights, is perhaps the most telling pronouncement the ancient world made concerning the problem of the human personality and the dignity of the individual.—Compare A.-H. Chroust, "The Function of Law and Justice in the Ancient World and the Middle Ages," in: *Journal of the History of Ideas*, vol. VII (1946), no. 3, p. 302 ff.; This Roman definition of the proper function of the legal order, however, is but an outgrowth of a legal polity which sees in the law primarily an instrument devised to secure certain personal interests. It is not, as it is with the mediaeval thinkers, the cogent result of man's divine ordination, the inescapable outgrowth of the belief that each and every human individual is essentially the holy vessel of an immortal soul destined to an everlasting life of heavenly bliss. This novel Christian conception of the individual and his absolute worth endows the classical Roman idea of giving every one his own with an infinitely profounder significance. Compare A.-H. Chroust, *op. cit.*, p. 331.
8. Compare O. Gierke, *Das Deutsche Genossenschaftsuct* (Berlin, 1881), III, 514.
9. Marsilius of Padua, *Defensor Pacis* II, 24.
10. Compare Johannes Andreae Mugellanus, *Novella in Decretales Gregorii IX*, chap. 4, I, 1, 13: "*ecclesia universalis est unum Christi corpus . . . cuius caput est Romana ecclesia . . . inferiores ecclesiae sunt huius capitis membra quae sunt vel membra ex capite vel membra ex membris sicut in corpore humano a brachio manus, a manu digiti, a digitis ungulae proveniunt.*" See also St. Bernard, *De Consideratione* III, p. 82; Marsilius of Padua, *Defensor Pacis* II, 24.
11. Rodrigo Sanches de Arévalo, *Defensorium Ecclesiae et Status Ecclesiastici*, fol. 35v, in: *Cod. Vat. Lat.* 4106 Ir-238. —Compare also St. Thomas Aquinas, IV. *Sent.*, dist. 18, quaest. 1, art. 1; *Summa Theologica* I, quaest. 60, art. 1; Alexander of Hales, *Summa Universae Theologiae* IV, quaest. 35; John of Torquemada, *Summa Ecclesiae* (edit. Venetiis 1561) II, 113.
12. *De Institutione Laicali* II, 20, in: *Patrol. Lat.* vol. 106, 211.
13. Guido Vernani, *De Reprobatione Monarchiae* 11 (edit. Jarro).
14. Marsilius of Padua, *Defensor Pacis* I, 2; I, 5.
15. *De Institutione Regia*, prooem.

16. Dominicus de Dominicis Venetus, *De Potestate Papae,* in: *Cod. Vat. Lat.* 4123, fol. 58r. Compare also St. Thomas Aquinas, I. *Sent.* dist. 20, quaest. 3, art. 1; *Summa Theologica* I, quaest. 42, art. 3.

17. Ptolomaeus of Lucca, *De Regimine Principum* II, 26. See also St. Thomas Aquinas, *Summa contra Gentiles* III, 76 ff.; Engelbert of Volkersdorf, *De Regimine Principum* III, 21: "*in ordinatione debita et proportione ad invicem . . . partium. . . .*"

18. Dominicus de Dominicis Venetus, *De Potestate Papae,* in: *Cod. Vat. Lat.* 4123, fol. 58r; Jacobus de Viterbo, *De Regimine Christiano* p. 131. (edit. Arquillière).

19. St. Thomas Aquinas, *Lectio 2 ad Romanos* 12.

20. Ptolomaeus of Lucca, *De Regimine Principum* II, 23. —Compare also John of Salisbury, *Policraticus* V, 2; Marsilius of Padua, *Defensor Pacis* I, 2; Alvarus Pelagius, *De Planctu Ecclesiae* I, 63; William of Occam, *Octo Quaestiones,* quaest. I, 1; quaest. VIII, 5.

21. Marsilius of Padua, *Defensor Pacis* I, 5; I, 2. Marsilius distinguishes between several *officia,* that is, the several functions of the various clearly defined organs of the body politic. Compare also Engelbert of Volkersdorf, *De Regimine Principum* III, 16; John of Salisbury, *Policraticus* V, 2; Ptolomaeus of Lucca, *De Regimine Principum* II, 23.

22. Compare O. Gierke, *op. cit.,* p. 582.

23. St. Thomas Aquinas, *Summa Theologica* I, quaest. 96, art. 4. Compare Ptolomaeus of Lucca, *De Regimine Principum* IV, 23; Marsilius of Padua, *Defensor Pacis* I, 17.

24. Remigio de' Girolami of Florence, *Contra Falsos Ecclesiae Professores* 37 (fol. 164v).

25. St. Thomas Aquinas, *Summa Theologica* I, quaest. 96, art. 4.—Compare also *Summa contra Gentiles* IV, 76.

26. Ptolomaeus of Lucca, *De Regimine Principum* IV, 23.

27. Marsilius of Padua, *Defensor Pacis* I, 17.—Compare also John of Paris, *Tractatus de Regia Potestate et Papali* (written in 1303), 1; Petrus de Andlo, *De Imperio Romano-Germanico* I, 3.

28. Compare Alvarus Pelagius, *De Planctu Ecclesiae* I, 7; I, 13; I, 36.

29. Dante, *De Monarchia* I, 15.—Compare Petrus de Andlo, *De Imperio Romano-Germanico* I, 3.

30. Compare Hincmar of Reims, *Pro Ecclesiae Libertatum Defensione* 1, in: *Patrol. Lat.,* vol. 125, 1049; Peter Damian, *Liber Gratissimus* 39, in: *Monumenta Germ. Hist., Lib. de Lite* I, 72; Lambert, *Annales ad Annum* 1074, in: *Monumenta Germ. Hist., Scriptores, Rer. Germ.,* p. 199; Ennodius, *Liber pro Synodo,* in: *Monumenta Germ. Hist., Auct. Ant.* VII, 52; *Decretum Gratiani* I, D. 40.

31. *De Institutione Regia* 7. Compare also Jonas of Orleans, *Historia Translationis,* prooem., in: *Patrol. Lat.,* vol. 106, 389.

32. John of Salisbury, *Policraticus* IV, 1 ff.; IV, 5; St. Thomas Aquinas, *De Regimine Principum* I, 14; Dante, *De Monarchia* I, 12.

33. Hugo Floriacensis, *Tractatus de Regia et Sacerdotali Dignitati* I, 4.

34. St. Thomas Aquinas, *De Regimine Principum* I, 14; Alvarus Pelagius, *De Planctu Ecclesiae* I, 62; Ptolomaeus of Lucca, *De Regimine Principum* II, 5 ff.; Hugo Floriacensis, *Tractatus de Regia et Sacerdotali Dignitate* I, 4; I, 6; I, 7; Manigold of Lautenbach, *Tractatus adversus Wenricum* (written in 1085), in: *Monumenta Germaniae, Libelli de Lite* I, p. 301; Engelbert of Volkersdorf, *De Regimine Principum* II, 1 ff.; Antonius de Rosellis, *Monarchia sive de Potestate Imperatoris et Papae* I, 64; Petrus de Andlo, *De Imperio Romano-Germanico* I, 3; II, 16 ff.

35. See *Monumenta Germaniae, Legum.* sect. IV I, p. 346, *et al.* "Thus at the Councils of Paris and Worms in 829 it was held that all rulership is only a *ministerium a Deo commissum.*" It was also stated that the term "*rex*" must be derived from "*recte agere,*" and that ceasing to rule righteously and justly any *rex* becomes a *tyrannus.*

36. Hervaeus Natalis (Brito), *De Potestate Papae* 2;—

Fulbert of Chartres had already declared that the secular rulers are *vicarii Christi.* See *Epistola* 30, in: *Patrol. Lat.,* vol. 141, 216. Compare also Sedulius Scotus, *De Rectoribus Christianis* I, 11.

37. See John of Salisbury, *Policraticus* IV, 1 ff.; IV, 5; Ptolomaeus of Lucca, *De Regimine Principum* III, 11: "*regnum non est propter regem, sed rex propter regnum.*" Engelbert of Volkersdorf, *De Regimine Principum* V, 9: "*procuratio reipublicae inventa est ad utilitatem eorum qui commissi sunt, et non eorum qui commissionem susceperunt.*" Dante, *De Monarchia* I, 12: "*non enim cives propter consules, nec gens propter regem, sed e converso consules propter cives et rex propter gentem.*"

38. Compare Jean de Menun, *Roman de la Rose* V, 5297 ff.

39. Engelbert of Volkersdorf, *De Regimine Principum* I, 10; Dante, *De Monarchia* I, 12; St. Thomas Aquinas, *Summa Theologica* I, quaest. 96, art. 4; William of Occam, *Octo Quaestiones,* quaest. III, 5.—Every breach of these duties turns the rulership into an outright tyranny. See note 138. *supra.* Compare also Hugo Floriacensis, *Tractatus de Regia et Sacerdotali Dignitate* I, 7 ff.; *Petrus Blesensis* (died 1200), *Epistola,* in: Migne, *P. L.,* vol. 200, 476; John of Salisbury, *Policraticus* III, 17 ff.; Ptolomaeus of Lucca, *De Regimine Principum* III, 11; St. Thomas Aquinas, *De Regimine Principum* I, 3 ff.; Vincent of Beauvais, *Speculum Doctrinale* VII, 8, Occam, *Dialogus* III, tract. 1, Book 2, chap. 6 ff.; *Octo Quaestiones,* quaest. III, 14.

40. Obviously, then, the rightfulness of command is determined by the fact whether or not it is in agreement with the commands of God. Compare St. Augustine, *De Civitate Die* XIX, 14; St. Thomas Aquinas, *Summa Theologica* I, II, quaest. 91, art. 2; quaest. 94, art. 1–6; quaest. 97, art. 1; *ibid.* II, II, quaest. 57, art. 2; Aegidius Romanus Colonna, *De Regimine Principum* III, pars 2, cap. 29; Vincent of Beauvais, *Speculum Doctrinale* VII, 41 ff.; X, 87; William of Occam, *Dialogus* III, tract. 1, lib. 2, chap. 6; tract. 2, Book 2, chap. 26 ff.; Baldus de Ubaldis, *Commentarius in Usus Feudorum* I, 3, 24 ff.

41. St. Augustine, *De Diversis Quaestionibus* I, 53, 2; *ibid.* 31, 1 ff.; *De Trinitate* XII, 15; St. Thomas Aquinas, *Summa Theologica* I, II, quaest. 91, art. 1; art. 2; art. 4; art. 5; William of Auxerre, *Summa Aurea* III, tract. 7, chap. 1, quaest. 3; Alexander of Hales, *Summa Universae Theologiae* III, quaest. 27, membr. 1, art. 1; art. 2; *Anonymous Cod. Borgh.* (*saec.* XIII, *Lib. Vat.* no. 139) folio 97 ff., quoted in: A.-H. Chroust, "The Philosophy of Law from St. Augustine to St. Thomas Aquinas," in: *The New Scholasticism,* vol. 20 (1946) no. 1, p. 51 ff. and footnote.

42. St. Augustine, *Ennar. in Psalm.* IX, 8, in: *Patrol. Lat.,* vol. 36, 120 ff.

43. St. Thomas Aquinas, *Summa Theologica* I, II, quaest. 90, art. 3; quaest. 97, art. 3; Ptolomaeus of Lucca, *De Regimine Principum* II, 8; III, 8; IV, 1; Engelbert of Volkersdorf, *De Regimine Principum* I, 10; I, 11; William of Occam, *Dialogus* III, tract 1, lib. 2, chap. 6; Petrus de Andlo, *De Imperio Romano-Germanico* I, 8; John of Salisbury, *Policraticus* IV, 2; Aegidius Romanus Colonna, *De Regimine Principum* III, pars. 2, cap. 2.

44. Compare St. Thomas Aquinas, *Summa Theologica* I, quaest. 96, art. 4.

45. See Aegidius Romanus Colonna, *De Regimine Principum* III, pars. 2, cap. 2: "*totus populus magis dominatur. . . .*" Compare also Nicolaus of Cues, *De Concordantia Catholica* II, 9 ff.; II, 20; III, praef.; III, 41.

46. Marsilius of Padua, *Defensor Pacis* I, 7; I, 8; I, 12; I, 13; I, 15; I, 17.

47. See Koch, J., *Durandus de S. Porciano, Forschungen zum Streit um Thomas von Aquino zu Beginn des 14. Jahrhunderts,* vol. I, p. 172; 173.

48. Patricius of Siena, *De Institutione Reipublicae* I, 1. Compare also Marsilius of Padua, *Defensor Pacis* I, 17; William of Occam, *Dialogus* III, tract. 1, Book 2, chap. 2.

49. Nicolaus of Cues, *De Concordantia Catholica* III, 4: "*tunc divina censetur, quando per concordantiam communem a subiectis exoritur.*"

50. *De Investigatione Antichristi* 38.
51. Nicolaus of Cues, *De Concordantia Catholica* II, 12; II, 13; III, 4; III, 41.

30

Feudalism in Russia

George Vernadsky

I

In spite of the fact that so much work has already been devoted to the study of feudalism in Russia, the problem as a whole needs reconsideration, especially since the definition of feudalism in Soviet historiography is too vague to be of real service to the student of the problem. A twofold approach to the problem of feudalism is possible: first, a broad sociological approach which tends to define the most essential traits of feudalism by confronting feudalizing tendencies in the history of different epochs and different countries; second, a characterization of the main features of the feudalism of the Romano-Germanic countries of mediaeval Europe as a standard or "ideal" type of feudalism.

Feudalizing processes have been observed by historians and sociologists throughout the ages almost the world over. We have accustomed ourselves to speak of feudalism in China and Japan; of Turco-Mongol feudalism; of feudalism in Moslem countries; of feudalism in the "Middle Ages" (roughly, the fifth to the fifteenth century A.D.); or of feudalism in the Homeric epoch (roughly, the first half of the first millennium B.C.).[1]

There is always a danger, by expanding the range of the term too much, to label by the same name social processes which are outwardly similar, but inwardly stand widely apart. While Japanese feudal institutions show striking similarity with those of mediaeval Europe, the feudalizing tendencies among the Turks and the Mongols, or in the Moslem countries, did not have the same effect on the building up of the whole social structure as in Europe.[2]

Recently a careful attempt to construct a definition of feudal trends in different countries has been

made by Otto Hintze.[3] According to Hintze, there are three factors which in their combination produce feudalism or, in other words, there are three functions through which feudalism expresses itself. These are the following: (1) the military aspect: the establishment of a well-developed order of warriors (*Kriegerstand*) bound to the ruler by an oath of fealty which has the nature of a private contract (*Privatvertrag*); (2) the economic and social aspect: the establishment of a manor with the bound husbandry which provides the privileged warriors' order with rent income; (3) the establishment of the noble warriors as local rulers and their self-assertion with regard to the supreme state authority.

While Hintze's definition of feudalism has been cautiously couched in fairly general expressions, it still is not broad enough in the sense that, by retaining the classical definition of feudal economics based on agriculture, Hintze excludes the possibility of the development of a "nomadic feudalism" upon which some Soviet orientalists now insist. On the other hand, Hintze's definition is, in my opinion, too broad in the sense that some essential traits of European feudalism have found no place in his scheme.

For the purpose of my present article I find it more practical to dwell first on the essential characteristics of the Romano-Germanic feudalism in the Middle Ages, which still might be considered the standard type of feudalism.

The task of formulating the fundamentals of the concept of European feudalism is not so easy either. Has not Charles H. McIlwain recently made a rather melancholy statement that "the word 'feudalism' is little more than a rough generalization"?[4] Has not Alfons Dopsch succeeded in considerably shaking, if not completely destroying, some of the old opinions as to the foundations of social and economic life of mediaeval Europe, e.g., such as that of the

From George Vernadsky, "Feudalism in Russia," *Speculum*, XIV (1939), 303–305, 313–323. Reprinted by permission of the publisher.

prevalence of a "closed economy" in the early Middle Ages?[5] And yet it seems essential to come to an agreement concerning at least some general traits of a feudal régime as typical for Romano-Germanic countries of mediaeval Europe. A tentative outline of these traits greatly helps us in discussing the problems of Russian social development.[6]

The following four points might be mentioned here with regard to the main prerequisites for the growth of feudal institutions: the fusion of public and private law; the dismemberment of political authority; the prevalence of a natural economy; interdependence of both political and economic administration. As to a developed feudal régime, the following three items seem to be the most essential: (1) "political feudalism": mediatization of supreme political authority; establishment of a scale of greater and lesser rulers (suzerain, vassals, subvassals) bound by personal contract; reciprocity of such a contract; (2) "economic feudalism"; the establishment of the manorial régime with a restriction of the legal status of the peasants; distinction between the *dominium directum* and *dominium utile;* (3) the feudal nexus: an indissoluble fusion of personal and territorial rights, the control of the land by the vassals being stipulated by the service rendered to their seignior.

On the ground of these general considerations, let us now attempt to give a more specific description of the organization of the feudal world. We may approach this task by considering one by one the three following aspects of the feudal structure: (I) The lower feudal group; (II) The mutual relations between feudal groups; and (III) The feudal state.

I. It still might be recognized that the basis of a primary feudal group is land. In its economics feudal society is dependent chiefly upon agriculture; the methods of control and use of the land result in the formation of two main social groups: a landed aristocracy and peasants. Thus, the seigniory, or manor, is the primary cell of the whole feudal structure. Economically speaking, it consists of a demesne farm superimposed over the village community. If the seignior would grant part of his land to some noble holder, to be held by military service and not by labor service, such holder would be his vassal and the land controlled by him a fief and not a *censiva.* In such case the seigniory would assume a more complex character. Its social agents would be: (1) The seignior; (2) his villeins; (3) his vassals; (4) the villeins of the vassals. The seignior had authority over both his vassals and his villeins, but it was a different kind of authority. While both the villeins and the vassals had to swear an oath of fealty to

the seignior, only the vassals had their holdings guaranteed by the reciprocity of the contract.

II. Each elementary feudal group, being a unit in itself, is not an isolated social group. Its intercourse with kindred groups results on one hand in the formation of a general class of feudal aristocracy all over mediaeval Europe. On the other, the interrelations among the elementary feudal units result in the establishment of a network of feudal units connected among themselves more or less tightly. The seignior of a lower feudal group would pledge vassal fealty to a stronger lord, and as a concomitant result his manor would become part of a larger seigniory. His vassals would become subvassals with regard to the new lord. It is in that way that a scale of greater and lesser seigniors comes into being, and the whole feudal world assumes a more complex political aspect.

III. The feudal state as a whole is characterized by the following traits: (1) The authority of each lord is of conditional nature; a lord might be simultaneously a seignior with regard to both his vassals and villeins, and a vassal of a greater lord (the suzerain); (2) the degree of authority of each lord is adapted to the position of his seigniory or his fief in the feudal scale of the possessions; (3) there exists a far-reaching dismemberment of the political sovereignty, each lord possessing but a fraction of it. . . .

The Mongol administration in Russia had as its main objectives the collection of taxes for the Khan's treasury and the drafting of recruits into the Khan's army. A census of population was, therefore, introduced in Russia under the same methods as were applied by the Mongols in other provinces subject to their domination. Part of South Russia along the middle course of the Dnieper River was directly subjected to Mongol governors (*daruga* or *baskak*). This territory was divided into a number of taxation units, each district being known as *tuma* (*tuman*). The population of each district was organized in communes with the mutual guarantee of the members of paying the right amount of taxes.[7]

In the remaining Russian provinces, both in the West and in the East, the native princes were allowed to stay under the provision of their absolute submission to the Khan's will. Each prince had to receive a special patent (*yarlyk*) from the Khan and to be inducted to his throne by the Khan's envoy (*elchi; posol* in Russian). The native princes were obliged to assist the Mongol agents in collecting taxes. Later on, the Grand Duke of Moscow was commissioned by the Khan to collect taxes under his responsibility. It was this commission which contributed a great deal to the ascendancy of the authority of the Grand Duke to Moscow.

In the next section we shall deal with the developments in Eastern Russia, and now confine our comments to Western Russia. The period of Mongol domination in Western Russia lasted a little over one hundred years. In the middle of the fourteenth century, most of the West Russian provinces recognized the authority of the Grand Duke of Lithuania in order to escape that of the Khan.[8] The grand duchy of Lithuania was, politically speaking, a loose federation of both Lithuanian and West Russian principalities and provinces organized along lines strikingly similar to the feudal patterns of the Romano-Germanic countries.[9]

In order better to understand the graduation of dependency of the local princes and lords (*pany*) on the Grand Duke, it would not be amiss to state briefly the territorial division of the grand duchy of Lithuania with respect to the distribution of political authority of the Grand Duke. There was, first, the grand duchy of Lithuania proper, composed of those lands which came under the sway of the Grand Duke in the period of the original formation of the grand duchy. This original domain was comprised of most of the Lithuanian and of some of the West Russian lands incorporated into the grand duchy at the end of the thirteenth and in the beginning of the fourteenth century. It was divided into two duchies: that of Vilno and that of Troki. The second group of lands was the federated principalities which recognized the authority of the Grand Duke in the second half of the fourteenth century or in the first half of the fifteenth. One of such affiliated dominions was the Lithuanian province of Zhmud. All of the others were West Russian principalities as follows: Polotsk, Vitebsk, Smolensk, Kiev, Volyn, Podolie and Chernigov-Sever. It was only within the grand duchy proper that the Grand Duke was able to exercise his immediate control. Even within the boundaries of the grand duchy proper only part of the territory was left to the Grand Duke as his own domain. The other part was held by feudal lords—princes and boyars.

Though pledging an oath of personal fealty to the Grand Duke, each local prince was a ruler over his own province. As to the boyars, the Grand Duke granted them the control of their estates on condition of military service as well as the performance of some other duties as provided in the patents (*privilei*). In addition to the patrimonial boyar estates, there also developed another type of conditional grants of land either for life or for the term at the Grand Duke's discretion. Such lands were known as *pomestie*[10] Similar régimes came into being in each of the federated principalities. Some of the provincial princes were descendants of the Grand Duke Gedymin (1316–1341); others belonged to the old house of Kiev. The provincial prince, himself a vassal of the Grand Duke, had his own vassals, both the local princes and the *pany* (boyars). The provincial prince was a seignior in his own domain and a suzerain with regard to the minor local princes, each of whom had his *votchina* as well.[11]

As a result of such arrangements, a feudal scale of greater and lesser rulers bound by a mutual contract established itself in the grand duchy as a whole. The Grand Duke was the supreme suzerain, comparable to a feudal king of continental Europe or even to the King of England. His higher vassals, the provincial princes, corresponded to the German and French dukes; both the local princes and the major boyars constituted the bulk of the feudal landowning class comparable to the counts, barons, and knights of Central and Western Europe.

It is necessary to bear in mind that Latin was one of the two official languages of the Grand Duke's chancery, the other being Russian. The Grand Duke's charters, when issued in Latin, adapted western feudal terminology to the political régime of the grand duchy. In that way the feudal aspects of the political and social structure of the grand duchy were even more sharply emphasized.

Turning to social conditions, we notice the establishment of the typical manorial régime throughout the country. The legal status of the peasants was subject to gradual restrictions, both with regard to those peasants who cultivated the Grand Duke's domanial estates and those who were laboring on the princely and boyars estates. In 1447 the Grand Duke issued a patent (*privilei*) forbidding the peasants to shift from a princely or a boyar estate to that of the Grand Duke. This amounted to the official recognition of serfdom.

While we have sufficient reason to call the sociopolitical régime of the Grand Duchy of Lithuania feudalism, we now point to some divergent tendencies in its development. The owners of the larger feudal estates, both princes and boyars, attempted gradually to enforce their respective authority over their lands in such a way that they would receive full property rights over their estates not subject to any restrictions with regard to their suzerain. On the other hand, the political authority of the Grand Duke was more and more limited by the parliament (*Seim*). By the middle of the sixteenth century, this twofold transformation of the political and social structure of the grand duchy went a considerable distance toward undermining its feudalizing tendencies. The union of Lublin with Poland (1569) was an important landmark in this regard, signalizing the increase of the patrimonial rights of the gentry.[12] The Commonwealth (*Rzeczpospolita*) which resulted from the political union of the Crown (Poland) and the grand duchy (Lithuania) was an aristocratic republic, but it was no more a feudal confederation.

II

While the Mongol domination in Western Russia was in the fourteenth century replaced by the control of the Grand Dukes of Lithuania, Eastern Russia continued to remain under the Khan's authority for one more century, and it was not until the middle of the fifteenth century that the Grand Duke of Moscow emancipated himself from the Khan's control. The princes of Eastern Russia lost their independence after the Mongol conquest and recognized the Khan's suzerainty, or, as the contemporary terms put it, placed themselves under the Khan's hand, became his *podruchniki* (literally "underarmmen." i.e., vassals).[13]

As has been already mentioned, . . . the Khan issued patents (*yarlyk*) to the native princes in Russia. A prince provided with such yarlyk enjoyed the Khan's support against other claimants. In case such prince would apportion part of his principality to his son or his younger brother, the latter would rule over his portion as a subordinate (*podruchnik*) of the main prince of the province. In that way there was established a hierarchy of princes within each province. At the head of it was the Grand Duke (literally, Grand Prince, *veliki knyaz*, in Turkish *ulug beg*) provided with the Khan's patent.[14] The local princes were subordinated to the Grand Duke, some of them directly, others indirectly.

The main grand ducal provinces of Eastern Russia were Vladimir, Tver, Ryazan, Suzdal, Nizhni Novgorod. From the end of the thirteenth century the princes of Moscow advanced their claims to the grand duchy of Vladimir. Their aspirations collided with those of the princes of Tver. A stubborn struggle started between the princes of Moscow and Tver for obtaining the Khan's patent (*yarlyk*) covering the grand duchy of Vladimir. From 1329 the grand duchy remained in the hands of the Prince of Moscow. The next move of the princes of Moscow, now Grand Dukes of Vladimir, was to extend their suzerainty over the Grand Dukes of other provinces of Eastern Russia as well. Since the Grand Duke of Moscow and Vladimir succeeded in receiving the Khan's commission to collect taxes for the Khan's treasury, he had ample opportunity to improve his own financial affairs considerably which placed him in an advantageous position with regard to the other princes.

According to the treaty of 1375, the Grand Duke of Tver, Michael, recognized himself a *podruchnik* of the Grand Duke of Moscow, Dimitri.[15] The result of this policy was the gradual concentration of political authority over most of the East Russian principalities in the hands of the Grand Duke of Moscow. While Moscow was in ascendancy, the Golden Horde was in decline, and in the middle of the fifteenth century the former became practically independent of the latter. Owing to the disintegration of the Golden Horde at that time, part of the Tatar princes now recognized the suzerainty of the Moscow Grand Dukes. The creation of the vassal Tatar principality ("Tsardom") of Kasimov (about 1452) was a masterpiece of Moscow policy.[16] In that way, the political and social intercourse between the Turko-Mongol world and Eastern Russia was only strengthened. To the princes of the Kiev house a number of Mongol and Tatar princes ("Tsars" and "Tsareviches") were now added as vassals of the Grand Duke of Moscow and Vladimir.

The political structure of Eastern Russia thus assumed some aspects of similarity to both Western Russia and Europe. It is necessary to bear in mind, however, that a boyar, Russian or Tatar, still could not become a prince. On the other hand, the authority of a boyar as a landlord was increasing. The manor as an institution gradually consolidated itself. The manor administration and the manor courts claimed authority over the peasant population originally not connected with it. Reservation should be made, however, that the typical boyar *votchina* (patrimonial estate) of the period was a manor of a simple type and not a developed seigniory. The *votchina* consisted of the boyar's demesne and of the plots of land settled by peasants, the latter being subject to some control by the boyar. This in itself presented but a nucleus of a developed seigniory if compared with the western patterns. As has been already mentioned, a fully developed western seigniory used to comprise not only the seignior's demesne and the village community, but the vassal fiefs as well.[17]

Now it was not so common for a boyar to apportion part of his *votchina* estate as a *pomestie* (land grant under provision of service) to one of his servitors. Such practice was indeed usual with the princes and ecclesiastical lords or monasteries. We have, however, to keep in mind that the institution of *pomestie* in itself was not identical with that of the fief. The boyar's authority over his manor, as well as that of the ecclesiastical dignitaries and monasteries over the church *votchina,* was strengthened by the practice of the Grand Dukes in granting immunity charters to the *votchina* owners, guaranteeing them the privilege of manorial justice and exemption from taxation. Such immunity charters were often known as *tarkhan,* which implies the presence of the Turko-Mongol roots of this institution in Eastern Russia. The patents, or *yarlyk,* granted by the Khans of the Golden Horde to the Russian church, formed the background for the *tarkhan* charters of the Moscow Grand Dukes in favor of the monastery *votchina.*[18]

As to the peasants tilling the lord's land, they were not yet his serfs, and the peasant commune had as yet not become a universal institution. Some tendencies may, however, be noticed as preparing the ground for the coming of serfdom. In case a peasant's family stayed on the lord's land for more than a generation, they were considered "old settlers" (*starozhiltsy*) and were not expected to leave the manor freely and without notice.[19] The indebtedness of the peasant who would need a loan for buying cattle and farming implements was another way in which the peasant lost his freedom.[20] The institution of indentured labor assumed stricter forms under Turko-Mongol influence. The man receiving a loan had to work for his creditor until the loan was paid back. According to the new type of agreement, his work covered only the interest on the loan and not the principal. It is obvious that under such arrangements the debtor had to work for life and never was able to repay the principal unless he received a new loan from another creditor. This was known as *kabala* slavedom which developed in Eastern Russia under the apparent influence of Uigur law.[21]

While the manor type of agriculture was making rapid progress in Eastern Russia of the Mongol period, the smaller farms of the freemen (*lyudi, svoezemtsy*) were still existent, although their numbers steadily decreased. It was in the province of Novgorod that they stood their ground more firmly, but in 1479 Novgorod was annexed to Moscow and all private land estates in Novgorod were confiscated by the Moscow Grand Dukes, who granted these estates to Moscow nobles as *pomestie.*[22] While both the hierarchical organization of the princely power and the growth of the manor were important features of feudalizing tendencies in Eastern Russia during the Mongol period, no comprehensive feudal régime was established. The very essence of the feudal nexus was lacking. There was no implicit connection between the institutions of "political feudalism" and those of "economic feudalism." The authority of the boyar as the lord of his manor was not dependent upon his service to the prince of the Grand Duke. The Russian manor of this period was the boyar's patrimonial estate (*votchina*) and not his fief. The boyar would not lose his estates in case he left his prince and enrolled in the service of another prince.

In order to tighten their control over the administration of their state, the Moscow Grand Dukes attempted, from the early fourteenth century, to build up a new class of servitors to whom land would be granted upon condition of service only. Such lands became known as *pomestie.* The *pomestie* system, however, assumed no general significance before the sixteenth century, and accordingly will be dealt with in the next section.

III

By the beginning of the sixteenth century the Grand Duke of Moscow and Vladimir had extended his control over all Eastern Russia. This meant the political unification of the so-called Great-Russian branch of the Russian nation.[23] In 1547, Ivan IV assumed the title of Tsar to emphasize both his independence from outside rulers and his sovereignty at home. The Tsardom of Moscow absorbed in itself the remnants of the former grand duchies and principalities of Eastern Russia. The former provincial Grand Dukes and local princes lost their independence or even their autonomy. They now became known as mere *knyazhata,* "the princes' sons," and joined the ranks of the Moscovian boyardom. The central power was rapidly concentrating in the hands of the Tsar. The *knyazhata* made a disorganized attempt to recompense themselves for the loss of political power in provinces by claiming their share in central government. In that they were supported by some old Moscow boyar families. The Moscow Duma did not succeed, however, in establishing itself as a constitutional council similar to the *Pany-Rada* of the grand duchy of Lithuania and Western Russia.

Tsar Ivan the Terrible ruthlessly crushed the boyar opposition by organizing the so-called *oprichnina.*[24] As a result of the *oprichnina* terror, parts of the princely and boyar families were deprived of their patrimonial estates. The boyar class was badly shaken, thus opening the way for the ascendancy of the new class, that of the *pomeshchik.* The *pomestie* was a land grant issued by the Tsar on condition of the military service of the recipient of the grant (the *pomeshchik*). In case no service was rendered by the recipient the grant was revoked.[25] Not all of the boyar patrimonial estates (*votchina*) were confiscated during the *oprichnina* régime, and part of those confiscated were later returned to the former owners or their descendants. New *votchina* grants were also made for some special service, e.g., to reward officers of the army for defending the city of Moscow against the Poles in 1618.[26] Thus patrimonial estates were not entirely replaced by *pomestie* estates even in the seventeenth century. But the *pomestie* now became the standard type of land grant and the patrimonial estates (*votchina*) were now more or less adjusted to the *pomestie* type. In that way military service was required by the Tsar from the owners of the *votchina* estates to the same extent as from the holders of the *pomestie* estates.

The discretionary powers of the owner of the *votchina* with regard to his landed property were likewise somewhat limited, as for example in the matter of inheritance.[27] On the other hand, the social authority of the *pomestie* holder within his estate was gradually increasing on the basis of the privileges possessed by the *votchina* owner, with the result that from the point of view of social and economic function the *pomestie* was gradually merging with the *votchina*.

Freedom of the peasants, on both *votchina* and on *pomestie* estates, was restricted by the ukas (1581) forbidding them to quit the landlords' estates on certain years proclaimed as "prohibitive" (*zapovedny*).[28] By the middle of the seventeenth century, serfdom became a universal institution in the Tsardom of Moscow.[29]

We may notice that the régime of serfdom established itself in Eastern Russia almost two centuries later than it did in Western Russia, but even there it came later than in Romano-Germanic countries. The Russian peasants became serfs at a time when there were only remnants of serfdom in both France and England. It is for this reason that some scholars speak of an "inverted process" in the social developments of Russia and Eastern Europe.[30]

The Moscow *pomestie* régime has many traits in common with western feudalism, especially with the centralized feudalism of the Norman period in England. In the sixteenth and the seventeenth century we have in Moscow what seems to be one of the essential features of a feudal régime, i.e., holding of land estates by members of the military class on condition of service rendered. For that reason P. B. Struve even considers the sixteenth and the seventeenth centuries as the actual period of the establishment of feudalism in Moscow Russia. His argument is

hardly valid. The similarity between the Moscow *pomestie* régime and the regulated feudalism of the English type is an outward one only. The Moscow régime, while establishing the nexus between military service and landholding, lacked another essential trait of western feudalism. There was no reciprocity of contract between the Tsar and the *pomeshchik*. The latter was not the Tsar's vassal; he was merely the Tsar's servitor.

IV

Such similarity as there was between the Russian *pomestie* régime and feudalism came to a close in the eighteenth century. The essential trend in Russian social development from the semi-feudal monarchy of the seventeenth century toward the absolutist Empire of the eighteenth century was the gradual merging of the original two different types of landholding, the patrimonial estate (*votchina*) and the conditional grant (*pomestie*) into one new type— that of the real estate (*nedvizhimoe imenie*) owned on a full property basis.[31]

If, as has been mentioned, the Tsar intended to equate the patrimonial *votchina* to the *pomestie* in requiring equal military service from both, the *pomestie* holders attempted to increase their discretionary powers over the *pomestie* land they held in such a way that they would enjoy at least some of the authority of the *votchina* owners. According to the original plan, a *pomestie* grant was strictly personal. However, the recipient of such a grant usually attempted to secure it to his descendants. A *pomestie* could not be, strictly speaking, a subject of legacy, but it soon became customary that, in case the holder had male descendants, the *pomestie* grant was transferred to the name of his eldest son when the original holder became too old for military service. In case the *pomestie* holder died during his service term and left no male heirs, the estate or any portion of it could be left to his widow for her use until she died or married again, or to his daughter until her marriage. In this latter case the daughter's husband could expect that the estate would be given to him to hold on condition of his service to the Tsar.

By the slow process of such gradual adjustment there was established, by the end of the seventeenth century, a habit of leaving the *pomestie* for the use of the same family whenever there was the slightest pretext for arranging it. To all practical purposes, there was at the beginning of the eighteenth century little difference between the rights of a *pomestie* holder and those of a *votchina* owner with respect to their respective estates.

Important changes in the land régime resulted from Peter the Great's thorough reconstruction of both the military and civil service statutes. He required personal service from all members of the gentry class without any discrimination by virtue of the type of their landholding. On the other hand, Peter to a recognizable extent considered all types of land estates as being subject to direct control of the government. All timber on private estates, as on crown lands, was under option to the government for the building of the navy. The owner had no right to cut it without governmental permit. The same was true with regard to mining. It would not be an undue modernization to suggest that Peter intended to establish what is now termed a totalitarian state. However, following his death (1725) the gentry attempted to recover their individual freedom and property rights, in which effort they finally succeeded.

By the law of 1731, the legal distinction between *pomestie* and *votchina* was finally abolished and the real estate (*nedvizhimoe imenie*) was recognized as the property of the owner. The estates were still for some time liable to state encroachments, e.g., for timber and mining. These were cancelled by Catherine II, and by her Charter of the Gentry (1785) she solemnly guaranteed full property rights to the gentry on their land. Meanwhile, the gentry were excused from obligatory service to the state (1762).

The authority of the gentry over the peasant population, however, was not yet abrogated. In the sixteenth and seventeenth centuries the gentry used laborers of two different categories. Some of the laborers were slaves (used chiefly for household service); the others were serfs (used exclusively for tilling the land). The serfs were considered bound to the estate, but not to the owner of the estate personally. The slaves were the private property of the owner. The distinction between the two groups was abolished by Peter the Great, who ordered both serfs and slaves drafted into his army. This resulted in the merging of the two groups into one, that of the serfs.[32]

While slavedom was thus abrogated, the position of the serfs was not improved. With the expansion of gentry privileges in the course of the eighteenth century the authority of the landlord over his serfs even tended to increase. There was some inner contradiction in granting to the gentry full property rights on their estate while the serfs legally were still considered as attached to the estate and not to the person of the owner.

Serfdom was originally introduced in Russia in order to supply the military landholders (the *pomeshchik*) with labor, and thus enable them to devote themselves to the Tsar's service. Now that obligatory service was abrogated, the land estate became full property of the former owner. There seemed to be no logical ground for continuing to keep the peasants in the state of serfdom.[33] It was not, however, until 1861 that the peasants were emancipated. By the provisions of the emancipation act each estate was divided into two parts, one retained by the lord and the other transferred to the peasants.[34] In this way the legacy of the *pomestie* régime was at last liquidated.

V

We now have to sum up the main results of the preceding argument.

Three distinctive types of socio-political structure may be taken into consideration when discussing the problem of feudalism in Russia. These are: (1) the *votchina* régime; (2) the *pomestie* régime; (3) standard feudalism of western type.

1. The *votchina* régime is characterized by the growth of the manorial power of the lord of the estate over the laboring population working on the estate or merely settled around it. Such power could be enforced by immunity privileges. The *votchina* estate may be owned by a political ruler (prince) or by private persons, or else by the church. While representing to a certain extent the social aspects of feudalizing processes the *votchina* régime has no direct political counterpart for it.

The political power superimposed upon the *votchina* plan of society might assume feudalizing traits, such as the building up of the scale of suzerain and local rulers, but there is no formal connection between the vassal's service and the control of the land.

2. The *pomestie* régime tends to make the control of the land dependable upon service rendered to the state by the holder of the land estate. There is no partition of political power in this régime as it grew up in the Muscovite state of the sixteenth and seventeenth centuries. The power was concentrated in the person of the supreme ruler, the Tsar.

3. For the development of the standard type of feudalism in which some characteristics of both the *votchina* and the *pomestie* régimes are combined, certain traits are essential which are lacking in either the *votchina* régime or the *pomestie* régime, or in both.

Like the *votchina* régime, the standard type of

feudalism presupposes the expansion of manor and the growth of the manorial rights of the lord. On the other hand, like the *pomestie* régime, feudalism of the standard type is characterized by the conditionality of rights on the land. The control of the land by the lower class landlord is dependable on his service rendered to the seignior.

The important point of difference between the *pomestie* régime and feudalism of the standard type is that, while in the former the political power is concentrated in the hands of the supreme ruler, for the latter the partition of political authority is typical. Greater and lesser rulers each has his respective share in it. The suzerain, the vassals, and the sub-vassals form a continual political chain, all bound as they are by reciprocal feudal contracts.

It is only in Western Russia as organized by the Grand Dukes of Lithuania in the fourteenth and to the sixteenth centuries that we have been able to establish the existence of the standard feudalism of western type. The *votchina* régime was existent in the Kievan period but was not prevalent then. It is in Eastern Russia of the Mongol period (thirteenth to fifteenth century) that the *votchina* régime assumed full significance.

While the *pomestie* régime first took root in the Mongol period, its full development occurred in the Muscovite Tsardom of the sixteenth and the seventeenth centuries. By the eighteenth century the *pomestie* system, as has been seen, was dead, and only some scanty repercussions of it can be traced as far down as the middle of the nineteenth century.

NOTES

1. See, for example, articles on "Feudalism" in the Russian Encyclopedia published by Brockhaus & Efron, *Enciklopedičeskij slovar,* Half Volume LXX (1902) (hereafter quoted as *ES*), and in the *Encyclopedia of Social Sciences,* Volume VI (1931) (hereafter quoted as *ESS*).
2. On Japanese feudalism see K. Asakawa in *ESS,* VI, 214 ff. On Saracen and Ottoman feudalism see A. H. Lybyer, *ibid.,* pp. 210 ff.; see also p. 312, n. 3. Bibliographical references on the so-called Turco-Mongol feudalism are given on p. 312, n. 1.
3. O. Hintze, "Wesen und Verbreitung des Feudalismus," *Sitzungsberichte der preuss. Akad. der Wiss.,* Jahrgang 1929, pp. 321 ff. There is a revised edition of this study which appeared in *Die Welt als Geschichte,* Heft 2/3 (1938), pp. 157 ff.
4. C. H. McIlwain, "Medieval Estates," *Cambridge Medieval History,* VII (1932), 664.
5. A. Dopsch, *Wirtschaftliche und soziale Grundlagen der europäischen Kulturentwicklung,* I–II (2d ed., Vienna, 1923); there is now a somewhat abridged English edition in one volume under the title *The Economic and Social Foundations of European Civilization* (New York and London, 1937). Cf. D. M. Petruševski, "Strittige Fragen der mittelalterlichen Verfassungs- und Wirtschaftsgeschichte," *Zeitschrift für die gesamte Staatswissenschaft,* LXXXV (1928), 468 ff.

6. In my attempt to formulate the essential characteristics of the feudal régime I have in mind Continental Europe chiefly, leaving English feudalism aside. I wish to make it plain that in presenting such an outline I lay no claim of producing anything new or definitive in the general field of the study of feudalism. My purpose is simply to establish some landmarks for approaching the problem of feudalism in Russia. Since I have to compare the peculiarities of the Russian development with the institutions of the Romano-German feudalism, I prefer to let the reader know just what I consider the standard type of feudalism. Nor do I intend to give here a selected bibliography of feudalism. I only wish to point out some of the best general outlines of the problem as well as some of the important recent monographs which I have found of special use for my purpose. These remarks will suffice for suggesting the following references: Ivan Grevs, "Sušénost feodalizma i ego proischoždenie," *ES,* 70, pp. 494 ff. (an admirable survey summing up the results of the study of feudalism prior to 1902); Paul Vinogradoff, "Feudalism," *Cambridge Medieval History,* III (1930), 458 ff.; Marc Bloch, "Feudalism: European," *ESS,* VI, pp. 203 ff.; Otto Hintze (cf. p. 303, n. 3); Heinrich Mitteis, *Lehnrecht und Staatsgewalt* (Weimar, 1933). Cf. also Max Weber, "Wirtschaft und Gesellschaft," *Grundriss der Sozialökonomik,* III (Tübingen, 1922), especially pp. 148 ff. The Société Jean Bodin has published three valuable symposiums, one on the "Liens de vassalité," *Revue de l'Institut de Sociologie,* XXII (1937), 7–118, the second on serfdom: *Le Servage* (Brussels: Université Libre, Institut de Sociologie Solvay, 1937), and third on *La Tenure* (Brussels: Nouvelle Société d'Editions, 1938).
7. G. Vernadsky, *ZRK,* I, 158 ff. and 162; N. Molchanovski, *Očerk izvesti o podolskoi zemle do 1436 goda* (Kiev, 1885), pp. 156 ff.
8. G. Vernadsky, *PDH,* pp. 114 ff.; M. Ilruševskyj, *IUR,* IV (Lvov, 1903).
9. See M. Lyubavsky's article "Feodalizm v litovsko-russkom gosudarstve," *ES,* 70, pp. 550 ff., and his general outline of the history of the Lithuanian-Russian State: *Očerk istorii litovsko-russkogo gosudarstva* (2d ed., Moscow, 1915).
10. See Section III, below.
11. See Sections II and III, below, for the *votčina* régime.
12. It is necessary to bear in mind that, while mediaeval Poland was a land of large estates of the manorial type, there was no "political feudalism" in Poland. Cf. Z. Wojciechowski, "Le problème de la féodalité en Pologne au Moyen Age," *Revue Historique de Droit,* 1933, pp. 206–207.
13. See G. Vernadsky, *PDH,* Chs. IX to XII and A. Presnyakov, *Obrazovanie velikorusskogo gosudarstva* (Petrograd, 1918), for details concerning the attitude of the Khan toward East Russian princes and the latter's interrelations.
14. See V. Bartold, *Istorija kulturnoi žizni Turkestana* (Leningrad, 1927), p. 96, for the parallels between the scale of appanage rulers in Mediaeval Russia and Turkestan. Cf. also his study *Ulugbek i ego vremja* (Petrograd, 1918), p. 10.
15. The text of the treaty has been first printed in *Sobranie gosudarstvennych gramot i dogovorov,* I (1813), No. 28 (the date as referred to there is wrong); cf. A. Presnyakov (p. 315, n. 2), pp. 305–360.
16. There is an excellent monograph on the Khanate of Kasimov by V. Velyaminov-Zernov, *Izsledovanie o kasimovskich tsarjach i tsarevičach,* 4 vols (St. Petersburg, 1863–1887). Cf. G. Vernadsky, *PDH,* pp. 140, 145 ff.
17. Compare Section II, above.
18. V. Grigoryev, *O dostovernosti chanskich jarlykov* (Moscow, 1842); M. Priselkov, *Chanskie jarlyki* (Petrograd, 1916); D. Meichik, *Gramoty XIV i XV vv. moskovskogo archiva Ministerstva Justicii* (Moscow, 1883), Ch. I.
19. M. Dyakonov, *Očerki obščestvennogo i gosudarstvennogo stroja drevnej Rusi* (4th ed., St. Petersburg, 1912)

(hereafter quoted as *Očerki*), pp. 327 ff.; P. Belyaev (as cited p. 301, n. 1), p. 173 and *passim*.

20. M. Dyakonov, *Očerki*, pp. 320 ff.

21. M. Dyakonov, *Očerki*, pp. 362 ff.; G. Vernadsky (as cited, n, 7).

22. V. Sergeyevich, *Drevnosti russkogo prava*, III (St. Petersburg, 1911); cf. G. Vernadsky, "The Heresy of the Judaizers and the Policies of Ivan III of Moscow," *Speculum*, VIII (1933), 445 f.

23. G. Vernadsky, *PDH*, Ch. XIV.

24. G. Vernadsky, *PDH*, pp. 169 ff. Cf. H. von Staden, *Aufzeichnungen über den Moscauer Staat*, ed. F. Epstein (Hamburg, 1930).

25. M. Vladimirski-Budanov, *Obzor*, pp. 566 ff.; K. Nevolin, *Polnoe sobranie sočineni*, IV (St. Petersburg, 1857), 191 ff.

26. M. Vladimirski-Budanov, *Obzor*, pp. 562 ff.; K. Nevolin, *op. cit.*, IV, 156 ff.

27. Cf. G. Vernadsky, "Studies in the History of Moscovian Private Law," *Studi in memoria di Aldo Albertoni*, III (Padova, 1937), 444 ff.

28. B. Grekov, "Jurjev den i zapovednye gody," *Izvestija* of the Academy of Sciences of U.S.S.R., 1926, pp. 67 ff.; I. Polosin, "Le servage russe et son origine," *Revue Internationale de sociologie*, 36 (1928), pp. 608 ff. A. Eck, "L'asservissement du paysan russe," *Le Servage* (as cited p. 304, n. 3), pp. 256–257.

29. M. Dyakonov, *Očerki*, pp. 336 ff.

30. G. I. Bratianu, "Servage de la glèbe et régime fiscal," *Annals d'histoire économique et sociale*, V (1933), 445 ff.

31. M. Vladimirski-Budanov, *Obzor*, pp. 580 ff.

32. *Ibid.*, pp. 409 ff.

33. See V. O. Klyuchevski, *Kurs russkoi istorii*, IV (2d ed., Moscow, 1915), 431 ff.; English edition, *A History of Russia*, IV (London and New York, 1926), pp. 339 ff. Cf. G. Vernadsky, "Zamečanija o juridičeskoi prirode krepostnogo prava," *Mélanges Pierre Struve* (Prague, 1925), pp. 253 ff.

34. A. Kornilov, *Kurs istorii Rossii v XIX veke*, II (Moscow, 1918), pp. 181 ff. American edition: *Modern Russian History* (New York, 1924), II, 45 ff.; G. T. Robinson, *Rural Russia under the Old Régime* (London, New York, Toronto, 1932), Chapter V.

31

Some Aspects of Japanese Feudal Institutions

K. Asakawa

The starting point of my discourse should be the *shō*. *Shō* . . . was the generic name applied to several species of private domains—such as *shō* in the narrower sense, *sono, maki, soma,* and the like, after their conditions had been more or less equalized—whose nature as an institution defies an exact definition. Being a slow, unpremeditated growth under circumstances of considerable diversity, the *shō* may better be described and analyzed than briefly defined. When they made their modest appearance in the eighth century, the *shō* were few in number and of an irregular and varying institutional character; but they all shared in common at least the following aspects: (1) each *shō* contained, as its chief element, a tract of land that had been newly brought under cultivation; (2) the *shō* was under the patronage of some person of influence or of an institution, known as the *hon-ke* . . . and *ryō-ke*, . . . to whom we shall hereafter apply the word "seignior"; (3) some *shō* enjoyed or claimed and all *shō* aspired for fiscal immunity in whole or in part, the extent of immunity being coincident with the degree to which their revenues were diverted from the fiscus of the state to the private coffer of the seignior. In the course of the next four hundred years, *shō* so far increased in number and in immunity at the expense of the state, that, at the end of the twelfth century, their extent probably equaled that of the public domain, and their practical influence upon the political and economic life of the nation overshadowed that of the government. At the same time, the *shō* underwent as remarkable an internal development. It is the first requisite for the student of Japanese feudalism to gain an understanding of the nature of the *shō* from a comparative point of view.

We shall imagine ourselves visiting a typical *shō* about the year 1150, for then the *shō* as an institution had attained its full maturity. Here we find our *shō* already immune or nearly so from taxation and from the intrusion of public officials. More or less autonomous, the *shō* is under the shadowy rule of an absent seignior, who is a court noble at Kyōto or perhaps a great temple; his interest is in the keeping of his agent residing in the *shō*. Under these agents range themselves in order the various tenures of land and the classes of people who hold them. As we set about

From K. Asakawa, "Some Aspects of Japanese Feudal Institutions," *Asiatic Society of Japan, Transactions*, XLVI, Part I (1918), 83–101. Reprinted by permission of the publisher.

studying the tenures and classes, however, we find them always covered under a ubiquitous institution, called *shiki,* . . . which at first mystifies and baffles us. After an effort, the veil is torn, the *shiki* is exposed, and the whole life of the *shō,* with all its classes and tenures, is revealed before us. What, then, is a *shiki?*

Suppose that you own a piece of land, and let it to a tenant; that he plants rice on it, and, when the harvest is gathered, divides the crop into two parts, keeping one for himself and rendering the other to you as rent; and that you, too, divide your share, and give up a part to the government as a tax. Here we have a distribution between the State, the proprietor, and the tenant, of rights and interests relative to a single piece of land. These rights and interests may be distributed differently, and be further divided and vested in more parties; and still they will all be derived from the same piece of land. A *shiki* of land is a separate right or profit derivable from it that is vested in a person—after whom it is named; as, for instance: the seignior-*shiki,* proprietor-*shiki,* tenant-*shiki,* or the like.

Of all the *shiki*-holders of a given piece of land, it is evident that the highest in rank will be its titular head; while, at the same time, the one whose control over the land is the most real will be he, whatever his title and *shiki,* who actually possesses and exploits the land. The former is the seignior, and the latter the producer; the seignior has secured the public immunity of the *shō,* and the producer bears ultimately all its private financial burden.

True to their genius for adaptability, the Japanese of the Middle Ages displayed a remarkable flexibility in their disposition of the *shiki* of *shō.* They divided and redivided landed interests, it would seem, as far as they dared, and conveyed them from person to person with great freedom. So long as the dues were forthcoming to the seignior and others who were entitled to them, there was naught to prevent the *shiki* of the same tract of land being held by or circulated among many people, and the same person controlling *shiki* of different grades and qualities derived from many pieces of land, even in different seigniories.

Of this singular phenomenon, I shall later offer an interpretation; but even a reflection will show that, in an age of unrest, this freedom about *shiki* must have been a powerful aid to the smaller proprietors in their struggle to retain their possession of the use of land; for, even after they had been obliged, for self-protection, to yield to others many *shiki,* they would thus still be able to reserve for themselves and their heirs the *shiki* of actual exploitation. The

mobility of *shiki* did more: it enabled the chief holders in *shō* to transfer some of their *shiki* to potent seigniors whose immune character could then accrue to the *shō* as a whole. What *shō* would not seek to avail itself of this attractive opportunity to make itself tax-free?

Here, let us understand clearly that *shiki* and "tenures" coincided with each other to a certain extent, but were not identical. *Shiki* were more readily divisible, detachable from land, and movable among individuals, than tenures; for *shiki* were not so much, like tenures, the terms under which land was held, as profits derived from land, irrespective as to whether land was actually held or not. Tenures were primarily conditions; *shiki* chiefly meant incomes. Rights, rather than obligations, were innate in the ideal of *shiki.* As a consequence, while the word "tenure" would seem inappropriate when it was applied to the holding of the warrior lord, the term *shiki* was as strictly germane to the status of the seignior as to that of the tenant farmer.

A counterpart of the idea of *shiki* was, however, not unknown to Europe. In fact, it may be said that it was a kind of forced application of a similar notion to church lands in France after the eighth century that caused the creation of the *precarium* for the knight which later became the *beneficium* and the fief. But the European *shiki,* if I may use the term, seem always to have been more closely connected with land, and never to have been so far detached and sublimated and so freely conveyed about as in Japan. I shall have occasion later to suggest that there was an underlying cause for this significant difference, and that the difference produced far-reaching consequences that made the two systems of feudalism divergent in important respects throughout their history. . . .

The *shō* of the twelfth century is not feudal: it is neither a manor nor a fief. And the difference from these European institutions gives rise to two important problems for the student of comparative institutions. The typical manor in Europe possesses features that resemble those of a village community: its arable land is laid out in strips of a rectangular shape and of certain regular sizes, and its cultivation, as also the management of the meadows, pastures and woods of the manor, is under the joint supervision of lord and tenants; and the tenants hold these strips in tenures that are stationary, for each strip is encumbered with definite customary services; moreover, the lower tenants are strictly tied down to their strips and their tenures, and are forbidden to shift. The *shō,* on the contrary, as we have seen, consists, where the ground is cultivated, of plots irregular, not only in position, but also in shape and size, and managed independently by their holders; and many of these holders will, so long as the seignior's fiscal rights are not affected, dispose of their *shiki* as they please, and so continue to make the tenures more intricate and changeable. If, therefore, a chief problem of the origin of the manor concerns its elements of village community, the first great question of the *shō* must relate to its growth as a congeries of shifting interests and relations loosely bundled together under an absent seignior. This is the first of the two problems to which we shall address ourselves.

The other problem arises from the comparison of the Japanese *shō* with the European fief. Though both are economic and political units that are largely autonomous, their difference in other respects is fundamental. There is an immeasurably greater coherence in the personal relation between the lord and his armed servitors in the fief than between the seignior and any class of the inhabitants of the *shō*. In the fief, the lord and vassal are bound together for services of war and council, and the vassal receives his grant of land because he serves the lord, instead of serving the lord because he receives the land. Usually, also, the lord of a fief is himself a vassal of a higher lord; and, in the whole chain of these relative positions, the fief or sub-fief is incapable of alienation without special sanction, for the tenure is personal; even though the fief has by custom been made hereditable and subinfeudable, the original personal character of the tenure is still clearly retained in the formality of a new investiture that is repeated at each succession. How different are conditions in a *shō*! Here the relations between seignior and tenants are primarily fiscal, not personal; the freer tenants are very nearly absolute owners of their holding, which are not only divisible and inheritable, but also alienable without restraint; the lower *shiki* of "cultivation" does not imply a servile status of its holder, but is often held by a person of note and is as mobile as all other *shiki;* even about those who are lowest in the social scale—the laborers on the soil—we are not certain that they are not men privately hired for wages by the individual holder of the "cultivator"-*shiki*. For a parallel with the *shō,* one should not go to the French fief, but rather to the Roman *saltus;* and even there the resemblance will be superficial. And yet—and this is a marvel in institutional history—despite all the radical difference at the beginning, the *shō* of the twelfth century will be seen in the fifteenth to have become, or to have been replaced by, an institution that is charged with all the essential marks that characterize the European fief. Here, then, is

our second problem: How did the *shō* become a fief?

The remainder of my lecture will be concerned chiefly with these two great problems.

If we would understand the origin of the characteristics of the *shō* that differentiate it from the manor, we must, I believe, return to those peculiarities of Japanese agriculture that distinguished it from the beginning of the historic ages. Of these, I would single out two as the most vital and far-reaching in their effects upon Japan's institutional life: the comparative absence of pasture, and the cultivation of rice as the chief agricultural industry.

Rice-culture is practised in paddies that are terraces made perfectly level, and is available only on lowlands that can be so used and irrigated. It is, therefore, practised only in plots that are so small and of such irregular shapes as are determined by the lay of the land and by the need of irrigation. What is even more important, the nature of the industry is strongly conducive to an early development of individual ownership of rice-land, whether by person or by family; for, as is well known, rice-culture requires, during a considerable space of time each year, an investment of personal labor that is more varied, intensive, and unremitting, than do other kinds of husbandry known to early agriculture. And this tendency will be emphasized if, for any reason, rice is, as was the case in Japan at least from the seventh century, of high economic value, and is used as the standard of value and as the chief article in a system of taxation that has the person or the family as a basis of its assessment.

Individual ownership may, however, be retarded even with rice-fields, if pasture is everywhere present beside them, as seems to be the case in some parts of Java, and of ancient China; for the interference of the community that is imperative in the use of the common pasture and meadow will conceivably react upon the use of the rice-land as well. I cannot help thinking that the juxtaposition of pastures and arable lands that characterized the typical manors of Europe was a great cause for the presence of that side of their life that resembled a village community. Without going further into other allied circumstances which I would discuss if I had time, I call your attention to the fact that Japan was under no special need of having so many pastures as would enter into all communities as their integral parts. If we now consider the various effects together, it will not be difficult to see that Japanese rural communities before the seventh century were not *Dörfer,* or, village communities, but rather *Einzelhöfe,* or, "scattered farms," which comprised irregular plots of arable land, and of which at least the rice-land was under individual ownership and independent management. This state of things may be fairly substantiated from the records.

In defiance of this condition, the government of the seventh and the early eighth centuries took the bold measure, fashioned after the written laws of China, of arranging the free taxable population of Japan in artificial communities of fifty families, and of imposing upon it a system of equal allotment of rice-land subject to a periodical redistribution.[1] Then the older native institutions of individual ownership and "scattered farms" quickly reappeared around newly tilled lands. These, under the patronage of private seigniors, absorbed land and people from public districts, and grew with such ominous facility that their importance threatened to outweigh that of the areas which still remained under the control of the state and were fast being swallowed by the new domains. These new domains were the *shō*. The *shō* was the old *Einzelhof* revived on new grounds under new conditions. Among the new conditions that confronted the holders of new lands were the existence of the seignior who would tighten his control over land and men, and the social unrest and insecurity abroad that was growing worse and that irresistibly drove the independent landholders, in spite of themselves, to seek the protection and the immunity of the seignior. Notwithstanding the pressure of the circumstances, however, these men would, if they could, retain in their hands the substance, if not the outer form, of their familiar rights over the fields. They naturally, and perhaps unconsciously at first, in their struggle to maintain the real possession and use of land and to secure its immunity from public taxation, had recourse to the division and the conveyance of detached *shiki* of land, with the resultant looseness and flexibility of tenures and classes that we have seen. The excessive mobility of *shiki* seems to me to indicate behind it a great effect of the want of pasture and the prevalence of rice-culture; namely: personal proprietary right of cultivated land in Japan that was already so securely intrenched, prior to her beginning in feudal formation, as to prevent the appearance of a manorial organization, and to resist the encroachment by the seignior upon the freedom of individual possession—an important condition which we should bear in mind if we would grasp the difference of feudalism in Japan from that in Europe.

Having briefly dealt with one of the two problems we set before ourselves, I now turn to the other. With what changes can a *shō* be made over into a fief? Evidently, first, its tenures and classes must be so simplified, rearranged, and tightened, that there should appear distinct classes, one rendering service in arms which is considered noble, and another or others engaged in productive labor and holding land in tenures that are regarded as ignoble; and, secondly, the seignior or his intendant should himself be a warrior, and the armed men of the domain should be in direct personal relations with him. These two changes—the reconstruction of tenures and classes, and the advent of the military seignior—with the other far-reaching effects that would flow from them, made a substantial progress in the first feudal period, known as the Kamakura (the late twelfth to the early fourteenth century), but was completed only in the next period.

I shall give a tentative view of the process as it began in the Kamakura period. From a study of documents of this period, I am led to conclude with a degree of confidence that the seignior, even a religious seignior, went a long way toward attaining his object to assimilate the freer tenures with the more precarious. He now dared to confiscate *shiki* of offending "landholders" and "cultivators," and grant them to others in more dependent tenures. He also achieved similar results through awards in lawsuits that had been brought before his court, and through loans and purchases in which he himself was not seldom engaged. Even commended lands were now, in unusual instances, handed back likewise as grants. For reasons I need not specify, the conveyance of *shiki* was in general very frequent in this period, and often ended in their finally reposing in the hands of the seignior in some title or other. Such being the case even in religious *shō,* it may well be imagined that the freer tenures under military seigniors or intendants must have fared worse. It is significant that the suzerain decreed in 1270 that neither the hereditary possessions nor the granted lands of his tenants-in-chief could be alienated without his sanction, though still heritable and sub-infeudable; thirty-eight years before, hereditary domains, as distinguished from granted holdings, had been alienable.

At the same time, the classes of people in the *shō* I find to be shifting toward a new alignment. The old "resident" officials of the *shō* were gradually replaced by agents appointed or specially despatched by the seignior, whose service was rewarded either with grants of land or with stipends of rice or money. They were expected to be more subservient to the seignior, and yet the inhabitants were taught to look up to them as nobler, than the earlier local representative chiefs. The evolution of this process is sometimes seen vividly through documents.

I see an equally significant change in the status of the so-called "cultivators." They were becoming more dependent as regards the seignior, pledging themselves to a faithful performance of their duties and directly paying taxes to him (which I assume to be a new condition); but, on the other hand, the "cultivators" had been made, in relation to the "landholders" under whom they had in theory held their *shiki,* more independent and secure than in the twelfth century, for they had been brought under a more direct control of the seignior and could not be dislodged with impunity. Many, I should not say all, "cultivators" had become the sole exploiters of the soil, bearing ultimately all its fiscal burdens, and had advanced to the position where the "landholder" had been. The distinction between the two was disappearing. Below them, we again have occasional glimpses of menial laborers, but little can be gathered of their position from the rare references that occur.

If the status at least of armed men in the *shō* could be made nearly uniform, and if the tillers of the soil could be sharply distinguished from the warriors and bound down to simple, fixed tenures, there would result a counterpart of the fief. But the Japanese *shō,* even under a military seignior, does not seem to have attained in the Kamakura period even the first half of that state; only, as we have seen, a fair beginning for progress in that general direction had been made. And it is highly instructive to reflect that this progress had at once been facilitated to that point and was restrained from going further by that characteristic Japanese institution, *shiki.* For its flexibility at the same time helped the seignior in his interference with the freer tenures, and also aided the possessor of land to cling to his last right of usufruct when all other *shiki* had been taken away from him.

For the next period, two things would seem clear: —(1) That for the completion of the organization of the fief, something was needed that should be sufficiently strong to break down the subtilty of the *shiki;* and (2) that, even if that should take place, the historic proprietary right in Japan over land might be expected to hold its own. The divided *shiki* might largely be obliterated, but would hardly be replaced by servile tenures only.

From the second quarter of the fourteenth century, Japan entered upon the dark ages of a protracted civil war that, with interruptions, lasted till the end of the sixteenth. Amid the utmost decentralization that ensued, the period witnessed certain momentous changes taking place as if by concert in the institutional life of the whole country. Among these the most important for our present study are three parallel processes—two of them begun more or less in the earlier period, but the one completely and

the other nearly finished in this period; and a third begun only now but matured after 1600.

The first of these movements may be characterized as the consummation of the feudalization both of the administrative functions and of the land-tenure of Japan. The double process was necessarily long and many-sided, and is still largely obscure, but the results stand out in bold outlines. We may well say that the governmental machinery was at length completely feudalized when, as we find in 1600, most of the *shō* under civil control and all the public offices of civil origin in the provinces had been seized by groups of warriors held together by personal ties of vassalage. Similarly, it is just to say that land-tenure was finally feudalized when the conquering war-lord assumed a free disposition of the domains he had won at the point of his sword, and without scruple reduced the multiple tenures of the military tenants that he found therein into a nearly uniform tenure— a tenure which, though normally capable of heredity and subinfeudation, was, under his dictatorial control, subject to a re-investiture at succession and liable to confiscation for an offence, and entailed upon its tenants definite personal services toward him. The peculiarly loose and complex *shō,* such as we found in the twelfth century, was no more, at least under military control: the average *shō* had, to all intents and purposes, been converted into a veritable fief.

The year 1600 saw this double transformation practically accomplished; it witnessed another movement continued but not completed. That was a growing differentiation of the military from the agricultural class. It will be remembered that a tendency in that direction was already perceptible in the Kamakura period. The process was greatly accelerated during the next centuries of incessant civil strife. The use of the sword as the chief weapon, and then of the spear, had caused tactical operations to be somewhat more extended than before; but under the impact of the terrific struggle for ascendency among the leaders of this age, followed by the introduction of gunpowder about 1542, organized tactics in Japan made sudden and great progress. Warriors had become professional, and now tended to reside near the lords' castles, instead of squatting as before in poorly defensible mansions in their small rural domains; the service they offered was in an increasing number of cases rewarded, not with land, but with rice or money; not with fiefs, but with stipends. A growing separation of arms from land was a natural consequence. This left the peasants on the fields at once less protected, because more exposed and unarmed, and freer in status and in feeling, because more independent of immediate military control, than before. Nothing better illustrates the changed position of the peasantry of this period than the interesting history of the term *hyaku-skō*, . . . and I regret I have no time even to outline it.

The improved position of the peasant was coincident with a third movement of the age, which, in fact, he embraced and nursed. I refer to the tendency now begun among the peasants to reverse the earlier habit of subdividing landed rights and interests, and to unite them once more with land itself. The simplification of tenures and *shiki* was apparently congenial to the spirit of the age; as the lord reduced his vassals' tenures to mere grants in fee, so the peasants showed a decided tendency to regard *shiki* as something rooted in the soil and disposable as a whole. Nominally, their tenures, too, were grants of rents,[2] but, inasmuch as they were alone on the field and treated their real rights as one with land, their actual status was remarkably free. Scarcely had the lord imagined that he had succeeded in reducing the peasants into a dependent tenant, when the latter placed himself on the road to become the practical owner of the land which, under the name of a grant by favor, he in fact exploited, passed on to his heir, and disposed of with much freedom.

Below this new peasantry, we gain a clear view of another new class—that of real tenants. They were tenants pure and simple, paying the "economic rents," but not taxes, which fell on the landlord, and were therefore not the institutional descendants of the earlier taxpaying "cultivator," but a natural economic class that would come into being without a special historic antecedent. The tenants formed a relatively small class, for the taxes on land being disproportionately high and the margin of rent being relatively small as a consequence, there could be but few great landlords.

In this period, also, we are at last able to prove positively that in the lowest rank of the agricultural population were domestic farm hands hired for wages. They were, of course, not serfs, if indeed there ever had been a large class of people deserving that name at any time in the history of the *shō* and fief in Japan.

I shall conclude this period with a word of comparison with European feudalism. It would seem that the European system offers parallels to all the changes that I have noted but one. In the feudalization of government, in the formation of the fief, and in the comparative simplicity and fixity of tenures, the student of the one system will find in the other, institutions so familiar as to seem almost disconcerting. But the relative freedom of the Japanese peasant strikes a strange note that does not chime with the Western system. How can we account for this difference? The time is approaching that I must close. Remember, at one end, the comparative security of the proprietary right of rice-land that had characterized Japanese agriculture throughout the historic ages, and, at the other end, the relatively late and sudden progress in organized tactics, in the sixteenth century, that cleared the fields of the squatting warriors. I leave you to fill in the intermediate gap between these two ends of the process.

The third and last period of Japan's feudal history, 1600–1868, may be dismissed with a few words. Remember the main currents of the institutional movements of the past ages: the consolidation of land with landed interest already begun, the separation of land and arms almost accomplished, and the complete feudalization of land-tenure and of local government. A little reflection will show that no régime would remain purely feudal, if its peasants were too free and if too many of its warriors were detached from land; the same forces that had carried to its consummation the feudal organization of Japan, had also created conditions subversive of it. And yet the new rulers of the seventeenth century fully admitted these tendencies, and made them the foundation of the remarkable government that they elaborated. Having at last unified all Japan torn for centuries by civil war, the Tokugawa suzerain was concerned more with the problem how to preserve the peace and power he had earned, than with the question how to make his régime purely feudal; it was, in fact, certain that peace and power could not be maintained if the régime were forced back to feudalism. He, therefore, frankly extended to his rule of the whole the principles of feudal government and feudal land-tenure that had developed separately in its parts: he regarded the entire realm as a vast domain, as it were, with its control centralized as far as was practicable in his council at Edo; and carved four-fifths of the total area into some three hundred feudatories, many of them arbitrarily, and assigned them, under the name *han,* to as many barons, as fiefs held of him, with the familiar forms of fealty and re-investiture. In the remaining fifth, which the suzerain retained as his own domain, his policies, both about the warrior and about peasant classes, were, if anything, even more pragmatic. As regards the warriors, he deliberately increased the proportion of landless stipendiaries. As for the peasantry, he, on the one hand, gave a generous measure of self-government to its communities, and, on the other, treated the modest land holdings of the peasants as definite unitary possessions, and as such safeguarded them with great care, keeping the rural population in a state of mild contentment and fairly equalized poverty. And the example was largely copied by the barons in their respective fiefs. The result was a régime in which were combined and balanced with unusual skill both feudal and non-feudal elements of society, and centralizing and decentralizing tendencies and forces of government. The system was, of course, no longer purely feudal, either on the whole or in its parts, either in its warrior class or in its peasantry.

NOTES

1. An imperfect discussion of those reforms will be found in my *Early Institutional Life of Japan,* Tokyo, 1903.
2. From the middle of the fifteenth century at least, "culti-vator"-*shiki* are often, on the face of documents, revocable grants, accompanied at times with specific dues and profits.

32

The Decline and Fall of English Feudalism

Helen M. Cam

The operation of the laws of inheritance and descent had brought about a vast accumulation of estates, the administration of which necessitated the organisation of a great household system consisting of a host of paid dependents. The more efficiently a magnate administered his franchise, or exploited the material resources of his domains, the greater were the potentialities of his personal influence. To this must be added the effects of the wars in Scotland and France, which led to the growth of the system whereby lords contracted to supply the government with troops which they themselves secured by indenture, a practice, as has been recently shown, at least as old as 1297.[1] John of Gaunt's Register for 1370 to 1373 contains numerous examples of these contracts by which knights and squires bound themselves for life to a great lord, at a retaining fee in time of peace, augmented in time of war, with wages by the day for the duration of the campaign and supplemented by a fixed share of the profits arising from prisoners' ransoms or loot. But the retainers of a fourteenth-century magnate were not all soldiers; they ranged from legal experts "feed of the lords council" to any humble neighbour who might be useful. The 600 liveried retainers of Thomas Lancaster in 1314 included knights, squires, clerks and grooms. The practice of clothing your adherents in a livery or uniform has been traced by Mrs. Stenton as far back as 1218, when a certain north-country robber was reported as buying 100 marks' worth of cloth to clothe his following of fifteen men "as if he had been a baron or an earl." The Cambridge parliament of 1388 was the first to legislate on the subject; and by 1393 it had become necessary to forbid yeomen below the rank of squire to wear livery of company unless they were resident in their lord's household.[2] It is not necessary to-day to insist upon the psychological importance of uniform-wearing. The abuses that became associated with the practice are forcibly expressed in the oath taken by all the members of parliament in 1433 from the king downwards—"that no lord, by colour nor occasion of feoffment or of gift of movable goods shall take any other men's cause or quarrel in favour supportation or maintenance, as by word, by writing or by message to officer, judge, jury or party, by gift of his clothing or livery or taking into his service the party, nor conceive against any judge or officer indignation or displeasure for doing of his office in form of law."[3] Oaths and statutes were equally vain: the citizen who petitioned against the practice found himself forced to rely on it for self-protection and to "get lordship." Society was honeycombed by these new feudal contracts whereby a man in effect commended himself to a lord, and bound himself to love what he loved and loathe what he loathed.

The contrast between this new feudalism and the old lay firstly in the fact that from the legal point of view the contract between lord and man was no

From Helen M. Cam, "The Decline and Fall of English Feudalism," *History,* XXV (1940–1941), 224–233. This article was reprinted in *Liberties and Communities* issued by The Merlin Press in 1964. Reprinted by permission of the editor of *History,* the author, and The Merlin Press.

longer secured by land, and the stability of the tenurial relationship was thus lacking; and secondly that from the constitutional point of view the relationships operated not as a substitute for a national governmental system but within the framework of that system. The lord protected his dependent not by excluding government officials from his franchise, but by intimidating juries; by controlling sheriffs; by nominating justices of the peace or of oyer and terminer, or by getting himself put on the commissions. The dependent rendered his service in the shire court, on a jury, or in the witness-box, no less than as a member of an armed gang. The writs might run in the king's name, and the justices, sheriffs and juries might swear to uphold his government, but in fact the machinery of royal government was manipulated by the magnates, without liberties as well as within. If this is to be called feudalism, it is a parasitic institution, deriving its strength from a system hostile to itself, cut off from its natural roots in the soil, and far removed indeed from the atmosphere of responsibility, loyalty and faith which had characterised the relationship of lord and vassal in the earlier middle ages.

Sir John Fortescue put his finger on the economic basis of this power. His proposal for the resumption of franchises by the crown was no way original; for sixty years a succession of acts with that purpose were being passed, but all loaded with exemptions that made them as futile as the measures against livery and maintenance. No effective remedy could come from a parliament dominated by the lords who were the first beneficiaries of the system which the commons bewailed. The Yorkists made a beginning,[4] but it was left to the Tudors to destroy the ascendancy of the landed aristocracy, to restore the effective, as against the nominal ascendancy of the law, within liberties as well as without, and to make royal administration so efficient that the king's revenue was, as Fortescue had demanded, greater than that of his wealthiest subject.

Of the means employed for this end the suppression of livery and maintenance by Star Chamber methods and the confiscation of lands of attained rebels are familiar. Harrington in his *Oceana* indicated the legislation by which economic and thus ultimately political power was transferred from the old aristocracy to the new squirearchy.[5] The aspects of Tudor policy which are examined below are the insistence on the rights of the crown as feudal suzerain, the invocation of a stricter interpretation of the legal theory of *quo warranto,* and the abolition or absorption of those franchises which sheltered lawlessness or opposed a barrier to the effective sovereignty of the crown.

Fortescue had recommended a stricter enforcement of the royal rights of wardship and marriage, and Richard III had anticipated Henry VII in the sending out of commissioners to inquire into all "lordships, manors, lands, advowsons, wards, marriages, reliefs, escheats, and escapes of felons concealed from the king, and all alienations of land without licence."[6] From 1485 to 1508 these inquests, in effect a revival of the oldest articles of the general eyre, were being held from county to county,[7] including, as Mr. Stewart Brown pointed out, the county palatine of Chester.[8] Their efficiency and unpopularity are attested by the protests of parliament and by the surprised comments of the Venetian ambassadors on the amount of revenue derived from this source, as well as by the enthusiasm with which the fall of Edmund Dudley was greeted when Henry VIII disgraced him, as the indictment put it, "for procuring of false inquests of alienation to be found, making out that manors were held in chief of the crown that were not, refusing livery of seisin to heirs holding of the crown when they came of age unless they paid extortionate fines."[9] But Henry VIII had his own methods for achieving similar results; as Plucknett and Holdsworth have shown, the Statute of Uses in 1536 was the outcome of a long struggle with the aristocracy to prevent the evasion of feudal dues by the device of enfeoffment to uses,[10] a device employed as early as 1405 and unsuccessfully attacked by Henry VII in the statutes of 1489 and 1504. The statute of 1536 fixed the responsibility for the payment of feudal dues on the beneficiary of the use, and Miss Brodie has shown that the court of Wards and Liveries, set up in 1540 to take over from Chancery the administrative, fiscal and judicial work of enforcing the feudal incidents, had been anticipated by Henry VII's short-lived *supervisor of the Prerogative* who fell with Empson and Dudley.[11]

The second line of attack on feudal irresponsibility can also be associated with Edmund Dudley, though it did not originate with him. His law-reading on the Statute of Quo Warranto, discovered by Miss Putnam and now being edited by Miss Brodie,[12] might well be a programme for the attack upon the franchises by the Tudor judges. But the campaign had begun before he gave his lecture; Keilwey's *Reports* and Brooke's and Fitzherbert's *Abridgements* contain the cases on which his doctrine is based. Miss Thornley has told of the struggle with the sanctuaries,[13] beginning under the Yorkists by administrative methods such as registration, but carried on by Henry VII with the collaboration of pope and of lawyers. A philosopher like More might defend sanctuary as a refuge for the political offender; practical statesmen could only applaud the judgement in Stafford's case in 1487, which abolished the protection which had been legally accorded to the traitor by the special sanctuary since 1388.[14] To pardon treason, the judges declared, belongs to the king alone, and no sanctuary can give more than temporary protection in treason.[15] This was only one of the series of judgements by which the legal basis of title to franchise was being restricted under Henry VII. Dudley's doctrines[16] as to the forfeiture of liberties for non-use, for abuse, for non-claim, for false claim, for failure to prove prescription for one type of liberty, to produce a charter in another or to establish allowance in the eyre for yet another can all be illustrated in the Yearbooks. The case of the Abbot of Battle in 1494,[17] for instance, when it was ruled that a charter of William the Conqueror gave no title because it was before the time of legal memory, and that a recent allowance of the liberty in the Common Bench gave no title because it was not in the general eyre, forms a significant contrast to the case of St. Martin's le Grand in 1440, when the two chief justices had said that allowance of the liberty in eyre was unnecessary since the king could not resume a franchise granted by William the Conqueror.[18] Thus interpretations of the law of Quo Warranto far stricter than those of Edward I's or Edward II's justices were threatening the existence of the franchises well before Henry VIII and Cromwell launched their direct attack in the Reformation Parliament.

The note of battle is first sounded in the undated report on the northern franchises sent in to Cromwell in 1534, which stated that "the king's rights are attacked by all manner of liberties, his felons and outlaws are clothed and maintained by stewards and bailiffs of liberties, so that his process has no place, and his laws are not dreaded."[19]

The Welsh marcher franchises were, however, the first to be tackled. Four acts of 1534 struck at their practice of sheltering escaped felons, giving the neighbouring county officials and J.P.s power to demand the surrender of such fugitives.[20] In 1536 the act "for making the laws of Wales the same as those of England," extinguished the Custom of the March, absorbed some 136 lordships into five new shires and brought both old and new shires under the English administrative and judicial system.[21]

In February 1536 Cromwell had noted as matters to be discussed with the king for parliament "specially to speak of the utter destruction of sanctuary. Item for the dissolution of all franchises and liberties throughout the realm, especially the franchise of spirituality."[22] By April, besides the Welsh act, there had been passed an act drastically restricting, though not utterly destroying, sanctuary rights,[23] and the

act "for recontinuing certain liberties heretofore taken from the crown," by which the power to pardon crimes, the power to appoint justices in eyre, justices of assize, justices of gaol delivery and justices of the peace and power to issue writs, original or judicial, was taken away from every subject.[24] Henceforth no man could be said to break the peace of any one but the king. "The most ancient prerogatives and authorities of justice appertaining to the imperial crown of this realm that had been taken from it by sundry gifts of the king's progenitors to the detriment of the royal estate and the hindrance and delay of justice" were restored to it. The palatinates had lost their viceregal character; henceforth all stewards and bailiffs of franchises were to come under the same regulations as the ordinary officials of the shire. The surrender of the greater monasteries in the years 1536–1539 wiped out the greater number of the ecclesiastical liberties, for the lay successors to the abbots' lands received them with greatly lessened privileges.

Revolutionary as was the work of the Reformation Parliament, feudal and franchisal administration had still a long period of life and, one must suppose, usefulness before it. The courts of the duchy of Lancaster, of Chester, of Durham and of Ely were expressly retained by the act of 1536, though the writs of the local chanceries ran in the king's name and the justices were appointed by him. Chester and Lancaster, as we have seen, were in the hands of the crown; Durham would probably have been converted into an ordinary shire on the death of its bishop if he had not happened to outlive Henry VIII. But in fact it was not until the nineteenth century that these "peculiars" in local government ceased to function. The clue to their survival is to be found in the protest of the inhabitants of Durham in 1688 against the abolition of the palatinate: they said, "We were and are born to the sure use and enjoyment of the laws of the county (which are and always have been conformable to the laws of the land) distributed at our doors."[25] In fact, 5,084 writs issued out of the Durham Chancery between 1825 and 1836 and 150 pleas were heard in the Palatinate Court.[26] So, in 1771, Bentham could write of the bishop of Ely's court of pleas that "for the bishop it was a matter of prestige rather than profit, but for the inhabitants it was a matter of great convenience since they had justice administered, as it were, at their very doors in all pleas of the crown; and in most civil cases they need not, unless they thought fit, have recourse to any other place for justice than the bishop's court."[27] The same argument applies to the Courts of Great Sessions which functioned for Wales after the abolition of the marcher lordships, and to the Court of Duchy Chamber of Lancaster which continued to function down to 1835. Until the county courts were set up in the nineteenth century, the courts of the franchises were undoubtedly serving a useful purpose, and the enduring quality of medieval administrative arrangements is attested by the fact that the boundaries of the old monastic franchises are still retained in some cases for the county administrative districts of to-day.[28]

One feature of the palatinates of special interest is their relation to parliament. We have seen that the commons had complained in the fourteenth century that residents in the franchises did not bear their fair share of members' expenses. In Cambridgeshire the contribution of the Isle of Ely was already held to be a third in 1331, and this was compounded for by a payment of £200 in 1431.[29] In the county of Lancaster the practice of representation was established before the creation of the palatinate, and the charter of 1351 empowered the duke to send two members to parliament for the county and two for the borough. Mr. Richardson has recently shown how John of Gaunt applied this privilege.[30] Wales and the Welsh Marches were given representation by the act of 1536, and seven years later, the inhabitants of the county palatine of Chester petitioned for representation and obtained it.[31] Durham remained unrepresented until the Commonwealth. Down to 1603 the residents in the palatinate had been exempt from taxation also, in consideration of their hazards and services in Scottish wars, but the Union had removed that pretext. Petitions for representation in 1614, 1623 and 1627, in which the plea of "no taxation without representation" was urged by the inhabitants of the palatinate 150 years before the American colonists, were rejected.[32] A petition of 1653 was successful, but in 1660 the inhabitants again lost their members and a fresh agitation began in 1666.[33] Bishop Cosin resisted their demand vigorously, informing them that they were very lucky to be exempt from representation: a bill introduced into parliament was defeated in 1668 by sixty-five to fifty, and it was only during the vacancy of the see that occurred after his death that the borough and county of Durham finally obtained representation in 1672.[34]

The history of Scottish feudalism[35] is illuminating in its similarities and contrasts with English feudalism. The legal theory is more clear cut, the beginning and ending of the system more definite, and the political importance is greater, because the crown failed to secure its own position either by evolving a strong central bureaucracy, or by retaining or recovering an adequate royal demesne. Something like the *Leihe-zwang* of the Empire seems to be operative. The lords to whom rights of public justice were granted by the Scottish kings in the twelfth century not only retained their regalities intact, but kept the right to delegate those powers which the English barons lost before the end of the twelfth century; they retained the power to hear appeals from their vassals' courts which the English barons lost in the thirteenth century; they retained down to the seventeenth century the power to hear pleas of the sword and to inflict capital punishment by gallows and pit.[36] Dalrymple, writing in 1758, said, "In the declension of almost every part of the feudal system the English have gone before us." An act of 1455 to prohibit further grants of jurisdiction was not observed; at the time of the Reformation the forfeited ecclesiastical franchises were re-granted undiminished to the new secular landlords; Cromwell's attempt to discipline the feudal courts was only partially successful,[37] and it took two Jacobite risings to bring about the abolition of hereditary jurisdictions in 1747.

Undoubtedly the greater activity both of the regalities (the Scottish equivalents of the palatinates), and of the baronies with less exalted jurisdiction is partly due to the absence of a royal judicial system comparable to the English. The chief justiciarship of Scotland was hereditary down to the eighteenth century; the justice of the peace was only introduced into Scotland in 1609. If the rolls of the Scottish barony courts of the sixteenth and seventeenth centuries be compared with those of contemporary English manorial courts their greater competence and activity are at once evident; the technique of the feudal court is functioning effectively in dealing with the problems of local justice and local administration where in England, in spite of the additional duties imposed on the leet jury by Tudor legislation,[38] the business tends to become more and more formal. Neither the presentment of nuisances by a jury nor the transfer of copyholds before a steward involved judicial activity; in the seventeenth century feudal jurisdiction in England was really a thing of the past, whilst the feudal incidents whose existence had been artificially prolonged by Tudor policy, having contributed to the unpopularity of James I's and Charles I's government, were finally abolished in 1660 as part of the financial settlement of Charles II.

To what extent, then, are we to consider feudalism as an operative reality in England from the fourteenth to the seventeenth centuries?

To the administrative historian it is clear that

during the later Middle Ages the monarchy preserved feudal forms of government to serve its own ends. As in the earliest days of feudalism, conditions in the north and west still demanded decentralisation and devolution of government, both military and civil. But the fact that a national system of royal government existed made it possible to enforce the feudal contract by non-feudal machinery when necessary. Only on the Welsh Marches is there any real retrogression; Edward I's claim that the powers of the marcher lords derived from royal grant and not from conquest, and that the law of England was superior to the Custom of the March was not upheld. In the south and east the feudal and franchisal jurisdictions were part and parcel of the national system of administration, their functions being recognised and utilised by the royal government.

But if we turn from the framework of government to the forces moving within it, it is clear that the French wars had produced a revival of the political and social power of the landed aristocracy which in its turn exploited the forms of national government and abused and distorted royal justice. Royal officials became the tools of baronial power. Not till the crown had recovered control of its own machinery could the "new feudalism" be exorcised. Then the Tudors could with one hand enforce half-obsolete feudal obligations on their tenants in chief, and with the other resume those regalities which, like the privileges and alien loyalties of the church, endangered the unique sovereignty of the crown. Their modifications of the land law and their redistribution of landed property released new social and economic forces which operated in the same direction.

The legislation of Henry VII and VIII, followed by the suppression of the two great northern rebellions, killed political feudalism and dealt a mortal blow to economic and social feudalism. The forms of feudalism survived in administration till the nineteenth century and in the land law till the twentieth century. But the real forces of national life were moving in other channels, and if a traditional deference to the great landholders dominated English society well into the nineteenth century, the balance of economic and political power had long before that been transferred to other hands.

NOTES

1. Denholm-Young, *Seignorial Administration*, pp. 23, 167–168.
2. *Stat. of Realm*, II, 84.
3. *Rot. Parl.*, IV, 421–2.
4. *E.g.*, by the resumption of some of the northern franchises and the creation of the palatinate of the Western March under Richard of Gloucester in 1482. (*Rot. Parl.*, VI, 204.)
5. 4 Hen. VII, c. 12, 19; 7 Hen. VII, c. 2; J. Harrington, *Oceana* (1700), p. 69.
6. *Pat. Rot. Cal.*, 1476–1485, p. 543.
7. See D. Brodie in *Trans. R. Hist. Soc.* for 1932, pp. 156–158; and *Pat. Rot. Cal.*, 1485–1494, pp. 133–134, 415; 1494–1509, pp. 33, 66, 420–424.
8. *Eng. Hist. Rev.*, 1934, pp. 676 ff.
9. Coke, *Fourth Inst.*, c. 35.
10. *Trans. R. Hist. Soc.* for 1936, pp. 121 ff.; Holdsworth, *Hist. of Eng. Law*, IV, 443–467, 579–580.
11. *Trans. R. Hist. Soc.* for 1932, pp. 158–159; Holdsworth, *H.E.L.*, I, 409; *Pat. Rot Cal.*, 1494–1509, p. 591.
12. I am deeply in Miss Brodie's debt both for many valuable references and for her great kindness in allowing me to consult her transcript of Dudley's Reading, from Camb. Univ. Lib. M.S. Hh. 3. 10.
13. *Tudor Studies*, ed. F. Seton Watson, pp. 199 f.
14. *Journal of Brit. Arch. Ass.*, 1933, p. 306.
15. *Year Book 1 Hen. VII*, Pasch., pl. 15; Trin., pl. 1.
16. C. U. L. MS. Hh. 3. 10, ff. 11d–17.
17. *Year Book 9 Hen. VII*, Mich. pl. 6; cf. *2 Hen. VII*, Mich. pl. 1, *16 Hen. VII*, Trin. pl. 17.
18. B.M. MS. Lansdowne 170, ff. 95–95v. Cited by Miss Thornley, *Journal of Brit. Arch. Ass.*, 1933, p. 310.
19. *Letters and Papers of Henry VIII*, VII, no. 1669.
20. 26 Hen. VIII, cc. 4, 5, 6, 11.
21. 27 Hen. VIII, c. 26.
22. *Letters and Papers of Henry VIII*, X, no. 254.
23. 27 Hen. VIII, c. 19.
24. 27 Hen. VIII, c. 24.
25. W. Hutchinson, *Durham*, I, 561.
26. *Parl. Papers*, 1836, XLIII, 161–162.
27. Jas. Bentham, *History and Antiquities of Church of Ely*, 1812, Appendix, p. 25*.
28. *E.g.*, the Isle of Ely, the Soke of Peterborough, and Western Suffolk (Bury St. Edmunds).
29. *Rot. Parl.*, IV, 382.
30. *Bulletin of John Rylands Library*, 1938, pp. 175–222.
31. 34 Hen. VIII, c. 13 (*Stat. Realm*, III, 911).
32. *Vict. County Hist. of Durham*, II, 167 f.
33. W. Hutchinson, *Durham*, I, 539–547; *V.C.H. Durham*, II, 172.
34. 25 Car. II, c. 9 (*Stat. Realm*, V, 795).
35. For Scottish feudalism, see especially John Dalrymple, *An essay towards a general history of feudal property in Great Britain*, 1758 (2nd edit.); and W. C. Dickinson's introductions to *The Court Book of the Barony of Carnwath* and *The Sheriff Court Book of Fife*, Scottish Hist. Soc., 1937, 1938.
36. Dalrymple, *op. cit.*, p. 235; *Court Book of Barony of Carnwath*, pp. xxvi, iii.
37. See *Minutes of Barony Court of Stitchell* (1655–1807), ed. G. Green; *Forbes Barony Court Book* (1659–1678), ed. J. M. Thomson, Scottish Hist. Soc., 1905, 1919.
38. Holdsworth, *H.E.L.*, I, 137.

CHAPTER VIII

The Centralized Traditional Polity.
Bureaucratic Empires: Introduction

I

We pass now to the analysis of the most homogeneous, compact, and enduring types of premodern political systems—at least as homogeneous as the city-states and certainly much more compact and continuous than either patrimonial systems or tribal federations—namely, the imperial systems or, to be more precise, the centralized bureaucratic empires.[1]

The term "empire" has normally been used to designate a political system encompassing wide, relatively highly centralized territories, in which the center, as embodied both in the person of the emperor and in the central political institutions, constituted an autonomous entity. Examples of centralized, bureaucratic empires are to be found throughout history. The principal ones, which comprise the major historical societies, are as follows:

1. The ancient empires, especially the Egyptian, Babylonian (1900–641 B.C.), and possibly the Inca and Aztec (1100–1521 A.D.) as well.

2. The Chinese Empire from the Han period to the Ching (200 B.C.–1912 A.D.).

3. The various Iranian empires, especially the Sassanid (226–650 A.D.) and, to a smaller extent, the Parthian (600–330 B.C.) and Achaemenid (sixth to fourth century B.C.).

4. The Roman Empire (31 B.C.–527 A.D.) and the various Hellenistic empires.

5. The Byzantine Empire (330–1453 A.D.).

6. Several ancient Hindu states (especially the Maurya (327–174 B.C.) and Gupta (320–495 A.D.) and the Mogul empires (1526–1705 A.D.).

7. The Arab Caliphate (especially from the reign of the Abbasides [750–940] and Fatimides), the Arab Moslem states in the Mediterranean and Iran, and the Ottoman Empire (1451–1789).

8. European states during the age of absolutism and to some extent their initial colonial empires, especially insofar as they were built with the idea of the direct extension of the patrimony and its central authority and not as merchant colonies or purely colonization settlements of small groups. Of these, the Spanish-American Empire (early sixteenth century to eighteenth century) is probably the nearest to the ideal type of historical bureaucratic empire.[2]

The majority of these empires developed from one of the following types of political system: (*a*) patrimonial systems, such as Egypt or the Sassanid Empire; (*b*) patrimonial dualistic nomad-sedentary systems; (*c*) feudal systems, such as the European absolutist states; (*d*) city-states, such as the Roman and Hellenistic empires.

II

The different origins of these systems have necessarily greatly influenced the differential course of their history—the exact nature of their political symbolism, their international setting, their longevity or continuity—as well as the directions of their image. We have relatively full historical records of the origins of these systems, and it might, therefore, be worth while to examine the processes of their establishment.

Despite the great variety of historical and cultural settings, some common features in the first stages of the establishment of such polities can be found. The initiative for their establishment came from emperors, kings, or members of a patrician ruling elite (like the more active and dynamic element of the elite in republican Rome). In most cases either these rulers came from established patrician, patrimonial, tribal, or feudal families or they were usurpers from lower-class families who attempted to establish new dynasties or to conquer new territories. In some cases they were conquerors who tried to establish their rule over various territories.

In most cases such rulers arose during periods of unrest, turmoil, acute strife, or dismemberment of the existing political system. Usually their aim was the re-establishment of peace and order. They did not, however, attempt to restore the old order in its entirety, although for propagandist and opportunistic reasons they sometimes upheld such restoration as political ideology or slogan. The rulers always had some vision of the distinctly political goals of a unified polity. They aimed to establish a more centralized, unified polity in which they could monopolize political decision making and the setting of political goals without being bound by traditional —aristocratic, tribal, or patrician—groups.

Of crucial importance in shaping the activities of these rulers was the geopolitical situation of the polity they tried to organize, such as the specific geopolitical situation of Byzantium at the crossroads of Europe and Asia or the vast hydraulic arrangement of China and its special relation with steppe frontiers. These geopolitical factors indicated, in a sense, the nature of the specific international system to which these empires had to respond, as well as the range of problems to which the rulers were willing and able to address themselves.

The aims of the rulers were very often oriented against various social and political groups and encountered their opposition. These hostile elements, usually consisting of aristocratic groups or some of the more traditional urban and cultural elites, usually felt themselves menaced by the new aims and activities of the rulers. Accordingly, they worked against the rulers either in open political warfare or by infiltration and intrigues.

The rulers had to find allies, whether passive or active, in order to implement their aims in the face of these various aristocratic forces. Thus they had to forge instruments of power and policy with which to mobilize the resources they needed, whether economic resources, manpower, or political support. Naturally the rulers tried to find such allies among the groups and strata whose interests were opposed to those of the more traditional and aristocratic elements and who thus could benefit by the weakening of the latter and by the establishment of a more

unified polity. The rulers' allies were therefore of two principal kinds. The first were the more active (mostly urban) economic, cultural, and professional groups who, whether by origin or by their social interests and orientations, were opposed to the aristocratic-traditional groups. The second were the wider politically and socially more passive strata, especially peasants and (to a smaller extent) the urban lower classes.

It was from these various groups and strata that the rulers hoped to mobilize the resources they needed. But in order to do this they also had to forge instruments of political and administrative action on which they could rely and through which they could provide services to their potential allies. Most rulers were able to form an entourage by recruiting from established administrative and political bodies; even when such organs of administration were available, however, they had to be adapted to the rulers' particular purpose. Insofar as the existing personnel were related to the aristocratic forces, the rulers had to find replacements. They tried, as far as possible, to appoint persons who were loyal to them and had the necessary administrative qualifications. The rulers also attempted to control the administrative budget, making sure that it was adequate for official salaries as well as other running expenses. This control enabled them to emphasize the dependent position of the officials; they were to be "servants," either of the individual ruler or of the polity he wanted to establish.

Thus the development of an imperial system (in the sense of historical-bureaucratic empires) was dependent on two conditions. One condition was the existence in the preceding social structure of a relatively high level of societal differentiation, which limited the place of the basic ascriptive units, such as family, kinship, or traditional status groups, in the social division of labor and created many forces cutting across them. On the one hand, this differentiation created problems of integration that called for new solutions, while on the other hand, it provided the resources needed for new organizations that could attempt to deal with some of these problems. The second condition was the development of a new type of political leader and elite who had wider aims and perceptions of political authority and were able to serve as a focus of the new imperial authority and symbols and to articulate new, more differentiated, and broader political goals.

The existence of only one of these conditions was not sufficient for the institutionalization of an imperial system. In the city-states of Greece, for example, there did not develop such an internally new leadership.[3] Although such new leadership developed in the Carolingian and Mongol states (or empires), there was not sufficient differentiation; thus the imperial system could not become institutionalized, and these polities remained at the level of loosely integrated conquest empires in which the different groups (conquerors and conquered) were not integrated into a polity bound by common symbols of identity.[4]

III

As we have for all other systems we shall examine the scope of differentiation of political roles, organizations, and activities, the nature of the division of labor, and the relation between center and periphery that developed in these systems. We shall start with the last, because it is probably the most outstanding and crucial characteristic of these systems.

It is in these empires that we find the fullest differentiation, specification, and crystallization of centers in general and of political centers in particular as autonomous, structurally and symbolically distinct entities. This can be seen in many external manifestations in these empires, such as temples and palaces in which the basic conception of the centrality in relation to society and to the cosmic or cultural order could be found. But such monuments of centrality could probably be found also in many patrimonial regimes. The distinctiveness and autonomy of the imperial centers were manifest mainly in their symbolic and institutional crystallization.

In structural terms the autonomy and distinctiveness of the center were evident in its separation from other social units of the periphery, in its ability to develop and maintain its own specific criteria of recruitment and of organization, and in the consequent development of a relatively distinct ruling class, some of whose characteristics we have already mentioned.

Even more distinct was the symbolic articulation of the centers in general and of the political center in particular. The political center in all these empires was conceived as an autonomous, self-contained focus of the charismatic elements of the sociopolitical and often also of the cosmic cultural order; that is, as the major embodiment of the charismatic qualities of the cosmic order as they were reflected in the social order or related to it.

This symbolic—and structural—distinctiveness and autonomy of the centers was based on a growing conception of the distinctiveness of the different orders of human and social existence—the cosmic, religious, cultural orders and the sociopolitical ones—and on the growing rationalization and symbolic articulation of each of these symbolic spheres hitherto discussed.[5] The religious-cosmic order, conceived symbolically and as distinct from the social and political order, organized according to its own symbolism and criteria, thus attempted to establish its own links with the social and political order. This order, in its turn, was also already conceived as partially autonomous, as having some distinctiveness of its own, although necessarily closely related to the cosmic one.

But the very conditions that facilitated the development of the political center, such as the growing rationality of the symbolic sphere, also accounted for a multiplicity of such centers or at least facilitated their development.

Here it should be remembered that these empires were also the seat of the great universal religions—Christianity, Islam, Buddhism—of Confucianism, Hinduism, and the more "secular" ideological systems derived from the traditions of Greek and Roman city-states.[6] Hence, there usually developed in these systems a plurality or multiplicity of centers that were, on the whole, based on the same degree of symbolic and structural autonomy as the political center.

But in almost all these empires, with the partial exception of India, there was competition between the representatives of these orders about their nature, about their relative place in the over-all scheme of the world, and about the right of representation of these orders and of their symbols.

These tendencies were connected with the development of both a special ruling class on the one hand (on which we have already commented above), and a relatively independent autonomous religious or sometimes secular intelligentsia, on the other hand. It is in these empires that the more embryonic developments of special intellectual or intelligentsia groups, which can be discerned in some of the city-states, tribal federations, and feudal systems, tended to become more fully crystallized and organized.

The very multiplicity of the different centers and the higher level of social differentiation tended to give rise here to more autonomous intellectual and professional groups and to the possibility of development of some more autonomous religious intelligentsia.[7] Needless to say, the extent of autonomy of different centers in general and of the development of such intelligentsia in particular differed greatly among the different empires, which could be mainly explained in terms of difference in the relative strength of their basic constituent elements.[8]

The full-fledged development of such intelligentsia took place only in the West. But important comparative indications could also be found in other societies. India constitutes a special case in which the religious caste was organized as distinct from the political one but superior to it in terms of status and in which the religious caste constituted the main bearer of "great," country-wide traditions. Thus, while most Indian political entities can be seen as transitional between patrimonial and embryonic imperial systems, the strength, persuasiveness, and continuity of their "great tradition," focused in the ritual-status systems, caused many of the characteristics of imperial civilization also to be found there.

The autonomy of the different cultural centers in imperial systems can best be seen in their capacity for survival beyond the imperial systems; that is, in many cases, like most Christian, Islamic, and Buddhist organizations, the cultural centers outlasted the political systems of the empires in which they developed.

IV

These various centers—the political, religious, and cultural centers—constituted the focuses and loci of the various great traditions that developed in these societies. It is in these centers that the full autonomous symbolic and institutional development of great traditions, as distinct not only in content but also in the very symbolic and organizational structural characteristics from local traditions, tended to develop. In this development these societies greatly differed from other political systems hitherto analyzed. In the tribal federation and in city-states there did indeed often develop the symbolic aspects of such centers of great traditions, but as we have seen, their structural basis was very weak.

In most of the patrimonial systems there was little basic distinction between the central and local traditions, although in some cases—already bordering on the imperial systems, as in Egypt—these differences of degree indeed became differences of kind. It was mostly in the imperial systems that the specific characteristics of great traditions could become both institutionally and symbolically organized and could become located in the institutional centers of the social, political, and cultural orders.

These imperial centers tended to combine within them most of the components of center formation, with special emphasis on the crystallization of attributes of common identity, the development of collective goals, and the regulation of internal intergroup relations. But the extent to which any of these or other components were predominant in such a combination tended to vary greatly among them.

V

This multiplicity of centers and their structural and symbolic autonomy may explain the special relation between center and periphery and the specific structural characteristics of both. Two such characteristics are of crucial importance. First is the coexistence in the same social institution of different levels of differentiation, and second is the relatively greater—and yet limited—permeation of the periphery by the center and the concomitant impingement of the periphery on the center.

As we have seen, these systems were characterized by a relatively high degree of structural differentiation and especially by the relatively high extent of organizational autonomy of central political activities in general and of executive and administrative ones in particular.

But the extent of differentiation of political activities, organization, and goals was still limited in these political systems by several important factors. First, the legitimation of the rulers was usually couched in basically traditional-religious terms, even though the rulers tended to stress their ultimate monopoly of such traditional values and tried to deny that other (traditional) groups could also share in this monopoly. Second, the basic political role of the subject was not fully distinguished from other basic societal roles, such as membership in local communities; it was often embedded in such groups, and the subject exercised no direct political rights through a system of voting or franchise. Third, numerous traditional ascriptive units, such as aristocratic lineages or territorial communities, still performed many crucial political functions and continued to serve as units of political representation. As a consequence, the scope of political activity and participation was far narrower than in most modern and contemporary political systems.

The existence of both traditional and differentiated political orientations, activities, and organizations created in these empires a complex interrelation between the political institutions and other parts of the social structure. The rulers were in need of both traditional and more complex, differentiated political support and were dependent on both. The rulers' traditional dependence on other parts of the social structure was manifest in their need to uphold their traditional legitimation and the traditional, unconditional political attitudes and identifications of many groups. On the other hand, the rulers' tendency to political independence and autonomy made them dependent on types of resource that were not available through various ascriptive-traditional commitments and relations. In order to implement their various political goals, the rulers needed more flexible support and resources that could not be embedded in traditional, ascriptive groups or committed for more or less fixed goals.

Among these flexible resources the most important were economic and political ones. In the economic field the rulers needed manpower and goods that were not available through the fixed commitments of ascriptive kinship and status groups but which could be allocated directly. Among such economic resources the most important were man power (military and administrative) for services and for relatively free and flexible occupational choices and various goods and commodities needed by the rulers for direct spending or for payment for services.

In principle, such resources could have been the same as those used within the various ascriptive groups and in their fixed interrelations. But the very emphasis on their flexibility entailed the possibility of their greater mobility and hence of their necessary translatability into media of exchange such as money, credits, and their equivalents. Once some such media of exchange were established, it was highly necessary to maintain markets and organizational frameworks in which they could flow continuously. Similarly, it was very important to maintain conditions and frameworks in which possibilities of relatively free occupational choices and avenues of mobility could be realized.

A similar situation developed in the field of political support and organization. The rulers needed commitments and loyalties that could be made available without the restrictions of such ascriptive groups, and this requirement entailed the organization of new types of political organization and leadership that could mobilize such support. Parallel needs could also be found in the cultural, social, and religious fields.

The political demands made on the rulers by the various groups in the society were of both the traditional and the more complex, differentiated types. On the one hand, the rulers were expected to uphold ascriptive traditional rights and benefits; on the other, they were faced with demands for participation in the formulation of the political balance of power and even in the process of legitimating their own authority. Thus the authority of the rulers, traditional though it may have been, was no longer automatic; merely to raise the question of the rulers' accountability was to deny them fixed support.

These different types of political activity and orientation did not coexist in these political systems in separate "compartments," bound together only in some loose and unstable way. They were bound together in the same institutions, and the continuity of each type of political activity was dependent on the existence of both types of political orientation. Because of this unity, the activities of the rulers were, paradoxically, oriented to maintaining basic traditional legitimation and symbolism of the system.

VI

Closely related to but not identical with these patterns of differentiation, there developed the specific interrelations between the centers and the periphery that were characteristic of imperial systems. The distinctiveness of the center, related as it was to a broader, autonomous conception of the sociopolitical and cultural orders, implied a stronger permeation of the periphery by the center as well as some—although usually weaker—impingement of the periphery on the center.

The conception developed that the sociopolitical and the cultural order represented in the centers encompassed the periphery beyond its own specific local traditions. The very distinction of the center was indeed articulated in the ways in which broader groups and strata—the periphery—could become related to it.

In contrast to patrimonial systems, there developed the assumption that the periphery could indeed have some, at least symbolic, access to the new center. Such access was to a very large extent contingent on some undermining by the periphery of its social and cultural closeness and self-sufficiency and on its incorporating into itself some orientations to the social and cultural order represented by the center.

This permeation of the center into the periphery could be seen in the very widespread channels of communication and in the center's attempts to break through, even if in limited degree, the ascriptive ties of the groups of the periphery.

At the same time, however, this relative affinity between the center and the periphery emphasized the symbolic and structural difference of the center from the periphery and the uniqueness of the center or centers as the sole guardians of the tradition and legitimacy of the traditions of these societies. It was here that the symbolic and structural implications of traditionality outlined above[9] became most fully articulated. This articulation can be most clearly seen in the nature of the conception of cosmic and sociopolitical orders and of the respective centers that developed in these empires.

VII

The historical origins of the different patterns of political symbolism have been as varied as the historical origins of the empires themselves. But whatever their origin, there did develop in the confines of the empires some very important and interesting changes and transformations in such conceptions, as compared with those of their origins. These changes and transformations were mostly rooted in the specific structural and symbolic patterns of the empires, in the structural and symbolic autonomy of the centers, and in their distinctions from the periphery on the one hand and in the multiplicity of the centers on the other hand.

It is out of these basic poles of political symbolism that the conception of the tasks of the centers tended to develop in the imperial systems. This symbolism was focused around most of the components of center formation but especially around those that were predominant in the centers of most of these empires.

Thus the major poles or problems of such symbolism were, first, the maintenance and active cultivation of the great traditions and of the imperial settings with their specific political goals; second, the maintenance of sociopolitical order in the narrower sense with special emphasis on its technical aspects of such maintenance; and last—in a way most important and encompassing the former—the maintenance of the interrelation between these various orders through the special "mediating" or representative function of the political center.

One of the basic tests of any imperial order was whether it maintained these mediating or representative functions in a way that would assure the proper functioning of all the cultural and the sociopolitical orders alike. The Chinese conception of the Mandate of Heaven is one of the most outstanding illustrations of this assumption, but it is found in one way or another in most imperial traditions. In contrast to many patrimonial systems, the very maintenance of these orders was no longer conceived of as given but had also to be assured by special efforts—political and administrative as well as communicative and religious efforts and activities.

The relation of the periphery to these centers and orders was of special importance. With few exceptions—of which Western political thought has been the most outstanding example—there was relatively little emphasis on the active participation of the broader strata of the periphery in the formation of such orders and in the active upholding of their respective centers. But at the same time these orders were seen as encompassing all groups of the society, and the periphery was expected to participate in them, even though passively.

But all this did not assume the active participation of the ruled, of the periphery, in the center. Neither did it assume the full applicability or homology between private morality and public life, private and public morals of the ruler, and the private virtues of daily life in the periphery. The sharp articulation of responsibility of the ruler in both private and public life that could be found in many of the prophetic or city-state visions became greatly blunted or transformed into purely abstract or symbolic directions and usually played a secondary part in the whole panorama of political symbolism. It was because of the great emphasis on the distinctiveness of the center that the full conception of *raison d'état* applying often to both political and religious centers tended to develop in these systems.

Even in China, where the Confucian ethic seemingly prescribed such a parallel between the private and public movements, this ethic was much more in the nature of symbolic parallelism or of technical requirements of good rules than of accountability to the ruled in terms of their private behavior.

It was again only in the West and, paradoxically enough, in some parts of Indian tradition that some such orientation persisted in more than a purely secondary verbal form. In the West it was the tradition of the city-state politics and of legal responsibility of the rulers as well as of the prophetic vision of the Judaeo-Christian tradition and of the feudal tradition of multiple centers that upheld such orientation as a basic ingredient of political symbolism. In India the relatively extreme divorce between the religious and the political center tended to stress the purely secular nature of politics in an entirely different way and hence also may have facilitated some emphasis on the accountability of rulers in terms of sheer political efficacy.

In the non-Christian universalistic religions (Islam and Buddhism) there tended to develop a form of political symbolism that was different, although not entirely alien, from the Judaean-Christian prophetic orientation, namely, the conception of the ruler either as the "custodian" of the conditions of secular and of the religious orders also or as the epitome of these orders. This conception placed him in a position beyond any accountability and thus stressed the distinction between the public and private realms or between the *raison d'état* of the center and the private morality of the periphery.

This distinctiveness of the center can be found in another focus of political symbolism that developed in the empires: that dealing with the appropriate behavior of rulers and ruled. The most important types of document relevant to this problem are to be found in the various "Mirrors for Princes," one of the most outstanding of which is again the Indian Kautilya's Arthashastra.[10]

Here different components of center formation can already be discerned, as well as two major types of orientation, one focusing on the maintenance of the public order and the other on the political and administrative acumen. The extent to which these two orientations are differentiated varies greatly. By the nature of things the first tends to be more "moralistic" and overt, while the second is more Machiavellian and purely manipulative. Common to both these tendencies is their perception of the technical and symbolic autonomy of the political realm and centers.

VIII

These varied characteristics of the empires tend to explain the patterns of political struggle and, ultimately, of processes of change and transformation in them. These characteristics also enable us to distinguish between the main types of political organizations and leadership that developed in the empires.

The first is individual or group representation and petitioning on behalf of various concrete and discrete problems. It is found mostly among peasant and traditional communities. In this type of organization the "represented" individuals and groups cannot be said to participate fully in the political struggle as an independent (even if weak) force. They are rather a passive, petitioning force or group of forces which have no continuous independent role in the political activities, but tend to react only insofar as these activities touch them from time to time. This type of activity is connected with a leadership characterized by *ad hoc* representation before the rulers, in which the leaders appear as supplicants and petitioners.

A second type of political organization and activity that is very frequent in these societies is that of the court or bureaucratic clique. Such cliques are usually composed of various members of the ruling family, eunuchs, aristocrats, upper bureaucrats, and so on. This type of organization is similar in some respects to the previous type, despite the obvious difference in its proximity to the center of power and in its participation in the executive and administrative process.

In some cases, however, these cliques do represent already varied social forces and strata. Such cliques are therefore among the most important and continuous and active elements in the political struggle of most of these societies, especially insofar as there are but few legitimate channels and organizations for political struggle. These include the various offices of the "inner court," various controlling offices, and various semi-independent offices, or those that interlink with an independent organization and the harem.

The concrete aims and bones of contention of these cliques may develop into a different order than the issues about which the representatives of groups petition, even if their interests and the scope of their problems may sometimes differ only in degree and not in kind. The main types of such aims are influence over policy making and decisions on concrete issues affecting both immediate interests and, in some cases, wider and more permanent interests of various groups; the promotion of members of various groups into the bureaucracy both as an avenue of advancement and as a means of acquiring positions of power and influence that can be used for the benefit of the group; the execution of various types of policy and the determination of the concrete means of such execution; and the concrete definition of various goals of the polity insofar as they are related to the interests or values of the various groups. The most important focus of such struggles is the problem of succession to the throne. Under certain conditions such cliques, either in conjunction with more rebellious types of movement or on their own initiative, may aim not only at influencing the choice of a legitimate heir but also at the overthrow of a ruler or a dynasty.

A third type of political activity and organization is what may be called the continuous and semi-permanent representation of various groups in a special political framework. Such representation can vary in type and in degree of perpetuity and organization. The best examples can be found in the various representative or semirepresentative assemblies: the Senate at Rome and Byzantium and the assemblies of Estates in Europe. In a less articulated form, many religious institutions enjoyed such representation at the courts of the rulers by virtue of their social position.

The next type of social and political organization, which in a way both constitutes a new stage and cuts across former stages, is organization into social movements of various kinds. The chief common denominator of these movements is the ability to organize in a relatively unitary framework rather varying and divergent interests and groups. However, they differ greatly in extent of perpetuity, of organization, of articulation of political issues, and of homogeneity or heterogeneity of the strata participating in them.

In this general category two special subtypes should be mentioned. One is the "secret society," usually with some sort of religious focus, which engages in various types of clandestine activity and sometimes joins a rebellion or a popular outburst. The best examples of such societies can be found in China, although they occur elsewhere. The second subtype is the militant-religious sect or order that, in addition to its avowed religious purpose, aims also at the overthrow of a political system, the murder of a ruler, or sometimes the establishment of a "semiutopian" polity. The best example of this is the Moslem Order of Assassins.[11]

The next and—within the framework of the present analysis—the final stage of political organization in the societies under study is comprised of special and permanent groups organized around political aims and, to some extent, programs. In the imperial systems they tend to develop only in an embryonic form, especially in the transition to modernity.

This kind of social organization of political activities is closely connected with a new type of political leadership. Its main characteristics: are differentiation of levels of leadership unattached in a fixed way to any ascriptive group; the development of country-wide or society-wide contacts between leaders and groups; the development of special free-floating public opinion; the growth of semi-institutional competition among different groups of leaders. Examples can be found in England, France, and, to some extent, in the Spanish-American empire. To a much smaller extent, they can also be found in the circus parties of Byzantium and in late republican and early imperial Rome.

It is mostly in this type of organization that we find regular, organized attempts to mobilize the potential political support available in the various associations and nonascriptive groups in the society and from informal leaderships in various spheres of life. Some rudiments of such an approach occur in the less articulated form of political organization, but it is only in this final form that the approach becomes fully developed.

IX

Parallel to these types of political issues and organizations are the main channels through which the political struggle has been waged in these societies. Broadly speaking, we can differentiate between two types of channels. One type includes the informal channels that are not primarily envisaged as legitimate and institutionalized arenas of political struggle. The second includes institutions specifically designed as legitimate arenas of open political struggle.

The specific modes of organization of the means of political struggle are obviously related to some of the basic characteristics of the political systems. Most important from this point of view is the crucial significance of various types of "free-floating" resources and support, on the one hand, and of various attempts at controlling these resources, on the other. The main methods in the political struggle of the various strata and groups in these societies are:

1. Withdrawing resources directly from the rulers by various groups, including manpower, economic resources (through fighting, nonpayment of taxes, or nonperformance of various tasks and offices), or political support.

2. Undermining the bases of the supply of economic resources, manpower, or political support (through migration, submission to feudal lords, and so on).

3. Organizing such fluid resources, especially contingent political support, in various types of opposition to the policies and interests of the rulers.

4. Blocking the channels of communication, influence, and supply between various social strata and the central ruling elite.

In other words, in these societies the political institutions provided a framework for the development of activities of other groups. From a broad comparative point of view this indicates that the activities of various groups, the regulation of their interrelation, and so forth, cannot be fully worked out without reference to the framework of the central political institutions. The extent to which the various groups could influence the political elite differs greatly from one society to another, but the reference to the central political institutions seems to be general in all of them. This, however, means also that the political institutions and the activities of the rulers must be able to incorporate, in a relatively flexible way, some of the goals of the more active groups in the population.

It is these general issues and the more fully articulated and flexible types of policy and of political organization that enabled the various social groups and strata to organize themselves and to attempt to articulate and solve some of their own regulative and integrative problems, their political goals, and their relations toward other groups in the society. Through their participation in the "wider" aspects of the political process, various groups may attempt to find some ways of dealing with their own problems and of elaborating some norms that can regulate their interrelationship. By their very nature, these norms are to some extent flexible and thus may enable the continuous reorganization and rearticulation of these intergroup problems.

X

This great variety of political organizations and their issues, channels of political struggle, is another manifestation of the great complexity of imperial systems, and it brings us to the relation between the processes of political struggle and of change and transformation of these empires. As we shall see, it was these regimes—together perhaps with feudal systems—that evinced the greatest symbolic and institutional transformative capacities.

The processes of political struggle and change were focused around the interplay between the orientations of the rulers—their dependence on both traditional and differentiated resources—that greatly influenced their concrete policies and gave rise to some of the basic contradictions that developed in those policies. The rulers of these empires tended to develop three major types of basic political orientations. First, they were interested in the limited promotion of free resources and in freeing themselves from commitments to traditional aristocratic groups. Second, they were interested in controlling those resources and committing them to their own use. Third, the rulers tended also to pursue various goals—military expansions, for example—that alone could exhaust many of the available free resources. Among these various tendencies of the rulers serious contradictions easily developed.

Such contradictions, though not always consciously grasped by the rulers, were nevertheless implicit in their structural position, in the problems and exigencies with which they dealt, and in the concrete policies they employed to solve their problems.

The main sphere to exhibit these contradictions was that of legitimation and stratification. As we have seen, the rulers often attempted to limit the aristocracy's power and to create new status groups, but regardless of the extent of the monarchs' independent activities in this field, of the number of new titles created, and of the degree of encouragement of new strata, the symbols of status used by the rulers were usually very similar to those borne by the landed, hereditary aristocracy or by some religious

elites. The creation of an entirely new secular and "rational" type of legitimacy in which the social groups or universalistic principles would be the focuses of legitimation was either beyond their ability or against their basic interest. It would necessarily involve extending the sphere of political participation and consequently the growing influence of various strata in the political institutions. Therefore, the rulers were usually unable to transcend the symbols of stratification and legitimation borne and represented by the very strata whose influence they wanted to limit.

This failure limited the ability of the rulers to appeal to the lower strata of the population. Even more important, the emphasis on the superiority and worth of aristocratic symbols and values caused many middle or new strata and groups to identify with them and consequently to "aristocratize" themselves.

The contradiction between the ruler's policies and goals could develop also in a different direction. However tradition-bound the ruling elites may have been, their policies required the creation and propagation of more flexible "free" resources in various institutional fields. Here again the major types of free resources in the economic field were money and easily exchangeable goods, free manpower in general, and free "professional" manpower in particular, and in the political and social fields they were relatively free commitments and possibilities of support. The propagation of such free resources either gave rise to many religious, intellectual, and legal groups whose value orientations were much more flexible than the traditional ones, or else promoted such groups. Moreover, the orientations and values of the broader middle strata of the society sometimes were similar to those propagated by these more active elite groups. Although in many cases all these elements were very weak and succumbed to the influence of the more conservative groups and policies of the ruling elites, in other cases—as in Europe—they developed into relatively independent centers of power whose opposition to the rulers was only stimulated by the ruler's more conservative policies.

A similar contradiction existed between the long-range and short-range policies dealing with problems of administrative manpower. In many cases there was not enough manpower available for the execution of various administrative and political tasks, or inadequate communication and technical facilities made it very difficult to supervise such personnel effectively. It then became necessary to "farm out" various functions and positions either to local gentry and landowners or to officials, who gradually became aristocratized.

The best example of how the social groups created by the ruling elite became partially opposed to its aims and basic political premises is the development of the system of sale of offices, which was closely connected with the entire process of recruitment into the bureaucracy.[12] At first, this system was usually introduced by the rulers as a means of solving their financial problems and admitting new (nonaristocratic) elements into their service. But in time, in most of these societies the bureaucracy came to regard its offices as possessions and either transmitted them in the family or sold them in the market; in this way the rulers, despite many efforts, slowly lost control over these offices.

This development was usually connected with the tendency by the bureaucracy itself—the very instrument of power of the rulers—to aristocratize itself; that is, to acquire symbols of aristocratic status and to ally itself with aristocratic forces. In such cases the bureaucracy very often replaced its goals of service to the rulers with those of self-aggrandizement; its members, using their positions for enriching themselves and their families, thus became a growing burden on the economy and lost their efficiency.

This development necessarily affected the nature and extent of political activity and the scope of mobilization of political leadership. Insofar as the processes of aristocratization, outlined above, became intensified, they usually depleted the supply of political leaders to the central political institutions. The more active elements became alienated from the regime, whether their alienation took the form of succumbing to the aristocratic forces, falling into complete political apathy, or becoming centers of social and political upheaval.

XI

Similar contradictions tended to develop in the political attitudes and activities of the major strata in these societies. Several attitudes toward the basic premises of the political systems of these empires and toward the basic aims of the ruler can be distinguished.

The first attitude, evinced chiefly by the aristocracy, was one of opposition to these premises—an opposition that was often shared by the peasantry and sometimes also by other groups that were interested only in maintaining their own limited local autonomy and their immediate economic interests.

The second attitude consisted of basic identification with the political premises of the imperial system combined with a willingness to fight for one's own interests within the framework of existing political institutions. This attitude was to be found mostly among the bureaucracy and among various elements of the urbanized professional and cultural elites.

The third attitude, found mainly among the more differentiated urban groups and professional and intellectual elites, favored changes in the extension of the scope of political systems. This attitude, which was most clearly evinced by the European middle class and intellectual groups at the end of the eighteenth century,[13] was manifested in various attempts to change the basic value premises of the political system, to widen the patterns of political participation in it, and to find referents of political orientation that transcended the given political system.

These attitudes often overlapped in concrete instances and varied by group and stratum in different societies and periods. Moreover, the attitudes of any one group were never homogeneous and stable, and they could change greatly according to political conditions. The various political attitudes of the major social groups greatly influenced the extent of their political participation and the scope and the nature of the political leadership that tended to develop from within them. Here again, the most significant factor from the point of view of the continuity of the imperial system was the bureaucracy's tendency to aristocratize itself and thus undermine the very conditions of such continuity. But no less important was the possibility that the very administrative organs created for the implementation of the rulers' policies could develop autonomous orientations and activities that might become opposed to the basic premises of the imperial system.

XII

All these conflicts and focuses of political struggle were closely related to processes of change as they developed in the empires and to the different directions of their possible transformation.

The policies of the rulers and the political orientations and activities of the major social groups in the empires were greatly influenced by two major sources (both external and internal) of pressure and change. As we have seen, the external, geopolitical factors, in the broadest sense, not only provided the general setting for these polities but also constituted sources of many concrete pressures, such as external pressures of population and problems of military security or of adjustment to international trade.

The geopolitical setting indicated the nature of the international system within which the rulers of the empires worked and the types of problem to which they were especially sensitive. It has been rightly claimed that in many of these empires there existed, because of their basic structural characteristics, what has been called *Primat der Aussenpolitik*,[14] or the priority of foreign policy. This priority implied a much greater sensitivity to external pressures than was the case in many other types of political systems.

External pressures were very often connected with internal problems. Thus, for instance, there obviously developed close relations between problems of international trade and the situations and activities of merchant groups, or between military problems and recruitment of manpower. It was, therefore, the combination of external and internal pressures that constituted the major focuses of change in the empires.

In more concrete terms, the main factors generating processes of change in these empires were the continuous needs of the rulers for different types of resources and especially their great dependence on various flexible resources; the rulers' attempts to maintain their own positions of control in terms of both traditional legitimation and effective political control over the more flexible forces in the society; the great and continuous sensitivity of the internal structure of these societies to various external pressures and to political and economic developments in the international field; the consequent needs of the rulers to intensify the mobilization of various resources in order to deal with problems arising out of changes in military, diplomatic, and economic international situations; the development of various autonomous orientations and goals among the major strata and their respective demands on the rulers.

Insofar as there developed strong contradictions between these different factors, and especially insofar as the rulers emphasized very expensive goals that exhausted the available economic and manpower resources, the rulers found themselves in various dilemmas. In such situations the special sensitivities of these political systems were brought out, and forces were generated that could undermine the delicate balance between political participation and apathy on which the continuity of these systems depended. This meant that the ruler's tendency toward maintenance of active control over different strata could become predominant and thus increase the power of traditional forces, sharpen the conflicts between them and the more flexible, differentiated strata, and either deplete or alienate the more "free"

groups and strata from the rulers. This depletion may have taken varying forms: outright reluctance to have children (or "demographic apathy," as it is sometimes called), weakening of the more independent economic elements and their subordination to more conservative, aristocratic-patrimonial (or feudal) elements, and depletion or flight of mobile capital.[15]

These processes were usually closely connected with the aristocratization or ossification of the bureaucracy, with its growing parasitic exploitation of the economy, and with the depletion of active political leadership identified with the regime. Such parasitic exploitation of the economy by the rulers was in a way an intensification of the usual economic activities of the rulers of the empires. The special parasitic nature of their activities during periods of decline—or of the setting in of decline—was evident not so much in the mere extension of the demands for taxes or for manpower as in the fact that the resources mobilized by the rulers were used for the creation of new ascriptive positions and groups. Instead of promoting conditions that could have encouraged the extension of free resources through trade or the facilities for training professional manpower, the rulers depleted their resources by adding to their already overdeveloped bureaucracies.

Thus there often developed a continuous flux of foreign elements into the centers of the realms. Initially mere merchants, hirelings, and personal helpers of the rulers, these foreign military groups gradually infiltrated into some of the most important political posts and finally totally usurped the supreme political power. This was made possible by the depletion of native strata and the mounting internal and external crises.

XIII

Here some of the basic differences between various imperial systems become especially pertinent. Despite their structural similarities, the empires did, of course, have many differences. Perhaps the most important external indicator of their differences was their longevity.

The differences in longevity were not entirely random or accidental; they were found not only in the exigencies of external events but also in the ability to deal with them. This ability was related, at least to some extent, to the variabilities in their internal structures. Their differences could become especially manifest in the exact ways in which the basic conditions for change developed in them and in the exact basic processes that caused them. The processes varied in different empires according to the specific constellation of their structural characteristics, the various external processes that impinged on them, and their unique historical circumstances.

Among the more accidental or external factors that influenced the processes of change we should mention different extents of external pressure, major movements of population, conquests of nomads, international economic fluctuations, and the degree of native ethnic heterogeneity. Of equal importance was the specific geopolitical situation of any polity, such as the special geopolitical situation of Byzantium at the crossroads of Europe and Asia.

Among the internal aspects of the social structure of these empires that influenced the processes of change was the nature of the goals of the rulers. These goals might be chiefly military and expansionist, or more oriented to the maintenance of a cultural order, or concerned mainly with economic advancement. In any case, each kind of goal made different demands on the various types of resource available in the society.

The processes of change and disintegration were also set in motion by the policies the rulers developed for the implementation of their goals and the repercussions of those policies on the relative strength of different social strata; changes in the relative strength of such strata as a result of internal economic, religious, or political developments; and the development of various internal and external crises and the ways in which the policies developed to deal with them influenced the strength of different groups.

The structural outcomes of these processes of change were greatly influenced by several aspects of the social structure of the empires and especially by the relations between the different centers that developed in them, the different conception of cosmic, cultural, and social order, and the relations between them.

We may distinguish between those centers in which these orders were symbolically and structurally embedded in one another and those in which they were concerned and organized in a more autonomous way.[16] Concurrently we may distinguish, as in patrimonial regimes, between strong and weak centers. These differences have greatly influenced the patterns of legitimation, of broader participation, of the intensity of political struggle, of the processes of change, of survival, and of the transformative capacities and directions in these regimes.

If there were relatively weak centers in such systems or if the pressure of international exigencies was great, then these regimes could not usually subsist and tended to revert to simpler patrimonial or feudal units. Insofar as such centers were relatively strong but the autonomy of the different centers small, and the stronger the dominant center was, the better was its control over its internal and external environment and, given propitious external circumstances, this center had a greater ability to control internal changes and to minimize their impact—but also a lesser ability to deal with new types of change and their transformative abilities.

Thus, to give only some very preliminary examples, the fact that in China various invasions, rebellions, and the famous dynastic cycles[17] did not undermine for a very long period of time the basic institutional structure of the Chinese Empire (from the Han to the Ching) can be understood if one remembers its geographical position, which made it relatively immune to the heavy impact of external forces. Furthermore, in China the relative weakness of the aristocracy and the predominance of the gentry tended to enhance the position of the centralized rulers; and the Confucian literati and bureaucracy, who constituted the backbone of the social and political structure, intervened between the central government and the major social strata and provided an indispensable framework of continuity and unity for the empire.[18] At the same time the absence of autonomy decreased their adaptability to the impingement of modernity.

The internal transformation of the imperial societies was greatly facilitated by the autonomy of strong social, cultural, and political institutions. In the cultural order, autonomy facilitated the development of new symbols supporting and legitimizing central institution building. Yet in the sphere of social organization autonomy facilitated the crystallization of viable new organizational nucleuses without disrupting the whole pre-existing order; a fact that has enabled the new order to rely, at least to some extent, on the forces of the old one. The relatively strong internal cohesion of broader social strata and of family groups, with some status autonomy and openness toward the center, has helped to develop positive orientations toward the new centers and willingness to provide the necessary support and resources.

This tendency can be seen especially in the transition to modernity. The illustrations of Europe[19] and Japan[20] and to some extent of India[21]—in each of which some type of multiplicity of centers can be discerned—are very significant.

Whatever the differences in the processes of change of these systems, in general the imperial systems and the feudal systems evinced greatest transformative capacities, that is, the greatest capacities for creating from within themselves new types of political systems.

NOTES

1. For fuller exposition and analysis of these systems, see S. N. Eisenstadt, *The Political Systems of Empires* (Glencoe: The Free Press, 1963).

2. On Russia in this period, see especially M. Beloff, *The Age of Absolutism* (London: Hutchinson House, 1954), Ch. 6; B. H. Sumner, "Peter the Great," *History*, XXXII (1947), 39–50; Sumner, *A Short History of Russia* (New York: Harcourt, Brace, 1949); M. Beloff, "Russia," in A. Goodwin, ed., *The European Nobility in the Eighteenth Century* (London: Adam and Charles Black, 1953); I. Young, "Russia," in J. O. Lindsay, ed., *The New Cambridge Modern History*, VII (Cambridge: Cambridge University Press, 1957), 318–338; M. Raeff, *Origins of the Russian Intelligentsia: The Eighteenth Century Nobility* (New York: Harcourt, Brace, and World, 1966); J. Blum, *Lord and Peasant in Russia* (Princeton: Princeton University Press, 1961). On China in this period, see especially Etienne Balazs, *Chinese Civilization and Bureaucracy: Variations on a Theme* (New Haven: Yale University Press, 1964); Derk Bodde, "Feudalism in China," in R. Coulborn, ed., *Feudalism in History* (Princeton: Princeton University Press, 1956), pp. 49–92; W. Eberhard, *A History of China* (London: Routledge and Kegan Paul, 1960); Eberhard, *Conquerors and Rulers: Social Forces in Medieval China* (New York: Heineman, 1965); J. K. Fairbank, ed., *Chinese Thought and Institutions* (Chicago: University of Chicago Press, 1957); D. S. Nivison and A. F. Wright, eds., *Confucianism in Action* (Stanford: Stanford University Press, 1959); K. A. Wittfogel, *Oriental Despotism: A Comparative Study of Total Power* (New Haven: Yale University Press, 1957); A. F. Wright, ed., *Studies in Chinese Thought* (Chicago: University of Chicago Press, 1953). On Indian civilization with special reference to the caste system, see Max Weber, *The Religion of India*, trans. Hans H. Gerth and Don Martindale (Glencoe: The Free Press, 1958); L. Dumont, *Homo Hierarchicus—Essai sur le système des castes* (Paris: Gallimard, 1966). See also the nine issues of *Contributions to Indian Sociology* ed. L. Dumont (The Hague: Mouton, 1957–1966); Milton Singer, "The Social Organization of Indian Civilization," *Diogenes* XLV (Winter 1964), 84–119; Singer, ed., *Traditional India: Structure and Change* (Philadelphia: American Folklore Society, 1959). Some of the earlier exposition of the caste system can be found in J. H. Hutton, *Caste in India* (London: Cambridge University Press, 1946); H. M. C. Stevenson, "Status Evaluation in the Hindu Caste System," *Journal of the Royal Anthropological Institute*, LXXXIV (1954), 45–65; E. A. H. Blunt, *The Caste System of Northern India* (London: Oxford University Press, 1931). On Europe, see especially Beloff, *op. cit.*; Lindsay, *op. cit.*, Vol. VII; G. Clark, *The*

Seventeenth Century (Oxford: Oxford University Press, 1929, 1959); Clark, *Early Modern Europe (1450–1720)* (London: Oxford University Press, 1957); Goodwin, *op. cit.*; B. Barber and E. G. Barber, eds. *European Social Class: Stability and Change* (New York: Macmillan, 1965).

3. For Greece, see M. T. Finley, *The Ancient Greeks* (New York: Viking, 1963); A. W. Gomme, "The Working of the Athenian Democracy," *History*, XXXVI (1951), 12–28. For Rome, see A. E. R. Boak, *History of Rome to 565 A.D.* (New York: Macmillan, 1955); R. Syme, *The Roman Revolution* (Oxford: Basil Blackwell, 1939).

4. For the Carolingian Empire, see L. Halphen, *Charlemagne et l'empire Carolingien* (Paris: Albin Michel, 1949). For the Mongol Empire, see O. Lattimore, *The Inner Asian Frontiers of China* (New York: Capitol, 1951); G. Vernadsky, "The Scope and Contents of Genghis Khan's Yasa," *Harvard Journal of Asiatic Studies*, III (1938), 337–360; H. H. Vreeland, *Mongol Community and Kinship Structure* (New Haven: Yale University Press, 1954).

5. See R. N. Bellah, "Religious Evolution," *American Sociological Review*, XXIX (June 1964), 358–375; C. Geertz, "Ideology as a Cultural System," in D. Apter, ed., *Ideology and Discontent* (New York: The Free Press, 1964), pp. 47–77.

6. See S. N. Eisenstadt, "Religious Organization and Political Process in Centralized Empires," *Journal of Asian Studies*, XXI, No. 3 (May 1962), 271–295.

7. See in greater detail S. N. Eisenstadt, *The Political Systems of Empires*, especially Chs. VI–VIII.

8. *Ibid.*

9. See Chapter III, above, in the present volume.

10. Rudrapatna Shammasatry, ed., *Kautilya's Arthashastra* (5th ed.; Mysore: Mysore Printing and Publishing House, 1960).

11. M. G. S. Hodgson, *The Order of Assassins* (The Hague: Nijhoff, 1955).

12. K. W. Swart, *Sale of Offices in the Seventeenth Century* (The Hague: Nijhoff, 1949).

13. Beloff, *op. cit.*

14. F. Altheim, *Gesicht von Abend und Morgen* (Frankfurt: 1955).

15. See Eisenstadt, *The Political Systems of Empires*, Ch. 12.

16. S. N. Eisenstadt, "Transformation of Social, Political and Cultural Orders in Modernization," *American Sociological Review*, XXX, No. 5 (October 1965), 659–673; Eisenstadt, *The Political Systems of Empires*, pp. 361–371.

17. Balazs, *op. cit.*

18. Max Weber, "The Chinese Literati," in H. H. Gerth and C. Wright Mills, eds., *Essays in Sociology* (New York: Oxford University Press, 1958), pp. 416–444; and Balazs, *op. cit.*

19. Beloff, *op. cit.*; Robert N. Bellah, *Tokugawa Religion* (Glencoe: The Free Press, 1956).

20. Albert M. Craig, *Choshu in the Meiji Restoration* (Cambridge: Harvard University Press, 1961).

21. Singer, "The Social Organization of Indian Civilization"; Myron Weiner, "India's Two Political Cultures," in Weiner, *Political Change in South Asia* (Calcutta: Firma K. L. Mukhopadhyay, 1965), pp. 115–153.

INTRODUCTION
TO THE READINGS

The material presented on centralized imperial systems is divided into five sections. Some general analyses of the basic characteristics of these systems are presented in the first section. This is followed by selections which illustrate the basic world view, especially of the ideal political institutions as they developed in these systems. The third to fifth sections contain analyses of contemporary scholars dealing respectively with the bases of legitimation of these empires, some aspects of their social and political structure, and processes of change in them.

The first section consists of Wittfogel's article, which presents his conception of the imperial system as equivalent to the system of oriental despotism rooted in the needs of a "hydraulic" society. He explains how an agricultural society which is located around a river in a semiarid region needs complex arrangements of water supply which require over-all territorial regulations. These needs enhance the establishment of a regime with a strong center that undermines the authority of local communities.

Wittfogel claims that the penetration of the center into the periphery in this type of political organization is limited to functional purposes and is therefore only partial. The policies of the rulers are mainly coercive and aim at the exploitation of the population. In spite of the pressure of the center on the periphery, the latter remains quite undifferentiated, and the traditional kinship units continue to exist unchanged. This view of Wittfogel's idea of the purely exploitative and coercive nature of the policies of the rulers of "hydraulic" societies has been often abused. Thus, for instance, in a review of his work I have proposed that:

> The functions of the bureaucracy are not only to administer the hydraulic works and to mobilize resources for the ruler and for themselves. Even in order to be able to do this, the bureaucracy has to perform various functions for the different groups in the society, and to mediate to some extent between such various groups. And in such mediation it must sometimes uphold the interests of these groups against the wishes of the rulers, or to find some modus vivendi between the two even if this modus vivendi is greatly biased in favour of the rulers.*

* S. N. Eisenstadt, Review Article: "The Study of Oriental Despotism as Systems of Total Power," *Journal of Asian Studies,* XVII (1958), 445, and the introduction in this book to the section on imperial societies.

The second section presents selections from various historical sources illustrating the basic world view and especially the conception of the ideal political institutions which developed in these imperial systems. Ch'eng-hao's "Ten Matters Calling for Reform" emphasizes that change in the imperial political systems is rooted in and limited by traditional writings. According to the Indian scholar Mahaviracarita, the ideal king follows the Indian ideal which blames the use of force. Another Indian book, *Digha Nikaya,* also bases ideal rulership on moral qualities and loyalty to the religious requirements.

The selection "The Conduct of Kingship" by Kai Ka'us Ibn Iskandar deals with the conduct of the king and stresses the importance of his authoritative as well as moral qualities. The emphasis in this document is on firm but just rulership.

All these sources emphasize the special role of the emperor in this political system as a focus of identification and as a sole ruler who has immense power over all his subjects. But this ruler is always legitimized by religious values and is justified only as long as he proves both his loyalty to religious norms and his political acumen.

The third section presents contemporary analyses of the nature of legitimation in different empires. Bodde's article, "Authority and Law in Ancient China," proves that though Chinese rule was sanctioned by the concept of "The Mandate of Heaven (*T'ien Ming*)," there was an "insistence on the fact that Heaven may conceivably transfer the Mandate from one ruling house to another." He deals also with the epoch of the establishment of Confucianism as the basis of legitimation in China. Thus he explains the possibility of dynastic change in China without undermining the traditional legitimation.

Dumont's article discusses the unique case of the Indian conception of kingship. "The function of the king in India has been *secularized,*" and there existed a clear-cut differentiation between the religious role of the Brahmans and the political tasks of the Kshatria. This rendered a great extent of autonomy to the political sphere and enabled it to change greatly without affecting the total social order.

In the fourth section, Liu's article describes the social and political environment and the administrative problems in China under the Sung.

The strengthening of the decentralistic tendencies in the form of aristocratization in Byzantium is analyzed by Charanis in his "Aristocracy in Byzantium in the Thirteenth Century." The emperor tried

263

to overcome these tendencies by attaining control over the aristocracy through his establishment and control of military estates.

Ghoshal's article on ancient Indian political institutions shows the implication of separation between state and religion for the exercise of power by the monarch. The political institutions in India were largely autonomous, yet their power was greatly restricted by the religious order and especially by the caste order.

The reign of the Hohenzollerns in Prussia, as presented by the selection from Rosenberg, exemplifies the success of the emperor in subjugating and directing the nobility for his own purposes. They succeeded in establishing a highly centralized bureaucracy, which operated according to universalistic criteria based on a competitive system of achievement. This bureaucracy was entirely committed to the emperor, and it formed a "new" high stratum. Its success compelled the nobility to try to enter bureaucratic service in order to maintain their position in society. This tendency was the basis of change into modernity and emphasized the growing importance of the middle classes and the establishment of a new type of secular center.

In the fifth section, two articles analyze some of the structure and orientation of various processes of change in the imperial system. Levy describes and analyzes the "Yellow Turban Religion and Rebellion" during the last years of the Han dynasty. Lewis' article on the decline of the Ottoman Empire shows how uneven differentiation in various institutional spheres causes the decline of the imperialistic regime. The existence of a rather modern army in an economy with a small extent of differentiation raises problems which could not be solved in the institutional organizations of the Ottoman Empire. The far-reaching cleavage between the differentiated center and the undifferentiated periphery enhanced the processes of decline, as the periphery was unable to produce enough resources for the center.

All these passages show that the maintenance of equilibrium between the traditional orientations and the relatively limited "free-floating" resources was the major condition for the existence of these empires.

a. THE BASIC SOCIAL AND POLITICAL CHARACTERISTICS OF GREAT EMPIRES

33

Chinese Society: An Historical Survey[1]

Karl A. Wittfogel

I. Traditional China—A Hydraulic ("Oriental") Society[2]

Traditional China was an agrarian society which experienced a significant development of handicraft and commerce. In this respect, China was similar to medieval Europe and to certain pre-Hellenistic civilizations of the northern and western Mediterranean.

However, while these Western agrarian civilizations ultimately lost their societal identity, Chinese society perpetuated its basic features for millennia. And while medieval Europe saw a commercial and industrial revolution that led to the rise of an industrial society, traditional China never underwent such changes.

Obviously, when characterizing societal structures, it is not enough to speak of agriculture, handicraft, and trade in general. We must consider their ecological and institutional setting and the specific human relations involved in their operation.

From Karl A. Wittfogel, "Chinese Society: An Historical Survey," *Journal of Asian Studies*, XVI, No. 3 (May 1957), 343–344, 348–358. Copyright 1957 by the Association for Asian Studies, Inc. Reprinted by permission of the publisher.

Chinese society originated in the Yellow River basin under semi-arid conditions. In this setting agricultural man created a stable economy by manipulating water productively and protectively (for the purposes of irrigation and flood control); and whenever these tasks transcended the strength of individuals or local groups, he did so by means of large work teams directed by the government. I suggest that farming based on large-scale waterworks be designated "*hydraulic* farming," and that it be differentiated from "*hydro*-agriculture" (small-scale irrigation farming), and, of course, from rainfall farming. I also suggest that a government managing such an agriculture be designated a "hydraulic government," and a society dominated by it a "hydraulic society."

Thus hydraulic society is a special type of agrarian society. Its peculiarities rest on five major conditions:

1. Cultural: the knowledge of agriculture.
2. Environmental: aridity or semi-aridity and accessible sources of water supply, primarily rivers, which may be utilized to grow rewarding crops, especially cereals, in a water-deficient landscape. A humid area in which edible aquatic plants, especially rice, can be grown is a variant of this environmental pattern.
3. Organizational: large-scale co-operation.
4. Political: the organizational apparatus of the hydraulic order is either initiated, or quickly taken over, by the leaders of the commonwealth who direct its vital external and internal activities—military defense and maintenance of peace and order.
5. Social: stratification separating the men of the hydraulic government from the mass of the "people." The rise of a professional, full-time bureaucracy distinguishes *primitive* hydraulic society (headed mostly by part-time functionaries) from the state-centered forms of hydraulic societies (headed by full-time officials), which may have no important secondary classes based on mobile and immobile private property (*simple* hydraulic society), or which may have secondary classes based on mobile private property, such as craftsmen or merchants (*semi-complex* hydraulic society), or secondary classes based on both mobile and immobile private property (*complex* hydraulic society).

The hydraulic type of an agrarian society was not confined to China. Historical evidence indicates that agrarian civilizations with government-directed water control originated several thousand years before the Christian era in the Near East, in Egypt, and in Mesopotamia. Similarly structured societies emerged early in India, Persia, Central Asia (Turkestan), many parts of Southeast Asia, and in Java, Bali, and ancient Hawaii. . . .

IV. Imperial China

A. Institutional Roots and Patterns

The constructional, organizational, and acquisitive operations of hydraulic society are fairly well documented for the periods of the Spring and Autumn Annals and the Warring States. During this time the despotic claims of the Chou dynasty lost their reality, except within the Chou domain itself, while the oriently despotic order assumed a more flexible, and more effective, shape in the territorial states, especially in the country of Ch'in, which ultimately unified China.

CONSTRUCTIONAL OPERATIONS: In China, as in India, large-scale government-managed hydraulic activities combined with many small and medium-sized enterprises[3] to produce a "loose" subtype of the hydraulic system. Having previously given a comprehensive survey of this system,[4] I need only note here that the Chinese hydraulic economy includes large territorial and interterritorial waterworks. This pattern (Loose I) differs from the less impressive variant of a loose hydraulic pattern (Loose II), of which ancient Mexico is an outstanding example.[5]

In addition to productive and protective hydraulic installations, China built enormous communicational hydraulic works, among them the world's largest artificial waterway, the Grand Canal. Some of the large non-hydraulic constructions, such as city walls, palaces, and temples, are documented since the early Chou days. Others, such as state highways and "long walls," appeared spectacularly at the close of the Chou period.

ORGANIZATIONAL OPERATIONS: The large-scale constructions of hydraulic society led to the development of organizational methods which, properly modified, could be applied also to military affairs and communications.

Since the start of the Chou dynasty, standard armies were orderly bodies with a center and two wings; and discussions of the art of war—as alien to feudalism as they are typical of advanced hydraulic societies—became a general feature in Chou China at least from the sixth century B.C. on. Significantly, the Japanese, who readily repeated what certain Chou authors, such as Sun Tzu, had said on this subject, seriously discussed the art of war only after their feudal period came to an end, that is, under Tokugawa absolutism.[6] In Europe, writings on the art of war appeared first in the Greek city-states that had integrated citizen armies, and then again, much later, after the close of the feudal period.

At the end of the Chou period, state highways and the state post were fully developed.[7] In Europe, it was only under post-feudal conditions that a system of highways, a state post, navigation canals, and census-taking became significant.[8]

ACQUISITIVE OPERATIONS: All hydraulic bureaucracies commandeer a substantial part of the labor and/or the products of labor of their subjects. The most numerous group, the peasants, either rendered corvée labor on "public" land or paid taxes. In Chou China the public fields, as an integral element of a system of regulated village land, was a widespread, although probably not a universal institution.[9] In the fourth century B.C. this system of land tenure was abolished in the territorial state of Ch'in. We do not know whether any, or all, of the other territorial states acted similarly before they were conquered, since the final victor, Ch'in, destroyed their records. But we do know that, in the unified empire, land was bought and sold freely.[10] Among the secondary institutional developments of China the establishment of private landownership at the end of the Chou dynasty is perhaps the most important one. Unfortunately, it is the least clearly documented.

The rise of independent artisans and merchants seems to have preceded the spread of private landownership by several centuries. The literary records suggest that up to the period of the Spring and Autumn Annals the majority of the professional traders were attached to the various courts and administrative centers.[11]

Thus after a primitive (tribal) hydraulic beginning China moved very slowly from a "simple" hydraulic society (with a regulated land system and little private handicraft and commerce) to a "semi-complex" hydraulic society (which still had a regulated land system, but increased private handicraft and trade) and then quickly to a "complex" hydraulic society with a considerable development of both mobile and immobile private property. Except for a temporary regression to a regulated land system, which lasted from the fifth to the eighth century A.D., China perpetuated itself as a complex hydraulic society throughout the imperial period, that is, roughly speaking, for almost two thousand years.

B. The Dominant Socio-Political Ideology: Confucianism

Our institutional analysis makes it easy to understand why Confucius, who lived at the end of the Spring and Autumn period, so strongly influenced the ideas of post-Chou China. In his days the relations between the Son of Heaven and the territorial rulers were greatly weakened; but Confucius' pious wish that the Son of Heaven should rule supreme[12] fitted well the realities of the unified empire.

Confucius' political world was a world of territorial rulers in which hierarchies of imperfect officials served equally imperfect princes. This was the situation that Confucius wanted to improve. Drawing a picture of the perfect gentleman-bureaucrat, he trained his disciples for just that role. No wonder that his principles have enabled innumerable generations of Chinese officials to serve in an agrodespotic government as qualified members of the ruling bureaucracy.

Confucius viewed the good family as the cornerstone of the good society. In order to make the members of the family both exercise and accept authority in the proper spirit, the relations between father and son, husband and wife, and the elder and younger brothers had to be clearly understood and carefully cultivated. The father-son relationship indicates the political implications of family authority: a son who obeys his father is well prepared to obey his government.[13]

A wise government will be careful not to upset the father's authority over his family unnecessarily. The prince of a small Central Chinese state praised the "upright" son who, if his father stole a sheep, bore witness against him. Confucius preferred another kind of conduct. "In our part of the country, those who are upright are different from this. The father conceals the misconduct of the son, and the son conceals the misconduct of the father."

Confucius' formula expresses in a normative way a basic feature of Oriental despotism. Fulfilling only semi-managerial functions, the representatives of such a regime, although exerting total *political* power, are unable to control the everyday life of the individual. Nor can they direct the activities of such social groups as the family, the village community, the guilds, and the secondary religions. They permit these groups some degree of self-government; but they hold their headmen responsible for the behavior of the members. By bolstering the authority of these men, the government builds up an army of unpaid aides.

The maintenance of such secondary patterns of authority is more important than the solution of a minor crime. In stressing this point, Confucius defined an important aspect of the rulers' rationality optimum.[14]

C. Secondary (Politically Insignificant) Forms of Self-Government

Under the unified empire the elaborate kinship system that had arisen in pre-Chou and Chou times persisted. Although the main operational kin unit was the small family, the clan often performed a number of ceremonial and social tasks. In China's traditional hydraulic order, which was less densely staffed with government officials than such "compact" hydraulic civilizations as Pharaonic Egypt and the Inca empire, family authority bulwarked state authority in a very vital way. In hydraulically "loose" India the priests of the dominant religion fulfilled similar functions.

Another secondary group of great importance in China was the village community. Even after the dissolution of the regulated land system, the rural community still fulfilled a variety of tasks, and probably with greater latitude than previously.

The organizations of artisans and merchants (guilds) became conspicuous at a relatively late date —to judge from the known evidence only in Sui and T'ang times. Under the T'ang and Sung dynasties the guilds seem to have been more closely attached to the government. Obviously they had greater autonomy under the last dynasty, Ch'ing, but they still lacked political importance. A government edict of 1898[15] boasted that, prior to that year, the government had not allowed associations. The statement implies that the rulers did not consider the traditional guilds politically significant.

Among the tolerated secondary religions,[16] Buddhism and Taoism were most important. Under the last two dynasties the adherents of these creeds were not free to propagandize their views; nor were they permitted to determine the number of their priests. But the same government that restricted these religious groups also permitted them to worship according to their beliefs.[17]

Under some of the earlier dynasties Buddhism importantly supplemented the old Chinese state religion. The Mongol conquerors favored Buddhism as the dominant creed.[18] And the Ch'i-tan masters of another conquest dynasty, Liao, practiced their shamanistic cults as they had done in an earlier day in the steppe regions of Mongolia and Manchuria.[19]

D. Conquest Dynasties and Conquest Societies

Reference to the Mongols and the Ch'i-tan reminds us of the fact that, during the era of the imperial dynasties, conquest played a substantial role in shaping China's societal order. To be sure, Inner Asian tribes had invaded the "Middle Country," *chung-kuo,* in Chou and pre-Chou times. But the "barbarian" pastoralists became a serious threat only when horseback riding increased their mobility (the technique spread to the Far East by 500 B.C.). They became a truly formidable threat when the stirrup increased their firing and hitting power.[20] During a period of transition, increasingly powerful "barbarians" moved into Chinese territory—in part invited, in part just pushing ahead—to infiltrate and then overpower their Chinese neighbors. The empire of the Northern Wei (386–534) is an example of such an "infiltration dynasty."[21]

The Sui emperors again unified the empire, which had been split into a Chinese South and a barbarian North under the Southern and Northern dynasties. A reorganized and revitalized bureaucracy consolidated China, until a cyclical internal crisis caused the collapse of the T'ang dynasty. On its ruins, the Ch'i-tan tribesmen established on the northeastern periphery of China the first major conquest dynasty, Liao.

The Sung dynasty defended the greater part of China against the Liao armies. But it was less successful against the Jurchen, the tribal successors of the Ch'i-tan, who set up in North China a second conquest dynasty, Chin. Interestingly, they stopped at the edge of the rice area, which before them the Toba (T'o-pa) horsemen had also found hard to cross.

Even the much stronger Mongols were at the start unable to carry their conquest of China beyond the rice line. But when Kublai Khan overran Southern Sung, the northern "barbarian" conquerors for the first time seized the whole country.

After the collapse of the Ming dynasty this extraordinary feat was repeated by the Manchus, the most sinicized of the barbarian invaders. Different from the essentially pastoral Ch'i-tan and Mongols, but like the Jurchen, the Manchus in their pre-dynastic days engaged in agriculture as well as animal husbandry. In fact, they practiced irrigation farming before they crossed the Great Wall to conquer China.[22]

There would be no need in a sketch of Chinese society to take more than fleeting notice of these waves of conquest if the Chinese had always absorbed their conquerors. That they did so has been claimed by many scholars who found that soon after the establishment of their power the barbarian rulers began to adopt Chinese culture. Conquest, however, is a military and political phenomenon, and to test the validity of the absorption theory we must first determine whether or not the tribal conquerors of China lost their military and political identity after they became the masters of a part or the whole of China.

Examination of the pertinent facts reveals that this failed to happen either in the four major conquest societies of Liao, Chin, Yüan, and Ch'ing,[23] or in such earlier infiltration dynasties as the Toba Wei. In the case of the four later dynasties we can say that in all of them the conquerors maintained a special military machine composed mainly of reliable tribesmen: under the Liao dynasty the *ordu* ("horde");[24] under the Chin dynasty the *meng-an mo-k'o*;[25] under the Yüan dynasty the Mongol troops;[26] and under the Ch'ing dynasty the "banners."[27]

The tribal conquerors also reserved for themselves the political key positions; and, as a rule, they forbade intermarriage between the conquering group and the Chinese. Thus national distinctions became social distinctions; and the customary Chinese class structure was complicated by new strata, a ruling tribal nobility that ranked above, but worked closely with, the Chinese bureaucracy (which remained indispensable for controlling the Chinese population), and the tribal commoners who, a barbarian nation in arms, stood apart from and above the Chinese commoners.

Summing up, the conquerors, who in varying degrees adopted Chinese culture and folkways, never gave up their superior socio-political position nor, for that matter, their religion. Even the Manchu rulers who faithfully performed the sacred ceremonies of the Chinese state religion continued within the walls of their residences to worship their tribal gods.[28]

The motive for maintaining a distance between the two national and social groups lost its purpose when the conquest dynasty collapsed. Then those members of the former ruling nationality who did not choose to return to their tribal homelands were indeed gradually assimilated. Absorption became a reality, not while the conquest situation lasted, but when it had ceased to exist.[29]

All this has been fully documented. And in consequence serious scholars have recognized the untenability of the absorption theory. But the consolidation of Chinese Communist power has given new life to an absorption myth that makes the consequences of the Communist victory seem less frightening. If the Chinese have always absorbed their conquerors—as wishful thinkers like to maintain—then they can also be expected to assert themselves successfully against their Communist conquerors.[30]

The reasoning is faulty, not only because the Chinese did not always absorb their conquerors, but also—and essentially—because the Chinese Communists conquered China, not from without but from within. True, Moscow's guidance and aid were essential for the rise of the Chinese Communists; but the success of their movement culminated, not in the occupation of China by the Russians, but in the establishment of a new Chinese ruling class.

NOTES

1. The original draft of this article was written for the *Handbook on China* prepared by the Human Relations Area Files (HRAF) for the U.S. Army. I wish to thank the guiding spirit of the *Handbook,* Professor Hellmut Wilhelm (University of Washington), for his generous co-operation, and HRAF for permission to publish my contribution independently.

The following abbreviations are used in the footnotes:

Bloch—Marc Bloch, *La société féodale* (Paris, 1949).

Chang—Chang Chung-li, *The Chinese Gentry, Studies on Their Role in Nineteenth-Century Chinese Society,* with Introduction by Franz Michael (Seattle, 1955).

Engels—Friedrich Engels, *Der Ursprung der Familie, des Privateigenthums, und des Staats,* 20th ed. (Stuttgart, 1921).

Ganshof—F. L. Ganshof, *Feudalism,* trans. Philip Grierson (London, 1952).

Legge—James Legge, *The Chinese Classics,* rev. ed., 7 vols. (Oxford, 1893–1895).

Michael—Franz Michael, *The Origin of Manchu Rule in China* (Baltimore, 1942).

Wittfogel 1931—Karl A. Wittfogel, *Wirtschaft und Gesellschaft Chinas,* Erster Teil (Leipzig, 1931).

Wittfogel 1957—Karl A. Wittfogel, *Oriental Despotism, A Comparative Study of Total Power* (New Haven, 1957).

Wittfogel and Fêng—Karl A. Wittfogel and Fêng Chiashêng, *History of Chinese Society, Liao,* Transactions of the American Philosophical Society, XXXVI (Philadelphia, 1949).

2. Most of the phenomena discussed in this essay have been systematically treated in Wittfogel 1957. I therefore ask the interested reader to consult this volume for fuller analysis, argument, and documentation.

3. See Wittfogel 1931, pp. 411–415, 433 ff., 446 ff.

4. Wittfogel 1931, pp. 187–300, 410–456.

5. Wittfogel 1957, pp. 166 f.

6. Delmer M. Brown, "The Impact of Firearms on Japanese Warfare, 1543–98," *FEQ,* VII (1948), 236 ff. According to a communication from Dr. Marius Jansen (University of Washington) on this topic, "the first integrated treatment of the subject [the art of war] comes in a work by Takeda Shingen [1521–73]."

7. *Kuo yü* (Shanghai, 1935), 2, 22 f.

8. In Japan an incipient—and frustrated—early hydraulic development produced elements of an orientally despotic system of communications and census-taking. But the rising feudal order prevented the growth of these elements. Like the art of war, they gained in vigor only after the close of the feudal period. See Wittfogel 1957, pp. 198 ff.

9. Wang Kuo-ting, *Chung-kuo t'ien-chih shih* (Nanking, 1933), pp. 51 ff.

10. *Han shu* (Po-na ed.), 24A.14b.

11. Ch'ü T'ung-tsu, *Chung-kuo feng-chien she-hui* (Shanghai, 1937), pp. 200 f.

12. Legge, I, 310.

13. Legge, I, 138.

14. For this concept, see Wittfogel 1957, pp. 128 ff.

15. *Peking Gazette*, October 11, 1898.
16. As contrasted with the dominant state religion. See Wittfogel 1957, pp. 115, 121.
17. J. J. M. de Groot, *Sectarianism and Religious Persecution in China* (reprinted 1940), I, 109–116.
18. Herbert Franz Schurmann, *Economic Structure of the Yüan Dynasty*, Harvard-Yenching Institute Studies XVI (Cambridge, 1956), p. 6.
19. Wittfogel and Fêng, pp. 217 ff.
20. Wittfogel and Fêng, pp. 505 ff.
21. Wittfogel, "General Introduction" in Wittfogel and Fêng, pp. 15 ff.
22. *Ibid.*, p. 10. For the bureaucratization of the Manchus in the course of the conquest of China, see Michael, passim.
23. "Introduction," Wittfogel and Fêng, pp. 5–14.
24. Wittfogel and Fêng, p. 568.
25. "History of Chinese Society, Ch'in-Han," MS. (in preparation by the Chinese History Project).
26. O. Franke, *Geschitche des chinesischen Reiches*, IV (Berlin, 1948), 561 ff.
27. Michael, pp. 66 ff.
28. "Introduction," Wittfogel and Fêng, p. 14.
29. *Ibid.*, p. 15.
30. The fallacy of this argument has been stressed by Richard L. Walker, *China under Communism: The First Five Years* (New Haven, 1955), p. 293.

b. THE SYMBOLIC CONCEPTION OF IMPERIAL AUTHORITY

34

Ten Matters Calling for Reform

Ch'eng Hao

This memorial, presented by Ch'eng Yi's elder brother to the Emperor Shen-tsung (r. 1068–1085), opens with the characteristic assertion that despite the need for adapting institutions to the times there are certain underlying principles of Confucianism which remain valid even for later dynasties like the Sung. He then details ten evils of the day which require bold action. Some of these are urgent problems from almost any point of view—unequal distribution of land, population pressure, inadequate educational facilities, the expense and ineffectiveness of a professional army, the danger of famine and need for increased grain storage, and the need for conservation of natural resources. Other reforms are more doctrinaire in character, though from the Confucian point of view they are the most fundamental of all. These involve the ritual functions of government, and reflect the Confucian conviction that all human evils are attributable in some basic way to improper government. Conversely the moral reformation of mankind is believed possible through the maintenance of a perfectly ordered hierarchy of offices, ranks, and rites. It was, therefore, precisely this belief in the perfectibility of man and society which dictated complete conformity to the ancient pattern.[1]

Your servant considers that the laws established by the sage-kings were all based on human feelings and in keeping with the order of things. In the great reigns of the Two Emperors and Three Kings, how could these laws not but change according to the times and be embodied in systems which suited the conditions obtaining in each? However, in regard to the underlying basis of government, to the teachings by which the people may be shepherded, to the principles which remain forever unalterable in the order of things, and to that upon which the people depend for their very existence, on such points there has been no divergence but rather common agreement among the sages of all times, early or late. Only if the way of sustaining life itself should fail, could the laws of the sage-kings ever be changed. Therefore in later times those who practiced the Way [of the sage-kings] to the fullest achieved perfect order, while those who practiced only a part achieved limited success. This is the clear and manifest lesson of past ages. . . .

But it may be objected that human nature today is no longer the same as in ancient times, and that

From Ch'eng Hao, "Ten Matters Calling for Reform," in I. De Bary, ed., *Sources of Chinese Tradition* (New York: Columbia University Press, 1960), pp. 453–458. Reprinted by permission of the publisher.

what has come down to us from the early kings cannot possibly be restored in the present. . . . Now in ancient times all people, from the Son of Heaven down to the commoners, had to have teachers and friends in order to perfect their virtue. Therefore even the sages—Shun, Yü, [King] Wen, and [King] Wu—had those from whom they learned. Nowadays the function of the teacher and preceptor is unfulfilled and the ideal of the "friend-minister" is not made manifest. Therefore the attitude of respect for virtue and enjoyment in doing good has not been developed in the empire. There is no difference between the past and the present in this matter.

A sage-king must follow Heaven in establishing the offices of government. Thus the functions relating to Heaven, earth, and the four seasons did not change throughout the reigns of the Two Emperors and the Three Kings, and for this reason all the regulations were carried out and everything was well ordered. In the T'ang dynasty these institutions were still preserved in attenuated form, and in its [initial] period of peace and order, the government and regulations of the T'ang had some semblance of correctness. Today, however, the offices and ranks have been thrown into great confusion, and duties and functions have not been performed. This is the reason why the ideal of peace and order has not been achieved. There is no difference between the past and present in this matter.

Heaven created men and raised up a ruler to govern and to guide them. Things had to be so regulated as to provide them with settled property as the means to a flourishing livelihood. Therefore the boundaries of the land had to be defined correctly, and the well-fields had to be equally distributed—these are the great fundamentals of government. The T'ang dynasty still maintained a system of land distribution based on the size of the family.[2] Now nothing is left, and there is no such system. The lands of the rich extend on and on, from this prefecture to that subprefecture, and there is nothing to stop them. Day by day the poor scatter and die from starvation, and there is no one to take pity on them. Although many people are more fortunate, still there are countless persons without sufficient food and clothing. The population grows day by day, and if nothing is done to control the situation, food and clothing will become more and more scarce, and more people will scatter and die. This is the key to order and disorder. How can we not devise some way to control it? In this matter, too, there is no difference between past and present.

In ancient times, government and education began with the local villages. The system worked up from [the local units of] *pi, lü, tsu, tang, chou, hsiang, tsan,* and *sui.*[3] Each village and town was linked to the next higher unit and governed by them in sequence. Thus the people were at peace, and friendly toward one another. They seldom violated the criminal law, and it was easy to appeal to their sense of shame. This is in accord with the natural bent of human feelings and, therefore, when practiced, it works. In this matter, too, there is no difference between past and present.

Education in local schools was the means by which the ancient kings made clear the moral obligations of human relationships and achieved the ethical transformation of all under Heaven. Now true teaching and learning have been abandoned, and there is no moral standard. Civic ceremonies have ceased to be held in the local community and propriety and righteousness are not upheld. Appointments to office are not based upon the recommendation of the village communities, and the conduct [of appointees to high office] not proven by performance. The best talents are not nurtured in the schools, and the abilities of men are mostly wasted. These are matters clearly evident, and there is in them no difference between the past and the present.

In ancient times, government clerks and runners were paid by the state, and there was no distinction between soldiers and farmers. Now the arrogant display of military power has exhausted national resources to the limit. Your servant considers that if the soldiery, with the exception of the Imperial Guards, is not gradually reconverted to a peasant militia, the matter will be of great concern. The services of government clerks and runners have inflicted harm all over the empire; if this system is not changed, a great disaster is inevitable. This is also a truth which is most evident, and there is no difference between the past and the present.

In ancient times, the people had to have [a reserve of] nine years' food supply. A state was not considered a state if it did not have a reserve of at least three years' food. Your servant observes that there are few in the land who grow food and many who consume it. The productivity of the earth is not fully utilized and human labor is not fully employed. Even the rich and powerful families rarely have a surplus; how much worse off are the poor and weak! If in one locality their luck is bad and crops fail just one year, banditry becomes uncontrollable and the roads are full of the faint and starving. If, then, we should be so unfortunate as to have a disaster affecting an area of two or three thousand square *li,* or bad harvests over a number of years in succession, how is the government going to deal with it? The distress then will be beyond description. How can we say, "But it is a long, long time since anything like that has happened," and on this ground trust to luck in the future? Certainly we should gradually return to the ancient system—with the land distributed equally so as to encourage agriculture, and with steps taken by both individuals and the government to store up grain so as to provide against any contingency. In this, too, there is no difference between past and present.

In ancient times, the four classes of people each had its settled occupation, and eight or nine out of ten people were farmers. Therefore food and clothing were provided without difficulty and people were spared suffering and distress. But now in the capital region there are thousands upon thousands of men without settled occupations—idlers and beggars who cannot earn a living. Seeing that they are distressed, toilsome, lonesome, poor, and ill, or resort to guile and craftiness in order to survive and yet usually cannot make a living, what can we expect the consequence to be after this has gone on for days and years? Their poverty being so extreme, unless a sage is able to change things and solve the problem, there will be no way to avoid complete disaster. How can we say, "There is nothing that can be done about it"? This calls for consideration of the ancient [system] in order to reform the present [system], a sharing by those who have much so as to relieve those who possess little, thus enabling them to gain the means of livelihood by which to save their lives. In this, too, there is no difference between the past and the present.

The way the sages followed the will of Heaven and put things in order was through the administration of the six resources.[4] The responsibility for the administration of the six resources was in the hands of the Five Offices. There were fixed prohibitions covering the resources of hills, woodlands, and streams. Thus the various things were in abundance and there was no deficiency in the supply. Today the duties of the Five Offices are not performed and the six resources are not controlled. The use of these things is immoderate and the taking of them is not in due time and season. It is not merely that the nature of things has been violated, but that the mountains from which forests and woods grow have all been laid bare by indiscriminate cutting and burning. As these depredations still go uncurbed, the fish of the stream and the beasts of the field are cut short in their abundance and the things of nature [Heaven] are becoming wasted and exhausted. What

then can be done about it? These dire abuses have now reached the extreme, and only by restoring the ancient system of official control over hills and streams, so as to preserve and develop them, can the trend be halted, a change made, and a permanent supply be assured. Here, too, there is no difference between the past and the present.

In ancient times, there were different ranks and distinctions observed in official capping ceremonies, weddings, funerals, sacrifices, carriages, garments, and utensils, and no one dared to exceed what he was entitled to. Therefore expenses were easily met and people kept their equanimity of mind. Now the system of rites is not maintained in practice, and people compete with each other in ostentation and extravagance. The families of officials are unable to maintain themselves in proper style, whereas members of the merchant class sometimes surpass the ceremonial display of kings and dukes. The system of rites is unable to regulate the human feelings, and the titles and quantities[5] are unable to preserve the distinction between the noble and the mean. Since there have been no fixed distinctions and proportions, people have become crafty, deceitful, and grasping; each seeks to gratify his desires and does not stop until they are gratified. But how can there be an end to it? This is the way leading to strife and disorder. How, then, can we not look into the measures of the ancient kings and adapt them to our need? Here, too, there is no difference between the past and the present.

The above ten points are but the primary ones. Your servant discusses these main points merely to provide evidence for his belief that the laws and institutions of the Three Dynasties can definitely be put into practice. As to the detailed plans and procedures for their enactment, it is essential that they conform to the instructions contained in the Classics and be applied with due regard for human feelings. These are fixed and definite principles, clearly apparent to all. How can they be compared with vague and impractical theories? May your sage intelligence deign to consider them.

NOTES

1. From *Ming-tao wen-chi*, SPPY ed., 2:6a–7b; *Sung-Yüan hsüeh-an*, 14:332.
2. Under the equal land system of the T'ang, each adult was entitled to hold 30 *mu* of hereditary land and 80 *mu* on assignment from the state.
3. Units of local administration in ascending order as described in the classic *Rites of Chou*.
4. That is, fire, water, metal, wood, earth, and grain.

35

The Ideal King

Mahaviracarita

The Jain attitude of rulership and government varied considerably. The state is a necessary feature of society in the period of decline in which we now find ourselves. It maintains the social order and is conducive to the good life, leading to liberation. In this respect Jain thought differs very little from that of Hinduism. In fact Jain writers set much the same ideals before rulers as do those of Hinduism, and their thought on the subject has few original features. A sample of typical Jain advice to kings is given later. Exceptional ideas, however, are to be found in the writings of Hemachandra, who appears to have had real influence on politics, which may still be indirectly felt in India to the present day. This teacher, the greatest doctor of Jainism, was born in or about 1089 in Gujarat. Entering the Jain order as a boy, he rapidly acquired a great reputation for learning, and was much patronized by the powerful king of the Chaulukya dynasty, Jayasimha (1094–1143), despite the fact that the latter was an orthodox Hindu. Jayasimha died childless, and was succeeded by Kumārapāla (1143–1172) a distant relation who seized the throne by force. Under Hemachandra's influence Kumārapāla became a Jain, and if we are to believe later Jain sources, enforced ahimsā so rigorously that two merchants were mulcted of all their wealth for the crime of killing fleas. There is no doubt that Kumārapāla did attempt to enforce ahimsā quite stringently, under the guidance of his Jain mentor, who composed several works in his honor. Hemachandra died a little before his pupil at the age of eighty-four, by fasting to death; Kumārapāla is said to have died in the same manner. His successor, Ajayapāla, introduced something of an orthodox reaction, and is referred to by the Jains as a violent persecutor of their faith.

Hemachandra was evidently a man of great versatility; among his works are philosophical treatises,

grammars of Sanskrit and Prākrit, lexica of both languages, a treatise on poetics, and much narrative poetry which, if judged according to the canons of the time, is often very beautiful and brilliantly clever. The longest of his poems is *The Deeds of the Sixty-three Eminent Men* (*Triṣaṣṭiśalākāpuruṣacarita*), an enormous work telling the stories of the twenty-four Tīrthankaras and of other eminent figures in Jain mythology, including the patriarchs and various legendary world emperors. The last section of this forms an independent whole, *The Deeds of Mahāvīra*, and records the life story of the historical founder of Jainism. In its course Mahāvīra is said to have prophesied in his omniscience the rise to power of Hemachandra's patron Kumārapāla, and to have forecast the reforms he would inaugurate. It will be seen that Hemachandra's ideal king is a rigorous puritan, and that he has a rather pathetic faith that man could be made good by legislation.

[From *Mahāvīracarita*, 12.59–77]

The vows, especially those concerning . . . food,
He will keep regularly, and he will be generally celibate.
The king will not only avoid prostitutes
But will encourage his queen to remain chaste. . . .

He will not take the wealth of men who die sonless[1]—
This is the fruit of insight, for men without insight are never satisfied.

Hunting, which even the Pāndus[2] and other pious kings did not give up,
He will abjure, and all men will do likewise at his command.

When he forbids all injury there will be no more hunting or other cruel sports.
Even an untouchable will not kill a bug or a louse.

When he puts down all sin the wild deer of the forest
Will ever chew the cud unharmed, like cows in a stall. . . .

Even creatures who eat meat by nature, at his command,
Will forget the very name of meat, as an evil dream.[3]

From Mahaviracarita, "The Ideal King," in I. De Bary, ed., *Sources of Indian Tradition* (New York: Columbia University Press, 1958), pp. 86–87. Reprinted by permission of the publisher.

NOTES

1. According to earlier Hindu law books, if a man died sonless and without male relatives the king was entitled to appropriate his property, though he was responsible for the maintenance of the widow and the dowering of the dead man's daughters. In accordance with the precept of the *Yājñavalkya Smṛti* Kumārapāla allowed the widow to inherit in such cases.

2. The heroes of the *Mahābhārata*.

3. It was a commonplace of Indian thought that the king had jurisdiction not only over the human beings of his kingdom, but also over the animals. His virtue or lack of it, moreover, was supposed directly to affect the course of nature.

36

The Ideal of Government and the Decay and Growth of Civilization (from *Digha Nikaya*)

The following *Discourse,* again attributed to the Buddha, attempts . . . to account for the origin of crime and evil, but it gives a different answer. According to a former passage crime began in the state of nature, and kingship was introduced to suppress it. Here government precedes crime. The golden age has its governments and indeed its conquests, but they are not conquests by the sword. It seems more than likely that this account of the Universal Emperor's peaceful victories over his neighbors is in some way linked with Ashoka's "Conquest by Righteousness," and we are inclined to believe that the present passage is post-Ashokan. Note that sin and crime, and the consequent lowering of the standards of civilization and of human conditions generally, are said to be due to the shortcomings of the ruler, and especially to his failure to continue the policy of his predecessors in caring for the poor. Hence crime appears, morality declines, and with it the standards of life deteriorate, until, after a brief period of complete anarchy, human love and fellowship again prevail, and gradually restore the golden age. Interesting is the reference to Metteya (Sanskrit, *Maitreya*), the future Buddha. This indicates that the *Discourse* is a comparatively late one. Our version is considerably abridged.

[From *Digha Nikaya,* 3.58 ff.]

In the past . . . there was a king called Dalhanemi. He was a Universal Emperor . . . a king of Righteousness, a conqueror of the four quarters, a

From *Digha Nikaya,* "The Ideal of Government and the Decay and Growth of Civilization," in I. De Bary, ed., *Sources of Indian Tradition* (New York: Columbia University Press, 1958), pp. 136–142. Reprinted by permission of the publisher.

protector of his people, a possessor of the Seven Jewels—the Wheel, the Elephant, and Horse, the Gem, the Woman, the Householder, and the General.[1] He had over a thousand sons, all heroes brave of body, crushers of enemy armies.[2] He conquered the earth from ocean to ocean and ruled it not by the rod or by the sword, but by the Law of Righteousness.

Now after many thousands of years King Dalhanemi ordered one of his men thus: "When you see that the Divine Wheel has sunk or slipped from its place, come and tell me." . . . And after many thousand years more the man saw that the Divine Wheel had sunk . . . and went and told the King. So King Dalhanemi sent for his eldest son, and said: "Dear boy, the Divine Wheel has sunk, and I've been told that when the Wheel of a Universal Emperor sinks he has not long to live. I have had my fill of human pleasure—now the time has come for me to look for divine joys. Come, dear boy, you must take charge of the earth. . . ." So King Dalhanemi duly established his eldest son on the throne, shaved his hair and beard, put on yellow robes, and left his home for the state of homelessness. And when the royal sage had left his home seven days the Divine Wheel completely vanished.

Then a certain man went to the King, the anointed warrior, and told him that it had vanished. He was beside himself with sorrow. So he went to the royal sage his father and told him about it. "Don't grieve that the Divine Wheel has disappeared," he said. "The Wheel isn't an heirloom, my dear boy! You must follow the noble way of the Universal Emperors. If you do this and keep the fast of the full moon on the upper terrace of your palace the Divine Wheel will be seen again, complete with its thousand spokes, its tire, its nave, and all its other parts."

"But what, your Majesty, is the noble way of the Universal Emperors?"

"It is this, dear boy, that you should rely on the Law of Righteousness, honor, revere, respect, and worship it. You should be yourself the banner of Righteousness, the emblem of Righteousness, with Righteousness as your master. According to Righteousness you should guard, protect, and watch over your own family and people, your armed forces, your warriors, your officers, priests and householders, townsmen and country folk, ascetics and brāhmans, beasts and birds. There should be no evil-doing throughout your domains, and whoever is poor in your land should be given wealth. . . . Avoid evil and follow good. That is the noble way of the Universal Emperors."

"Very good, your Majesty," the King replied, and he followed the way of the Universal Emperors, until one day the Divine Wheel revealed itself . . . complete and whole. And he thought: "A king to whom the Divine Wheel reveals itself thus becomes a Universal Emperor—so may I now become such a Universal Emperor." He uncovered one shoulder, took a pitcher of water in his left hand, and sprinkled the Divine Wheel with his right, saying: "Roll on, precious Wheel! Go forth and conquer, lordly and precious Wheel!"

Then the precious Wheel rolled on toward the east, and the King followed it with his fourfold army. Wherever the Wheel stopped the Universal Emperor encamped with his army, and all the kings of the east came to him and said, "Come, your Majesty! Welcome, your Majesty! All this is yours, your Majesty! Command us, your Majesty!" And the Universal Emperor said, "Do not take life; do not take what is not yours; do not act basely in sexual matters; do not tell falsehoods; do not drink spirits.[3] Now enjoy your kingdoms as you have done in the past." And all the kings of the east submitted to him.

Then the Divine Wheel plunged into the eastern ocean, and rose again and rolled towards the south. And so the Wheel conquered the south, west, and north, until it had covered the whole earth from sea to sea. Then it returned to the capital, and stood at the door of the Universal Emperor's private apartments, facing the council hall, as though fixed to the place, adorning the inner palace.

With the passage of many thousands of years other kings did as this one had done, and became Universal Emperors—and it all happened as it had done before. But one day a Universal Emperor left

his palace to become an ascetic, and his son, who succeeded him, heard that the Divine Wheel had vanished, but, though grieved at its disappearance, did not go to his father, the royal sage, to ask about the noble way of the Universal Emperors. He ruled the land according to his own ideas, and the people were not governed as they had been in the past; so they did not prosper as they had done under former kings who had followed the noble way of the Universal Emperors.

Then the ministers and counsellors, the officers of the treasury, the capitals of the guard, the ushers, and the magicians, came to the King in a body and said: "The people do not prosper, your Majesty, because you govern them according to your own ideas. Now, we maintain the noble way of the Universal Emperors. Ask us about it and we will tell you." The King asked them about it and they explained it to him. When he had heard them he provided for the care and protection of the land, but he did not give wealth to the poor, and so poverty became widespread. Soon a certain man took what had not been given to him, and this was called stealing. They caught him and accused him before the King.

"Is it true that you have taken what was not given to you?" asked the King.

"It is, your Majesty," replied the man.

"But why did you do it?"

"Because I'd nothing to live on, your Majesty."

Then the King gave him wealth, saying, "With this keep yourself alive, care for your father and mother, children and wife, follow a trade, and give alms to ascetics and brāhmans, to help yourself along the way to heaven."

"I will, your Majesty," he replied.

And another man stole and was accused before the King, and the King rewarded him in just the same way. People heard of this and thought that they would do the same in order to receive wealth from the King. But when a third man was brought before the King and accused of theft the King thought: "If I give wealth to everyone who takes another man's property theft will increase. I'll put a stop to this! I'll sentence him to execution and have him beheaded!"

So he ordered his men to tie the culprit's arms tightly behind him with a strong rope, to shave his head with a razor, to lead him from street to street and from square to square to the strident sound of the drum, and to take him out of the southern gate of the city, and there to cut off his head. And they did as the King commanded.

But when people heard that thieves were to be put to death they thought: "We'll have sharp swords made, and when we steal we'll cut off the heads of those we rob." And they did so, and looted in village and town and city, besides committing highway robbery.

Thus, where formerly wealth had been given to the poor, poverty became widespread. Hence came theft, hence the sword, hence murder . . . and hence the span of life was shortened and men lost their comeliness, until where the fathers had lived for eighty thousand years the sons lived for only forty thousand.

Then it happened that a certain man stole and was accused, and when the King asked him whether it was true that he had stolen he replied, "No." Thus lying became widespread, and where the fathers had lived for forty thousand years the sons lived for only twenty thousand.

And again, when a certain man took what was not given him, another man came to the King and said: "So and so has taken what was not given him, he has committed . . . theft." Thus he spoke evil of the thief. So speaking evil of others became widespread, until where the fathers had lived for twenty thousand years the sons lived for only ten thousand.

Now some people were handsome and some ugly. And the ugly were jealous of the handsome, and took to committing adultery with other men's wives. So base conduct in sexual matters became widespread, and men's life-span and comeliness diminished until where the fathers had lived for ten thousand years the sons lived for only five thousand.

Next abusive speech and foolish gossip increased, and so where the fathers had lived for five thousand years the sons lived some for two thousand five hundred and some for two thousand years. Then cupidity and ill-will increased, and the life-span became only one thousand years. With the growth of false doctrines it fell to five hundred, and then incest, inordinate greed, and unnatural lust spread, and hence the span of life dropped to two hundred and fifty or two hundred years. Finally three further sins—disrespect for father and mother, disrespect for ascetics and brāhmans, and refusal to heed the head of the family—reduced man's life to one hundred years.

A time will come when the descendants of these people will live for only ten years, and when girls will reach puberty at the age of five. Then there will not be even the taste of ghee, butter, sesamum oil, sugar, or salt, and the finest food of the men of that time will be mere millet, where now it is rice and curry. Among those men . . . good deeds will entirely disappear, and evil deeds will flourish exceedingly— there will not even be a word for good, much less anyone who does good deeds. Those who do not

honor mother and father, ascetic and brāhman, and those who do not heed the head of the family will be respected and praised, just as today those who do these things are respected and praised.

Among those people there will be no distinction of mother or aunt or aunt-by-marriage or teacher's wife —society will be just as promiscuous as goats and sheep, fowls and pigs, dogs and jackals. There will be bitter enmity one with another, bitter ill-will, bitter animosity, bitter thoughts of murder, and parents will feel toward their children, children toward parents, brothers toward their brothers . . . as a hunter feels toward a deer.

Then there will be a transitional period of the Seven Days of the Sword, during which men will look upon one another as wild beasts, and with sharp swords in their hands will take one another's lives. . . . But a few will think: "We don't want anyone to kill us and we don't want to kill anyone. Let us hide in grassland, in jungle, in hollow trees, in river-marshes, or in the high places of the mountains, and live on the roots and fruits of the forest."

And thus they will survive. And after the Seven Days of the Sword are passed they will come out and embrace one another, and with one accord comfort one another, saying, "How good it is, my friend, to see you still alive!" Then they will say: "We have lost so many of our kinsfolk because we took to evil ways—now we must do good! But what good deed can we do? We must stop taking life— that is a good custom to adopt and maintain!"

They will do this, and increase in both age and comeliness. And their virtues will increase until once more they live to the age of eight thousand years and girls reach puberty at the age of five hundred. . . . India will be rich and prosperous, with villages and towns and cities so close together that a cock could fly from one to the next. India will be as crowded then as purgatory is now, as full of people as a thicket is of canes or reeds. Vārānasī . . . will be a rich and prosperous capital, full of people, crowded, and flourishing, and there will be born Sankha, a Universal Emperor, who will . . . like Dalhanemi . . . conquer the earth from ocean to ocean and rule it . . . by the Law of Righteousness.

And among those people will be born the Lord Metteya, the perfected being, the fully enlightened, endowed with wisdom and virtue, the blessed, the knower of all the worlds, the supreme guide of willing men, the teacher of gods and men, a Lord Buddha, even as I am now. Like me, with his own insight, he will know the world and see it clearly, with its spirits, with Māra, with Brahmā, with its ascetics and brāhman, with its gods and men. He will teach the Law of Righteousness in spirit and in letter, lovely in its beginning, lovely in its middle, lovely in its end, and he will live the pure life of celibacy in all its completeness, just as I do now. But he will have thousands of monks as his followers, where I have only hundreds.

NOTES

1. A Universal Emperor (Pāli, *Cakkavatti;* Skt. *Cakravartin*) is a figure of cosmic significance, and corresponds on the material plane to a Buddha on the spiritual.

thus, according to the legend of the Buddha, it was prophesied at the birth of Siddhārtha Gautama that he would either become a Buddha or a Universal Emperor. Universal Emperors invariably have the Seven Jewels, which are perfect specimens of their kinds, and are the magical insignia of their owners. The Woman is of course the chief queen. In most lists the Crown Prince takes the place of the Householder.

2. The Universal Emperor is not thoroughly adapted to the ethics of Buddhism, and though he conquers by force of character even the Buddhist author cannot disconnect him wholly from the usual militancy of the Indian king.

3. These are the five precepts which all Buddhist laymen must do their best to follow.

37

The Conduct of Kingship

Kai Ka'us Ibn Iskandar

If you become king some day, my son, be God-fearing; keep eye and hand away from other Muslims' women-folk and let your robe be unspotted, for the unspotted robe means unspotted religion. In every undertaking let your own opinion be wisdom's servitor, and, in every task you propose, first consult with wisdom, for wisdom is the king's prime minister. As long as you see any possibility of leisurely action avoid haste; and, whenever you propose to enter upon an undertaking, first ascertain the way by which you will emerge from it—before you have considered the end, do not consider the beginning.

Be circumspect; where an undertaking can succeed only with the exercise of circumspection, embark upon it only circumspectly. Never consent to injustice and scrutinize every deed and word with the eye of discrimination, so that you may be able to distinguish the true from the false in all matters. If a king fails to keep the eye of discrimination and wisdom open, the way of truth and falsehood will not be revealed to him.

Be ever one that speaks the truth, but speak rarely and laugh rarely, so that those subjects to your sovereignty may not become emboldened against you. It has been said that the worst auguries for a king are audacity in his subjects, disobedience

amongst his retainers and the failure of his rewards to reach those who have earned them.

Expose yourself to the general gaze only rarely, and so prevent yourself from becoming a spectacle commonplace in the eyes of your troops and people, taking heed not to esteem yourself too poorly. Be merciful towards God's creatures, but be merciless against them that exercise no mercy; maintain stern discipline, more especially with your vizier, towards whom you should in no circumstances show yourself mild-mannered. Never be completely dependent upon his counsel. Hearken to what he has to say about persons or about the courses to be taken in any affair, but do not make an immediate reply. Say, "Let us consider the matter, after which we will issue appropriate commands." Then make inquiry into the circumstances of the case to ascertain if it is your welfare he is seeking or his own benefit, and when all is known to you give him such reply as you think proper. Thus he will be unable to regard you as being governed by his views.

Whether you are young or elderly, have an old man as your vizier and do not grant the vizierate to a young man. . . . Whoever it is upon whom you bestow the vizierate, grant him full powers in his office to ensure that progress in the affairs of your kingdom shall not be hindered. Be generous towards his kinsmen and adherents to the extent that there shall be no parsimony in any provision made for them or in any largesse granted them. But never

From Kai Ka'us Ibn Iskandar, *A Mirror for Princes,* ed. and trans. by Reuben Levy (London: Cresset Press, 1951), pp. 222–226. Reprinted by permission of the publisher.

appoint to office the vizier's kinsmen and adherents (the whole of the fat tail may not be given to the cat at once), for he will not in any circumstances render a true account of his adherents' dealings nor condemn his kinsmen to penalties for the benefit of your revenues. There is the further reason that those related to the vizier, relying upon their kinship with him, can make exactions from fellow-Muslims so great that no stranger would dare to do one-hundredth part as much.

Have no compassion upon robbers and never allow a pardon for them, nor grant any forgiveness to the shedder of blood. It behoves you to exercise caution where he is concerned, for if he deserves retaliatory punishment and you pardon him, you will be associated with him on the Day of Resurrection for the crime of bloodshed and will be held accountable for it. Yet be merciful towards your own henchmen, for the chieftain is like the shepherd, with the lesser men as his flock; if the shepherd is without compassion for his own sheep and fails to guard them from wild beasts, they will soon perish. Albeit, do not place reliance upon every person for whom you have made provision merely because you have done so.

Assign to every man a task and grudge no man employment, for the earnings which men thereby make they add to their own allotted portions and thus exist without lack of anything, while you are relieved of anxiety about them. Adherents are maintained for the purpose of working, yet when you make an appointment be careful to allot it to the man adapted to it and not one lacking the needful capacity. Do not, for example, give the position of wine-butler to the man fitted only for household work, nor the treasuryship to a man fitted to be wine-butler, nor the office of chamberlain to him that is suitable to be treasurer. Not every duty can be assigned to every man; as the Arabic proverb says, "Every task has its man and every occasion its speech."

By acting according to this rule you will avoid having the tongues of cavillers extended against you and no injury will be done to your interests. Obviously, if you assign a servant to a duty about which he is ignorant, he will never in his own interest admit to his lack of knowledge, although undertaking the work, which will consequently be badly done. Give the work, therefore, to one who is expert in it and thus avoid annoyance. As the poet says:

> This gift on thy behalf of God I ask:
> That you appoint men fitted for their task.

Accordingly, if you have an interest in a particular person's career and you wish to enhance his importance, you may assign him benefits and advancement without (unnecessarily) appointing him to an office, thus not providing the world with evidence of your folly.

In the course of your kingship, never permit your commands to be treated with indifference. The king's solace and pleasure lie in giving commands; in other respects the king is like his subjects, and the difference between them is that the king issues commands while the subjects obey.

38

Authority and Law in Ancient China

Derk Bodde

Lack of space compels us to focus our attention almost exclusively on the China of the Chou dynasty, that is, on the span of eight centuries beginning late in the eleventh century B.C. and ending abruptly in 221 B.C. with creation of a new centralized form of empire.[1] Even within these chronological limits, moreover, we must concentrate, at the risk of possible distortion, on the evolution of but a few concepts. Concerning the many philosophical theories which, during the second half of the dynasty (sixth century B.C. onward), arose out of the breakup of the old way of life that then took place, we can say extremely little.

Feudalism is the word commonly, and with considerable justice, applied to the political system that operated during the early centuries of the Chou. Only a small part of the country was directly ruled by the Chou kings themselves. The remainder was divided into a host of petty states or principalities, held by titled nobles who were linked to the house of Chou by ties of vassalship. Within each state, most of the land was in turn subdivided among relatives, officials and courtiers of the presiding noble. Beneath this ruling class lived the great mass of commoners, most of whom were peasant serfs hereditarily bound to the lands they cultivated for their overlord proprietors.[2]

The entire population was thus, in theory, integrated into an ascending pyramid capped by the Chou monarch, whose claim to universal sovereignty is graphically expressed in the following passage from the *Book of Odes* (Ode 205):

Everywhere under vast Heaven
There is no land that is not the king's.

To the borders of those lands
There are none who are not the king's servants.

A characteristic feature of this political system was its reliance on custom and personal relationships rather than on any clearly defined body of law. Its resulting arbitrariness, however, was to some extent tempered by certain moral and religious considerations. The aristocracy, for example, were expected to live according to an elaborate but (in early Chou times) unwritten code of politeness and honor known as *li*—a word that may be variously rendered as rites, ceremonies, traditional mores, customary morality, etc. These *li*, however, were excessively refined and laborious to learn, so that it is questionable whether they affected the commoners, save indirectly, to any great extent at this time.

Among the psychological factors giving the aristocracy its power and prestige, probably none was more important than the cult of the ancestors. Unlike the commoners (who at this period bore no surnames), each aristocratic clan maintained genealogies through which it traced descent from famous ancient heroes. To the spirits of these heroes the clan members offered periodic solemn sacrifice, in return for which they received powerful aid and protection.

The dominance of this cult probably goes far to explain one of the most striking differences between early China and many other ancient civilizations: the absence in the former of a universal church or a significant priesthood. For this there is a two-fold explanation. In the first place, the ancestral sacrifices of each clan were necessarily offered only to its own clan ancestors, not to those of any other clan. Secondly, these sacrifices, in order to be effective, had to be performed by the clan members in person, not by priestly proxies. As a result, the ancestral cult was inevitably divisive rather than unifying in its

From Derk Bodde, "Authority and Law in Ancient China," *Journal of the American Oriental Society,* Supplement, LXXIV (1954), 46–55. Reprinted by permission of the publisher.

effects. It could not readily develop into a national religion with a powerful organized priesthood.

Peculiar to the Chou ruling house was a further important religious sanction for its sovereignty, embodied in the theory of T'ien Ming, "the Mandate of Heaven." Ming, rendered as Mandate, literally means "command." T'ien or "Heaven," the supreme Chou divinity, was undoubtedly originally conceived of in anthropomorphic terms. Already early in the dynasty, however, there are numerous instances in which we find the word depersonalized into the name for a non-anthropomorphic divine power identified as the blue vault of the sky, or even secularized entirely into the everyday designation for the physical sky.[3] According to one plausible explanation, T'ien was perhaps originally a word simply meaning "great man." Then in historic Chou times it came to be used by the Chou more specifically as a collective designation for their own "great men" of the past, i.e., the Chou departed ancestors. Finally it became the name for the realm occupied by these ancestors, i.e., the heavens or sky.[4]

In essence, the T'ien Ming theory asserts that a ruler's political legitimacy depends upon whether Heaven approves of his rule by conferring on him its Ming or Mandate. Thus when the Chou overthrew the preceding dynasty of Shang (also known as Yin), they justified their act by asserting that the final Shang king had been a dissolute tyrant; that he had therefore forfeited Heaven's Mandate; and hence that they themselves, in destroying him, were simply executing the will of Heaven. This idea appears clearly, for example, in the following exhortation addressed by the Chou to the adherents of the fallen dynasty very shortly after the conquest:

Oh ye numerous officials who remain from the Yin! Heaven, unpitying and implacable, has majestically sent down its disaster on Yin, and we of the Chou have [merely] acted to support its Mandate (Ming). Assisting its brilliant awesomeness, we have effectuated the royal punishment and have correctly dealt with Yin's [Heavenly] Mandate. . . . Oh, ye numerous officials, it is not our small state that has dared aspire to the Mandate held by Yin, but rather it is Heaven that has denied you its trust . . . and has given us its support. . . . How could we ourselves have presumed to seek the throne? . . . It is simply that what we, the people here below, have done, represents the brilliant awesomeness of Heaven.[5]

The vital feature distinguishing this T'ien Ming theory from superficially similar theories elsewhere, such as that of the Divine Right of Kings, is the Chinese insistence on the fact that Heaven may conceivably transfer the Mandate from one ruling house to another. That is to say, even after Heaven has once conferred its Mandate on a certain ruling house, it may thereafter withdraw it at any time, should that house prove to be unworthy. This distinction is important, because it means that in ancient China, unlike some other early civilizations, the king was definitely not regarded as a divine being. On the contrary, he was a man like other men, though one who, because of his superior qualities, had been chosen by Heaven to carry out its divine purpose.[6] This explains why in later times the theory was repeatedly invoked to justify the numerous changes of dynasty that have taken place in China, and why even today the Chinese term for revolution is *ko ming,* which literally means "transferring the Mandate."

The heavy burden of moral responsibility such a doctrine could impose upon a ruler is vividly illustrated by the following statement, issued in the name of the youthful second Chou king (trad. 1115–1079 B.C.) by his regent uncle, the revered Duke of Chou, at a time when the new dynasty was threatened by rebellion:

Unpitying Heaven sends down injury on our house. . . . I am not perfected or wise, leading the people to tranquillity; how much less then should I be able to comprehend the Mandate of Heaven? Yes, I am but a little child; I am like one who must cross deep water. . . . Alas indeed for the widowers and widows! In performing Heaven's service I have been remiss, and have greatly thrown trouble on my person. Yet I, the young one, have no self-pity. . . .[7]

This is the prototype of a long series of penitential edicts in which kings and emperors of China, sometimes as recently as the past hundred years, have held themselves accountable not only for human disorders, but also for floods, droughts and other disorders in the world of nature.[8]

The ethical ideas introduced by the T'ien Ming theory were, with the coming of Confucianism (sixth century B.C. onward), enormously strengthened and elaborated. Mencius (379?–281? B.C.), for example, declared flatly that "the people are the most important element" in a state, and that a tyrannical ruler no longer deserves to be called ruler, but should be removed, by force if need be. Heaven, he said, does not actually speak itself, but reveals its choice of a ruler by the manner in which that ruler, through his own exemplary conduct, succeeds in gaining the support of his people. As evidence, Mencius cited the great sage-kings of antiquity who, through sheer force of virtue alone, induced all men to be their subjects. In short, for Mencius (and for all the Confucianists), the ruler's goodness, together with the popular support it elicits, becomes *the* great criteria for judging whether or not he enjoys the Mandate of Heaven.[9]

The championing of these ideas by the Confucianists had two important practical effects. On the one hand, it contributed to the dream, emerging in late Chou times, of a universal empire, ruled by a single Chinese monarch, whose benevolent sway extends to all under Heaven. On the other hand, it contributed to the belief that this monarch should be guided in his rule by an intellectual élite (the Confucian scholars), who through their moral training and knowledge of history are best qualified to interpret to him the meaning of the Heavenly Mandate. This dream and this ideal were partially realized in post-Chou times with the creation of a unified empire whose administrators, aside from the emperor himself, consisted of non-titled, non-hereditary scholar-bureaucrats, recruited through the famous examination system. The cultural egocentrism engendered in this politico-cultural system, with its far-flung empire fringed by tributary dependencies, was to prove one of the major causes for conflict when China entered on large-scale contacts with the West during the nineteenth century.

Before leaving this topic of the Mandate of Heaven, we should stress that the conception of Heaven as an unpitying punishing power—a conception exemplified in the early Chou texts quoted above—becomes greatly softened and even transformed in the thinking of many of the late Chou philosphers. By these men the universe comes to be regarded as an organism that is self-contained, harmonious, and in essence good. It functions solely because of its own inner necessity, without dependence on any kind of an external volitional power. T'ien, therefore, no longer constitutes such a presiding power in this new kind of cosmos. Rather, it becomes simply the name for the non-human aspects of the universe (somewhat equivalent to our word Nature), while T'ien Ming, the Mandate of Heaven, becomes one of several metaphorical designations for its dynamic pattern. The highest function of the ruler in such a universe is to maintain the state of harmonious equilibrium believed to exist between the interlocking spheres of man and nature. To do this, however, he does not, like the Hebrew prophets, rely on personal divine revelation. Instead, he studies the way of the ancient sages, for they above all are the men who, through their superior wisdom, were first able to comprehend the organic oneness of man and nature, and on its basis to create our human

civilization.[10] Such is the rationalistic and humanistic interpretation which Chinese philosophy, with increasing clarity, gradually gives to the old religious ideas.[11]

It is curious that this philosphical conception of a harmonious universe should have begun to develop precisely during those later centuries of the Chou when intensified interstate wars, coupled with growing social and economic change, were rapidly liquidating the old order. The Chou kings had by now become mere figureheads; most of the little principalities of early Chou times had been annexed by their neighbors, leaving only a handful of giants to struggle for supremacy; men of aristocratic birth had lost their lands and become impoverished, while some of the peasantry, at least, were gaining a measure of emancipation from their age-old serfdom. Such is the background of crisis from which sprang the first Chinese written law codes of which we have definite knowledge, those promulgated in the years 536, 513 and 501 B.C. Unfortunately, these codes have not been preserved. Judging from what is recorded concerning them, however, it is clear that they arose in response to purely secular needs, and were primarily penal in character.[12]

It was not until the fourth and third centuries B.C., however, that a group of statesmen and political theorists known as the Legalists took the final step of exalting law as the one and only arbiter of human conduct. In place of the flexibly interpreted *li* of antiquity—the traditional mores—they wished to institute a single body of clearly defined law to which all men high and low should be equally subject. In so doing, they were motivated by no burning desire to protect the rights of the individual. On the contrary, their aim was to create an all-powerful state authority which could forcibly put an end to the prevailing disorder. They rejected the concept of a harmonious universe, ridiculed the Confucian ideal of government through virtue, and persistently urged the need for absolutist controls with which to curb what they regarded as the essential selfishness of human nature. Law, in their hands, was merely one of several such controls; others advocated by them included state rewards for public informers; the use of secret police, institution of group responsibility for crime, and suppression of allegedly seditious literature. Thus the law of the Legalists was used to uphold a scale of values very different from the usual morality. Though its exact provisions have not come down to us, we know that they went so far as even to punish privately performed acts of public welfare, provided these had not been specifically authorized by the state.

The Legalists had their triumph in 221 B.C. when the state of Ch'in, employing these principles, subdued its last military opponent and for the first time in Chinese history created a genuinely unified and centralized empire. The triumph was shortlived, however, for the very harshness of the Ch'in brought its speedy collapse. Under the following dynasty Legalism was gradually displaced by Confucianism; government by law was subordinated to government by moral precept. In the words of the late Professor Duyvendak: "While profiting from its work, China has rejected the doctrines of the Law School [the Legalists]. The gulf between law and ethics, created by the Law School, was bridged by again restricting law to merely penal law. . . . Law became again firmly embedded in ethics; it never acquired authority as an independently regulating norm of conduct."[13]

The Confucian theory that has since prevailed has been democratic in the sense that it has consistently emphasized the ideal of government *for* the people, has tried to counter absolutism by the weight of a morally educated non-hereditary bureaucracy, and has sanctioned occasional political change as an escape from tyranny. It has been undemocratic, however, in the sense that it has never recognized the need of government *by* the people as a whole, has always regarded such government as the particular preserve of a small ruling élite, and has sanctioned political change only in terms of shifting personalities, not of basic change in the social and political order.

It is understandable why the Confucianists, with their memories of what happened in Ch'in times, should ever afterward refuse to magnify law lest in so doing they cause moral principle to become subordinated to legal form. We may sympathize with their contention that no government is better than the men who operate it, and hence that the moral training of such men counts for far more than any amount of purely legal machinery. The mistake of the Confucianists, however, as of all advocates of benevolent paternalism, was their belief that a ruling group, even when free from checks such as would be imposed on it by the presence of influential social groups and forces external to itself, can nevertheless long remain true to its ideals. In Confucian China such checks were weak because, aside from the scholar-official class itself, no such influential social group existed. There was in China nothing comparable to the rise of the urban bourgeoisie of the modern West.

Under these circumstances it is scarcely surprising, therefore, that the noble Confucian ideal of government by merit has, despite many triumphs, too often degenerated into a government by privilege. There is a partial similarity at this point between Confucianism and the ideology of the men who today control the destinies of China. For these men too, like the Confucianists, proclaim the people's welfare to be their highest aim, yet at the same time insist, again like the Confucianists, that the achievement of this aim depends on the leadership of an élite controlling group—in their case the Chinese Communist Party.[14] This is but one of several significant parallels to be found between these two seemingly sharply antithetical ideologies.[15]

NOTES

1. The Chou is traditionally said to have been founded in 1122 B.C., but the actual date was probably almost a century later. Though the dynasty officially ended in 256 B.C., the really decisive break between it and later epochs came only in 221, when its successor dynasty, the Ch'in, achieved the unification of all China.

2. For a detailed account of this system, see the writer's "Feudalism in China," in Rushton Coulborn, ed., *The Place of Feudalism in History* (Princeton, 1956).

3. Numerous examples of all three usages can be found in the *Book of Odes*: (*a*) As an anthropomorphic divinity (Ode 236): "Heaven (T'ien) gazed below. . . . Heaven made for him a match, . . . fair as a sister of Heaven. . . . There came a command from Heaven, ordering this King Wen," etc. (*b*) As a non-anthropomorphic supreme power identified with the blue vault of heaven (Ode 121): "O blue Heaven so far away, when will this all be settled?" (*c*) As the everyday name for the physical sky (Ode 178): "Swoop flew that hawk straight up into the sky (T'ien)." Cf. trans. of Arthur Waley, *The Book of Songs* (Boston and New York, 1937), pp. 262, 156 and 128 respectively.

4. See H. G. Creel, *The Birth of China* (New York, 1937), pp. 342–344. The ancient graph for T'ien clearly represents a human figure with outstretched arms and legs, i.e., "the great man." A transition such as this is quite conceivable in a language like Chinese, which has no inflection and hence no ready means for distinguishing gender, number, etc.

5. *Book of History*, V, 14. Cf. translations (here modified) of J. Legge in *Sacred Books of the East*, Vol. III (Oxford, 2nd ed., 1899), pp. 196–197, and of B. Karlgren in *Bull. of Museum of Far Eastern Antiquities*, No. 22 (Stockholm, 1950), p. 55.

6. The fact that, beginning in Chou times, the Chinese sovereign was traditionally known as T'ien Tzu, lit. "Son of Heaven," might at first sight seem to point to a different conclusion. The term becomes readily understandable, however, if we accept Creel's theory, mentioned above, that T'ien had first been the collective designation for the Chou royal ancestors, and only later became transformed into a more generalized divinity.

7. *Book of History*, V, 7 (Legge, *op. cit.*, pp. 157–159; Karlgren, *op. cit.*, pp. 36–37).

8. Cf. the edict of August 22, 1862, issued in the name of the youthful T'ung-chih Emperor by the two co-regent Empresses Dowager: "During the night of the fifteenth of the seventh month, a flight of many shooting stars was suddenly seen moving toward the southwest; on the nights of the twenty-sixth and twenty-seventh, a comet appeared twice in the northwest. That Supreme Blue One [Heaven], when thus sending down its manifestations, does not produce such

portents in vain. Moreover, beginning last month and continuing without abatement until now, an epidemic has been rife in the capital. Truly, though we be of tender years, we are filled with deepest dread and apprehension. By the Empresses Dowager we have been instructed that these warnings, transmitted by Heaven to man, are surely indicative of present deficiencies in our conduct of government. . . ." Cf. also the penitential edict of the Kuang-hsü Emperor, issued February 14, 1901, after the disastrous Boxer Rebellion, in which he says that he and the Empress Dowager had wished to commit suicide at the time of their flight from Peking in order to "offer atonement to the spirits of our imperial ancestors." For texts of these edicts, see the *Ta-Ch'ing Li-ch'ao Shih-lu* (Veritable Records of the Great Ch'ing Dynasty for Successive Reigns) [Tokyo, 1937], Mu-tsung Sect., *chüan* 35, pp. 33b–34b, and Te-tsung Sect., *chüan* 477, pp. 13a–16b; English paraphrases in J. O. P. Bland and E. Backhouse, *China under the Empress Dowager* (London, 1910), pp. 486 and 376–381 respectively (where the dates are inexactly given as 1861 and February 13, 1901). I am much indebted to Mr. Joseph Wang, of the Division of Orientalia, Library of Congress, for kindly locating these edicts in the Library's copy of the *Shih-lu,* and copying them for me.

9. *Mencius,* esp. Ib, 6 and 8; Va, 5–6; Vb, 9; VIIa, 31; VIIb, 14.

10. Typical of this point of view is the account in Appendix III, *passim,* of the *Book of Changes,* describing how the ancient sages, basing themselves on their examination of natural phenomena, created the eight trigrams and sixty-four hexagrams as graphic symbols of these phenomena, and then proceeded from these symbols to get the ideas of inventing plows, boats, bows and arrows, houses, and other artifacts of civilization. Cf. transl. of Legge in *Sacred Books of the East,* Vol. XVI (Oxford, 2nd ed., 1899), esp. pp. 353–354, 360–361, 371–374, 377–378, 382–385.

11. For a detailed survey of this world view, which became the dominant one in later Chinese philosophy, see the writer's "Harmony and Conflict in Chinese Philosophy," in Arthur F. Wright, ed., *Studies in Chinese Thought* (University of Chicago Press, 1953), pp. 19–80. It should be stressed that

this was the world view of philosophical sophisticates, not necessarily shared by all non-philosophical writers. Even among later philosophical writers themselves, in fact, throwbacks to the earlier, more personalistic ways of thinking can sometimes be found. A good example is Tung Chung-shu (179?–104? B.C.). Cf. *ibid.,* pp. 43–44, 71.

12. Cf. the *Tso Chuan* (Legge, *Chinese Classics,* V [Hongkong, 1872], pp. 609, 732, 772). The codes of 536 and 501, belonging to the state of Cheng, were inscribed on bronze vessels and bamboo tablets respectively; that of 513, belonging to the state of Chin, was inscribed on iron tripods.

13. J. J. L. Duyvendak, *The Book of Lord Shang* (London, 1928), pp. 128–129. This is not to deny, of course, that there have been numerous and bulky law codes in later China. They were, however, primarily penal, and played a much less prominent role in Chinese life than that held by law in the West. Professional lawyers, for example, were virtually nonexistent in China prior to recent times. For a comprehensive discussion of Chinese law, see Jean Escarra, *Le droit chinois* (Peiping, 1936).

14. The word "partial" in the preceding sentence deserves stress, in that the Chinese Communists, unlike the Confucianists, not only explicitly advocate, but even insist on, the active participation of the common man in public affairs. Granted that such participation is usually confined to local matters, and is carefully guided from above along lines which severely limit its scope and freedom, it has nevertheless given to many Chinese a hitherto unknown feeling that they have a necessary and appreciated public role to play. Illustrative of the differing Confucian and Communist attitudes toward the people is the Communist slogan, made with regard to their army, that "the soldiers are fish and the people water," as contrasted with the orthodox statement of the Confucian, Hsün Tzu (ca. 298–ca. 238 B.C.), that "the people are the water and the ruler is the boat; the water can support the boat but it can also sink it." Cf. John K. Fairbank, *The United States and China* (Harvard University Press, 1948), p. 205.

15. This thesis is developed with great skill, though sometimes to excess and with over ingenuity, by C. P. Fitzgerald in his *Revolution in China* (New York, 1952).

39

The Conception of Kingship in Ancient India

Louis Dumont

Comparative Significance of the Fact

The complex and characteristic relation between priesthood and kingship, Brahmanas and Kshatriyas, is fundamental in itself and in its implications, and a brief reflection will be useful for locating it in a comparative perspective. The fact has surprised

From Louis Dumont, "The Conception of Kingship in Ancient India," in Louis Dumont and D. Pocock, eds., *Contributions to Indian Sociology* (The Hague: Mouton; Paris: Ecole Pratique des Hautes Etudes; December 1962), VI, 53–56, 75–77.

modern authors, most of whom, without conceiving it clearly, have tried to explain it as the result of a hypothetical struggle between the two classes, and have interpreted in that sense certain legends to which we shall turn hereafter. They have written of a struggle for the first rank (Lassen), or for "the presidency, even spiritual" of the society (Dumézil), or, conversely, of a struggle for "practical power" (*Vedic Index*). They are not all of one mind; however, among the different tendencies, one is the persistent rationalist and "anticlerical" mentality according to which the priests are suspected of having "usurped" something (James Mill). If the idea that there has been a struggle between Brahmans and Kshatriyas at one or the other period of ancient Indian history is found in the works of indologists, it flourishes still more freely in secondhand considerations. This shows that we encounter here a deep-rooted inclination of western minds when confronted with the Indian institution, as for instance when the guarded pronouncements of Hopkins on the subject are interpreted by the sociologist O. C. Cox in a rigid and affirmative fashion.[1]

Let us take a different path and look at the relation between king and priest, not as a contingent trait for which a conjectural historical struggle might account, but as a necessary institution. The first obstacle we encounter lies in the way we conceive the hierarchy of a society. As we live in an egalitarian society, we tend to conceive of hierarchy as a scale of commanding powers—as in an army— rather than as a gradation of statuses. One may note *en passant* that the combination of the two aspects seems to have been anything but easy in a number of societies, for there are many instances of sovereigns whose eminent dignity was coupled with idleness. Precisely, the Indian case is one in which the two aspects are absolutely separated, and this apparently was the first reason of surprise. Further, the very word hierarchy, and its history, should recall that the gradation of status is rooted in religion: the first rank normally goes, not to power, but to religion, simply because religion represents, for those societies, what Hegel has called the Universal, i.e. absolute truth, in other words because hierarchy integrates the society in relation to its ultimate values.

This is borne out, I think, by the exceptional place of Indian society in a comparison bearing on kingship. In most of the societies in which kingship is found, it is a magico-religious as well as a political function. This is commonplace. In Ancient Egyptian or Sumerian kingship, or in the kingship of the Chinese empire for instance, the supreme religious functions were vested in the Sovereign; he was the Priest *par excellence* and those who were called the priests were only ritual specialists subordinate to him. Comparing this with the Indian situation, there seems to be a simple alternative: either the king exerts the religious functions which are generally his, and then he is the head of the hierarchy for this very reason, and exerts at the same time political power, or, this is the Indian case, the king depends on the priests for the religious functions, he cannot himself operate the sacrifice on behalf of the king-

dom, he cannot be his own sacrificer, instead he "puts in front" of himself a priest, the *purohita,* and then he looses the hierarchial preeminence in favour of the priests, retaining for himself power only.

This is, I think, the point which most modern philologists have failed to grasp, and for this they cannot be blamed, since modern anthropologists too have sometimes thought that the rank of the king depended more on his exercise of power than on his religious qualifications.

Through this dissociation, the function of the king in India has been *secularized*. It is from this point that a differentiation has occurred, the separation within the religious universe of a sphere or realm which is opposed to the religious, and roughly corresponds to what we call political. As opposed to the realm of values and norms it is the realm of force. As opposed to the *dharma* or universal order of the Brahman, it is the realm of interest or advantage, *artha*. We shall follow some developments in which the implications of this fundamental fact become apparent. All these can, in my view, be traced back to this initial step. In other words, they would have been impossible if the king had not from the beginning left the highest religious functions to the priest.

Incidentally, one might ask whether the king, while not having the first role in the brahmanical, the so to say official ritual, did not nevertheless retain something of the magico-religious aspects which universally adhere to his function and person. We shall see that the texts answer this question positively.

But to return to supposed evolutions or changes, we may say, speaking comparatively, that in India the king has lost his religious prerogatives. It is not impossible that this happened through a process which would have taken place in the vedic period. If the Brahmans may be said to have "usurped" anything, it would be that, and that only. On the contrary, from the time of the Brahmanas until our days, the stability of the formula shows that neither the Brahman nor the king has arrogated anything belonging to the other. It happened that certain Brahmans became kings, blending in their person, on first sight, the two functions. (But this is only an appearance, since in actual fact there is no reason to suppose that a Brahman king did not employ a Brahman priest to perform the sacrifice on his behalf. But in the matter of principle, the Brahmans as such have never claimed political power. Even in our days, they are content in essentials with guaranteeing spiritual merits to acts which are materially profitable to themselves and of which the *gift* is the prototype. To give to Brahmans is basically to exchange material goods against a spiritual good, merits. The gift embodies in its particular way the very relationship with which we are dealing.

Conclusion

I have tried to set in a global and comparative perspective some well-known data about the way kingship was conceived in ancient India. This led me to emphasize two main events or stages. The first event, which really sets the stage for Indian history, is the secularization of kingship laid down in the *brahman-ksatra* relationship. It invites us to revise some current notions about the relation between hierarchy and power. The second event, or stage, is more complex. It has appeared to us under two forms: on the one hand in the idea of contractual kingship, which appears to emanate from renouncers, on the other in the theory of *artha,* not unconnected with the renouncers' individualism and their negation of brahmanical values, but constituting a politico-economic domain. This domain is, in the dominant tradition, *relatively* autonomous with regard to absolute values. In so far as it is autonomous, there is at this stage a rough parallel with the modern western development, and this leads to a generalizing hypothesis, namely that such a domain as we know it necessarily emerges in opposition to and separation from the all-embracing domain of religion and ultimate values and that the basis of such a development is the recognition of the individual.[2]

Certainly, the similarities with the West are the more striking, when the wide differences in the context are kept in mind: difference in the point of departure as recalled above, difference in the genesis and situation of the individual, . . . difference also in the final result: in India the autonomy of the domain remains relative, and within it economics and politics remain undifferentiated. It would seem that, here as regarding religion, . . . the difference with the West lies less in the development itself, or its principle, than in the fact that, on the Indian side, the development took place *within* the given framework without altering it or emancipating itself from it. To stress the point, let me anticipate on another study and say that in the West, the political sphere, having become absolutely autonomous in relation to religion, has built itself up as an absolute: comparatively, the modern "nation" embodies its own absolute values. This is what did not happen in India. It could not happen, I suppose, as long as the politico-economic realm was only relatively autonomous, and this in turn could not be otherwise while the individual remained, in essence, outside the social world.

I shall not engage here on the wide question of Indian history, to which we hope to return in these pages, but only note a welcome paradox. Here, as when dealing with religion, while primarily concerned with permanent characteristics, I have been led to recognize an historical development, I mean a development which is not only chronological, but meaningful in the Indian set-up as compared with the Western. Furthermore, while far from assuming at the start that Indian history should be reducible to Western schemas, . . . I end by stating a parallelism. This is in strong contrast with the approach of some modern historians. They follow Marx but on one point: where—quite rightly from his point of view—he saw stagnation they want to find movement, even if only that of physical change instead of meaningful change. They appear to attempt to vindicate India's reality in Western terms. I think it is better to try and curb our terms to India's reality. The search for meaning delivers development; the search for changes does not deliver history.

Let me end by drawing attention to some of the limitations of this attempt and to their reasons. I have not considered factual happenings, as distinct from ideas, and as in the main the inscriptions can reveal them. But, apart from questions of fact, I have been impelled to leave out many aspects of the matter for a quite different reason, which may cause some surprise. It is because they show the need for a formulation of the Western phenomena themselves sociologically more satisfactory than that at present available, at least to my knowledge. At first sight, it would seem that our side of the picture is better known, and that all the effort has to be directed at the Indian side. But, if this is in a sense true, it is also a fact that our institutions and forms of thought have rarely been formulated in comparative terms. Actually, it is only because the Indian situation is, on some points, so clear-cut and logical that one is emboldened to put forward the beginning of a comparative view. But one is very soon made to acknowledge that, to proceed any further, one should begin with sweeping one's own doorsteps. The comparative task imposes itself, whether in considering religion we discuss the type of ultramundaneity and the place of monachism in Christianity; whether, here itself, we touch on the assumed struggle between "temporal" and "spiritual" agencies, or, to refer to a notion of which great use is being made at present, when we speak of feudalism (which should be analysed into clearly defined features).

The time has perhaps come when the mirror which anthropologists direct at other societies should be turned back by them on ourselves, when we should try to formulate our own institutions in comparative language, i.e. in a language modified by what we have learnt of different societies, however incomplete it still is. About the difficulty of the task there is no doubt. But this might well be the royal road for the advancement of sociological understanding.

NOTES

1. See mainly J. Muir, *Sanskrit Texts,* 2d ed., I, pp. 287 sq., and Keith and Macdonell, *Vedic Index,* II, pp. 249, 255–256; G. Dumézil, *Jupiter, Mars, Quirinus,* p. 43; E. W. Hopkins, "Ruling Caste," *Journ. Amer. Or. Soc.,* 13, 1889, pp. 57–376; O. C. Cox, *Caste, Class and Race,* New York, 1948, pp. 102 sq.; also C. Bouglé, *Régime des Castes,* p. 181.

2. The main point in this hypothesis is to formulate a relation between two domains or "systems" with which the anthropologist busies himself. One apparent difficulty, which has been cursorily mentioned here itself (p. 59) and in another context (*Contrib.* V, p. 37, § 3), should perhaps be more explicitly discussed here. It can be objected that the very word of polity (politics, political) comes to us from the Greek *polis,* and that, even if we lay aside its actual political constitutions, ancient Greece confronts us, in the thought of its philosophers, with a political domain which is neither opposed to religion as a system of ultimate values nor based on the individual. But precisely Greek speculation is markedly different from that of Machiavelli and Hobbes, it differs from it as political philosophy from political science; the one, essentially normative, starts from the society or state, the other, in principle at any rate empirical, starts from the individual. In philosophy as in religion, everything is governed by ultimate values, and this is why Plato's ideal state is a hierarchical society. In other terms, philosophy is, or at any rate begins, within the sphere of religion (or more precisely of ultimate values of the general type), the political domain as the moderns think of it is not yet there. At the same time, philosophy differs from religion in that ultimate values are not given from revelation, tradition or faith, but discovered or established by the sole use of human reason. (There is nothing new here regarding the relation between philosophy and religion, cf. Hegel, *Vorlesungen in die Geschichte der Philosophie,* ed. Michelet, Stuttgart, 1940 [*Sämtliche Werke,* Band 16], I, p. 92.) As reason argues in fact through particular men, the recourse to reason could not but lead to the recognition of the individual, as with the Stoics, and with the Moderns reason was to become the weapon of the individual.

It is not passing a value judgement on ancient philosophy, nor denying the part it played in the genesis of the individual in the West, to say that political philosophy, and that of the Greeks in particular, represents on the whole, between the two extremes I have been considering, an intermediary stage in so far as the yardstick it applies to society and state is not the individual but is derived from all-embracing ultimate values, as in the religious sphere. It might then be asked whether it is advisable to define the political sphere as narrowly as I have done. As this is the (dominant) modern conception of it, within which we live, and which the sociologist or anthropologist consciously or not carries with him, I think it is at any rate necessary to distinguish it, under one name or another, if confusion is to be avoided.

‖ d. THE SOCIAL AND POLITICAL STRUCTURE OF CENTRALIZED EMPIRES

40

Sung Roots of Chinese Political Conservatism: The Administrative Problems

James T. C. Liu

The Sung period (960–1279), as is generally recognized, shaped the pattern of China's develop-

From James T. C. Liu, "Sung Roots of Chinese Political Conservatism: The Administrative Problems," *Journal of Asian Studies,* XXVI, No. 3 (May 1967), 457–463. Copyright 1967 by the Association for Asian Studies, Inc. Reprinted by permission of the author and the publisher.

ment for the last millennium. Carrying forward the trends originating in late T'ang, it integrated both the traditional and the new ingredients into a distinctive way of life which gradually permeated the entire society down to the level of the average villager. The result was a broadly based, deeply rooted, stable, but conservative culture.[1] Remarkable economic advancement and social reconstruction took place. The same was generally true, though to a lesser extent, of political institutions and thought: the bureaucratic empire was now thoroughly centralized under a generally attentive and restrained absolutism; great gains were achieved in the number, quality, and especially the status of the nonaristocratic scholar-officials; the enriching variety of theoretical formulations known as neo-Confucianism carried increasing weight. Government administration in particular, the most effective ever to exist in China itself, was probably the best in the world then and for several centuries to come.[2] Improvements made by the Ming and the Ch'ing, after the intervening period of the Mongols, were more or less within this general pattern.

One should not, however, overstate the case. The forward momentum of the Sung period did not last too long. A great deal of energy was lost in political strife, in efforts to introduce perhaps ill-advised changes, in determined oppositions to these and other proposed alterations, and in ensuing vacillations, all of which were accompanied by demoralizing tendencies. After the disastrous invasion at the end of the Northern Sung, the political atmosphere was never quite the same. Confined to the Yangtze Valley and the areas below it, the Southern Sung succeeded in withstanding both external threats and internal strains with considerable stability; but it was a stability that suffered from a political standstill, even creeping deterioration. Not only did the administration and the various policies as a whole come to reflect a conservative outlook, but even the political critics, while full of complaints and lamentations, provided few constructive alternatives to the prevailing conditions. The trend of utilitarian thought, so dynamic in the Northern Sung, was carried on by only a minority of outstanding scholars, none of whom was ever in power.[3] Most scholar-officials realized, it seems, that numerous practical difficulties in running the government stemmed from deepseated diseases for which there could be no easy cure. For example, the various malpractices of the government clerks were common knowledge; yet only a handful of books ever took up the subject, though the Confucianists were assumed to have prepared themselves well for the profession of career bureaucrats.[4]

This critical decline from surging dynamism to lame conservatism is open to varying interpretations. There are, of course, a number of plausible explanations, such as certain basic socioeconomic injustices, the evils of absolutism, selfish interests of the ruling class, and other situations usually considered factors contributing to the well-known dynastic cycle. Valid as they may be, these reasons do not quite explain why, after the end of the Southern Sung, the new rulers of the succeeding dynasties took over much of the old administrative system without many significant changes. It is submitted here that the particular reason may be found in the specific area of the administration itself, often in the mundane aspects of daily routine, which were cumulatively of crucial consequence.

Administration, even in routine matters, always runs into operational problems, principally the task of selection among feasible alternatives. Given this frame of reference, we may for the sake of illustration briefly examine a few outstanding administrative problems during the Sung period.

1. The choice between government by law and government by moral influence, with the difficulties attendant on both. Most career bureaucrats of the Sung period, especially in Southern Sung, accepted the reality that "the state rules by law" (*fa-chih*),[5] though as Confucianists they would cling, at least theoretically, to the ideal of government by morality (*te-chih*) through the inducing effects of moral examples and persuasion. The resultant dualism was expressed in various ways. For instance, it was often said that "it is most desirable to govern according to the laws, except it would not be advisable to leave everything to the laws."[6] Another ambivalent formula maintained that the best government would "entrust good men to enforce the laws."[7] Even then, those laws that did not agree with the social reality or did not find ready acceptance among the population in general could not possibly be enforced effectively. It was pointed out, for example, that "decorations of inlaid emerald and gold embroidery have been repeatedly banned by imperial edicts . . . yet they are being openly displayed by the stores in market places."[8] Apparently the art of government was no easy task, whether one relied on the laws, or on moral influence, or both. Most Sung scholar-officials, it must be emphasized, were fairly realistic and not nearly so concerned with the theoretical conflict between the two different ways of government as one might gather from their formal writings and pronouncements. What troubled them basically was rather the frustration they encountered in either alternative. It was realized that moral influence "can make inroads among the people only gradually" and that "it would take a very long time before it could achieve the best order [of *t'ai-p'ing*]."[9] Was this process not in fact a treadmill? For it was also recognized that in the meantime the legal institutions would degenerate, "gradually waning and ebbing."[10]

In other words, before government by moral influence could possibly become effective, government by law would already have begun to break down.

2. The "Parkinsonian tendency" of the laws. The proliferation of the laws was inevitable, especially in Sung times, given the growing complexity of economic and social developments. Every now and then, the government found it necessary to bring the legal codes and the administrative regulations up to date by issuing revised editions. Each revision would run into dozens of chapters (*chüan*), but no matter how exhaustive their provisions became, they could not readily cover all cases. In the year 1103, for example, the Department of Finance dealt with about 51,000 cases, each involving some aspects of criminal offense. While a number of cases were presumably of a routine nature, the rest would require or depend upon an interpretation of the relevant laws.[11]

There was another trouble with the laws. From time to time, exceptions were made and exceptions once made automatically became precedents. And precedents would invariably be cited by analogy, similarity, or comparability, from one standpoint or another. As this snowballing process went on, it was said that "the laws are being broken [to pieces] by resorting to the precedents" and therefore "the Department of Personnel (*li*) has been nicknamed the department of precedents (*li*)."[12] To make matters worse, many offices "could no longer ascertain what had been in their old records and files," which had become a jungle of papers.[13] The burden of paper work was such that the bureaucrats in charge of these offices would "merely sign endless documents without having the time to give them proper perusal or consideration."[14] Under these circumstances, they found an easy way out by "listening to the clerks" who were familiar with the laws, the exceptions, the precedents, and some other ways of circumventing the legal provisions. The saying was that "it is a world [in the hands] of the clerical staff" in which "the officials are not feudalistic (*feng-chien*), but the clerks are," in the sense that their entrenchment was permanent by virtue of their local origin, practically a life tenure of their position, and in many cases the hereditary occupation of the family.[15] In spite of all its pronounced defects, the Sung administration with its heavy reliance upon law interlaced with some moral persuasion remained better than any other then conceivable alternative. In any event, it limped along as best it could be expected to.

3. The dilemma between attempting reforms and following the established ways. Improvements were much easier discussed than made. As early as 1001, a councilor observed that "unless there are ten advantages, do not change the laws." "Is it worth the trouble of making changes," he asked, "only to discover that they would be subject to many abuses?"[16] Without discussing the minor reform of 1043–1044 and the major reform under Wang An-shih a quarter of a century later, let it suffice to mention a common complaint on both occasions, that "the changes that were intended to erase malpractices became on the contrary malpractices themselves."[17] The Southern Sung, having learned this lesson, decided to remain cautious and conservative. Kao-tsung, its first emperor, repeated the statement quoted above with additional emphasis: "Unless there are a hundred advantages, do not change the laws."[18] He found "the laws set up by the founding fathers to be quite adequate" and denounced "the careless changing of the established ways . . . for causing a great deal of chaos and vacillations."[19] Nonetheless the laws he followed included a number of changes that had previously been put into effect by Wang An-shih, and were now an integral part of the accepted system. In other words, changes that had been established were now routine; only further changes were to be discouraged.

Beginning in the middle part of the Northern Sung and more so in the Southern Sung, conservatism also justified itself or found a convenient rationalization in the concept of gradual approach [to improvement or perfection] (*hsün-chih*) whereby with gradual improvements in implementation the established ways would be sufficient to produce a good order over a long period of time. However, Yeh Shih, a leading Southern Sung scholar much respected for his institutional analysis and utilitarianism, made the penetrating criticism that the trouble with the gradual approach is that "in the end it does not reach the assumed goals at all."[20] As a matter of fact, a number of officials long before Yeh Shih had admitted quite frankly that the gradual approach in theory was none other than the conservative approach in practice. It merely aimed at "keeping things quiet and under control and otherwise getting rid of only those defects which happen to be excessively bad," without really entertaining the illusion of ever reaching a good order.[21]

4. The search for the best possible examination standards. This issue was of great concern to all Confucian scholars, since the renowned Sung civil service examination system was the major avenue to the officialdom. Originally, the Confucian philosophy placed its emphasis not so much upon literary skills as moral conduct. Yet a brief attempt by Ts'ai Ching in late Northern Sung to have the local government recommend candidates according to eight

specific categories of exemplary behavior degenerated into a miserable failure of abusive favoritism. The written examinations, being impersonal and objective, remained far more satisfactory. Yet, what were their standards? Without going into the details here, it may be said that there were several shifts of emphasis during the Northern Sung. At the beginning, the stress was upon the memorization of the ancient classics and their official commentaries as well as upon the composition of poems and poetic-prose in the parallel style. By mid-eleventh century, emphasis shifted to prose in the ancient style which permitted far greater freedom of expression, with value placed upon the discussion of statecraft problems. Under the reformer Wang An-shih, the examination standards favored the interpretations of the classics and the application of their principles to statecraft. These successive changes did not have the intended result of producing many more useful opinions for better government, nor necessarily a larger number of superior administrators than before. On the contrary, one major ill effect was the excessive amount of divergent opinions, which further intensified existing factional controversies.[22] In any event, such prose also came to be written, like poetry and poetic-prose, "by resorting to trite patterns . . . without necessarily having real skill."[23] The Southern Sung finally reverted to the original emphasis upon poetry and poetic-prose, in part because the candidates from the lower reaches of the Yangtze River excelled in these elegant genres and in part because such compositions were capable of demonstrating a thorough mastery of their rigorous rules as well as an artful creativity in spite of them. They might be said to have been a kind of proficiency and intelligence test.

At the root of the problem, as Su Shih (Su Tung-p'o) had pointed out, was the lack of either ideal examination standards or a sure way of identifying useful talents. After all, no matter what the standards happened to be, the candidates would simply do their best to conform. And whatever was written on paper, no matter how well it read, had little bearing upon administrative ability which could be proven only in deeds, not in the words of the candidates who had as yet no experience in administration whatsoever. When the problem of the examination standards was again brought up later during the Southern Sung, the responsible officials reported to the court that "since the system has been in use for such a long time, it is difficult [even] to discuss how to change it."[24] One comment openly admitted the fact that, as no feasible alternative

seemed to have worked, it proved that "nothing can be done about it."[25]

5. The difficulty of civil service evaluation. The civil service system established in the early years of the Sung was a great improvement over the lack of careful regulations in the preceding period of the Five Dynasties. T'ai-tsu, the founding emperor, proudly asserted: "I am sending more than a hundred scholarly officials with administrative skill to take over the various regional government offices. Even if all of them should turn out to be corrupt, their corruption would hardly be as bad as that of a single corrupt military man."[26] When Jen-tsung, the fourth emperor, wondered why there was a higher percentage of corruption cases among the non-scholarly officials who came up through the ranks than among those who were degree-holders, Wang Tseng reminded him that "the scholarly officials had been educated to value their integrity and honor."[27] In short, Confucian education definitely helped the quality of government. Nonetheless, administrative talent was a different matter. Wang Tan, an exemplary councilor in early Northern Sung, had no illusion that an honest Confucianist would necessarily be a capable official. "If among the ten men selected," he said, "two or three prove to be capable, that is already plentiful."[28] Later estimates were more confident and one of them put the optimum as high as fifty per cent.[29] Apparently, the recruitment of the Sung civil service was satisfactory enough. However, once administrators had been recruited through the examination system, there arose the problem of continuing evaluation. Mere seniority was obviously an inadequate criterion. Recommendations and sponsorship by superiors proved sometimes satisfactory but was often open to the charge of favoritism. The system of rating the performance at the post tended to degenerate into a formality, as many officials chose to overlook each other's faults; it was a common saying that "the officials are mutually protective" (*kuan kuan hsiang hu*). Hsiao-tsung, the second emperor of the Southern Sung, emphasized this: "These evaluations required by the regulations would soon after their initial implementation relapse into mere formalities on paper." On another occasion, he observed that "repeating previous orders and calling for strict enforcement of the regulations are of no use." The urgent problem was, in his opinion, to find ways of identifying genuine ability other than the routine of annual evaluation.[30] But neither he nor any one else could come up with a solution that would serve the purpose without producing such troubles as favoritism, factionalism, in-

gratiating, cheating, slanderous attacks, and other similar abuses.

It is hoped that these five illustrations demonstrate the need to study such administrative problems. Nor is the value of such studies confined to the Sung period. For example, if we skip the relatively short period of the Yüan, what was the condition in the Ming and the Ch'ing? As compared with the Sung, they were far greater in area, more populous and prosperous, with many fine accomplishments of the Chinese civilization reaching what was probably their utmost limit. But how did the Ming and the Ch'ing fare administratively? Did they solve the numerous administrative problems that had baffled the Sung scholar-officials? It would appear that, in broad terms, there are two seemingly contradictory but actually concomitant aspects for consideration: one, that the later empires did make considerable headway in solving some administrative problems, in reducing the degree of difficulties in others, and in keeping all of them under relatively more effective control; second, such progress was after all rather limited; yet it took China many centuries to achieve even that, let alone any major breakthrough in the administrative system. One might perhaps combine these two points to advance the hypothesis that while the Ming and the Ch'ing were more advanced than the Sung, they did not go beyond the limits of the neo-traditional pattern previously set by the Sung; that they produced many splendors but only on top of a basic stagnation; that their great cultural enrichment paradoxically reinforced conservatism; and that in effect these accomplishments made the neo-traditional pattern all the more inflexible save in a total breakdown.

In appealing for more studies of these administrative problems, the suggested approach is of course quite different from the manner of traditional scholarship dealing with the formal system of the bureaucratic posts, known as the study of *kuan-chih*. In fact, we should seek to go beyond the type of scholarship which treats the administration with some descriptions and analyses but merely as a part of the general political system. Would it not be fruitful to use a problem-oriented approach, asking such questions as what administrative problems were encountered? What solutions were proposed and which ones were tried? And what were the feed-back effects upon the administrative system itself? In short, in taking China as a leading example of the historical bureaucratic empires, we need to know more about how its administrative system worked through the sequence of problems, solutions, and net results. This knowledge will help us explain why it had numerous changes but did not escape a basic stagnation.

NOTES

NOTE. Some keys to often-cited sources:

HCP —Li T'ao, *Hsü Tzu-chih-t'ung-chien ch'ang pien* (reprint)
HNYL—Li Hsin-chuan, *Chien-yen i-lai hsi-nien yao-lu* (KHEPTS)
SHY —*Sung hui-yao chi-kao* (Shanghai, 1936); or reprint)
WHTK—Ma Tuan-lin, *Wen-hsien t'ung-k'ai* (WYWK ed.)

1. James T. C. Liu, "Note on the Neo-Traditional Period (ca. 800–1900) in Chinese History," *JAS*, 24:1 (Nov. 1964), 105–107; cf. John Meskill, *The Pattern of Chinese History* (Boston, 1965).
2. Among several contributions by Professor E. A. Kracke, Jr., see his latest, "The Chinese and the Art of government," in *The Legacy of China*, ed. Raymond Dawson (Oxford, 1964), pp. 309–339.
3. Professor Hsiao Kung-ch'üan in his best standard work on Chinese political thought, being translated by my colleague Frederick W. Mote, *Chung-kuo cheng-chih ssu-hsiang-shih* (Shanghai, 1946), 2:143–167, has probably overstated the case of the utilitarian trend during the Sung, as little is mentioned about its decline.
4. See various works by Miyazaki Ichisada and Sudō Yoshiyuki, among other authors. A forthcoming article of mine will deal with the Sung views on the control of the clerks, principally the ones in the central government.
5. Yeh Shih, *Yeh Shih chi* (Peking, 1961), 3:806–807.
6. WHTK, 32:301; see also Chu Hsi, *Chin-ssu lu* (Taipei, 1957 ed.), 9:248–250.
7. Same as note 5.
8. HNYL, 128:6.
9. Ou-yang Hsiu, *Ou-yang Yung-shu chi* (TSCC ed.) 8:17.
10. HCP, 53:6; see also Lo Ts'ung-yen, *Lo Yü-chang chi* (*Cheng-i-t'ang chüan-shu*), 5:7–8 and Wang Fu-chih, *Sung lun* (SPPY ed.), 4:4.
11. SHY: *chih-kuan*, 59:12.
12. *WHTK*, 38:365.
13. *SHY, chih-kuan*, 4:45–51.
14. *Ibid.*, 8:34–35.
15. Yeh Shih, *Shui-hsin chi* (SPPY ed.), 3:15.
16. HCP, 48:5.
17. WHTK, 38:360.
18. HNYL, 122:5.
19. *Ibid.*, 174:2.
20. Yeh Shih, *Shui-hsin chi*, 5:3.
21. HNYL, 174:20; see also 200:23 as well as HCP 77:11.
22. Wang Fu-chih, *Sung lun*, 4:21–24.
23. WHTK, 31:293; see also 32:302.
24. HNYL, 189:9.
25. WHTK, 32:301; see also Wang Feng-yüan, *Kwang-ling Hsien-sheng chi* (Chia-hsing ed.), 14:2.
26. HCP, 1:4–15; also found in *T'ai-p'ing chih-chi t'ung-lei*, (*Shih-yüan ts'ung-shu*), 2:13.
27. HCP, 104:1.
28. HCP, 84:18.
29. HCP, 82:13 and *Chung-hsing liang ch'ao sheng cheng* (*Wan wei pieh ts'ang ed.*), 55:17–18.
30. *Chung-hsing liang h'ai sheng cheng*, 15:9 and 22:15.

41

The Aristocracy in Byzantium in the Thirteenth Century

Peter Charanis

From the very beginning the large estate had been a feature of Byzantine society. The complicated and burdensome fiscal administration effected by the reorganization of the Empire following the political and economic crisis of the third century worked in such a way as to give impetus to the growth of the large estates. The society revealed by the papyri and the great legislative monuments of the fifth and the sixth centuries is a society dominated by these estates. *Coloni,* reduced into serfs, composed the vast majority of the agrarian population, although the free peasant proprietors did not disappear completely.

The situation changed in the seventh century. The military reorganization of the Empire, more especially the establishment of a system of military estates, designed to check the advance of the Saracens and the incursion of the barbarians, was chiefly responsible for this change. These military estates, small in size and granted to soldiers in return for military service, became the opening wedge in the formation of a new class of small peasant proprietors. The soldiers themselves constituted the nucleus of this class, but others gradually were added. For while the eldest son of a soldier inherited his father's plot together with the obligation of military service, the rest of the family were free to reclaim and cultivate the land that was vacant.[1]

The new peasantry thus developed was not only numerous, but also seems to have been the dominant element of Byzantine agrarian society during the eighth and ninth centuries. In the course of the ninth and tenth centuries, however, the landed aristocracy forged forward and began to extend its holdings at

an alarming rate.[2] In the tenth century a serious attempt was made to check the growth of the large estates, but the various laws enacted by the socially minded emperors of that century ended in failure.[3] These laws with one exception, that of the law of the *allelengyon,* which had been issued by Basil II, were never repealed, but neither were they enforced. Basil II was the last emperor who seriously tried to check the growth of the large estates. With his death all checks to this growth ceased to operate. It is true that during the eleventh century the struggle between the central government and the provincial aristocracy still raged, but it had lost its social aspect and it became wholly political in nature. The aim of the central government was no longer to prevent the growth of the large estates because they threatened to absorb all the landed property of the Empire and thus to eliminate completely the small peasant proprietors, but to remove the military from the key positions in the administration.[4] It was a struggle for the demilitarization of the political life of the Empire. The attempt was made to replace the aristocracy which had been nurtured in the great military tradition of the Empire by a new body of functionaries trained in law and in philosophy. The profession of the soldier, which in the great days of Byzantium carried with it prestige, honor, and position, was made to have no longer any value, and so, as Scylitzes puts it, "the soldiers put aside their arms and became lawyers or jurists."[5]

But this effort against the aristocracy as a military class was no more successful than had been the efforts of the emperors of the tenth century against the same aristocracy as a landed class. In both cases it was the aristocracy which finally triumphed. The accession of Alexius Comnenus to the throne in 1081 usually is considered as marking the final and complete ascendency of the landed aristocracy in the political, economic, and social life of the Empire. The provincial aristocracy became henceforth the

From Peter Charanis, "The Aristocracy in Byzantium in the Thirteenth Century," in P. R. Coleman-Norton, ed., *Studies in Roman Economic and Social History in Honor of A. C. Johnson* (Princeton: Princeton University Press, 1951), pp. 336–341, 345–346, 349–355. Reprinted by permission of Princeton University Press. Copyright 1951 by Princeton University Press.

prop of the political system of the Empire.[6] Alexius was anxious to create a coterie of friends, with the members of his family as the nucleus, upon whom he could rely and to whom he could entrust the administration and defense of the Empire. The result was that throughout the twelfth century the central government came to depend more and more upon those who enjoyed wealth and privileges. These were the *archontes* who after the catastrophe of 1204 sought to organize resistance against the conquerors in Asia Minor, Thrace, Epirus, and the Peloponnesus.

The political revolution which the Fourth Crusade induced did not affect radically the social structure of the lands, which had formerly belonged to the Byzantine Empire. When they took over the Empire, the Latins found its social structure substantially not very different, at least in its outer forms, from their society in the west and they were content to let it stay as it was, satisfied with the taxes and *corvées* exacted from the peasants. The state property was confiscated and many of the Greek magnates were dispossessed, but many also were not disturbed. This was particularly true of the Morea and of the lands which came under the domination of the Venetians. In 1207 the island of Corfu was granted by Venice to Angelo Acotonto and Petro Michaeli and in the agreement it was stipulated that the status of everyone in the island should remain the same and that no one should be required to pay more than he used to pay at the time of the Greek emperors.[7] A similar stipulation was included in the treaties which Venice concluded with Ravano dalle Carceri and his successors in 1211 and 1216 respectively concerning the island of Negropont (Euboea).[8] In the Morea also a general understanding between the French and the Greek magnates was reached, providing for the retention of most of their possessions by the latter.[9] It is not improbable also, although it is nowhere mentioned by the sources, that the agreement which the inhabitants of the Thracian cities finally reached with the Latins of Constantinople, whereby they submitted to them, included a clause which safeguarded their property.[10] For it is doubtful if they would have submitted otherwise, especially since they stipulated—and this stipulation was accepted by the Latins—that the Greek, Theodore Branas, should be placed over them as their governor. Thus the political upheaval of 1204 did not radically affect the social and economic system. Many of the Greek magnates were left untouched, provided they swore allegiance to the new masters. Nor were the peasants affected radically by the political changes. Their position remained the same and they continued to be

subject to the same charges as before. Still less were the changes in those lands which were retained by the Greeks. The aristocracy remained, as before, the strongest prop of the political and social system. Theodore Lascaris was raised to the throne of Nicaea by the military, civil and ecclesiastical dignitaries; and throughout the period of the Empire of Nicaea the aristocracy was strengthened rather than weakened. This was achieved by a liberal distribution of revenue-producing grants, usually but not always land, known as *pronoeae* or *oeconomeae*.

The *pronoea* was a development of the eleventh century and its wide use is connected with the period of the Comneni.[11] It was the principal means which they adopted to recuperate much of the deserted land, to reconstitute the class of soldiers with landed interests, to reward many of their partisans. A *pronoea* was granted to an individual for a specific period of years, usually his lifetime, in return for services rendered or to be rendered. It was never hereditary, unless it was specifically declared so by a special measure.

The distribution of *pronoeae* was one of the foundation stones of the political and military system of the Empire in the thirteenth century. Some of the grants were very extensive, others less so, but the general effect of all was to increase the power and influence of the aristocracy and to lessen the hold of the central government over the agrarian population. For the holders of *pronoeae* exercised over the population important financial and judicial powers which were granted to them along with the land.[12] The documentary evidence of the thirteenth century makes it possible to some extent to identify some of the holders of *pronoeae* and to determine their privileges, powers, and influence. . . .

To this limited list of important personages holding *pronoeae* or possessing large estates of their own in Asia Minor others may be added. Some of these were military officers; the status of others is not known, but there is no doubt that they belonged to the aristocracy; still others were civil functionaries. Among the officers may be mentioned George Petritzes, who bore the title of *sebastos;* George Manteanos, characterized in the sources as most glorious (μεγαλοδοξότατος); Nicephorus Pharissaeos, who is described as most manly (ἀνδρικώτατος).[13] Among the others were Manuel Ducas,[14] the *vestiarites* Rabdokanakis,[15] Theodore Branas, called most noble (πανευγενέστατος),[16] Michael Comnenus Branas, a relative of the emperor.[17] The large estates, indeed, were particularly numerous in the region of Smyrna. They were to be found on every side of the properties of the monastery of Lembo, whose monks repeatedly complained that their owners violated the rights of the monastery.[18] But the situation was doubtless the same everywhere in Asia Minor. Lack of documentary evidence, however, makes it impossible to know conditions precisely and in detail.

In the European possessions of the Empire the situation was not different. There too the large estates, whether acquired by imperial grants or by other means, predominated. . . .

What was true of Thessaly with respect to the aristocracy was also true of Macedonia and Thrace. There were located the vast estates of the powerful Byzantine families, whose members dominated the political life of the Empire—the Angeli, the Cantacuzeni, the Tzamblaci, the Synadeni, and others. Their great holdings, the existence of which is well attested by the sources of the fourteenth century, were doubtless already in their possession in the thirteenth century. The Tzamblaci, who in the fourteenth century possessed vast domains in the region of Christopolis and Serres and Thessalonica, were in the service of Michael Palaeologus and doubtless were included among those who were rewarded by that emperor.[19] This is also true of the Angeli. It is known from a document dated 1306 that Manuel Angelus, described as a relative of the emperor, possessed a number of villages in the neighborhood of Serres and Thessalonica. These villages had already belonged to his father, having been granted to him by an imperial chrysobull.[20] Similar grants had been awarded to Demetrius Spartanus, who bore the title of *pansebastos sebastos*. Demetrius Spartanus must be the Spartanus who figured among the conspirators who in 1246 paved the way for the occupation of Thessalonica by John Vatatzes.[21] In a document, dated 1265 and signed by the sons of Spartanus, the latter stated that the village of Lozikion had been granted to their father by an imperial chrysobull. The emperor who made this grant was doubtless John Vatatzes. The grant had been inherited by the sons of Spartanus, for in 1265 Demetrius Spartanus was dead while his sons considered themselve masters of this property.[22] The possessions of the Cantacuzeni in Thrace were fabulous and those of the Synadeni were considerable. Both the Cantacuzeni and the Synadeni were in the service of the Lascarids and the Palaeologi and they were doubtless amply rewarded. The Synadeni are known to have possessed important properties in the region of Serres, which had been granted to them by an imperial chrysobull, and the vast wealth of John Cantacuzenus had already been in the possession of the family by the end of the thirteenth century.[23]

Thus in every region of the Empire the landed possessions of the aristocracy predominated. These possessions had been accumulated by inheritance and purchase and imperial grants. Their holders dominated the political life of the Empire. Like the Comneni and the Angeli before them, the Lascarids, with the possible exception of Theodore II Lascaris, based the foundation of the central government upon the support of the aristocracy. They themselves had belonged to the aristocracy and their rise to power they owed to that class. The Nicene Empire was indeed the creation of the Greek lay and ecclesiastical magnates of Asia Minor and those of Thrace who had fled to Nicaea.[24] From the literary sources it is known that among the aristocratic families which throughout the thirteenth century dominated the Empire were included the Palaeologi, the Vatatzae, the Nostongi, the Tarchaneiotae, the Philanthropeni, the Caballarii, the Kamytzae, the Rauli, the Cantacuzeni, the Angeli, the Apreni, the family of Theodore Philes and others. From the same sources it is also known that to these families the Lascarids distributed important titles and high positions. The official documents of the thirteenth century, such as imperial chrysobulls and orders, and various monastic acts reveal further that the same families were the beneficiaries of important land grants. By means of these documents it has been possible to show that to many of these families, as, for instance, the Nostongi, the Angeli, the Apreni, the Tarchaneiotae, the Rauli, the family of Theodore Philes and others, were made important land grants in Asia Minor, in Macedonia, in Thrace. However, the grants of land and privileges which the Lascarids made to these and other families were, with rare exceptions, temporary, perhaps for the duration of the holder's life, and could not be transmitted from father to son. This policy was changed by Michael Palaeologus.

Michael Palaeologus, as already has been stated, had come to the throne by way of usurpation and murder. But it would have been difficult, if not impossible, to achieve this end without the support of the powerful families of the aristocracy. It so happened that the situation from that point of view was very favorable, for the aristocracy was discontented with the political arrangement which Theodore II Lascaris had made just before his death. Theodore II Lascaris had never trusted the aristocracy. Soon after he came to power he removed from office the nobles who during the reign of John Vatatzes occupied the most important positions. Included among these were Alexius Strategopoulus and his son, Constantine Tornikes, Theodore Philes, the Rauli, Nicephorus Alyates, and others. The son of

Strategopoulus, Theodore Philes and the Rauli were blinded, while the son of Tornikes was executed and the tongue of Alyates was cut off.[25] But what caused greater discontent was the appointment of the Muzalon brothers, men of obscure origin, who "were not worth three cents," according to Acropolites, to the most important offices of the government.[26] This discontent increased still more when it was learned that just before his death Theodore II had designated George Muzalon regent and supreme ruler of the Empire until his son, who was then eight years old, came of age. It was this discontent which Michael Palaeologus exploited in order to rise to power. But he had to make important concessions which included among other things the enlargement of the land grants (*pronoeae*) held by the aristocracy and the military. What was more significant for the future than the enlargement of these grants, however, was the fact that these were made hereditary.[27] Land grants in absolute ownership were not unknown in Byzantium, but they were not very frequent.[28] Michael Palaeologus made them *en masse* and his policy accelerated the process of feudalization which had begun in the eleventh century. Henceforth the nobility was not content with grants for a definite period. It asked and almost always obtained that they be made hereditary.[29]

Grants made to the aristocracy sometimes included whole regions. In such cases the grant consisted not of the land itself, unless that land belonged to the state, but of the public revenues obtained from the regions granted. In a region thus granted the status of the private land located in it did not change. Whoever owned it continued to own it as before, but he now paid his taxes for it not to the imperial treasury but to the grantee. The classical example of such a grant is the one which Alexius I made to his brother Adrian. The grant consisted of the entire peninsula of Cassandra and included all the public land located in that peninsula and all the public revenues obtained from the land which was privately owned.[30] Another such grant was also made by Michael Palaeologus. It was made to his brother John and consisted of the islands of Rhodes and Mitylene and of extensive territories located on the continent.[31] Such also must have been the grant which was held by Syrgares under the Lascarids, for it is known that peasants who lived in the villages granted to him were proprietors of their land and paid their taxes to him. Grants of this sort were, of course, potentially dangerous to the power of the central government and for that reason they were made infrequently and usually only to members of the imperial family. But they could still be danger-

ous. Michael Palaeologus revoked the grant which he had made to his brother, John, because he came to fear that John, whose power and influence and wealth were increased by this grant, might become a rival of Adronius, Michael's son, for the throne.[32] In the fourteenth century grants of this sort were not only more frequently bestowed, but in some instances they were made hereditary. It is known, for example, that in 1356 John V granted Christopolis, Anactaropolis and the island of Thaso κατὰ λόγον γονικότητος, i.e., the grantees were made absolute masters with the right of transmitting their grant to their heirs.[33] The making of such grants marks the final step in the feudalization of the Empire.

Throughout the reign of Michael Palaeologus the aristocracy was, more than ever before, the dominant element of the society of Byzantium. Its members had wealth, position, influence, power. Michael Palaeologus made every effort to identify their interests with those of his house. Hence the almost boundless liberality which he showed toward them. He was especially liberal with the distribution of titles. Pachymeres mentions the most important personages to whom titles were granted, but he adds that many others were also honored. Michael raised his brother John to the dignity of *despot*, his other brother Constantine to that of *caesar*. Constantine Tornikes, the father-in-law of John, Michael's brother, was named *sebastocrator*; Alexius Strategopoulus, *caesar*; John Raul, *protovestarios*; Alexius Philes, *megas domesticos*; Alexius Philanthropenus, *protostrator*; a certain Angelus, the brother of Michael's mother-in-law, *megas primicerios*; Michael Nostongus, *protosebastos*; Michael Palaeologus, a nephew of the emperor, *mysticos*.[34] But he did more than distribute titles. He sought to bind the great families to his house by a series of marital alliances. He himself was married to a member of the Vatatzes family, Theodora, granddaughter of Isaac Ducas, the brother of the emperor John Vatatzes.[35] His brother John was married to the daughter of Constantine Tornikes;[36] his other brother, Constantine, had taken his wife from the Branas family;[37] his sister Eulogia was married to a Cantacuzenus;[38] the husband of his other sister, Maria, was Nicephorus Tarchaneiotes.[39] These alliances were further extended by the marriages of Michael's nieces which Michael himself arranged. Eulogia's daughters, Theodora and Maria, he gave to John Raul and Alexius Philes respectively,[40] while Theodora, the daughter of his other sister, Maria, was given to Balaneidiotes, who was raised to the position of *megas stratopedarches*.[41] Maria's son, Michael, was married to the daughter of Alexius Philanthropenus.[42] In the discussion connected with the large land estates it was found that the Cantacuzeni, the Angeli, the Nostongi, the Rauli, the Tarchaneiotae, the family of Theodore Philes, the Branae and others were the great landed proprietors of the Empire. These are precisely the families which Michael Palaeologus sought to attach to his house by favors and marital alliances. One may say that never before was the Byzantine Empire dominated and ruled by a number of great families, families which were related to each other and to the ruling dynasty.

NOTES

1. P. Charanis, "On the Social Structure of the Later Roman Empire" in *Byzantion*, XVII (1946), pp. 41ff.; G. Ostrogorsky, "Agrarian Conditions in the Byzantine Empire in the Middle Ages" in *The Cambridge Economic History* (Cambridge, 1941), 1, pp. 196ff.

2. A measure which promoted the growth of large estates was the law issued by Leo VI (886–911), which made it virtually legal for provincial functionaries, except the governors, to acquire property either by purchase or gift while in office. P. Noailles and A. Dain, *Les novelles de Léon VI le sage* (Paris, 1944), p. 283.

3. V. Vasilievsky, "Materialy k vnutrennej istorii vizantijskago gosudarstva" in *Zurnal Ministerstva Narodnago Prosvieshcheniia*, CCII (1879), pp. 160–230; G. Testaud, *Des rapports des puissants et des petits propriétaires ruraux dans l'empire byzantine au Xe siècle* (Bordeaux, 1898); F. Dölger, "Die Frage des Grundeigentums in Byzanz" in *Bulletin of the International Committee of Historical Sciences*, v (1933), pp. 5ff.; A. Andreades, "Floraison et décadence de la petite propriété dans l'empire byzantine" in *Mélanges offerts à Ernest Mahaim* (Paris, 1935), i, pp. 261–266.

4. Charanis, *op. cit.*, pp. 58ff. On the position of the Empire in the eleventh century the two fundamental books are: (1) C. Neumann, *Die Weltstellung des byzantinischen Reiches vor den Kreuzzügen* (Leipzig, 1894) [French translation (Paris, 1905)]; (2) N. Skabalanovich, *Vizantiiskoe gosudarstvo i tserkov v XI viêkiê* (St. Petersburg, 1884).

5. Cedrenus-Scylitzes, *Hist. Comp.* (Bonn, 1839), II, p. 652.

6. G. Ostrogorsky, *Geschichte des byzantinischen Staates* (München, 1940), pp. 258ff. But see also G. Rouillard, "Notes et discussions: À propos d'un ouvrage récent sur l'historie de l'état byzantin" in RP, XVI (1942), pp. 119ff.; Charanis, "The Monastic Properties and the State in the Byzantine Empire" in *Dumbarton Oaks Papers*, IV (1948), pp. 69ff.

7. G. L. F. Tafel and G. M. Thomas, *Urkunden zur älteren Handels- und Staatsgeschichte der Republik Venedig* (Wein, 1856), II, p. 57: *Quos omnes et alios in ipsis insulis consistentes debemus in suo statu tenere, nichil ab aliquo exigentes, quam quod facere consueuerant temporibus Grecorum Imperatorum.*

8. *Ibid.*, II, pp. 95, 183. *Grecos autem tenebo in eo statu, quo domini Emanuelis Imperatoris tempore tenebantur. Faciam etiam, quod omnes, qui per me sunt in insula et erunt in antea, et Latini et omnes magnates Greci, uobis iurent fidelitatem.*

9. *The Chronicle of Morea*, ed. J. Schmitt (London, 1904), p. 112, ll. 1641–1650.

10. Geoffroi de Villehardouin, *La conquête de Constantinople*, ed. N. de Wailly (Paris, 1872), p. 253; Nicetas Choniates, *Historia* (Bonn, 1835), p. 830.

11. The two fundamental works on the Byzantine *pronoea* are: (1) P. Mutafčiev, "Vojniski zemi i vojnici v Vizantija prez XIII/XIV v" in *Spisanije na Bulgarskata Akademija*,

XXVII (1923) [in Bulgarian], pp. 37ff.; (2) T. Uspenskij, "Značenie vizantijskoj južnoslavjanskoj pronii" in *Sbornik V.J. Lamanskomu* (St. Petersburg, 1883), pp. 1–32. See also A. A. Vasiliev, "On the Question of the Byzantine Feudalism" in *Byzantion*, VIII (1933), pp. 590f.; Ostrogorsky, *Geschichte des byzantinischen Staates*, pp. 262f., 344f.; C. Diehl *et al.*, *L'Europe Orientale de 1081 à 1453* [*Histoire du moyen age*, IX.1], (Paris, 1945), pp. 30, 80.

12. Lawsuits involving property disputes among the inhabitants of a *pronoea* were judged by the *pronoetes* with the help of the κρείττονες, i.e., the more distinguished elements of the *pronoea*. F. Miklosich and J. Müller, *Acta et Diplomata Graeca* (Wien, 1871), IV, p. 81. Lawsuits involving a *pronoetes* or the *paroikoi* of a *pronoetes* with another party not included in the *pronoea* were judged by the military governor of the region. *Ibid.*, IV, pp. 239f., 36ff., 419.

13. *Ibid.*, IV, p. 128; George Petritzes as *sebastos*, *ibid.*, IV, p. 159. The family of Petritzes was rather important in the region of Smyrna. Cf. *ibid.*, IV, pp. 92, 95, 130, 161.

14. *Ibid.*, IV, p. 141.

15. *Ibid.*, IV, p. 199.

16. *Ibid.*, IV, pp. 122, 178.

17. *Ibid.*, IV, pp. 178, 273.

18. *Ibid.*, IV, p. 256.

19. Pachymeres, *Histozia* (Bonn, 1835), I, p. 319. On the Tzamblaci see N. Bănescu, "Peut-on identifier le Zamblacus des documents ragusains?" in *Mélanges Charles Diehl* (Paris, 1930), I, pp. 31–35.

20. *Actes de l'Athos: V. Actes de Chilander*, ed. R. P. Louis Petit, Appendix, in *Vizantiiskij Vremennik*, XVII (1910), p. 50.

21. Acropolites, *Opera*, ed. A. Heisenberg (Leipzig, 1903), I, pp. 79f.

22. *Actes de l'Athos: V. Actes de Chilander*, p. 15.

23. *Ibid.*, pp. 17, 123ff., 259.

24. Acropolites, *op. cit.*, I, p. 11.

25. *Ibid.*, I, pp. 154f.

26. *Ibid.*, I, p. 124.

27. Pachymeres, *op. cit.*, I, pp. 97f.; cf. also p. 92. *The Chronicle of Morea*, p. 84, ll. 1240–1241, about the distribution of *pronoeae* by Michael VIII Palaeologus.

28. Rouillard, *op. cit.*, p. 177.

29. Most of such requests are of the fourteenth century. See, for instance, Miklosich and Müller, *op. cit.*, v, pp. 89–90, 107.

30. The chrysobull whence this information is derived was edited first by Vasilievsky in *Vizantiiskij Vremennik*, III (1896), p. 121. It has been reëdited by G. Rouillard and P. Collomp, *Actes de Laura* (Paris, 1937), pp. 104ff.

31. Pachymeres, *op. cit.*, I, p. 321. The grant of the island of Euboea (Negropont) made to Licario by Michael VIII was another such grant. Marino Sanudo Torsello, *Istoria del regno di Romania*, ed. C. Hopf, *Chroniques gréco-romanes* (Berlin, 1873), p. 123: "ed allora l'Imperator, acciò il detto Mega Duca li fusse più leal e lo servisse più fedelmente, li fece dono di tutta l'isola di Negroponte pigliandosi, e li fece il Privilegio di questo amplissimo, con obbligazion di servirlo con 200 Cavallieri; li diede ancora per Moglie una Nobile dell'Imperio con Grandi entrate e ricchezza."

32. Pachymeres, *op. cit.*, I, p. 321.

33. *Actes de l'Athos: II. Actes du Pantocrator*. Appendix, *Vizantiiskij Vremennik*, X (1903), IX, 9. See also Stein, "Untersungen zur spätbyzantinischen Verfassungs-und Wirtschaftsgeschichte" in *Mitteilungen zur Osmunischen Geschichte*, II (1925), p. 23, n. 2.

34. Pachymeres, *op. cit.*, I, pp. 108f.

35. Acropolites, *op. cit.*, I, p. 101.

36. *Ibid.*, I, 173; Pachymeres, *op. cit.*, I, p. 108.

37. Pachymeres, *op. cit.*, I, p. 97.

38. *Ibid.*, I, p. 108.

39. Acropolites, *op. cit.*, I, p. 55.

40. Pachymeres, *op. cit.*, I, p. 108.

41. *Ibid.*, I, p. 109.

42. *Ibid.*, I, p. 206.

42

Some Aspects of Ancient Indian Political Organization[1]

U. N. Ghoshal

Monarchic Constitutions

In the first millennium and a half and more of our country's ancient history (c. 1500 B.C.–A.D. 300) monarchic States dominated the political stage at the expense of republican constitutions arising in their midst from time to time, while they held exclusive sway in the following millennium (c. A.D. 300–1300). This was due to the operation of a number of historical forces. Among these may be mentioned in the first place the teachings of the Brāhmaṇa canonists who recognized in their Law-Books (*Smṛitis or Dharmaśāstras*) the king as an essential unit of their social system. To this we have to add the view of the authors of the science of polity (*Arthaśāstra*), who held the sovereign to be one (and in general the first) of a group of seven constituents of the State. Without pressing the analogy too far we may find a parallel in European history where the main political tradition ever since the downfall of the Roman Republican constitution and until the rise of the French Revolutionary Republic has been monarchical, and the cause of this phenomenon has been traced in the first instance to the two great factors of the Roman Empire and the Christian Church. (H. A. L. Fisher, *The Republican Tradition in Europe*, pp. 3, 5, 7, 16, 34, 88.) It is evidently not possible in the course of a short paper to trace the history of the Indian monarchic State through all the centuries of its existence as mentioned above. We propose instead to analyse some of the leading and much-discussed features of this type of polity in the light of a dispassionate survey of the available material as far as possible.

Firstly, as regards the rules and principles of the works on Dharmaśāstra and Arthaśāstra in relation to the King's office. We have to mention two extreme views that have been put forward on this subject, one dismissing the above as "admonitions of text-book writers about the duties of the ideal King," and the other acclaiming the same as "constitutional laws" limiting the King's authority. A careful examination of the relevant data proves both these views to be erroneous. On the one hand the *Smṛiti* rules and principles relating to the obligation of the temporal ruler towards his subjects partook of the nature of solemn injunctions imposed upon the King by the sacred canon as part and parcel of a comprehensive scheme of duties of the constituent units of the social system, and they were supported as such by the highest moral and spiritual sanctions. Although from the nature of the case the similar rules and principles of the *Arthaśāstra* tradition were lacking in such high authority, they could not but carry great weight as reflecting the judgment of the great masters of the science of polity. On the other hand the *Smṛiti-Arthaśāstra* rules and principles fall short of the requirements of "constitutional laws" even after general standards. For, in the first place, the Indian scheme of duties and obligations of the temporal ruler claims to lay down the law for the King's guidance irrespectively of the conditions of place and time, thus missing its practical application as the organic law of a particular state or group of states at any definite period. In the second place, the Indian scheme failed, as we shall presently see, to provide an effective constitutional machinery to enforce its observance by the King. The most convincing evidence of the ineffectiveness of the *Smṛiti-Arthaśāstra* restraints on the ruler's authority in actual practice is furnished by the objective pictures of the misrule of Kings which lie scattered throughout our ancient literature. As regards the general tendencies and characteristics of the directions laid down for the ruler's guidance by our ancient authors, we have to mention that these rest throughout on the two mutually complementary principles,

From U. N. Ghoshal, "Some Aspects of Ancient Indian Political Organization," prepared for the International Commission for a History of the Scientific and Cultural Development of Mankind, and published in *Journal of World History*, VI, No. 2 (1960), 223–234.

namely those of the King's authority and his obligation. It is remarkable that even the greatest development of the principle of authority of the temporal ruler in the *Manu-smṛiti* and in the didactic extracts of the *Mahābhārata* is accompanied by the clear recognition of the right of resistance against the evil ruler belonging to the *Brāhmaṇas* (*Manu-smṛiti*), or the community in general along with the Brāhmaṇa order (*Mahābhārata*). The above discussion is sufficient to disprove the contention that "the Brāhmaṇical people" were "always content" with autocracy. On the other hand, such interpretations of the King's obligations as that he was regarded as "the servant of the State" (or "of the people"), that he was bound by his coronation oath and that his office was held to be a trust, rest, as has been shown by the writer in another place, upon the evidence of one set of texts to the complete exclusion of other and at least equally authoritative passages.

Secondly, as for the influence of ministers and other high officials upon the King's administration. The high status of a number of officials of the King's household and administration is repeatedly brought out in the dogmatic exposition of the great ceremonies of royal and imperial consecration in the late Vedic *Saṃhitās* and the *Brāhmaṇas*. These consist especially of the two groups *Sūta* (minstrel)—*Grāmaṇī* (village headman) and *Kshattṛi* (carver)—*Saṃgrahitṛi* (charioteer) who ranked (as we learn from some references in the description of the Horse-sacrifice (*Aśvamedha*) ceremony as the superior and the inferior social order immediately below the *Rājaputras* (princes) and the *Rājanyas* (nobles); the *Sūta* and the *Grāmaṇī* again along with the *Kshattṛi* and the *Saṃgrahitṛi* are included in a list of eleven or more *Ratnins* (jewel-holders) at whose residences the King is required to make offerings to the appropriate deities on successive days at the ceremony of the *Rājasūya*. The two groups of officers are included in another place in a list of eight *Vīras* (persons of distinction). The importance of the *Ratnins* in the late Vedic polity is indicated by their designation in some texts as "limbs of the ruling power" and as "givers and takers of the Kingdom," while the high position of the *Vīras* is hinted at in another passage where they are said to sustain the kingly power. The *Sūtas* and the *Gramaṇīs* are described elsewhere as "non-royal King-makers" in contrast with the princes and the nobles who are "the royal King-makers." The function of these King-makers is illustrated in one place by making them proclaim the newly consecrated king at the ceremony of the Great Consecration of Indra. The cumulative evidence set forth

above tends to show that the officials exercised a considerable influence in the late Vedic polity. On the other hand, the contention that the *Ratnins* "probably formed the King's council" is not only unsupported by facts, but is on general grounds inadmissible.

The creation of an organized bureaucracy in the monarchic States is one of the great achievements of the pre-Maurya period. This consisted of a class of officials called *amātyas* in Kautilya's *Arthaśāstra*, and *mahāmāttas* (Skt. *mahāmātras*) in the Pali canonical literature, who were divided into various categories. The fullest account is preserved in Kautilya's work, which gives a classified and graded list of a large number of officials on the King's establishment and discusses various methods of recruitment and selection of the *amātyas*. At the head of the list stand the high ministers (*mantrins* in Kauṭilya's and *mantri-mahāmāttas* in the Pali Canonists' nomenclature). Alongside the *mantrins* there was in Kauṭilya's system a council of lesser ministers called the *mantri-parishad*. Kauṭilya likewise gives detailed accounts of the working of various administrative offices which were run by officers called *adhyakshas* following a detailed administrative procedure. References are found even in the imperfect records of the Imperial Mauryas and their immediate successors to the institution of the *parishad* (mor fully the *mantri-parishad*) and the *amātyas*. Of the constitutional status of these ministers and other high officials unfortunately not much can be said with certainty. Attempts, which have been made in recent times to prove their high authority in relation to the King, must be pronounced unsuccessful. Thus as regards the view that the King was prevented by "the law and the principle of the Hindu constitution" from acting without the approval and co-operation of the Council of Ministers, all that can legitimately be concluded from the texts is that the King's consultation with his ministers was held by the authors to be an act of his ethico-religious obligation, or else of sound policy. The King indeed, it was recognized, was his own master in the selection of his ministers, and what is more, he was allowed considerable discretion in following their advice. In the particular instance of Aśoka, the passages from his inscriptions which have been taken to signify that the ministers had the authority to bind the sovereign by their decision, as has been shown by the writer elsewhere, do not bear out this interpretation. Similarly, the view crediting Aśoka's ministers with the right of discussing and even rejecting the Emperor's orders is not supported by the evidence of his inscriptions. Again, neither the *Smṛiti* texts nor the Buddhist tradition nor the historical inscriptions bear out the interpretation that the King was incompetent to make gifts in disregard of his ministers. The alleged refusal of the ministers of a Śaka ruler to sanction his demand for money-grants out of the State treasury is based upon a misunderstanding of the record in question, while the alleged act of Aśoka's ministers in depriving him of his sovereignty in defence of "the constitutional laws of the realm" is not borne out either by the evidence of his own inscriptions, nor that of the Buddhist traditions about his later career.

From the rise of the Imperial Guptas (c A.D. 320) in Northern India and from the advent of the Western Chālukyas of Bādāmi as well as the Pallavas of Kāñchi in the South in the middle and the last quarter respectively of the sixth century after Christ, we have the invaluable evidence of contemporary inscriptions pointing to a large number of officers of the central and the local governments. These officers —who were called by their appropriate titles, were in charge of different departments. Unfortunately our records are almost completely silent about the relation of these ministers and other high officials to the King. Leaving aside instances of usurpation of the royal authority by ambitious individuals of this class, we have one historical example deserving mention in this connection. We refer to the election (c. A.D. 750) of Gopāla, the founder of the Pāla dynasty of Eastern India, by the *prakṛitis* (meaning probably in this context "the chief officials of the time") to end the prevailing anarchy in the land. That this momentous event was barren of constitutional results is the strongest evidence of the absence of a regularly constituted public body at that time.

Thirdly, as for the influence of popular assemblies in the central and the local administration. A distinguishing feature of the Vedic polity is that the King was assisted by two Popular Assemblies called the *Samiti* and the *Sabhā*, which enjoyed (unlike other ancient tribal assemblies) the right of freedom of debate. According to the consensus of opinion among scholars the *Samiti* was the tribal or the folk-assembly of the Vedic Aryans, while the *Sabhā* was a more select body with restricted functions. Evidence has been given by the writer elsewhere to indicate that the *Sabhā* functioned as the royal council and court by the side of the large popular assembly of the *Samiti*. The texts leave us in no doubt that the *Samiti* in particular was sufficiently important to make it the King's most valuable asset. Nevertheless there is not sufficient evidence to prove, as has been alleged, that the *Samiti* was "the sovereign assembly" of Vedic times, or that it "met

on all important occasions," or that it "exercised considerable control over the military and executive affairs of the State," or that it "decided all questions of policy," while the reference to its alleged right of legislation is a lamentable historical anachronism. It remains to mention that the complete disappearance of the Vedic assemblies was not due, as has been alleged, to the inherent incapacity of the Indians to develop popular institutions, but resulted from the operation of historical forces tending towards concentration of all governmental authority in single or selected hands.

Coming to another point we have to mention that our knowledge of the working of the village administration in the Vedic period is exceedingly scanty, although the *Grāmaṇī* (who was the village leader in peace and in war) is known to have occupied a position of a great importance. We may, however, presume from the existence of powerful popular assemblies as noted above at the centre that the local affairs of villages were usually decided by the villagers themselves. In the following period we notice a strong tendency towards organisation of the local administration on bureaucatic lines. Reference is made in a *Smṛiti* passage to the King's officer in charge of villages and towns, and in other passages to a chain of such officers with jurisdictions extending from single villages to larger and larger village-groups. The parallel system of the *Arthaśāstra,* with its sharp division between the government of the rural and the urban areas, shows a similar, but not identical pattern of local administration. The detailed account in Kauṭilya's work further indicates the stringent control exercised by the central government over the cultivators in the rural areas for the sake of maximum output from the fields and by the town-authorities over the citizens in the interests of municipal sanitation as well as of state security and public safety. The contemporary account of Chandragupta Maurya's administration from the pen of the Greek ambassador Megasthenes mentions in general terms the same type of local administration, with separate staffs of royal officers in charge of the rural and the urban areas. By contrast the references in these authorities even to village-assemblies are surprisingly few. A few narratives in the *Jātakas* ("Birth-stories of the Buddha"), however, suggest that village-assemblies for the transaction of local affairs were in working order at the time.

The first clear references to the association of representatives of important trades and professions with the town administration are found in some inscriptions of the Imperial Guptas belong to North Bengal in the fifth and sixth centuries after Christ.

The records of various dynasties in Northern and Western India in the post-Gupta period contain sporadic references to village-assemblies as well as town-councils with representatives of interests and classes (or even to whole town assemblies with adequate functions). Our fullest account of self-governing village-assemblies relates to South India during the period of supremacy of the Imperial Cholas ranging from the ninth to the thirteenth century A.D., although instances of such assemblies with elected executive committees are found earlier in the records of the Imperial Pallavas of Kāñchi and the Pāṇḍyas of Madurā. Under the Imperial Cholas there were two types of autonomous village-assemblies, namely the ordinary type (*ur*) associated generally with non-Brāhmaṇa residents, and the special type (*sabhā*) which was inhabited by Brāhmaṇa house-holders. From a famous inscription of the time of the Chola King Parāntaka I, we learn that the *sabhā* of the particular village repeatedly framed its own rules for constitution of its committees by a mixed method of lot and election, or else by lot alone. The *sabhā* in the Chola Empire exercised a wide range of powers which comprised maintenance of records of village rights, deciding disputes, granting lands, maintaining the local irrigation-works, founding and maintaining hospitals, and supervising the charitable endowments. They controlled a number of taxes which they could assign or remit at their pleasure. They had their own staff of officials, who took down the proceedings of the assembly without sharing in its deliberations.

The above facts undoubtedly point to a progressive development of municipal self-government, and still more of self-governing village assemblies in the country during the period of the Imperial Guptas and their successors. On the other hand, we have no reason in the light of the available data to conclude with a recent author that there was from early times a conscious extension of self-government "from the top through all grades and strata of society down to the lowest classes in the villages," so as to make "every village" a self-governing unit and the whole country "a vast rural democracy." Equally untenable is another view of the planned extension of administrative decentralisation so as to invest the ancient Indian town and village councils with greater powers than those enjoyed by similar bodies elsewhere. We have, lastly, to mention that in the absence of direct evidence of the organized resistance of the local bodies against royal tyranny and misrule, they cannot be called, as has been held, "the most effective and practical checks upon the King's powers."

Fourthly, and lastly, as regards the influence of caste and other groups upon the King's administration. Beginning with the Vedic period, we may state two fundamental doctrines of the Vedic Aryans, which were followed by the Brāhmaṇa canonists in all later times. These were concerned, firstly, with the precedence of the Brāhmaṇas over the other classes by Divine ordination, and secondly, with the separation of the spiritual from the temporal power. The former doctrine was accompanied in the Vedas by stringent claims of immunity of person and property on behalf of the privileged order. These claims were developed in the *Smṛitis* into the doctrine of immunities and privileges of the Brāhmaṇas and crystallised in their discriminatory clauses of the civil and criminal law favouring the Brāhmaṇas while imposing disabilities upon the rest of the population (and specially the śūdras). What is more, the Brāhmaṇa's right of resisting the evil or the incompetent ruler is recognised (as we have seen) alike in the authoritative *Manu-smṛiti* and the didactic extracts in the *Mahābhārata*. It would, therefore, seem that the Brāhmaṇas counted as one of the most important factors in the State administration. It is, however, a curious fact that historical instances of constitutional opposition of Brāhmaṇas against unpopular Kings or their acts are surprisingly few. In Kalhana's great chronicle of Kashmir . . . we are told that the Brāhmaṇa residents of villages as well as Temple priests often resorted to success to a bloodless passive resistance in the form of solemn fast as a protest against unpopular measures of the State administration. The author, however, although himself a distinguished Brāhmaṇa, shows a singular want of sympathy for the actors in the scenes who repeatedly, according to his own account, allowed themselves to be won over by bribery, or else made use of their weapon for blackmail. Only on one memorable occasion, when the Brāhmaṇa assemblies were summoned by a commander-in-chief for the purpose of electing a successor to the vacant throne, they justified themselves by setting aside the claims of the foolish commander-in-chief, and electing a poor but wise Brāhmaṇa, Yaśaskara, who became the founder of a new dynasty. In attempting a possible explanation of the failure of the Brāhmaṇas to make the fullest use of their potential strength we may mention, apart from the lapses of individuals or groups, two principal factors. The Brāhmaṇa order, to begin with, was wanting in the strength of an organised Church. Lacking a corporate body with a permanent head and unsupported by permanent contributions from the people, it could present no united front even for the vindication of personal rights of its members.

The Brahmanical order, again, by deliberately cutting itself off from intermixture with the ruling and fighting classes, was deprived of the strength arising from the infusion of fresh blood.

No account of the influence of castes upon the state administration will be complete without some reference to the privileges enjoyed by these and other groups in the branch of law and justice. We have a very full recognition of the customs of groups as the secondary source of the State law in an old *Smṛiti* work (*Gautama-Dharmaśāstra* XI, 19.21). Here the author, after requiring the king to regulate his administration of justice by the Veda and its auxiliaries, declares the customs of regions, sub-castes and families (*deśa, jāti* and *kula*) also to have authority, provided these are not opposed to the canon. What is more, cultivators, traders, herdsmen, money-lenders and artisans are declared by him to be authorities for their respective groups, and the King is asked to give his decision after ascertaining the law from the accredited leaders of those groups. In the parallel system of Kauṭilya's *Arthaśāstra* the customs and practices of *deśas, jātis* and *kulas* as well as *saṁghas* (communities) are required to be registered by the officer-in-charge of the State records, evidently for the purpose of their application in the King's Court (II, 7). A concrete illustration of this kind is given by the author at the end of his chapter on the law of partition and inheritance (III, 7). What is more, reference is made in the early Buddhist literature to caste-councils (called *sabhā* or *parisā*) functioning as courts for the hearing of civil and criminal cases after the approved procedure of interrogation of witnesses. Again, courts of *kulas, śreṇīs* (economic guilds) and *gaṇas* (otherwise called *pūgas*) (assemblies of residents of villages and towns) are mentioned in this order in an ascending hierarchy of such bodies leading to the courts of the King's representative and the King himself in the later authoritative *Smṛitis*. The period extends from the fourth to the ninth century after Christ. We have no means of judging how these important institutions worked at any definite time or place. But in so far as they were in operation, they undoubtedly served as a most important means of associating the people with the official administration.

Republican Constitutions

In the long history of ancient Indian political organization we may distinguish three principal periods which were marked by the rise of republics. These are, firstly, the period of the early Buddhist literature (sixth and fifth centuries B.C.); secondly,

the period of decline and fall of the Achaemenid power in the Indus Valley (from the fifth to the third quarter of the fourth century B.C.); and thirdly, the period of foreign conquests and settlements (during the first two centuries before and after Christ).

Beginning with the first period we have to state that the epoch of the rise of Buddhism saw a number of republics flourishing in Eastern India, which were gradually swallowed up by the neighbouring monarchic States in their struggle for supremacy. The literature of this period acquaints us with a generic term *saṁgha* and its synonym *gaṇa* ("community of living beings"), and the division of this genus into various species, namely, religious, economic, military and political. To take a few instances, the great grammarian Pāṇini mentions not only *saṁgha* and *gaṇa*, but also its particular type called the *āyud-hājivi-saṁgha* (*saṁgha* living by the profession of fighting). Kauṭilya distinguishes between two types of *saṁghas*, namely, the *vārtāśāstropajīvi-saṁghas* (saṁghas living by economic and military pursuits) and *rājaśabdopajīvi-saṁghas* (probably meaning "saṁghas appointing their executive heads for a high property qualification"). It is the type of the political *saṁgha* or *gaṇa* which signifies the republican constitution. From the detailed references in Kauṭilya's work, we learn that both types of *saṁghas* had high executive officers (*mukhyas*) and princelings (*kumārakas*) as well as the popular assembly. In the corresponding account of the *Mahābhārata*, we are similarly told, that the *gaṇas* had their *mukhyas* as well as their general assembly. Recent discussions about the political *saṁghas* or *gaṇas* have led to very different views of their characteristic features. They have been described broadly as "democracies," or else as a generic type consisting, according to one account of the three varieties of aristocracies, democracies and mixed constitutions, and according to another account of two varieties of oligarchies and democracies, each of which is further subdivided into a unitary and a federal sub-type. These views have been shown by the writer elsewhere to be untenable, and the *saṁgha-gaṇa* of this period has been explained to mean an aristocratic clan-republic in the sense that the supreme power in the State was held by the appropriate Kshatriya-clans.

Let us now turn to the much discussed question of application of the known rules for the transaction of ecclesiastical acts among the early Buddhist monastic order to the deliberative procedure of the contemporary or nearly contemporary republican assemblies. On this point, independent evidence has been given by the writer in the same context to show that the assemblies, while enjoying complete freedom of discussion of momentous issues of the State, used to reach their decision by unanimous consent, and in default by the voice of the majority. It has also been suggested that the business procedure of the republican assemblies bore a general resemblance to that of their Buddhist counterparts, subject to such difference as is inevitable in the contrast between a sovereign political assembly and an ecclesiastical gathering of monks. From this general statement a three-fold corollary has been drawn in respect of republican procedure. Firstly, as in the Buddhist monastic gatherings the official proposal was normally brought forward in the form of a motion which, being put to the vote once or thrice (as the case might be), was declared carried if there was no opposition, and in the contrary case was referred to a committee of the assembly and was decided in the last resort by an appeal to the majority vote. Secondly, the assemblies like their Buddhist counterparts followed definite rules about the quorum, the recording of absentee votes and so forth, but unlike them required the proposals to be moved by the chief magistrate (or other high officers) periodically holding office. Thirdly, the method of settlement of disputed questions in the assemblies, being necessarily accompanied by political sanctions, differed in degree as well as in kind from those known to the Buddhist gatherings.

We may wind up our discussion of the general characteristics of the republics of the period with a short notice of their two most important historical examples. In the case of the Lichchhavis of Vaiśālī the relevant *Jātaka* text has been interpreted by different scholars to mean that they formed a unitary republican State ruled by a selected body of hereditary nobles, a republic of a complex type with each member of the ruling assembly forming a State in miniature and a federal State with autonomy for each constituent principality. On the other hand, the constitution of the Śākyas of Kapilavastu has been taken, mainly on the authority of various *Jātaka* texts, to have been a republic with a sovereign clan-assembly and an elected President, or else a republic of the supposed Lichchhavi type and, or lastly, a hereditary monarchy with a King ruling over the whole State. A careful consideration of the older and more authentic canonical texts on this point has led the writer in the context quoted above to a different conclusion. The Lichchhavi constitution, it has been proved, had according to the most authentic texts two elements, namely an executive head (*senāpati*) and a general assembly. The *senāpati* was chosen by free election of the assembly, and he held office for an unknown term. The assembly had full

rights of sovereignty over the community and the decrees of the republic were issued jointly in the names of the *senāpati* and the *gaṇa*. It has further been shown that the Śākyas had a mixed constitution consisting of hereditary monarchy and a ruling clan-assembly, which was interpreted by the later writers in such a way as to bring it into line with the familiar type of the (political) *saṃgha*.

Passing to the second period we may begin by stating that, following the downfall of Achaemenid rule in the country, the Punjab was parcelled out among a number of monarchies and republics which held the field until they were all overthrown by the invasion of Alexander of Macedon (326 B.C.). In the case of the republics we have advantage of their description by competent Greek observers in Alexander's train, who distinguished between the two types, aristocracies and democracies. In the context from which we have quoted above, it has been suggested by the writer, on the basis of the available information, that the two types had three elements of the constitution in common, namely, a magistrate (or board of magistrates), a council of elders, and a sovereign assembly. The supreme executive was evidently elected by the assembly, but the composition and functions of the council are not precisely known. The composition of the assembly was apparently limited to the ruling Kshatriya class in the case of the aristocracies, one particular aristocracy having been stated to consist of five thousand members (councillors) selected by the peculiar property qualification of contribution of an elephant to the State by each one. In the case of the democracies the assembly may be presumed to have been open to all qualified freemen. Altogether in a class by itself stood a State in the Indus delta with a mixed constitution consisting of monarchic and aristocratic elements. It had, we are told, two hereditary kings of different houses who had the command in war, and a council of elders ruling the whole State with paramount authority, thus offering to the Greek observers a parallel to the familiar Spartan constitution.

We now come to the republics of the third and the last period. The decline and fall of the Greek Kingdom in India gave the opportunity to a number of ancient peoples (the Kunindas, the Audumbaras, the Yaudheyas, the Ārjunāyanas, and Rājanyas) in the Eastern Punjab and the upper Gaṅgā basin to establish republics as well as kingdoms, which were called after their respective States or rulers on their coins. In the late second, the third and the early fourth centuries of the Christian era, another revival of republican freedom took place in the Punjab and Rajputana in the wake of the downfall of the foreign

Kushāṇa power in Northern India. Among the republican peoples of this phase we may mention the names of the Kunindas, the Yaudheyas, and the Mālavas, who issued coins in the names of their respective republics (*gaṇas*) or States (*janapadas*). In the inscriptions of some of these peoples as well as in an interesting discussion of this type of polity in the *Mahābhārata* we may detect a tendency towards concentration of the ruling and deliberative authority in the hands of a select few. This was evidently due to the urgent necessity of safeguarding the independence of the republics against the ambition of neighbouring powerful kings. The end came in the first half of the fourth century after Christ when all the republics of Northern India, along with a number of minor monarchies, were absorbed in the Empire of the Imperial Guptas.

NOTES

1. The present paper is based upon a number of the writer's previous publications, where full references are given throughout. These are, in the first place, *A History of Hindu Public Life, Part I* (Period of the Vedic *Saṁhitās*, the *Brāhmaṇas*, and the Older *Upanishads*), *Studies in Indian History and Culture* (Chapters VIII, IX, X and XI entitled "The Genius of Ancient Indian Polity," "The Vedic Ceremonies and Their Political and Constitutional Significance," "Vedic Political Institutions," "The Ancient Indian Republican and Mixed Constitutions from the Sixth Century B.C. to the Third Century A.D.," and "The Status and Functions of the King's Ministers in Ancient Indian Polity"), and *A History of Indian Political Ideas* (Chapters II, III, IV, V, VI, VII, VIII, IX, X). To the above have to be added the writer's chapters on "Political Theory and Administrative Organisation," in Volumes III, IV and V of the work *History and Culture of the Indian People* (edited by R. C. Majumdar) as well as his chapter on "Political Organisation (Post-Mauryan)" in the work *A Comprehensive History of India*, Vol. II (edited by K. A. Nilakanta Sastri).

43

The New Bureaucratic Elite

Hans Rosenberg

The composition of the civil and military service elites of the Hohenzollern state was indicative of some of the major social changes which crystallized everywhere with the growth of the monarch's personal powers and of bureaucratic organization on a large scale. Since absolute government and the expansion of the dynastic labor market opened up fresh sources of differentiation, the stratification of society grew more complex. By giving rise to novel segments of the governing class, absolutism disturbed and confused the old social system, built on birth and privilege, on hierarchy and hereditary estate distinctions (*ständische Gesellschaft*).

The new civil and military bureaucracies constituted professional classes of great functional and political importance. Hence they were recognized by their creator, the sovereign ruler, as superior status groups. Having like organizational state and a common way of life as "royal servants," they formed two distinct occupational estates (*Berufsstände*), an estate of administrative government officials (*Beam-*

tenstand) and an estate of military officers (*Offiziersstand*). These hierarchies of appointed and removable dynastic employees did not fit into the neatly defined divisions of the traditional society of northeastern Germany, the essential features of which had been the rigorous partition into hereditary estates (*Geburtsstände*), into closed, caste-like legal classes. In such a society "man was not man"; he was either superior, common, or inferior.

The nobility, being superior to all other groups in power, privilege, and prestige, had formed the First Estate (*Adelsstand*), the upper class. The commoners or burghers, i.e., the permanent town residents subject to municipal law and administration, being only "second class people" in influence and rights, had constituted the Second Estate (*Bürgerstand*), the middle class, inferior to the nobility but superior to the peasantry. At the bottom of the scale had stood the "inferiors," the Third Estate (*Bauernstand*), identical with the rural masses, mostly peasant serfs.[1]

The formation of new upper class strata, made up of the holders of the higher positions in the civil and military bureaucracies, complicated social rankings. But their emergence also reacted on the relations between social stratification and political hierarchy. By their very existence and by virtue of the heterogeneous social antecedents of their personnel, the service estates challenged the complacent illusion that inherited superior status and ownership of a landed estate as such assured the right to rule as well as fitness for leadership and managerial ability.

Even titled aristocrats were now impelled, before they were entrusted with definite duties, to give the impression of competence. This requirement often aroused hurt feelings in the circles of the large landed proprietors, infuriated by any violation of noble privileges, especially where "places" and the "right of the native-born" were at stake.[2]

The competitive struggle for professional advancement and individual social success among the bureaucratic partisans of absolute government gave birth to a type of functionary more opportunistic and more "rational" than the *Ständestaat officier* had been. Within the royal service careful calculation of personal chances and the adoption of rules of behavior designed to outwit and trip up rivals by shrewdness, superior performance, intrigue, or eel-like maneuvering, came to be typical ingredients of "personal ability," "special skills," and "efficiency."[3] For the persevering climber it was not enough to learn self-discipline. He had to make a methodical attempt to appraise his professional colleagues and superiors in terms of their fluctuating "value" and the influence of their relatives, friends, and cliques. In short, he had to be a special kind of social and political arithmetician. He could not get ahead without the favor of prominent influence peddlers in the good graces of the absolute prince, the chief dispenser of power, emoluments, social prestige, and other favors.

The "new bureaucrat," as a social type, was well represented by the aides of Frederick William, the Elector, and of his immediate successor. These restless, intensely selfish men played their cards with cold-blooded efficiency. They were ardent collectors of tips, bribes, and valuable gifts. They had to be unscrupulous, ever suspicious, sharp-witted careerists to come out on top for a while in the turmoil and controversy following the harrowing decades after the Thirty Years' War. The "servants" of King Frederick William I were certainly not superior in intelligence or energy, let alone in forcefulness of personality to the early pioneers, but they had grown conscious of the burdensome proprieties of "Prussian Puritanism."

Although the nobles of descent continued to enjoy great initial advantage, their rise in the official hierarchy was often impeded or blocked by the successful competition of "immodest" commoners of some distinguishing personal quality. This trespassing on traditional class functions and monopolies and the ensuing rivalry between nobles and non-nobles were a notable phenomenon only in a little, though extremely important niche of the social order: in the realm of dynastic employment. Here, from the outset, a major problem presented itself, the problem of the compatibility of two coexistent, disparate social ladders of advancement.

In view of this situation, some *modus vivendi* had to be found between the antagonistic claims to social position which arose from the old, simple way of equating noble birth with superior social worth and personal excellence and the new, more individualized and more fluid practice of rating man on the basis of his vocational qualities, political utility, and official grade in the state service.

The ancient social rank order was regulated by inherited privilege, landownership, and genealogical considerations. The new service rank order was determined by office, function, and the will of the autocratic prince. In government employment, official position as a fountain of social esteem and self-respect competed with rank derived from exalted birth. Men of "poor extraction" frequently became the supervisory or commanding officers of old-established aristocrats.

This impertinent innovation, the growth of "unfair competition," gave rise to new and knotty relationships between nobles and commoners. Unabating irritation and friction were bound to emanate from the fact that the holding of significant posts under the authority of the crown became an important determinant of social status. In accordance with the novel yardstick for gauging merit and excellence, the upper service grades and the more imposing official titles *per se* became conspicuous symbols of high social standing. Thus organizational status, relative to hereditary prestige, gained vastly in significance as a social ranking device with the rise of the modern bureaucratic state.

NOTES

1. These social status divisions continued to prevail until 1807 when they were largely liquidated by the famous October Edict. As for the numerical strength of the hereditary estates and the occupational estates on the eve of the Stein-Hardenberg reforms, see Leopold Krug, *Abriss der neuesten Statistik des preussischen Staats* (Halle, 1804), 18.

2. For a typical illustration, see *Urkunden und Aktenstücke zur Geschichte des Kurfürsten Friedrich Wilhelm*, XVI (1899), 1004ff., 1014.

3. For descriptive detail, see M. Philippson, *Der Grosse Kurfürst Friedrich Wilhelm von Brandenburg*, III (Berlin, 1903), 14–15, 40–55; C. Hinrichs, *Friedrich Wilhelm I,*

111ff.; Theodor Fontane, *Wanderungen durch die Mark Brandenburg*, II (Berlin, 1868), 90ff. A penetrating generalized comment on this process of readjusting the modes of social behavior to the trend of political centralization under dynastic leadership, in Norbert Elias, *Ueber den Prozess der Zivilisation*, II (Basel, 1939), 370ff. See also Max Handman,

"The Bureaucratic Culture Pattern and Political Revolution," *The American Journal of Sociology*, XXXIX (1933), 301–313; Alexander Rüstow, *Ortsbestimmung der Gegenwart. Eine universalgeschichtliche Kulturkritik*, I (Erlenbach-Zürich, 1950), 241–246.

|| e. REBELLIONS AND CHANGE IN THE EMPIRES

44

Yellow Turban Religion and Rebellion at the End of Han

H. S. Levy

Rebellion

Rebellion first arose in the east. The leader of the Yellow Turban Taoists there was Chang Chüeh. Over a ten-year period, he enjoyed a phenomenal success in enlisting the services of an estimated 360,000 followers from eight provinces.[1] One reason for the rapid growth of this movement may have been the series of economic misfortunes suffered by the peasantry. A Chinese historian implies that the uprisings were caused by the collaboration of the eunuch clique at court,[2] but economic factors might also explain why people blocked the roads in their rush to support Chang Chüeh. The floods of 175 were followed by drought in 176, 177, 182 and 183, while epidemics caused further suffering in 173, 179 and 182, the critical years before the Taoist uprising.[3] The alternation of flood, famine and epidemic led to a dispossessed peasantry, ready to flock to the standards of anyone who offered to alleviate its misery.[4] The Chang brothers, while versed in faith-healing, may also have known of efficacious herbalistic and medical remedies which would either cure or lessen the sufferings of their innumerable patients.

From H. S. Levy, "Yellow Turban Religion and Rebellion at the End of Han," *Journal of the American Oriental Society*, LXXVI (1956), 219–224. Reprinted by permission of the publisher.

A minister named Yang Tz'u warned the emperor in a memorial that more and more people were giving their allegiance to Chang Chüeh. Because of the mass support which Chang Chüeh enjoyed, Yang Tz'u feared that an outright attack on the eastern Taoists might prove disastrous to the empire. He advised instead that Emperor Ling-ti prevent the incipient rebellion by forcing all vagrants to return to their original homes.[5] The vagrancy alluded to by Yang Tz'u may have resulted from the occurrence of the devastating floods and famine. These economic misfortunes created a vast reservoir of displaced persons, from whom Chang Chüeh might amply replenish his ranks.

Another official warned Ling-ti that Chang Chüeh was plotting to usurp the throne, but the emperor remained unconcerned and undertook no overt action.[6] Rumors of a coming uprising spread throughout the provinces. The eastern Yellow Turbans agreed to stage a coordinated revolt and to strike both from within and without the imperial palace on the fifth day of the third month (April 4, 184).[7] Grand Adept Ma Yüan-i[8] was employed by the Yellow Turbans as an espionage agent in the capital of Lo-yang. He compiled confidential reports and entered into secret compliance with eunuch officials.[9] However, the court rebels were betrayed in the winter of 184 by a former disciple of Chang Chüeh called T'ang Chou.[10] Ma Yüan-i was captured and condemned to a terrible death. He was dismembered by being tied to two carts which were then started in opposite directions. More than one thousand Yellow Turban sympathizers were seized and executed. The emperor ordered that Chang Chüeh be apprehended, but Chang discovered this imperial directive emanating from Lo-yang in time to escape. Riding day and night, Chang Chüeh and his confederates called on all disciples to rise in revolt, and to burn and plunder official residences.[11] The ministerial hierarchy at Lo-yang was dismayed by the enthusiastic mass response to the Yellow Turban rebellion. At first there was imperial indecision as how to effectively extirpate the rebels, owing to the wrangling which ensued between the rival Confucian and eunuch cliques. The emperor allegedly was partial to the eunuchs, once stating that eunuch Chang Jang was his father and eunuch Chao his mother.[12] Although several eunuchs were implicated in the Yellow Turban plot,[13] Emperor Ling-ti included them in a general amnesty from which Chang Chüeh alone was excluded.[14]

Imperial forces led by Huang-fu Sung,[15] Chu Chün[16] and Lu Chih[17] set forth to quell the rebels. Chu Chün was defeated at Ying-ch'uan Commandery (in modern Honan) by the Yellow Turban leader Po Ts'ai;[18] Huang-fu Sung defended Ch'ang-sha District, also in Ying-ch'uan Commandery. Po Ts'ai surrounded him there, but he turned defeat into victory by setting fire to the grass encircling the rebel encampment and then routing the panicked enemy.[19] Ts'ao Ts'ao,[20] who later ruled Wei Kingdom, joined forces with Huang-fu Sung. Ts'ao Ts'ao first gained prominence as an antagonist of the Yellow Turbans, battling them victoriously in the summer of 184. The imperial commanders pressed their victories, and pursued and defeated various Yellow Turban leaders.[21] However, while Lu Chih and Tung Cho[22] engaged the troops of Chang Chüeh in combat, they were forced to retreat before them.

Chang Chüeh's younger brother Chang Liang fought Huang-fu Sung to a standstill at Kuang-tsung District (in modern Hopei).[23] Huang-fu noted that his adversaries had relaxed their defenses, and ordered an attack at daybreak. In the ensuing battle, Chang Liang was decapitated along with an estimated 30,000 rebels, a figure which is obviously unreliable. When Huang-fu Sung discovered that Chang Chüeh had died previously of illness, he broke his coffin, severed the head of the corpse and transmitted it to the capital. Chang Pao, the youngest and last survivor of the brothers, also was decapitated.[24] It is asserted that many of the 100,000 corpses of his Yellow Turban cohorts were stacked

and covered over with dirt, forming a mound so high that the capital could be seen from it. This grisly mound was called the Capital Observatory (*ching-kuan*).[25] Huang-fu Sung thus quelled the three Chang brothers and brought temporary peace to the bloodied land. The relieved peasants celebrated his achievements by composing the following ballad:

> Great chaos in the empire,
> The markets were desolate.
> Mothers could not protect children,
> Wives lost their husbands.
> Depending on Huang-fu,
> Again we live in peace.[26]

The emperor ordered that his reign style be changed from Brilliant Harmony (*kuang-ho*) to Central Pacification (*chung-p'ing*),[27] believing that the period of rebellion had ended with the death of the Chang brothers. However, sporadic uprisings of small groups of Yellow Turbans and others continued to harass the central government.[28] By the end of 188, there were those who believed that Lo-yang might soon become the scene of unremitting conflict. While this fear proved to be unfounded, Taoist-inspired Yellow Turban revolts did hasten the downfall of the Han and encouraged the fortunes of warlords who seized power as a consequence of military exploits against the rebels.

The Taoist State in the Southwest

With the death of Chang Chüeh, the main scene of Taoist activities shifted towards the southwest. The mantle of Taoist leadership in the Szechwan region was assumed by Chang Lu, the grandson of Chang Ling. Two later writers allege that Chang Chüeh's plans for rebellion had been coordinated with those of his distant Taoist confederate and ally Chang Lu. Both were accused of advocating the wearing of yellow turbans and Taoist clothing, of deceiving their followers, and of plotting jointly to overthrow the state.[29] It was further asserted that Chang Chüeh's rebellion in the winter of 184 had been carried out in collaboration with the distant Chang Lu.[30] However, as the Japanese scholar Fukui Kōjun has noted, this statement is probably in error, since one would expect the father Chang Heng rather than his son to have been active in 184, the year of Chang Chüeh's short-lived rebellion.[31]

The connecting link between the Neo-Taoists of east and west may have been supplied several years after the death of Chang Chüeh by a Yellow Turban rebel named Ma Hsiang.[32] Ma Hsiang was from

Liang Province (in modern Kansu). About the summer of 189, he staged an uprising at Mien-chu District (in modern Szechwan). Ma Hsiang called himself a Yellow Turban, and in a few days succeeded in recruiting several thousand emaciated followers. He killed the local magistrate and, backed by over ten thousand civilians and officials, crushed three commanderies in Szechwan within a ten-day period. Ma Hsiang proclaimed himself emperor, but he was routed and his following dispersed soon afterwards at the eastern border of Chien-wei Commandery. Thus, all of Ma Hsiang's movements during the height of his rebellion took place in Szechwan, stronghold of the southwestern Taoism popularized by Chang Ling and his successors.

After the official Liu Yen[33] was appointed Magistrate (*mu*) of I Province, he moved his administrative center to Mien-chu District in order to regain the allegiance of the local inhabitants who still cherished thoughts of rebellion. While within this district, he and his subordinates undoubtedly came into contact with remnants of Yellow Turban teachings propounded there by the former disciples of Ma Hsiang.

Liu Yen probably became a Taoist adept.[34] He favored the Taoist Chang Lu,[35] assigned an important military post to him,[36] and directed him to join forces with another military commander named Chang Hsiu.[37] Chang Lu and Chang Hsiu were to launch a concerted attack on Su Ku, the Great Defender of Han-chung Commandery (in modern Shensi). However, Chang Lu attacked and killed Chang Hsiu, secured his troops and conquered the Han-chung area.[38] He transformed it into a Taoist community, instructing the inhabitants through the "ways of the demons."[39] His teachings are described as being in general accord with those of the eastern Yellow Turbans. Chang Lu called himself Lord of the Teachers (*shih-chün*),[40] escaped annihilation, and administered a state within the Chinese state for about thirty years.

Chang Lu maintained the popularity of his doctrine by having his Libationers erect public houses (*i-she*) along the roads, stocked with provisions of rice and meat.[41] Passers-by could freely enter and take enough food to satisfy their hunger, but it was proclaimed that anyone who took more food than he actually needed would be afflicted with demoniacal possession. This food distribution policy undoubtedly increased the number of converts, rice-Taoists though they might have been. The Yellow Turbans of the west abolished Han imperial institutions, killed official envoys and refused to tolerate the assignment of imperial magistrates to the Han-chung area. Their places were taken by the Libation-

ers appointed by Chang Lu. The barbarians were said to have been delighted with the Taoist administration.[42]

The objectives of Chang Lu and his associates were twofold. On a political plane, they wished to replace all imperial authorities with their own disciples. Their religious aim was to initiate the Taoist novice into increasingly complex religious practices.[43] Titles and grades were instituted on the basis of relative advancement. Beginners might be called the Sons of the Tao (*tao-nan*) or the Daughters of the Tao (*tao-nü*). Superior grades were those of the Male Bonnet (*nan-kuan*) and Female Bonnet (*nü-kuan*), while further progress enabled a disciple to be entitled a Father of the Tao (*tao-fu*) or Mother of the Tao (*tao-mu*).[44] The attitude towards women was in advance of the rest of second-century Chinese society, for these titles were accessible to both men and women. Chang Ling, while accused of being a wife deserter, was also credited with speaking favorably of the intellectual potentialities of unmarried women fourteen years of age and above.[45] No distinction in the conferring of titles seems to have been made on the basis of sex. However, there was no feminine counterpart for the supreme title of Teacher of Heaven (*t'ien-shih*).[46]

The Han dynasty, at this late stage of its decline, could not effectively oppose these revolutionary innovations in the southwest. Since the court could not subjugate Chang Lu, it resorted to the expedient of entitling him as a loyal official.[47] Chang Lu agreed to send yearly tribute to the court as a token of nominal submission. His position was of such eminence that he once considered proclaiming himself the independent King of Han-ning, but decided against it.[48] The warlord Ts'ao Ts'ao invaded the Han-chung area in 215. Chang Lu's younger brother Chang Wei stubbornly resisted the invasion, but was routed with his troops.[49] Chang Lu did not oppose Ts'ao Ts'ao.[50] Pending his arrival, he refused to allow his subordinates to destroy, pillage or plunder.[51] Ts'ao Ts'ao treated Chang Lu more as an honored compatriot than as an enemy, and enfeoffed him and his five sons.[52] He also arranged a marriage between one of his daughters and one of Chang Lu's sons. Chang Lu must have enjoyed considerable prestige among his people to have received such preferential treatment from the warlord Ts'ao Ts'ao.

Concluding Remarks

The Taoist revolt in the east and west thus encountered varying fortunes. The revolt in the east was eliminated; its western counterpart enjoyed a relative independence. The western revolutionaries therefore were able to institute religious and political innovations, some of which survived at least until the fifth century.[53] The Taoist religion in this early stage was undoubtedly influenced by Buddhism,[54] although the insinuation that Chang Ling became a Buddhist sounds more like clerical propaganda than established fact.[55] However, after the close of the Han dynasty the Taoist religion assumed its place alongside Buddhism and Confucianism as an independent doctrine of major importance and mass attraction. The later Buddhists criticized the Taoist religion for having fostered false concepts, while the historians and upholders of imperial orthodoxy reviled it as a vehicle of subversion. From the time of Chang Ling onwards, the Confucians felt that the worst crime of the Taoist pontiff was his claim to be Teacher of Heaven. Since in Confucian eyes no one was greater than the Son of Heaven or emperor, this Taoist assertion must have seemed an insolent affront. Despite the accusations hurled against it by many antagonists,[56] the Taoist religion during and after the Yellow Turban uprisings was accepted by the common people as a consoling religious faith. The question of Buddhist-Taoist cross-fertilization remains a frutiful potential field of inquiry.

NOTES

1. HHS, 8, 14b. The commentary to this passage notes that the *Hsü Han-shu* records more than 360,000 men. This signifies that a large number of people followed the Yellow Turbans, but the unverifiable figure itself is probably exaggerated. HHS, 61, 1b states that in over ten years Chang Chüeh's followers came to number several hundred thousand. W. Eichhorn, op. cit., 327, does not quote a reference to support his contention that ". . . in somewhat more than ten years he (i.e. Chang Chüeh) gathered round him several tens of thousands of adherents."

2. HHS, 8, 15a informs us that the eunuch clique returned from its places of concealment after Emperor Ling-ti issued a general amnesty on April 5, 184. The commentary adds that the official Lu Chiang advised the emperor not to amnesty the eunuchs because they had plotted together with the Yellow Turbans. Nevertheless, the emperor forgave all of the eunuchs allegedly because he feared them.

3. See the following references: HHS, 15, 7a–b; Ibid., 16, 6b–7a, 12a; Ibid, 17, 11a. Ibid., 47, 5a records the successive years of famine which occurred during the reign of Ling-ti. In the two years preceding the Yellow Turban rebellion of 184, a great epidemic in the winter of 182 was followed by famine that summer. Great famine was suffered again in the summer of 183. (Ibid., 8, 14a–b.) The possibility remains that the disastrous nature of these calamities was exaggerated in order to indicate Heaven's displeasure with the eunuch-dominated administration of Emperor Ling-ti.

4. The eleventh century historian Ssu-ma Kuang asserted that over ten thousand people failed to reach the Yellow Turbans because they died of illness along the way. (*Tzu-chih t'ung-chien*, 58, 5a.)

5. The contents of this memorial offered to the throne by Yang Tz'u are recorded in HHS, 44, 26b–27a.

6. During the year preceding the rebellion, the official Liu T'ao fruitlessly reiterated the contentions of Yang Tz'u to the emperor. (For details, consult HHS, 47, 11b–12a.)

7. This date for the anticipated Yellow Turban rebellion is recorded in HHS, 61, 2a.

8. The Yellow Turban spy Ma Yüan-i had formerly recruited thousands of followers from Ching and Yang Provinces. (HHS, 61, 2a.)

9. Ma Yüan-i travelled back and forth between his stronghold in Yeh District (modern Honan) and Lo-yang, and secured the compliance of eunuchs Feng Hsü, Hsü Feng and others to a projected palace revolution. (HHS, 61, 2a.)

10. T'ang Chou was a native of Chi-nan Commandery (in modern Shantung). He informed the emperor in writing of the Yellow Turban plot to usurp the throne. (Ibid., loc. cit.) Fukui Kōjun, *Dōkyō Seiutou Izen no Ni-San no Mondai" Tōyō Shisō Kenkyū* No. 1, 19, 1937, p. 115 observes that the *Hou Han-chi* speaks of T'ang K'o rather than T'ang Chou in this connection.

11. According to HHS, 8, 14b, 360,000 Yellow Turban followers of Chang Chüeh rose up in rebellion on the same day. The uprising occurred during the second month and first year of Central Pacification (*chung-p'ing*) (Feb. 29–Mar. 29, 184). The men of An-p'ing (in modern Hopei) and Kan-ling (in modern Shantung) seized their rulers and then joined the rebels. (Ibid., loc. cit.)

12. See HHS, 68, 33a for this statement attributed to the emperor.

13. One official charged that the Yellow Turban rebellion was brought about by the connivance of the eunuch faction. Eunuchs Chang Jang and Chao Chung were specifically accused of communicating with Chang Chüeh. (HHS, 68, 31a–b; consult the combined biography of these eunuchs in Ibid., loc, cit., 30a–34b.)

14. The general amnesty excluding Chang Chüeh was issued on April 5, 184 (HHS, 8, 15a), or one day after the date originally scheduled for the Yellow Turban revolt (See note 7).

15. Huang-fu Sung achieved military distinction as a successful antagonist of the Yellow Turban and Yüeh-chih rebels. For further information, see HHS, 61, 1a–11a; G. Haloun, "The Liang-Chou Rebellion, 184–221 A.D." *Asia Major*, 1949, pp. 121–123.

16. Chu Chün's biography is in HHS, 61, 11a–21a.

17. General Lu Chih was separately despatched in the spring of 184 and ordered to subjugate Chang Chüeh. (HHS, 8, 15a; consult Ibid., 54, 14b–22a for his biography.)

18. I have no information on the rebel Po Ts'ai. However, in the spring of 184 a fellow rebel named Chang Man-ch'eng attacked Nan-yang Commandery and killed Ch'u Kung, the Commandery Defender (*chün-shou*) (HHS, 8, 15a). Since Nan-yang Commandery bordered Ying-ch'uan Commandery to the northeast the assault by Chang Man-ch'eng may have been coordinated with that launched by Po Ts'ao. The Yellow Turbans in nearby Ju-nan and Kuang-yang Commanderies also defeated their imperial opposition (Ibid., 15b).

19. When Po Ts'ai's troops first enveloped the city of Ch'ang-sha, Huang-fu Sung's forces within the city became frightened because their own numbers were so few. Huang-fu exhorted his soldiers not to lose hope, supporting his argument with relevant historical precedents. When a wind arose, the besieged then took advantage of it by setting fire with torches to the grass around the rebel camp, and defeated the rebels (HHS, 61, 3a–b).

20. Ts'ao Ts'ao's biography is in *SKC Wei*, 1.

21. After the rebels were put to flight at Ch'ang-sha, Huang-fu Sung, Ts'ao Ts'ao and Chu Chün combined forces. They then inflicted a serious defeat on the Yellow Turbans, although the assertion that they decapitated several tens of thousands is probably exaggerated. Royal troops then attacked the Yellow Turbans of Ju-nan and Ch'en-kuo (in modern Honan), pursued Po Ts'ai to Yang-ti and P'eng

T'o to Hsi-hua (both districts in Honan), and crushed the two leaders. Chang Man-ch'eng was decapitated in the summer of 184 by Tsou Hsieh, the Great Defender of Nan-Yang (*HHS*, 8, 15b).

22. The birth of a two-headed child in Lo-yang supposedly accompanied the failure of Tung Cho to defeat Chang Chüeh (*HHS*, 8, 16a). To the Chinese historian, there was an obvious supernatural connection between these events. (Tung Cho's biographies are in *HHS*, 62; *SKC Wei*, 6, 1a–14b.)

23. Lu Chih was first sent to Kuang-tsung, but during his siege of the city the eunuchs at court slanderously accused him of procrastination and duplicity. Thus incriminated, he was killed at the behest of Emperor Ling-ti (*HHS*, 8, 16a; also commentary).

24. Chang Pao was decapitated during the defeat of his troops by Huang-fu Sung at Ch'ü-yang District (in modern Hopei) in the winter of 184 (*HHS*, 8, 16b).

25. Commentary and text in *HHS*, 61, 4b.

26. *HHS*, 61, 4b–5a. The same reference notes that the emperor granted Huang-fu Sung's request that the land tax from Chi Province (in modern Hopei) be remitted because the peasantry there was starving.

27. The reign style was not changed to Central Pacification until the twelfth month and day *chi-ssu* of the seventh year of Brilliant Harmony (Feb. 16, 185). However, the twelve months of the seventh year of Brilliant Harmony were considered retrospectively as belonging to the first year of Central Pacification, and therefore the seventh year or any portion thereof is omitted in the histories.

28. In the spring of 185, Chang Niu-chüeh of Ho-shan (in modern Honan) and over ten of his confederates rose up with their followers in rebellion. The rebellion of the *Yüeh-chih* leader Pei-kung Po-yü and others prior to his pacification in the winter of 185 is detailedly described by G. Haloun, op. cit., 119–121. A soldier from Hupei named Chao Tz'u rebelled in the spring of 186 and killed Tsou Hsieh, the Great Defender of Nan-yang. The year closed with Hsien-pei depredations along the border provinces. Other rebellions by self-styled Yellow Turbans occurred during the next two years (see *HHS*, 8, 17b–21b).

29. *Tui Fu I fei Fo-seng-shih*, 24a, as cited in *KHMC*, 11; *Chui-tui Fu I fei Fo-seng-shih*, 6b–7a, as cited in *KHMC*, 12.

30. *Tui Fu I fei Fo-seng-shih*, loc. cit.

31. Fukui Kōjun, op. cit., 66.

32. Ma Hsiang's activities are briefly outlined in *SKC Shu*, 1, 2a–b; see also Fukui Kōjun, op. cit., 117–120.

33. Liu Yen's biographies are in *HHS*, 65, 1a–8a and in *SKC Shu*, 1, 1a–3b.

34. Liu Yen trusted Chang Lu because he was adept in the "ways of the demons" (*kuei-tao*). He was also intimate with Chang Lu's mother (*HYKC*, 2, 3a).

35. Chang Lu's biography is in *SKC Wei*, 22b–25b.

36. The military post Chang Lu received was that of Marshal Who Controls Righteously (*tu-i ssu-ma*) *SKC Wei*, 8, 22b; *HYKC*, 2, 3a).

37. See Fukui Kōjun, op. cit., 62, for arguments that the person Chang Hsiu killed by Chang Lu was unrelated to the Chang Hsiu whose name was mentioned in a philosophical connection.

38. Chang Lu exercised dictatorial control over the Han-chung area, killing Han envoys on several occasions. Liu Yen reported that Chang Lu had severed the roads (as a mode of transportation) (*HYKC*, 2, 3b). In light of these facts, W. Eichhorn's assertion (op. cit., 331) that "it (i.e. the Taoist state) seems to have replaced by reason of its popularity the official system of the Han government in many areas . . ." is open to question. The Taoists may have replaced the central government not only by reason of their popularity, but rather because in areas such as Han-chung they were able to exercise totalitarian control and forcibly exclude Han officials.

39. *SKC Wei*, 8, 23a.

40. Ibid., op. cit. W. Eichhorn, "Description of the Rebellion of Sun En and Earlier Taoist Rebellion" *Mitteilungen des institus für Orientforschung*, II (Berlin, 1954), 330, translates *shih-chün* as "master of teachers."

41. The public houses were comparable to the arbors in existence at the time of the *SKO* compilation (circa fourth century). The free provisions of rice in the public houses may have been secured from the five pecks of rice which the families of patients treated by the Taoists gave up to cover the costs of confinement.

42. *SKC Wei*, 8, 23a.

43. In my opinion, the statement by W. Eichhorn (op. cit., 328) that Chang Lu's faith-healing methods were more complicated than those practiced by Chang Chüeh is not necessarily valid. In view of the scarcity of primary materials, one can only say that more information is available concerning Chang Lu's faith-healing methods as compared with those attributed to the eastern Yellow Turban leader.

44. H. Maspero, *Le Taoisme* (Paris, 1950), 156; for a list of similar titles, accompanied by a brief commentary, see *Pien-huo-lun*, 5a, as cited in *HMC*, 8.

45. *Pien-cheng-lun*, 23b, as cited in *KHMC*, 13. The three wives of Chang Ling, Chang Heng and Chang Lu were referred to as the Three Ladies (*san fu-jen*) (*Hsiao-Tao-lun*, 28a as cited in *KHMC*, 9).

46. The title Teacher of Heaven was first assumed by Chang Ling (*Pien-huo-lun*, 2a, 4b, as cited in *HMC*, 8).

47. Chang Lu was entitled General of the Inner Worthies Who Protects the People (*chen-min chung-lang-chiang*) and as Great Defender of Hanning (*Han-ning t'ai-shou*) (*SKC Wei*, 8, 23b). The envoys sent to Lo-yang by Chang Lu are accused of arrogant behavior. While the court was unable to retaliate, Liu Yen's son and replacement Liu Chang killed the mother and younger brother of the alleged usurper Chang Lu. Liu Chang then remained a mortal enemy of Chang Lu (*HYKC*, 2, 3b, 4a). Chang Lu's younger brother Chang Wei escaped death at the hands of Liu Chang.

48. The people wished to elevate Chang Lu as king after a jade seal had been uncovered in the earth. Chang Lu's councillor Yen Fu cautioned him against acquiescing to the popular will. Yen Fu said: "The people of Han-ch'uan have over 100,000 households, a wealth of resources and fertile land, and are secure on all sides. If His Highness aids the Son of Heaven, then he shall become comparable to (Duke) Huan (of Ch'i) and (Duke) Wen (of Sung); next he shall attain to (the prestige of) Tou Yung (of the Eastern Han). You shall not lose your wealth and eminence. Now, your decrees are accepted and your offices established. Your prestige is sufficient to decapitate and sever, and you are not troubled by the (Han) king. I request that you do not declare yourself (king), and thereby do not bring disaster to your ancestral line." (*SKC Wei*, 8, 24a; *HHS*, 65, 7a–b.)

49. There are two different versions of the invasion by Ts'ao Ts'ao. According to one version, when Ts'ao Ts'ao invaded the passes at Yang-p'ing, he was opposed by Chang Wei and his troops. Chang Wei's brother Chang Lu, however, wished to surrender. Ts'ao Ts'ao first issued orders to retreat, but two of his generals confusedly advanced and routed the defenders. (*SKC Wei*, 8, 24a; commentary, loc. cit., 24a–b.)

A different account is recorded in *SKC Wei*, 1, 40a–41a. Here we are informed that Chang Lu sent his younger brother Chang Wei and others to oppose [the] Ts'ao Ts'ao invasion. When the defenders suffered defeat, Chang Wei escaped in the darkness while Chang Lu also fled in disorder. The claim is set forth in *Chüeh-tui Fu I fei Fo-seng-shih*, 11a, as cited in *KHMC*, 12, that Chang Lu was executed by Ts'ao Ts'ao. This is probably in error, as it contradicts the earlier evidence.

50. Chang Lu is reported as having once said that he would rather be Ts'ao Ts'ao's slave than an honored guest of Liu Pei, who also wished to conquer this area (*HYKC*, 2, 4a).

51. Chang Lu retired to Han-chung, in compliance with

his minister's advice. Others among his associates wanted to burn all valuables, but Chang Lu objected and sealed up the treasury, awaiting the arrival of Ts'ao Ts'ao (*SKC Wei*, 8, 24b).

52. Ts'ao Ts'ao, delighted because the valuables at Pa-chung had not been tampered with, sent a messenger to comfort Chang Lu. Ts'ao Ts'ao entitled Chang Lu either as the General Who Protects the South (*chen-nan chiang-chün*) (*HHS*, 65, 7b) or as the General Who Protects the People (*chen-min chiang-chün*) (*SKC Wei*, 8, 25a). Chang Lu was enfeoffed either as the Marquis of Lang-chung (in modern Szechwan) (*HHS*, 65, 7b; *SKC Wei*, 8, 25a) or as the Marquis of Hsiang-p'ing (in modern Fengtien) (*HYKC*, 2, 4a).

53. W. Eichhorn, op. cit., 331–352, describes the Taoist rebellion led by Sun En towards the end of the fourth and beginning of the fifth centuries. The Sun En rebellion had many of the characteristics of its Yellow Turban predecessors.

54. Practices which the Taoists might have copied from their Buddhist contemporaries were the burning of incense, the bestowal of free food in the public houses, the memorizing of texts, the prohibition of wine drinking and the killing of animals in certain seasons, and the instructions to Taoist penitents to kowtow and reflect on past transgressions. (See Fukui Kōjun, op. cit., 138–142.)

55. *Tui Fu I fei Fo-seng-shih*, 8a–b, as cited in *KHMC*,
56. "Chang Ling was falsely called Teacher of Heaven. He thereby ridiculed and insulted man and the spirits, and his body suffered retribution. . . . By dealing in death, he (Chang Ling) profited in life; such was his deception of heaven and earth." (*Pien-huo-lun*, 2b–3a, as cited in *HMC*, 8.) "Chang Ling and Chang Lu deceitfully spoke demoniacal words and falsely composed prophetical books . . . (Chang Lu and Chang Chüeh) deceived and misled the foolish people." (*Chüeh-tui Fu I fei Fo-seng-shih*, 6b–7a as cited in *KHMC*, 12.) "Chang Ling . . . composed Taoist books, called himself the Primordial Origin of Great Purity (*t'ai-ch'ing hsüan-yüan*) and thereby deluded the common people." (*HYKC*, 2, 3a. "The Taoist faith-healing methods were really without efficacy for curing illness. However, because of their lewdness and delusion, the petty people stupidly and ignorantly competed as one to serve them." (Commentary to *SKC Wei*, 8, 23b.) "He (Chang Chüeh) changed the aspect (of his teachings) towards deceit and delusion." (*HHS*, 61, 1b. "(Chang) Chüeh despatched his disciples throughout the four regions, and they went about deluding and deceiving." (*Tzu-chih t'ung-chien*, 58, 5a.) "Prior to this, the Yellow Turban master Chang Chüeh and others grasped the ways of heterodoxy and called themselves Great Worthies (*ta-hsien*) in order to deceive and dazzle the common people." (*HHS*, 44, 26b).

45

Some Reflections on the Decline of the Ottoman Empire

Bernard Lewis

During the sixteenth century three major changes occurred, principally of external origin, which vitally affected the entire life of the Ottoman Empire. The first of these has already been mentioned—the halting of the Ottoman advance into Europe. This was an event comparable in some ways with the Closing of the Frontier in the United States—but with far more shattering impact. The Ottoman state had been born on the frontier between Islam and Byzantine Christendom; its leaders and armies had been march-warriors in the Holy War, carrying the sword and the faith of Islam into new lands. The Ottoman gazis and dervishes, like the pioneers and missionaries of the Americas, believed themselves to be bringing civilization and the true faith to peoples sunk in barbarism and unbelief—and like them

reaped the familiar rewards of the frontier warrior and the colonist. For the Ottoman state, the frontier had provided work and recompense both for its men of the sword and its men of religion and, in a deeper sense, the very *raison d'être* of its statehood. True, by the sixteenth century that state had already evolved from a principality of march-warriors into an Empire, but the traditions of the frontier were still deeply rooted in the military, social, and religious life of the Ottomans, and the virtual closing of the frontier to further expansion and colonization could not fail profoundly to affect them. The Ottoman systems of military organization, civil administration, taxation, and land tenure were all geared to the needs of a society expanding by conquest and colonization into the lands of the infidel. They ceased to correspond to the different stresses of a frontier that was stationary or in retreat.[1]

While the great Ottoman war-machine, extended beyond its range, was grinding to a standstill in the

From *The Emergence of Modern Turkey* (London: Oxford University Press, 1968), pp. 26–36. Published under the auspices of the Royal Institute of International Affairs. Reprinted by permission of the publisher.

plains of Hungary, the life and growth of the Ottoman Empire were being circumvented, on a far vaster scale, by the oceanic voyages of discovery of the Western maritime peoples, the ultimate effect of which was to turn the whole Eastern Mediterranean area, where the Empire was situated, into a backwater. In 1555 the Imperial ambassador in Constantinople, Ogier Ghiselin de Busbecq, one of the acutest European observers of Turkey, could still comment that the Western Europeans basely squandered their energies "seeking the Indies and the Antipodes across vast fields of ocean, in search of gold," and abandoning the heart of Europe to imminent and almost certain conquest.[2] But in about 1580 an Ottoman geographer, in an account of the New World written for Murad III, gave warning of the dangers to the Islamic lands and the disturbance to Islamic trade resulting from the establishment of Europeans on the coasts of America, India, and the Persian Gulf; he advised the Sultan to open a canal through the isthmus of Suez and send a fleet "to capture the ports of Hind and Sind and drive away the infidels."[3] By 1625 another Ottoman observer, a certain Ömer Talib, could see the danger in a more pressing form:

> Now the Europeans have learnt to know the whole world; they send their ships everywhere and seize important ports. Formerly, the goods of India, Sind, and China used to come to Suez, and were distributed by Muslims to all the world. But now these goods are carried on Portuguese, Dutch, and English ships to Frangistan, and are spread all over the world from there. What they do not need themselves they bring to Istanbul and other Islamic lands, and sell it for five times the price, thus earning much money. For this reason gold and silver are becoming scarce in the lands of Islam. The Ottoman Empire must seize the shores of Yemen and the trade passing that way; otherwise before very long, the Europeans will rule over the lands of Islam.[4]

The effects on Middle Eastern trade of the circumnavigation of Africa were by no means as immediate and as catastrophic as was at one time believed. Right through the sixteenth century Eastern merchandise continued to reach the Ottoman Empire, coming by ship to Red Sea ports and Basra and overland across Persia, and European merchants came to Turkey to buy. But the volume out of international trade passing this way was steadily decreasing. From the seventeenth century, the establishment of Dutch and British power in Asia and the transference of the routes of world trade to the open ocean deprived Turkey of the greater part of

her foreign commerce and left her, together with the countries over which she ruled, in a stagnant backwater through which the life-giving stream of world trade no longer flowed.[5]

The European voyages of discovery brought another more immediate blow, as violent as it was unexpected. The basic unit of currency of the Ottoman Empire had been the silver *akçe,* or asper, in which all the revenues and expenditures of the state had been calculated. Like other Mediterranean and European states, the Ottoman Empire suffered from a recurring shortage of precious metals, which at times threatened its silver-based monetary system. To meet these difficulties, the Ottoman Sultans resorted to such well-tried measures as controlling the silver mines, discouraging the export and encouraging the import of coin and bullion, extending the non-monetary sector of the state economy, and alternately debasing and reissuing the currency.

This situation was suddenly transformed when the flow of precious metals from the New World reached the Eastern Mediterranean. American gold, and, to a far greater extent, American silver had already caused a price revolution and a financial crisis in Spain. From there it passed to Genoa and thence to Ragusa, where Spanish coins of American metal are first reported in the 1580's.[6] Thereafter the financial impact on Turkey of this sudden flow of cheap and plentiful silver from the West was immediate and catastrophic. The Ottoman rulers, accustomed to crises of shortage of silver, were unable to understand a crisis of excess, or adequately to tax the new commercial inflow; the traditional measures which they adopted only served to worsen the situation. In 1584 the asper was reduced from one-fifth to one-eighth of a dirham of silver—a measure of devaluation which unleashed a continuous financial crisis with far-reaching economic and social consequences. As the price of silver fell, that of gold rose. Turkish raw materials became very cheap for European traders, and were exported in great quantities—including, despite prohibitions, even corn. Local industries began to decline, and the import of European manufactures expanded. Fiscal pressure and economic dislocation, accentuated by large-scale speculation and usury, brought distress and then ruin to large sections of the population. Before long there was a vast increase in coining, coin-clipping, and the like; the rate of the asper fell from 60 to the ducat to over 200, and foreign coins, both gold and silver, drove the debased Ottoman issues even from the internal markets. Twice in the seventeenth century the Ottoman government tried to stem the inflationary tide by the issue of a new silver currency; first, the *para,* which appeared as a silver coin in the 1620's, then the piastre, or *kuruş,* which appeared in the 1680's, in imitation of the European dollar. Both followed the asper into debasement and devaluation.[7]

Precisely at this time of monetary and financial crisis, the government was compelled to embark on a great expansion in its salaried personnel and a great increase in expenditure in coin. When Mehmed the Conqueror had faced a monetary crisis, he had reduced the numbers of paid soldiers and increased the numbers of cavalry sipahis, whose services were rewarded with fiefs and not coin.[8] But in the changed conditions of warfare of the sixteenth and seventeenth centuries this had ceased to be possible. The greatly increased use of firearms and artillery necessitated the maintenance of ever larger paid professional armies, and reduced the relative importance of the feudal cavalryman. Both Koçu Bey and Hacı Halife note and deplore the decline of the sipahis and the increase in the paid soldiery which, says Hacı Halife, had increased from 48,000 in 1567 to 100,000 in about 1620.[9] Both writers are aware of the harmful financial and agrarian effects of this change. Understandably, they miss the point that the obsolescence of the sipahi had become inevitable, and that only the long-term, professional soldier could serve the military needs of the time.

The price was appalling. Faced with a growing expenditure and a depreciating currency, the demands of the treasury became more and more insatiable. The underpaid and over-sized salaried personnel of the state—civil, military, and religious— had growing difficulties in making ends meet, with the inevitable effects on their prestige, their honesty, and their further recruitment. Though the feudal cavalryman was no longer the main strength of the army, his decline was sorely felt in the countryside, as the old Ottoman agrarian system, of which he had once been the foundation, tottered and collapsed. In place of the sipahi, who resided in or near the fief in which he had a hereditary interest, palace favourites, parasites, and speculators became the recipients of fiefs, sometimes accumulating great numbers of them, and thus becoming, in effect, absentee owners of great latifundia. Other fiefs reverted to the Imperial domain.[10] But the growing inefficiency and venality of the bureaucracy prevented the formation of any effective state system for the assessment and collection of taxes. Instead these tasks were given to tax-farmers, whose interposition and interception of revenues became in time a prescriptive and hereditary right, and added to the number of vast and neglected latifundia.

The shrinking economy of the Empire thus had to support an increasingly costly and cumbersome superstructure. The palace, the bureaucracy, and the religious hierarchy, an army that in expenditure at least was modern, and a parasitic class of tax-farmers and absentee landlords—all this was far more than the medieval states or even the Roman Empire had tried to support; yet it rested on an economy that was no more advanced than theirs. The technological level of agriculture remained primitive, and the social conditions of the Turkish countryside after the sixteenth century precluded the appearance of anything like the English gentleman-farmers of the seventeenth and eighteenth centuries whose experiments revolutionized English agriculture.

These developments are not peculiar to Turkey. The fall in the value of money, the growing cost of government and warfare, the sale of offices and farming of taxes—all these are known in other Mediterranean and adjoining states, where they contributed to the rise of a new class of capitalists and financiers, with a growing and constructive influence on governments.

In Turkey too there were rich merchants and bankers, such as the Greek Michael Cantacuzenos and the Portuguese Jew Joseph Nasi—the Fugger of the Orient, as Braudel called him.[11] But they were never able to play anything like the financial, economic, and political role of their European counterparts. Part of the cause of this must undoubtedly be found in the progressive stagnation of Ottoman trade, to which allusion has already been made. But that is not all. Most if not all of these merchants were Christians or Jews—tolerated but second-class subjects of the Muslim state. However great their economic power, they were politically penalized and socially segregated; they could obtain political power only by stealth, and exercise it only by intrigue, with demoralizing effect on all concerned. Despite the scale and extent of their financial operations, they were unable to create political conditions more favourable to commerce, or to build up any solid structure of banking and credit, and thus help the Ottoman government in its perennial financial straits. In England too finance and credit were at first in the hands of alien specialists, who have left their name in Lombard Street. But these were ousted in time by vigorous and pushful native rivals. In Turkey no such rivals arose, and in any case, in the general decline of the seventeenth century, even the Greek and Jewish merchant princes of Constantinople dwindled into insignificance. Fortunes were still made in Turkey, but their origin was not economic. Mostly they were political or fiscal in origin, obtained through the holding of public office. Nor were they spent on investment or development, but consumed or hoarded, after the fashion of the time.

Reference has often been made to the technological backwardness of the Ottoman Empire—to its failure not only to invent, but even to respond to the inventions of others. While Europe swept forward in science and technology, the Ottomans were content to remain, in their agriculture, their industry, and their transport, at the level of their medieval ancestors. Even their armed forces followed tardily and incompetently after the technological advances of their European enemies.

The problem of agriculture in the Ottoman Empire was more than one of technical backwardness, however. It was one of definite decline. Already during the reign of Süleyman the Magnificent, Lûtfi Paşa gave warning of the dangers of rural depopulation, and urged that the peasantry be protected by moderation in taxation and by regular censuses of village population, as a control on the competence of provincial government.[12] Koçu Bey reinforces these arguments; but by 1653 Hacı Halife reports that people had begun to flock from the villages to the towns during the reign of Süleyman, and that in his own day there were derelict and abandoned villages all over the Empire.[13]

Much of this decline in agriculture can be attributed to the causes named by the Ottoman memorialists: the squeezing out of the feudal sipahis, the mainstay of the early Ottoman agrarian system, and their replacement by tax-farmers and others with no long-term interest in peasant welfare or land conservation, but only an immediate and short-term interest in taxes. Harsh, exorbitant, and improvident taxation led to a decline in cultivation, which was sometimes permanent. The peasants, neglected and impoverished, were forced into the hands of moneylenders and speculators, and often driven off the land entirely. With the steady decline in bureaucratic efficiency during the seventeenth and eighteenth centuries, the former system of regular land surveys and population censuses was abandoned.[14] The central government ceased to exercise any check or control over agriculture and village affairs, which were left to the unchecked rapacity of the tax-farmers, the leaseholders, and the bailiffs of court nominees. During the seventeenth century some of the more permanently established lease-holders began to coalesce with the landowners into a new landed aristocracy—the *ayan-i memleket* or country notables, whose appearance and usurpation of some of the functions and authority of government were already noted at the time.[15]

While agriculture declined, industry fared little better. The corporative structure of the guilds fulfilled a useful social function in expressing and preserving the complex web of social loyalties and obligations of the old order, and also, though to a diminishing extent, in safeguarding the moral level and standards of craftsmanship of the artisan. Their economic effects, however, were restrictive and eventually destructive. A man's choice of profession was determined by habit and inheritance, the scope of his endeavour limited by primitive techniques and transport, his manner and speed of work fixed by guild rule and tradition; on the one hand a sufi religious habit of passivity and surrender of self, on the other the swift fiscal retribution for any sign of prosperity, combined to keep industrial production primitive, static, and inert, utterly unable to resist the competition of imported European manufactures.[16]

Some have sought the causes of this backwardness in Islam or in the Turkish race—explanations which do not satisfy, in view of the previous achievements of both. It may, however, be possible to find part of the explanation of Ottoman lack of receptivity—perhaps even of Ottoman decline—in certain evolving attitudes of mind, inherited by the Ottomans along with the classical Islamic civilization of which they had been the heirs and renovators.

Classical Islamic civilization, like others before and after it, including our own, was profoundly convinced of its superiority and self-sufficiency. In its earliest, primitive phase, Islam had been open to influences from the Hellenistic Orient, from Persia, even from India and China. Many works were translated into Arabic from Greek, Syriac, and Persian. But with the solitary exception of the late Latin chronicle of Orosius, not a single translation into a Muslim language is known of any Latin or Western work until the sixteenth century, when one or two historical and geographical works were translated into Turkish.[17] For the Muslim of classical times, Frankish Europe was an outer darkness of barbarism and unbelief, from which the sunlit world of Islam had nothing to learn and little to fear. This view, though becoming outdated towards the end of the Middle Ages, was transmitted by the medieval Muslims to their Ottoman heirs, and was reinforced by the crushing victories of Ottoman arms over their European opponents. On the warlike but open frontier one could still exchange lessons with one's counterpart on the other side; through renegades and refugees new skills could still reach the Islamic Empire. But the willingness to learn these lessons was not there, and in time the sources also dried up. Masked by the still imposing military might of the

Ottoman Empire, the peoples of Islam continued to cherish the dangerous but comfortable illusion of the immeasurable and immutable superiority of their own civilization to all others—an illusion from which they were slowly shaken by a series of humiliating military defeats.

In the military empire, at once feudal and bureaucratic, which they had created, the Muslims knew only four professions—government, war, religion, and agriculture. Industry and trade were left to the non-Muslim conquered subjects, who continued to practise their inherited crafts. Thus the stigma of the infidel became attached to the professions which the infidels followed, and remained so attached even after many of the craftsmen had become Muslim. Westerners and native Christians, bankers, merchants, and craftsmen, were all involved in the general contempt which made the Ottoman Muslim impervious to ideas or inventions of Christian origin and unwilling to bend his own thoughts to the problems of artisans and vile mechanics. Primitive techniques of production, primitive means of transportation, chronic insecurity and social penalization, combined to preclude any long-term or large-scale undertakings, and to keep the Ottoman economy at the lowest level of competence, initiative, and morality.[18]

This apathy of the Ottoman ruling class is the more striking when contrasted with the continuing vigour of their intellectual life. An example of this may be seen in the group of writers who memorialized on the decline of the Empire, which they saw so clearly but were powerless to stop. We may point also to the brilliant Ottoman school of historiography, which reaches its peak of achievement in the work of Naima (1655–1716); to the Ottoman traditions of courtly and religious poetry, two of the greatest exponents of which, Nedim and Şeyh Galib, lived in the eighteenth century; to the Ottoman schools of architecture, miniature, and music. It is not until the end of the eighteenth century and the beginning of the nineteenth that we can speak of a real breakdown in the cultural and intellectual life of Turkey, resulting from the utter exhaustion of the old traditions and the absence of new creative impulses. And even then, behind the battered screen of courtly convention, the simple folk arts and folk poetry of the Turks continued as before.

In the late Middle Ages, the Ottoman Empire was the only state in Europe which already possessed the territory, the cohesion, the organization, the manpower and the resources to carry the new apparatus of warfare, the crushing cost of which was outmoding the city-states and feudal principalities of medieval Europe, as surely as modern weapons have

outmoded the petty sovereignties of Europe in our own day. In part perhaps because of that very primacy, it failed to respond to the challenge which produced the nation-states of sixteenth-century Europe, and the great commercial and technological efflorescence of which they were the scene.

Fundamentally, the Ottoman Empire had remained or reverted to a medieval state, with a medieval mentality and a medieval economy—but with the added burden of a bureaucracy and a standing army which no medieval state had ever had to bear. In a world of rapidly modernizing states it had little chance of survival.

NOTES

1. The significance of the frontier and of the frontiersman in Ottoman government and society has been demonstrated by Paul Wittek. The whole question of the frontier as a cultural entity, with some reference to F. J. Turner's famous thesis on the significance of the frontier in American history, has been re-examined by Owen Lattimore in his "The Frontier in History" (published in *Relazioni*, i, 105–38, of the Tenth International Congress of Historical Sciences, Rome 1955).

2. *The Turkish Letters of Ogier Ghiselin de Busbecq*, tr. by C. T. Forster and F. H. B. Daniell (1881) i, 129–30.

3. *Tarih al-Hind al-Garbi* (Constantinople, 1142/1729), fol. 6b ff.

4. The observations of Ömer Talib, written on the margins of a manuscript of the *Tarih al-Hind al-Garbi* in Ankara (Maarif Library 10024), were published by A. Zeki Velidi Togan, *Bugünkü Türkili (Turkistan) ve Yakin Tarihi*, i (1947), p. 127.

5. On these questions see the important studies of Köprülü (in his additional notes to the Turkish translation of Barthold's *Muslim Culture (Islam Medeniyeti Tarihi*, 1940), pp. 255 ff.) and Inalcık in *Bell.*, no. 60 (1951), pp. 661 ff.

6. I am informed by Professor R. B. Serjeant that cheap silver of Portuguese provenance is reported slightly earlier in Southern Arabia, where it caused a drop in the rate of silver to gold.

7. The effects on wages, prices, and currencies of the flow of American bullion, first studied for Spain in the classic monograph of Earl J. Hamilton (*American Treasure and the Price Revolution in Spain, 1501–1650*, 1934), were examined on a larger scale for the whole Mediterranean area in the great work of F. Braudel, *La Méditerranée et le monde méditerranéen à l'époque de Philippe II* (1949). Braudel's pointers on events in Turkey (especially pp. 393–394, 419–420, 637–643) were taken up and developed by Inalcık in his illuminating study. "Osmanli Imparatorlugunun Kurulus ve Inkisafi devrinde Türkiye' nin Iktisadi Vaziyeti üzerinde bir tetkik münasebetile," *Bell.*, no. 60 (1951), 656 ff. See further the review of Braudel's book by Barkan in *R. Fac. Sci. Éc. Univ. Ist.*, xi (1949–1950), 196–216.

8. Inalcık, in *Bell.*, no. 60, 656 ff.

9. *Düstur al-'Amal li-Islah al-Halal* (Ist., 1280/1863, as an appendix to the *Kavanin-i Al-i Osman* of Ayn-i Ali), pp. 131–132; German trans. by Behrnauer in *ZDMG*, xi (1857), 125. In this little treatise, written in about 1653, Hacı Halife examines the causes of the financial and other troubles of the Ottoman Empire. On changes in the Ottoman armies, see *EI*[2], "Bārūd iv" and "Harb iv" (by V. J. Parry).

10. From the late sixteenth century onwards the cadastral registers in the Ottoman archives show a steady decrease in the number of *timars*, and a corresponding increase in the extent of Imperial domain.

11. Braudel, p. 567.

12. Lûtfi Paşa, *Asafname,* ch. 4. Lûtfi Paşa's treatise, written after his dismissal from the office of Grand Vezir in 1541, sets forth rules on what a good Grand Vezir should do and, more urgently, on what he should avoid. In this booklet, written at a time when the Ottoman Empire was still at the height of its power and glory, the writer shows deep concern about its fate and welfare, and is already able to point to what, in later years, became the characteristic signs of Ottoman decline.

13. Haci Halife, ch. 1.

14. See for example the list of *tapu* registers for the Arab provinces, given in B. Lewis, "The Ottoman Archives as a Source for the History of the Arab Lands," *JRAS* (1951), pp. 149 ff. The great majority of the registers listed there are of the sixteenth century. After 1600 the surveys become less and less frequent, and the resulting registers more and more slipshod.

15. cf. the remarks of Hüseyin Hezarfen, writing in 1669 (R. Anhegger, "Hezarfen Hüseyin Efendi'nin Osmanlı devlet teskilâtina dâir mülâhazalari," *TM,* x (1951–1953), 372, 387. The *ayan-i vilayet* already appear occasionally in *Kanuns* of the sixteenth century (Barkan, *XV ve XVI inci asırlarda . . . Kanunlar,* i (1943), index).

16. Sabri F. Ülgener, *Iktisadî Inhitat Tarihimizin Ahlak ve Zihniyet Meseleleri* (1951). Much light is thrown on these questions by Professor Ülgener's attempt to apply the methods of Weber and Sombart to the study of Ottoman social and economic history.

17. See further B. Lewis, "The Muslim Discovery of Europe," *BSOAS,* xx (1957), 415; also B. Lewis and P. M. Holt, eds., *Historians of the Middle East* (1962), pp. 180–191, where some earlier references to Western sources are discussed.

18. Ülgener, pp. 193 ff.

PART THREE

MAJOR TYPES OF MODERN POLITICAL SYSTEMS: POLITICAL MODERNIZATION AND THE POLITICAL SOCIOLOGY OF THE MODERN STATE

INTRODUCTION TO CHAPTERS 9–12

I

We come now to the last stage in our exploration —the analysis of modern political systems. As we have seen in our introductory chapter, modern sociology in general and political sociology in particular have developed in the context of the emergence of the modern socio-political order in western and central Europe, and it was these developments that have had the greatest impact on the initial *Problemstellung* of political sociology. And yet the problems of political sociology in general and of modern political systems in particular range far beyond these initial *Problemstellung*. The spread of modernity beyond western Europe has greatly varied the extent and scope of these problems, as did later (twentieth-century) developments in Europe and North America. In order to be able to explore them it might be worth while to point out some of the background of the spread of modernity as well as its basic characteristics.[1]

Modernization is probably the most overwhelming and most permeating feature of the contemporary scene. Most nations are now caught in its web, either becoming modernized or continuing their own traditions of modernity. As it spreads throughout the world, both its common features and its different characteristics in various countries stand out. Historically, modernization is the process of change toward those kinds of social, economic, and political systems that developed in western Europe from the seventeenth century to the nineteenth and then spread to other European countries, to North America, and in the nineteenth and twentieth centuries to the South American, Asian, and African countries.

Modern or modernizing societies have evolved from a great variety of different traditional premodern societies. In western Europe they developed from feudal or absolutist states with strong urban centers and in eastern Europe from more autocratic states and less urbanized societies. In the United States and the English-speaking Dominions they developed through colonization and immigration; some of the colonies were rooted in strong religious motivations and organized in groups of religious settlers, while others were based mostly on large-scale immi-gration oriented mostly to economic opportunity and greater equality of status.

In Latin America more fragmentary modern structures developed from oligarchic conquest-colonial societies in which there existed strong division between the white conquering oligarchy and the indigenous subject population. In Japan it developed from a centralized feudal state of unique characteristics, and in China from the breakdown of the most continuous imperial system in the history of mankind, a system based on special types of "literati-bureaucratic" institutions.

In most Asian and African societies the process of modernization began in colonial frameworks, some (especially in Asia) based on preceding more centralized monarchical societies and elaborate literary-religious traditions, others (especially in Africa) mostly on tribal structures and traditions. These different starting points greatly influenced the specific contours of development and the problems encountered in its course. And yet beyond these variations there also developed many common characteristics that constitute perhaps the major core of modernization of a modern society, and it would be well to start our analysis with a review of those characteristics.

II

The most salient aspects of modernization have often been summarized under two broad categories: sociodemographic and structural. The broad demographic and structural corollaries of modernization as they develop in the major institutional spheres are now well known.

Perhaps the best over-all summary of the sociodemographic indices of modernization has been coined by Karl Deutsch in the term "social mobilization." He has defined modernization as "the process in which major clusters of old social, economic, and psychological commitments are eroded and broken and people become available for new patterns of socialization and behaviour," and he has indicated that some of its main indices are exposure to aspects of modern life through demonstrations of machinery, buildings, consumers' goods, response to mass media,

317

change of residence, urbanization, change from agricultural occupations, literacy, growth of per capita income, and the like.[2]

Similarly, the major structural characteristics of modernization have been identified as the development of a high extent of differentiation, of free resources not committed to any fixed ascriptive (kinship, territorial, and such) groups, of specialized and diversified types of social organization, of wide nontraditional, "national," or even supernational group identifications, and, in all major institutional spheres, of specialized roles and special wider regulative and allocative mechanisms and organizations, such as market mechanisms in economic life, voting and party activities in politics, and diverse bureaucratic organizations and mechanisms in most institutional spheres.[3]

These varied processes of differentiation and social mobilization have developed side by side with basic structural changes in all major institutional phases of social life of modern or modernizing societies. In the economic sphere proper these developments have been characterized by growing specialization of economic activities and occupational roles, by the development of units of production oriented to the market, and by the growth of the scope and complexity of the major markets—the markets for goods, labor, and money.[4]

In the sphere of social organization the characteristic features of modern society are the large number of functionally specific organizations, the division of labor between functionally specific and more solidary or culturally oriented associations, the weakening of the importance of the kinship and narrow territorial bases of specialized associations on the one hand and of various "specialized" associations and of broad ascriptive-solidary groups on the other.

This structural differentiation had several repercussions in the area of social stratification, the most important of which has been the development of an ambiguous status system. The tendency found in many premodern societies for most property, power, and status relations either to coalesce or to be segregated in a rigid hierarchical order tends to break down with the process of modernization.[5] This can be seen first in the high importance of criteria of universalism and achievement in all major institutional spheres. The social positions held by anyone in different social spheres were no longer necessarily identical, and there was no necessary coalescence between them. One's place in the political or "social" sphere was not so assured as in many premodern societies by virtue of one's economic or occupational standing, or vice versa. Although strong tendencies

to some such coalescence exist in all modern societies, they are usually counteracted as a result of the relative independence of the different—deference—relevant distributions. Moreover, mobility in modern societies is not only of individuals and families moving between relatively given and fixed structural positions; there is also a creation of new structural positions as a result of new types of business enterprises, labor organization, or political or administrative organizations, and of new criteria of evaluation of such positions.

Another very important aspect of the system of stratification that tended to develop with processes of modernization was the growing dissociation between elite and broad status groups (strata, classes) on the one hand and among the different elites on the other hand. In all these spheres there have developed categories of groups or of people whose members are leaders in various institutional spheres without at the same time being confined to definite strata or classes. This applies to the bureaucracy, the economic entrepreneurs, the military, the intellectuals, and the different political elites alike, as well as to various local elites.

If the different elite groups became continuously dissociated from broader status groups on the one hand and more autonomous on the other, a continuous differentiation took place among the elites themselves. One such important differentiation was that between elites oriented to more general, collective or cultural, diffuse goals and activities that focused on the promotion of various symbols of solidarity, such as the political and intellectual (especially the literary, journalistic) and the more specialized elites, such as various professional, technical, or managerial ones. Of no smaller importance was the growing differentiation within each of these broad types of elites.[6]

The educational channels themselves have changed from agencies oriented mainly toward the education of an elite and agencies of sponsored mobility to agencies concerned with the spread of education, with cultural mobilization of wider strata, and with problems of social mobility in general and occupational mobility in particular.[7]

In the cultural sphere, a modern society is characterized by a growing differentiation of the major elements of the major cultural and value systems: that is, religion, philosophy, and science; the spread of literacy and secular education; and a more complex intellectual institutional system for the cultivation and advancement of specialized roles based on intellectual disciplines. These developments have been very closely related to the expansion of media of communication, the growing permeation of such central media of communication into the major groups of the society, and the wider participation of these groups in the cultural activities and organizations created by the centrally placed cultural elites.[8]

The culmination of these developments has been the development of a new cultural outlook—perhaps the most pervasive aspect of modernization—even if its spread and permeation have been intermittent and very uneven. It has been characterized by an emphasis on progress and improvement, on happiness and the spontaneous expression of abilities and feeling, on individuality as a moral value, and concomitant stress on the dignity of the individual and on efficiency.[9]

This has been manifest in the development of some new personality orientations, traits, and characteristics: greater ability to adjust to the broadening societal horizons; and the development of some ego flexibility, of widening spheres of interest, and of growing potential empathy toward other people and situations; as well as a growing evaluation of self-advancement, increased mobility, and a growing emphasis on the present as the meaningful temporal dimension of human existence.[10]

III

In the political sphere modernization has been characterized first by growing extension of the territorial scope and intensification of the power of the central, legal, administrative, and political agencies of the society.

Second, it has been characterized by the continuous spread of potential power to wider groups in the society—ultimately to all adult citizens—and their incorporation into a consensual moral order.

Third, modern societies are in some sense democratic or at least populistic societies. They are characterized by the decline of traditional legitimation of the rulers with reference to powers outside their own societies (God, reason) and by the establishment of some sort of ideological and usually also institutional accountability of the rulers to the ruled, who are alleged to be the holders of the potential political power.

All these characteristics are connected, of course, with the greater fluidity of political support and with considerable weakening, sometimes almost total disappearance, of ascriptive political commitment to any given ruler or group. Thus, in order to maintain themselves effectively in power and receive support for the specific goals they propagate and for the policies they want to implement, the rulers believe they must cultivate continuously the political support of the ruled, or at least of large or vocal parts of them, through elections, plebiscites, and acclamatory surrogates.

The difference between modern democratic or semidemocratic and totalitarian political systems lies not in the genuineness of these beliefs, but in the extent to which they are given institutional expression in pluralistic political organizations, in public liberties, and in welfare and cultural policies.

Modernity has also been related to a marked change in the symbols of common national, social and cultural identity. These symbols were no longer chiefly traditional, defined in terms of kinship, tribal, or traditional and restricted status groups. Although the new national symbols usually had a distinct territorial referent, they were much less traditional and included many more subgroups of various kinds. Among many strata there developed some measure of differentiation, but not rigidly ascribed, identification with common cultural symbols that were neither entirely limited to any one territorial or kinship unit nor mediated by it.

This attitude toward symbols is very closely related to the tendency toward the establishment of a civil order—an order in which all citizens, regardless of kinship, status, or territorial belonging, participate in and share the same set of central institutions.

IV

Modern societies are characterized, however, not only by the various sociodemographic and structural characteristics outlined above, but also by the propensity to create continuously in all institutional spheres new levels of differentiation and new types of structural organization.[11] However, neither of these varied sociodemographic and structural characterictics, nor even the propensity to continuous structural change, exhausts the basic nature of society in general and of modern sociopolitical orders in particular. In order to be able to analyze the very core of modernity, it might be worth while to look back at the genesis of modern sociopolitical orders.

The emergence or creation of modern polity has been always an outcome of a revolutionary act—the Great Rebellion or Glorious Revolution in England,[12] the American and French revolutions in the eighteenth century,[13] the various European and Latin-American revolutions in the nineteenth and twentieth centuries,[14] the anticolonial, national, and communist revolutions in Asia and Africa.[15] These revolutionary events differed in many ways from the processes of change that characterized premodern types of polities, with the partial exception of the city-states.

Unlike the processes of change in premodern societies, the revolutions that ushered in modern polities were more or less consciously oriented at changing the basic contours of the societal center; the changes in these contours were not just an aftereffect of other changes. Thus from its very beginning modernity has been connected with a revolutionary concept and imagery, and even the most reformist or conservative tendencies and orientations that tend to develop in modern settings are from the very beginning set in the framework of such revolutionary imagery and symbolism.

These revolutionary orientations, whatever their concrete contents, are directed toward a complete transformation of the nature of the centers of society, of participation and access to them, and of the relation between centers and periphery. These basic transformations can be discerned both in the contents of these centers and in the pattern of participation in them and access to them. From the point of view of content, the major transformation has been in the growing secularization of the centers and of the "opening up" of their contents—that is, the nonacceptance of the givenness of these contents and the assumption that these contents can indeed be formulated anew.

This transformation was closely connected with changes in the structure of the centers and the relations among them, with the growing multiplicity of such centers—political, cultural, social—the growing autonomy of each of them, as well as the growing interpenetration and independence among them. It was also connected with crucial changes in the patterns of participation of the periphery in the center, and of its access to the center. From this point of view modern polities are characterized by the growing impingement of the periphery on the center, by the permeation of the periphery by the center, and by the concomitant tendency toward the obliteration of at least the symbolic differences between center and periphery and the equalization of membership in the collectivity with participation in the center.

Whatever the exact details of this process of drawing wide groups into the central institutional spheres of the society, they all epitomize the growth and concretization of the demand for equality. Equality has thus become not only an abstract ideal but also an overwhelming demand for growing concrete participation of all groups in all spheres of life.[16]

In the political and cultural fields this impingement on the center can best be seen in the fact that the broader groups and strata of society tended more and more to claim access to the central institutions not only by making various demands on it but also by aspiring to participate in the very crystallization of the center, its symbols, and its institutional contours. All the major social movements—be they national, social, or cultural—that developed with the onset of modernization manifest, in varying degrees and scope, this tendency.[17]

V

The preceding discussion indicates that the core of the modern sociopolitical order can be seen in the breakdown of traditionality as we have defined it above.[18]

Within the sociopolitical order the distinction between a traditional and a modern political or cultural order does not lie in the development within any institutional sphere of the specific structural characteristics that have often been identified as modern, whether it is the industrial labor force and free markets in the economic sphere or a centralized administration and unified legal system in the political sphere. Rather it may be seen in the extent to which the basic symbolic and cultural premises of traditionalism with their structural and cultural limitations are or are not maintained on the central levels of the societal and cultural orders.

The most important among these premises in the political field are the continuing symbolic and cultural differentiation between the center and periphery and the concomitant limitation on the access of members of broader groups to the political center or centers and on participation in them.

In traditional regimes these premises were closely connected to the fact that the legitimation of the rulers was couched in basically traditional religious terms. There was no distinction between the basic political roles and the subject societal roles, such as membership in local communities. Such membership was often embedded in such groups, but the citizens or subjects exercised no actual direct or symbolic political rights through a system of voting or franchise.

In the cultural sphere, the basic premises of traditionality, common to all "traditional" societies however great the differences between them, were the acceptance of tradition, of the givenness of some past event, order, or figure (whether real or symbolic) as the major focus of their collective identity, of the scope and nature of their social and cultural order, as the ultimate legitimizer of change, and as the delineator of the limits of innovation.

The most important aspects of such traditionality were limitation in terms of reference to some past event of the scope, contents, and degree of changes and innovations; limitation of access to positions, the incumbents of which are the legitimate interpreters of the scope of the contents of the traditions; and limitation of the right to participate in these centers and in forging the legitimate contents and symbols of the social and cultural orders.

Whatever the extent and scope to which the various traditional forms of life in various spheres of society persist, it is insofar as changes in the connotation of tradition on central levels have taken place that we witness the breakthrough, which may be gradual or abrupt, to some sort of modern sociopolitical or cultural order. If such changes in the connotation of tradition on central levels have not taken place, whatever the extent of structural changes or possible transformation of tradition in different parts of the society, then we still have some type of traditional order.

Thus the breakthrough to modernity is focused on the change in the contents of the symbols of the center, of their secularization, on the growing emphasis on values of human dignity and social equality, and on the growing possibility of the participation, even if in an intermittent or partial way, of broader groups in the formulation of its central symbols and institutions.

It is such changes in the connotations of tradition and its major structural implications that provide the impetus to continuous processes of change and to the perception of change as a positive value in itself and which create the problem of the absorption of change as the major challenge of modernization.[19]

The preceding analysis brings out perhaps the most central characteristics and problems of modern societies: their basic mass-consensual orientation and their predisposition to continuous change. The consensual or mass aspect of modern society is rooted in the growing impingement of broader strata on the center, in their demands to participate in the sacred symbols of society and in their formulation, and in the displacement of the traditional symbols by new ones that stress these participatory and social dimensions.

This tendency to mass consensuality does not, of course, find its fullest institutionalized expression in all types of modern society. During the first stages of modernization it may be weak or intermittent, while totalitarian regimes tend, of course, to suppress its fullest expression. But even totalitarian regimes attempt to legitimize themselves in terms of such values, and it is impossible to understand their policies, their attempts to create symbols of mass consensus, without assuming the existence of such

consensual tendency among its strata and its acknowledgment by the rulers.

VI

As a result of these developments, we find in modern polities a paradoxical tendency toward the obliteration of the differences between center and periphery apparently similar to that of primitive societies. Although in purely structural terms modern societies are characterized by the greatest distinctiveness of centers from periphery, many of the modern ideologies—and especially the socialist-Communist and utopian ones—have envisaged the ultimate culmination of revolutionary tendencies in modern society as a return to the basic tenets of primitive communism.

This similarity between the modern and primitive orders is in a sense an optical illusion, and in a way its basic characteristics are the reverse of what has been found in primitive societies. The obliteration of the differences between center and periphery in modern societies, insofar as it is taken seriously at all, is mostly confined to the symbolic field—to the symbolic, ideological claims of the possibility of the embodiment of the true, good, over-all social and cultural order in all the centers of society, in which all the members of the society can fully participate.

But given the basic structural characteristics of modern societies—their high level of complexity and differentiation of organic division of labor—the tendency to obliterate the differences between center and periphery cannot be attained in the structural field proper; it cannot result in the setting up of a structural equivalence and homology between the center and the periphery. From the structural point of view, modern societies probably constitute the culmination of the trends of specialization and distinctive organization of the center and of its differentiation from the periphery. Hence the many attempts of the ideological trends to obliterate such a distinction could not be successful without destroying the very structural bases of these centers.

But it is this combination of the structural distinctiveness and autonomy of the center with the growing tendency to the obliteration—at least the symbolic obliteration—of the differences between center and periphery that provides the major poles and focuses of political symbolism and process in modern societies, especially as it developed in Western political traditions. It is in the framework of these developments that some of the basic dimensions of the problem of the "quality" of modern society—such as those of freedom, stability and change, which have been analyzed, and of the Western conception of the dichotomy of state and society —have developed.

These developments had some very interesting implications for certain aspects of political symbolism in modern—especially Western—societies. Perhaps one of the most interesting of these implications was the transformation of the relationship between the symbolic and the more technical aspects of political order.

Because of the tendency to obliterate at least the symbolic distinction between the center and the periphery, we witness here—especially in Western societies—the almost total demise of the autonomous ideological concern with purely technical aspects of political life, their full subsumption under the symbolic order, and also a growing emphasis on the homology between public and private morality. Modern regimes differ greatly as to which aspect is the most important and predominant. This is perhaps most clearly seen in the structure of modern constitutions in which the technical and the symbolic aspects of the political order are very often most closely interwoven.

It is from the meeting between the symbolic aspects and the basic pattern of participation and conception of centers that the major types of orientations of protest evolved in modern societies.

VII

In modern societies these orientations are not purely intellectual exercises. They are very closely related to the structural and symbolic aspects of participation and center building and to the general political process that developed in modern societies. The common denominator of these orientations was first that they aimed at the transformation of the newly emerging social and political centers, their symbols, and the broader social structure; and second that they were relatively widespread among the major articulate groups and strata of the society.

The first basic theme was the search for principles of social order and justice and of the legitimation of the center in general and the ruling groups in particular in terms of nontraditional values acceptable to broader strata and to some extent shared and even created by them. These values could be social, that is, related to some of the problems of distributive justice referred to above or to the representation of the symbols of the over-all collectivity, of efficiency, or of legality.[20] Problems of the allocation of resources —power, wealth, status—and of access to various positions in the society by different groups and strata were also central.[21]

The second theme focused on the nature of the emerging over-all civil, political, and cultural community, especially on finding new common symbols in which various groups of the society could find some sense of personal and collective identity.[22] The problem of the relevance of the tradition and history of the community to the problems attendant on modernization and to the new institutional setting became a very important focus of debate. Closely connected to this question of relevance was the search for symbols and roles that would combine both general universal orientations—inherent in basic cultural orientations of modernity—with the particular national traditions and would, within the last, find the bases for the maintenance of a civil order.[23]

The third major theme of protest was focused around the possibility of attaining full expression of human and cultural creativity, of personal dignity, and of true or pure interpersonal relation within the specialized and differentiated frameworks attendant on modernization and the complex division of labor involved. Basic to this theme was the problem of so-called "alienation"; that is, the assumed loss, by individuals, of direct relation to and identification with their work, their social setting and other people.[24]

Around all these focal themes of protest there could develop different basic views or orientations, which often tended to overlap. One such orientation, usually called the "rightist" one, was rooted in the continuous feeling by different groups of being ousted from existing positions and values, of losing their place in the society, and the consequent development of demands for upholding or restoring traditional order and values. The second extreme, what may be called the "leftist" view, was oriented to effecting far-reaching change in the social structure, in the basic principles of allocation in favor of groups or classes that allegedly were deprived of advantageous position or full participation. These groups could be social classes, occupational categories, regional groups in any society, or special over-all national or tribal subgroups in a broad (imperial, colonial) or international social and political order.[25]

Both these orientations could become interrelated in different ways with the search for direct, "pure," unalienated human relations and attachments to primordial symbols. Traditionalists would claim that such relations are possible only under relatively stable, ordered conditions undiluted by the disrupting forces of growing differentiation, democratization, and mass society. Political radicals, on the other hand, could claim that such relations can be achieved only by overthrowing the order and establishing a new one whose institutional arrangements would entirely coalesce with nonalienated relations. More nonpolitical radicals could claim that such relations can be attained only outside of both traditional and any modern, formalized power order.

Such orientations of protest, aiming at the transformation of the major symbols of community, also developed in the cultural sphere proper; but it would be beyond the scope of our discussion here to dwell on them in any detail. It might be worth while to mention that throughout different stages of modernization the major themes that developed in this sphere were those of traditionalism as against more autonomous forces of cultural creativity and of the relation of both to the possibility of erosion of cultural creativity and standards.[26]

These social and cultural orientations and symbols of social justice and tradition and the various attempts to define the over-all cultural and political community in terms of these values and symbols developed not only within each national community but also very largely with respect to the international sphere. First, many of the modern social movements, such as socialist, Communist, or national movements, were international in scope and orientation. Second, with the growing interrelations and interdependence between nations and with the unification of the international scene, international relations became more and more conceived in terms of distributive justice.

This development perhaps had its roots in the nature of the encounter between the latecomers to modernization and the firstcomers (especially England and France) in general, between the Asian and African nations and the Europeans in particular, and in the colonial situation that has developed as one of the main patterns of interrelations between them. Hence the self-perception of many New Nations, beginning with "the first New Nation—the United States"[27]—in terms of social justice and cultural attainments, was not only or even mainly directed inward but was also conceived in terms of their interrelation to other nations and their international standing.

VIII

As we have pointed out above, the orientations of protest were not purely academic or utopian, however strong these ingredients might have been in them and in the elites and the movements that helped to develop and articulate them. They were most closely related to the political processes in modern societies, and it was in this that the political process in modern societies greatly differed from that of other types of society, again with the partial exception of some of the city-states.

In modern societies these protests and demands manifest themselves in two closely interwoven ways. One is the search for ways of regulating the varied, discrete, and often conflicting interests of different groups. The other is the search for and attempts to crystallize new major symbols of personal and of collective (usually national) identity.[28]

Perhaps even more significant than either of these problems is the growing interconnection between them. The discrete and concrete interests of various groups—whether economic, religious, or political problems—tended more and more, although in different degrees in different places, to be perceived and defined not only in terms of their immediate, concrete settings but also in broader terms of social justice, of participation in the broader collectivity, and of the primordial images of this collectivity.

Many of the objects of protest and demands constituted some of the major focuses of political struggle and were, as we have seen, objects of social policies developed by the ruling elites. This means that the orientations of protest and the movements of demand related to them have to be seen as more extreme manifestations of the regular workings of the political institutions, and they therefore have to be analyzed in this context.

These various demands are articulated and aggregated in the major types of political organization prominent in modern societies analyzed above: in interest groups, movements, public opinion, and political parties.[29] The interest groups tend to emphasize the more restricted, discrete interests of different groups. Restricted social movements and public opinion tend to emphasize demands for the reformation of existing political institutions, while the more extreme social movements emphasize demands for total transformation of political regimes. Different party or partylike organs may evince, of course, different degrees of predominance of each of these types of organization and of their respective political orientations. But whatever such relative predominance, the integration of each element into the frameworks of parties is never complete; and interest groups, social movements, and different organs of public opinion tend to develop autonomous orientations. In many situations they tend often to "burst" the frameworks imposed on them by the parties. They tend to maintain their autonomous orientations by presenting their own demands directly to the central political institutions—the executive, legislative, or bureaucratic—without the mediation of any given party, by attempting to mobilize support and resources for themselves directly, and by attempting to interpret within their own frameworks different political demands.

The possibility of the persistence and transformation of protest in its different manifestations has thus been inherent in modern institutional settings, no matter how well organized they might have become. It is mostly these autonomous expressions of interest groups, public opinion, and social movements that constitute the major focuses of perspective of social protest in the political field.

IX

The preceding discussion brings out some of the most salient characteristics and problems of modernization. First, it is the breakthrough from a traditional sociopolitical order in the direction of a mass-consensual one that contains within itself the specific characteristics of social changes in modernity, the propensity to system transformation, and the persistence of demands for change, protest, and transformation. These demands to change could develop, of course, in different directions; they could be reformatory, demanding the improvement of existing institutions, or they could aim at total transformation of a system.

Second, modernization evinces two closely connected and yet distinct aspects. The first is the development of a social structure with a great variety of structural differentiation and diversification; of continuously changing structural forms, activities, and problems; and of propensities to continuous change and to system transformation. But the mere development of these propensities does not in itself assume the development of an institutional structure capable of dealing in a relatively stable way with continuous changes and of assuring the maintenance of a civil order.

The second and crucial problem that modernization creates is whether or not the emerging social structure can deal with such continuous changes; that is, can it develop an institutional structure capable of "absorbing" continuously changing problems and demands?[30] This constitutes the central problem and challenge of modernization.

X

Thus it is the extent of their ability to absorb continuous changes, to institutionalize sustained growth, to combine some measure of stability and

order with such absorption of change that is the most central problem common to all modern and modernizing societies. But if the problem has been common, the answers have been greatly diversified.

Modern regimes and political systems varied greatly with regard to their ability to absorb change and in the types of institutional arrangements—in the types of political regime—they developed. The two need not be the same, although much of the Western political tradition has assumed that only one type of regime—the pluralistic constitutional regime—has been really capable of institutionalizing sustained growth. Moreover, most of the typologies of political systems that can be found in the literature of political science and even of political sociology, at least until the growing concern with the problems of New States arose, have been focused mostly around the distinction among the constitutional-institutional aspects of regimes—among democratic, autocratic, totalitarian regimes—and on differences in each of these "types."[31]

Even the more recent developments in political sociology that combine the analytical, comparative, and behavioral approaches we mentioned in the General Introduction, some of which will be presented in the following selections, have gone beyond such typologies, but still retain some of the assumptions on which these typologies were based. In most of them we still find, even if only implicitly, the assumption that there exists a strong relation between the type of regime defined in such constitutional terms and the ability to institutionalize sustained growth.

All the evidence indicates that this is not the case. This assumption is to some extent true in the sense that most of these regimes, especially those of western Europe, northern Europe, the United States, and the White Dominions, have indeed evinced the longest history of such sustained growth. But some pluralistic regimes, such as the political systems of France and Italy, of Weimar Germany, and of many Latin-American countries that have adopted the external paraphernalia of pluralistic regimes, did not evince such capacity for sustained growth. On the other hand, some nonpluralistic regimes, such as Soviet Russia, postrevolutionary Mexico, and Turkey, seem to have evinced a relatively high degree of such capacity.[32]

Moreover, the parallel assumptions often found in large parts of the literature, even if implicitly, that the formal constitutional features of a regime also embody its qualities in terms of personal and public liberties and possibilities of participation in the political process, and that these various aspects of liberty—or the lack of it—go together, have been disproved by recent history. The limitation of these assumptions tended to become obvious as more attempts were made to apply these typologies to more recent developments in Western societies as well as to the study of non-European regimes, especially to the so-called New Nations.

A quotation from a recent review article by L. Stone brings out some of these limitations, especially, but not only, as they apply to Western regimes.

To-day, however, the question of the authoritarian versus the democratic way seems much less fundamental, not because we care less about liberty in the Sixties than in the Fifties, but because the constitutional forms seem both superficial and temporary. Our study of primitive and traditional societies has revealed ways of achieving consultation and consent unknown to Anglo-Saxon constitutional lawyers, and Marx's view of legal institutions as epiphenomena dependent on social structure and economic relationships has merely been strengthened by the test of time. Fascism and Stalinism both now look like short-term transition phases rather than as permanent and deep-seated structural phenomena. To-day, the three ex-fascist states, Italy, West Germany, and Japan, have settled down to a democratic way of life, with safeguards for liberty which are not to be despised. Russia seems to be edging gingerly toward a more relaxed view of personal freedom, and the role of public opinion and pressure groups in determining policy seems to be increasing.

On the other hand, many democratic states of the 1950s are moving in the opposite direction. Greece, once the pride of the architects of the Truman Doctrine, is in the grip of a régime whose authoritarian brutality is only mitigated by its stupidity. In France, political liberty is closely controlled by the manipulations of a paternalistic autocracy, although personal liberty survives (except where it runs counter to Madame de Gaulle's Victorian notions of sexual prudery). In the U.S., it is not yet clear whether the formal processes of democratic government will be capable of dealing with the two basic issues of the day: the desire by a powerful section of the élite to make America take on the job of policeman of the world, and the interrelated problems of the Negro and the city. After a bad scare during the McCarthyite days of the Fifties, personal liberty seems fairly secure for the moment. In England, personal liberty is perhaps better protected than anywhere in the world, but the political role and prestige of the representative institution is in rapid decline, and democratic control is becoming confined to the power to turn the rascals out every five years or so. . . .[33]

The limitations of these assumptions became even more explicit in the study of New Nations. This does not mean—as has sometimes been claimed—that the basic concepts and variables employed in these studies of Western political systems could be applied to the non-European political systems. Rather, it means that there developed new specific constellations of these variables that could not be accounted for by the basic—even though implicit—assumptions of many of these studies. The most important of these assumptions are the existence of a relatively strong center and a concomitant national community and the image of a strong center in which almost all components of center formation were combined with the special predominance of developing new attributes of collective identity, upholding collective goals, and regulating intergroup relations.

The various patterns of political participation and the cleavages considered in most of these studies were perceived as taking place in relatively strong centers; that is, they were institutionally strong and also served as important reference points for these societies. These centers could indeed be broken down by various cleavages and conflicts, yet they retained their basic strength and vitality. But these studies did not envisage the possibility of the development of weak centers or centers with different constellations of components of center formation; nor did they see explicitly the processes and conditions under which strong, as against weak, modern centers or modern centers with different constellations of components tend to develop; nor the different implications of seemingly similar patterns of political participation, organization in the settings of weak and strong centers, or centers with different types of components.

XI

Thus we come to the problem of the conditions under which different types of modern or modernizing regimes, that is, modern regimes characterized by different types of centers, political conditions, and the ability to sustain continuous change, can develop. On the most general level of analysis it can be assumed that at least some of the differences are rooted in the different ways in which the forces of modernity impinged on these societies and in which their own social and cultural structure influenced their paths to modernity; that is, to the breakdown of traditional legitimation and of the ascriptive ties of the periphery to the center, to the development of various new types of nontraditional elites, and to the quest for new nontraditional legitimation.

But beyond this common core there are many

differences among the various modern and modernizing societies. In order to be able to understand these differences we must first distinguish between several aspects of modernity. We must distinguish between the impingement of forces of modernity and the consequent undermining of the existing traditional settings, the breakthrough to modernity on the structural and cultural levels, and the ways in which the new emerging social systems tend to deal with these problems, and their capacity to deal with them.

Given the historical spread of modernity from the seventeenth and eighteenth centuries until today, almost all traditional societies have been, or are being, caught up in it in the sense that modern forces impinge on them, undermining their existing settings in at least three different ways.

First, they impinge on many of the bases of the various existing traditional institutional spheres— economic, political or community life, or social organization—making various new demands on them and opening up new vistas before their members. There are obviously very great differences among various modern and modernizing societies with regard to the intensity of this impingement and its specific institutional location.

Second, these forces create a new international system in which differences in strength in modern (economic or political) terms is a major determinant of relative international standing. Here too, however, there are great variations in the extent of the impingement of these international forces on different traditional societies and in the extent to which they are exposed to it.

Third, the forces of modernity tend to impinge on many traditional societies by creating the vogue or demand for a growing participation of the citizens in the center, most clearly manifested in the tendency to establish universal citizenship and suffrage and some semblance of a "participant" political or social order.

These different forces may impinge on varied constellations in different historical cases, and each of these constellations tends to create different types of breakthrough to modernity and institutional and cultural problems with which these societies and their newly emerging structures have to deal. Such transition or break-through to modernity may take place under a variety of conditions. It may, of course, take place under different structural conditions, or different types of impingement of modern forces on the basic institutional spheres—the economic and political, or that of social organization and stratification.

Such a breakthrough to modernity may occur in societies whose groups and elites evince different degrees of adaptability or resistance to change, of erosion of wider normative commitments, and of transformative capacities, and where the new centers evince different degrees or kinds of strengths or weaknesses. It may take place under different degrees of structural differentiation with broad strata evincing a relatively high level of resistance to change in the new setting and of erosion of normative commitments, or, conversely, a high level of adaptability to it; with secondary elites and especially with more central elites that may be resistant to change, that is, "traditionalistic" in a militant or an erosive way; with elites that are highly adaptable to the new settings, with but few transformative orientations; or with elites that have transformative capacities in either a flexible or a coercive way.

It may take place under different temporal sequences of development in different institutional spheres, and such different temporal sequences may greatly influence both the problems these societies face and their responses to them. These various structural and temporal differences greatly affect the nature of the concrete problems that arise in these societies, including the levels of aspirations and conflicts of various groups as well as some aspects or conditions of the ability of the central elites to deal with these problems and especially the level of economic, organizational, and educational resources available for the crystallization of new institutional settings.

Each constellation of these processes tends to create the impetus to the breakthrough to modernity in the sociopolitical and cultural order, and the concomitant impetus to intensive continuous change. But each such specific constellation tends also to create different types or patterns of such a breakthrough, different types of institutional and cultural problems with which these societies and their new emerging structures have to deal, as well as the patterns of institutional response to the problem of continuous change, different degrees and types of ability or lack of ability to deal with these problems, and the crises specific to each type of modern or modernizing society.

XII

But these are necessarily very general and preliminary indications; they do not as yet explain how such different concrete impingements of modernity have been connected with the development of different types of modernizing regimes. There is quite an abundant literature about the conditions of development and continuity of modern democratic-pluralistic, and to some extent also of some modern (European), authoritarian regimes.[34]

Many of the insights of these analyses have been applied to a more general framework of modernization and have given us many important indications about some of the general conditions that facilitate the development of institutions capable of dealing with some aspects of continuous change. Of special importance are the initial patterns of the establishment of central institutional modern frameworks, the relative tempo of modernization, and processes of and the extent of structural flexibility of strategic groups and elites in the society.

The establishment and continuity of flexible political symbols and central, political and legal frameworks, of common symbols of political-national identification, and of organs of political struggle, legislation, and administration are basic prerequisites for the development of a sense of modern, differentiated political identity and affinity among the different groups and strata that are drawn into the context of modern political community.

The nondevelopment of such frameworks may reinforce the closeness of the various modern elites, as manifested by their lack of ability to forge new, cohesive symbols and by the development of policies incapable of forging new interlinking mechanisms in the society and creating cohesive symbols and frameworks. These factors may be of crucial importance in the development and institutionalization of adequate regulative mechanisms that can deal with new emerging problems.

Of special importance in this context has been the establishment and institutionalization—whether formal or informal—of certain rules of the political game, such as systems of election or less formal institutional devices of different types that establish some procedural consensus in the society. Similarly, such successful institutionalization has been usually greatly dependent on, and related to, the development of a relatively flexible and differentiated legal system that, whatever its social or political underpinnings, could assure some basic legal rights to individuals, some protection in the undermining of long-term commitments and activities, and some minimal rights of the citizens.

All such developments greatly facilitate the development of a more cohesive and flexible modern institutional center that is capable of both promoting and regulating change and that can be responsive to various needs and demands without becoming totally ineffective. But the effectiveness and continuity of these central symbols and institutions as agents of

political socialization are not given or assured through their mere establishment, although this very establishment is, as we have seen, of great importance. Such effectiveness and continuity are greatly dependent on several additional factors or conditions.

Among these, of great importance (beyond the structure of elites and ideological transformation analyzed above) are several aspects of the general tempo of modernization; and the differential tempo of modernization in different institutional spheres becomes very significant. The importance of these variables lies in the fact that they may greatly influence the extent to which various groups become modernized in such a way that they are able to develop both various new regulative frameworks through which their problems can be dealt with and general positive orientations to wider modern frameworks and developed symbols.

Of great importance is the continuity of economic development and progress. The greater such continuity, the greater, naturally, is the positive adjustment of various groups and strata to the new, modern settings. But this is only one indication of the more general importance of the tempo of modernization in general and of the relative tempo of modernization in different institutional spheres in particular.

It has been shown that the general tempo of modernization tends greatly to influence its smooth progress and that on the whole the slower the tempo, the smoother the process of modernization because, other conditions being equal, the greater is the ability of the institutional structure to deal with problems generated by these processes. It has also been shown that the temporal spread of modernization over different institutional spheres usually facilitates the smooth progress of modernization, while the temporal convergence of modernization in several institutional spheres may undermine, through the accumulation of problems and tensions, such a smooth process.

Of no smaller importance is the analysis of the relative tempo of modernization within different institutional spheres; that is, the extent to which modernization takes place in different degrees and in a certain temporal sequence in different institutional systems. Thus, insofar as the modernization of the central political institutions takes place before that of the periphery without at the same time continuously blocking the incorporation of the periphery, the greater the chances for sustained development. Similarly, these changes are greater insofar as the internal religious and ideological transformation of social groups on the one hand and their integration in modern economic frameworks on the other take place before their full politicization in terms of the development of excessive political demands. Similarly, the successful development of internal regulative mechanisms is greater insofar as internal values and status transformation come side by side with economic differentiation or at least do not lag far behind it.

Of no less crucial importance is the extent to which there develops in a society a flexibility of the status system, as evident in the autonomy and mutual openness of various elites and social group in terms of their status symbols.[35] Perhaps the clearest illustration of such status autonomy has been found among many of the Protestant groups that were among the initial modernizers in western Europe. They evinced a combination of two characteristics or orientations. First was their openness toward the wider social structure, which was rooted in their "this-worldly" orientation, which was not limited only to the economic sphere, and which gradually extended also into demands for wider political participation and for the setting up of new, wider political frameworks and criteria. Second, they were characterized by a certain autonomy and self-sufficiency from the point of view of their status orientation.

Some of the ingredients of such autonomy can be found, as we have seen in the preceding analysis of the various cases, in many other societies, although in different forms.

This relative autonomy and flexibility of status orientation tend to influence greatly the interrelation between different groups and strata. They may enable the development of some new status criteria and groups without a great disruption of the cohesion of the older groups. They may greatly facilitate the development of new elites willing to learn new modern roles in the economic, organizational, and political spheres.

Such new elites (or the members of the old elite who learned new tasks and patterns of behavior) can often acquire an established place in the structure of the societies and so find some sort of *modus vivendi* with the older ones. The new criteria of status (that is, of economic achievement and specialization, of participation in a political party or youth movement) often overlap with many of the older, traditional ones without creating close groups constituted only according to one type of criterion, and in this way enable a relatively continuous development of varied organizations within a relatively common structure.

However, the cohesiveness and openness of vari-

ous groups and strata—and especially of the elite groups that we have found to be of crucial importance for the development of institutional flexibility—depend not only on the various broader processes analyzed above but also on the placement of these elites and groups in the broader social frameworks as well as on their internal transformative forces—on what may be called their ideological or value transformation. Such transformation is very important for the development of commitments to the specific value orientation of modernity as well as for the sustenance of those structural mechanisms that facilitate the development of continuous structural flexibility. Of crucial importance is the development of cohesive elites that are able to develop new, viable, modern centers as against those elites that are weak, easily succumb to manifold pressures, and are unable to develop such centers.

Thus it becomes obvious that the processes of transformation of elites are very closely connected with the development of different types of modern centers, that is, relatively strong and weak centers or those with different combinations of components of center formation. As we have seen, this has been one of the most neglected—and yet most crucial—aspects of the study of modernization. In the following pages we shall attempt to give some preliminary indications about the nature of the conditions under which weak as opposed to strong modern centers tend to develop and about the nature of some of the differences of political process in modern regimes.

We may take off from the analyses of the conditions of transformation of patrimonial, feudal, and imperial societies presented above and from the concluding part of the introduction to the section on Centralized Empires.

As we have already indicated, all modern polities were ushered in by some revolutionary event. But not all revolutions created new, strong, viable centers, and here the influence of the preceding setting might have been very great.

Some of the aspects of the social structure of modernizing societies in their premodern settings, especially the relative strength of their respective centers and the relative autonomy of different political, cultural, and social centers, may be of special importance. Most of the preindustrial societies—with the exception of the African and, to some extent, Latin-American ones—began modernizing, or were pushed into it, with a relatively complex, differentiated institutional structure. In the great historical and imperial civilizations, for example, centralized, differentiated structures and organizations already existed together with some relative autonomy of the basic institutional spheres—

political, religious, or ideological—and social organization and stratification.

Both the centralized frameworks and the relatively autonomous institutional spheres could be crucial to the transformative capacities of these societies, for they could facilitate the initial modernization and help make the new modern centers and frameworks work efficiently. Different constellations of these characteristics, however, may have greatly influenced the general level of the transformative capacity as well as the particular institutional forms that modernization may take on in each case.

The internal transformation of the imperial societies was greatly facilitated by the relative autonomy of strong social, cultural, and political institutions. In the cultural order autonomy facilitated the development of new symbols supporting and legitimizing central institution building, while autonomy in the sphere of social organization facilitated the crystallization of viable new organizational nucleuses without disrupting the whole pre-existing order, thus enabling the new order to rely, at least to some extent, on the forces of the old one.

The illustrations of Europe and Japan and to some extent of India—in each of which some type of multiplicity of centers can be discerned—are very significant; and they tend also to indicate that it is such conditions that may facilitate—although they do not assure—the development of pluralistic regimes.

Insofar as there existed in the premodern imperial regimes a small degree of autonomy of the different centers, the process of modernization was much more fraught with difficulties and crises, which led ultimately to more coercive, monolithic types of centers—totalitarian or authoritarian, yet not devoid of some capacities for sustained growth.

As against these historical cases there are those of breakthroughs to modernity from semi-imperial, semipatrimonial regimes such as most east European ones, purely patrimonial ones like many Southeast Asian ones, weak provincial centers like the Latin-American ones, or from tribal, almost entirely centerless societies like many of the African ones.

Most of these societies were brought into processes of modernization under the impact of external forces, and indeed the history of the spread of modernization in the nineteenth and twentieth centuries from its initial centers in western Europe has been, to a very large extent, the history of the impingement of these centers on new countries in the Americas, eastern and southern Europe, Asia, and Africa. Some of these societies have never—at least, not yet—gone beyond what may be called the stage of adapting to these external impingements. Many

of them have not evinced a very high degree of internal adaptability after having started on the road to modernity.

In many of these cases there developed situations of ineffective transition from traditional to modern society, when the undermining of traditional frameworks and the erosion of traditional commitments tended to result in nonadaptive traditionalistic attitudes virtually torn off from any commitment to accepted, meaningful traditional order or in unregulated demands for various new modern goals. These attitudes may then give rise to a much wider scope of apathy and withdrawal from participation in the broader settings and to a growing level of unregulated conflicts among them.

In almost all these cases there tended to develop initially some very weak modern centers. The centers were characterized by what may be called pure "modern" patrimonialism; that is, the establishment or continuation of new political and administrative central frameworks that have a tendency to maintain the external contents of traditional or of modern symbols without simultaneously maintaining any strong commitments to them. At the same time, such centers tended to display almost exclusive concern for the preservation of the existing weak frameworks of power, thus giving rise to a continuous succession of weak centers.[36]

The formal-institutional type of regime that tended to develop in such centers was probably to no small degree dependent on conditions not dissimilar from those in the framework of strong centers. Insofar as there existed in these societies a relative plurality and some autonomy of different groups and (even if weak) centers, there could develop in them some sort of semipluralistic regime.

Insofar as such autonomous units either did not exist because of the weakness of these centers or were abolished by some semirevolutionary form, there tended to develop various types of regimes with very strong authoritarian and totalitarian orientations, as in Egypt or Burma.

XIII

The major difference between these regimes and seemingly similar ones that developed in the framework of strong centers was in their low ability to mobilize effectively new political forces and to create viable modern institutional frameworks capable of dealing with problems of absorption and change. These differences tended to become manifest both in some of the types of political organization and in the nature of the crises specific to each such type of regime.

Perhaps the best illustrations of such differences can be seen in the functions of parties, voting, and political participation, all of which tend to develop in all types of modern centers and yet whose significance in the political process differs greatly among them. To take just a few illustrations, more of which can be found in the various selections presented in the following sections, the functions of parties seem to vary greatly among them. The tendency to monolithic but not totalitarian parties or to single nontotalitarian party regimes in many new states indicates that many of these parties may be more instruments for forging collective identities for the struggle between different contenders of power representing different interests or ideological orientations. This struggle seems to take place more inside the parties than among them.

Concurrently, bureaucracies may often be not only administrative branches of the center or small contending groups or cliques in it but also custodians of whatever common symbols such centers may represent and whatever civil order they may be able to maintain. Just because of this they may compete with the parties for the full representation of the center—a fact that can perhaps to some degree explain the quick succession of a party regime by a military regime—with each regime maintaining some of the organizational frameworks and activities of the former.

Similarly, in many of these states voting and suffrage may be only a manifestation of some broad, not fully articulated, orientation to a center and not of total identity with the regime, as in totalitarian regimes, or an expression of specific concrete interests or ideologies as in many of the pluralistic-constitutional regimes.

The differences between strong and weak centers can also be seen in the nature—and especially in the outcomes—of crises and breakdowns that may occur in them. The general reasons and symptoms of such crises and breakdowns—the rifts and cleavages between different types of elites, between the central and the parochial symbols and identities, between precontractual and contractual symbols, between classes and regions—are to a large extent common to all of them.[37] But the nature of the crises and their outcomes tend to differ. Although in regimes with strong centers such crises usually tend to focus around problems of integrating new groups in such centers, the situation is different in the societies with weak centers.

The specific crises or problems faced by regimes with weak centers are their effectiveness on the new modern international scene, the upsurge of un-regulated demands of various broader groups that are very often fostered by these elites, and the concomitant waste of resources. They are confronted with potentially continuous conflicts in the elite and the new centers. The crises and problems that may develop out of the great intensity of the conflicts between traditionalistic and more modern elites, the new modern ways in which the claims of many of these groups are being made, and the contradictory assumptions of these groups about the nature of the center itself and the bases of its legitimation may minimize the possibilities of establishing new, stable, and viable centers of any kind.

Similarly, the outcomes seem to differ. In societies with strong centers the tendency is more toward a "total," dramatic breakdown of the center, possibly leading to its reconstitution on a new level. Societies with weak centers face the possibility of a continuous succession of such weak, patrimonial centers, together with economic regression and growing political apathy.

But beyond these differences between weak and strong centers, the study of New Nations opens up before us possibilities of different kinds of contents of modern centers. The various differences in political organization and participation may connote not only differences in the strength of the center in terms of the people's present or future commitment to it but also different types of content in the different centers—the political, cultural, and societal centers—and their interrelationship. In many of these countries we find a lesser symbolic autonomy of the specific cultural or political center and a greater extent of segregation between the different types of center, each of which may also encompass a different geographical boundary.

These features may be very closely connected with the development of different patterns of political ideology and with types of relations between the conception of the political and the cosmic cultural orders and between technical, administrative, and symbolic aspects of political order and of the behavior of rulers, which differ greatly from those that developed in the framework of European tradition.

These patterns may give rise to patterns of collective identity and political participation and struggle different from those that developed in the European or in other postimperial centers. They may also give rise to regimes in which there is a much smaller identity between political and cultural centers; that is, in which the nation-state no longer constitutes the natural unit of a modern political order.[38]

The patterns of breakdown that may tend to develop here may be different from those found in countries under the influence of such European political conceptions. They all may lead to the development of new types of nontraditional centers—weak and yet viable—based on nontraditional legitimation but not having attained a high level of internal transformation.

XIV

But such weak centers need not always remain weak, as the illustrations of Mexico, Turkey, and to some extent Chile attest. The crucial event that changed such weak centers into relatively strong ones was some successful ideological-revolutionary process attained either through a violent revolution, as in Mexico, or through a combination of revolution and *coup d'état,* as in Turkey, or, as has been attempted in Chile or Venezuela, a more gradualistic process.

Why elites with orientations toward change and the ability to implement relatively effective policies emerged either in the initial or in later stages of modernization in some countries (such as in Turkey, Mexico, India; in a somewhat different way in Russia; and earlier in Japan and western Europe) while they did not emerge in these initial phases in other countries (such as in Indonesia, Pakistan, or Burma), or why elites with similar differences tended to develop also in later stages of modernization is one of the most baffling problems in comparative sociological analysis. There are but few available indications to deal with this problem. Very tentatively it may be suggested that it has to some degree to do with the placement of these elites in the preceding social structure, according to the extent of their internal cohesiveness and of their internal transformation of their own value orientation. These indications can probably be best examined in relation to the societies whose basic features developed in the second stages of modernization.

In all these societies the new, modernizing elites were greatly alienated from the preceding (colonial or traditional) sociopolitical systems and tended to emphasize the development of new values and ideologies as a very important part of their modernizing orientations. But in most of these countries the elites were mostly composed of intellectuals, and in many cases they constituted the only initially available modern elite. They had very few social and ideological contacts or identifications (even if ambivalent ones) either with the bearers of pre-existing traditions or with the wider groups of the society. The modernizing orientations of these elites were focused mostly on the political and much less on the economic sphere. Surprisingly enough, they were also very often less focused on the cultural sphere, in the sense of redefinition and reformation of their own basic internal value orientation. Consequently, they were not able to establish a strong internal cohesiveness and strong ideological and value identifications and connections with other, potentially modernized groups and strata.

Similarly, in many of the Latin-American countries the various political elites or leaders, whether the more oligarchic or more demagogic ones, tended to be more dissociated, even though in a different way, from the various broader groups that were continuously coming into the society or impinging on its central institutions. The process of selection and formation of these elites was a relatively rigid and restricted one, bringing in relatively weaker elements and intensifying their alienation from the broader group as well as from their internal insecurity and lack of cohesion. Similar and even more intensive rifts between different elites developed, as is well known, in various European countries in the nineteen-twenties and thirties.

On the other hand, the elites in Turkey, Japan, Mexico, and India and some of the more cohesive elites in countries of later stages of modernization, however great the differences between them, had some contrary characteristics in common. They were not usually composed only of intellectual groups entirely alienated from the preexisting elites and from some of the broader groups of the society but were also to some extent placed in secondary elite positions in the preceding structure and had somewhat closer relations with many active broader groups.

In the ideological and value spheres they aimed at the development of a new, more flexible set of symbols and collective identity that, while not negating the traditions, would also provide some new meaning for the new processes of change. Hence they tended to be more cohesive while at the same time they effected some internal value transformation in the broader groups and strata.

All these considerations—preliminary as they are —necessitate the revision of the basic typologies of political regimes, and they all constitute challenges for further vistas in political sociology, as yet largely unexplored.

XV

The preceding remarks provide only very tentative indications as to the conditions under which such different types of elites, with different orientations to change and different center-forming and institution-building capacities, tend to develop. And although the systematic research of these problems is as yet in its beginning stages, it might perhaps be worthwhile to present here a tentative hypothesis based on the present state of research and illustrated by the selections and analyses throughout this book.

Psychological and sociological research seem to indicate that several sets of variables and their interrelations are of greatest importance in this context. One such set of variables which appears to influence the extent of resistance to change or of adaptability to it seems to be the extent of internal solidarity and cohesion of any such group within the social system. Another set of such variables, amply illustrated in the selections presented above, includes the rigidity and uniformity of the internal division of labor and of the social structure and cultural order of any group or society, the degree of autonomy of their various components, and the openness or closeness of any given group toward other groups and toward the broader society and social and cultural orders.

The extent of structural flexibility or rigidity of the major institutional spheres can be measured both by the extent to which such different institutional tasks are differentiated and performed in specific situations, group roles, and institutional frameworks and by the extent to which each such group, role, or situation is governed by some autonomous criterion of its own goals and values or, conversely, is dominated by those of another sphere.

The flexibility or rigidity of the symbolic orders of the cultural tradition of society has to be measured, first, in the extent to which the contents of each of these spheres in the major realms of social and cultural order—the realm of cosmic and cultural order, the social collectivity and the social order, and the sociopolitical centers—are closed, that is, fixed and rigid, or relatively open. Second, it has to be measured by the respective closeness or openness of the participation of different groups in these different orders; and, third, by the nature of their symbolic—and to some extent organizational and institutional—interrelations and interdependence.

Here several possible constellations can be distinguished. First is the case in which each symbolic sphere is seen as autonomous but closely interrelated with the others, such that participation in one enables access to another without the imposition of criteria or orientations. The second possibility is that of relative closeness of each order and of purely adaptive, or "power," interrelations among them. Finally, and sometimes connected with the former, there is the possibility of one of these predominating over the

others by being able both to regulate access to them and to impose on them its own values and symbols.

The exact nature or contents of such institutional and symbolic flexibility or rigidity necessarily differs greatly between different types of societies. Thus, in primitive societies, such rigidity is manifest especially in the close interdependence of their various units (clan, kinship group), in the organizational and symbolic overlapping, or even identity, of definition of these units—there being little differentiation between the symbols of belonging to one or another institutional sphere (political, economic or ritual) and between the situations and roles in which they are enacted. In more complex societies in which there already exists a much higher degree of organizational differentiation of institutional and symbolic spheres, such flexibility or rigidity is especially evident in the institutional autonomy (that is, in terms of their specific goals) of such spheres as against a relatively tight symbolic or institutional control of some central sphere over all the other spheres.

Beyond such interrelations of the symbolic and institutional orders, an additional set of variables, which also has been amply illustrated in our selections, and which is of great importance in influencing the development of adaptability or resistance to change, is the contents and organization of a cultural tradition.

Of special importance in this context is, first, the extent to which any given tradition entails an active commitment to its values and symbols on the part of individuals, as well as the nature of such commitment—that is, whether such commitments are relatively open or ritualistically closed or prescribed. Closely related to this is also the distinction between weak and strong centers.

XVI

These major sets of variables—the extent of solidarity of a social group or system, the extent of autonomy of different institutional and symbolic systems, and the weakness or strength of different centers—tend greatly to influence the attitudes toward change mentioned above.

It seems that the general predisposition to change is influenced by some combinations of two of these sets of variables, namely, the scope of solidarity of a system and the degree of its institutional flexibility. Most available data show that the lower the solidarity and cohesion of any given social system, the lower also is the adaptability to change of its members. It has been adequately documented in social and psychological research that the maintenance of the cohesion of primary groups, and to some extent of their solidarity links to wider social settings, is of crucial importance for the ability of their members to face new, even adverse, conditions; and the destruction of such solidarity may greatly impair this ability. Most of these studies have, however, dealt with primary groups within larger, formal organizations, especially as regards modern societies. Therefore, the problem arises of the relation of these variables to those that deal with more formal aspects of micro- or macro-societal structures. The importance of rigidity or of flexibility for the development of adaptability of different social systems to situations of change is best seen here. In general, it seems that such adaptability is greatly facilitated by the extent of flexibility and autonomy of the social, cultural, and political institutions and of the major symbolic orders of a society.

Comparative research on this problem, which is indeed only in the beginning of its systematic development, indicates that such autonomy of the cultural and social spheres facilitates the development of a relatively high degree of general predisposition to change and of a positive attitude toward change.

The greater the autonomous interrelations among the various symbolic orders and the more non-ritualistic the precepts of the tradition of a given society, the more flexible are the status images which tend to develop among its members, who, therefore, may similarly evince a greater adaptability or predisposition to change. Conversely, insofar as such autonomy is absent and the social, cultural, and political orders are closely identified with one another, the greater the propensity for resistance to change. The closer are the various symbolic orders and the more rigid and ritualistic their precepts, the greater the tendency for ritual status images to develop among members, who evince less of a tendency to develop adaptability to change or, in other words, a greater resistance to change.

Obviously there are many more permutations among these various elements of cultural traditions, and they, as well as their influence on processes of change, have to be analyzed more fully and systematically in further research.

Thus it would appear that group cohesion and solidarity, on the one hand, and rigidity or flexibility of the social and cultural order, on the other hand, are similar in their influence on the adaptability or transformative capacity of the members of any group and that they tend to go together and reinforce one another in their influence on processes of change. But a closer examination of the data indicates that this need not always be the case. While it may be true that a low degree of solidarity and cohesiveness in a group tends to enhance its members' lack of ability to adapt to situations of change, and while relatively strong internal cohesion of groups with some internal flexibility, status autonomy, and openness toward the wider society tends to develop positive orientations to change, between these two extreme types the picture is not so simple.

A relatively high degree of group solidarity may be connected with a relatively rigid internal division of labor and need not necessarily denote the lack of organizational adaptability to change (although the adaptation which it may foster is of a rather special kind).

In general—and in a very tentative way—it seems that it is the extent of solidarity of a group or structure which tends to influence the degree to which individuals or groups with some organizational ability develop from within it, while it is the extent of flexibility of its structure that influences the nature of the general attitude toward change that may develop within a given society or part thereof. It is here that the relative focus of solidarity—the cohesion of various groups and their structural characteristics in relation to the social framework of the society, and especially the possibility of the extension of this solidarity to new fields of instrumental activities and patterns of participation in new social spheres—becomes very important.

XVII

But neither of the sets of variables does as yet explain the extent to which there develops from within various societies or sectors thereof the ability to crystallize new, effective, institutional frameworks as well as the concrete contours of such frameworks. Here, as has been cited several times before, the crucial variable seems to be the extent to which there develops in different institutional fields different types of entrepreneurial and/or charismatic elites and groups.

The process of social change or the undermining of existing patterns of life, social organization, and culture, accompanied as it often is by structural differentiation, gives rise, by its very impetus, to a great variety of new groups which, of course, differ greatly in their basic organizational features from the older ones, as well as among themselves. By their very nature most such new occupational, religious, political, or status categories or groups of elites undertake to perform new tasks and new types of activities and to develop orientations to new organizational settings. These tasks and activities naturally differ greatly according to the characteristics of the new emerging system; for instance, there is a great difference between an imperial system with a predominant agrarian base and some mercantile and factorial bases, and a modern-industrial and/or democratic system.

But beyond these differences, they vary greatly as to the extent of their general organizational ability, their adaptive, innovative, or transformative capacities in their own direct sphere of activities, and with regard to broader groups of society and its more central institutions.

What then are the conditions which tend to influence the development of such different types of elites? Of special importance, in addition to the variables outlined above, is the third set of variables, which concerns the contents of a cultural tradition and the existence within it of a strong or weak center. It seems that the relative strength or weakness of the major centers of any social or cultural orders has several structural repercussions on the cohesion and orientations of its major elites in general and of the intellectual strata in particular. Weak centers tend to generate or to be connected with the development of new elites with little internal autonomy and cohesion, restricted in their social orientations, and evincing a tendency towards dissociation from one another and from the broader strata of the society. Strong centers, on the other hand, tend mostly to be connected with or to generate more cohesive elites and intellectual strata, which tend to have relatively close interrelations among them. The nature of such interrelations (whether coercive, hierarchical, or autonomously interdependent), as well as of their relations with broader groups and strata, depends greatly on the exact structure and contents of such centers and especially on the flexibility and openness of its symbolic contents.

XVIII

It is the interrelation among degrees of solidarity of different groups and strata, of structural and symbolic autonomy of different social spheres (that is, the degree of rigidity or flexibility of these spheres), the strength or weakness of the major centers of the symbolic orders (that is, the social, political, and cultural, and, in the case of traditional societies, religious centers) that can best—even if yet in a limited and preliminary way—explain the development within a given society of elites and groups with different degrees of organizational, innovative, and transformative capacities. In any one society,

and especially in the more differentiated ones, these relations are rather complex and heterogeneous; and this very complexity—the multiplicity of different traditions and groups within them—necessarily gives rise in situations of change to a great variety of elites and groups with diverse capacities. These tend to compete strongly among themselves for relative predominance in the emerging social structure. It would be impossible here to go into all the possibile variations, we shall, therefore, present only some general hypotheses in terms of very rough and general tendencies. Only further research will enable us to go beyond these very rough generalizations.

On the basis of the various variables presented above and some of the materials in the selections, it can be postulated that in a society, or parts thereof, characterized by relatively high solidarity but low flexibility, relatively traditionalistic but well-organized groups will tend to develop. On the other hand, in a society, or parts thereof, which are characterized by a high level of flexibility but a relatively low level of solidarity, several relatively adaptable but not very well-organized groups or strata may develop. When a high level of solidarity exists in such a society, we might expect the development of relatively well-organized and adaptable groups or elites.

But the extent to which such elite groups are able to influence their broader institutional settings, and especially the more central institutional cores of the society, depends primarily on the types of centers which exist within their societies and on their relations to these centers. The capacity to affect the broader institutional settings will be smaller among elites which are relatively noncohesive, which are alienated from other elites and the broader groups and strata of the society, and which are very distant from the existing center and/or able to totally monopolize it to the exclusion of other groups and elites. In terms of center-building, most such groups will tend to emphasize the maintenance of some given attributes of collective identity together with the regulation of internal and external force.

In those societies, or parts thereof, in which there exists a high level of rigidity of the social system and/or of the symbolic orders, that is, where there is but relatively little symbolic distinction between the different social and cultural orders, together with relatively weak centers (as seems to have been the case in many South East Asian patrimonial regimes), there will tend to develop relatively traditionalistic, nontransformative elites, which may yet evince a certain organizational capacity and some predisposition for limited technical innovation.

Side by side with such elites, there may also develop under such conditions, especially within the less cohesive sectors of the societies, various new ideological or political groups with some positive orientations to change but with relatively small transformative capacities beyond the adaptation of new ideologies or symbols and with but little ability for continuous institutional activity.

Both types of elites which develop under such conditions will tend to develop a closeness in their social and status perception, a ritual emphasis on certain specific and very limited types of status orientations, and will conceive of their own legitimation in terms of maintaining these restricted ranges of status symbols.

Most elites which develop under such conditions, insofar as they attempt to be active in center-formation, tend to emphasize one component of center-building—especially the maintenance of symbols of common identity or the regulation of external and internal force—and to place less stress on the other components, especially the regulation of center-group relations and the development of *new* goals and symbols of common identity. Insofar as rigidity of the social and cultural order and the concomitant resistance to change coexist with a rather strong center there might also develop from within some sectors—probably from within those groups not too distant from the center and enjoying some internal solidarity—militant elites with strong innovative but coercive orientations. The more center-oriented among such elites tend to accomplish their center-building activities, both the *combination* of the development of common identity and force and the development of new collective goals, with but a small degree of noncoercive regulation of intergroup relations.

The existence within societies, or sectors thereof, of a great degree of structural and cultural autonomy and flexibility, especially when connected with the high cohesion of social groups, may facilitate the development of elites with a relatively high level of adaptability to change but not necessarily with great transformative capacities.

The extent to which more transformative elites may develop is once again dependent, in large measure, on the symbolic and institutional structure of the centers, their strength or weakness. Insofar as such conditions of flexibility exist together with strong—and almost, by definition, open—centers, the possibility of the development of highly transformative elites seems greater.

Under such conditions, as research on inactive elites within various micro- and macro-societal settings indicates, such transformative capacities are to be found mostly among elites which are relatively cohesive with a strong sense of self-identity, and especially among secondary elites which, while somewhat distant from the central ruling one, either maintain positive solidary orientations to the center and are not entirely alienated from the preexisting elites and from some of the broader groups of the society, or manage to function within relatively segregated institutional spheres. Such elites also tend to develop simultaneous orientations to collective ideological transformation and to concrete tasks and problems in different "practical" fields, and they perceive their own legitimation in terms of such wider changes and not only in terms of providing various immediate benefits or status symbols to other groups. It is such elites which tend, from the point of view of center-building, to assure the larger degree of flexibility in terms of combining various components of the center. They tend especially to emphasize the combination of a relatively noncoercive regulation of intergroup relations with the creation of new symbols of common identity and possibly also with the development of new types of collective goals.

Insofar as in such conditions of relatively high flexibility of the social structure there exist relatively weak centers, the development of such transformative elites is usually greatly impeded. Instead, a variety of both traditionalistic and highly adaptable elites, each with different orientations, may develop. If no balance of power develops among them, such multiplicity may jeopardize the successful institutionalization of a viable new institutional structure. The centers that may be built up by these elites may then be characterized by a high level of ability of coalition building but by a much smaller ability to develop binding, common attributes of identity or to crystallize collective goals.

XIX

The preceding analysis of the conditions of the development of different types of elites and of their center-building activities may seem to have been put in a rather deterministic way; this was, however, far beyond our intention. As has already been pointed out, in every complex society there always exist rather heterogeneous conditions and a variety of sectors, each of which may produce different kinds of elites. Among such elites there usually develops a strong competition as to their relative predominance; the emerging situation and the result of such competition never fully predetermined. The relative lack of predetermination is emphasized even more if we bear in mind the importance of the international setting and its relations to the developmet of various elites.

Throughout our discussion we have stressed the crucial importance of various secondary elites or movements as potential bearers of sociopolitical transformation. But the structural locations of these elites seem to differ greatly among the various types of political regimes, mainly according to the nature of the division of labor prevalent within a society, on the one hand, and the relative placement of these elites within the internal system of the societies, or within the international settings of their respective societies, on the other.

In general, it seems that insofar as the division of labor within any given social system is either "mechanical" and/or based on a center which is focused mostly on regulation or force and/or on the upholding of symbols of common identity, a change-oriented or transformative cultural or political elite will probably develop, mainly within some of the international enclaves *around* such a society and to a lesser extent *within* the society. The probability of its effecting such change would depend, however, on the breakdown of the center because of some external or internal forces and/or the finding of some secondary internal groups or elites which would, for either ideological or interest factors, tend to become its allies.

On the other hand, insofar as a social system is characterized by a higher degree of organic solidarity and/or an emphasis within its center on the combination of all components of center-building (especially on the regulation of intergroup relations and of common symbols of identity), there then exists the probability that a change-oriented elite will develop, to some extent at least, from within such a society, although being also closely related to broader international settings and enclaves. The probability of its becoming effective would then depend more on some of the interrelations (briefly discussed above) among them and existing centers on the one hand and the broader groups on the other.

XX

It is only natural at this stage of our discussion to inquire whether the development of these different types of elites depends not only on the "formal" structure of the social and cultural orders but also on their contents, for instance, value orientations and system of beliefs.

We cannot deal with this problem here in detail. It might, however, be worthwhile to present some tentative conclusions about these problems, which have been derived from a reexamination of Weber's Protestant Ethic thesis.[39]

According to this analysis, the central aspects of the Protestant religion and value orientations, which created as it were its transformative potential, were, first, a strong combination of "this-worldliness" and transcendentalism—a combination which orients the individual behavior to activities within this world but at the same time does not ritually sanctify any of them, either through a mystic union or any ritual act—as the final point of religious consummation or worthiness; second, a strong emphasis on individual activism and responsibility; third, the unmediated, direct relation of the individual to the sacred tradition—an attitude which, while strongly emphasizing the importance and direct relevance of the sacred and of tradition, minimizes the extent to which this relation and individual commitment can be mediated by institutions, organizations, or textual exegesis. Hence, it opened up the possibility of continuous redefinition and reformulation of the nature and scope of such tradition, a possibility which was further enhanced by the strong transcendental attitude which minimizes the sacredness of any "here and now."

These religious orientations of Protestantism and Protestants (and especially Calvinists) were not, however, confined only to the realm of the sacred. They were closely related to, and manifested in, two major orientations: in most Protestant groups' conception of the social reality and of their own place in it, that is, in what may be called their status images and orientations. Of crucial importance here was first their openness towards the wider social structure rooted in their this-worldly orientation, which was not limited only to the economic sphere but also, as we shall see later, could encompass other social fields. Second, they were characterized by a certain autonomy and self-sufficiency from the point of view of their status orientation; they evinced little dependence—from the point of view of the crystallization of their own status symbols and identity—on the existing political and religious centers.

A full comparative application of these insights to other religions is still before us, but here again some preliminary hypotheses can be presented.

Thus, it seems that the effects of transformative capacities of religious or ideological ideas and movements on the motivational level—that is, in the direction of development of strong motivations to undertake new types of nonreligious roles—seem to be greater when the transcendental and this-worldly orientations of these religions or ideologies are stronger and when they evince more ideological autonomy with regard to any given social or communal order. Conversely, such transformative effects are smaller when their immanent (whether this- or other-worldly) orientation is stronger and more embedded in the existing political and social order and/or when their negative, apathetic attitude toward it is greater.

The transformation of new central symbols and frameworks is, in its turn, greatly dependent on the extent to which the religious (or ideological) systems evince a relatively high level of both ideological and organizational autonomy while at the same time being oriented to participation in the sociopolitical order.

The more autonomous the religious organizations are, and the less they are identified with the existing political order, the more able they are to develop new types of central political and cultural symbols.

Similarly, the greater the extent to which a given polity and state constituted a basic referent of religious activity, the smaller was the extent to which there could develop from within it movements and systems of reform oriented to the redefinition of the central spheres of the society. Conversely, the stronger the universalistic and transcendental elements within these religious orientations, the greater were the possibilities of such developments.

Finally, the more the activist orientations within the religious value-orientation were mainly other-worldly oriented, the smaller was the extent to which they, no matter what reformatory movements developed within them, tended to orient themselves to the recrystallization of the central spheres of the society.

Conversely, the greater the extent to which these orientations emphasized involvement in the secular world and the stronger the specific ideological formulations of these orientations, the greater was the possibility of such transformative effects.

NOTES

1. For a fuller exposition, see S. N. Eisenstadt, *Modernization, Protest and Change* (Englewood Cliffs: Prentice-Hall, 1966).

2. Karl Deutsch, "Social Mobilization and Political Development," *American Political Science Review*, LV (September 1961), pp. 493–515. See Selection 61 in this volume. See also United Nations, *Report on the World Social Situation* (New York: United Nations, 1961).

3. Some of the most important studies dealing with these problems can be found in D. Lerner, *The Passing of Traditional Society* (Glencoe: The Free Press, 1958); B. F. Hoselitz, "Non-Economic Factors in Economic Development," *American Economic Review*, XLVII (May 2, 1957), 28–71; W. Moore, "The Social Framework of Economic Development," in R. Braibanti and J. J. Spengler, eds., *Tradition, Values, and Socio-Economic Development* (Durham: Duke University Press, 1961), pp. 57–83; J. J. Spengler, "Theory, Ideology, Non-economic Values and Politico-Economic Development," *ibid.*, pp. 3–56. A good summary is provided by J. A. Kahl, "Some Social Concomitants of Industrialization and Urbanization," *Human Organization*, XVIII, No. 2 (Summer 1959), 53–75. See also A. H. Leighton and R. J. Smith, "A Comparative Study on Social and Cultural Changes," *Proceedings of the American Philosophical Society*, XCII, No. 2 (April 1955), 79–88; R. Firth, F. J. Fischer, and D. C. Macrae, "Social Implications of Technological Change in International Social Science Council," in *Social and Economic and Technological Changes: A Theoretical Approach* (Paris: UNESCO, 1958).

4. See Moore, *op. cit.*; W. Moore and A. Feldman, eds., *Labor Commitment and Social Change in Developing Areas* (New York: Social Science Research Council, 1960).

5. M. Tumin, "Competing Status Systems," in *ibid.*, pp. 277–288; L. Fallers, "Equality, Modernity and Democracy in the New States," in Clifford Geertz, ed., *Old Societies and New States* (New York: The Free Press, 1963), pp. 158–219.

6. Karl Mannheim, *Man and Society in an Age of Reconstruction* (London: Kegan Paul, Trench, Trukner & Co., 1940).

7. See J. Floud and A. Halsey, "The Sociology of Education, A Trend Report and Bibliography," *Current Sociology*, VIII, No. 3 (1958); A Halsey, J. Floud, and C. Anderson, eds., *Education, Economy and Society* (New York: The Free Press, 1961); S. N. Eisenstadt, "Education and Political Development," in Don C. Piper and Taylor Cole, eds., *Post-Primary Education and Economic Development* (Durham: Duke University Press, Commonwealth Studies Center, 1964), pp. 27–48.

8. Mannheim, *op. cit.*; L. Pye, ed., *Communication and Political Development* (Princeton: Princeton University Press, 1963).

9. Lerner, *op. cit.*

10. E. Shils, "Centre and Periphery," in *The Logic of Personal Knowledge,* essays presented to Michael Polanyi (London: Routledge and Kegan Paul, 1961); A. Inkeles, "Industrial Man: The Relation of Status Experience, Perception and Value," *American Journal of Sociology*, LXVI, No. 1 (July 1960), 1–31.

11. On this point, see in greater detail Eisenstadt, *Modernization, Protest and Change.*

12. See A. D. Lindsay, *The Modern Democratic State* (London: Oxford University Press, 1963).

13. S. M. Lipset, *The First New Nation: The United States in Historical and Comparative Perspective* (New York: Basic Books, 1963); D. Thomson, *Europe since Napoleon* (New York: Knopf, 1962).

14. P. Robertson, *Revolutions of 1848: A Social History* (New York: Harper and Row, 1960); K. Silvert, *The Conflict Society: Reaction and Revolution in Latin America* (New Orleans: Hauser, 1961); H. Davis, ed., *Government and Politics in Latin America* (New York: Ronald, 1958); E. Lieuwen, *Arms and Politics in Latin America* (New York: Frederick A. Praeger, 1960).

15. See on this in greater detail Eisenstadt, *Modernization, Protest and Change;* G. Barraclough, *An Introduction to Contemporary History* (New York: Basic Books, 1965), Ch. 6.

16. Shils, *op. cit.*

17. William Kornhauser, *The Politics of Mass Society* (New York: The Free Press, 1959); and in greater detail in Eisenstadt, *Modernization, Protest and Change.*

18. See "Major Types of Breakthrough from Preliterate Societies: Introduction" in this volume.

19. See on this, in greater detail, Eisenstadt, *Modernization, Protest and Change*, especially Ch. 3.

20. On the variety of modern social and especially socialist thought, see, for instance, A. Fried and R. Sanders, eds., *Socialist Thought* (New York: Doubleday, 1964).

21. On the variety of modern political thought, especially as related to problems of legitimation, see, for instance, W. Ebenstein, ed., *Man and the State: Modern Political Ideas* (New York: Holt, Rinehart, and Winston, 1947).

22. *Ibid.,* Ch. 14.

23. E. Shils, "Tradition and Liberty: Antinomy and Interdependence," *Ethics,* LXVIII, No. 3 (April 1958), 153–165.

24. T. B. Bottomore and M. Rubel, eds., *Karl Marx: Selected Writings in Sociology and Social Philosophy* (London: C. A. Watts, 1961), pp. 167–177.

25. Fried and Sanders, *op. cit.*

26. See in greater detail Eisenstadt, *Modernization, Protest and Change,* Ch. 2.

27. Lipset, *op. cit.*

28. E. Kedourie, *Nationalism* (London: Hutchinson, 1961).

29. G. Almond, "Introduction: A Functional Approach to Comparative Politics," in G. Almond and J. S. Coleman, eds., *The Politics of the Developing Areas* (Princeton: Princeton University Press, 1960), pp. 3–64.

30. E. Shils, *Political Development in the New States* (New York, Humanities Press, 1964); M. Halpern, "The Rate and Costs of Political Development," *Annals of the American Academy of Political and Social Science* CCCLVIII (March 1965), 21–28. See also Eisenstadt, *Modernization, Protest and Change.*

31. See the bibliographical indications given in the General Introduction and in the bibliography.

32. See on this, in greater detail, Eisenstadt, *Modernization, Protest and Change.*

33. L. Stone, review of "Barrington Moore Jr.: Social Origins of Dictatorship and Democracy," in *New York Review of Books,* IX, No. 31 (August 24, 1957), 32.

34. See S. M. Lipset, "Some Social Requisites of Democracy," in Lipset, *The First New Nation;* J. Linz, "An Authoritarian Régime: Spain," in E. Allardt and Y. Littunen, eds., *Cleavages, Ideologies and Party Systems.* Transactions of the Westermarck Society (Helsinki: Academic Bookstore, 1964), Vol. X.

35. On all this see in greater detail Eisenstadt, *Modernization, Protest and Change.*

36. Guenter Roth, *Personal Rulership, Patrimonialism and Empire Building in the New States* (Sixth World Congress of Sociology, International Sociological Association, Evian, France, 1966) in *World Politics,* XX (January 1968), 194–206; A. R. Zolberg, "Patterns of National Integration in Tropical Africa" (Brussels; International Political Science Association, 1967).

37. See S. N. Eisenstadt, "Breakdowns of Modernization," in William J. Goode (ed.), *The Dynamics of Modern Society* (Chicago: Atherton Press, 1966), pp. 434–439.

38. R. Bendix, *Nation Building and Citizenship* (New York: Wiley, 1966); R. Emerson, *Political Modernization—The Single Party System* (Denver: University of Denver, Monograph 1, 1963–1964).

39. On this see in greater detail S. N. Eisenstadt, "The Protestant Ethic Thesis in an Analytical and Comparative Framework," in S. N. Eisenstadt, ed., *The Protestant Ethic and Modernization* (New York: Basic Books, 1968).

CHAPTER IX

The Basic Characteristics of Political Modernization

INTRODUCTION TO THE READINGS

The passages included in this part of the book aim at presenting, first, the various symbolic and structural conditions of modernization in different parts of the world and, second, the types of modernizing and modern regimes which emerge under such conditions. They attempt to show how different social conditions influence the concrete process of center formation and of different modern political regimes.

The first section in this chapter deals with the revolutionary origins of the modern state, in which there evolved a secular legitimation of the political order. First come political ideological texts representing the political thought in the first modern societies. Jefferson's letter to Colonel W. Stephens Smith, the French "Declaration of the Rights of Man and Citizen," and passages from the *Communist Manifesto* represent the various revolutionary approaches on the symbolic level.

Then come excerpts which analyze the characteristics of the social and political revolutions that ushered in the first historical types of modernization. Gentz compares the French and American revolutions and emphasizes how the strength of the emerging center determines the process of crystallization of a new social order and how the lack of congruence between its ideological and structural aspects prevents the formation of a new stable social order. Lindsay shows how the traditional premise of the Divine Right of Kings was undermined by the Puritan revolution; that is, from within the fold of

a religious movement which ushered in the more secular type of legitimation of political regimes and was based on the individual's responsibility, on the one hand, and on the state's accountability to the conscience of the individuals, on the other. In this, his analysis parallels Weber's famous Protestant Ethic thesis. Schieder analyzes the ubiquity and limits of revolution in modern society, especially the differences between the revolutions of the nineteenth and twentieth centuries.

In the next section, entitled "Transformation of Legitimation in Modern Political Systems," some of the major political philosophies are presented which questioned the basic premises of traditional legitimation and suggested a new "true" legitimation that required change of all the social institutions. Excerpts from only a few of the most famous treatises which addressed themselves to the problem of the legitimation of the political order could be presented in this book. From among the older classicists we have selected excerpts from Hobbes and Rousseau; from the later ones an excerpt from J. S. Mill.

These selections all deal, on an ideological level, with one of the central problems of mode; namely, of how a sociopolitical order which is based on its acceptance by individuals and is continuously judged by them is possible at all. However great the differences among these answers, all of them stress the continuous tensions between the individual and the social order.

The ideologies that carried on the revolutions of the twentieth century were, like their predecessors, secular in their nature. Yet many of them, and mainly the Communist ideology, were totalistic in their approach, stressing to a much larger degree than the former the necessity of submerging the individual in the social order. These ideologies demanded, like the rules of various religious orders, total commitment of the individual; and they justified coercion as a means of implementing political and social change. The passages from Lenin's *The State and Revolution* describe this attitude and try to justify the idea of "revolutionary dictatorship of the proletariat."

Sukarno's "Lecture to the Students of Hasanuddin University" shows that a new ideology emerged in the second state of modernization—that is, in postcolonial Africa and Asia. He attempted to combine democratic and Communistic ideas into a new value system, which suggests a "guided democracy" as an ideal form of government. Nkrumah's "Background to Independence" represents a similar approach, and thus these two passages serve as an example of the ideas that developed in the emerging New Nations.

Hodgkin's "Note on the Language of African Nationalism" attempts to analyze the ways by which the transformation of legitimation has linked modern national ideas with the symbols and the collectivist African precolonial past.

a. THE REVOLUTIONARY ORIGINS OF THE MODERN STATE

46

Rebellion and Liberty: From a Letter to William Stephens Smith, November 13, 1787

Thomas Jefferson

The British ministry have so long hired their gazetteers to repeat and model into every form lies about our being in anarchy, that the world has at length believed them, the English nation has believed them, the ministers themselves have come to believe them, and what is more wonderful, we have believed them ourselves. Yet where does this anarchy exist? Where did it ever exist, except in the single instance of Massachusetts? And can history produce an instance of rebellion so honourably conducted? I say nothing of its motives. They were founded in ignorance, not wickedness. God forbid we should ever be twenty years without such a rebellion. The people cannot be all, and always, well informed. The part

which is wrong will be discontented in proportion to the importance of the facts they misconceive. If they remain quiet under such misconceptions it is a lethargy, the forerunner of death to the public liberty. We have had thirteen states independent for eleven years. There has been one rebellion. That comes to one rebellion in a century and a half, for each state. What country before ever existed a century and a half without a rebellion? And what country can preserve its liberties if their rulers are not warned from time to time that their people preserve the spirit of resistance? Let them take arms. The remedy is to set them right as to facts, pardon and pacify them. What signify a few lives lost in a century or two? The tree of liberty must be refreshed from time to time with the blood of patriots and tyrants. It is its natural manure.

Reprinted from Thomas Jefferson, "Rebellion and Liberty," in William Ebenstein, ed., *Man and the State* (New York: Holt Rinehart & Co., 1947), pp. 10–11.

47

The French "Declaration of the Rights of Man and Citizen," August 27, 1789

The representatives of the French people, organized in National Assembly, considering that ignorance, forgetfulness, or contempt of the rights of man are the sole causes of public misfortunes and of the corruption of governments, have resolved to set forth in a solemn declaration the natural, inalienable, and sacred rights of man, in order that such declaration, continually before all members of the social body, may be a perpetual reminder of their rights and duties; in order that the acts of the legislative power and those of the executive power may constantly be compared with the aim of every political institution and may accordingly be more respected; in order that the demands of the citizens, founded henceforth upon simple and incontestable principles, may always be directed towards the maintenance of the Constitution and the welfare of all.

Accordingly, the National Assembly recognizes and proclaims, in the presence and under the auspices of the Supreme Being, the following rights of man and citizen.

1. Men are born and remain free and equal in rights; social distinctions may be based only upon general usefulness.

2. The aim of every political association is the preservation of the natural and inalienable rights of man; these rights are liberty, property, security, and resistance to oppression.

3. The source of all sovereignty resides essentially in the nation; no group, no individual may exercise authority not emanating expressly therefrom.

4. Liberty consists of the power to do whatever is not injurious to others; thus the enjoyment of the natural rights of every man has for its limits only those that assure other members of society the enjoyment of those same rights; such limits may be determined only by law.

5. The law has the right to forbid only actions which are injurious to society. Whatever is not forbidden by law may not be prevented, and no one may be constrained to do what it does not prescribe.

6. Law is the expression of the general will; all citizens have the right to concur personally, or through their representatives, in its formation; it must be the same for all, whether it protects or punishes. All citizens, being equal before it, are equally admissible to all public offices, positions, and employments, according to their capacity, and without other distinction than that of virtues and talents.

7. No man may be accused, arrested, or detained except in the cases determined by law, and according to the forms prescribed thereby. Whoever solicit, expedite, or execute arbitrary orders, or have them executed, must be punished; but every citizen summoned or apprehended in pursuance of the law must obey immediately; he renders himself culpable by resistance.

8. The law is to establish only penalties that are absolutely and obviously necessary; and no one may be punished except by virtue of a law established and promulgated prior to the offence and legally applied.

9. Since every man is presumed innocent until declared guilty, if arrest be deemed indispensable, all unnecessary severity for securing the person of the accused must be severely repressed by law.

10. No one is to be disquieted because of his opinions, even religious, provided their manifestation does not disturb the public order established by law.

11. Free communication of ideas and opinions is one of the most precious of the rights of man. Consequently, every citizen may speak, write, and print freely, subject to responsibility for the abuse of such liberty in the cases determined by law.

12. The guarantee of the rights of man and citizen necessitates a public force; such a force, therefore, is instituted for the advantage of all and not for the particular benefit of those to whom it is entrusted.

13. For the maintenance of the public force and for the expenses of administration a common tax is indispensable; it must be assessed equally on all citizens in proportion to their means.

14. Citizens have the right to ascertain, by themselves or through their representatives, the necessity of the public tax, to consent to it freely, to supervise its use, and to determine its quota, assessment, payment, and duration.

15. Society has the right to require of every public agent an accounting of his administration.

16. Every society in which the guarantee of rights is not assured or the separation of powers not determined has no constitution at all.

17. Since property is a sacred and inviolable right, no one may be deprived thereof unless a legally established public necessity obviously requires it, and upon condition of a just and previous indemnity.

48

The Communist Manifesto

Karl Marx and Friedrich Engels

A spectre is haunting Europe—the spectre of Communism. All the powers of old Europe have entered into a holy alliance to exorcise this spectre: Pope and Tsar, Metternich and Guizot, French Radicals and German police-spies.

Where is the party in opposition that has not been decried as communistic by its opponents in power? Where is the Opposition that has not hurled back the branding reproach of Communism, against the more advanced opposition parties, as well as against its reactionary adversaries?

Two things result from this fact:

1. Communism is already acknowledged by all European powers to be itself a power.

2. It is high time that Communists should openly, in the face of the whole world, publish their views, their aims, their tendencies, and meet this nursery tale of the spectre of Communism with a manifesto of the party itself.

To this end, Communists of various nationalities have assembled in London, and sketched the following manifesto, to be published in the English, French, German, Italian, Flemish and Danish languages:

I: Bourgeois and Proletarians

The history of all hitherto existing society is the history of class struggles.

Freeman and slave, patrician and plebeian, lord and serf, guild-master and journeyman, in a word, oppressor and oppressed, stood in constant opposition to one another, carried on an uninterrupted, now hidden, now open fight, a fight that each time ended, either in a revolutionary reconstitution of society at large, or in the common ruin of the contending classes.

In the earlier epochs of history, we find almost everywhere a complicated arrangement of society into various orders, a manifold gradation of social rank. In ancient Rome we have patricians, knights, plebeians, slaves; in the Middle Ages, feudal lords, vassals, guild-masters, journeymen, apprentices, serfs; in almost all of these classes, again, subordinate gradations.

The modern bourgeois society that has sprouted from the ruins of feudal society has not done away with class antagonisms. It has but established new classes, new conditions of oppression, new forms of struggle in place of the old ones.

Our epoch, the epoch of the bourgeoisie, possesses, however, this distinctive feature: it has simplified the class antagonisms. Society as a whole is more and more splitting up into two great hostile camps, into two great classes directly facing each other—bourgeoisie and proletariat.

From the serfs of the Middle Ages sprang the chartered burghers of the earliest towns. From these burgesses the first elements of the bourgeoisie were developed.

The discovery of America, the rounding of the Cape, opened up fresh ground for the rising bourgeoisie. The East-Indian and Chinese markets, the colonisation of America, trade with the colonies, the increase in the means of exchange and in commodities generally, gave to commerce, to navigation, to industry, an impulse never before known, and thereby, to the revolutionary element in the tottering feudal society, a rapid development.

From Karl Marx and Friedrich Engels, *The Communist Manifesto*. English translation of 1888, edited by Friedrich Engels.

The feudal system of industry, in which industrial production was monopolised by closed guilds, now no longer sufficed for the growing wants of the new markets. The manufacturing system took its place. The guild-masters were pushed aside by the manufacturing middle class; division of labour between the different corporate guilds vanished in the face of division of labour in each single workshop.

Meantime the markets kept ever growing, the demand ever rising. Even manufacture no longer sufficed. Thereupon, steam and machinery revolutionised industrial production. The place of manufacture was taken by the giant, modern industry, the place of the industrial middle class, by industrial millionaires, the leaders of whole industrial armies, the modern bourgeois.

Modern industry has established the world market, for which the discovery of America paved the way. This market has given an immense development to commerce, to navigation, to communication by land. This development has, in its turn, reacted on the extension of industry; and in proportion as industry, commerce, navigation, railways extended, in the same proportion the bourgeoisie developed, increased its capital, and pushed into the background every class handed down from the Middle Ages.

We see, therefore, how the modern bourgeoisie is itself the product of a long course of development, of a series of revolutions in the modes of production and of exchange.

Each step in the development of the bourgeoisie was accompanied by a corresponding political advance of that class. An oppressed class under the sway of the feudal nobility, an armed and self-governing association in the mediaeval commune; here independent urban republic (as in Italy and Germany), there taxable "third estate" of the monarchy (as in France); afterwards, in the period of manufacture proper, serving either the semi-feudal or the absolute monarchy as a counterpoise against the nobility, and, in fact, corner-stone of the great monarchies in general, the bourgeoisie has at last, since the establishment of Modern Industry and of the world market, conquered for itself, in the modern representative State, exclusive political sway. The executive of the modern State is but a committee for managing the common affairs of the whole bourgeoisie.

The bourgeoisie, historically, has played a most revolutionary part.

The bourgeoisie, wherever it has got the upper hand, has put an end to all feudal, patriarchal, idyllic relations. It has pitilessly torn asunder the motley feudal ties that bound man to his "natural superiors,"

and has left no other nexus between man and man than naked self-interest, than callous "cash payment." It has drowned the most heavenly ecstasies of religious fervour, of chivalrous enthusiasm, of philistine sentimentalism, in the icy water of egotistical calculation. It has resolved personal worth into exchange value, and in place of the numberless indefeasible chartered freedoms, has set up that single, unconscionable freedom—Free Trade. In one word, for exploitation, veiled by religious and political illusions, it has substituted naked, shameless, direct, brutal exploitation.

The bourgeoisie has stripped of its halo every occupation hitherto honoured and looked up to with reverent awe. It has converted the physician, the lawyer, the priest, the poet, the man of science, into its paid wage-labourers.

The bourgeoisie has torn away from the family its sentimental veil, and has reduced the family relation to a mere money relation.

The bourgeoisie has disclosed how it came to pass that the brutal display of vigour in the Middle Ages, which reactionaries so much admire, found its fitting complement in the most slothful indolence. It has been the first to show what man's activity can bring about. It has accomplished wonders far surpassing Egyptian pyramids, Roman aqueducts, and Gothic cathedrals; it has conducted expeditions that put in the shade all former Exoduses of nations and crusades.

The bourgeoisie cannot exist without constantly revolutionising the instruments of production, and thereby the relations of production, and with them the whole relations of society. Conservation of the old modes of production in unaltered form, was, on the contrary, the first condition of existence for all earlier industrial classes. Constant revolutionising of production, uninterrupted disturbance of all social conditions, everlasting uncertainty and agitation distinguished the bourgeois epoch from all earlier ones. All fixed, fast-frozen relations, with their train of ancient and venerable prejudices and opinions, are swept away, all new-formed ones become antiquated before they can ossify. All that is solid melts into air, all that is holy is profaned, and man is at last compelled to face with sober senses his real conditions of life and his relations with his kind.

The need of a constantly expanding market for its products chases the bourgeoisie over the whole surface of the globe. It must nestle everywhere, settle everywhere, establish connections everywhere.

The bourgeoisie has through its exploitation of the world market given a cosmopolitan character to production and consumption in every country. To the great chagrin of reactionaries, it has drawn from under the feet of industry the national ground on which it stood. All old-established national industries have been destroyed or are daily being destroyed. They are dislodged by new industries, whose introduction becomes a life and death question for all civilised nations, by industries that no longer work up indigenous raw material, but raw material drawn from the remotest zones; industries whose products are consumed, not only at home, but in every quarter of the globe. In place of the old wants, satisfied by the production of the country, we find new wants, requiring for their satisfaction the products of distant lands and climes. In place of the old local and national seclusion and self-sufficiency, we have intercourse in every direction, universal interdependence of nations. And as in material, so also in intellectual production. The intellectual creations of individual nations become common property. National one-sidedness and narrow-mindedness become more and more impossible, and from the numerous national and local literatures there arises a world literature.

The bourgeoisie, by the rapid improvement of all instruments of production, by the immensely facilitated means of communication, draws all, even the most barbarian, nations into civilisation. The cheap prices of its commodities are the heavy artillery with which it batters down all Chinese walls, with which it forces the barbarians' intensely obstinate hatred of foreigners to capitulate. It compels all nations, on pain of extinction, to adopt the bourgeois modes of production; it compels them to introduce what it calls civilisation into their midst, i.e., to become bourgeois themselves. In one word, it creates a world after its own image.

The bourgeoisie has subjected the country to the rule of the towns. It has created enormous cities, has greatly increased the urban population as compared with the rural, and has thus rescued a considerable part of the population from the idiocy of rural life. Just as it has made the country dependent on the towns, so it has made barbarian and semi-barbarian countries dependent on the civilised ones, nations of peasants on nations of bourgeois, the East on the West.

The bourgeoisie keeps more and more doing away with the scattered state of the population, of the means of production, and of property. It has agglomerated population, centralised means of production, and has concentrated property in a few hands. The necessary consequence of this was political centralisation. Independent, or but loosely connected provinces, with separate interests, laws, governments and systems of taxation, became lumped together into one nation, with one government, one code of laws, one national class interest, one frontier and one customs tariff.

The bourgeoisie, during its rule of scarce one hundred years, has created more massive and more colossal productive forces than have all preceding generations together. Subjection of nature's forces to man, machinery, application of chemistry to industry and agriculture, steam-navigation, railways, electric telegraphs, clearing of whole continents for cultivation, canalisation of rivers, whole populations conjured out of the ground—what earlier century had even a presentiment that such productive forces slumbered in the lap of social labour?

We see then; the means of production and of exchange, on whose foundation the bourgeoisie built himself up, were generated in feudal society. At a certain stage in the development of these means of production and of exchange, the conditions under which feudal society produced and exchanged, the feudal organisation of agriculture and manufacturing industry, in one word, the feudal relations of property became no longer compatible with the already developed productive forces; they became so many fetters. They had to be burst asunder; they were burst asunder.

Into their place stepped free competition, accompanied by a social and political sway of the bourgeois class.

A similar movement is going on before your own eyes. Modern bourgeois society with its relations of production, of exchange and of property, a society that has conjured up such gigantic means of production and of exchange, is like the sorcerer who is no longer able to control the powers of the nether world whom he has called up by his spells. For many a decade past the history of industry and commerce is but the history of the revolt of modern productive forces against modern conditions of production, against the property relations that are the conditions for the existence of the bourgeoisie and of its rule. It is enough to mention the commercial crises that by their periodical return put the existence of the entire bourgeois society on its trial, each time more threateningly. In these crises a great part not only of the existing products, but also of the previously created productive forces, are periodically destroyed. In these crises there breaks out an epidemic that, in all earlier epochs, would have seemed an absurdity—the epidemic of over-production. Society suddenly finds itself put back into a state of momentary barbarism; it appears as if a famine, a universal war of devastation had cut off the supply of every means of subsistence; industry and commerce seem to be destroyed. And why? Because there is too much civilisation, too much means of subsistence, too much industry, too much commerce. The productive forces at the disposal of society no longer tend to further the development of the conditions of bourgeois property; on the contrary, they have become too powerful for these conditions, by which they are fettered, and as soon as they overcome these fetters, they bring disorder into the whole of bourgeois society, endanger the existence of bourgeois property. The conditions of bourgeois society are too narrow to comprise the wealth created by them. And how does the bourgeoisie get over these crises? On the one hand by enforced destruction of a mass of productive forces; on the other, by the conquest of new markets, and by the more thorough exploitation of the old ones. That is to say, by paving the way for more extensive and more destructive crises, and by diminishing the means whereby crises are prevented.

The weapons with which the bourgeoisie felled feudalism to the ground are now turned against the bourgeoisie itself.

But not only has the bourgeoisie forged the weapons that bring death to itself; it has also called into existence the men who are to wield those weapons—the modern working class—the proletarians.

In proportion as the bourgeoisie, i.e., capital, is developed, in the same proportion is the proletariat, the modern working class, developed—a class of labourers, who live only so long as they find work, and who find work only so long as their labour increases capital. These labourers, who must sell themselves piecemeal, are a commodity, like every other article of commerce, and are consequently exposed to all the vicissitudes of competition, to all the fluctuations of the market.

Owing to the extensive use of machinery and to division of labour, the work of the proletarians has lost all individual character, and, consequently, all charm for the workman. He becomes an appendage of the machine, and it is only the most simple, most monotonous, and most easily acquired knack, that is required of him. Hence, the cost of production of a workman is restricted, almost entirely, to the means of subsistence that he requires for his maintenance, and for the propagation of his race. But the price of a commodity, and therefore, also of labour, is equal to its cost of production. In proportion, therefore, as the repulsiveness of the work increases, the wage decreases. Nay, more, in proportion as the use of machinery and division of labour increases, in the same proportion the burden of toil also increases, whether by prolongation of the working hours, by increase of the work exacted in a given time, or by increased speed of the machinery, etc.

Modern industry has converted the little workshop of the patriarchal master into the great factory of the industrial capitalist. Masses of labourers, crowded into the factory, are organised like soldiers. As privates of the industrial army they are placed under the command of a perfect hierarchy of officers and sergeants. Not only are they slaves of the bourgeois class, and of the bourgeois state; they are daily and hourly enslaved by the machine, by the over-looker, and, above all, by the individual bourgeois manufacturer himself. The more openly this despotism proclaims gain to be its end and aim, the more petty, the more hateful and the more embittering it is.

The less the skill and exertion of strength implied in manual labour, in other words, the more modern industry becomes developed, the more is the labour of men superseded by that of women. Differences of age and sex have no longer any distinctive social validity for the working class. All are instruments of labour, more or less expensive to use, according to their age and sex.

No sooner is the exploitation of the labourer by the manufacturer so far at an end that he receives his wages in cash than he is set upon by the other portions of the bourgeoisie, the landlord, the shopkeeper, the pawnbroker, etc.

The lower strata of the middle class—the small tradespeople, shopkeepers, and retired tradesmen generally, the handicraftsmen and peasants—all these sink gradually into the proletariat, partly because their diminutive capital does not suffice for the scale on which modern industry is carried on, and is swamped in the competition with the large capitalists, partly because their specialised skill is rendered worthless by new methods of production. Thus the proletariat is recruited from all classes of the population.

The proletariat goes through various stages of development. With its birth begins its struggle with the bourgeoisie. At first the contest is carried on by individual labourers, then by the work people of a factory, then by the operatives of one trade, in one locality, against the individual bourgeois who directly exploits them. They direct their attacks not against the bourgeois conditions of production, but against the instruments of production themselves; they destroy imported wares that compete with their labour, they smash to pieces machinery, they set factories ablaze, they seek to restore by force the vanished status of the workman of the Middle Ages.

At this stage the labourers still form an incoherent mass scattered over the whole country, and broken up by their mutual competition. If anywhere they unite to form more compact bodies, this is not yet the consequence of their own active union, but of the union of the bourgeoisie, which class, in order to attain its own political ends, is compelled to set the whole proletariat in motion, and is moreover yet, for a time, able to do so. At this stage, therefore, the proletarians do not fight their enemies, but the enemies of their enemies, the remnants of absolute monarchy, the land-owners, the non-industrial bourgeois, the petty bourgeoisie. Thus the whole historical movement is concentrated in the hands of the bourgeoisie; every victory so obtained is a victory for the bourgeoisie.

But with the development of industry the proletariat not only increases in number; it becomes concentrated in greater masses, its strength grows, and it feels that strength more. The various interests and conditions of life within the ranks of the proletariat are more and more equalized, in proportion as machinery obliterates all distinctions of labour, and nearly everywhere reduces wages to the same low level. The growing competition among the bourgeois, and the resulting commercial crises, make the wages of the workers ever more fluctuating. The unceasing improvement of machinery, ever more rapidly developing, makes their livelihood more and more precarious; the collisions between individual workmen and individual bourgeois take more and more the character of collisions between two classes. Thereupon the workers begin to form combinations (trades' unions) against the bourgeois; they club together in order to keep up the rate of wages; they found permanent associations in order to make provision beforehand for these occasional revolts. Here and there the contest breaks out into riots.

Now and then the workers are victorious, but only for a time. The real fruit of their battles lies, not in the immediate result, but in the ever expanding union of the workers. This union is helped on by the improved means of communication that are created by modern industry, and that place the workers of different localities in contact with one another. It was just this contact that was needed to centralise the numerous local struggles, all of the same character, into one national struggle between classes. But every class struggle is a political struggle. And that union, to attain which the burghers of the Middle Ages, with their miserable highways, required centuries, the modern proletarians, thanks to railways, achieve in a few years.

This organisation of the proletarians into a class, and consequently into a political party, is continually being upset again by the competition between the workers themselves. But it ever rises up again, stronger, firmer, mightier. It compels legislative recognition of particular interests of the workers, by taking advantage of the divisions among the bourgeoisie itself. Thus the ten-hours' bill in England was carried.

Altogether, collisions between the classes of the old society further in many ways the course of development of the proletariat. The bourgeoisie finds itself involved in a constant battle. At first with the aristocracy; later on, with those portions of the bourgeoisie itself, whose interests have become antagonistic to the progress of industry; at all times with the bourgeoisie of foreign countries. In all these battles it sees itself compelled to appeal to the proletariat, to ask for its help, and thus to drag it into the political arena. The bourgeoisie itself, therefore, supplies the proletariat with its own elements of political and general education, in other words, it furnishes the proletariat with weapons for fighting the bourgeoisie.

Further, as we have already seen, entire sections of the ruling classes are, by the advance of industry, precipitated into the proletariat, or are at least threatened in their conditions of existence. These also supply the proletariat with fresh elements of enlightenment and progress.

Finally, in times when the class struggle nears the decisive hour, the process of dissolution going on within the ruling class, in fact within the whole range of old society, assumes such a violent, glaring character that a small section of the ruling class cuts itself adrift and joins the revolutionary class, the class that holds the future in its hands. Just as, therefore, at an earlier period, a section of the nobility went over to the bourgeoisie, so now a portion of the bourgeoisie goes over to the proletariat, and, in particular, a portion of the bourgeois ideologists, who have raised themselves to the level of comprehending theoretically the historical movement as a whole.

Of all the classes that stand face to face with the bourgeoisie to-day, the proletariat alone is a really revolutionary class. The other classes decay and finally disappear in the face of modern industry; the proletariat is its special and essential product.

The lower middle class, the small manufacturer, the shopkeeper, the artisan, the peasant, all these fight against the bourgeoisie, to save from extinction their existence as fractions of the middle class. They are therefore not revolutionary but conservative. Nay, more, they are reactionary, for they try to roll back the wheel of history. If by chance they are revolutionary, they are so only in view of their impending transfer into the proletariat; they thus defend not their present, but their future interests; they desert their own standpoint to place themselves at that of the proletariat.

The "dangerous class," the social scum, that passively rotting mass thrown off by the lowest layers of old society, may, here and there, be swept into the movement by a proletarian revolution; its conditions of life, however, prepare it far more for the part of a bribed tool of reactionary intrigue.

In the conditions of the proletariat, those of old society at large are already virtually swamped. The proletarian is without property; his relation to his wife and children has no longer anything in common with the bourgeois family relations; modern industrial labour, modern subjection to capital, the same in England as in France, in America as in Germany, has stripped him of every trace of national character. Law, morality, religion, are to him so many bourgeois prejudices, behind which lurk in ambush just as many bourgeois interests.

All the preceding classes that got the upper hand, sought to fortify their already acquired status by subjecting society at large to their conditions of appropriation. The proletarians cannot become masters of the productive forces of society, except by abolishing their own previous mode of appropriation, and thereby also every other previous mode of appropriation. They have nothing of their own to secure and to fortify; their mission is to destroy all previous securities for, and insurances of, individual property.

All previous historical movements were movements of minorities, or in the interest of minorities. The proletarian movement is the self-conscious, independent movement of the immense majority, in the interest of the immense majority. The proletariat, the lowest stratum of our present society, cannot stir, cannot raise itself up, without the whole superincumbent strata of official society being sprung into the air.

Though not in substance, yet in form, the struggle of the proletariat with the bourgeoisie is at first a national struggle. The proletariat of each country must, of course, first of all settle matters with its own bourgeoisie.

In depicting the most general phases of the development of the proletariat, we traced the more or less veiled civil war, raging within existing society, up to the point where that war breaks out into open revolution, and where the violent overthrow of the bourgeoisie lays the foundation for the sway of the proletariat.

Hitherto, every form of society has been based, as we have already seen, on the antagonism of oppressing and oppressed classes. But in order to oppress a class, certain conditions must be assured to it under which it can, at least, continue its slavish existence. The serf, in the period of serfdom, raised himself to membership in the commune, just as the petty bourgeois, under the yoke of feudal absolutism, managed to develop into a bourgeois. The modern labourer, on the contrary, instead of rising with the progress of industry, sinks deeper and deeper below the conditions of existence of his own class. He becomes a pauper, and pauperism develops more rapidly than population and wealth. And here it becomes evident that the bourgeoisie is unfit any longer to be the ruling class in society and to impose its conditions of existence upon society as an overriding law. It is unfit to rule because it is incompetent to assure an existence to its slave within his slavery, because it cannot help letting him sink into such a state, that it has to feed him, instead of being fed by him. Society can no longer live under this bourgeoisie; in other words, its existence is no longer compatible with society.

The essential condition for the existence and for the sway of the bourgeois class is the formation and augmentation of capital; the condition for capital is wage-labour. Wage-labour rests exclusively on competition between the labourers. The advance of industry, whose involuntary promoter is the bourgeoisie, replaces the isolation of the labourers, due to competition, by their revolutionary combination, due to association. The development of modern industry, therefore, cuts from under its feet the very foundation on which the bourgeoisie produces and appropriates products. What the bourgeoisie therefore produces, above all, are its own grave-diggers. Its fall and the victory of the proletariat are equally inevitable.

The Communists everywhere support every revolutionary movement against the existing social and political order of things.

In all these movements they bring to the front, as the leading question in each, the property question, no matter what its degree of development at the time.

Finally, they labour everywhere for the union and agreement of the democratic parties of all countries.

The Communists disdain to conceal their views and aims. They openly declare that their ends can be attained only by the forcible overthrow of all existing social conditions. Let the ruling classes tremble at a Communist revolution. The proletarians have nothing to lose but their chains. They have a world to win.

Working men of all countries, unite!

49

The French and American Revolutions Compared

Friedrich Gentz

The contrast between the French and American revolutions, when you compare them with each other in respect to their *objects* is no less striking than that which has resulted from the comparison of their *origin* and *progress*. As the utmost precision of object, and consequently of principles and of means, distinguished the American revolution through its whole duration, so the utmost want of precision in the object, and consequently a perpetual mutability in the choice of the means and in the modification of principles has been one of the most stubborn, one of the most essential, and certainly one of the most terrible characteristics of the French revolution. Its history was nothing but a long series of uninterrupted developments of this extraordinary phenomenon; single and unexampled in its whole compass as this circumstance may be, it will not much astonish the man, who shall reflect upon its origin, and its nature. For so soon as in a great undertaking, a step is taken wholly out of the boundaries of definite rights, and every thing is declared lawful, which imaginary necessity, or unbridled passion inspires, so soon is the immeasurable field of arbitrary will entered upon; and a revolution, which has no other principle than to attack the existing constitution, must necessarily proceed to the last extremities of imagination and of criminal guilt.

When, by the impotence and the faults of the government, and by the success which crowned the hardiness of its first antagonists, the old constitution of France was dissolved, all those who took an interest in favour of the revolution (and their number was infinitely great, precisely because no one knew exactly what he meant by a revolution) concurred, that an essential and wide spreading alteration must be effected in the whole political constitution of the state. But how far this alteration should extend, how far the old order of things should be preserved, and how the new one should be organized, with regard to all this, no two persons of the

From Friedrich Gentz, *The French and American Revolutions Compared* (Chicago: Gateway Editions, Inc., 1955), pp. 79–95.

legions, who thought themselves called to public activity, were agreed. If we confine ourselves merely to the opinions of those, who in this interval of unbounded anarchy, publicly wrote, or spoke, we shall soon be convinced, that there were then in France, not three, or four, or ten, but thousands of political sects and parties. The impossibility of taking notice of so many individual variations, distinctions, sub-distinctions, and shades of every kind, compelled the contemporaries, and especially those immediately interested in the great spectacle, to class the infinite mass of opinions under certain known principal titles, and thus erase the names of *pure royalists,* of whole and half *monarchists,* of *feuillants,* of *jacobins,* of every degree, &c. Each of these parties, however, could have exhibited almost as many subordinate parties as it contained members.

In this number of political systems, some were built upon a limited monarchy, in the British sense of the word, others upon a thousand-fold new modification of a constitution, monarchical only in name; some wished from the beginning, to treat the revolution merely as a passage to the utter abolition of the monarchy. These pronounced sentence of death upon all the privileges of the higher orders; others wished to leave them the prerogatives of rank. One was for reforming the constitution of the churches; another for extirpating religion: one would have shewn mercy in this general overthrow, at least to the rights of property; another was for passing all positive right, under the sickle of equality. The constitution of 1791, was a desperate and impotent attempt to reconcile together, by a sort of general capitulation, all these contending theories, and the infinitely multiplied motives of interest, of ambition, and of vanity, connected with them; this attempt of course failed, for in the absolute and total indefiniteness, and I might add, the impossibility of ascertaining the last object of the revolution, every individual in France felt but too well, that he had as much right to maintain his private opinion, and to carry through his private purposes, as the members of a committee had to establish theirs; it

348

was, besides, more than doubtful, whether, even the immediate authors of this impracticable constitution, seriously considered it as a last result.

Under the shelter of the inexpressible confusion, in which the storm of these first debates involved the whole country, arose, at first, more timid, but from the last months of the year 1791, growing constantly bolder, and more powerful, the only consistent party; that which had always been of opinion, that it was folly to prescribe to the French revolution, any bounds whatsoever. This party had, indeed, like all the rest, a multitude of subdivisions, and of systems peculiarly modified, and often at violent strife with each other; but all who declared themselves for it, concurred in the great and decisive point of view, that the revolution was to be considered, not as a local transaction, but as one of those, which give a new form to civil society, and which must draw all mankind within its vortex. For the ambition, or for the enthusiasm of this insatiable party, the theatre, which France offered to their thirst for destruction, was too small; they wished to tear up the world from its poles, and commence a new aera for the whole human race. That this was their purpose, from the very breaking out, and even before the breaking out of the French revolution, we need not learn from proselyting tales and imaginary cabals of the illuminati; the writings in which they have unfolded their principles in plain terms, have proved it beyond all contradiction.

To draw near the execution of so gigantic a plan, they had first of all to destroy the last trace of a monarchical form of government in France. It would be hard to maintain, that, after all what had happened since 1789, they had not nearly about the same right to found a republic, as the monarchists, so called, had to introduce a royal democracy. The only thing which seemed against them, in point of right, was the oath which, in common with all the rest, they had taken, to support the constitution of 1791. But, after so many bands had been torn, none but weak heads could flatter themselves, that an empty form would arrest the torrent in its course. At the very time, while, with the cry of "The constitution or death!" they hushed a few credulous souls to repose, they were working with restless activity the mine, which in one instant was to blow up the whole fabric.

But, precisely at this great and important moment, the absolute indefinitude of object, that inextinguishable character of the French revolution, discovered itself in a new and terrible light. The republic had been proclaimed; but this republic was a word without definite meaning, which every one believed he might explain, according to his inclinations, and according to the fantastic whims, which he called his principles. There were just as many republican systems contending for the mastery, as there had been monarchical parties. France was drenched in blood, to decide the great question, whether Brissot, or Marat, the federalists, or the unionists, the Girondists, or the mountaineers, the Dantonians, or the Hebertists, should prescribe a republican constitution. Force alone could determine the issue of this horrible contest; and the victory must necessarily remain to the most resolute. After having torn, for nearly a year, the inmost bowels of their country, without being able to agree upon the form of their republic, a daring faction, at length, fell upon the strange expedient of settling and organizing the revolutionary state itself, as a provisional government, and, under the name of a revolutionary government, brought into play what was called the system of terror; a monstrous and unexampled monument of human error and human frenzy, which in the eyes of posterity will almost degrade the history of our times to a fable. A less cruel faction overthrew and murdered the inventors of this gigantic wickedness; not long afterwards, another devised a new code of anarchy, which was called the constitution of the third year. It is well known, by what an uninterrupted series of revolutions, and counter-revolutions, this constitution was likewise conducted to the unavoidable catastrophe of its destruction.

Just at the period, when the republican party obtained possession of the supreme power, the bloody contest broke out between them and the greatest part of the European states. They had denounced the destruction of all governments; they had declared, that between their revolution and those who rejected it, no further intercourse could exist; they had solemnly absolved all subjects from obedience to their governments. The revolution prepared against Europe, and Europe against the revolution, a war, with which only the most dreadful religious wars, that ever scourged the world, can be compared. On the side of the coalesced powers, the proper object of this war could not be doubtful; and if, unfortunately, it often was, at least it ought never to have been so. But, on the side of France, it was always as indefinite as the object of the revolution itself. Some, as for instance, Robespierre, wished for the present, only to maintain the right of turning their own country into a butchery, with impunity, and to reduce by one half the number of its inhabitants; others had projected extensive plans of conquest, and wished to realize for the French republic, all the dreams, which the ambition of Lewis the XIVth, had formerly inspired; others yet had sworn never to lay down their arms, until they should have led the principles of the revolution in triumph over the whole civilized world, or *have planted, at least,* the tree of liberty, from Lisbon to the frozen sea, and to the Dardanelles.

This war has now, with short and local intervals of insecure and treacherous peace, already desolated the earth eight years long; it has, undoubtedly, for some time past, lost much of its extent, and very much of its original character, and has now nearly declined to a common war; yet when and how it will end, is still a problem, which puts all human penetration to the blush. The fate of the French revolution is, in a great measure, connected with the fate of this war; but its last result depends, besides, upon an infinity of other combinations. There has, perhaps, never yet been a man, who could even imagine, with any clearness, what this result will be. When one of the great masses of the physical world is suddenly started from its quiet centre of gravitation, and hurled with a prodigious impetus into the empty space of air, the point at which it will stop is much harder to conceive, than the continuance of its motion. And, in truth, after the serious question, Who could have a right to begin such a revolution? has remained unanswered, nothing is more difficult than to answer that, which is equally serious: to whom belongs the right of ending it?

4. The American revolution had a mass of resistance, comparatively much smaller to combat, and, therefore, could form and consolidate itself in a manner comparatively much easier, and more simple: the French revolution challenged almost every human feeling, and every human passion, to the most vehement resistance, and could therefore only force its way by violence and crimes.

The American colonies had already, before their revolution, attained a high degree of stability; and the supremacy of the British government in America, was the relation, not so much of an immediate sovereign, as of a superior protector. Hence, the American revolution had more the appearance of a foreign, than of a civil war.

A common feeling of the uprightness of their cause, and a common interest in its issue must necessarily have animated a great and overpowering majority of the inhabitants of North America. The royal governors, the persons more immediately connected with them, and the inconsiderable number of royal troops constituted the only permanent and great opposition party. If a certain number of independent citizens, from principle, or from inclination took the side of the ministry, they were however much too weak to become dangerous to the rest; and their impotence itself protected them against the hatred and intolerance of their countrymen.

There were in the interior of the colonies no sort of zeal or personal prerogatives, and no other distinction of ranks, than what proceeded from the exercise of public functions. Property owing to the novelty of civil society in the country, was much more equally distributed than can be the case in old countries, and the relations between the wealthy and the labouring classes were more simple and therefore more beneficent. As the revolution altered little in the internal organization of the colonies, as it only dissolved an external connection, which the Americans must always have considered rather as a burden, than an advantage; there was nobody, except the few, who took a share in the administration at the head of the country, who was immediately and essentially interested in the preservation of the ancient form. What this form contained of good and useful remained untouched; the revolution only removed that in which it had been oppressive.

How infinitely different was in this point of view the situation of France! If the French revolution had been content merely to destroy with violent hands the old Constitution, without making any attack upon the rights and possessions of private persons, it would, however, have been contrary to the interest of a numerous, and in every respect important class of people, who by the sudden dissolution of the old form of Government, having lost their offices, their incomes, their estimation and their whole civil existence, would of themselves have formed a powerful opposition—But, when in its further progress, it no longer spared any private right whatsoever, when it declared all political prerogatives to be usurpations, deprived the nobility not only of their real privileges, but likewise of their rank and title, robbed the clergy of their possessions, of their influence, and even of their external dignity; by arbitrary laws took from the holders of estates half their revenues; by incessant breaches of the rights of property, converted property itself into an uncertain, equivocal, narrowly straitened enjoyment, by recognizing publicly principles of the most dangerous tendency, held the sword hovering over the head of every one, who had any thing to lose, and aggravated the essential wretchedness, which it every where spread by the ridicule and contempt it shed over every thing that bore the name of possessions, or privileges— then truly it could not fail to accumulate against itself a mass of resistance, which was not to be subdued by ordinary means.

Should the friends of the French revolution declare this important circumstance to be merely accidental; should they impute solely to the good fortune of the American nation, that they found no domestic impediments in the way to their new constitution; and to the ill fortune of the French, that they had to struggle with so many obstinate antagonists; should they consider the former case only as enviable, and the latter only as deserving compassion, yet will the impartial observer, never forget how much merit there was involved in that good, and how much guilt in this ill fortune. The Americans were wise enough to circumscribe themselves within the bounds, which right, on one side, and the nature of things, on the other, had drawn round them. The French in their giddiness no longer acknowledged the prescriptions of the clearest right, nor the prescriptions of nature. They were so proud as to think they could bend impossibility itself, under the arm of their violence, and so daring that they thought the clearest right must yield to the maxims of their arbitrary will. The resistance of which they complained, was with perfect certainty to be foreseen; it lay in the unalterable laws of human feelings, and human passions; it was just, it was necessary; it was impossible to believe that it would not take place. Those, who had called it forth by the most cruel injuries, did not fail to be sure to declare it punishable, and did punish thousands, whose only crime consisted in refusing to rejoice at their own ruin. But this double injustice prepared a new resistance, which could be overcome only by new acts of violence. Thus at last, in the barbarous law book of the revolution, suffering itself was made an unpardonable offence; the fear of a just reaction drove the authors of these oppressions to measures of still deepening cruelty against the victims of their first crimes; and the presumption of the natural and inevitable hatred, which these crimes must every where rouse against them, was a sufficient ground to them to treat as an offender deserving death, every man, who did not immediately and actively associate with them.

Although the American revolution never involved itself in this horrible labyrinth, where voluntary iniquities can only be covered by necessary misdeeds, and where every earlier crime became the only justification of an hundred later ones; yet did it not altogether escape the misfortune, which seems inseparable from all sudden and violent changes in the civil and political relations of society. The smallness of the resistance it met with, and the moderation of those who conducted it, preserved it from a multitude of cruel, desperate, and dishonorable measures, which have sullied other revolutions; but its warmest friends will not venture to maintain that it was wholly exempt from injustice and violence. The

bitterness against the English government, often degenerated into a spirit of persecution, and involved those, who were suspected of a punishable indifference, or of secret connivance, in the sentence of proscription pronounced against tyranny. The hatred between the friends of independence, and the partizans of the ministry, the whigs and the tories, as they were distinguished by names taken from old English parties, broke out, especially amidst the dangers of the war, sometimes in violent scenes, which tore to pieces the internal harmony of neighbourhoods, and sometimes even of families. The reciprocal cruelties, which from time to time were practised upon prisoners, called to mind the peculiar character, which had never wholly abandoned a civil war. The rights of property likewise were often violated by single communities and single states, and, in some few instances, with the co-operation of the supreme authority. The history of the descendants of the great and benevolent Penn, driven from the paradise, which he had created, and compelled, like other loyalists, to take refuge in the generosity and magnanimity of England, is no honorable page in the annals of North-America.

But what are all these single instances of injustice and oppression, compared with the universal flood of misery and ruin, which the French revolution let loose upon France, and all the neighbouring countries. If, even in America, private hatred, or local circumstances threatened property or personal security; if here and there even the public authorities became the instruments of injustice, of revenge, and of a persecuting spirit, yet did the poison never flow into every vein of the social body; never, as in France, was the contempt of all rights, and of the very simplest precepts of humanity, made the general maxim of legislation, and the unqualified prescription of systematic tyranny. If in America, the confusion of the moment, the impulse of necessity, or the eruption of the passions, sometimes inflicted misfortune upon innocence, never at least, never as in France, did reason herself, abused, desecrated reason, ascend the theatre of misery, solemnly to justify, by cold blooded, criminal appeals to principles and duties, these revolutionary confusions; and if in America, single families and districts, felt the heavy hand of the revolution and of war, never at least, as in France, were confiscations, banishments, imprisonments, and death, decreed in a mass.

When the American revolution was concluded, the country proceeded with rapid steps to a new, a happy, and a flourishing constitution. Not but that the revolution had left behind it many great and essential ravages: the ties of public order, had, in a long and bloody contest, been on all sides more or less relaxed; peaceful industry had suffered many a violent interruption; the relations of property, the culture of the soil, the internal and foreign trade, the public and private credit, had all considerably suffered by the revolutionary storms, by the insecurity of the external relations, and especially by the devastations of paper money.[1] Even the morals and the character of the people, had been essentially, and not in every respect advantageously affected by the revolution. Although we can draw no conclusion from this circumstance with regard to futurity, yet history must remark with attention, and preserve with care, the confession, which comes from the pen of a calm and impartial witness, the best of all the writers upon the American revolution hitherto (Ramsay): "That by this revolution, the *political, military,* and *literary* talents of the people of the United States, were improved, but their *moral* qualities were deteriorated."

A picture of the condition in which the revolution has left France, is by far too great, too complicated, and too formidable a subject to be touched upon even transiently here. The idea itself of a final result from such a revolution as this, must still be in some sort an indefinite, and perhaps a hazarded idea. Thus much, however, may be asserted with confidence, that between the results of the American and those of the French revolution, no sort of comparison can so much as be conceived.

I might have continued the above parallel through many other respects, and perhaps into single points of detail. I believe, however, that the four principal points of view in which I have treated it, with regard to the *lawfulness of the origin, character of*

the conduct, quality of the object, and *compass of resistance,* sufficiently answer the purpose, I proposed to myself, and it appears, at least to me, evident enough, that every parallel between these two revolutions, will serve much more to display the *contrast,* than the *resemblance* between them.

NOTE

1. In no one point is the analogy between the conduct of the revolutionary leaders in America and in France, so striking as in this; yet it must not be forgotten, that the Americans failed partly from inexperience and partly from real necessity; whereas in France they knew very well what they were about, and opened and widened the precipice with design.

The history of the American assignats, is almost word for word, only upon a smaller scale, and not attended with circumstances of such shocking cruelty, as the history of the French ones. The sudden start from two millions to two hundred millions of dollars; the credulity with which the first assignats were received, the undeserved credit which they for a time enjoyed, their subsequent rapid fall, so that in the year 1777, they already stood with specie in the proportion of 1 to 3; in 1778, of 1 to 6; in 1779, of 1 to 28; in the beginning of 1780, of 1 to 60; fell immediately afterwards to that of 1 to 150, and finally would pass for nothing at all; the attempt to substitute a new emission of assignats, instead of those which were worn out, continued until at last it became necessary to establish a formal depreciation; the harsh laws made to support the value of the paper; the regulation of the price of provisions (the maximum) and the requisitions, which they occasioned; the general devastation of property, and disturbance of all civil intercourse; the wretchedness and immorality which ensued upon them—all this goes to compose a picture, which the French revolutionary leaders seem to have taken for a model. It is remarkable, that they closely copied the Americans only in two points, of which one was the idlest, and the other the most objectionable of any throughout their revolution; in the declaration of the rights of man, and in paper-money.

50

The Modern Democratic State

A. D. Lindsay

The immediate answer to the problem of political obligation in the new State was, strangely enough, the theory of the divine right of kings. All the re-

From A. D. Lindsay, *The Modern Democratic State* (London: Oxford University Press, 1943), pp. 73–81. Reprinted by permission of the present Lord Lindsay of Birker, son of the author, who holds the copyright.

ligious authority which had been behind law and church was transferred to the King. Men had been accustomed for generations to regard their loyalty to the organs of government as an essential element in their religion. They retained the notion of the religious duty of obedience, but its concentrated object was now the King. He and he alone had God's authority. As God's authority was now thought of as that of an absolute sovereign and not as the authority of divine law: so the authority of his Vicar was the same. "The King is in the room of God," said Tyndale, "and his law is God's law."[1]

The theory was strongest when no reasons were given for it. It represented men's gratitude for the efficiency of the new monarchy, put into religious terms which were for most men the most natural. When men tried to rationalize it, their reasons were so silly that their defence of it weakened it. It seems to us now a strange and fantastic doctrine, though the way in which "German Christians" talk of Hitler should make us more capable of understanding it. But it was clearly an impossible *Christian* defence of the new monarchy. Christianity is too intimately connected with moral values and with the universalism of the Gospel for Christians to support such blasphemies for long. In more recent times men have found other Gods to worship—the nation or the people—and have found in such worship religious emotions which can inspire irrational obedience with less qualms.

Further, if the real inspiration for the divine right of kings was gratitude for the benefits of the new monarchy, the religious embodiment of that gratitude could not long outlive its inspiration. Such irrational religions demand success from their Gods. But while it lasted, the religious character of the sentiment did something which the utilitarian theories could not do. The belief in the *divine* right of Kings made men separate their feelings for the King's divinity from the gratitude which had largely inspired it and they could go on suffering evil at the King's hands for a considerable time without their devotion being impaired. As we shall see later, a rational calculation of individual advantage will not produce the necessary steadiness and universality of obedience which a political society needs. Reasoned individual selfishness is not enough. Obedience to the state may be in our general interest. It is often not in our particular interest. A sense of interest has somehow to be translated into a sense of obligation. The doctrine of the divine right of kings, however irrational it may appear, gave obedience just the touch of absoluteness which is needed and is not supplied by a sense of interest. That is why this irrational doctrine had in practice far more effect than all Hobbes's cleverness.

These new monarchies were supported, in France and England at least, by the growing consciousness of nationality. But it took some time before nationalism was essential to them. At first, as has been said, the reverence which had been given to the church and the law of nature, was concentrated in the king. The divine right of kings does really express what was for a short time the operative ideal of the state. All the spiritual capital built up by the civilization of medieval Christendom was devoted to the embodiment by the new state in the person of the king. The principle by which the religious problem was settled in Germany shows this clearly. *Cujus regio ejus religio.* Any territory with its inhabitants belonged to someone. "Whosoever's territory it is"; he will be either Protestant or Roman Catholic. Let the people on that territory have his religion. The king or ruler is all: the people are nothing. It has been said that John Knox's remark to Queen Mary marked the beginning of democracy as we know it.

" 'What have ye to do,' said she, 'with my marriage? Or what are ye within this Commonwealth?' 'A subject born within the same, Madam,' said he. 'And albeit, I neither be Erle, Lord, nor Barronn within it, yett has God made me (how abject that even I be in your eyes) a profitable member within the same.' " But that was an early premonitory flash. Mary's obstinate and pedantic son held on to the doctrine of divine right with fatal consequence to his son. "I am the Husband, and the whole isle is my lawful wife; I am the Head, and it is my Body," he said to his first English Parliament.

The feelings of unquestioning and unreasoning authority which thus supported the new absolutism could not last. The first attempt at totalitarianism failed partly because of its own inefficiency. The techniques of a totalitarian state had not yet been invented. The new states were always in money difficulties. It was not till the twentieth century that the weapons were invented which gave a comparative few control over a vast population. Hobbes could still say that men were equal because any one of them might kill any other. But the ideas on which absolute government rested were gradually undermined and especially by three things, all of which had had at first something to do with the coming into being of the new order.

Failure of Absolutism

The doctrine of the divine right of kings, as the quotation from Tyndale suggests, had been largely the product of Protestantism, putting forward the absoluteness of the king against the absoluteness of the pope. The further development of Protestantism in the Puritan sects destroyed it. Hobbes makes clear how akin to absolutism the temper of the new sciences could be. But the widespread development of scientific inquiry produced a state of mind very remote from belief in a doctrine like the divine right of kings. The effects of capitalism we shall consider later. It is enough now to notice that while the monied classes were undoubtedly behind the new monarchy, they were soon behind the revolt against it. On the whole, commerce and industry since the seventeenth century till the end of the nineteenth put a premium on adventurous enterprise and initiative. Regulations and government help were on the whole and in the long run a handicap. Capitalism which began by supporting the new absolutism ended by demanding *laissez-faire*.

These three movements, the Reformation and in particular Puritanism, the progress of science and capitalism all worked against the new absolutism. They destroyed its totalitarianism. Puritanism led to revolution and the independence of the church or the churches on the state. The progress and spread of scientific thinking gradually produced a new something, Science with a capital S, wanting to be let alone and go its own way with its own values and its own drive. The progress of industrialism produced the new world of business, with *its* own values, and its own momentum and its own non-political concentrations of power, growing, partly for good and partly for evil, its own international world: substituting the internationalism of business for the internationalism of the Catholic Church.

These all destroyed the traditional authority, on which, when transferred to the king, the new absolutism rested, by the universal spread of what came to be known as individualism. That particular word was not invented till the nineteenth century. It first occurs in de Tocqueville's *Democracy in America,* but the phenomenon made its first striking appearance in the seventeenth century. Of the distinction of society into several spheres with its consequent limitation of the function of the state we shall have more to say in the next chapter. It is more important to notice at this point the fundamental difference between the individualism fostered by Protestantism and that fostered by science and capitalism. An understanding of that difference will provide a clue to many ambiguities in democratic theory. It will occupy us at greater length when we discuss in a later chapter the distinction between mass democracy and Christian democracy. But the distinction is already apparent in the seventeenth century.

Protestant Individualism

Protestant or Puritan individualism depends on the full acceptance of the fundamental Protestant doctrine of the priesthood of all believers. That doctrine is but an emphatic assertion of the fundamental Christian doctrine of the absolute worth of the individual soul. All men are equal in the sight of God—not because they are indistinguishable, "the very hairs of their head are numbered"—but because each in his separate individual existence is dear to God. Any one of them is at any rate "the least of these my brethren." In Puritan theology every believer is a priest because he has been called by God. That fact, common to all believers, is so all important that it overshadows and renders relatively unimportant the difference which it does not deny. The equality of the elect is therefore the equality of a society in which all count, and in which all are recognized to have different gifts. "There are diversities of gifts but the same spirit, and there are differences of administration but the same Lord, and there are diversities of operations but it is the same God which worketh all in all."

Secondly, believers are called into a fellowship, and the fellowship according to the Puritans of the left must be a small one. The congregation is the church, a small community in which democratic practice is easy: in which individuals could be treated as individuals with their separate gifts and callings, with their separate message from God. Hence the exaltation of the small society in which the individual man in close community with his fellows can find shelter from the pressure of Leviathan. Hence comes, as we shall see, the new view of the function of the state as concerned to cherish and protect the voluntary association in which the most precious things in society may develop.

Scientific Individualism

The new sciences which came into being in the seventeenth century and have gone on growing in prestige ever since began with a repudiation of final causes. That repudiation is the denial of the authority of ethics in science. The new sciences were as energetic as the new politics in denying the supremacy of morality. The anti-moral claims of the new politics, though they are, as at present we sadly know, reasserted from time to time, have been energetically rebutted. The similar claims of the new sciences have been so triumphant that we now hardly notice them. So much is their acceptance taken for granted.

This repudiation of final causes has this further effect. The new sciences substituted for the authority of a whole rational system which no one individual can grasp in its entirety, which therefore depends on the acceptance of the authority of others, the authority of the individual experiment. The experiment can be tested by any one who understands scientific method. Descartes, the first philosopher of the new sciences, finds truth, not in a system, but in clear and *distinct* ideas, truths separately and distinctly grasped. As the nature of the new sciences and the place of experiment in them come to be better understood, the authority of the separate repeatable experiment took the place of the clearly and distinctly perceived idea. Few things are more striking in Descartes than his apparently genuine belief that his scientific discoveries were due, not to any special abilities of his own but solely to his having found the proper method of scientific discovery. He implies that all who follow his method will be able to make scientific discoveries as he has done. The new realm of science is not a preserve for the gifted, but a democratic commonwealth, open to all who will learn its laws, where each can make his contribution and where there is work for all. There had of course been scientists before the seventeenth century but there could not have been before modern times what may be called the "ordinary scientific mind," or the widespread assumption about what sort of things can be proved and what cannot, or the disbelief in anything which cannot be verified by experiment. That implies the existence in a community of a fair number of ordinary men who have learnt scientific method and done some scientific investigation for themselves.

This is the subjective side of scientific individualism—the personal individualism of the scientist. It is not so unlike the individualism of the Puritan. Its individuals, as has been said, are members of a fellowship. Science gradually built up a new internationalism, the internationalism of scientific research, which helped to produce in the nineteenth century a strange Utopian flower, the free commonwealth of universities all over the world. It is, like Puritanism, committed to the idea of infinite progress and for that reason concerned that room should be found for free inquiry and the free mind.

But there is another and a very different side of scientific individualism. The scientific revival of the seventeenth century not only repudiated final purposes. It revived atomism. The triumphs of physics rested on the assumption that reality in the last analysis consisted of an infinite number of identical repeatable atoms: that all qualitative differences were reducible to quantitative variations of such atoms; that analysis could reduce all the apparent wealth and colour of the visible world to this quantitative reality. The triumphant prestige of physics made many thinkers anxious to extend the same method to the analysis and understanding of society. When men are regarded as objects of scientific inquiry so conceived, they are regarded as atomistic individuals, not as personalities. Society is regarded as analysable into a collection of independent, isolable, alike atoms. The doctrine of human equality when held as it is by Bentham, for example, means that men are regarded as for all *practical* purposes identical. They are like the replaceable parts of a machine. This analytical method, borrowed from physics, applied the same assumptions to man's mind, reducing it in associationist psychology to a collection of independent ideas, with only external relations between them. Men with minds thus conceived are at the mercy of their accidental desires and are only capable of acting according to the pull of their desires, according therefore to their self-interest as thus accidentally determined.

As we shall see, this atomistic individualism has had a far-reaching effect upon democratic theory. It is well to notice that it is in its essence profoundly undemocratic. The natural sciences which arose in the seventeenth century gave man unprecedented power over nature. The physicist regards nature as something which in virtue of his atomistic analysis he can manipulate. His analysis is an instrument of power. So when the mechanical hypothesis is applied to society there is implied throughout, whether it be stated or not, the distinction between the creative power of the planner and the mass of atomistic individuals to be planned. Hitler's distinction between the master minds and the servile masses is only the logical conclusion of this fundamental attitude, and Hitler's destruction of the freedom of scientific enquiry is the nemesis of the narrowness of this whole mechanical hypothesis.

The same conflict between creative individualism and mass individualism showed itself in the development of capitalism. Capitalism first supported the seventeenth-century totalitarian state, then revolted against it and then in the twentieth century sometimes supported totalitarianism again. The entrepreneur wanted to be free from restraints on his powers. He also wanted to retain power over the men he employed. When he praised individualism and freedom of enterprise he was thinking of the freedom of himself and his kind, the masterful enterprising industrial planners. But in the application of "scientific" methods to industry he thought of his workpeople as "factors of production" to be co-ordinated efficiently and scientifically along with the other material factors of production. He came to resist their democratic organization and freedom as stoutly as he demanded democratic freedom for himself and his kind. The development of industrialism gradually produced an organization of industry where the qualitative differences between masses of men were not wanted and were discouraged; where craftsmanship decayed and nothing more was wanted to the majority of those employed but repetitive standardized actions. Planning and organization became the monopoly of the few.

51

Revolution in the Nineteenth Century

Theodor Schieder

Karl Marx's conception of revolution occupies a position between social-economic determinism and political activism. The final uncertainty in which his whole political system wavers was transmitted to those Socialist parties that were his followers, and it resulted not merely in fluctuations in theory but in very great feebleness in their political strategy and tactics. If we take for example the strongest among them, German Social Democracy, we see clearly to what extent the dilemma at the heart of Marxist revolutionary theory affected its political effectiveness. August Bebel was no ordinary revolutionary leader of the workers; he fought passionately for the downfall of "sabre and class rule" and never denied that he was a "social revolutionary." But the more his thought became permeated with Marxist conceptions, the less real became his determination for violent revolution. As Social Democracy gained strength he and his party increasingly stressed the more immediate aim of the politically organised working class—the achievement of democracy by means of electoral agitation and parliamentary opposition. The testing time for the tactics of formal legalism was the period of the anti-Socialist laws; and by the retention of these tactics the Social Democrats even earned some measure of rebuke from Marx and Engels. This formal legalism was, however, very far from being collaboration; for Social Democracy under Bebel, without overstepping the limit of parliamentary opposition or obstruction or using any revolutionary or terrorist methods, retained its attitude of uncompromising non-co-opera-

From Theodor Schieder, *The State and Society in Our Times* (London: Thomas Nelson & Sons Ltd., 1962), pp. 24–32. Reprinted by permission of R. Oldenbourg Verlag, publisher of the original German edition.

tion with the German state created by Bismarck. In his "Social Democratic catechism" of 1893 Kautsky described it as the "party that is revolutionary but does not make a revolution."[1] And German Social Democracy does indeed occupy a position between the English trade-union movement with its social policy of practical reform and the Russian Socialists' programme of underground activity and terror.

The opponents of the Social Democrat party had difficulty in even comprehending this sort of policy —indeed, its own leaders were not all fully conscious of its significance—and it by no means lacked critics. We today are only at the outset of the impartial historical analysis which would enable us to assess its worth.[2] Bismarck saw nothing in it but its purely negative attitude to the state he had built up, and called the Social Democrat programme the "gospel of negation."[3] But he did not clearly discern the revolutionary tactical method that lay behind it and he took no trouble to do so, for he thought he had explained it sufficiently by analogy with the social-revolutionary movement in neighbouring countries. Bebel gave him what might have been a hint on two quite separate occasions. The first was during the first session of the Reichstag in May 1871, when he called the Commune revolt in Paris "a small skirmish on the outposts" and expressed the assurance "that the main events in Europe are still to come; before many decades the war-cry of the Paris proletariat: War on the palaces, peace for the humble homes, death to poverty and idleness—this war-cry will be that of the whole proletariat of Europe." The second time came during the discussion on the anti-Socialist laws, and just before the murder of Czar Alexander in 1881. Bebel, in much more guarded and moderate language, was defending an article in the Zürich newspaper *Sozial-demokrat* which spoke of the need for "self-help" and vindicated the attack on the Czar's life.[4] The Commune revolt in Paris and the subversive policy of Russian anarcho-nihilism form the background against which Bismarck saw the German Socialists and their policy. In 1878, when the hasty anti-Socialist laws were being forced through, he observed that since the reference to the Commune—he could not recall exactly whether by Bebel or Liebknecht—he had regarded the Social Democrat elements as an enemy against whom the state, indeed society, had to defend itself.[5] Social Democracy, he once put it later, "lives at war with us, and so soon as it feels itself strong enough, it will begin the attack, just like the French."[6] In the great debate of 9 May 1884 Bismarck did indeed stress that "conditions [in Germany and Russia] were as the poles asunder"; but his object here was merely to show that Germany was at an *advanced* stage of revolution. "The Russians have not yet to fear that the masses may join with the Nihilists in opposing the government. The sole enemy force there is still the dagger and the revolver of the single murderer, whereas with us it is a public opinion that is being harmed and poisoned."[7]

While one should never discount the tactical significance of these and similar utterances, it appears certain that Bismarck did believe in an impending revolutionary movement, as Metternich had done at the beginning of the century, and that he was firmly convinced of Social Democracy's subversive aim, of "the Social Democrat revolution." He could even work himself up into a frantic fear of revolution and was then haunted by a kind of "cauchemar des révolutions"—to turn his own phrase on himself. His repressive policy in the anti-Socialist laws, mistaken in both origin and outcome, is attributable to this, to political motives, to the interests of the state which he had established and which he now led, and not to personal spite—though this was a point on which he felt attack on himself and his policy most keenly.

In passing any fair judgment on the policy it must be remembered that in France the twice-repeated suppression of Socialist movements with fire and sword in 1848 and 1871 had been far more brutal; for there, thousands of combatants were deported and many, whether participants or not, were done to death.[8] Friedrich Engels, praising the dignity and firmness of purpose shown by the French, wrote to Bebel (14 November 1879): "The storm that broke over the French Socialists after the Commune was quite a different thing from the commotion in

Germany about Nobiling."[9] At the same time it should not be forgotten that Bismarck himself always regarded his own social measures of the 1880s as the necessary positive counterpart to his policy of repression towards Social Democratic ideas; and he was prepared to endure the accusation of "Socialism" made against him by the middle-class Liberals, the opponents of those measures. But what really led to disaster was this unhappy linking of a noble pioneering experiment in state social reform (incidentally, except for the formulation of the Imperial Codes of Law, it is the only legislative inheritance of Bismarck's Empire that is still extant, though in a much altered form) with a piece of political emergency legislation. It made it extremely difficult, if not psychologically and politically impossible, for the Social Democrats to give their support to it; and they could hardly avoid a sterile attitude of arid rejection. And thus the course events had taken in England, where independent evolution in their working conditions had led on to the proletariat's initiation into political responsibilities, was finally blocked in Germany. It is highly significant that the Revisionist wing of the Social Democrat party, prepared to take a more conciliatory course, particularly in matters of social policy, failed to gain official control and was outlawed at the Party Congress in Dresden in 1903.[10] The success of this wing would have achieved an ideological superiority for the evolutionary over the revolutionary principles. But its victory was prevented by the prodigious hardening of opinion on both sides in Germany which on the one hand led the Socialist working class within the Empire to hold itself completely aloof from politics, and on the other led the rest of the nation to treat it as a pariah. It must be admitted, however, that the strengthening of the trade unions opened up an alternative way for the Revisionist wing to assert itself, and actually the veto against its policies amounted more and more to a *reservatio mentalis.*

It is characteristic of developments in Germany that up to the moment of the military collapse of the Empire, despite savage emergency legislation, no extremist revolutionary policy emerged, and that the political working-class movement, for all its "purely formal radicalism,"[11] never took the final step into revolutionary action. Karl Kautsky, who had come into prominence as one of the most determined leaders in the struggle against the Revisionists, wrote his *Die proletarische Revolution und ihr Programm* at this stage in events. In it he put forward the opinion, so much reviled by the radical Communist left wing, that Marx's phrase "the revolutionary dictatorship of the proletariat" (referring to the period covering the revolutionary transformation from a capitalist to a Communist state) ought rather "in view of recent events" to read: "Between the eras of the purely middle-class and the purely proletarian control of the democratic state there lies a period of transformation leading from the one to the other. And to this there corresponds a period of political transition when the control will generally be assumed by some form of coalition."[12]

The problem of revolution repeatedly brings one back to a view embracing world history. This explains why the next stage of our investigation deals with Russia and not Germany; for it was in Russia that the revolutionary aspects of the Marxist doctrine of history and society were most fully explored. It might be true to say that within the lands of German culture the political and intellectual system of Restoration and reaction had led to the elevation of counter-revolution to almost axiomatic validity; but for Russian thought it was revolution, not only as a political but as positively an ethical and religious principle, which occupied this position. No other nation—not even the French, the "demiurge" of bourgeois revolution—had embraced the idea of revolution in the same manner as did the Russian intelligentsia about the turn of the century, when they prophetically interpreted the whole of Russian history as a coming revolution[13] and created the revolutionary as a human type whose very outward appearance is at variance with his surroundings and who submits himself to the forms of a sort of monastic life. It is worth reflecting on this phenomenon. One of its causes is the particular form of the Russian state whose autocratic despotism drove criticism and opposition to take on the forms of underground conspiracy, of violent revolt by individuals or smaller secret societies, of personal acts of terrorism against isolated representatives of a system which could not be overthrown *in toto*.[14] This is why as early as the '60s the Russian intelligentsia were already debating the moral right to take terrorist action—what Karl Nötzel called the "social act of desperation"—which was still unacceptable in the West outside small anarchist circles.[15] Michael Bakunin, the "Don Quixote of the Revolution," praised the destructive urge as at the same time "a creative urge";[16] and he sought God in the revolution[17] and exalted the brigand as the true and only revolutionary in Russia. He saw Western European anarchism, largely a theoretical product, as a force of nature which had something sinister about it for Western Europeans. "What a man!" as Caussidière, the French fighter on the barricades, is said to have exclaimed; "on the first day of the revolution he is invaluable, but by the second you simply must shoot him."[18] It was Bakunin who had wanted to make the International into a "revolutionary general staff" made up of a handful of coconspirators devoted to himself; and this brought him into the sharpest conflict with Marx.[19] His aim, then, was to put revolution into the hands of an élite of professional revolutionaries, and not into that of a party of the masses. Nicolai Chernyshevsky portrayed this kind of professional revolutionary in his *What Now?*, a social novel of the future. The concept added a further element of "nihilistic" anarchism to the Russian revolution that followed.

But it was not only in reaction from Czarist despotism but also in response to social conditions that the Russian intelligentsia gave themselves over (at first in theory and later also in practice) in an unprecedented manner to the spirit of the revolution. Serfdom, social bankruptcy in the rural districts contrasting with the splendid existence of an upper stratum that lacked nothing, filled large sections of the youth of the country with a sense of social guilt which assumed such varied forms of "social asceticism" as renouncing one's family inheritance, turning from reputable professions, and living among and with the people.[20] Such emotions, nowhere else so intense or so general, must surely spring in the first place from some religious source; indeed, the Russian revolution has at times been referred to as a "pseudo-morphism" of Russian religious feeling.[21] I cannot undertake an assessment of how correct this statement is from the point of view of doctrinal history; but might it not be true in a country whose Church has "retained the eschatological character of early Christendom in perhaps the greatest degree"[22] and has always revered asceticism and the person of the ascetic?[23] Nihilism had only to pervert the doctrine of love, so alive in the Eastern Church, into a doctrine of hatred, and then ascribe the professional revolutionary's withdrawal from a world ripe for destruction to social asceticism. The most striking evidence of this conception is surely the *Revolutionary Catechism* taken to be the work of Bakunin and his pupil Sergei Netchaev, and a sort of nihilist revolutionary ordinance. It contains such passages as the following:

> The revolutionary is a dedicated being. He has neither personal interests nor concerns nor feelings nor preferences nor even a name. Everything about him is absorbed by one single exclusive interest, one single passion: revolution. In the depths of his being he has not merely renounced but actually severed every tie binding him to the bourgeois and indeed to the civilised

world, to law, to morals, and to generally accepted obligations. He is its implacable foe, and if he continues to live in this world, it is only to be more certain of destroying it. . . . The revolutionary is a dedicated being. He is pitiless in his attitude to the state in general and towards the whole of civilised society, and he need expect as little pity in his own case. He and society are engaged in a life and death struggle, both openly and in secret, endless and remorseless. He must accustom himself to martyrdom.[24]

However sharply Bolshevism as the most radical product of Marxism dissociated itself from this irrational revolutionary romanticism, it was unable really to deny its debt to earlier Russian revolutionary faith with its religious, indeed chiliastic, features. The first Russian Socialists who tried to follow on from Marx, men like Peter Lavrov and in particular G. V. Plechanov,[25] took over the social-economic automatism of his revolutionary thought. This led at once to the question whether in Russia the course of revolution would have to go through the whole process of the build-up of capital and the resulting creation of the working class, or whether the Socialist revolution there could not take over directly from the primitive communistic elements in the Russian agrarian system—thus omitting the whole stage of the bourgeois revolution.[26] In the labyrinth of such speculative reflections the practical impulse in Russian Socialism was in danger of faltering and failing; and none saw this more clearly than Lenin, for whom every theoretical opinion was merely material for his radical revolutionary will. And so in drafting his revolutionary programme of action he completely cut out all economic fatalism and concentrated on Russia's particular needs: revolutionary action *before* capitalism should have created a class-conscious proletariat in Russia; mobilisation also of the peasants' revolutionary energy; organisation of a revolutionary spearhead composed like Bakunin's of a general staff of professional revolutionaries and not drawn from the crowd of lukewarm hangers-on.[27] What he was attempting here was a radical rationalisation of Russian revolutionary doctrine, the application of Marxist revolutionary theory to conditions in Russia, and at the same time the stressing of all its activist elements. In the final form of Lenin's *State and Revolution* (1917), the plan of action which he brought out immediately before the actual outbreak of the revolution, fragments of Marxist revolutionary concepts are drawn together to form a coherent exposition of the revolutionary process then being translated into action; and here it is categorically stated: "The replacement of the bour-

geois by the proletarian state is impossible without revolution by force." And later: "Every Marxist has to accept class warfare for the recognition of the dictatorship of the proletariat." Earlier, in 1905, at the end of the first Russian revolution, Lenin had revived another significant conception of Marx's: "We stand for permanent revolution!"[28] And this, like all the words uttered by this man of will and power with his hatred of everything indecisive, acquired a new steely ring and sounded an unmistakable note of determination. Permanent revolution, that is the form which the proletariat's existence took on in the period after the democratic revolution. It is another name for the dictatorship of the proletariat, the vindication of force which should pave the way for a "classless society." No longer confined to Russia, its latest phase passes into world revolution.

Such is the prospect with which the revolutionary thought of the nineteenth century leaves us. Here it had reached its furthest limit where the means became an end, the form the substance; and it has swept on towards crises in which in fact the bewildered eye of the contemporary often misses the real significance not merely of the aim but of the course of events, the convulsion itself. The immanence of revolution has gone on growing vaster, more threatening; and what when the century opened had seemed only a bogy conjured up by political hypochondriacs had by its end drawn close indeed.

That century has bequeathed the problem of revolution to us, and with it the question of its objective and subjective causes; and this inheritance has grown before our eyes to gigantic proportions. Standing on the ruins of a shattered world and, like those who lived through the Terror of 1793, dreadfully conversant with the demoniac raging of revolutionary passion, we inquire with a deeper urgency than before into the moral justification for revolution, into its tangle of freedom and necessity, that is to say, of guilt and fate, into the possibility of avoiding it by reading the signs of coming crises and applying timely remedies before the outburst occurs. Since 1917, after the stupendous revolutionary convulsions of the last generation, the problem of revolution which obsessed the whole of the nineteenth century faces us in our turn in a totally different sense.

NOTES

1. Quoted by E. Matthias in *Kautsky und der Kautsky-anismus*, p. 163.

2. See principally H. Heidegger, *Die Deutsche Sozialde-mokratie und der nationale Staat 1870–1920* (Göttingen 1956); P. Gay, *Das Dilemma des demokratischen Sozialis-mus. Eduard Bernsteins Auseinandersetzung mit Marx* (Nürn-berg 1954); Carl E. Schorske, *German Social Democracy 1905–1917. The Development of the Great Schism* (Cam-bridge, Mass., 1955).

3. Reichstag speech of 9 October 1878. For the whole problem from a present-day standpoint see G. A. Rein, *Die Revolution in der Politik Bismarcks* (Göttingen 1857), pp. 284ff.

4. This speech of 21 March 1881 was again mentioned in the Reichstag discussions on the renewal of the anti-Socialist laws. Bebel once more stressed the conditional sense of his words: "Monarchy would naturally be struck were the same means to be employed as are now customary in Russia. And naturally so! And I herewith state that in that case I would be one of the first to lend a hand if the same conditions were to obtain here." Bismarck interpreted this as approval of the assassinations by the Russian nihilists and as a qualified recognition of political murder, especially of a ruler.

5. Reichstag speech of 9 October 1878.

6. Reichstag speech of 28 May 1889.

7. This speech affords a very accurate and informed analysis of Russian nihilism about the close of the century; for the rest it is tactically conditioned by the endeavour to refute the arguments by the opposition that a repressive policy in Germany would surely lead to the same manifesta-tions as in Russia.

8. There is an echo of this in Bismarck's Reichstag speech of 9 October 1878, during which the Chancellor recalled that "the Communards were all condemned by the courts-martial to be shot out of hand or deported, with a ruthlessness of which no other nation but the French is capable."

9. Printed in A. Bebel, *Aus meinem Leben*, vol. iii, p. 70f.

10. On this point see H. Herkner, *Die Arbeiterfrage* (8th ed., 1922), vol. ii, pp. 396ff.

11. A. Rosenberg, *Geschichte der deutschen Republik* (1928), p. 16f.

12. K. Kautsky, *Die proletarische Revolution und ihr Programm* (1922), p. 106.

13. The intellectual bases of the Russian revolution are examined by Peter Scheibert in his comprehensive work, *Von Bakunin zu Lenin. Geschichte der russischen revolutionären Ideologie 1840–1895* (Leiden 1956). So far only the first volume has been published.

14. On this whole question the best source is still Karl Nötzel, *Die Grundlagen des geistigen Russlands* (Jena 1917).

15. Cf. Valentin Gitermann, *Geschichte Russlands* (Ham-burg 1949), esp. vol. iii, Part 8, pp. 191ff.; on the beginnings of the Terror see pp. 219f., 235f.

16. No. 251 (21 Oct. 1842) in the series of articles en-titled "Die Reaction in Deutschland," in the *Deutsche Jahr-bücher für Kunst und Wissenschaft:* "Let us put our trust in the eternal spirit which destroys and annihilates only because it is the unfathomable and ever-creative source of all life. The destructive urge is at the same time a creative urge!" Published under the pseudonym of Jules Elysard.

17. Quoted by P. Scheibert, *Von Bakunin zu Lenin*, vol. i, p. 275.

18. V. Gitermann, *Geschichte Russlands*, vol. iii, p. 222.

19. In the articles of the Alliance de la démocratie socialiste et l'association internationale des travailleurs (1873) Bakunin declared that though there was no need to call the army of the revolution into being—that army could never be anything but the people themselves—"still, there must be a kind of revolutionary general staff. This must comprise dedicated, forceful, and gifted men who above all love the people without either ambition or vanity and are able to build a bridge between the revolutionary idea and the instinctive longings of the people. There is no need for any very large number of such men. For an international organisation covering the whole of Europe one hundred revolutionaries bound in one fixed and earnest common aim would suffice. Two to three hundred revolutionaries are enough to organise even the largest country." Quoted by P. Eltzbacher, *Der Anarchismus* (Berlin 1900), p. 123. On Bakunin's quarrel with Marx see also *Karl Marx oder Bakunin? Demokratie oder Diktatur?*, a new edition of the Report to the Socialist International by K. Marx and Fr. Engels, ed. W. Blos (Stutt-gart 1920). On his quarrel with the International see also G. Mayer, *Fr. Engels*, vol. ii, chap. 7.

20. See especially K. Nötzel, *Die Grundlagen des geistigen Russlands*, p. 187ff., on "social mourning." The work by Peter Scheibert already mentioned has not yet dealt with this question, but see vol. i, p. 17. A vital relevant article is that by F. F. Seeley, "The Heyday of the 'Superfluous Man' in Russia," in *The Slavonic and East European Review,* 31 (1952), pp. 92ff.

21. In this connection see especially Fedor Stepan and Nikolai Berdyaev; in *Sinn und Schicksal des russischen Kommunismus* (Luzern 1937), p. 139, the latter speaks of the revolution as a "lesser apocalypse," a "judgment of God within the limits of history."

22. Quoted from *Das orthodoxe Christentum* by the Bul-garian theologian Zankow, cited by Freidrich Heiler in his *Urkirche und Ostkirche* (München 1937), p. 228.

23. See F. Heiler, op. cit., p. 365ff.

24. In Michail Dragomanov, *Michail Bakunins sozialisti-scher Briefwechsel mit Alexander von Herzen und Ogarov,* ed. Boris Minzès (Paris 1894), pp. 371ff.

25. Cf. V. Gitermann, *Geschichte Russlands*, vol. iii, pp. 317f, 324ff.

26. Vera Zasulic (who is remembered because of her sensational acquittal on a political murder charge) put this whole question to Marx in a letter in February 1881, and after composing numerous versions he sent her an extremely guarded reply (published in the *Marx-Engels Archiv*, ed. D. Rjazanov, vol. i, pp. 309ff.: *Vera Zasulic und Karl Marx*). In its final form, 8 March 1881, it reads: "L'analyse donnée dans le *Capital* n'offre donc de raisons ni pour ni contre la vitalité de la commune rurale, mais l'étude spéciale que j'en ai faite, et dont j'ai cherché les matériaux dans les sources originales, m'a convaincu que cette commune est le point d'appui de la régéneration sociale en Russie, mais afin qu'elle puisse fonctionner comme tel, il faudrait d'abord éliminer les influences délétères qui l'assaillent de tous les côtés et ensuite lui assurer les conditions normales d'un développement spontané." In the preface to the Russian edition of the Communist Manifesto, the joint work of Marx and Engels, which Zasulic prepared, there is a similar conditional statement: "If the Russian revolution should be-come the signal for a revolution of the workers in the West also, so that each supplements the other, then the system of common property in Russia today can serve as the starting point for a Communist development." From V. Gitermann, *Geschichte Russlands*, vol. iii, pp. 318f.

27. See Georg Lukacs, *Lenin* (Berlin 1924).

28. Lenin, *Collected Works*, vol. viii, p. 248.

52

The General Will

J. J. Rousseau

That the General Will Is Indestructible

As long as several men in assembly regard themselves as a single body, they have only a single will which is concerned with their common preservation and general well-being. In this case, all the springs of the State are vigorous and simple and its rules clear and luminous; there are no embroilments or conflicts of interests; the common good is everywhere clearly apparent, and only good sense is needed to perceive it. Peace, unity, and equality are the enemies of political subtleties. Men who are upright and simple are difficult to deceive because of their simplicity; lures and ingenious pretexts fail to impose upon them, and they are not even subtle enough to be dupes. When, among the happiest people in the world, bands of peasants are seen regulating affairs of State under an oak, and always acting wisely, can we help scorning the ingenious methods of other nations, which make themselves illustrious and wretched with so much art and mystery?

A state so governed needs very few laws; and, as it becomes necessary to issue new ones, the necessity is universally seen. The first man to propose them merely says what all have already felt, and there is no question of factions or intrigues or eloquence in order to secure the passage into law of what every one has already decided to do, as soon as he is sure that the rest will act with him.

Theorists are led into error because, seeing only States that have been from the beginning wrongly constituted, they are struck by the impossibility of applying such a policy to them. They make great game of all the absurdities a clever rascal or an insinuating speaker might get the people of Paris

From Jean J. Rousseau, *The Social Contract, Discourses* (London: Sonnenschein, 1895), Book IV, Chap. I–II, pp. 85–89.

or London to believe. They do not know that Cromwell would have been put to "the bells" by the people of Berne, and the Duc de Beaufort on the treadmill by the Genevese.

But when the social bond begins to be relaxed and the State to grow weak, when particular interests begin to make themselves felt and the smaller societies to exercise an influence over the larger, the common interest changes and finds opponents: opinion is no longer unanimous; the general will ceases to be the will of all; contradictory views and debates arise; and the best advice is not taken without question.

Finally, when the State, on the eve of ruin, maintains only a vain, illusory, and formal existence, when in every heart the social bond is broken, and the meanest interest brazenly lays hold of the sacred name of "public good," the general will becomes mute: all men, guided by secret motives, no more give their views as citizens than if the State had never been; and iniquitous decrees directed solely to private interest get passed under the name of laws.

Does it follow from this that the general will is exterminated or corrupted? Not at all: it is always constant, unalterable, and pure; but it is subordinated to other wills which encroach upon its sphere. Each man, in detaching his interest from the common interest, sees clearly that he cannot entirely separate them; but his share in the public mishaps seems to him negligible beside the exclusive good he aims at making his own. Apart from this particular good, he wills the general good in his own interest, as strongly as any one else. Even in selling his vote for money, he does not extinguish in himself the general will, but only eludes it. The fault he commits is that of changing the state of the question, and answering something different from what he is asked. Instead of saying, by his vote, "It is to the advantage of the State," he says, "It is of advantage to this or that man or party that this or that view should prevail." Thus the law of public order in assemblies is not so much to maintain in them the general will as to secure that the question be always put to it, and the answer always given by it.

I could here set down many reflections on the simple right of voting in every act of Sovereignty—a right which no one can take from the citizens—and also on the right of stating views, making proposals, dividing and discussing, which the government is always most careful to leave solely to its members; but this important subject would need a treatise to itself, and it is impossible to say everything in a single work.

Voting

It may be seen . . . that the way in which general business is managed may give a clear enough indication of the actual state of morals and the health of the body politic. The more concert reigns in the assemblies, that is, the nearer opinion approaches unanimity, the greater is the dominance of the general will. On the other hand, long debates, dissensions, and tumult proclaim the ascendancy of particular interests and the decline of the State.

This seems less clear when two or more orders enter into the constitution, as patricians and plebeians did at Rome; for quarrels between these two orders often disturbed the comitia, even in the best days of the Republic. But the exception is rather apparent than real; for then, through the defect that is inherent in the body politic, there were, so to speak, two States in one, and what is not true of the two together is true of either separately. Indeed, even in the most stormy times, the *plebiscita* of the people, when the senate did not interfere with them, always went through quietly and by large majorities. The citizens having but one interest, the people had but a single will.

At the other extremity of the circle, unanimity recurs; this is the case when the citizens, having fallen into servitude, have lost both liberty and will. Fear and flattery then change votes into acclamation; deliberation ceases, and only worship or malediction is left. Such was the vile manner in which the senate expressed its views under the emperors. It did so sometimes with absurd precautions. Tacitus observes that, under Otho, the senators, while they heaped curses on Vitellius, contrived at the same time to make a deafening noise, in order that, should he ever become their master, he might not know what each of them had said.

On these various considerations depend the rules by which the methods of counting votes and comparing opinions should be regulated, according as the general will is more or less easy to discover, and the State more or less in its decline.

There is but one law which, from its nature, needs unanimous consent. This is the social compact; for civil association is the most voluntary of all acts. Every man being born free and his own master, no one, under any pretext whatsoever, can make any man subject without his consent. To decide that the son of a slave is born a slave is to decide that he is not born a man.

If then there are opponents when the social compact is made, their opposition does not invalidate the contract, but merely prevents them from being included in it. They are foreigners among citizens. When the State is instituted, residence constitutes consent; to dwell within its territory is to submit to the Sovereign.[1]

Apart from this primitive contract, the vote of the majority always binds all the rest. This follows from the contract itself. But it is asked how a man can be both free and forced to conform to wills that are not his own. How are the opponents at once free and subject to laws they have not agreed to?

I retort that the question is wrongly put. The citizen gives his consent to all the laws, including those which are passed in spite of his opposition, and even those which punish him when he dares to break any of them. The constant will of all the members of the State is the general will; by virtue of it they are citizens and free.[2] When in the popular assembly a law is proposed, what the people is asked is not exactly whether it approves or rejects the proposal, but whether it is in conformity with the general will, which is their will. Each man, in giving his vote, states his opinion on that point; and the general will is found by counting votes. When therefore the opinion that is contrary to my own prevails, this proves neither more nor less than that I was mistaken, and that what I thought to be the general will was not so. If my particular opinion had carried the day I should have achieved the opposite of what was my will; and it is in that case that I should not have been free.

This presupposes, indeed, that all the qualities of the general will still reside in the majority: when they cease to do so, whatever side a man may take, liberty is no longer possible.

In my earlier demonstration of how particular wills are substituted for the general will in public deliberation, I have adequately pointed out the practicable methods of avoiding this abuse; and I shall have more to say of them later on. I have also given the principles for determining the proportional number of votes for declaring that will. A difference of one vote destroys equality; a single opponent destroys unanimity; but between equality and unanimity, there are several grades of unequal division, at each of which this proportion may be fixed in accordance with the condition and the needs of the body politic.

There are two general rules that may serve to regulate this relation. First, the more grave and important the questions discussed, the nearer should the opinion that is to prevail approach unanimity. Secondly, the more the matter in hand calls for speed, the smaller the prescribed difference in the numbers of votes may be allowed to become: where an instant decision has to be reached, a majority of one vote should be enough. The first of these two rules seems more in harmony with the laws, and the second with practical affairs. In any case, it is the combination of them that gives the best proportions for determining the majority necessary.

NOTES

1. This should of course be understood as applying to a free State; for elsewhere family, goods, lack of a refuge, necessity, or violence may detain a man in a country against his will; and then his dwelling there no longer by itself implies his consent to the contract or to its violation.

2. At Genoa, the word "Liberty" may be read over the front of the prisons and on the chains of the galley-slaves. This application of the device is good and just. It is indeed only malefactors of all estates who prevent the citizen from being free. In the country in which all such men were in the galleys, the most perfect liberty would be enjoyed.

53

Leviathan, or the Matter, Form and Power of a Commonwealth, Ecclesiastical and Civil

Thomas Hobbes

Of the Causes, Generation, and Definition of a Commonwealth

The final cause, end, or design of men, who naturally love liberty, and dominion over others, in the introduction of that restraint upon themselves, in which we see them live in commonwealths, is the foresight of their own preservation, and of a more contented life thereby; that is to say, of getting themselves out from that miserable condition of war, which is necessarily consequent, as hath been shown (Chapter XIII), to the natural passions of men, when there is no visible power to keep them in awe, and tie them by fear of punishment to the performance of their covenants, and observation of those laws of nature set down in the fourteenth and fifteenth chapters.

For the laws of nature, as justice, equity, modesty, mercy, and, in sum, doing to others, as we would be done to, of themselves, without the terror of some power, to cause them to be observed, are contrary to our natural passions, that carry us to partiality, pride, revenge, and the like. And covenants, without the sword, are but words, and of no strength to secure a man at all. Therefore notwithstanding the laws of nature (which every one hath then kept, when he has the will to keep them, when he can do it safely) if there be no power erected, or not great enough for our security; every man will, and may lawfully rely on his own strength and art, for caution against all other men. And in all places, where men have lived by small families, to rob and spoil one another, has been a trade, and so far from being reputed against the law of nature, that the greater spoils they gained, the greater was their honour; and men observed no other laws therein, but the laws of honour; that is, to abstain from cruelty, leaving to men their lives, and instruments of husbandry. And as small families did then; so now do cities and kingdoms which are but greater families, for their own security, enlarge their dominions, upon all pre-

Reprinted from Thomas Hobbes, *Leviathan, or the Matter, Form and Power of a Commonwealth, Ecclesiastical and Civil* (London: Basil Blackwell, 1946), pp. 109–113.

tences of danger, and fear of invasion, or assistance that may be given to invaders, and endeavour as much as they can, to subdue, or weaken their neighbours, by open force, and secret arts, for want of other caution, justly; and are remembered for it in after ages with honour.

Nor is it the joining together of a small number of men, that gives them this security; because in small numbers, small additions on the one side or the other, make the advantage of strength so great, as is sufficient to carry the victory; and therefore gives encouragement to an invasion. The multitude sufficient to confide in for our security, is not determined by any certain number, but by comparison with the enemy we fear; and is then sufficient, when the odds of the enemy is not of so visible and conspicuous moment, to determine the event of war, as to move him to attempt.

And be there never so great a multitude; yet if their actions be directed according to their particular judgments, and particular appetites, they can expect thereby no defence, nor protection, neither against a common enemy, nor against the injuries of one another. For being distracted in opinions concerning the best use and application of their strength, they do not help but hinder one another; and reduce their strength by mutual opposition to nothing: whereby they are easily, not only subdued by a very few that agree together; but also when there is no common enemy, they make war upon each other, for their particular interests. For if we could suppose a great multitude of men to consent in the observation of justice, and other laws of nature, without a common power to keep them all in awe; we might as well suppose all mankind to do the same; and then there neither would be, nor need to be any civil government, or commonwealth at all; because there would be peace without subjection.

Nor is it enough for the security, which men desire should last all the time of their life, that they be governed, and directed by one judgment, for a limited time; as in one battle, or one war. For though they obtain a victory by their unanimous endeavour against a foreign enemy; yet afterwards, when either they have no common enemy, or he that by one part is held for an enemy, is by another part held for a friend, they must needs by the difference of their interests dissolve, and fall again into a war amongst themselves.

It is true, that certain living creatures, as bees, and ants, live sociably one with another, which are therefore by Aristotle numbered amongst political creatures; and yet have no other direction, than their particular judgments and appetites; nor speech, whereby one of them can signify to another, what he thinks expedient for the common benefit: and therefore some man may perhaps desire to know, why mankind cannot do the same. To which I answer,

First, that men are continually in competition for honour and dignity, which these creatures are not; and consequently amongst men there ariseth on that ground, envy and hatred, and finally war; but amongst these not so.

Second, that amongst these creatures, the common good differeth not from the private; and being by nature inclined to their private, they procure thereby the common benefit. But man, whose joy consisteth in comparing himself with other men, can relish nothing but what is eminent.

Third, that these creatures, having not, as man, the use of reason, do not see, nor think they see any fault, in the administration of their common business; whereas amongst men, there are very many, that think themselves wiser, and abler to govern the public, better than the rest; and these strive to reform and innovate, one this way, another that way; and thereby bring it into distraction and civil war.

Fourth, that these creatures, though they have some use of voice, in making known to one another their desires, and other affections; yet they want that art of words, by which some men can represent to others, that which is good, in the likeness of evil; and evil, in the likeness of good, and augment, or diminish the apparent greatness of good and evil; discontenting men, and troubling their peace at their pleasure.

Fifth, irrational creatures cannot distinguish between *injury,* and *damage;* and therefore as long as they be at ease, they are not offended with their fellows: whereas man is then most troublesome, when he is most at ease: for then it is that he loves to shew his wisdom, and control the actions of them that govern the commonwealth.

Last, the agreement of these creatures is natural; that of men, is by covenant only, which is artificial: and therefore it is no wonder if there be somewhat else required, besides covenant, to make their agreement constant and lasting; which is a common power, to keep them in awe, and to direct their actions to the common benefit.

The only way to erect such a common power, as may be able to defend them from the invasion of foreigners, and the injuries of one another, and thereby to secure them in such sort, as that by their own industry, and by the fruits of the earth, they may nourish themselves and live contentedly; is, to confer all their power and strength upon one man, or upon one assembly of men, that may reduce all their wills, by plurality of voices, unto one will: which is as much as to say, to appoint one man, or assembly of men, to bear their person; and every one to own, and acknowledge himself to be author of whatsoever he that so beareth their person, shall act, or cause to be acted, in those things which concern the common peace and safety; and therein to submit their wills, every one to his will, and their judgments, to his judgment. This is more than consent, or concord; it is a real unity of them all, in one and the same person, made by covenant of every man with every man, in such manner, as if every man should say to every man, *I authorize and give up my right of governing myself, to this man, or to this assembly of men, on this condition, that thou give up thy right to him, and authorize all his actions in like manner.* This done, the multitude so united in one person, is called a COMMONWEALTH, in Latin CIVITAS. This is the generation of that great LEVIATHAN, or rather, to speak more reverently, of that *mortal god,* to which we owe under the *immortal God,* our peace and defence. For by this authority, given him by every particular man in the commonwealth, he hath the use of so much power and strength conferred on him, that by terror thereof, he is enabled to form the wills of them all, to peace at home, and mutual aid against their enemies abroad. And in him consisteth the essence of the commonwealth; which, to define it, is *one person, of whose acts a great multitude, by mutual covenants one with another, have made themselves every one the author, to the end he may use the strength and means of them all, as he shall think expedient, for their peace and common defence.*

And he that carrieth this person, is called SOVEREIGN, and said to have *sovereign power;* and every one besides, his SUBJECT.

The attaining to this sovereign power, is by two ways. One, by natural force; as when a man maketh his children, to submit themselves, and their children to his government, as being able to destroy them if they refuse; or by war subdueth his enemies to his will, giving them their lives on that condition. The other, is when men agree amongst themselves, to submit to some man, or assembly of men, voluntarily, on confidence to be protected by him against all others. This latter, may be called a political commonwealth, or commonwealth by *institution;* and the former, a commonwealth by *acquisition.* And first, I shall speak of a commonwealth by institution.

54

Considerations on Representative Government

John Stuart Mill

A good despotism means a government in which, so far as depends on the despot, there is no positive oppression by officers of state, but in which all the collective interests of the people are managed for them, all the thinking that has relation to collective interests done for them, and in which their minds are formed by, and consenting to, this abdication of their own energies. Leaving things to the Government, like leaving them to Providence, is synonymous with caring nothing about them, and accepting their results, when disagreeable, as visitations of Nature. With the exception, therefore, of a few studious men who take an intellectual interest in specu-

lation for its own sake, the intelligence and sentiments of the whole people are given up to the material interests, and, when these are provided for, to the amusement and ornamentation, of private life. But to say this is to say, if the whole testimony of history is worth anything, that the era of national decline has arrived; that is, if the nation had ever attained anything to decline from. If it has never risen above the condition of an Oriental people, in that condition it continues to stagnate. But if, like Greece or Rome, it had realised anything higher, through the energy, patriotism, and enlargement of mind, which as national qualities are the fruits solely of freedom, it relapses in a few generations into the Oriental state. And that state does not mean stupid tranquillity, with security against change for the

Reprinted from John Stuart Mill, *Considerations on Representative Government* (London: Parker, Son, and Brown, 1861), pp. 138–144.

worse; it often means being overrun, conquered, and reduced to domestic slavery, either by a stronger despot, or by the nearest barbarous people who retain along with their savage rudeness the energies of freedom.

Such are not merely the natural tendencies, but the inherent necessities of despotic government; from which there is no outlet, unless in so far as the despotism consents not to be despotism; in so far as the supposed good despot abstains from exercising his power, and, though holding it in reserve, allows the general business of government to go on as if the people really governed themselves. However little probable it may be, we may imagine a despot observing many of the rules and restraints of constitutional government. He might allow such freedom of the press and of discussion as would enable a public opinion to form and express itself on national affairs. He might suffer local interests to be managed, without the interference of authority, by the people themselves. He might even surround himself with a council or councils of government, freely chosen by the whole or some portion of the nation; retaining in his own hands the power of taxation, and the supreme legislative as well as executive authority. Were he to act thus, and so far abdicate as a despot, he would do away with a considerable part of the evils characteristic of despotism. Political activity and capacity for public affairs would no longer be prevented from growing up in the body of the nation; and a public opinion would form itself not the mere echo of the government. But such improvement would be the beginning of new difficulties. This public opinion, independent of the monarch's dictation, must be either with him or against him; if not the one, it will be the other. All governments must displease many persons, and these having now regular organs, and being able to express their sentiments, opinions adverse to the measures of government would often be expressed. What is the monarch to do when these unfavourable opinions happen to be in the majority? Is he to alter his course? Is he to defer to the nation? If so, he is no longer a despot, but a constitutional king; an organ or first minister of the people, distinguished only by being irremovable. If not, he must either put down opposition by his despotic power, or there will arise a permanent antagonism between the people and one man, which can have but one possible ending. Not even a religious principle of passive obedience and "right divine" would long ward off the natural consequences of such a position. The monarch would have to succumb, and conform to the conditions of constitutional royalty, or give place to some one who

would. The despotism, being thus chiefly nominal, would possess few of the advantages supposed to belong to absolute monarchy; while it would realise in a very imperfect degree those of a free government; since however great an amount of liberty the citizens might practically enjoy, they could never forget that they held it on sufferance, and by a concession which under the existing constitution of the State might at any moment be resumed; that they were legally slaves, though of a prudent, or indulgent, master.

It is not much to be wondered at if impatient or disappointed reformers, groaning under the impediments opposed to the most salutary public improvements by the ignorance, the indifference, the intractableness, the perverse obstinacy of a people, and the corrupt combinations of selfish private interests armed with the powerful weapons afforded by free institutions, should at times sigh for a strong hand to bear down all these obstacles, and compel a recalcitrant people to be better governed. But (setting aside the fact, that for one despot who now and then reforms an abuse, there are ninety-nine who do nothing but create them) those who look in any such direction for the realisation of their hopes leave out of the idea of good government its principal element, the improvement of the people themselves. One of the benefits of freedom is that under it the ruler cannot pass by the people's minds, and amend their affairs for them without amending them. If it were possible for the people to be well governed in spite of themselves, their good government would last no longer than the freedom of a people usually lasts who have been liberated by foreign arms without their own co-operation. It is true, a despot may educate the people; and to do so really, would be the best apology for his despotism. But any education which aims at making human beings other than machines, in the long run makes them claim to have the control of their own actions. The leaders of French philosophy in the eighteenth century had been educated by the Jesuits. Even Jesuit education, it seems, was sufficiently real to call forth the appetite for freedom. Whatever invigorates the faculties, in however small a measure, creates an increased desire for their more unimpeded exercise; and a popular education is a failure, if it educates the people for any state but that which it will certainly induce them to desire, and most probably to demand.

I am far from condemning, in cases of extreme exigency, the assumption of absolute power in the form of a temporary dictatorship. Free nations have, in times of old, conferred such power by their own choice, as a necessary medicine for diseases of the body politic which could not be got rid of by less violent means. But its acceptance, even for a time strictly limited, can only be excused, if, like Solon or Pittacus, the dictator employs the whole power he assumes in removing the obstacles which debar the nation from the enjoyment of freedom. A good despotism is an altogether false ideal, which practically (except as a means to some temporary purpose) becomes the most senseless and dangerous of chimeras. Evil for evil, a good despotism, in a country at all advanced in civilisation, is more noxious than a bad one; for it is far more relaxing and enervating to the thoughts, feelings, and energies of the people. The despotism of Augustus prepared the Romans for Tiberius. If the whole tone of their character had not first been prostrated by nearly two generations of that mild slavery, they would probably have had spirit enough left to rebel against the more odious one.

There is no difficulty in showing that the ideally best form of government is that in which the sovereignty, or supreme controlling power in the last resort, is vested in the entire aggregate of the community; every citizen not only having a voice in the exercise of that ultimate sovereignty, but being, at least occasionally, called on to take an actual part in the government, by the personal discharge of some public function, local or general.

To test this proposition, it has to be examined in reference to the two branches into which . . . the inquiry into the goodness of a government conveniently divides itself, namely, how far it promotes the good management of the affairs of society by means of the existing faculties, moral, intellectual, and active, of its various members, and what is its effect in improving or deteriorating those faculties.

The ideally best form of government, it is scarcely necessary to say, does not mean one which is practicable or eligible in all states of civilisation, but the one which, in the circumstances in which it is practicable and eligible, is attended with the greatest amount of beneficial consequences, immediate and prospective. A completely popular government is the only polity which can make out any claim to this character. It is pre-eminent in both the departments between which the excellence of a political constitution is divided. It is both more favourable to present good government, and promotes a better and higher form of national character, than any other polity whatsoever.

Its superiority in reference to present well-being rests upon two principles, of as universal truth and applicability as any general propositions which can be laid down respecting human affairs. The first is, that

the rights and interests of every or any person are only secure from being disregarded when the person interested is himself able, and habitually disposed, to stand up for them. The second is, that the general prosperity attains a greater height, and is more widely diffused, in proportion to the amount and variety of the personal energies enlisted in promoting it.

Putting these two propositions into a shape more special to their present application; human beings are only secure from evil at the hands of others in proportion as they have the power of being, and are, self-*protecting;* and they only achieve a high degree of success in their struggle with Nature in proportion as they are self-*dependent,* relying on what they themselves can do, either separately or in concert, rather than on what others do for them.

The former proposition—that each is the only safe guardian of his own rights and interests—is one of those elementary maxims of prudence, which every person, capable of conducting his own affairs, implicitly acts upon, wherever he himself is interested. Many, indeed, have a great dislike to it as a political doctrine, and are fond of holding it up to obloquy, as a doctrine of universal selfishness. To which we may answer, that whenever it ceases to be true that mankind, as a rule, prefer themselves to others, and those nearest to them to those more remote, from that moment Communism is not only practicable, but the only defensible form of society; and will, when that time arrives, be assuredly carried into effect. For my own part, not believing in universal selfishness, I have no difficulty in admitting that Communism would even now be practicable among the *élite* of mankind, and may become so among the rest. But as this opinion is anything but popular with those defenders of existing institutions who find fault with the doctrine of the general predominance of self-interest, I am inclined to think they do in reality believe that most men consider themselves before other people. It is not, however, necessary to affirm even this much in order to support the claim of all to participate in the sovereign power. We need not suppose that when power resides in an exclusive class, that class will knowingly and deliberately sacrifice the other classes to themselves: it suffices that, in the absence of its natural defenders, the interest of the excluded is always in danger of being overlooked; and, when looked at, is seen with very different eyes from those of the persons whom it directly concerns. In this country, for example, what are called the working classes may be considered as excluded from all direct participation in the government. I do not believe that the classes who do participate in it have in general any intention of sacrificing the working classes to themselves. They once had that intention; witness the persevering attempts so long made to keep down wages by law. But in the present day their ordinary disposition is the very opposite: they willingly make considerable sacrifices, especially of their pecuniary interest, for the benefit of the working classes, and err rather by too lavish and indiscriminating beneficence; nor do I believe that any rulers in history have been actuated by a more sincere desire to do their duty towards the poorer portion of their countrymen. Yet does Parliament, or almost any of the members composing it, ever for an instant look at any question with the eyes of a working man? When a subject arises in which the labourers as such have an interest, is it regarded from any point of view but that of the employers of labour? I do not say that the working men's view of these questions is in general nearer to the truth than the other: but it is sometimes quite as near; and in any case it ought to be respectfully listened to, instead of being, as it is, not merely turned away from, but ignored. On the question of strikes, for instance, it is doubtful if there is so much as one among the leading members of either House who is not firmly convinced that the reason of the matter is unqualifiedly on the side of the masters, and that the men's view of it is simply absurd. Those who have studied the question know well how far this is from being the case; and in how different, and how infinitely less superficial a manner the point would have to be argued, if the classes who strike were able to make themselves heard in Parliament.

It is an adherent condition of human affairs that no intention, however sincere, of protecting the interests of others can make it safe or salutary to tie up their own hands. Still more obviously true is it, that by their own hands only can any positive and durable improvement of their circumstances in life be worked out. Through the joint influence of these two principles, all free communities have both been more exempt from social injustice and crime, and have attained more brilliant prosperity, than any others, or than they themselves after they lost their freedom. Contrast the free states of the world, while their freedom lasted, with the contemporary subjects of monarchical or oligarchical despotism: the Greek cities with the Persian satrapies; the Italian republics and the free towns of Flanders and Germany, with the feudal monarchies of Europe; Switzerland, Hol-

land, and England, with Austria or ante-revolutionary France. Their superior prosperity was too obvious ever to have been gainsaid: while their superiority in good government and social relations is proved by the prosperity, and is manifest besides in every page of history. If we compare, not one age with another, but the different governments which co-existed in the same age, no amount of disorder which exaggeration itself can pretend to have existed amidst the publicity of the free states can be compared for a moment with the contemptuous trampling upon the mass of the people which pervaded the whole life of the monarchical countries, or the disgusting individual tyranny which was of more than daily occurrence under the systems of plunder which they called fiscal arrangements, and in the secrecy of their frightful courts of justice.

It must be acknowledged that the benefits of freedom, so far as they have hitherto been enjoyed, were obtained by the extension of its privileges to a part only of the community; and that a government in which they are extended impartially to all is a desideratum still unrealised. But though every approach to this has an independent value, and in many cases more than an approach could not, in the existing state of general improvement, be made, the participation of all in these benefits is the ideally perfect conception of free government. In proportion as any, no matter who, are excluded from it, the interests of the excluded are left without the guarantee accorded to the rest, and they themselves have less scope and encouragement than they might otherwise have to that exertion of their energies for the good of themselves and of the community, to which the general prosperity is always proportioned.

Thus stands the case as regards present well-being; the good management of the affairs of the existing generation. If we now pass to the influence of the form of government upon character, we shall find the superiority of popular government over every other to be, if possible, still more decided and indisputable.

This question really depends upon a still more fundamental one, viz., which of two common types of character, for the general good of humanity, it is most desirable should predominate—the active, or the passive type; that which struggles against evils, or that which endures them; that which bends to circumstances, or that which endeavours to make circumstances bend to itself.

55

The State and Revolution

V. I. Lenin

The Transition from Capitalism to Communism

"Between capitalist and communist society, [Marx continues] there lies a period of revolutionary transformation from the former to the latter. A stage of political transition corresponds to this period, and the State during this period can be no other than the *revolutionary dictatorship of the proletariat.*"

This conclusion Marx bases on an analysis of the role played by the proletariat in modern capitalist society, on the facts of the development of this society and on the irreconcilability of the antagonistic interests of the proletarian and the capitalist class.

Earlier the question was put thus: To attain its emancipation the proletariat must overthrow the capitalist class, conquer political power and establish its own revolutionary dictatorship. Now the question is put somewhat differently: The transition from capitalist society developing towards Communism, to a Communist Society, is impossible without a period of "political transition," and the State in this period can only be the revolutionary dictatorship of the proletariat.

What, then, is the relation of this dictatorship to democracy?

We saw that *The Communist Manifesto* simply places side by side the two ideas: the "conversion of the proletariat into the ruling class" and the "conquest of Democracy." On the basis of all that has been said above, one can define more exactly how democracy changes in the transition of Capitalism to Communism.

In capitalist society, under the conditions most favourable to its development, we have a more or less complete democracy in the form of a democratic republic. But this democracy is always bound by the narrow framework of capitalist exploitation, and, consequently, always remains, in reality, a democracy only for the minority, only for the possess-

From V. I. Lenin, *The State and Revolution* (London: George Allen & Unwin Ltd., 1919), pp. 88–94. Reprinted by permission of the publisher.

ing classes, only for the rich. Freedom in capitalist society always remains more or less the same as it was in the ancient Greek republics, that is freedom for the slave owners. The modern wage-slaves, in virtue of the conditions of capitalist exploitation, remain to such an extent crushed by want and poverty that they "cannot be bothered with democracy," have "no time for politics"; that, in the ordinary peaceful course of events, the majority of the population is debarred from participating in public political life.

The accuracy of this statement is perhaps most clearly proved by Germany, just because in this State constitutional legality has lasted and remained stable for a remarkably long time—for nearly half a century (1871–1914); and the Social-Democracy during this time has been able, far better than has been the case in other countries, to make use of "legality" in order to organise into a political party a larger proportion of the working class than has occurred anywhere else in the world.

What, then, is this highest proportion of politically conscious and active wage-slaves that has so far been observed in capitalist society? One million members of the Social-Democratic Party out of fifteen millions of wage-workers! Three millions industrially organised out of fifteen millions!

Democracy for an insignificant minority, democracy for the rich—that is the democracy of capitalist society. If we look more closely into the mechanism of capitalist democracy, everywhere—in the so-called "petty" details of the suffrage (the residential qualification, the exclusion of women, etc.), in the technique of the representative institutions, in the actual obstacles to the right of meeting (public buildings are not for the "poor"), in the purely capitalist organisation of the daily press, etc., etc.—on all sides we shall see restrictions upon restrictions of Democracy. These restrictions, exceptions, exclusions, obstacles for the poor, seem slight—especially in the eyes of one who has himself never known want, and has never lived in close contact with the oppressed classes in their herd life, and

369

nine-tenths, if not ninety-nine hundredths, of the bourgeois publicists and politicians are of this class! But in their sum these restrictions exclude and thrust out the poor from politics and from an active share in democracy. Marx splendidly grasped the *essence* of capitalist democracy, when, in his analysis of the experience of the Commune, he said that the oppressed are allowed, once every few years to decide which particular representatives of the oppressing class are to represent and repress them in Parliament!

But from this capitalist democracy—inevitably narrow, stealthily thrusting aside the poor, and therefore to its core, hypocritical and treacherous—progress does not march along a simple, smooth and direct path to "greater and greater democracy," as the Liberal professors and the lower middle-class Opportunists would have us believe. No, progressive development—that is, towards Communism—marches through the dictatorship of the proletariat; and cannot do otherwise, for there is no one else who can *break the resistance* of the exploiting capitalists, and no other way of doing it.

And the dictatorship of the proletariat—that is, the organisation of the advance-guard of the oppressed as the ruling class, for the purpose of crushing the oppressors—cannot produce merely an expansion of democracy. *Together* with an immense expansion of democracy—for the first time becoming democracy for the poor, democracy for the people, and not democracy for the rich folk—the dictatorship of the proletariat will produce a series of restrictions of liberty in the case of the oppressors, exploiters and capitalists. We must crush them in order to free humanity from wage-slavery; their resistance must be broken by force. It is clear that where there is suppression there must also be violence, and there cannot be liberty or democracy.

Engels expressed this splendidly in his letter to Bebel when he said, as the reader will remember, that "the proletariat needs the State, not in the interests of liberty, but for the purpose of crushing its opponents; and, when one will be able to speak of freedom, the State will have ceased to exist."

Democracy for the vast majority of the nation, and the suppression by force—that is, the exclusion from democracy—of the exploiters and oppressors of the nation: this is the modification of democracy which we shall see during the *transition* from Capitalism to Communism.

Only in Communist Society, when the resistance of the capitalists has finally been broken, when the capitalists have disappeared, when there are no longer any classes (that is, when there is no difference between the members of society in respect of

their social means of production), *only then* "does the State disappear *and one can speak of freedom*." Only then will be possible and will be realised a really full democracy, a democracy without any exceptions. And only then will democracy itself begin to wither away in virtue of the simple fact that, freed from capitalist slavery, from the innumerable horrors, savagery, absurdities and infamies of capitalist exploitation, people will gradually *become accustomed* to the observation of the elementary rules of social life, known for centuries, repeated for thousands of years in all sermons. They will become accustomed to their observance without force, without constraint, without subjection, without the *special apparatus* for compulsion which is called the State.

The expression "the State withers away," is very well chosen, for it indicates the gradual and elemental nature of the process. Only habit can, and undoubtedly will, have such an effect: for we see around us millions of times how readily people get accustomed to observe the necessary rules of life in common, if there is no exploitation, if there is nothing that causes indignation, that calls forth protest and revolt and has to be suppressed.

Thus, in capitalist society, we have a democracy that is curtailed, wretched, false; a democracy only for the rich, for the minority. The dictatorship of the proletariat, the period of transition to Communism, will, for the first time, produce a democracy for the people, for the majority, side by side with the necessary suppression of the minority constituted by the exploiters. Communism alone is capable of giving a really complete democracy, and the fuller it is the more quickly will it become unnecessary and wither away of itself. In other words, under Capitalism we have a State in the proper sense of the word: that is, a special instrument for the suppression of one class by another, and of the majority by the minority at that. Naturally, for the successful discharge of such a task as the systematic suppression by the minority of exploiters of the majority of exploited, the greatest ferocity and savagery of suppression is required, and seas of blood are needed, through which humanity has to direct its path, in a condition of slavery, serfdom and wage labour.

Again, during the *transition* from Capitalism to Communism, suppression is *still* necessary; but in this case it is the suppression of the minority of exploiters by the majority of exploited. A special instrument, a special machine for suppression—that is, the "State"—is necessary, but this is now a transitional State, no longer a State in the ordinary sense of the term. For the suppression of the minority of exploiters, by the majority of those who were *but yesterday* wage slaves, is a matter comparatively so easy, simple and natural that it will cost far less bloodshed than the suppression of the risings of the slaves, serfs or wage labourers, and will cost the human race far less. And it is compatible with the diffusion of democracy over such an overwhelming majority of the nation that the need for any *special machinery* for suppression will gradually cease to exist. The exploiters are unable, of course, to suppress the people without a most complex machine for performing this duty; but *the people* can suppress the exploiters even with a very simple "machine"— almost without any "machine" at all, without any special apparatus—by the simple *organisation of the armed masses* (such as the Councils of Workers' and Soldiers' Deputies, we may remark, anticipating a little).

Finally, only under Communism will the State become quite unnecessary, for there will be *no one* to suppress—"no one" in the sense of a *class,* in the sense of a systematic struggle with a definite section of the population. We are not utopians, and we do not in the least deny the possibility and inevitability of excesses by *individual persons,* and equally the need to suppress such excesses. But, in the first place, for this no special machine, no special instrument of repression is needed. This will be done by the armed nation itself, as simply and as readily as any crowd of civilised people, even in modern society, parts a pair of combatants or does not allow a woman to be outraged. And, secondly, we know that the fundamental social cause of excesses which violate the rules of social life is the exploitation of the masses, their want and their poverty. With the removal of this chief cause, excesses will inevitably begin to "wither away." We do not know how quickly and in what stages, but we know that they will be withering away. With their withering away, the State will also wither away. Marx, without plunging into Utopia, defined more fully what can *now* be defined regarding this future epoch: namely, the difference between the higher and lower phases (degrees, stages) of Communist society.

56

Lecture to the Students of Hasanuddin University[1]

Sukarno

Jefferson and Marx

. . . The British philosopher Bertrand Russell divides mankind at present into two groups, following two different philosophies. One group has faith in the Declaration of Independence of Thomas Jefferson, while the other group believes in the Communist Manifesto of Karl Marx. . . .

Bertrand Russell is not partial to one or the other group. He only hopes that the competition between the followers of these two philosophies would not be determined on the battlefield. It should not be solved through the destruction of men by men, because of the signs we see now and which have also been observed by themselves, but at the end they want to

Reprinted from Sukarno, "Lecture to the Students of Hasanuddin University," in Paul E. Sigmund, ed., *The Ideologies of the Developing Nations* (New York: Frederick A. Praeger, 1963), pp. 57–62.

prove their stand by fighting one another, destroying one another in war.

Bertrand Russell said: Compete with each other, but do not try to reach a solution on the battlefield. Compete in a field that brings prosperity to mankind. Please compete and try to achieve prosperity of mankind by applying your respective ideas. Followers of Thomas Jefferson, please try to establish the prosperity of men according to your world of thought, and followers of Karl Marx, please try to bring prosperity to mankind. Those who will bring the greatest prosperity to men will prove to be the victors in this competition. . . .

I do not agree with Bertrand Russell when he said that humanity only consists of these two groups. There is a third group, which numbers more than a billion, maybe even more than one and a half billion people—namely, the people who live under the flags of nationalism in Asia and Africa.

Those are the people whose hearts throb eagerly, who are very anxious to realize their national independence by establishing a just and prosperous society without getting involved in any way with the two ways of thought mentioned by Bertrand Russell. These three groupings I regard as a phenomenon of the twentieth century: the group of Thomas Jefferson, the group adhering to the Communist Manifesto, and the group of Asian and African nationalism. . . . We not only advocate the coexistence of what is known as the Western bloc and the Communist bloc—the bloc of the United States and that of the Soviet Union, we not only want coexistence between these two blocs, but we also suggest that these two blocs should coexist with Asian-African nationalism. I suggest this because I have seen that Asian-African nationalism, the third group, is always disturbed and attacked by people from outside. It is not respected by people from outside. People even try to suppress and destroy it.

It is my sincere hope, and this hope I put on all the Indonesian students, that we should not, as a nation that has just been established as a state, that is eager to establish a just and prosperous society, a nation that is eager to build up, a nation that thus needs to look at the experiences of the outside world, indulge in too many theories and look for the small mistakes in other people's ideas, so that at the end we only see these mistakes. This attitude is useless. . . . We do not have to look deliberately for errors in the Declaration of Independence, concentrate and pounce on it when we have found one. Neither do we look only for the mistakes of Karl Marx and Friedrich Engels and doggedly criticize and analyze them. It is of no use for the community we are building. We are looking for the experience of other nations outside of Indonesia, especially in these later periods; we use their good experiences to build up our community and country, and cast away the bad experiences.

That is why it is so important to send our scientists, cadres, and youth to other parts of the world. If our government had enough money, I would ask Pak Prijono, the Minister of Education, to send as many students as possible to the United States, to the Soviet Union, to Canada, to the People's Republic of China—everywhere—to get experience.

Do not say first, I do not want to go to the United States, as it follows the world of thought of Thomas Jefferson. Or do not say, I do not want to go to the People's Republic of China, as it is within the world of thought of Karl Marx. This kind of opinion is wrong. I have mentioned earlier that the world of thought of Thomas Jefferson has a great number of

followers. It is impossible for human beings not to be rational, not to see some good things in the world of thought of Thomas Jefferson. Because of the existence of some good points in the world of thought of Thomas Jefferson, that world of thought has tens of millions, hundreds of millions of followers, because human beings have sound minds. The same applies to Karl Marx. . . .

The problem our country faces now is in the first place to provide our people with a good living. Therefore, the present is no time for us for too much theorizing. We had better be practical and pick out whatever is good from the ideas of Thomas Jefferson as well as those from Karl Marx—without, however, taking sides. In politics, this attitude is known as our independent and active policy. But I would like this attitude to be taken in the field of science, too. . . .

Guided Democracy

For reconstruction, three basic requirements are needed:

First, capital. It is clear that one cannot build up without capital. Furthermore, capital, if possible, should be our own capital—national capital—owned and raised by the Indonesian people themselves. If our own capital is not sufficient, we can contract loans from abroad. If we cannot obtain enough loans, then only can we invite foreign capital to invest here, but remember, my friends, I mention capital investment as number three here. Firstly, we have to get our own capital. Whenever it is not enough, there is nothing we can do except to borrow, to borrow capital which we will repay in terms. Only when it is necessary, foreign capital has to be imported.

Second, managerial know-how. One cannot build without the knowledge of how to organize. That is the reason why we make a blueprint, that is the reason why we established this university, to train and educate cadres—as many as possible. . . . We are grateful that at present we have 30,000 students in the whole of Indonesia. But that is not enough yet. I think that we need more than 150,000 students whose spirits are alert and whose minds are filled with practical, managerial, and applied sciences.

Third, a political atmosphere which is conducive to reconstruction. Even though we possess capital (the first requirement), although we possess managerial know-how (the second requirement), if the political atmosphere is not conducive to reconstruction, development cannot be carried out smoothly. How is our political atmosphere at present? I have said over and over again, our political atmosphere is an unhealthy one, a liberal political atmosphere, an atmosphere of "free-fight liberalism." An atmosphere in which we continuously fight and quarrel, each claiming to be right, looking for mistakes of one another. It is a situation where there is no order and no unity, no one yielding to the other. One is eager to destroy the other. We must abandon this free-fight liberalism completely, if we want to develop and build up in the right way.

Indeed, the delegations which I sent have come back with an answer from the people of the countries they visited. Indonesia is richer than those countries. The Indonesians do not lack intelligence or brains. We also know that the Indonesian people have enough spirit. But why do we not build up speedily, why are we lagging behind? That is why, on the 17th of August, 1957, I said that the political atmosphere in Indonesia had to be changed. That is why I suggested that the free-fight liberalism which gives us this unhealthy atmosphere has to be abandoned. In order to draw up a blueprint, I suggested what is called democracy with leadership.

The day before yesterday, in Bogor, I was visited by a large delegation of 260, representing cooperative bodies of the whole of Indonesia. Their spokesman said the following: "Mr. President, with our cooperatives we have been able to raise the standard of living of the people a little. And for your knowledge, we would like to inform you that in the world of cooperatives, democracy with leadership or guided democracy is applied. In the world of cooperatives . . . we have a clear aim, a clear-cut way of working and distribution of profit—everything is clearly under leadership."

Within the world of cooperatives, then, guided democracy is applied. If the blueprint of the National Planning Council is finished, the execution thereof could not be carried out smoothly without guided democracy, without leadership. The number-one leader is the blueprint itself. One cannot carry out a blueprint and at the same time debate about it, after it has been approved by parliament. This blueprint becomes the property of the Indonesian people, becomes national property. . . . This blueprint has to be carried out, and its principles cannot be debated again.

I am myself a qualified engineer. Very often, when I was in the construction business, I received blueprints of things to be built. I carried out those blueprints as they were. I did not argue why, for instance, certain lines went a certain way, why a certain thing should be made of concrete and not of wood, why its stories were that high when they were not lower. It was a blueprint entrusted to me,

for me to carry out, and I would carry it out. The blueprint was my guide, and I myself guided and led the employees. As a qualified engineer, I had under me superintendents and foremen. I was their leader, and I had conferences with them. But my conferences with them were not of that type of free-fight liberalism. I conferred with them about the execution of the blueprint. I asked the superintendents: These things have to be made out of concrete; what would be the best way to get them done? One superintendent would suggest: Pak, I think this is the best way; get stones, gravel, sand, and cement, call a lot of people—twenty, a hundred—and have everything mixed by hand. I then asked another superintendent what his opinion was. He answered: No, do not work by hand, Bung, this building is too large for that; buy a concrete mixer at once; with that we can mix concrete for this building and others. I conferred with my foremen—I practiced democracy with them—I asked for their opinion. I also discussed the choice of the materials; I conferred with my men. On all aspects of the execution of the blueprint, I held discussions, but these discussions were under guidance—the guidance of the blueprint, my guidance, the constructor of the building.

That is why it is wrong when people say that guided democracy is a false democracy, that it is a form of dictatorship. I even said in my statement of October 28, 1958, that democracy with leadership is a true Indonesian democracy. This is the danger you are facing, the danger that many of you become copyists. You have heard of the word "democracy"; democracy is indeed good. What does America say about democracy? It is to be found in certain American books. What does England say, France, the Netherlands, Germany? They each have their own reference books. Well, one of them must be the genuine democracy. Thus, you then try to apply in Indonesia democracy as it is practiced in America, Germany, France, England, the Netherlands, the U.S.S.R., or in other countries? You are only trying to copy!

No, as I have said before, we have to return to our own personality; we want to return to our own identity. Do not let us become a carbon-copy nation. We have had a democracy since olden times. I do not imply that we should remain as we were then. But the things of former times are good material for us today to refer to, because we are going to establish democracy in our own country.

How was democracy of former times in Indonesia? It still is practiced today in the villages in Java, Minangkabau, Sulawesi, Lombok, Bali, and other places—namely, in their laws and their system of *musjawarah* and *mufakat* (discussion and agreement). Every village practices democracy. But do they in these village meetings apply the practice of voting? Of free-fight liberalism, where half plus one is always right? No, the *musjawarah* is held under the guidance of Lurah, the Chief of the Elders, of Nini Mamak, the guidance of whoever is leader. Everybody says something different until at one time a compromise is achieved out of all these different opinions, without voting. This is what is called *mufakat* (agreement)—that by *musjawarah* (discussion) without voting, a joint compromise is achieved. There is no dictatorship in *musjawarah* and *mufakat*. That is why democracy with leadership is a true, original Indonesia democracy. This is one of the most important sources for us from which we can draw material to find a new, clear democracy—not American democracy, Dutch, French, British, German, or Soviet, or anybody else's democracy. Let us find a democracy which is suitable for our own identity. And use sources and material which are to be found in our own country.

Regarding our own democracy, I initiated the idea, calling on the people to join to fight the diseases that were the results of free-fight liberalism. I called on the people to destroy free-fight liberalism completely, and to change it into Indonesian democracy, guided democracy, or democracy with leadership. If people asked me to explain in detail what it means, I would not be able to give a proper answer. No, I want this guided democracy to become the property of the Indonesian people again. That is why I suggest to the people, especially the experts, scientists, students, to think. Please think and rethink, make and remake. Think, carry it out so that as a joint result we can achieve a new democratic system which I call democracy with leadership, or guided democracy, which is suitable for conditions in Indonesia. . . .

NOTE

1. Translated and published by the Ministry of Information, Djakarta, Indonesia, 1959.

57

Background to Independence

Kwame Nkrumah

Independence for the Gold Coast was my aim. It was a colony, and I have always regarded colonialism as the policy by which a foreign power binds territories to herself by political ties, with the primary object of promoting her own economic advantage. No one need be surprised if this system has led to disturbances and political tension in many territories. There are few people who would not rid themselves of such domination if they could.

At this time, I devoted much energy to the study of revolutionaries and their methods. Those who interested me most were Hannibal, Cromwell, Napoleon, Lenin, Mazzini, Gandhi, Mussolini, and Hitler. I found much of value to be gleaned and

From *Ghana: The Autobiography of Kwame Nkrumah* (London: Thomas Nelson and Sons, Ltd., 1957). Copyright 1957 by Thomas Nelson and Sons. Reprinted by permission of the publisher.

many ideas that were useful to me later in my own campaign against imperialism.

At first I could not understand how Gandhi's philosophy of nonviolence could possibly be effective. It seemed to me to be utterly feeble and without hope of success. The solution of the colonial problem, as I saw it at that time, lay in armed rebellion. How is it possible, I asked myself, for a revolution to succeed without arms and ammunition? After months of studying Gandhi's policy and watching the effect it had, I began to see that, when backed by a strong political organization, it could be the solution to the colonial problem. In Jawaharlal Nehru's rise to power I recognized the success of one who, pledged to socialism, was able to interpret Gandhi's philosophy in practical terms.

The Gold Coast revolt against colonialism is not a new thing. Its roots are deep. There was the Confederation of 1868, when certain chiefs came together to defend themselves not only against their tribal kin, the Ashantis, but also against political encroachments from abroad. After the bond of 1844, which gave Britain trading rights, the Gold Coast had come increasingly under her control.

The next great move of political cohesion and conscience was the formation of the Aborigines Rights Protection Society by chiefs and literate Africans with the object of defending Gold Coast land. When this collapsed—because of an ever-widening rift between the chiefs and the educated people—the latter, binding themselves together and supported by their educated brothers in other West African territories, established the National Congress of British West Africa. This was the first indication of West African nationalism. However, because it lacked the support of the masses, it disintegrated in 1930.

The vacuum that this left in Gold Coast politics was eventually filled by the formation of the United Gold Coast Convention by the merchant and lawyer class of the country. It was when I realized that this movement was doomed to failure because it ignored the interests of the masses that I broke away, in 1949, and formed the Convention People's Party.

I saw that the whole solution to this problem lay in political freedom for our people; for it is only when a people are politically free that other races can give them the respect that is due them. It is impossible to talk of equality of races in any other terms. No people without a government of their own can expect to be treated on the same level as peoples of independent sovereign states. It is far better to be free to govern or misgovern yourself than to be governed by anybody else.

The formation of the CPP coincided with a political reawakening among the workers and young people of the country. Ex-servicemen who had taken part in World War II returned to the Gold Coast dissatisfied with their position after having been given the chance of comparing their lot with that of other peoples, and they were prepared to take up any line which would better their conditions. There was a general dissatisfaction with the British colonial policy that had been adopted until that time, especially the policy of indirect rule which so encouraged tribal feudalism. Again, the Russian Revolution and its aftermath had left its mark by spreading ideas of workers' solidarity, trade-union movements, freedom and independence. Events in Asia also added a glow to the political awakening.

The CPP was not merely a mass movement. Mass movements are well and good, but they cannot act with purpose unless they are led and guided by a vanguard political party. And when the time comes for a ruling power to accord self-government, it will do so more willingly if it can hand over to a properly constituted political party with a majority backing, rather than to a revolutionary nationalist movement. Rallying around me all those who genuinely wished for progress, I resisted both the opportunist element and the reactionary forces, and sought to establish the CPP as the democratic instrument of the people's will and aspirations. We were freely elected to power in 1951. Three years later, and again in 1956, the same confidence was shown by the country.

The first objective then is political independence, for which I believe the organization itself must take two forms. First there is the period of "positive action"—a combination of nonviolent methods with effective and disciplined political action. At this stage, open conflict with the existing colonial regime is inevitable, and this is a test of strength for the organization. Since it is marked by nonviolence, and since the forces of might are on the side of the colonial power, there is little chance of complete success in this period.

The second stage is one of "tactical action"—a sort of contest of wits. From now on, the movement must make its ideology clear and convincing. The ideology of my party may be formulated as follows: No race, no people, no nation can exist freely and be respected at home and abroad without political freedom.

Once this freedom is gained, a greater task comes into view. All dependent territories are backward in education, in science, in agriculture, and in industry. The economic independence that should follow and maintain political independence demands every effort from the people, a total mobilization of brain and manpower resources. What other countries have taken three hundred years to achieve, a once dependent territory must try to accomplish in a generation if it is to survive. Unless it is, as it were, "jet-propelled," it will lag behind and thus risk everything for which it has fought.

Capitalism is too complicated a system for a newly independent nation. Hence the need for a socialistic society. But even a system based on social justice and a democratic constitution may need backing up, during the period following independence, by emergency measures of a totalitarian kind. Without discipline, true freedom cannot survive. In any event, the basis must be a loyal, honest, hard-working, and responsible civil service on which the party in power can rely. Armed forces must also be consolidated for defense. . . .

I concentrated on finding a formula by which the whole colonial question and the problem of imperialism could be solved. I read Hegel, Marx, Engels, Lenin, and Mazzini. The writings of these men did much to influence me in my revolutionary ideas and activities, and Marx and Lenin particularly impressed me as I felt sure that their philosophy was capable of solving these problems. But I think that of all the literature that I studied, the book that did more than any other to fire my enthusiasm was *The Philosophy and Opinions of Marcus Garvey* . . . with his philosophy of "Africa for the Africans" and his "Back to Africa" movement.

58

A Note on the Language of African Nationalism

Thomas Hodgkin

I have been obliged to think recently about the language of African nationalism; in particular to ask what light the language of African nationalists throws on their theory; whether indeed there is what can reasonably be called a "theory" of African nationalism, which can be distinguished from other theories —and, if there is, what this theory asserts. My practical interest in these questions arose out of disagreement with two prevailing opinions: the view, expressed by the Prosecution in the South African Treason Trial, that in so far as those who talk the language of African nationalism are moved by any political theory it must be a "Communist" theory; and the view that African nationalism lacks any genuine theoretical basis—that such ideas as it makes use of are merely gadgets, borrowed to give an appearance of respectability. This note attempts to formulate, in a preliminary way, a different view.

For the most part African national movements have developed within the artificial frontiers determined by the European Powers—Britain, France, Belgium, Portugal, Germany, Italy, and to a very minor extent, Spain—during the last quarter of the nineteenth century. With the disappearance of Germany from the ranks of the colonial Powers after World War I, and of Italy World War II, and given the lack of opportunity for political organization in the Portuguese territories, national movements in Africa south of the Sahara have in practice been largely confined to countries in which either English or French is the dominant language—for administrative, judicial, educational, journalistic, and similar purposes. (Somalia, within the zone of Italian linguistic influence, is an important exception.) In these territories indigenous languages are, of course, widely used for purposes of political agitation and debate, especially where—as in the case of Swahili in Tanganyika—a particular African language serves as a *lingua franca* throughout a territory. But most of the literature of these national movements—newspapers, periodicals, pamphlets, broadsheets, programmes and policy statements, reports, biographical and autobiographical works, studies of specific problems—is in either English or French. (This generalization does not apply to Arab North Africa, where the Arabic literature is probably more important than the French.) Hence, although an adequate account of nationalist language would be bound to pay attention to material—in the form of speeches, songs, poetry, journals, et cetera—in the various African languages, a good deal can be learned from a study of the literature existing in English and French.

If one considers the output of national movements of sub-Saharan Africa only, whether in English or French, over the past fifteen years, one point is immediately clear: there is, to a large extent, a common political language; common themes continually recur. These themes might be summarized as follows:

1. The people inhabiting a given colonial territory constitute a "nation," or a nation in process of

From Thomas Hodgkin, "A Note on the Language of African Nationalism," in Kenneth Kirkwood, ed., *St. Antony's Papers No. 10* (London: Chatto and Windus Ltd., 1961), pp. 22–24, 31–32, 39–40. Copyright 1961 by Thomas Hodgkin. Reprinted by permission of Chatto and Windus Ltd., and the Southern Illinois University Press.

becoming (Ghanaian, Cameroonian, Tanganyikan, Congolese, for example).

2. This "nation" is governed by an "imperialist" Power, which seeks its own, predominantly economic, interests and advantages.

3. The relationship between the "imperialist" Power and the African "nation" is essentially one of "domination," in its political aspect; of "exploitation," in its economic aspects; and of "racialism," or "racial discrimination," in its human aspect. A system in which such relationships predominate is described as "colonialism."

4. The members of a subject Africa "nation" have an "inalienable right" to govern themselves.

5. In order to substitute "self-government," or "independence" for "colonialism," or "colonial bureaucracy," a "national liberation movement" has to be generated.

6. The "national liberation movement" expresses itself through a political organization, which may be either a "Congress" or *Rassemblement* or a "Party," with linked functional associations—of women, youth, Trade Unionists, and the like. Though led by an élite, it attracts to itself "the masses," and seeks as its primary aim "the conquest of political power."

7. The organization which serves as the instrument for national liberation possesses a double legitimacy. Historically it is the successor to the pre-colonial African States whose power was broken during the period of "imperialist" penetration. Morally it is the expression of the "popular will," the will of the emergent African "nation." Thus, on both historical and moral grounds, it enjoys an authority superior to the merely legal authority, backed by physical sanctions, of the colonial state.

8. In its effort to achieve "political emancipation," this organization will be found to pursue, and justified in pursuing, a "dynamic," aggressive, strategy in its dealings with the colonial Government and Administration, involving, on occasion, the use of "positive action"—which should, however, as far as possible be "non-violent."

9. Since the "national liberation movement" is, by definition, a "progressive" force, it will be bound also to seek to weaken, and eventually to eliminate, such "reactionary" forces as exist within the "nation" and are liable to retard the process of "political emancipation." The most important of these forces are restricted ethnic loyalties ("tribalism") and chiefly power, in many of its various forms (sometimes labelled "feudalism")—surviving from the pre-colonial period, but generally fostered by "colonialism," and liable to assert themselves in opposition

to the organization expressing the "popular will" during the period of transition from "colonialism" to "independence."

10. The new form of independent African state which the "national liberation movement" seeks to bring into being will be "democratic"—in the sense, particularly, that its government will be responsible to a popular assembly elected on the principle of "one man, one vote"; and "socialist," in the sense that it will develop a planned economy, in the interests of the "masses."

11. The "national liberation movement" in any given African state should co-operate with similar movements in other African states, with a view to the total elimination of "colonialism" throughout the African continent, the avoidance of political fragmentation, or "Balkanization," and the realization, in the first place, of large and durable African systems—adequate to withstand external pressures—and, eventually, an "African Commonwealth." . . .

* * *

In some cases African nationalist borrowings from Marxist sources are scarcely more than linguistic: echoes, without any particular political significance. It is indeed natural that the rhetoric of Marx, the prophet of the doom of capitalism, should be easily adaptable to the requirements of the contemporary prophets of the doom of imperialism. Two such echoes from *The Communist Manifesto* occur in the concluding sentences of Dr. Nkrumah's early pamphlet, *Towards Colonial Freedom:*

> Thus the goal of the national liberation movement is the realization of complete and unconditional independence, and the building of a society of peoples in which the free development of each is the condition of the free development of all. PEOPLE OF THE COLONIES, UNITE: the working men of all countries are behind you.[1]

Similarly, the opening sentence of the original manifesto of the *Rassemblement Démocratique Africain*, from 1946 until 1958 the dominant anti-colonial organization in French Africa, "La réaction agite devant l'opinion un épouvantail: celui du mouvement des peuples d'Outre-Mer vers la liberté,"[2] is reminiscent of the opening sentence of *The Communist Manifesto:* "A spectre is haunting Europe— the spectre of Communism."

More important is the use of Marxist categories of explanation. One obvious example is the concept of "imperialism." The theory that "the imperialist powers need the raw materials and cheap native labour of the colonies for their own capitalist industries; through their system of monopolist control they eliminate native competition, and use the colonies as dumping grounds for their surplus mass-produced goods";[3] that "the whole policy of the colonizer is to keep the native in his primitive state and make him economically dependent,"[4] and that this form of "economic imperialism" at the same time corrupts the European masters and degrades the African servants, is "a cult which is just as offensive as the abuse of the leopard society"[5]—this theme, or some variation upon it, recurs constantly in the literature of African nationalism. I suspect that there are few radical nationalists who would not agree with the essentials of the argument. It is, however, important to note that what is accepted is the assertion that there is a direct causal relationship between capitalism—or, more specifically, "monopoly capitalism"—and modern imperialism; not the orthodox Leninist account of the genesis of imperialism in its entirety, with its thesis that it is primarily the pressure of "finance capital" for new outlets for investment that generates the imperialist drive to dominate colonial and semi-colonial territories.[6]

So far the argument has been somewhat negative, merely seeking to define the extent to which Marxist ideas have been embodied in African nationalist theory and expressed in its literature. Is it possible to say anything more positive about the content of this theory? Consider some of its basic ideas: the conception of an undifferentiated African people as the legitimate source of power; the emphasis upon the moral purposes which government should seek to realize (the restoration of African "dignity," for example); the strongly egalitarian, levelling outlook —"il n'y a pas des surhommes"[7]—the insistence on equality of rights for Africans, Asians, and Europeans, commoners and chiefs; the notion of the nationalist party, and thus the state—once the party has taken hold of it and remoulded it according to

party principles—as the expression of the popular will; the idealization of the pre-colonial, pre-capitalist, collectivist African past; the linking of the ideas of national renaissance and international, particularly inter-African, brotherhood. The analogies with some of the central theses of Jean-Jacques Rousseau seem remarkably close. I would not argue that Rousseau's direct influence has been of special importance: I would doubt whether, even in the case of French-speaking African leaders, this is so. It is rather, perhaps, that a certain kind of historical situation, certain fundamental human problems to be resolved, tend to stimulate a particular way of thinking about the situation and the problems. Nor, of course, is African nationalist theory simply Rousseau transplanted, any more than it is simply Marx transplanted (though it is certainly less misleading to regard it as the former than the latter). I would argue only that it belongs to a family of theories— which might be labelled "revolutionary democratic theories"—and that within this family Rousseau's teachings occupy a special and original place. In order to be able to say what are the distinctive characteristics of the various versions of African nationalist theory—how they differ from one another and from other non-African members of the family —a great deal more exploration would be necessary.

NOTES

1. Kwame Nkrumah, *Towards Colonial Freedom* (republished London, 1957), pp. 32–33.
2. RDA, *Manifeste* (Paris, 1946, published in *Le Rassemblement Démocratique Africain dans la Lutte Anti-impérialiste* (Au Service de l'Afrique Noire, 1948), p. 23.
3. Kwame Nkrumah, *Autobiography,* pp. 46–47.
4. *Ibid.*
5. Nnamdi Azikiwe, *Before Us Lies the Open Grave* (Lagos, 1947).
6. V. I. Lenin, *Imperialism, the Highest Stage of Capitalism.*
7. From Sékou Touré: compare J-J. Rousseau—"Man is the same in all ranks; that being so, the ranks which are most numerous deserve most respect."

CHAPTER **X**

The Social Conditions of Political Modernization

INTRODUCTION TO THE READINGS

This chapter deals with the broad social-structural conditions of modernization that create the basic propensity to change in modern societies. The first section is devoted to the analysis of the structural conditions of modern societies and the spread of political participation.

The excerpt from Weber explains the crucial importance of representation as one of the specific mechanisms through which the center and the periphery are linked in modern societies. At the same time it shows the fragility of this link from the point of view of the institutional stability of modern political regimes.

The excerpt from de Tocqueville stresses the importance of equality in its different structural aspects—as related to property and family tradition—for the crystallization of the modern sociopolitical order.

Deutsch's article spells out the broad structural-demographic characteristics of modernization with emphasis on the process of "social mobilization."

Rokkan's contribution analyzes the structural implication of the different types of extensions of suffrage for the creation of the conditions for modernization and sustained change.

The article by Bellah stresses the propensity to systemic transformation and to sustained change which is, as we have seen, central to the understanding of modernization. Bellah underlines the cultural roots and problems of this tendency.

The second section of the chapter deals with the process of elite formation. This is one of the broad structural conditions of modernization, and, as we have seen above special importance is to be attached to it.

Aron's article analyzes the differences between the ruling class—the elite—and the social class in different types of modern societies, while Shils's stresses the importance of intellectuals in the formation of modernity.

The articles by Walzer, Smith, Benda, and Weiner analyze different types of modernizing elites in different periods and situations of modernization.

Walzer analyzes one of the first of such elites, the Protestant (especially Calvinist) intellectual elite, which was certainly not modernizing in intent but only in consequence. The importance of this elite for modernization was originally stressed in Weber's famous Protestant Ethic thesis.

Smith analyzes the unusual case of the relatively successful modernizing aristocratic-oligarchic elite that guided the transition to modernity in Japan.

Benda analyzes the emergence of intellectual elites in Southeast Asia and the problems which they face—and which they pose for their societies by virtue of their being almost the only modernizing elite in their setting.

The article by Weiner presents an analysis of the development of new types of political elite in one of the relatively most stable of New States—India.

59

Representation

Max Weber

The Principal Forms and Characteristics of Representation

The primary fact underlying representation is that the action of certain members of a group, the "representatives," is binding on the others or is looked upon as legitimate so that its result must be accepted by them. In the organization of authority in corporate groups, however, representation takes a variety of typical forms.

1. Appropriated representation. In this case the chief or a member of the administrative staff holds appropriated rights of representation. In this form it is very ancient and is found in all kinds of patriarchal and charismatic groups. The power of representation has a traditionally limited scope. This category covers the sheiks of clans and chiefs of tribes, the headmen of castes in India, hereditary priests of sects, the patel of the Indian village, the *Obermärker,* hereditary monarchs, and all sorts of similar patriarchal or patrimonial heads of corporate groups. Authority to conclude contractual agreements and to agree on binding rules governing their relations is found permitted to the elders of neighbouring tribes in what are otherwise exceedingly primitive conditions, as in Australia.

2. Closely related to appropriated representation is that on a basis of socially independent grouping.[1] This does not constitute representation so far as it is a matter primarily of representing and enforcing their own appropriated rights or privileges. It may, however, have a representative character and be recognized as such, so far as the effect of the decisions of such bodies as estates extends beyond the personal holders of privileges to the unprivileged groups. This may not be confined to the immediate dependents of the members of the class in question but may include others who are not in the socially privileged class. These others are regularly bound by the action of the privileged group, whether this is merely taken for granted or a representative authority is explicitly claimed. This is true of all feudal courts and assemblies of privileged estates, and includes the *Stände* of the late Middle Ages in Germany and of more recent times. In Antiquity and in non-European areas this institution occurs only sporadically and has not been a universal stage of development.

3. The radical antithesis of this is "instructed" representation. In this case elected representatives or representatives chosen by rotation or lot or in any other manner exercise powers of representation which are strictly limited by an imperative mandate and a right of recall, the exercise of which is subject to the consent of those represented. This type of "representative" is, in effect, an agent of those he represents. The imperative mandate has had for a very long time a place in the most various types of groups. For instance, the elected representatives of the communes in France were almost always bound by the *cahiers des doléances.* At the present time this type of representation is particularly prominent in the Soviet type of republican organization where it serves as a substitute for immediate democracy, since the latter is impossible in a mass organization. Instructed mandates are certainly to be found in all sorts of organizations outside the Western World, both in the Middle Ages and in modern times, but nowhere else have they been of great historical significance.

From Max Weber, *The Theory of Social and Economic Organization,* ed. Talcott Parsons, trans. Talcott Parsons and A. M. Henderson. (New York: Oxford University Press, 1947), pp. 416–423. Reprinted by permission of the editor.

4. Free representation. The representative, who is generally elected though he may actually or formally be subject to rotation, is not bound by instruction but is in a position to make his own decisions. He is obligated only to express his own genuine conviction, and not to promote the interests of those who have elected him.

Free representation in this sense is not uncommonly an unavoidable consequence of the deliberate object of choice. In so far as this is true, the representative, by virtue of his election, exercises authority over the electors and is not merely their agent. The most prominent example of this type is modern parliamentary representation. It shares with legal authority the general tendency to impersonality, the obligation to conform to abstract norms, political or ethical.

As a feature of the representative bodies of modern political organization of parliaments, the function of this type of representation is not understandable apart from the voluntary intervention of parties. It is the party groups which present candidates and programmes of the politically passive citizens. They also, by the process of compromise and balloting within the parliament, create the norms which govern the administrative process. They subject the administration to control, support it by their confidence, or overthrow it by withdrawal of confidence whenever, by virtue of commanding a majority of votes, they are in a position to do this.

The party leader and the administrative staff which is appointed by him, consisting of ministers, secretaries of state, and sometimes undersecretaries, constitute the political administration of the state, that is, their position is dependent upon the electoral success of their party, and an electoral defeat forces their resignation. Where party government is fully developed they are imposed on the formal head of state, the monarch, by the party composition of the parliament. The monarch is expropriated from the actual governing power and his role is limited to two things. On the one hand by negotiation with the parties, he selects the effective head, and formally legitimizes his position by appointment. On the other hand, he acts as an agency for legalizing the measures of the party chief who at the time is in power.

The "cabinet" of ministers, that is the executive committee of the majority party, may be organized in a monocratic or a more collegial form. The latter is unavoidable in coalition cabinets, whereas the former is more precise in its functioning. The cabinet protects itself from the attacks of its followers who seek office and its opponents by the usual means, by monopolizing official secrets, and maintaining solidarity against all outsiders. Unless there is an effective separation of powers, this system involves the complete appropriation of all powers by the party organization in control at the time. Not only the top positions but often many of the lower offices become benefices of the party followers. This may be called parliamentary cabinet government.[2]

Where the appropriation of power by the party government is not complete but the monarch or a corresponding elected president enjoys independent power especially in appointments to office, including military officers, there is a "constitutional" government. This is particularly likely to be found where there is a formal separation of powers. A special case is that where an elective presidency is combined with a representative parliament.

It is also possible for the government of a parliamentary organization to be chosen by a process of election of the executive authorities or the chief executive by the parliament, which would be a purely representative form of government.

The governing powers of representative bodies may be both limited and legitimized where direct canvassing of the masses of members of the groups is permitted through the referendum.

1. It is not representation as such but free representation in conjunction with the presence of parliamentary bodies which is peculiar to the modern Western World. Only relatively small beginnings are to be found in Antiquity and elsewhere in such forms as assemblies of delegates in the confederations of city states. But in principle the members of these bodies were usually bound by instructions.

2. The abolition of imperative mandates has been very strongly influenced by the positions of the monarchs. The French kings regularly demanded that the delegates to the Estates General should be elected on a basis which left them free to vote for the recommendations of the king. If they had been bound by imperative mandates, the king's policy would have been seriously obstructed. In the English Parliament, as will be pointed out below, both the composition and the procedure of the body led to the same result. It is connected with this fact that right up to the Reform Bill of 1867, the members of Parliament regarded themselves as a specially privileged group. This is shown clearly by the rigorous exclusion of publicity as late as the middle of the eighteenth century. Heavy penalties were laid upon newspapers which reported the transactions of Parliament. The theory came to be that the parliamentary deputy was "a representative" of the people as a whole and that hence he was not bound by any specific mandates, was not an "agent" but a person in authority.

This theory was already well developed in the literature before it received its present connotation in the French Revolution.

3. It is not possible at this point to analyse in detail the process by which the English king and certain others following his example came to be gradually expropriated by the unofficial cabinet system which represented only party groups. This seems at first sight to be a very peculiar development in spite of the universal importance of its consequences. But in view of the fact that bureaucracy was relatively undeveloped in England, it is by no means so "fortuitous" as has often been claimed. It is also impossible to analyse the peculiar American system of functional separation of powers combined with electoral representation and the place in it of the referendum which is essentially an expression of mistrust of corrupt legislative bodies. Also Swiss democracy, and the related forms of purely representative democracy which have recently appeared in some of the German states, will have to be left aside for the present. The purpose of the above discussion was only to outline a few of the most important types.

4. So-called "constitutional monarchy," which is above all characterized by appropriation of the power of patronage including the appointment of ministers and of military commanders by the monarch, may concretely come to be very similar to a purely parliamentary regime of the English type. Conversely, the latter by no means necessarily excludes a politically gifted monarch like Edward VII from effective participation in political affairs. He need not be a mere figurehead.

5. Groups governed by representative bodies are by no means necessarily "democratic" in the sense that all their members have equal rights. Quite the contrary, it can be shown that the classic soil for the growth of parliamentary government has tended to be an aristocratic or plutocratic society. This was true of England.

The relations of the different forms of representation to the economic order are highly complex and will have to be analysed separately later on. For the present primary purposes only the following general remarks will be made:

1. One factor in the development of free representation was the undermining of the economic basis of the older estates. This made it possible for persons with demagogic gifts to pursue their own inclinations without reference to their social position. The source of this undermining process was the development of modern capitalism.

2. Calculability and reliability in the functioning of the legal order and the administrative system is vital to rational capitalism. This need led the middle classes to attempt to impose checks on patrimonial monarchs and the feudal nobility by means of a collegial body in which the middle class had a decisive voice, which controlled administration and finance and could exercise an important influence on changes in the legal order.

3. At the time when this transition was taking place, the proletariat had not reached a stage of development which enabled it to become an important political factor which could endanger the position of the bourgeoisie. Furthermore, there was no hesitation in eliminating any threat to the power of the propertied classes by means of property qualifications for the franchise.

4. The formal rationalization of the economic order and the state, which was favourable to capitalistic development, could be strongly promoted by parliaments. Furthermore, it seemed relatively easy to secure influence on party organizations.

5. The development of demagogy in the activities of the existing parties was a function of the extension of the franchise. Two main factors have tended to make monarchs and ministers everywhere favourable to universal suffrage, namely, the necessity for the support of the propertyless classes in foreign conflict and the hope, which has proved to be unjustified, that, as compared to the bourgeoisie, they would be a conservative influence.

6. Parliaments have tended to function smoothly as long as their composition was drawn predominantly from the classes of wealth and culture, that is, as they were composed of political "amateurs." Established social status rather than class interests as such underlay the party structure. The conflicts tended to be only those between different forms of wealth, but with the rise of class parties to power, especially the proletarian parties, the situation of parliaments has changed radically. Another important factor in the change has been the bureaucratization of party organizations, with its specifically plebiscitary character. The member of parliament thereby ceases to be in a position of authority over the electors and becomes merely an agent of the leaders of the party organization. This will have to be discussed more in detail elsewhere.

Representation by the Agents of Interest Groups

A fifth type of representation is that by the agents of interest groups. This term will be applied to the type of representative body where the selection of members is not a matter of free choice without regard to occupational, social, or class status, but where the body consists of persons who are chosen on the basis of their occupations or their social or class status, each group in the social system being represented by persons of its own sort. At the present time the tendency of this type is to representation on an occupational basis.

This kind of representation may, however, have a very different significance, according to certain possible variations within it. In the first place, it will differ widely according to the specific occupations, social groups and classes which are involved, and, secondly, according to whether direct balloting or compromise is the means of settling differences. In the first connection its significance will vary greatly according to the numerical proportions of the different categories. It is possible for such a system to be radically revolutionary or extremely conservative in its character. In every case it is a product of the development of powerful parties representing class interests.

It is, at least, the theory that this type of representation weakens the dominance of the play of party interests in politics, though, if experience so far is conclusive, it does not eliminate it. It is also theoretically possible that the role of campaign funds can be lessened, but it is doubtful to what degree this is true. Representative bodies of this type tend to be unfavourable to individual leaders. The professional representative of an interest group can only be a person who devotes his whole time to this function. In classes without independent means the function hence devolves on the paid secretaries of the organized interest groups.

1. Representation where compromise has provided the means of settling differences is characteristic of all the older historical bodies of "estates." To-day it is dominant in the trade unions and everywhere where negotiation between the various advisory and executive authorities is the order of the day. It is impossible to assign a numerical value to the "importance" of an occupational group. Above all the interests of the masses of workers on the one hand and of the increasingly smaller number of entrepreneurs, who are likely both to be particularly well informed and to have strong personal interests, somehow have to be taken account of regardless of numbers. These interests are often highly antagonistic, hence voting by units which are made up of elements which in social and class status are highly heterogeneous, is exceedingly artificial. The ballot as a basis of final decision is characteristic of settling the conflicts and expressing the compromise of parties. It is not, however, characteristic of the estates.

2. The ballot is adequate in social groups where the representation consists of elements of roughly equal social status. Thus the so-called Soviets are made up only of workers. The prototype is the Mercadanza of the time of the conflict between guilds. It was composed of delegates of the individual guilds who decided matters by majority vote. It was, however, in fact in danger of secession if certain particularly powerful guilds were out-voted. Even the participation of "white-collar workers" in Soviets raises problems. It has been usual to put mechanical limits to their share of votes. If representatives of peasants and craftsmen are admitted, the situation becomes still more complicated, and if the so-called "higher" professions and business interests are brought in, it is impossible for questions to be decided by ballot. If such a body is organized in terms of equal representation of workers and employers, the tendency is for "yellow" unions to support the employers and certain types of employers to support the workers. The result is that the elements which are most lacking in class loyalty have the most decisive influence.

But even purely proletarian "Soviets" would in settled times be subject to the development of sharp antagonism between different groups of workers, which would probably paralyze the Soviets in effect. In any case, however, it would open the door for adroit politics in playing the different interests off against each other. This is the reason why the bureaucratic elements have been so friendly to the idea. The same thing would be likely to happen as between representatives of peasants and of industrial workers. Indeed any attempt to organize such representative bodies otherwise than on a strictly revolutionary basis comes down in the last analysis only to another opportunity for electoral manipulation in different forms.

3. The probability of the development of representation on an occupational basis is by no means low. In times of the stabilization of technical and economical development it is particularly high, but in spite of this it does not follow that "partisanship" will be greatly reduced. Unless there is reason to believe that it will be reduced, it is obvious that occupational representative bodies will fail to eliminate parties. On the contrary, as can be clearly seen at the present time, all the way from the "works councils" to the Federal Economic Council in Germany, a great mass of new benefices for loyal party henchmen are being created and made use of. Politics is penetrating into the economic order at the same time that economic interests are entering into politics. There are a number of different possible

value attitudes toward this situation, but this does not alter the facts.

Genuine parliamentary representation with the voluntary play of interests in the political sphere, the corresponding plebiscitary party organization with its consequences, and the modern idea of rational representation by interest groups, are all peculiar to the modern Western World. None of these is understandable apart from the peculiar Western development of social stratification and class structure. Even in the Middle Ages the seeds of these phenomena were present in the Western World but only there. It is only in the Western World that "cities" in the peculiar corporate sense "estates" (*rex et regnum*), "bourgeois," and "proletarians" have existed.

NOTES

1. *Ständische Repräsentation.*
2. The facts are in many respects best presented in the brilliantly polemical attack on the system by W. Hasbach which has erroneously been called a "political description." The author in his own essay, *Parlament und Regierung im neugeordneten Deutschland,* has been careful to emphasize that it is a polemical work which has arisen out of the particular situation of the time.

60

Social Conditions of the Anglo-American

Alexis de Tocqueville

Among nations whose law of descent is founded upon the right of primogeniture, landed estates often pass from generation to generation without undergoing division; the consequence of this is that family feeling is to a certain degree incorporated with the estate. The family represents the estate, the estate the family, whose name, together with its origin, its glory, its power, and its virtues, is thus perpetuated in an imperishable memorial of the past and as a sure pledge of the future.

When the equal partition of property is established by law, the intimate connection is destroyed between family feeling and the preservation of the paternal estate; the property ceases to represent the family; for, as it must inevitably be divided after one or two generations, it has evidently a constant tendency to diminish and must in the end be completely dispersed. The sons of the great landed proprietor, if they are few in number, or if fortune befriends them, may indeed entertain the hope of being as wealthy as their father, but not of possessing the same property that he did; their riches must be composed of other elements than his. Now, as soon as you divest the landowner of that interest in the preservation of his estate which he derives from association, from tradition, and from family pride, you may be certain

From Alexis de Tocqueville, *Democracy in America* (New York: Alfred A. Knopf, 1945), I, 49–57. Reprinted by permission of the publisher.

that, sooner or later, he will dispose of it; for there is a strong pecuniary interest in favor of selling, as floating capital produces higher interest than real property and is more readily available to gratify the passions of the moment.

Great landed estates which have once been divided never come together again; for the small proprietor draws from his land a better revenue, in proportion, than the large owner does from his; and of course he sells it at a higher rate.[1] The reasons of economy, therefore, which have led the rich man to sell vast estates will prevent him all the more from buying little ones in order to form a large one.

What is called family pride is often founded upon an illusion of self-love. A man wishes to perpetuate and immortalize himself, as it were, in his great-grandchildren. Where family pride ceases to act, individual selfishness comes into play. When the idea of family becomes vague, indeterminate, and uncertain, a man thinks of his present convenience; he provides for the establishment of his next succeeding generation and no more. Either a man gives up the idea of perpetuating his family, or at any rate he seeks to accomplish it by other means than by a landed estate.

Thus, not only does the law of partible inheritance render it difficult for families to preserve their ancestral domains entire, but it deprives them of the inclination to attempt it and compels them in some measure to co-operate with the law in their own extinction. The law of equal distribution proceeds by two methods: by acting upon things, it acts upon persons; by influencing persons, it affects things. By both these means the law succeeds in striking at the root of landed property, and dispersing rapidly both families and fortunes.[2]

Most certainly it is not for us, Frenchmen of the nineteenth century, who daily witness the political and social changes that the law of partition is bringing to pass, to question its influence. It is perpetually conspicuous in our country, overthrowing the walls of our dwellings, and removing the landmarks of our fields. But although it has produced great effects in France, much still remains for it to do. Our recollections, opinions, and habits present powerful obstacles to its progress.

In the United States it has nearly completed its work of destruction, and there we can best study its results. The English laws concerning the transmission of property were abolished in almost all the states at the time of the Revolution. The law of entail was so modified as not materially to interrupt the free circulation of property. The first generation having passed away, estates began to be parceled out; and the change became more and more rapid with the progress of time. And now, after a lapse of a little more than sixty years, the aspect of society is totally altered; the families of the great landed proprietors are almost all commingled with the general mass. In the state of New York, which formerly contained many of these, there are but two who still keep their heads above the stream; and they must shortly disappear. The sons of these opulent citizens have become merchants, lawyers, or physicians. Most of them have lapsed into obscurity. The last trace of hereditary ranks and distinctions is destroyed; the law of partition has reduced all to one level.

I do not mean that there is any lack of wealthy individuals in the United States; I know of no country, indeed, where the love of money has taken stronger hold on the affections of men and where a profounder contempt is expressed for the theory of the permanent equality of property. But wealth circulates with inconceivable rapidity, and experience shows that it is rare to find two succeeding generations in the full enjoyment of it.

This picture, which may, perhaps, be thought to be overcharged, still gives a very imperfect idea of what is taking place in the new states of the West and Southwest. At the end of the last century a few bold adventurers began to penetrate into the valley of the Mississippi, and the mass of the population very soon began to move in that direction: communities unheard of till then suddenly appeared in the desert. States whose names were not in existence a few years before, claimed their place in the American Union; and in the Western settlements we may behold democracy arrived at its utmost limits. In these states, founded offhand and as it were by chance, the inhabitants are but of yesterday. Scarcely known to one another, the nearest neighbors are ignorant of each other's history. In this part of the American continent, therefore, the population has escaped the influence not only of great names and great wealth, but even of the natural aristocracy of knowledge and virtue. None is there able to wield that respectable power which men willingly grant to the remembrance of a life spent in doing good before their eyes. The new states of the West are already inhabited, but society has no existence among them.

It is not only the fortunes of men that are equal in America; even their acquirements partake in some degree of the same uniformity. I do not believe that there is a country in the world where, in proportion to the population, there are so few ignorant and at the same time so few learned individuals. Primary instruction is within the reach of everybody; superior instruction is scarcely to be obtained by any. This is not surprising; it is, in fact, the necessary consequence of what I have advanced above. Almost all the Americans are in easy circumstances and can therefore obtain the first elements of human knowledge.

In America there are but few wealthy persons; nearly all Americans have to take a profession. Now, every profession requires an apprenticeship. The Americans can devote to general education only the early years of life. At fifteen they enter upon their calling, and thus their education generally ends at the age when ours begins. If it is continued beyond that point, it aims only towards a particular specialized and profitable purpose; one studies science as one takes up a business; and one takes up only those applications whose immediate practicality is recognized.

In America most of the rich men were formerly poor; most of those who now enjoy leisure were absorbed in business during their youth; the consequence of this is that when they might have had a taste for study, they had no time for it, and when the time is at their disposal, they have no longer the inclination.

There is no class, then, in America, in which the taste for intellectual pleasures is transmitted with hereditary fortune and leisure and by which the labors of the intellect are held in honor. Accordingly, there is an equal want of the desire and the power of application to these objects.

A middling standard is fixed in America for human knowledge. All approach as near to it as they can; some as they rise, others as they descend. Of course, a multitude of persons are to be found who entertain the same number of ideas on religion, history, science, political economy, legislation, and government. The gifts of intellect proceed directly from God, and man cannot prevent their unequal distribution. But it is at least a consequence of what I have just said that although the capacities of men are different, as the Creator intended they should be, the means that Americans find for putting them to use are equal.

In America the aristocratic element has always been feeble from its birth; and if at the present day it is not actually destroyed, it is at any rate so completely disabled that we can scarcely assign to it any degree of influence on the course of affairs.

The democratic principle, on the contrary, has gained so much strength by time, by events, and by legislation, as to have become not only predominant, but all-powerful. No family or corporate authority can be perceived; very often one cannot even discover in it any very lasting individual influence.

America, then, exhibits in her social state an extraordinary phenomenon. Men are there seen on a greater equality in point of fortune and intellect, or, in other words, more equal in their strength, than in any other country of the world, or in any age of which history has preserved the remembrance.

Political Consequences of the Social Condition of the Anglo-Americans

The political consequences of such a social condition as this are easily deducible.

It is impossible to believe that equality will not eventually find its way into the political world, as it does everywhere else. To conceive of men remaining forever unequal upon a single point, yet equal on all others, is impossible; they must come in the end to be equal upon all.

Now, I know of only two methods of establishing equality in the political world; rights must be given to every citizen, or none at all to anyone. For nations which are arrived at the same stage of social existence as the Anglo-Americans, it is, therefore, very difficult to discover a medium between the sovereignty of all and the absolute power of one man: and it would be vain to deny that the social condition which I have been describing is just as liable to one of these consequences as to the other.

There is, in fact, a manly and lawful passion for equality that incites men to wish all to be powerful and honored. This passion tends to elevate the humble to the rank of the great; but there exists also in the human heart a depraved taste for equality, which impels the weak to attempt to lower the powerful to their own level and reduces men to prefer equality in slavery to inequality with freedom. Not that those nations whose social condition is democratic naturally despise liberty; on the contrary, they have an instinctive love of it. But liberty is not the chief and constant object of their desires; equality is their idol: they make rapid and sudden efforts to obtain liberty and, if they miss their aim, resign themselves to their disappointment; but nothing can satisfy them without equality, and they would rather perish than lose it.

On the other hand, in a state where the citizens are all practically equal, it becomes difficult for them to preserve their independence against the aggressions of power. No one among them being strong enough to engage in the struggle alone with advantage, nothing but a general combination can protect their liberty. Now, such a union is not always possible.

From the same social position, then, nations may derive one or the other of two great political results; these results are extremely different from each other, but they both proceed from the same cause.

The Anglo-Americans are the first nation who, having been exposed to this formidable alternative, have been happy enough to escape the dominion of absolute power. They have been allowed by their circumstances, their origin, their intelligence, and especially by their morals to establish and maintain the sovereignty of the people.

The Principle of the Sovereignty of the People of America

It dominates the whole society in America —Application made of this principle by the Americans even before their Revolution —Development given to it by that Revolution—Gradual and irresistible extension of the elective qualification

Whenever the political laws of the United States are to be discussed, it is with the doctrine of the sovereignty of the people that we must begin.

The principle of the sovereignty of the people, which is always to be found, more or less, at the bottom of almost all human institutions, generally remains there concealed from view. It is obeyed without being recognized, or if for a moment it is brought to light, it is hastily cast back into the gloom of the sanctuary.

"The will of the nation" is one of those phrases, that have been most largely abused by the wily and the despotic of every age. Some have seen the expression of it in the purchased suffrages of a few of the satellites of power; others, in the votes of a timid or an interested minority; and some have even discovered it in the silence of a people, on the supposition that the fact of submission established the right to command.

In America the principle of the sovereignty of the people is neither barren nor concealed, as it is with some other nations; it is recognized by the customs and proclaimed by the laws; it spreads freely, and arrives without impediment at its most remote consequences. If there is a country in the world where the doctrine of the sovereignty of the people can be fairly appreciated, where it can be studied in its application to the affairs of society, and where its dangers and its advantages may be judged, that country is assuredly America.

I have already observed that, from their origin, the sovereignty of the people was the fundamental principle of most of the British colonies in America. It was far, however, from then exercising as much influence on the government of society as it now does. Two obstacles, the one external, the other internal, checked its invasive progress.

It could not ostensibly disclose itself in the laws of colonies which were still forced to obey the mother country; it was therefore obliged to rule secretly in the provincial assemblies, and especially in the townships.

American society at that time was not yet prepared to adopt it with all its consequences. Intelligence in New England and wealth in the country to the south of the Hudson . . . long exercised a sort of aristocratic influence, which tended to keep the exercise of social power in the hands of a few. Not all the public functionaries were chosen by popular vote, nor were all the citizens voters. The electoral franchise was everywhere somewhat restricted and made dependent on a certain qualification, which was very low in the North and more considerable in the South.

The American Revolution broke out, and the doctrine of the sovereignty of the people came out of the townships and took possession of the state. Every class was enlisted in its cause; battles were fought and victories obtained for it; it became the law of laws.

A change almost as rapid was effected in the interior of society, where the law of inheritance completed the abolition of local influences.

As soon as this effect of the laws and of the Revolution became apparent to every eye, victory was irrevocably pronounced in favor of the democratic cause. All power was, in fact, in its hands, and resistance was no longer possible. The higher orders submitted without a murmur and without a struggle to an evil that was thenceforth inevitable. The ordinary fate of falling powers awaited them: each of their members followed his own interest; and as it was impossible to wring the power from the hands of a people whom they did not detest sufficiently to brave, their only aim was to secure its goodwill at any price. The most democratic laws were consequently voted by the very men whose interests they impaired: and thus, although the higher classes did not excite the passions of the people against their order, they themselves accelerated the triumph of the new state of things; so that, by a singular change, the democratic impulse was found to be most irresistible in the very states where the aristocracy had the firmest hold. The state of Maryland, which had been founded by men of rank, was the first to proclaim universal suffrage and to introduce the most democratic forms into the whole of its government.

When a nation begins to modify the elective qualification, it may easily be foreseen that, sooner or later, that qualification will be entirely abolished. There is no more invariable rule in the history of society: the further electoral rights are extended, the greater is the need of extending them; for after each concession the strength of the democracy increases, and its demands increase with its strength. The ambition of those who are below the appointed rate is irritated in exact proportion to the great number of those who are above it. The exception at last becomes the rule, concession follows concession, and no stop can be made short of universal suffrage.

At the present day the principle of the sovereignty of the people has acquired in the United States all the practical development that the imagination can conceive. It is unencumbered by those fictions that are thrown over it in other countries, and it appears in every possible form, according to the exigency of the occasion. Sometimes the laws are made by the people in a body, as at Athens; and sometimes its representatives, chosen by universal suffrage, transact business in its name and under its immediate supervision.

NOTES

1. I do not mean to say that the small proprietor cultivates his land better, but he cultivates it with more ardor and care; so that he makes up by his labor for his want of skill.

2. Land being the most stable kind of property, we find from time to time rich individuals who are disposed to make great sacrifices in order to obtain it and who willingly forfeit a considerable part of their income to make sure of the rest. But these are accidental cases. The preference for landed property is no longer found habitually in any class except among the poor. The small landowner, who has less information, less imagination, and less prejudice than the great one, is generally occupied with the desire of increasing his estate: and it often happens that by inheritance, by marriage, or by the chances of trade he is gradually furnished with the means. Thus, to balance the tendency that leads men to divide their estates, there exists another, which incites them to add to them. This tendency, which is sufficient to prevent estates from being divided *ad infinitum*, is not strong enough to create great territorial possessions, certainly not to keep them up in the same family.

61

Social Mobilization and Political Development

Karl W. Deutsch

Social mobilization can be defined, therefore, as the process in which major clusters of old social, economic and psychological commitments are eroded or broken and people become available for new patterns of socialization and behavior. As Edward Shils has rightly pointed out,[1] the original images of "mobilization" and of Mannheim's "fundamental democratization" imply two distinct stages of the process: (1) the stage of uprooting or breaking away from old settings, habits and commitments; and (2) the induction of the mobilized persons into some relatively stable new patterns of group membership, organization and commitment. In this fashion, soldiers are mobilized *from* their homes and families and mobilized *into* the army in which they then serve. Similarly, Mannheim suggests an image of large numbers of people moving away *from* a life of local isolation, traditionalism and political apathy, and moving *into* a different life or broader and deeper involvement in the vast complexities of modern life, including potential and actual involvement in mass politics.[2]

The first and main thing about social mobilization is, however, that it does assume a single underlying process of which particular indicators represent only particular aspects; that these indicators are correlated and to a limited extent interchangeable; and that this complex of processes of social change is significantly correlated with major changes in politics. . . .

From Karl W. Deutsch, "Social Mobilization and Political Development," *American Political Science Review*, LV, No. 3 (September 1961), 494–495, 497–502. Reprinted by permission of the publisher and the author.

Some Implications for the Politics of Development

In whatever country it occurs, social mobilization brings with it an expansion of the politically relevant strata of the population. These politically relevant strata are a broader group than the elite: they include all those persons who must be taken into account in politics. Dock workers and trade union members in Ghana, Nigeria, or the United States, for instance, are not necessarily members of the elites of these countries, but they are quite likely to count for something in their political life. In the developing countries of Asia, Africa and parts of Latin America, the political process usually does not include the mass of isolated, subsistence-farming, tradition-bound and politically apathetic villagers, but it does include increasingly the growing numbers of city dwellers, market farmers, users of money, wage earners, radio listeners and literates in town and country. The growth in the numbers of these people produces mounting pressures for the transformation of political practices and institutions; and since this future growth can be estimated at least to some extent on the basis of trends and data from the recent past, some of the expectable growth in political pressures—we may call it the potential level of political tensions—can likewise be estimated.

Social mobilization also brings about a change in the quality of politics, by changing the range of human needs that impinge upon the political process. As people are uprooted from their physical and intellectual isolation in their immediate localities, from their old habits and traditions, and often from their old patterns of occupation and places of residence, they experience drastic changes in their needs. They may now come to need provisions for housing and employment, for social security against illness and old age, for medical care against the health hazards of their crowded new dwellings and places of work and the risk of accidents with unfamiliar machinery. They may need succor against the risks of cyclical or seasonal unemployment, against oppressive charges of rent or interest, and against sharp fluctuations in the prices of the main commodities which they must sell or buy. They need instruction for themselves and education for their children. They need, in short, a wide range and large amounts of new government services.

These needs ordinarily cannot be met by traditional types of government, inherited from a precommercial and preindustrial age. Maharajahs, sultans, sheikhs and chieftains all are quite unlikely to cope with these new problems, and traditional rule by land-owning oligarchies or long established religious bodies most often is apt to prove equally disappointing in the face of the new needs. Most of the attempts to change the characteristics of the traditional ruling families—perhaps by supplying them with foreign advisers or by having their children study in some foreign country—are likely to remain superficial in their effects, overshadowed by mounting pressures for more thoroughgoing changes.

In developing countries of today, however, the increasingly ineffective and unpopular traditional authorities cannot be replaced successfully by their historic successors in the Western world, the classic institutions of 18th and 19th century liberalism and laissez-faire. For the uprooted, impoverished and disoriented masses produced by social mobilization, it is surely untrue that that government is best that governs least. They are far more likely to need a direct transition from traditional government to the essentials of a modern welfare state. The developing countries of Asia, Africa and parts of Latin America may have to accomplish, therefore, within a few decades a process of political change which in the history of Western Europe and North America took at least as many generations; and they may have to accomplish this accelerated change almost in the manner of a jump, omitting as impractical some of the historic stages of transition through a period of near laissez-faire that occurred in the West.

The growing need for new and old government services usually implies persistent political pressures for an increased scope of government and a greater relative size of the government sector in the national economy. In the mid-1950s, the total government budget—national, regional and local—tended to amount to roughly 10 per cent of the gross national product in the very poor and poorly mobilized countries with annual per capita gross national products at or below $100. For highly developed and highly mobilized countries, such as those with per capita gross national products at or above $900, the corresponding proportion of the total government sector was about 30 per cent. If one drew only the crudest and most provisional inference from these figures, one might expect something like a 2.5 per cent shift of national income into the government sector for every $100 gain in per capita gross national product in the course of economic development. It might be more plausible, however, to expect a somewhat more rapid expansion of the government sector during the earlier stages of economic development, but the elucidation of this entire problem—with all its obvious political implications—would require and reward a great deal more research.

The relationship between the total process of social mobilization and the growth of the national income, it should be recalled here, is by no means symmetrical. Sustained income growth is very unlikely without social mobilization, but a good deal of social mobilization may be going on even in the absence of per capita income growth, such as occurs in countries with poor resources or investment policies, and with rapid population growth. In such cases, social mobilization still would generate pressures for an expansion of government services and hence of the government sector, even in a relatively stagnant or conceivably retrograde economy. Stopping or reversing in such cases the expansion of government or the process of social mobilization behind it—even if this could be done—hardly would make matters much better. The more attractive course for such countries might rather be to use the capabilities of their expanding governments so as to bring about improvements in their resources and investment policies, and an eventual resumption of economic growth. To what extent this has been, or could be, brought about in cases of this kind, would make another fascinating topic for study.

The figures just given apply, of course, only to non-Communist countries; the inclusion of Communist states would bring the average in each class of government sectors higher. It would be interesting to investigate, however, whether and to what extent the tendency toward the relative expansion of the government sector in the course of social mobilization applies also, *mutatis mutandis,* to the Communist countries.

A greater scope of governmental services and functions requires ordinarily an increase in the capabilities of government. Usually it requires an increase in the numbers and training of governmental personnel, an increase in governmental offices and institutions, and a significant improvement in administrative organization and efficiency. A rapid process of social mobilization thus tends to generate major pressures for political and administrative reform. Such reforms may include notably both a quantitative expansion of the bureaucracy and its qualitative improvement in the direction of a competent civil service—even though these two objectives at times may clash.

Similar to its impact on this specific area of government, social mobilization tends to generate also pressures for a more general transformation of the political elite. It tends to generate pressures for a broadening and partial transformation of elite functions, of elite recruitment, and of elite communications. On all these counts, the old elites of traditional chiefs, village headmen, and local notables are likely to prove ever more inadequate; and political leadership may tend to shift to the new political elite of party or quasi-party organizations, formal or informal, legal or illegal, but always led by the new "marginal men" who have been exposed more or less thoroughly to the impact of modern education and urban life.

Something similar applies to elite communications. The more broadly recruited elites must communicate among themselves, and they must do so more often impersonally and over greater distances. They must resort more often to writing and to paper work. At the same time they must direct a greater part of their communications output at the new political strata; this puts a premium on oratory and journalism, and on skill in the use of all mass media of communication. At the same time rapid social mobilization causes a critical problem in the communications intake of elites. It confronts them with the ever present risk of losing touch with the newly mobilized social strata which until recently still did not count in politics. Prime Minister Nehru's reluctance to take into account the strength and intensity of Mahratti sentiment in the language conflict of Bombay in the 1950s and his general tendency since the mid-1930's to underestimate the strength of communal and linguistic sentiment in India suggest the seriousness of this problem even for major democratic leaders.

The increasing numbers of the mobilized population, and the greater scope and urgency of their needs for political decisions and governmental serv-ices, tend to translate themselves, albeit with a time lag, into increased political participation. This may express itself informally through greater numbers of people taking part in crowds and riots, in meetings and demonstrations, in strikes and uprisings, or, less dramatically, as members of a growing audience for political communications, written or by radio, or finally as members of a growing host of organizations. While many of these organizations are ostensibly nonpolitical, such as improvement societies, study circles, singing clubs, gymnastic societies, agricultural and commercial associations, fraternal orders, workmen's benefit societies, and the like, they nevertheless tend to acquire a political tinge, particularly in countries where more open outlets for political activities are not available. But even where there are established political parties and elections, a network of seemingly nonpolitical or marginally political organizations serves an important political function by providing a dependable social setting for the individuals who have been partly or wholly uprooted or alienated from their traditional communities. Such organizations may serve at the same time as marshalling grounds for the entry of these persons into political life.

Where people have the right to vote, the effects of social mobilization are likely to be reflected in the electoral statistics. This process finds its expression both through a tendency towards a higher voting participation of those already enfranchised and through an extension of the franchise itself to additional groups of the population. Often the increase in participation amongst those who already have the right to vote precedes the enfranchisement of new classes of voters, particularly in countries where the broadening of the franchise is occurring gradually. Thus in Norway between 1830 and 1860, voting participation remained near the level of about 10 per cent of the adult male population; in the 1870s and 1880s this participation rose rapidly among the enfranchised voters, followed by extensions of the franchise, until by the year 1900, 40 per cent of the Norwegian men were actually voting. This process was accompanied by a transformation of Norwegian politics, the rise to power of the radical peasant party *Venstre,* and a shift from the earlier acceptance of the existing Swedish-Norwegian Union to rising demands for full Norwegian independence.[3] These political changes had been preceded or accompanied by a rise in several of the usual indicators of social mobilization among the Norwegian people.

Another aspect of the process of social mobilization is the shift of emphasis away from the parochialism and internationalism of many traditional cultures to a preoccupation with the supralocal but far less than worldwide unit of the territorial, and eventually national, state.

An as yet unpublished study of American communications before the American Revolution, which has been carried on by Richard Merritt, shows how during the years 1735–1775 in the colonial newspapers the percentage of American or all-colonial symbols rose from about 10 to about 40 per cent, at the cost, in the main, of a decline in the share of symbols referring to places or events in the world outside the colonies and Britain, while Britain's share in American news attention remained relatively unchanged. Within the group of American symbols, the main increase occurred among those which referred to America or to the colonies as a whole, rather than among those referring to particular colonies or sections.[4]

More recent experiences in some of the "development countries" also suggest a more rapid rise of attention devoted to national topics than of that given to world affairs, on the one hand, and to purely local matters, on the other. This, however, is at present largely an impression. The nature and extent of attention shifts in mass media, as well as in popular attitudes, in the course of social mobilization is a matter for research that should be as promising as it is needed.[5]

Some data on the flow of domestic and foreign mails point in a similar direction. Of five development countries for which data are readily available the ratio of domestic to foreign mail rose substantially in four—Egypt, Iran, Nigeria, and Turkey—from 1913 to 1946–1951; the fifth, Indonesia, was an exception but was the scene of internal unrest and protracted warfare against the Dutch during much of the latter period. The trend for Egypt, Iran, Nigeria, and Turkey is confirmed in each case by data for the intermediate period 1928–1934, which are also intermediate, in each case, between the low domestic-foreign mail ratio for 1913 and the high ratios for 1946–1951. Many additional development countries—including the Gold Coast (now Ghana), the Belgian Congo, Malaya, French Morocco, Kenya-Uganda, Tanganyika, Mozambique, and Malaya—for which data were found only for the 1928–1934 to 1946–1951 comparison, show upward trends in their ratios of domestic to foreign mail.[6] Here again, a relatively moderate investment in the further collection and study of data might lead to interesting results.

According to some data from another recent study, a further side effect of social mobilization and economic development might possibly be first a substantial expansion, and then a lesser but significant reduction, of the share of the international trade sector in the national economy. Thus, in the course of British development, the proportion of total foreign trade (including trade to British overseas possessions) rose from an average of 20 per cent in 1830–1840 to a peak of 60 per cent in 1870–1879, remained close to that level until 1913, but declined subsequently and stood at less than 40 per cent in 1959. Similarly, the proportion of foreign trade to national income rose in Germany from about 28 per cent in 1802–1830 to a peak of 45 per cent in 1870–1879, declined to 35 per cent in 1900–1909, and by 1957 had recovered, for the much smaller German Federal Republic, to only 42 per cent. In Japan, the early proportion of foreign trade to national income was 15 per cent in 1885–1889, rising to peaks of 11 per cent in 1915–1919 and 40 per cent in 1925–1929; but by 1957 it stood at only 31 per cent. Data for Denmark, Norway, France and Argentina give a similar picture, while the same foreign-trade-to-national-income ratio in the United States fell, with minor fluctuations, from 23 per cent in 1799 to less than 9 per cent in 1958.[7] Here again the evidence is incomplete and partly contradictory, and the tentative interpretation, indicated at the beginning of this paragraph, still stands in need of confirmation and perhaps modification through additional research.

The problem of the ratio of the sector of internationally oriented economic activities relative to total national income—and thus indirectly the problem of the political power potential of internationally exposed or involved interest groups *vis-à-vis* the rest of the community—leads us to the problem of the size of states and of the scale of effective political communities. As we have seen, the process of social mobilization generates strong pressures towards increasing the capabilities of government, by increasing the volume and range of demands made upon the government and administration, and by widening the scope of politics and the membership of the politically relevant strata. The same process increases the frequency and the critical importance of direct communications between government and governed. It thus necessarily increases the importance of the language, the media, and the channels through which these communications are carried on.

Other things assumed equal, the stage of rapid social mobilization may be expected, therefore, to promote the consolidation of states whose peoples already share the same language, culture, and major social institutions; while the same process may tend to strain or destroy the unity of states whose population is already divided into several groups with different languages or cultures or basic ways of life. By the same token, social mobilization may tend to promote the merging of several smaller states, or political units such as cantons, principalities, sultanates or tribal areas, whose populations already share substantially the same language, culture and social system; and it may tend to inhibit, or at least to make more difficult, the merging of states or political units whose populations or ruling personnel differ substantially in regard to any of these matters. Social mobilization may thus assist to some extent in the consolidation of the United Arab Republic, but raise increasing problems for the politics and administration of multilingual India—problems which the federal government of India may have to meet or overcome by a series of creative adjustments.[8]

In the last analysis, however, the problem of the scale of states goes beyond the effects of language, culture, or institutions, important as all these are. In the period of rapid social mobilization, the acceptable scale of a political unit will tend to depend eventually upon its performance. If a government fails to meet the increasing burdens put upon it by the process of social mobilization, a growing proportion of the population is likely to become alienated and disaffected from the state, even if the same language, culture and basic social institutions were shared originally throughout the entire state territory by rulers and ruled alike. The secession of the United States and of Ireland from the British Empire, and of the Netherlands and of Switzerland from the German Empire may serve in part as examples. At bottom, the popular acceptance of a government in a period of social mobilization is most of all a matter of its capabilities and the manner in which they are used—that is, essentially a matter of its responsiveness to the felt needs of its population. If it proves persistently incapable or unresponsive, some or many of its subjects will cease to identify themselves with it psychologically; it will be reduced to ruling by force where it can no longer rule by display, example and persuasion; and if political alternatives to it appear, it will be replaced eventually by other political units, larger or smaller in extent, which at least promise to respond more effectively to the needs and expectations of their peoples.

In practice the results of social mobilization often have tended to increase the size of the state, well beyond the old tribal areas, petty principalities, or similar districts of the traditional era, while increasing the direct contact between government and governed far beyond the levels of the sociologically superficial and often half-shadowy empire of the past.

This growth in the size of modern states, capable of coping with the results of social mobilization, is counteracted and eventually inhibited, however, as their size increases, by their tendency to increasing preoccupation with their own internal affairs. There is considerable evidence for this trend toward a self-limitation in the growth of states through a decline in the attention, resources and responsiveness available for coping with the implicit needs and explicit messages of the next marginal unit of population and territory on the verge of being included in the expanding state.[9]

The remarks in this section may have sufficed to illustrate, though by no means to exhaust, the significance of the process of social mobilization in the economic and political development of countries. The main usefulness of the concept, however, should lie in the possibility of quantitative study which it offers. How much social mobilization, as measured by our seven indicators, has been occurring in some country per year or per decade during some period of its history, or during recent times? And what is the meaning of the differences between the rates at which some of the constituent subprocesses of social mobilization may have been going on? Although specific data will have to be found separately for each country, it should be possible to sketch a general quantitative model to show some of the interrelations and their possible significance.

NOTES

1. Edward Shils, at the Social Science Research Council Conference on Comparative Politics.

2. Karl Mannheim, *Man and Society in an Age of Reconstruction* (New York, 1940).

3. See Raymond Lindgren, *Norway-Sweden: Union, Disunion, Reunion* (Princeton, Princeton University Press, 1959); and K. W. Deutsch *et al., Political Community and the North Atlantic Area* (Princeton University Press, 1957).

4. Richard Merritt's monograph, "Symbols of American Nationalism, 1735–1775," which is to cover eventually one or more newspapers from Massachusetts, New York, Pennsylvania and Virginia, respectively, will be published in due course.

5. For examples of pioneering contributions of this kind, see the series of Hoover Institute Studies by Harold Lasswell, Ithiel Pool, Daniel Lerner and others, and particularly Pool, *The Prestige Papers* (Stanford, Stanford University Press, 1951).

6. See charts 1, 3, and 4 in Karl W. Deutsch, "Shifts in the Balance of Communication Flows: A Problem of Measurement in International Relations," *Public Opinion Quarterly*, Vol. 20 (Spring 1956), pp. 152–155, based on data of the Universal Postal Union.

7. See Karl W. Deutsch and Alexander Eckstein, "National Industrialization and the Declining Share of the International Economic Sector, 1890–1957," *World Politics*, Vol. 13 (January 1961), pp. 267–299. See also Simon Kuznets, *Six Lectures on Economic Growth* (Glencoe, 1959), esp. the section on "The Problem of Size" and "Trends in Foreign Trade Ratios," pp. 89–107.

8. For more detailed arguments, see Deutsch, *Nationalism*

and Social Communication, and Deutsch *et al., Political Community and the North Atlantic Area;* see also the discussions in Ernst B. Haas, "Regionalism, Functionalism and Universal Organizations," *World Politics,* Vol. 8 (January 1956), and "The Challenge of Regionalism," *International Organization,* Vol. 12 (1958), pp. 440–458; and in Stanley

Hoffmann, *Contemporary Theory in International Relations* (Englewood Cliffs, N.J., Prentice-Hall, 1960), pp. 223–240.
   9. *Cf.* Karl W. Deutsch, "The Propensity to International Transactions," *Political Studies,* Vol. 8 (June 1960), pp. 147–155.

62

Nation-Building and the Structuring of Mass Politics

Stein Rokkan

The extraordinary growth in the number of legally independent units of government during the 1950s and 1960s has prompted a wide variety of scholarly efforts toward description, analysis, and theorizing. The literature generated through these efforts is voluminous and dispersed and has so far never been subject to systematic codification.[1] In this brief treatment there can be no question of doing justice to the entire range of approaches to the comparative study of state formation and national development. Only a few lines of attack will be singled out for discussion, and even these will not be evaluated in any great detail: the purpose is not to review the past literature, but to define priority tasks for future cooperative data processing and interpretation.

Imbalances in Current Research

There are curious discontinuities in the history of the comparative study of national development. Karl Deutsch published his pioneering study of *Nationalism and Social Communication* in 1953 and focused all but one of his quantitative analyses of rates of assimilation and mobilization on European nations. Two of these were post-World War I nations: Czechoslovakia and Finland. The third was a nation but not a sovereign state: Scotland. And only the fourth was a new nation of the underdeveloped world: India. These analyses appeared just a few

years before the great onrush of new state formations in Africa and Asia: the UN added some fifty new states to its roster of members from 1953 to the end of 1966.

This extraordinarily rapid wave of decolonization and state formation deeply affected the priorities in the social science community from the mid-1950s onward: vast investments were made in research on the political and the economic developments in this "third world," and a great phalanx of scholars were able to familiarize themselves with the intricacies of these many cases of state formation and initial nation-building. These efforts went beyond mere fact-finding: the great wave of "third world" studies also triggered impressive efforts of theory construction.

Perhaps the most influential of these efforts of conceptualization and theorizing was the series of studies of political development organized by the Almond-Pye Committee of the American Social Science Research Council:[2] these studies represented a persistent and systematic endeavor to identify crucial variables in a generic process of change from the traditional tribal polity to the modern "bureaucratic-participant" state and have exerted a great deal of influence on the structure and the style of current research on the politics of the developing countries.

But the very success of these efforts of research on the developing areas of the world threatened to disrupt the continuity of scholarly concern with processes of state formation and nation-building: the theories of the late 1950s and the early 1960s tended to concentrate exclusively on the experiences and the potentialities of the polities just emerging from colonial status and showed only minimal concern with the early histories of nation-building in Europe

From "The Structuring of Mass Policies in the Smaller European Democracies," *Comparative Studies in Society and History,* X, No. 2 (January 1968), 173–210, reprinted by permission of Cambridge University Press, the copyright holder; and "Models and Methods in the Comparative Study of Nation-Building," *Acta Sociologica,* XIII (1969), reprinted by permission of Unesco, the copyright holder.

and in the European-settled territories. The idea of the participant nation-state was European in origin and had been exported to the developing world through colonization and ideological diffusion; yet there was a great deal of reluctance to draw directly on the rich European experience in developing models for the explanation of the processes of change inherent in the growth of national polities. There were many reasons for this reluctance: the great complexity of the European developments, the linguistic difficulties, the low level of communication between historians and generalizing social scientists. It was easier to deal in comparative terms with the less history-burdened, less documented, and less scrutinized countries of the developing world: the working languages were fewer because of the colonial inheritance, and there were fewer professional historians around to question the interpretations and the classifications of the social scientists.

There are many signs of uneasiness about this gap. A number of comparisons across the developed and the developing polities have been published in recent years, and still more are under way and will help to pave the way for a *rapprochement*.[3] The Committee on Comparative Politics has itself given increasing attention to the peculiarities of the developments in Europe and has encouraged attempts to incorporate the variations in Europe in a broader model of political modernization.[4] A number of attempts have been made at comparisons across pairs or multiples of contrasting polities in the West and the East: among the most important of these are Reinhard Bendix's work on aspects of nation-building in Germany, Russia, Japan, and India,[5] Robert Holt and John Turner's paired comparisons of England and Japan, France and China,[6] Barrington Moore's analysis of the economic basis of political development in England, France, the United States, and Germany, Russia, China, India, and Japan.[7] Seymour Martin Lipset's attempt at a comparison of the early stages of nation-building in the United States with the current efforts of integration and consolidation in the newest states of Africa and Asia[8] points in the same direction, and so does Samuel Huntington's current work on contrasts in the timing of social and political modernization.[9] Karl Deutsch and his team at Yale, since 1966 at Harvard, have extended the program of research implicit in the 1953 volume: Deutsch has not only deepened his analysis of conditions and varieties of nation-building through his work on the Swiss case[10] but also built up, with his colleagues, an important computer archive of data on the new as well as the old units of the expanding international system.[11]

These varied attempts at bridge-building across the great gap in the comparative study of political development have helped to clarify the priorities of further research, but have barely scratched the surface of the vast masses of data to be processed in any serious and systematic effort to test alternative models and hypotheses.

There are still marked imbalances in the ranges of cases and variables covered in comparative analysis of processes of political development:

1. *The large-nation bias.* Most comparisons, whether in the West or with developing polities, have limited themselves to the larger and more influential units[12] and have tended to neglect the richly varied experiences of the smaller polities, particularly the many European "secession states" after 1814, 1830, and 1918 and their histories of nation-building: these are, after all, the units most immediately comparable to recently formed states of the "third world."

2. *The "whole-nation" bias.* Most comparisons have been limited to institutional or aggregate statistical data for each nation as a unit and have tended to neglect highly significant variations in the rates of growth among competing economic, political, or cultural centers and between such centers and the rural peripheries.[13]

3. *The "economic growth" bias.* Most comparisons have limited themselves to the most easily accessible time series data from censuses and economic bookkeeping statistics and have neglected a wide range of less complete data series for levels and rates of social, educational, and cultural mobilization, all processes of crucial importance in the study of nation-building.

This article will discuss alternative strategies in coping with these deficiencies in the data bases for comparative developmental analysis: (*a*) it will first review salient features of recently advanced *models of nation-building;* (*b*) it will pass on to a listing of *priority variables* for comparative data collation and analysis; and (*c*) it will wind up with some suggestions for *international action* to accelerate the development and testing of different models through a series of encounters between historians and social scientists.

A Sample of Models

Models of political development vary along a variety of dimensions: in their logical structure and their openness to direct empirical testing, in the number and precision of the variables, and in the possibilities of adequate matching with actual or potential data sources, in the ranges of historically given variations they seek to explain.

Let us, to simplify the mapping of variations in the organization of models, try to locate a few of the best-known ones in a two-dimensional diagram inspired by Talcott Parsons.[14] See Figure 62–1.

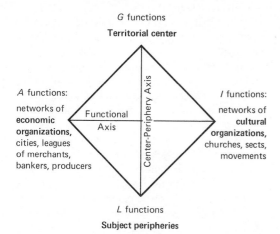

Figure 62–1

Karl Deutsch focuses on the center-periphery axis. His model is primarily designed to predict variations in the extent of territorial-cultural integration through the joint, but not necessarily parallel, processes of national standardization and social mobilization. His dependent variables bear on *nation-building,* and his model simply assumes some initial level of state formation through interelite coalitions.

The Deutsch model is particularly appropriate in the study of the actual or potential breakup of multilingual empires; it is no accident that his four examples of quantitative analysis bear on such linguistically divided territories as Finland (Finnish vs. Swedish), Bohemia-Moravia-Silesia (Czech vs. German), Scotland (Gaelic vs. English) and India-Pakistan (Hindi vs. other vernaculars vs. English).

The model posits a *center* and a *leading group of active "nation-builders"* and seeks to specify the conditions for the development, in the territory controlled from this center or reached by this group, of a *culturally cohesive, or at least complementary, community* clearly distinct from the surrounding populations.[15]

The core of the model explores the interrelations between two rates of change in the process of nation-building or nation-fragmentation: (*a*) the rate of *assimilation,* defined as an increase or decrease from t_1 to t_2 in the subset (*A*) of the territorial population (*P*) who have become speakers of the pre-

dominant ("nation-building") language; (*b*) the rate of *mobilization,* defined as an increase or decrease from t_1 to t_2 in the subset (*M*) of *P* who are no longer exclusively tied to the traditional, locally bounded communication environments and have in some sense entered the broader, urban, if not nationwide, system of social communication.[16]

At any one point in time t_i after the initial drive the extent of unification or integration may be measured by the sizes of the four cross products of these two dichotomies:

the *mobilized and assimilated* (M_A);
the *mobilized but still differentiated* (M_D);
the *underlying but assimilated* (U_A);
the *underlying and differentiated* (U_D).

The rise and fall in these shares of the territorial population from one point in time to another will obviously be affected by the interaction between the two processes of change, but the character of this interaction will vary over time and as a function of the levels already reached on each variable. A number of extraneous variables will also affect the interrelations of assimilation and mobilization: differential fertility and mortality, the economic or military strength of alternative centers of clusters of nation-builders, the extent of exogenous mobilization through economic, ecclesiastical, or other cultural networks.

There is no attempt in *Nationalism and Social Communication* to spell out in any formal detail the consequences of this simple model: there is a brief mathematical appendix on the relationships between the principal rates of change distinguished,[17] but there are no explicit formulations of functional relationships between the rates of assimilation and mobilization and the finally generated national structure. There is a series of illuminating applications to concrete historical developments but no easily identifiable generalizations for empirical testing across a broad range of nations. Karl Deutsch's model is essentially heuristic: it suggests a priority in comparative data collection and then simply exhorts us to develop generalizations inductively through the processing of such materials.

The Deutsch model fired the imagination of a number of scholars: it was a first attempt to apply notions from information theory and cybernetics to the study of political development, and it pointed to exciting possibilities of empirical testing through the construction of quantitative indicators from historical statistical data. But the core of the model limited itself to *mass effects:* the focus was primarily on the incorporation of peripheral populations in some form of national community, much less on the actual political or administrative measures of nation-building at the territorial centers or on the conflicts among competing elites and organizations over such policies.

A variety of difficulties, terminological, conceptual, empirical, confront the student of processes of center formation. In this quick review we shall focus on attempts to cut across the historically inherited confusions of national terminologies through the identification of discriminating variables and through the development of models for the cross classification of cases and the establishment of distinctive syndromes and configurations.

Much of the literature in this field focuses on single cases of center formation and nation-building and offers only *ad hoc* comparisons: outstanding examples are Lipset's interpretation of the United States as *The First New Nation* and Ralf Dahrendorf's *Gesselschaft und Demokratie in Deutschland*.[18] Conceptually and empirically much more taxing, but of greater potential value in the development of systematic macrotheory, is the strategy of *paired comparisons* attempted in a number of recent writings. Such confrontations of pairs of contrasting cases of center formation and nation-building may not only offer opportunities for a deepening of insights into the dynamics of each system but also offer springboards for further model-building across a broader range of cases.

This strategy is well known in comparative economic history: consider Clapham's classic study of the French and the German economies,[19] Habakkuk's pathbreaking study of technological developments in Britain and the United States,[20] Kindleberger's attempt at a systematic confrontation of data on society and economy in Britain and France.[21] Students of comparative political development have found the method of paired contrasts of great value, both as a device in the ordering and evaluation of data and as a procedure in the generation of hypotheses and insights. Possibly the best example of a collective effort of this type is the symposium organized by the Almond-Pye Committee on contrasts in the development of the Japanese and the Turkish political system.[22] Excellent examples of the use of this strategy in a broader context of theory development are Reinhard Bendix's work on the development of territorial systems of public authority in Prussia/Germany and Russia and in India and Japan[23] and Robert Holt and John Turner's[24] paired comparisons of two early industrializers, England and Japan, with two late industrializers, France and China. Both these works focus on variations in the distinctiveness, the strength, and the cohesion of the center-forming collectivities in each territory: the

aim is to pinpoint contrasts in the characteristics of the agencies of territorial decision-making and control and to develop models for the explanation of such contrasts. Bendix's analysis focuses on the tactics of center-forming collectivities, dynastic bureaucracies, and military organizations in breaking down local solidarities and creating direct links between the territorial nation and its individual subjects through the development of universalistic criteria of citizen rights and citizen obligations. The study by Holt and Turner is organized around a distinctive hypotheticodeductive model: it seeks to test a set of propositions about the likelihood of economic innovations under different conditions of administrative centralization.

These studies help to underscore the importance of the "center" variables for an understanding of contrasts in nation-building processes. Nationalization processes in the territorial peripheries are clearly conditioned by circumstances of cultural as well as physical distance and by the possibilities of concerted mobilization of local resources against the standardizing agencies, but the *contents* of the communications spread through the actual or potential national territory are primarily determined by the center-forming collectivities. No typology of nation-building processes can be developed without an analysis of variations in the structures and the functions of the territorial centers. Among recent attempts at classifications of such structures two deserve particular attention: Samuel Huntington's analysis of the contrast between the United States and what he calls "Europe," in fact primarily England, France, Prussia, and Sweden, and Peter Nettl's effort to identify dimensions of "stateness." Huntington's much-discussed article focuses on the origins of the marked differences in the speed of political modernization between England and France on the one hand, the United States on the other. This dependent variable is a composite of several indicators of organizational complexity: the extent to which traditional, familial, religious, and ethnic authorities have been replaced by a single, secular, nation-centered political authority, the extent of differentiation in the political and the bureaucratic machinery, and the extent of the development of parties and interest associations for the channeling and mobilization of popular participation.[25] His explanatory variables are essentially social-structural: the higher levels of centralization and administrative differentiation characteristic of a number of European polities can be understood only against the background of long histories of feudal resistance and of secular-religious conflicts; the "fusion of functions" and the "division of power" characteristic of the United

States could emerge only in a settler society freed from any legacy of feudalism and unencumbered by entanglements with a dominant supranational church.[26] Peter Nettl goes one step further: relying heavily on Weber's analysis of the growth of bureaucratic organizations, he suggests a scheme for the rank ordering of historically given political systems on a number of dimensions of "stateness."[27] He does not attempt any detailed ordering of a wide range of polities along such dimensions, but concentrates his attention on four particularly significant cases: Prussia/Germany, France, and the United States. The continental polities were built around increasingly autonomous bodies of territorial administrators, the British polity around coalitions of elite "establishments" embodied in parties while the American polity stuck to what Huntington calls the "Tudor constitution" in its heavier emphasis on the integrative role of the courts and the legal profession. Schemes of this type clearly have to be spelled out in greater detail before they can be subjected to tests against empirical indicators; among the most obvious ones would be time series data on the growth of full-time administrative personnel in each territory, on the economic resource bases of each category of administrators, their family and kin links to local power-holders, the distinctiveness of their education, the standardization of criteria of entry and promotion. The marked variations in administrative structures in the "developed" world have never been adequately mapped: Huntington and Nettl tend to group together in their "European-Continental" category markedly different cases of center-formation. Clearly, we cannot expect much progress in the empirical testing of models of political development without some concerted action to organize confrontations between generalizing social scientists and students steeped in the administrative histories of pairs or triples of developed systems, smaller as well as larger.

The great merit of Nettl's analysis in this context is his systematic insistence on the logical and empirical independence of the variables "stateness" and "nationness": there have been many examples of nonnational states, and there are a great number of national polities without any "intrasocietal" state apparatus. A territorial nation need not be built around an autonomous state in the Weberian sense. "What constitutes nations is surely the organized diffusion of common experience, and this may be structured and experienced by a King, leader, church, party, army *or* state—or all of them."[28] In this style of conceptualization the term "nation-state" is an unfortunate misnomer: "If the entry of the third world onto the stage of modern socio-scientific consciousness has had one immediate result (or should have had), it is *the snapping of the link between state and nation*."[29] In the language of our Parsonian diagram the national center can be organized around collectivities and coalitions varying markedly in power resources and styles of legitimation; the national center need not constitute a "state" except in the elementary sense that it is the locus of external representation.

This is the great thrust of Barrington Moore's pathbreaking analysis of the center-forming coalitions of the leading powers of the modern world.[30] He proposes a model of "polity-building" options and seeks to substantiate a set of propositions about the consequences of such options for the structuring of the central institutions in each territory.

Moore's model posits four sets of actors in the historical process of change from traditional to modern society: the central dynasty and its bureaucracy, the trading and manufacturing bourgeoisie in the cities, the lords of the land, and the peasantry. None of these four sets of actors is strong enough to constitute a center-forming collectivity on its own; the model forces them to enter into coalitions by pairs or triples, and at least one set of actors will be left outside to form an opposition front against this "nation-building alliance."

Moore does not attempt any formalization of his model, but the underlying combinations are easily spelled out. The system mathematically allows six two-against-two and four three-against-one coalitions. Four of these are highly unlikely to occur in any historical situation: the likelihood of any form of bourgeois-peasant co-operation is very small, and so is a direct landowner-peasant front against the others. Of the remaining six coalitions, Moore singles out four for detailed study: these are the ones he uses in his attempts to explain the variations among seven of his eight leading polities and at the same time constitute the alternatives he finds it most fruitful to concentrate on in his analysis of the one deviant case, India.

Table 62–1 sets out schematically the four alliance options and their consequences in the seven empirical cases.

This schema obviously cannot do full justice to Moore's richly faceted comparative analysis, but it does help to bring out the structure of the argument. In the language of a Parsonian diagram the Moore model concentrates on variables on the *G–A–L* side: on options on the economic front. Linguistic and religious variations enter only marginally into the discussion. True enough, Moore does analyze the weight of religious traditions in the structuring of elite coalitions and peasant reactions in his

Table 62–1 Four Alliance Options and Their Consequences

Type of Coalition	Cases	Decisive Modernizing Revolution	Consequences for Structure of Polity
Urban with *landed* interests	Britain	Puritan Rev. 1640–1660: subordination of dynastic bureaucracy	Weak, elite-dominated bureaucracy, rule through alternation of parties
	U.S.	Civil War 1860–1865: defeat of Southern "Junkers"	Weak, dispersed bureaucracy; rule through pluralist bargaining between courts and established interests
Urban with *landed* interests *and* with *bureaucracy*	France	Great Rev. 1789–1815; abolition of feudal privileges, but increased openings for bourgeois landownership and strengthened peasantry	Strongly centralized egalitarian-competitive bureaucracy; oscillation between plebiscitarian rule and fragmented multiparty bargaining
Landed interests with *bureaucracy*	Prussia/ German *Reich*	No "bourgeois" revolution: failure in 1848. Modernization from above: alliance of bureaucracy, armed forces and Junker landowners	Strong, elite-dominated bureaucracy, autocratic rule leading to mass dictatorship
	Japan	No revolution: Imperial Restoration in 1868 through action of modernizing landowners	Feudalized bureaucracy, autocratic rule leading to period of fascist-military domination
Bureaucracy with *peasantry*	Russia	October Rev. 1917: temporary coalition of peasantry with party bureaucracy against the old "agrarian bureaucracy," the landowners and the (weak) bourgeoisie	Strong centralizing bureaucracy, single-party rule
	China	Long March 1934: party-peasantry coalition against traditional gentry-scholar bureaucracy	Single-party rule

comparison of India, Japan, and China, but he quickly comes to the conclusion that the inherited system of beliefs and ritual was less important than the style of center formation: in India continuous segmentation through the operation of caste codes, in Japan fragmentation of peasant oppositions through the feudal control system, in China a much higher level of vulnerability to peasant mobilization because of the heavy concentration of power in the "agrarian bureaucracy." Moore is anxious to keep his model free of redundancies: the merit of his analysis lies exactly in the parsimony of his selection of explanatory variables. But this leaves the question of the *range of variations to be accounted for* in any such model of center formation and nation-building. Moore argues strongly for a concentration of attention on leading nations: his model focuses on the variations among the eight economically and politically most powerful polities of the modern world and explicitly leaves out of consideration all the smaller and less influential units of the international system. He even goes so far as to question the possibility of any general model of political development: ". . . a general statement about the historical preconditions of democracy or authoritarianism covering small countries as well as large would very likely be so broad as to be abstractly platitudinous."[31]

Moore is probably right in questioning the possibility of constructing empirically models for cross-polity variations at all levels of size *across all cultural regions of the world:* this may work, as he has so ably shown, for large and powerful units, but the smaller political systems tend to be so heavily dependent on their cultural contexts that there are likely to be very small pay-offs in attempts at indiscriminate comparisons across distinctive cultural regions. This still leaves one important strategy open: the development of *region-specific models* for the explanation of variations in center formation and nation-building. Such regionally focused models cannot fruitfully be restricted to the large and powerful leader polities: on the contrary, the purpose is to account for variations among *all* the distinctive polities in the region, and this requires direct attention to the possible consequences of such factors as size, economic resource potential, and location in the international power system.

Region-Specific Models

A model of this type has been sketched out for one cultural region of the world: it differs markedly from Moore in its dependent variable, but is astoundingly similar in its logical structure. Seymour

Martin Lipset and I presented a first version of this model in our Introduction to the volume *Party Systems and Voter Alignments.*[32] We developed a scheme of successive "option points" in each nation-building history to account for variations in the party systems which emerged in western Europe with the extension of the suffrage to all adult men. In my further work on "the politics of the smaller European democracies,"[33] I have tried to extend the model to account for variations in the entire process of mass mobilization: differences in the sequences and the timing of measures of democratization as well as differences in the aggregation of party fronts across historically given cleavage lines.

By contrast to Moore's schema, this model posits initial variations on both sides of the Parsonian diagram: the *G–A–L* side as well as the *G–I–L* side. The model proceeds in two steps: at the first step it maps variations in the *preconditions* for actual or potential nation-building in the period *before* the decisive thrusts toward mass mobilization in the wake of the French Revolution; at the second it traces options at a number of choice points in the early histories of mass politics in each country.

Again very schematically, Table 62–2 sets out the determining variables of the model.

These variations in nation-building history serve in the next round as parameters in propositions about steps in the democratization process and about the generation of party systems. The "precondition" variables help to predict variations in the timing of decisions on democratization, the "system option" variables to account for variations in party systems. In a fuller statement of the model the linkages between the early preconditions and the later system options will be spelled out in greater detail: in this context our primary concern is to bring out the similarities and the differences in structure between Moore's model for the eight world powers and this model for eleven smaller and five larger polities of western Europe.

Moore's model focuses on the *L–A* option, but at a different stage in the development of each system: he seeks to characterize the conditions for alliances between rural and urban interests in the centuries before the national and the industrial revolutions and tries to generate propositions about the chances for competitive pluralist democracy or authoritarian monolithic rule given the variations in such initial conditions. In our model these early alliance conditions were not brought in to explain variations in the stages and the timing of the decisions on democratization: the *L–A* alternatives were not included among the "preconditions" variables, but only at the

Table 62–2 Region Specific Model

I Precondition Variables	Location in Diagram	Alternative States of System
1. Territorial	G–L	Timing of territorial consolidation/secession: —before 1648 —after Napoleonic wars

2. Cultural	L–I	Cultural dependence on outside metropolitan center:
		    —high (same language)
		    —divided
		    —low

	G–I	State-Church settlement:
		    —All Protestant
		    —Catholic minority
		    —Independent Catholic (France)
		    —Counter-Reformation
		      State-Church alliance

3. Economic	G–A	Centralization of urban network:
		    —monocephalic
		    —polycephalic

4. Political	G	Structure of central decision-making organs:
		    —continuous history of corporate participation/representation (city councils, estate assemblies)
		    —significant period of absolute monarchic rule

II. System Options	Location in Diagram	Critical Juncture	Alternatives
1. Cultural	L–I	"Reformation": identification of culture and territory	—one standard national language, suppression of alternatives —one or more minor (subject) languages tolerated —two standard languages
	G–I	National Revolution: control of educational agencies	—national church allied to secular state —supranational church (Roman Catholic Church) allied to national state —secular state opposed to supranational church
2. Economic	L–A	Industrial Revolution: agricultural versus commercial-industrial interests	—State allied to agricultural interests (high corn tariff) —State allied to commercial-industrial interests (low tariff)
	G–A	Industrial Revolution: owner versus worker interests	—protect rights of owners/employers —protect rights of workers—propertyless

level of elite options accounting for the structuring of the national party systems (II.2, Table 62–2). This difference in the strategy of explanation has obvious consequences for the classification of empirical cases. Moore contrasts the English and the Prussian developments on the basis of the alliance choice of the landowners, while our party systems model groups the two together because they constitute a configuration unlikely to lead to distinctive agrarian party formations.[34] All this finally comes down to a decision about the ranges of dependent variables to be accounted for in the model. Our eleven plus five country scheme restricts itself rigorously to the tasks of predicting variations in the steps taken toward full-suffrage democracy and in the character of the national party systems by the 1920's. Such a model does not necessarily generate propositions about the *stability* or the *vulnerability* of such full-suffrage system.[35] This is a different task: Moore has pointed to a possible scheme of explanation for the larger powers, but has made no effort to account for variations among polities at varying levels of size and economic strength; in fact, he rejects this task as unworthy of his intellectual efforts. To students of comparative nation-building this constitutes a real challenge: the small nations have developed their own distinctive strategies of consolidation and survival, they have accumulated a wealth of experiences of conflict resolutions and institution-building, and there are enough of them to tempt the ingenuities of all manner of generalizers and model builders.

We are, it is true, still far from any sort of general consensus on procedures in such comparative studies of nation-building. A number of enthusiasts have tried to develop schemes for world-wide comparisons of the nation-building process. Karl Deutsch's data bank was organized for this purpose; Arthur Banks and Robert Textor included all UN members in their *Cross-Polity Survey*;[36] Gabriel Almond, Lucian Pye, and their colleagues have proposed paradigms for the comparison of nation-building processes wherever they might occur.[37] Our objectives in constructing a model for the eleven smaller and the five larger countries of western Europe were much more restricted: our model is confined to the territories of Europe affected by the drive toward state formation and the struggle with the supranational church in the sixteenth and seventeenth centuries and serves to identify only the minimum of elements in the histories of these countries which help to predict the later variations in electoral arrangements and party systems. These are deliberate and programmatic restrictions; they serve to increase

the possibilities of operationalization and empirical testing, but for that very reason do not claim validity for polities developed from other initial conditions or for other ranges of dependent variables. It is hoped, of course, that this is a case of *reculer pour mieux sauter:* similarly region-specific models are under construction for Latin America[38] and could certainly be developed for other parts of the world. Whether in the end it will be possible to validate universal, world-wide models of political development must still remain an open question: a great deal of hard work will have to be done, not only on the internal logic of each effort of model-building, but even more on the systematic coding of information country by country to test the alternative derivations of the models already advanced.

Nation-Building and Mass Politics: The Four Revolutions

So much for the general rationale of this Europe-centered model. Let us now add some flesh and blood to the skeleton by spelling out some of its concrete empirical implications for the comparative study of mass politics. We shall try to show, at least for the eleven smaller democracies of western Europe, how our typology of nation-building sequences helps to generate propositions about variations in cleavage fronts and party systems. Our aim is to reduce to the smallest possible number the range of explanatory variables required to account for the variations in electoral alternatives among our countries:

Why did some polities develop party oppositions over issues of *ethnic-cultural identity* while others left such issues to be settled *within* broader party fronts?

Why did some polities develop strong parties for the defense of the rights of *organized churches and religious movements,* while some developed only small or short-lived parties of this type, and others were able to keep religious divisions completely out of politics?

Why did the *peasantry* organize their own parties in some countries or regions, while in others they never found this necessary?

Why did the *working classes* develop strong and unified political movements in some countries, much weaker ones in other countries, and deeply divided organizations in still others?

It is easy enough to spin out strings of explanations for one country at a time: the task is to develop a unified scheme of accounting that will hold up across a maximum of empirically extant cases.

In our attempt at accounting for the marked variations in the timing, the speed, and the scope of the measures taken to institutionalize competitive mass politics we started out from a typology of the *initial conditions of nation-building:* the character of the medieval organization of the given territory, the exposure to absolutist centralization, the final definition of the territorial nation-state through the processes of secession and consolidation after the Napoleonic upheavals, and, finally, the size of each resultant polity and its position in the international interaction system.[39]

In our attempt at an explanation of the variations in the structuring of partisan polities we have found it fruitful to proceed through a parallel series of steps to generate a developmental typology:

1. We first identify four *"critical junctures"* in the sequences of nation-building.

2. We next identify the principal *cleavage lines* generated by the decisions taken at each critical juncture.

3. And we finally generate from each of the possible cleavage structures *core systems of parties* and test these predictions against the historically given cases.

The gist of the argument has been summarized in the schema of developmental linkages in Table 62–3. Table 62–4 sets out the four "critical junctures" and seeks to locate six larger and eleven smaller European polities within the resulting $2 \times 2 \times 2 \times 2$ attribute space. Table 62–5 presents the cleavage structures to be expected for five of the sixteen initial types and identifies the "core" party systems generated for each structure through a set of uniform assumptions about probabilities of coalition and aggregation: these "generated" systems are finally tested against the historically extant cases, and the principal deviations are listed.[40]

This exercise in developmental typology may appear forbiddingly schematical. These extraordinarily varied territorial and national histories clearly cannot be summarized in a developmental typology at this level of simplicity. But this is not the purpose: the object is to single out in the multifaceted flow of events in each unit those choice points which proved most significant for the generation of similarities and differences in cleavage structures and in party systems.

In fact it is not very difficult to translate the succession of "revolutionary junctures" into a straight-

Table 62–3 A Schema of Developmental Linkages: Revolutions, Issues, and Cleavages

Critical Juncture	Crucial Issue	Resultant Cleavages
I. *Reformation:* the 1648 settlement and the nineteenth and twentieth century secessions	Consolidation of territorial state	1. Peripheries vs. centre subject ethnicities/ language groups against central dominance 2. Moralist/religious rejection of central culture
II. *National Revolution:* post-Napoleonic nation-building	Control of territorial standardization media: primarily mass education	Church vs. Secular State
III. *Industrial Revolution:* 1850's onwards	1. The primary economy: protection vs. modernization (tariff issue) 2. The secondary economy: freedom of enterprise vs. state control; rights of owners/employers vs. rights of workers/ employees	1. Rural/agricultural vs. urban/industrial interests 2. Worker-owner cleavage
IV. *International Revolution:* Russian Revolution and after	Integration of underprivileged strata in national community	1. Communism *vs.* Socialism 2. Pacifism neutralism *vs.* commitment to nation/ larger alliance

Table 62–4 A 2 x 2 x 2 x 2 Typology of Cleavage Structures and Its Fit with the Empirical Cases in Western Europe

	1. National State Church								2. State(s) Allied With RC Church							
I. Reformation	1. National State Church								2. State(s) Allied With RC Church							
II. National Revolution	11. Strong Prot. Dissent				12. Strong RC Dissent				21. Secularizing Revolution				22. State-RC Alliance			
III. Industrial Revolution	111. State Close to Split		112. State Close to		121.		122.		211.		212.		221.		222.	
IV. International Revolution	1111. Landed Int. Minor (Split)	1112. Urban Int. Major	1121. Landed Int. Minor	1122. Urban Int. Major	1211. Landed Int. Minor	1212. Urban Int. Major	1221. Landed Int. Minor	1222. Urban Int. Major	2111. Landed Int. Minor	2112. Urban Int. Major	2121. Landed Int. Minor	2122. Urban Int. Major	2211. Landed Int. Minor	2212. Urban Int. Major	2221. Landed Int. Minor	2222. Urban Int. Major

Nearest empirical examples

	1111	1112	1121	1122	1211	1212	1221	1222	2111	2112	2121	2122	2211	2212	2221	2222
Large Early	G.B. (Excl. Irel.)				G.B. (Incl. Irel.)				Spain				France			
Late	Prussia				*Reich*								Hapsb. Empire			
Smaller Early			Denm. Swed.				Neth. Switz.									
Late			Nor. Finl. Icel.										Austria Ireland		Belg. Lux.	

Table 62–5 Cleavage Structures and Party Systems: The Eleven Smaller European Democracies

Type in Table 4	Characteristic Cleavages					Generated "Core" System of Parties		Deviant Cases
	Periphery-Center	Church-State	Urban-Rural	Worker-Owner	International-National	Early	Late	
1121	xx					Cons. "Left"		DENMARK: a) No Prohibitionist split b) Georgist party
			xx				Radical Prohibitionist Agrarian	SWEDEN: Split Radical-Prohibitionist party 12 years (1922–1934). Minor Christian party 1964.
				xxx		Soc. Dem.		
					x		CP (weak)	
1122	xxx					Cons.		FINLAND: Old Finns vs. Young Finns (Independence struggle); Swedish party ICELAND: Merger Cons./Lib. Independence party
						Left	Radical; Christian	
			xxx				Prohibitionist: Agrarian	*Only in Norway*
				xxx		Soc. Dem.		NORWAY: Labour with Comintern party 20s, CP weak except 1945.
					xxx		CP (strong)	
1221	xxx					Lib./Rad. Orthodox Prot.		NETH.: Lib. CHU, Anti-Rev. Cath. Minor SWITZ.: Rad. Lib.-Dem. (regional) Cath.-Cons. Regional
		xxx				Cath.		
			xx				Agr. (weak)	
				xxx		Soc. Dem.		
					x		CP (weak)	
2211	xxx					Pro-larger unit		AUSTRIA: Pan-Germans vs. Cath.-Cons. IRELAND: *Fine Gael* vs. *Fianna Fail* *No church party.*
		xxx				Cath.		
			xx				Agr. (weak)	*Landbund* (regional, I. Rep.) Minor
				xxx		Soc.		Strong Weak
					x		CP (weak)	
2221	xxx						Regionalists	BELGIUM: Flemish party, *Volksunie* LUXEMBOURG: None
						Lib.		
		xxx				Cath.		
				xxx		Soc.		
					x		CP (weak)	

forward account of events at four critical junctures in the political history of western Europe:

I. The great upheavals of the *Reformation and the Thirty Years' War* left western Europe divided into three parts:

(*a*) a wholly Protestant North (Denmark-Norway, Sweden-Finland, Prussia);

(*b*) a broad belt of religiously mixed territories from Ireland toward the Alps (Britain-Ireland, the Low Countries, the Rhineland, large sections of France until 1685, the Swiss cantons);

(*c*) the Counter-Reformation countries in the East and the South (the Habsburg territories, Spain and the Italian territories, France after 1685).

II. The *National Revolution* triggered off in territory after territory in the wake of the Napoleonic Wars produced very different sorts of cleavages in the three parts of western Europe:

(*a*) in the Protestant North the decisive cleavages tended to be territorial-cultural: the awakening peasantry and the defenders of ethnic peripheries allied themselves with outgroups within the urban elite and developed broad "Left" fronts against the established administrative and religious bureaucracy;

(*b*) in the broad "border belt" conflicts developed on two fronts: peripheral protest and Protestant dissent on the one side, movements for the defense of Catholic minorities on the other;

(*c*) in Counter-Reformation Europe a deep division between Radical-Liberal secularizers and Catholic defenders of the privileges of the church.

III. The *Industrial Revolution* added further dimensions to each national cleavage structure:

(*a*) in the Protestant North and in the Protestant regions of the "border belt" the growth of industrial production generated increasing tension between rural and urban interests, but this cleavage did not always find expression in the organization of distinct agrarian parties:

1. in economies dominated by large estates (England, Scotland, Prussia) the rural interests tended to be aggregated within broader Establishment fronts;

2. in countries and regions with larger proportions of smaller, family-sized farms distinct agrarian parties were more likely to emerge;

(*b*) in the Counter-Reformation countries the emerging Catholic mass parties found most of their support within the devout peasantry and were able to aggregate the agrarian interests without too much difficulty.

IV. The Industrial Revolution also generated in each country deepening cleavages between workers and salaried employees on the one hand, employers and owners on the other, but these cleavages did not always generate unified political movements: the leaders of the last stratum of the population to be given regular rights of political citizenship were torn between their commitment to the *historical nation* they were part of, and their commitment to the *international solidarity* of their class; this was an old-established line of cleavage in most working-class movements, but the dilemma became particularly acute when one country, the Soviet Union, made itself the champion of international working-class solidarity and generated splits within each national movement.

Of the five cleavage lines singled out in the model the first, what we have called the *center-periphery cleavage,* generates most diversity in the systems of party constellations. This is not at all surprising. With two or possibly three exceptions (Sweden and the Netherlands, Denmark a limiting case) our eleven smaller countries have all been marginal in the European structure, all highly dependent on the inflow of political, economic, and cultural resources from outside. Such situations of dependence tend to produce deep cleavages. With the spread of literacy, urbanization, and economic growth, the elites closest to the external center come under increasing pressures from nationalist-separatist counterelites. Depending on the geopolitical situation, such cleavages may generate elite factions or opposed mass parties, or lead on to a fight for territorial secession. A critical consideration in all such sequences of "nation-accentuating" politics is the extent of metropolitan settlement in the peripheral territory: had there been a history of colonization from the dominant center? how large, how strong, how concentrated was this settlement? how closely was its elite tied in with the fate of the metropolis?

Let us try out a classification of our cases in these terms and see whether we can detect any regularity in the resulting party divisions: Table 62–6 represents a first attempt in this direction.

The table excludes the oldest and the ethnically most homogeneous of our eleven smaller polities: Sweden, Denmark, the Netherlands, and Luxembourg. Of these, Sweden has been least afflicted by ethnic-territorial cleavages (the Danish territories to the south and the Norwegian ones to the west were incorporated well before mass literacy and therefore proved much less resistant to the national standardization process). Denmark has had a long history of border disputes with the Germans, and its politics was for decades dominated by this issue: it has not, however, produced any major party division (apart, of course, from the persistence until recently

Table 62–6 The Political Consequences of Liberation/Secession Struggles: Dimensions of Territorial Conflict in Seven Smaller European Nations

Status of Settlement	Dependence on Metropolis	Case	Situation	Expression in Party System
Total core area "Metropolitan": part of larger area of ethnic/cultural identity	Competitive metropolis, later dependent on larger unit	Austria	Dominant within old Empire, dependent after rise of Prussian *Reich* (defeat in 1866)	Pan-Germans *vs.* Catholics
Territorially concentrated settlement from metropolis	Highly dependent	Ireland	English/Scottish settlement in East, North	*Secession* of six Northern countries; party division over acceptance/rejection of secession: *Fine Gael* pro-Commonwealth solution, *Fianna Fáil* pro-total separation from metropolis
Same	Once dependent, later disrupted	Finland	Double front: Swedish settlement in Southwest; struggle for independence from Russia	*No secession* of Swedish areas (problem of Aland Islands). Separate Swedish party. Early Finnish party division over external strategy: Constitutionalists (Young Finns) *vs.* Compliants (Old Finns)
Weak concentration	Slow disruption of cultural ties	Norway	Danish cultural influence in East and in cities	Left-Right opposition over culture, language, religion
No territorial concentration	Distant, weak	Iceland	Diffuse Danish impact on bureaucracy, patriciate	Original division over speed of liberation soon overcome; new party structure after 1925
Cultural/ethnic division of national territory	Divided dependence: one major center outside, one minor	Belgium	French-speaking elite, Flemish-speaking subject population	No direct expression of territorial cleavage in party system before 1920's: Flemish separatists, *Volksunie*
Same	Divided dependence: two major centers outside	Switzerland	Major language groups: German, French	No direct expression of territorial cleavage in party system (except Jura area of Berne in 1950's–60's)

of the minor German party in Schleswig). The Netherlands solved its major ethnic-territorial problem through the secessions of Belgium and Luxembourg in 1831–1839: the remaining South-North opposition was contained within the church-state cleavage. Luxembourg, finally, requires no separate discussion in this context. Territorial-cultural conflicts never counted in this small border polity: it was caught between pressures from two major powers, but the issues of foreign policy were continuously kept out of party politics.

The other seven polities all had to face potentially disruptive conflicts over issues of ethnic-cultural dominance. Of these seven, the Swiss Confederation stands out as most successful in integrating so many historically distinct ethnicities and cultures. The contrast between Switzerland and Belgium has given rise to much speculation. The differences in geopolitical location and in religious structure stand out as immediately relevant: in Switzerland the two leading languages both enjoyed high international prestige; in Belgium the one was distinctly an elite language, the other not. In Switzerland the upper and the lower strata of each territory spoke the same language, but the linguistic cleavage was cross-cut by two powerful churches. In Belgium the established elite identified with the French language throughout the country, and the Flemish opposition expressed a class cleavage as much as a territorial-cultural cleavage: the Liberal associations and the Catholic hierarchy were for a long time able to maintain channels of communication between the two cultures, but could not prevent the foundation of regionalist-federalist parties after World War I.

It is indeed impossible to analyze the translation of territorial-cultural cleavages into party oppositions without considering the religious context of nation-building: the *church-state* cleavage. The prudent federalism of the Swiss can be understood only against the experiences of the war against the Catholic *Sonderbund:* the legitimation of the Catholic opposition and the later incorporation of Catholic representatives in the Federal Executive were an essential response to pressures of territorial fragmentation. By contrast to the Swiss *Sonderbund,* Belgium and the Catholic counties of Ireland did manage to secede from a dominant Protestant power. Why, then, such remarkable differences between the two party systems? In some ways the *Fianna Fail* opposition in Ireland corresponded to the Flemish movement against the predominance of French culture: as Rumpf has shown through his historical cartography, the early strength of the Anti-Treaty Republicans increased along a Northeast-Southwest gradient, while the Pro-Treaty Conservatives were stronger in the English Pale and the old "Land of Peace" counties.[41] What distinguishes the Irish from the Belgian, and, for that matter, all the other Catholic cases in Europe, is the absence of any party-political expression of a church-state opposition.

It is easy to say that the Irish Catholic Church did not need any party to defend it: the state-builders and the church were natural allies, and the secession of the Northern counties had made the territorial population nearly completely Catholic. But this does not explain the absence of a strong secular-religious cleavage of the type that generated party divisions in all the other Catholic countries. Two factors seem important here: first, the very low level of urbanization in Ireland; second, the very close ties between the church and the peasantry and the absence of any opposition over church lands. As the historian J. G. A. Pocock has put it:

> Being a hierarchical and bureaucratic organization more or less coterminous with the geographic nation, [the Church] exerted a structurally unifying influence, and historical circumstances ensured that it was identical neither with the legal sovereign (the Crown of England) nor with the governing . . . aristocracy (the Anglo-Irish settlers). An accidental but very important benefit of English rule to Ireland was that the Church never became a major landowner; and in this and other ways it differed from the Counter-Reformation norm. Growing up in the very adverse circumstances of the 17th and 18th centuries . . . it emerged as a bureaucratic and popular structure nowhere organically linked with a ruling aristocracy.[42]

In these terms the Irish deviation does not confirm the prediction of the model, but simply helps to specify the conditions for the emergence of a significant church-state conflict and the articulation of church interests in an explicit party front. Irish politics remained at the level of territorial-cultural polarization typical of the Protestant secession state: there are remarkable parallels between the early party divisions for and against the Treaty of 1922 and the split in Norway over the acceptance of the cultural dominance of the East,[43] and there is an equally intriguing similarity with the conflict in Finland over liberation strategies in the double front between the Swedish settlement and the Russian political supremacy.[44] The East-West gradient brought out for Ireland by Rumpf has its counterpart in the contrast between Eastern center and South/Western counterculture in Norway and in the clear-cut demarcation in Finland between the conservative Finnish nationalism of the West and the radical democratic independence movement of the East.

None of these cleavages can be analyzed in isolation: what counts is the distinctive system of interdependence generated in each country. The center-periphery and the state-church cleavages feed into the cleavages produced by the *Industrial Revolution*. The Catholic political movements have throughout continental Europe proved able to cross-cut the cleavages between rural and urban economic interests generated by the Industrial Revolution: distinctly Agrarian parties have rarely if ever emerged in countries or regions with strong Catholic parties. The Agrarian parties in the Austrian First Republic (the *Landbund*), in Switzerland, and in the Netherlands have had very little success beyond the Protestant or secularized regions. Ireland is a very interesting case just from this point of view: in the only Catholic country *without* a distinctive Catholic party sizable groups of farmers *have* found it to their advantage to put up their own candidates and organize for separate political action (the Farmers' party won fifteen seats in 1923, eleven in 1927, but disappeared and was followed by a Center party and the *Clann na Talmhan* which won fourteen seats in 1943, eleven in 1944, but petered out by 1961).

In the Protestant countries the likelihood of the emergence of distinctive Agrarian parties was essentially a function of the concentration of agricultural wealth and the size of the agricultural labor force: the larger the estates, the greater the incentive to develop urban-rural alliances; the greater the number of family-sized but market-oriented farms, the greater the pressures for organized action against the urban-industrial interests. This goes far to explain the contrasts between the five Scandinavian countries on the one hand and the British-Prussian cases on the other.[45]

The Industrial Revolution produced very different results in the other sectors of the economy: while the conflicts generated in the *commodity* market resulted in wide divergencies of party development across the European countries, the conflicts triggered off in the *labor* market proved much more uniformly party forming. All countries of western Europe developed lower-class mass parties at some point or other before World War I. The decisive *contrasts* among the Western party systems clearly reflect differences in *the territorial histories of state formation, nation-building, and land tenure systems;* the worker-owner cleavage generated through the process of industrialization tended to bring the party systems *closer to each other.*

This, of course, says nothing about the *character* of these working-class movements: the Industrial Revolution produced lower-class parties of one sort or another throughout the West, but these differed conspicuously in strength, in organizational unity, in ideological orientation, and in the extent of their integration into, or alienation from, each historically given polity. These variations were clearly conditioned by the earlier histories of state formation and national, cultural, and economic integration in each country: the decisive contrasts among the systems had emerged before the entry of the rural and the urban proletariats into the political arena, and the character of the emerging mass parties for lower-class protest was heavily influenced by the constellations of ideologies, organizations, and alliances they had to confront in that arena.

To aid in the mapping of these variations in the character of working-class politics our model posits a fourth "critical juncture," an *International Revolution*. The conflict between proletarian internationalism and "nation-accepting" socialism emerged early in the history of the working-class movement. The dramatic events of World War I and the Russian Revolution deepened the split in the movement and produced not only militant factions but distinct and competing working-class parties. The final row of dichotomies in Table 62–4 simply sorts party systems by the strength of these split-off movements in the 1920's or later. Empirically the pattern of variations is clear enough, but the theoretical derivation of the predictions is still much in doubt.

In the Protestant and the Mixed countries the differentiating criterion appears to be the *recency of the nation-building process:* the less settled the issues of national identity and the deeper the ongoing conflict over cultural standardization, the greater the chances of radicalization and fragmentation in the working class.

In the Catholic countries a similar process seems to have been at work but in different terms: the deeper and more persistent the church-state conflicts, the greater the fragmentation of the working class: the closer the historical ties between the ecclesiastical hierarchy and the secular "nation-builders," the less the chances of left-wing split-offs.

The Empirical Testing of the Model

Space will not allow me to pursue in further detail this review of parallels and contrasts in nation-building sequences, cleavage structures, and party systems in western Europe. I hope that I have gone far enough in my presentation of the model to give

Table 62–7

	Unified "Domesticable" Labour Movements		Deep Splits in Labour Movements (strong CP wings)	
	Early consolidation		*Late independence, unification*	
	Smaller	*Larger*	*Smaller*	*Larger*
Protestant countries	Denmark Sweden	Britain	Norway (1920's) Finland Iceland	
Mixed countries	Netherlands Switzerland			Reich
	Initial Church-State Alliance		*Marked State-Church Cleavage*	
Catholic countries	Austria Belgium Luxembourg Ireland			France Italy Spain

an impression of the rich opportunities for detailed developmental comparisons across these countries. My work with the eleven cases has made me more and more convinced that further efforts of formalization and testing of models of the type I have sketched may not only help us build better theories of comparative political development at the *macro-level* but also prove directly useful in our continued efforts to make sense of the similarities and the differences found in comparative analyses at the *micro-level*.

In fact, the model I have suggested seeks to specify invariances at four different levels: at the level of critical options for each territorial system as a whole—the four "Revolutions"; at the level of solidarities and conflicts within the territorial population—the five "cleavage lines"; at the level of the system of electoral alternatives presented by organized parties; and finally and not least important, at the level of *the individual citizen and his behavior* within the limits set by the past and the present configurations of his polity.

I believe we shall find in the future testing of models of this type that the hypotheses generated at the higher levels will have very direct consequences for our priorities in developmental analysis of statistics at the microlevel (this would include analysis of recall data from surveys as well as the typical ecological analyses of time series by locality): the five cleavage lines differentiated in Tables 62–4 and 62–5 constitute as many top-priority variables in the development study of partisan strength in our European countries.

To get closer to an understanding of the processes at work in the translation of sociocultural cleavages into party systems, we shall have to start out with multivariate analyses of the weight of our five core variables in the determination of the strength of each party:

1. We need to know how heavily *territorial, ethnic,* or *linguistic* divisions counted in the production of given distributions of votes.

2. We need to know how strongly the distributions were influenced by variations in *church membership* and in *religious activity*.

3. We need information about the differences by *rates and levels of urbanization* and by the character of the *primary economy* (land tenure systems, strength of forestry, fisheries sectors).

4. We need more details about the variations, from locality to locality and from period to period, in the *class basis* of the vote.

5. We shall have to pin down in the same detail the factors making for *splits within the working-class vote,* particularly in the early 1920's and during the period of peak CP strength after World War II.

Work along these lines is far advanced in some countries and has hardly begun in others. We can safely predict that a great deal of further effort will be made in this direction during the next few years. A major accelerating factor will be the development in country after country of *data archives* for computer processing of early election and census records.[46] There is every reason for us to push ahead with such work, but it is very important that we do this in the broader perspective of comparative development, of comparative nation-building. We clearly shall not be assembling such sets of analyses just to test hypotheses about individual behavior. We shall also do so to establish important benchmark data for a typology of the macrocontexts of political behavior: in fact, any such analysis of the weight of the core variables in the production of votes for each party will help us to characterize the differences among the historically given "packages" still facing these different national citizenries. Our "ultrageneralist" friends will say that this is outright surrender to abject "configurationism": my reply is that we have to live with comparisons of unique configurations, but can still make headway in comparative electoral research by resolutely tackling the task of identifying the critical dimensions of variation across the historically given systems of political interaction.

NOTES

1. These are probably the most complete bibliographical listings: Koppel S. Pinson, *A Bibliographical Introduction to Nationalism* (New York: Columbia University Press, 1935); Karl W. Deutsch, *An Interdisciplinary Bibliography on Nationalism, 1935–1953* (Cambridge: M.I.T. Press, 1956); Karl W. Deutsch and R. L. Merritt, *Nationalism: An Interdisciplinary Bibliography, 1935–1956* (Cambridge: M.I.T. Press, 1968). For a useful review of major writings from 1953 through 1965 see K. W. Deutsch, *Nationalism and Social Communication*, 2nd ed. (Cambridge: M.I.T. Press, 1966), pp. 1–14.

2. The initial formulations appeared in G. A. Almond and James S. Coleman, eds., *The Politics of the Developing Areas* (Princeton: Princeton University Press, 1960). The Committee on Comparative Politics has so far published six volumes in the series *Studies in Political Development* (all with Princeton University Press): L. W. Pye, ed., *Communications and Political Development*, 1963; J. LaPalombara, ed., *Bureaucracy and Political Development*, 1963; R. E. Ward and D. A. Rustow, eds., *Political Modernization in Japan and Turkey*, 1964; J. Coleman, ed., *Education and Political Development*, 1965; L. W. Pye and S. Verba, eds., *Political Culture and Political Development*, 1965; J. La-Palombara and M. Weiner, eds., *Political Parties and Political Development*, 1966.

3. Cf. especially J. LaPalombara, "Parsimony and Empiricism in Comparative Politics: An Anti-Scholastic View," in R. Holt, ed., *Essays on Comparative Methods*, in press, 1968.

4. Several of the publications flowing from the Committee or its individual members evidence interest in the theoretical implications of the variations in Europe and the West; see especially G. Almond and S. Verba, *The Civic Culture* (Princeton: Princeton University Press, 1963), and G. Almond and G. B. Powell, Jr., *Comparative Politics: A Developmental Approach* (Boston: Little, Brown, 1966).

5. R. Bendix, *Nation-Building and Citizenship* (New York: Wiley, 1964).

6. R. Holt and J. Turner, *The Political Basis of Economic Development* (Princeton: Van Nostrand, 1966).

7. Barringtone Moore, Jr., *Social Origins of Dictatorship and Democracy: Lord and Peasant in the Making of the Modern World* (Boston: Beacon, 1966).

8. S. M. Lipset, *The First New Nation* (New York: Basic Books, 1963).

9. Samuel P. Huntington, "Political Development and Political Decay," *World Politics*, XVII, No. 3 (April 1965), 386–430; "Political Modernization: America *vs.* Europe," *ibid.*, XVIII, No. 3 (April 1966), 378–414.

10. K. W. Deutsch and H. Weilenmann, "The Swiss City Canton: A Political Invention," *Comparative Studies in Society and History*, VII, No. 4 (July 1965), 393–408, and *United for Diversity: The Political Integration of Switzerland*, 1969.

11. B. Russett et al., *World Handbook of Political and Social Indicators* (New Haven: Yale University Press, 1964); cf. the further discussion in R. L. Merritt and S. Rokkan, eds., *Comparing Nations* (New Haven: Yale University Press, 1966).

12. Cf. a typical remark by Moore, *op. cit.*, pp. xii–xiii: "This study concentrates on certain important stages in a prolonged social process which has worked itself out in several countries. As a part of this process new social arrangements have grown up by violence or in other ways which have made certain countries political leaders at different points in time during the first half of the twentieth century. The focus of interest is on innovation that has led to political power, not only the spread and reception of institutions that have been hammered out elsewhere, except where they have led to significant power in world politics. *The fact that the smaller countries depend economically and politically on big and powerful ones means that the decisive causes of their politics lie outside their own boundaries. It also means that their political problems are not really comparable to those of larger countries. Therefore a general statement about the historical preconditions of democracy or authoritarianism covering smaller countries as well as large would very likely be so broad as to be abstractly platitudinous*" (our italics). Clearly, there are as good intellectual reasons for studying diffusion and reception as for analyzing conflict and innovation in major centers: after all, most of the units open to comparative research are "follower" nations rather than leaders. But this surely is not always and exclusively a matter of size: Greece and Israel produced the greatest innovations of the ancient world, and Sweden, the Netherlands, and Switzerland can hardly be fruitfully studied as passive victims of exogenous pressures.

13. For discussions of the "whole nation" bias in the draft version of the Russett *et al.* World Handbook see Part III of Merritt and Bokkan, eds., *Comparing Nations, op. cit.* Also B. J. L. Berry, "By What Categories May a State Be Characterized?" *Economic Development and Cultural Change*, XV, No. 1 (October 1966), 91–94.

14. This "hierarchization" of the Parsonian A–G–I–L scheme of functional differentiation was first presented in the Introduction to S. M. Lipset and S. Rokkan, eds., *Party Systems and Voter Alignments* (New York: The Free Press, 1967). For a further utilization of this imagery in the study of the *inter*national system see P. J. Nettl and R. Robertson, *International Systems and the Modernization of Societies* (London: Faber, 1968), pp. 162–168.

15. Deutsch, *Nationalism*, 2nd ed., pp. 101–104.

16. See the definitions *ibid.*, Ch. 6. For a further elaboration of the concept of mobilization see Karl Deutsch, "Social Mobilization and Political Development," *American Political Science Review*, LV, No. 3 (September 1961), 493–514. A similar listing of variables is discussed in S. Rokkan, "Electoral Mobilization, Party Competition and National Integration," in LaPalombara and Weiner, *op. cit.*

17. *Nationalism*, 2nd ed., Appendix V.

18. R. Dahrendorf, *Gesellschaft und Demokratie in Deutschland* (Munich: Piper, 1965); cf. the parallel analysis of central political institutions in K. D. Bracher, "Staatsbegriff und Demokratie in Deutschland," *Pol. Vierteljahresschrift*, IX, No. 1 (1968), 2–27.

19. J. H. Clapham, *The Economic Development of France and Germany* (Cambridge: Cambridge University Press, 1921).

20. H. J. Habakkuk, *American and British Technology in the 19th Century* (Cambridge: Cambridge University Press, 1962).

21. Ch. P. Kindleberger, *Economic Growth in France and Britain, 1851–1950* (Cambridge: Harvard University Press, 1964).

22. Ward and Rustow, *op. cit.*

23. Bendix, *op. cit.*

24. Holt and Turner, *op. cit.*

25. Huntington, "Political Modernization," *op. cit.*, p. 378.

26. *Ibid.*, pp. 401–408.

27. J. P. Nettl, "The State as a Conceptual Variable," *World Politics*, XX, No. 4 (1968), 559–592.

28. *Ibid.*, pp. 565–566; Nettl's italics.

29. *Ibid.*, p. 560; our italics.

30. Moore, *op. cit.*

31. *Ibid.*, p. xiii.

32. S. M. Lipset and S. Rokkan, "Cleavage Structures, Party Systems and Voter Alignments: An Introduction," in Lipset and Rokkan, *op. cit.*, pp. 1–64.

33. On this project see V. R. Lorwin, "Historians and Other Social Scientists: The Comparative Study of Nation-Building in Western Societies," in S. Rokkan, ed., *Comparative Research across Cultures and Nations* (Paris: Mouton, 1968). A first report on an attempt at a systematization of data on electoral arrangements and party systems in these eleven countries (the five Nordic countries, the three BE–NE–LUX ones, Ireland, Switzerland, and Austria) will be found in S. Rokkan, "The Structuring of Mass Politics in the Smaller European Democracies," *Comparative Studies in Society and History*, X, No. 2 (1968), 173–210.

34. Lipset and Rokkan, *op. cit.*, pp. 44–46.

35. Cf. the discussion of the conditions for the breakdown of European multiparty systems in Lipset and Rokkan, *op. cit.*, pp. 50–56.

36. A. Banks and R. Textor, *A Cross-Polity Survey* (Cambridge: M.I.T. Press, 1963).

37. See the volumes listed in footnote 2 and especially Lucian Pye, *Aspects of Political Development* (Boston: Little, Brown, 1965), and "Political Systems and Political Development," in Rokkan, ed., *Comparative Research across Cultures and Nations, op. cit.*, pp. 93–101.

38. Cf. O. Cornblit, T. DiTella and E. Gallo, "A Model for Political Change in Latin America," *Social Science Information*, VII, No. 2 (1968), 13–48.

39. See Rokkan, "The Structuring," *op. cit.*, pp. 180–197.

40. For a full statement of the assumptions and an initial discussion of the fit for the larger polities, see Lipset and Rokkan, "Cleavage Structure," *op. cit.*, pp. 36–50.

41. E. Rumpf, *Nationalismus und Sozialismus, op. cit.*, Ch. 2.

42. J. G. A. Pocock, "The Case of Ireland Truly Stated: Revolutionary Politics in a Context of Increasing Stabilization," Paper, Department of History, Washington University, St. Louis, 1966.

43. See S. Rokkan, "Geography, Religion and Social Class: Cross-Cutting Cleavages in Norway," in Lipset and Rokkan, *Party Systems, op. cit.*

44. See especially E. Jutikkala, "Political Parties in the Elections of Deputies to the Estate of Burgesses and the Estate of Farmers," *Sitzungsber. der finn. Akad. Wiss.* (1960), pp. 167–184, particularly at p. 175 ("one of the most striking examples of a geographical division of public opinion in any European country in modern time"); also O. Rantala, "The Political Regions of Finland," *Scandinavian Political Studies*, II (1967), 117–140. Erik Allardt has based a number of his ecological factor analyses on the regional demarcation originally established on the basis of the votes for Old Finns vs. Young Finns.

45. For further details see Lipset and Rokkan, "Cleavage Structures," *op. cit.*, pp. 44–46. Barrington Moore, Jr., focuses his theory of the conditions for the emergence of stable representative democracy on the alternative options for land-industry-state alliances; see Moore, *op. cit.*, especially Ch. 7.

46. See Rokkan, "Electoral Mobilization," *op. cit.*, and S. Rokkan, ed., *Data Archives for the Social Sciences* (Paris and The Hague: Mouton, 1966).

63

Values and Social Change in Modern Japan

Robert N. Bellah

To me the real heroes of this early Meiji period, the real beginning of the whole modernization of Japan and of real democracy, are those who questioned the basic value system of Edo society and who sought to reform the fabric of social relations inherited from that society. In this context I would be inclined to value the enlightenment thinkers, *Keimō Shisōka*, quite highly and probably consider them more highly than any thinkers of the *Jiyū-Minken Undō*. Also I would include the Christians

who, as you know, played such an important role in many aspects of life in the Meiji period in questioning the old assumptions and in working for reforms at all kinds of levels. I would include in my list of heroes Ueki in his role of reformer of society, more than in his role of political ideologist of the *Jiyū-Minken Undō* and I especially think that Fukuzawa Yukichi is worthy of very serious attention. He is guilty of an explicit utilitarianism with respect to "Fukoku kyōhei," and yet I feel that his position goes much deeper than any such surface expression, that he was expressing a really revolutionary way of thinking about human relations basically in a non-political way, that he is not to be evaluated primarily as a political thinker but in terms of his role as a

From Robert N. Bellah, "Values and Social Change in Modern Japan," in Kiyoko Cho, ed., *Asian Cultural Studies* (Mitaka Tokyo: International Christian University, 1962), pp. 52–56. Reprinted by permission of the publisher and the author.

representative of a whole new way of thinking about action in society. Certainly we find that when very many of the leaders of the *Jiyū-Minken Undō* had become imperialist, a band of committed Christians and others devoted to some principle transcending society, remained loyal to democratic ideas. Christians too were among those who defected to imperialism in this period of the last years of the century. But, Uchimura Kanzō and Kinoshita Naoe, though they were somewhat maverick Christians, were nevertheless, I think, representatives of a real sea change in Japanese history and these are the kind of people that I would tend to evaluate most highly in this early period. I evaluate them so highly because I think they are the people who explicitly or implicitly stood for the dimension of transcendence, questioned the assumptions of the traditional value system, and worked, through many different kinds of movements, movements for women's equality, for a democratic family, for the reform of morals, and so on, to realize a new way of phrasing human relations. These people did not deify a new social structure, the people as such, or any class or party in place of the old deified social structure characteristic of traditional Japanese society, and I think it is from these people that the seeds of a healthier, more really modern, in the sense I use the term, value system, "kachi taikei," came.

However, in the middle of Meiji it is clear that the seeds were very few and the sprouts were yet very young and weak. In one sense, Japanese society was becoming modernized, that is, in its economy and many other more immediately tangible ways, very rapidly. Society was becoming penetrated by compulsory education, literacy, mass communication, and so on. At the same time, the developing economy was disrupting traditional forms and leading to a questioning of traditional values. All this was happening, especially in the decade of the 1890s, in the great industrial revolution in Japan, but at the same time a really meaningful modern value system had not been fully developed and even in so far as it was developed it yet had little meaning to the great majority of the Japanese people. I think we have to remember what a relatively small group the enlightenment thinkers were compared to the vast mass of the people who were still in the villages or, if they were in the cities, were still encased almost entirely in village mentality. So we have a situation in which the people, though increasingly separated from traditional structure of family and village, and undergoing changes in consonance with the modern economy, nevertheless were not really ready for a modern value system.

I think it is in this framework that we have to explain the rise of the Emperor system (*Tennō sei*) and the nationalism of the Meiji twenties and thirties.

I think we must ask the question, if the emperor was not to be the basis of the new constitution, that is the source of ultimate sovereignty, then what was? I think if one honestly thinks what the alternatives were in terms of the real situation of Japan, alternatives that would have any hope of meaning to the mass of the people, one will see that they were not very numerous. The society was, in fact, committed to the traditional value system. That traditional value system could without great difficulty be put into forms of mass culture in terms of the Emperor system. This new ideology served the dual function of integrating Japanese society which had been shaken by the industrial revolution and unifying Japan against external danger which was still great at the end of the 19th century and unfortunately also of unifying Japan for external expansion. It was, I think, basically unmodern and anti-democratic in spirit but it left room for a certain degree of healthy development. I do not think it was the same thing as fascism. Many diverse modes of thought continued, especially in areas not directly associated with politics, and contributions to Japan's modern thought continued to be made by such people as Natsume Sōseki, Nishida Kitarō, and so on. Of course, the Meiji solution was not ideal, but it is difficult to imagine that a much more radical solution would have worked. The Emperor system had the virtue of maintaining social solidarity while modernization proceeded more or less rapidly in various areas.

Under the aegis of a basically unmodern value system, modernization yet continued. The balance, I think, was very delicate and easily influenced by outside forces. During the first World War, with extremely favorable economic conditions from outside as well as the political alignment with western democracy, the circumstances were favorable and shifted the balance in the direction of democratic development in Japan. In the late twenties the world situation, economically and politically, became very unfavorable and the balance was tipped strongly the other way. I do not believe that the outcome was inevitable from the point of view of Japanese development alone. That is, I do not think that the Meiji Emperor system made fascism inevitable in the thirties and early forties. I certainly think it raised few barriers against that development. Because it was not a democratic system it left the ground open, given certain kinds of circumstances for that outcome, but it is at least conceivable that had general world circumstances been different, healthy developments out of Taishō democracy could have been achieved without the tragic events of the thirties.

The Meiji thirties and forties saw the emergence of something new on the scene, namely the socialist movement, and this becomes the second great positive force for present day Japanese intellectuals. But just as I cannot see in the Emperor system (*Tennō sei*) an absolutely negative picture, so I am not convinced that there is a ground for evaluating the socialist movement in absolutely positive terms, although I certainly sympathize much more closely with the values and ideals of that movement than with those of the conservative government. Though many important programs were proposed by the socialists and many contributions made to the development of democracy in Japan, here again I have a basic doubt which is essentially the same as in the case of Ueki. For example, I cannot but feel that Kōtoku Shūsui's position was potentially as dangerous as that of the government which killed him. An unbroken commitment to the political process such as he had, no matter how progressive the aim, always contains the seeds of demonic fanaticism. I believe that a really democratic, in the present sense, modern value system must have a transcendental reference in terms of which the political process itself can be judged. Lacking that, and we have a number of examples in this century, the progressive socialist movement can become the mirror image of its enemy. This is the basis of my schematism comparing Buddhism and Confucianism with Christianity and socialism. The transcendent, critical, religious element in the kind of Buddhism that Shinran was speaking for, relative to the affirmation of the social system in Confucianism, is somewhat comparable to the transcendent reference of Christianity relative to the socialist belief which makes the social system absolute. Of course, this comparison was far from exact because there were Christian socialists and actually, of course, the early Japanese socialists were mainly Christians. And there are principled socialists who do not make an absolute commitment to a party or a class. Nevertheless, I think Kōtoku and others are examples which indicate that a danger to Japanese democracy existed and still exists from the fanatical left, as well as from the conservative right.

In conclusion, this analysis has certain implications for the present. I think they are rather obvious, but let me just mention two in particular.

I think in the present situation, granted that one is committed to modernization, there are two areas above all which need attention. First of all, I think the cultural area, especially the problem of values. The reconstruction of the Japanese value system is of course a long, slow process, which has been going on since early Meiji and is still going on. I do not think it can be accomplished without some sort of healthy union of elements from the traditional Japanese past and the western tradition. Here, I want to stress that very deep study needs to be made of both sides. Japan today cannot be considered an Asiatic or East Asian culture. Deep now, after a hundred years, deep in Japanese culture are ideas, values, ways of handling human relations which ultimately, historically go back to the western traditions, to Greece and to Israel. In many ways the lines that separate people living in America from those distant lands in the Eastern Mediterranean are also rather tenuous. Japan now participates in the tradition of western culture and since it does it must, as we must in America or in Europe, constantly reevaluate those sources, become aware of the meaning of those traditions in which we now all participate.

And, also of course deep study is to be made of the East Asian tradition, just as we in America need to study that tradition. I think the kind of activity that Kiyo Takeda Cho is undertaking here is part of this enterprise. In particular the Japanese tradition must be studied in order to discover those elements in it which can provide fruitful soil for the development of democratic institutions in Japan. In somewhat different ways men like Ienaga Saburo and Kōsaka Masaaki are engaged in this task.

The second area is that of the structural reform of Japanese society, but in a somewhat different sense from that of Mr. Eda. I think the effort to make democratic the various groups which actually exist, the family, various kinds of work groups, and so on, is a very primary task, which the intellectuals have to engage in right at home, in a literal sense, and also in the university where they work, where so-called feudal attitudes in human relations remain very strong. This problem is not, of course, limited to the intellectuals but the labor unions and the socialist party itself are in need of a good deal of structural reform. The effort to develop voluntary organizations to meet the needs of everyday life, I think, needs to be pressed very much more than it has been, and is an important obligation of all democratic and progressive people. Tenant councils, neighborhood councils, organizations to meet the thousand and one needs of everyday life, which are constantly bearing down on people in this country and about which people complain so much, are needed because through organizations and through democratic forms of voluntary association those thousand and one problems can begin to be handled. I believe that politicization in the sense of concern with the national political struggle in Japan is partly a danger. An exclusive concentration on national and international issues can hinder the development of a local structure of democratic, voluntary organizations. The real framework of a modern, democratic society is a complex, imbricate structure of voluntary associations and here I think much needs to be done. If the real structural reform at this level were achieved then Diet politics would almost automatically take a healthier form. Here I want to stress again that I think there is a danger in the polarized image of the absolutely good and absolutely bad forces in Japan today. The enemy is at home and within as well as in the "reactionary forces" and this is, of course, as true in America as it is in Japan. There is no democratic society which does not need constantly to be remaking and reforming itself.

And finally I want to suggest two means towards these ends. First of all, social theory. Analytical theory is important because the use of such theory is one of the best means for avoiding the possible danger of mistakes from ideological distortion. Here again much is being done in Japan that is very exciting.

And secondly, I think the essence of modernization from the personal point of view is courage. The courage to oppose the government in mass demonstrations is important, but I think more important and the hardest of all is the courage to stand utterly alone if need be. In this sense, Uchimura Kanzo is the real symbol of what is needed, even though I differ from him on both theological and political grounds. That kind of courage always has a transcendental reference; it can make its affirmation only through what Ienaga calls the logic of denial and not because it attributes ultimate righteousness to any group or system.

b. ELITE FORMATION IN MODERN STATES

64

Social Structure and the Ruling Class[1]

Raymond Aron

The object of these articles is to try to combine in a synthesis the sociology which is based on Marxist ideas and that which derives from Pareto and, from that starting point, to outline a few general ideas on the evolution of modern societies.

Why, it may be asked, should I choose Marx and Pareto, whose works were, in one case, written nearly a century, and in the other, several decades ago? Does recent literature offer nothing more scien-

tific? I have no doubt that more accurate empirical studies could be found than those scattered through Marx's books or concentrated in the *General Treatise on Sociology*, but I do not think that any theory has been elaborated which can take the place of either of those doctrines.

For a Marxist, the determining factor is the opposition between the owners of the means of production and workers who hire out their labour. The "alienation" of the workers is the origin of all social ills, the opposition between the classes the root of all human conflicts. History is a dialectical process by which, from contradiction to contradiction, we

From Raymond Aron, "Social Structure and the Ruling Class," *British Journal of Sociology*, I, No. 1 (March 1950), 1–2, 5–11, and I, No. 2 (June 1950), 141–143. Reprinted by permission of the author.

are brought to a classless society and a self-reconciled humanity.

For Pareto and his followers, on the other hand, the exercise of power by a minority is a constant factor in any social order. The constitution and character of governing minorities, or, to use the usual term, the "élites," change; the privileged are replaced by others. But there is always a minority, holding the key-posts in society, which appropriates to itself a more or less disproportionate share of the national income.

These two views of historical philosophy—on the one hand a dialectical process tending towards a classless society and, on the other, a permanent division between the masses and the élite—are reflected in the two most influential political ideologies of our time, Communism and Fascism. The Marxists justify the revolutionary desires of the proletariat by the need to put a stop to the alienation of labour by overcoming class struggles. The followers of Pareto have often justified the revolutionary spirit of a non-proletarian party by the need to replace weak, degenerate, democratic élites by strong and ruthless élites. On the one hand, there is revolution to eradicate the class system; on the other, revolution to restore to communities that strength and prosperity which are always dependent on the virtue, in the Machiavellian sense, of the few who rule the multitude.

Our study will, therefore, be concentrated on that delicate point where the analytical method touches political ideology. The problem of combining in a synthesis "class" sociology and "élite" sociology is a scientific one. It can be reduced to the following question: "What is the relation between social differentiation and political hierarchy in modern societies?" We shall find the answer by considering the facts, i.e. by comparing the various types of society. The consideration of the facts, however, does not by itself lead to a political ideology. Whether policy should work towards the elimination of classes or towards replacing the élite, will depend on one's estimate of values and of the future course of history. All that scientific analysis can give us is a criticism of political ideologies in so far as they pervert or distort reality. The refusal of the Marxists to take into account the political hierarchy which existed before, and survives, the division of society into classes is an attempt to mystify, and is disclosed as such by sociological analysis. The refusal of the Fascists to take into account social differentiation is a similar or contrasting attempt to mystify, and is also so discovered by scientific analysis. When the true nature of the

ideologies have thus been disclosed, however, there is still ground for the two conflicting revolutionary desires. Sociology shows men what they truly desire and what will be the probable results of their actions; it never indicates to them what they ought to desire. . . .

The analysis of the structure of a society aims at distinguishing its various groups. Such an analysis is infinitely more complex and more subtle than that which is generally made by merely applying a scheme drawn from some philosophy of history. Indeed, the distinction between these groups can be made on many different criteria, which do not give the same results.

This is what I mean. A group may be characterized by a particular standard of life, a particular type of life, the nature of its professional activities, its legal status or by the degree of unity recognized in it by society or of which it is conscious.

Let us take as our starting point the standard of life. Individuals enjoying a similar standard of life are not by any means uniform in the way they live or in their mental outlook. A clerk does not necessarily earn more than a skilled workman; a "stiff-collared" proletarian, as the Germans say, does not consider himself a member of the same group as the horny-handed working man. Comparative surveys of family budgets have shown that the clerk does not spend his income in the same way and that he allows more for housing and keeping up his position and less for food. There is a still greater difference in psychology and the outlook on life when the town worker is compared with the country worker or the skilled worker with the smallholder, even when their real incomes are the same.

We may also consider professional activities or occupations. The differences within the industrial proletariat have been increased by technical developments. In 1940, out of 51,000,000 persons actively employed in the United States, there were less than 9,000,000 unskilled workers, i.e. workers without any real professional training, including 3,530,000 agricultural workers, 1,193,000 of whom were members of the farmers' own families. The proportion of absolute proletarians was therefore down to 18 per cent in 1940, whereas in 1910 it had been over 25 per cent.

What is even more important is the division of the workers between the various sectors of economic activity. Colin Clark, in his book on the *Conditions of Economic Progress,* has taught us to distinguish between three basic sectors: that of primary activities (agricultural production and raw materials); that of secondary activities (the manufacture of goods); and that of tertiary activities (the public services, commerce and administration). We know that in modern industrial societies there is an initial phase in which the secondary activities expand at the expense of the primary activities; then in their turn the tertiary activities develop at the expense of the secondary. In the United States at the present day more than half the working population is employed in tertiary activities and about 35 per cent in secondary activities. In other words, the Marxist type of industrial worker will not represent the bulk of society for the future but a decreasing fraction of the population.

No doubt we might pursue the analysis of professional differentiation. In the tertiary group of activities there are some manual workers, in the secondary group some clerical workers. The tendency is, however, very clear. We are moving towards a civilization made up of clerical workers rather than towards a civilization of manual workers. Planning, organization, administration and distribution are becoming increasingly complicated and absorbing an increasing number of men. We are living in the administrative age no less than in the machine age.

It is evident that this distinction between the three sectors cannot claim to correspond to the dividing lines between the conscious social groups. The psychological boundaries, which are in any case indeterminate, are based in essence on three types of influence: horizontal economic community of interests, i.e. interests of agriculture in opposition to industry, or of grain producers in opposition to producers of dairy products, or of industries working for the internal market in opposition to export industries; the social status of an occupation according to public opinion or in the eyes of the persons involved (in European societies there is still a prejudice against manual work, and the son of a middle-class or lower middle-class family feels that he loses less prestige if he finds a post as a clerk than if he has to work with his hands, even when he earns the same amount); and lastly a person's legal status as a wage-earner or independent worker. The opposition of certain liberal professions, such as the medical profession, to schemes for a National Service, is partly due to the loss of prestige which they consider would be involved in giving up their independent position to become salaried officials.

We could easily continue such analyses, which are only intended to illustrate what I call the law of social differentiation and to support the following proposition: if it is the standard or type of life, the nature of the profession, the legal status or collective psychological outlook which is considered, the social groups will be defined differently in each case. The structure of contemporary society is characterized, firstly, by the elimination of the barriers between the "Orders," founded on birth or the traditional hierarchy and, secondly, by the numerous distinctions maintained by differences between professions and standards of life, and in prestige.

This elementary analysis marks the first stage of a sociological study. Should we stop there and be content with merely listing the groups? Certainly not. After the microscopic examination comes what we might call the macroscopic examination, that is, an endeavour to find new embracing wholes. Which groups have a common destiny? Which groups are conscious of that community? The communities which exist are discovered by economic analysis and the consciousness of community is discovered by sociological and political analysis.

It is easy to show that such a community and consciousness of community do not necessarily coincide. When the market mechanism is unhampered, the workers' remuneration varies with the prosperity of the branch of industry in which they are employed. A community of practical interests frequently links together the employers and employees of one branch of industry rather than the employees in competing branches. Similarly, it is to the advantage of skilled workers that there should be increasing differentiation of wages and consequently that independent trade unions should be set up to protect the higher wage scales. The idea of working-class solidarity, however, generally transcends conflicts between divergent interests.

It is usual to divide society into three wholes: the industrial workers or wage-earners, the middle class, and the bourgeoisie or upper class. This division might be used politically, but has little scientific value, because none of these so-called classes possesses a real unity. The middle class consists of those who receive salaries rather than wages, but this distinction is more one of psychology than of economics. At the same time the middle class includes men from professional occupations (what we call *les professions libérales*) like physicians, who are (or were), in an economic sense, independent; and it also contains small industrialists or shopkeepers, who belong to the category of the owners of means of production. It would perhaps not be impossible to observe a few tendencies which seem common to all the intermediary groups: medium income, liking for independence, in some cases leaning towards intellectual tastes. But it is not enough to bring about economic solidarity. In the same way, the upper class possesses neither a unity of interests nor of ideology.

It is not a criticism of Marxism to say that the community of interest of wage-earners is often a fiction, for Marxism defines the common interests of wage-earners or proletarians less as existing within the present organizations, than in opposition to it. Their common interest, or rather their historical mission, it to destroy the wage system. Once more the proletariat as such comes into existence only when it refuses to accept its position. Class, in the philosophic sense which Marxism gives to the word, is defined only in relation to a classless society. But what can a classless society be?

According to the analysis which we have just made, a classless society is obviously not a society without social groups. The differences in types of life, standards of life and sectors of activity still remain. The distinctions founded on barriers associated with the social value of occupations and the survival of traditional prestige could be reduced. Admittedly the differences in legal status will disappear. When the means of production are nationalized, the economic and social category of the owners of the means of production is automatically destroyed; there is no longer any entrepreneur's profit or ground rent. All workers become the employees of a single employer—the State. In this sense, it is perfectly true that there are no classes in a society of the Soviet type. But it does not follow that economic inequalities therefore disappear. It all depends on the hierarchy of remuneration established, nominally to meet the requirements of production, by those in power in the State.

In a society where there are no classes, as in one where there are, there are unskilled and skilled workers, clerks, engineers and managers; there is one part of the national income for current consumption and another for capital investment. The distribution of the national resources between consumption and investment and between the various grades in the hierarchy is theoretically decided by the planning office. Differences in fortune are necessarily lessened by the fact that the means of production are not held as private property and that the saving necessary for investment is largely achieved by the State's own action and not through the medium of private incomes. Individual incomes may, however, remain as unequal as in a society with numerous classes, if the rulers think it desirable for the community or for their own interests.

Indeed the first discovery which the Soviet rulers made was that nothing can take the place of self-interest as an incentive. Piece wages are more general than in any capitalist country. The managers receive a large share of the profits of any undertaking, so that it is to their personal advantage to improve production. The economic inequality which was eliminated by the abolition of acquired fortunes is coming back through the hierarchy of social functions and in order to encourage production.

Inequality in political power is in no way eliminated or diminished by the abolition of classes, for it is quite impossible for the government of a society to be in the hands of any but a few. In a society where there are no classes, as in one where there are, all do not share to the same extent in the administration and government of the society. When people speak of the proletariat's seizing power, they are using a metaphor or symbol. Power never can be in the hands of millions of men. There is government *for* the people; there is no government *by* the people.

There may be two types of changes in the society: one type affects the constitution of the élite (let me explain once for all that by "élite" I mean the minority which, in any society, performs the function of ruling the community), the other, recruitment to the élite.

In my opinion, the élite in a modern society is sub-divided into five groups: political leaders, government administrators, economic directors, leaders of the masses and military chiefs. In the British, American or French democracy, everyone distinguishes between Parliamentary Members, civil servants, business managers or proprietors, trade union secretaries and Generals or Admirals. I pass over the question of how far this scheme could be applied to the societies before capitalism or what alterations would be necessary to make it generally applicable. There seems to me to be no doubt at all that it fits modern societies.

In all modern societies these five groups correspond to essential functions. The differences lie in the degree of separation between the groups and their relative strength. For example, in France the principal officials are seldom drawn from the ranks of the directors of private industry: public opinion would immediately rise against the annexation of the State by the two hundred families. In the United States, on the other hand, the chief administrators are appointed for specific tasks and frequently come from private business and return to it after their service to the State. Similarly, the Parliamentary representatives come, to a varying degree in different countries, from business and the trade unions. There were many personal links between Members of

Parliament and economic leaders in the Conservative party in Britain and there are also many personal links between Members of Parliament and trade union leaders in the Labour Party. In France before the war the Parliamentary representatives were not so much associated either with the capitalist or with the trade unionist but were drawn from the middle classes and particularly from the liberal professions. With regard to the military leaders, in Great Britain their part in politics is no greater than that of other officials. In Spain and the South American Republics they are still an essential and active part of the ruling class.

For the first time I have used the word of the ruling class. My reason for avoiding it till yet is that in classic sociological theory the ruling class is always considered more or less as a unity. For example, Pareto tended to characterize every ruling class by the psycho-social type to which it belonged and the means it used to remain in power. He distinguished between cunning and violent élites, between élites who prefer to use artifice, argument, ideology, and financial manipulation, and those who are more ready to resort to force and constraint. The former speak of democracy, peace and humanitarianism, the latter of national greatness and conquest. James Burnham, who in *The Managerial Revolution* has also outlined a synthesis of the theory of classes and that of élites, contrasts the managerial society with the capitalist society, as that in which the managers instead of the owners of the means of production control those means.

The analysis of the groups included in the élites is, in my view, more useful because the structure of the élite is as characteristic of the society as the structure of the social groups. By structure of the élite I mean the relation between the various groups in the élite which is peculiar to each society. Indeed, although there are everywhere business managers, government officials, trade union secretaries and ministers, they are not everywhere recruited in the same way and they may either form one coherent whole or remain comparatively distinct from one another. The fundamental difference between a society of the Soviet type and one of the Western type is that the former has a unified élite and the latter a divided élite.

In the U.S.S.R. the trade union secretaries, the business managers and the higher officials generally belong to the Communist party. If they do not belong to the party they are non-political technicians, working in isolation and with little opportunity of organizing as an independent body. The Generals were the only people who might have been able to constitute a power more or less independent of the Party-State. Stalin appointed himself a Marshal, a party member was made Minister of War and the Generals who were too popular were scattered through the vast spaces of the Union; the unity of the élite has been entirely restored.

This unity obviously does not prevent competition between administrative departments or rivalry between individuals, which are inherent in the organization of every human society, but this competition and rivalry is not openly declared and does not take the form of a struggle between independent bodies; they can hardly operate except through plots. This explains how, in mass-societies, we find recurring personal struggles around the inner sanctum.

On the other hand democratic societies, which I would rather call pluralistic societies, are full of the noise of public strife between the owners of the means of production, trade union leaders and politicians. As all are entitled to form associations, professional and political organizations abound, each one defending its members' interests with passionate ardour. Government becomes a business of compromises. Those in power are well aware of their precarious position. They are considerate of the opposition because they themselves have been, and will one day again be, in opposition.

The foregoing analyses are to be used for three possible functions. First, in order to study the structures of the social group and of the élite in a particular society. Secondly, in order to determine different types of social events or of societies—as example, one could try to differentiate between various revolutions, in showing to what extent each one has brought about a change, either in the relations between the social groups, or in the relations between the subgroups of the élite, or in the way in which an élite maintains its power. The 1830 revolution, in France, has given to industrialists and bankers a stronger position, weakened the landlords' influence, partly renewed the political personnel, but it remained almost without action upon the social structure. On the contrary, a revolution like the 1917 revolution, in Russia, has suppressed the whole aristocracy, given power to a wholly new set of individuals, modified the method of government and upset the social structure. Thirdly and lastly, one could try to distinguish the successive moments of the evolution of a civilization. In other words, this system of concepts could be the instruments of a synthesis between analytical sociology, the sociology of social types and the interpretation of history. . . .

It is not surprising, after all, that the Catholic nations should be attracted by an ideology speaking of salvation from the existing State and the building of a future State to restore the unity of the temporal and spiritual realms. It is not an accident that philosophers who want to be more or less Marxist go back to the writings of the young Marx, in which the desire for revolution is expressed in the language of Hegelian dialectics, very far removed from the tone of economic and social determinism. The message which tells of the end of alienation may be raised again in the name of a spiritual desire instead of as the expression of a material necessity. This interpretation of Marxism, however, also becomes involved in contradictions, for if, in order to put an end to the alienation of the worker by the owner of the means of production, the worker is handed over body and soul to a bureaucratic élite, is he, in the last resort, set free or enslaved?

The time has come to sum up the results of these analyses, which have been both too short and too long.

First of all, I hope I have shown you a method of analysis, combining familiar methods which are seldom used in conjunction: analysis of the economic structure, the social structure, the structure of the groups within the élite, and, it should be added, the structure of the constitutional system; all these elements are of equal importance in any theory of sociology which wishes to understand society as a whole.

Secondly, I hope I have convinced you that one of the most characteristic features of any society's structure is the structure of the élite, that is, the relationship between the groups exercising power, the degree of unity or division between these groups, the system of recruiting the élite and the ease or difficulty of entering it. No doubt its constitutional system is characteristic of any society. The real nature of a constitutional system, however, can only be understood when the men who in fact operate the system are taken into account. The aristocratic parliaments of the nineteenth century were fundamentally different from the popular parliaments of our own century, even when no point in the constitution has been altered. The parliaments elected by proportional representation on the continent, the battlefield on which communists and anti-communists carry on their wordy fight before they fight on another field, are profoundly unlike the British and American parliaments, in which the representatives of the various interests try to arrive at practicable compromises and observe the rules of the game.

Thirdly, I hope I have shown you the significance of the classless society in history. The unified élite deriving from the proletariat offers to fulfill the office which should have been fulfilled by capitalism, in cases where a weak or degenerate élite fails to eliminate the surviving traces of feudalism and to provide its country with industrial equipment. It offers to carry out the task which sometimes seems beyond the strength of socialistic democracies in countries which have been rich and are to-day impoverished; the adherents of the classless society would unhesitatingly impose all those measures which democratic socialism is unwilling to impose—compulsory saving, investment, discipline, incentives—because they would have the material and moral means necessary: unlimited power in the State and an ideology to justify them.

Thus, through many different channels, we come to a synthesis of Marxist ideas with those of Pareto. A society cannot be characterized only by the class which owns the means of production or by the psychological and social nature of the élite. The power and influence in the State of the industrial and financial leaders varies between different capitalistic countries with the constitutional machinery and the power of the political rulers. The distribution of power changed radically in Germany between the time of the Kaiser's Empire, the Weimar Republic and the Third Reich, even although the owners of the means of production remained in their places. Changes in the relative strength of the groups included in the élites are a typical sign of political and social evolution. The definition of the post-capitalist organization as the replacement of the owners of the means of production by the new class of managers, is inadequate, for the character of the society is entirely different if those managers come to power within a pluralistic society or if they do so through the seizure of power by a unified élite. The managers are one of the groups in any modern élite. They are never, as managers, the ruling group. In both capitalism and socialism there are, above the managers, mass leaders or politicians who fix the targets for the managers and hold the secret of securing obedience from the masses.

Neither does the idea of an élite working by force or guile, or that of the substitution of an élite using force for an élite using guile represent reality in all its complexity. It is true that both the fascist and communist revolutions are a sign of the strengthening of the means of compulsion and the abandonment of slow and more subtle methods by which men are convinced, for the adoption of ruthless methods of policing and propaganda by which they are compelled. Pareto was therefore certainly right in his interpretation of one aspect of contemporary history, but when we say that an élite decays it is a fact more than an explanation. There are many ways by which élites may be renewed, transformed or disintegrated. A typical form of disintegration at the present day is paralysis due to internal strife. The democratic method of elections to parliament and free trade unions means that representatives of the mass of the people come to take part in the work of administration. This phenomenon, which is comparatively recent in history, gives a new meaning to the law of the succession of élites. It offers a hope that fortunate societies may succeed, renewing their élite gradually, without a revolutionary upheaval. It involves the danger to which unfortunate societies and nations who prefer ideology to wisdom fall victim, that there may be fatal conflicts which only the dictatorship of one group can succeed in overcoming. The substitution of one élite for another, which is an essential point in Pareto's treatise, can be explained to a large extent by phenomena of economic and social change which Marxism has accustomed us to consider of primary importance. The Marxist type of revolution, involving the seizure of power by the party deriving from the proletariat, can be fitted into both Pareto's scheme and that of Marx, being, as it is, the victory of one élite and the elimination of the owners of the means of production. Those who see in it only the elimination of the capitalists and teach that a State in control of the whole economy will wither away, whereas in fact it grows stronger, and that a classless society knows no master, when in fact it has a single omnipotent master, are deliberately trying to mystify the people. But those who see only the substitution of one master for another and forget that the disappearance of the private owners of the means of production involves a far-reaching change in the social atmosphere and the hierarchy of men and values, also try to mystify.

I told you at the beginning that sociology helps us to know what is at stake in political struggles but never provides us with a judgment. I am afraid that my own convictions may have become apparent. I should merely like to add that the choice cannot be decided by the mere analysis of the social machinery which I have tried in this study. A single factor never decides the whole nature of society, but the consequences of the fact that an élite is united or divided, and of the question whether the rulers of the State also control the economy or not, and whether the hierarchy is based on technical skill, a single party or numerous groups, are tremendous.

A classless society may be efficient and imposing, it may give millions of men, who feel sure that they are building the future, joy and pride and even the feeling of fulfilling themselves in their activity, which may be called a sense of freedom. Such a society breeds soldiers, workers, devotees, but I am afraid it may stifle the individual man, responsible to his conscience and master of his own fate. Leaving out of account this argument, which is above politics, the theory of divided and united élites brings us back to the old idea that freedom depends on a system of checks and balances. That theory must, however, be transferred from the constitutional organization to society as a whole. A unified élite means the end of freedom. But when the groups of the élite are not only distinct but become a disunity, it means the end of the State. Freedom survives in those intermediate regions, which are continually threatened when there is moral unity of the élite, where men and groups preserve the secret of single and eternal wisdom and have learnt how to combine autonomy with co-operation.

NOTE

1. These articles are a reproduction, with minor amendments, of the text of three lectures delivered at the London School of Economics. I am fully conscious of the deficiencies of these "*essais.*" But it would have been impossible to give them a really scientific character without going beyond the limits of a paper designed to review the general field.

65

The Intellectuals and the Powers: Some Perspectives for Comparative Analysis

Edward A. Shils

Laity and Intellectuals

In religion, in art, in all spheres of culture and politics, the mass of mankind in all hitherto known societies have not, except for transitory interludes, been preoccupied with the attainment of an immediate contact with the ultimate principles implicit in their beliefs and standards. The directly gratifying ends of particular actions, the exigencies of situations, considerations of individual and familial advantage, concrete moral maxims, concrete prescriptions and prohibitions, preponderate in the conduct of the majority of persons in most societies, large and small. The systemic coherence and the deeper and more general ground of beliefs and standards only intermittently hold their attention and touch on their passions. Ordinary life in every society is characterized by an unequal intensity of attachment to ultimate values, be they cognitive, moral, or aesthetic, and an unequal intensity of the need for coherence. Ordinary life shuns rigorous definition and consistent adherence to traditional or rational rules, and it has no need for continuous contact with the sacred. Ordinary life is slovenly, full of compromise and improvisation; it goes on in the "here and now."

In every society, however, there are some persons with an unusual sensitivity to the sacred, an uncommon reflectiveness about the nature of their universe, and the rules which govern their society. There is in every society a minority of persons who, more than the ordinary run of their fellow-men, are enquiring, and desirous of being in frequent communication with symbols which are more general than the immediate concrete situations of everyday life, and remote in their reference in both time and space. In this minority, there is a need to externalize this quest in oral and written discourse, in poetic or plastic

From Edward A. Shils, "The Intellectuals and the Powers: Some Perspectives for Comparative Analysis," *Comparative Studies in Society and History*, I, No. 1 (1958), 5, 7–11, 21–22. Reprinted by permission of the publisher.

expression, in historical reminiscence or writing, in ritual performance and acts of worship. This interior need to penetrate beyond the screen of immediate concrete experience marks the existence of the intellectuals in every society. The moral and intellectual unity of a society, which in the size of its population and its territory goes beyond what any one man can know from his average first-hand experience, and which brings him into contact with persons outside his kinship group, depends on such intellectual institutions as schools, churches, newspapers, and similar structures. Through these, ordinary persons, in childhood, youth, or adulthood, enter into contact, however extensive, with those who are most familiar with the existing body of cultural values. By means of preaching, teaching, and writing, intellectuals infuse into sections of the population which are intellectual neither by inner vocation nor by social role, a perceptiveness and an imagery which they would otherwise lack. By the provision of such techniques as reading and writing and calculation, they enable the laity to enter into a wider universe. The creation of nations out of tribes, in early modern times in Europe and in contemporary Asia and Africa, is the work of intellectuals, just as the formation of the American nation out of diverse ethnic groups is the achievement of teachers, clergymen, and journalists. The legitimation of the reigning authority is naturally a function of many factors, including the tendencies within a population towards a submission to and rejection of authority, the effectiveness of the authority in maintaining order, in showing strength and dispensing a semblance of justice. The legitimacy of authority is however a function of what its subjects believe about it; beliefs about authority are far from resting entirely on first-hand experience, and much of what is believed beyond first-hand experience is the product of traditions and teachings which are the gradually accumulated and attenuated product of the activities of intellectuals.

Through their provision of models and standards, by the presentation of symbols to be appreciated, intellectuals elicit, guide, and form the expressive dispositions within a society. Not that the expressive life of a society is under the exclusive dominion of its intellectuals. Indeed the situation has never existed—and in fact could never exist—in which the expressive life of a society, its aesthetic tastes, its artistic creations, or the ultimately aesthetic grounds of its ethical judgments fell entirely within the traditions espoused by the intellectuals of the society. Societies vary in the extent to which the expressive actions and orientations are in accordance with what is taught and represented by the dominant intellectuals. Within these variations much of the expressive life of a society, even what is most vulgar and tasteless, echoes some of the expressive elements in the central value system represented by the intellectuals.

The first two functions treated above show the intellectuals infusing into the laity attachments to more general symbols and providing for that section of the population a means of participation in the central value system. Intellectuals are not, however, concerned only to facilitate this wider participation in certain features of the central value system. They are above all concerned with its more intensive cultivation, with the elaboration and development of alternative potentialities. Where creativity and originality are emphatically acknowledged and prized, and where innovation is admitted and accepted, this is perceived as a primary obligation of intellectuals. However, even in systems where individual creativity is not seen as a positive value, the labor of powerful minds and irrepressible individualities working on what has been received from the past, modifies the heritage by systematization and rationalization, and adapts it to new tasks and obstacles. In this process of elaboration, divergent potentialities of the system of cultural values are made explicit and conflicting positions are established. Each generation of intellectuals performs this elaborating function for its own and succeeding generations, and particularly for the next succeeding generation.

These specifically intellectual functions are performed not only for the intellectuals of a particular society but for the intellectuals of other societies as well. The intellectuals of different societies are ordered in a vague hierarchy, in which the lower learn from the higher. For South East Asia, the Indian intellectuals, in the Middle Ages and early modern times, performed this function. The intellectuals of Republican and Imperial Rome learned from Greek intellectuals. For Japan, for a time, Chinese intellectuals performed this function. In modern times, the British intellectuals through Oxford, Cambridge, and the London School of Economics, have formed the intellectuals of India, Africa, and for a long time the United States. In the 19th century, German academic intellectuals provided a worldwide model, just as in the 19th and 20th centuries, French artistic and literary intellectuals have provided models of development for aesthetically sensitive intellectuals all over the civilized world. In the 18th century, the intellectuals of the French Enlightenment inspired their confrères in Spain, Italy, Prussia, and Russia. This function is performed for the intellectual community above all. The laity only comes to share in it at several removes and after a lapse of time.

The function of providing a model for intellectual activity, within and among societies, implies the acceptance of a general criterion of superior quality or achievement. The pattern of action of a certain group of intellectuals comes to be regarded as exemplary because it is thought to correspond more closely to certain ideal requirements of truth, beauty, or virtue. Such standards are never the objects of complete consensus, but they are often widely accepted over very extensive areas of the world at any given time.

The process of elaborating and developing further the potentialities inherent in a "system" of cultural values, entails also the possibility of "rejection" of the inherited set of values in varying degrees of comprehensiveness. In all societies, even those in which the intellectuals are notable for their conservatism, the diverse paths of creativity, as well as an inevitable tendency towards negativism, impel a partial rejection of the prevailing system of cultural values. The very process of elaboration and development involves a measure of rejection. The range of rejection of the inherited varies greatly; it can never be complete and all-embracing. Even where the rejecting intellectuals allege that they are "nihilistic" with respect to everything that is inherited, complete rejection without physical self-annihilation is impossible.

It is practically given by the nature of the intellectuals' orientation that there should be some tension between the intellectuals and the value-orientations embodied in the actual institutions of any society. This applies not only to the orientations of the ordinary members of the society, i.e., the laity, but to the value-orientations of those exercising authority in the society, since it is on them that the intellectuals' attention is most often focussed, they being the custodians of the central institutional system. It is not this particular form of "rejection" or alienation which interests us most at the moment.

Rather it is the rejection by intellectuals of the inherited and prevailing values of those intellectuals who are already incorporated in ongoing social institutions. This intra-intellectual alienation or dissensus is a crucial part of the intellectual heritage of any society. Furthermore it supplies the important function of moulding and guiding the alienative tendencies which exist in any society. It provides an alternative pattern of integration for their own society, and for other societies the intellectuals of which come under their hegemony (e.g. the Fabian Socialists in Britain and the Indian intellectuals, or the French and British constitutional liberals of the early 19th century and the intellectuals of many countries in Southeastern Europe, in South America, Asia, etc.).

It is not only through the presentation of orientations toward general symbols which reaffirm, continue, modify or reject the society's traditional inheritance of beliefs and standards that intellectuals leave their mark on society. The intellectuals do not exhaust their functions through the establishment of a contact for the laity with the sacred values of their society. They fulfill authoritative, power-exercising functions over concrete actions as well. Intellectuals have played a great historical role on the higher levels of state administration, above all, in China, in British and independent India, in the Ottoman Empire and in modern Europe. Sovereigns have often considered a high standard of education, either humanistic or technical-legal, confirmed by diplomas and examinations, necessary for the satisfactory functioning of the state. The judiciary too has often been a domain of the intellectuals. In private economic organizations, the employment of intellectuals in administrative capacities has been uncommon to the point of rarity. Nor have intellectuals ever shown any inclination to become business enterprisers. It is only since the 19th century that business firms, first in Germany, then in America, and latterly in other industrialized countries, have taken to the large-scale employment of scientists in research departments and to a much smaller extent in executive capacities.

Equal in antiquity to the role of the highly educated in state administration is the role of the intellectual as personal agent, counsellor, tutor, or friend of the sovereign. Plato's experience in Syracuse, Aristotle's relations with Alexander, Alcuin's with Charlemagne, Hobbes and Charles II prior to the Restoration, Milton and Cromwell, Lord Keynes and the Treasury, and the "Brains Trust" under President F. D. Roosevelt, represent only a few of numerous instances in ancient and modern states,

Oriental and Occidental, in which intellectuals have been drawn into the entourage of rulers, their advice and aid sought, and their approval valued. Again there are many states and periods in which this has not been so. The Court of Wilhelm II for example drew relatively little on the educated classes of the time; important episodes of Chinese history are to be seen as a consequence of the intellectuals' reaction to the ruler's refusal to draw them into his most intimate and influential circle of counsellors; American administrative and political history from the time of the Jacksonian Revolution until the New Liberalism of Woodrow Wilson was characterized by the separation of intellectuals from the higher administrative and the legislative branches of government. Intellectuals have emerged occasionally in monarchies at the highest pinnacles of authority, through sheer accident or at least through no deliberate process of selection. Asoka, Marcus Aurelius, Akhnaton are only a few of the scattered coincidences of sovereignty and the concern with the highest truths. In the last century and a half under conditions of liberal-democratic party politics, Benjamin Disraeli, William Gladstone, F. M. Guizot, Woodrow Wilson, Jawaharlal Nehru, Thomas Masaryk, et al. have provided impressive instances of intellectuals who have been able, by their own efforts and a wide appreciation for their gifts of civil politics enriched by an intensity of intellectual interest and exertion, to play a notable role in the exercise of great political authority. This has not been accidental; liberal and constitutional politics in great modern states and liberal and "progressive" nationalist movements in subject territories have to a large extent been "intellectuals' politics."

Indeed in modern times, first in the West, and then in the 19th and 20th centuries at the peripheries of Western civilization and in the Orient, the major political vocation of the intellectuals has lain in the enunciation and pursuit of the ideal. Modern liberal and constitutional politics have largely been the creation of intellectuals with bourgeois affinities and sympathies, in societies dominated by land-owning and military aristocracies. This has been one major form of the pursuit of the ideal. Another has been the promulgation and inspiration of politics, i.e. revolutionary politics working outside the circle of constitutional traditions. Prior to the origins of ideological politics, which came into the open with the European Reformation, conspiracies, putsches, and the subversion of the existing regime, although they often involved intellectuals, were not the object of a particular affinity between intellectuals and revolutionary tendencies. In modern times however, with the emergence of ideologically dominated political activities as a continuously constitutive part of public life, a genuine affinity has emerged.

Not by any means all intellectuals have been equally attracted by revolutionary politics. Moderates and partisans in civil politics, quiet apolitical concentration on their specialized intellectual preoccupations, cynical anti-political passivity, and faithful acceptance and service of the existing order, are all to be found in substantial proportions among modern intellectuals, as among intellectuals in antiquity. Nonetheless the function of modern intellectuals in furnishing the doctrine of revolutionary movements is to be considered as one of their most important accomplishments.

In Conclusion

Intellectuals are indispensable to any society, not just to industrial society, and the more complex the society, the more indispensable they are. An effective collaboration between intellectuals and the authorities which govern society is a requirement for order and continuity in public life and for the integration of the wider reaches of the laity into society. Yet, the original impetus to intellectual performance, and the traditions to which it has given rise and which are sustained by the institutions through which intellectual performance is made practicable generate a tension between intellectuals and the laity, high and low. This tension can never be eliminated, either by a complete consensus between the laity and the intellectuals or by the complete ascendancy of the intellectuals over the laity.

Within these two extreme and impossible alternatives, a wide variety of forms of consensus and dissensus in the relations of the intellectuals and the ruling powers of society have existed. The discovery and the achievement of the optimum balance of civility and intellectual creativity are the tasks of the statesman and the responsible intellectual. The study of these diverse patterns of consensus and dissensus, their institutional and cultural concomitants, and the conditions under which they have emerged and waned are the first items on the agenda of the comparative study of the intellectuals and the powers.

66

The Revolution of the Saints

Michael Walzer

III

The Puritan ministers provide, perhaps, the first example of "advanced" intellectuals in a traditional society. Their exile had taught them the style of free men; its first manifestation was the evasion of traditional authority and routine. The doctrine of the objective Word reflected the new style; exclusive reliance upon the Word symbolized the intellectuals' escape from the corporate church, in effect, their self-reliance, for the Word was self-taught. It was lawful for men "to try whether the church's determinations be according to the Word and to reject them if they be otherwise."[1] The consequence of such

From Michael Walzer, *The Revolution of the Saints* (Cambridge: Harvard University Press, 1965), pp. 121–130, 140–143. Copyright 1965 by the President and Fellows of Harvard College. Reprinted by permission of Harvard University Press and Weidenfeld and Nicolson Ltd., London.

a trial, however, was no mere personal eccentricity; the radical intellectuals did not disperse, but rather formed new associations. The Word gave birth to the Cause, and it was as representatives of a Cause that the returning exiles confronted corporate and feudal England.[2] The effect of this new role was to depersonalize political conflict and to challenge the traditional forms of organization: the clique, the entourage, familial connection. In dramatic fashion, the preacher John Penry publicly announced the impersonal character of his devotion to the Puritan cause. In the late 1580's a warrant was issued for his arrest; he immediately published a treatise defending not himself but the reformation for which he labored. Had the accusation "reached no further than my own person," he wrote, "it were my duty in regard of the quietness of our state to put it up"—that is, to yield silently. "But seeing that *it doth not touch me at all* . . . and wholly striketh at that truth, in the defense whereof it pleased the Lord to use my weak and polluted hands," he fled the Queen's police and published his defense.[3]

In England many of the exiles found themselves once again members of some near-feudal entourage, caught up in an intricate system of connection and loyalty. Some of them, including the well-known Anthony Gilby, were protected by the Huntingdon faction; others discovered patrons in Lady Bacon's circle of friends and relatives. Leicester offered valuable support and, though the Genevan exile Thomas Wood told him bluntly that he was not sufficiently wholehearted, most of the ministers would gladly have accepted a reformation wrought by his hands.[4] There were later to be saints who connived at a reformation wrought by the even less godly hands of Essex and Buckingham. Despite all this, however, Protestant aristocrats never assumed such importance among the Puritans as did their French counterparts among the Huguenots. Nor were the ministers ever entirely satisfied with the comfort and assistance they found within the old order—not least, of course, because the assistance was never sufficient for their purposes.

Their own associations were not feudal factions at all, but gatherings of men familiar less with each other than with Scripture. Only such associations, argued two of the ministers, were truly safe. The old ties of neighborhood and kindred, they warned, would fail, but allies chosen for their "virtue and godliness" could be trusted. "Be faithful," wrote Thomas Taylor some years later, "especially in the fellowship of the gospel."[5] Insofar as Puritanism spread among the gentry, the old feudal ties were supplemented by the new gospel fellowship. Thus Sir Richard Knightley writing to Leicester: "You have . . . gotten you such friends as would be ready to venture their lives with your lordship *in a good cause,* even such as would not do it so much in respect of your high calling. . . ."[6] But such "friends" were still relatively rare among laymen; it was more significantly among the ministers that ideological commitment replaced personal loyalty. And the clerical saints came to identify their new *impersonal* organizations as the necessary forms of English life. Instinctively, as it were, with the sensitivity of hostile strangers, they pointed to the decay of the traditional order and suggested alternatives.

They were estranged not only from the corporate church and the feudal system, but also from the rapidly developing secular and aristocratic culture of London. For, in fact, these two coexisted without undue tension. Renaissance exuberance, in and of itself, did not involve any significant attack upon the traditional order of the church (or of the state); it did not provide any basis, surely no programmatic basis, for religious reconstruction or social discipline. It seemed, indeed, to intensify the disorder which attended the gradual decline of the traditional political and religious worlds; it symbolized the breakdown of the old norms and gave expression to the brilliant, often "fantastical" and bizarre individuality which that breakdown permitted. But the exciting and open city did not point the way, as the ministers sought to do, toward a new discipline.[7] No revivifying morality, no stream of selfless men flowed from London to the country. The movement of men was in the other direction, toward what Puritans felt was the decadence and corruption of the swelling, prosperous city. Their anxious response to the pleasure-seeking urban crowd is apparent in the attack upon the theaters, more so in the fierce condemnation of Renaissance extravagance in dress.[8] The purely individual preoccupation with fashion and style, the new interest in conspicuous consumption —these were worries also of traditional moralists, but Puritan concern was more nervous, more intense. The ministers constituted, as it were, an advance guard in the middle-class repudiation of Renaissance sensuality and sophistication.

Themselves the members of a clerical third estate, the Puritan ministers tended to anticipate the intellectual and social characteristics of a secular third estate. Their "plain speaking" and matter-of-fact style; their insistence upon education and independent judgment; their voluntary association outside the corporate church; their emphasis upon methodical, purposive endeavor; their narrow unemotional sense of order and discipline—all this clearly suggested a life-style very different from that of a feudal lord, a Renaissance courtier or even an Anglican archbishop. This new style was first developed and tested on the margins and in the interstices of English society by men cut off from the traditional world, angry and isolated clerics, anxiously seeking a new order. It was by no means the entirely spontaneous creation of those sturdy London merchants and country gentlemen who later became its devoted advocates; it was something they learned, or rather, it was something some of them learned. The automatic burgher values—sobriety, caution, thrift— did not constitute the significant core of Puritan morality in the seventeenth century; the clerical intellectuals had added moral activism, the ascetic style, and the quality of high-mindedness and taught these to their followers.[9]

In politics, too, the "advanced" intellectuals, committed representatives of a Cause, developed a new style and taught it to those who came after. Years before English merchants and gentlemen were ready for an independent venture in politics and religion, the ministers had arrived in the political world and were already active, energetic, creative.[10] Their earliest organizations were made up almost entirely of clergymen; it was some time before Puritanism spread into the country and the clerical saints found themselves saddled with powerful allies. In this interval they experimented with many of the techniques of what came to be called modern politics; the politics of free assembly, mass petition, group pressure, and the appeal to public opinion. All this was illegal or at best semilegal in Elizabethan England; political experimentation required then, as it often has since, a willful disdain for lawful procedures. It was precisely their disdain which turned the "advanced" intellectuals into successful entrepreneurs. The methods with which they experimented were determined in part by their situation as political outsiders; in larger part, perhaps, by the new ideas that they had brought home from exile. While friendly but hesitant gentlemen held back, ardent Puritans were already insisting that politics was a public business and that the public was a great impersonal association of saints.

A group as small and as isolated as this radical band of clerics, however, can rarely play an important part in political history. A certain balance of social forces made Puritan innovation possible; it turned the disdain of the "advanced" intellectual into an effective political method; it set the saints free. In a society where the old feudal aristocracy no longer dominated political life, in which the patronage of intellectuals was no longer an exclusive prerogative of king's court, noble house or corporate church, and yet in the absence of well-established, politically sophisticated professional and commercial classes—in such a society the influence and power of an intelligentsia possessed with new ideas was quite out of proportion to its possession of land and —wealth. "The elite of the word tries to establish its ascendancy where there is no elite of any kind"[11]— or, for this was the situation in England in the late sixteenth century, where the decay of the old elite and the immaturity of a new one, result in a certain tense equilibrium. Until the gentry had seized secure hold of the House of Commons, there was no energetic, clearly dominant social group that could give a decisive lead to the creation of new forms and institutions. Social stalemate temporarily freed the men of ideas from their usual role as spokesmen and apologists for one or another established power.[12]

A closely united group of intellectuals—like the Puritan clergy—could then move into those social interstices where power and prerogative were indeterminate. The Puritans were protected by dissident elements in the aristocracy, but they never became dependent members of a feudal entourage, defended, as Wycliffe was, by such an "overmighty subject" as John of Gaunt. For they also found shelter, and then disciples, among the politically untrained and unorganized members of new and growing social groups. In contrast to the poor priests of the Lollards, for example, Puritan ministers moved easily among the merchant classes of the towns and among the country gentry.[13] Their ideas were adopted and helped eventually to form strong men, confident enough to challenge the old order. In its search for support, a radical intelligentsia may thus help to organize the inchoate political forces of the classes to which it makes its appeal. For the moment, however, neither the Merchant Adventurers of London, nor the godly members of the country gentry, nor even the Puritan "chorus" in the House of Commons could compromise the resolute independence of the ministers.

The demands they made were on their own behalf, developed in direct proportion to their isolation and independence—which is to say, to that superiority over their contemporaries that their "advanced" ideas led them to claim. Clerical pretensions were therefore greater among the English ministers of the sixteenth century than they were in the seventeenth, when Puritanism had far more support in the country at large and the ministers had to reckon with the lay saints. They reached their highest point in both periods among the Scottish Presbyterians who lived in one of the most backward of European societies.[14] Before merchants and gentlemen could demonstrate their social power, the ministerial mind constructed a Calvinist hierarchy, a tightly disciplined social order, dominated by the "elite of the word," ruled according to those objective and absolutist criteria which appealed to the new intellectual. The ministers were, in a sense, the predecessors of those merchants and gentlemen, but at the same time their would-be rulers.

IV

In the course of the last three decades of the sixteenth century, the Puritan ministers attained a surprising independence in both organization and ideology, and developed a radical and innovating politics. They continued the work of the Marian exiles—John Field, one of their leaders, was Knox's literary executor in England[15]—but the revolutionary quality of their thinking was blunted against the amorphous Protestantism of the Elizabethan establishment. The ministers admitted that salvation was possible in the new English church; they even accepted Anglican benefices. But they were never integrated into the establishment and they continually sought to evade its discipline: ruse and deceit were among the first weapons of the radical. The returning exiles and their followers continued to associate—openly whenever possible, secretly whenever necessary—outside the church and to maintain among themselves the discipline that the Queen abhorred. The "prophesyings," held for mutual edification and criticism, kept alive their party spirit. They constituted an exile, so to speak, at home—and if this were true then the later "conferences" might well be called an underground organization.[16]

These secret clerical meetings represent an early form of the voluntary association. They indicate the tendency of Puritanism to set men outside the conventional patterns of Elizabethan England, much as it had set them outside the actual boundaries of Marian England. The "conferences" were planned in the form of a loose Presbyterian system: ministers met together in their local areas, and several times sent representatives to London for a "national synod." The synods were timed to coincide with parliamentary sessions—thus forming a kind of ministerial lobby. The various meetings throughout the country were informally coordinated by John Field, who served as secretary for the Puritan ministers in the 1580's. Field collected large amounts of written material, apparently planning some sort of propaganda campaign. His "registers" have survived and suggest the extent of the clerical effort: they include drafts of parliamentary bills, broadsides and pamphlets, political doggerel, and numerous examples of "supplications" (petitions) drafted by the ministers and circulated among country gentlemen. In the conferences themselves, the ministers debated fine points of theology and casuistry, but they also discussed parliamentary matters and the more secular aspects of their own affairs: money, relations with parishioners, troubles with bishops. The movement was, in effect, a substitute establishment, "in which things were compassed, which legally were never conceived."[17] "They have combined themselves together into a strange brotherhood," wrote the future archbishop Richard Bancroft; "they challenge to their unlawful and seditious assemblies the true and most proper name of the church. . . . For a full conclusion of their attempts [they] will take upon them . . . to discharge the estate of bishops and to direct their

commissioners to her most excellent majesty. . . ."[18]

Bancroft, the alarmed conservative, was probably right. The political activity of the ministers was marked by an extraordinary carelessness about the established channels and procedures of Elizabethan government.[19] Church convocation was avoided altogether after 1563. Contrary to all custom, the ministers discussed parliamentary affairs in their conferences; proposals and petitions were adopted and sent on to London. And at the London sessions of the House of Commons the ministers explored the techniques of lobbying: "[they] were wont . . . to attend the House of Commons door," a contemporary writer reports, "making legs to the members *in transitu,* praying their worships to remember the Gospel."[20] An effort was also made to organize public pressure upon the members of Parliament. The clerical conferences compiled a parish by parish survey of the established church, itemizing its supposed deficiencies; they published it for the parliamentary session in 1584 and circulated it along with numerous petitions from sympathetic gentry. It was an attempt, writes Neale, to create the appearance, at least, of "spontaneous, widespread discontent."[21] These efforts to influence parliamentary decisions and even to organize a following in the Commons represent a major development in English political history. Many of the tactics of the lay saints and parliamentarians of the 1640's were anticipated and tested by the ministers of the 1580's. . . .

VII

The career of a seventeenth-century Puritan minister, and of an increasing number of Puritan gentlemen, usually began at one of the universities. Cambridge and Oxford came to provide, less an education, than a crucial bit of social space where the alliance of ministers and lay saints could be worked out. It was at school that the saint's "spiritual struggle" and final conversion took place, though more often under the impact of town preaching than of university teaching. As among other groups of "advanced" intellectuals, a more important education was offered by the institutions and publications of the Cause than could yet be secured in the universities. The curriculum at both Cambridge and Oxford continued through the early seventeenth century to follow the old scholastic pattern. Ramus, perhaps, had replaced Aristotle for many of the tutors in logic, and the new categories may have lent support to Calvinist theology. But it is hard to discover anything in the subject matter of an academic education in the seventeenth century that would have turned a careless young man into an ardent Puritan. Perhaps the mere fact of a university education speeded the transformation, for Calvinism undoubtedly encouraged the pretensions of the newly educated, and English society was hardly ready to accommodate those pretensions or to provide some outlet for the ambitions of the godly graduate.[22]

The sudden influx of gentlemen's sons into the universities in the late sixteenth and early seventeenth centuries helped to free the Puritan dons and divinity students from Anglican discipline and to provide an alternative source of patronage and support. Men like Chaderton and Preston, masters of Emmanuel, trained a whole generation of young ministers and godly gentlemen. Among the pupils of Preston were many future members of the Long Parliament and a number of officials of the Protectorate.[23] In the university such men associated more or less freely with the future ministers—especially when their social status was the same—establishing connections often maintained for many years. Students boarded together at the home of a Puritan tutor, studied together and undoubtedly exchanged information as to their respective spiritual conditions. Or, they indulged together in that "wildness" and "dissipation" that were conventionally supposed to precede conversion. The influence of such associations can hardly be weighed; what is clear is that something of the style of the future ministers was acquired by men who looked forward to secular careers.

The alienation from the traditional forms of English life which the ministers had long felt, now came to be shared by many young gentlemen. They too learned to behave in a somber, unemotional fashion according to the dictates of the objective Word; they adopted the ascetic style and carried it outside the church; they devoted themselves to the Cause with a resolute highmindedness. From among these university students came the first Puritan lay intellectuals. Milton, for example, attended Christ's College in Cambridge during the 1620's. He had planned to enter the church; instead, as Haller writes, he was one of the first to bring to the profession of letters an evangelical sense of commitment and activism.[24] Men like Cromwell—who had been tutored by the Puritan minister Thomas Beard before he came to Cambridge—carried this same commitment into politics. It brought with it that freedom from convention and routine that had previously been imparted to the ministry by the self-confident possession of "advanced" truths.

In a letter of 1638, Oliver Cromwell described his condition before the spiritual crisis of his final conversion. He had led, it should be said, an ordinary enough existence, undistinguished at the university and occupied thereafter with his lands and his family. "You know what my manner of life hath been," he wrote to his cousin, the wife of the lawyer St. John, "Oh, I lived in and loved darkness and hated light; I was a chief, the chief of sinners." There was a certain perverse egotism in this, though Cromwell was undoubtedly sincere. That the most usual forms of English upper-class life suddenly seemed monstrous—this was a function of the enormous distance the reborn Oliver felt he had traveled. Now, he went on, "my soul is with the congregation of the first-born, my body rests in hope; and if here I may honor my God either by doing or by suffering, I shall be most glad."[25] But there was as yet no opportunity for godly "doing" in England; the highmindedness and self-importance of the lay Puritan led only to frustration and bitterness. And so Cromwell's spiritual journey was a kind of internal emigration, a withdrawal from old England. It recapitulated the actual experience of the clerical intellectuals, an experience that had already become a part of Puritan imagery, and in whose terms many young gentlemen had been taught to think.

"Alas poor souls," one of the ministers had written, "we are no better than passengers in this world, our way it is in the middle of the sea."[26] The earthly home of the "first-born" was not yet determined. Cromwell would have deserted an England in which Laud was finally triumphant; many others fled a land in which he seemed to triumph—they turned their spiritual alienation into a physical withdrawal. The persecution of the 1630's reproduced, to some extent, the conditions of the Marian exile; this time, however, not eight hundred but more than twenty thousand fled England's shores. Between 1629 and 1640 some one hundred Cambridge men emigrated to New England; thirty-three of these were Emmanuel bred. Another thirty-two emigrants came from Oxford.[27] These were the intellectual and political leaders of the rush to America; they continued the sixteenth-century tradition of exile and escape. The long effort to transform the old order seemed now to have failed and the Calvinist sense of "unsettledness" deepened into that profound pessimism which characterizes the Caroline period. "I saw the Lord departed from England . . . and I saw the hearts of most of the godly set and bent that way [toward the new world]," wrote Thomas Shepard in his *Autobiography,* "and I did think I should feel many miseries if I stayed behind." His view was shared by such a pious gentleman as John

Winthrop. "All other churches of Europe are brought to desolation," he wrote to his wife, "and it cannot be but a like judgment is coming upon us."[28] With the dissolution of Parliament in 1629, the last channels of opposition were closed; the choice of ministers and lay saints was between radical conspiracy and emigration. Why should they stay, engaging in illegal activity and filling the prisons, asked Shepard, "when a wide door was set open of liberty otherwise?"[29]

Emigration was but one outcome of the Puritan's spiritual estrangement from old England; revolution was another. Not until 1640 did the Lord open the second "door." But even before that date the lay Puritan, trained by the godly ministers, had begun his own revolutionary career. Alongside the large-scale emigration, there reappeared in the 1630's (for the first time since the 1580's) the whole apparatus of radical politics: the illegal press, organized book smuggling, a rough underground network. Ministers like Henry Burton participated in the new illegal Puritanism, but increasingly leadership fell into other hands. The emergence of Prynne, Lilburne, and Bastwick—lawyer, cloth-merchant's apprentice, and physician—opened a new era in political history. Soon Cromwell and his friends would honor their God "by doing."

NOTES

1. John Penry, *A Brief Discovery of the Untruths and Slanders . . . Contained in a Sermon by D. Bancroft* (n.p., 1588), p. 35.
2. The manner in which intellectuals "objectify" social conflicts, intensifying the struggle by depersonalizing its purposes, is discussed by Lewis Coser in *The Functions of Social Conflict* (Glencoe, Ill., 1956), pp. 111–119. It is only necessary to add that this seems the achievement specifically of *modern* intellectuals, and that it is especially significant when they are attacking a society in which personal and corporate connections play an important part. Ideological commitment is a powerful solvent of traditional order.
3. John Penry, *A Treatise Wherein is Manifestly Proved That Reformation and Those That . . . Favor the Same Are Unjustly Charged to be Enemies Unto Her Majesty and the State* (n.p., 1590), sig. 4 verso.
4. *Diary of Lady Margaret Hoby, 1599–1605,* ed. Dorothy M. Meads (London, 1930), Introduction, pp. 5ff.; A. F. Scott-Pearson, *Thomas Cartwright and Elizabethan Puritanism: 1535–1603* (Cambridge, 1925), p. 345; *Letters of Thomas Wood,* pp. 18–22.
5. See John Dod and Robert Cleaver, *A Plain and Familiar Exposition of the Thirteenth and Fourteenth Chapters of the Proverbs of Solomon* (London, 1609), p. 119; Thomas Taylor, *The Progress of Saints to Full Holiness* (London, 1630), p. 341.
6. Quoted in *Letters of Thomas Wood,* p. xxviii (emphasis added).
7. The enthusiasm of Renaissance writers for the London underworld may have led them to exaggerate the viciousness and disorder which prevailed in the city. See, for example, George Whetstone, *A Mirror for Magistrates of Cities* (London, 1584), and Thomas Dekker, *The Seven Deadly Sins of London* (London, 1606). A Puritan version of this sort of thing, without the enthusiasm, is Philip Stubbes, *The Anatomy of Abuses* (1583; repr. by F. J. Furnival, London, 1879).
8. "Attacks upon plays as such may be regarded as little more than skirmishes in the larger campaign against audiences." Alfred Harbage, *Shakespeare's Audience* (New York, 1941), p. 11. On the new styles in dress, see Stubbes, *Anatomy,* p. 34, discussing "gorgeous apparel" and concluding: "This is a great confusion and a general disorder: God be merciful unto us!"
9. Much of the literature cited by Louis Wright in his *Middle-Class Culture in Elizabethan England* (Ithaca, 1935) suggests that the immediate tendency of new gentlemen and merchants was toward an imitation of the old aristocracy; see especially pp. 138–139. It would appear that Puritanism had a major part in establishing a new and alternative style; see Ruth Kelso, *The Doctrine of the English Gentlemen in the Sixteenth Century,* University of Illinois Studies in Language and Literature (Urbana, Ill., 1929), vol. XIV, no. 1–2, p. 107.
10. See the description of the country gentlemen in Parliament under Elizabeth, in W. M. Mitchell, *The Rise of the Revolutionary Party in the English House of Commons, 1603–1629* (New York, 1957), p. 2ff.
11. Suzanne Labin, "Advanced Intellectuals in Backward Countries," *Dissent,* 6:240 (1959).
12. For the "usual role," see Karl Marx, *German Ideology* (New York, 1947), p. 39. Karl Mannheim's picture of the intelligentsia as a "socially detached stratum" would seem to describe its position only at particular and relatively rare historical moments. Even at such moments, it is doubtful that the intellectual achieves any sort of "objectivity." (See Mannheim, *Ideology and Utopia* [New York, n.d.], pp. 156ff.) At any rate, objectivity could hardly be claimed for the nervously self-regarding Puritan minister. He does achieve *originality;* he can be an innovator—in the absence of a superior social force. The introduction of new political ideas by the clerical exiles may be paralleled by the introduction of new economic techniques by Flemish and Dutch Protestant refugees; see F. A. Norwood, *The Reformation Refugees as an Economic Force* (Chicago, 1942). For a comprehensive view of Elizabethan England as a "backward" society, open to foreign inspired innovation, see Thorstein Veblen, *Imperial Germany and the Industrial Revolution* (New York, 1942), ch. iv.
13. Cartwright provides a useful example; see Scott-Pearson, *Cartwright,* pp. 168ff., 345, and *passim,* for the social connections of the sixteenth-century Puritan leader.
14. For examples of Presbyterian pretension, see W. L. Mathieson, *Politics and Religion: A Study in Scottish History from the Reformation to the Revolution* (Glasgow, 1902), I, 265 and *passim.* Cf. H. R. Trevor-Roper, "Scotland and the Puritan Revolution," in *Historical Essays: 1600–1750: Presented to David Ogg,* ed. H. F. Bell and R. L. Ollard (London, 1963), pp. 82–83.
15. *The Second Part of a Register,* Introduction, p. 15. See Field's eulogy of Knox: "so worthy and notable an instrument of God . . . what a heroical and bold spirit he was. . . ." Knox, *An Exposition upon Matthew IV* (London, 1574), Introduction, p. 91.
16. See Neale, *Parliaments: 1587–1601,* pp. 18ff. The "prophesyings" were described by the contemporary minister William Harrison; see *Harrison's Description of England in Shakespeare's Youth,* ed. F. J. Furnival (London, 1877), I, 17ff.
17. R. G. Usher, ed., *The Presbyterian Movement in the Reign of Queen Elizabeth* (London, 1905), Introduction, p. xxiii. This book contains the "Minute Book of the Dedham Classis," which is the best source of information on the clerical conferences. On Field see Patrick Collinson, "John Field and Elizabethan Puritanism," in *Elizabethan*

Government and Society: Essays Presented to Sir John Neale, ed. S. T. Bindoff et al. (London, 1961).

18. Bancroft, *Dangerous Positions and Proceedings* (London, 1593), pp. 126, 127.

19. Frere and Douglas, *Puritan Manifestoes,* Introduction, p. xiv. Knappen treats Puritan parliamentary tactics as "ordinary"—excluding from this category, however, the appeal to public opinion (*Tudor Puritanism,* p. 234). In fact, these tactics were quite unprecedented—this was apparent to men like Bancroft and of course to the Queen, as it is today to conservative historians like J. E. Neale.

20. Quoted in Irvonwy Morgan, *Prince Charles' Puritan Chaplain* (London, 1957), p. 111. For another description of lobbying, see Thomas Fuller, *Church History of Britain* (London, 1845), V, 83.

21. Neale, *Parliaments: 1587–1601,* p. 61. See *Second Part of a Register,* for copies of the petitions.

22. Mark Curtis, "The Alienated Intellectuals of Early Stuart England," *Past and Present,* no. 23 (November 1962), especially pp. 27–28. On university life in general, see William Haller, *The Rise of Puritanism* (New York, 1957),

ch. ii, and Mark Curtis, *Oxford and Cambridge in Transition: 1558–1642* (Oxford, 1959).

23. Morgan, *Prince Charles' Puritan Chaplain* (a life of John Preston), pp. 28–40.

24. Haller, *Rise,* pp. 293ff. See Milton's own statement of his commitment in his *Second Defense* (1654), *Works,* VIII, 119ff.

25. Thomas Carlyle, ed., *Oliver Cromwell's Letters and Speeches* (London, 1893), I, 79–80.

26. William Perkins, *Works* (London, 1616), I, 398; quoted in H. O. Porter, *Reformation and Reaction in Tudor Cambridge* (Cambridge, Eng., 1958), p. 312.

27. S. E. Morison, *The Founding of Harvard College* (Cambridge, Mass., 1935), appendix B, pp. 359–410.

28. Shepard, *Autobiography* (Boston, 1832), pp. 42–43; quoted in H. W. Schneider, *The Puritan Mind* (Ann Arbor, 1958), pp. 78–79; on Winthrop see E. S. Morgan, *The Puritan Dilemma: The Story of John Winthrop* (Boston, 1958), p. 40.

29. Quoted in Perry Miller, *Orthodoxy in Massachusetts 1630–1650* (Boston, 1959), p. 100.

67

Japan's Aristocratic Revolution

Thomas C. Smith

"An aristocracy," Alexis de Tocqueville wrote, "seldom yields [its privileges] without a protracted struggle, in the course of which implacable animosities are kindled between the different classes of society." Despite our democratic partialities, most of us would add, "And why should it?" To know the exalted pleasures of power, and the grace of refined taste with the means of satisfying it; to believe oneself superior on the only evidence that gives conviction—the behavior of others; and to enjoy all this as birthright, with no vitiating struggle, nor any doubt that one's privileges are for God, King, country, and the good of one's fellow man—what happier human condition, for a few, have men devised?

Yet, not all aristocracies have behaved as one fancies they must. Japan's warrior class, a feudal aristocracy though it differed from European aristocracies in crucial respects, did not merely surrender its privileges. It abolished them. There was no democratic revolution in Japan because none was necessary: the aristocracy itself was revolutionary.

Consider the bare outlines of the case. Until 1868, Japan was ruled by a class of knights who alone had the right to hold public office and bear arms and whose cultural superiority the rest of the population acknowledged. A party within this aristocracy of the sword (and swagger) took power in 1868 and embarked on a series of extraordinary reforms. Where there had before been little more than a league of great nobles, they created an immensely powerful central government: they abolished all estate distinctions, doing away with warrior privileges and throwing office open to anyone with the education and ability to hold it; they instituted a system of compulsory military service, although commoners had previously been forbidden on pain of death to possess arms; they established a system of universal public education; and much else. The result was a generation of sweeping and breathless change such as history had rarely seen until this century. I believe, though of course I cannot prove, that these decades brought greater changes to Japan than did the Great Revolution of 1789 to France.

Why was the Japanese aristocracy—or part of it—revolutionary? Why did it abandon the shelter of its historic privileges for the rigors of free competition, which, incidentally, many warriors did not

From Thomas C. Smith, "Japan's Aristocratic Revolution," *Yale Review,* L, No. 3 (Spring 1961), 370–383. Copyright 1961 Yale University Press. Reprinted by permission of the publisher.

survive? Its behavior, like that of a man who takes cold baths in the morning, requires a special explanation.

Two general lines of explanation have been offered; though no bald summary can do them justice, even on fuller accounts they leave much unexplained.

One might be called the prescient patriot theory. That is, the foreign crisis—to be quite specific, the unamiable Yankee, Commodore Perry, and the Americans, English, and Russians who followed him —stimulated the patriotism of the warriors and demonstrated to them the inadequacy of existing institutions, prompting them to make revolutionary innovations in the name of national salvation. This I believe is quite true in a way. But it takes for granted what most needs explaining. Communities in danger do not necessarily seek safety in innovation; commonly they reaffirm tradition and cling to it the more resolutely. Such was the first response to the challenge of the modern West in China and Korea; it also had intelligent and patriotic spokesmen in Japan.

The other explanation may be called the Western analogue theory. It emphasizes (in the century before Perry's arrival) the improvement of transport, the growth of towns, the development of trade, and the rise of a wealthy merchant class—all important developments which add much to our knowledge of pre-modern Japan. But, suggestive as they are, these developments would better explain, keeping the Western analogy in mind, an aristocracy being overthrown or reluctantly forced to share power with a rising new class, than an aristocracy conducting a social revolution.

Differences, rather than analogies, would seem more to the point. The man who takes cold baths is made of different stuff from most of us; and the Japanese warrior differed from the European aristocrat in ways that throw light on his seemingly odd class behavior. I wish to discuss three such ways that any satisfactory explanation of the aristocratic revolution, as I will call it, would have to take into account. One has to do with the relations of the warrior to the merchant class; another with social and economic distinctions within the warrior class; and the third with the relations of the warrior class to land and political power.

My earlier statement that there was no democratic revolution in Japan because the aristocracy was revolutionary has an important corollary: had there been a democratic revolution, the aristocracy would not have been revolutionary. Nothing unites an aristocracy so quickly and firmly in defense of its privileges as an attack from below, by classes in which it can perceive neither distinction nor virtue.

Unlike the Western bourgeoisie, townsmen in Japan never challenged aristocratic privileges, either in practice or theory. They were seemingly content with a secondary political role, finding apparent satisfaction in money-making, family life, and the delights of a racy and exuberant city culture. This political passivity is puzzling. It is not to be explained by numerical weakness (Tokyo was a city of a million people in the late eighteenth century, and Osaka was only slightly smaller); nor by poverty, nor illiteracy, nor political innocence. Least of all is it to be understood as reflecting an absence of resentment at the warriors' smug and strutting pretensions. There was resentment aplenty and there were many instances of private revenge; but for some reason resentment never reached the pitch of ideology, never raised petty private hurts to a great principle of struggle between right and wrong. For whatever reasons, townsmen acknowledged the political primacy of the warrior, leaving him free to experiment without fear that to change anything would endanger everything.

But, one may suppose, no ruling group ever launches on a career of radical reform merely because it is free to do so; there must be positive incentives as well. In the Japanese case these incentives were in part born of differences within the aristocracy. Such differences were not unique to Japan, of course, but they can rarely have been more pronounced anywhere.

On the one hand were a few thousand families of superior lineage and very large income, with imposing retinues and magnificent houses, who in practice, though not in law, monopolized the important offices of government; some offices in effect became hereditary. On the other hand was the bulk of the warrior class, numbering several hundred thousand families, who were cut off from high office and lived on very modest incomes; many in real poverty, pawning their armor and family heirlooms, doing industrial piecework at home to eke out small stipends, and resorting to such pitiful tricks as sewing strips of white cloth to the undersides of their collars so people might take them to be wearing proper undergarments. As warrior mothers proudly taught their children, a samurai might have an empty belly but he used a toothpick all the same.

But it was not so much the contrast between his own and the style of life of his superior that moved the ordinary warrior to fury. It was, rather, the impropriety of the merchant's wealth. Surely it was a perversion of social justice, that the warrior, who gave his life to public service, should live in want and squalor, while men who devoted themselves to money-making lived in ease and elegance, treated him with condescension and even rudeness, and in the end not infrequently found favor with the lord.

The merchant himself was not to blame since he merely followed his nature. Though he was feared and hated for that, ultimate responsibility lay with the effeminate high aristocrats who, through idleness or incompetence, failed to use their inherited power for the proper ends of government. No secret was made of the failure, either. Political writings were full of charges of the incompetence and corruption of government, of the fecklessness and indifference of princes; and the only remedy, it was said, lay in giving power to new men—men of lower rank, who were close to the people and whose characters had been formed by hardship. This was no revolutionary doctrine. It called for a change of men, not institutions; but the men it helped to power were in fact radical innovators.

This brings me to the final difference—or rather to two differences—between the Japanese warrior class and European aristocrats. Japanese warriors did not own land, and their political power was to a greater extent bureaucratic. I want to say more on these points, but first it will be helpful to see how a once feudal aristocracy had come to be without private economic or political power.

We must go back to the late sixteenth century. At that time warriors were scattered over the land in villages where they were overlords, levying taxes, administering justice, and keeping the peace. To defend their territories and lessen the hazards of life, they had long since banded together into regional military organizations consisting of a lord and his vassals. The normal state among such groups was war or preparation for war, that being the most direct means of increasing territory and territory of increasing strength and security.

Then, about the turn of the century, Tokugawa Ieyasu, a man of authentic genius, who had the remarkably good fortune of having two brilliant predecessors who had already half done what he intended, succeeded in conquering the country. Instead of destroying the feudal leagues or groups, however, he chose to use them to govern, taking care only to establish his own firm control over them. Seemingly a compromise between order and chaos, the resulting political structure, surprisingly, kept the peace for two and a half centuries.

These long years of orderly government, which favored economic growth and urban development, brought profound changes to the warrior class, alter-

ing not so much, however, the fact of warrior power (which remained uncontested) as the nature of it. I would like to mention three such changes in particular.

First was a change in the relation of warriors to the land. The lord, in order better to control his vassals and to achieve greater uniformity of administration within the territory he dominated, gradually restricted his vassals' power over their fiefs. He forbade them to administer local justice; he moved them from the land into a town which now grew up around the castle; he decreed what taxes they might collect and at what rates, then decided to collect the taxes himself and in return to pay them stipends in money or kind from his treasury.

There were local exceptions to the rule, but taking the country as a whole, fiefs in land disappeared. Land and the seignorial rights associated with it, once widely dispersed through the warrior class, were now consolidated in the hands of a few hundred noble families. The typical warrior had become a townsman living on a salary paid him by the lord, with the townsman's disdain for the country and country people. Both his juridical and social ties with the land were gone. If his fief was still an identifiable piece of land at all, it was rarely more than a unit of account, with other land, under the lord's common administration.

Second was the resulting bureaucratization of government. The lord, having taken into his hands his vassals' political and judicial functions, now governed an average population of about 100,000. To police so large a population, to collect its taxes and regulate its trade, to give it justice and maintain its roads and irrigation works, required a small army of officials and clerks. The lord, of course, used his vassals to perform these functions, to man the expanding and differentiating bureaucracy under him. The warriors who manned the bureaucracy exercised far more power over the rest of the population than warriors ever had before; but it was a new kind of power. Formerly power was personal and territorial: it pertained to a piece of land and belonged to a man as inherited right. Now it was impersonal and bureaucratic: it pertained to a specialized office to which one must be appointed and from which he might be removed.

There is unmistakable evidence of the increasingly bureaucratic nature of power in the more and more impersonal criteria for selecting officials. However writers on government might differ on other matters, by the late eighteenth century they were in astonishingly unanimous agreement that ability and specialized knowledge should take precedence over lineage and family rank in the appointment and promotion of officials. To this end they devised tests for office, job descriptions, fitness reports, official allowances, salary schedules, and pensions.

It was only in the lower ranks of officials that the ideal of impersonality came close to realization. Nevertheless, men of low rank were sometimes promoted to high office; merchants and occasionally even peasants with specialized qualifications were ennobled that they might hold office; and promotion in the bureaucracy became for warriors an important means of improving status. If the highest offices usually went to certain well-placed families, this was looked on as an abuse rather than proper recognition of rank, and an abuse that struck at the very foundations of good government. Moreover, many families of high rank were without office, and office rather than rank or wealth gave power.

Thus a group of young samurai who met on the morrow of Perry's first alarming visit to Japan, to consider what they might do for their country, were exhorted by their leader to do what they could *even though none held office.* One cried out: "But what *can* we do without office!" No one, it seems, complained of the lack of age, wealth, or high rank in the group.

The third change I would like to mention followed very largely from the second. The relationship between vassal and lord was slowly, silently, and profoundly transformed. It had been an intimate, intensely emotional relationship, based in no small part on the personal qualities of the lord, a relationship which existed between men who had fought side by side, grieved together at the loss of comrades, whose safety and families' safety depended on their keeping faith. During the centuries of peace and urban living, however, the relationship lost much of its emotional significance. It became distant and formal; it was hedged about by ceremonies and taboos; the vassal came to look on his lord less as a leader in war (for there was no war) than as an administrative head.

One sees this change in the changing concept of the ideal warrior. Once a strong, stout-hearted fellow, quick and warm in his sympathies, generous to the weak and unyielding to the strong, he becomes a man whose native intelligence has been disciplined in the classroom, who gets on harmoniously with his colleagues, who deals with matters within his jurisdiction without fear or favor. Loyalty is still the highest virtue for him; but where once it had meant willingness to follow the lord to death, now it meant giving the lord disinterested advice and conducting

oneself in a way reflecting credit on his administration. Qualities of the ideal bureaucrat had come to be viewed as the very essence of the warrior.

Moreover, the power of the lord as administrative head increasingly became merely symbolic; actual power passed to lower echelons of officials. Partly this was a result of the growing complexity of government, but in greater measure it was because the lord's position was hereditary and as time passed fewer and fewer of his breed were men of force and intelligence, fit for the top job. Vassals who still looked on the lord with awe were likely to be men who regarded him from a distance; those who saw him closer, despite all outward deference, could often scarcely conceal their contempt.

Indeed some hardly tried. An anonymous author, writing about 1860, calls the lords of his day timeservers; men brought up by women deep in the interior of palaces where no sound of the outside world penetrated; surrounded from childhood by luxury and indulged in every whim, they were physically weak and innocent of both learning and practical experience. But it was not revolution that was called for, only better education for rulers, that they might choose better officials. "The secret of good government," the writer confidently declared, "lies in each official discharging his particular office properly, which in turn depends on choosing the right man for the right job."

To summarize up to this point: the two and a half centuries of peace after 1600 brought great changes to the warrior class. They brought a change in the warrior's relationship to the land, which became purely administrative; in his relationship to political power, which became bureaucratic; and in his relationship to his lord, which became distant and impersonal.

I should like now to show, as concretely as I can, the connection between these changes and some aspects of the economic and social transformation of the country after 1868—my so-called aristocratic revolution.

Consider the creation in the years immediately after 1868 of a highly centralized government. This was a brilliant achievement which permitted the new leaders who came to power to formulate for the first time a national purpose and to call up energies that did not before exist. Political power had lain scattered in fragments over the map, each lord collecting his own taxes, maintaining his own army and navy, even following an independent foreign policy. Then, with astonishing speed the fragments were pulled together; a central government created; the entire country subjected to a single will. Feudal lords and their miniature kingdoms were swept away and one bureaucratic empire emerged in their place.

This change was possible in part because warriors had long since been removed from the land and stripped of seignorial rights. Had these interests remained, the warrior must first have been dispossessed of them—the base of his power and source of his pride. Whoever might eventually have succeeded in this would not likely himself have been a warrior, nor have accomplished the feat without a long and bitter struggle. As it was, only the great lords had to be deprived of their power, and the deed was sooner done because their powers had come to be exercised, in fact, by officials who might trade them for similar powers within a vastly larger organization.

But what of the vaunted loyalty of the samurai? One would think this must have prevented liquidation of the great territorial lords by their own vassals. The unconditional loyalty to the lord as war leader, however, had shrunk to the conditional loyalty of the administrative subordinate to his chief —a loyalty valid only so long as the chief performed his duties efficiently. That the great lords had long ceased to do this was known to all. Meanwhile a new and higher loyalty emerged, sanctioning—indeed, those who prevailed thought, demanding—the transfer of all power to a central government. This was loyalty to the Emperor, in whose name the aristocratic revolution was carried out. Nor was the emergence of this new loyalty unconnected with the decline of the older one: one suspects that men brought up in the cult of loyalty to the lord, as an absolute obligation and the noblest of human ideals, needed some escape from the disloyalty they felt in their hearts.

Second, consider how the new central government used its power to liquidate the four estates of which society was legally composed. Each estate—warrior, peasant, artisan, and merchant—was theoretically closed, and subject to detailed restrictions concerning occupation, residence, food, and dress peculiar to itself. The new government swept away such restrictions, and endowed men with extensive civic, though not political, rights. Henceforth anything that was legally permissible or obligatory for one, was permissible or obligatory for all; moreover, a system of free public schools very soon gave this new legal dispensation concrete social meaning. The warrior lost his privileges and immunities and was forced to compete in school and out with the sons of tradesmen and peasants. Even his economic privileges were done away with. Warrior stipends were commuted into national bonds redeemable in twenty years, after which time warriors, as such, had no claim on the national income.

Now, how is one to explain a ruling class thus liquidating its privileges, and not by a series of forced retreats but at a single willing stroke? Surely part of the answer lies in warrior privileges not being bound up with the ownership of land. To restrict or even abolish them, therefore, did not arouse fears for the safety of property, or stir those complicated emotions that seem to attach peculiarly to land as a symbol of family continuity and an assurance of the continuing deference of neighbors. Few ruling classes have ever been so free of economic bias against change. Warrior power was based almost exclusively on office-holding, and this monopoly was not immediately in danger because no other class had yet the experience, education, and confidence to displace warriors in administration. The striking down of barriers between estates, on the other hand, opened up to warriors occupational opportunities formerly denied them, a not insignificant gain in view of the large number of warriors who, with more than normal pride but neither property nor important office, were nearly indigent.

This brings me to a third aspect of the revolutionary transformation of Japanese society after 1868: the explosion of individual energies that followed the sudden abolition of status distinctions. Until then opportunity was very limited; men looked forward to following the occupations of their fathers, and even to living out their lives in their same villages and towns and houses. After it, everything seemed suddenly changed, and young men strove with leaping hope and fearful determination to improve their characters, to rise in the world, to become something different from their fathers.

For warriors the abolition of status restrictions meant finding new occupations and new roles in society. Few had enough property after the commutation of stipends to live without work, and not all could continue in the traditional occupations of soldier, official, policeman, and teacher. A very large number were forced either to suffer social eclipse or become merchants, industrialists, lawyers, engineers, scientists; or they saw in these occupations exciting new opportunities for wealth and fame.

In any case, there was a grand redirection of warrior talent and ambition. Despite the traditional warrior aversion to money-making and the merchant's love of it, for example, most of the first generation of modern entrepreneurs, above all the earliest and most daring, came from the warrior class. Nor is this to be explained merely by the occupational displacement of the warrior. Part of the explanation lies in the warrior's aristocratic background—his educational preferment under the old regime, his cult of action, and (at his best) his intense social idealism.

Okano Kitaro, a man born in a warrior family of low rank, who founded an important provincial bank, illustrates the point. He writes in his autobiography: "I lost my wife and third daughter in the earthquake of 1923. They were on their way to a resort hotel when the great quake struck, and their train plunged into the sea. When news of the accident reached me my courage failed, but after a while my sense of responsibility returned and I thought to myself, 'You are head of the Suruga Bank! You must discharge your duty as a banker in this time of trouble! Compared to that, your personal loss is a trifling matter!' My whole body trembled."

Other classes were scarcely less affected than warriors. Finding themselves suddenly free to become whatever wishes, effort, and ability could make them, with not even the highest positions in society closed to competition, they responded with an heroic effort at self-transcendence. Freedom of this kind must always be heady; but one wonders if it is not especially so when it comes suddenly, in societies with a strong sense of status differences, where the social rewards of success are more finely graded and seem sweeter than in societies less schooled to such distinctions.

In a charming little anecdote in his autobiography, Ito Chubei, the son of a peasant who became a leading industrialist, gives some hint of the poignancy of the hopes for success he shared with other peasant boys of his generation. Upon graduating from elementary school not long after 1868, the first boy in his village to do so, Ito called on the headmaster to take leave. He was not surprised to meet with an angry scolding, since he had been far from the model boy. After the master finished his scolding, however, he spoke glowingly of Ito's future and predicted that, despite his rebelliousness, he would be a success. "You will make your mark in the world, I know it!" he exclaimed. And at this the young boy, unable to hold back his tears, wept aloud. Years later, in recounting this incident to a reunion of his classmates, Ito was so affected that he wept again, and his gratitude to his former teacher was no less when, after the meeting, he discovered that all of his classmates had been sent off with exactly the same exhortation!

Such hopes were real because, though not everyone was equal in the competition for wealth and honor, the privileged estate under the old regime had no prohibitive or enduring advantage. In respect to income, for example, warriors were at no advantage over the rest of the population, and though they were the most literate class in society, literacy was very widespread among other classes as well, and it rapidly became more so through the new schools. But most important, perhaps, warriors could not for long claim a cultural superiority, compounded of superior education, elegance, and taste, to act as a bar to the achievement of others, or to divert others from achievement in the pursuit of aristocratic culture. Indeed, by the twentieth century, one can scarcely speak of an aristocratic culture in Japan, despite the peerage created by the government in 1885. Whether a young man came of warrior family could no longer be reliably told from his speech, manners, or social ideas; moreover, his origins were far less important to his self-esteem and the good opinion of others than whether he had a university diploma and where he was employed. I want to return to this point.

In hope of making its revolutionary behavior less puzzling than must otherwise appear, I have discussed three ways the Japanese warrior class differed from Western aristocracies—its relation to other classes, its internal divisions, and its relation to economic and political power. I should like now to suggest, very briefly, some of the ways in which Japanese society seems to be different because its modern revolution was aristocratic rather than democratic.

First, a point so obvious it need only be mentioned in passing: the aristocratic revolution, despite the civil equality and economic progress it brought, has not made for a strong democratic political tradition—but the contrary.

Second, more than any other single factor, perhaps, that revolution helps explain Japan's rapid transition from an agrarian to an industrial society. How different the story must have been had the warriors behaved as one would expect of an aristocracy, if they had used their monopoly of political and military power to defend rather than change the existing order.

Third, as there was no aristocratic defense of the old regime, there was no struggle over its survival; no class or party war in which the skirmish line was drawn between new and old, revolutionaries and conservatives. There was, of course, tension between traditional and modern, Japanese and Western, but not a radical cleavage of the two by ideology. All parties were more or less reformist, more or less traditional, and more or less modern; excepting perhaps the Communists, whose numbers were insignificant, no pre-war party thought of the past, as such, as a barrier to progress. It was a barrier in some respects, in others a positive aid. Modernization therefore appeared to most Japanese who thought about it at all, not as a process in which a life-or-death confrontation of traditional and modern took place, but as a dynamic blending of the two. I wonder if this does not account in large part for what has seemed to many people the uncommon strength of tradition in the midst of change in modern Japan.

Fourth, status-consciousness is relatively strong in Japan in part because there was no revolutionary struggle against inequality, but for that reason class-consciousness is relatively weak. These attitudes are by no means contradictory. The nervous concern of Japanese for status is quite consonant with their relatively weak feeling about classes—higher-ups to some extent being looked on as superior extensions of the self. This is an attitude familiar to us elsewhere. It is illustrated in Jane Austen by the servant who fairly bursts with pride when his master is made a baronet; and by Fielding's story of Nell Gwynn. Stepping one day from a house where she had made a short visit, the famous actress saw a great mob assembled, and her footman all bloody and dirty. The fellow, being asked by his mistress what happened, answered, "I have been fighting, madam, with an impudent rascal who called your ladyship a whore." "You blockhead," replied Mrs. Gwynn, "at this rate you must fight every day of your life; why, you fool, all the world knows it." "Do they?" the fellow said in a muttering voice; "They shan't call me a whore's footman for all that."

Finally, and this brings me back to an earlier point about the absence of an aristocratic culture in modern Japan, since warriors were never thrown on the defensive by the hostility of other classes, they never felt the need to make a cult of their peculiar style of life, either as evidence of virtues justifying their privileges or as compensation for loss of them. One wonders if Western aristocracies did not put exceptional value on leisure, gambling, dueling, and love-making, as aspects of the aristocratic way of life, in good part because they were a dramatic repudiation of bourgeois values.

In any case the warrior did not have the means of supporting a leisurely and aesthetic style of life. The revolution found him separated from the land, living on a government salary rather than on income from property; he therefore carried no capital inheritance from his privileged past into the modern age. He had no country estates, no rich town properties, no consols to spare unbecoming compromises with the crass new world of business. On the contrary, warriors were the chief makers of this world and they scrambled for success in it to escape social and economic oblivion.

Then too, this new world was irrevocably bound up with Western culture, whence came (with whatever modifications) much of its technology and many of its conventions. Success in it had very little to do with traditional skills and tastes, and much to do with double-entry bookkeeping, commercial law, English conversation, German music, French painting, and Scotch whiskey. Traditional arts were not forgotten, but they were never identified with a particular social class, least of all perhaps the upper class. It is significant, for example, that the pre-war Peer's Club in Tokyo, located within easy walking distance of the Foreign Office and the Ministry of Finance, was a great ugly stone building with marble stairways, thick carpets, mahogany bar, wallpaper, glass chandeliers, and French cuisine. In respect to such things all classes of Japanese, during the first generation or two after 1868, were born cultural equals. One could not learn of these things at home, any more than one could learn there a foreign language or the calculus. Such subjects were taught only in the schools, and the schools were open to anyone.

68

Non-Western Intelligentsias as Political Elites

Harry J. Benda

In the course of the past century, the non-western world has experienced a series of revolutionary changes, most, if not all, of them caused by the impact of western civilization on the traditional societies of Asia, Africa and the Middle East (and to some lesser extent also of Latin America). Since 1914, political evolution has proceeded at an accelerated rate, leading in recent times to the creation of new political, national entities, either by internal revolution or by the voluntary or forced withdrawal of western political control. In these states new political élites have come to power in many parts of the non-western world, and a pattern is emerging which allows some preliminary classifications of the new ruling groups.

I

Non-western societies can broadly be divided into two categories, those that have so far remained outside the orbit of westernization or have, at best, barely or only superficially embarked upon it; and those that have travelled along the road of westernization to a more or less marked and significant degree. The first group is fairly rapidly dwindling; its hallmarks are a continuation of the old socio-political moulds and *mores,* with political authority continuing to be vested in traditional élite groups. Some Arab sheikdoms, including (for the time being at least) Saudi Arabia, and the tribal societies in many parts of Negro Africa are the prototypes of this group.

Within the other category, that of westernizing non-western countries, two main types can be discerned. There are, first, those countries in which westernization—to whatever degree it has been or is being achieved—has actually been accomplished by traditional ruling classes, so that the revolutionary changes that have taken place in the process of adaptation have left the pre-revolutionary power pattern more or less intact. One of the outstanding examples of this type was, of course, nineteenth century Japan, which achieved the fullest degree of westernization attained anywhere in the non-western world through the guidance of the *samurai,* a military-feudal class that adapted itself, and directed the adaptation of the rest of the country, to a modern economic and political order without abdicating its intrinsic control, even though in time it came to share power with other classes, notably a new economic middle class.[1]

Other examples of this type can be found in more and more isolated instances in the Middle East, as *e.g.* Iran and (until recently) also Iraq. But the most numerous instances occur in the areas of the erstwhile Spanish and Portuguese empires in Latin America and Asia (mainly the Philippines). Spanish and Portuguese colonialism, an overseas extension of a feudal, pre-industrial west, through Christianization and cultural assimilation, called into existence a distinct social pattern whose main beneficiary was a class of either Spanish or *mestizo* landowners. It was they who either won independence from the mother countries (as in Latin America), or who at any rate gained social and economic prominence (as the *cacique* in the Philippines), where they only assumed political control under American aegis, after Spain had forfeited political control. By origin and education westernized, they naturally proceeded to lead in the further—but, compared to Japan, very slow—process of modernization while retaining political power in most parts of the former Spanish and Portuguese realms. The Mexican revolution of 1910 marked the first successful challenge to this socio-political *status quo,* to be followed by incidental upheavals in other parts of the area, notably Uruguay, Peru, and quite recently, in Cuba. As yet, however, the old pattern predominates. The fact that military dictatorships are such a common political institution in Latin America should not obscure the fact that in most cases (including Juan Perón until 1945) these military *juntas* are an offshoot of, and

From Harry J. Benda, "Non-Western Intelligentsias as Political Elites," *Australian Journal of Politics and History,* VI, No. 2 (November 1960), 205–208. Reprinted by permission of the publisher and the author.

tend to govern in the interest of, the traditional ruling classes of *hacienderos*.

In contrast to this prototype, political power in the second category is exercised by essentially new ruling groups. These new élites are the products of revolutionary changes of more profound significance, of social as well as of political revolutions. This second category consists of western-trained intellectuals and military leaders; for reasons which will presently be discussed, they can be subsumed under the more general, generic term of "intelligentsia." It is with these élites that the present paper is primarily concerned.

What distinguishes such non-western intelligentsias from most intellectuals in western societies is that they wield political power as it were independently, *i.e.,* they wield it in their own right, *as* intelligentsias, rather than as spokesmen for entrenched social forces. In other words, these intelligentsias are a *ruling class,* or rather *the* ruling class *par excellence,* whereas elsewhere intellectuals do not as a rule constitute a socio-political class of their own so much as an adjunct to other classes or groups in society. Representatives of this group can be easily identified throughout the non-western world. Among intellectuals as rulers are men like Nehru, Bourguiba, Kwame Nkrumah in Ghana and Francisco Madero in Mexico; among the "military intelligentsia," men like Nasser, al-Kassem in Iraq, Ne Win in Burma and also Argentina's Perón in his later years. In several non-western areas there has, moreover, been a tendency—recently demonstrated in Pakistan, Burma, and the Sudan—for the military to take over from civilian leaders within this intelligentsia.

A third category should, perhaps, be added to this list, *viz.* the communist élites in the Soviet Union, China and other non-western countries. To some extent they, in fact, historically fall within the categories listed above, for Lenin and several, if not most, of the early bolshevik leaders belonged to the intellectual prototype. While in the Soviet Union intellectuals as wielders of political power are now an anachronism,[2] the Chinese communist élite and its Asian variants (North Korea and North Viet Nam) are still largely recruited from among the intelligentsia of the early twentieth century; but the Chinese élite (as, for that matter, that of Yugoslavia) is, even by early Soviet standards, a unique intelligentsia in that it combines within itself "ideological" with "military" qualities that, among non-communist élites, tend to be divided into two, often competing, branches of the new non-western ruling classes. In this essay, communist élites will only receive peripheral consideration.

II

To avoid confusion, we should distinguish between two kinds of non-western intellectuals, *viz.* the "old" and the "new" intellectual. The first bears a distinct resemblance to the intellectual of the pre-industrial west, especially—though neither invariably nor exclusively—to the "sacral" intellectual of mediaeval times.[3] For purposes of our present analysis, this group is of relatively minor importance, since it does not furnish the new political élites of contemporary non-western nation states. This is not to deny that it has played, and in some significant ways continues to play, important political roles. But for one thing, the "old" intellectuals' role, like that of their western counterparts, has almost invariably been limited to an ancillary function, a political task delegated to them, so to speak, by more or less powerful classes in their societies. Not infrequently these intellectuals (in west and non-west) were actually members of the ruling classes themselves and did not exercise independent political power *qua* intellectuals (priests, scholars, etc.) as such.[4] Admittedly there were at all times also members of this "old" intelligentsia—such as Buddhist monks and Muslim *ulama*—who here and there allied themselves with the "outs" rather than the "ins," and who thus attained political significance by resisting the indigenous *status quo* and, in modern times, western colonialism. On the whole, however, the "old" intellectuals of the non-western world have suffered, and are suffering, a decline in their prestige, great as it may still be in areas hitherto untouched by modernization, especially the countryside, where the "new" intelligentsia's influence is only slowly penetrating.[5]

These "new" intellectuals are a recent phenomenon, for they are for the greater part the product of western education during the past few decades. But though western-trained and therefore in several respects kin of their western counterparts, they also differ from the western intellectuals in some very significant respects. In the first place it is not literacy *per se* but westernization that stamps the non-westerner as the "new" intellectual. To the traditional tasks of manipulating the tools of communication have now been added the tasks of what Toynbee has aptly called the "human transformer." He, so Toynbee says, has "learned the tricks of the intrusive civilization . . . so far as may be necessary to enable their own community, through [his] agency, just to hold its own in a social environment in which life is ceasing to be lived in accordance with the local tradition."[6] Since, then, the criteria of westernization and "transforming" are their hallmarks, non-western intelligentsias will tend to include wider categories than has been the case of western intelligentsias. Westernization—thinking and acting in western, rather than traditionally indigenous ways—can extend to types of social activity that in the west have not, as a rule, formed part of intellectual activity as such.

The most common, and historically also most significant, representative of this category is the new military group, the "Young Turks" so to speak, of the non-western world.[7] Nor is this at all surprising, since one of the prime contacts between west and non-west during the past century-and-a-half has been military in nature. As a result, the desire to attain equality with the west has often found expressions in terms of military equality, and officers were often the first social group to receive western training. Thus very frequently military westernizers, or westernized officers, have played a leading—at times a preponderant—role as independent political leaders in non-western countries. What distinguishes them as prototypes from traditional military rulers or dictators is, first, the fact that they are consciously using the means of coercive, military power for the attainment of essentially non-military, ideologically conceived social ends. And, second, unlike *e.g.* the military *juntas* of Latin America, the twentieth century military leaders in Asia and the Middle East are almost invariably social revolutionaries whose coming to power signals the end of the *status quo* and the eclipse of the traditional ruling classes. In some isolated instances of the twentieth century, non-western military leaders can be found who combine these ideological ends with the qualities of charismatic leadership. The Peróns, the Nassers, and the Castros are thus yet another phenomenon of the "new" non-western intelligentsia.

Second, to a degree unparalleled in the west, non-western intellectuals are very frequently an isolated social group in indigenous society. This is largely due to the fact that this "new" intelligentsia is not, as in the west, a product of organic social growth, but rather a product of alien education more or less precariously grafted on indigenous non-western societies.[8] Unlike the "old," predominantly sacral, intellectuals most of whom represented or spoke for the powers-that-were, and who thus performed the ancillary political roles usually assigned to intellectuals throughout the world, non-western intelligentsias do not, sociologically speaking, as a rule represent anyone but themselves. It is the exception rather than the rule that the young aristocrat, the landowner's son or for that matter even the scion of

a newly established bourgeois class, once he has acquired a western education of any kind, becomes the defender and spokesman of the class of his social origin. In turn, it is equally the exception rather than the rule that these "new" intellectuals will be supported by traditional social classes with a vested socio-economic interest in non-western societies.

In short, non-western intelligentsias, insofar as they are politically active—and, as will be seen, most of them are so to a far higher degree than in the west—tend to be social revolutionaries whose ideological aims as often as not militate against the *status quo*. Since, by definition, most of these aims are western-derived and transplanted to a social environment inherently still far more conservative than is true of the more advanced societies of the west, the task of social engineering becomes far more radical, and its proponents, the only group with a vested ideological interest in change, may find themselves driven to the use of radical reforms in order to hasten the approximation between reality and ideal.

There is, third, an additional reason for the relatively high incidence of radicalism among non-western intelligentsias, and it is connected both with their numbers and employability. As for size, it is on the whole relatively smaller than in industrialized western societies, for the number of persons able to afford western education, at home but particularly abroad, is more limited, and democratization of education has—with the exception of Japan—not yet paralleled that in the west. Yet, in spite of the smallness of non-western intelligentsias, the supply by far exceeds social demand. This unhappy phenomenon of the overproduction and underemployment of intellectuals is in part doubtless conditioned by the social, psychological and ideological traditions of most non-western societies.

Since education, in these predominantly pre-industrial communities, still enjoys great traditional prestige, western education has automatically attracted large numbers of non-westerners; but in spite of the fact that the process of modernization and industrialization would indicate the need for technical, vocational and scientific training, the aristocratic or gentry bias common to pre-industrial societies has, in fact, led non-western students to bypass these fields in favour of humanistic and legal studies. Thus, while a crying shortage exists almost everywhere in Asia, the Middle East, Africa and even Latin America for physicians, engineers and scientists, the bulk of non-western intellectuals can be found in the humanities and the law, both of which appear to promise status satisfaction in traditional terms. In fact, it is predominantly graduates in these fields that compose the present-day political élites of so many non-western states.

The absorptive capacity for this kind of intellectual is, however, severely limited in non-western societies. As a result, intellectual unemployment—a phenomenon by no means unknown in some western countries—has social and political consequences of great importance, for non-western intelligentsias are by and large politicized to a degree unknown in the west. Particularly in areas recently freed from western colonial control, where national liberation has invariably led to a rapid expansion of western-style education, the steady growth of a largely unemployable "intellectual proletariat" presents a very real political threat to stability and social peace.[9] There, the "new" intellectual-rulers are thus, paradoxically enough, threatened by their own kind.

Finally, there is a fourth factor of great importance, that of ideological causation. In opposing the *status quo* of traditional non-western societies, most of the "new" intellectuals also tend to oppose the *status quo* of a world which either directly or indirectly can be held responsible for the internal social and political conditions that form the prime target of the intelligentsia's attack. Thus "feudalism" as well as colonialism—rule by entrenched native classes or rule by foreigners—can be blamed on the political, military and economic preponderance of the western world. It is, therefore, not surprising that socialist and communist teachings have found far more fertile soil among non-western intellectuals than among their western counterparts. If it is symptomatic that the first statues ever erected for Marx and Engels stand on Russian soil, it would be equally fitting to find statues, say of Harold Laski gracing the main squares of New Delhi, Colombo, Rangoon, Accra, and even Baghdad.

Indeed, it is not too surprising that modern socialism has so profoundly attracted intellectuals all over the world. In the most highly industrialized countries of the west, it is, in fact, among intellectuals, rather than among the proletariat itself, that this social philosophy has found its most numerous adherents. This is very likely due to the fact that socialism, especially Marxism, is the most recent, and perhaps also the most coherent and intellectually most respectable version of the philosopher king, the social engineer ruling in the interest of abstract social justice *par excellence*. An intelligentsia thus not only has a vested intellectual interest in socialism, it also has a vested social and political interest in it. In spite of the Marxian theory of the class struggle as the major social determinant of history,

in spite even of the quasi-humility at times exhibited by Marx and his later followers in terms of their willingness to be "guided by," and "learn from," the proletariat, programmatic, "scientific" socialism has always, as Lenin himself bluntly stated, been the product of a bourgeois intelligentsia.[10] It is the "vanguard" of the proletariat, not the proletariat itself, that is cast for the crucial role of governing, and for quite obvious reasons: in proclaiming the rule of social justice, the socialist intellectual is proclaiming rule by his own kind.

But whereas in the west the Marxist intellectual's political aspirations have as a rule encountered great difficulties, at least in working-class movements dominated by, or at least highly dependent upon, union leaders,[11] the non-western socialist intellectual can in the absence of a sizable proletariat (as well as of other organized socio-economic forces) actually become ruler in his own right. Socialism, in addition to providing the desired combination of anti-western—*i.e.*, anti-capitalistic—westernization also provides the non-western intellectual with a justification for rule by the intelligentsia. In embracing it, he feels *ipso facto* justified in looking askance at political competition from other segments of society, such as "old" intellectuals, aristocracies, and landowners, but also nascent capitalistic middle classes.[12] Planning in the name of socialism means planning with the intelligentsia as planners, irrespective of whether they be the military intellectuals of Nasser's stamp or the "pure" intellectuals of the Nehru variety.

III

Up to this point we have drawn no distinction between the military and the civilian, or "pure," intellectual; yet this distinction is of great analytic significance. It is by no means a matter of historic accident whether a non-western country, insofar as it has become westernized and undergone change, is ruled by either one or the other prototype. The existence of a military group of young officers in itself depends on the political status of a country; it depends, that is to say, on the fact of political (though not necessarily economic) independence. It is, therefore, only in non-colonial countries that westernization has been primarily channeled through military leaders. Kemal Ataturk, Yüan Shih-k'ai and the Satsuma and Choshu *samurai* are good examples, as are the many military régimes in Latin America and the newly emerging élite groups in the Middle East.

Wherever, then, the impact of the west did not

lead to outright political domination, wherever a non-western society was given a chance of adjusting to the demands of the modern era by internal adaptation without suffering direct political control from the outside, there the officer has almost invariably emerged as the modern political non-western leader. Since he as a rule possesses a monopoly of physical power, he can fairly easily grasp control in a society where he represents the most powerful—even if numerically weak—social group with a vested interest in modernization and change.[13]

Westernization as well as the *status quo* prevailing in these countries, have, as we said, combined to stamp many, if not most of these younger military leaders with an ideological orientation not usually found among the professional soldiers in the west, or for that matter among the older generation of officers in independent non-western states. While this orientation is at times fairly close to the socialism so prevalent among non-western intelligentsias in general, while as a rule little love is lost between them and either the aristocracies, clergies or the nascent capitalist classes in their lands, their political goals tend to center around the creation of strong, "socially just" régimes rather than around the creation of parliamentary régimes. In their distrust of the professional politician, including the "civilian" intelligentsia, non-western military leaders like the Japanese *samurai* of the nineteenth century and Colonel Nasser of today bear a recognizable similarity to the military prototype of modern societies in the west. Under a military régime "pure" intellectuals play a subordinate role as political leaders, if indeed they are at all tolerated by their military colleagues. In some of the contemporary non-western military dictatorships the intellectual as an independent political actor is politically as ineffectual as he was in, say, Meiji Japan. He has the choice between playing auxiliary to the new powers-that-be and being doomed to political impotence.

If the military intelligentsia has emerged as the most universal revolutionary phenomenon in the non-colonial countries of the non-western world, the "pure" intellectual has made his appearance as political ruler in many areas recently freed from western colonialism. This is an interesting phenomenon, for, unlike the military, the "pure" intellectual does not *a priori* command the means of physical coercion that have, throughout history, made military power so significant a factor. It is, indeed, a phenomenon rooted in modern western colonialism itself. The absence of an indigenous military élite proper is one of the most significant sociological aspects of colonialism of all times. Since military

power rests with the alien ruling class, this occupation is closed to the indigenous population.[14] Nineteenth century colonialism had other stultifying effects on social growth as well, particularly in preventing or retarding the development of a sizable bourgeoisie within the populations of many areas. This is particularly true of the plural societies of South-East Asia and parts of Africa, in which the introduction of capitalist economies has tended to benefit foreign rather than indigenous entrepreneurs.

It is this stunted social growth that turned the western-trained intellectuals—the doctors, the lawyers, the engineers, the professors and the students —into the only sizable group with a vested interest in political change. Unlike their military counterparts in non-colonial areas, however, the intellectuals of colonial Asia and Africa remained politically impotent as long as colonialism lasted, *i.e.*, they had no instruments for physically seizing power, and had to content themselves with the weapons of ideological warfare, political organization and nationalist protest within the limits set by their alien overlords. As the westernized leaders of nationalism and anti-colonialism, these non-western intelligentsias formed a numerically very small, and in most cases also very weak, élite group. In some few areas, like British India, where indigenous entrepreneurs had gained a measure of economic strength, they have supported the intelligentsia in order to bolster their position *vis-à-vis* foreign competition. In most cases, however, the nationalist leadership did not have such support at its disposal. Smarting under the constant vigilance of colonial masters, it was vociferous rather than politically entrenched. It is doubtless true that these intellectuals—as westernized intelligentsias throughout the non-western world—have sought identification with the rural mass of the population and the "nation" at large, but this identification rests, as we will presently discuss, on slender roots. Partly this is due to the very westernization of these urban élite groups and partly to the fact that in virtually all colonies access to the peasantry was rendered extremely difficult, if not impossible, by the colonial authorities. Only in British India again did the urban intelligentsia—largely through Gandhi—succeed in forging a link with the peasantry.

Thus, whereas military leaders were able to grasp political control in non-colonial areas whenever the opportunity arose from the internal power constellation—as *e.g.* in China after 1911, in Japan after 1867, in Turkey in 1918, in Thailand in 1931, etc.— the "pure" intellectuals had to wait for external liberation from colonial rule to step into the political arena as actual rulers in their own right. It is not coincidental that the Japanese occupation of South-East Asia performed this act of liberation for the intellectuals of Burma and Indonesia[15] and that the train of post-war liquidations of colonial possessions has paved the way for the intelligentsia elsewhere, as in India, Ghana, Tunisia and to some extent also in Malaya. In the social and political vacuum created by modern colonialism, the western-trained intellectual was, at the crucial hour, the only politically and ideologically trained élite group on whom political power could devolve.

But if there is historic logic in the emergence of "civilian" intellectuals as rulers in post-colonial non-western areas today, continuation of this fairly unique phenomenon is fairly problematical. The demise of colonialism itself has brought with it the breaking down of the artificial barriers to social growth that were, as we said, one of its most significant sociological aspects. In the newly independent countries of Asia and Africa the "pure" intellectual is now free to search for non-intellectual avenues to social status and prestige, and some of them—Aung San of Burma is an excellent example—have rapidly turned towards a military career. In this sense, colonial countries are socially "coming of age," and are demonstrating the adaptability of non-western intelligentsias to new social conditions, an adaptability previously exhibited by Leon Trotsky and some members of the Chinese communist intelligentsia in a non-colonial setting.

Second, quite apart from this incidental transformation of individual "pure" intellectuals, independence, and in particular the revolutionary struggle against colonialism—in South-East Asia, conscious Japanese policies[16]—have given rise to a distinct group of military leaders, who socially, educationally and often also ideologically stand apart from the western-trained academic intellectuals of the colonial era. Having played a significant role in the liberation of their countries and having gained access to military power, they have also created a political following, both among their subordinates and, quite often, among the public at large. The military, in short, have become a competing élite which has increasingly come to challenge the "civilian" intelligentsia's monopoly of political power in formerly colonial non-western countries.

As the struggle between Sun Yat-sen and Yüan Shih-k'ai symbolically showed, the contest between "pure" intellectuals and military leaders is, because of the latter's physical superiority, fraught with grave dangers to the civilian leadership. But the new military élites, it must be remembered, are for the greater part not simply war lords or "strong men" only.

To a large extent, they, too, make ideological appeals—if nothing else, appealing for national unity in the face of disunited civilian leadership—that render them truly formidable political opponents.[17] In recent times, military leaders have taken over from civilian intelligentsias in the Sudan, in Burma and in Pakistan,[18] while in Indonesia army leaders appear to be gaining increasing political influence.[19]

The apparent ease with which civilian régimes are being replaced by military ones points to the inherent weakness and instability of rule by "pure" intellectuals. The causes of these are not far to seek. In the first place, the "pure" intellectual, however well versed he may have been in the politics of opposition to colonialism, very rarely possesses actual administrative experience that could make him an effective and efficient statesman. Second, the democratic or parliamentary institutions imported by western-trained intellectuals are as a rule operating in a social and political vacuum, with no organizational framework connecting the new edifice at the center with the country at large. It is true that many non-western intellectuals are stressing the intrinsically democratic nature of traditional village government in their countries; but it may be doubted whether this "village democracy"—whatever its merits—can serve the purpose of providing an adequate underpinning for a modern, viable constitutional state.

Finally, the political parties functioning under most non-western parliamentary systems do not as a rule represent organized social forces so much as factions centered around personalities. The temporary unity exhibited before the attainment of independence thus tends to wane once nationhood has been achieved, and to give way to fierce factional struggles.[20] It is these struggles, accompanied by lack of central purpose and achievement, that leave the intellectual in a precarious position, and thus render the appeal of the military so forceful.

The substitution of a military for a civilian régime does not necessarily involve more than a change within the intelligentsia, and thus a structural change in the façade of government. The short-cut solution of the military *coup* does no more than eradicate the often anaemic institutional forms of a western-style political system; it does not substitute more viable forms in their stead. If the "pure" intellectuals encounter almost insuperable obstacles in realizing their goals, the military leadership, moving into the *terra incognita* of politics, may find it at least equally difficult to translate their long-term aspirations into reality.

If the difficulties besetting non-western intelligentsias as ruling classes of both types appear formidable, they are in many areas partly offset, or at least obscured, by the "countervailing" power of *charisma* embodied in individual members of both the civilian and the military, such as Nehru, Nasser, Nkrumah, Sukarno and Castro, to mention but a few outstanding examples.[21] The simultaneous appearance of charismatic leadership in Asia, Africa, the Middle East and Latin America is perhaps one of the most important phenomena accompanying the political readjustments in the contemporary non-western world.[22] It is the charismatic leader who by force of sheer personality can apparently bridge the gap between the westernized élites and the rural population, and who can serve as the symbolic link between the ruler and the ruled.

It is a moot point whether the presence of such leadership alone can suffice to guarantee a measure of political stability or to extract the co-operation required to set sustained modernization and economic improvement in motion. It is similarly a moot point whether an intelligentsia, bereft of its charismatic leader, will produce adequate cohesion to continue in power.[23] At any rate, there can be little doubt that the charismatic leader is already a deviant from the standard pattern of the western-educated intelligentsia, whether civilian or military: insofar as the charismatic appeal is politically important in the non-western world it is so not because of these leaders' western training and ideological orientation, but perhaps in spite of them. In the eyes of the general population, the charismatic leader may well be *malgré lui*, the reincarnation of the "old," sacral intellectual rather than the modernizer and westernizer he claims to be.

IV

An intelligentsia ruling in its own right as a ruling class or group is, strictly speaking, not necessarily a specific non-western phenomenon only. In the course of western history, there have been brief episodes when intellectuals—sacral, secular and military—have performed similar functions, as for example Calvin, Cromwell, the Jacobins, or the Puritan founders of Massachusetts. This random list indicates that rule by intelligentsias has almost invariably been the hallmark of revolutionary eras in the west. It may thus be suggested that the differences between western and non-western history—leaving aside the specific characteristics of the new non-western élites discussed in the preceding pages—are quantitative rather than qualitative. In other words, since the non-western social and political revolution of the twentieth century is a virtually global phenomenon following the wake of historically well-nigh simultaneous dissolutions of tradi-

tional social moulds, what in the west have been chronologically and geographically disparate, local and sporadic incidents, have now assumed the proportions of a world-wide socio-political phenomenon. If, then, western history is to serve as a measuring rod, it could be further argued that rule by contemporary intelligentsias in parts of Asia, Africa, the Middle East and Latin America may represent an interim stage in the political evolution of the non-western world, and that sooner or later it will be superseded by other élites and new forms of political organization.

Suggestive as such a hypothesis may be, it needs to be qualified. The brevity of revolutionary régimes led by intellectuals in western history was intimately connected with the presence of powerful social and economic classes bent on eliminating the "dictatorship of the intellectuals" imposed on their societies. These opponents may have belonged to entrenched social interests (as *e.g.* the Genevan bourgeoisie or the much-discussed English gentry of the 1640s), or, more paradoxically, to groups born of, or vastly strengthened by, the very changes inaugurated by the intelligentsia (as *e.g.* the French bourgeoisie or the *nouveaux riches* landowners and businessmen in Massachusetts). *Mutatis mutandis,* a very similar process led to the elimination of the original core of bolshevik intellectuals by a new generation of party bureaucrats and managers in the 1930s, a process anticipated by Trotsky, and later described by both Milovan Djilas and Arthur Koestler. In the west, intellectuals have only been able to rule in the intervals between the breakdown of an old social and political order and the establishment of a new one (or, as in the *terra nova* of Massachusetts, between the birth of a new order and its normalization, so to speak). Their régimes have usually been ended by "counter-revolutionary" movements instigated by social classes who, in the proper Marxian sense, have commanded wealth and power, as a rule based on control over important sectors of the economy, and who were thus able, sooner rather than later, to displace the intellectual as wielder of independent political power. This done, the intelligentsia invariably found itself reduced to its more "normal" and ancillary role in politics, *i.e.,* it reverted to the task of verbalizing or ideologizing the political interests of other classes or groups, either those in power or those opposing them.

It is not unlikely that intelligentsias represent a similar intermediate stage in the non-western political evolution. But it is probable that their displacement is not a matter of the immediate future, even though, as we have seen, there exists an apparently growing trend for power to devolve upon the military within these non-western intelligentsias. Members of older social groups, such as landowners[24] or sacral intellectuals—as *e.g.* the Muslim Brotherhood in Egypt, the Hindu Mahasabha in India, or the Darul Islam in Indonesia—though they may here and there exert significant political influence, seem as a rule to be lacking in strength or social dynamism to constitute a real threat to the new order. The urban bourgeoisie is numerically and often also economically too weak to challenge the new intelligentsia-rulers. And, finally, the revolutions are of too recent date to have laid the groundwork for the growth of other social groups able and willing to form a viable opposition, in terms of economic strength at least.

For quite some time to come, non-western intelligentsias may therefore be expected to retain their virtual monopoly of political power. To a large extent this continuity seems to be assured by the fact that the national polities over which they rule are of recent date, and, indeed, of the intelligentsias' own making. Essentially, these are modern governmental edifices superimposed on societies which, as yet, do not nourish them by established channels of political communication. The political process in non-western societies is thus, to a far greater extent than is true of most western societies, a superstructure without viable underpinning.[25] This state of affairs, for sure, cannot but be transitional. But as long as it lasts, intelligentsias are very likely to remain the prime political actors in many non-western countries. Political changes are likely to take place within these élites rather than to affect their predominance as ruling classes.

NOTES

1. In spite of the fact that the Meiji Restoration of 1868 marked a break with the preceding political order, in terms of élite structure it signified a change within the *samurai* class rather than a social revolution.

2. See for example "L," "The Soviet Intelligentsia," *Foreign Affairs*, XXVI (1957), 122–130.

3. On "sacral" and "secular" intellectuals see Edward Shils, "The Intellectuals and the Powers: Some Perspectives for Comparative Analysis," *Comparative Studies in Society and History*, I (1958–1959), 5–22.

4. This is basically true also of the Chinese scholar-gentry, in spite of the fact that entry into that élite group was—in theory and partly also in practice—open to all. To some extent, the scholar-gentry, by representing the state cult of Confucianism, also fulfilled some of the functions of the sacral intellectual, in competition with the Buddhist priesthood.

5. For a fuller discussion, see the present writer's essay, "Revolution and Nationalism in the Non-Western World," in Warren S. Hunsberger, ed., *New Era in the Non-Western World* (Ithaca: Cornell University Press, 1957), pp. 17–51.

6. Arnold J. Toynbee, *A Study of History*, Abridgement of Volumes I–VI by D. C. Somervell (New York, 1947), p. 394.

7. Toynbee, *ibid.*, p. 395, specifically includes the military leaders in the category of the intelligentsia.

8. *Cf.* E. Shils, "The Culture of the Indian Intellectual," *Sewanee Review* (1959), pp. 3–46. Shils seeks to minimize the extent of the Indian intellectuals' "alienation."

9. *Cf.* Justus M. van de Kroef, "The Educated Unemployed in Southeast Asia," *Journal of Higher Education*, XXXI (1960), 177–184.

10. The fact that the intelligentsia is the actual ruling group in the early stages of communism has never been admitted in Marxist analysis. For a recent re-statement, *cf.* Oscar Lange, *Some Problems Relating to the Polish Road to Socialism* (Warsaw, 1957), p. 28: "Wherein lies the specific character of the intelligentsia? In the fact that it is not really a class. Its position comes from the superstructure and not from production relations. . . . Its very essence prevents it from being an independent force; it can only express the opinions and wishes of the working class. . . . It can help, but it is not the social force which by itself can bring about social change. . . ."

11. Lenin encountered such opposition and crushed it after the Kronstadt revolt, thereby subjugating the workers to the control of the party intelligentsia. By contrast, Harold Laski was never able to play a truly decisive role in the British Labour Party.

12. *Cf.* the following comment connected with the governing intellectual élite group in Indonesia: "Speaking to the Constituent Assembly on November 10, 1956 [Sukarno] expressed his fears at the recent emergence of a great many prospective Indonesian capitalists. . . . [He] believed that the development on the Indian model would mean, as Sukarno sees it, permitting the growth of a group of capitalists; in other words the *oligarchy of the educated* who now control the society would have to share power with a private entrepreneurial group . . . with different interests. To have economic development on either the Russian or the Chinese model would obviate the need to surrender power." (Italics added.) Leslie H. Palmier, "Sukarno, the Nationalist," *Pacific Affairs*, XXX (1957), 117–118.

13. See *e.g.* Dankwart A. Rustow, *Politics and Westernization in the Near East* (Princeton, N.J., 1956), pp. 26–33.

14. This does not mean that the western colonial powers did not recruit soldiers among the native population. But, for one thing, colonial armies were almost invariably officered by westerners, and, for another, in many instances the soldiers were purposely recruited from among ethnic and/or religious minority groups in the colony.

15. In Thailand (a non-colonial country) and the Philippines (where Spanish rule had created a quasi-feudal social system), the Japanese did not vitally affect the pre-war socio-political structure. In the former country the military oligarchy retained power; in the latter the landowning class. Only among the anti-Japanese Filipino underground did potential new leaders, like Ramon Magsaysay and Huk leader Luis Taruc, come to the fore. Magsaysay's presidency in the 1950s constituted the first major breach in the Philippine political scene, in that it temporarily brought to power an intelligentsia, partly military in character, and based on widespread peasant support centered on the charismatic leadership of the president. Since Magsaysay's sudden death, the pre-war *status quo* seems to have been more or less restored.

16. For Indonesia, see the present writer's *The Crescent and the Rising Sun; Indonesian Islam during the Japanese Occupation, 1942–1945* (The Hague/Bandung/New York, 1958), pp. 138–141, 172–173, 203.

17. As we said earlier, it is so far only among Asian communist élites that a more or less complete merger has apparently been effected between "pure" and military intelligentsias. It was, in fact, Russian advice and aid that had helped to produce a similar merger within the Kuomintang

leadership in the 1920s. In the measure that the Kuomintang in later years de-emphasized ideology and political organization it dug, so to speak, its own political grave by yielding supremacy to the Chinese communists who excelled in combining military striking power with organizational and ideological strength.

18. Burma and Pakistan are not, strictly speaking, identical cases. The civilian régime displaced in Pakistan was not a régime of intellectuals so much as of landowners. Schematically, Pakistan's case is thus comparable to that of Iraq rather than that of Burma.

19. *Cf.* Guy J. Pauker, "The Role of Political Organizations in Indonesia," *Far Eastern Survey,* XXVII (1958), 141–142.

20. *Cf.* Richard L. Park, "Problems of Political Development," in Philip W. Thayer, ed., *Nationalism and Prospects in Free Asia* (Baltimore, Md., 1956), pp. 103–104, and Vera M. Dean and others, *The Nature of the Non-Western World* (New York, 1958), pp. 212–213.

21. On charismatic leadership see also George McT. Kahin, Guy J. Pauker, and Lucian W. Pye, "Comparative Politics in

Non-Western Countries," *American Political Science Review,* XLIX (1955), 1025, and Gabriel L. Almond, "Comparative Political Systems," *Journal of Politics,* XVIII (1956), 401.

22. Charismatic leadership is, nonetheless, not a *sine qua non* of political modernization as witness its absence in Meiji Japan, republican China and in communist countries. Stalin's "cult of the individual" or Mao's all-pervading presence is by no means synonymous with *charisma.*

23. The assassination of Aung San in Burma was followed by gradual dissolution of the party headed by him, until the civilian intelligentsia surrendered power voluntarily to the military.

24. Their political influence appears to be stronger in formerly Hispanic lands than elsewhere. Moreover, it is very likely that in Latin America they have been able to obtain aid from abroad, as witness the short-lived régime of Col. Arbenz in Guatemala.

25. See also the illuminating essay by Lucian W. Pye, "The Non-Western Political Process," *Journal of Politics,* XX (1958), 469–486.

69

Congress Party Elites[1]

Myron Weiner

Modernizing societies typically create conditions which encourage individuals who have not previously participated in politics to do so. Both mass media and mass public education create a new public awareness, and as the state itself takes on new functions more and more individuals seek to influence what the state will do. Peasants may press for more irrigation works or resist new taxes, a linguistic minority may feel threatened by a government's language policy in the schools, tenants may agitate for security of tenure, and the educated unemployed may clamor for jobs. These demands become strains upon a political system not simply because a stray individual here or there becomes interested in political matters, but because whole social groups and whole communities now want something out of the political system.

Not all governmental elites welcome the demands of new groups, nor are they willing to share power. Indeed, European history is replete with accounts of governmental elites who refused to share power and who used repressive means to maintain their monopoly of authority. In the developing areas

From Myron Weiner, *Congress Party Elites* (Bloomington: Carnegie Seminar on Political and Administrative Development, University of Indiana, 1966), pp. 1–19. Reprinted by permission of the author and the Carnegie Seminar.

today few governing elites have been willing to share power or to admit the legitimacy of opposition parties. Though many elites utilize a populist, nationalist, and socialist rhetoric, they repress the opposition and in practice restrict the admission of new elites into the government. Needless to say, some systems have been more open than others, the varieties and reasons for restricting entrance into the elite are complex and varied, and a policy of sharing power has not necessarily ensured stability or rapid modernization.

Nonetheless, there is reason to believe that governments which institutionalize channels of political participation are likely to create a population which is loyal to both the political system and the nation. In the developing areas today India has thus far been one of the few successful political systems in the handling of new political participants. Considering the extraordinary ethnic diversity, the vast gaps in income, and the hierarchical character of the social system, it is remarkable that the country has been plunged neither into civil war nor revolution and that insurgency movements have been confined to a few tribal areas. Surely the reason is not public apathy or the absence of social conflict, for social tensions have been great and political participation, both at the mass and elite level, has been high. Voting turnout is considerable—over 55 per cent for state assemblies and parliament. Moreover, there have been intense conflicts between hills and plains people, linguistic groups, religious groups, and between peasant proprietors and tenants.

The single most important institution in India through which new participants, both elite and mass, have entered the political system is the Congress Party. Since 1885, when it was formed as India's nationalist movement, it has been the vehicle through which many social groups have sought to achieve their economic, political, and social aims. Ever since India became independent, the Congress Party—unlike most nationalist movements—has continued to provide opportunities for new participants. How and why this is so is the major concern of this essay. In particular we shall explore the changing pattern of recruitment to Congress in selected local areas, partly to show how the party has adapted itself to new social groups, but also, and more generally, to specify some of the conditions which have made it possible for Congress to absorb new political elites.

Indian Social Organization and Elite Change

In any analysis of changing elite recruitment within the Congress Party, it is first important that we distinguish among different kinds of social groups in Indian society whose patterns of political participation have been changing. It is a common error to associate political participation in India, as in other developing areas, simply and exclusively with membership or involvement in the nationalist movement, for to do so is to neglect significant types of political involvement. Indeed, as we speak of changing patterns of political participation and elite recruitment in India, it is rare to see shifts from total non-involvement to involvement. Rather, we find changes from one form of political action to another. The issue, thus, is not so much why apathetic people become political participants, but rather why the levels of political action change. Using this framework we can discern at least four major social groups whose patterns of political activity have changed in India in recent years, with a significant bearing on Congress Party elite recruitment.

1. In the pre-independence period there existed in many parts of the subcontinent powerful local elites who can be said to have had a virtual monopoly over both political authority and land—maharajas, samindars, watandars, jagirdars, and other titled powerholders. These elites exercised power in the village, the taluka, the district, and the state, and their influence was felt mainly in administration and upon executive authority. In recent years, though most of these men have lost their titled power and much of their landed property, many have shifted from closed administrative politics to open electoral politics. In Orissa and Rajasthan, for example, Congress has absorbed many of the ruling families, and in other regions ex-rulers and large landholders have joined opposition parties.

2. A second type of political elite includes the urban professional classes—the journalists, lawyers, academicians, and administrators. These were among the earliest supporters of the nationalist movement and, indeed, could be described as the initial organizers of the movement. Sections of this class joined the British administrative structure and, in a sense, shared power with the British, while other sections sought to undercut British power. As the nationalist movement under Gandhi's leadership grew in mass character and reached into the countryside, the influence of the urban elite upon the movement and subsequently upon government declined.

3. By the mid-1930's the small landholding rural gentry in the countryside and the bazaar merchants in the towns became increasingly active in the nationalist movement. This group often had exercised considerable power in panchayats, municipal councils, and quasi-governmental cooperatives, but not until the mid-thirties in many areas did they extend their political participation into the nationalist movement and into the state government. We speak today of "rising castes"—that is, of the Reddis and Kammas in Andhra, the Nadars and other non-Brahmins in Madras, the Lingayats in Mysore, and the Jats in Rajasthan—as if they were new to politics. The important point, however, is that these "new" elements at the state level have always been politically active at the local level. They are "new" political participants only in the sense that the level of their participation has changed and that they are now engaged in party, not simply personal, politics.

Among these groups it has been the rural gentry with massive electoral backing which has moved readily into state politics, gradually displacing the more educated urban classes. The critical factor in this development is the growing importance of numbers in an electoral system, particularly when the numerically large groups are also in possession of some economic means. Thus neither the numerically large, poor lower castes nor the small, wealthy upper castes are now as important as the middle castes, who are both large and moderately prosperous.

4. The last type of political activist can appropri-

ately be described as traditionally nonactivist at any level of politics. Here we have in mind the lowest castes—the landless laborers, tenant farmers, the sweepers and others in the city performing menial tasks, and the unskilled factory laborers. Unlike the rural gentry and bazaar merchants, who played an active part in local affairs even before they moved into state politics, these social groups rarely participated, even in local affairs. These elements are now prodded into political life because the establishment of adult suffrage has made them a target of political parties and ambitious politicians. In the general elections special seats are reserved for members of scheduled castes and tribes, and the Congress Party and the Communists have made a special effort to win electoral support from these communities. In a few instances these communities have produced their own political leadership, who have become sufficiently influential, although rarely in proportion to their size, to make their support or lack of support a critical factor in some states. In Andhra, for example, the selection of a Jarijan Chief Minister by the Congress Party was an important factor in the movement of Jarijan landless laborers away from the Communist Party in the 1962 general elections of state assembly and parliament. In Gujarat the Swatantra Party succeeded in attracting the leadership of the Bariya community, a group of lower castes, away from Congress, thereby winning enough seats to establish itself as a formidable opposition party in the state.

When the so-called lower classes enter politics, they often do so not by moving into the local political arena but by leapfrogging directly into state politics. Landless laborers may hesitate to oppose their employers for control over local government, but need not fear sanctions if they support opposing candidates for more remote state assembly and parliamentary seats. Thus in Andhra the landless laborers almost never have fought for control over village panchayats, but often have given their votes to Communist assembly and parliamentary candidates. Finally, it should be noted that the lower classes, like other communities, do not necessarily enter politics as a cohesive force, but typically split into factions which in turn are allied to existing factions within political parties.

Congress Party Cadres

The changing relationship of landlords, the urban middle classes, peasant proprietors and the lower castes have had important consequences for the

Congress Party, especially at the local level where recruitment occurs. Therefore, in order to see how recruitment patterns change, it is essential that we first look at the local Congress Party organization. Congress is divided into approximately four hundred district organizations, each covering a population of a million or more and each subdivided into units known as taluka and mandal committees. As part of a study of the Congress Party, I examined five district Congress committees and their subunits in some detail, data from three of which will be reported briefly here. These three districts are predominantly rural, though each has several larger towns. For each of the three districts we have some data on the age, sex, residence, occupation, and in many instances the caste and language of party workers. In one of the districts we can compare membership data of the late 1950's with membership data of the early 1950's, and therefore can analyze with some statistical precision questions such as whether the party is aging, whether the social composition is becoming more or less diverse, and whether the party is becoming more or less rural. We also have sought to interject a longer historical dimension by a comparative examination, where such data were available, of the social backgrounds of the present district leadership and the party leadership in the mid-1930's.

Though it is not easy to generalize from these three districts to India as a whole, two factors strengthen our willingness to generalize. One is that our findings are in accord with what I and others have more superficially noted in other local units of the Congress Party around the country. The second is that there are many similarities in the patterns of elite development in the three district organizations (despite the fact that the social organization and economic patterns of the three districts vary considerably) and these similarities suggest that there are factors at work transcending local differences. Moreover, in addition to these three rural districts, I have examined closely the recruitment patterns of Congress in two Indian cities, and my two urban studies support many of the generalizations I shall make about the three rural areas.

The three districts are in three different regions of India. Belgaum district is in Mysore State, south of the city of Bombay; Guntur district is in Andhra State, north of Madras; Kaira district is in Gujarat, near the city of Ahmedabad. For each district I shall describe briefly some of the main features of local social organization before going on to a description of the party cadres.

Belgaum District

Belgaum is a bilingual district in Mysore State, bordering on Goa and Maharashtra in the west-central portion of India. The district has nearly two million people in an area of 5,553 miles. Approximately two thirds of the population speak Kanarese and one fourth speaks Marathi. The district was part of Bombay State until 1957 when it was transferred to the predominantly Kanarese-speaking state of Mysore. As a result of the transfer, the Marathi-speaking element in the northern portions of the district has been demanding that the district be partitioned. Since the Kanarese speakers, who oppose partition, control the Congress Party in the district, the party has lost support among Marathi speakers.

Within the Kanarese-speaking population the largest single community is the Lingayats, a group of castes mainly engaged in agriculture and sharing a common set of religious beliefs and rituals. Some scholars have classified the Lingayats as a distinct Hindu sect. Within the district as a whole, slightly more than 30 per cent are Lingayats, but in the Kanarese-speaking areas the percentage is higher.

The Brahmins are few in number, perhaps only 4 per cent of the Hindu population (90 per cent of the district is Hindu, 10 per cent is Muslim), but they hold important posts in medicine, law, and journalism, and as landlords. In the past they were politically the most powerful community, partly because of their positions as landlords and partly because traditionally they held posts as village land record keepers under the British and under local maharajas. The shift in power from the Brahmins to the Lingayats during the last thirty years is one of the most significant political developments in the district.

Landholdings in Belgaum are more concentrated than elsewhere in India. The district has approximately 2.5 million acres of cultivated land; of this more than 1.5 million acres are in units of less than thirty acres and are owned by a quarter of a million people. The remaining acreage (under 1 million acres) is in holdings of above thirty acres and is owned by 13,695 landowners. In other words, there is a small class of landowners—about 5 per cent of those who own land—who have holdings exceeding thirty acres. This economic fact assumes great political importance, since almost all the important political leaders in the district, including a large proportion of the Congress Party cadres, are recruited from this small class of landowners. It should also be noted that only half the population owns land, while another quarter are tenant cultivators or agricultural laborers and the remainder are engaged in nonagricultural activities.

I have analyzed membership data for five of the ten talukas (subdivisions) within the district for the years 1952 and 1959. During this seven-year period the number of active party cadres rose from 224 to 512. Since I have given detailed statistical findings elsewhere, here I shall simply provide a brief summary of the results.

1. The average Congressman, both in 1952 and 1959, comes from a Kanarese-speaking area, is in his late thirties, is an agriculturalist, and is a resident of a small town or village.

2. As one might expect, the majority of party workers are agriculturalists, but there are also a number of white-collar workers, businessmen, and artisans. During this seven-year period agriculturalists have had a slight proportional increase, and non-agriculturalists now come from a wider variety of occupations. Thus, the occupational structure of party cadres has become more representative of the occupational distribution in the district.

3. Between 1952 and 1959 recruitment into the party was substantial in all age groups. The greatest increase came in the 46–50 year-old group, and the next greatest in the 20–25 year-old group. The average age of the cadres increased slightly—from 38.3 to 39.8 years of age—during this seven-year period. The party is obviously sustaining itself with new recruits.

4. The linguistic controversy between the Kanarese and the Marathi speakers and the identification of the district Congress organization with the Kanarese position have led to a decline in Marathi membership and a corresponding rise of Kanarese membership. Since the Marathi-speaking politicians were more often businessmen from urban settlements, the decline in membership of their linguistic group has meant a decline in the number of businessmen and cadres from large towns and a corresponding increase, reflecting the demographic and occupational characteristics of the Kanarese community, in agriculturalists and cadres from the smaller towns and villages.

As we examine the top positions within the party, several other trends are apparent. I have analyzed the social backgrounds of seventeen MP's, MLA's, and senior party officials in the district for whom education and past political and social work data were available. While it is difficult to generalize on the basis of so few cases, we can tentatively conclude that the younger Congressmen differ in several important ways. They are slightly less educated, have had more experience in social service work than the older Congress group, and are less apt to be professionals (doctors, lawyers, teachers). The most significant change, however, is that the younger Congressmen are more likely to have been born in rural areas and to represent rural constituencies, while the older Congressmen tend more to have urban backgrounds and to represent urban constituencies.

The changes in the caste and occupational structure during the past decade have not been nearly so great as those which occurred before independence. Indeed, a major shift in power within Congress took place in the mid-thirties. Until 1936 every president of the District Congress Committee had been a Brahmin and a lawyer. In 1936 an agriculturalist belonging to the Reddi caste was elected, and the next year a lawyer who was a member of the Lingayat caste succeeded him. Thereafter—that is, since 1940—every president has been an agriculturalist, and from 1947 to 1960 every president was also a member of the Lingayat community.

In short, the party in Belgaum has become more representative—that is to say, more rural: the party is increasingly dominated by agriculturalists who are from the middle and upper castes and, in the main, are peasant proprietors but not great landowners. These generalizations are further confirmed by an analysis of 114 Congress Party officers in the district, including members of the District Congress Committee Executive and presidents of the smallest mandal units. Seventy-two people were agriculturalists, seventeen were businessmen, seven were landlords, and nine were pleaders. The caste distribution shows Lingayats making up almost 50 per cent with fifty-six, while there are now only eleven Brahmin officers.

The growing representative character of the party in the district is reflected in the election returns. In 1962, out of sixteen state assembly seats, Congress won ten, an opposition party in the Marathi-speaking area where Congress has few cadres won five, and an independent won one seat.

Guntur District

Guntur is one of the most densely populated rural districts in India. It is located on the eastern shore line of Andhra and has a population of more than three million in an area of 5,795 square miles. About 20 per cent of the people live in towns; the rest, in rural areas. It grows a number of commercial crops such as tobacco and cashew nuts, and is also a paddy surplus area.

Politically, socially, and economically, the most important castes have been the Brahmins, the Kammas, and the Reddis, the latter two being the traditional agricultural castes of the district. By rough projection from the 1920's when the census indicated caste, we estimate that about 6 per cent now are Brahmins, 9 per cent are Reddis, and 18 per cent are Kammas. A third agricultural caste, the Telagas, comprises about 9 per cent; the two largest untouchable castes make up another 11 per cent; the Indian Christian community, 9 per cent.

Two aspects of the socio-economic structure are of great importance in the analysis of party elites. One is that the proportion of tenants and agricultural laborers is higher than in other parts of India (37 per cent of the labor as against 30 per cent for India as a whole), and the other is that the price of land and the earnings from land are higher than in most of India. In some parts of the district, land sells for $1,000 an acre and can bring in a profit (when under paddy) of $60 a year. A landowner with fifty acres thus can earn $3,000 a year, an extraordinarily high income in a country where the average per capita yearly income is only about $65. Only a small number owns such large holdings, but a substantial number of farmers—unfortunately no reliable data are available to tell us precisely how many—own five or ten acres. It is these men who constitute the rural gentry class of Guntur and from whose ranks the political activists are recruited.

One scholar (Selig Harrison) has argued that the major political division in the Andhra delta is between the Reddi caste, which dominates the Congress Party, and the Kamma caste, which dominates the Communist Party. Though there is some evidence that the Reddi caste is the strongest supporter of Congress in the delta and elsewhere in the state, there is also evidence that members of the Kamma caste, who outnumber the Reddis in Guntur, give considerable support to Congress. The Kammas have held more leadership positions within the Congress Party in Guntur than any other caste, including the Reddis. From 1935 to 1962 seven of the ten District Congress Committee presidents were Kammas, and within the seventeen-man executive committee, six are Kammas, three are Reddis, three belong to a subcaste of the Kammas, and each of the remaining five seats is held by a member of a different caste. Indeed, a close examination of conflicting groups within the district, both within Congress and between parties, suggests that politicians have affiliations with factional groups that are typically multicaste and that these groups are the units of political action, both within the party and the village.

Unfortunately, detailed statistical data on party cadres are not available for this district, and there are no detailed historical records of the leadership or composition of the party in the 1930's or earlier. But we do know that until the mid-1930's the predominant leadership in the district was, as in Belgaum, Brahmin.

The factional conflict that we now find within the Reddi and Kamma castes was duplicated within the Brahmin community in the 1930's, and it is this factional conflict which, strangely enough, helps explain the transformation in the composition of the party. Throughout the early 1930's the Congress movement in Andhra was torn between two distinguished and powerful Brahmin politicians, each contending for control over the nationalist movement in the area. The details of this struggle need not detain us here, but what is important to note is that in their effort to defeat one another, each sought support from outside his own small group and, therefore, outside the Brahmin caste. Throughout much of South India in what is now Madras, Andhra, and Mysore, and also in Maharashtra, the non-Brahmin agricultural castes were opposed to what they felt was their social and political domination by the Brahmin community. Strong and emotional anti-Brahmin movements developed, permeated in some instances with antinorthern sentiment, antireligious overtones, and equalitarian elements. Many upper-caste non-Brahmins remained outside the nationalist movement in the South since the movement had strong Brahmin support. It is not surprising that the Brahmins, as the urban-educated professional classes, were among the first to join the nationalist movement against the British. Many members of the peasant proprietor castes in the South—the Kammas and Reddis in Andhra, the Lingayats and Okkalingas in Mysore, the Marathas in Maharashtra—were reluctant at first to participate in what appeared to them to be a Brahmin-dominated nationalist movement. Many joined antinationalist organizations—the largest was a group known as the Justice Party. The non-Brahmin castes, as they were generically called although the phrase meant only selected, higher non-Brahmin castes (the movement, for example, received no significant support from among the untouchables), were first active in local politics. In fact, in much of southern India the Justice Party gained control of the district local boards and the provincial assemblies. In the 1937 elections for the provincial assemblies the Congress Party successfully displaced the Justice Party. There are many reasons for the Congress victory, not the least of which is that before the elections the non-Brahmin castes entered the nationalist movement. The striking feature about their entry was that it was welcomed, rather than opposed, by the Brahmin Congress leaders, partly because the Brahmin Congressmen saw the British as the major enemy and were eager to win mass and therefore non-Brahmin support, but also partly because each Brahmin faction wanted to increase support for itself and therefore sought recruits from among the non-Brahmin castes.

Factional struggles continue today within Congress and, as in the past, each faction is seeking support from groups not currently actively aligned with Congress.

Prior to the 1961 elections a major struggle took place between two major factions for control over the office of Chief Minister. The two groups were so evenly balanced in 1960 that to agree they finally chose someone outside either group, a Harijan member of the state cabinet. The Harijan Chief Minister —incidentally the first of his caste to become Chief Minister of an Indian state—took steps to provide benefits for his own community. He was instrumental in building more schools for Harijan, providing housing sites and employment in the state administration for them, and, above all, in instilling in his community some sense of pride that one of their own had achieved a position of prominence. In late 1961 a faction led by a Reddi had enough support among the Congress candidates for the state assembly to displace him, so an opposing faction sided with the Harijan Chief Minister. Again, the details of the election campaign need not detain us. The important point is that one faction of Congress, working with a prominent Harijan, sought support among the Harijans in order to defeat the other Congress faction. There is good reason to believe that, until the 1962 elections, a rather substantial percentage of the Harijan vote had been given to Communist candidates; it was the struggle *among* Congressmen, rather than the struggle *between* Congressmen and Communists, that, ironically enough, eroded Communist strength among the Harijans. The Communist vote in the district dropped from a high of 40.8 per cent in the 1955 elections to only 26.1 per cent in 1962, and though there are many reasons for this decline, and though it probably occurred within many social groups, there is strong evidence to believe that a substantial shift occurred within the Harijan castes.

Kaira District

Kaira district is our third and last rural example, and it provides us with some of the richest data on active party membership. The district is located in the state of Gujarat in the northwest corner of India.

Kaira is a cash crop area, one of the more developed agricultural regions of the subcontinent. The district is half the size of Guntur or Belgaum, with only 2,621 square miles, but its population, two million, equals that of Belgaum. It is, then, a densely populated rural area.

In 1959 Kaira had 741 active party members, compared with 485 in 1953. Slightly more than half (57.5 per cent) of the party workers live in villages of less than 5,000 people, while 69.5 per cent of the population at large lives in villages of this size. However, while every town in the district has party workers, only 24 per cent of the villages has an active Congressman. These villages, however, happen to be the larger ones of the district, so, of the actual district population, half live in towns or villages where Congress is represented.

Since data were available on how each village voted, it is possible to study the effectiveness of party workers in winning votes for the Congress Party. The Congress vote in Kaira is lowest in the smaller villages—those with low literacy and no school or post office—and high in the reverse situation—that is, in larger villages with great literacy, schools, cooperatives, and a nearby post office. These latter units are where Congress concentrates its resources and where Congress workers can usually be found. In 1952 Congress won 89 per cent of all the villages in which it had Congress workers, as against 70 per cent of the villages in which it had none. The Congress vote dropped in 1957, but even then Congress won 77 per cent of the villages with workers, as against 64 per cent of the villages where no workers were present. The age of Congress workers didn't seem to have much effect on their success in the 1952 elections, but in the 1957 elections the younger Congressmen (under 35) carried their villages in 85 per cent of the cases, as against 73 per cent for the older Congressmen.

The most striking measure of success, however, is in the caste of the Congress workers. Traditionally, the most influential caste in the district is the Patidars. This community owns much of the land and has a reputation for being one of the most enterprising agricultural communities in India, with a keen interest in new agricultural methods and in expanding into nonagricultural activities. The Patidars have always provided leadership in the district—in the large dairy cooperative, in the district and local government bodies, and in the Congress Party. While in the other districts we have studied there has been a reasonably close fit between the distribution of castes within the party and caste distribution in the district, in Kaira this is not the case. Twenty per cent of the population are Patidars, while 45 per cent of the party workers are Patidars. Moreover, the President of the District Congress Committee and the most prominent and influential Congressmen are Patidars.

The most numerous caste in Kaira is a group known as the Bariyas. The term is loosely used and actually covers a number of related castes, most of whose members are tenants or landless laborers. Throughout the late 1950's this community became increasingly active politically, partly because land reform legislation made it aware of its political opportunities, partly because improvement in communication and education made Bariya leaders aware of the relative backwardness of their community, and partly because Rajput leaders—members of a small (in this district) but high-status landowning community—successfully forged an alliance with the Bariyas by persuading them that both communities belonged to the Kshatriya or traditional warrior class. Rajput leaders thus appealed to the status aspirations of prominent Bariyas and together they formed their own association known as the Kshatriya Sabha which, before the 1962 elections, generally supported Congress candidates. At one point the Kshatriyas made an effort to increase their power within the Congress Party, but in 1959 only fifty-four Congress Party workers (7.3 per cent) were Kshatriyas.

Together the Patidars and Kshatriyas constituted slightly more than half of the party workers. What is striking is that these two groups were generally more successful in carrying their villages and towns than were other Congress workers. In 1952, 94 per cent of the villages and towns with Patidar cadres and 100 per cent of the communities with Bariya or Rajput cadres voted Congress. Bariyas remained in Congress through the 1957 elections, but it was widely reported in the district that many of the Bariya Congressmen actually supported opposition candidates; even then 75 per cent of the villages and towns with Kshatriya party workers (there were actually only a dozen in all) gave a majority of their vote to Congress.

In the 1962 elections the Kshatriya Sabha turned against the Congress Party and, although there were still many Kshatriya Congressmen, the most influential leaders of the community joined the opposition Swatantra Party. The results were startling. Congress lost both parliamentary seats and ten (all to Swatantra) out of fifteen assembly seats. The Congress vote for state assembly seats dropped from 50 per cent to 43.8 per cent, and the Swatantra Party, contesting for the first time, won 50 per cent of the vote for the assembly and 51.7 per cent for the two parliamentary seats.

Unfortunately we do not have any data on the relationship between caste and occupation, so we cannot say with any precision which occupations are engaged in by the Kshatriyas and which by the Patidars. Among Congress workers Kshatriyas were almost all agriculturalists—81.5 per cent—as against 75 per cent of all party workers and 71 per cent of the district population in general. It also seems that, generally speaking, Congress Party activists are representative of the upper strata agriculturalists —that is, those who own land—and not of the landless tenants and farm laborers who comprise about 25 per cent of the population.

In one sense, of course, the occupations of the Kshatriyas make little difference. Since they constitute some 40 per cent of the population, their defection from Congress was bound to result in a Congress defeat. It should be noted, however, that while the loss of Kshatriya support accounts for the Congress defeat, the Congress vote dropped from only 50 to 44 per cent. Even if we assume that the decline is all within a single community, these figures suggest that Congress still retains some support among the Kshatriyas. Even in Kaira district, therefore, where Congress tends to recruit its cadres more from a single community than it does elsewhere in India, the fact is that Congress still substantially recruits cadres from other, including lower, castes and that its electoral strength is widely dispersed among different castes and occupations.

Patterns of Elite Recruitment and Mass Political Participation

Though patterns of recruitment into the Congress Party are affected in each district by the peculiar features of local social organization, there are some remarkably similar patterns in all three of our rural districts. As we have seen, in Kaira the Patidars, a high caste of prosperous peasant proprietors and merchants, predominate in the party, though they are challenged now by lower castes. In Guntur, the Reddis and Kammas, two agricultural castes, have gradually displaced the Brahmins as the most active elements in the party. In Belgaum a linguistic controversy led many Marathi-speaking cadres to leave the party, but the number of Kanarese-speaking cadres, especially from the Lingayat community, has increased with the result that there are now fewer businessmen and more agriculturalists, more cadres from the smaller towns and correspondingly fewer cadres from the larger, more densely settled towns. In all three districts recruitment has shifted from the urban centers to the smaller towns and larger vil-

lages, and there has been a general decline in the preponderance of the most educated higher castes and a corresponding increase in agriculturalists, in cadres of more varied educational level, and in the so-called middle castes. Today, in the main, the district party organizations are run by peasant proprietors of middle and upper castes—but not Brahmins—who are men who own property or, in some instances, are town merchants. The lowest castes, the nonpropertied, may and do vote for the party, but they provide few of the party leaders or cadres.

It would be reasonable to generalize that it is the local power elite which joins and dominates the local party organization, but to this generalization two very important qualifications must be added. One is that not all members of the local power structure join Congress, and the other is that the local power structure is itself in flux.

Insofar as the local dominant elites are torn by internal factional conflict, it is impossible for Congress to recruit all local leaders into their organization. Once one faction joins Congress, the opposing faction invariably joins an opposition party. It is for this reason that Congress is subjected to party competition locally throughout almost all of India. Though Congress wins three quarters of the seats in the national parliament and in most state assemblies, it typically receives no more than half the vote in any single assembly and parliamentary constituency.

The presence of conflict within local village elites makes it possible, and indeed necessary for the pro-Congress group to appeal to other groups in the community. It is this feature of local factional struggle which makes the factions within the local Congress non-exclusive in character. The local Congress leadership tries to win support from factions within villages, and, particularly since the establishment of universal adult suffrage, the party leadership must try to win support from many sections of the community. Thus, universal adult suffrage plays an important role in breaking down ascriptive patterns of traditional local political leadership.

Turning now to our second qualification, it is important to note that the power structure of rural India has been changing and that, more fundamentally, patterns of social stratification are in a process of great change. In this brief paper we cannot document the wide range of changes now occurring or the reasons for these changes, except to make two points. One is that, although there is some individual mobility in India, in the main social mobility involves the changing position of rather large social groups. Thus, it would be impossible to understand the changes that occurred within the Congress Party in the three districts we have discussed without being aware of the changing social and economic positions of the Brahmins, the Kammas, the Reddis, and the Lingayats since the 1930's, or, more recently, of the Bariyas and the Rajputs. The second point is that to a large extent social mobility or the desire for social mobility is a consequence of government policy. Thus, the establishment of universal adult suffrage, the vast expansion of schools and colleges, the passage of land reform legislation, the creation of new institutions of local government, and government-sponsored economic development activities in rural areas have all unsettled relatively established patterns of social relations. Though India still remains the deferential society *par excellence,* at the local level it is no longer as clear as it once was to whom deference is to be given.

Today the local Congress Party organizations are faced with a changing local power structure and considerable local conflict. We have seen the consequences of these developments in our three districts: how the Lingayat, Kamma, and Reddi castes displaced the Brahmins in Guntur and in Belgaum, and how the Patidars are now threatened by the Rajputs and Bariyas in Kaira. However, the matter is not simply one of a caste or group of castes being replaced by another, but rather, it is one of a growing diversification of the castes and occupations of party cadres. The important point is that Congress is not a vehicle simply for those who exercise power, as the governing party typically is in new nations, but it also is a vehicle for those who seek power.

Sometimes it is only after castes or factions have gained some local power by winning control of local government bodies and quasi-governmental institutions that they seek to gain control of the Congress Party organization. Congress district leaders will often approach newly elected panchayat presidents to urge them to join the party, and it is common for Congress leaders to explain away a party defeat in municipal or state assembly elections on the grounds that they failed to nominate the local influentials. The district party leadership thus often is torn between two incongruent goals. On the one hand the party leadership wants to attract to the party men of local power and social groups whose support is necessary to win the local, assembly, and parliamentary elections. On the other hand, the party leadership is also concerned lest it lose its own position within the party. Thus in Kaira the Patidar Congress leadership feared that the Rajput and Bariya politicians might gain control of the party.

While the reaction of the party to new groups varies considerably from district to district, as one looks at the elite composition of the party during the last two decades one is struck by the success of aspiring social groups in gaining a share of power within the local Congress Party.

The Institutionalization of Political Participation

We began this paper by pointing to the challenge to developing political systems from new elites who seek to share power, and we suggested that in India the Congress Party has been the most important single instrument for the absorption of new political elites and their followers. It now remains for us to specify what the conditions are which have made it possible for Congress to perform this function. Our task is twofold: we must explain why aspiring elites choose Congress as their vehicle for gaining political power, and we must explain why existing elites within the party have been prepared to share their power.

The first explanation is easier to find than the second. Congress is, after all, the government party and Congressmen therefore have great access to policymakers and administrators. They have more influence over the distribution of patronage, the allocation of development funds, and the administration of government regulations than other political parties do. Political aspirants, therefore, are likely to seek power first within Congress, and, only after having failed, to join the opposition. Congress is thus given the option of first refusal. In Kaira, for example, the Rajput and Bariya castes joined Swatantra only after they failed to win the power they sought within Congress. There are few prominent opposition leaders in India, whether at the national, state, or district levels, who have not at one time or another been Congressmen. In short, one might say that the capacity of Congress to provide rewards is a key factor in the willingness of aspiring elites to seek power first within Congress.

It is, however, the response of the elite within Congress which is more critical, for in most political systems it is the unwillingness of the established elites to share power that turns aspiring elites to revolutionary channels and alienated politics. We have already referred to one reason for the accommodating character of the Congress leadership—the degree of competition within Congress at the local level. If the local Congress Party was not so torn by internal factional disputes, Congressmen would be less eager to seek further support. One faction may seek support from a minority religious group, an aspiring caste, or another faction, not simply because the Congress faction wants to win an election against the opposition—although this is obviously a consideration—but often because the faction wants to strengthen its position vis-à-vis another faction within Congress. To generalize, we might say that competition within the local governing elite, whether within a single party or between parties, is an important factor in the capacity of that elite to accommodate the demands of aspiring elites for power.

A corollary of this proposition is that competition within the aspiring elite also facilitates its admission into the governing party. If the aspiring elite is united, the dominant elite is often fearful that it may be completely displaced. If, on the other hand, the aspiring elite is divided, factions within the dominant elite can each compete for sections of the aspiring elite. This is why, strangely enough, the capacity of Negroes in the American South to influence the outcome of elections may be greater if Negroes are divided and all candidates must seek their support than if they vote as a bloc—in which case the candidate who does not receive their support need make no concessions and is likely to appeal to white voters to keep Negroes out of office. Similarly, the Kammas who entered Congress in Guntur in the 1930's were very much divided, and each Kamma faction was able to ally itself with a Brahmin faction in the party. It was precisely because the Kammas were divided that each Brahmin faction was eager to solicit Kamma support. In contrast, Patidar factions within the Congress Party of Kaira each feared Bariya and Rajput domination, since these two castes were united in their own association and were clearly trying to exercise power as a bloc within Congress.

A third factor in the capacity of Congress to absorb new elites is that even when some Congressmen are reluctant to allow new elements in the party, it is difficult to stop new elites from coming in. Party membership is, after all, open, and once a large number of people join the party they can begin to elect their own members to positions of importance within the party and can influence the selection of candidates for assembly and parliamentary constituencies. Moreover, once suffrage is extended, new participants generally will first try to enter the most powerful party if its doors are even remotely open. Again, the American example is illuminating. Even in the South Negroes are trying to enter the Democratic Party, despite its racist character, be-cause the Democratic Party controls most of the state and local governments.

Finally, the fourth and perhaps most important factor in the willingness of Congressmen to share power with aspiring elites is that the amount of power to be shared has been growing. For the past thirty years the amount of power available to Congressmen has grown as a result of the increase in the amount of power within the Indian political system, and this increase has made it possible for existing elites to share power without the fear that they may be totally displaced. The British India Act of 1935 gave greater powers to provincial governments and, for the first time, Congressmen fought for control over these governments, with the result that more offices were available to Congressmen. It was during this period, especially around the time of the 1937 elections, that the elite composition of Congress became so diversified. After independence, in 1947, when a Congress government replaced the British and men moved out of party offices and out of the jails into the state and national governments, there was a second wave of expanding power. Moreover, the expansion of the functions of national and state governments since independence, the establishment of new district and taluka local governments, the growth in the powers of village panchayats, the transfer of community development powers and finances from the state administration to elected local bodies, the establishment of two-house state assemblies and large cabinets—these all have meant an expansion of the supply of power and of offices to meet the growing demand. In a situation in which power is confined to a central government which is itself weak—a typical pattern in most new nations—it would be far more difficult and far more threatening for an elite to share power. In traditional societies there is often a zero-sum view of the political process—that is, there is a belief that the expansion of power for some people must mean a contraction of power for others. In modern political systems, or at least in modern democratic systems, there is rather the belief that power, like national income, is expandable: just as one can grant higher wages without necessarily reducing profits, so it is possible for state and local governments to expand their functions without necessarily reducing the power of the national government, and so it is also possible for new participants to enter the political system without necessarily displacing other participants. Thus, the more developed a political system, the greater its capacity to handle the demands of new groups. The increasing supply of governmental power in India at all levels—local, state, and national—is a significant factor in the capacity, and therefore in the willingness, of local elites within the Congress Party to cope with the growing demand of aspiring elites for the sharing of power. In this respect the Indian political system is clearly more developed than that of many other new nations in the developing areas.

NOTE

1. This paper draws heavily from *Party Building in a New Nation: The Indian National Congress* (University of Chicago Press, 1967), and from my introductory chapter to *State Politics in India,* Myron Weiner, editor (Princeton University Press, 1968).

CHAPTER XI

The Process of Center Formation in Modern States

INTRODUCTION TO THE READINGS

These selections should be read together with the various excerpts on legitimation and revolutionary origins that were presented in Chapter IX.

The excerpts in the second part of this section that deal with the structural aspects of center building are all focused around a common theme—that of state and nation building. They deal, however, with this problem in different settings; that is, in the European setting as well as in the New Nations. The very diversity of the concrete problems to which they address themselves emphasizes the great differences in the process of center building and of the meaning of nationhood, statehood, and so forth, in these different settings.

Symmons-Symonolewicz's article is an attempt at a comparative analysis of the different and most important types of rational movements from the point of view of center formation.

The rest of the selections in the second section provide analyses of the formation of national identities and centers in different types of modern society. S. M. Lipset analyzes this process in the *First New Nation*—the United States. Hans Rogger analyzes this process in modern Russia, where the formation of a modern political center was already caught up in the contradiction between the existing traditional state and modern nationalism on the one hand and the revolt against the "West"" on the other. The general theme of the revolt against the West and its effect on political development beyond Europe is taken up by Barraclough.

The various threads presented here reappear again in the next section which deals with the different types of modern political regime.

70

Pact of Fraternity of Young Europe

Giuseppe Mazzini

Humanitarian Nationalism

1. *Young Europe* is an association of men believing in a future of liberty, equality, and fraternity, for all mankind; and desirous of consecrating their thoughts and actions to the realisation of that future.

General Principles

2. One sole God; One sole ruler,—His Law; One sole interpreter of that law,—Humanity.

3. To constitute humanity in such wise as to enable it throughout a continuous progress to discover and apply the law of God by which it should be governed, as speedily as possible: such is the mission of *Young Europe*.

4. As our true well-being consists in living in accordance with the law of our being, the knowledge and fulfilment of the law of humanity is the sole source of good. The fulfilment of the mission of *Young Europe* will result in the general good.

5. Every mission constitutes a pledge of duty. Every man is bound to consecrate his every faculty to its fulfilment. He will derive his rule of action from the profound conviction of that duty.

6. Humanity can only arrive at the knowledge of its Law of Life through the free and harmonious development of all its faculties. Humanity can only reduce that knowledge to action through the free and harmonious development of all its faculties. Association is the sole means of realising this development.

7. No true association is possible save among free men and equals.

8. By the law of God, given by Him to humanity, all men are free, are brothers, and are equals.

9. Liberty is the right of every man to exercise his faculties without impediment or restraint, in the accomplishment of his special mission, and in the choice of the means most conducive to its accomplishment.

10. The free exercise of the faculties of the individual may in no case violate the rights of others. The special mission of each man must be accomplished in harmony with the general mission of humanity. There is no other limit to human liberty.

11. Equality implies the recognition of uniform rights and duties for all men—for none may escape the action of the law by which they are defined—and every man should participate, in proportion to his labour, in the enjoyment of the produce resulting from the activity of all the social forces.

12. Fraternity is the reciprocal affection, the sentiment which inclines man to do unto others as he would that others should do unto him.

13. All privilege is a violation of Equality. All arbitrary rule is a violation of Liberty. Every act of egotism is a violation of Fraternity.

14. Wheresoever privilege, arbitrary rule, or egotism are introduced into the social constitution, it is the duty of every man who comprehends his own mission to combat them by every means in his power.

15. That which is true of each individual with regard to the other individuals forming a part of the society to which he belongs, is equally true of every people with regard to humanity.

16. By the law of God, given by God to humanity, all the peoples are free—are brothers and are equals.

17. Every people has its special mission, which will co-operate towards the fulfilment of the general mission of humanity. That mission constitutes its *nationality*. Nationality is sacred.

18. All unjust rule, all violence, every act of egotism exercised to the injury of a people, is a violation of the liberty, equality, and fraternity of the

From "Pact of Fraternity of Young Europe" (1834); reprinted in *Life and Writings of Joseph Mazzini, III* (Smith, Elder and Co., 1905).

peoples. All the peoples should aid and assist each other in putting an end to it.

19. Humanity will only be truly constituted when all the peoples of which it is composed have acquired the free exercise of their sovereignty, and shall be associated in a Republican Confederation, governed and directed by a common Declaration of Principles and a common Pact, towards the common aim—the discovery and fulfilment of the Universal Moral Law.

71

The German Idea of Freedom

Ernst Troeltsch

The German idea of freedom possesses its own characteristic traits. Undoubtedly it has been affected by French and English ideas of liberty. Locke and Rousseau have influenced theory, whereas the English constitution and self-government and the French Revolution have been of tremendous practical impact. However, these ideas have been thoroughly transformed in the real core of German development, in the institutions which go back to Baron von Stein, Scharnhorst and Boyen, and in the philosophical, idealistic interpretation of state and history from Kant, Fichte and Hegel to the contemporary philosophical idealists. Here, too, liberty is the key word, but this liberty has its own meaning, determined by German history and the German spirit.

Liberty as creative participation in the formation of state authority means to us, not the bringing forth of governmental will out of individual wills, not control of the mandatory by the principal, but the free, conscious and dutiful dedication of oneself to the whole, as it has been molded by history, state and nation. The whole as the expression and incarnation of collectivity is to be willed freely and always re-created anew in personal activity. Thus, prince and officials consider themselves as the first servants of the state, and citizens think of themselves as members of the state. They are all organs of the one sovereign whole which they bring forth anew in ceaseless self-

From Ernst Troeltsch, "The German Idea of Freedom," in William Ebenstein, ed., *Man and the State* (New York: Holt, Rinehart & Co., 1947), pp. 256–257. Reprinted by permission of J. C. B. Mohr, Tübingen, copyright holders of the article which first appeared in *Deutscher Geist und Westeuropa*, 1925.

devotion. Liberty consists more in duties than in rights, or, rather, in rights which are simultaneously duties. The individuals do not compose the whole, but identify themselves with it. Liberty is not equality, but service of the individual in his station organically due to him. In this, lie the dignity and active participation of the individual, but also his restraint, and all modern achievements of national unity, equality before the law, parliaments and universal military service, are molded by this spirit. This is the "state mysticism" (*Staatsmystik*) which our great thinkers and historians have felt in common with Plato. It has been rejected as philosophically meaningless by Bishop Welldon and his English nominalism, and it has been defined as immoral by the English ideal of independence. But Hegel saw in it the philosophy of freedom, and it has become evident, more or less consciously, more or less coherently, in all great German creations of the century. As everything in this world, this "state mysticism" has its dangers, and can obviously degenerate in face of fear of responsibility and bureaucratic rule of officials. But where its most characteristic nerve is alive in autonomous, dutiful, self-dedication and participation combined with vigilance and responsibility, it leads to a joining of initiative with devotion, pride with discipline, creative energy with public spiritedness and sacrifice. This spirit has created all that is great in the past German century, it characterizes two expressions of life so contrary to one another as the German army and the socialist party. It has also absorbed, and digested, Bismarck's realism.

72

The Concept of "The Political"

Carl Schmitt

The definition of the concept of the "political" can be arrived at only through the discovery of the specifically political categories. Politics stands as an independent sphere of its own, apart from other, relatively independent, spheres of human thought and action, such as morals, esthetics, economics, the complete enumeration of which is not required here. Politics must, therefore, possess its own, ultimately independent, distinguishing characteristics, to which all specifically political action can be traced back. Let us assume that, in the province of morals, these distinctions are Good and Evil; in esthetics, Beautiful and Ugly; in economics, Useful and Harmful, or Profitable and Unprofitable. The question then remains whether a specific and self-evident distinguishing characteristic exists in the realm of politics, and what it is.

The specifically political distinction to which political acts and motivations may be traced back, is the distinction of *friend* and *enemy*. It corresponds, in politics, to the relatively independent distinctions in other fields: Good and Evil in morals; Beautiful and Ugly in esthetics, etc. This distinction is independent, i.e., it cannot be deduced from any of these other distinctions, singly or combined. Just as the contrast between Good and Evil is not identical with, nor reducible to, that of Beautiful and Ugly, or of Useful and Harmful, it must not be confused or mixed up with any of these other contrasts. The distinction between friend and enemy can subsist, in theory and practice, without applying, at the same time, moral, esthetic, economic, or other distinctions. The political enemy need not be morally evil nor esthetically ugly; he need not appear as an economic competitor, and it may, in fact, be advantageous to do business with him. He is the other, the stranger, and his nature is sufficiently defined if he is, in an

intense way, existentially different and strange; in case of conflict, he constitutes the negation of one's own kind of existence, and must therefore be repulsed or fought, in order to preserve one's own way of life. In psychological reality, the enemy is easily treated as evil and ugly, because politics, like any autonomous area of human life, gladly calls on the help which it can receive from the distinctions of other spheres. This does not change the independence of such specific distinctions. As a consequence, the opposite is valid, too: what is morally bad, esthetically ugly, or economically harmful, need not be the enemy; what is morally good, esthetically beautiful, and economically useful, does not become, necessarily, the friend in the specifically political meaning of the word. The basic autonomy and independence of politics is evident in the possibility of distinguishing such a specific contrast of friend and enemy from other contrasts, and to conceive of it as an independent category.

The concepts of friend and enemy are to be understood in their concrete meaning of existence, not as symbols or metaphors, nor fused with, or weakened by, economic, moral and other ideas, nor as the expression of private feelings and tendencies. They are not normative or "spiritual" contrasts. Liberalism has transformed the enemy, from the economic side, into a competitor, and from the ethical side, into a debating adversary. In the sphere of economics, it is true, there are no enemies, but only competitors, and in a world suffused with morals and ethics, there are only debating contestants. However, the enemy is something entirely different. It makes no difference whether one considers it a reprehensible and atavistic residue of barbarian ages or not, that men still separate each other as friends and enemies, or whether one entertains the hope that this distinction will disappear, one day, from the earth, or whether it is good and advisable to construe the fiction, for educational reasons, that there are no more enemies. What is at stake, are not fictions and prescriptions of what ought to be, but real existence and the real possibility of this distinction of friend and enemy.

From Carl Schmitt, "Politics: The Struggle with the Enemy," in William Ebenstein, ed., *Man and the State* (New York: Holt, Rinehart & Co., 1947), pp. 299–302. Reprinted by permission of the author and J. C. B. Mohr, Tübingen, copyright holders of the article which first appeared in *Archiv für Socialwissenschaft und Socialpolitik*, Vol. LVIII (September 1927).

One may share those hopes and pedagogical efforts. But one cannot rationally deny that nations have been able to line up, till now, according to the distinction of friend and enemy, and that it constitutes as a real possibility for every politically existent nation.

The enemy is, thus, not the competitor or opponent in general. Nor is he the private opponent whom one hates. "Enemy" is only a collectivity of men who eventually, i.e., as a real possibility, will *fight* against a similar collectivity of people. Enemy is only the public enemy, because everything that relates to such a collectivity, especially a whole nation, becomes *public*.

The genuine concept of the enemy thus implies the eventual reality of a struggle. One should abstract, from this term, all accidental changes inherent in the historical evolution of the techniques of war and armaments. War is armed struggle between nations. The essential characteristic of "the weapon" is the fact that it is a means of physical killing of human beings. The word "struggle," like the term "enemy," is to be taken here in its original meaning. It does not mean competition, nor the "intellectual" struggle of discussion, nor the symbolic struggle, which, after all, every person fights, and be it only with his inertia. The terms "friend," "enemy," and "struggle" obtain their real significance from their relation to the real possibility of physical killing. War follows from enmity, because the latter is existential negation of another being. War is only the most extreme negation of enmity. As long as the concept of the enemy retains its meaning, war need not be an everyday, normal occurrence, nor need it be felt as an ideal, but must subsist as a real possibility.

The conceptual characteristics of politics imply the pluralism of states. Political unity presupposes the real possibility of an enemy and, thus, of another, co-existing political unity. Therefore, as long as there is a state, there will always be several states on earth, rather than one world "state" comprehending the whole world and all of humanity. The political world is a pluriverse, not a universe. To this extent, every theory of the state is pluralistic, though in a different sense from the pluralism of Laski. The very nature of political organization makes its universality impossible. If the various nations and human groupings of the earth were all so united as to make a struggle among them actually impossible, if the distinction between friend and enemy ceases to operate even as a mere eventuality, then all that is left is economics, morals, law, art, etc., but not politics or a state.

73

"The Four Freedoms," Message to Congress on the State of the Union, January 6, 1941

Franklin D. Roosevelt

I address you, the Members of the Seventy-Seventh Congress, at a moment unprecedented in the history of the Union. I use the word "unprecedented," because at no previous time has American security been as seriously threatened from without as it is today.

Since the permanent formation of our government under the Constitution, in 1789, most of the periods of crisis in our history have related to our domestic affairs. Fortunately, only one of these—the four year War between the States—ever threatened our national unity. Today, thank God, one hundred and thirty million Americans, in forty-eight States, have forgotten points of the compass in our national unity.

It is true that prior to 1914 the United States often had been disturbed by events in other Continents. We had even engaged in two wars with European nations and in a number of undeclared

From Franklin D. Roosevelt, "The Four Freedoms," in William Ebenstein, ed., *Man and the State* (New York: Rinehart & Co., 1947), pp. 74–81.

wars in the West Indies, in the Mediterranean and in the Pacific for the maintenance of American rights and for the principles of peaceful commerce. In no case, however, had a serious threat been raised against our national safety or our independence.

What I seek to convey is the historic truth that the United States as a nation has at all times maintained opposition to any attempt to lock us in behind an ancient Chinese wall while the procession of civilization went past. Today, thinking of our children and their children, we oppose enforced isolation for ourselves or for any part of the Americas.

That determination of ours was proved, for example, during the quarter century of wars following the French Revolution.

While the Napoleonic struggles did threaten interests of the United States because of the French foothold in the West Indies and in Louisiana, and while we engaged in the War of 1812 to vindicate our right to peaceful trade, it is, nevertheless, clear that neither France nor Great Britain nor any other nation was aiming at domination of the whole world.

In like fashion from 1815 to 1914—99 years—no single war in Europe or in Asia constituted a real threat against our future or against the future of any other American nation.

Except in the Maximilian interlude in Mexico, no foreign power sought to establish itself in this Hemisphere; and the strength of the British fleet in the Atlantic has been a friendly strength. It is still a friendly strength.

Even when the World War broke out in 1914, it seemed to contain only small threat of danger to our own American future. But, as time went on, the American people began to visualize what the downfall of democratic nations might mean to our own democracy.

We need not over-emphasize imperfections in the Peace of Versailles. We need not harp on failure of the democracies to deal with problems of world reconstruction. We should remember that the Peace of 1919 was far less unjust than the kind of "pacification" which began even before Munich, and which is being carried on under the new order of tyranny that seeks to spread over every continent today. The American people have unalterably set their faces against that tyranny.

Every realist knows that the democratic way of life is at this moment being directly assailed in every part of the world—assailed either by arms, or by secret spreading of poisonous propaganda by those who seek to destroy unity and promote discord in nations still at peace.

During sixteen months this assault has blotted out the whole pattern of democratic life in an appalling number of independent nations, great and small. The assailants are still on the march, threatening other nations, great and small.

Therefore, as your President, performing my constitutional duty to "give to the Congress information of the state of the Union," I find it necessary to report that the future and the safety of our country and of our democracy are overwhelmingly involved in events far beyond our borders.

Armed defense of democratic existence is now being gallantly waged in four continents. If that defense fails, all the population and all the resources of Europe, Asia, Africa, and Australasia will be dominated by the conquerors. The total of those populations and their resources greatly exceeds the sum total of the population and their resources of the whole of the Western Hemisphere—many times over.

In times like these it is immature—and incidentally untrue—for anybody to brag that an unprepared America, single-handed, and with one hand tied behind its back, can hold off the whole world.

No realistic American can expect from a dictator's peace international generosity, or return of true independence, or world disarmament, or freedom of expression, or freedom of religion—or even good business.

Such a peace would bring no security for us or for our neighbors. "Those, who would give up essential liberty to purchase a little temporary safety, deserve neither liberty nor safety."

As a nation we may take pride in the fact that we are soft-hearted; but we cannot afford to be soft-headed.

We must always be wary of those who with sounding brass and a tinkling cymbal preach the "ism" of appeasement.

We must especially beware of that small group of selfish men who would clip the wings of the American eagle in order to feather their own nests.

I have recently pointed out how quickly the tempo of modern warfare could bring into our very midst the physical attack which we must expect if the dictator nations win the war.

There is much loose talk of our immunity from immediate and direct invasion from across the seas. Obviously, as long as the British Navy retains its power, no such danger exists. Even if there were no British Navy, it is not probable that any enemy would be stupid enough to attack us by landing troops in the United States from across thousands of miles of ocean, until it had acquired strategic bases from which to operate.

But we learn much from the lessons of the past years in Europe—particularly the lesson of Norway, whose essential seaports were captured by treachery and surprise built up over a series of years.

The first phase of the invasion of this Hemisphere would not be the landing of regular troops. The necessary strategic points would be occupied by secret agents and their dupes—and great numbers of them are already here, and in Latin America.

As long as the aggressor nations maintain the offensive, they—not we—will choose the time and the place and the method of their attack.

That is why the future of all American Republics is today in serious danger.

That is why this Annual Message to the Congress is unique in our history. That is why every member of the Executive branch of the government and every member of the Congress face great responsibility—and great accountability.

The need of the moment is that our actions and our policy should be devoted primarily—almost exclusively—to meeting this foreign peril. For all our domestic problems are now a part of the great emergency.

Just as our national policy in internal affairs has been based upon a decent respect for the rights and dignity of all our fellow-men within our gates, so our national policy in foreign affairs has been based on a decent respect for the rights and dignity of all nations, large and small. And the justice of morality must and will win in the end.

Our national policy is this:

First, by an impressive expression of the public will and without regard to partisanship, we are committed to all-inclusive national defense.

Second, by an impressive expression of the public will and without regard to partisanship, we are committed to full support of all those resolute peoples, everywhere, who are resisting aggression and are thereby keeping war away from our Hemisphere. By this support, we express our determination that the democratic cause shall prevail; and we strengthen the defense and security of our own nation.

Third, by an impressive expression of the public will and without regard to partisanship, we are committed to the proposition that principles of morality and considerations for our own security will never permit us to acquiesce in a peace dictated by aggressors and sponsored by appeasers. We know that enduring peace cannot be bought at the cost of other people's freedom.

In the recent national election there was no substantial difference between the two great parties in respect to that national policy. No issue was fought out on this line before the American electorate. Today, it is abundantly evident that American citizens everywhere are demanding and supporting speedy and complete action in recognition of obvious danger.

Therefore, the immediate need is a swift and driving increase in our armament production.

Leaders of industry and labor have responded to our summons. Goals of speed have been set. In some cases these goals are being reached ahead of time; in some cases we are on schedule; in other cases there are slight but not serious delays; and in some cases—and I am sorry to say very important cases—we are all concerned by the slowness of the accomplishment of our plans.

The Army and Navy, however, have made substantial progress during the past year. Actual experience is improving and speeding up our methods of production with every passing day. And today's best is not good enough for tomorrow.

I am not satisfied with the progress thus far made. The men in charge of the program represent the best in training, ability, and patriotism. They are not satisfied with the progress thus far made. None of us will be satisfied until the job is done.

No matter whether the original goal was set too high or too low, our objective is quicker and better results.

To give two illustrations:

We are behind schedule in turning out finished airplanes; we are working day and night to solve the innumerable problems and to catch up.

We are ahead of schedule in building warships; but we are working to get even further ahead of schedule.

To change the whole nation from a basis of peace time production of implements of peace to a basis of war time production of implements of war is no small task. And the greatest difficulty comes at the beginning of the program, when new tools and plant facilities and new assembly lines and ship ways must first be constructed before the actual matériel begins to flow steadily and speedily from them.

The Congress, of course, must rightly keep itself informed at all times of the progress of the program. However, there is certain information, as the Congress itself will readily recognize, which, in the interests of our own security and those of the nations we are supporting, must of needs be kept in confidence.

New circumstances are constantly begetting new needs for our safety. I shall ask this Congress for greatly increased new appropriations and authorizations to carry on what we have begun.

I also ask this Congress for authority and for funds sufficient to manufacture additional munitions and war supplies of many kinds, to be turned over to those nations which are now in actual war with aggressor nations.

Our most useful and immediate role is to act as an arsenal for them as well as for ourselves. They do not need man power. They do need billions of dollars' worth of the weapons of defense.

The time is near when they will not be able to pay for them in ready cash. We cannot, and will not, tell them they must surrender, merely because of present inability to pay for the weapons which we know they must have.

I do not recommend that we make them a loan of dollars with which to pay for these weapons—a loan to be repaid in dollars.

I recommend that we make it possible for those nations to continue to obtain war materials in the United States, fitting their orders into our own program. Nearly all of their matériel would, if the time ever came, be useful for our own defense.

Taking counsel of expert military and naval authorities, considering what is best for our own security, we are free to decide how much should be kept here and how much should be sent abroad to our friends who by their determined and heroic resistance are giving us time in which to make ready our own defense.

For what we sent abroad, we shall be repaid, within a reasonable time following the close of hostilities, in similar materials, or, at our option, in other goods of many kinds which they can produce and which we need.

Let us say to the democracies: "We Americans are vitally concerned in your defense of freedom. We are putting forth our energies, our resources and our organizing powers to give you the strength to regain and maintain a free world. We shall send you, in ever-increasing numbers, ships, planes, tanks, guns. This is our purpose and our pledge."

In fulfillment of this purpose we will not be intimidated by the threats of dictators that they will regard as a breach of international law and as an act of war our aid to the democracies which dare to resist their aggression. Such aid is not an act of war, even if a dictator should unilaterally proclaim it so to be.

When the dictators are ready to make war upon us, they will not wait for an act of war on your part. They did not wait for Norway or Belgium or the Netherlands to commit an act of war.

Their only interest is in a new one-way international law, which lacks mutuality in its observance, and, therefore, becomes an instrument of oppression.

The happiness of future generations of Americans may well depend upon how effective and how immediate we can make our aid felt. No one can tell the exact character of the emergency situations that we may be called upon to meet. The Nation's hands must not be tied when the Nation's life is in danger.

We must all prepare to make the sacrifices that the emergency—as serious as war itself—demands. Whatever stands in the way of speed and efficiency in defense preparations must give way to the national need.

A free nation has the right to expect full cooperation from all groups. A free nation has the right to look to the leaders of business, of labor, and of agriculture to take the lead in stimulating effort, not among other groups but within their own groups.

The best way of dealing with the few slackers or trouble makers in our midst is, first, to shame them by patriotic example, and, if that fails, to use the sovereignty of government to save government.

As men do not live by bread alone, they do not fight by armaments alone. Those who man our defenses, and those behind them who build our defenses, must have the stamina and courage which come from an unshakable belief in the manner of life which they are defending. The mighty action which we are calling for cannot be based on a disregard of all things worth fighting for.

The Nation takes great satisfaction and much strength from the things which have been done to make its people conscious of their individual stake in the preservation of democratic life in America. Those things have toughened the fibre of our people, have renewed their faith and strengthened their devotion to the institutions we make ready to protect.

Certainly this is no time to stop thinking about the social and economic problems which are the root cause of the social revolution which is today a supreme factor in the world.

There is nothing mysterious about the foundations of a healthy and strong democracy. The basic things expected by our people of their political and economic systems are simple. They are:

Equality of opportunity for youth and for others.

Jobs for those who can work.

Security for those who need it.

The ending of special privilege for the few.

The preservation of civil liberties for all.

The enjoyment of the fruits of scientific progress in a wider and constantly rising standard of living.

These are the simple and basic things that must never be lost sight of in the turmoil and unbelievable complexity of our modern world. The inner and abiding strength of our economic and political systems is dependent upon the degree to which they fulfill these expectations.

Many subjects connected with our social economy call for immediate improvement.

As examples:

We should bring more citizens under the coverage of old age pensions and unemployment insurance.

We should widen the opportunities for adequate medical care.

We should plan a better system by which persons deserving or needing gainful employment may obtain it.

I have called for personal sacrifice. I am assured of the willingness of almost all Americans to respond to that call.

A part of the sacrifice means the payment of more money in taxes. In my budget message I recommend that a greater portion of this great defense program be paid for from taxation than we are paying today. No person should try, or be allowed, to get rich out of this program; and the principle of tax payments in accordance with ability to pay should be constantly before our eyes to guide our legislation.

If the Congress maintains these principles, the voters, putting patriotism ahead of pocketbooks, will give you their applause.

In the future days, which we seek to make secure, we look forward to a world founded upon four essential human freedoms.

The first is freedom of speech and expression—everywhere in the world.

The second is freedom of every person to worship God in his own way—everywhere in the world.

The third is freedom from want—which, translated into world terms, means economic understandings which will secure to every nation a healthy peace time life for its inhabitants—everywhere in the world.

The fourth is freedom from fear—which, translated into world terms, means a world-wide reduction of armaments to such a point and in such a thorough fashion that no nation will be in a position to commit an act of physical aggression against any neighbor—anywhere in the world.

That is no vision of a distant millennium. It is a definite basis for a kind of world attainable in our time and generation. That kind of world is the very antithesis of the so-called new order of tyranny which the dictators seek to create with the crash of a bomb.

To that new order we oppose the greater conception—the moral order. A good society is able to face schemes of world domination and foreign revolutions alike without fear.

Since the beginning of our American history we have been engaged in change—in a perpetual peaceful revolution—a revolution which goes on steadily, quietly adjusting itself to changing conditions—without the concentration camp or the quicklime in the ditch. The world order which we seek is the cooperation of free countries, working together in a friendly civilized society.

This nation has placed its destiny in the hands and heads and hearts of its millions of free men and women; and its faith in freedom under the guidance of God. Freedom means the supremacy of human rights everywhere. Our support goes to those who struggle to gain those rights or keep them. Our strength is in our unity of purpose.

To that high concept there can be no end save victory.

74

Nationalist Movements: An Attempt at a Comparative Typology

Konstantin Symmons-Symonolewicz

Although all the forms of nationalism have undoubtedly certain characteristics in common, they could be logically divided into two distinct categories: (1) *nationalism of majorities* which hold political power in their respective realms, and (2) *nationalism of the subject peoples* which strive for political and cultural emancipation. This last category includes genuine minorities as well as political minorities, i.e., groups which may constitute majorities in their respective territories, but may find themselves in a position of minorities with respect to the states to which they belong. The dynamics of development of nationalism as an individual as well as social phenomenon is different in each case.

In the first case, nationalism is usually a consequence of the country's international relations (such as conflicts over the boundaries, political and economic rivalry, military defeats, etc.) or a reaction against the nationalist stirrings among the country's minority peoples.[1] In the second case, it is usually a reaction to the status of inferiority, to the denial of political and cultural self-expression and to the imposition of alien rule and custom. Only this category can be legitimately described as nationalist movements, i.e., social movements aiming at a national liberation.

Although nationalism among the majority peoples may at times take the form of a social movement,[2] it is for the most part represented by regular political parties or by the state itself. In the case of "minority peoples," on the other hand, nationalism must of

necessity follow the pattern of a typical social movement.

A social movement is defined by sociologists as a "large-scale, widespread, and continuing, elementary collective action in pursuit of *an objective that affects and shapes the social order in some fundamental aspect.*"[3] For nationalist movements, this fundamental objective is represented by the emancipation from the restrictions of the foreign rule, cultural and political.[4]

Nationalist movements constitute a variety of social movements which has two distinguishing characteristics: (1) their appeal is, by the very nature of their goals, limited to the potential supporters among the "natives,"[5] and (2) their success is not assured even when they command an unqualified support from the groups which they claim to represent.

The purpose of the present paper is to consider various types of nationalist movements and to suggest their general typology.

Before attempting this, however, it is necessary to discuss some classifications which were developed previously by various authors. These can be grouped under three headings: (1) those presented by the historians of nationalism; (2) those advanced by the students of the "developing" countries; and (3) those suggested by the sociologists.

The historical studies in the origin and growth of nationalist movements and ideologies were inaugurated by the events of World War I.[6] They have continued as an active field ever since.[7] During the inter-war period they were confined largely to Europe, but already as early as the late 1920's the most important nationalisms of Asia were also brought into their purview.[8]

The period of colonial emancipation and "nation-

From Konstantin Symmons-Symonolewicz, "Nationalist Movements: An Attempt at a Comparative Typology," *Comparative Studies in Society and History,* VII (1965), 221–230. Reprinted by permission of the publisher.

building" which followed World War II brought into the field many political scientists who became interested in the emerging nationalisms of the colonial and post-colonial world. This contributed to the development of a broader comparative framework for the analysis of nationalist movements.[9]

Both historians and political scientists, although concerned primarily with the task of clarifying the course of events and describing groups and personalities involved in nationalist movements, were drawn into generalizing about nationalism and both have come up with some interesting classifications.

The historians approached this task well equipped with facts but somewhat handicapped by at least two difficulties of conceptual nature: (1) their preoccupation with the problem of moral evaluation of nationalism and (2) their tendency to view it as primarily a "state of mind" or ideology, and not a social movement.

The first of these tendencies was reflected in such historical typologies as the frequently quoted distinction between *original* and *derived* nationalism suggested by Carlton J. H. Hayes,[10] or the even more popular dichotomy between "Western" and "Non-Western" nationalism developed by Hans Kohn.[11] Hayes's distinction, although involving a moral judgment, is clearly universal in its outlook:

> Every subject or oppressed nationality has begun its nineteenth-century agitation for national liberty and union in the spirit of a Mazzini, a Condorcet, or a Herder. It has put before itself and its members an ideal of justice and self-sacrifice. It has been revolutionary. . . . It has sympathized with similar efforts elsewhere. . . . In many instances, however, a nationality which has once been "oppressed," but which has obtained its freedom, transforms its "original" nationalism into a "derived" nationalism which renders it reactionary, militarist and imperialist.[12]

Kohn's dichotomy is an attempt to establish a rather similar distinction on the basis of a contrast between the two socio-political environments in which nationalism had to grow and develop. However, it is hardly more than an explanation of why the Western nationalism in its travel Eastward lost so much of its democratic content and absorbed various local admixtures. As Kohn writes,

> In the Western world, in England and in France, in the Netherlands and in Switzerland, in the United States and in the British dominions, the rise of nationalism was a predominantly political occurrence; it was preceded by the formation of the future national state, or . . . coincided with it. Outside the Western

world, in Central and Eastern Europe and in Asia, nationalism arose not only later, but also at a more backward stage of social and political development . . . (it) grew in protest against and in conflict with the existing state pattern . . . (and) found its first expression in the cultural field. . . . (Nationalism in the West arose in an effort to build a nation in the political reality and the struggles of the present without too much sentimental regard for the past; nationalists in Central and Eastern Europe created often, out of the myths of the past and the dreams of the future, an ideal fatherland, closely linked with the past, devoid of any immediate connection with the present, and expected to become sometime a political reality. Thus they were at liberty to adorn it with traits for the realization of which they had no immediate responsibility, but which influenced the nascent nation's wishful image of itself and of its "mission." While Western nationalism was, in its origin, connected with concepts of individual liberty and rational cosmopolitanism current in the eighteenth century, the later nationalism in Central and Eastern Europe and in Asia easily tended towards a contrary development.[13]

This ostensibly geographical typology is open to criticism on several counts: (1) it disregards any manifestations of anti-democratic, i.e., "non-Western" nationalism in the "West" as understood by Kohn;[14] (2) it discounts all the manifestations of democratic, i.e. "Western" nationalism among the nations which he places in the "non-Western" category;[15] and (3) it throws into one basket all the nationalisms which do not meet his criteria of respectability, no matter how otherwise they differ from each other, e.g. German and Indian.

From this point of view a more discerning effort at a typology of nationalism is another well-known classification by Hayes which is focused exclusively on ideology, yet is based on a sound empirical observation that nationalism does not exist in any "pure" form, but represents always a blend in which certain nationalist ingredients are fused with various other ideological elements. This ideological precipitate which has much to do with the final form of a given "nationalism" may range widely, from monarchism to communism, or from religious orthodoxy to racism.

According to Hayes, since the 18th century when modern nationalism seems to have emerged, the Western World has experienced at least five of its doctrinal varieties: humanitarian, Jacobin, traditional, liberal and integral—depending on other ideological components which were involved in each particular case.[16]

This scheme of Hayes's is not only useful in

tracing the successive stages in the development of various European nationalisms,[17] but could also serve as a guide for interpretation of some new peculiar blends of nationalism which have appeared on the post-colonial scene. It is subject, however, to all the limitations of a classification based on ideology alone.

The weakness of such exclusively "ideological" approach to the whole field of social movements was pointed out some years ago by R. Heberle.[18] If we are to understand a given social movement, we cannot treat it as a contending system of philosophy but as an *action group* striving to attain some definite objectives.

The theoretical contributions made by the students of the developing countries might be summarized under two headings: (1) the definition of the phenomena to be recognized as "nationalist" and (2) the classification of various partially overlapping and partially contending group loyalties operating in the colonial and post-colonial areas.

The students of European nationalism were not seriously concerned with the problem of defining whether a particular movement should or should not be considered nationalist.[19] By the time nationalist movements became an important political factor, most of the European nationalities had clearly advanced beyond the stage of any local or tribal loyalties. The situation was quite different in Africa, where the "Spring of Nations" came before the nations were even formed, and where the term "nationalism" was applied indiscriminately to every manifestation of resistance against colonial rule, no matter how primitive in nature.

Some observers of African developments[20] defend this indiscriminate usage of the term arguing that it is virtually impossible to separate the political movements aiming at self-government from all other forms of opposition to European control. Other students, however, notably Rupert Emerson, prefer to restrict the term to the organized movements of resistance led by the Westernized middle classes, and to relegate other forms of anti-colonial sentiment and action to more archaic forms of xenophobic defense of the old order.[21] This suggestion seems valuable not only for Africa, but also from a comparative point of view, because the occurrence of xenophobic reaction as an archaic type of protest against foreign encroachment and interference is an almost universal antecedent of modern nationalism.[22]

As for the classification of African nationalism, at least four of its varieties have been distinguished: *linguistic, territorial, regional* and *Pan-African*. The first two seem to represent nationalism in its true

sense, even if not yet fully mature; the other two belong to the pan-movement, a rather separate category. Linguistic nationalism falls into the same category as the younger ethnic nationalisms of Europe; territorial nationalism is an attempt to develop a broader modern superethnic community corresponding to the area of a particular colony or former colony.

To this series of typologies of nationalism may be added one more perceptive classification suggested by a sociologist. Almost thirty years ago, Louis Wirth published in the *American Journal of Sociology* his well-known article "Types of Nationalism."[23] In it he distinguished four basic types: an expansionist variety or *hegemony nationalism,* a separatist variety or *particularistic nationalism,* a virulent borderland variety or *marginal nationalism,* and the *nationalism of minorities.* This last type was discussed by him later in a separate article[24] where he broke it down into three basic orientations: *pluralistic,* seeking cultural autonomy and civic equality; *secessionist,* seeking separation from the dominant majority; and *militant,* seeking domination over this majority with support from aggressive co-nationals from across the border.[25]

Wirth's classification was based predominantly on *the aims* of particular nationalist or minority movements, but it was lacking somewhat in consistency; for example, marginal nationalism, from this point of view, is hardly a separate variety. It also posed the question of whether a satisfactory typology could be built upon the aims of various movements. The true aims of a given movement may be concealed for tactical reasons; they also may change with changing circumstances. Thus, the types of nationalism set forth by Wirth may be interpreted, as he himself was willing to admit, not so much as its distinct varieties, but rather as "various stages of the same nationalistic movement."[26]

The typology which is suggested below is narrower than those proposed by Wirth and others in that it does not attempt to classify all the varieties of nationalism as a sentiment, an ideology or a political program. It is limited, as was already pointed out, to the *nationalist movements* and does not include the nationalisms of the majorities, regardless of their particular form or the dynamics of development.

I define nationalism as *the active solidarity of a group claiming to be a nation and aspiring to be a state.*[27] I am using the term in an ethically neutral sense. Thus conceived, nationalism is neither good nor bad, neither liberal nor illiberal, neither democratic nor undemocratic. When seen as a movement, nationalism represents a series of stages in the struggle of a given solidary group to achieve its basic aims of unity and self-direction.[28]

The proposed typology is based on the assumption that the aims of all movements rooted in exclusive loyalty to a given group are essentially similar. Whether the movement expresses the resentment of an ethnic group against alien rule or that of a regional group against the administration set up by their own mother country, it would naturally tend to aim at some degree of autonomy. Only such an autonomy could bring the subordinate group a measure of "self-determination," that is, self-government. When this goal is definitely denied, a demand for secession must follow, whether the group is, or is not, a separate ethnic entity. Thus, the differences between particular movements representing various oppressed groups or minorities are not a matter of their aims, but rather of the objective conditions determining their opportunities in achieving these aims. These conditions consist primarily of such factors as their numerical strength, their geographic location, cultural development, economic advancement, and current political situation.

Proposed Typology of Nationalist Movements

I. Minority Movements
   A. Perpetuative
      1. Segregative
      2. Pluralistic
   B. Irredentist
II. Liberation Movements
   A. Restorative
   B. Revivalist
   C. Ethnic
   D. Autonomist-Secessionist
   E. Anti-Colonialist
   F. Nativist

The proposed classification distinguishes broadly between two kinds of nationalist movements: *minority* and *liberation*. The minority movements are basically movements aiming at self-preservation. We include here only the real minorities, groups which are so weak, or so territorially located, that the aim of "liberation" from the majority rule is for them utterly inconceivable. The liberation movements are those which either are capable of achieving the goal of independence, or conceive of themselves as being able to do so. They include several types of modern nationalism and at least one archaic variety. Both categories as well as their subdivisions are, of course, ideal types.

Within the first category, the main distinction is drawn between the *perpetuative-segregative* and *perpetuative-pluralistic types*. Both are interested in preserving their cultural identity, but the pluralistic type strives also for full civic equality for its members, while the other wants only to be left alone. Medieval Jewish ghettos, or the imperial Ottoman millet system, are examples of a solution which would be satisfactory to the first type of orientation. Minority rights, as envisaged in the so-called Minority Treaties of the post-Versailles Europe, would be a solution satisfactory to the second type of orientation.[29]

Since our category of minorities was restricted by definition to the genuine "minorities" whose chances for independence are nil, the third type included in this category, the *irredentist,* refers only to those border groups which strive for secession, even though they represent only a minority in a given area and could not possibly achieve this goal on their own. This could happen only in the situation when their desires are shared and supported by an expansionist neighboring state which claims them as its co-nationals.

Within the category of liberation movements, the distinctions are drawn in terms of the historical development of various groups and the kind and degree of their unity. The *restorative* movements are those which involve nations whose independent existence was interrupted relatively recently and which managed to retain their social structures in a relatively intact form. Typical examples here would be Poland or Hungary of the 19th century.

The *revivalist* movements are those which involve the ethnic communities which lost their political identity some centuries ago and which have to rebuild not only their historical tradition, but also their social structure. Having lost their leading classes, they find themselves reduced socially and intellectually to the level of the lower social strata. The examples here would be such nationalities in the 19th century as the Flemish, the Catalonians, the Finnish or the Lithuanians.

The *ethnic* movements are those which involve the ethnic communities which possess no tangible historical tradition but whose feeling of solidarity has been activated by increased external pressure or awakened by educational progress or by the spread of such ideologies as democracy, self-determination, etc. The examples would be such European nationalities of the 19th century as the Latvians or the Estonians or such linguistic groups in contemporary Africa as the Somalis or the Kikuyu.

The *autonomist-secessionist* type refers to the

regional entities which, in spite of their numerous ties to their mother groups, develop about themselves a certain distinctiveness which is expressed in their demand for some degree of autonomy. When this demand is rejected, separation rather than autonomy becomes their goal. These movements are rather nationalisms *in statu nascendi* than true nationalisms, but they evolve rapidly in this direction, once their aim of separation is achieved. The movements which created the United States of America and many Latin American states are a good example. The attempted secession of the Confederate States, or the movements aiming at autonomy of such ethnically Russian territories as Siberia or Don Cossack's region, are examples of unsuccessful movements of the same type.

The *anti-colonialist* type is even farther removed from genuine nationalist movements. They are "nationalist" movements behind which there are still no nations,[30] not even cultural or ideological unities from which such nations could easily develop. Their unity is predominantly of a negative type—it rests on their common opposition to, and rejection of, colonial rule. Thus, it is rather brittle. This is suggested not only by such notorious examples as the Congolese "nationalism," but also by a considerable internal dissension in such countries as Indonesia or Burma, even India or Pakistan.

The final variety in this category, the *nativist* movements, represents really not modern nationalism at all, but one of its most primitive components— xenophobic tribalism, or in Toynbeean terms, a reaction of the "zealots" to conquest and disruption of the old order. An example here would be not only various millenarian movements which attracted the attention of some anthropologists and sociologists,[31] but also such movements as the struggle of the Caucasian mountaineers under Shamyl against Russia in the 19th century or that of the mountaineers of the Riff under Abdelkrim against Spain and France in the 20th century.[32]

It is important to observe in conclusion that our typology of nationalist movements, as any other classification conceived in terms of ideal types, tends to draw the lines separating particular varieties more sharply than they may appear in empirical reality. For example, the distinction between the revivalist type and the ethnic type is rather clear when we contrast the peoples who preserved some traditions of their historical identity, such as the Ukrainians or the Greeks of the 19th century, with various contemporary African groups whose identity is based exclusively on their ethnic or linguistic unity. Some other groups, however, such as the Slovaks or the Albanians, might be harder to place properly, especially in the earlier stages of their national evolution.

NOTES

1. Occasionally, nationalism of the majority may be spurred by the mere presence of an unassimilable minority, especially if it is large or influential.

2. Such examples as Italian Fascism or German National Socialism readily suggest themselves, but even in these cases nationalism was only one of the important ideological ingredients. For an interesting discussion of the difficulties which a genuine nationalist movement may encounter in a country ruled by a quasi-nationalist autocracy see H. Rogger, "Nationalism and the State: A Russian Dilemma," *Comparative Studies in Society and History,* IV, 253–264.

3. K. and G. E. Lang, *Collective Dynamics* (New York, 1961), p. 490. Italics are ours.

4. Much was made by some historians of the predominantly cultural nature of early nationalism in Central and Eastern Europe, but even such typical cultural nationalists of the pre-Napoleonic Germany as Herder deplored their nation's political disunity and divisions. Cf. R. R. Ergang, *Herder and the Foundations of German Nationalism* (New York, 1931).

5. Only exceptionally may they attract some idealists from the other side who may recognize that the demands of the nationalists are morally justified.

6. The war and the peace treaties produced a large number of books on nationalism, both in England and in the United States, but the credit for initiation of systematic investigations of national movements in various European countries belongs to Carlton J. H. Hayes and his pioneering volumes, *Essays in Nationalism* (New York, 1926) and *The Historical Evolution of Modern Nationalism* (New York, 1931).

7. For bibliography of works on nationalism, see K. S. Pinson, *A Bibliographical Introduction to Nationalism* (New York, 1935); K. W. Deutsch, *An Interdisciplinary Bibliography on Nationalism, 1935–1953* (Cambridge, Mass., 1956); and B. C. Shafer, *Nationalism: Interpreters and Interpretations* (New York, 1959 and 1963).

8. Cf. H. Kohn, *A History of Nationalism in the East* (New York, 1929).

9. Cf. R. Emerson, *From Empire to Nation: The Rise to Self-Assertion of Asian and African Peoples* (Cambridge, Mass., 1960); G. A. Almond and J. S. Coleman, eds., *The Politics of the Developing Areas* (Princeton, 1960); K. H. Silvert, ed., *Expectant Peoples: Nationalism and Development* (New York, 1963); and K. W. Deutsch and W. J. Foltz, eds., *Nation-Building* (New York, 1963).

10. C. J. H. Hayes, "Two Varieties of Nationalism, Original and Derived," *Proceedings of the Association of History Teachers of the Middle States and Maryland,* XXVI (1928), 70–83.

11. H. Kohn, *The Idea of Nationalism: A Study in Its Origins and Background* (New York, 1944) and elsewhere. Cf. also L. L. Snyder, *The Meaning of Nationalism* (New Brunswick, N.J., 1954), Chapter V.

12. Hayes, *loc. cit.,* pp. 73–74. Similar distinctions were made also by other students of nationalism, e.g., M. H. Boehm in his "Nationalism," *Encyclopaedia of the Social Sciences,* XI, 231. Some scholars, yielding to the growing tendency to identify nationalism with its more common and more virulent contemporary variety, have suggested that the use of the term be limited to this variety and that the more humanitarian forms of nationalism be described as national consciousness. However, this would hardly be a terminological improvement.

13. Kohn, *op. cit.,* pp. 329–330.

14. A similar tendency to clean the record of truly "West-

ern" nationalism of any "tribal" impurities is shown by H. Arendt in *The Origins of Totalitarianism* (New York, 1951).

15. He was chided for this by H. Gerth in his review of *The Idea of Nationalism* in the *American Journal of Sociology*, LI, 341.

16. Cf. Hayes, *The Historical Evolution of Modern Nationalism*.

17. Cf. J. D. Clarkson, " 'Big Jim' Larkin: A Footnote to Nationalism," *Nationalism and Internationalism*, ed. by E. M. Earle (New York, 1950), pp. 45–63.

18. R. Heberle, *Social Movements* (New York, 1951), Ch. I.

19. Although the existence or non-existence of some "nations" represented by particular nationalist movements was sometimes argued about.

20. E.g., T. Hodgkin in his *Nationalism in Colonial Africa* (New York, 1957).

21. Cf. R. Emerson, *From Empire to Nation*. J. S. Coleman applies to both the term "nationalism" but distinguishes between its *traditional* and *modern* forms. Cf. his *Nigeria: Background to Nationalism* (Berkeley, 1963).

22. For a general view of various reactions to conquest, cf. A. Toynbee, *The World and the West* (New York, 1953).

23. L. Wirth, "Types of Nationalism," *American Journal of Sociology*, XLI (1936), 723–737. This article was recently reprinted in the Bobbs-Merrill reprint series.

24. L. Wirth, "The Problem of Minority Groups," *The Science of Man in the World Crisis*, ed. by R. Linton (New York, 1945). This article was recently reprinted in *Theories of Society*, ed. by T. Parsons and others.

25. Wirth mentions also the fourth orientation found among some minority groups, namely the desire to be completely assimilated to the dominant group, but since this orientation, if adopted by the whole group and accepted as desirable by the dominant majority, would eventually lead to the disappearence of a given minority, it cannot be considered a minority "movement" in the same sense of the term as the other three. It is also an extremely rare phe-

nomenon, if considered in reference to whole minority groups, not just individuals, but it does occur. An example of such a minority group which is not interested in preserving its distinct identity is the American Negroes.

26. Wirth, *American Journal of Sociology*, XLI, 725.

27. Following in part F. Znaniecki and in part R. M. MacIver.

28. I have attempted to discuss some of the problems of such an approach to nationalism in my paper "Nationalism Considered as a Social Movement" presented at the Annual Meeting of the Midwest Sociological Society in Milwaukee (1963).

29. I am not concerned at this point with the nature of the state in which one or the other solution is possible.

30. Cf. R. Emerson, *From Empire to Nation*, p. 95 and passim.

31. Cf. R. Linton, "Nativistic Movements," *American Anthropologist*, XLV (1943), 230–240; A. F. C. Wallace, "Revitalization Movements," *ibid.*, LVIII (1956), 264–281; P. M. Worsley, "Millenarian Movements in Melanesia," *Rhodes-Livingston Journal*, XXI (March, 1957), 18–31; B. Barber, "Acculturation and Messianic Movements," *American Sociological Review*, VI (1941), 663–669. Cf. also *Millennial Dreams in Action*, ed. by S. L. Thrupp (The Hague, 1962), and *The Pursuit of the Millennium* by N. Cohn (New York, 1961).

32. It seems inadvisable to include among the varieties of nationalist movements another category which is frequently distinguished, especially by students of African developments, namely regional or pan-continental "nationalisms," Pan-movements, when not the instruments of the policy of some aggressive power (as was the case with Pan-Germanism or Pan-Slavism), are usually to be considered a way of bolstering the nationalisms developing among a number of related weaker nationalities which on their own could hardly hope to achieve their aims of independence and unity. They belong rather to another level of group solidarities, those that reach beyond the limits of a nationality or a nation.

75

Formulating a National Identity

Seymour Martin Lipset

All states that have recently gained independence are faced with two interrelated problems, legitimating the use of political power and establishing national identity. And if it is a democratic polity they seek to establish, they must develop institutional and normative constraints upon efforts to inhibit organized opposition or to deny civil liberties to individual critics of those in power.

This section has explored ways in which these

From Seymour M. Lipset, *The First New Nation: The United States in Historical and Comparative Perspective* (New York: Basic Books, 1963), pp. 90–98. Copyright 1963 by Seymour M. Lipset. Reprinted by permission of the publishers, Basic Books and Heinemann Educational Books Ltd.

problems were confronted in the early history of the United States. National identity was formed under the aegis, first of a charismatic authority figure, and later under the leadership of a dominant "left wing" or revolutionary party led successively by three Founding Fathers. The pressures in new nations to outlaw opposition movements were reduced in America by the rapid decline of the conservative opposition. The revolutionary, democratic values that thus became part of the national self-image, and the basis for its authority structure, gained legitimacy as they proved effective—that is, as the nation prospered.

The need to establish stable authority and a sense of identity led the leaders of the United States to resist efforts by "old states" to involve the young nation in their quarrels. But at the same time that Americans rejected "foreign entanglements," they clearly used the Old World as both a negative and a positive point of reference, rejecting its political and class structures as backward, but nevertheless viewing its cultural and economic achievements as worthy of emulation. The intellectuals in particular expressed this ambivalence, since they played a major role in establishing and defining the state; but they then found that the task of operating and even living in it required them to conform to vulgar populist and provincial values.

In specifying those processes in the evolution of the first new nation that are comparable to what has been taking place in the societies of Asia and Africa in our own time, I am relying upon analogy. It ought to go without saying that: "We cannot assume that because conditions in one century led to certain effects, even roughly parallel conditions in another century would lead to similar effects. Neither can we be sure, of course, that the conditions were even roughly parallel."[1] It is fairly obvious that conditions in the early United States were quite different from those faced by most of the new nations of today. Many of the internal conditions that hamper the evolution of stable authority and a unifying sense of national identity in the new nations of the twentieth century were much less acute in the early United States. But the evidence suggests that despite its advantages, the United States came very close to failing in its effort to establish a unified legitimate authority. The first attempt to do so in 1783, following on Independence, was a failure. The second and successful effort was endangered by frequent threats of secession and the open flaunting of central authority until the Civil War. The advantages which the early United States possessed, as compared with most of the contemporary new states, then, only show more strongly how significant the similarities are.

There were other American advantages that should be mentioned. Although internal conflicts stemming from attitudes toward the French Revolution disrupted the young American polity, there was no world-wide totalitarian conspiracy seeking to upset political and economic development from within, and holding up an alternative model of seemingly successful economic growth through the use of authoritarian methods. Also the absence of rapid mass communication systems meant that Americans were relatively isolated, and hence did not immediately

compare their conditions with those in the more developed countries. The United States did not so urgently face a "revolution of rising expectations" based on the knowledge that life is much better elsewhere. The accepted concepts of natural or appropriate rights did not include a justification of the lower classes' organized participation in the polity to gain higher income, welfare support from the state, and the like. And whatever the exaggeration in the effects frequently attributed to the existence of an open land frontier, there can be little doubt that it contributed to social stability.

Internal value cleavages, which frustrate contemporary new nations, were comparatively less significant in young America. Shils points out that in today's new nations "the parochialism of kinship, caste and locality makes it difficult to create stable and coherent nation-wide parties."[2] None of these parochialisms was as strong in the United States which was formed by a relatively homogeneous population with a common language, a relatively similar religious background (although denominational differences did cause some problems), and a common cultural and political tradition.

American social structure did not possess those great "gaps" which, in the contemporary new states, "conspire to separate the ordinary people from their government."[3] The culture with which the educated identified contrasted less strongly with that of the uneducated. The ideology in the name of which America made its revolution was less alien to prevailing modes of thought than some of today's revolutionary creeds. Perhaps most important, the class structure of America, even before the establishment of the new nation, came closer to meeting the conditions for a stable democracy than do those of the new nations of our time—or, indeed, than those of the Old World at that time. Writing shortly before Independence was finally attained, Crèvecoeur, though sympathetic to the Tory cause, pointed up the egalitarianism of American society:

> The rich and the poor are not so far removed from each other as they are in Europe. . . . A pleasing uniformity of decent competence appears throughout our habitations. . . . It must take some time ere he [the foreign traveler] can reconcile himself to our dictionary, which is but short in words of dignity, and names of honor. . . . Here man is as free as he ought to be; nor is this pleasing equality so transitory as many others are.[4]

The ability to work the institutions of a democratic nation requires sophistication both at the elite level and the level of the citizenry at large. And as Carl

Bridenbaugh has well demonstrated, the America of revolutionary times was not a colonial backwater.[5] Philadelphia was the second largest English city— only London surpassed it in numbers. Philadelphia and other colonial American capitals were centers of relatively high culture at this time: they had universities and learned societies, and their elite was in touch with, and contributed to, the intellectual and scientific life of Britain.

In this respect, the political traditions that the American colonists held in common were of particular importance since they included the concept of the rule of law, and even of constitutionalism. Each colony operated under a charter which defined and limited governmental powers. Although colonial subjects, Americans were also Englishmen and were thus accustomed to the rights and privileges of Englishmen. Through their local governments they actually possessed more rights than did most of the residents of Britain itself. In a sense, even before independence, Americans met a basic condition for democratic government, the ability to operate its fundamental institutions.[6]

> It requires, not only efficient administration, but an independent judiciary with high professional standards and, in all branches of government, a scrupulous respect for rules, written and unwritten, governing the exercise of power. What these rules are must be known to more people than those who actually have the power supposed to be limited by these rules, and it must be possible to lodge effective complaints against those people who are suspected of breaking the rules. This means that there must be, in the broad sense, constitutional government.[7]

In many contemporary new nations, a potentially political powerful military class, who have a patriotic, national outlook, may use the army to seize power if it becomes impatient with civilian leadership.[8] When the United States was seeking to establish a national authority, it was not bedeviled by such a class. The entire army in 1789 consisted of 672 men; and even after a decade of threats of war, there were only 3,429 soldiers in 1800. The potential military strength was, of course, much larger, for it included various state militia reserves. The latter, however, were simply the citizenry, and as long as the government had the loyalty of the general population, it had no need to fear its professional soldiers.[9]

Of great significance in facilitating America's development as a nation, both politically and economically, was the fact that the weight of ancient tradition which is present in almost all of the contemporary new states was largely absent. It was not only a new nation; it was a new society, much less bound to the customs and values of the past than any nation of Europe. Crèvecoeur well described the American as a "new man," the likes of which had never been seen before.[10]

Religion, of course, may be viewed as a "traditional" institution which played an important role in the United States. But in the first half-decade of the American Republic, as we have seen, the defenders of religious traditionalism were seriously weakened, as the various state churches—Anglican in the South and Congregationalist in New England —were gradually disestablished. Moreover, the new United States was particularly fortunate in the religious traditions which it did inherit. Calvinistic Puritanism, which was stronger in the colonies than in the mother country, was not as "uncongenial to modernity" as are some of the traditional beliefs inherited by new nations today. A positive orientation toward savings and hard work, and the strong motivation to achieve high positions that derives from this religious tradition, have been seen as causes of the remarkable economic expansion that made possible the legitimation of equalitarian values and democratic government. Max Weber, the most prominent exponent of the thesis that ascetic Protestantism played a major role in the development of capitalism in the Western world, argued that "one must never overlook that without the universal diffusion of these qualities and principles of a methodical way of life, qualities which were maintained through these [Calvinist] religious communities, capitalism, today, even in America, would not be what it is. . . ."[11] Calvinism's "insistence that one's works were signs of eternal grace or damnation" has been transformed into a secular emphasis upon achievement.[12]

Other Puritan influences on American development have perhaps not been sufficiently emphasized. As Richard Schlatter has pointed out in a recent summary of the researches on this subject, the Puritan tradition involved a respect for learning which led to the establishment of schools and universities on a scale that surpassed England.[13] The opportunities for learning thus created, and the pressures for widespread education that equalitarian values implied,[14] led to a wide distribution of literacy. The census of 1840 reported only 9 per cent of the white population twenty years old and over as illiterate.[15]

The Puritan tradition may also have made it easier to legitimize American democracy as the rule of law. Tocqueville saw the special need of an egalitarian and democratic society for a self-restraining value system that would inhibit the tyranny of the majority, a function supposedly once fulfilled in the European societies by a secure and sophisticated aristocratic elite. In a democracy only religion could play this role, and therefore the less coercive the political institutions of such a society, the more it has need for a system of common belief to help restrict the actions of the rulers and the electorate. As he put it:

> But the revolutionists of America are obliged to profess an ostensible respect for Christian morality and equity, which does not permit them to violate wantonly the laws that oppose their designs; nor would they find it easy to surmount the scruples of their partisans even if they were able to get over their own. . . . Thus while the law permits Americans to do what they please, religion prevents them from conceiving, and forbids them to commit, what is rash or unjust.[16]

While Tocqueville pointed out that Catholicism was not necessarily incompatible with democratic or egalitarian values, since "it confounds all the distinctions of society at the foot of the same altar," he describes the "form of Christianity" in early America as "a democratic and republican religion."[17] It would indeed seem that the Calvinistic-Puritan tradition was particularly valuable in training men to the sort of self-restraint that Tocqueville felt was necessary for democracy. By making every man God's agent, ascetic Protestantism made each individual responsible for the state of morality in the society; and by making the congregation a disciplinary agent it helped to prevent any one individual from assuming that his brand of morality was better than others.[18]

Puritanism had been associated with the movement of the squirearchy for political recognition in England. As Trevelyan has put it:

> Under Elizabeth the increasing Puritanism of the squires introduced a new element. The fear and love of God began to strive with the fear and love of the Queen in the breast of the Parliament men. . . . Protestantism and Parliamentary privilege were already closely connected, before even the first Stuart came to trouble [the] still further seething waters [of Cromwell's rebellion].[19]

So that, as Schlatter has pointed out, the Puritan tradition implied a concern for "constitutionalism and limited government," as well as a belief "that they are a peculiar people, destined by Providence to live in a more perfect community than any known in the Old World. . . ."[20]

In establishing its identity, the new America quickly came to see itself, and to be perceived by others, as a radical society in which conservatism and traditionalism had no proper place. The religious traditions on which it drew stressed that it was to be different from European nations. But its really radical character derived from its revolutionary origins.

The political scientist Clinton Rossiter has described the effects of the revolution on the political ideologies of the nation in explaining why conservatism as a doctrine is weak in America:

> The reason the American Right is not Conservative today is that it has not been Conservative for more than a hundred years. . . .
>
> Conservatism first emerged to meet the challenge of democracy. In countries like England it was able to survive the rise of this new way of life by giving way a little at a time under its relentless pounding, but in America the triumph of democracy was too sudden and complete. It came to society as well as to politics; it came early in this history of the Republic and found the opposition only half dug in. . . . The result was a disaster for genuine, old-country Conservatism. Nowhere in the world did the progressive, optimistic, egalitarian mode of thinking invade so completely the mind of an entire people. Nowhere was the Right forced so abruptly into such an untenable position. If there is any single quality that the Right seems always and everywhere to cultivate, it is unquestioning patriotism, and this, in turn, calls for unquestioning devotion to the nation's ideals. The long-standing merger of "America" and "democracy" has meant that to profess Conservatism is to be something less than "one hundred per cent American"; indeed, it is to question the nation's destiny. Worse than that, this merger has doomed outspoken Conservatism to political failure.[21]

From Tocqueville and Martineau in the 1830's to Gunnar Myrdal in more recent times, foreign visitors have been impressed by the extent to which the values proclaimed in the Declaration of Independence have operated to prescribe social and political behavior. And the legitimacy which the American authority structure ultimately attained has been based on the assumption that as a nation it is dedicated to equality and to liberty, to the fulfillment of its original political objectives.

As Frank Thistlethwaite put it a few years ago:

> In the mid-twentieth century the American people still pursue their Revolutionary ideal: a Republic established in the belief that men of good will could voluntarily come together in the sanctuary of an American wilderness to order their common affairs

according to rational principles; a dedicated association in which men participate not by virtue of being born into it as heirs of immemorial custom, but by virtue of free choice, of the will to affirm certain sacred principles; a community of the uprooted, of migrants who have turned their back on the past in which they were born; . . . a society fluid and experimental, uncommitted to rigid values, cherishing freedom of will and choice and bestowing all the promise of the future on those with the manhood to reject the past.[22]

NOTES

1. Karl W. Deutsch, S. A. Burrell, R. A. Kann, M. Lee, Jr., M. Lichterman, R. E. Lindgren, F. L. Loewenheim, R. W. Van Wagenen, *Political Community and the North Atlantic Area* (Princeton: Princeton University Press, 1957), p. 11.

2. Edward Shils, "The Military in the Political Development of the New States," in John J. Johnson, *The Role of the Military in Underdeveloped Countries* (Princeton: Princeton University Press, 1962), p. 14.

3. *Ibid.*, p. 29.

4. J. Hector St. John Crèvecoeur, *Letters from an American Farmer* (New York: Dolphin Books, n.d.), pp. 46–47.

5. Carl Bridenbaugh, *Rebels and Gentlemen, Philadelphia in the Age of Franklin* (New York: Reynal and Hitchcock, 1942).

6. See John Plamenatz, *On Alien Rule and Self Government* (New York: Longmans, Green, 1960), pp. 47–48.

7. *Ibid.*, p. 51.

8. Shils, "The Military . . . ," *op. cit.*, p. 40.

9. James R. Jacobs, *The Beginning of the U.S. Army, 1783–1812* (Princeton: Princeton University Press, 1947); see also Deutsch *et al.*, *Political Community and the North Atlantic Area*, p. 26.

10. What then is the American, this new man . . . ? He is an American, who leaving behind him all his ancient prejudices and manners, receives new ones from the new mode of life he has embraced. . . . He becomes an American by being received in the broad lap of our great *Alma Mater*. The American is a new man, who acts upon new principles; he must therefore entertain new ideas and form new opinions." Crèvecoeur, *Letters from an American Farmer*, pp. 49–50.

11. Max Weber, "The Protestant Sects and the Spirit of Capitalism," in *Essays in Sociology*, translated by Hans Gerth and C. W. Mills (New York: Oxford University Press, 1946), pp. 309, 313.

12. Robin Williams, *American Society* (New York: Knopf, 1957), p. 313.

13. Richard Schlatter, "The Puritan Strain," in John Higham, ed., *The Reconstruction of American History* (New York: Harper, 1962), pp. 39–42. See also Bernard Bailyn, *Education in the Forming of American Society* (Chapel Hill: University of North Carolina Press, 1960), for a discussion of the influence which the multiplication of numerous sects by the eve of the Revolution had upon the spread of education. The promotional and propagandizing possibilities of education made it an instrument of survival among competing sects. "Sectarian groups, without regard to the intellectual complexity of their doctrine or to their views on the value of learning to religion, became dynamic elements in the spread of education, spawning schools of all sorts, continuously, competitively in all their settlements; carrying education into the remote frontiers." Bailyn, pp. 40–41.

14. "What strikes one most forcibly about the Puritans' efforts in education is the expectation of uniformity. Every family, without regard to its fortunes and the accomplishment of its head, and every town, without regard to its condition or resources, was expected to provide an equal minimum of education—for who, in what place, should be exempt from the essential work of life? . . . the quest for salvation . . . this was an occupation without limit, in the proper training for which all were expected to join equally, without regard to natural ability and worldly circumstance." Bailyn, *op. cit.*, p. 81.

15. Bureau of the Census, *A Statistical Abstract Supplement, Historical Statistics of the U.S. Colonial Times to 1957* (Washington: 1957), p. 214. The census of 1840 was the first to report literacy.

16. Tocqueville, *Democracy in America*, I, 316.

17. *Ibid.*, p. 311.

18. Williams, *American Society*, p. 312.

19. G. M. Trevelyan, *History of England* (Garden City, N.Y.: Doubleday Anchor Books, 1954), II, 143–144.

20. Schlatter, "The Puritan Strain," *op. cit.*, p. 42.

21. Rossiter, *Conservatism in America* (New York: Vintage, 1962), pp. 201–202.

22. Thistlethwaite, *The Great Experiment* (New York: Cambridge University Press, 1955), pp. 319–320.

76

Nationalism and the State: A Russian Dilemma

Hans Rogger

The title of the panel at which this paper was originally presented—"Nationalism and the Growth

From Hans Rogger, "Nationalism and the State: A Russian Dilemma," *Comparative Studies in Society and History*, IV, No. 3 (April 1962), 253–264. Reprinted by permission of the publisher.

of States," at the 1960 meeting of the American Historical Association in New York City—suggested a concern with nationalism as a political phenomenon. We were not speaking primarily about love of country, the cultivation of a national style or hatred of the foreigner, but about political convictions, atti tudes or movements and their relation to the state. The dilemma of nineteenth-century Russian nationalism, so defined, consists in this—that it could only with difficulty, if at all, view the tsarist state as the embodiment of the national purpose, as the necessary instrument and expression of national goals and values, while the state, for its part, looked upon every autonomous expression of nationalism with fear and suspicion.

The Russian experience in this regard is in sharp contrast with that of the West. There, the transition from the dynastic to the national state, the dissolution of old loyalties and allegiances had, by the nineteenth century, made nationalism a major factor of political loyalty and social integration. Nationalist sentiments, ideologies and movements had helped to throw bridges across conflicts of class and religion, had created common bonds between individuals and groups and had reconciled society and its members to the state to a surprising degree. This reconciliation between what many nineteenth-century thinkers, from all parts of the political spectrum, felt to be irreconcilables survived severe trials, such as the first World War, and helped to diminish the bitterness of political strife in the long-established nation-states. Nationalism had become more than a vague sentiment or an intellectual abstraction. It had become the expression of a substantial degree of agreement about the arrangements by which the society lived. As the state had become more national, nationalism had become more state-minded and had transformed itself from a romantic vision or a millennial hope into a harsher and hardier phenomenon. It had come not only to accept but to affirm the state.

This did not happen in Russia. Modern Russia did not develop a nationalism that was capable of reconciling important segments of Russian society to one another and to the state. In spite of the extraordinary preoccupation of Russian thought with the problem of national identity, culture or mission, nationalism as an ideology or political movement was plagued by contradictions and tensions that kept it from playing a decisive political or social role in the last century of the Empire's existence, that made its relationship with the state one of fateful ambivalence and caused it for the most part to remain a cultural and psychological rather than a political phenomenon. Among the masses, nationalism remained very much at the level of instinct, often violent and anarchic, while among the cultural elite it was predominantly a problem of personal and cultural identity. And the nationalism of this elite was as likely to be a criticism as an affirmation of Russian reality and the Russian state. As the government, after

1825, came increasingly to be preoccupied with the preservation of the status quo and its own security, there could be no sustained agreement between the state, its bureaucracy and its upholders and the spokesmen for society about the nature and content of Russian nationalism. The lack of such agreement prevented nationalism from performing the integrative function it had carried out elsewhere.

What was it that had kept nationalism from being a unifying force in Russia at precisely the time when it had created broad areas of agreement in other countries? One of the most frequent explanations offered by Russians themselves came in the form of a criticism of the intelligentsia, and of much of educated Russian society, for its cosmopolitanism, its infatuation with the West, its estrangement from the people and the national community, its indifference to the state and to its task.[1] "Patriotism and nationalism," wrote Peter Struve, "mean love for one's people and state,"[2] a proposition which was far from acceptable to the majority of the intelligentsia. It was not that they thought themselves deficient in nationalism or love of country, but they felt that the state was, and that a nationalism acceptable to society would not have found favor in the eyes of the state.

It is the root problem of Russian nationalism in the nineteenth century that too often the state did not reflect in its actions the aspirations of society, and that even when it did so it was fearful of enlisting society in a common effort born of common needs. It was the state which kept itself apart from society, the state which time and again withdrew into a sphere of its own, jealously preserving its prerogatives, careful to keep all initiative in its own hands. The state distrusted nationalism much more than did the intelligentsia, and its bureaucracy realized that an unpredictable nationalism, with its admixture of instinct, emotion, Utopian or liberal yearnings might well conflict with a cautious, controlled and rationalistic policy.

That the tsarist state was wary of nationalist ideologies and exalted sentiments long before the nineteenth century, before one can properly speak of nationalism, and that these sentiments frequently had anti-state implications, has been shown by Professor Michael Cherniavsky in his study of the epithet "Holy Russia."[3] It must also be noted that the creation of the Muscovite state, the ingathering of the Russian lands, had been the achievement of a ruling house which had viewed this as a dynastic undertaking, the recovery by the tsars of their rightful patrimony. Even when in 1612 the nation took an independent initiative for the preservation of its state which had virtually disintegrated during the "Time of Troubles," it restored the autocracy and soon relapsed into muteness and submission; it did not press a claim to share in the exercise of power as a reward for its deed of national salvation. It is, I think, one of the decisive facts of Russian history which deeply influenced the character of Russian nationalism, that the work of national territorial consolidation was completed before nationalism became a major fact of Russian life, and that this consolidation brought with it no extension of political rights, no interpenetration of state and society, no lasting accommodation between them.

On what basis then could a Russian nationalism have arisen which would have served to link society and the state, to bridge the deep gulf that divided them? The question became an urgent one when Russia became deeply involved in the politics of Europe and when the rise of nationalism gave to Western states a degree of internal cohesion and external dynamism that was disturbing and threatening to governments which rested on more traditional foundations.

There had been a time, in the eighteenth century, when state and society had been willing partners in a common effort, when the state had not only seemed to share the national purpose but had taken a dynamic lead in its formulation and realization. Then the state had fostered the development of a national culture in the European image and society had shared the state's concern with power and its drive for Westernization. Then, clerics like Feofan Prokopovich, the historian Tatishchev, poets like Lomonosov and Derzhavin had not only served the state and its rulers; they had celebrated it with patriotic pathos as the manifestation and the guarantee of the nation's destiny and greatness. In the eighteenth century too, there had been those, like Prince Mikhail Shcherbatov, who were driven in their criticism of the West's impact on Russia to criticize the state which was itself Western and the spearhead of Western influence; but these first instances of a critical nationalism do not yet constitute a break with the state or with its task. They concerned rather the manner of its execution and the protection of privileges, and for much of the eighteenth century the educated classes, the precursors of the nineteenth-century intelligentsia, still identified their strivings for modernization, reform and Westernization with the activities of the state. And in their country's strength and greatness, in its new standing among the powers, they found a source of personal pride.[4]

This community of interests began to weaken when with Catherine II the state turned increasingly to the bureaucracy as its main support and associate; when the coming of the French Revolution made it appear doubtful whether continued Westernization was a safe policy and when, after a brief interval of hope during the early years of Alexander I's reign, the government was entirely handed over to a bureaucracy which looked with misgivings even upon the cultural activities of society. The Decembrist uprising of 1825 widened the breach, which was never fully healed and which made it appear unlikely that the autocracy and the articulate portion of society could ever again find common ground in a program of Westernization and reform. The European revolutions of 1830 and 1848 made nationalism even more suspect in the eyes of the state and raised the question whether the tsarist state could be nationalistic, whether it could ever assent to a definition of nationalism which went beyond self-preservation. The record of most of the nineteenth century suggests that it could not. This was the case not only when the state was confronted by versions of nationalism formulated by radicals or liberals but even, and here the dilemma is most strikingly expressed, when it was defined by those who were most vocal in their support of the established order.

The reign of Nicholas I (1825–1855) set the pattern. From the very start, the Tsar and his government sensed that the nationalist teachings of the Slavophiles were at variance with official definitions of the content and direction of national life. And the Slavophiles, for their part, though they were far from radical or even liberal in any consistent, political sense, denied that the state created by Peter stood in any intimate, organic relationship to the people over which it ruled. For them, the essence of nationality was the people, the peasants, a people which might accept the state as a necessity but had no state element in itself. The autocracy was to be accepted; it might even be regarded as a Muscovite tradition that ought to be revered, but it could never be embraced, and the more it departed from its truly national bases and became more like its formalistic, Western counterparts, the less national it became. The state would always be the principle of unfreedom and, no matter what its form, a lie which denied the liberty of a truly Christian community of love.[5]

The Slavophile endorsement of an autocracy of Muscovite stamp in which, presumably, tsar and people had enjoyed a direct communion, undisturbed by the intervention of a meddling state apparatus, constituted in effect an indictment of the state of Nicholas I. This, and not merely a delineation of the spheres of activity reserved to government and to society, is the meaning of the memorandum addressed by Konstantin Aksakov to Alexander II on the latter's accession. To ask, as Aksakov did, that the ancient harmony between government and people, the state and the land, be reestablished on the basis of mutual respect and non-interference,[6] was not merely romantic; it could be taken as revolutionary. It was so taken by Bakunin who said that Aksakov's hostility to the state far exceeded his own anarchism.[7] One of Nicholas' officials found that "the Moscow Slavophiles mixed with their attachment to the Russian past principles which cannot exist in a monarchical state,"[8] after which they had considerable difficulty getting their writings past the censor. The Aksakovs, A. S. Khomiakov and Iurii Samarin all had a brush with officialdom which had little sympathy for their criticisms of Peter and Peter's state and their praise of the primitive democracy of old Russia. To denounce the Slavophiles as Russian Saint-Simonians, as did some of their opponents on the Right,[9] was clearly absurd; and theirs, moreover, was a Utopia that looked to the past. But Utopias, of whatever kind, might be subversive of constituted authority and therefore suspect.

This suspicion could also extend to such loyal and political-minded exponents of official nationality as the historian Pogodin and his friend and associate Shevyrev, for the very intensity of their nationalism, the very grandeur of their vision of Russia—a vision which definitely included the state—challenged the state's conception of itself. They wanted to bring Russia to the starry firmament of glory; Nicholas was more concerned with order, efficiency and stability. Nationalism would have proved disruptive of these; it was not merely different from official nationality, it was its antithesis. Whether it was their opposition to serfdom or to the German bureaucrats in Russian service, their Pan-Slav sentiments or their hopes that Russia would accept the mission of Christian enlightenment, such views were bound to set these men apart from the state and the Emperor whom they wished to serve. If Russian achievements were a miracle to Pogodin, Nicholas would rather place his trust in a strong army and an effective police.[10]

Even such a dedicated conservative as the diplomat and poet Fedor Tiutchev came to speak of the alien absolutism with its instinctive hatred for all things Russian that ruled at St. Petersburg,[11] hoped that Russia would regain her true identity,[12] and was at one point led to the radical conclusion that an autocracy devoid of nationality made no sense at all.[13] Official Russia, he feared, had lost all sense and

understanding of her historical mission, and in an ultimate condemnation of a bureaucratic obtuseness that would not hear the call to greatness, he wagered that people would be found in St. Petersburg on judgment day who would insist that they had not been informed.[14] St. Petersburg would not heed the visionary and Utopian notes of Tiutchev's call for a Slavic Empire which was to be more than merely a state—this would be a new world, a new dispensation to resolve all problems.[15]

Nicholas I made it all but impossible that nationalism could ever become official policy or that the unofficial nationalism of society would lose the ambivalence (or outright hostility) toward the state that was part of its essence. The problematic nature of the relationship between nationalism and the state affected every thinker who dealt at all seriously with the question of Russia's nature and destiny. Men like Dostoevskii and Danilevskii were suspect among broad circles of the educated classes because of their political conservatism or occasional chauvinism, while the grand and visionary sweep of their ideas made them equally unacceptable as the spokesmen of an anxious official nationalism. They too accepted the state, but the scope of their hopes exceeded anything that a government chancellery would have found comfortable or even comprehensible.

Danilevskii and other proponents of Pan-Slavism did, it is true, carry into Russian nationalism a new militancy and a political realism that made it appear as if their doctrine would, in the words of Bernard Pares, become "a weapon in the armoury of Russian foreign policy";[16] but it was a weapon on which the government never relied and which, at best, it handled with great caution, for it retained too much of the Slavophile legacy. The new-found appreciation of Realpolitik did not keep Danilevskii from expecting that the ultimate Slavic contribution would be to provide the masses with a just solution of social and economic problems;[17] it kept neither him nor other Pan-Slavists from viewing the peasant commune as the matrix of a more egalitarian, morally superior social order which stood in sharp contrast to the life of the West and to such Western principles in Russian life as political coercion and conflict.[18] And in its stress on Orthodoxy as an integral and definitive element of Slavic civilization, Pan-Slavism revealed its hesitation before a purely political nationalism. Even Danilevskii asked how a government could be free from Christ, and Ivan Aksakov, though the most crudely nationalistic of the Slavophiles, with more conviction denied that nationality stood above faith.[19] Dostoevskii remained deeply Christian even when he was most chauvinistic. His goal was the building of a universal Church, and although the Russian state might temporarily enclose the Church, it would eventually be transformed by it, perhaps abandoned as a constraint on man's freedom. Russia to him seemed less a state—republican, Jacobin or communist—than the embodiment of the soul of that Orthodoxy in which the peasants lived.[20]

It would be placing too great a strain on the evidence to deny that Pan-Slavism as a heightened form of Russian nationalism had political dimensions or to assert that it denied the state. The essential point, however, is that the state and the majority of the Pan-Slavists were inspired by fundamentally different goals. The state's primary objective was security, conceived exclusively in traditional military and diplomatic terms, and for the sake of security it always stood ready to sacrifice an exalted nationalism that might lead to unwanted difficulties with the European powers. Although Pan-Slavists were to be found in official circles, their teachings never became government doctrine, and even at the height of nationalist fervor during the Balkan crisis of 1875–1878, the government did not identify itself with the movement but dissociated itself from it and at times penalized it.[21]

In the face of the greatest demonstration of popular enthusiasm for a cause that should have united them, the state antagonized those who would have been its firmest supporters. Ivan Aksakov was made nearly desperate by what he considered the timidity of official Russia. Before the declaration of war against Turkey he castigated government and the bureaucracy for their indifference to the fate of the Balkan Slavs, for the anxious regulation of popular efforts on their behalf; during the war, he blamed Russian reverses on official obscurantism, on the censorship, on fear of the revolutionary élan of the popular movement; and after the war, his attacks on the "servile folly" of the diplomats whom he called the true Nihilists of Russia for their conduct at the Congress of Berlin, and even on the Tsar himself, gained him disfavor and temporary banishment from Moscow.[22]

The fear which Aksakov attributed to the government, that the general sympathy for the Slavic cause might be mixed with revolutionary expectations and give rise to unsupervised social action, was not without foundation. There were revolutionary populists and Bakuninists who not only acclaimed the rebellion of the Southern Slavs as a fight for national liberty against a foreign despotism, but saw in it a means for reviving revolutionary movement in Russia by linking it with that of the Slavs and for

acquiring insurrectionary experience. A small number of these men actually fought the Turks as volunteers, and some of them died while doing so.[23] The populist leader Mikhailovskii was momentarily led to give voice to the hope that to destroy Turkey meant to resolve the social question,[24] a position which made him sound curiously like Dostoevskii who also expected much that was "new and progressive" from war with Turkey, "the last great struggle which will bring about the great regeneration of mankind."[25]

If the record of the reign of Alexander II was one of only partially fulfilled hopes, there had at least been cause for hope, and in the great reforms of the sixties and in Russian sponsorship of the Slavic cause there lay the seeds of a grand reconciliation between state and society. The reforms in particular made it appear to moderate men like the St. Petersburg jurist Gradovskii that Russia, by becoming more progressive, had also become more national, that a freer press and a less constrained social life would create a national intelligentsia no longer captivated by an abstract cosmopolitanism, that Slavophiles and Westernizers could find common ground in support of a state which was truly national because it responded to national needs and national aspirations.[26] The government of Alexander III did not even give rise to such hopes, and although it loudly proclaimed its nationalism, this was little more than official nationality with a vengeance. Even if this nationalism of the regime had been more nearly in tune with that of society in its purposes, it could hardly appeal in view of its rigid, repressive and purely bureaucratic methods which, as some of its critics pointed out, had largely been borrowed abroad.[27]

The ideological defense of bureaucratic absolutism as a national institution was even more difficult under Alexander III than it had been under Nicholas I. For all its Slavophile windowdressing, it was constrained to be a defense of what Konstantin Pobedonostsev, its only theorist of note, called arbitrary government, though he wished also that it be rational and humane. Among the defenders of the government of Alexander III this was even more true of the publicist M. N. Katkov than of the statesman Pobedonostsev, for Katkov's reactionary tirades, where they were not purely opportunistic, were directed as much against native institutions (such as the communal village) as against Western importations.[28] Pobedonostsev himself, though more profound and consistent, also revealed the difficulties of a purely static, purely governmental nationalism, for his opposition to alien intrusions into Russian life ought logically to have extended to that Western innovation over which he presided, the Holy Synod, and to the whole St. Petersburg system itself. He not only admired Peter the Great and his work while deploring the activity of Alexander II, but he even expressed his contempt for the qualities of the national character and tradition of which the government was to be the guardian and reflection. "Don't you yourself see," the philosopher Vladimir Soloviev wrote to him in 1892, "that you have pushed your system to the extreme absurdity?"[29] An example of this absurdity was that so fervent and loyal a nationalist as Ivan Aksakov, shortly before his death in 1886, could be accused by the government of "a lack of genuine patriotism,"[30] and that society became less nationalistic as official policy became ostensibly more so.

The defeat of the working class risings in 1905, the political concessions made by the government in that year and the more active policy of Stolypin in the field of agrarian reform, appeared initially to bring closer the possibility of a reconciliation between the state and at least the moderate elements of society. But the turning point came too late and was, moreover, felt to be insufficiently decisive by much of society to overcome the heritage of antagonism left by the previous century. The experience of the World War revealed that the constitutional experiment had not in its short life succeeded in removing it.

The coming of the war brought with it an unprecedented outburst of nationalist fervor, a closing of ranks behind the government that was hardly expected by anyone. But the government, aware that the enthusiasm for war against German militarism in alliance with the Western democracies was fed by hopes of domestic reform, did not make full use of this enthusiasm. The Tsar's wish to be in perfect union with his people during this time of national trial,[31] remained no more than a pious utterance, and even right-wing nationalists like V. V. Shulgin were eventually driven into the opposition along with the liberals.[32] By their failure to recognize the nature and the opportunities of the war, because they saw the conflict as not much more than another dynastic struggle in which all direction and initiative had to come from the center, state and bureaucracy alienated the nationalism of society which could be employed effectively only if it were given a measure of self-definition and autonomy. The state demonstrated again its alienation from society, its incapacity or unwillingness to become the instrument of a truly national purpose.

The Russian state might have succeeded in enlisting the nationalism of society on its behalf, in making nationalism a public as well as a private sentiment, if it could have continued to be, unequivocally and successfully, the instrument of modernization and reform; or if, through a scrupulous respect for the civil and political liberties which it had granted, it could have diminished society's revulsion or indifference for the state and created the soil for a viable political movement which could have hoped to become part of the state and to nationalize it. Failure to pursue either course consistently or successfully, a failure for which the unyielding radicalism of the opposition must share some responsibility, made the Russian dilemma insoluble. There was no lasting agreement about the tasks of the national community, their order of priorities or the manner of their solution. In the absence of such agreement, most calls for support of the state and for a return to hazily defined national foundations and the national spirit were fated to fall on deaf ears. A nationalism which would have been satisfied with such formulas was for most educated and politically conscious Russians an impossibility.

It is significant that one of the very last attempts to determine the content of Russian nationalism, Dmitrii Muretov's "Studies in Nationalism" (1916),[33] evaded the difficulty of relating it to the concrete issues of Russian life by defining it as Eros in politics: neither virtue nor vice, but a blind creative force. It was a definition which even those who were most in sympathy with Muretov's aims could not accept.[34] The essence of the problem had been stated with the utmost clarity by Vladimir Soloviev: the national question in Russia was no longer one of national survival or existence; it now concerned the purpose of that existence and its ethical justification.[35] On that question, there was too wide a divergence of answers. There was no class or group in nineteenth-century Russia which felt strong and confident enough, as had the Third Estate in France, to speak not only on behalf of the nation, but *as* the nation; which could feel certain that a nation had in fact come into being to replace the system of antagonistic estates which tended to deal with the state separately and which were held together by the predominance of state power. In the years after 1905, attempts at a liberal nationalism (Struve) as well as at a national socialism (The Union of Russian People) failed equally to find a wide public resonance because of the stumbling block of the state and the diversity in interests and outlook between the various sectors of Russian society. It is conceivable, though it must for long remain a matter of speculation, that the Soviet regime, by reducing this diversity and by its ruthless policy of industrialization and modernization, has gone further in bridging the gulf between itself and the nation than the more easy-going autocracy of tsarist days.

Alexander Herzen had written in 1857 that the social problem and that of Russia were essentially one. "Russia is for us more than the fatherland."[36] For the intelligentsia of the nineteenth century, even for its more or less conservative wings, nationalism was always part of a larger conception—either of a Christian vision or a secular Utopia. In either form, its very boldness was an indictment of Russian reality or an escape from it. The integrative role that nationalism played in other societies, where common interests and common action forged common loyalties, it could not play in Russia where communication between various social and political forces was so poor and where the state could win respect neither for its benevolence nor its efficiency. Russian nationalism remained for the most part the striving of the articulate portion of society for its own identity, an effort to overcome its sense of futility and isolation in a hostile or indifferent environment. The state hindered rather than helped that effort and in doing so deprived itself of a potential source of support.

NOTES

1. See the famous collection of essays edited by M. O. Gershenzon in Moscow in 1909, *Vekhi* ("Signposts") and written by him, Nicholas Berdiaev, Sergei Bulgakov, Peter Struve and others; also, Bulgakov's *Dva Grada* (Moscow, 1911), II, 291–292, where he states that "each manifestation of Russian national consciousness is met with distrust and hostility, and this boycott, or self-boycott, of Russian self-awareness reflects its spiritual weakness."

2. P. B. Struve, "Bliudenie sebia," *Russkaia Mysl'*, 1916, no. 1, 140–142.

3. Michael Cherniavsky, " 'Holy Russia': A Study in the History of an Idea," *American Historical Review*, LXIII (April 1958), 617–637.

4. Hans Rogger, *National Consciousness in Eighteenth-Century Russia* (Cambridge, Mass., 1960), 253–262.

5. Konstantin Aksakov, *Polnoe sobranie sochinenii*, I (Moscow, 1889), 241: "The foremost minds of the West are beginning to realize that the lie lies not in one or another form of state, but in the state itself as an idea, as a principle that one ought not to speak of which form is worse and which better, which true and which false, but about the fact that the state, *qua* state, is a lie." Cf. N. V. Riasanovsky, *Russia and the West in the Teaching of the Slavophiles* (Cambridge, Mass., 1952), 121.

6. The text of Aksakov's memorandum is given in L. Brodskii, *Rannie slavianofily* (Moscow, 1910), 69–102. R. C. Tucker, in his article "Dual Russia" in C. E. Black, ed., *The Transformation of Russian Society* (Cambridge, Mass., 1960), 587–605, describes Aksakov's program as one designed to make possible a peaceful coexistence between an absolutist government and an apolitical people. Even this more limited statement of Aksakov's aims implies the removal of the state to the periphery of national life. See also Riasanovsky, *Russia and the West*, 152.

7. Emanuel Sarkisyanz, *Russland und der Messianismus des Orients* (Tübingen, 1955), 156, note 11, and Tucker, *loc. cit.*, 593.

8. P. N. Miliukov, "Slavianofily," *Entsiklopedicheskii slovar' Brokgaus*, XXX, 311, and V. N. Riasanovsky, *Nicholas I and Official Nationality* (Berkeley-Los Angeles, 1959), 226.

9. In the periodical *Vest'*. See Thomas G. Masaryk, *The Spirit of Russia* (London, 1919), I, 328.

10. Riasanovsky, *Nicholas I*, 142–144, 150, 167, 219.

11. Letter to A. F. Aksakova, in K. Pigarev, "F. I. Tiutchev i problemy vneshnei politiki tsarskoi Rossii," *Literaturnoe Nasledstvo*, no. 19/21 (1935), 246. The letter is dated 1 Dec. 1870.

12. Letter to P. Chaadaev (1853) in Hans Kohn, *The Mind of Modern Russia* (New Brunswick, N.J., 1955), 92.

13. George Florovsky, "The Historical Premonitions of Tyutchev," *Slavonic Review*, III (1924–1925), 338.

14. I. S. Aksakov, *Biografiia F. I. Tiutcheva* (Moscow, 1886), 163, quotes a letter from Tiutchev to a Russian friend in France, dated 15 July 1872, in which Tiutchev speaks of the general decline of the dynastic sentiment without which, he felt, there could be no monarchy. Speaking of the possibility of a republican era in Russia he adds: "Il n'y a que la Russie, où le principe dynastique a de l'avenir, mais c'est à la condition sine qua non que la dynastie se fasse de plus en plus nationale, car en dehors de la nationalité, d'une énergique et consciente nationalité, l'autocratie russe est un nonsens."

15. Kohn, *The Mind of Modern Russia*, 92, 94, and Peter Scheibert, *Von-Bakunin zu Lenin* (Leiden, 1956), I, 290.

16. Bernard Pares, *Russia* (Washington-New York, n.d.), 72. Hans Speier, in a review paper presented at the 1958 Arden House Conference (see Black, *Transformation of Russian Society*, 655), described the anti-Westernism of Dostoevskii and Danilevskii as an expression of individual views rather than of public opinion, while Prof. Barghoorn, in the same volume (p. 576), states that the extreme nationalism of Danilevskii, Dostoevskii and Strakhov was not representative either of official policy or of Russian public opinion.

17. N. Ia. Danilevskii, *Rossiia i Evropa*, 5th ed. (St. Petersburg, 1895), 538–539.

18. *Ibid.*, 191, 202, 526.

19. *Ibid.*, 525, and Michael B. Petrovich, *The Emergence of Russian Panslavism, 1856–1870* (New York, 1956), 92.

20. Unpublished fragment from "The Possessed" in N. Brodski *et al.*, *Der Unbekannte Dostojewski* (München, 1931), 240. See also R. Lauth, "Die Bedeutung der Schatow-Ideologie für die philosophische Weltanschauung Dostojewskis," *Münchener Beiträge zur Slavenkunde. Festgabe für Paul Diels* (= *Veröffentlichungen des Osteuropa Institutes München*, Band IV) (1953), 240–252.

21. Michael Karpovich, "Russian Imperialism or Communist Aggression," *New Leader*, June 4 and 11, 1951, and Hans Kohn, *Pan-Slavism; Its History and Ideology* (University of Notre-Dame Press, 1953), 141, 170.

22. O. K. (Olga Novikova), *Russia and England* (London, 1880), 24–35, 53–60, 98–106, reproduces extensive excerpts of three of Ivan Aksakov's speeches delivered in Moscow during this period. R. F. Byrnes, "Pobedonostsev on the Instruments of Russian Government," in E. J. Simmons, ed., *Continuity and Change in Russian and Soviet Thought* (Cambridge, Mass., 1955), 119, characterized a famous conservative's view of popular sympathy for the Slavic cause in the following words: ". . . he soon realized that the government would have to control all such popular movements or face the danger that they might turn against the state in distrust and then in enmity."

23. J. H. Billington, *Mikhailovskii and Russian Populism* (Oxford, 1958), 99–101, and Franco Venturi, *Roots of Revolution* (London, 1960), 559–562.

24. Billington, *Mikhailovskii*, 100.

25. Kohn, *Pan-Slavism,* 169.
26. A. D. Gradovskii, *Sobranie Sochinenii,* VI (St. Petersburg, 1901), 359–362.
27. *Ibid.,* 360.
28. Sarkisyanz, *Russland,* 157.
29. Konstantin Pobedonostsev, *L'autocratie russe* (Paris, 1927), 627. A measure of the difficulty faced by a Russian statesman who wished to be both a nationalist and a defender of the undiminished authority of the state is Pobedonostsev's assertion that the state was an expression of the national will and of the national faith and his belief that there could be no institution or individual whose power did not derive from that of the state, which was absolute. There was, in reality, no opportunity for the national will or national tradition to define or assert themselves unless one assumed that these were always identical with the will of the state. Even Pobedonostsev could not claim that such an identity always existed, and he was highly critical of Nicholas I for the alienation of his court from the people and of Alexander II for the introduction of non-Russian principles into Russian life.
30. Peter Struve, "My Contacts and Conflicts with Lenin," *Slavonic Review,* XII (April 1934), 575. Compare also Riasanovsky's *Russia and the West,* 199, concerning A. Kireev's restatement of Slavophilism.
31. A. A. Kornilov, *Modern Russian History* (New York, 1943), II, 340. The domestic political implications of a statement by the poet Leonid Andreev were unmistakable: "If the German be our enemy, then this war is necessary; if the English and the French be our friends and allies, then this war is good and its purpose is good." (*Ibid.,* 346.)
32. V. V. Shul'gin, *Dni* (Belgrade, 1925).
33. D. Muretov, "Etiudy o natsionalizme," *Russkaia Mysl',* 1916, no. 1, 64–72.
34. E. N. Trubetskoi in *Russkaia Mysl',* 1916, no. 4, 79–87.
35. V. S. Soloviev, *Sobranie Sochinenii,* V (St. Petersburg, 1883–1897), i.

77

The Revolt against the West

Geoffrey Barraclough

The development of the nationalist movements in Asia and Africa occurred in three stages. The first can be identified with the "proto-nationalism" we have already considered. It was still preoccupied with saving what could be saved of the old, and one of its main characteristics was the attempt to re-examine and reformulate the indigenous culture under the impact of western innovation. The second stage was the rise of a new leadership of liberal tendencies, usually with middle-class participation—a change of leadership and objectives not inappropriately described by Marxist historiography as "bourgeois nationalism." Finally, there was the broadening of the basis of resistance to the foreign colonial power by the organization of a mass following among peasants and workers and the forging of links between the leaders and the people. Not surprisingly these developments proceeded at different paces in different countries, and could be complicated by the impact of an exceptional personality, such as Gandhi, who fitted uneasily into any recognized category of revolutionary leadership. They took place more slowly in countries such as India,

which pioneered the revolutionary techniques, and more quickly in countries where nationalist movements developing after the process of decolonization had begun could benefit from the precedent and example of the older areas of discontent. In Burma, for example, nationalist developments which in India lasted for almost three-quarters of a century were telescoped into the decade between 1935 and 1945,[1] while in the Belgian Congo, less than four years before it became independent in 1960, Lumumba was still content to ask for "rather more liberal measures" for the small Congolese *élite* within the framework of Belgian colonialism, and it was not until 1958 that he founded the first mass party on a territorial basis, the *Mouvement National Congolais.*[2] Nevertheless there is a clear pattern running through the nationalist movements, and the sequence observable in Asia and Africa seems in all essentials to be the same; in most cases, also, the three stages of development can be identified with the policies and actions of specific leaders.

The process of change is clearest in India. Here the representative names are Gokhale, Tilak and Gandhi, and the stages of development correspond fairly accurately to the three periods in the history of Congress: 1885–1905, 1905–1919, 1920–1947. In its earlier phase Congress was little more than a large-scale debating society of upper-class membership, content to pass resolutions proposing specific piecemeal reforms, and Gokhale, like other early Congress leaders, accepted British rule as "the inscrutable dispensation of providence," merely asking for greater liberalism in practice and a larger share in government for educated Indians.[3] With Tilak, after his rise to prominence between 1905 and 1909, this upper middle-class reformism was abruptly challenged. Tilak rejected liberal reform under British overlordship, and demanded nothing less than independence; he also rejected constitutionalism and advocated violent methods. Yet on social questions Tilak was essentially conservative, while his nationalism—unlike that, for example, of the elder Nehru—was backward looking, postulated upon a purified Hindu ethic which he opposed to that of the west. Tilak, in fact, marked an intermediate stage—the stage of nationalist agitation on a relatively narrow middle-class basis, with the disaffected students as a spearhead and little effort at systematic mobilization of the masses.

What propelled the Congress movement into a new stage was the return of Gandhi to India in 1915, his assumption of leadership in the following year, the substitution for non-co-operation, which affected only a few special groups—lawyers, civil servants, teachers, and the like—of mass civil disobedience, which brought in the whole population, and the reorganization of Congress by the Nagpur constitution of 1920, as a result of which it became an integrated party with links from the village to the district and province and thence to the top. This is not the place to discuss Gandhi's complex and in many ways enigmatic character. Over the long run it was perhaps his greatest achievement to reconcile and hold together the many disparate interests of which Congress was composed—a task it is highly improbable that anyone else could have accomplished. But there is no doubt that his outstanding contribution in the phase immediately following the First World War was to bring Congress to the masses and thus to make it into a mass movement. It was when Gandhi launched his first national civil disobedience campaign in 1920 that "India entered the age of mass politics."[4] He did not, of course, work single handed, and the efforts of his lieutenants, particularly Vallabhai Patel and Jawaharlal Nehru, should not be underestimated. It was Patel, a superb political manager, who organized the Kheda and Bardoli campaigns which galvanized the peasant masses into action; it was Nehru who combatted the right-wing elements in Congress and maintained the impetus to social reform without which

popular support might have flagged.[5] But although it was the new radical *élite* which took in hand the task of organizing the masses politically, it is fair to say that it was Gandhi who made them aware of the importance of the masses.[6] One significant result was that a nationalist movement which had originated in Bengal and long retained a Bengali imprint spread throughout the whole sub-continent and became, except in areas dominated by the Moslem League, an all-Indian movement; another was that Congress, which at the time of the First World War was "a floating but vocal *élite* with few real ties to its followers," had acquired by the time of the Second World War "an effective organizational structure reaching from the Working Committee down through several levels of territorial organization to the villages."[7]

The pattern we can trace in India can be seen, not without appreciable variations, in China. Here the three stages of nationalist development may be identified with Kang Yu-wei, Sun Yat-sen and Mao Tse-tung, their sequence represented by the Hundred Days (1898), the revolution of 1911, and the reform and reorganization of the Kuomintang in 1924.

Unlike Kang Yu-wei, who hoped to reform China within the framework of the Manchu monarchy, Sun Yat-sen was a true revolutionary. It is true that, in 1892 or 1894, he had founded a reformist society, which aimed no higher than the establishment of constitutional monarchy; but after the disillusionment of 1898 and the bloody suppression of the Boxer revolt in 1900 Sun definitely threw over constitutional methods and in 1905 organized a revolutionary group which was the forerunner of the National Party, or Kuomintang. Its objects were essentially political—the expulsion of the Manchus and the establishment of a republic—and although as early as 1907 Sun made reference to the third of his famous three principles, "the People's Livelihood" (*Min sheng chu-i*), social problems and particularly the agrarian question played little part in practice in his programme at this stage.

Sun was, in fact, a liberal and an intellectual, who believed that China's political salvation lay in the attainment of democracy on the western model; before 1919, he was not hostile to the western powers and was prepared to leave the unequal treaties intact. But the failure of the republic after 1911 showed the limitations of this "moderate" approach. It also revealed Sun's essential greatness as a leader. In terms of actual achievement Sun counted for little during the first ten years of the republic; he had difficulty in retaining a foothold in Canton and the principal role in the revolutionary movement appeared to be passing to the leaders of the Fourth of May movement. But Sun was one of those rare men—in this respect not unlike Gladstone—who became more radical with age. Disillusioned with the western powers, and stimulated by the nationalist enthusiasm of the Fourth of May movement and the workers' strikes which followed on 5 June,[8] Sun reorganized his party at the end of 1919, made contact with the Russian Bolsheviks, and set to work to revise his programme. From this time, Sun was a pronounced and open anti-imperialist, preaching passive resistance on the Indian model and a boycott of foreign goods. More important, he now placed the economic question at the head of his programme, allied himself with the Chinese communist party, which was busy under Mao Tse-tung organizing the peasants of Hunan, and carried through a major reorganization of the Kuomintang with the object of turning it into a mass party with a revolutionary army as its spearhead.

This reorganization of 1924 was a turning-point in the Chinese revolutionary movement. It marked the arrival of the third stage, namely the combination of nationalism and social reform and the broadening of the basis of resistance by the mobilization of the peasant masses. From this point, however, the revolutionary movement in China diverged from that of India. The death of Sun Yat-sen in 1925 meant that there was no one to hold together, as Gandhi did in India, the divergent elements in the national party; in China the businessmen, financiers and landlords on the right wing of the movement allied with the army under Chiang Kai-shek and turned against the communists and the left. The rest is well known. Encouraged and financed by a group of Shanghai businessmen, Chiang in 1927 liquidated all communists within reach, finally forcing the remnant to withdraw in 1934–1935 to a remote area in the north-west where they were out of reach of the nationalist armies. The Kuomintang itself, under the control of reactionary groups, put aside all thought of land reform, and gradually the initiative passed to the communists under Mao. Their strength lay in the fact that they did not shrink from social revolution. In his testament, composed a few days before his death, Sun Yat-sen had written that forty years' experience had taught him that China would only attain independence and equality when the masses were awakened.[9] Because Mao succeeded in translating this conviction into practice, it was he, rather than Chiang, who emerged as Sun's true heir. "Whoever wins the support of the peasants," Mao declared, "will win China; whoever solves the land question will win the peasants."[10]

In the agrarian revolution they launched in 1927 in the rural border areas of Kiangsi and Hunan and which ten years later they carried from their mountain retreat at Yenan into northern Hopei and Shansi, the communists provided the peasants with a leadership and organization without precedent in Chinese history. They organized local government by soviets, in which the poor and landless peasants had the major voice; they distributed land taken from the landlords to this rural proletariat; they welded them into a revolutionary army waging guerrilla warfare against the privileged groups and classes. In short, they tapped the great human reservoir of China, and in this way they carried through an irreversible social transformation, which brought the work begun by Sun to its logical conclusion. "The political significance of mass organization," it has truly been said, "was the primary factor that determined the success of the communists and the failure of the Kuomintang."[11]

What we see, both in the Gold Coast and in Nigeria, is a characteristic evolution, from loose and often informal associations for reform within the existing colonial system, through middle-class parties with limited popular contacts, to mass parties which mobilized support by combining national with social objectives for the attainment of which the whole people could be stirred into action. This evolution is clearly parallel to that which, for the most part, had already occurred in Asia; indeed, it has been said that, with the founding of the National Congress of West Africa in 1920, there began in Africa the period which India had entered towards the end of the nineteenth century and left in the years immediately following the First World War, and that the foundation of the U.G.C.C. and the N.C.N.C., in 1947 and 1944 respectively, started British West Africa on the road travelled by south-east Asia in the two decades of the inter-war period.[12] There are also clear parallels between the evolution of African political parties and the movement towards mass democracy which had begun, as we have seen, three or four decades earlier in Europe. But the movement proceeded further and more logically in Asia and Africa, because there the development of mass parties was not hampered by the survival of earlier traditions of parliamentary government. Nevertheless it could only be carried through by new leaders less inhibited both in their relations with the colonial government and in their social outlook than the older leadership. As Nkrumah put it, "a middle-class *élite,* without the battering-ram of the illiterate masses," could "never hope to smash the forces of colonialism."[13] In other words, social revolution was the necessary counterpart of national emancipation; only in this way and through the strict discipline of tightly organized national parties could a mass resistance be built up, against which the colonial governments would ultimately be helpless.

Only a brief summary is possible of the steps by which this transformation took place. Their background was the period of rapid economic and social change during and after the Second World War to which allusion has already been made. Of this the most spectacular aspect—parallel in many ways to what was going on simultaneously in Soviet Asia—was the growth of towns; and the new towns generated both a social life of their own, unlike any that had previously existed in Africa, and a spirit of African radicalism which provided a ready-made material for the new generation of nationalist leaders, of whom Nkrumah is perhaps the typical example. Elisabethville almost trebled in population between 1940 and 1946; Bamako doubled and Léopoldville more than doubled in the same short span of time; Dakar rose from 132,000 in 1945 to 300,000 in 1955.[14] Four main consequences ensued. First, the towns threw up a new stratum of tough, emancipated, politically active men, ready to follow a bold leadership, which knew where it was going. Secondly, they provided a mass audience. Thirdly, they acted as new focuses of national unity, which cut through tribal divisions and formed an urban network binding together Africa's scattered rural communities. And, finally, the tremendous improvement in communications which economic progress necessitated enabled the leaders to forge organizations which covered the whole country.

As in Indonesia, it was the return from abroad of a new generation of leaders, schooled in politics, confident of their ability to handle western political techniques, and aware of the potentialities of the new situation, that made it possible to exploit these changes. The older generation was hampered by a sense of insufficiency. As one of them confessed during the constitutional debate in the Gold Coast in 1949, under colonial government their limbs had become "atrophied through disuse"—"we want faith and confidence in ourselves."[15] They were also chary of seeking popular support, conscious that the political mobilization of the masses would weaken their own position. As Nkrumah scornfully remarked, "the party system was alien to them," and he recounts how, when he took up his duties as general secretary of the U.G.C.C. in 1948, only two branches had been established "and these were inactive."[16] The return of Nkrumah from England in 1948 thus marked a turning-point in Gold Coast politics, just

as the return of Azikiwe to Nigeria in 1937 had opened a new period.[17] Like Azikiwe, Nkrumah realized that "there is no better means to arouse African peoples than that of the power of the pen and of the tongue."[18] His *Accra Evening News* performed the same function of inflaming racial and national feeling in Ghana as Azikiwe's *West African Pilot* did in Nigeria. At the same time—again like Azikiwe—he threw himself with intense energy into touring the countryside, addressing meetings, issuing membership cards, collecting dues, founding branches. Nkrumah himself has told how, within six months of arriving in the Gold Coast, he established five hundred branches of the U.G.C.C., how this enlistment of the rank and file alienated the Working Committee of the U.G.C.C.—"it went completely against their more conservative outlook"—and how, when the latter refused to endorse his policy of "Positive Action," he broke away and formed the Convention People's Party.[19]

The C.P.P. was from the first a mass party, but it was not merely a mass party, for, as Nkrumah said, "mass movements are well and good, but they cannot act with purpose unless they are led by a vanguard political party."[20] Nevertheless its victory in 1956 was due to its organization of the masses and to the strict discipline imposed on its members; it "marked the ascendancy of an egalitarian, nationalist, mass party over a traditionalist, regionalistic, and hierarchical coalition."[21]

The success of the C.P.P. in Ghana is only one of the more striking examples of a policy which other leaders were applying elsewhere in Asia and Africa. Trained in the United States, London, Paris, and sometimes in Moscow, they built up mass parties on the model of what they had observed in the west, with a pyramid of units running from local branches to national conferences, with a central office and a permanent secretariat, with their own newspapers, emblems, flags and slogans, and with cars, helicopters, loud-speaker trucks and all the other paraphernalia of political organization and propaganda. This was the type not only of the Convention People's Party in Ghana, but also of the Action Group in Nigeria, of Julius Nyerere's Tanganyika African National Union, of the *Rassemblement Démocratique Africain* and the *Bloc Populaire Sénégalais*. Their leaders knew, as Nkrumah recorded in his autobiography, "that whatever the programme for the solution of the colonial question might be, success would depend upon the organization adopted."[22] They were right. It was this perception that distinguished them from the earlier generation of nationalist leaders and enabled them to

ιιobilize the forces which the impact of westernization had released in Asian and African society. On
the whole, we can fairly say that those who mobilized
the new social forces succeeded, those who held back
and fought shy of mass agitation and social action
did not. In essence, it was because it failed to cope
with the agrarian problem and thus to meet the basic
needs of the people that the Kuomintang missed its
opportunity in China and was superseded by the
Chinese Communist party under Mao Tse-tung and
Chou En-lai. In India the outcome was the opposite
because Congress, though originating like the
Kuomintang in the middle classes, made contact
with the peasantry and, through the organizing
genius of V. J. Patel, built a party machine which
mobilized the masses, in the countryside as well as
in the towns, behind the struggle for independence
until it was won. In the end, the revolt against the
west, both in Asia and in Africa, merged into a
greater revolt still—the revolt against the past. Political independence, as Nkrumah said, was only "the
first objective";[23] what gave it strength, and won it
overwhelming popular support, was the determination to use independence to build a new society
designed to serve the needs of the people in the
modern world.

NOTES

1. Mansur, *op. cit.*, p. 83.
2. Cf. Patrice Lumumba, *Congo, My Country* (London, 1962), p. 182; Lumumba's political evolution is discussed by Colin Legum in his foreword to this revealing book.
3. Cf. P. Spear, *India, Pakistan and the West* (London, 1961), p. 200. Nehru, in his autobiography (e.g., 48–49, 63–64, 137, 366, 416), has much to say on the middle-class bias of Congress at this time and later.
4. M. Weiner, *Party Politics in India* (Princeton, 1957), p. 7.
5. There are good assessments of Patel's and Nehru's roles in the movement in R. L. Park and I. Tinker, *Leadership and Political Institutions in India* (Princeton, 1959), pp. 41–65, 87–99.
6. Cf. Mansur, *op. cit.*, p. 71.
7. Cf. Park and Tinker, *op. cit.*, p. 185.
8. For the Fifth of June, important as the first political strike by the urban workers in Chinese history, and as a link between the intellectual and working-class patriotic movements, cf. Chow Tse-tsung, *op. cit.*, pp. 151–158.
9. Cf. Franke, *op. cit.*, p. 208.
10. Cf. Shao Chuan Leng and Norman D. Palmer, *Sun Yat-sen and Communism* (London, 1961), p. 157.
11. Cf. Ping-chia Kuo, *China, New Age and New Outlook* (revised ed., Penguin Books, 1960), p. 63.
12. Cf. Mansur, *op. cit.*, p. 56.
13. *Autobiography*, p. 177.
14. For these and other figures, cf. T. Hodgkin, *Nationalism in Colonial Africa* (New York, 1957), p. 67. There are figures for the Gold Coast, based on the 1931 and 1948 census, in Apter, *op. cit.*, p. 163. In this period Kumasi more than and Accra and Sekondi-Takoradi almost doubled in population.
15. Cf. Apter, *op. cit.*, p. 178.
16. *Autobiography*, pp. 57, 61.
17. For "Zik," cf. Coleman, *op. cit.*, pp. 220–224.
18. Cf. N. Azikiwe, *Renascent Africa* (Accra, 1937), p. 17.
19. *Autobiography*, pp. 61, 79, 82, 84.
20. *Ibid.*, p. vii.
21. Mansur, *op. cit.*, p. 88.
22. Nkrumah, *Autobiography*, p. 37.
23. *Ibid.*, p. vii.

CHAPTER XII

Patterns of Response: The Major Types of Modern Regime and Their Sociological Frameworks

INTRODUCTION TO THE READINGS

In this chapter we present several articles dealing with the actual institutional responses to the general problems of modernization that were analyzed in the preceding sections. These patterns of response differed greatly among various modern and modernizing regimes, and there exists no fully adequate typology of such regimes.

In the following excerpts we shall follow the usual distinctions, classifying these regimes as pluralistic, authoritarian, totalitarian, and those regimes of the New States that developed in the later stages of modernization, emerging after World War II. All these regimes, in spite of their differences, have much in common with one another.

The first section presents articles dealing with various aspects of the pluralistic regimes. These regimes—characterized by a combination of strong centers and a large scope of political freedom and considered capable of the absorption of sustained growth—emerged mainly in the states that were modernized during the first phase of modernization; that is, in western Europe and in the United States. This type continues to emerge, to some degree, in some posttotalitarian states, such as Germany and Japan; but this development is due to external influence.

The first three articles in the first section deal with various aspects of the most crucial concern of these types of regimes—the development of dissent within them and their ability to absorb dissent. The excerpts from Lipset's *Political Man* analyze the reasons for the development of leftist and rightist orientations among intellectuals. Allardt's article analyzes both the roots of radicalism in Finland and the far-reaching capacity of the Finnish political system to absorb and change the pluralistic regime. It also shows how the Communist party with its totalitarian orientation was well integrated into the pluralistic political framework. Michels' classic essay on "The Origins of Anti-Capitalist Mass Spirit" deals with some major issues of protest that develop in the various stages of modernization and industrialization. Alford's conclusions from his research data on voting behavior in Australia, Canada, England, and the United States show that social polarization endangers the pluralistic regime.

The other articles in this section provide us with a series of analyses of the changing constellations of the characteristics of pluralistic regimes. The passages from Lindsay's *The Modern Democratic State* analyze the problems of securing an efficient control by the community over the government in an industrialized country with a high degree of professional and technical differentiation. Medina Echavarría analyzes the varying structural patterns in different types of democratic regimes, with special emphasis on the differences in the conditions between the early stages and later stages of modernization in European countries on the one hand and between European and non-European (especially Latin-American) settings on the other hand.

The selections in the section on authoritarian regimes deal first with the less extreme types of authoritarian systems, with what may be called the authoritarian—as distinct from the totalitarian—regimes of the right. Analyses of these regimes are best exemplified here by Linz's article on the Spanish regime and, to some degree, by Morse's article on the ideology of some of the Latin-American regimes.

The section also deals with totalitarian regimes of the right—the fascist regimes—such as those that developed in Italy, Germany, and Japan in the wake of the breakdown of initially pluralistic regimes. Maruyama considers the ideological and structural background of the rise of Japanese fascism from within the more flexible situation of the thirties. Seton-Watson's article presents an over-all comparative analysis of fascist regimes.

These articles should be compared and taken together with those of Carl Schmitt and Troeltsch in Chapter XI.

In the third section, which deals with the modern totalitarian regimes of the left, the two major concrete types—the Russian and the Chinese—are discussed. The ideological orientations of these regimes—which should again be taken together with that of Lenin presented above—are represented by the excerpt from Mao Tse-tung. The articles by Brzezinski, Schwartz, and Lowenthal present sociological and political analyses of the origin and dynamics of these systems, seen mostly as specific types of response to the general problem of modernization.

The selections in the last section of this chapter deal with the patterns of response to the problems of modernization, that is, with patterns of center formation in the so-called New Nations or developing areas. Roth's article provides a general analysis of the theme of the emergence of the modern patrimonial regimes and a description of the appropriate use of the term "patrimonialism" in the analysis of these regimes. The other selections bring out the great diversity of the processes of center formation in the later stages of modernization and especially the possibility of the development of weak centers. Emerson's article analyzes the single-party system, especially as it developed in Africa, as a pattern of the response to modernization that attempts to create the framework of a modern regime. This is done in a setting in which some of the basic prerequisites of modernity—such as a strong center and cohesive national communities—are lacking and in which the single party is more concerned with the creation of such preconditions than with the usual party activities that can be found in the pluralistic or even the totalitarian regimes that they may attempt to copy.

The papers by Germani and Silvert, Feith, Silverstein, and Mazrui analyze different patterns of attempts to create modern frameworks in different settings of late non-European modernization. All of them stress the great diversity of the conditions and of the responses to the challenges of modernization.

78

American Intellectuals: Their Politics and Status

Seymour Martin Lipset

The Move to the Right

This analysis of the sources of contemporary anti-intellectualism, and of the dominant politics of American intellectuals, has produced some curious paradoxes. I have argued that anti-intellectualism has been particularly widespread among conservatives because intellectuals have not been distributed more or less equally among the different political parties and tendencies. American intellectuals have accepted the equalitarian ideology of the United States, and this has both eliminated conservatism as a real alternative for them and also led many of them to regard themselves as underprivileged because they do not receive the overt deference that the more class-bound European societies give their Continental colleagues. The very success of the liberal ideology which most American intellectuals espouse reinforces their feelings of deprivation, which then become an additional source of their reformist zeal; and that zeal in turn stimulates political attacks on intellectuals by conservatives, and furnishes further support for the intellectuals' left-of-center political tendencies.[1]

However, this self-supporting cycle, which would keep American intellectuals on the left and right-wing groups on the offensive against them indefinitely, has shown some signs of breaking down in the last few years. American intellectuals as a group seem to have shifted toward the center, although most of them probably remain to the left of that imaginary line; and a significant minority have become conservative in their thinking. Many circumstances underlie this shift. Clearly one of the most important is the social consequences of prolonged

postwar prosperity. Another is the reaction of liberal leftist intellectuals in America, as elsewhere, to the rise of Communism as the main threat to freedom. Faced with a society far worse than the one which now exists in the West but one which claims to be fulfilling the values of the American and French revolutions, such intellectuals, including many of the socialists among them, now have for the first time in history a conservative ideology which allows them to defend an existing or past society against those who argue for a future utopia. Like Burke, they have come to look for sources of stability rather than of change. The very social classes which the intellectual reformer saw as the carriers of the good society—the lower classes, especially the workers—back the new despotism, and not only the despotism of the left, but, as McCarthyism and Peronism showed, often of the "radical right."[2] Furthermore, the very success of moderate forms of leftism—the New Deal in this country, democratic Socialism in the British Commonwealth and Scandinavia—has removed programs for economic reform from the category of a utopia to that of a reality with imperfections and inconsistencies.

And while changing political events have everywhere destroyed the utopias of the democratic left, prolonged prosperity, with its concomitant improvement of the relative positions of workers and intellectuals, has reduced the visible reasons for an intense concern with economic reform. The political issue of the 1950s has become freedom versus Communism, and in that struggle many socialist and liberal intellectuals find themselves identifying with established institutions. This identification comes hard to intellectuals who feel called upon to reject conventional stupidities, and results in a feeling of malaise which takes the form of complaining that everyone, including the intellectuals, is too conformist. Many American liberal intellectuals in the

1950s know that they should like and defend their society, but they still have the uneasy feeling that they are betraying their obligation as intellectuals to attack and criticize. Their solution to this dilemma is to continue to feel allied with the left, but to vote Democratic; to think of themselves as liberals—and often even as socialists—but to withdraw from active involvement or interest in politics and to concentrate on their work, whether it be writing poetry or scholarly articles.

It is important to emphasize that this evidence on the changes in many intellectuals' attitudes does not support the assumption, thrown out by the few who still remain in the extreme left, that McCarthyism or other forms of intimidation have silenced the radicals and created a frightened or bought group of conformists. An opinion survey of the attitudes of American social scientists supplies strong evidence that those who thought the spirit of the academic profession was crushed by McCarthyism were wrong. In general, the liberals among them stood up for the rights of unpopular minorities and continued to exercise their own right of free expression, even though they felt apprehensive about the threats to intellectual activity. As Lazarsfeld and Thielens remark about the behavior of the social science professors they interviewed: "There is indeed widespread apprehension among these social science teachers, but in general it is hardly of a paralyzing nature; the heads of these men and women are 'bloody but unbowed.' "[3]

The courage and liberalism of the university professor is actually constantly reinforced by his relations with his confreres. "While outside forces such as legislative committees may have harsh and definite means to do him damage, he cannot underestimate the subtle deprivations to which his immediate professional environment could subject him."[4] Men live in small communities, not simply in the great society, and the small community both reinforces its own attitudes to and punishes deviations from group norms. Thus the liberal consensus within the intellectual community has served to intimidate conservatives much more than outside prying and criticism has inhibited those left-of-center.[5] Today the larger social forces pushing the intellectual community as a whole in a conservative direction may also reduce this internal consensus on liberal political values and allow the release of more latent conservatism than has yet been apparent.

Even more significant evidence that the decline of intellectual leftist sentiment in America is not primarily a result of coercion is that a similar reconciliation between imperfect democratic society and leftist intellectuals has lately taken place in a number of other Western countries, where the pressures linked to internal security programs and anti-Communism have been much less. In Britain, the London School of Economics, once regarded as a stronghold of the Labor party, now contains a Conservative voting majority among its faculty, according to a number of reports.[6] In Canada, the *Canadian Forum,* the organ of Socialist writers and academics for three decades, ceased being a Socialist magazine within the past five years. One can point to similar changes in Scandinavia. And in France and Italy many intellectuals have moved from Communism to Socialism.

Only time will tell whether a permanent change in the relation of the American intellectual to his society is in process. In spite of the powerful conservatizing forces, the inherent tendency to oppose the *status quo* will still remain. As Edward Shils, a Chicago sociologist, has written: "In all societies, even those in which the intellectuals are notable for their conservatism, the diverse paths of creativity, as well as an inevitable tendency toward negativism, impel a partial rejection of the prevailing system of cultural values. The very process of elaboration and development . . . of the potentialities inherent in a 'system' of cultural values . . . involves a measure of rejection."[7] Any *status quo* embodies rigidities and dogmatisms which it is the inalienable right of intellectuals to attack, whether from the standpoint of moving back to traditional values or forward toward the achievement of the equalitarian dream. And in so doing the intellectual helps to maintain the conflict which is the lifeblood of the democratic system.

NOTES

1. R. C. Bruckberger, "An Assignment for Intellectuals," *Harper's,* CCXII (February 1956), 70 (emphasis in original).
2. An earlier alliance between the intellectuals and the lower-class based Democratic party broke down in the 1840s because a noneconomic issue, slavery, became the principal liberal intellectual cause, and the masses and the Democrats were on the wrong side. Many political intellectuals allied themselves with the "upper class" or Republican Tory liberalism discussed in the previous chapter, or with small left-wing parties. They began their return to the Democrats with Wilson's New Freedom and completed it with the New Deal.
3. Paul F. Lazarsfeld and Wagner Thielens, *The Academic Mind* (Glencoe: The Free Press, 1958), p. 95.
4. *Ibid.,* p. 104.
5. Morris Freedman, "The Dangers of Nonconformism," *American Scholar,* XXVIII (1958–1959), 25–32.
6. See William C. Havard, "The London School of Economics Revisited," *South Atlantic Quarterly,* LVIII (1959), 108–123.
7. Edward Shils, "The Intellectuals and the Powers: Some Perspectives for Comparative Analysis," *Comparative Studies in Society and History,* I (1958), 8.

79

The Radical Vote and the Social Context: Traditional and Emerging Radicalism

Erik Allardt

Political radicalism on the left and radical leftist voting are usually interpreted as reflections of discontent and deprivation among the lower classes. It has also been assumed that a large Communist vote in non-socialist countries is an indication of political instability. While these assumptions are reasonable and supportable in many contexts by research findings, it also seems clear that they can be questioned and need to be made specific. Deprivation associated with a radical vote can be of different kinds, and Communism has different implications in different contexts.

Finnish data and research findings are useful for dealing with these questions.[1] This paper presents some findings about the social sources of Communist voting strength in Finland, and also contains a discussion of the theoretical implications of the results.

Several reasons why Finland provides a good case for testing propositions about the social sources of radical political movements on the Left are:

1. The Communist movement in Finland has had rather heavy mass support. During the period after World War II the Communists have received between 20.0 and 23.5 per cent of the total vote in national elections.

2. The Communists have had strongholds in very diverse social and economic regions. Since World War II the Communist vote has been large in some communities in the industrialized and developed Southern and Western parts of the country as well as in some communities in the more backward, but now developing Northern and Eastern parts of the country.

3. The working class vote is divided between the Communists and the Social Democrats. During the elections from 1945 to 1962 the Social Democrats and the Communists got about equal shares of the

working class vote but in the most recent elections of March 1966 the Social Democratic vote surpassed the Communist. A total of 80 per cent of those working class voters who actually vote in the elections support either the Social Democrats or the Communists. Accordingly, one can say that class based voting is high in Finland but it should be pointed out that class-based voting in itself is by no means something rare or unusual in the Scandinavian countries. This is clearly seen from Table 79–1 in which voting by social class in Finland and Sweden is compared.

There are some differences in the classifications used, and the table can hardly be used for very detailed comparison. However, if class-based voting is defined either by the proportion of working class voters who vote for a working class party or by the proportion of middle and upper class voters who do not vote for a working class party it is obvious that class-based voting is by no means higher in Finland than in Sweden. The most striking difference, however, is that the Communists are much stronger in Finland than in Sweden, and that the working class voters in Finland are divided between a more radical and less radical alternative.

The assumption that the Communists are more radical than the Social Democrats is, however, in its general form dubious. From all that is known the leadership and the party platforms demand more radical social change among the Communists than the Social Democrats. It is, however, difficult to make the same contention without qualifications when focussing on rank-and-file members and ordinary voters. Survey studies of class identification indicate that the Social Democratic voters classify themselves more often as workers than the Communist voters. A segment of the Communist voters classify themselves as farmers which is a reflection of the fact that the Communists receive a heavy vote from individuals who are both small farmers and

Printed by permission of Professor Erik Allardt of the University of Helsinki.

Table 79–1 Party Preference by Social Class in National Samples in Finland Immediately after the Elections in 1966, and in Sweden Immediately after the Elections in 1964[2]

Parties or Combination of Parties	Social Class by Occupation							
	Farmers		Working Class		Middle Class		Upper Class	
	Finland (384)	Sweden (297)	Finland (651)	Sweden (1,397)	Finland (232)	Sweden (995)	Finland (133)	Sweden (160)
Communists (in Finland in coalition with a small group of dissenting Social Democrats)	7%	—	26%	4%	7%	2%	4%	—
Social Democrats	11	6	45	61	32	35	13	7
Agrarians (in both Finland and Sweden called the Center Party)	57	58	6	8	9	7	8	3
Bourgeois Parties	16	25	12	11	49	40	73	77
Non-voters, or Information Lacking	9	11	11	16	3	16	2	13
	100%	100%	100%	100%	100%	100%	100%	100%

lumberjacks. At least one can say that there is nothing to indicate that the Communist voters are more class-conscious than the Social Democratic voters. Surveys, however, indicate that the Communist voters more often than the Social Democratic voters refer to grievances of an economic nature when asked what is wrong in Finnish society.[3] A much greater proportion of the Communist than of the Social Democratic voters also express discontent with the leadership in Finnish society, with the courts, with the armed forces, etc. It seems clear that the Communist vote clearly is more of a protest than the Social Democratic vote. However, as will be shown in this paper, there are strong and almost conventional elements in Finnish Communism. To some extent the Communist alternative functions almost as an institutionalized channel of protest in Finnish politics.

Industrial and Backwoods Communism

The Communism in the Southern and Western parts of Finland is often labeled "Industrial Communism" whereas the Communism in the North and the East is known as "Backwoods Communism." As the names suggest, Industrial Communism exists in regions which are industrialized and developed whereas Backwoods Communism is concentrated in less developed, rural regions. The problem here is to specify under what conditions Industrial and Backwoods Communism are strong. Their background is

of course different as regards the degree of industrialization in the communities in which these two forms of Communism exist but the question is whether there are also other differences.

The social background of these two kinds of radicalism has been studied both through survey studies and ecological research. The data units in the ecological analyses have been the 550 communes in the country. The communes, both the rural and urban ones, are the smallest administrative units in Finland, and they have a certain amount of self-government. Due mainly to the long historical tradition of local self-government the communes form natural areas in the sense that the communes are important for people's identification of themselves. The communes are also the territorial units for which statistical data are easiest to obtain. In the analyses a file of 70 quantitative ecological variables referring to conditions in communes in the 1950's were used as a starting point.[4]

In analyzing the data factor analysis was mainly used although the correlation matrices reveal from the start many consistent patterns. Since a single factor analysis is not always interesting—it gives just a structure or a conceptual framework—the communes were divided into five groups. For each of the five groups of communes (called communities) in what follows separate correlational and factor analyses were done. Of the five groups three represented the more developed regions in Southern and Western Finland, and two the more backward regions in Northern and Western Finland:

Groups of Developed Communities

1. Cities and towns
2. Rural communities with a Swedish-speaking population along the Southern and Western Coast of Finland
3. Rural communities in Southern and Western Finland

Groups of Less Developed Communities

4. Rural communes in Eastern Finland
5. Rural communes in Northern Finland

The intention of making separate analyses for the five different regions was to inquire whether Communist voting strength is explained by different or similar background factors in different regions.

The comparisons of the findings for the five regions reveal some quite consistent patterns. The background factors of Communist strength in the three developed regions are very similar, and so are the background factors in the two less developed regions. However, the background factors in Communist strength in the developed regions, on one hand, and in the backward regions, on the other hand, seem to be very different.

In the developed regions the Communists are strong in communities in which:

1. *political traditions* are strong. This is indicated mainly by the fact that the Communists tend to get a heavy vote in those communities in which there are *stable voting patterns*.
2. *economic change* is comparatively *slow*. This is mainly indicated by the fact that communities with a strong Communist support have had a rather slow rise in per capita income during the 1950's. Those communities were modernized and industrialized in an earlier period.
3. *social security* is comparatively *high*. The communities with a heavy Communist vote are those in which there is no or very little unemployment and those in which the standard of housing is high.
4. *migration both into and out of the communities is small*. The communities with a heavy Communist vote have a very stable population.

The foregoing are the conditions prevailing in those developed communities in which the Communists get a heavy vote. When focussing on the background factors of Communist strength in the less developed and more backward communities a very different pattern is revealed. In the more backward communities the Communist vote is heavy when:

1. *traditional values,* such as the religious ones, have recently *declined* in importance.

2. *economic change is rapid.* In the backward regions the Communists are strong in those communities which have had a considerable rise in the per capita income during the 1950's and weak in those communities in which the income rise has been small.

3. *social insecurity prevails.* Communities with Communist strength are those in which unemployment has been common. It may be said that unemployment in Finland is mainly a question of agrarian underemployment. Unemployment strikes those who are both small farmers and lumberjacks.

4. *migration is heavy.* There is a heavy migration both into and out of the communities.

While Communist strength in the developed regions, the so-called Industrial Communism, seems to be associated with background factors reflecting stability almost the contrary is true for Backwoods Communism. It is strong under conditions of instability and change.

Observations of particular strongholds in the developed and in the backward communities strongly support the results of the statistical analysis. The strongest Communist centers in the developed regions are towns which industrialized comparatively early. They are often towns in which one or a few shops completely dominate the community. Some of the communities voting most heavily Communist in rural Finland are located in Finland's northernmost provinces of Lapland. These communities are usually those in which there are many indications of a rapid modernization process.

In order to correctly assess the social background of Industrial and Backwoods Communism it is important to observe also the background factors of the voting strength of the main competitors of the Communists. The Social Democrats are the competitors for the working class vote in the more developed regions in Southern and Western Finland. In the backwoods of the North and the East, however, the Agrarians are the ones who compete with the Communists for the lower class vote. The data and the findings clearly indicate that the Social Democrats in the South and in the West, on one hand, and the Agrarians in the North and the East, are strong in clearly different communities than the Communists. In the developed regions the Social Democrats are strong in towns and industrial centers undergoing rapid change and having a high amount of migration. In fact, workers who move from the countryside to the cities much more often vote Social Democratic than Communist. As has been shown, the Communists have their strength in communities with little migration. In the backward regions the Agrarians are strong in the most stable, the most traditional and the most backward communities. There are strong indications that a Communist vote in the more backward regions is a symptom of modernization. A switch of the vote from the Agrarians to the Communists is also a switch from traditional, particularistic loyalties to a more universalistic form of political thinking. In Northern and Eastern Finland the breakdown of regional barriers and loyalties is clearly associated with a tendency to vote Communist.

Traditional and Emerging Radicalism

The results reported so far all deal with Communist voting strength. The factor analysis of the ecological data of the Communist vote in 1954 has been the dependent variable. It is, however, interesting to compare these results with those we get if we focus instead on changes in the Communist vote over a period of time. The dependent variable in the analysis is now the change in the Communist vote from 1948 to 1958. During the period after World War II there has been some fluctuation in the Communist vote although Finnish voting patterns are generally very stable. In 1948 the Communists got 20 per cent of the total national vote but in 1958 it amounted to 23.2 per cent. In the overwhelming majority of the communities the Communist vote increased from 1948 to 1958. In any case, the dependent variable is a measure of the change in the Communist vote from 1948 to 1958, and it reflects mainly the amount of increase in the Communist vote.[5]

The results indicate that the change, primarily the increase in the Communist vote from 1948 to 1958 in all regions, is explained by the same kind of factors which are also related to Backwoods Communism. In all areas, also in the developed ones, the Communist increase was largest in communes characterized by rapid social change, relatively high insecurity measured by the rates of unemployment and housing conditions and a high amount of migration from one community to another. Of course, this result also means that the Communist increase from 1948 to 1958 in the developed regions most often occurred in communities in which the Communists did not earlier have a strong voting support. While in the backward regions, this increase most often occurs in communities in which the Communists earlier were strong.

The fact that increase in Communist strength is explained by the same background factors as Backwoods Communism makes it reasonable to assume that the differences in the social background of

Industrial and Backwoods Communism constitute a special case of a more general pattern. The difference may be assumed to reflect differences generally found when comparing radicalism of new and old origin. If we want some more general terms than Industrial and Backwoods Communism we could perhaps speak about *Traditional* and *Emerging Radicalism*.

There are additional grounds for regarding the Backwoods Communism as being emerging in type. Before the Second World War the population in the backward communities in the Northern and Eastern parts of Finland had the lowest voting frequencies in the whole country. After World War II the population in the Northern and Eastern regions has become politically conscious and politically mobilized. In fact, after World War II the highest voting frequencies are found among communities in the Northern and Eastern regions. It can be said that this mobilization to a great extent is due to Communist activity.

A Theoretical Model

The results can be summarized by formulating a simple theoretical model. The conditions associated with radicalism in the developed regions reflect hindrances of movement, strong group ties and strong social pressures. All of the conditions related to Industrial Communism, or in more general terms Traditional Radicalism, reflect, directly or indirectly, some kind of hindrances to people using their resources and abilities. The term *social constraints* may be used; in developed regions, radicalism tends to be strong in those communities in which there are strong social constraints. In the backward regions the contrary is true. Radicalism is strong in those communities in which the social constraints are weak. Accordingly, the results suggest a simple model according to which strong social constraints in developed and differentiated communities are apt to lead to discontent which expresses itself as political radicalism, whereas in undeveloped and undifferentiated communities lack of group ties and weak social constraints will have similar effects. The results may be expressed by simply cross-tabulating two dichotomized variables, the degree of the differentiation of labor (corresponding to the division in developed and undeveloped communities), and the degree of social constraints (see Table 79-2).

The fourfold table[6] has a resemblance to Emile Durkheim's[7] theory on the division of labor, and the terminology has also been chosen in order to comply with Durkheim's terminology. Cell 1 can

Table 79–2 Division of Labor

		Low	High
Social Constraints	Strong	1. Mechanical solidarity Low degree of radicalism (heavy agrarian vote in the backwoods)	3. Situation of coercion Industrial Communism
	Weak	2. Situation of uprootedness Backwoods Communism	4. Organic solidarity Low degree of radicalism (Heavy Social Democratic vote in the developed regions)

be characterized as a situation of mechanical solidarity and cell 4 as a situation of organic solidarity. Cell 2 may be taken as denoting a situation of uprootedness while cell 3 may be labeled a situation of coercion.

The model can be elaborated by distinguishing different types of social constraints and also different types of division of labor. Three important forms of social constraint might be mentioned:

1. Some societies, situations or communities can be characterized as having strictly enforced and severe social norms. There are non-specialized and diffuse pressures directed toward large, rather vaguely defined categories of ascriptive statuses.[8] These kinds of pressures can be found in undeveloped societies or in brutal dictatorships. Constraints of this type can, when the society becomes more differentiated, lead to very strong legitimacy conflicts. These kinds of situations are likely to exist in colonial and post-colonial situations.

2. Strong social constraints also exist in societies which are strongly stratified according to social class or social rank. In such societies lower class individuals are hindered by class barriers to improve their economic situation or their rank. If this situation occurs in industrialized and developed societies it is likely that there will exist strong intra-class communication, but a weak inter-class communication. In this situation there is a high likelihood for legitimacy conflicts and radicalism on the left.

3. Constraints may sometimes be particularly imposed on groups which earlier have had good social positions. There may exist middle-class groups who, because other groups have become more powerful, are losing in status or rank. They are likely to experience constraints imposed on them, and they will tend to develop aggressive political attitudes which are likely to be of the Fascist or the Radical Right type. If the statuses threatened are ascribed rather than achieved there is an increasing likelihood for a Radical Right reaction.[9]

Institutionalized and Diffuse Deprivation

According to the theoretical model cells 2 and 3 describe situations in which people are apt to feel discontent and deprivation. There is also a likelihood of legitimacy conflicts in these two situations. Discontent does not always of course lead to radicalism and feelings of the political system as illegitimate. The political effects of the discontent will depend very much on with whom the discontented compare themselves. This leads to a consideration of the reference group concept. The reference group concept is a tricky one because the concept has, as we know, many denotations. Of these denotations, however, two seem to be crucial. On one hand, a person's reference group is the group by which he identifies himself and from which he obtains his social norms and standards for social perception. On the other hand, the term also refers to a group by which a person compares himself when he evaluates his status, his abilities and his rewards. These two kinds of reference groups cannot always be empirically separated because the group for identification and the group for comparison often seem to be the same. In Festinger's well-known theory of social comparisons it is assumed, for instance, that the two kinds of reference groups usually coincide since a person tries to be similar to those he is comparing himself with.[10] It is obvious, however, that these two kinds of reference groups do not always coincide and that we need a specification under which conditions the groups for identification and the group for comparison are the same, different or altogether absent.

A preliminary answer to these queries can be

given in terms of the model presented. It seems reasonable to say that the two kinds of reference groups coincide in situations of organic and mechanical solidarity whereas this is not the case for the two other situations contained in the four-fold table:

In a society of mechanical solidarity the satisfaction of individuals and their ability to predict the behavior of others is mainly procured through similarity and strong attachment to specific social norms. Out-groups, and accordingly also, comparison groups are not available. As a result, the group for identification and for comparison tend to be the same.

In a society with a high degree of differentiation and division of labor individual satisfaction and also ability to predict how other people behave is obtained through intensive social exchange. People will feel satisfied if they are hindered as little as possible in exchanging rewards. They compare their rewards and inputs with those with whom they are in exchange, and they tend to regard their exchange partners as norm-senders.

There are of course many kinds of groups which can constitute reference groups but the ones which are most relevant in our discussion are social classes as reference groups. The case in which the group for identification is different from the group for comparison means then actually that discontented people will tend to identify themselves with one specific social class. Whereas in evaluating their rewards they will compare them with the rewards of those who are better off or belong to a higher class. This is what happens in cell 3. Strong social constraints will usually affect and hinder people in the lower classes in particular. They are the ones who will be deprived when making the comparisons. If this situation prevails for a longer period of time the deprivation felt because the rewards received are experienced as unjust will become institutionalized. Groups with a history of being deprived will tend to socialize their younger members to experience relative deprivation. The result can be labeled *institutionalized relative deprivation*.

The situation of uprootedness, cell 2, clearly leads to different forms of deprivation. The division of labor is undifferentiated, and the individuals have few opportunities for the social exchange of rewards. At the same time the social constraints are weak, and the individuals will experience difficulties in predicting the behavior of others. They have, so to speak, neither social norms nor the wishes of exchange-partners to rely on. The result is that groups both for identification and comparison tend to be lacking. In this situation the individual feels deprived because he cannot find relevant reference groups. The result can be labeled *diffuse deprivation*.

According to the theoretical model institutionalized relative deprivation is associated with Traditional radicalism, and diffuse deprivation connected with Emerging radicalism. Traditional radicalism exists in communities with stable voting patterns and a very stable population and it is natural to assume that people are reared into their radicalism. Emerging radicalism, on the other hand, exists in communities in which traditional values have been disappearing and in which the population is highly migratory, and it is natural to assume that people are searching for new footholds. The relationship between the two forms of radicalism and our two types of deprivation can also be substantiated by at least three independent observations:

1. The Communists in the South and the West have an efficient organizational network. According to the studies of some particular cities in the more developed parts of Finland it appears that there is a network of Communist organizations which corresponds to the national network of all associations and voluntary organizations. The Communist network performs for its members the same social functions as the national network for citizens in general. There are women's clubs, sports associations, children's clubs, etc. The situation is on this count very different in the North and the East. It is true that the population in the Northern and Eastern parts of the country has become politically alerted since World War II. This increase in the political consciousness is mainly displayed only during elections. It has not displayed itself as a general increase in social and intellectual participation. The Communist support in the North and the East is concentrated in groups in which the opportunities for social and intellectual participation are slight. A nationwide study of youth activities shows that the young Communist voters in the North and East belong to the most passive in the country as far as general social participation is concerned.[11]

2. Many observations of the Communist centers in the developed regions of the South and the West show how the Communist alternative in the elections is the conventional and respectable one. The Communist voters in these communities are well integrated in their communities and stable in their jobs.

3. According to survey findings the Communist voters in the more developed regions are the first to decide how to vote during election campaigns. Among the Communist voters in the North and the East, however, there is a very high proportion of

voters who make their decision at the last minute. According to a national survey in 1958 as many as 82 per cent of the Communist voters in the South and the West have made their voting decisions at least two months before the elections while only 56 per cent of the Communist voters in the North and East made their decision at that early moment. The latter was the lowest percentage in all groups established on the basis of party and geographical area.

Discussion: Social Functions of the Communist Vote

The Finnish electorate does not generally bring about great political changes. The Communist vote, too, is fairly stable. From the elections in 1945 to 1966 the Communists have obtained the following proportions of the popular vote:

1945	23.5%
1948	20.0
1951	21.6
1954	21.6
1958	23.2
1962	22.0
1966	21.2

Since the elections of 1966 the Communists have been represented in the Cabinet together with the Social Democrats and the Agrarians. Today the Communists have access to political power, and they cannot be regarded as politically disenfranchised in any sense. The Communists have become more and more integrated into the Finnish party system. One of the most decisive factors in bringing about this integration is the fact that there is a strong consensus around Finland's foreign policy. The relationship to Finland's eastern neighbour, the Soviet Union, is of course one of the most crucial factors influencing the formulation of goals in Finnish politics. If by goals we mean aims that are consciously promoted by those in the polity who make major decisions[12] it can be said that there is strong consensus around the goals of promoting friendly relations with Soviet Russia while at the same time retaining national independence. In Finland these two goals together are usually associated with the label of "neutrality." Finland has a pact of friendship and mutual aid with the Soviet Union but Finland has reserved its right to remain neutral in conflicts between the great powers unless the Soviet Union is attacked through Finnish territory. The friendship with the Soviet Union and the right to remain neutral are also constant themes in public

declarations by Finnish politicians. Survey studies indicate that this Finnish conception of neutrality has almost a unanimous support in the population. According to a nationwide survey in 1964, 91 per cent of all respondents expressed their approval of Finland's particular brand of neutralism while only 2 per cent were opposed to it. In the same fashion Finland's line in foreign policy is strongly approved in all sectors of the population. As many as 88 per cent of the respondents expressed the view that Finland's handling of foreign affairs has been done well whereas, again, a very negligible minority thought it had been handled badly. Likewise an overwhelming majority of the population thinks that Finland's foreign policy has been honorable for the country. Today Finland's line of neutrality is not only considered necessary but by all important segments of population is also conceived as right or good. For these crucial parts of the goal structure in Finnish politics there is consensus and almost unanimous support, and the Communist voters accept exactly the same goals as the voters of other parties. Accordingly, when focussing on some of the most crucial goals in Finnish politics, those embodied in the concept of Finnish neutrality, the Communist vote can hardly be taken as an indication of instability or lack of consensus.

There are of course other components in the goal structure than those related to external relations. The most important of these relate to the concept of Social Welfare. For the goals related to Social Welfare there is definitely more dissensus, and within the working class parties topics related to social welfare, social security and equality are often discussed in class terms. The Communist vote can, accordingly, be taken as an indication of class consciousness but the situation is complicated because it is difficult to say on many counts how the Communists differ from the Social Democrats. The difference between the Social Democrats and the Communists is often regional, and at least as far as Industrial Communism is concerned it is often deprivation experienced in the past which counts most. The Communists are, as has been reported, more prone to express their discontents with references to economic grievances than the Social Democrats.

It can, however, be argued that the Communists actually have accomplished the incorporation of large segments of the Finnish population into the Finnish political system. There is, of course, a difference between Industrial and Backwoods Communism. In some of the developed communities in the Southern and Western parts of Finland the population has nourished memories from grievances in the past. Through their support of the Communists they have gained a feeling of being a part of the Finnish political system.

The background factors of Backwoods Communism correspond more closely to the background factors conventionally mentioned as conditions for the rise of support for extremist political movements. According to the theory of mass society the supporters of so-called extremist movements are usually described as uprooted and without ties to secondary groups which in turn would bind the individuals to the community or society at large.[13] This description also goes for Backwoods Communism. While the theory of mass society does not explain Industrial Communism it contributes to an understanding of Backwoods Communism. However, it does not seem reasonable to let the matter rest with this conclusion. The voters in the backward Northern and Eastern regions have been politically alerted since World War II partly because of Communist activity, and they have been reared into the Finnish political system during the last twenty years while voting Communist. As has been shown, the lower class vote for the Communists in the North and the East is an indication of modernization and of the breakdown of many regional, particularistic barriers.

In countries in which the Communist party has had mass support over a longer period of time it does not seem well grounded to regard the Communist vote as an indicator of political instability or as a symptom that parts of the population are outside the political system. Communist mass support has different implications in different contexts. This is even often true for the Communist voting support within a single country. The difference between Industrial and Backwoods Communism is a case in point.

NOTES

1. There is a wealth of ecological and survey data about political behavior in Finland. Most of the original tables for the results discussed here cannot be presented in this paper. The data and statistical tables are found mainly in Erik Allardt, "Patterns of Class Conflict and Working Class Consciousness in Finland," in E. Allardt and Y. Littunen, eds., *Cleavages, Ideologies and Party Systems* (Helsinki: The Westermarck Society, 1964), pp. 97–131.

2. The Finnish data are from a poll by Finnish Gallup in April 1966. The Swedish data are from *Official Statistics of Sweden. The Elections to the Riksdag During the Years 1961–64* (Stockholm, 1965).

3. Allardt, *op. cit.,* pp. 109–110.

4. Erik Allardt and Olavi Riihinen, "Files for Aggregate Data by Territorial Units in Finland," in S. Rokkan, ed., *Data Archives for the Social Sciences* (Paris: Mouton, 1966).

5. The data for this particular analysis are mainly presented in Erik Allardt, "Institutionalized Versus Diffuse Support of Radical Political Movements," *Transactions of the Fifth World Congress of Sociology,* IX (1964), 369–380.

6. A slightly different formulation of the same model is presented in Erik Allardt, "A Theory on Solidarity and Legitimacy Conflicts," in William J. Goode, ed., *The Dynamics of Modern Society* (New York: Atherton, 1966), pp. 167–178.

7. Emile Durkheim, *The Division of Labor in Society* (Glencoe: The Free Press, 1960).

8. Ulf Himmelstrand, "Conflict, Conflict Resolution and Nation-Building in the Transition from Tribal 'Mechanical' Solidarities to the 'Organic' Solidarity of Modern (or Future) Multi-Tribal Societies." Paper presented at the Sixth World Congress of Sociology, 1966.

9. Johan Galtung, "Rank and Social Integration: A Multidimensional Approach," in Berger, Zelditch, Jr. and Anderson, *Sociological Theories in Progress* (New York: Houghton Mifflin, 1966), pp. 169–171.

10. Leon Festinger, "A Theory of Social Comparison Processes," *Human Relations,* VII (1954), 117–140.

11. Yrjö Littunen, "Aktiivisuus ja radikalismi, with an English Summary: Activity and Radicalism," *Politiikka* (A quarterly published by the Finnish Political Science Association) II, No. 4 (1960), 182–183.

12. See Bo Anderson and James D. Cockcroft, "Control and Cooptation in Mexican Politics," *Technical Report No. 16 from the Laboratory for Social Research, Stanford University,* 1965.

13. E.g. Hannah Arendt, *The Origins of Totalitarianism* (New York: Harcourt, Brace, 1951), or William Kornhauser, *The Politics of Mass Society* (Glencoe: The Free Press, 1959).

80

The Origins of Anti-Capitalistic Mass Spirit

Robert Michels

I. The Factory

The Development of "Psychological Mass" and Class Consciousness

The shift from the handicraft and domestic system to large-scale factory enterprise, from manual to machine labor, engendered a psychological change which in the long run gave the labor force a new and quite specific character. Before the industrial revolution, the working force was atomised into innumerable tiny units; its most striking trait was its parochialism and narrow individualism with all the good and bad this implies. This was true even of those workers who were grouped together in crafts or guilds. These individuals or small economic bodies were pushed into temporary cooperation only by suddenly enflamed political or, more frequently, religious passions, or under extreme stress of serious economic crises.

The new mode of [factory] production first created the modern concept of the working mass. . . . [It] taught the proletarians to work together in one shop on one piece. It compelled the combination of innumerable small production units into a far smaller number of large-scale units. In addition, it created new plants which were large-scale enterprises from the start. It hounded workers into factory towns and forced them to perform identical tasks in huge shops. Those who had lived as peasants or domestic workers, or as artisans in small towns and small shops, now became a compact mass, through the manner of their work and the absolute homogeneity of their condition. This mass, spatially and spiritually compact, may be called "psychological mass."

Among the urbanized workers there now emerged the first intimations of a collective feeling of "belonging together." The machine became the center.

From Robert Michels, "The Origins of Anti-Capitalist Mass Spirit," in *Man In Contemporary Society* (New York: Columbia University Press, 1955), pp. 740–745, 758–765. Reprinted by permission of the publisher.

This instrument demanded for its service a very large number of ever busy hands. The machine, one may say, is like a great general who gathers around him thousands of battle-ready soldiers in order to assign them their tasks. The machine brings about a militarization of the labor process, not only because it disciplines the dispersed individual units, but also because—in spite of the most thorough division of labor—it orients them towards the achievement of the single goal of maximum production. The mechanized enterprise thus creates a form of industrial cooperation which, in the purely technical realm, leads, without question, to a high degree of solidarity despite all the conflicts which it stimulates in the economic sphere between the managerial and capitalistic elements on the one hand and the wage-receiving element in the enterprise on the other. In other words: The human material of the "factory," while without a common interest in the distribution of income derived from production does, however, share an interest in the technical process of production itself.

The mechanized large-scale factory operates like a model school of solidarity on the tightly concentrated working force, united on the floor of the factory in identical tasks around identical tools. This solidarity is, at first, necessarily restricted to the work process. After finishing its daily stint the working mass of the large-scale enterprise dissolves into its innumerable molecules. When the gates of the factory close in the evening, solidarity is at an end. Individuality with its particularizing influences once more resumes its old and rightful place. However, when early next morning the heavy gates swing open once again, the iron duty of solidarity begins anew. The steady, systematic, eternal repetition of this process; the eternal close contact of working side by side to which the individuals are exposed in the factory; the ease with which workers get to know each other and talk to each other created by this process (on the way home or in the saloons); these encourage in the worker's soul the growth of a new feeling which is based no longer solely on technological, but also on economic, solidarity. One may say: Solidarity, the consciousness of belonging together, is transferred from the production process of labor into the spiritual life of the proletariat. When in the evening the shrill factory whistle sounds the worker now carries a feeling of identity of interests shared with his fellow workers from the giant plant along into his own home. Thus the modern production process itself embeds in the mentality of the proletarian the seed of that complicated and curious plant designated by the social psychologist as Class Consciousness. . . .

Isolation of the Masses by Their Spatial Separation from the Employer

While the workers were thus molded into a unit they were on the other hand, separated from the employer. First to disappear was the community home, residence at the same hearth. Then there disappeared the work community, the working together on the same piece or at least in the same room. In the mechanized, large-scale enterprise the entrepreneur lost his previous character as fellow worker. . . . Control over output was now entrusted to intermediaries. The entrepreneur became invisible to his workers. He was banished into closed-off, not always easily accessible offices. . . . He became a stranger to his workers with whom he no longer had anything in common beyond the labor contract. . . . The relationship between employer and employee was depersonalized, materialized. Some employers requested that their workers not greet them any longer in the street. Others demanded the workers' greeting but refused to return the salutation.

Already before the middle of the last century one could say that the only entrepreneurs who were interested in the personal fortune of their workers, apart from a few very large manufacturers whose great means permitted them philanthropic feelings, were the very small manfacturers who remained in the old patriarchal traditions of communal living. The relationship of workers to the overwhelming number of entrepreneurs was objectified. Between employee and employer the only connecting link left was the cash nexus. . . .

Thus the spatial separation of home and work through the relocation of the place of work and the differentiation of labor acted to divide, that is, to create new, classes. This phenomenon is complementary to the emerging solidarity of a shared way of life. There can be no doubt that the gradual disappearance of the employer from the shop floor and from the social horizon of the wage earners contributed to the emergence of a special proletarian class.

The class division [thus] brought about . . . paid little attention to the Saint-Simonian formula of class unity among producers, be they entrepreneurs or workers. To the wage worker the invisible and remote financier and capitalist were mythical personalities; his rage was directed quite concretely against the visible, tangible factory owner whose villa he saw before his eyes and whose method of enrichment he recognized by perceptible symptoms. It was the factory owner and *not* the financier living on unearned income who became for the worker the tormentor and exploiter, even though the worker saw that the owner also worked—sometimes the office lights burned far into the night.

At first, this separation did not lead to hatred, only to estrangement. The worker's hatred was reserved for the representative of the entrepreneur at the place of work, the foreman. Opposition to the employer was sharper rather than weaker if he himself had come from the ranks of the proletariat. Especially the proletarian turned factory owner (in France or England) was not distinguished by his humane reputation. In the latter case the worker did not even feel that natural respect which the lowborn had had for the highborn.

An equalizing, class-unifying element is present where the manner of living is equal or at least similar, even when other characteristics, such as property, income, and profession, are and remain heterogeneous. This is particularly true when this living in similar style proceeds in the same space, when therefore one can speak of a common life, of a living-together. During the French Revolution a struggle broke out almost immediately in almost all the realm's provinces between the landowning aristocracy and the small leaseholders and tenant farmers which led to the destruction of the manor houses and, finally, to the expropriation of the landed aristocracy and the partition of their estates. But in the Vendée, gentry and peasantry only closed ranks more tightly in a common defence of the monarchy against the Republic. One of the main reasons for the solidarity characterizing this latter case, according to the Marquis de Vaissière, may be found in the fact that absentee ownership was less prevalent among the gentry of the Vendée than in the rest of France. There in the Vendée the gentlemen worked their own fields, and participated in the feasts and carousals of the peasants and even invited them occasionally in a sociable manner to a visit at their manor houses.

Occasionally even the mere presence of certain

outwardly common features creates a certain degree of internal solidarity between classes. In the period between the publication of Adam Smith's *Inquiry into the Wealth of Nations* and the rise of the Chartist movement, German and Italian visitors to England were struck . . . by the uniformity of dress exhibited by Englishmen of all classes. Differentiation between classes, particularly on Sundays, was hardly noticeable. There were those who saw in the dress-democracy of Englishmen and the feeling of community deriving from it one of the reasons for the fact that the English social classes were not touched by the fever of the French Revolution. It must be remarked, however, that common manner of living, not to speak of common fashion and dress, alone are by no means sufficient to bridge class differences. Upon closer analysis of the factual relationships it becomes clear that this common manner of living usually is conditioned by other features, such as similarity of profession, distribution pattern, and education, which tend to overcome inequalities of psychological if not economic weight. The *gentilhomme campagnard* [country gentleman] and the *paysan* [peasant] are both members of the farmer group. . . .

The sharing of meals is today a characteristic of class membership. At the table classes divide. Those who by habit sit down to table with each other or invite each other to meals, belong to the same social class. Members of different classes do not associate socially with each other any more, at least not in their homes. In the domestic structure itself this division has taken place creating the same result by giving rise to class distinctions. The patriarchically shared table gave way to the banishment of the servants from the family's living room. The household members divide themselves at meal time according to their class membership. The master and mistress of the house eat in the dining room, the servants in the kitchen. The sharing of meals by master and servant at the long table of patriarchalism is a dying institution.

To the loosening spatial labor community must be added the loosening geographical community of habitation, operating in the same direction.

We may disregard . . . the suddenly rising factory town. While it represents a tremendous concentration in labor and habitation space, it is not of an exclusively proletarian nature and, more important, does not represent the segregation of the proletarian element from the rest of the population. The owners and managers of the industries are co-inhabitants of the city.

On the other hand, attention must be directed at the growth of workers' quarters, for there the proletarian element is to be found in almost complete isolation.

The peripheral location of factories within the urban area is conditioned not so much by the change of the city's core into an office and amusement center with corresponding weakening of the dormitory element and the movement of workshops from center to periphery; rather, to a much greater extent, it is due to the fact that factories were constructed, from the very start, at the urban periphery, drawing upon human material coming from the country, i.e., from the outside. At first factory location was tied to rivers by the technological reliance on water power. Factories were, therefore, located along river banks in the country. . . . [Steam] power emancipated the factories from . . . rivers and permitted establishment of plants at the very edge of the towns. Thus there arose the workers' suburb, the *Faubourg Ouvrier*, which was separated from the start by its peripheral location from the living quarters of the other classes of the population. The uniformity of these workers' quarters was only increased by their ugliness and accented by their lack of variety. No churches, no parks, no fountains, no squares, no statues! . . .

The misery, the unwholesomeness, and the dirt soon beginning to accumulate were not, however, the primary factors tending to create class consciousness. The workers' dwellings in the preindustrial era were superior to the later ones in only one respect: they had a more petty bourgeois character. The workers were emotionally attached even to their miserable furnishings. The bleakness of the modern factory hall, its nakedness, may very well be a secretly guilty contributor to the rise of modern class consciousness. . . .

This growth of workers' quarters seems to have led to protests on the part of the inhabitants themselves. Should the workers of a democratic state permit themselves to be crowded together in special streets and quarters similar to the ghetto which had just been abolished, apart from the homes of their fellow citizens and avoided by them? Was this not directly contrary to the dignity of the citizen and the equality of man? Even the opposition did not view the growth of workers' quarters with favor. They realized the political danger inherent in the crowding together of masses of men left to themselves. . . .

The first form which workers' houses took under modern industrialism was . . . the barrack-like tenement building. This, at least, is true of many parts of Germany, France, Italy, and other countries on the Continent. It has been said:

In Germany the greatest concentration of population, the highest average density of dwellings, is to be found in the suburbs, i.e., in the newly built-up city areas. The tenement houses with the most intensive crowding of inhabitants developed not on the scarce, highly priced real estate of the city centers, but rather on the plentiful land open to urban development. It is just these newly built-up districts with their plentiful, naturally most inexpensive ground which offer the greatest difficulties to building development. According to natural, economic laws the curve of suburban building should flatten out, just as the curve of ground rent flattens out.

Development of the new workers' dwellings was, of course, not restricted to private or speculative building activity. The employers themselves, for reasons which ranged from considerations of utility and power on one hand to pure charity on the other, either themselves built or supported the building of individual homes for their workers, usually in the immediate vicinity of the plant. The fact of the local segregation of the labor force and its separation from the residential quarters of the rich remained. It mattered little whether the workers rented their dwelling, which subjected them to the capitalist in his double capacity of factory owner and landlord, or whether they, through paying installments, had acquired the status and dignity of property ownership. . . .

But the nature of many types of labor tends in the same direction. Sombart, with justification, inquires how the worker in a factory producing insect powder or corn plasters or sulphuric acid can gain an inner relationship to his occupation. The bleakness and wretchedness characteristic of the majority of his labor functions are incapable of inculcating in the modern industrial worker an *esprit de corps,* a guild spirit, such as the artisans possessed. The effect of this is that his emotional needs are transferred from the unloved or indifferent occupation which has become nothing more than a means toward earning a living, to the wider sphere of his social life, to his class. Class consciousness becomes the ideal expression of the feeling of belonging, though not to a profession, yet to a branch of industry. The more severely industrialism damages and disturbs the workers' inner life the more important class consciousness becomes to them as an anchor of safety, as an ideal which particularly the most valuable elements among them embrace. Class consciousness is the refuge, once love for his work has

disappeared, which meets the worker's need for love and pride; love to his class comrades, pride towards the class strangers.

In this sense socialism is nothing else than the enlargement or rather continuation and realization of the human right theory. This theory (1789) states that every human being possesses from birth the inalienable right to equal position in society. While the theory contained the right to property, it was formulated without reference to advancement in the economic sphere of life. Thus its effect was at first political. It resulted in the political and juridical equalization of all before the law, a change which found its most forceful military expression in the slogan that every soldier carried the marshal's baton in his knapsack. Indeed, all civil posts and honors were theoretically, and in individual cases also practically, made available even to the poorest man from the people. Social stratification according to estate was destroyed by equality before the law (freedom of marriage, trade, and movement, availability of offices, declaration of human rights). The community of interests of modern classes became free and mobile, a fact that convinced the French democrats of the first half of the 19th century that classes had ceased to exist after the French Revolution. . . . Very soon it became clear, however, that the removal of all legal barriers which had impeded the rise of the proletarians was incapable of doing away with the presence of the initial economic stratification based on property. Even after the abolition of barriers between bourgeoisie and feudal aristocracy, high and low, enfranchised and disenfranchised persons, the difference between exploiters and exploited, loafers and workers, rich and poor, remained. Human rights suffered shipwreck, even in their political form, on the rock of economic inequality between the classes. The hungry worker was not in a position to make free decisions when selling his labor power. The right to the development of his gifts or the possibility of such a development proved to him just as worthless as, let us say, to the incurably sick person the right to recovery. Human rights are not what one *may* do but what one *can* do.

The difference in the points from which men start the race of life sets barriers to the equality of rights. The wellborn have an innate advantage over the lowly. It will only rarely be possible to make up for the advantage. Thus economics inhibits the process of natural selection in the Darwinian sense as the selection of the fittest in the struggle of life. It is due to the difference in starting points that the stupid, ungifted rich man may succeed with the help of good advice in improving his social position in life while the gifted poor man is not always able to bring about an important change in his. Based on this realization, an equalizing socio-political demand was raised at a very early date, gaining a particularly strong hold among militant labor since the efforts of Saint-Simon's follower, Bazard: the demand for the abolition of inheritance. In the International Workingmen's Association, Michael Bakunin paid special attention to it.

IV. Growth of Class Ethics

Introductory Remarks

The laborer is that proletarian who possesses the most highly developed feeling for human dignity and considers it below his dignity to beg, steal, or sell himself. Dignity is the mother of class consciousness; the class struggle presupposes "status consciousness." Gradually appeals to charity, understanding, the ultimate community of all interests cease; appeals which still dominated so profoundly the working class literature of the '48 period.

Class and Nation

Mankind seen as a whole does not form a uniform mass but can be divided into groups which possess the most diverse characteristics. The main lines which cut across mankind, dividing it into definite parts, may be traced according to two criteria. The first bases itself on the unit of living together, national feeling, race, language, the state, or in whatever other individual form the concept of "Volk" may be expressed. Humanity is here divided into some kind of nationally separate groups, such as Germans, Frenchmen, Italians, Russian, Englishmen. The lines of division are vertical: groups therefore lie alongside each other. According to the second, however, scientific analysis is instituted from other viewpoints, and bases research on a unit of different type. This unit is the social one. All of mankind, or at least the totality of European and American mankind, is divided along social categories, classes, occupational groups, income groups, etc. The lines of division running through the entity are horizontal. Groups lie on top of each other, are horizontally stratified. It is almost unnecessary to point out that the former type of division corresponds to the nationalist, the latter to the socialist philosophy of life. Groups analyzed on the basis of the first method include individuals of the most diverse economic and educational classes; those for which the second method is used, include individuals

of the most diverse languages, districts, races, and citizens of the most diverse states and worlds. No nationalist must overlook the economical and occupational stratification of the group "nation," nor must any socialist disregard the ethnic and linguistic mixture within the group "class." The fact that humanity as a whole is simultaneously divided by vertical and horizontal lines of differentiation is quite clear to both. The basic difference between the two viewpoints lies in the higher or lower rank which they assign to them. For the one, the concept of nation ranks in a superior position, that of class in an inferior one; for the others the concept of class is the primary, the concept of nation the secondary one. To put it differently: one believes that community of language and race, the close living together, the common fate of nations represent an ethnically and historically determining link compared to which all differences of status and style of life are bound to remain in the background. The other holds that equality of class position and way of life, identity of wealth and comfort on one hand, or of misery and aspiration on the other, and, finally, the identity of opposition, have created among the classes such a high degree of international solidarity that contrasts of a purely external kind, such as language and citizenship, are bound to be displaced by them. In both instances the term "are bound to" is used to convey what has been found to be the case as well as what ought to be. It is therefore to be taken as a scientific statement of fact as well as an ethical demand. To put it differently once more: both viewpoints base themselves on the same perceptions. It is only the allocation of stresses which differs.

Homogeneity of individual fortunes is by its very nature potentially without limit. It ignores the presence of states and may exceed in intensity the homogeneity created by linguistic, cultural, or national ties. That is why this homogeneity has led to international class formations. Christian Garve already remarked in 1786 that differences between peoples were smaller than the differences between the estates within the same people. A greater distance separated a German peasant from a German aristocrat, psychologically as well as economically, than separated a German peasant from a Polish peasant. Several observers picked up these thoughts once more half a century later with great force. Hardly another word of de Tocqueville has been proved truer than his statement that class differences within the same society were at times deeper than differences between nations. Each nation, in fact, was composed of two "nations" differing greatly from each other with regard to physical, psychological, and even ethnographic considerations. To this thesis corresponded also the social novel by Benjamin Disraeli (later Lord Beaconsfield) which carried the significant title: *Sybil, or the Two Nations* (1845). Karl Marx and Friedrich Engels then asked the "proletarians of all countries" in the *Communist Manifesto* (1847) to unite, as they had "nothing to lose" except their chains. The doctrine that the horizontal divisions among nations into social classes possessed greater dynamic power than the vertical division of mankind into nations represented, by implication, the theoretical foundation for the organization of the International Workingmen's Association.

Solidarity

Out of the proletarian socialist philosophy grew, spontaneously and apodictically, the demand for class solidarity as an ethical postulate. The commandment was formulated like this: the individual has the duty to subordinate himself to the whole; the single worker thus has the duty to subordinate himself to the concept of the working class or, at least, to that part of the working class employed in his factory, or rather its concretely measurable representation: the majority. Adherence to this duty is especially sacred in times of struggle, when a strike for improved wages is to be initiated or, after its completion, return to work is indicated. The most despicable type of worker, according to the ethical norms of social movements, is the strikebreaker who stabs his comrades in the back by remaining at work or prematurely going back to work, thus lessening their chance for victory. He is simply a scoundrel. No term is too low for him. . . .

The strikebreaker falls subject to defamation, thus social boycott. Defeated, he must put up with all sorts of tricks which are played on him, must formally apologize, or run through the city streets with a placard denoting his crimes. For him there are no excuses, no mitigating circumstances, even if he himself acted from the noblest personal motives (love for his children, loyalty to his employer); nor if he belongs to a more poorly rewarded stratum to whom the wage level seems sufficient where it appears intolerable to his striking fellow workers. For frequently strikers and strikebreakers belong to two different social strata which are fighting a "class struggle" with each other. In countries of more advanced working class organization, such as Germany and England, they can sometimes be aptly

differentiated by the terms organized and unorganized workers.

The military duty of the individual born into the working class is thus not merely fixed in an ethical code, but is also of a coercive nature analogous to the military duty to which the state subjects every citizen whether born within or without its frontiers. Punishment of the deserter is desired and takes the form, if necessary, of depriving him of life or property. The history of workers' movements is, in fact, everywhere characterized by the attempts, continued till the present day, on the part of those on strike, to use force against those who are willing to work, if peaceful persuasion by the workers manning the picket lines proves ineffective. In times of general strike and highest excitement the ethical demand for class solidarity of all class comrades, to be backed, if necessary, by force, has even been extended to the women who gain their livelihood by the sale of their bodies. During general strikes in Italian cities it has frequently occurred that excited masses of the population have marched in front of the *bordellos* and closed them, or at least posted guards before them. The reason given was that during the acute phase of the proletarian struggle for liberation it was the duty of the female proletarian sexually exploited by the bourgeoisie, namely the prostitute, to take a holiday; that, just as the male proletarians were intent on harming the ruling classes in their economic needs, the female proletarian should contribute her part in order to disturb the ruling class in the satisfaction of its sexual needs. As male workers crossed their arms, so the prostitutes should cross their legs. The basis of this demand is not merely the humane feeling of regard and pity for the girls, but also an instinct of class unity developed to its last logical consequence (even though the assumption that the customers of the prostitutes were exclusively recruited from the ranks of the bourgeoisie is not in accord with the facts).

For the maintenance of class discipline organized labor even uses tactics which do not shrink from utilizing employers who are or have been rendered willing to cooperate. Frequently special paragraphs of contracts or other industrial peace pacts, often after the ending of strikes, are used to force the employers to employ in their enterprises only union-organized workers and respectively to dismiss unorganized workers now employed. This is the method of the closed shop. The procedure, however, is not always directed at the achievement of solidarity through the creation of a unified, organized mass without regard to the person. In America the solidarity of white proletarians frequently halts before the color line. Black and yellow workers are frequently excluded from work by the organized white workers even when they ask for nothing better than to be permitted to join the organization, and thereby specifically recognize the duty to solidarity.

Socialism in Italy has at times achieved the highest degree of human solidarity. The events which accompany strikes there are expressive testimony of this. It was quite usual, when a strike started in one town, to remove first of all the children of the striking workers and distribute them among the working class families of the neighboring towns for free bed and board. It is true that this method did not lack an economic motive: there were some hundred or thousand fewer hungry mouths to feed. In other words: the chance for victory of the strikers increases. Yet the factor of class ethics weighs more heavily in this procedure: the warm feeling of solidarity, and the pity, touching in its humane expressions, for the innocent victims of the great modern struggles between warring interests. A frequent point in the programs of Italian political or industrial workers' organizations is the demand for a moral way of life. People about whose way of life there is some suspicion are refused acceptance. The demand for a Socialist's personal integrity has become the norm. Feeling of solidarity is here based on two factors: morality and class. Class solidarity resting on an ethical base sometimes reaches a pitch of intensity which reminds us of the days and psychology of early Christianity.

A Mantuan union of women landworkers stipulated in its program in 1902 as the main weapons in their struggle the duties of power of persuasion, comradeship, kindness, and love of neighbor. It obligated its members in case of spreading unemployment to take turns at handing over jobs to those comrades who had become unemployed. The members also were pledged to support their pregnant comrades not only through help from the union treasury but also through personal gifts. They were admonished to be good wives and mothers; to flee vice, though "love" was permitted to them. Furthermore they were duty bound not only to abstain from thefts in the fields themselves but also to prevent others from thieving wherever possible. The socialist sketches and novel fragments of the poet Edmondo de Amicis do not only represent the tenor of this program in their spirit. Their characters are also highly moral beings, and are not the fictional creatures of a poet's imagination but rather represent accurately the prevailing mood of the Italian proletarian mass movement between, say, 1893 and 1900.

In the field of the wage struggle the ethical form of class solidarity finds its most profound expression in the so-called sympathy strike. In it a locally or occupationally separate group of workers, at peace with their employers, voluntarily and sacrificially enter a strike in favor of another, distant (or, if local, then occupationally separate) striking group of workers whose prospects of victory may be in danger. The impelling motive is fraternity, class-determined love of one's neighbor. The immediate cause of the sympathy strike is the truly mass psychological eruption of excitement, sudden spread of the atmosphere of battle, "contagion." The latter is particularly true of the locally limited battle centers. Usually, admittedly, the sympathy strike is only a conscious tactic for the achievement of economic security by pressuring intimidated public opinion and orienting it towards the aims of the strike leaders; thus an attempt to increase the strike's chances of victory through its spread to unconcerned groups of workers who, due to their lack of personal contact, would from the viewpoint of mass psychology be otherwise hard to reach. Under this last category fall primarily sympathy strikes extending across national borders (dock workers, miners, etc.) in which, without doubt, local linguistic and national differences exclude the dominance of purely emotional motives among the workers.

Political Hatred as a Concomitant of Group Solidarity

The very intensity of feeling and firmness of institutions creating solidarity within the anticapitalist mass movement naturally tended to loosen its connection to human groups standing outside the particular association. If what Nietzsche says is true, that every ideal presupposes both love and hatred, admiration and contempt, but that in all these ideals the negative elements are to be considered the primary motivations, then it is clear that the workers' movement, born in opposition to the possessing classes, has expended its entire reservoir of love on itself. Only social democratic cant, based on fear of the propagandistic disadvantages of such a confession, and contemptible consideration for moralistic fellow travelers and nonpartisans, will deny the statement made by the Dutch Marxist Herman Gortner: the stronger the love to one's own class, the weaker the sympathy for the enemies of that class. The one excludes the other. The urge for sympathy is exhausted within one's own ranks. Thus the frequent note of hatred in the newspapers of the anticapitalist mass movement. However, other factors as well are responsible for this rudeness which has also been called "improper tone." Only those not acquainted with the laws of mass psychology will be surprised by it in view of the youthful nature of the movement, the educational level of the workers, and the need of the intellectuals attached to the movement to assert their leadership role and to prove the genuineness of their convictions before the followers through their supercilious behavior and coarseness of language vis-à-vis those of their colleagues who remained with the bourgeois parties. Furthermore, the contrast between labor's Cinderella-like position in the economic and political

sphere and the tremendous role which it has chosen for itself frequently tends to stimulate the feeling of bitterness and the violence of accent which accompany the spirit of battle. It is true, as Socialists always have claimed energetically, that theoretically hatred has nothing to do with the class struggle and that generally it is not being "preached." No unbiased person will, however, be able to deny that it usually accompanies the struggle. That this also projects hatred into the future must be clear as well. Hatred is a good means for the conquest of power, but serves as a poor basis for the treatment of men and things by those who have acquired power.

81

Some Consequences and Correlates of Class Polarization

Robert R. Alford

Australia and Great Britain—with fairly high levels of class voting and low regional or religious voting —may be called the more "class-polarized" political systems, while the United States and Canada may be called the less class-polarized systems. As might be expected, labor union membership is greater in the more class-polarized countries, although Australia and Britain are not differentiated in this respect, nor are Canada and the United States.[1] It seems probable that the relative strength of labor unionism is both a cause and a consequence of class politics. The level of self-identification of manual workers as "working class" is also in the same order as the level of class voting according to one study of three of these countries. Undoubtedly the integration of class and party serves to clarify the character of the stratification system, for workers at least.

A number of political and social processes seem to differ in a way logically related to these various measures of the extent to which these political systems are polarized around class bases. Localism, par-

ticularism, and informal bases for political action seem to be more prevalent in the less class-polarized systems, as will be described. No systematic evidence exists for these generalizations, but some suggestive regularities appear.

In the more class-polarized systems, Great Britain and Australia, politics has become bureaucratized, and "mass parties"—parties organized around branches, with individual membership, and a centralized, tightly organized form—have emerged. Australia and Great Britain have party systems organized around "mass" parties; the United States and Canada have party systems organized on a "cadre" or "honoratioren" basis.[2] The parties in the latter two nations are led by "notables" and lack the strength and solidarity of party organization characteristic of mass parties. Instead, party organization practically disappears between elections. Both of the major parties in Canada and the United States are more like "honoratioren" parties than either of the major parties in Australia and Great Britain, and it may be suggested that the rise of a working-class party organized along disciplined lines forces the more conservative party in each country to organize likewise in self-defense.

From Robert R. Alford, *Party and Society* (Chicago: Rand McNally & Co., 1963), pp. 292–302. Reprinted by permission of the publisher.

The effect of parties strongly organized on a class basis is to spread party organization to every political level. The parties in both Australia and Great Britain are far more likely to operate on local and city levels than are the parties in the United States and Canada.[3] The dominance of party and class also reduces the importance of informal pressure groups because political influence and decisions are more likely to be expressed through formal party and governmental organizations.

The contrast between the "hometown boy" politics of Canada and the United States, found in exaggerated form in the South, and rural politics in Australia is evident from a study of an Australian country constituency, Eden-Monaro, in the election of 1955. Few of the candidates benefited from their hometown votes, and the authors concluded that "there is no automatic process which gives a candidate an advantage in the district around his home, except perhaps over a very limited area indeed."[4] On the other hand, in spite of national centralization of the Canadian parties, "they have not always fought their engagements on purely national issues, and it has been by no means uncommon to have the fates of Dominion Governments decided by a series of local skirmishes which have borne little real relationship to each other."[5] Thus, localized issues and personalities in the United States and Canada probably have nationally decisive consequences far more than they do in Britain and Australia.[6]

It may be possible to ascribe differences in the operations of government bureaucracies and even the legal systems in these countries to differential pressure toward regionalism and decentralization (and therefore away from effective bureaucratization at the national level). A comparative analysis of parliamentary supervision of delegated legislation (rules enacted by government departments within a general framework of parliamentary legislation) in Britain, New Zealand, Australia, and Canada found that the efficacy of such supervision was greatest in Britain and least in Canada, the same order as that of class polarization.[7] Where regionalism is less evident, effective control of bureaucracies may be easier to establish. "Federalization" of bureaucracies undoubtedly increases what seem from an administrative point of view to be "inconsistencies" and "arbitrary decisions." It may be significant that Australia's system of supervision was judged to be more effective than Canada's. Federalism in and of itself apparently does not interfere with effective control of bureaucratic decision-making.

Particularism also penetrates the judicial systems of less class-polarized countries in various ways. To take only one example, choice of which United States Supreme Court justice is to write an opinion may sometimes be determined by his sectional, religious, or party identification. In one classic case, Justice Frankfurter was first assigned the writing of the opinion in a case overturning Texas' "white primary." The assignment was later given to Justice Reed, after Justice Jackson wrote a revealing letter to the Chief Justice which asserted that the combination of Frankfurter's being a Jew, from New England (the home of abolitionism) and not a strong Democrat might "grate on Southern sensibilities." Reed, in contrast, was a Kentuckian, a Protestant, and an old-time Democrat.[8] Such explicit revelations of the particularistic bases of judicial actions are infrequent, but they reveal something of the character of the legal and political system when they appear. The British courts, by contrast, undoubtedly consider the consequences of judicial actions for various regional and religious groupings, but probably do not take into account the personal characteristics of judges in such a manner.

Even such a purely legal process as judicial review, supposedly based on precedent and justice, may come to be influenced by considerations of "expediency" (which group a decision will affect and what its political consequences will be) rather than "principle" (which underlying values or precedents, applied to this case, will be accepted by most politically relevant groups) where regional and religious factors are more important than class. The courts in a consensual system cannot act as if laws have universal application or derivation when in fact they are not accepted by certain segments of the society. Class probably does not have the same effect because class interests can be more readily split, compromised, and handled than can regional and religious values.

The localism and particularism of the less class-polarized systems probably increase the proportion of the electorate likely to see informal pressure as effectively able to influence local politics. Persons in the United States are more likely than persons in Great Britain at every level of education to indicate that they would undertake political action through informal channels (Table 81–1). Where class is the dominant basis of political cleavage, parties and government tend to be less influenced by informal and particularistic loyalties. Decisions are taken as compromises between more or less "rational" interest considerations and reflect the pressures of formally organized groups, rather than informal ones.

Note also from Table 81–1 that in the United States, higher education increases the proportion

Table 81–1 "Local Competents" Who Would Enlist the Support of an Informal Group to Influence a Local Regulation They Thought Was Unjust, by Education, United States and Great Britain

Country	Per Cent Who Would Enlist Support, by Education				
	Primary or Less	Some Secondary	Some College or More	Total	Percentage-Point Range
United States	63	75	81	73 (747)*†	+18
Great Britain	41	46	45	43 (727)	+ 5
Percentage-point difference	+22	+29	+36	+30	

Source: Sidney Verba, "Political Participation and Strategies of Influence: A Comparative Study," *Acta Sociologica*, VI (1962), 31, 39. Other countries included in the study were Germany, Italy, and Mexico. The year the surveys were conducted was not given.

* To make the samples more comparable, the figures are only for persons considered politically "competent" from answers to questions concerning their political information.

† Total number of respondents is in parentheses.

willing to enlist informal support, while in Great Britain, education has no such effect. Despite the lower proportion of British citizens who view informal action as appropriate, better-educated Britishers are no more likely than poorly educated ones to use informal political channels. The difference between the United States and Britain is not, therefore, due to differences between low and high status persons; it is probably a true difference between the two political systems.

Differences between low and high status groups in political participation and in what might be called a sense of "political efficacy" are also smaller in the more class-polarized systems. A comparative study of Norway and the United States found no status differences in the proportion of politically active persons in the former country, but substantial differences in the latter. The authors interpreted this in terms of a difference of the institutional setting of participation in the two countries, particularly the difference in "status polarization" (or class-voting,

as I have termed it). They suggest that in more class-polarized countries, "citizens of little formal education and in lower-status occupations would be under a minimum of cross-pressures and would feel much less discouraged for taking on active roles in the political organizations they would give their vote."[9]

Further evidence that the usual differences in political participation between status-groups dwindle in more class-polarized systems is that lower status-persons in Great Britain are more convinced of the efficacy of political action than similarly placed persons in the United States. Persons with low education in Great Britain are considerably more likely to feel that they can "do something" about an unjust local law than persons with similar education in the United States, while persons with more education do not differ in the two countries (Table 81–2). Middle-class persons have a higher sense of political efficacy than lower-class persons do in both countries, and the difference between the countries appears only in the less-educated stratum.

Table 81–2 Respondents Who Say That They Can Remedy a Local Regulation They Consider Unjust, by Education, United States and Great Britain

Country	Per Cent Who Believe They Can Remedy a Local Regulation, by Education			
	Primary or Less	Some Secondary	Some College or More (Per Cent)	Total
United States	58	82	94	77 (970)*
Great Britain	73	84	92	77 (963)

Source: Sidney Verba, "Political Participation and Strategies of Influence: A Comparative Study," *Acta Sociologica*, VI (1962), 26, 38.

* Total number of respondents in parentheses.

Another consequence of the existence of mass parties based upon social classes seems to be an increase of universalism as a basic political principle. The non-rational and particularistic aspects of politics are probably less evident in the more class-polarized systems. One illustration of this may be differences in the degree of political corruption—nepotism and graft—between the Anglo-American countries. One analysis of Australian society suggests, "Although the extent of political corruption is difficult to estimate, the Australian record would appear to be reasonably good compared with that of the United States and the Latin American republics, but considerably poorer than that of Britain."[10] Since political corruption is particularly widespread in Canadian Quebec, the more class-polarized countries also seem to have less political corruption.[11] Universalism in political procedures may be associated with the bureaucratization and interest-cleavages more characteristic of class politics than of regional and religious politics.

Another aspect of universalism in politics is the way voters judge candidates. In the more class-polarized system of Great Britain, voters are much less likely to let particularistic factors influence their voting decision than are voters in the less class-polarized system of the United States. Some evidence for this is afforded by a 1958 Gallup survey in both countries which asked whether certain personal characteristics of political candidates (being a Catholic, a Jew, a "colored" person, a woman, or an atheist) would interfere with their voting for that candidate. On each score, voters in the United States were less likely to say that they would vote for such a candidate (Table 81–3). Whether a voter was Catholic or Jewish made the least difference to the voters of both countries, and this factor showed the least difference between the countries. The difference

between the countries was sharpest on the matter of atheism. Less than one-fifth of United States voters would vote for an atheist, while almost one-half of British voters would not care. Despite the differences between the countries, the rank order of importance of these personal characteristics of candidates was nearly the same in both countries, showing the similarity of social values in the two countries, despite the higher level of universalism in Great Britain.

The domination of class politics in countries such as Australia and Great Britain, which possess high degrees of effectiveness and legitimacy, has meant that both the major parties are pulled far to the Left.[12] On domestic economic and welfare issues, at least, the Right parties of Australia and Great Britain (the Liberal and Conservative parties, respectively) have accepted legislation which would be regarded as almost outright communism by many American voters.

Where the relative power of Left forces is greater, another consequence may be that lower-income groups are able to secure more of the national product than where the Left has less power. A preliminary study indicates that although Britain has a lower level of economic growth and development than the United States, the proportion of British national income going to workers is slightly higher. Political power may compensate somewhat for the relatively poorer economic situation of Britain.[13]

Another consequence of different levels of class polarization may have been a quicker shift to the Right in the more class-polarized systems. The conservative shift after World War II took place sooner in the countries with higher levels of class voting. In Australia, the Liberal party took power in 1949, and in Great Britain the Conservative party won in 1950, while the Republicans won in the United States in 1952, and the Progressive-Conservatives in Canada, in 1957. Assuming that the switch to a more conservative party reflects social trends in each country in the prosperous era after World War II, several characteristics of the social and political systems of these countries may account for this pattern.[14]

First, it may be suggested that a switch of a class-based system in a conservative direction because of prosperity, occurs more rapidly than a switch of a political system based upon regional, religious, and ethnic solidarities. Class-based political allegiances may actually change more readily than others once the demands of working-class groups (trade unions and parties) for legitimacy and bargaining rights are won.

Second, in societies which are more homogeneous, such as Australia and Great Britain, there are fewer

Table 81–3 People Willing to Vote for a Qualified Candidate Who Happens to Have Certain Social Characteristics, United States and Great Britain, 1958

Characteristic of the Candidate	Per Cent of Respondents		
	Britain	United States	Percentage-Point Difference
Catholic	82	68	+14
Jewish	71	62	+ 9
Woman	76	52	+24
Colored	61	38	+23
Atheist	45	18	+27

Source: BIPO release, November, 1958.

"solid seats," and fewer regional strongholds; therefore, a relatively smaller switch of group allegiances to a party produces quicker and more massive political consequences.

Another consequence of a high level of class polarization may be the reduction of either the number or the intensity of strikes, which may seem paradoxical. But, given the similar class structures and political cultures of these countries, we might expect to find that where class interests are not expressed explicitly through political parties, they are more likely to be demonstrated elsewhere—as in strikes. Where, on the contrary, a labor party exists and there is a relatively sharp political division of social classes, class issues will tend to be moved from the bargaining arena to the political arena.

Among these four countries, there should thus be a greater incidence or intensity of strikes in Canada and the United States than in Australia and Britain. On the other hand, the original factors producing class voting (in Chapter 5 class voting was found to be higher in relatively poorer countries with fewer educational opportunities and lower growth rates) would seem also to produce high strike rates. However, a study of strikes in fifteen countries found that in the United States and Canada there is a "moderately high propensity to strike as well as a relatively long duration" for those strikes that occur. In contrast, in the United Kingdom there is a "nominal propensity to strike and a low or moderate duration of strikes."[15] Australia has a unique pattern of numerous but short strikes. The authors attribute this to the lack of constitutional powers available to the Commonwealth government to carry out labor's objectives through political action. Therefore, Australian labor, unlike British labor, was unable to translate its potential power into effective intervention in the collective bargaining process.[16]

Both Britain and Australia have relatively short strikes; both Canada and the United States have relatively long ones. In the latter two countries, a grievance which reaches the point of a strike may tend to last longer in part because workers are under less political control than they are in the other countries. Not only does a labor party encourage compulsory collective bargaining, but it must restrain strikes as the price of respectability in a consensual system. Potential governmental power in such a system carries with it responsibilities not only to serve the workers but to discipline them.

To summarize, clear differences in the consequences and correlates of class polarization have been shown. The more class-polarized systems are more likely to have strongly organized and disciplined parties extending their influence even to the city level. Where workers have a party clearly appealing to their interests, their participation and sense of political efficacy is as great as middle-class persons. Where class polarization is greater, politics tends to be more universalistic, in the sense that political corruption is less evident and candidates are not as likely to be rejected on the grounds of personal characteristics. Political shifts may take place more readily in the more class-polarized systems, which are also more homogeneous and have fewer regional one-party bastions. Overt class conflict in the form of strikes is less evident in the class-polarized systems—which possess labor parties with greater control over collective bargaining, and have a higher level of trade union organization.

NOTES

1. The percentage of labor union membership in Great Britain, Australia, the United States, and Canada, respectively, listed in their order of class voting, was in 1957 approximately: 42, 45, 26, and 23 (using the total labor force as a base), and 19, 18, 10, and 9 (using the total population as a base). Figures were compiled from the *Worldmark Encyclopedia of the Nations* (New York: Worldmark, 1960).

2. The terms are those of Maurice Duverger and Sigmund Neumann. Duverger asserts that the distinction between cadre and mass parties "corresponds approximately with the distinction between Right and Left, Middle-class and Workers' Parties," and suggests that the rise of mass parties coincided with the rise of working-class movements seeking to gain political representation outside of the existing ruling elites. See Maurice Duverger, *Political Parties* (London: Methuen, 1954), pp. 63–71, and Sigmund Neumann, "Toward a Comparative Study of Political Parties," in S. Neumann, ed. *Modern Political Parties* (Chicago: University of Chicago Press, 1956), p. 401.

3. See Delbert C. Miller, "Decision-Making Cliques in Community Power Structures: A Comparative Study of an American and an English City," *American Journal of Sociology*, LXIV (November 1958), 299–310. In "English City," representatives of different institutions (party, economic, and others) function "in relatively independent roles," as contrasted with the American city, which has a highly stratified single elite (p. 310). I suggest that a part of these differences is due to the dominance of class in British politics. Many American cities undoubtedly exhibit the "British" pattern, although no such comparative studies have been published.

4. Donald W. Rawson and Susan M. Holtzinger, *Politics in Eden-Monaro* (Melbourne: Heinemann, 1958), p. 147. While local influences are important in Great Britain—especially in rather traditional Conservative-dominated towns such as Glossop—the parties are organized both for national and local elections. See A. H. Birch, *Small-town Politics* (London: Oxford University Press, 1959), pp. 98–100.

5. Robert MacGregor Dawson, *The Government of Canada* (2nd ed.; Toronto: University of Toronto Press, 1954), p. 497.

6. There may also be differential consequences for the attitudes of voters. W. E. Miller found that, in the United States, political motivations and attitudes of Democrats were quite different in strongly Republican counties than in Democratic counties, and vice versa. I would expect such "local" effects to be much less in Australia and Britain, but no studies have been done on this problem. See W. E.

Miller, "One-Party Politics and the Voter," *American Political Science Review*, L (September 1956), 707–725.

7. See John E. Kersell, *Parliamentary Supervision of Delegated Legislation* (London: Stevens & Sons, 1960). Kersell does not make an explicit general comparison, but his judgments concerning the relative immunity of political heads of departments from criticism (p. 4), and the elaborateness of the supervisory machinery and the date of its development (chap. vii) are consistent with the ordering above.

8. Quoted in Henry J. Abraham, *The Judicial Process* (New York: Oxford University Press, 1962), p. 187.

9. Stein Rokkan and Angus Campbell, "Norway and the United States of America," *International Social Science Journal*, XII (1960), 69–99. I have computed an index of class voting from their data, given in Table 9; the figure for the United States is +14; for Norway, +47 (combining the Socialist and Communist parties) (p. 88). Norway's class voting level is thus close to Britain's. The political distinctiveness of the working class in Norway is much greater than that of the British working class, however.

10. R. Taft and K. Walker, "Australia," in Arnold M. Rose, ed., *The Institutions of Advanced Societies* (Minneapolis: University of Minnesota Press, 1958), p. 159.

11. Since Quebec comprises one-third of Canada, its high level of political corruption may be considered evidence of the differential between Canada and the other English-speaking countries (if we may consider Canada as a nation—and therefore the attributes of its component parts as in some degree reflections of the whole). Trudeau considers Quebec corruption to reflect the lack of commitment by Quebecers to the institutions and morality of democracy. The manipulation of those institutions by the English in the early years of Canada produced such a reaction. See Pierre E. Trudeau, "Some Obstacles to Democracy in Quebec," in Mason Wade, ed., *Canadian Dualism* (Toronto: University of Toronto Press, 1960), pp. 244–247. Articles in *The New York Times*, November 19 and 22, 1959, following the death of Quebec Premier Maurice Duplessis, noted that observers did not expect a change in the spoils system characteristic of Quebec politics.

12. See M. Lipset, *Political Man* (New York: Doubleday, 1959), pp. 77–83.

13. See S. M. Miller and Herrington Bryce, "Social Mobility and Economic Growth and Structure," *Kölner Zeitschrift für Soziologie* (forthcoming). Britain was lower than the United States in percentage increase in national product (1900–1950), percentage increase in national product per capita (same years), and current product per man-hour (United States dollars); however, it was higher in percentage of national income paid to "employees."

14. Particular historical and political features of elections in each country obviously may have speeded up or slowed down conservative drifts. If Eisenhower had won on the Democratic ticket in 1952, clearly the Republican trend would have been invisible.

15. Arthur M. Ross and Paul T. Hartman, *Changing Patterns of Industrial Conflict* (New York: Wiley, 1960), pp. 72, 77.

16. Ross and Hartman agree that more and longer strikes should be associated with the absence of a labor party. Where no such party exists, collective bargaining is normally settled by a trial of economic strength. *Ibid.*, p. 163.

82

Democracy and the Common Life

A. D. Lindsay

The argument for democratic as contrasted with expert leadership is that political wisdom needs more than anything else an understanding of the common life; and that that wisdom is given not by expert knowledge but by a practical experience of life. If the defect of the expert is his onesidedness, the merit of the practical man of common-sense judgement will be his all-round experience. The simple agricultural societies where democracy flourishes and seems native to the soil produce naturally men of common sense and sound judgement, appraisers alike of men and horses. The men whom we readily think of as men of sound judgement though unlearned have often had that kind of training. The

From A. D. Lindsay, *The Modern Democratic State* (London: Oxford University Press, 1943), pp. 279–286. Reprinted by permission of the present Lord Lindsay of Birker, son of the author, the copyright holder.

part played by the village cobbler or blacksmith in the democratic life of a village has often been noticed. The inhabitants of a natural democracy like the New England township described in Mr. Winston Churchill's *Coniston* are independent, accustomed to act on their own, and to make judgements within the scope of their experience.

Modern industrialism has taken away from the great mass of men in an industrialized community their independence. It has condemned very many of them to specialized and narrow lives. Their lives are far more specialized and far narrower than the lives of the experts whom our democratic argument has been putting in their place, and they are without the expert's skill or knowledge or his partial independence. Where under such conditions are the common-sense qualities and sound judgement of the ordinary man to be found? How can we keep a modern industrial society from becoming not a community but a mob, not a society of persons capable of judging for themselves, discussing and criticizing from their experience of life the proposals put before them, but a mass played upon by the clever people at the top? These, nowadays armed with new psychological techniques, claim to be able to manipulate those masses to their will, make them believe what the rulers want, hate what the rulers want, and even fight and die for what the rulers want.

For the real issue between the democrats and the anti-democrats is that democrats think of a society where men can and do act as responsible persons. The anti-democrats talk of the mob, or the herd, or the crowd. What these latter say of mobs or herds or crowds is as true as what the democrats say of the sound sense of the ordinary man who acts and thinks as an individual. No one can read a book like Ortega y Gasset's *The Revolt of the Masses* without recognizing the strength of the forces in modern society which go to the making of men into masses or crowds; or without seeing that, if they prevail, mass democracy must produce, as it has in so many countries produced, totalitarianism. That is the greatest of the challenges to democracy which we shall have to consider when in the next volume we examine the modern challenges to democracy.

But . . . modern industrialism has supplied an antidote in the working-class movement. If we consider what gives that movement its vitality, we see that it creates innumerable centres of discussion. Trade union branches, co-operative guild meetings, W.E.A. classes and discussion groups of all kinds provide conditions as far removed as possible from those that produce a mob. The key to democracy is the potency of discussion. A good discussion can draw out wisdom which is attainable in no other way. The success of antidemocratic totalitarian techniques has depended on the suppression of discussion. If the freedom of discussion is safeguarded and fostered, there is no necessity for the most urbanized of constituencies becoming a mob. Those of us who have seen anything of the spread of discussion in England during the war, in the Army, in A.R.P. posts, in shelters, in all kinds of places where people come together have seen something of how in discussion the "plain" man can come into his own.

Government and Control

Finally, let us turn to the last of the questions which we noted for discussion in this chapter, the relation between the few who govern and the many who control. In a democratic state those who have power and expert knowledge are to serve the community and be controlled by the ordinary people who have neither power nor knowledge. The first problem of a democratic state is to ensure that government is kept to its proper task. Democracy is not, properly speaking, government *by* the people. For the people, if we mean by that, as we ought to mean, all the members of society in all their multifarious relations, cannot govern.

Government involves power and organization, administration, and decision. Even a small public meeting cannot administer or organize. It can only express approval or disapproval of the persons who govern or of their general proposals.

We talk of the Greek city states as governed by a public meeting. But those states recognized the incapacity of a meeting to govern. The typical Greek democratic device was not the control by the public meeting but that most remarkable institution—election by lot. All except the chief magistrates of the state were elected by lot. The citizens *en masse* could not govern, but they could take turns at it. Aristotle describes this as the principle of ruling and being ruled in turns. The officials who governed were prevented from dominating the state by being selected by the chance of the lot and given only a short time of governing. But that meant that they could only perform very simple and routine duties; that they could not possibly have any specialized skill or specialized training.

Clearly such a device is entirely inapplicable to any large society and particularly to the large nation state with its necessity for complex and skilled administration. We have in the jury system a relic of this device of what Professor Lowell has called sample democracy, but its extension to any but the simplest jobs is clearly impossible. The attempt to put it or something like it into practice under the influence of Jacksonian democracy produced the spoils system in America.

It is essential to any sound democracy to recognize what part the ordinary public can take in the government of a state and what it cannot. Experience has shown abundantly that, if in the name of democracy you ask the ordinary member of the public to do more than he can or will in fact do, the result is a sham. We must, therefore, distinguish between the various processes by which the government of a country is kept responsible to public opinion from the highly technical and specialized process of government itself. I propose to call the relation of the public to the government in a democratic country control; and keep the word government for the decisive, definite process of administering and commanding. The distinction is not always clear cut. The one function shades into the other, but the broad distinction remains and is important. There are, as we shall see, some forms of control of government, which are quite unlike commanding or governing, which are apt to be overlooked if we think of democracy as government by the people. . . . If the task of democracy is to make the organized power which is government subservient and sensitive to the whole complex common life of society, the expression of general approval or disapproval conveyed in votes will be sure to be only one among several ways of ensuring this control.

Let us begin by realizing how paradoxical is this problem of the democratic control of government. Organized power is to be a servant and not a master. "Ye know that the princes of the Gentiles exercise dominion over them, and they that are great exercise authority upon them. But it shall not be so among you: but whosoever will be great among you, let him be your minister; and whosoever will be chief among you, let him be your servant."

In recognition that that is the task of democratic government we call our real ruler a prime minister, and we call our armed forces the services. We can call them so but can we make and keep them so?

The problem is of course an old one, but its modern form is new. For before the days of modern weapons governments were comparatively weak. They had power only so long as it continued to be given them. This was true at least before the days of standing armies. The citizens all taken together were clearly stronger than the government, and both they and the government knew it. But millions and millions of men are helpless before a government which has a bombing air force at its command—or has tanks and artillery at its command. Walt Whitman says, "The great city stands, where the populace rise up at once against the never-ending audacity of elected persons." But if the elected persons can call upon a force equipped with modern weapons, the populace will repent its rising.

Though the difficulties in the control of armed force by a democracy illustrate the problem of the democratic control of power in its most acute form, the problem can be stated more generally. The organs of power in a democratic state are not and cannot well be themselves democratically organized. An army or navy or air force is of course not democratically organized. It could not be if it is to do its job properly. Any organization of men which is intended for rapid and decisive action must be hierarchic. It must be a disciplined instrument which can be moved quickly in this direction or in that. That means a disciplined force with a thought-out and accepted practice of giving and obeying orders. But the organization of a government department follows roughly the same pattern and for the same reasons. A hierarchical disciplined organization is much the most efficient way to secure technical efficiency. By technical efficiency I mean efficiency in achieving an end which is imposed from without and taken for granted.

An efficient organization of men is bound to be based on the division of labour, and that, as Plato pointed out long ago, is based on men's differences not on their equality. Further, the necessities of organization will exaggerate men's differences. In an efficient organization the ablest man should be put at the top and his mind should direct if possible the whole machine, if rapid action is essential. Of course there are differences of degree in the hierarchical character of technical organization. There is ground for supposing that if business organization were somewhat more democratic than it is, it would be more efficient. At present it wastes the abilities of the ordinary men and women whom it will only treat as unskilled labour. Even an army can be more or less democratic in some slight degree. But it remains true that these organs of government must have a largely hierarchical structure, that they must be subject to discipline, and that they will be concerned almost exclusively with means and not with ends. They are bound therefore to breed in their members an attitude of mind very different from that of the ordinary citizen. That is apparent, e.g. in the contemptuous way in which almost all soldiers talk of politicians. They ignore or do not understand the fact that politicians do the soldier's moral dirty work for him. The position of a soldier who has to obey orders and is not concerned with the ultimate reasons for the order is of course morally a simple one.

It has further to be noticed that without this disciplined organization which gives the services their peculiar character and their special mentality the democratic control of these services would be impossible. Their democratic control is effected by making their head responsible to the elected representatives of the people. But the cabinet minister cannot be responsible, cannot answer for his department, unless he has authority over it. If you arm a minority of the population with overpoweringly potent weapons and allow or encourage them to discuss what they ought to do with the state, their power will no longer be an instrument to be used in the service of the community. The traditions of the civil service bring out the same point. The civil service is a necessary instrument by means of which the general purposes approved by the electorate can be put into practice, translated into laws and administrative regulations. But that is only possible if the service is regarded, and regards itself, as an instrument, fit to carry out policies whose general character has been decided on by other people. The civil servant is therefore rightly limited in his political activities, and the good civil servant will often say, "But that is politics," in something of the same tone as the soldier will refer to "those damned politicians." But if the tradition that the organs of power must be taught to regard themselves as only organs—services in the strictest sense of the term—prevents a democratic community from being dominated by its own instruments, if the services think of themselves entirely as instruments and not as citizens, they may be tools in the hands of a government which is trying to subvert the constitution. One of the most sinister things which happened in the Spanish Civil War was the employment of Moroccan troops in a dispute between Spanish parties. How are we to ensure that the services are instruments, with no policy of their own to push, and yet citizens, ready to resist any attempt to use them as instruments to subvert the constitution? We seldom discuss these questions in either England or the United States, but the failure to keep the armed force of the state as loyal servants of the constitution was a major cause of the failure of democracy in Italy, in Germany, and in Spain.

The problem is made more difficult by the new tasks which modern conditions have put upon government. In early nineteenth-century democracy, i.e. the democracies of the United States and Switzerland, where society being mainly agricultural was naturally democratic, there was little need for any functions of government except the function of keeping order. A naturally democratic society had to be protected from violence from within and without. "Administrative nihilism plus the policeman" was an exaggerated but not hopelessly false description of the government required for such a society. The Industrial Revolution has entirely altered the situation. If government is to serve the community, and to help to make it more of a community, it has to take on, as it has taken on, all kinds of more positive and constructive functions. If it is true to say that the purpose of organized force is negative, to keep off forces which would disturb the free life of society, there is no such clear line to be drawn between the many other functions performed by a modern government and those performed by voluntary associations. There is a corresponding approach in the methods by which a government department performs these functions to the methods followed by voluntary associations. Compulsion fades into the background: consultation and deliberation takes its place. With this difference in the methods by which government performs its functions may go a corresponding difference in the methods of democratic control.

83

Changes in the Structure of Democracy

José Medina Echavarría

Changes in the Structure of Democracy

At the risk of being tiresome, we would repeat that it is only possible here to touch rapidly on essential points. It is generally acknowledged that—

From José Medina Echavarría, "Changes in the Structure of Democracy," in José Medina Echavarría and Benjamin H. Higgins, *Social Aspects of Economic Development in Latin America* (Paris: Unesco, 1963), pp. 124–137. Reprinted by permission of Unesco.

pending the appearance of a work transcending it—the best description extant of the changes that have taken place in the structure of democracy over the past few decades is that given by G. Leibholz,[1] which, despite an understandable emphasis on the experiences of his own country (Germany), is generally applicable to all other countries. To avoid the temptation of examining some of the technical questions that crop up, I prefer not to take this work as my reference but rather to have recourse to the general lines of another, by the same author.[2] This one is not intended for "experts" and colleagues but for the general public, and its main purpose is to point out some of the dangers inherent in the whole process as far as the maintenance and defence of individual freedoms are concerned. This is a subject to which it may only be worth while reverting later on, and then only in one context.

In the development of the situation with regard to individual freedoms, the following three stages may be noted: first, monopolization of legislative power by Parliament; second, replacement of liberal, representative democracy by the radical or egalitarian democracy of the party State; and third, the stage of the ever more marked development of the so-called Welfare State. Observing our promise to avoid the subject of safeguards for the individual, however, the two main concepts which we have to compare, in connexion with the evolution of democracy, are those pertaining to the second of the above-mentioned stages: that is to say, the old liberal and representative democracy, on the one hand, and the modern radical and egalitarian democracy of the party State, on the other. The terms in which this contrast is expressed are not, perhaps, altogether satisfactory, and it is therefore not easy, without going into detailed technicalities, to explain the significance of the differences between the two forms of democracy. They affect the actual internal structure of Parliament, co-operation between the traditional legislative and executive powers, and relations between Parliament and society in general. At the risk of making undue generalizations, let us try to explain as briefly as possible what this complex of relationships implies: in the first place, an increasing predominance of the executive and administrative branches over Parliament; in the second place, changes in the internal life of Parliament, in the "representation" and behaviour of the parties (of the parliamentarians themselves in the strict sense of the term) and the encroachment of administrative matters on Parliament's traditional sphere of activity; in the third place, the loss or diminution of Parliament's exclusive privilege of political participation, as other forms of participation have slowly developed within society itself.

Although the term "party State" is clear enough when definite political principles (not always existing everywhere) are accepted, mistakes may arise from the ascription of the quality of "representative"—without precise explanations—to the first form of democracy, since the second form possesses it in no less a degree.

Consequently, despite his predilection for exaggerated and even paradoxical expressions, the interpretation given by Siegfried Landshut[3] may clarify the subject for us from the sociological standpoint. In so far as democracy and parliamentary life may be considered as equivalent, the historical phases of the latter can help to explain the situation. According to Landshut, there is a first phase which he describes as that of the democratization of parliamentarism. The elements of this process are so well known that it is almost superfluous to recall them: the continual expansion of the electorate; the transformation of parties, from the flexible associations of notables which they were at the beginning into the disciplined and comparatively rigid organizations which they constitute at the present time; the transformation of the electoral system, from the original type of election by simple majority into the proportional representation type which now largely prevails.

The second phase, however, has been much less explored, and it is of particular interest to sociologists, precisely because it is characterized from the sociological point of view by changes in the social structure coinciding with the development of industrialization. These industrialized societies have seen a gradual levelling of many of the earlier social differences (incomes, living standards and forms of culture and group living) a fundamental consequence of which has been a decline of political imperatives in parliamentary democratic government. To some people this expression may seem exaggerated; it therefore needs to be carefully examined. From the political standpoint, the consequences of changes in the social structure have produced the following political phenomena, among others:

1. "The increasing levelling-out of social differences leaves even less room for a multiplicity of parties."[4] One result of this may be a dwindling of the significance attached to ideologies; this theory, maintained by various thinkers, was referred to earlier in this study.

2. Increasing preoccupation with the manifold State activities affecting the citizen in the spheres of economics, health, social security, education, etc., has led to "an atrophy of the political sectors of modern parliamentary democracies and a corresponding hypertrophy of the administration."[5]

3. The fact that a greater part is being played by individuals in a number of private organizations—whether or not pursuing purely material interests—focuses attention more and more on the political significance of such "interest groups," which certainly look "mainly towards the executive as the

centre of State activity."[6] (But this does not occur always or everywhere: e.g., the case of the United States of America.) However, the general thesis is clear and should not be overlooked, even in its apparently most extreme statement, namely, that the whole process signifies the simultaneous socialization of the government, on the one hand, and nationalization of society, on the other—all the more so when this process tends to be rounded off by awareness of the inadequacy of the traditional national and domestic policy, which leads to demands on all sides for supranational integration and the maintenance as far as possible of universal solidarity within the community of nations. It is very possible that all industrial societies (whether of one persuasion or the other, to return to a subject mentioned earlier) are moving in this direction, although no one can foresee either the rapidity of the movement or the variations which may occur in the general trend.

Significantly enough, if we look at a catalogue of the latest publications on political science, we find an intense preoccupation with certain subjects that have a direct or indirect bearing on the chief problems referred to above.

The inclinations of the different academic and national traditions exert an influence, as is natural. In addition, the North Americans (who invented the term), the Italians and the French are constantly adding to the studies on pressure groups. And the English and the Germans, who also do not despise these groups, are probably outstanding, the former for meticulous studies of parliamentary organization[7] and the latter for research on parties and their parliamentary interconnexions through fractional groups and technical committees. Nor should we be surprised at the revival of an old idea: the so-called representation of professional interests,[8] which aroused passionate interest a few years ago and is now being studied more thoroughly and with a fuller knowledge of the facts.

Pluralist Democracy

Despite all that has just been said, we shall be told (and rightly so) that we have not yet met with a formula expressing concisely the complex of ingredients comprised in modern democracy. Such a formula exists, however, and, whether or not its terms are happily chosen, enjoys general acceptance today. This formula is pluralist democracy.

An attempt at describing its content systematically and in detail would be out of place, not only as putting a further strain on time and patience but also as requiring a logical statement of each and every one of the phenomena mentioned above.

Nevertheless, we would recall very briefly that pluralist democracy consists essentially in the political acceptance of the social reality as a complex of highly diverse groups, each with its individual interests and therefore prone to conflicts and disputes with the other groups, but all complying with a common standard so as to seek the most fitting agreement and compromise in each case which arises—in consideration, of course, of its temporary character. This pluralism of interests and convictions, this outcome of tolerance, can only be attained if there is that agreement on fundamentals so skilfully discussed and explained by a great German-American authority on political science.[9]

Although, generally speaking, pluralist democracy now obtains in one form or another in the most advanced Western countries, it is perhaps in the Scandinavian countries that it has reached its fullest perfection. Anyone wishing to acquaint himself with it in such an advanced form would do well to have recourse to the experience of these Nordic countries, which have been so fortunate in this respect—although we should of course avoid the temptation to indulge in servile copying, to try (in the same way that we have covered our hot regions with Alpine chalets) to disguise our worthy Araucanos as Laplanders.[10]

Democracy and Planning

Notwithstanding the foregoing remarks on the most immediate concerns of present-day sociological and political research, it is a strange, not to say startling, fact that hardly any research has been conducted on a most important matter connected with modern democracy (at least from the Latin American point of view): the question of the relation between democracy and economic planning. For the very reason that it is so strange, we should be hard put to it to explain or interpret this lack. We shall therefore not attempt to do so.

Since the illustrious Karl Mannheim—the greatest of present-day sociologists since Max Weber—launched the theme of "planning for freedom," passionately devoting himself to the defence of the "third way," of what he called a militant democracy, it must be admitted that little progress has been made in this direction. His premature death, or the missionary spirit which dominated his last days (far removed from the intellectual intensity of his earlier years), prevented him from completing his task himself, as did also, perhaps, its severely technical character. Since then, a great deal has been said on the subject of democracy and planning and not with least cogency by its detractors.

Not long ago Gunner Myrdal[11] took up the subject, but without making much progress as regards practice; he did, however, draw an important distinction, which has not been duly followed up. Within the generalized trend towards the Welfare State, beside that dominant in the Soviet orbit, he distinguished two different forms of planning, according to whether the countries considered were wealthy (and his experience, of course, lay chiefly in Scandinavia) or underdeveloped. And Friedrich, likewise in the realm of general ideas, evolved a definition embodying the nodal point of planning in pluralist democracies:

> Planning, as the pluralist organization of a community, represents the direction and co-ordination of that community's activities under an over-all programme, with particular reference to the use of economic resources. This direction is achieved in conformity with the will of the community as expressed through the Constitution and the representative bodies.[12]

Since, here and there, the Welfare State has come into being, the fact should not be overlooked that the recognition of its existence has given rise to various problems, depending on the intensity with which its presence is felt or, again, on certain intellectual propensities. A very few examples will suffice. An Englishman like Richard M. Titmuss,[13] reflecting the temperament of his nation, prefers to take the most uncompromisingly practical topics (the English public health service, the family and industrialization, the pension system, exchanges of population, etc.), and to distil from his examination, as it were involuntarily, the delicate constitutional and legal problems involved in the launching of a Welfare State. On the other hand, a German like Ernst Forsthoff[14] prefers to go straight to the point and define, in abstract and systematic form, some of the most serious problems posed by the *Sozialstaat* to jurists. Drawing on another work by the same author, we give below an outline of these problems, at least in so far as they concern us at the moment.

1. There is an inconsistency between the constitutional structure of modern States (that is, parliamentary States) and the tasks proposed for them and imposed upon them. The matter of programming, whether in developed or in less developed countries, must obviously be included under this

point and is of particular importance to us in Latin America.

2. With the continual increase in the tasks devolving upon the administration, the practice of litigation, that is to say, the defence *vis-à-vis* the State of the rights of the individual, is becoming increasingly difficult—all the more so as the Welfare State, by reason of its distributive function, has to employ special procedures which, being subtle and complex, elude the traditional forms of legal control.

3. The advent of the Welfare State inevitably implies an increase in the Civil Service. Our first reaction to this bureacratic expansion is one of misgiving; we would like to see it curtailed as far as possible. But here we come across a paradox that cannot be ignored: the best safeguard for the individual *vis-à-vis* such a bureaucracy consists precisely in the fact that it is of the strictest integrity and therefore enjoys the greatest possible authority. None of these questions (which at a superficial glance might seem to be mere legal technicalities) can be evaded in any serious analysis of the relationship between economic planning and democracy. The past few years have seen a distinct advance in the Latin American countries towards a general recognition of the importance, from the point of view of the region's economic development, of a thorough reform of their administrative systems. Stress was laid on this matter in the discussions and recommendations of the Working Group which met in Mexico City in December 1960 to study the social aspects of economic development, as may be seen from the Group's *Report,* to which we have already referred on various occasions. A vigorous educational campaign has been carried out in this connexion (establishment of a number of schools of administration, seminars, publications, etc.), and evidence is not lacking that serious investigation has begun in several countries, under the sponsorship of international organizations.

Mention was made above of the question of litigation; it might therefore not be out of place to make a passing reference to a matter of concern to some Latin Americans (a concern shared by the author of the present study, himself formerly a jurist). In attempts to improve the situation with regard to our government services, which (with some exceptions, of course) is not very encouraging, it is customary to take as a model the North American public administration, which has developed so remarkably and so admirably in recent years. There can be no objection to this inspiration; since, however, our administrative tradition is based on the

Continental (and especially the French) pattern, the case presents some difficulties, apart from the high degree of sociological interest inherent in any problem of "reception" (cf., in the legal sphere, the famous "reception" of Roman law). The danger (even if it is only imaginary) is that what we assimilated previously may not be sturdy enough to enable us, in the new process of "reception," to save what is most valuable in the old tradition—its legal content, that is to say, administrative law itself. That venerable institution, law, has now fallen on such evil times everywhere that it would be deplorable if here too, in its administrative branch, its true essence were to disappear. Hence the fear entertained by some people that, with the precipitate reception of the aforesaid public administration system, the essential preoccupation (essential from the legal standpoint) with the question of litigation may remain a *capitis deminutio* because attention is devoted primarily to the question of efficiency and is overwhelmed by such things as diagrams and schemes for "organization and control." However, to avoid any misunderstanding, we would stress the fact that there is no objection in principle—quite the contrary, in fact—to the reasonable and well-assimilated "reception" of the techniques carefully developed by North American talent in an important discipline.

The foregoing question remains wide open to investigation and it presents a challenge to the younger generation. Some admirable research has been done, but, as far as we are aware, no definitive work has yet been published which describes technically the problems of economic planning in parliamentary democracies. Our countries, it appears, were the first to institute the so-called development corporations (or bodies with similar names). The idea of programming, once it had become general in those countries, also produced a crop of councils and boards. These bodies do not simply exist; they are concerned with a variety of parties, trade unions and interest groups. How can all these activities be co-ordinated, so as to achieve, through Parliament, a harmonized direction, representing, in accordance with Friedrich's definition, the national will?[15]

Is There Only One Form of Democracy?

The question put in the above heading might seem presumptuous and out of place in the present study if we did not categorically deny in advance any intention of considering it in its philosophical substance or its complete politico-sociological context. The last great philosopher who ventured upon the theme of the value of democracy in all its radical profundity was obliged to enlist the help of Reason (*Vernunft*) with a capital R, to defend democracy against the irrational alternatives offered by our times. Although we must resist the temptation to follow some of his brilliant (and, of course, complex) analyses, we may refer to one of his penetrating ideas—that democracy is not principally a pretension of man *vis-à-vis* the State, but a pretension of man *vis-à-vis* himself, the fulfilment of which is precisely what enables him to take part in democracy; and this pretension can be perceived from the following three standpoints: consciousness of responsibility, veneration for great men, ability for self-education.[16]

The lure of politico-sociological considerations (the relations between political systems with economic structures and with historical or ideological traditions) with respect to each country is easier to evade, at least for the reason that something has already been said on the subject in the present study. Let us return, then, to our original question in its simplest connotation and as a mere question of fact. There is an obvious parallelism between the question asked at the beginning of this paragraph and another question set forth earlier: Is there a single unitary model for economic development? In view of this parallelism, we may ask: Is there also a single model for democracy? The answer is negative in both cases. But the stubborn persistence—particularly on the part of textbooks—in taking as a model, in its own setting, the venerable English (or perhaps Anglo-Saxon) definition can only lead to an irremediable hopelessness. The subject has suddenly acquired great importance because of the interest now taken by politicians and scientists in the possible connexion between democracy and economic development in the newer countries. Perhaps, for this reason, and to guard against the rather emotional impatience of some Latin Americans, the Working Group in Mexico City was wise in recognizing the subject in all its simplicity and even in recommending some research in this connexion: What forms of democratic government are the most appropriate for societies at different levels of economic and social development?

Once more we come up against the fact that the situation in the Latin American countries is, as might be expected, very different from that obtaining in the bevy of new States; and consequently, some of the concepts and recommendations of current research are of little use to us—for instance, the general theoretical questions considered by R. Braibanti . . . : "The relevance of political science to the study of underdeveloped areas."[17] We venture to give below a few other brief examples.

Reference was made elsewhere to a classification of political systems of the new countries used by a group of young North American research workers.[18] There are apparently three "standard models of political systems": (*a*) the so-called "mobilization" system or type; (*b*) the "consociational" system; and (*c*) the system of "modernizing autocracies." These various types are not difficult to explain, but such an explanation is unnecessary at the moment. (We shall merely list, by way of illustration, the characteristics of the first type: (*a*) hierarchical authority; (*b*) total loyalty; (*c*) tactical flexibility; (*d*) unitarism; (*e*) ideological specialization.) It is interesting to note that each type corresponds to a different form of economic development. Broadening the horizon a little, a further interesting classification is to be found in another book, also mentioned earlier.[19] Its authors prefer a dichotomic distinction: (*a*) oligarchies, which are or can be modernist, colonial and racialist, conservative and traditionalist; and (*b*) democracies, which in turn correspond to one or other of the following types: political, tutelary and resulting from the liquidation of the colonial system. If time allowed, it would be worth while to examine in some detail cases where the Spanish language had fallen into disuse, or else one of the so-called "tutelary democracies" which are also of interest to some Latin American countries.

The Brazilian professor Helio Jaguaribe (who attended the meeting in Mexico City) has ventured to tackle the subject with reference to the Latin American world, following up the connexion, referred to above, between political forms and methods of economic development. His undeniably original and discerning study[20] is perhaps unnecessarily complicated by some questions of a geopolitical nature and it strikes here and there an extremely pessimistic note. In Professor Jaguaribe's view, there are three viable models or types: the model of national capitalism or capitalistic nationalism; the model of State capitalism; and the type of "developmentistic socialism." As will be seen, the classification here is politico-economic in character. A more attenuated and systematized expression of his thought is contained in the report of the above-mentioned Working Group:

In all probability, the structure of political models applicable to Latin American countries would include, *inter alia*, various combinations of the following preponderant factors:

1. National entrepreneurial *bourgeoisies* and or technocratic middle classes.

2. Parliaments with a predominance of parties supporting economic development as a fundamental political value on the basis of nationalist aspirations, or with a predominance of centralized political groups having a profoundly reformist outlook under the leadership of the technocratic group formed by the middle classes.

3. States responsible for the programming and control of an economic development activity carried out mainly by national entrepreneurs, or States performing themselves the function of entrepreneur on account of the insufficiency of private enterprise.[21]

While it was necessary to mention these opinions, it would be out of place to indulge in polemics. Our task for the moment is simpler; it does not aspire to offer even moderately satisfactory analyses, for these can only be attempted in a special study—which will have to be carried out some time.

In our view, Arnold Bergsträsser[22] is right in stating that, at this point in the twentieth century, there are still four fundamental types of rule existing side by side: primitive, class, constitutional or rule of law, and totalitarian.

Since gaining their independence, the Latin American countries have been, or have wanted to be, constitutional States, governed by the rule of law, although traces of their earlier class rule have persisted here and there. They have also been, or have wanted to be, democratic States. Because that democracy has not always functioned well, this is no reason for calling it in question. But in most cases there has been an endeavour to get nearer to democracy; and it is essential that, in the coming decades, which will be decisive for Latin America's economic growth, attempts be made to give it substance (in each country, according to its particular characteristics), even if the almost mythical ideal of the Anglo-Saxon model is not reproduced point by point. In regard to economic development and programming, it is hardly probable that the old "liberal-representative" democracy in Leibholz's classification can prove an effective instrument at the present time. Pluralist democracy, typical of the most modern industrial countries, can only now begin in some of the Latin American countries, if they are fortunate; that is to say, if they are in full take-off or are getting under way.

Democracy as a Participation Phenomenon

Some people may think that the system of the so-called "dominant party" (not to be confused with the "one party") is the most effective instrument for maintaining a programme and enlisting popular support. (By the foregoing, we mean that form of the classic parliamentary system in which we have a majority coalition exercising a modifying influence in both directions.) The essential point, however, is that the paradigm of democratic political life is not single but plural.

If, as has already been said, the economists have tried to define in an original way, "from within," the problems inherent in the Latin American situation, this is because, as is natural, they had in mind the fundamental concepts of their science, which are equally valid everywhere. The politicians and their advisers—the social scientists—have to bear in mind that there are also fundamental principles of democracy, if real meaning is to be attached to the term. These principles are well known, but they should perhaps be recalled briefly.

In the first place, there must be a minimum of representation, whatever the electoral procedure and the party system, and of respect for the sanctions (no re-elections, etc.) of public opinion. In the second place, there must be safeguards for the individual person and such safeguards must be maintained; without this liberal element, any democracy is bound to perish. And in the third place, there must be opportunities for effective social participation, in a greater or lesser degree.

Sociologists, while admitting the importance of the first and second of these principles, will be particularly anxious to stress the paramount value of the third. Sociologically speaking, democracy is, indeed, a manifestation of participation. This manifestation is not confined to election times, to the casting of a vote or the temporary fulfilment of other purely political functions; real democratic participation by the citizen extends throughout society and is expressed in a variety of group activities. The painful experiences of the past few decades have been needed to bring about a revival in one form or another—adapted, of course, to present circumstances—of some of Durkheim's ideas, expressed with such vigour in the preface to the second edition of his classic work *De la Division du Travail Social.* Nowadays, we speak rather of the structural importance of what are known as the intermediate groups, in the social and *a fortiori* in the political field. As the present author expressed it elsewhere:

> . . . it may be maintained that it is only possible to speak of full and real participation in those cases where the individual is genuinely involved, i.e., where he has direct or first-hand experience of the things that are important to him and from which he forms, even without meaning to do so, his own opinion. An individual is genuinely involved in his family, his occupation, his firm, in the trade union, the producers'

association, the parish, etc. An individual cannot act readily and judiciously when confronted with general, abstract situations, unless he is prepared for them by a gradual broadening of his limited, specific outlook. The means by which this gradual broadening of the outlook on life can be brought about is active participation in intermediate groups, of steadily increasing size, from the tiny family nucleus, at one end of the scale, to the entire State and its international connexions, at the other. Real and fairly responsible political participation is thus achieved through these various groups. That participation is direct in so far as the individual takes part in private decisions which, whether he wishes it or not, have general political repercussions; it is indirect in so far as he forms his general political opinions as a result of contact and exchanges of ideas and experience with the other members of his group.[23]

Such is the importance conceded today to this fact of democracy as a participation phenomenon that attempts have been made in a number of surveys to gauge it in different countries. And sometimes with surprising results. The vigour of economic development—deriving from that popular support so often mentioned—depends on the degree of effective participation existing at all these intermediate levels. And this brings us to a question about which nothing has been said up to the present: the vigour of trade union life. The importance of this fact, even from the standpoint of economic development, has been forcefully pointed out by some contemporary sociologists—André Philip, Goetz Briefs, etc.[24] A. Philip said recently[25] that there was coming to pass a transition from "participation democracy" to libertarian (or liberal) democracy. We need not discuss the felicity of the terms chosen. The second of them is meant to convey the idea that, as a result of modern working conditions (in the most highly industrialized societies, of course), the individual is in a position to participate to an ever greater extent in a large variety of organizations. While liberating himself, man also concentrates more narrowly on his interests and responsibilities. Perhaps for this reason political democracy may be becoming steadily weaker and more uncertain as far as purely "political" participation is concerned, but it does not on that account cease to be a democracy. In his own words:

> I wonder whether, instead of lamenting over the indifference, passivity and apathy of the masses, it would not be better to consider that this weakening implies a kind of liberation of the individual; we shall thus attain to a democracy which, though perhaps allowing of less participation, will, on the other hand, allow of greater controls, determination of limits and definition of spheres of action.

He adds the following, which is of particular interest for our present purpose:

> There can be no economic democracy without the provision of a continuing education for the whole population—a continuing education in keeping with conditions in the modern world . . . education for a people decreasingly interested in ideologies and philosophies of life and increasingly interested in definite technical realities at the same time as in the values in which they are reflected.

It was thus through the trade unions that was bound to arise the burning problem of economic democracy,[26] that is to say, the problem (as various definitions agree) of the extension to the economic sphere of the democratic principles which first appeared in the political sphere. But we have made so many digressions that one more would be unpardonable.

Moral Integrity. Latin America "farà da sè"

Would it be possible, or rather, are we able at this stage to tackle a last, thorny question? Up to now, the conviction has prevailed that the democratic system is capable of promoting economic development, and in some sort not only because of value judgements but also for technical reasons. These reasons provide at once for the prerequisites of growth, i.e., a sustained and adequate rate of growth, and the equitable and humane distribution of the fruits thereof. No one would deny in principle that the human intelligence is capable of determining the procedures required for democratic programming. It would, doubtless, be more difficult, though by no means impossible, to reconcile planning and democracy. Intellectuals may be provoked to great impatience at times by the delays and obstacles which their ideas encounter when applied to the complex situations of real life, though the experience of practical men may in due course contrive to damp down the intellectual's inherent intolerance. What may happen, however, is that a moment will come when the general conviction prevails that the democratic system is a failure, that Western ideas are exploded. The future is in the lap of the gods; and there is no point in our striving with Proteus now, to wrest his secret from him—the elusive sea-god will always escape us, so we had better give up any idea of prophecy.

Although the future is unforeseeable, we can in any case bear in mind the causes that may lead us to some such gamble with fate (as rejecting democracy).

In these last remarks on the viability of the democratic system, let us emphasize once more the significance of its two indispensable buttresses: legitimacy and efficiency. The democratic system can perish if it is wasted by inefficiency. But it can also perish if the vital force of its legitimacy is sapped by pernicious anaemia. It is important not to be mistaken about these two dangers; the second is much more serious and relentless than the first. There is always a hope that, even at the eleventh hour, men may arise who are able to turn inaptitude into efficiency, who are able, if need be, to perform a final, saving operation. On the other hand, the complete evaporation of beliefs, the moral collapse that may result from the dissolution of faith—the psychological disintegration of a whole society—can only lead to hopelessness and "extremism." Men cannot live without the stimulus of a lofty example. And, sometimes, ruling groups through their corruption may poison democracy instead of affording an example of devotion and steadfastness. But there is perhaps no deeper form of such corruption (for the very reason that it slowly and inexorably undermines) than the power, Machiavellism of public men, whether of their own country or of a foreign dominating country. It has rightly been observed that the Machiavellism of the Prince corrupts, at most, his little Court; but the mass Machiavellism of the great modern leaders saps, equally and inevitably, the moral fibre of all individual citizens. And democracy is basically a question of ethics, as has been so clearly explained by the philosopher Jaspers. Psychological disintegration implies, at the most, mere selfish resignation, content to gratify its most "human" and immediate interests, and, at the least, escape to an "ivory tower," represented, perhaps, by one of the world religions. Let us, then, face this possibility—as is fitting for adult, mature beings—and at the same time let us hope, and, still more firmly determine, that it be not translated into fact. In one of the most fateful moments in the history of Spain, her greatest leader was in a position to say: "*España farà da sè.*" He did not, however, do so, and therefore did not shatter the mystery that history preserves throughout its long course by reason of its secrets. Why should not that same hope be repeated here? We have no doubt that, in the era which is now dawning, Latin America, too, *farà da sè.*

NOTES

1. Gerhard Leibholz, *Strukturprobleme der modernen Demokratie*, Karlsruhe, C. F. Müller, 1958.
2. Gerhard Leibholz, "Die Bedrohung der Freiheit durch

die Gesetzgeber," in: *Freiheit der Persönlichkeit* (series of broadcasts by a team of lecturers), Kroner, Stuttgart, 1958.

3. S. Landshut, "Wandlungen der parlamentarische Demokratie," *Hamburger Jahrbuch,* Year 4, pp. 150–162.

4. *Ibid.,* p. 157.

5. *Ibid.,* p. 159.

6. *Ibid.,* p. 161.

7. See, for example, *Parliamentary Reform, 1933–58; a Survey of Suggested Reforms,* Hansard Society for Parliamentary Government, 1956.

8. J. H. Kaiser, *Die Repräsentation organisierter Interessen,* Berlin, Duncker und Humblot, 1956; valuable work which supersedes all earlier ones on the same subject.

9. Carl Joachim Friedrich, *Demokratie als Herrschafts- und Lebensform,* Heidelberg, Quelle und Meyer, 1959, Chapter VII. A development of some lectures given in Heidelberg, based on his previous book, *The New Belief in the Common Man.*

10. Bibliography on the subject is not scarce. There is a concise and very instructive study by Gunnar Heckscher, "Pluralist Democracy: the Swedish Experience," *Social Research,* December 1948. On the other hand, I am unacquainted (a common misfortune for intellectuals in our part of the world) with another book by this author which has been translated into French, bearing the extremely explicit title: *Démocracie Efficace: l'Expérience Politique et Sociale des Pays Scandinaves* (Paris, Presses Universitaires de France, 1957).

11. G. Myrdal, *Beyond the Welfare State,* New Haven (Conn.), Yale University Press, 1960.

12. *Ibid.,* p. 97.

13. R. M. Titmuss, *Essays on the Welfare State,* London, Allen and Unwin, 1958.

14. E. Forsthoff, *Verfassungsprobleme der Sozialstaats,* 1953.

15. Some interesting material on this subject has been collected in a book by the Chilean economist Luis Escobar Cerdá, *Organización para el Desarrollo Económico,* Santiago de Chile, Editorial Universitaria S.A., 1961. However, the task is only at its beginning.

16. Karl Jaspers, *Die Atombombe und die Zukunft des Menschen,* Munich, R. Piper, 1948, p. 441.

17. R. Braibanti and J. J. Spengler, eds., *Tradition, Values, and Socioeconomic Development,* Duke University Press, 1961, p. 139.

18. David E. Apter and C. Rosberg, "Some Models of Political Change in Contemporary Africa" in: *The Political Economy of Contemporary Africa,* Washington, D.C., National Institute of Social and Behavioral Sciences, edited by D. P. Ray, 1959, and in other writings, especially by the first of these authors.

19. See Almond and Coleman, eds., *The Politics of the Developing Areas,* Princeton University Press, 1960.

20. *El Desarrollo Económico Programado y la Organización Política* (ST/ECLA/CONF.6/L.C-2b and Add.1).

21. *Boletín Económico de América Latina,* VI, No. 1 (March 1961), p. 64.

22. See A. Bergsträsser, *Führung in der modernen Welt,* Freiburg, Rombach, 1961.

23. Lectures at the University of Córdoba, Argentina, mentioned earlier.

24. See an excellent general account by Alfred Christmann, "Die Gewerkschaften in der industriellen Gesellschaft," in: *Hamburger Jahrbuch,* Year. 5.

25. André Philip, "Les Syndicats et la Démocratie Économique," *Revue de l'Institut de Sociologie,* Brussels, Nos. 1–2, 1961.

26. The journal of the Institut Solvay (1961, Abs. 1–2) contains a number of contributions to a symposium held in Geneva (May 1960) on this subject. Some are very valuable. But for a Latin American, the most interesting perhaps is that by Alain Touraine, "Situations Ouvrières et Types de Démocratie Economique"—not only, of course, because he expressly mentions some Spanish-American phenomena (*loc. cit.,* p. 40).

b. AUTHORITARIAN REGIMES

84

An Authoritarian Regime: Spain

Juan J. Linz

Before defining an authoritarian regime, let us refer briefly to the conceptions of democracy and totalitarianism from which we start in our comparative analysis. This is particularly important since many authoritarian systems claim to be "organic," "basic," "selective," or "guided" democracies, or at least to govern for the people, if not in fact to be "people's" democracies. We consider a government democratic if it supplies regular constitutional opportunities for peaceful competition for political power

From Juan J. Linz, "An Authoritarian Regime: Spain," in Erik Allardt and Yrjo Littunen, eds., *Cleavages, Ideologies and Party Systems* (Helsinki: Transactions of the Westermarck Society, 1964), X, 295–297, 323–331, 334–341. Reprinted by permission of the author and publisher.

(and not just a share of it) to different groups without excluding any significant sector of the population by force. This definition is based on those of Schumpeter, Aron and Lipset,[1] with the addition of the last qualification to include censitary regimes of the nineteenth century, democracies in which the vote has been denied to some groups, but with real competition for support from a limited electorate. As long as new claimants to suffrage were not suppressed forcibly for more than a limited time, we can consider such regimes democratic.

As Schumpeter has stressed, the element of competition for votes makes the whole gamut of civil liberties necessary, since without them there could be no true free competition; this is the link between classical Liberalism and democracy. It could be argued that authoritarian regimes, even preconstitutional monarchies, have or had certain civil liberties, but we would not call them democracies for this reason. To give an example in recent years, legalization of a right to strike—perhaps not under that name—has been discussed in Spain, particularly since de facto strikes are tolerated and government officials participate in the negotiations between workers and employers despite their illegality. Similarly, the courts have assumed quite extensive control over administrative acts through the Law of Administrative Procedure, following the model of continental European administrative law and jurisprudence. Many elements of the Rechtsstaat are not incompatible with an authoritarian state and perhaps not even with a "secularized" totalitarian state. However, full civil liberties, including an unlimited right of association and assembly, for example, inevitably create pressures toward political democracy. In this sense, against a strong tradition in continental political theory, we can say that liberalism and democracy are inseparable.

In defining totalitarianism we also want to limit the term somewhat and reserve it for the unique new forms autocratic government has taken since World War I, without denying that similar tendencies existed in the past. Perhaps Kornhauser's characterization is as good as any other, even if it overstresses somewhat the arbitrary aspects, when he writes:

> Totalitarian dictatorship involves total domination, limited neither by received laws or codes (as in traditional authoritarianism) nor even the boundaries of governmental functions (as in classical tyranny), since they obliterate the distinction between State and society. Totalitarianism is limited only by the need

to keep large numbers of people in a state of constant activity controlled by the elite.[2]

C. J. Friedrich's well-known definition[3] includes the following five clusters of characteristics: an official ideology, often with chiliastic elements; a single mass party unquestioningly dedicated to the ideology; near complete control of mass media; complete political control of the armed forces; and a system of terroristic police control not directed against demonstrable enemies only. In another version central control and direction of the economy is added. This more descriptive definition provides a clearer yardstick, although in view of recent developments I would not give as much emphasis to the role of the police and terror.[4]

Definition of an Authoritarian Regime

Authoritarian regimes are political systems with limited, not responsible, political pluralism: without elaborate and guiding ideology (but with distinctive mentalities); without intensive or extensive political mobilization (except some points in their development); and in which a leader (or occasionally a small group) exercises power within formally ill-defined limits but actually quite predictable ones.

To avoid any confusion we want to make it clear that personal leadership is a frequent characteristic but not a necessary one, since a junta arrangement can exist and the leader's personality might not be the decisive factor. Furthermore, the leader does not need to have charismatic qualities, at least not for large segments of the population nor at all stages of development of the system. In fact he may combine elements of charismatic, legal and traditional authority in varying degrees, often at different points in time—though the charismatic element often tends to be more important than the legal authority, at least for some sectors of the population. . . .

Defining authoritarian regimes as a particular type of political system is only useful if we can show that such regimes handle the invariant problems of any political system in a distinctive way. We have already made passing reference to problems like the control of the armed forces, the problem of loyalty, etc., but it may be useful to focus in more detail on a few examples. One is the recruitment and characteristics of the political elite. Another set of questions can be asked about the conditions under which such regimes are likely to emerge and to be stable. Finally, a third set of problems appears when we consider the dynamics of such regimes: whether they will turn totalitarian or democratic, and under what conditions.[5]

The Authoritarian Elite

Let us start with a very specific problem: who constitutes the top elite in authoritarian regimes?

Limited pluralism makes the authoritarian elite less homogeneous than that of the totalitarian system in ideology and political style, and probably in career patterns and background as well. This does not mean that the personalities will be more forceful or colorful. The lieutenants of the totalitarian leader, who rose with him in the struggle for power, often share the demagogic qualities, the marginality and uniqueness, that frequently characterize him; brilliant intellectuals and journalists appear as ideologists in the totalitarian elite's first generation. In contrast, many in the authoritarian elite are less colorful, brilliant or popular; their military, professional and bureaucratic backgrounds do not breed such qualities.

In a sense both the democratic and totalitarian top elites are composed fundamentally of professional politicians, who live through if not for politics. In the totalitarian first generation, the decisive step was to join the party before it came to power; in most democratic countries there is a slow *cursus honorum* through elected or appointed offices, particularly when the parties are bureaucratized and well organized. The second generation of the totalitarian elite may combine a career in the party apparatus with some technical specialization, as reflected in the expression: "he did party work in agriculture." Research on totalitarian leadership has underscored its marginality[6] in terms of regional origin, religious affiliation, social mobility, stable work life and so on. In contrast, a significant part of the authoritarian regime's leadership had already participated actively in the country's political life as parliamentarians, and through seniority in the army, civil service, or academic world would have been assured a respectable position in the society under any regime. Given the non-ideological character of much authoritarian politics, the emphasis on respectability and expertise, and the desire to co-opt elements of established society, a number of those assuming power will have little previous involvement in politics. Occasionally, particularly at the second level, we find people who define themselves publicly as apolitical, just experts. The old fighters of the extremist groups which contributed to the crisis of the previous regime, who participated in the take-over, who hoped to take power, may find their claims rejected, and will have to content themselves with secondary positions. In some cases their political style, their ideological commitments, their exclusivism, may lead them to break away and retire to private life. This has been the destiny of many Falangist and extreme Carlist leaders under Franco.

Participation in the single party may not be a requisite for entering the elite, but it can be quite helpful combined with other qualifications: a brilliant academic or civil service career, identification with other groups in the pluralistic system such as religio-political interest groups. Such multiple affiliations give the elite member wider contacts and legitimize him in the eyes of the groups that will find themselves represented through him. Some biographies of members of Franco's cabinet, described later, will illustrate this point.

Since both totalitarian and democratic governments want to mobilize opinion, intellectuals play an important role as journalists and ideologists. Lasswell and Lerner have stressed that skill in the use of symbols is decisive. In Spain the only effective journalist in the cabinet was there as a minister without portfolio immediately after the war; a minister of labor with demagogic abilities held the ministry until 1957. Both came from the fascist wing of the system. The more rightist an authoritarian regime, the less place is there for the non-professional, non-academic intelligentsia. Without careful research it is difficult to know if some authoritarian regimes which are described as progressive owe their image to such men; their policies may actually not differ greatly from others not enjoying the same reputation.

Despite their tendency to elect national heroes, in democracies normally only a minority of non-military posts are occupied by officers, and even the defense ministries are often held by civilians. In totalitarian systems a politically neutralized or indoctrinated army may control its own affairs but few key positions outside that realm are held by military men. Authoritarian regimes that emerge as "commissary dictatorship" (to use Carl Schmitt's expression for those whose intent is to re-establish "order" and then transfer power to the constitutional government) tend to be, initially, exclusively or almost exclusively military: the classical junta. There, a balanced representation of the services, rank, and seniority are more important than personality or political beliefs. If such a regime retains power, shifts are likely to take place, either through reinforcement of a faction like the Free Officers of Egypt, or through the co-optation of civilians, as in the regimes of Primo de Rivera, Franco and Perón. These civilians may be professional politicians (as in Eastern Europe during the interwar years), civil servants or experts (Calvo Sotelo in Spain and Salazar in Portungal entered this way), leaders of interest groups or religious organizations (like Artajo, the lay head of Spanish Catholic Action in 1945), or fascists willing to forego a state dominated by a single party. Soon the balance of power may shift considerably toward the civilian element, which may even assume leadership as Salazar did, but it is unlikely that the equilibrium between civil and military power will be established at the same level as before. The absence of a relatively large, disciplined, dynamic revolutionary party, or the weakness or death of its leadership, is decisive for the establishment in this period of an authoritarian rather than a totalitarian regime. This was the case in Spain with the death of José Antonio (who probably never would have been a real totalitarian leader in any case) and the weakness and dissension in Falangist leadership described so well by Payne. In Rumania, one of the most authentic and revolutionary fascist parties had to play second fiddle in the regime of Marshal Antonescu after losing its leader Codreanu, finally to be ousted after four months of collaboration. The strength of the party also decides if the men co-opted from other groups will be able to maintain some degree of pluralism.

The persistence of the pre-crisis social order that goes with limited pluralism and co-optation means that the legal profession, so important in democratic politics and even under traditional rulers, will play a much greater role in authoritarian regimes than in totalitarian systems. The same is true of civil servants. Their presence may contribute to the strange combination of Rechtsstaat and arbitrary power, of slow legalistic procedure and military command style, that characterizes some of these regimes. This preoccupation with procedure ultimately becomes an important factor in the constant expansion of a state of law, with an increase in predictability and opportunities for legal redress of grievances. At the same time it may prevent political problems from being perceived as such, irreducible to administrative problems and not soluble by legislation. Legal procedures are often seen, particularly in the continental legal tradition, as an adequate equivalent of more collective, political expressions of interest conflicts.[7]

Stability and Change: Patterns of Entry

The top elite of an authoritarian regime, despite its limited pluralism, is likely to be more limited both numerically and in shades of opinion than the spectrum of government and opposition in democracies. The existence of a loyal opposition, and the greater dispersion of power, facilitate the training and emergence of new leaders. Limited pluralism allows new personalities to emerge in the shadows, but their political experience is often inhibited. This slows down renewal of leadership, and each successive generation is likely to have an even smaller activated constituency than those of the original group. The emphasis on stability and continuity in such regimes, one of their main claims to legitimacy against the previous "unstable" democratic system, also contributes to slow renewal. On the other hand a change in the elite's composition can go on more silently and smoothly than under totalitarianism, where changes in leadership are associated with crisis. Turnover in authoritarian elites, can take place without purges, by retiring people to secondary or honorary positions, if not to private life. The following incident illustrates how, even in the case of serious disagreement, a maximum of good manners is maintained within the elite: when two ministers were dropped from the Spanish regime's elite, the official announcement of the dismissal omitted the customary formula "thanking you for services rendered"; but a few days later a "corrected" version, including the phrase, was published.[8]

Venomous hatred of defeated elite members is not always absent, but the lack of ideological clarity, of self-righteousness, contributes to making this infrequent. On the other hand the more pluralistic, open structure of society may help make the loss of power less painful.

While the elite is relatively open, predictable ways of entry are lacking, which frustrates the ambitions of many. Because competition for power is not institutionalized effectively, paths to it are obscure: neither devoted partisan service and ideological conformity, nor a steady career through elected office, is available. Success in non-political spheres, identification with groups like religious associations, particularistic criteria of who knows whom, even accident, may be more important. These processes, which incidentally do not necessarily lead to the selection of incompetent people, exist in all systems, but normally they coexist with more universalistic recruitment criteria. With the increasing complexity of industrial society and increasing emphasis on achievement criteria, universalistic standards are used more and more, but there is no purposive planned cadre training or recruitment through youth organizations, party schools and so on such as the totalitarians employ. When the educational system is class biased, this depolitization of the elite results in less equalitarian recruitment than that afforded by totalitarianism; formally no one is excluded, but in fact educational requirements exclude many. On the other hand authoritarian regimes with their universalistic bureaucratic recruitment may be more open than conservative or bourgeois parties in a society at the same level of economic development. But as Kornhauser has rightly noted: ease of entry into elites, and ability to exert influence on them, are not the same thing and may not even vary together.[9]

The first generation totalitarian elite, having come to power together in a revolutionary group, are likely to represent the same generation and to be younger than their democratic counterparts. Authoritarian leadership is likely to be more heterogeneous, combining younger elements (who may have sought a more revolutionary regime) with older men co-opted into the system because of their experience or symbolic value. Obviously the age composition of an elite is likely to differ, depending on whether we are dealing with the period immediately after the conquest of power or years later when the revolutionary group has consolidated its position. From a sociological point of view it is the age at which the group first obtained office that matters. A very interesting problem is how each type of regime handles the problem of recruitment and succession. One interesting feature of the Franco regime, not unrelated to its pluralism, has been its ability to bring a significant number of younger men into the elite. This is the more surprising when we recall the political channels for selection and socialization into politics, youth organizations and the party, are so undeveloped, though this very fact enhances recruitment of the young, since it makes political careers less of a *cursus honorum*. So in the present cabinet there are two men, one of them playing an important role, who were under 17 when the Civil War ended. The average age of the "victory cabinet" (1939) was 46.1 years, but most have tended to be slightly older; the average for all ministers from 1938 through 1957 at the time of assuming office was 50.5. Significantly the average for the Republican ministerial elite was 50.8; in terms of age the Franco regime did not mean a great change, compared to that represented by the younger Peronist cabinets. The average age of the Nazi top hierarchy in 1933 was appreciably younger: 41.9 years, as we would expect in a revolutionary elite. It is only natural that in Spain the Minister Secretary General of the Movement should have, generally, the youngest members (average age 41) while the military ministries where seniority counts have been close to or above the middle fifties.

Political Pluralism in the Elite of the Franco Regime

I. The Cabinet

Using some data on the top Spanish elite I hope to illustrate and to some extent support some of the points made above. The most important decision-making body is the cabinet, both as a collective body and as individual members each in his area of competence. While cabinet members are not equally powerful, they all have control of significant sectors of administrative policy making, and have taken strong initiative in legislative processes. It therefore seems legitimate to concentrate on cabinet members from the first appointed in 1938 to the last sworn in in the summer of 1962, to explore elite pluralism. The number of persons involved is 67, though the number of incumbencies is higher since many have been holdovers from one government to the next and several have held different ministries at one time or another.

Let us start with the political orientations of these men, their former party affiliations, and the groups they may be said to represent. Since these identifications, a good index of pluralism, are not announced, and political allegiances are not always stable, this involves certain risks. Nevertheless such classifications are made by participants themselves, as the memoirs of Serrano Suñer reveal.[10] Similarly Arrese describes how, in a cabinet crisis, Falangists asked for and received various portfolios.[11]

Of the total, 39 per cent have been army officers; a number of them can be classified as pro-Falangist, pro-Traditionalist, or pro-monarchico-conservative, but their primary identification probably continues to be the army; in the case of 24 per cent no political tendency could be assigned easily. In order not to overestimate the role of the army, it is important to note that of the 26 military in the cabinet, 15 have held defense ministries. Professionals and civil servants without any particular group affiliations number at least ten, or 15 per cent. The Falange, in the strict sense, has contributed 17 members, or 25 per cent, of whom only eight had no other identification prior to the Civil War. Another four had been members of the CEDA (Gil Robles' center-right Catholic party) or close to demochristian organizations; four could be considered technical with Falangist leanings. The other official part of the fused party, the Traditionalists (heirs of the XIX century dynastic and ideological conflict between the liberals

Table 84–1 Political Background or Identification of Members of the Spanish Cabinet (1938 to 1962)

	Total	% of
Falange:		
Falange with no previous political background	8	12 %
Falange with CEDA background	5	7
Technical with Falangist orientation	4	6
Total Falange	*17*	*25*
Traditionalist	3	4.5
Acción Española and non-traditionalist Monarchist	2	3
Civil figure of the Primo de Rivera Dictatorship	3	4.5
Political Catholicism	3	4.5
Opus Dei	3	4.5
Technical or civil service apolitical	10	15
Military:		
With Falangist leanings	3	4.5
With Traditionalist leanings	1	1.5
With Acción Española or Opus Dei ties	2	3
With CEDA background	2	3
Former office holders under Primo de Rivera	2	3
With no particular identification	16	24
Total Military	*26*	*39*
TOTAL	67	100 %

and the legitimist-Catholic-conservatives) held three posts, particularly the ministry of Justice where they could enact the pro-clerical legislation in many mixed matters. Three civil figures who were already present in the Primo de Rivera dictatorship (1923–1929) together with two military of that period represent an important element of continuity. The small group of Acción Española, inspired largely by the Action Française of the 1930's, contributes several members, some of whom I have included in other groups with which they were later more closely identified. The CEDA, a party that in the February 1936 election was the second largest in Parliament with 88 of 473 seats, contributes three of its deputies, two of them military and one (Serrano Suñer) turned Falangist. Three other important figures are closely identified with the ACNDP (Acción Catolica Nacional de Propagandistas), a small elite group of political Catholics. From this group came a younger professor who as minister of education followed an interesting policy of liberalization. . . .

The academic world is represented by 8 (12 per cent) university professors, fewer than in the Republic which had 17, or 20 per cent. But the real change reflecting the lesser importance of the intelligentsia in the regime is the absence, with but two exceptions, of the secondary and primary educa-

tional system representatives. In summary the teaching professions contribute 13 per cent while they made up 30 per cent of the cabinet between 1931 and 1936. The health professions that contributed 8 men to the Republican cabinets, reflecting the leftist-laicist orientation of the medical profession in much of Europe, are absent. In contrast, naturally reflecting the more technical tasks of the government, the proportion of engineers and architects has increased from 7 per cent to 13 per cent. One of the greatest changes is the proportion of journalists: almost one fourth of the ministers of the Republic, but only a small minority (3) of those in the present regime would mention this as a major activity.

Military men holding civilian ministries constitute an important group, numbering 11, or 16 per cent; among them were a general secretary of the party, the undersecretary of the presidency, and a naval engineer who had a decisive role in the creation of the INI (Instituto Nacional de Industria), the state-owned industrial complex.

It would be interesting to continue with the analysis of the changes in the top elite, the early pluralism of the Consejo Nacional, the absence from the top elite, years later, of the Student Movement's youthful politicians, the rise of the technicians, etc., but the examples given so far must suffice.

II. The Elite in General

The political pluralism indicated by the data on the cabinet extends throughout the entire elite. Arrese, when he was secretary general of the party, presented in 1956 to the party's National Council some proposals for new constitutional laws that were received very critically. He felt compelled to defend himself against those who saw these proposals as an attempt by the party to gain greater strength. He wrote that "since some councillors have alluded to the excessive role of the original group of the Falange and of the JONS in the positions of the State and of the Movement," he would give the backgrounds of all levels of the elite at the time by their political origin before July 18, 1936. He stresses the following figures as the share of the Falange:

2 of 16 cabinet members	12.5%
1 of 17 undersecretaries	6.0
8 of 102 director generals	7.8
18 of 50 provincial governors (who are also heads of the provincial party organizations)	36.0
8 of 50 mayors of provincial capitals	16.0
6 of 50 presidents of provincial chambers	12.0
65 of 151 National councillors of the party	43.0
137 of 575 members of the legislature	24.0
133 of 738 provincial deputies	18.0
776 of 9,155 mayors	8.4
2,226 of 55,960 municipal councillors	9.0

Arrese continues: "I don't say this to make anyone despair, nor to justify anything, but for the benefit of so many speculators of politics who give as an explanation for not joining the Movement the worn-out excuse that the Falange did not leave a place for their honest desire to collaborate."[12]

In official circles one may hear persons described as "of the regime but not of the Movement," "Falangist against the Regime," "of the regime but apolitical," and so on through a vast variety of possible combinations which no one would say are meaningless descriptions of political views.

The Dynamics of Authoritarian Regimes

As a final point, let us turn to the dynamics of authoritarian regimes. It could be argued that they are unstable hybrids, subject to pressures and pulls in the direction of democracy or totalitarianism. Undoubtedly their limited ideological creativity makes them unattractive to those who look for logical consistency, meaning and purpose in political life, for real ideals even at great sacrifice. The intellectuals, the young, those intolerant of ambiguity, soon become disillusioned and turn to the two great political myths of our time, which are represented by the major powers of the world. The unfulfilled promises of authoritarianism may make them more susceptible to totalitarianism, which they believe to be more efficient and idealistic; the immobility of limited pluralism has already disillusioned some of them about the chances of speedy, far reaching reform under pluralism. Ideological elements from revolutionary movements like fascism and marxism are a source of tension when incorporated in such regimes and used as standards against which to measure their performance and their pragmatic, often dull, politics. In other cases instability comes from longstanding ideological commitments to constitutional democracy, to which the regime has had to pay lip-service, as in most of Latin America. The same is true in new countries where authoritarianism was introduced with the promise of preparing the ground for democracy, as in Turkey after World War I and now in the new states styling themselves "guided," "basic," or "presidentialist" democracies. Another source of tension is felt in countries relying on Catholic organic social theories; shifts in church policy may subject them to pressure. However, one should not overestimate the impact of ideological pulls, and instead pay some attention to the economic and social factors contributing to the stability of such regimes. After all, some of them have lasted several decades, even in the face of considerable hostility.

If we were to accept the interpretation that such regimes lie on a continuum between democracy and totalitarianism, we should find many examples of transitions from authoritarianism to one or the other without serious crises or revolutionary changes. This however does not seem to be the case; even when the transition to some kind of democracy has been done with little bloodshed, the democracy has often been unstable. Evolutionary cases are rare—Atatürk's Turkey and Vargas' Estado Novo come to mind and the process would deserve serious study. An initial commitment to democratic ideals, and self-definition as a preparatory stage for democracy, seem relevant, as the borderline case of Mexico also shows. Transitions to totalitarianism have not been frequent either unless we agree with the German conservatives (as I would not) that Hitler in 1933 was really pursuing an "autoritärer Staat" rather than a Nazi revolution. Another possible case would be Cuba, if we assume that Castro was initially willing to stop at a left-pluralist authoritarian system and not pursue totalitarianism. Perhaps Peronism is the most interesting case of a shift toward a more totalitarian conception from what was originally a military dictatorship. Political sociology should devote increasing attention to such problems of transition from one system to another, in the way that Bracher and his collaborators have offered a model for the breakdown of Weimar democracy and the process of Machtergreifung.

Another question is whether totalitarian regimes, whose transformation into the Western type of democracy no one expects, will look more like some of the present authoritarian regimes if their ideological impetus is weakened, apathy and privatization replace mobilization, and bureaucracies and managers gain increasing independence from the party. Some such tendencies are in sight and undoubtedly the difference between some authoritarian regimes and the Soviet Union today is less than in the Stalinist period. I would even venture to say that a country like Poland seems more authoritarian than totalitarian, but my knowledge of that system is too superficial to document this idea.

A dynamic description of authoritarian regimes should locate factors influencing the development of political and social pluralism and mobilization. It is essential to understand the historical constellations from which such regimes emerge: the breakdown of existing democracy, of a traditional society, or of colonial rule. This limits the alternatives open to the authoritarian ruler, the appeals he may use, the type of legitimacy he can claim, and so on, often independently of his own pragmatic or ideological preferences. But the present cannot be understood only in terms of origins. When these regimes began, their futures were generally very ill-defined (one has only to read the different manifestoes and speeches made in the first days of the Spanish Civil War to get a sense of this indeterminacy) and their relative openness makes for considerable shifts if the regime lasts. In the case of Spain it would be extremely misleading to interpret the present only in terms of the past; particularly the forces at play in the late 30's and early 40's, for the simple reason that a considerable part of the second level elite of today was not yet adult at the time, and close to half of the population was not even in their teens. In some of these regimes the bulk of existing information deals with their take-over phase and interest dwindles afterwards, which makes comparative study difficult.

Some of you may have missed a judgment about these regimes. I think that as a social scientist I should not express one. As an individual I could, but as a social scientist I would suggest that the problem be broken down into many sub-problems, examining the positive and negative implications of such regimes from many points of view. A number of cases would be required to give a general idea of their functions and dysfunctions for social change, but even so the observer's final evaluation of them would depend much on his own hierarchy of values.

Authoritarian regimes can be evaluated on a variety of dimensions: their ability to create stable political institutions articulating the conflicting interests of society, especially in countries where the regime came to power because of the heat of ideological and interest conflicts; their capacity to handle the succession problem; their ability to foster rapid economic development, both rural and industrial, compared to democratic and totalitarian societies under comparable conditions and considering the costs, both social and economic. We might examine the social and political consequences of some typical authoritarian labor policies: stability of employment vs. aggressive wage policy; imposed or voluntary company welfare benefits vs. a more general state or municipal policy; great emphasis on social security legislation combined with limited autonomy of labor organizations. Problems like these require cooperation between sociologists and economists, and I feel that today we have no good studies along these lines.

Among the most difficult questions of all is that posed by the leaders of authoritarian regimes, when they say that national unity can only be maintained or achieved by excluding open expression of political cleavages through political parties.[13] It has been expressed as follows:

> In face of the fundamental problems, the union, the unity of the country is indispensable. Now, without any doubt, the multiplicity of parties ends creating national disagreement about the great questions. No; democracy has nothing to do with regime of parliamentary assemblies and the agitation of rival political parties. Democracy consists in searching the will of the people and in serving that will.[14]

> We don't want democracy to be a source of cleavages, of childish struggles in the course of which the better part of our energies would be wasted. We want . . . to pursue in peace and in union the work of national construction.[15]

> Guinea's political unity has been proved by the referendum, and has been growing stronger ever since. It is not our intention to squander this chance of unity by adopting a system which would only reduce our political strength. What Africa needs is a fundamental revolution. It is not too much to ask that all our strength be mobilized and directed toward

a common goal. A political system based on two parties would be a certain check on our revolution. The revolutionary dynamism doesn't need any other stimulant than our needs, our aspirations, and our hopes.[16]

Certainly the activation of cleavages in a society where the basic consensus is shattered—as it was in Spain after the October revolution of 1934—or where it has not developed, as in some of the new nations, creates serious problems. Social scientists would have to know much more about the conditions under which the balance of cleavage and consensus required for democratic politics can emerge. Studies of the integration of new sectors into the society under different political and social institutions, particularly by Bendix and Guenther Roth,[17] suggest how difficult it is to weigh the consequences of following one or another path. A comparative analysis of the aftermath of different authoritarian regimes, for example those of Vargas and Perón, would be most important in exploring how authoritarianism can be combined with the expansion of citizenship which characterizes our time.

Evaluation of each authoritarian regime depends finally on the answer to these questions: could alternative systems work in the societies now under authoritarian rule? What conditions are necessary for these alternative systems, and how could they be created? At what cost? I for one have no definitive answers for Spain.

NOTES

1. Joseph Schumpeter, *Capitalism, Socialism and Democracy* (New York: Harper, 1947), pp. 232–302, esp. 269; Raymond Aron, *Sociologie des Sociétés Industrielles. Esquisse d'une théorie des régimes politiques* (Paris: La Centre de Documentation Universitaire, "les cours de la Sorbonne" Sociologie, 1958), p. 38; Seymour M. Lipset, *Political Man* (Garden City, N.Y.: Doubleday, 1960), Chap. II, "Economic Development and Democracy," p. 46.

2. William Kornhauser, *The Politics of Mass Society* (Glencoe, Ill.: The Free Press, 1959), p. 123.

3. There is no point in referring in detail to the extensive literature on totalitarianism since the works of C. J. Friedrich and Z. K. Brzezinski, Sigmund Newmann, Franz Neumann, Emil Ledere, H. Arendt, Barrington Moore, Jr., Adam B. Ulam, Raymond I. Bauer and Alex Inkeles, are well known. A recent review of the problem with references to the non-American literature can be found in the articles by Otto Stammer, G. Schulz, and Peter Christian Ludz, in *Soziale Welt*, Vol. 12, No. 2, 1961, pp. 97–145; Karl D. Bracher, *Die Auflösung der Weimarer Republik* (Stuttgart: Ring-Verlag, 1957); and K. D. Bracher, Wolfgang Sauer, Gerhard Schulz, *Die Nationalsozialistische Machtergreifung* (Köln: Westdeutscher Verlag, 1960), both sponsored by the Berlin Institut für Politische Wissenschaft, incorporate much of recent German scholarship on the breakdown of democracy and the establishment of Nazi totalitarianism. These monumental works should be used to supplement—and in my opinion modify—much of the dated but classic *Behemoth* of Franz Neumann.

4. Friedrich's definition was formulated in "The Nature of Totalitarianism," Symposium on Totalitarianism in Carl Friedrich, *Totalitarianism* (Cambridge: Harvard University Press, 1954), pp. 52–53, and then expanded and slightly modified in C. J. Friedrich and Z. K. Brzezinski, *Totalitarian Dictatorship and Autocracy* (Cambridge, Mass.: Harvard University Press, 1956), pp. 9–10.

5. Political sociology has centered its attention on the relationship between social structure and political institutions, but with important exceptions has tended to neglect the analysis of how different political systems handle the "invariant problems," and, even more so, the dynamics of political change. While the three aspects are closely interrelated they cannot be reduced to the relationship of society and political institutions. In this paper we have consciously attempted to focus on the organizational aspects and the political process without seeing them fundamentally as reflections of social bases. In a study of specific authoritarian systems and even more their emergence, evolution and breakdown, we would have to give more attention to the interaction between social bases and the political structure; or, to put it graphically, to add to a Weberian approach a more Marxist one.

6. On this marginality see mainly Daniel Lerner, *The Nazi Elite* (Hoover Institute Studies, Stanford: Stanford University Press, 1951), pp. 84–90.

7. [On] the typical political mentality—ideology—of the bureaucrats, see Karl Mannheim, *Ideology and Utopia* (New York: Harvest Books, 1936), pp. 118–119.

8. See Clark, *op. cit.*, I, 289, in the case of José Larraz and Pedro Gamero del Castillo, ministers of finance and without portfolio, at the time of the change of government on May 19, 1941, while the dismissal of other officials contained the phrase.

9. Kornhauser, *op. cit.*, p. 52.

10. Ramón Serrano Suñer, *Entre Hendaya y Gibraltar* (*Noticia y reflexion frente a una lejenda sobre nuestra politica en dos guerras*) (Madrid: Ediciones y Publicaciones Españolas S.A., 1947), pp. 60–64, 123–125.

11. Personal interview, materials of which were incorporated into Chapter 16 of Stanley Payne's *Falange, A History of Spanish Fascism* (Stanford: Stanford University Press, 1961).

12. Arrese, "Nacia un meta," *op. cit.*, pp. 212–213.

13. Social scientists raise similar questions, so Immanuel Wallerstein in *Africa. The Politics of Independence, op. cit.*, writes: "The choice has not been between one-party and multiparty states; it has been between one-party states and either anarchy or military regimes or various combinations of the two" (p. 96), and:

"At present many Africans cannot determine the limits of opposition, do not understand the distinction between opposition and secession. This is what the African leaders mean when they argue that 'our oppositions are not constructive.' It is not that they tend to be destructive of the government in power; this is the purpose of an opposition. It is that they tend to destroy the state in the process of trying to depose the acting government.

"This is particularly true because, in almost every African country the opposition takes the form of a claim to regionalism—a demand for at least decentralization in a unitary state, federalism in a decentralized state, confederation in a federation, total dissolution in a confederation. Regionalism is understandable because ethnic loyalties can usually find expression in geographic terms. Inevitably, some regions will be richer (less poor) than others, and if the ethnic claim to power combines with relative wealth, the case for secession is strong. . . . But every African nation, large or small, federal or unitary, has its Katanga. Once the logic of secession is admitted, there is no end except in anarchy. And so every African government knows that its first problem is how to hold the country together when it is threatened by wide disintegration" (p. 98); and we could continue quoting.

I would surmise that Franco, or the supporters of the Yugoslav-Serbian authoritarian regimes, would fully agree with these arguments. And in the case of Spain one cannot deny a certain legitimacy to the argument if one considers the behavior of a large part of the Socialist party in the opposition during the October days of 1934, or that of Companys, the head of the Generalitat of Catalonia during those days, or the activities of the Basque nationalists, or those of the extreme Right opposition to the Republic. . . . The distinction between opposition to the government, the regime and even the state, was certainly not clear to many Spaniards. (I am sure that Wallerstein would not agree with my application of his conclusions, but then I would suggest that those writing on authoritarian, single-party regimes, the role of the army as modernizer, etc., in underdeveloped areas, would specify further, how in the long run, such regimes will evolve differently from those in the semi-developed regions of the West.)

14. From the declarations of Franco to the correspondent of *Le Figaro* on June 12, 1958, *ABC* (Madrid) June 13, 1958. The text quoted was important enough to deserve the headlines of the newspaper. Similar statements could be found throughout the political statements of Caudillo.

15, 16. These quotations are respectively from Camille Alliali, Secretary General of POIC (Ivory Coast) and Sekou Toure (Guinea), quoted by Szymon Chodak in a paper on "The Societal Functions of Party Systems in Sub-Saharan Africa."

17. Reinhard Bendix, "Social Stratification and the Political Community," *European Journal of Sociology*, I, No. 2 (1960), 3–32; "The Lower Classes and the Democratic Revolution," *Industrial Relations*, I, No. 1 (October 1961), 91–116; and R. Bendix and Stein Rokkan, "The Extension of National Citizenship to the Lower Classes: A Comparative Perspective," a paper submitted to the Fifth World Congress of Sociology, Washington, 1962. His study *Work and Authority in Industry* (New York: Wiley, 1956) is also relevant. See also the study by Guenther Roth, *The Social Democrats in Imperial Germany. A Study of Working-Class Isolation and National Integration* (Totowa, N.J.: Bedminster Press, 1963). These studies as well as the comparative research on labor movements, like those of Calenson, should be taken into account before such ideas of unity, rather than painful integration by conflict, are accepted.

BIBLIOGRAPHIC NOTE. There is no sociological or even political science analysis of the institutions and operations of the Franco regime. Most of the literature on contemporary Spain deals with the historical background of the Civil War, the well-known books by: Gerald Brenan, *Spanish Labyrinth* (Cambridge: Cambridge University Press, 1943); Salvador de Madariaga, *Spain. A Modern History* (New York: Praeger Paperbacks, 1958); Hugh Thomas, *The Spanish Civil War* (New York: Harper, 1961); Franz Borkenau, *The Spanish Cockpit;* D. C. Cattell, *Communism and the Spanish Civil War* (Berkeley: University of California Press, 1955). None of these works is written with a pro-Franco point of view. For that the reader has to turn to Joaquin Arraras, *Historia de la Cruzada Española* (Madrid, 1940—3, 35 vols.) and his *Historia de la Segunda Republica Española* (Madrid: Editora Nacional, 1956).

For a good general history of modern Spain until the Republic see: Vicens Vives, J. Nadal, R. Ortega, M. Hernandez Sanchez Barba, Vol. IV of the *Historia Social de España y America* (Barcelona: Editorial Teide, 1959).

A very important book whose analysis of the early stages of the Franco regime is better documented than most sources in English—that focus on the Republican side—is Carlos M. Rama, *La Crisis Española del Siglo XX* (Mexico: Fondo de Cultura Económica, 1960).

The literature on Spain after the civil war, both journalistic and scholarly, is largely focused on Spanish foreign policy, but does not add much to the understanding of domestic politics. While, as the title indicates, this is also the focus of Arthur P. Whitaker, *Spain and the Defense of the West. Ally and Liability* (New York: Praeger Paperbacks, 1962), it contains a lot of material on the basis of the regime, the opposition groups, from the semitolerated ones to the Communists, economic policies, etc. We mentioned already the important work of Stanley Payne, *Falange,* but by focusing on only one element in the system, it can only give an incomplete picture. Ebenstein's study of the Church is also useful. Richard Pattee, *This Is Spain* (Milwaukee: Bruce, 1951), is a presentation from a point of view friendly to Catholic political forces within the Regime, but has no scholarly pretensions. For the basic constitutional texts of the Regime until 1945 see Clark, *op. cit.,* translations in English.

85

Toward a Theory of Spanish American Government

Richard M. Morse

The Viceregal Period and Its Antecedents

The purpose of this essay is neither fully to analyze the political experience of Spanish America

From Richard M. Morse, "Toward a Theory of Spanish American Government," *Journal of the History of Ideas,* XV (1954), 71–82, 85–90. Reprinted by permission of the publisher and the author.

nor to construct a mature theory which will comprehensively illuminate it. The histories of these eighteen countries are, taken singly, too fragmentary and, taken jointly, too uncorrelated to permit of so systematic a project. In this as in most areas of New World studies the elements for conclusive synthesis are still unavailable. Therefore a heuristic device will be used, which will be to examine certain formal European notions in the hope, not that they will concisely epitomize Spanish American political experience, but that they may be "played off against" that experience—contrapuntally, perhaps—in a way to evoke corresponding themes. . . .

Spanish American preceded British colonization by more than a century, and thus belongs to an era that antedates not only the Lockean rights of man but also the Bousset- and Hobbes-type apology for the absolutist national state. It is the Catholic kings, Ferdinand and Isabella, who symbolize Spanish America's political heritage.

Isabella in a sense prefigures the divine-right monarch. Her thwarting of the nobles and of the Cortes wherein they formed an estate; her royal agents and administrative reforms that centralized the government; her replacement of feudal levies with a modern army; her use of the faith to further political unity—all have been cited to identify her as a precursor of the Hobbesian autocrat. Yet it must be remembered that for three centuries after Isabella's death the Spanish empire retained, in comparison at least with the burgeoning capitalist countries, many hall marks of the medieval, hierarchical state.

The "common law" of Isabella's Castile was the *Siete Partidas,* drawn up c. 1260 and promulgated in 1348, [which] . . . assumed the nuclear element of society to be, not Lockean atomistic man, but religious, societal man: man with a salvable soul (*i.e.,* in relationship with God) and man in a station of life (*i.e.,* having mutual obligations with fellow humans, determinable by principles of Christian justice). The ruler, though not procedurally responsible to the people or the estates, was bound, through his conscience, to be the instrument of God's immutable, publicly ascertainable law. The *Partidas,* in fact, specifically excoriated the tyrant who strove to keep his people poor, ignorant and timorous and to forbid their fellowship and assemblies.

As mistress of the hierarchical Castilian state whose governance was largely by immanent justice and specially ceded privileges (*fueros*), Isabella found constant occasion to make inter- as well as intra-national assertion of her spiritual authority. Unlike Aragón—from whose border the Moorish menace had been lifted in the thirteenth century and whose rulers were therefore indifferent to the Reconquest—Castile directly confronted Moorish Granada until 1492. Furthermore, it was Cisneros, the Queen's confessor, who largely animated the African campaigns against the infidel Turks and

Moslems. And it was with the Castilian sovereign that the expeditions which claimed dominion over millions of pagan Amerinds were initially associated. In her major foreign ventures, therefore, Isabella's policy reflected not only politico-military vicissitudes of statecraft but also spiritual responsibilities in the face of non-Christian multitudes. After Columbus had assigned three hundred Indians to forced labor, it was as the imperious agent of the Church Universal that Isabella demanded: "By what authority does the Admiral give my vassals away?"

If Isabella, in her enterprises to the south and overseas to the west, symbolizes the spiritualist, medieval component of the emergent Spanish empire, then Ferdinand, whose Aragón was engaged to the east and north, represents a secular, Renaissance counterpart. His holdings (the Balearics, Sardinia, Sicily, Naples) and his Italian and Navarrese campaigns confined his problems of rule, alliance and warfare to the European, Christian community. Isabella presented the unity of spiritually intransigent Christendom to infidel and pagan. Ferdinand was committed to the shifting, amoral statecraft of competing Christian princes in maintenance and expansion of a domain which, within its Christian context, was diversely composed.

Ferdinand ruled under transitional conditions which precluded resorting for authority to Isabella's Thomistic sanction or to statist apologetics. Managing with sheer personal verve and cunning, he was, in the fullest sense, Machiavellian. . . .

Spanish conquistadors, colonizers and catechizers, then, carried with them to American shores this dual heritage: medieval and Renaissance, Thomistic and Machiavellian. . . . For half a century after Isabella's death in 1504 Spanish New World administration hovered between medieval and Renaissance orientations. . . . After Philip II came to power in 1556, the structure of the Spanish American empire assumed the cast which, for purposes of this essay, it kept until c. 1810. That cast I describe as dominantly Thomistic, with recessive Machiavellian characteristics. . . .

In the 1570's, by extending the Inquisition to America and by declaring Church patronage inalienable from the crown, Philip set his governance definitively within a larger framework of divine law, imbuing his own and his agents' directives with spiritual purpose. No entry was left for the atomistic tolerance that England, despite its state religion, had already begun to evince. . . .

The crown considered the political and social hierarchy to be energized at every level and in every department. As Indian peoples were absorbed, for example, they were not indiscriminately reduced to a common stratum. Certain of their leaders retained prestige in the post-conquest society, and many low-born Spaniards raised their own status by marrying caciques' daughters. . . .

To be sure, the social hierarchy had its anomalies. Creoles (American-born whites or near-whites) rarely received the prestige and the economic and political opportunities that were officially assured them. Mestizos, mulattoes, Indians and Negroes, on the contrary, occasionally found a social fluidity that they could not officially have expected. Broadly speaking, however, a man's status was defined somewhat fixedly by his occupation and by his place and condition of birth. Transferral from one status to another (*e.g.:* an Indian who passed from mission to *encomienda,* a Negro from slave to free status, or a mestizo to the creole nobility) generally entailed official sanction and registration.

The multiplicity of judicial systems underscored the static, functionally compartmented nature of society. The fact that they—like the several hierarchies of lay and clerical administrators—constantly disputed each other's spheres of influence only served to reaffirm the king's authority as ultimate reconciler. Nuclear elements—such as municipalities or even individual Indians—as well as highly placed officers could appeal directly to the king, or to his proxy, the viceroy, for redress of certain grievances. The king, even though he might be an inarticulate near-imbecile like Charles II, was symbolic throughout his realm as the guarantor of status. In Thomistic idiom, all parts of society were ordered to the whole as the imperfect to the perfect. This ordering, inherently the responsibility of the whole multitude, devolved upon the king as a public person acting in their behalf, for the task of ordering to a given end fell to the agent best placed and fitted for the specific function. . . .

The Spanish empire, to be sure, could scarcely avert contagion from the post-medieval world in which it existed and for which it was in part responsible. The Jesuits, who had received extensive privileges overseas for the very purpose of bolstering the empire's moral and religious base, were outstandingly versed in modernism. An "enlightened" Bourbon regime expelled them in 1767 less for their reactionary perversity than for their shrewd, disciplined commercial activities and their faith-defying "probabilist" dialectics.

Spanish American bullion was a lodestar for foreign merchants. Introduced as contraband or else covertly within the Spanish system itself, the wares of Dutch, French and English were temptingly cheap, well-made and abundant. They, like the fiscal demands of the mother country, were a constant incentive for creoles to organize local economies from which bullion and exportable surplus might readily be factored out. The calculating acquisitiveness of capitalism, if not its institutions for unlimited accrual, was frequently in evidence.

Moreover, Indian and Negro burden-bearers were, unlike the medieval serf, never fully identified with the historical and cultural ethos of their masters. For this reason they suffered more from the emergent exploitative psychology than, perhaps, post-medieval peasants who remained bound to the land. The African received no comprehensive protective code until 1789. And the very laws that assured the Indian status in return for fixed services could in practice be perverted, rendering him servile to an *encomendero* or a royal agent (*corregidor*). Indeed, the existence of Thomistic guarantees for the common man can be confirmed only by examining Spain's New World experience in selected eras and locales, or by comparing it en bloc with other European ventures in the Antilles and North America.

Yet however strongly such "recessive" Machiavellian, proto-capitalist or secularistic traits might erupt, the underpinning of the empire—social, economic, political, intellectual—bore a rubric of the earlier era. Eighteenth-century Bourbon reforms (the notable ones being those of Charles III, 1759–88) did little to alter this generalization. Some reforms—like the intendant system—were superimposed on the old structure, [and] caused added confusion. . . . Others—like the Caracas Company, a more modern and enterprising trade monopoly—found harsh opposition because their services entailed strict enforcement of regulations which a more adaptive, personalistic regime of local control had traditionally winked at.

The hierarchical, multiform, pre-capitalist Spanish America of 1800 was ill prepared for the ways of enlightened despotism, still less for those of Lockean constitutionalism.

The Republican Period

That the heterogeneous Spanish American realm was for three centuries relatively free from civil strife and separatist outbreaks must largely be explained by a steadfast loyalty to the politico-spiritual symbol of the crown. Even the sporadic Indian revolts of the eighteenth century were directed not against the Catholic sovereign and imperium but against malfeasance of local agents. . . .

Not until 1809, during Spain's Napoleonic interregnum, did local juntas appear overseas. Yet even then their autonomy, in expectation of a legitimist restoration, was provisional. Only when the ad hoc "liberal" Cortes, established in unoccupied Spain, tried to reduce Spanish America from viceregal to colonial status did the independence campaign, championed by a few firebrands, gather momentum.

Ferdinand VII was restored in 1814. But in the face of the independence movement, his character and policy discredited both himself and the Church, whose support he retained. For Spanish America the Thomistic keystone had been withdrawn. Efforts to supplant it, on a continental basis or even within regional blocs, were vain. No creole caudillo and no prince of European or Inca lineage could command universal fealty or age-old spiritual sanction. A Thomistic sovereign could not be created *ex nihilo,* and Spanish America's centrifugal separatism was for the first time unleashed.

Another idiom than the Thomistic is therefore needed to be played off against the republican experience. Hitherto the most satisfying analyses have been those that attribute Spanish American instability to the imposition of French-, British- and American-type constitutions upon peoples whose illiteracy, poverty, provincialism, political inexperience and social inequalities rendered ineffectual the mechanisms of constitutional democracy. This somewhat negative view, however, does not fully draw one into the fabric of Spanish American politics. If postulates of the Enlightenment were not relevant to that milieu, how, in a positive sense, may we comprehend it?

The answer this essay proposes is that at the moment when the Thomistic component became "recessive," the Machiavellian component, latent since the sixteenth century, became "dominant.". . .

Machiavelli was born into an "Age of Despots." Italian city states had lost their moral base; they no longer shared a common Christian ethos. The pope had become one of many competing temporal rulers. Machiavelli perceived that the mercenary "companies of adventure" of his time, unlike national militias, were undependable since they lacked any larger loyalty. They could be used to further intrigues of statecraft, but not to wage open and steady warfare. The Italian was effective only in duelling and individual combat.

Like Machiavelli, the Spanish American nationbuilder of c. 1825 had to contend with nucleated "city states," the rural masses being passive and inarticulate. The absence of any communities intermediate between such nuclei and the erstwhile imperium had been revealed by the autonomous urban juntas of 1809–10. Only the somewhat arbitrary boundaries of colonial administration defined the new nations territorially. Only virulent sectionalism could define them operatively. The Church, once coterminous with the State, had become the intruding handmaiden of a hostile sovereign power (Spain). For lack of a politico-spiritual commonalty, sources and directions of leadership were wholly fortuitous. The consequent emergence of opportunist caudillos—as of Italy's city tyrants—deranged the predictable interplay of hierarchical class interests.

The Spanish American who held to constitutionalism and avowed the existence in fact of a state-community was swept away before winds of personalism. Mexico's Gómez Farías, vice-president under Santa Anna, was a statesman who, despite his energy and dedication, would not infract "the principles of public and private morality," before which, wrote his contemporary, Mora, vanished "his indomitable force of character." Why did he not cast out the treacherous Santa Anna? "Because the step was unconstitutional [:] . . . a famous reason which has kept the reputation of Señor Farías in a very secondary place at best and caused the nation to retrogress half a century."[1]

A similar case was Rivadavia, Argentina's first president and proponent of bourgeois democracy and economic liberalism. His plans and principles had been no match for provincial *caudillismo.* The exiled statesman wrote sadly from Paris in 1830 (shortly before the personalist tyranny of Rosas):

> In my opinion what retards regular and stable advance in those republics stems from the vacillations and doubts that deprive all institutions of that moral force which is indispensable to them and can be given only by conviction and decision. It is evident to me, and would be easy to demonstrate, that the upheavals of our country spring much more immediately from lack of public spirit and of cooperation among responsible men in sustaining order and laws than from attacks of ungovernable, ambitious persons without merit or fitness and of indolent coveters.[2]

Machiavelli's writings are the handbook *par excellence* for the leader who could cope with "lack of public spirit and of cooperation among responsible men." . . . On nearly every page of Machiavelli appears practical advice which almost seems distilled from the careers of scores of Spanish American caudillos. Of crucial importance is the leader's commanding physical presence. In time of sedition he should ". . . present himself before the multitude with all possible grace and dignity, and attired with all the insignia of his rank, so as to inspire more respect. . . . [For] there is no better or safer way of appeasing an excited mob than the presence of some man of imposing appearance and highly respected" (*Discourses,* I, liv). Among countless leaders and incidents one recalls the moment when Bolivia's ruthless Melgarejo, with six men, entered the palace where his rival, Belzu, was celebrating a coup d'état. The intruder, icily calm, shot the President, then with imperious presence faced and overawed the mob in whose throats the shouts of victory for Belzu had scarcely died away.

The personalist leader must be physically disciplined, skilled in warfare, and "learn the nature of the land, how steep the mountains are, how the valleys debouch, where the plains lie, and understand the nature of rivers and swamps" (*Prince,* XIV; see also *Discourses,* III, xxxix). This is almost a page from the autobiography of Páez, who knew Venezuela's vast *llanos* (inland plains) like the palm of his hand, a knowledge that confounded the royalists in 1817 and later earned respect for him as caudillo of the new republic. Writing of an assault against the Spaniards, Páez recalled:

> Necessity obliged us not only to fight men but to challenge the obstacles opposed by nature. Counting on these, we proposed to turn to our advantage the impediments that gave the enemy surety and trust in his position, for to no one would it occur that in that season cavalry troops could sortie from the lower Apure to cross so much inundated terrain and especially the many streams and five rivers, all at the period of overflow.[3]

This telluric, earthbound quality so vital to Spanish American leaders was matched in Argentina's Quiroga and San Martín, Uruguay's Artigas, Mexico's Pancho Villa, Venezuela's Bolívar, Peru's Santa Cruz and innumerable others. Their guerrilla warfare was a far cry from the chessboard strategy and diplomatic power alignments of Europe. . . .

[But] how is it . . . that Spanish American caudillos or governments have in certain countries and eras, achieved political stability in the face of this New World brand of social and moral centrifugalism? I define three essential modes of stability, which are categorized here merely for schematic purposes and with the understanding that the "pure" type never occurs. By way of further analogy I suggest a correspondence between these types and the three "legitimations of domination" which Max Weber distinguishes in his essay, "Politics as a Vocation."[4]

The first mode of stability is furnished by the Machiavellian leader who asserts himself by dynamic personalism and shrewd self-identification with local "original principles," though without ever relinquishing government, as Machiavelli would have wished, "to the charge of many." The system remains subordinate to the man and unless a suitable "heir" is available, which happens infrequently, it falls with him. Here we perhaps have Weber's charismatic leader with the personal gift of grace, who flouts patriarchal traditionalism and the stable economy, whose justice is Solomonic rather than statutory, who maintains authority "solely by proving his strength in life." One recent writer, Blanksten, holds that the caudillo and charismatic types correspond.[5] George S. Wise, on the other hand, claims that the "stratagem and chicanery" of at least one caudillo (Venezuela's Guzmán Blanco) revealed an insecurity and lack of purpose precluding the oracular, prophetic qualities that he attributes to charismatic legitimacy.[6] Weber's specific consideration of the condottiere type leads me to feel, however, that charisma need not invariably imply "anointment."

The charismatic leader may be dedicated to molding the self-perpetuating traditions of a state-community—for example, Bolívar's vision of federated Andean republics, Morazán's Central American union, the constitutionalism of Mexico's Juárez and perhaps the quasi-theocracy of Ecuador's García Moreno. Or, which is more usual, he may set about exploiting the country as his private fief. In the decades after independence such a caudillo would win the army's allegiance (or create his own plebeian militia), then assert control over the several classes by blandishment, personal magnetism or threat of force—the method depending, in the case of each segment of society, on "original principles" and the leader's own antecedents. Examples are Argentina's Rosas, Mexico's Santa Anna, Guatemala's Carrera, Paraguay's Francia. (Venezuela's Páez seems to fall between the two sub-types.)

Toward the end of the century the exploitation of new sources of mineral and agricultural wealth, together with a strong influx of foreign investments, gave caudillos more dependable leverage for control. Though force and personalism did not go in the discard, financial resources and the protective favor of foreigners allowed the leader to govern by "remote control." He adopted bourgeois bon ton and even paid lip service to constitutionalism. Such men were Venezuela's Guzmán Blanco, Mexico's Porfirio Díaz, Guatemala's Barrios.

Intensified economic activity might also give rise

to a second type of state: a modified version of laissez-faire democracy. This development, which Weber calls legitimation through bureaucratic competence and public respect for rational legal statutes, has been rare in Latin America, even in hybrid form. Argentina affords an example. In that country after 1860, and especially after 1880, the pampas experienced a torrential land rush, occasioned by a world demand for meat and grains and by improved methods of husbandry, transportation and refrigeration. Though the lion's share of the benefits accrued to an oligarchy of large proprietors, many immigrants took small homesteads in the northern provinces; moreover, the expanding economy created niches for articulate, middle-class city dwellers. Argentines were, relative to Latin America, homogeneous and white. A growing nucleus identified its interests with the stability and prosperity of the nation-community, even though the positions of highest socio-economic authority were already preempted.

Given Argentina's economic direction and momentum, it remained for a series of statesmen-presidents merely to encourage and guide its development, in tolerable conformance with the Lockean Constitution of 1853. Eventual malfeasance in high office led, not back to tyranny, but to the emergence in 1890 of the Radical (liberal, middle-class) Party, to free suffrage and the secret ballot, and finally to Radical control of the presidency (1916–1930). Twentieth-century Radical leaders, however, reined back certain socio-economic forces from a natural course by acquiescing in the continued entrenchment of the landowning oligarchy. Only then did thwarted urban classes fall prey to demagoguery of an ominous breed—and to Juan Domingo Perón.

A third solution for anarchy has been a full-scale implementing of the Machiavellian blueprint. A personalist leader emerges (as in the first case), but goes on successfully to create a system, larger than himself, that is faithful to "original principles." In Spanish America such a system is larger than the leader, to frame a paradox, only when it *recognizes* the leader to be larger than itself. This statement has Thomistic implications, and the more successful Spanish American constitutions have translated into modern idiom certain principles under which the viceroyalties enjoyed three centuries of relative stability.

This solution, insofar as it reinvigorates the body social by setting its classes, or "estates," into centrally stabilized equilibrium, is a neo-traditionalism reminiscent of Weber's third category: "the authority of the eternal yesterday." Of Mexico's present Constitution—brought into being in 1917 by Carranza, a shrewd, opportunist caudillo—Frank Tannenbaum has written:

> By implication, the Constitution recognizes that contemporary Mexican society is divided into classes, and that it is the function of the State to protect one class against another. The Constitution is therefore not merely a body of rules equally applicable to all citizens, but also a body of rules specially designed to benefit and protect given groups. The community is not made up of citizens only; it is also made up of classes with special rights within the law. What has in fact happened is that the old idea of the "estates" has been re-created in Mexican law. The pattern of the older Spanish State, divided into clergy, nobility, and commons, has been re-created in modern dress, with peasants, workers, and capitalists replacing the ancient model. This is not done formally, but it is done sufficiently well to make it evident that a very different kind of social structure is envisioned in the law, even if only by implicit commitment, than that in a liberal democracy. . . .

> The Revolution has certainly increased effective democracy in Mexico. It has also increased, both legally and economically, the dependence of the people and of the communities upon the federal government and the President. The older tradition that the king rules has survived in modern dress: the President rules. He rules rather than governs, and must do so if he is to survive in office and keep the country at peace.[7]

I have reserved any mention of Chile until now because its history usefully illustrates our three political types as well as a twentieth-century variant which has yet to be considered. Like its sister nations, Chile fell after independence into anarchic factionalism. A revolution of 1829–30, however, brought the conservatives into power; at their head was Diego Portales who, as a business man, was atypical among Spanish American nation-builders. Portales appreciated more keenly than most the need for disciplined, predictable conditions of life and was more empirical in perceiving that liberal slogans and mechanisms were meaningless within an aristocratic, agrarian society. His views were reflected in the centralized, quasi-monarchic Constitution of 1833 which, by recognizing Chile's hierarchic social anatomy and at the same time guaranteeing status and justice for the component members, lent the government a supra-personalist sanction. Portales himself did not become president, but wisely designated a military hero, General Prieto, whose prestige, aristocratic bearing and benevolence, traditionalism and religiosity further enhanced the office with an aura of legitimacy.[8] None of Chile's presidents was overthrown for sixty years, while the Constitution lasted nearly a century.

Portales, alone among his Spanish American contemporaries, brought to fulfillment the policy of "the compleat Machiavellian." As the century advanced, however, a leavening took place within the system he had fathered. A law of 1852 abolished primogeniture, infusing new blood and interests into the landed oligarchy. Mineral exploitation in the north and the activities of German immigrants in the south posted new directions for economic change and opportunity. The consequent desire for more effective economic competition provided a rallying cry for enthused liberals emerging from the new (1843) University. So too did growing dissatisfaction with the constitutional ban on public exercise of non-Catholic religions.

At length the Chilean élite, larger and more diversely composed than in 1833, revolted against centralized, one-man rule by ejecting President Balmaceda from office in 1891. This élite then governed through its congressional representatives, and the fitfulness of public policy for the next thirty years reflected the jostling of private economic interests.

As in Argentina, however, the modified laissez-faire state could not indefinitely subsist if it was to victimize the increasingly self-aware lower classes, such as, in Chile's case, the copper and nitrate workers. The little man eventually found his champion in President Arturo Alessandri (1920–1925, 1932–1938).[9]

Alessandri's and subsequent administrations represent an attitude toward government that has in this century become universal throughout Spanish America. It has in varying degrees infiltrated the three earlier systems, or combinations thereof, wherever they exist. Essentially, it is a recognition of the need to build into public policies a dynamics for socio-economic change. This need stems from two interrelated phenomena: first, the urbanization and industrialization of hitherto extractive economies; second, the growing self-awareness and articulateness of the citizenry at large.

The Spanish American leader, whether dictator or democrat, is fast adopting a broader, more sophisticated view of how modern political power must be won, maintained and exercised. He also knows that, regardless of any nationalistic rhetoric to which he may be committed, he must import more and more blueprints and technical solutions from abroad. Such solutions, however—whether socialism, fascism, exchange control or river valley authorities—take

on a new complexion as they flash into amalgam with conditions of life wholly different from those by which they were engendered. Not only is the receiving ethos broadly speaking *sui generis,* but in a strictly technological sense the particular juxtapositions of ancient and modern in Spanish America are quite beyond the experience of any of the capitalist countries. Therefore slogans of foreign systems ring far differently upon Spanish American ears than their originators imagine.

In fact, Peru's *Aprista* movement and Mexico's forty-year-long "Revolution" attest that Spanish America is starting to generate its own credos. Sometimes, as with Perón's *justicialismo,* they are heartlessly cynical rhetoric. At best they designate, as did our own New Deal, a piecemeal pragmatism, uncommitted to the mysticism or fixed morality prescribed for the New World by Hegel. Yet the fact that Spanish America is by tradition accustomed and by economic necessity forced to rely heavily on official planning, intervention and protection has on occasion led its statesmen to a "total view" (to be distinguished carefully in nature and intent from a totalitarian view). From such views flow social, economic and cultural agenda which, however imperfect of execution, uniquely contribute to an understanding of man-in-community.

Co-existent, indeed, with Spanish America's atomism . . . is a sense of commonalty, however latent, deriving in large part from its Catholicity (in the ingrained, cultural sense) and from its agrarian, Negro and Indian heritage. Native to this commonalty is an ethic upon which the hyper-rationalist logos of the industrial world seems able to make only limited and conditional encroachments. The prediction is sometimes heard among Spanish Americans that this logos will in the long run exhaust itself; that their descendants will be freer to weave certain principles of a pre-Machiavellian age into the new patterns of an entering one; that the promise which erratically flashes in the travail of twentieth-century Mexican democracy is yet to be realized.

NOTES

1. José María Luis Mora, *Ensayos, ideas y retratos* (Mexico City, 1941), xx, 184.

2. Bernadino Rivadavia, *Páginas de un estadista* (Buenos Aires, 1945), 137 (letter to a politician of Upper Peru, 14 March 1830).

3. José Antonio Páez, *Autobiografía,* 2 vols. (New York, 1946; re-issue of 1869 edition), I, 132.

4. H. H. Gerth and C. W. Mills (eds.), *From Max Weber: Essays in Sociology* (London, 1947), 78ff.

5. George I. Blanksten, *Ecuador: Constitutions and Caudillos* (Berkeley and Los Angeles, 1951), 35–36.

6. George S. Wise, *Caudillo, A Portrait of Antonio Guzmán Blanco* (New York, 1951), 161–163.

7. Frank Tannenbaum, *Mexico: The Struggle for Peace and Bread* (New York, 1950), 101, 118.

8. Ricardo Donoso, *Las ideas políticas en Chile* (Mexico City, 1946), 64–114; Alberto Edwards Vives, *La fronda aristocrática en Chile* (Santiago, 1936), 39–47.

9. The dictatorial interregnum of Carlos Ibáñez (1925–1931) can be considered as Chile's nearest approach to the first, or pure caudillo type of rule. His advent is partially explained by the post-World War I collapse of the world nitrate market, which impaired the mainspring of parliamentary, laissez-faire government and left Chile (since Alessandri had not yet given shape and momentum to his social democracy) in its primordial anarchy. Ibáñez, though sometimes referred to as a "man on horseback," effectively used modern technocratic methods and was not a caudillo of the old stamp—to which his re-election in 1952 bears witness.

86

The Ideology and Dynamics of Japanese Fascism

Masao Maruyama

What mainly characterizes the formation of the Japanese radical fascist movement from the Blood Pledge Corps Incident until the February Incident is that until the very last its practical managers had no mass organization and showed no particular zeal for organizing the masses. Rather they made it from first to last a movement of a limited number of "patriots." The heroism, or the consciousness of the "patriot" bound up with the Japanese fascist movement, acted as a check on its development on a mass basis. For example, Tachibana Kōsaburō in his *Principles of the Japanese Patriotic Reformation* writes as follows:

> What I now emphasize, and ask you all to engrave on your hearts, is the cardinal fact that a nation-wide social reformation can be initiated only by a group of patriots who are capable of pursuing the great aim of saving the country and relieving the people in accordance with the will of Heaven. . . . Needless to say, the number of patriots who can be found to initiate this great task at the sacrifice of their lives will never be large. But it is also a fact that scattered among all classes of society there are patriots who can carry out the will of Heaven if it chooses them to do so. . . . People who call for reformation must be willing to sacrifice their lives for the people. Only a group of patriots who would sacrifice their lives for the great aim of saving the country and relieving the people can be the leaders of a national reform movement. In view of the present state of Japan, such patriots can be found only among you military men,

and it is above all the farmers who will respond to your call. This is why I must ask you to contemplate deeply and to make an iron decision.

In this way Tachibana whipped up the strong patriotic spirit of the military class, which was already imbued with what Nietzsche called "the pathos of distance."

Because of this basic idea the movement naturally developed as the visionary idealism of a minority and failed to organize and mobilize the masses. This was allied to other distinctive characteristics of the Japanese fascist movement, such as its extreme fantasy, abstraction, and lack of plan. The radical fascist movement was always governed by the mythological optimism that, if patriots led the way by destructive action, a future course would become clear. For instance, the thought of Inoue Nisshō, the leader of the Blood Pledge Corps Incident, is described in the court judgement as follows:

> To overthrow the old system of organization is a destructive or negative act. To establish the new system of organization is a constructive or positive act. Without destruction, however, there can be no construction. Since ultimate denial is the same as genuine affirmation, destruction is itself construction, and the two are one and inseparable.[1]

During the trial Inoue himself stated: "It is more correct to say that I have no systematized ideas. I transcend reason and act completely upon intuition." He deliberately rejected any theory for constructive planning after the rising. . . .

Thus the pattern of the radical fascist movement was almost invariably characterized by fantasy and

From Masao Maruyama, *Thought and Behavior in Modern Japanese Politics* (London: Oxford University Press, 1963), pp. 52–53, 56–58, 76–83. Reprinted by permission of the publisher.

lack of realism. This is best revealed by the fact that the mobilization of one thousand six hundred troops in the February Incident resulted in nothing more than the murder of a few elderly men.

This point also marks a clear difference between fascism in Japan and Germany. As a result of the strong survival in its ideology of a medieval Bakumatsu patriotism of the type exemplified by Kumoi Tatsuo, this sort of patriotism came to appear in the concrete fascist movement as well. Democracy was flatly rejected by Japanese fascism, but not by the Nazis. The Nazis decried Weimar democracy, but not democracy in general. Rather the aim of the Nazis was to stigmatize Weimar and Anglo-American democracy as a Jewish plutocracy and to proclaim themselves a "true" Nordic democracy. Of course this claim was simply "the democratic disguise for dictatorship," to borrow the words of Professor Miyazawa. However, the fact that it was constrained to appear in a democratic disguise reveals that even in Germany democracy had already struck ineradicable roots in the political ideology of the nation.

Hitler was strongly opposed to the monarchism of some Junkers, and was himself fundamentally a republican. In *Mein Kampf* he sharply distinguishes monarchic patriotism from the patriotism that loves the Fatherland and the people, and he ridicules the tendency to worship State power for its own sake as animalian worship. He maintained that "States exist for men, and not men for States." Such a way of thinking is accepted as a matter of course only after the experience of a *bourgeois* democratic revolution. This naturally gave the Nazi movement a clear mass character from the outset. Again, it is stated in *Mein Kampf* that "the previous Pan-Germanism was splendid as an ideology but failed because it did not possess a mass organization."

But the Japanese fascist movement from below remained to the last a movement of a small number of patriots—visionary, fanatic, and lacking in plan. These are the striking tendencies in the formation of the Japanese fascist movement. Of course mythological elements and the idea of an *élite* are common to all fascist ideologies. The differences in the degree to which these were held in Japan, however, are so marked as to amount to qualitative differences.

Distinctive Characteristics in the Social Support of Japanese Fascism

If the military and the bureaucracy were the driving forces of fascism, which social classes showed a positive sympathy towards its development? In Germany and Italy, as everywhere else, fascism was a movement of the lower-middle class. With obvious exceptions a large proportion of the intellectuals were also positive supporters of Nazism and fascism.

Roughly speaking, we can say that the middle strata provided the social support for the fascist movement in Japan as well. But in the case of Japan a more elaborate analysis is necessary. The middle or petty *bourgeois* stratum in Japan can be divided into the following two types: first, the social class that comprises small factory owners, building contractors, proprietors of retail shops, master carpenters, small landowners, independent farmers, school teachers (especially in primary schools), employees of village offices, low-grade officials, Buddhist and Shinto priests; secondly, persons like urban salaried employees, so-called men of culture, journalists, men in occupations demanding higher knowledge such as professors and lawyers, and university and college students. The distinction between these two types is especially significant when we consider the fascist movement in Japan.

In Japan it is mainly the first type that provides the social foundation of fascism. If the second group represents intellectuals in the proper sense, the first group might be called the pseudo- or sub-intellectuals. It is the pseudo-intellectuals that create the so-called voice of the people. Of course among Japanese intellectuals of the second type the number of people who persisted in an openly anti-fascist attitude to the last was comparatively small. Most people adapted themselves to the process of fascization and followed in its wake. On the other hand, they were certainly not positive advocates or the driving force of the fascist movement. Rather their mood was generally one of vague antipathy towards it, an antipathy that amounted almost to passive resistance.[2]. . .

Why in Japan did fascism from below, the fascist movement that arose among civilians, fail to grasp hegemony? This is a crucial question and any answer must emphasize the following point. In the process of fascization the strength of influences from the lower stratum of society is prescribed by the extent to which a democratic movement has taken place in the country concerned.[3] In Italy before the March on Rome the Socialist Party was the leading party in the Assembly. In the case of Germany we note again the powerful influence of the Social Democratic and Communist Parties just before the Nazi revolution. Both the Nazis and the Fascists could draw in the masses only by flaunting themselves as the exponents of true socialism and as the party of the workers. This bespeaks the power of the mass movement in Germany and even in Italy, and is the reason that popular bases had to be preserved to some extent in the fascist organization, if only for deception.

How does this compare with the situation in our country? Of course in Japan too the labour movement had made an unprecedented advance from about 1926, and, because of the crisis in rural tenancy disputes, had increased rapidly year by year. As we have seen, the Japanese fascist movement flourished in the background of these conditions and appeared on the scene as a reaction to the left-wing movement. In this respect it can be said to follow the rules. But today it is quite clear to any observer that the left-wing movement did not in fact permeate to the workers and farmers to a degree comparable with that in Germany and Italy. It would be going too far to suggest that the overwhelming influence of Marxism was a phenomenon confined to the educated class—to the lecture platforms and journals that this class supported; its power was felt in many other areas also. Yet it is doubtful whether the menace of bolshevism in Japan was ever as real as the ruling class and the conservative circles proclaimed.[4]

The progress of Japanese fascist transformation was very gradual. There was no March on Rome and no 30 January 1933; this suggests the weakness of resistance from below. There were no organized labour or proletarian parties to be smashed. Here we should note the form of Japanese monopoly capital itself.[5] When we consider the population structure in 1930, directly before the Manchurian Incident when the Japanese fascist movement suddenly became vigorous, we find that the number of labourers employed in workshops of five or more people was 2,032,000, and the number of casual workers 1,963,-000. In contrast, employees in commerce numbered 2,200,000, government officials and company employees 1,800,000, and small traders 1,500,000. One understands how small in numbers the true proletariat was compared with the medium and small businessmen and the salaried class. As another example, in the *League of Nations Statistical Yearbook* for 1926 Japan's industrial population (including domestic industries) is given as 19.4 per cent of the total population. When this is compared with, for example, Britain (39.7 per cent), France (33.9 per cent), Belgium (39.5 per cent), Holland (36.1 per cent), and Germany (35.8 per cent), it becomes clear how inferior the industrialization of Imperial Japan was compared with that of the European capitalist nations.

At the peak of the Japanese social structure stood monopoly capital, rationalized to the highest degree. But at its base were crammed together minute-scale agriculture with production methods that had scarcely changed since feudal times and household industries almost entirely dependent on the labour of members of the family. The most advanced and the most primitive techniques existed side by side in a stratified industrial structure. Production forms of different historical stages overlay and supplemented each other. This was a decisive obstacle to the growth of an organized democratic movement in Japanese politics. On the one hand there was the stubborn rule of absolutism, on the other the development of monopoly capital, both in agreement and reinforcing each other.

This may also have determined the fate of the Japanese fascist movement as we have observed it above. Here is revealed the internal weakness of the fascism from below in Japan. In the Japanese right wing, pedigrees ranged from the most advanced Nazi type to the almost pure feudal *rōnin* type distantly connected with the Dark Ocean Society. Few of them had ever received the baptism of modernity. The dominant type was not so much fascist as Bakumatsu *rōnin*.[6] As Freda Utley points out in *Japan's Feet of Clay*, the right-wing leaders were a cross between the *rōnin* of the feudal period and Chicago gangsters.

The character of the right-wing movement is epitomized by the fact that a personality like Tōyama Mitsuru was one of its most prominent figures. If we compare the way of life of Hitler and Mussolini with that of Tōyama, we should find that the factor of rational planning in the lives of the former was lacking in Tōyama's case. *A True Portrait of the Venerable Tōyama Mitsuru*[7] records various statements by Mr. Tōyama; the following is written about his younger days:

> That was when I was about twenty-six, in the prime of my youth. Coming up to Tokyo, I rented a house with five or six companions. Starting with umbrella and shoes, gradually everything disappeared. Even the bedding disappeared. But I was the only one who went naked; the others had to have something on. I took a lunch-box and ate it. I didn't pay. So the waitress from the lunch-box shop came to dun me. When I came out of the cupboard stark naked, she jumped with fright and withdrew. Even if I didn't eat for two or three days, I thought nothing of it.

He feels a kind of pride in not returning borrowed money and in repulsing people by such methods. He also speaks of warding off high-interest moneylenders in this way. However we may regard him, he does not belong in the category of the modern man. There is no trace of modern rationality here. In this respect Tōyama is typical of rightist personalities.

When we look at the internal construction of right-wing groups, we find that they mostly have a paternal boss organization. As we have seen, a united front never emerged from the right-wing movement in spite of fairly advantageous conditions. Unity was constantly intoned, but as soon as they had joined together, they split and exchanged abuse. Since they were associations centered on a paternal boss, they could only be small-scale; each struggled to elevate its own deity. Many groups emerged, each centered on its small master. Among them were gangs of ruffians in disguise. In the case of the Nazis, too, the storm-troops were strongly tinged by the gang element; still, for better or for worse, they had organizational rationality and did not constantly unite and divide as in Japan.

This pre-modern character may be attributed not only to the right-wing groups but to the reforming officers who joined them and played important roles. The base in which they fabricated their plots was almost always a house of assignation[8] or a restaurant. While drinking saké and bewailing the depraved state of the country, they no doubt secretly cherished in their hearts the image of the Bakumatsu patriot who sang: "Drunken, I lay my head in a beautiful girl's lap. Waking, I grasp the power of the whole realm."

In the final analysis it was the historical circumstance that Japan had not undergone the experience of a *bourgeois* revolution that determined this character of the fascist movement. From a different angle it reveals the marked continuity between the period of party government and the fascist period in Japan. The pre-modern character of right-wing leaders and organizations is a characteristic that can also be found to a lesser extent in the established political parties. The Japanese political parties, instead of behaving as the champions of democracy, had from an early date compromised with the absolutist forces, adapted themselves to it, and were contented with a sham constitutional system. Hence the oligarchic structure that had existed since the Meiji era was able to transform itself into a fascist structure without the need for a fascist "revolution."

When the Nazis got control, they eradicated not only the socialist political parties but also the Central Party and all other existing political forces. But in Japan the forces that had previously held sway were not eradicated (*gleichschaltet*). The previous political forces were mostly left as they were and

absorbed into the fascist structure. As we have seen, almost all the established political parties were absorbed into the Imperial Rule Assistance Political Association. This is why those who were purged after the war included so many members of the established pre-war political parties and the bureaucracy.

It cannot be clearly stated from what point of time the fascist period began. The totalitarian system gradually came to completion within the framework of the State structure determined by the Meiji constitution. The established political parties had neither the spirit nor the will for an all-out war against fascism. Instead they frequently performed the role of actively promoting it. For example, the Seiyū Kai Cabinet of April 1927 to July 1929 headed by General Tanaka Giichi was supposed to be a purely political party Cabinet. Yet in domestic policy it put severe pressure on the left-wing movements and further restricted freedom of speech, publication, and association by revising the Law for the Maintenance of Public Peace in the form of the Emergency Decree. Abroad it adopted the Tanaka "positive diplomacy," dispatching troops to China on the occasion of the Tsinan Incident. Until it collapsed after getting entangled in the assassination of Chang Tso-lin, its course of action almost appears to be that of a fascist government. These domestic and overseas measures are extremely significant in the light of the later domination of fascism. Thereafter, the Seiyū Kai also pressed the Hamaguchi Cabinet fiercely on the issue of the infringement of the supreme command involved in the London Disarmament Treaty. Again, when the organ theory of the Emperor became an issue, the Seiyū Kai President, Mr. Suzuki, personally led the movement for the clarification of the national polity in the House of Representatives.

It is no exaggeration to say that the Seiyū Kai made important contributions to the fascist transformation of Japanese politics; for it is well known that the issue of the infringement of the supreme command was a great stimulus to the fascist movement. Again, in the circumstances described above, the issue of the organ theory implied a denial of the theoretical basis of party government. For a political party to take the lead in rejecting the theory was nothing less than suicide. Such was the tragi-comic role of the established political parties.

The Hamaguchi and Wakatsuki Minsei Tō Cabinets, which succeeded the Tanaka Cabinet, have the strongest complexion of *bourgeois* liberalism in the recent history of Japanese politics. Yet they crumbled just after the Manchurian Incident because of fascist trends from within the Cabinet in the form of the coalition Cabinet movement by the Home Minister, Mr. Adachi, and his supporters. Needless to say, the anti-fascist stand of the Minsei Tō does not suffice to draw a clear line between it and the Seiyū Kai. For example, when the Anti-War Pact was ratified by the Tanaka Cabinet, the Minsei Tō as the party in opposition joined the right-wing groups in a vigorous attack on the government on the grounds that the words "in the name of the people" were incompatible with the national polity.

It seems that the Seiyū Kai took its revenge over the issue of the London Disarmament Treaty. Both parties stopped at nothing in the struggle for political power, and joined hands with any forces to overthrow a government of the other party. This greatly encouraged the growing political influence of the various semi-feudal forces which were already strong and independent of the Diet. The part played by the right wing of the Socialist Party in Germany and Italy was played by the Seiyū Kai and the Minsei Tō in Japan.

Of course in Japan too one cannot overlook the significance of the conversion to fascism within the proletarian movement. As I have said before, this was performed by the Akamatsu and Kamei group in the Social Mass Party and groups like Asō's, which led the Labour-Peasant Party and its successors. But from the point of view of the political parties that controlled the Diet, Japan must be regarded as having diverged one stage from Germany and Italy. With the decline of party politics in Japan the social elements that had made up the lobbyist groups largely flowed into the right-wing societies. On the other hand, in Italy for example, it was the supporters of anarchism and syndicalism who later became the centre of fascist organization.

Thus we can see that a major characteristic separating Japanese fascism from the European form was the gradation of its development. Fascism did not burst on the scene from below as it did in Italy and Germany. The leaders of Japanese fascism were not obliged to manipulate or counter any strong proletarian movement; and, in the absence of a *bourgeois* democratic background, they were able to effect a comparatively smooth consolidation of State power from above by amalgamating supporting groups that were already in existence.

To see in the political developments of the 1930s a sudden, fortuitous break, an historical perversion, in the "evolution towards democracy" is not only to overlook the fundamental continuity with the preceding period of "party government." Such a view fails to take into account the distinctive under-

current in thought and social structure that had existed in Japanese political life since the Meiji Restoration and that sanctioned the advance of Japanese fascism.

NOTES

1. Inoue was a Nichiren priest and the present proposition is derived from Buddhist philosophy.

2. In my description of the part played by the intelligentsia, too much concern with their mental posture towards the fascist movement can lead to an over-estimation of so-called negative resistance. The need at present is rather for a detailed study of the process by which, though the actions of the intelligentsia of the time were varied, they were all alike in moving towards an acquiescent acceptance of the ruling structure. A view of the intelligentsia more or less common to radical fascists can be seen in the *Prison Papers* (*Gokuchū Shuki*) of Yasuda Masaru, a defendant in the February Incident. In an analysis of the existing state of Japan, under the heading "A Discussion of the Mental Decadence of the Middle Class," he stated: "The learned classes timidly take refuge in the pursuit of personal happiness and lack the courage to act faithfully according to their beliefs, which are largely confined to the gospel of Marx. The ordinary *petit bourgeois*, on the other hand, are indulging in sensual pleasures. This must be considered a great cause in misleading the country." An inquiry was carried out in 1943 by the Tokyo Thought Measures Study Association (Tōkyō-to Shisō Taisaku Kenyū Kai) into the thought of teachers and secondary school boys in the city of Tokyo. According to this inquiry, the attitude of teachers towards the wartime education system could be broadly divided into attitudes of approval or of criticism *vis-à-vis* existing conditions. The latter could again be divided into the way of thought (which the inquiry calls a "radical attitude") which complained that educationalists were not fully aware of the present situation, that a wartime educational system should be more positively promoted, and so forth; and the one (which the inquiry calls a "conservative attitude") that was opposed to the "extremes" of the system as a whole, saying that teaching was at present excessively controlled, that it would lapse into formalism, that miscellaneous duties were too numerous and prevented study, and so forth. Leaving aside those who approved of the existing conditions (about 50 per cent of those investigated), we find that among those with a critical attitude the radicals were comparatively numerous among the younger stratum of normal school instructors (over 55 per cent).

3. This is not the only cause that determines the type as "from above" or "from below" in the process of fascist advance. See below, "Fascism—Some Problems."

4. "Bolshevization" was felt by the ruling class to be a profound menace to Imperial Japan, but it is quite another question whether the material conditions existed for a proletarian revolution. The nervous reaction to "bolshevization" occurred in the first place because it was tied up with the image of infiltration by the influence of neighbouring Russia. (In this sense the credit for bringing out the symbol of "indirect aggression," long before the American Secretary of State, Mr. Dulles, did so, goes to the Japanese ruling class.) The reason that the young officers were out-and-out anti-communists despite their resentment against the *zaibatsu* was their conception of the national polity (discussed above) and their almost instinctive sense of vocation which made it impossible for them to separate their thoughts on communism from their military-strategic standpoint towards Russia. A second factor that contributed to the fears of the ruling class was that "bolshevization" was believed to be penetrating the sons of prominent men, the intelligentsia and the university students, who formed the true *élite* of Imperial

Japan or who would do so in the future. In the *Summary of Incidents* (*Shojiken Gaiyō*), the investigation of the Police Bureau of the Home Ministry into the causes of right-wing terrorism, it is stated: "We see the importation of socialist and communist thought influenced by the Russian Revolution. . . . After the Great Earthquake [1923] graduates from colleges and high schools, the so-called educated class, were most susceptible to the baptism of bolshevist thought, and finally we see the succession of members of the Japan Communist Party who even advocate the overthrow of our splendid national polity. This has even appeared within the Imperial Army." A situation in which the organization of the workers and farmers was so slight as to present no problem, but in which the *élite* and educated class had become "bolshevized," is completely abnormal according to the laws of Marxism, and it is ironical that this abnormality should have been regarded as a fearful menace by the ruling class of Japan. As we see in the *Konoe Memorial to the Throne* (*Konoe Jōsō Bun*), what gave the rulers of Imperial Japan nightmares until the last was the "bolshevization" of the State from within rather than revolution from below. Moreover, even the so-called bolshevization of the educated class and of children from good homes had certainly not gone far enough to be alarming from the point of view of the system as a whole. The question must therefore be carried forward to the spirit and structure of Imperial Japan, which gave rise to immediate allergic reactions to the phenomena of ideological dissemination. On this point see above, "Theory and Psychology of Ultra-Nationalism."

5. Any systematic treatment of this subject must examine the distinctive characteristics of the Imperial government structure and the mechanism of the process by which loyal Imperial subjects were fostered, a process of intense homogenization and de-politicization. In Imperial Japan the two supports of structural stability were de-politicization at the bottom of society (government by men of repute, which was the basis of "good morals and manners," and the Japanese version of local self-government, which ensured it) and

trans-politicization at the apex (the transcendence of the Emperor and his officials over all political rivalries). There was a powerful inclination to regard as dangerous all trends towards political and ideological diversity that might interfere with the homogeneity of the community (the "spirit of harmony"). This tendency becomes strong in direct proportion to the acceleration of a sense that the structure is in danger. In this sense the pet saying of the fascists and national polity advocates, that "liberalism is the hotbed of communism," has a special validity. It is a general law of fascism that it always concentrates its attack on marginal ideologies in concrete situations. But since the first task of fascism—i.e. the destruction of the vanguard organizations of revolution—had already been effected in Japan under political party Cabinets, the Japanese right-wing and national polity movements were bound at an early stage to change the chief target of their attack from communism and socialism to liberalism (the "hotbed"). This distinctive character was extremely significant in Japanese political and social processes after 1932–3.

6. Bakumatsu Period: The last part of the Tokugawa Period, 1603–1867. *rōnin:* originally referred to disenfeoffed samurai (e.g. the Forty-Seven Rōnin), but later came to apply in general to adventurers, soldiers of fortune, and others who lived by their wits, courage, and readiness to break the law.

7. *Tōyama Mitsuru O no Shimmemmoku.*

8. House of assignation (*machiai*). Sometimes incorrectly described as "geisha houses," these are places traditionally used by a certain type of Japanese politician for behind-the-scenes political dealings. "Machiai politics," referring to political negotiations conducted in these houses, have a strong connotation of shadiness and corruption. Since the Meiji Period, geishas, who met their customers in these houses, frequently established close ties with Japan's political and military leaders, and some of the more intelligent ladies of this class were in a position to exert a good deal of influence.

87

Fascism, Right and Left

Hugh Seton-Watson

Twenty years after the destruction of the Third Reich, the essence of fascism is still elusive. There are at least two governments in existence today, in Spain and Portugal, which can plausibly be described as fascist. The first owed its victory in large measure to the support of Mussolini and Hitler, and in both countries official spokesmen were at one time proud

From Hugh Seton-Watson, "Fascism, Right and Left," in Walter Laqueur and George L. Mosse, eds., *International Fascism, 1920–1945* (New York: Harper & Row Publishers, 1966), pp. 183–197. Copyright 1966 by the Institute for Advanced Studies in Contemporary History. Reprinted by permission of Harper & Row, Inc., and Weidenfeld & Nicolson Ltd.

to identify themselves with fascism. Apart from this, communists freely use "fascist" as a smear-word, designed not so much to identify anything specifically fascist as to discredit persons or groups which appear, for whatever reason, to be hindering communist purposes. The word is also often used as a term of abuse by woolly-minded persons of "left-wing" views, many of whom are too young personally to have suffered, or to have faced serious danger, as a result of fascism.

Polemical and inexact use of the word has inevitably discouraged scholars. Some may be tempted to argue that it can only usefully be applied to one party and regime which have a limited but important place in the history of one country, Italy. Yet there remains a complex political and social phenomenon of the first half of the twentieth century which historians have the duty to examine. There remains a family relationship between a number of movements which had a part to play in the 1930s and 1940s. One could perhaps describe them by some neutral jargon phrase like "non-Marxist totalitarianism." But it seems to me preferable to use the word "fascism" in full awareness of its subjective and emotional elements. Scientific precision is not at present attainable, and one may doubt whether it ever will be. One can pursue a more modest aim, to throw some light, by the comparative method, on a trend and a period in history of which imprecision, irrationality, and passion are inescapable features.

Let us begin not with a definition but with an attempt to narrow the field of discussion. All fascist movements combine, I suggest, in varying proportions, a reactionary ideology and a modern mass organization. Their leaders, when in opposition, extol traditional values, but they appeal for support to the masses, and exploit any form of mass discontent that is available. In their original ideas they often closely resemble old-fashioned conservatives, but their methods of struggle, indeed their whole notion of political organization, belong not to the idealized past but to the modern age. Their outlook may be nostalgic, and it is certainly elitist, but as a political force they are more democratic than oligarchic. The study of fascism requires an understanding both of nineteenth-century European conservatism and of the social conflicts within both the advanced industrial and the underdeveloped economies which coexisted within Europe between the world wars.

There is a vast literature on European conservatism, covering its ideas, its personalities, and its political action. But comparative study has certainly not yet exhausted its possibilities. A recent publication of great merit in this field is a symposium on *The European Right,* edited by Professors Hans Rogger and Eugen Weber of the University of California in Los Angeles.[1] Though the following arguments are not a summary of its contents, and indeed I do not always agree with the interpretations of its contributors, I must express my appreciation of this book, and recommend it to all readers of this journal.

The word "reactionary," perhaps even more than the word "fascist," has become a term of abuse in political propaganda. Yet the word has a perfectly clear and legitimate meaning. A reactionary is one who wishes to resurrect the past, and reactionary ideologies are based on visions of the past, usually more mythical than real, which are intended to inspire political action in the present. A conservative, by contrast, should be one whose aim is not so much to resurrect the past as to conserve what he believes to be valuable in the traditions and institutions which still exist. In practice the difference between reactionaries and conservatives has been blurred. Reactionaries have usually called themselves conservatives. The Right in most European countries has had a reactionary wing, in some cases forming a distinct faction, in others operating within a larger conservative group.

Those ideas derived from the European Right which have been important in the intellectual formation of the leaders of fascism have been essentially nostalgic and reactionary. They may be briefly examined under the four main headings of religion, the state, the social structure, and the nation.

The identification of the church with reactionary ideas, and the tendency for reactionary spokesmen to take their stand on religion, to denounce their political opponents as enemies of God, and indeed to regard most modern ideas and institutions as works of the devil, can be found to some extent almost everywhere, but is most marked in Catholic and Orthodox countries. In England the official church was respectable and conservative, but hardly reactionary. In Germany the Lutheran church, like the Hohenzollern monarchy, was more reactionary, yet as a political factor too vacillating to be a strong bulwark of reaction. In Spain, France, Austria, and Italy the church was a powerful reactionary force. There were of course variations. In France there was always a strong minority trend towards Catholic democracy, and the task of Catholic reactionaries was complicated by the difficulty of deciding which of the mutually hostile secular reactionary groups they should support. Austrian Catholicism abandoned oligarchic for demagogic procedures with the rise of Karl Lueger's movement, yet can hardly be said to have much modified its reactionary political outlook. Italian Catholicism after 1870 was in a sense the most reactionary of all, since it was committed to hostility to the Italian State as such. In the only Orthodox State with centuries of continuous independence behind it, the Russian Empire, the political attitude of the church was overwhelmingly reactionary. The outstanding spokesman was of course Pobedonostsev. But the role of the church was diminishing, as the secular reactionaries were not only losing their own religious faith but paying less attention to it as an influence on the people. On the other hand there were a few dissident voices, believers who rejected the existing secular social and political order. They were not many, but they included men of the stature of Vladimir Solovyov, Berdyaev, and Struve. In the new Balkan states the Orthodox church by no means always stood for reaction. The reason was that the church had been emotionally committed to the struggle for liberation from the Turks, which was inescapably linked with democratic ideas. This was least true of Rumania, whose liberation was more the result of war and diplomacy by the Great Powers, and less of her people's own efforts, and in which the social structure was more rigid and oligarchical than in Serbia, Bulgaria, or Greece.

Reactionaries aim to restore a past political system as well as to restore religious belief. In this sense there can hardly be said to have been any reactionaries in England. No one aimed to return to the age before Simon de Montfort's parliament, or to restore Stuart despotism, or even to undo the Reform Bills of 1832 or 1867. At most one can quote the dislike of Milner, Chesterton, or Belloc for modern political parties. In France, however, the desire to undo the work of 1789, to bring back the Kings who had made France great, was long a powerful emotion, even if it was held only by a minority. The Carlists in Spain, and the supporters of the Bourbon monarchy in the Italian South, left their mark on the political scene in both countries. In Prussia and Austria the task was rather to conserve privileges and obstruct reform than to restore the good old days of the Holy Roman Empire. In Russia we have the paradox that in the nineteenth century those who held the purest reactionary views about the State were reformers, and those who upheld the autocracy as it was were to some extent modernizers. The early Slavophils wished to return to a mythical past, in which they claimed that the people, represented by its *zemskii sobor,* had enjoyed a happy communion with the Tsar. The germanized bureaucracy created by Peter the Great and his successors must be abolished, the peasants freed from serfdom, and educated men from censorship and police rule. By contrast, the bureaucrats of the Tsars, resolutely opposed to all liberty, viewed with realism the need to bring Russia into the modern world of industry and conscript armies. Only in the last decades of the Empire after the reforming zeal of the Slavophils had been worn away by decades of official obstruction, and their intellectual descendants had been carried away by russifying nationalism, did a new reactionary synthesis of demagogic autocracy begin to appear. The reactionary view of the social structure had two main

elements, a dislike of the industrial urban economy and a belief in a common interest uniting the old ruling class with the masses against the capitalists. The myth of a golden age of rural harmony in the past was usually an important feature of such doctrines. Their exponents came sometimes from the upper classes but more often from the professions —from writers, academics, soldiers, or government officials, often though not always derived from families of the lesser nobility or provincial gentry. It is worth stressing the strength of traditional anti-capitalist and anti-liberal values, which survived within the educational systems and within the intellectual elites long after industrial capitalism had become dominant in the economy, and even after socialism had arisen and gained strength as a force challenging liberal and capitalist values from the base of the social pyramid and from a post-industrial point of view. The cliché of successive feudal, capitalist, and socialist stages greatly distorts the historical reality. The three stages overlapped. The combination of the two sorts of anti-capitalism, from above and from below, looking to the past and looking to the future, is an essential trend in modern European history, still under-rated by historians, still blurred by the conventional wisdom of Western democracy, and especially important for the origins of fascism. It was important even in England, the classical home of the capitalist ethos and bourgeois values. In the synthesis of capitalist and traditionalist outlooks promoted by the Victorian "public schools" —whose function was to draw the children of the new rich into the upper class—it is by no means clear which element was the stronger. The idea of the common interest between old elite and common people against money-grubbing materialism is found in "Young England," in Disraeli, in Milner, and in G. K. Chesterton, to take only a few obvious names. Something similar can even be found in the United States, whether in New England or the Old South. In France and in Prussia anti-capitalism of both kinds was even stronger, but cooperation between them was inhibited by a fiercer hatred between classes. The memories of 1793, 1848, and 1871 in France, and the contempt of the Prussian Junker for the mob, made almost impassable barriers.

It must also be noted that everywhere in western Europe capitalism and industry were defeating the pre-capitalist ruling class. The capitalists became rich, and acquired social and political power. They were now a large part of the ruling class. But essentially they were conservatives, not reactionaries. They wanted to preserve and secure their own power, not to restore the past. The social programme of the reactionaries was different—to limit or even reverse industrialization, and to build on the solid foundations of the peasant class, allegedly the heir to the best moral and spiritual values. An important distinction should be made here. In the countries of southern and eastern Europe whose economy was still agrarian, and the bulk of whose population lived in villages, the peasant problem was the problem of the masses, and peasant discontent was the main potential force of social revolution. But in the industrial countries the advocacy by intellectuals of the simple virtues of peasant society was reactionary utopianism. It was not of much importance in England, to whose problems it was demonstrably irrelevant, or even in the three western Latin countries, where the cultural tradition was overwhelmingly urban. But it was a factor of great importance in Germany.

The cementing force in reactionary ideologies from the end of the nineteenth century onwards was nationalism. This is of course something of a paradox. The doctrine of nationalism is essentially a product of the Enlightenment and of 1789. To place above all the interests of the nation is to reject traditional concepts of legitimacy, to diminish the claims of God and the King. In the age of Metternich, reactionaries were against nationalism. But in the decades that followed the unification of Italy and Germany they made a bid to take over the national idea for themselves. It no longer made sense to argue that the community, within which elite and people were united against materialist money-grubbers, was simply the community of the King's subjects: the right word was the Nation. The outstanding doctrinaire was Charles Maurras, whose *nationalisme intégral* became a model for nationalist intellectuals in many lands.

It is worth noting some different aspects of nationalism, depending on the situations in which different nations found themselves. It is a paradox that it was in France, whose national identity was centuries old and whose national independence was not threatened, that an intellectual doctrine of nationalism was formulated. The explanation can perhaps be found in the sense of humiliation resulting from the defeat of 1870. In the other country of ancient national identity, England, there has never been any function for a nationalist movement or doctrine to perform, and it can hardly be said that either has existed. In Italy and Germany the sense of national identity was still precarious after 1870, and it is understandable that intellectuals in both countries should have felt obliged to emphasise it. There is a vast difference between the Latin word

"nation," with its background of Roman church and law and modern Enlightenment, and the Germanic word "folk," with its suggestion of dark emotions, tribal loyalties, and Teutonic forests. But the similarity of the post-1870 status of both nations is important, and was reinforced by the German defeat and Italian disillusion in 1918. Further east in Europe nationalism was a simpler and more straightforwardly revolutionary force. There were nations demanding independence (Poles, Czechs, Slovaks, Croats, Balts, Finns, Ukrainians), or demanding that their incomplete independence should be perfected by union with their unredeemed brothers (Greeks, Serbs, Rumanians, Bulgarians). There were other nations again whose aim was to prevent their multi-national subjects from breaking away, by imposing their own nationality on them. Such were the Hungarians and Russians, and to a lesser extent the Prussians and Austrian Germans.

A special case were nations which had attained, at least for a large part of their number, an independent State, but still felt themselves to be dominated by foreigners. This was especially the case in the agrarian states of eastern Europe, where the growing industries were largely owned either by foreigners or by members of economically more advanced alien minorities in their midst. Greeks in Rumania, Germans in Hungary, formed such minorities, but far more important were the Jews. It is not possible simply to correlate the intensity of anti-semitism with the economic power of the Jewish minority. Maurras denounced Jews and Protestants as alien bodies in France, and the Dreyfus Affair was the greatest anti-semitic event in nineteenth-century Europe. But it cannot seriously be argued that Jews dominated the cultural or economic life of France. This could however certainly be argued of Hungary; yet before 1914 Hungarian Jews had little cause to complain. The rulers of Hungary from 1867 were landed noblemen whose leaders had grown up with liberal ideas. As the years passed their liberalism waned, but they had no motive to deprive the Jews of the liberties they had originally granted them. They wanted Hungary industrialized, but did not themselves want to go into business: the Jews did a necessary job for them. For their part the Hungarian Jews became ardent Hungarian patriots. Hostility to the Jews came from peasants, and from the small but growing number of peasant children entering business or the intellectual professions, especially among the non-Hungarian nationalities. In Vienna, where Jewish influence in business and in the professions, though very great, was still less than in Budapest, anti-semitism was much stronger. The reason is that the

German middle classes of Vienna, both business and intellectual, were not only numerous but politically influential, and their interests were in direct conflict with those of the Jewish middle classes. In Germany the proportion of Jews in the population, and their economic and cultural influence, were relatively far less than in Vienna, but were sufficient to provoke hostility from the German upper and middle classes. To nostalgic reactionary intellectuals the Jews were an obvious object of dislike, a symbol of the urban materialist corruption which threatened the idyllic medieval Germanic peasant virtues. But the area of most widespread anti-semitism was the belt of heavy Jewish settlement extending from Lithuania through eastern Poland, western Ukraine, Slovakia, Bukovina, and Moldavia, from the Baltic to the Black Sea. Most of this territory was within the Russian Empire until 1917; part was within Hungary and Rumania. Hungarians and Russians were not much inclined to anti-semitism, but among Poles, Ukrainians, Slovaks, and Rumanians it was very strong.[2] The artificial social structure of the Jewish community, which was excluded from agriculture and government service, and thus confined to business, the intellectual professions, and employment in crafts or factories, deepened the gulf between the Jews and their neighbours. To the peasant, the Jew was the shopkeeper who took his small cash income; to the official, the rootless half-educated fanatic who peddled ideas; to the would-be indigenous small capitalist, his successful established rival who prevented him from getting a footing in business; to the government, the most active element in the discontented urban proletariat. In the eastern belt, despotic governments, reactionary ideologues, discontented peasants, and to some extent also industrial workers could unite in hating the Jew, blaming their various fears and sufferings on him, the foreign exploiter and agent of subversion.

Reactionary ideologies and political programmes, varied mixtures of religious intolerance, historical myth, social utopia, nationalism and anti-semitism, were present in most European countries around 1914. But fascism is more than a reactionary ideology: it is a movement, based on substantial mass support. The significant fascist movements all started in opposition to existing regimes. All had to struggle for power, and some were severely persecuted. All regarded their victories (some of which were of brief duration) as triumphs of a revolutionary idea. None aimed at restoring the past. Their ideologies were essentially reactionary, but they cannot correctly be described as "counter-revolutionary," for they did not seek to replace something overthrown by a previous revolution. They were essentially revolutionary movements. The fact that their aims and policies were distasteful to me entitles me to call them evil revolutions, but not to deny their revolutionary character.

The 1930s and 1940s were the period of fascist success. Inevitably fascist policies and institutions were aped by others. Obvious examples are Hungary under Gömbös, Yugoslavia under Stojadinovic, and Rumania under King Carol. But in these cases no fascist revolution took place. The existing regimes were only superficially changed, and even the anti-Jewish measures were comparatively mild. The true fascists were not deceived. Arrow Cross, Ustashe, and Iron Guard bided their time, and when it came they showed, in orgies of butchery, that they were men of a different stamp.

There are some marginal cases. The regime of Dollfuss in Austria was copied from the Italian model. But it was introduced from above, without any forcible seizure of power, and it never succeeded in organizing much genuine mass support. It was without doubt reactionary, but it is hard to say whether it was fascist. The Spanish case is also obscure. During the civil war there were revolutionary fascists on Franco's side, but after victory they lost much of their influence. At least by the 1960s Franco's Spain looked less like fascism than like an old-fashioned military dictatorship with bureaucratic and capitalist support. As for Italy itself, it may even be paradoxically argued that it was "less fascist" than some other regimes. Certainly it never attained the totalitarian perfection which Mussolini proclaimed as his goal.

Of the Nazi regime in Germany, all that need be noted here is that no simple formula will describe it. Hitler got money from German capitalists, but once in power he subjected them to his will, even if he left them good profits. Among his supporters were not only "petty bourgeois" (whatever that may mean) and peasants but also hundreds of thousands of workers (even if a minority of the working class as a whole). Hitler had no plan for social revolution, but the totalitarian regime which he installed not only exterminated hundreds of thousands of German Jews (as well as millions of Jews outside Germany), but transformed the life of every individual and every class of the German people. To deny the epithet "revolutionary" to this monstrous process is doctrinaire perversity.

The impact of fascism on the social structure of eastern Europe was different. It became a powerful force in Rumania, Hungary, and Croatia, and a considerable factor in Poland and Slovakia. In these countries in the 1930s the dominant social group was the bureaucracy. In Hungary and Poland large land-owners were also powerful. Capitalists were in all five countries becoming more important, and included a large proportion of Jews. The bulk of the population were peasants, mostly very poor. There was a small skilled working class in a few established industrial centres, and a rapidly growing unskilled element flocking into the cities from the overpopulated countryside. The situation was in general similar to that of Russia at the turn of the century. As in Russia, the leadership of political movements challenging the regime came from the intelligentsia, in particular from students, professors, lawyers, and journalists, to a lesser extent from school-teachers. It is misleading to speak of "the middle class": there were three distinct middle classes, separated by vertical compartments—bureaucrats, business men, and intelligentsia. The first of these formed the hard core of the regime, the second either supported the regime or was politically neutral, and opposition came essentially from the third. The intelligentsia was a definite social group with a distinct political role of its own. It was not part of a bourgeoisie: no culturally homogeneous bourgeoisie, in the West European sense, existed in these countries. The intelligentsia provided the leadership of all radical or revolutionary movements, and mass support came from the peasants and the unskilled workers. The skilled workers, for example the printers, and a section of the intelligentsia, remained loyal to social-democracy in Hungary, and virtually the whole industrial working class in Poland was socialist.[3] The unskilled workers in Hungary and the Balkans were on the whole divided between communists and fascists.

In Hungary and Rumania fascism was a powerful mass movement. In both countries it is arguable that a majority of peasants remained loyal to democratic parties, but certainly a very large minority of Hungarian peasants seeking a distribution of the great landed estates, and of Rumanian peasants demanding relief from the appalling poverty of the Depression years, were attracted by fascism. Both fascist movements also won working-class followers. The coal-mines of the Pecs area were a stronghold of the Arrow Cross, the Malaxa Works in Bucharest of the Iron Guard. The Croatian Ustashe and the Slovak People's Party are rather different: here the driving force was plain nationalism, the social composition broad but the working-class element almost completely lacking. The Ustashe specialized in assassination, and once in power they achieved a record of butchery comparable with that of Hitler himself. They operated in a smaller area, but the proportion of victims to total population was probably surpassed only in occupied Poland and Ukraine. In Poland convinced fascists (as opposed to conservative politicians aping fascist slogans) were numerous in the intellectual youth, but almost completely failed to attract peasant or working-class support.

Rumanian fascism attracted to its leading cadres not only thugs but also young people who were both honourable and intelligent. There was in Rumania a fascist populism which recalls the "going to the people" in Russia in the 1870s. I saw something of this phenomenon at the end of the 1930s in both Rumania and Yugoslavia. The young Serbian *narodniki* were Marxists, and some were disciplined Communist Party members: the young Rumanian *narodniki* were fascists, and some were disciplined members of the Iron Guard. The social types, and the emotional attitudes, were very similar. The different orientation is not hard to explain. Rumanians feared Russia, and the capitalist enemy in their midst was often a Jew. The Third Reich was against both their internal and their external enemy, Hitler appeared their protector, and they swallowed his doctrines. Serbs feared Germany and loved Russia, and there was no Jewish problem in their country. Marxism offered answers to their difficulties, and was backed by the might of the Slav elder brother. The two trends went different ways. All the talents and idealism of the one group were burned out in a series of ignoble crimes and repressions, and ended with their country's defeat. The similar gifts of the young Serbs were used to glorious effect in the War of Liberation, and the survivors have built a new Yugoslavia. It is easy to sneer at the Rumanian dead, or to praise the Yugoslavs for better judgment. But both were to a large extent victims of their environment. A historian should aim at deeper compassion than this, and I at least remember with equal affection my friends in both countries.

An obviously important feature of fascism which often gets left out, and which can perhaps never be well explained, is the charismatic leader. Mussolini, Degrelle, and José Antonio Primo de Rivera were clearly men of outstanding abilities. Szalasi and Codreanu were complex personalities, combining ruthlessness with strange flashes of nobility of character. Hitler still defies analysis. It is true, but not enlightening, that he came from the "petty bourgeoisie." More significant is that he came from the morally and culturally uprooted drifting population of the great city. Lacking the discipline of a systematic education or of membership in an organized class, profession, or church, driven by ambition and obsessed by a few crude hatreds, he pursued his aims with relentless logic and tireless effort. Hate propaganda was of course nothing new, but Hitler did not stop at words: he went ahead and exterminated six million Jews, and made preparations to uproot and exterminate many more millions of Poles, Ukrainians, and Russians. This was something new: the crimes of the religious wars and the conquest of the Americas were on a smaller scale, and the massacres of Djengiz Khan lacked the hideous trappings of modern science. These horrors started from an apparently insignificant little unsuccessful painter from Vienna, assisted by other colourless uprooted men, from Himmler down to the concentration camp commandants. It is worth noting that the other great mass exterminator of our age was also a half-educated, classless, uprooted figure. Tiflis and Baku were different from Vienna, and simplified Marxism was different from a hotch-potch of Austrian reactionary ideology and anti-semitism, but the figures of Hitler and Stalin have many features in common which deserve serious study. One may hope that the like of these two men will never be seen again, but that the uprooted, classless, faceless hordes of the big cities of Europe and America have other monsters in store for us is pretty certain.

We still do not know enough about fascism; indeed we have hardly begun to study it. This is not just a task for academic scholars. The nagging questions remain, "Has fascism a future?" and less simply, "What social and political movements of the present or the near future can be better understood by a better knowledge of fascism?"

The Spanish and Portuguese regimes retain undoubted elements of fascism, but both appear to be in decline, and neither offers much inspiration to other countries. The only strong fascist regime to appear since the end of the Third Reich was in Argentina. Perón held power for ten years, enjoyed powerful support from the working class, and progressed a long way from old-fashioned Latin American military dictatorship towards stream-lined modern totalitarianism. In the end the church and the army were too strong for him, but his personal myth and his brand of fascism still enjoy mass support. In the Middle East the Moslem Brotherhood, with its combination of religious fundamentalism, terrorism, and populism, bore some resemblance to the Rumanian Iron Guard in its early days. The Young Officers' group of Nasser were certainly not fascists in their conspiratorial

days, but the regime built by Nasser in the last ten years appears to have its similarities with fascist totalitarianism. President Soekarno's constant aping of Mussolini, in his personal style, his slogans, and his formal institutions, can hardly be unconscious. But the reality of fascist organization is missing: the only disciplined forces are the Communist Party and the national army. In Japan there are right-wing movements which may yet revive, in some modified form, the revolutionary terrorism of the 1930s.[4] The new African dictatorships pride themselves on being "socialist." Yet the fact that they recite Marxist formulas, and seek the friendship of the Soviet Union, or China, may prove less important than it at first appears. Revolutionary nationalist regimes, applying techniques of mass mobilization, injecting into their quasi-socialist ideologies strong doses of racialism and of historical mythology, and moving from simple dictatorship ever further towards totalitarianism, may end up nearer to the Third Reich than to the Soviet or Chinese model. As for their leaders, the Osagyefo certainly seems to possess more of the hysteria of Hitler and the vanity of Mussolini than of the cold genius of Lenin.

Anti-semitism is not at present a major factor in world politics. But it is worth noting a limited but significant analogy. The Jews were the outstanding case of a community of commercially and intellectually gifted people set in the midst of more numerous and more backward nations. This made them symbols of foreign exploitation or spiritual corruption, and offered them as ideal scapegoats to demagogues. There are other such communities. The Greeks and Armenians of the Arabic-speaking successor states of the Ottoman Empire, the Chinese of South-East Asia, the Indians of Burma and of some surviving British island colonies, the Lebanese of West Africa, are the main examples. But the analogy can even be extended to cover all communities of white-skinned business-men or technicians in Asia and Africa. The doctrine of "neo-colonialism" deliberately concentrates hatred against these ready-made scapegoats. All that is wrong in new states can be attributed to them by demagogues, as all that was wrong in Hungary and Rumania was once attributed to the Jews. The argument is the more effective because it contains a good deal of truth: European capitalists *do* still largely dominate new states in Asia and Africa, and North American capitalists older states in Central and South America, just as Jewish capitalists, both Rumanian and foreign citizens, largely dominated the Rumanian economy.

In the Western democracies there is not much sign

cf fascism today. There are of course persons, both Jewish and Gentile, who with a mentality which can only be compared with that of Hitler's race-experts, insist that Germans are by their birth or by their blood inescapably and eternally aggressive, totalitarian, and Jew-hating. Happily the reality of Germany today gives small support to them. In France the danger of a fascist movement based on returned Algerian *colons* and on the submerged remnants of followers of Darnand and his kind seems to have passed. In the United States McCarthyism seems to have been connected with a coincidence of increased social mobility with the dismayed discovery that America was no longer invulnerable. Something rather similar has occurred in Britain—a small but significant increase in social mobility coinciding with the collapse of the British Empire and a steady decline of Britain's status in the world.[5] But this has so far produced nothing more dangerous than "angry" literature and journalism. Potentially more serious might be some sort of Negro fascism in the northern United States, or a totalitarian trend within Québécois nationalism. The tragic pressures on the white South Africans, who once for all their bitter resentments formed a democratic community, seem to be pushing them towards some form of fascism.

The purpose of these observations was not to offer definitions or to provide final answers, but simply to note a number of aspects of the movements which it is still best to call fascist. Comparative study of fascism is much needed today, not only to fill gaps in historical knowledge but to warn new generations of old dangers before they recur.

NOTES

1. *The European Right: a Historical Analysis,* editors Hans Rogger and Eugen Weber, University of California Press, 1965, pp. 589, $9.50. The book suffers to some extent from the diversity of approach which seems to be inevitable in works by many authors (in this case, ten). The distinction between the traditionalist and the modern "Rights," between classical conservatism and "right radicalism," is not always clear. Some contributors concentrate on the ideas of the period before the emergence of fascist movements. Others have given surveys of political history rather than political or social analysis. Outstanding in my view are the three contributions by Professor Weber—a general Introduction and a chapter each on France and on Rumania. I must also mention Mr. Deak's chapter on Hungary, which has perhaps less depth than Mr. Weber's but is both perceptive and clear.

2. Russian anti-semitism in fact was concentrated in the Ukraine and Bessarabia, and though its leaders regarded themselves as Russians, they were mostly of Ukrainian, Polish, or Rumanian origin. In the central Muscovite core of Russia anti-semitism had much weaker roots.

3. There was a minority among the Polish workers who followed the illegal Communist Party, but virtually no Polish workers were fascists.

4. Whether the right-wing terrorists should be called fascists is arguable. See Richard Storry's admirable book *The Double Patriots.* See also *Thought and Behaviour in Modern Japanese Politics,* by Masao Maruyama. I must confess to some disappointment with these essays by the outstanding Japanese authority on fascism. Learned and enlightening on the Japanese scene, he seems to lose his bearings when generalising on a wider scale: in particular, though he has clearly studied German sources carefully, he seems to me to have missed the essence of Hitler's national-socialism.

5. An increase in social mobility inevitably creates bitterness among those who enter the elite but find no social acceptance. This problem existed in England in the early nineteenth century. However the *parvenus* were soon absorbed in a country which was at the height of its economic and political power. The failure of the post-Second World War elite to absorb a new influx of *parvenus,* and consequent poisoned atmosphere of contemporary British public life, is due to the fact that the influx coincided with a period of rapid decline in Britain's position in the world.

88

The Chinese Revolution: The New Democratic Culture

Mao Tse-tung

The Chinese Revolution Is Part of the World Revolution

The historical feature of the Chinese revolution consists in the two steps to be taken, democracy and socialism, and the first step is now no longer democracy in a general sense, but democracy of the Chinese type, a new and special type—New Democracy. How, then, is this historical feature formed? Has it been in existence for the past hundred years, or is it only of recent birth?

If we only make a brief study of the historical development of China and of the world we shall understand that this historical feature did not emerge as a consequence of the Opium War, but began to take shape only after the first imperialist world war and the Russian October Revolution. Let us now study the process of its formation.

Evidently, the colonial, semi-colonial and semi-feudal character of present-day Chinese society determines that two steps must be taken in the Chinese revolution. The first step is to change a society that is colonial, semi-colonial and semi-feudal into an independent, democratic society. The second step is to develop the revolution further and build up a socialist society. In the present Chinese revolution we are taking the first step.

The preparatory period for taking the first step began from the Opium War in 1840, *i.e.* from the time when Chinese society started to change from a feudal into a semi-colonial and semi-feudal society.

The movement of the T'aip'ing Heavenly Kingdom, the Sino-French War, the Sino-Japanese War, the Reformist Movement of 1898, the Revolution of 1911, the May 4 Movement, the Northern Expedition, the War of the Agrarian Revolution and the present Anti-Japanese War—these numerous stages have altogether taken up a whole century and, from a certain point of view, represent the first step taken by the Chinese people on different occasions and in various degrees to fight against imperialism and the feudal forces, to strive to build up an independent, democratic society and to complete the first revolution. The Revolution of 1911 was the beginning of that revolution in a fuller sense. In its social character, that revolution is bourgeois-democratic rather than proletarian-socialist. That revolution is not yet completed and great efforts are still required because the enemies of the revolution are still very strong. When Dr. Sun Yat-sen said: "The revolution is not yet completed, all my comrades must strive on," he was referring to such a bourgeois-democratic revolution.

A change, however, occurred in the Chinese bourgeois-democratic revolution after the outbreak of the first imperialist world war in 1914 and the founding of a socialist state on one-sixth of the globe through the Russian October Revolution in 1917.

Before these events, the Chinese bourgeois-democratic revolution belonged to the category of the old bourgeois-democratic world revolution, and was part of that revolution.

After these events, the Chinese bourgeois-democratic revolution changes its character and belongs

Reprinted from Mao Tse-tung, *Selected Works* (London: Lawrence and Wishart Ltd., 1954), pp. 109–114, 141–142.

to the category of the new bourgeois-democratic revolution and, so far as the revolutionary front is concerned, forms part of the proletarian-socialist world revolution.

Why? Because the first imperialist world war and the first victorious socialist revolution, the October Revolution, have changed the historical direction of the whole world and marked a new historical era of the whole world.

In an era when the world capitalist front has collapsed in one corner of the globe (a corner which forms one-sixth of the world), while in other parts it has fully revealed its decadence; when the remaining parts of capitalism cannot survive without relying more than ever on the colonies and semi-colonies; when a socialist state has been established and has declared that it is willing to fight in support of the liberation movement of all colonies and semi-colonies; when the proletariat of the capitalist countries is freeing itself day by day from the social-imperialist influence of the Social-Democratic Parties, and has also declared itself in support of the liberation movement of the colonies and semi-colonies—in such an era, any revolution that takes place in a colony or semi-colony against imperialism, *i.e.* against the international bourgeoisie and international capitalism, belongs no longer to the old category of bourgeois-democratic world revolution, but to a new category, and is no longer part of the old bourgeois or capitalist world revolution, but part of the new world revolution, the proletarian-socialist world revolution. Such revolutionary colonies and semi-colonies should no longer be regarded as allies of the counter-revolutionary front of world capitalism; they have become allies of the revolutionary front of world socialism.

Although in its social character the first stage of, or the first step taken in this revolution in a colonial and semi-colonial country is still fundamentally bourgeois-democratic, and although its objective demand is to clear the path for the development of capitalism, yet it no longer belongs to the old type of revolution led by the bourgeoisie with the aim of establishing a capitalist society and a state under bourgeois dictatorship, but belongs to the new type of revolution which, led by the proletariat, aims at establishing a new-democratic society and a state under the joint dictatorship of all the revolutionary classes. Thus this revolution exactly serves to clear a path even wider for the development of socialism. In the course of its progress such a revolution further falls into several stages because of changes in the enemy's conditions and in the ranks of its allies; but its fundamental character will remain unchanged.

Such a revolution deals unrelenting blows to imperialism, and hence is disapproved and opposed by imperialism. But it meets the approval of socialism and is supported by the socialist state and the socialist international proletariat.

Therefore, such a revolution cannot but become part of the proletarian-socialist world revolution.

The correct thesis that "the Chinese revolution is part of the world revolution" was propounded as early as 1924–7 during the period of China's First Great Revolution. It was propounded by the Chinese Communists and approved by all who participated in the anti-imperialist and anti-feudal struggle of the time. But at that time the meaning of this theoretical proposition was not yet fully expounded, and consequently it was only vaguely understood.

This "world revolution" refers no longer to the old world revolution—for the old bourgeois world revolution has long become a thing of the past—but to a new world revolution, the socialist world revolution. Similarly, to form "part" of the world revolution means to form no longer a part of the old bourgeois revolution but of the new socialist revolution. This is an exceedingly great change unparalleled in the history of China and of the world.

This correct thesis propounded by the Chinese Communists is based on Stalin's theory.

As early as 1918, Stalin wrote in an article commemorating the first anniversary of the October Revolution:

> The great world-wide significance of the October Revolution chiefly consists in the fact that:
> (1) It has widened the scope of the national question and converted it from the particular question of combating national oppression in Europe into the general question of emancipating the oppressed peoples, colonies and semi-colonies from imperialism.
> (2) It has opened up wide possibilities for their emancipation and the right paths towards it, has thereby greatly facilitated the cause of the emancipation of the oppressed peoples of the West and the East, and has drawn them into the common current of the victorious struggle against imperialism.
> (3) It has thereby erected a bridge between the socialist West and the enslaved East, having created a new front of revolutions against world imperialism, extending from the proletarians of the West, through the Russian revolution to the oppressed peoples of the East.

Since writing this article, Stalin has again and again expounded the theoretical proposition that revolutions in colonies and semi-colonies have already departed from the old category and become part of the proletarian-socialist revolution. The article that gives the clearest and most precise explanation was published on June 30, 1925, in which Stalin carried on a controversy with the Yugoslav nationalists of that time. This article, entitled "The National Question Once Again," is included in a book translated by Chang Chung-shih, published under the title *Stalin on the National Question*. It contains the following passage:

Semich refers to a passage in Stalin's pamphlet *Marxism and the National Question*, written at the end of 1912. It is stated there that "the national struggle under the conditions of *rising* capitalism is a struggle of the bourgeois classes among themselves." By this he is evidently trying to hint that his own formula defining the social meaning of the national movement in present historical conditions is correct. But Stalin's pamphlet was written before the imperialist war, at a time when the national question in the eyes of Marxists had not yet assumed world significance, and when the basic demand of the Marxists, the right to self-determination, was judged to be not a part of the proletarian revolution, but a part of the bourgeois-democratic revolution. It would be absurd to ignore the fact that the international situation has radically changed since that time, that the war on the one hand and the October Revolution in Russia on the other have converted the national question from a part of the bourgeois-democratic revolution into a part of the proletarian-socialist revolution. As early as October, 1916, Lenin in his article "The Discussion on Self-Determination Summed Up," said that the fundamental point of the national question, the right of self-determination, had ceased to form part of the general democratic movement and that it had become converted into a component part of the general proletarian-socialist revolution. I will not mention later works of Lenin and of other representatives of Russian Communism on the national question. In view of all this, what interpretation can be placed on Comrade Semich's reference to a certain passage in a pamphlet by Stalin written in the period of the bourgeois-democratic revolution in Russia, now that, as a result of the new historical situation, we have entered a new era, the era of the world *proletarian* revolution? The only interpretation that can be placed on it is that Comrade Semich is quoting without reference to space and time and without reference to the actual historical situation, and that he is thereby violating the most elementary demands of dialectics and failing to take account of the fact that what is correct in one historical situation may prove incorrect in another historical situation.

New-Democratic Culture

We have explained above the historical features of Chinese politics in the new period and the question of the new-democratic republic. We can now proceed to the question of culture.

A given culture is the ideological reflection of the politics and economy of a given society. There is in China an imperialistic culture which is a reflection of the control or partial control of imperialism over China politically and economically. This part of culture is advocated not only by the cultural organisations run directly by the imperialists in China but also by a number of shameless Chinese. All culture that contains a slave ideology belongs to this category. There is also in China a semi-feudal culture which is a reflection of semi-feudal politics and economy and has as its representatives all those who, while opposing the new culture and new ideologies, advocate the worship of Confucius, the study of the Confucian canon, the old ethical code and the old ideologies. Imperialist culture and semi-feudal culture are affectionate brothers, who have formed a reactionary cultural alliance to oppose China's new culture. This reactionary culture serves the imperialists and the feudal class, and must be swept away. Unless it is swept away, no new culture of any kind can be built up. The new culture and the reactionary culture are locked in a struggle in which one must die so that the other may live; there is no construction without destruction, no flowing without damming and no moving without halting.

As to the new culture, it is the ideological reflection of new politics and new economy, and is in the service of new politics and new economy.

. . . Chinese society has gradually changed its character since the emergence of capitalist economy in China: it is no longer an entirely feudal society but a semi-feudal one, though feudal economy still predominates. In contrast to feudal economy, such capitalist economy is a new economy. The new political forces which have emerged and grown simultaneously with this capitalist new economy are the political forces of the bourgeoisie, the petty bourgeoisie and the proletariat. And what ideologically reflects these new economic and political forces and is in their service, is the new culture. Without capitalist economy, without the bourgeoisie, the petty bourgeoisie and the proletariat, and without the political forces of these classes, the new ideology or new culture could not have emerged.

All the new political, new economic and new cultural forces are revolutionary forces in China which are opposed to the old politics, old economy and old culture. The old things are composed of two parts: one is China's own semi-feudal politics, economy and culture and the other is imperialist politics, economy and culture, with the latter heading the alliance. All these are rotten and should be completely destroyed. The struggle between the new and the old in Chinese society is a struggle between the new forces of the broad masses of the people (the various revolutionary classes) and the old forces of imperialism and the feudal class. Such a struggle between the new and the old is a struggle between revolution and counter-revolution. This struggle has taken a full hundred years if dated from the Opium War, and nearly thirty years if dated from the Revolution of 1911.

But as has been said before, revolutions also can be differentiated into old and new, and what is new in one historical period will become old in another.

The century of China's bourgeois-democratic revolution can be divided into two main stages—a first stage of eighty years and a second of twenty years. Each has a basic historical feature: China's bourgeois-democratic revolution in the first eighty years belongs to the old category, while that in the next twenty years, owing to the change in the international and domestic political situation, belongs to the new category. Old democracy—the feature in the first eighty years. New Democracy—the feature in the last twenty years. This distinction holds good in culture as well as in politics.

89

The Nature of the Soviet System

Zbigniew Brzezinski

II

The Soviet system has now existed for more than forty-three years, and its political history has been closely identified with three major Communist leaders, each of whom symbolizes a distinct, but also a related, stage of development of that system. Broadly speaking, the phase of Leninism after 1917 can be said to have involved primarily the consolidation of the Communist Party's rule over society and the internal transformation of the party from a revolutionary vanguard into a more disciplined ruling elite. While some small measure of internal diversity remained within the party, especially at the top, perhaps the most enduring achievement of Leninism was the dogmatization of the party, thereby in effect both preparing and causing the next stage, that of Stalinism.

The Stalinist phase, particularly during the years 1928–41, was the time of what might be called the totalitarian "break-through," that is the all-out effort to destroy the basic institutions of the old order and to construct at least the framework for the new. The postwar period, that is, 1945–53, was in some respects a repetition of the preceding period and an extension of it. The process of postwar reconstruc-

tion again meant a conflict with society, destruction of established ways, and an extension of earlier efforts to build "socialism" in agriculture, through industrialization, in the arts and sciences, and so forth. The political consequences of these efforts, especially as they were shaped by Stalin's own personality, were the decline in the importance of the party, the personalization of leadership, the growth of the secret police, and the reliance upon terror as the crucial, most characteristic feature of the system. Indeed, Stalin's totalitarian edifice could be said to have rested on three supporting columns: the secret police, the state bureaucracy, and the party, with all three co-ordinated by the old dictator's personal secretariat. At the same time, the party reached perhaps its lowest point since the seizure of power. Weakened and demoralized by the purges, it became less and less the instrument of social revolution. Decline in zeal, dogmatic stagnation, and bureaucratization were the familiar consequences.

During the fourth phase, which began with several years of instability within the Kremlin but can still be associated with the name of Khrushchev, there occurred a gradual lessening of the conflict between society and the regime coupled with a certain maturation, and social acceptance, of the new order. This phase was made possible by the Stalinist liquidation of all nonpolitically directed social groups, and hence the regime could afford the luxury of

From Zbigniew Brzezinski, "The Nature of the Soviet System," *Slavic Review*, XX, No. 3 (October 1961), 354–368. Reprinted by permission of the publisher and the author.

diminished violence. Thus Stalinism paved the way for the relative leniency of the post-Stalinist phase. It has been characterized by the re-emergence of the party apparatus as the dominant political force and by Khrushchev's increasing emphasis on linking technical-economic achievement with broad and intensive ideological indoctrination. The revitalization of the party and the renewed emphasis on ideology marked an effort to make the system "move again" (to borrow a phrase made popular in the recent election), and the personal success of Khrushchev is in large part due to his instinctive perception of the organizational compulsion of the party towards ideology-action. Stagnant in Stalin's later days, the party almost naturally responded to a man whose appeal involved a reactivation of the party's historical role.

As the preceding remarks suggest, Khrushchev's political system is not the same as Stalin's, even though both may be generally described as totalitarian. Therefore, the next step in examining the nature of the Soviet system of 1960–61 is to find clues to important continuities and changes by looking more closely at certain key dynamic aspects of its political regime. Three seem to be most revealing: the role of the party; the role of ideology; the role of violence. (Because of limitations of space, each will be considered very briefly and only certain issues highlighted.)

Perhaps the most important single development of the last few years in Soviet politics has been the revitalization of the party and the reassertion of its dominant position in Soviet life. One by one, the secret police, the state administration, the army, as well as the planners, the intelligentsia, and the youth learned—sometimes painfully—this lesson. A direct relationship between the leadership and the masses has thus been reasserted—the relationship of access and mobilization.[1]

But the implications of the recent assertion of the party's role may be broader still. Certain conclusions reached by sociologists concerning the comparative roles of specialized experts and managers in large-scale American enterprises may be highly relevant to the Soviet totalitarian system. These studies have implied that experts are unable to provide the "integration" which a large-scale, diversified organization requires, since such integration is often incompatible with the narrower, highly specialized focus of the expert and requires a high degree of skill in human relations which an expert rarely possesses. Studies of the two groups have further suggested the following important differences between them: personality types; background and promotion procedures; orientations and goals.[2]

It would not be far-fetched to suggest that the role of manager in the Soviet system, if that system as a whole is seen as a large goal-oriented enterprise, is performed by the *apparatchiki* of the party. They are the ones who are skilled in human relations or in social organization; they are the ones who have a sufficiently wide perspective (if one can call their ideology that) to provide broad integration; they are the ones who rise from the ranks with their minds and skills focused on the over-all objective of the organization—the fulfillment of its historical purpose. They thus enjoy an inherent advantage over the expert, whether he is a technocrat or a professional bureaucrat. This picture is confirmed by the valuable studies of Soviet political and managerial elites carried out in recent years by Armstrong and Granick.[3]

A certain amount of technical expertise does not handicap a manager, but rather makes him more able to cope with his sometimes recalcitrant experts. This is true also of the party. The growing penetration of its ranks by technically and professionally trained persons will not necessarily transform its organizational values or sap its vitality. A local party secretary who can now deal with a recalcitrant expert by cajoling and arguing with him may get better results than his ignorant predecessor of twenty-five years ago achieved by threats and curses. What is essential, however, is that this political goal-orientation of the party be maintained. The recent intensification of indoctrination within the party suggests that the leadership intends to maintain it. The stress on *agitprop* activity and the size of the staffs engaged in it indicate the importance attached to this task by the regime. Technical proficiency and doctrinal sophistication were secrets of the Jesuits' success. It is important and revealing to note the CPSU's efforts to use the same methods.

In discussing the changing role of the party, it is also revealing to touch on the problem of leadership conflicts within it. The character of the contestants, the issues over which they fought, and the methods used to resolve the struggles cast light both on continuities and changes within the party and the system. In this connection, it is instructive to ask: who, what about, and how? For example, take the difference between some of the major party opponents of Stalin and Khrushchev. Trotsky symbolized the revolutionary, almost anarchistic, traditions of communism. To defeat him, Stalin skillfully exploited the instinct of self-preservation of the party, which was far from willing to sacrifice itself on the altar of world revolution. No contrast could be sharper than that between the flamboyant revolutionary and the quiet, dull Malenkov—a party *apparatchik* who perhaps in spite of himself became the symbol and maybe even the spokesman of the managerial technocracy. Similarly, when the time came for Stalin to move forward with domestic reforms, he was opposed by the brilliant and articulate Bukharin. Is it just a coincidence that his counterpart thirty years later was the hulking, sullen, and anything but effervescent Kaganovich? The change that has taken place within the top elite is well symbolized by the men who failed in the struggle for power; and this change is as significant as any of the similarities that one might find between the victors.

The "what about" of the conflicts is also revealing. The issues at hand no longer involve basic questions of the very survival of the Communist regime. The problem now is how to promote a venture that has been eminently successful but that cannot stand still (much like a prospering business in a competitive environment). Domestically, the major challenge to the ruler's power does not come from the visionaries and revolutionaries. To succeed, a challenger must be able to work within the ruling organization, and this successful organization, even while compulsively requiring ideology-action, does not wish to undertake reckless adventures. The greater threat comes from the dogmatic conservatives and the undogmatic managerial and technical intelligentsia. To the former, all necessary wisdom of theory and practice is to be found in the experience of the years 1928–53. The latter tend to equate the construction of "socialism" with the process of building a technically advanced industrial society, and to consider that after the process is completed, the further operation of society can be handled by the technical cadres of experts and specialists. But to each group the other group is a greater threat than Khrushchev leadership, and hence the two neutralize each other, much in the same way that the Left and Right did in Stalin's early days. Nonetheless, the characteristics of both groups indicate that the ruling party is no longer faced by fundamental questions of life and death, that the revolutionary phase of the great dilemma of principle and practice is finished.

The "how" of the conflicts serves, however, as a timely warning against premature conclusions concerning any fundamental change in the internal political practices of the party. In both cases, the victorious contestants skillfully combined their perception of the innate collective interest of the ruling elite with effective manipulation of the party's *apparat,* particularly through the secretariat. It would be misleading, however, to attribute Khrushchev's success merely to his control of the secretariat. After all, his opponents were strong in it as well. The case was similar, as Deutscher shows in his *Prophet Unarmed,*

in Stalin's struggle with Trotsky. Khrushchev as well as Stalin employed muted appeals for support and perceptive appreciation of the dominant aspirations of the ruling elite. And in both cases there were inherent pressures towards centralization of power in the hands of a single individual, pressures which he could exploit but which he alone could not have generated. Considering Khrushchev's age, it is well to be alert for signs of the struggle for succession that is likely soon to begin or has already begun, and in doing so one can learn a great deal not only about the power struggle itself but also about the *Gestalt* of the ruling party.

A discussion of the role of the party as a dynamic factor in Soviet politics leads directly into a consideration of the political function of ideology.[4] One of the most distinctive features of the Soviet system, and particularly of its ruling regime, is its conscious purposefulness. Everything it does—in fact, its very existence—is related to a conscious striving towards an announced but not exactly defined goal. Since this action is focused necessarily on the immediate task facing the party, whether it is collectivization and class struggle or the further limitation of the individual's opportunity for personal ownership, different aspects of the ideology may be emphasized at different times. These varying emphases provide clues to the changing preoccupations of the regime. As noted above, much of the ideological emphasis today is centered on making Russia, a highly advanced, technically skilled nation, and the party a rational, efficiency-oriented organization. But it is one thing for the party to be "rational" in its operation and another thing if this rationality begins to affect the utopian ends of political action and makes the efficient functioning of the system an end in itself. It is the party and the ideology together that provide the system with its inbuilt momentum. The decline of either would force the regime to rely almost exclusively on terror, as Stalin did, or face the prospect of far-reaching transformation of the system.

Internal indoctrination within the party is therefore a prime necessity. It is important that power within the party should not gravitate into the hands of "experts," but that broad purposeful "generalizers" remain at the helm, assisted on the one hand by loyal party "experts" (Gosplanner or manager) and on the other by the watchdogs of ideological purity. The split between these extremes is more "objective" than "subjective." Both are loyal and dedicated, but with the modernization and development of Soviet society the party, as noted, has necessarily absorbed the new, highly trained elite, with the concomitant danger of gradual change of orientation within its ranks. In part to balance this, in part almost by a process of reaction, there has developed within the party a professional cadre of "ideologues," a group of specialists in doctrinal matters, who bear little resemblance to the creative revolutionaries of the twenties. Yet the growth of the *agitprop,* its professionalization, is in itself an indication of the process of change which, in this case, involves strenuous efforts to maintain the commitment of the party membership to the party ideology and to express that commitment in action.

At the risk of excessively speculative generalization, one may perhaps suggest that the present relationship between the party members and the ideology is as follows: the very top of the party hierarchy is generally staffed by "ideology-action generalizers," men like Khrushchev, Aristov, Kozlov, with the extremes of technical "experts" (who may be said to specialize in aspects of action alone) and of "ideologues" (who specialize in ideology) represented. It would appear that among the probable successors to Khrushchev the ideology-action generalizers still predominate. (Of the various individuals that one may mention, Kozlov, Polyansky, Brezhnev, Aristov, or Suslov, only the last one is an ideologue, and none are narrow experts of the Kosygin type.[5]) On the intermediary level, we can note two broad categories: the professional party bureaucrats, the *apparatchiki,* from among whom the top level "generalizers" eventually emerge, but to whom on the whole the ideology has become internalized and is not a matter of continuous preoccupation; and, secondly, the large staffs of the *agitprop,* containing the often dogmatic, doctrinaire, and conservative professional ideologues. They are the ones who most often view any new departure as a betrayal. In the lower echelons, it is more a matter of simple stereotypes and formulas than fanatical commitment, although some cases of the latter can be observed even by a casual visitor to the USSR. However, it is to be remembered that all three levels operate within a system whose institutions already reflect the basic notions of the ideology and that therefore a more assured mood prevails than in the period of struggle against the old order.

Another aspect of the role of ideology is the almost frenetic effort of the regime to indoctrinate the masses. It is not an exaggeration to say that indoctrination has replaced terror as the most distinctive feature of the relationship of the regime to society, and perhaps even of the system itself as compared to others. With the completion of the destruction of organized intermediary groups between the regime and the people, with the basic outlines of the new society erected, the emphasis on class struggle has given way to a massively organized effort to instill in the Soviet people the values of the ruling party. The closer one studies the Soviet political system, the more one becomes impressed by the totality of the effort and the energy and resources committed to it. There is just no example elsewhere comparable to this total effort (in *Pravda*'s words on September 14, 1960) "to rear the new man." While the party meets often with major difficulties because of boredom, hostility towards uniformity and absence of free contacts with the West, disbelief or just formal acquiescence, it is able to exploit a very great advantage, namely, that it is in a position to link the process of ideological indoctrination to technical modernization of society, which in our age has become the universally accepted good. It is not an accident that in all recent discussions of propaganda the party, as already noted, has been stressing the need to link the two, and because of its monopoly of power the party can make modernization appear to be the consequence of its ideologically inspired action. The organizational compulsion of the party for ideology-action thus becomes the source and the means of modernization, thereby strengthening the party's social legitimization.

Ideology has thus the important effect of transforming the party's power into authority, and of replacing terror as a major buttress for the party's power. This is a major change from Stalin's days. It is now clear that terror has to be seen as a manifestation of a particular stage in the development of the system. In its most intense form, terror manifests itself during the "break-through" stage of totalitarianism, when the old order is being destroyed and the new erected. At that stage, the secret police emerges as the crucial organ of the regime, dominating the political scene. Given the objective of total reconstruction, terror quickly pervades the entire society and the police becomes supreme. If the dictator is inclined to a personal appreciation of violence, such terror can be in some respects even more extreme and sadistic. However, it is doubtful that the social impact of Soviet terror in the thirties would have been much less even if Stalin did not, as has been alleged, derive enjoyment from the physical liquidation of his enemies and friends. As terror mounts, the apparatus of violence becomes institutionalized and develops a vested interest in continuing its own operations. Terror is therefore difficult to halt suddenly; the ruling elite is naturally aware of the accumulation of social hostility that has been aroused and becomes fearful that abandoning terror might bring about a violent upheaval. Terror thus tends to perpetuate itself even after the regime's felt need for it recedes.

The abandonment of terror was facilitated by the involvement of the terror machine in the struggle for succession after Stalin's death. Although it is likely that terror would have declined anyway, the desperate need to decapitate the secret police lest it decapitate the various heirs-apparent precipitated a more rapid decline of the secret police than perhaps would otherwise have been the case. It is quite conceivable that Stalin's successors were pleasantly surprised to find that their system could work, and work as well or even better, without terror, and that the social response was not a revolution but gratitude. They thus pushed the process forward, and today one may justifiably say that terror is no longer a dominant feature of the system. To be sure, the potential is there and it acts as a restraining force. But it no longer pervades society, and it is certainly no longer one of the central means for effecting social change.

Instead, organized coercion performs the function of enforcing societal conformity. The acceptance of the new forms of society by a large part of at least the urban population permits the regime to utilize social orthodoxy for the purpose of enforcing ideologically desirable behavior. The Comrades' Courts, the Citizens' Militia, staffed by narrow-minded and intolerant low-level activists, are all forms of organized mass coercion designed to stifle politically dangerous individualism which might threaten the pattern of positive indoctrination discussed earlier. For that purpose, the potential of political terror in the background and organized social intolerance in the forefront is sufficient. A voluntarist totalitarianism can be far more effective than a terrorist one.

The theme running through the three aspects discussed earlier is the organizational compulsion of the party towards enforcing social integration around its overt dogmatic beliefs. To abandon these efforts to "ideologize" society, even if this process is already highly ritualized and may no longer involve general individual commitment, would signal the first real step in the direction of the transformation of the system. The regime has shown that it can rule with far less violent means than were used under Stalinism, but the kind of power it needs to continue changing society, even if at a decreasing pace, demands a degree of social integration that can be achieved only if a sense of purpose, organizationally expressed, is energetically maintained.[6] Only then can the emergence of alternative values be avoided;

only then can the appearance of groups showing alternative goals be prevented. Only then can the individual be faced with this politically paralyzing dilemma of the one alternative—to be against the regime is to be against everything and for nothing.

III

In recent years a great deal has been said about the socio-economic development of Soviet society. It has been argued that the achievement of the highly literate and economically mature society would necessarily cause a profound transformation of the political order, and in this connection the words "liberalization" or "democratization" have often been used. It has been suggested in the preceding pages that politics are still supreme within the Soviet system, but such political supremacy cannot be viewed as existing in a vacuum, independent of the socio-economic context. The role of the dynamic factors in shaping Soviet politics must be seen within a framework which relates them to the significant changes that have taken place in the USSR over the last few decades, and the preceding discussion has borne that in mind.

There can be no doubt that several sectors of Soviet society have particular relevance to a discussion of the Soviet political system and pose special problems for it. The relationship between the regime and four such sectors, namely, agriculture, the industrial organization, the intelligentsia, and the evolving public organizations, deserves special note.

In recent years agriculture has been in the forefront of domestic policy discussions. The failure of Stalinist policies to improve appreciably agricultural production forced the succession leadership to re-examine some hitherto sacred tenets concerning the untouchability of the MTS's and to adopt urgent measures to expand the acreage of arable land, to improve productivity, to increase individual incentives for the deplorably underpaid *kolkhozniki,* and last but not least to strengthen the direct control of the countryside by the party. Both the extremity of the crisis and the fluid situation in the leadership quickly led to the emergence of alternative positions, and the Central Committee plenums which attempted to deal with the situation (starting with the September, 1953, plenum and including both the 1958 and the 1959 meetings) also became arenas of bitter political conflict, with consequent political casualties at the very top. However, what is particularly interesting is that, although ample evidence has been cited by the Soviet leaders as well as by the recent statistical yearbook to show that productivity on private plots far outdistances the "socialist sector," all the solutions offered, both the conservative and neo-Stalinist as well as the innovating Khrushchevist ones, specifically excluded any alternative which could increase agricultural production at the cost of the ideology. Furthermore, the least controversial measures have been those which resulted in the taking of highly successful steps to politicize fully for the first time the agricultural sector. The present trend toward the amalgamation of collective farms, their increasing formation into state farms, and the liquidation of private plots and livestock, suggests that efforts to improve production and the lot of the collective farmer by making him in essence like an industrial worker, involve conscious political direction based on ideological considerations. In effect, the way of life of roughly 50 per cent of the Soviet population is still being actively and profoundly changed by political action.

The situation in the industrial sector is somewhat different. Here, too, the question of reforms was linked with serious political conflict, as was openly admitted after the July, 1957, plenum, particularly at the December, 1958, plenum. However, the policy issues and the measures taken in the industrial sector were much less, if at all, related to the dilemma of ideology versus efficiency, and brought no further politically directed changes in the way of life of the urban proletariat. Instead, the issues centered on the problem of planning and managerial organization, and their relationship to effective party control. The solution adopted, namely the system of *sovnarkhozy,* is familiar. In many individual cases it certainly involved important changes in the accustomed mode of life. A bureaucrat's family, moving from Moscow to Irkutsk, may have perhaps reflected, in the course of the long train ride on the Siberian railway, on the relationship of political decisions to their way of life. However, a more significant consequence of the reforms was that increased efficiency of operations (achieved, it is claimed, by debureaucratization) was linked to a consolidation of direct party control over the industrial sector. The party remained as the only source of social and political cohesion in Soviet society, and on all levels of the industrial organization direct party participation in the decision-making process was assured. A party secretary, Brezhnev, personally supervised the reorganization, and it is the responsibility of republican and regional party secretaries to make certain that increasingly frequent manifestations of *mestnichestvo* are subordinated to over-all national objectives as set by the top leadership.

The relationship with the intelligentsia is more difficult to define. As a group it enjoys special privileges, and many of its members, particularly among the intellectuals, have direct access to the leadership circles. As a result, it can make its influence felt perhaps even to a disproportionate degree. Furthermore, the experience of recent years, particularly of 1956–57, shows that there is restlessness and even dissatisfaction among a great many Soviet students, writers, and poets. The intellectuals have always been the carriers of new ideas, either indigenously conceived or adopted from abroad. However, in order to disseminate ideas on a politically significant scale, they must live in an environment which is actively, or at least passively, receptive.[7] By and large, one is forced to conclude that those intellectuals who are inclined to question the existing taboos have not found the Soviet Union to be either actively or passively receptive. With the possible exception of the small artistic communities in Moscow and Leningrad (within which a novel like *The Trial Begins* could be created), the regime has so far been able to prevent the development of anything like the intellectuals' clubs of Warsaw or Budapest, and it has successfully maintained its general monopoly on all means of communication.[8] Furthermore, the first generation of urban dwellers of the USSR are not paragons of intellectual tolerance; and the regime successfully appealed in 1956–57 to the anti-intellectual bias of the masses when it needed to intimidate the intellectuals. Beyond that, party control over *nomenklatura,* over publications, rewards and awards, has served to contain occasional individual violations of the politically determined limits.

Insofar as the intelligentsia as a whole is concerned, the prevalent tendency seems to be towards professionalization, towards a compartmentalization of interests. An engineer or a doctor is given relatively unlimited opportunities for advancement on the basis of merit, provided he meets certain minimum political criteria. Party membership, but not necessarily activism, is often a necessary condition for a position of major professional responsibility, but as long as formal behavior is in accord with the political norm and the expected degree of ideological competence is demonstrated, the regime does not impose heavy and objectionable demands. To the extent that such a relationship can be appraised, it would appear that there is at present mutual satisfaction with this arrangement.

A relatively new phenomenon in the regime-society relationship is the emphasis placed on the public organizations which are to absorb certain state functions in view of the latter's gradual "withering away" in the course of the transition to communism. Although as yet little of major significance has passed into the hands of such "public organizations," there appear to be three major objectives for stressing them: to revitalize public zeal and to stimulate interest in the transition to communism; to develop through popular participation a form of citizen's control over bureaucratic operations; to enforce societal conformity over wayward behavior. All three suggest that the regime is increasingly confident that it enjoys some measure of popular support and that if it is to increase the scope of social initiative, it will do so at the bottom, where ideological intolerance and social conformity are probably the strongest. At the same time, the regime will be in a better position to appraise popular moods (recent Soviet interest in public opinion polls is revealing) and will therefore be better prepared for the difficult task of both running and changing a large and at least a semi-modern society.

The Soviet political system thus involves one-party dictatorship, with its outstanding characteristic being the active indoctrination of the society in the party's ideology and the shaping of all social relations according to that ideology. For this reason, words such as "liberalization" and "democratization" are somewhat misleading. They are, after all, terms used to describe a process of political, social, and economic change that took place in Western societies under entirely different conditions—organically, often spontaneously, usually pluralistically.

Any consideration of the process of change within a totalitarian society must take into account the means used to modernize the existing society, since the means that have been used tend to affect the longer-range patterns of development. In the Soviet Union, a primitive society was to a degree industrialized and modernized through total social mobilization effected by violent, terroristic means wielded by a highly disciplined and motivated political elite. The very nature of this process is inimical to the emergence of a separate managerial class (not to speak of the even more amorphous concept of a "middle class"), which would be a first step towards limiting of the party's power. Furthermore, a society that has developed under total political direction has a need for continued political integration on a national scale since the liquidation both of the private economic sector and of all informal leadership groups creates a vacuum that must be filled. In such conditions, the party—its discipline, morale, and zeal—remain the determinants of change.

Assuming that this ruling party desires to maintain continued mobilization of society, it may even be argued that a modern industrial society provides that party with the most sophisticated tools of social control available and permits it to maintain that mobilization. Indeed, one may even say that the more modern and developed the society, the more malleable it is. Terror and violence may be necessary to change rapidly a primitive, uneducated, and traditional society. Persuasion, indoctrination, and social control can work more effectively in more highly developed societies. Czechoslovakia as compared to Poland and Hungary would be a good example. Students of Soviet scientific development have already noted ominous indications that even more sophisticated techniques of psychological and social manipulation are in the offing. Gide's observation, cited at the beginning of this essay, remains applicable.

The present Soviet discussions of what the future Communist society will be like offers us a revealing picture which, if past experience is a guide, should not be ignored. Professor S. G. Strumilin, the Soviet expert on the transition to communism, assures us (in *Novyi mir,* July, 1960): "Any Soviet citizen who enters the world will automatically be enrolled in a nursery, transferring to an established children's home and then, according to age, placed in a boarding school. His transition to productive life or to further special studies will also be arranged." The Professor adds: "Too much parental love often has catastrophic results for the children, hindering the development of the children. We are absolutely opposed to the old tradition which regarded children as the 'property' of the parents." People will live together in large communes, eating together; their children will play only with communal toys: "personal property in toys, ice skates, bicycles, and so forth will not be recognized in the commune. All gifts received by the children will go into the 'common pot' and be there for everybody." Everyone will be dedicated; behavior will be enforced by the sheer weight of communal orthodoxy, which necessarily excludes individual self-assertion. Dachas and automobiles will no longer be the objects of an individual's ambition, and public servants will toil with a dedication deeply rooted in the Communist ideology.

It may be comforting to dismiss all this as sheer fantasy, but to the extent that the stability of the present regime depends on the continuous, even if gradual, implementation of the ideology, such descriptions are a good guide to the understanding of the goals of a party ruling an increasingly mature and voluntarist totalitarian system. They suggest that the CPSU has not yet resigned itself to playing the role merely of a Soviet Chamber of Commerce! Indeed, all indications are that Soviet society is again on the eve of momentous changes, the execution of which is not likely to weaken the party's power.

It is at this point that a consideration of the interaction between external and domestic affairs becomes particularly relevant. Many past cases of such interaction can be cited: for instance, in 1926, the China policy and the domestic struggle for power; in 1936, Stalin's conviction of the West's basic hostility and his decision to give the Soviet society another taste of "war communism," that is, radical political and economic policies; in 1956, the general situation in the Soviet bloc and anti-Stalin campaign. It could be argued, however, that in some ways the relationship is becoming increasingly significant. In the past Stalin's regime was basically inward-oriented and isolationist, but today the USSR is deeply involved both in world politics and in the complex process of running an international Communist empire. This involvement on the one hand strengthens the role of the ruling party, since it seems to demonstrate its claim that it is leading the USSR to greatness. At the same time, what happens abroad is now much more relevant to domestic Soviet politics. That is why Kennan's thesis that political containment could lead to a domestic mellowing or breakdown of the Soviet system was at least premature. It assumed a relationship between external affairs and domestic politics that did not exist in Stalin's time. It exists today, however, but in a much different way.

The emerging diversity within the Communist orbit, and the necessary Soviet adjustment to it, means that the hitherto uniform ideology tends increasingly to be expressed and emphasized in different ways. Furthermore, the recent admonition that war is not inevitable and that a nuclear war would be a universal catastrophe necessarily challenges the conception of an immutable and objective historical process and makes a subjective and perhaps even an irrational factor, namely, someone's decision to start a war, a deciding factor in the historical process. The domestic ideological uniformity of the system may thus be threatened either by the penetration of competitive ideas or by the relativization of the ideology as a result of its varied interpretations in different Communist states. In either case, there is a danger of the gradual domestic erosion of the absolutist ideological commitment. The officially admitted fear of war, stemming in large part from the objective "factor"—the destructiveness of nuclear weapons, is closely related to the increasing domestic social desire to enjoy the "good life." In the history of the regime there has

always been a tension between the regime's genuine desire to improve the lot of society and its fear that doing it too quickly would be politically and economically disastrous. With the "victory" of socialism in the USSR finally assured, the regime finds itself increasingly able to respond to social pressures for a better life. However, it would be politically very dangerous if both at home and abroad a mood of general social relaxation were to prevail. The sense of dynamism must be preserved. The need for the party's dictatorship and therefore for its ideology-action must be demonstrated.

The present response is a compromise both at home and abroad. It is no longer a matter of violent large-scale social revolution at home, but "the extensive transition to communism," with its hopes for the good life, does mean that the march forward is being continued. And abroad, it is not a matter of outright violent hostility towards the enemy, since that carries with it the danger of total destruction. Rather again a compromise: acceptance of the "peaceful co-existence" of systems but an offensive in ideology, including the encouragement of radical nationalist revolutions that are made possible by the peaceful and paralyzing mutual nuclear blackmail of the USSR and the United States. Peace with victories will serve to strengthen the party's claim that history is still unfolding, that it must continue its mission, that there is no fraternization with the enemy—but all without war.

Nonetheless, relativization of the ideology is implicit in such adjustments and carries with it dangerous internal implications. The domestic power of the totalitarian system depends on the commitment to an absolutist ideology. But such conviction cannot be provided by an ideology which is right only in some places for some people and at some times. If the ideology becomes a relative one, it will be deprived of the fanaticism and dogmatic conviction which provided the momentum for sacrifice, forceful action, and internal unity. History teaches that relativization is the first stage in the erosion of dogmatic ideas.

The appearance of diversity within international communism, a diversity that the Soviet regime initially desired to restrict to institutions and not to extend to ideology, carries with it the danger that varying ideological emphases may result either in splits within the bloc or in the development of a silent agreement to disagree. That is a novel situation for a movement that has matured in the belief that ideological unity and organizational unity are absolutely essential. It also suggests that if gradual erosion of either kind of unity is to take place, and if as a result the Soviet political system is to change fundamentally, the change will have to come primarily from the outside and not from the inside. Originating in bona fide Communist states and formulated within the framework of the common ideology, alternative and more tolerant notions might gradually penetrate the ruling elite and only afterwards affect the society as a whole.[9] However, if one considers what it took and how long it took for foreign ideas to penetrate the far less controlled Tsarist Russia, to merge with domestic trends and eventually to emerge supreme, and weighs all this against the power of the Communist regime, one may well be justified in cautioning that this erosion must be awaited with a great deal of patience.

NOTES

1. For a theoretical analysis of this relationship see William Kornhauser, *The Politics of Mass Society* (Glencoe, Ill.: Free Press, 1959).

2. For discussion see Amitai Etzioni, "Authority Structure and Organizational Effectiveness," *Administrative Science Quarterly*, Vol. IV, No. 1 (1959), as well as the following sources cited therein: Robert Dubin, *Human Relations in Administration* (New York, 1951); Melville Dalton, "Conflicts Between Staff and Line Managerial Officers," *American Sociological Review*, Vol. XV, No. 3 (1950); A. W. Gouldner, "Cosmopolitans and Locals: Toward an Analysis of Latent Social Roles," *Administrative Science Quarterly*, Vol. II, No. 3 (1957) and No. 4 (1958).

3. John A. Armstrong, *The Soviet Bureaucratic Elite: A Case Study of the Ukrainian Apparatus* (New York, 1959); David Granick, *The Red Executive* (New York, 1960).

4. I have tried elsewhere to define what I mean by ideology and in what way I think it affects the conduct of Soviet leaders. I will not therefore cover the same ground here. See chapter xvi of my *The Soviet Bloc: Unity and Conflict*

(Cambridge, Mass., 1960), and "Communist Ideology and International Affairs," *Journal of Conflict Resolution*, September, 1960.

5. It may be tentatively posited that the ideology-action generalizers at the apex are usually in a closer relationship to the ideologues than to the more subordinate experts. On lower levels, the party *apparatchiki* are usually in a closer relationship to *agitprop* than to the experts. (By closer relationship is meant less direct subordination of latter by former.) In revolutionary times (in early post-1917 Russia or even in China today) there tends to be a relative fusion between the ideology-action generalizers and the ideologues (symbolized by Lenin or Mao Tse-tung). With stability a process of differentiation took place, and in some respects the *apparatchiki* came closer to the experts. In recent years Khrushchev has been trying to counteract this process by stimulating increased activity by the *agitprop* and by assigning greater responsibility to the *apparat*, thus compensating for the necessarily greater importance of the experts, given Soviet industrial-technical development.

6. One may add that an older example of the expression of the survival instinct of a goal-oriented movement through such organizational compulsion towards indoctrination and social integration is provided by church history.

7. By the former is meant that type of community which because of a continuous and often competitive interplay of groups is necessarily responsive to the impact of new ideas. New York and Paris are good metropolitan examples of actively receptive communities. By a passively receptive society is meant one which does not set up purposeful impediments to the inflow of new ideas.

8. The political experience of intellectual unrest in Hungary and Poland on the one hand and in China on the other might be relevant here. In the former it was closely associated with demoralization in the party and led to an eruption. In the latter it did not penetrate the party and the regime could quickly suppress it.

9. There might be an analogy here to the political history of religiously oriented societies. It was only after the Protestant and Catholic states learned to coexist with one another and, for that matter, with non-Christian states, that Protestants, Catholics, and others learned to live with one another *within* given states. An "interfaith council" in the United States is thus not only an example of conscious toleration but also of a decline in absolutist commitment.

90

Modernization and the Maoist Vision—Some Reflections on Chinese Communist Goals

Benjamin Schwartz

What can be said at this point about the broad goals and motivations of the present Chinese Com-

From Benjamin Schwartz, "Modernization and the Maoist Vision—Some Reflections on Chinese Communist Goals," *China Quarterly*, No. 21 (January–March 1965), pp. 3–19. Reprinted by permission of the publisher.

munist leadership? The question is, of course, distressingly imprecise and begs further definition. Is the leadership a monolithic group? Have its goals remained constant and unchanging? Is there a rigid Chinese Communist "goal structure," etc.?

On the question of leadership I shall simply adhere to the conventional hypothesis that Mao Tse-tung and those closest to him have played a leading role in determining basic policy shifts during the last fifteen years. There may have been moments when his presence has receded from the centre of the stage. In the early years after 1950, his role may have been somewhat inhibited by the awesome presence of Stalin. His influence may have flagged at the Wuhan meeting at the end of 1958 and after the retreat from the great leap forward. On the whole, however, one perceives the imprint of his outlook (probably developed in close collaboration with Liu Shao-ch'i) at almost every crucial turning point from the land reform campaign of 1950 to the present frenzied drive for "socialist education."

On the matter of goals, while there is certainly no rigid static "goal structure," while the relationship among goals has undoubtedly been enormously complex, problematic and shifting over time, it may nevertheless be possible to speak of a certain range of broad goals which has remained fairly constant and which may have set certain outer limits to the possibilities of policy choice. This does not mean, one should hasten to add, that the whole history of Communist China during the last fifteen years can be understood in terms of an unproblematic implementation of the leadership's goals. Unyielding objective conditions, unforeseen events and contingencies, and the recalcitrances of human nature have certainly been just as decisive as the goals of the leadership in shaping the history of China since 1949. Interpretations of events in Communist China have often swung wildly from the view that China is an inert clay in the hands of the leaders who shape it as they will to the view that everything that has happened is a result of an iron "objective necessity" which shapes all the leadership's decisions. All that will be urged in this article is that the goals of the leadership have been one of the factors shaping the course of events.

There has been much discussion of Chinese Communist goals during the last decade and a half and there is a certain range of broad assumptions which can be discerned in most analyses of the Chinese scene whether written by academic experts poring over Chinese Communist media or visitors who have been there. One such widely shared assumption is that the overriding, indeed, all-embracing goal of the Chinese Communist leadership is to achieve the modernisation of China or—put somewhat differently—everything that is happening in Communist China is an aspect of the process of modernisation. There is also the assumption that the basic goal of the leadership is the achievement of a certain vision of

society spelled out in the scriptures of Marxism-Leninism-Maoism. This vision may involve aspects of what is called "modernisation" in the West, but modernisation is conceived of as a part of a much larger whole defined by the ideology. This view of the goals of the leadership is, of course, the avowed view of the leadership itself but is also shared by many others who may be ardently attracted to the vision or violently repelled by it. Another view places central stress on nationalism—on the goal of national power and prestige and on the achievement of world power status as quickly as possible. It is of course true that to the protagonists of the modernisation school nationalism is simply an "aspect" or "function" of some all-inclusive modernisation process and hence not to be considered under a separate rubric. To others it must be considered as a force in its own right. There is another view which may be said to concern motivation more than goals —namely, that the Chinese Communist leadership is essentially engrossed in the limitless "totalitarian" aggrandisement of its own power, both within China and in the world at large. There are undoubtedly other assumptions which can and have been made concerning the goals and motives of the leaders, but I shall confine my attention to these.

Power

Turning first of all to the view that all the policies and decisions of the leadership are designed to maximise its power, we find that in recent years, particularly since the death of Stalin, there has been a distinct decline in the popularity of the "theory of totalitarianism" or all theories which stress the power drives of the leadership. There has, in fact, been a tendency on the part of some to brush aside the relevance of power considerations entirely on grounds which are a shade too facile. Power, we are told, is not an end in itself. It is functional to goals which lie beyond it or it plays a certain function in the larger social system, etc. It must always be explained in terms of "larger" social, historic and economic forces of which it is the mere instrument. One might say that for the whole course of human history power has always been "functional." It has always led to objective results, bad or good, which have survived its pursuit. This is just as true of Rameses and Ch'in Shih Huang-ti as it is of Mao Tse-tung. This by no means precludes the fact that it has also been pursued as an end in itself and that this pursuit has played its own role in human history. "Objectively" Macbeth may have been a most successful Scottish "state-builder" but this by no means proves that the side of him which Shakespeare chooses to depict is irrelevant to a discussion of his day-to-day political behaviour. Power has always been functional and always been demonic and the end is not yet in sight. What vitiates the narrow "power approach" is the assumption that a concern with the maintenance or expansion of power is necessarily incompatible with the pursuit of more general goals. If the Chinese Communist Party is conceived of as the sole effective instrument for achieving a certain vision of the good society or for making China a great world power or for consummating the process of modernisation, then the general goals and power considerations may actually reinforce and enhance each other.

Those who deny the relevance of power considerations might at this point maintain, however, that if power considerations and objective goals often move in the same direction why assign any particular causal weight to power considerations? In fact, however, at given points in time they may by no means move in the same direction. If one assumes that one of the basic domestic aims of the "hundred flowers" campaign was to provide the intelligentsia (a term which, of course, includes both professionals and academic and literary intellectuals) with an opportunity to participate more fully and freely in the economic and scientific development of China; if a reasoned judgment had been made that further economic and scientific development required the more positive participation of the intelligentsia, one can hardly say that the experiment was given time to prove itself. The fact that Mao Tse-tung was still vigorously supporting the programme in February 1957 only to allow himself to be won over to the opposition (which had undoubtedly been strong in the Party from the outset) within the next few months can hardly be due to its failure to produce spectacular economic results in the early months of 1957. The drive was speedily terminated when it seemed to involve a threat to the unlimited political power of the leadership. Similarly, while the purges of Kao Kang and Jao Shu-shih in 1954 and of P'eng Teh-huai in 1959 undoubtedly involved policy differences from the outset, it is quite clear that in the end these "anti-party elements" were associated with a threat to power. The vehemence with which the ideological remoulding of the army was carried on in the 1960–62 period can hardly be disassociated from this threat to power.

All of these instances, of course, involve not so much a concern for the expansion of power as for the preservation of power in being and it may well be one of the defects of the theory of totalitarianism

that it dogmatically assumes that the concern for power must always be a concern for its maximisation. It makes no allowance for the possibility that a concern for the maintenance of power in being may, at times, outweigh the concern for its maximisation in the future. Nevertheless, the power approach reminds us that we are dealing with a group of men who know and savour power and its uses as much as any ruling group that has ever existed. They are not merely the embodiment of a social vision, or the destiny of China, or the process of modernisation. Mao's spectacular projection of his own authority in the Communist bloc and the world at large and the present hysterical cult of Mao in China may serve a certain vision of the world or be in line with certain policies but also admirably feed his limitless *hybris*. The factor of power is relevant to a discussion of all these policies and shifts in policy. Indeed, at points where the implementation of policy may seem to endanger power interests, it may be the most relevant factor of all.

Modernisation

If the ever-present concern with power by no means precludes the pursuit of broader goals—what are these broader goals? One widely accepted response is that the goal is the modernisation of China. One could, of course, devote volumes to a discussion of the meaning of this term and yet there does seem to be a kind of common core of shared meaning which is implicit at least in most American discussions. In general, it tends to mean something approximating Max Weber's conception of the process of rationalisation in all those spheres of social action—economic, political, military, legal, educational—which lend themselves to the application of *"Zwecksrationalität."* It involves the sustained attention to the most appropriate, "rational" and efficient methods for increasing man's ability to control nature and society for a variety of ends. Economists often treat it as being co-extensive with industrialisation and it is indeed in this area that the meaning of the term "rationalisation" can be most concretely elucidated. Weber himself in spite of his tendency to use the cover term "capitalism" (presumably an economic category) was just as much concerned with political bureaucracy, military development and legal "rationalisation." It tends to involve the notion of a highly developed division of labour of "functional specificity" with the corollary that men should have a degree of autonomy and authority within their various areas of competence. It also involves a stress on norms of universality rather than ascription and thus, should involve social mobility—the opening up of careers to talents. Looking at the whole concept from the point of view of China, one is inclined to stress that it also may involve a sober respect for objective conditions. The technician and, for that matter, the professional bureaucrat will be very conscious of the limits imposed by his materials and by the imperatives of the situation within which he operates.

Actually one can distinguish two versions of the concept of modernisation which may have quite different implications. One version treats the "process of modernisation" as a vast, indeed, an all-embracing impersonal historic force. Revolutions, ideologies, nationalism and the policies of governments are all surface eruptions of this underlying process which is independent of the wills of men and operates behind their backs very much like Hegel's "*Weltgeist*" or Marx's "mode of production." In the other version, modernisation becomes a conscious project or consciously entertained goal of large or small groups of men. The two versions may have quite different consequences for an analysis of the behaviour of the Chinese leadership. If modernisation is an all-enveloping force which controls all the acts both conscious and unconscious of the leadership, all their acts must be explained as a "function" of the modernisation process. The leadership may explicitly profess concern with other matters; it may even sincerely be concerned "subjectively" with other matters. In fact, all its behaviour is determined by the imperatives of the modernisation process. If, on the other hand, modernisation is a goal consciously pursued, it is not impossible that it may compete in the minds of the leadership with other goals. In fact, the decisions of the leadership may have something to do with shaping the order of priorities and strategies of the modernisation process itself.

The adherents of the monistic modernisation theory seldom if ever raise questions about the goals of modernisation itself. It is assumed that the goals are immanent in the process and that we know what they are. Among many Americans there is in fact the latent assumption that a fully modernised society will look exactly like the United States with all its social and cultural specificities. Even if we assume that modernisation is leading in the end of days to some universal homogenised human condition, *in processu* it is quite compatible with quite different conceptions of the priority of ends to be served. A highly advanced industrial society may be able to lavish equal resources on state power and prestige and welfare. A less developed society will have to make choices in this area and these choices

may have a most profound effect on the strategy of modernisation.

Nationalism

Viewed in this light nationalism may be much more than a "function" of the modernisation process. Where it occupies a central place, it may actually determine the strategy of modernisation. To assume that Stalin's lop-sided emphasis on heavy industrial development was a function of Soviet nationalism seems to make much more sense than to assume that it was the only rational strategy of industrialisation in an underdeveloped area. Similarly one must assume that the apparent priority granted to nuclear development in China through all the recent shifts in economic strategy is related fundamentally to its nationalist goals rather than to any obvious imperative of the modernisation process.

The Chinese leadership's unquestioning adoption of this model after 1950 was due not simply to the fact that it was the orthodox Marxist-Leninist model of economic development but also to the fact that Stalin had in this model already bent Marxism-Leninism to national power purposes. As perfervid Chinese nationalists the Chinese leadership shared the preoccupations which lay behind Stalin's own choice of model. They were genuine Stalinists in their whole-hearted acceptance of Stalin's accommodation of Marxism-Leninism to the interests of a nation-state. It is thus entirely meaningful to stress that the speedy achievement of nationalist goals has been one of the unchanging central goals of the leadership which has shaped the priorities and strategy of the modernisation process itself. This does not mean that the leadership is not committed to the welfare goals which we associate with modernisation—with living standards, public health, literacy, etc.—but the relative priorities seem quite clear.

During the years from 1949 to 1956 there can be little doubt that the goal of modernisation *on the Soviet model* was assiduously pursued by the Chinese Communist leadership in many sectors. After the Korean War we have a gradual implementation of the Soviet model of economic development. There is a movement towards the creation of a state structure with a modern bureaucratic apparatus and the professionalisation of the army on a Soviet model is vigorously pursued. It has indeed become the tendency among some to regard this eminently Soviet phase of Chinese development as the "modernising" phase *par excellence* as opposed to the irrationalities of subsequent phases. Yet as we know, the relationship of the whole Soviet development to the supposed prerequisites of modernisation has itself been the subject of endless, unresolved debates. Ideology is also deeply implicated in the whole Soviet development. What is mainly implied is that the Soviet model involves a stress on professionalisation, on a degree of autonomy for professional hierarchies, particularly in the industrial, state administrative and military spheres. Franz Schurmann has, for instance, stressed the emphasis during this period on the Soviet conception of managerial responsibility in industry (without necessarily regarding it as pre-eminently rational).

One of the most striking facts of recent Chinese Communist history (particularly since 1956) has been the gradual departure from the Soviet model of modernisation. Some have leaped to the conclusion that this marks the departure from a "rational" approach to modernisation. Yet it might well be argued that, in part, the departure from the Soviet model of modernisation was due to the realisation that this model was not applicable to China's real situation. The Chinese could not reduce the peasantry to a subsistence level and then ignore the agricultural sector. To keep their vast population alive at the barest subsistence level it became obvious that a maximum attention to agriculture was imperative. In the strictly economic sphere one might argue that the economic policy pursued after 1960 with its emphasis on "agriculture as the base" has been much more rational in terms of China's conditions than the model of the 1953–56 period. In fact, one might argue that during the whole period from the "Hundred Flowers" campaign to the present campaign for "socialist education" all policies have borne some relationship to the problems of modernisation.

The Maoist Vision of the Good Society

It nevertheless seems to me that if we are to understand some of the modes of response to these problems which have emerged since 1956, we must introduce another broad goal area which might be called ideological but which I shall refer to as the Maoist vision of the good society.

The vision involves not only a conception of the good society of the future but also a sanctified image of the methods by which this vision is to be achieved. Certainly Marxist-Leninist-Stalinist ideology is one of the main sources of this vision, but this does not preclude the possibility that in some of its aspects it coincides with certain traditional Chinese habits of thought and behaviour. It draws above all on the actual experience of the Commu-

nist movement during the thirties and forties, and the interpretation of this experience enshrined in the Yenan writings of Mao Tse-tung and Liu Shao-ch'i. As has often been pointed out, the "Yenan syndrome" seems to occupy a central, hallowed place in the vision of Mao Tse-tung and most of the elements which form part of the Maoist vision first appear, at least in their embryonic form, during this period.

The phrase "Maoist vision" seems to describe a static frame of reference and almost suggests something like an "operational code" which may provide a key to all the shifts and twists of Party policy since 1949. On the contrary, there is absolutely no reason to assume that it provided Mao with any prevision of the circumstances which were to give rise to the "Hundred Flowers" campaign or the "great leap forward" campaign, or to the circumstances which were to lead to their abrupt demise. Not all elements of the vision have been equally prominent at all times and some of them have only been made fully explicit in the course of time. Many elements of the vision are highly ambivalent ("dialectic") lending themselves to the support of quite opposing policies. And yet when viewed in the abstract, there is a kind of rough coherence among them.

Not only has the pursuit of this vision often cut across other goals of the leadership but has with varying degrees of intensity conditioned the manner in which these other goals have been pursued. Some elements of the vision have had an obvious and almost unremitting impact on reality. The enormous energies invested since 1949 in the effort to achieve the spiritual transformation of the entire Chinese people whether in the form of "study" (*hsüeh-hsi*), "thought reform," "remoulding," "education through labour" or "socialist education" is one of the most obvious instances. At another level, some elements of the vision have been invoked and made most explicit in connection with certain specific campaigns—such as the notion of "contradictions among the people" at the time of the "Hundred Flowers" campaign or the emphasis on "subjective forces," "revolutionary romanticism" and "man as the decisive factor" at the time of the "great leap forward." One is tempted to say that, when invoked in this way, these ideological themes simply serve to confirm the infallibility of the "thought of Mao Tse-tung" in the face of all shifts and twists in line, and —particularly since 1956—to confirm ever more emphatically the autonomy and originality of the "Chinese path." Undoubtedly they do serve this purpose. Yet while these themes are hardly the "sufficient causes" of the campaigns of 1956, 1958 or other new departures, the genuine belief in the assumptions implicit in them may well explain the high confidence and élan with which these campaigns are pressed. One simply has to peruse Mao's comments in such works as *The Socialist Upsurge in China's Countryside* (1955) to appreciate the fervour of his belief in those "facts" which seem to support his vision. At another level, however, elements of the vision are obviously manipulated simply as ideology in the narrowest sense. Thus the fact that the slogans of the "Hundred Flowers" movement and of the great leap continue to live on into periods when they no longer apply is obviously a device designed to prove that Mao's contributions to the storehouse of Marxism-Leninism are irrevocable and cumulative.

Consensus and Collectivism

What are some of the essential elements of the Maoist vision? There is first of all the overriding commitment to a society united by something approaching a total consensus and a society marked by radical collectivism. It may seem superfluous to speak of the collectivist goal of a Communist society, and yet the image of collectivity which has emerged in China, particularly since 1958, seems somewhat different in kind from that projected in the Soviet Union. The emphasis on the individual's total self-abnegation and total immersion in the collectivity as ultimate goods; the frequent reference to the model of military life with its nostalgic allusions to the heroic and idyllic guerrilla bands of the past are particular characteristics of the Maoist projection of the future. Lenin's own projection of Utopia in *State and Revolution* still draws heavily on Marx's own meagre and vague descriptions which, as we know, speak in terms of the total liberation and self-fulfilment of the individual. Whether this language makes Marx a sort of ultimate liberal as some of his interpreters would have us believe, may be open to serious doubt, yet there is the fact that the individual and his situation does play a central role in Marx's Utopia. While the Soviet official ideology has been as deeply suspicious of the whole notion of alienation in the young Marx as the Chinese, a somewhat crasser form of the concern with the interests of the individual can nevertheless be discerned in its projection of Communism. The Maoist version on the other hand projects a kind of collectivist mysticism. Commenting on the European and Soviet discussions of Marxism, Chou Yang states "that in advocating the return of Man to himself they are actually advocating absolute individual freedom and asking the people who live

under Socialism to return to the human nature of bourgeois individualism and to restore the capitalism by which it is fostered."[1]

Even more characteristic has been the enormous emphasis on the power of spiritual transformation (indoctrination seems to be far too weak a term) to bring about this society of collective man. The hope is that of a kind of internalised total consensus achieved mainly by spiritual methods. The ultimate roots of this emphasis may be sought in Lenin's own emphasis on the conscious factor (further extended by Stalin) perhaps fed to some extent by the Confucian faith in the power of moral influence. Its more immediate background is to be sought in the circumstances of the Yenan period when the methods of "remoulding" were first applied to members and prospective members of the Communist Party. The notion was later vastly extended to include the whole "people" including the "national bourgeoisie" however defined. The doctrine that all can be saved—even some "counter-revolutionary elements"—has, of course, always been heavily qualified by the retention of the class notion. People of the wrong classes are not easily transformed, and continue to generate poisons of wrong thought. Yet they *can* be transformed while those of good class background *can* be led astray. In the end the main criterion for assigning persons to the "people" or "non-people" is to be sought in their spiritual attitudes rather than in the facts of their class origin. The doctrine of salvation stresses simultaneously that almost all men may be saved; that salvation is enormously difficult for all men, and that backsliding is an ever present possibility. Paradoxically the emphasis on spiritual transformation may lend itself to quite disparate policies. The "Hundred Flowers" campaign may have been predicated on the genuine belief that the intelligentsia had been basically transformed during the 1949–55 period, while the "anti-rightist" campaign of 1957 was based on precisely the opposite assumption. The "great leap forward" may have been based on the assumption that the "masses" (unlike the intelligentsia) had been basically transformed and that their "subjective forces" were at the disposal of the leadership while the present campaign of "Socialist education" seems to be predicated on the assumption that there is still much work to be done.

"Populism"

The emphasis on spiritual transformation is closely linked to the "populist" theme—because the whole people (defined as a union of four classes) can be transformed, the whole Chinese people can participate in the building of Socialism and Communism. This doctrine finds its formal institutional expression in the coalition structure of government, and can, of course, be harnessed to the nationalist goals of the régime as well as to project the Chinese model to the "emerging world" where there is such an obvious political need to "unite with whom one can unite." The obverse side of the formula—the notion that the "people" is not homogeneous but composed of different classes which still engender "non-antagonistic" (and even antagonistic) contradictions, has, however, been of equal importance. It has justified the need for constant vigilance and unremitting indoctrination, but was also used to justify the vaguely defined legitimate area of "blooming and contending" of the "Hundred Flowers" period. On this side, it is particularly closely linked to another element of the Maoist vision, namely, the enormous stress on struggle, conflict and high tension as positive values. Mao Tse-tung's commitment to these values probably preceded his conversion to Marxism-Leninism and has, as we know, even coloured his vision of the utopian future which he seems reluctant to think of in terms of stasis and total harmony. When directed against those defined as the outer enemy, struggle makes for solidarity "within the people." On another level, however, the enemy must be conceived of as ever present in the minds of the people itself in the form of "bourgeois thought." The struggle against this bourgeois thought is not only a negative factor. "Fighting against wrong ideas is like being vaccinated—a man develops greater immunity from disease after the vaccine takes effect. Plants raised in hot-houses are not likely to be robust."[2] At the time when it was uttered, this doctrine was linked to the lenient policies of the "Hundred Flowers" period. One can easily see how the same doctrine can be given a much more draconic interpretation.

Another element of the vision which is closely linked to the emphasis on spiritual transformation and collectivity is the stress on man rather than weapons or tools as the "decisive force in history." By transforming men's minds and consolidating their collective energies one can achieve enormous results in spheres where others have relied on material power. Here again the Yenan experience provides the shining example. Where one has mobilised the collective energies of men, motivated by the Maoist vision, economic advancement, national power and social transformation are no longer purely dependent on "material prerequisites."

Another theme which has been stressed, with varying degrees of intensity, is the necessity of contact with the masses, and "participation in physical labour" on the part of intellectuals, students, professionals and lower bureaucrats. This may reflect the genuine belief that "participation in labour" is a form of thought reform which will induce respect for physical labour and keep these elements from over-weening pretensions. At the same time it is made crystal clear that one is not free to find among the masses any view of reality which contradicts the Maoist vision.

The Role of the Communist Party

Finally there is the enormous pivotal role of the Communist Party as the "proletarian" vanguard of society. Again, we seem to be dealing here with standard Marxist-Leninist doctrine, but as has been pointed out by many, the Party has probably played a more crucial and concrete role in China than in the Soviet Union at least during the lifetime of Stalin. The transformation of the Chinese people must be carried out by the Party. Ideally speaking, the Party maintains its supremacy not simply by dint of its organisational machinery but by its ability to internalise its "proletarian nature" into every party member. The "proletarian nature" of the Party no longer resides, of course, primarily in the industrial workers but has become a kind of spiritual essence embodied in the Party and yet still endowed with all those transcendental and universal qualities which Marx attributes to the working class. It is this idea of the "proletarian nature" of the Party which sets strict limits to the whole populist drift of the Chinese vision. In fact since the beginning of the Sino-Soviet conflict, the Party has stressed its proletarian nature more than ever. The Party does not derive its transcendent moral status and historic role in China or in the world at large from the fact that it merely represents the Chinese people, but from a higher source. The Party may serve the interests of Chinese nationalism but it does so from a supranational stance.

Within China itself the Party ought to be the nervous system of society and should play a commanding role in every sphere of social and cultural endeavour. The ideal Communist cadre is not only a paragon of selflessness but potentially omnicompetent. Ideally it is also the Party which is in direct communication with the "worker-peasant-soldier" masses and which reflects what the masses want and need or rather what they ought to want and need in a Maoist universe. Thus whenever there is a stress on the "mass line," one may assume that the decision-making function of the local party faction is being stressed. Yet all of this still leaves open the possibilities that the Party ranks, as opposed to the

Supreme leader, are vulnerable to error and backsliding.

Mao's Vision and Modernisation

These it seems to me are some of the more salient elements of the Maoist vision. What have been the relations of this vision to the goal of modernisation?

The official view of the present leadership is that the vision—no matter how its interpretation may fluctuate—not only provides the most effective means of achieving modernisation, but is also an end in itself. The only desirable modernisation is a modernisation which can be incorporated into the Maoist vision. At the other extreme, we have the view that the vision runs completely athwart the prerequisites of modernisation or that it is a sort of rationalisation of the failures and difficulties of modernisation in China. One makes a virtue of necessity according to this view because the necessity is intractable. Where weapons and capital are scarce what is to be lost in stressing the organisation of human energies? Where material incentives are not available, why not stress the "Communist ethic"? Oddly enough, the official ideology also seems to stress the relation of necessity to virtue. It was, after all, the peculiarities of Chinese conditions which made possible the stress on guerrilla warfare. It is the "poverty and blankness" of China, Mao insists in 1958, which makes possible the achievement of Communism long before the insidious corruptions of capitalism and revisionism have set in. The fact that "virtue" is associated with necessity by no means implies that the belief in virtue may not be genuine and fervent particularly since the belief is also linked to the power interests of the leadership.

Surveying the history of the People's Republic since 1949, we find that various elements of the vision play an enormous role in the enormous effort of the first few years to bring about political and ideological consolidation. "Study," "thought reform," "confession," etc., were applied on various levels not only to prospective party members but to the "people" as a whole. The "small group" technique and the technique of mass organisation were universally applied. The Party seemed to be proving that totalitarian consolidation of a people could be carried out effectively by relying on "man" rather than technology. Except for those defined as counter-revolutionaries and reactionaries, there was considerable reason for belief that the spiritual transformation was succeeding. Some parts of the vision seemed, and seem, to be quite compatible with certain aspects of modernisation. Many tasks of public health, police work, social control and even economic undertakings, which depend primarily on labour intensivity, lend themselves to Maoist methods.

The Relevance of the Soviet Model

However, while the vision did permeate large sectors of political and social activity, in the areas most crucial to the modernisation effort—particularly as related to state power goals—it was the Soviet model which was followed. This involved some retreat in the concept of Party omnicompetence, considerable emphasis on a "rational" division of labour and professionalisation and some emphasis on the need for a professional state bureaucracy. This does not mean that one should see an absolute antagonism between the Soviet model of modernisation and the Maoist vision. Obviously the gravitation toward the total nationalisation of industry and the collectivisation of agriculture was entirely in line with both. In fact, it may well have been high confidence and exuberance (as well as a desperate sense of haste) induced by the success of his vision in the political and social spheres which led Mao and those closest to him in 1955 to feel that collectivisation could be speedily consummated in China without the dire effects it had produced in the Soviet Union. The fact remains, however, that on the whole Mao modestly deferred to the "superior experience" of the Soviet Union in these areas.

With the beginning of the "Hundred Flowers" experiment, the picture becomes more complex. On the one hand the experiment seems to mark a further concession to the requirements of modernisation. This can be discerned in the effort to give professionals and specialists a greater sense of security and freedom, in the rectification campaign directed against the Party with the implied admission that in some areas the specialists knew more than the Party and even in the new concern with legal codification. The campaign also seems to have coincided, however, with some dawning doubts about the complete applicability of the Soviet model of modernisation to Chinese conditions. These doubts were certainly encouraged by the death of Stalin and the new winds blowing in the Communist bloc itself. This new emphasis on the requirements of modernisation as well as the doubts about the Soviet model did not, however, necessarily diminish the role of the Maoist vision. On the contrary, the "Hundred Flowers" formula was presented as a precious new contribution of Mao Tse-tung (the first since 1949) to the storehouse of Marxism-Leninism and it is, of course, quite easy to see how many ambivalent elements of the vision lent themselves to the "soft" interpretation of this period. In fact, Mao may have genuinely believed that in the course of thought reform "the political outlook of the Chinese intellectuals has undergone a fundamental change."[3] The growing doubts about the complete applicability of the Soviet model of modernisation may have even encouraged the view that the Maoist vision was applicable in areas where "Soviet experience" had hitherto reigned supreme.

In fact the "great leap forward" and commune movement of 1957–1959 mark the high tide of the application of the Maoist vision to the very tasks of modernisation. If the intelligentsia had shown its fundamental untrustworthiness, the subjective forces of the masses[4] were still available for heaven-storming feats. The emphasis on man as the decisive factor, on the negligible role of "material prerequisites," on the superior efficacy of collective subjective forces and on the omnicompetence of the Party all enter into this experiment, and give it its utopian, apocalyptic flavour.

Contraction and Revival

The retreat from the great leap in 1960–1962 again seems to mark a return to a sober estimate of the requirements of modernisation but no longer on an exclusively Soviet model. It also seems to mark a contraction in the influence of the Maoist vision even though the new economic model with its emphasis on "agriculture as the base" was quite distinctly Chinese. One may, in fact, argue as has been suggested that the modernisation policies of this period are much more "rational" in terms of Chinese realities than the policies of the Soviet period. They have led, it would appear, to a substantial economic recovery. Yet, as we know, ever since the end of 1962 there has again been a rising crescendo of emphasis on "socialist education." At this very moment the Maoist vision, in one of its most extreme formulations, again occupies the centre of the stage. The beginnings of this new revival are perhaps to be discerned in the crisis surrounding the army in the 1959–1962 period. As we know, P'eng Teh-huai, who seems to have become the spokesman of military professionalism and perhaps of professionalism in general, had also become an "anti-party" element, that is a menace in the realm of power, while the crisis of morale in the army revealed in the *Bulletin of Activities* (*Kung-tso T'ung-hsun*) documents suggested that the threat to the vision, at least in this sphere, was also regarded as a threat to power. Thus the campaign of "Socialist education" was begun

very early in the army, and having been judged a success, we find the army projected as a model for society as a whole. Here again we note what Stuart Schram has called Mao's "military deviation"—his tendency to think of a well-indoctrinated army as providing a paradigm of Communist life.

The return of large numbers of students to the countryside involving as it did the frustration of hopes for advancement in urban society, also created a serious problem of morale which seemed to call for drastic therapy in terms of spiritual transformation. Beyond this, the growing intensity of the Sino-Soviet conflict has strongly impelled the leadership to project the Maoist vision onto the world at large as the very embodiment of "true Marxism-Leninism."

Above all, however, there is the fact that the aging Mao and those closest to him are genuinely concerned with the survival of the vision. The whole current fervid campaign of "Socialist education" is permeated more by a kind of pervasive anxiety than by a mood of high confidence. The leadership may be quite optimistic about China's present economic situation and posture in the world at large, but it is precisely in the ideological sphere that one detects a mood of concern. The intelligentsia had shown its unreliability at the time of the "Hundred Flowers" campaign. Even the masses had shown their inability to live up to Mao's expectations at the time of the "great leap forward." Indeed, it is now implied that the spontaneous inertial movement of things runs counter to the vision.

> The restoration of capitalism [states Chou En-lai (and here he is undoubtedly the spokesman of Mao Tse-tung)], is not inevitable. In China we have a firm and fighting Marxist-Leninist Party, a proletarian Power which is increasingly consolidating itself, a powerful and revolutionary People's Liberation Army, an enormous number of cadres, a people of high political consciousness and a glorious revolutionary tradition. Of especial importance is the fact that our Party and State can count on a leading nucleus guided by the thought of Mao Tse-tung. All of this makes the restoration of capitalism very difficult in our country.[5]

There is here, of course, an oblique implication that the Soviet Union lacks these reassuring features. The whole thrust of the passage suggests, however, that what mainly stands between China and the "restoration of capitalism" is the Maoist vision. It is noteworthy that there is no reference to the "Socialist structure" of Chinese society as one of the factors preventing such a restoration.

While the "Socialist education" campaign has,

however, fallen with an enormous weight on the literary, artistic and cultural spheres and perhaps on all non-vocational areas of social life, while the cult of Mao has been raised to unprecedented heights, it is still not clear whether it has again been allowed to affect the strategy of modernisation, particularly in the economic sphere. In fact, one may speculate that in the areas of highest priority—such as nuclear development—the Maoist vision has never been allowed to interfere with the requirements of technology. As far as one can judge at the present, experts are now expected to be diffused with redness even while devoting a maximum of attention to expertise and the system of higher education is more oriented than ever to the production of experts. Yet all this may change. It would certainly be the gravest of errors to assume that because the 1960 economic strategy has proven fairly successful, economic considerations will necessarily override the concern with the "succession to the revolutionary heritage."

The leadership's concern is probably justified. It is difficult to believe that the vision will survive at least in its present extreme form. It is difficult to believe not only, or even primarily, because in some of its aspects it runs counter to the requirements of modernisation. Even more immediately, it involves such a constricted and terribly simplified view of human life that one is inclined to doubt whether it is hu-

manly viable. In terms of modernisation, however, it is difficult to believe that the vision will be allowed in the long run to interfere particularly with those aspects of modernisation most relevant to the achievement of national power. While the vision may retreat, however, we are in no position to foresee the extent of the retreat or to predict what will remain. Modernisation may not be fully compatible with the Maoist vision but neither has it been fully compatible with Jeffersonian democracy. China may depart from the Maoist vision yet still move into a future uniquely its own. As long as Mao and those close to him remain at the helm, we may expect them to be as much concerned with the vision as with any of the other goals of the régime.

NOTES

1. *Peking Review,* "Fighting Task of Workers in Philosophy and Social Science," January 3, 1964.
2. "Correct Handling of Contradictions among the People," Bowie and Fairbank, *Communist China 1955–59* (Cambridge, Mass.: Harvard University Press, 1962), p. 289.
3. Lu Ting-yi, "Let a Hundred Flowers Blossom; Let a Hundred Schools Contend," Bowie and Fairbank, *op. cit.,* p. 154.
4. Whatever may have been the discontents revealed in 1956–1957, the peasants had, after all, been collectivised without producing anything resembling the effects of collectivisation in the Soviet Union.
5. "Report on the Work of the Government," *Peking Review,* January 1, 1965.

91

The Logic of One-Party Rule

Richard Lowenthal

To what extent are the political decisions of the Soviet leadership influenced by its belief in an official ideology—and to what extent are they empirical responses to specific conflicts of interest, expressed in ideological terms merely for purposes of justification? The phrasing of the question at issue suggests the two extreme answers that are prima facie con-

From Richard Lowenthal, "The Logic of One-Party Rule," in Abraham Brumberg, ed., *Russia under Khrushchev: An Anthology from Problems of Communism* (New York: Frederick A. Praeger, 1962), pp. 27–32, 35–37, 42–45. Reprinted by permission of Frederick A. Praeger and Methuen & Company Ltd., London.

ceivable—on the one hand, that ideology provides the Kremlin with a ready-made book of rules to be looked up in any situation; on the other, that its response to reality takes place without any reference to ideology. Yet any clear formulation of this vital issue will show that both extremes are meaningless nonsense.

A ready-made book of rules for any and every situation—an unvarying road map to the goal of Communism, which the Soviet leaders must predictably follow—cannot possibly exist, both because the situations to be met by them are not sufficiently predictable, and because no government behaving in so calculable a manner could conceivably retain power. On the other hand, empirical *Realpolitik* without ideological preconceptions can exist as little as can "empirical science" without categories and hypotheses based on theoretical speculation. Confronted with the same constellation of interests and pressures, the liberal statesman will in many cases choose a different course of action from the conservative—and the totalitarian Communist's choice will often be different from that of either.

It seems surprising, therefore, that at this late stage of discussion, Professor Sharp is apparently in earnest in defending the extreme of the *Realpolitik* interpretation and in denying completely the relevance of the Communist ideology for the formation, and hence the understanding, of Soviet foreign policy. The latter, he assures us, can be adequately understood in terms of national interest, just as it can in any other state. When reminded by Mr. Carew Hunt of certain irrational features of Soviet foreign policy, he replies that what matters is not any outsider's concept of Soviet interests, but the Soviet leaders' own. Yet this reduces his thesis to a tautology: He "proves" that national interest motivates Soviet foreign policy by the simple device of labeling whatever motivates it "national interest."

Surely Professor Sharp cannot have it both ways. Either there are objective criteria of national interest, recognizable by the scholar—and then the view that these interests explain Soviet actions is capable of proof or refutation; or else it is admitted that different statesmen may interpret national interest in different but equally "legitimate" ways—and then a consideration of the internal structures of different national communities and of the "ideologies" reflecting them becomes indispensable for an understanding of their foreign policies.

The latter observation does not, of course, apply to Communist states alone, although it is only reasonable to expect the influence of the monopolistic ideology of a single-party state to be specially pervasive. George Kennan, in his 1950 lectures on American diplomacy, has convincingly shown the relevance of ideological factors to an understanding of modern United States foreign policy as well. To deny this influence a priori and to admit, as Professor Sharp apparently would, only the *Ding an sich* of national interest on the one side, and the accidental element of human error or pathology (such as Hitler's "death wish") on the other, seems to this writer to be an unjustifiable renunciation of one of the limited roads to understanding that are available to present-day political science.

The Function of Doctrine

Assuming, then, that the Soviet leaders' ideology is relevant to their conduct, the real problem remaining is to discover which are the actual operative elements in it and in what way they affect policy decisions. Clearly, it would be folly to expect that Soviet policy could be predicted solely from an exegetic study of the Marxist-Leninist canon. Not only is it impossible for any group of practical politicians to base their decisions on an unvarying book of rules; there is any amount of historical evidence to show that the rules have been altered again and again to fit the practical decisions ex post facto. Moreover, there are vast parts of the Communist ideological structure, such as the scholastic refinements of "dialectical materialism" or the labor theory of value, that in their nature are so remote from the practical matters to be decided that their interpretation cannot possibly affect policy decisions. They may be used in inner-Party arguments to *justify* what has been decided on other grounds, but that is all.

How, then, are we to distinguish those elements of Soviet ideology that are truly operative politically from those that are merely traditional scholastic ballast, linked to the operative elements by the historical accident of the founding fathers' authorship? The answer is to be found by going back to the original Marxian meaning of the term "ideology"— conceived as a distorted reflection of social reality in the consciousness of men, used as an instrument of struggle. The fundamental, distinctive social reality in the Soviet Union is the rule of the bureaucracy of a single, centralized, and disciplined party that wields a monopoly of political, economic, and spiritual power and permits no independent grouping of any kind. The writer proposes as a hypothesis that the operative parts of the ideology are those that are indispensable for maintaining and justifying this state of affairs. "Marxism-Leninism" matters inasmuch as it expresses, in an ideologically distorted form, the logic of one-party rule.[1]

Totalitarian Parallels

There are a few interconnected ideological features common to all the totalitarian regimes of our century—whether of the nationalist-fascist or of the Communist variety. We may designate them as the elements of chiliasm, of collective paranoia, and of the representative fiction. Each totalitarian regime justifies its power and its crimes by the avowed conviction, first, that its final victory will bring about the millennium—whether defined as the final triumph of Communism or of the master race—and second, that this state of grace can only be achieved by an irreconcilable struggle against a single, omnipresent, and multiform enemy—whether Monopoly Capitalism or World Jewry—whose forms include every particular opponent of the totalitarian power. Each also claims to represent the true will of the people—the *volonté générale*—independent of whether the people actually support it, and argues that any sacrifice may be demanded from the individual and the group for the good of the people and the defeat of its devilish enemies.

The Communist version of these basic beliefs is superior to the Nazi version in one vital respect. Because the appeal of racialism is in its nature restricted to a small minority of mankind, the Nazis' goal of world domination could not possibly have been attained without a series of wars, preferably surprise attacks launched against isolated opponents. Because the appeal of Communism is directed to all mankind, it can be linked with the further doctrine of the inevitable victory of the rising forces of socialism over the imperialist enemy that is disintegrating under the impact of its own internal contradictions. This central ideological difference, and not merely the psychological difference between Hitler and the Soviet leaders, explains why the latter are convinced that history is on their side and that they need not risk the survival of their own regime in any attempt to hasten its final triumph: They believe in violence, revolutionary and military, as one of the weapons of policy, but they do not believe in the inevitability of world war.

Awkward Aims and Claims

Yet the Communist version of totalitarian ideology also suffers from some weaknesses and contradictions from which the Nazi and fascist versions are free. In the first place, its vision of the millennium has more markedly utopian features—the classless society, the end of exploitation of man by man, the withering away of the state—which made awkward yardsticks for the real achievements of Communist states. Second, in a world where nationalism remains a force of tremendous strength, an internationalist doctrine is bound to come into conflict with the interests of any major Communist power or with the desire of smaller Communist states for autonomy.

Third, by rejecting the "Führer principle" and claiming to be "democratic," Communist ideology makes the realities of Party dictatorship and centralistic discipline more difficult to justify; yet because

appeal to blind faith is not officially permitted, justification is needed in "rational" terms. It is precisely this continuous need for the pretense of rational argument—the awkward heritage of Communism's origin from revolutionary Western democracy—that has led to the far greater elaboration of its ideology, compared to that of "irrationalist" right-wing totalitarianism, and that gives its constant interpretation so much greater importance in preserving the cohesion of the Party regime. Due to the fictions of democracy and rationality, the morale of Party cadres has been made dependent on the appearance of ideological consistency.

The result of these inherent weaknesses of Communist ideology is that the doctrines dealing with the "dictatorship of the proletariat," the Party's role as a "vanguard" embodying the "true" class consciousness, "democratic centralism," "proletarian internationalism," and the "leading role of the Soviet Union" become focal points of ideological crises and targets of "revisionist" attacks whenever events reveal the underlying contradictions in a particularly striking way. Yet these are the very doctrines the regime cannot renounce, because they are the basic rationalizations of its own desire for self-preservation.

We can expect, then, that Communist ideology will have an effective influence on the policy decisions of Soviet leaders when, and only when, it expresses the needs of self-preservation of the Party regime. We can further expect that ideological changes and disputes within the Communist "camp" will offer clues to the conflicts and crises—the "contradictions"—that are inseparable from the evolution of this, as of any other, type of society. The fruitful approach, in this writer's view, consists neither in ignoring Communist ideology as an irrelevant disguise, nor in accepting it at its face value and treating it as a subject for exegesis, but in using it as an indicator of those specific drives and problems that spring from the specific structure of Soviet society—in regarding it as an enciphered, continuous self-disclosure whose cipher can be broken by sociological analysis. . . .

Yalta—A Historic "Misunderstanding"

The crucial example to illustrate the role of ideology in Soviet foreign policy, however, remains the history of the postwar division of Europe. The writer is not concerned here with the political controversy over whether this division, as first laid down in the wartime agreements at Teheran and Yalta, was inevitable in the light of the military situation as seen at the time or whether the Western statesmen committed an avoidable mistake of disastrous dimensions. What matters in the present context is the different meaning attached by the Western and Communist leaders, in concluding these agreements, to the concept of "spheres of influence," and the consequences of this "misunderstanding."

That great powers are in a position to exert a measure of influence over their smaller neighbors, and that they use this influence in one way or another to increase as far as possible their security against attack by other great powers, is a general experience in the politics of sovereign states and unlikely to be superseded by any amount of declamation about "equality of rights"; hence, the fact that the wartime allies, in drawing a military line of demarcation from north to south across the center of Europe, should have tried to agree about their postwar spheres of influence is, by itself, proof of realistic foresight rather than morally reprehensible cynicism.

To Roosevelt and Churchill, however, these spheres of influence meant what they had traditionally meant in the relations of sovereign states—a gradual shading over from the influence of one power or group of powers to that of the other, which might even be loosely described in terms of "percentages of influence," ranging from 50–50 to 90–10. To the Soviets, "spheres of influence" meant something completely different in the framework of their ideology—the ideology of the single-party state. To them there could be no securely "friendly" government except a government run by a Communist party under their discipline; no sphere of influence but a sphere of Communist rule; no satisfactory percentage short of 100. Hence the consistent Soviet efforts, which began even before the end of the European war, to impose total control by Communist parties in every country on their side of the demarcation line—an effort that was finally successful everywhere but in Finland and Eastern Austria; hence also the indignant protests of the Western powers that the Soviets had broken the agreements on free elections and democratic development, and the equally indignant Soviet retort that they were only installing "friendly governments" as agreed, that theirs was the truly "democratic" system, and that they had kept scrupulously to the essential agreement on the military demarcation line.

A large section of Western opinion has concluded from this experience that agreements with the Soviets are useless in principle, because "you cannot trust them"; and Professor Sharp's insistence on national interest as the sole key to Soviet policy is probably at least in part a reaction against this

emotional and moralizing approach. In fact, any interpretation of the postwar experience overlooking the fact that the Soviets have, for reasons of national self-interest, kept to the "self-enforcing" agreement on the demarcation line, would be as seriously one-sided as one overlooking the fact that they have, for reasons of ideology or party interest, broken every agreement on "percentages" and free elections.

There is no need, however, to base future policy on either of two one-sided views equally refuted by experience. Nobody in the Western world has argued more powerfully against the "moralizing" approach to foreign policy, and for a return to the give and take of diplomacy based on real interests, than George Kennan; yet in his 1958 Reith lectures, as before, he has insisted that the specific ideological distortion in the Soviet leaders' image of the world, far from being magically cured by such a return to diplomacy, has to be taken into account continuously in judging which kind of agreements are possible and which are not. After all, the peoples of Eastern Europe are still paying for the illusion of the West that the Soviet Union was a state like any other, pursuing its power interests without regard to ideology. . . .

The "Permanent" Revolution

Among the most revealing of these variables are Soviet doctrines dealing with the economic role of the state and with the "class struggle" within Soviet society. The underlying reality is that a revolutionary party dictatorship, once it has carried out its original program and thus has contributed to the emergence of a new privileged class, is bound to disappear sooner or later—to fall victim to a "Thermidor"—unless it prevents the new upper class from consolidating its position by periodically shaking up the social structure in a "permanent revolution from above." The ideological expression of this problem is the classical doctrine that the dictatorship of the proletariat should gradually "wither away" after it has succeeded in destroying the old ruling classes; thus, if continued dictatorship is to be justified, new goals of social transformation must be set and new "enemies" discovered.

In the early period of Stalin's rule, the new "goal" was the forced collectivization of the Russian countryside; the prosperous peasants—the kulaks—took the place of the former landowners and capitalists as the "enemy class" that had to be liquidated. Summing up the achievement in 1937, Stalin wrote in his *Short Course* on Party history that collectivization had been a second revolution, but a revolution carried out from above, by state power "with the help of the masses," not just by the masses from below. The ideological groundwork was thus laid for assigning the state a function of continuous economic transformation from above, not just a once-for-all revolutionary function.

The second step, also taken by Stalin in 1937, at the height of the Great Blood Purge, consisted in proclaiming the doctrine that the "class struggle" in the Soviet Union was getting more acute as the "construction of socialism" advanced, because the "enemies" were getting more desperate. This was the ideological justification of the Purge itself; at the same time, it was a veiled indication that another revolution from above was in effect taking place, although this time Stalin refrained from trying to define the "enemies" in social terms. In fact, what Stalin accomplished was a mass liquidation of both the bearers of the Party's older revolutionary tradition—considered unsuited to the tasks of a bureaucratic state party—and of the most confident and independent-minded elements of the new privileged bureaucracy; the end result was a transformation of the Party's social and ideological composition through the mass incorporation of the surviving frightened bureaucrats.

Stalin's final ideological pronouncement was contained in his political testament, *Economic Problems of Socialism,* published in 1952. In this work he mapped out a program for the further revolutionary transformation of Soviet society, with the taking over of kolkhoz property by the state as its central element.

Khrushchev's Formula for Perpetual Rule

The first major renunciation of these Stalinist ideological innovations was made by Khrushchev in his "secret speech" at the Twentieth Congress. Apart from his factual disclosures concerning Stalin's crimes, he denounced Stalin's doctrine of the sharpening class struggle with the advance of socialist construction as dangerous nonsense, calculated to lead to the mutual slaughter of loyal Communists after the real class enemy had long been liquidated. This statement affords the master clue to the puzzle of why Khrushchev made the speech: It was a "peace offering" to the leading strata of the regime in the Party machine, army, and managerial bureaucracy alike—a response to their pressure for greater personal security. But by his concession, Khrushchev reopened the problem that Stalin's doctrine and practice had been intended to solve—that

of preserving and justifying the Party dictatorship by periodic major shake-ups of society.

By the spring and summer of 1957, Khrushchev showed his awareness of the practical side of the problem: His dismantling of the economic ministries, breaking up the central economic bureaucracy, and strengthening the power of the regional Party secretaries, was another such revolutionary shake-up. By November, he responded to the ideological state of the problem. First he repeated, in his solemn speech on the fortieth anniversary of the Bolshevik seizure of power, his rejection of Stalin's doctrine of ever-sharpening class struggle and ever-present enemies, thus indicating his wish to avoid a return to Stalin's terroristic methods even while following his social recipe of permanent revolution. Then he proceeded to develop his own alternative justification for maintaining the Party dictatorship—a unique argument that equated the strengthening of Party control with the "withering away of the state" predicted by Lenin.

Reviving this formula for the first time since it was buried by Stalin, Khrushchev explained that the military and police apparatus of the state would have to be maintained as long as a hostile capitalist world existed outside; but he added that the economic and administrative functions of the state bureaucracy would henceforth be steadily reduced by decentralization and devolution, thus strengthening the organs of regional self-government and of national autonomy within the various republics. At the same time, he quietly took steps to strengthen the control of the central Party Secretariat—his own seat of power—over the republican and regional Party organs, thus following the old Leninist principle that the fiction of national autonomy must be balanced by the fact of centralized discipline within the ruling party.

In short, the same aim of maintaining the social dynamism of the Party dictatorship and justifying its necessity, which Stalin achieved by exalting the economic role of the state, is pursued by Khrushchev by means of the reverse device of claiming that the state's economic functions have begun to "wither away." On the face of it, this doctrinal manipulation seems to reduce the role of ideology to that of ingenious trickery, obscuring rather than reflecting the underlying social realities. Yet in fact, the very need for a change in the ideological argument, and its further elaboration by Khrushchev in his report to the Twenty-first Party Congress, reflects the change that is taking place in the underlying social situation—the resistance against a return to naked terrorism, the growing desire for a lessening of state pressure, and a greater scope for local activity. Whether in industry or agriculture, in the control of literature or in relations with the satellite states, the basic conditions that the regime needs for its self-perpetuation have remained the same—but they can no longer be assured in the same way. That, too, is reflected in the variables of the official ideology.

NOTE

1. While this comes close to the position outlined in Mr. Carew Hunt's paper, I cannot follow him in his assumption that the totalitarian party monopoly is a by-product of the attempt to establish collectivist economic planning or to achieve the speedy industrialization of a backward country. This neo-Marxist view, held by such otherwise divergent authors as Professor Hayek and Milovan Djilas, is con-tradicted by the fact that the Bolshevik Party monopoly, including the ban on inner-Party factions, was fully established by Lenin at the time of the transition to the New Economic Policy (1921), when economic planning was reduced to a minimum and forced industrialization not yet envisaged. Independent of the concrete economic program, totalitarianism was implicit in the centralized, undemocratic structure of a party consciously created as an instrument for the conquest of power, and in the ideological characteristics resulting (to be discussed further in this article). Of course, totalitarian power, once established, favors total economic planning and the undertaking of revolutionary economic tasks by the state; but this is a consequence, not a cause. Marx never developed a concept of total planning, and even Lenin never imagined anything of the kind before 1918. But Marx, in his youth at least, equated the "dictatorship of the proletariat" with the Jacobin model, and Lenin followed this model throughout.

‖ d. THE EMERGING OF NEW NATIONS IN LATE MODERNIZATION

92

Personal Rulership, Patrimonialism, and Empire-Building in the New States

Guenther Roth

The concrete lessons of recent history have helped us to appreciate the paramount importance of the political preconditions of social and economic development in the new states. The basic problem of political stability must be solved before all others —or everything else may be in vain. For this reason, some of the scholarly attention that used to be focused on social and economic development has shifted to political organization and has given prominence to terms such as "nation-building," "political culture," and "democratization." At the same time efforts have been made to modify the usual evolutionary and dichotomous conceptions of social and political development. The two-faced nature of tradition and modernity has come under scrutiny again.

Two basic theoretical choices have been made in the face of the complexity of the subject matter: one choice has been to resort to a relatively novel terminology that is intended to transcend Western historical connotations—witness the attempt by Gabriel Almond and his collaborators to adapt the Parsonian scheme; the other has been to re-examine older terms for their contemporary usefulness and to work with historically more specific concepts—an approach prominently pursued by Reinhard Bendix.[1]

I shall follow the latter path because I should like to reconsider a neglected part of Max Weber's typology of *Herrschaft,* the notion of patrimonial rule, for it seems to me that many of the features of legal-rational modernity may not appear in the new states and that certain basic modes of administration persist, even though traditionalist legitimacy has disintegrated in most cases. From the beginning, it should be clearly understood that Weber's sociology

From Guenther Roth, "Personal Rulership, Patrimonialism, and Empire-Building in the New States," *World Politics,* XX, No. 2 (January 1968). Reprinted by permission of the publisher and the author.

of *Herrschaft* deals not only with beliefs in legitimacy but also with the actual operating modes and administrative arrangements by which rulers "govern," not just "rule" (to paraphrase Adolphe Thiers's constitutional theory). This is made abundantly clear in his historical analyses of patrimonialism, sultanism, feudalism, the routinization of charismatic rule, hierocracy, and the city-state. If you wish, Weber tried to find out "how systems really work." It is true that he organized his great opus *Economy and Society* around a typology of social action and of legitimacy, but both in the terminology exposition (in Part I) and in the more descriptive analyses (in the older Part II) he always dealt with *Herrschaft* in terms of both legitimacy and the typical staff arrangements of the various kinds of rulers.[2] Here lies the great difficulty of translating *Herrschaft,* which in English is usually rendered either as "authority" (Parsons) or "domination" (Bendix, Rheinstein, Shils). Patrimonial rulers, for example, endeavor to maximize their personal control. Like all rulers, they are continually engaged in a struggle with their staff over ultimate control. In this regard, traditionalist legitimacy may be a burden as well as a help for them (as both Weber and Eisenstadt have shown).[3] Such legitimation may fetter them and prevent them from mobilizing the resources needed for empire-building, a handicap that Eisenstadt has considered the fatal flaw of the "historical bureaucratic societies." Rulers, then, avail themselves of various political and administrative devices that transcend the bases of their legitimacy. Patrimonial rulers resort to "extrapatrimonial" recruitment, which may retain the fiction of patriarchal subordination but may in fact be based on a feudal-contractual, bureaucratic-contractual, or merely personal relationship.

Traditionalist Patrimonialism and Personal Rulership

Lately, some attempts, primarily in the field of African studies, have been made to remember the meaning of patrimonialism; yet by and large Weber's broader typology of *Herrschaft* has been underutilized and, in fact, reduced to the dichotomy of bureaucracy and charisma. Not only patrimonialism but also collegial government and rule by notables have been disregarded.

I wish to distinguish two kinds of patrimonialism. One is the historical survival of traditionalist patrimonial regimes; the foremost example is Ethiopia, where the researcher, if he gains access at all, can almost perform the feat of travelling into the past.[4] The second type of patrimonialism is personal ruler-ship on the basis of loyalties that do not require any belief in the ruler's unique personal qualification, but are inextricably linked to material incentives and rewards. This second variant has been submerged in much of the literature through the indiscriminate use of the term "charismatic." As long as patrimonialism is considered to rest exclusively on traditionalist legitimation and hereditary succession, the category obviously loses applicability to the extent that these phenomena decline. Personal rulership, however, is an ineradicable component of the public and private bureaucracies of highly industrialized countries; some of the newer states lack the institutional matrix (whether pluralist or totalitarian) of these countries to such an extent that personal rulership becomes the dominant form of government. In terms of traditional political theory, some of these new states may not be states at all but merely private governments of those powerful enough to rule; however, this only enhances the applicability of the notion of personal rulership (in the sense of detraditionalized, personalized patrimonialism). Such personal governance easily evokes notions of opportunism and corruption from the perspective of charismatic or legal-rational legitimation.[5] Traditionalist as well as personal patrimonial regimes differ from charismatic rulership in that the patrimonial ruler need have neither personal charismatic appeal nor a sense of mission; they differ from legal-rational bureaucracies in that neither constitutionally regulated legislation nor advancement on the basis of training and efficiency need be predominant in public administration.

Also, personal rulership should not be mistaken for "authoritarianism," which has little to do with "authority" as such. After the First World War, the doctrine of authoritarianism was developed by right-wing nationalists, who championed the autonomy of the state apparatus as against parliament with its parties and interest groups and even as against the dynastic families and their loyalist supporters. Nowadays, however, the term is usually applied to the many political regimes that lie between democratic and totalitarian ones. These regimes base themselves on a limited structural pluralism, which admits of some interest-group articulation; strategies of *divide et impera* are usually more important than legitimation or ideological integration, and for that reason authoritarian regimes may be less stable and have less "authority" than democratic and totalitarian states.

Many authoritarian regimes have features of traditional and personal patrimonialism, which may be more important than charismatic appeals, the belief in legal rationality, and bureaucratic practices. Typologically, however, it would be inadvisable to equate "patrimonial" with "authoritarian." The latter term has been useful in establishing a continuum ranging from pluralist democracy to totalitarianism; the former category properly belongs to a typology of beliefs *and* organizational practices that can be found at any point of such a continuum.[6]

Personal Rulership in Industrialized Countries

In order to emphasize that personal rulership transcends the dichotomy of tradition and modernity, I shall first illustrate its continued functioning in industrialized countries, before turning to some African and Asian regimes. In the older political science literature the phenomenon has been subsumed under terms such as "machine" and "apparatus," or even "clique" and "faction"; organization analysts have rediscovered some aspects under the names "primary groups" and "informal relations," and they customarily contrast these with the formal structure of bureaucracy, which is usually and misleadingly called the Weberian model (as if Weber had not scrutinized patrimonial bureaucracies and modern higher civil servants as status groups and vested interests).

The old urban machines are a familiar example. They had, of course, some kind of traditionalist legitimation because of the immigrants' Old World ties, but they functioned primarily on the basis of personal loyalty—plebeian, not feudal—and material reward; offices were distributed by a noncharismatic and nonbureaucratic ruler, and occupying them amounted to holding a benefice. The boss might have had great power, but his legitimacy was precarious; thus he had little authority and had to envelop his "clients" in an intricate web of reciprocities.[7]

The old machines have largely disappeared, but personal rulership has not. Instead of the Irish bosses of yesteryear there is the Kennedy "clan" with its charismatic appeals to the electorate. However, the organizational power of the Kennedys has been based on an apparatus that only recently brought its patrimonial character to public attention during the Judge Morrissey affair in Boston.[8] For that matter, every American President, in order to be effective, cannot merely rely on his constitutional (legal-rational) powers, the institutionalized charismatic aura of his office, or any personal charismatic appeals to the public, but must build his own personal apparatus out of the so-called in-and-outers, who efficiently take the place of a permanent civil service of the British kind (as Richard E. Neustadt showed in his comparison of cabinet and presidential government, much of which reads like a description of personal governance).[9] Even the authority of the presidential office does not suffice to hold this apparatus together, and "authoritarian" imposition easily misfires.

The phenomenon of personal rulership is no less important in a totalitarian state than in a pluralist one. Nikita Khrushchev's fabled personal apparatus, which he took from Moscow to the Ukraine and back, served him well until defection eroded it. In the spring of 1966, his successor, Leonid I. Brezhnev, managed to enlarge to thirteen full members and seven candidates the number of Central Committee members who hailed from, or had connections with, the Ukrainian Dnepropetrovsk region, where he was born and began his career. Some of these are said to have been old friends from before World War II. At the same time, Kremlinologists identified another ascending group made up of Byelorussians and headed by Politburo member Kirill T. Mazurov, which is alleged to have made unusual gains on the Central Committee and to have taken over important positions.[10]

Far from being a vanishing phenomenon, personal rulership in public bureaucracies is apparently enlarged by the extension of government functions in industrialized countries. Both in Western Europe and in the United States, there are an increasing number of semipublic agencies and corporations in which such patrimonial relationships emerge and officials tend to become "benefice-holders." In the literature on industrial bureaucracies, this development is referred to by the wholly imprecise term of "industrial feudalism," which indicates the appropriation of managerial functions and prerogatives. Such prerogatives include the use of expense accounts, representation funds, official residences, limousines, and first-class tickets. The contractual character of the civil-service relationship may be changed because some officials cannot be dismissed *de jure* or *de facto*. Such officials may also be able to co-opt candidates and thus displace universalist criteria of formalized recruitment. However, along another universalist dimension, the hiring of highly qualified friends (from law school or graduate school days) can be very efficient. Finally, such patrimonial organizations may even be able to levy indirect taxes.

Revolutionary Legitimacy and Patrimonial Practice

It is my contention that in some of the new states patrimonial features in the detraditionalized sense are more important than bureaucratic and charismatic ones, and hence that it is too simplified a typology to contrast, for example, "the charisma of party" with "the bureaucracy of the military."[11]

Neglect of the patrimonial dimension of government has also led to a tendency to interpret all political leadership as charismatic. Both analytical trends usually ignore Weber's point that bureaucracy and charisma are not necessarily exclusive of each other and that, in fact, bureaucracies can be superior instruments for charismatic leaders.[12] Moreover, the treatment of almost all political leaders in the new states as "charismatic" has been misleading on at least two counts: it has obscured the difference between "charismatic authority" and "charismatic leadership,"[13] and it has taken at face value the international propaganda claims of some of the new leaders. Most heads of government in the new states do not have the magic of personal charisma for many groups in the society, nor do they have the kind of impersonal, institutional charisma that Edward Shils has stressed as a basic requirement for organizational stability.[14] The political situation in many African and Asian countries is so fluid exactly because leadership is merely personal and lacking in both charismatic qualities, that is, personal as well as office charisma.

For an outside observer it is very hard to gauge to what extent the international charismatic imagery of men like Nkrumah, Sukarno, Ben Bella, and Nasser has had substance for the various strata in their countries. At any rate, the sudden downfall of such men or slow attrition of their leadership shows that they lose power in the same way in which patrimonial rulers have often lost it: by a palace coup, especially by intervention of the army.[15] For reasons of legitimation some of them may be retained as figureheads; this is perhaps a good measure of charismatic efficacy, although in the case of Sukarno in 1966 the military's calculated "neutralization" of the head of state may have been as important a motive for his retention as his charismatic halo in the eyes of millions of Indonesians. At any rate, the successors of these charismatic leaders tend to have a more pragmatic bent—another patrimonial feature.

Much has been written about armies in underdeveloped countries as a major, and sometimes the only, modern bureaucracy and force for modernization. They certainly are hierarchical organizations, and some of them indeed approach the bureaucratic realities of a Western army, but most of them have personal patrimonial traits that facilitate the takeover of government; that is, the troops are more loyal to their immediate commanders than to the governmental leaders. Significantly, some of the more stable countries (Morocco, Iran, Ethiopia, Thailand) still have armies in which the belief in

traditionalist legitimacy is alive. However, such legitimation has never been sufficient insurance against the overthrow of the ruler, partly because of the administrative strategies of patrimonial regimes. One such strategy has been the creation of a military force that differed in social, ethnic, or tribal composition from the population, so that the social distance between apparatus and subjects would be maximized. However, this strategy could easily put the ruler at the mercy of his troops. (Weber took his major historical examples for this double-edged role from the Near Eastern armies, particularly the Mamelukes and Janissaries.)[16]

There seems to be a parallel here to the dilemma of present-day nationalist leaders, who want to have a "national" army free from regional and tribal ties. The course of events has proved that they can quickly lose control over their own instrument, either because regional or tribal elements in the army resist or because a "nationalized" army becomes the only nationally effective force in an otherwise fragmented state. In the Near East as well as in Africa the pattern of military takeover that was typical of traditional regimes is repeating itself. Some sub-Sahara kingdoms, for example, used to be unstable because army units tended to be more loyal to their immediate commanders (princes or other members of the ruling families) than to the king. In some of these areas political instability is part of the precolonial tradition, not just a phenomenon of transition and modernization.

It should be clearly understood that such patrimonial loyalties are compatible with universalist components. Among the Bantu, where interregnum wars and princely usurpations were frequent, patrons selected their clients among commoners according to administrative and military ability. Conversely, under British control the modern Bantu bureaucracy, which had been modeled after the British civil service, at times had to be "corrupt" (i.e., particularist) in order to reconcile conflicting values.[17]

Once in power, army leaders tend to become personal rulers: we can think of the extremely precarious position of the South Vietnamese corps commanders ("Baby Turks"), with their practices of appointment by loyalty and taxation by discretion, or of their much more entrenched neighbors in Thailand.[18] Several years ago Edgar L. Shor considered Thailand an unusual case, but actually the overall pattern he pictured has frequently been repeated. Shor perceived a transitional corruption of the civil service model, which had been borrowed from England in the 1880's, a corruption that would eventually be overcome. Like many others, his standard was the "classic Weberian model"; however, his description of the "aberrations" in the administrative realities of Thailand amounted to what I mean here by "personal governance":

> Deprived of the traditional deference accorded the morally legitimized monarchy, governments have relied upon the disposition of offices and shared material rewards to obtain the support of key leaders. . . . In the Thai bureaucracy, patterns of authority relationship are habitually hierarchical, predominantly personal, and inherently unstable. . . . The personal clique, based on a feudal-like system of personal obligation, provides the principal focus of bureaucratic loyalty and identification. Bonds of reciprocal obligation, reminiscent of earlier patron-client structures in the traditional social system, informally align a number of dependent subordinates with individual political and administrative leaders in more or less cohesive informal structures. In contrast to primary group ties in some other Asian countries, the clique groupings in Thailand are substantially independent of family or kinship relations. . . . Since the clique generally consists of a ranking superior and his subordinates within the organization, it usually coincides with the legal structures. . . . The dependence of careers on political and personal favor apparently dictates an entrepreneurial career strategy for the ambitious.[19]

The importance of personal loyalties and of material rewards does not exclude a peculiar mixture of reform-mindedness and "corruption" in such regimes. In his vivid description of the Young Turks' patrimonialism—which he never called by this name —Dankwart Rustow pointed to the "uninterrupted chain that links the Kemalists to the Young Turks, to the men of the Tanzimat, and to the classical Ottoman Empire—the sponsors of modernity in the twentieth century with the founders of tradition in the thirteenth." If the Ottoman Empire was "in essence a military camp and an educational institution," it is still true that "the sentiments persist among younger military officers that only an authoritarian regime under military aegis can accomplish the necessary tasks of social, cultural, and economic reform."[20] Rustow's portrayal of Turkish bureaucracy reveals a patrimonial administration that has not changed much since the Ottoman Empire adopted a formal French pattern; then as now there exists what is imprecisely known as "corruption": "connections" count, favoritism prevails, and for the few there is abundant profit in real-estate dealings. Corruption in the conventional sense varies with the strength of puritanical sentiment among reformist or revolutionary functionaries—officeholders or aspirants. However, reforms do not seem to change the largely personal character of loyalty patterns.

In sum, nowadays the nationalist leaders of the new states claim revolutionary legitimacy. Most of them embrace some variation of national socialism, which in the 1930's often came close to Nazism and Japanese fascism and later moved toward communism. Frequently, the same men have made the switch without drastically changing their outlook, whether they were Indonesian or Arab nationalists. Behind the ideological veneer lie goals and means that are closer to native traditions of government than tends to be apparent to the leaders themselves and to many an outside observer. Europeanization, Americanization, Westernization, and simply modernization—there is no similarly accepted term for the influence of Russian or Chinese communism— provide so many influential ideological and institutional models, but are not necessarily dominant in administrative practice.

Personal Rulership and Empire-Building

One of the major reasons for the predominance of personal rulership over legal-rational legislation and administration in the new states seems to lie in a social, cultural, and political heterogeneity of such magnitude that a more or less viable complementary and countervailing pluralism of the Western type, with its strong but not exclusive components of universality, does not appear feasible. Even the total victory of a totalitarian minority merely leads to a highly centralized variant of personal governance under which the ruler has maximum discretion (what Weber called "sultanism"). The foremost task of these states is the political integration of greatly disparate elements—ethnic, tribal, religious, linguistic, or even economic. Structurally, much of what is today called nation-building should perhaps be called, more precisely, empire-building, if the political connotations of the term do not make it too difficult to use it in a strictly sociological, value-neutral sense. The problem of empire is the problem of establishing political order in the face of social and cultural heterogeneity. By contrast, nation-building finds its historical matrix in the European nation-state, which aimed at the integration of a population with a common culture, especially a common language and common historical legacies shared by various strata. It is no accident that pluralist democracy has been successful, on a larger scale, only in fairly homogeneous countries.[21]

An empire in the sense meant here was the Austro-Hungarian Double Monarchy, which introduced parliamentary government only for each of its halves and not for the whole realm. Even Imperial Germany faced a substantial problem of integrating diverse cultural and political elements, but because of compensating homogeneous forces this task was ideologically perceived as that of building a nation.[22]

The problem of empire is not one of bigness as such, and the absolute number of people is not decisive. China is commonly called an empire by virtue of a combination of sheer size, historical longevity, military power, and expansionist ideology, but smaller African countries, for instance, face "empire problems" similar to those of India and Indonesia, because they have more tribal fragmentation on a smaller geographical scale and perhaps because they have a smaller "critical mass" of elites. In fact, Weber used his model of patrimonialism for African petty kingdoms as well as for the great empires of history.[23]

Despite technological progress—in particular, vastly increased communication facilities—many of the problems that troubled the patrimonial states of the past persist or recur. The agonies of Indonesia provide a stark example: Sukarno adhered to a rhetoric of the nation-state and of racial unity that simply denied the facts of an exceedingly complex pluralism and particularism. In a well-focused community study of social change and economic modernization in Indonesia, Clifford Geertz recognized several years ago what I call the problem of empire and stated it succinctly:

> The ideologies of modern nationalism, arising as they do out of intense concern with massive social reconstruction, show a strong tendency toward a neglect, even an outright denial, of important variations in domestic cultural patterns and of internal social discontinuities. . . . With regard to national economic planning this leads to a failure to cast proposals in a form which attempts to take maximum advantage of the peculiarities of various local traditions, to an unwillingness even to consider differentiated plans for different cultural and social groups. . . . In the overconcern with national integration, conceived in a wholly monistic sense, the very construction of such integration . . . may be undermined.[24]

Personal rulerships can be more responsive to cultural and social diversity than intensely ideological leaders are willing to be. But this does not imply that such regimes are much more likely to solve the "problem of empire" in the direction of faster economic growth and modernization. A country's diversity may amount to an inflexible pluralism that is not amenable to integration through the compromise strategies of personal rulers. Moreover, radical intellectuals deny legitimacy to ideologically uninspiring forms of personal rulership and in the long run can undermine them in both domestic and international politics. Since such intellectuals have taken over from traditional ones the role of legitimizers, personal rulerships are likely to have precarious legitimacy, and this is one reason for the pattern of frequent coups and countercoups. If self-proclaimed charismatic leadership with its ideological preoccupation fails to achieve the necessary amount of economic growth, personal rulership may fail to sustain political stability despite its pragmatic tendencies, and hence may also retard economic growth. This vicious circle may make it impossible for many of the new states to solve urgent problems of modernization, not to speak of catching up with the highly industrialized countries in the foreseeable future.

This skeptical conclusion is intentionally set in opposition to the predictions of those who, like Clark Kerr, envisage "the age of total industrialization" and anticipate that "by the middle of the twenty-first century, industrialization will have swept away most pre-industrial forms of society, except possibly a few odd backwaters."[25] It is equally possible to foresee a century in which the past will repeat itself and issues of personal rulership and empire-building will persist.

NOTES

1. See, for example, Gabriel Almond and Bingham Powell, *Comparative Politics* (Boston 1966). For Bendix, see his *Nation-Building and Citizenship* (New York 1964), 2, and "Modernization and Inequality," a paper prepared for Session I, Sixth World Congress of Sociology, ISA, mimeographed, 52ff.

2. See Part I, chap. 3, and Part II, chaps. 10–16, of my forthcoming variorum edition of *Economy and Society* (Totowa 1968).

3. See S. N. Eisenstadt, *The Political Systems of Empires: The Rise and Fall of the Historical Bureaucratic Societies* (New York 1963).

4. See Donald N. Levine, "Ethiopia: Identity, Authority, and Realism," in Lucian W. Pye and Sidney Verba, eds., *Political Culture and Political Development* (Princeton 1965), 245–281; also Levine, *Wax and Gold: Tradition and Innovation in Ethiopian Culture* (Chicago 1965). Levine's fascinating accounts disregard the literature on patrimonialism. For a detailed description of personal rulership and palace intrigues, see Richard Greenfield, *Ethiopia* (London 1965). On the much more precarious Iranian case, see Leonard Binder, *Iran: Political Development in a Changing Society* (Berkeley 1962); and now also Norman Jacobs, *The Sociology of Development: Iran as an Asian Case Study* (New York 1966).

5. For one of the latest examples, see Conor Cruise O'Brien, former member of the Irish delegation to the United Nations and vice-chancellor of the University of Ghana from 1962 to 1965, "The Counter-revolutionary Reflex," *Columbia Forum*, IX (Spring 1966), 21f.

6. For an excellent discussion of authoritarianism, see Juan J. Linz, "An Authoritarian Regime: Spain," in E. Allardt and Y. Littunen, eds., *Cleavages, Ideologies and Party Systems* (Helsinki 1964), 291–341. Linz argues that "Max Weber's categories can and should be used independently of the distinction between democracy, authoritarianism, and totalitarianism. Within each of these systems the legitimacy of the ruler, for the population or his staff, can be based on one or another of these types of belief. . . . While we want to stress the conceptual difference between authoritarian regimes and traditional rule, we also want to suggest that they sometimes have elements in common and that the students of such regimes could gain as many insights from Weber's analysis of patrimonial rule and bureaucracy as those of totalitarianism have gained from his thinking about charisma" (pp. 319, 321). My approach differs from Linz's suggestion in that it treats patrimonialism not only as a type of traditional belief but also as a strategy of rulership.

For another treatment of authoritarianism, which does not emphasize the issue of personal rulership, see Lewis A. Coser, "Prospects for the New Nations: Totalitarianism, Authoritarianism, or Democracy?" in Coser, ed., *Political Sociology* (New York 1966), 247–271.

7. In his discussion of patriarchalism and patrimonialism, Weber pointed out that traditionalist authority is not sufficient to ensure conformity with the directives of a patriarchal head; the ruler must be particularly responsive to his group as long as he does not have an efficient staff; once he has it, he must be responsive to his staff, lest he risk his power or even his position. In the language of the pattern variables, patrimonial organizations are particularist, but I shall show below that this is not necessarily so; on the other hand, Parsons himself long ago stressed the inherent instability of universalist orientation within legal-rational bureaucracy (*The Social System* [New York 1951], 268).

8. Almost forgotten are the charges of liberal Democrats in 1960 that J. F. Kennedy "bought" the nomination of his party, meaning that he had such great financial resources that he could build an overpowering nationwide machine.

9. "White House and Whitehall," *Public Interest,* I (Winter 1966), 55–69.

10. See Harry Schwartz, "Brezhnev Favors Old Colleagues," *New York Times,* July 15, 1966.

11. See Irving Louis Horowitz, *Three Worlds of Development* (New York 1966), 263.

12. Weber's example was Gladstone and Chamberlain's Liberal party machine, to which he gave much attention. See Weber, "Politics as a Vocation," in H. H. Gerth and C. Wright Mills, eds., *From Max Weber* (New York 1958), 106; on the relation of Weber's position to Michels' "Iron Law of Oligarchy," see Guenther Roth, *The Social Democrats in Imperial Germany* (Totowa 1963), 255f.

13. The distinction between charismatic authority and leadership is embedded in Weber's work, but was made explicit in Reinhard Bendix. *Max Weber* (New York 1960), 301, and was elaborated independently in Robert Bierstedt, "The Problem of Authority," in Morroe Berger and others, eds., *Freedom and Control in Modern Society* (New York 1954), 71f.

14. "Charisma, Order, and Status," *American Sociological Review,* xxx (April 1965), 199–213.

15. For the first major study of Nkrumah's downfall, see Henry L. Bretton, *The Rise and Fall of Kwame Nkrumah: A Study of Personal Rule in Africa* (New York 1966).

16. *Economy and Society,* Part II, chap. 12: 5.

17. See Lloyd Fallers, *Bantu Bureaucracy* (Chicago 1965, first published 1956), 241f., 248f. In spite of his recognition of universalist elements in traditional relationships, Fallers continues to think in terms of the dichotomy of bureaucracy and charisma (p. 250).

18. See Denis Warner's account of the practices of the South Vietnamese commanders in *The Reporter* (May 5, 1966), 11f.

19. "The Thai Bureaucracy," *Administrative Science Quarterly* (June 1960), 70, 77, 80. See also Fred W. Riggs, *Thailand: The Modernization of a Bureaucratic Polity* (Honolulu 1966).

20. "Turkey: The Modernity of Tradition," in Pye and Verba, 172f., 187.

21. The term "state-building" can perhaps substitute for "empire-building," but it does not imply equally well the integration of disparate elements. In Weber's terminology, which is applied here, the state is defined as a group that asserts an effective monopoly of legitimate force over a given territory; this definition does not specify the cultural and social aspects of the problem of political integration. The United States and the Soviet Union, which face tasks of international integration, can be called great or global empires (*Weltreiche*); expansionist states may be called "imperialist" in the conventional sense.

22. It should not be forgotten, however, that Imperial Germany remained a federation of states under the hegemony of Prussian constitutional monarchism (or monarchic constitutionalism), which combined dominant features of traditionalist patrimonialism with subordinate legal-rational (constitutional and bureaucratic) arrangements.

23. Weber and Eisenstadt have been almost alone among sociologists in giving systematic attention to the phenomenon of empire. Weber dealt with it throughout his career: in his book *Roman Agrarian History and Its Importance for Public and Civil Law* (1891), in his essay "The Social Causes of the Decline of Ancient Civilization" (1896), in his book *The Agrarian Conditions of Antiquity* (1909), in the major body of *Economy and Society* (1911–1913), and in the collected *Essays in the Sociology of Religion*. Eisenstadt applied structural functionalism to the great "patrimonial-bureaucratic" empires, as Weber called them. Both writers have been particularly concerned with the reasons for the empires' ultimate failure, the causes of stagnation and disintegration.

24. *Peddlers and Princes* (Chicago 1963), 155f. For an informative analysis of neo-traditionalism in Indonesia, see Ann Ruth Willner, *The Neotraditional Accommodation to Political Independence: The Case of Indonesia,* Center of International Studies, Princeton University, Research Monograph No. 26 (Princeton 1966).

25. Clark Kerr and others, *Industrialism and Industrial Man* (New York 1964), 3, 221.

93

Political Modernization: The Single-Party System

Rupert Emerson

I

The problem of modernization, be it political or otherwise, arises from the fact that a few of the world's societies have in the last centuries forged ahead to achieve riches and power which enabled them to overrun most of the rest of the world, establishing their imperial domination. To counter this power by coming to a level of equality with it and to secure their share of the more ample life which had now become possible, other peoples found themselves confronted by the necessity of rebuilding their societies on the model of those who had both stolen a lead and often the other peoples' countries as well. The most decisive push in this direction came as an unintended by-product of imperialism and more particularly of colonial rule.

It is startling to remember that the entire range of the last great forward surge of Western imperialism and its demise are embraced within the lifetime of anyone who has now reached the age of eighty or beyond. A conventional date for the beginning of this wave of imperialism is the Berlin Conference of 1884–1885 which formally opened the scramble for Africa. Its end is marked by no such specific event but it follows close after World War II, although the forces working to overturn Western imperialism were obviously gathering in the interwar decades. The opening phases of the anti-colonial drive are marked by the independence in Asia of the Philippines and India, and in Africa of Morocco and Tunisia, the Sudan and Ghana, promptly followed by the extraordinary liberating sweep of 1960.

Save for scattered and isolated colonial dots on the map and the gravely threatening mass of southern Africa which remains white-dominated, the colonial era has come to an end with amazing suddenness and finality. Despite the warnings in some quarters against the threat of neo-colonialism, a

recrudescence of colonialism in anything even remotely reminiscent of its familiar guise is profoundly unlikely. It is indicative of the change which has taken place that it has become one of the major preoccupations of the United Nations, now largely in the hands of the new countries, to see that every vestige of colonialism vanishes. Where in the very recent past imperial power was a proud symbol of greatness and strength it has now been translated into evidence of sin which must be immediately eradicated. Disinterested observers are inclined, however, to the view that, while exceptions must be made on both sides and the weighting of the scales is difficult, territories under Western colonial rule, for all its evils and shortcomings, have made a more effective advance toward modernization than have comparable countries which somehow managed to evade becoming dependencies.

An examination of the problems of political modernization requires no elaborate survey of the early stages of Western imperialism, but two or three points may be singled out which have a significant bearing on the main theme. An essential ingredient of the contemporary problem is that with the rarest of exceptions training for self-government on modern lines is a very recent matter. It is, of course, true that some of the contacts of the European powers with southern Asia, from which empires later developed, date back to the beginning of the seventeenth century or even earlier. The connections of the British with India, of the Dutch with Indonesia, and of the Spanish with the Philippines were old-established by the time the partitioning of Africa got under way. In that part of the world the renewed burst of imperialism which characterized the three or four decades preceding World War I was largely an extension or consolidation of earlier imperial activities and acquisitions, involving both a rounding out of territorial holdings and an intensification and rationalization of European rule and economic exploitation. The modern colonial system which set the stage for a take-over by the presently independent governments was in good part a product of this

From Rupert Emerson, "Political Modernization: The Single-Party System," *Monograph Series in World Affairs*, Monograph No. 1 (Denver: Department of International Relations, University of Denver, 1963–1964), pp. 1–30. Reprinted by permission of the publisher and the author.

more recent phase, even though some of the colonial relationships date much further back.

In Africa even in those very limited areas in which the full extent of the conventional figure of eighty years is relevant the period of Western overlordship or tutelage is still brief. Actually in the great bulk of Africa, south of the Sahara, Western administration penetrated beyond occasional and hesitant footholds on the coast only at a considerably later time than the Berlin Conference, and in many rural areas it had had only a minimal impact even by the time of independence. Throughout Africa, as in Indonesia and elsewhere under colonial auspices, only a handful of people participated significantly in the management of their countries although the numbers increased in the last years of colonialism, and only when independence was almost in sight was substantial responsibility vested in the people of the country.

It would, of course, be ridiculous to lump all the colonial regimes together and assume that they all produced similar results. The colonial policy and administrative practice of the different powers varied greatly, and the same power operated in quite different fashions in different circumstances, as, for example, in territories where there was or was not a sizable body of white settlers. The range of difference is reflected in such summary observations as that the Americans assumed from the outset that the Philippines should move toward self-government, the British in due course eased the entry of Indians into the Indian Civil Service and expanded their political participation particularly at the local and provincial level, the French in principle moved to assimilate their colonial subjects into French culture and a single far-flung French Republic, and the Belgians held all power in their own hands while cautiously raising the general Congolese level of education and economic employment.

If the period of effective colonial tutelage was brief, the time which has elapsed since independence is almost inconsequential in terms of any effort to assess the probable course of political evolution in the new countries. Colonial rule, whether it be seen as oppression and exploitation or as benevolent introduction to the modern world, is a shattering experience, and it will be many years before the peoples exposed to it can be expected to find their own solid footing. The processes of adaptation to a radically different style of life which were started under imperialist and other pressures must now be taken over by the people and turned to their own purposes. Both independence and development bring new forces into play which seem inevitably destined to bring about basic readjustments of the balance between generations, interests, and classes. Externally the new countries must somehow fit themselves into a world whose own foundations have been shaken by wars and revolutions and by an unceasing flow of revolutionary scientific discoveries which are fundamentally changing the relation of men to each other and to their environment. The transition from the pre-colonial traditional societies through the decades or centuries of alien-imposed colonial rule to a fully achieved and stable independence is more likely than not to be a painful and turbulent one. On the face of it, it is more realistic to expect drastic and seemingly erratic changes of direction than straightforward advance along the lines laid out by the first post-colonial generation.

The currently fashionable adjective used to describe the new countries is "emerging," but whether the term is "backward," "underdeveloped," "developing," or some other such, the implication is the same. The peoples are assumed to be emerging both from the colonial regimes to which they have been subjected and from the social systems in which they have traditionally lived; and what they are emerging into is the modernity whose content and pattern have been shaped in Western Europe in the last two or three centuries. The bearing of the now discarded term "backward"—nicer words are constantly introduced to cover harsh realities—was that the peoples so described had lingered far behind the "advanced" peoples who had set in motion the dominant civilization of the 19th and 20th centuries. To "develop" or "emerge" is to join the ranks of those in the West who have achieved a hitherto undreamt of power over both man and nature, an unparalleled prosperity, and, for a time, the imperial leadership of mankind at large. For a time—a time which may perhaps reach well beyond the era of Western imperial domination—the standards by which all men were judged were those which reflected the civilization brought into being in a small corner of Western Europe and carried abroad by its migrant sons.

The West is often accused of attempting, in parochial arrogance, not only to force its own values and systems down the throats of other peoples but also to label as inferior all those who fail to adopt these values and systems for themselves. No doubt there is justice in such a charge. Certainly the imperial supremacy which the West established over so vast a segment of the world invited the bitter resentment which colonialism has evoked, and discrimination on the basis of race and color has been a constant feature in one or another guise.

The West can be attacked for its arrogance but the

story has other sides as well. The most significant consideration is that the revolution which the West brought to men's affairs did in fact furnish an unprecedented power and made possible a material well-being which no other society had been able to approach. It is arguable that once such forces had been loosed in the world they were irresistible and that no people which wanted to lead an independent life could expect to survive unless it took over key elements of this revolution as its own. I have contended elsewhere that future analysts may find the most lasting consequence of colonialism to have been the spread of the new-style Western civilization accompanied by all its virtues and vices.[1]

At all events, whatever the validity of these propositions, it is the "backward" peoples themselves, or their leaders speaking for them, who are producing the most convincing demonstration of the assumption that to "emerge" is to adopt the characteristic features which distinguish the West from other and earlier civilizations. What makes "modernization" modern is the ability to live, to think, to produce, to organize, in substantially the same fashion as the Western countries whose imperial hold has now been almost totally broken. With the rarest of exceptions the men who have thrust themselves forward as the governing elites of the Asian and African states have explicitly aimed at coming to terms of equality with the West by taking over its science, its techniques, its institutions. Certainly these elites have also demonstrated their pride in the inherited culture of their people and have made it clear their desire to preserve and promote it; but the greater emphasis is on modernization as defined by the Western model. To this end foreign aid and technical assistance are eagerly sought through international and bilateral channels. It is obviously desirable that the modernization should be adapted as closely as possible to the local scene and its particular cultural inheritance, but the point of importance is far less the special elements of adaptation than the attainment of equality with the West—or, better yet, superiority to it—through utilization of the West's own concepts and instruments. In passing it might be noted that it has so far been a losing stern chase since the pace of development in the emerging countries has been constantly outstripped by the continuing advance of the West, even apart from the constant danger that any material gains which are secured will be devoured by the multiplication of population, most notably in Asia.

Political modernization has been sought no less than economic and other forms of development, and is certainly of no less importance. Indeed, it has become increasingly apparent that the existence of an effective political and administrative system is a prior condition for the attainment of economic development. It is, however, somewhat more difficult to determine precisely what is meant by political modernization and to make an objective assessment of it than in the case of other types of modernization.[2] Presumably the easiest of all to identify and to measure is economic development for which a number of objective quantifiable criteria are readily available, such as the gross national product, per capita income, the type and quantity of agricultural and industrial production, the rate of economic growth, the number of workers drawn into wage employment, etc. In the field of transport and communications or of hygiene and medical care similar sets of statistics likewise yield good evidence as to the progress which is being made, and advances in education are shown in the number of schools, teachers, and pupils at different levels in the educational system.

The assessment of political development is a more problematical matter for a variety of reasons. One major point of confusion is that the "advanced" Western standard against which development is to be measured is itself dubious and controversial. If the problem is approached in terms of political structure, there is surely no particular model which can be set up as representing an agreed ideal or a necessary, or even a peculiarly favorable, precondition for economic and social development. Indisputably advanced countries have, even in the present century, experimented with more or less every form of government that is likely to appear in the new states, short of the improbable event that the latter revert to feudalism or an outright tribalism. In the last decades the name of democracy has been most frequently invoked as representing the most desirable mode of government, but democracy has developed so many variants and been used to cover so large a multitude of sins as to become almost meaningless unless it is closely defined.

The advanced West has known one-party, two-party, and multi-party democracies; it has known monarchies and dictatorships, including the modern inventions of fascism and communism; and it has tried out such hybrid forms as de Gaulle's Fifth Republic which has presumably been influential in promoting the vogue of strong presidential regimes in ex-French Africa. The available evidence appears to indicate that a variety of radically different governmental forms are compatible with, or may positively promote, economic and other types of development. Great Britain, Germany, Italy, Switzerland, the United States, Japan, and the Soviet Union are all to be counted in the ranks of the advanced. It would be a quite arbitrary matter to pick out one among the strikingly divergent political systems which they have evolved as the model by which the degree of modernization of the emerging countries should be judged. We have, indeed, no reason whatsoever to assume that some of the new countries may not devise other and radically different forms of government, perhaps more closely related to their indigenous tradition, which will prove to be equally effective instruments for development.

A further complication is that in almost every instance the new countries come to independence already endowed with constitutions which must be characterized as specifically "modern" and are usually closely akin to the political system of the imperial power from which they have just separated. Thus, all the colonial territories which have moved to independence have either started their new life with constitutions designed for them by the colonial power, usually in some measure of agreement with the nationalist leaders, or have devised constitutions drawn essentially from Western models as soon as they have become free or shortly thereafter. This is not to contend that, say, the 1945 constitution of Indonesia, re-introduced by Sukarno, or the post-independence constitutions of Ghana and Tanganyika have no elements of novelty in them or are uninfluenced by local tradition, but the general proposition still holds that the new countries have drawn almost exclusively on Western constitutional models, perhaps making an eclectic combination of forms. Constitutionally speaking, therefore, political modernization has been achieved before or coincident with the end of colonial status.

In such circumstances the significant element is likely to be the way in which the constitutional structure is actually utilized, the political style in which public affairs are managed. In the emerging countries no less than in the advanced what is important is not the elegance of the constitutional or legal façade, but the reality of political behavior which lies behind it. As the West well knows, the gap between formal governmental institutions and actual political operations may be immense; and it is a gap which is likely to be larger in the new than in the older established states because of the heavy borrowing by the former of alien and still unfamiliar political forms, developed elsewhere in different climes and circumstances. To dig beneath the outward forms and discover where power actually rests and how it is manipulated is by no means always easy. It will be a substantial time before the newly independent countries break away from the impact of their former colonial regimes and from the temptation—perhaps one should say, the necessity—to copy the West as furnishing in its manifold guises the only authentic models of what modernization means. It is more plausible than not that in due course these countries will develop political institutions which are more specifically their own, unless the determinist position is accepted that their development along modern economic lines will necessarily bring them the same kind of political institutions as have accompanied economic development in the West.

Although the constitutional foundations associated with modernity are too varied to permit any simple identification, five characteristic features of any modern political system can be summarily stated. (1) Political leadership must be so organized as to make reasonably firm and swift decisions possible. (2) There must be a rationalized and reasonably noncorrupt civil service whose members are selected primarily on the basis of merit and ability and who can be counted on, in the ordinary course of events, to obey orders. (3) The government's financial affairs must be regularized and separated from the private financial affairs of those who are in political or administrative control. (4) There must be a judiciary and courts of law which administer some reasonable approximation of even-handed justice. (5) The writ of the government must run, in principle at least, throughout the entire country, even though at any given moment there may be substantial pockets of resistance or noncompliance.

The most trustworthy indices of the success of any political system in achieving modernization are to be found in the results for the society of which it is in charge. The maintenance of law and order internally and the preservation of the state's identity and integrity externally are the minimum and indispensable requirements. Assuming that these requirements are met, if the economy is advancing and the standard of living improving, if public health is making headway and education is spreading, it is a reasonable presumption that the government is doing its job well.

The responsibilities and aspirations of the governments of the emerging countries are as extensive as are the difficulties by which they are confronted. They are charged with, or have taken upon themselves, the immense task of bringing their people as speedily as possible to the level of the advanced, despite the fact that they are at best only meagerly equipped with the tools needed for the task. Since the transition to independence has generally taken place peacefully, they have usually inherited the colonial administrative systems as going concerns, although European civil servants have often left in substantial numbers as the nationalists took over. The functioning of the ex-colonial regimes has been grievously impaired only in the surprisingly rare instances of bitter and protracted revolutionary war, as in Indonesia, Vietnam, and Algeria, or where the parting was marked by a fit of bad temper as in the French reaction to Guinea's vote of "No" in the referendum on the de Gaulle constitution of 1958. Even where the colonial governmental machinery is inherited intact, however, it was the creation of the imperial authorities and is therefore unlikely to meet the new national demands satisfactorily. Although the colonial governments had come to reach well beyond the provision of the minimum services of law and order, the new governments have universally taken on a large array of broader functions which may be lumped under the general headings of economic development and the promotion of social welfare, plus entry into the wholly new field of international representation and action.

The purposes and scope of a colonial regime, manned in all its commanding heights by expatriate officials, are inevitably different from and more limited than those of a national government, and particularly a national government which takes over in a first surge of enthusiasm for its new-found power and responsibilities. Since the leaders in the new countries are virtually all men who have a substantial familiarity with the progressive programs and practices of the West, they set off from the assumption that it is their responsibility to see that their people are furnished with social welfare facilities of a type comparable with those existent elsewhere, even though the social and economic foundations of the societies which they govern have not begun to approach the level of the advanced societies which are taken as the model. Thus, to pick a single example, it is assumed, despite the heavy costs of many kinds that universal education should be provided in the earlier grades and secondary and higher education greatly expanded. In aspiration, at least, the new countries set as their more or less immediate goal the achievement of the whole apparatus of the advanced states which, in glaring contrast to themselves, are already equipped with highly developed economies and administrations.

Of particular moment is the fact that universally the new countries look to the government to carry the main burden of economic development. The general absence of a supply of indigenous entrepreneurs, the lack of capital or at least its unavailability for productive and developmental purposes, and the scarcity of private groupings and associations which might carry some of the burden all contribute to the belief that the government should play the major role. Deriving in good part from the experience of capitalism under the colonial regimes—seen as represented by alien concerns exploiting the local populace—there is a fear and suspicion of private enterprise, which is bolstered by wide acceptance of the theory that imperialism is an inevitable product of capitalism. In almost every country the view is dominant that socialism is the appropriate label for the kind of social-economic system which is desired. Socialism in this sense has no necessary connection with Marxism, and far less with the specific Marxist variant of Communism, but is rather a general term to cover a system adapted to local conditions and traditions, in which there will be a cooperative pulling together rather than an unleashing of the anti-social forces of private profit-making. In the large it may be said that the community is valued more than the individual. To put it in the simplest terms, socialism is a good word, and capitalism a bad one. In order to arrive at the socialist society and the planning which is incident to it, the government must take over the direction of economic life—but the extent to which the government actually intervenes varies greatly from state to state.

It is one of the ironies of the situation that the modernizing role of governments has undergone a decided expansion just at the time when the trained and "modernized" manpower available to them has been sharply reduced through the removal of at least some of the alien civil servants who have staffed the colonial regimes. Or, alternatively, where the expatriates have in fact stayed on, the new governments are left in the anomalous position of having to rely on this alien contingent, often in key posts, at a time of maximum national self-assertion. This has been peculiarly the case in most of the former French African territories which have remained so closely tied to France through the continued presence of French personnel and through financial and economic reliance on France as to open them to the charge of having secured only an outward show of independence.

A partial and temporary answer to the lack of expertise can be found in the utilization of externally supplied technical assistance and similar devices, but this is no answer for the long haul. In many countries great efforts are being made to train and recruit the administrators, but it is inevitably a slow and costly process, entailing much loss and inefficiency on the way by. At the same time every country has been plagued by the problem of trying to keep the official payroll clear of the multitude of people who feel that they are entitled to a place on it, either because of family connections or their education or merely because it is their country, no longer under alien rule and now obligated to take care of its own. These are the growing pains of new states and must be borne with, but they do not ease the already extraordinarily difficult processes of modernization and development.

The difficulties are, of course, compounded by the fact that nowhere are adequate revenues available to the governments to meet the costs of the expansive programs which they would like to introduce. The vicious circle of poverty perpetuating poverty, where riches multiply wealth, is an inescapable limiting factor. Again, foreign aid from a variety of donors or lenders can somewhat ease the situation but the basic reliance must be on home resources, particularly when private foreign enterprise and investment are likely to be eyed with suspicion, despite official pronouncements of welcome to the foreign investor. The full mobilization of home resources is often made very difficult, or for immediate purposes impossible, by the ability of the well-to-do to evade taxation, not infrequently on the assumption which has cropped up in many other parts of the world that their prosperity, far from imposing obligations on them, entitles them to special privileges.

A major cause of difficulty and even of potential disaster for the emerging countries is that they so often rest upon the unstable foundation of populations which are internally divided. Only rarely does one find in these countries the kind of homogeneity and national solidarity with which at least wishful thinking endows the modern state. As Edward Shils has put it:

> In almost every aspect of their social structures, the societies on which the new states must be based are characterized by a "gap." It is the gap between the educated and the uneducated, between the townsman and the villager, between the cosmopolitan or national and the local, between the modern and the traditional, between the rulers and the ruled. It is the gap between a small group of active, aspiring, relatively well-off, educated, and influential persons in the big towns, and an inert or indifferent, impoverished, uneducated, and relatively powerless peasantry.[3]

An even more dangerous threat to unity and stability appears when to this list are added the gaps which derive from the inclusion within a single political system of different tribal, caste, religious, and linguistic communities.

To seek to enlist the active participation of the people in creating a viable state and setting the processes of development in motion becomes a hazardous enterprise when substantial segments of the population are perhaps only dubiously aware of the existence of the new state and its government and certainly are moved by no overriding loyalty to them. The ability of the government to make its writ run throughout the entire territory may be decisively challenged, and even the continued unity of the state placed in jeopardy. To give a single example, the government of Burma has never been able since winning independence in 1947 to have unhampered access to, and establish its control over, all parts of the country. The disorders which tribalism has inflicted on the Congo need no elaboration.

The most evident lack is the failure to have achieved a feeling of national identity in some deeper sense of belonging together and sharing a common destiny than can be expected to flow from the superimposed fact of common membership in a recently constructed state. A few Asian and African countries, such as Japan and divided Korea and Vietnam, match up passably well to the ideal type of the nation which can be abstracted from the experience of a small number of West European peoples, but many can claim virtually nothing more than the tenuous roots with which a brief encounter with colonialism has endowed them. A cursory glance at their history furnishes the reason why this should be so, but an understanding of how they arrived where they are does not change the fact that they can often be given no more than a courtesy title of nationhood. Much is heard of nationalism and of the nationalist leaders who carry on the anti-colonial struggle, but for the most part the nations themselves are at the best only beginning to be shaped.

Africa south of the Sahara is a classic example of this situation since the multiplicity of states into which it is being divided are almost all colonial inventions, designed with cavalier disregard for the tribes and peoples which compose them. Even at the time when independence came, substantial parts of tropical Africa might have been given a different political shape, as most notably in the maintenance of the two big French federations of West and Equatorial Africa instead of "balkanization" into a dozen political entities. The magnitude and vigor of the drive for pan-African solutions indicate the lack of satisfaction with the present political division of the continent. In Asia, although Indonesia and the Philippines can claim a somewhat greater antiquity as political entities than their African counterparts, their boundaries are those which were established by the colonial powers. Even India had known little, if any, unity before the British *raj* enforced it, while Pakistan was barely dreamed of before the 1930's.

Where there has been no significant prior unity of a national variety the fact of organizing a nationalist movement and carrying on a revolutionary struggle has a significant effect in stimulating the spread of national awareness and loyalty. In a number of recent instances, however, the imperial authorities have been so ready to relinquish their hold that they have granted independence well before there was any effective and organized demand for it, much less an irresistible revolutionary drive. Although future legends may require a different and more heroic version, independence has in fact often been peacefully conceded on the basis of an agreed timetable and program. One of the results is that many of the ex-colonial peoples have not undergone such national welding together as might have come to them from the experience of concerting their forces to wage political and perhaps military warfare against the colonialists. The contemporary campaign against the dangers of neo-colonialism can be traced in part to the need to rouse a sense of nationalist fervor in peoples who were able to find an easy path to freedom, or to re-arouse it for those whose memory of the anti-colonial struggle is fading.

Where the population of a country is relatively homogeneous a nationalist movement or the attainment or near approach of independence will ordinarily have a unifying effect, but where the population is diverse the effect may be to call attention to differences and points of incompatibility. With the coming of independence it becomes increasingly impossible to evade the question, which perhaps hardly came to the surface under alien imperial rule, as to who will wield power in the new dispensation. In the interest of which nationality, tribe, or religious community will the new state function? The issue is perhaps most unmistakably clear where white settlers are involved, as in Algeria, Southern Rhodesia, or, at its most terrifying, in South Africa, in all of which independence for the native majority or the white minority means the subordination of the other. In India as independence neared, a large segment of the Muslim minority found intolerable the thought of Hindu domination, and in Ceylon the aftermath of freedom was the clash of Sinhalese and Tamils. The transition to independence of Ghana was threatened by the reluctance of the Ashanti to accept rule by other tribes, and Kenya's independence has been delayed by the fears of the lesser tribes for their future under Kikuyu and Luo supremacy. British Guiana's political advance has been plagued by the feud which increasing self-government has stirred up

between those of African and of Indian descent. Other parts of the British West Indies have, however, been able to take self-government and independence in their stride, and the extraordinary example of Malaya, whose interracial alliance between Malays, Chinese, and Indians may still prove too good to last, establishes that the ending of colonial rule need not aggravate tensions even when racial diversity is great.

The emerging countries are all of them in one or another stage of transition from a past which can be determined with considerable accuracy to a future of which only dim outlines can be discerned. Some clues as to what lies ahead of them can perhaps be derived from an examination of their political evolution to date, and particularly of their experience with democracy, to which almost all have expressed their devotion but in fashions which many democrats may feel inclined to repudiate as wholly unacceptable.

II

Before the current wave of colonial emancipation got under way it appears to have been widely taken for granted by both the colonial-nationalists and their backers in the imperial centers and elsewhere that the societies which were about to be liberated would surely give full expression to democracy. This reflected not only a general belief in progress but more specifically an optimistic faith that underdogs who achieved the freedom to which they were entitled could be counted on to run their societies in accord with the dictates of freedom. To doubt this proposition and its corollaries was to open up the entire foundations of liberal anti-colonialism to skeptical or hostile reexamination. The main opponents of such a view were indeed those who were convinced opponents of the whole swing toward colonial independence and took for granted the contrary proposition that only trouble lay ahead of peoples who were so obviously incompetent to manage their own affairs. At the extreme, the European who saw the African as having just come down from the trees was not likely to be impressed by his ability to rule himself on acceptable modern lines.

For the others, however, it was something of an article of faith both that democracy in its Western guise represented the highest form of political life and that the peoples who were achieving freedom would be satisfied with nothing less than the best. The imperial authorities were assailed because they had failed to live up to the democratic convictions of the mother countries in their dealings with the dependent peoples, imposing on them instead autocratic and bureaucratic rule. One of the principal criteria of political advance in the colonies was the grant of an increasing measure of democratic participation in the governmental process through elective councils and legislatures whose enhanced control over the executive began to break the exclusive hold of the expatriate officials. It was a logical presumption that with the coming of independence full power would be vested in the representatives of the people, elected on the basis of universal suffrage. The nationalists based themselves on their claim to speak for their own people as against the alien colonial masters, and had become familiar with democracy and its values in the course of their Western-style education at home or abroad. It may also have played a role that the spokesmen for the imperial powers made it clear that a democratic form of government could be managed only by a mature and advanced people; "natives" were not to be trusted with such a complex and delicate instrument. For the colonial peoples it became therefore a matter of pride and prestige to demonstrate that they as well as their erstwhile colonial rulers could make democracy work.

As has been seen, when the nationalist heirs of the colonial regimes took over, they operated for the most part under constitutions which were either a continuation of the colonial structure, modified to meet the requirements of an independent state, or had been hammered out in agreement with the imperial authorities prior to independence. In other instances, such as those of India and Indonesia, new constitutions were drafted by a constitutional convention or the political leaders. With only trivial exceptions the political systems under which the new states started their lives were quite evidently drawn from Western democratic models and were assumed to set the countries for which they were designed on a political path strictly comparable to that of the formerly dominant Western powers.

The optimistic faith with which the emerging countries started on their new careers has not been justified by the results as far as the maintenance of democratic rule is concerned; but it may be that the standards and expectations set for them and which their leaders set for themselves were improper and ill-designed. At all events in country after country, with or without drastic constitutional revision, the original democratic presuppositions have given way to quite different systems of centralized and authoritarian control in military or civilian hands. The countries which have maintained an acceptably Western style of democratic constitutionalism are a

small minority of those which have come to independence since World War II; and the earlier example of the twenty Latin-American republics does not lend much encouragement. Certainly in terms of sheer size, and perhaps in accomplishment as well, India heads the list despite those critics who point to the unbroken dominance of the Congress, the hold of the caste system, and other anomalies and shortcomings. In neighboring Southeast Asia both the Philippines and Malaya have maintained a respectable record of democratic performance. In the Middle East, Israel and Lebanon, balanced uneasily on its confessional division, would be the leading candidates. Among all the African states Nigeria has the best claim to have preserved a measure of multi-party constitutional democracy but the disturbances in the Western Region and the treason trials involving major opposition leaders have somewhat tarnished the Nigerian record. The occasional claims of Southern Rhodesia and South Africa to represent oases of parliamentary democracy in a continent overrun by authoritarian leaders and elites must be disallowed in view of their failure to give political expression to the bulk of the people of their countries.

I have deliberately expressed doubt as to the correctness of the standards and expectations which have been set and have referred to "an acceptably Western style" of democracy. What is involved is obviously a central and inescapable issue as to the meaning and structure of democracy. The alternative approach of discarding the concept of democracy itself and shifting to the assumption that some other social-political form than democracy is more effective and desirable has as yet made only slight headway. In the 1930's, when the Fascist regimes appeared to be making a great splash in the world, it was possible to share their scorn for democracy, but the presently available alternatives to democracy are not attractive; and Communism, of course, puts itself forward as embodying the true democracy in contrast to the oppressive rule of the bourgeoisie which masquerades as democracy in non-Communist societies. As a random sample of an opposing position, one J. Chuks Obi wrote that while it is fashionable to regard democracy as a panacea for all social and economic ills,

There is a real sense in which economic development demands leadership and direction from as *few* as possible. The astonishingly rapid transformation of Russia did not owe its achievements to a wellpacked House of Assembly. British capitalism and industrial leadership in the 19th century was not founded on government for the people and by the people. One cannot help thinking that when Dr. Sukarno advocated a "guided democracy" for Indonesia he had an eye on Nigeria where over 1,000 legislators for a population of about 33 millions (real text-book democracy) is proving an expensive luxury.[4]

As a matter of history a case can unquestionably be made for such a position, but in terms of present-day politics it is a position which finds few takers; and it is to be noted that Sukarno spoke of guided *democracy*.

The cardinal political assumption remains that the people rule, and that the governmental system runs on their behalf. Therefore democracy must figure in the title of the system; but what is democracy? Two major conceptions come immediately to mind, one deriving from the parliamentary systems of the West, and the other, also with Western origins but less reputable ones, which has found more favor in the emerging countries. Both share the great common ground of resting on a doctrine of popular sovereignty and on the acceptance, at least in principle, of universal suffrage. Although the differences run significantly deeper than this somewhat mechanical version of them would indicate, the breaking point comes where the Western liberal system requires the existence of two or more political parties, forming a government and an opposition, while Asian and African leaders have been moving more and more explicitly toward a single-party system, for which an impressive body of theoretical justification is being advanced.

The Western view sets off from the assumption that unless a variety of opinions, programs, and persons can be presented to the electorate for their approval or disapproval, the people are not in a position to make an informed choice between the alternatives which are open to them. Without full freedom for an opposition to canvass every possibility and to speak its mind, the sins and errors of the government cannot be brought to light, and, of even greater importance, nor can what may be wiser measures secure an adequate hearing. Only by establishing institutional safeguards for criticism and innovation, it is contended, is it possible to ensure that all viewpoints have been heard and that all means of achieving the public good have been explored. The opposition must therefore be free to organize and to publicize its views, to offer its candidates for election on the same terms as the governing party, and to take over the government if it wins public favor. The distinguished British authority Sir Ivor Jennings has put it succinctly: "If there is no opposition, there is no democracy,"[5]

and the Governor-General of Nigeria, Nnamdi Azikiwe, has made the same point slightly more elaborately: "Unless an opposition exists—as a 'shadow cabinet' capable of replacing the government—democracy becomes a sham. . . . Failure to tolerate the existence of an opposition party would be disastrous to the existence of democracy. It is the easiest invitation to dictatorship."[6]

However strong the case may be for this version of democracy, an overwhelming majority of Asian and African states have in the last few years moved away from it to embrace more authoritarian military or one-party, and usually one-man, regimes. By far the greatest of them, of course, is China which discarded the one-party authoritarianism of Chiang Kai-shek for the totalitarianism of Mao and the Communists, but the Communist pattern has so far been followed only in neighboring North Korea and North Vietnam, and in distant Cuba, although it has obviously had a significant influence elsewhere. The military have taken over in the Republic of Korea, Burma, Thailand, Pakistan, Egypt and from time to time other Arab countries, and the Sudan. In most of the rest of the Afro-Asian countries one-party political systems have been established, either *de facto* or through official outlawry of other parties. In a few instances parties have either never played a role, as in Ethiopia or Saudia Arabia, or have been reduced to insignificance, as in Egypt under Nasser or Indonesia under Sukarno, with the exception of the Communists in the latter case.

In order to make room for a more extensive survey of the justifications which the Asian and African leaders have themselves brought forward for the one-party system, only a brief listing will be attempted here of the major elements, for the most part already suggested in the preceding pages, which are usually regarded as responsible for the turn away from the liberal Western pattern. It might be added that while most external observers would agree on the items to be included in such a list they would be likely to disagree as to the weighting to be given them.

The easiest starting point is no doubt the gap which exists between the new elite which has become the heir to political power and the mass of the people in the emerging countries. The former have a substantial Western-style education, not infrequently including advanced degrees, are literate in at least one Western language which often serves as the *lingua franca* for the country, and are well acquainted with Western forms of government. The masses, on the other hand, are still illiterate, live close to the subsistence line, and have had no occasion to become familiar with any higher level of government than that which impinges on them locally, be it of a traditional variety or some modernized version brought in by the colonial or central authorities. These things are changing: education in many countries is spreading greatly, standards of living are slowly improving, universal suffrage in principle brings political activity to every corner of the country, and expanding governmental functions impinge more and more even upon the remote villages; but the gap between elite and mass remains great, though more intermediate groupings are coming into being. The usual meagerness and inadequacy of the network of mass communications also hinder the narrowing of the gap between governing elite and governed mass. It is typical that a highly educated and influential Pakistani intellectual should have told me the other day that at the most 10 per cent of the people of his country have any measure of political awareness and play any continuing political role.

The existence of the many other gaps which break up the homogeneity of the societies renders presently impossible the achievement of that basic consensus which most theorists of liberal democracy see as essential to its flourishing or even to its survival. The danger exists, not as an abstract threat for the future but as an inescapable present reality, that these gaps are likely to mean that any opposition party or movement of consequence bases itself on a tribal or other racial, linguistic, religious, or regional grouping which at least implicitly, if not quite openly, threatens the national unity which it is the goal of the dominant leaders to consolidate or bring into being. Given the lack of political experience of a modern type, the opposition is likely to conceive itself as the all-out enemy of the governing group and perhaps of the state itself rather than to grasp the subtle and sophisticated idea of becoming His Majesty's loyal opposition. It has frequently been said that in Ghana the word for "opposition" is "enemy."

A different order of considerations involves the ease with which the parliamentary system can be converted into an instrument for one-party rule. So long as the generally accepted political morality includes the assumption that two or more parties competing for power according to an implicitly agreed set of rules are an essential part of the political game democracy in the Western sense finds expression in the parliamentary forum. The entire situation changes if the emphasis is placed on the right of the majority not only to constitute the governnment, but also to take all power to itself without

regard for the minority. From the assumption that the majority rules with a firm hand and that the minority is no more than a tolerated nuisance, it is a relatively small step to seeing it as only a nuisance, no longer to be tolerated. In such circumstances opposition parties can be outlawed or by one or another device absorbed within the ruling "national" party; and what set out to be a parliamentary government on the Western model takes on a totally different hue. A convenient device for bringing the opposition into line is the provision adopted by several of the French-speaking African states that the entire country forms a single electoral constituency, and that the party whose national list secures the highest vote takes all the seats in the parliament. What emerges is executive predominance centered on the national leader.

As the leaders of the new countries themselves see it, it is only plausible to assume that their awareness of the gap between them and the masses is one of the key features of the situation. Their goal is to construct modern countries, and it would be obviously absurd to rely on the unmodern masses to undertake and guide their own transformation. The masses must be carried along in the process, but the controlling hand must be that of the contingent in the society which has itself achieved modernity. Contemporary democratic presuppositions make it unfashionable and perhaps politically unfeasible to come out openly with elitist doctrines but they occasionally make a more or less overt appearance. In a period less committed to full-scale democracy, Sun Yat-sen, as one of the first of those to confront the dilemmas involved in modernizing a society which very reluctantly abandoned its traditional ways, spoke out openly for a period of tutelage during which the people at large would be educated to assume their new democratic responsibilities. In his *San Min Chu I* he referred repeatedly to the inequality of men in ability and held the majority of the people to be without vision. Those of us who have a broader vision, he held, must guide the people into the right way and escape the confusions into which Western democracy has fallen.

The phrase which has come to be most widely used to designate this kind of tutelage is Sukarno's "guided democracy" which combines the conviction of the day that democracy is in order with the conviction that some people are more equal than others. In his first address as President of the United States of Indonesia, in December, 1949, Sukarno denied that democracy was anything new for Indonesia, but insisted that it differed from the democracy of others:

Eastern democracy—more clearly Indonesian democracy that has descended to us from generation to generation, is *democracy accompanied by leadership: democracy with leadership!* That is Eastern democracy, Indonesian democracy. *The leader carries a great responsibility,* the leader must know how to lead, the leader must lead.[7]

Although Sukarno has always related his political speculations and institutional proposals very closely to the Indonesian scene and its tradition many of the key propositions which he has emphasized turn up with regularity in a number of the other new countries. The heart of the matter is his repudiation of the notion of an opposition and of a majority which is automatically entitled to override a minority even though its margin of victory may be only a single vote. Democracy, if properly guided, has his blessing, but not the Western liberal version of it which he has derided as "free-flight democracy." The idea of an opposition he has lumped with liberalism and capitalism as alien to the Indonesian experience and outlook, serving to divide the community against itself rather than to unite. In his view, what Indonesian tradition renders desirable and feasible is the gathering together in the top councils of government of people representing as far as possible every viewpoint and every phase of the country's life. Their function is not to define the opposing positions more sharply and come to a vote in which one faction outnumbers the other, but to continue the discussion until all have collaborated in reaching a decision which all accept. Omnipresent in the background is Sukarno himself, prepared to take the decision which represents the popular will if agreement fails to emerge from the deliberations.

Time and again in a number of African countries surprisingly similar declarations of political principle have been made, denouncing the Western liberal-parliamentary conception of the opposition and insisting that African tradition calls for the slow ironing out of disagreement until the sense of the meeting has been arrived at. Thus in presenting the case for a one-party state in Ghana in 1962 Minister of Defence Kofi Baako told the National Assembly that the multi-party system was unfitting to Ghana where tradition called for a council of elders, approved by the people and with a chief to lead them. He continued: "There is no question of a deliberate division of that group, one side saying 'I am opposing' and another side saying 'I am governing.' All of them in fact govern and they govern by consultation and by deliberation."[8]

A different kind of objection to the multi-party system which has frequently been advanced in Africa, as, for example, by Sékou Touré in Guinea and Julius Nyerere in Tanganyika, is the contention that political parties developed in the West in response to the need of different classes to protect and promote their conflicting interests, whereas since Africa has produced no corresponding class differentiation it has no need of a multiplicity of parties. (There is here an interesting parallel to the Soviet claim that since the U.S.S.R. has arrived at a monolithic pattern of society without exploiting classes and other intermediate groupings, it requires only a single all-embracing party; but, on the other hand, Communist theorists are by no means prepared to accept the view that African societies are classless.)

A further step in the direction of the one-party system is made when the nationalist movements are brought into the argument. European and American parties, Nyerere has asserted, came into being as the result of internal social and economic divisions, one party arising to challenge the monopoly of political power of some aristocratic or capitalist group. In Africa, on the other hand, the function of parties was to challenge the external threat posed by the alien rulers: under such circumstances the parties represented not factions and divisions within the country, but "the interests and aspirations of the whole nation. . . . A Tanganyikan who helped the imperialists was regarded as a traitor to his country, not as a believer in 'Two-Party' democracy!"[9]

This introduction of the nationalist movements has served the one-party advocates well. With a heavy admixture of sarcasm they have confronted their Western and domestic critics with the question as to whether their countries, having achieved a nationalist consolidation of political forces against the colonial authorities, must now deliberately break down the unity which has been gained in order to satisfy the doctrinaire insistence of Western-style democrats on the existence of more than one party.

At this point the controversy is likely to swing back to what was suggested earlier as the fundamental distinction between the Western liberal approach to democracy and the variant approach which has spread so widely in other parts of the world. It is a characteristic difference that Western spokesmen are likely to stress the protection which their conception offers to minorities and to individuals, enabling diversity to flourish and encouraging the growth of a pluralistic society, while the emphasis in the new countries falls rather on the need for unity and a strong government which can take hold of the immensely difficult and urgent problems confronting it. It is felt that if the government has the popular approval of the mass it should be free to go about its business unhampered by checks and balances or other niceties of liberal constitutionalism. Madeira Keita of Mali has said of democracy that "in its naively original sense" it is "the exercise of public authority in conformity with the will of the masses."[10] In a cruder and more activist version of much the same proposition Castro protested in 1961 that the Cuban people had been deluded by a false democracy for sixty years:

> Speak to the people of elections and they will answer you that what interests them now is that the revolution advance rapidly and that no time be lost.
>
> For the first time the people hold power. For the first time it is the people who govern. It matters very little whether the formalities are observed. What counts is the essence of democracy, that is, that the people and public opinion determine the destiny of the country. We have need of all our time to push the revolution ahead, to develop our economy, to defend ourselves against imperialism.[11]

In Castro's statement there is at least a hint of what is probably the most frequent comment about the Western parliamentary system in general and the multi-party system in particular: These are luxuries which we cannot now afford; perhaps later on when we have caught up with the advanced countries we will be able to afford them. As the months and years have gone by, however, the tendency has been to postpone to a more and more remote future the time when such luxuries might prove desirable and to elaborate increasingly on the virtues inherent in the one-party system.

In the immediate here and now the most urgent task is almost certain to be seen not as the protection of individual and minority liberties but the realization in broad strokes of what is taken to be the community will—or perhaps what the elite feel it should be. The first order of business is not the creation of an opposition which can criticize but the establishment of a strong and vigorous government which can govern. Since so many of the emerging countries are in greater or less degree recent and artificial constructs whose inner solidarity rests on unstable foundations it is easy to comprehend why the leaders give priority to the consolidation of national unity through the prompt and decisive action of an effective government. Without such a government neither development nor a defense against disintegration or a return of colonialism is possible.

While it is evidently not necessarily the case that two or more parties should prejudice or disrupt the incipient national unity, it is reasonable to expect that they will not promote unity to the same extent as a single party, dedicated to that purpose; and national unity is regarded as a more real and desirable good than a pluralistic political freedom. The risks of disintegration which attach to a multi-party system are, of course, greatly enhanced where party loyalties and voting patterns are determined on the basis of particularistic racial, tribal, or other ethnic groups, as is so often the case in the Asian and African states. Furthermore, at least in principle, the one-party system avoids the dispersion of effort which an opposition involves and makes it possible to enlist all the limited expertise and leadership which is available for a combined attack upon the national problems. In practice, however, the solidarity of the ranks of the national leaders is gravely impaired in many countries by the substantial number of distinguished figures or potential contributors to national well-being who are held in preventive detention, are otherwise jailed, or have vanished into exile.

The apologists for the one-party state are not unlikely to play both sides of the street; that is, to assert that the single party can appropriately exist without violating democratic precepts because it is essentially a continuation of the national unity won in the anti-colonial struggle, and at the same time, perhaps less overtly, to plead the necessity of having a single party if the break-up of the society is to be prevented. The latter argument is bolstered by the charge that the imperialists and other external enemies foster the rise and activity of opposition parties in order to undermine the solidarity of the state which has so recently come to independence. Although the situation varies from country to country, it is in general more realistic to see the trend toward the authoritarian one-party system as deriving from the lack of national unity rather than as the expression of it. It is evidently the case in most instances that the single governing party is the same nationalist movement which won independence or is the direct descendant thereof, but one essential justification for the centralization of political control is that national unity is so tenuous as not be trusted to operate without the firmest of guidance from the top. The single party is an instrument to achieve the national solidarity which is otherwise conspicuous by its absence, and often it is the principal instrument available for that purpose.

One salient feature of the single-party system as it has functioned in practice is that in most instances the capstone of the structure has been the single charismatic leader. Indeed, it is often not going too far to see the ruling party as in fact the vehicle, or even an emanation, of the central figure who dominates the entire political landscape. At the present day their names have become household words and need no lengthy recitation: Gandhi and then Nehru, Sukarno, Chiang and then Mao, Bourguiba, Nkrumah, Sékou Touré, Houphouet-Boigny, Banda, Nyerere, to name only a few. A forthright expression of what is involved was made by the governing party in the Congo (Brazzaville) which contended that,

> While in Europe the rules of parliamentary behaviour are based on a relative or absolute majority. . . . parliamentary democracy in Africa is based on unanimity. One can truthfully say that an African state which is incapable of giving its undivided support to a unanimously acknowledged leader is, and will remain, a land deeply divided against itself, and to all intents and purposes ungovernable within the framework of the new institutions.[12]

This emergence of the strong heroic figure in new countries at a troubled time is nothing new in the historical record; it has of late been pointed out by several writers that what might be castigated as an abuse in the presently emerging countries found its close parallel in the unmeasured adulation of George Washington in the early days of the United States. The need of a visible symbol, and more than a symbol, of national identity and striving is very great. For the politically unsophisticated the whole paraphernalia of parliaments and cabinets, ministers and civil service hierarchies are remote, unreal, and confusing, while a single figure, visible in the flesh and constantly paraded before the public as the savior of his people, has an unmistakable and dramatic reality.

In constitutional terms the consequence has been a marked shift away from the European parliamentary pattern and toward the presidential system. After decades of finding few imitators the American constitution has again come into its own as a model for the new countries, although what has been taken over from it is far more the central national figure of the president than the host of checks and balances and countervailing institutions which plague the life of the American president. No occupant of the White House would recognize himself in the not overly exaggerated portrayal by a Tunisian newspaper of the "absolute supremacy" which Bourguiba has conquered for himself; "Everything converges toward the holder of power who, alone, exists, de-cides, and in expressing himself expresses the country and incarnates it."[13]

What has been sought is a direct and evident concentration of power in the hands of a single national leader. The division of power which at least appears to exist where a president is ceremonial head of state while a prime minister, surrounded by a cabinet and responsible to a parliamentary majority, actually controls the government has proved intolerable to countries which yearn for a simpler and more straightforward version of their new-found sovereignty. Considerations of the same sort have played a small role in persuading several of the newer members of the Commonwealth to become republics. Although nationalist pressures have been the most important, it has also been contended that the people find it difficult to comprehend an independence in which the Queen is still sovereign and in which her representative, the Governor-General, co-exists with the prime minister.

The swing to authoritarian single-party regimes has inevitably produced much controversy as to the extent to which political freedom has been impaired and whether and on what grounds such impairment can be justified. The extreme position, rarely stated in blunt terms and to be found most frequently among those who have undergone substantial exposure to Marxist thought, lays all its emphasis on the community as an integrated whole—Sékou Touré has spoken of Africa as being essentially *communaucratique*—whose general will, if guided by the right hands, must always be right. The mere fact that a minority opposes makes it immediately suspect and opens it to the charge of being a tool of the neo-colonialists.

On more pragmatic grounds, the accusation that the new states have abused the liberty of their people is met, particularly when it comes from Western critics, both by citing the abuses of colonialism and by pointing out that all countries have greatly tightened up the apparatus of control in time of war or other crises. The crisis deriving from the anti-colonial revolution and the setting in motion of an independent government and the drive for development are held amply to justify the restrictions of private liberty which have been imposed.

As a means of reconciling the demands of political freedom with those of one-party authoritarianism some reigning parties have adopted the familiar Communist device of democratic centralism which calls for full freedom of discussion at all levels as decisions are being reached and for unquestioning observance once they are made. This is a mode of procedure which has the advantage of being easily squared with the assumption of Sukarno and many others that the kind of democracy traditionally characteristic of Asian and African countries is a confrontation of all opinions in free discussion which ultimately achieves an agreed version of the community's will. As a statement of intent it is admirable and, if wholly lived up to, it could meet virtually all requirements, but the abyss which separates theory from practice is likely to be peculiarly great in this sphere. The formal promise of full freedom to oppose the leader and to challenge the desires of the party hierarchy is all too likely in reality to lead to political retaliation against the dissident faction. To make the voice of the village heard at the top is a difficult matter under any circumstances; the single party headed by a charismatic leader does not gladly suffer criticism; and within the single-party state it is hard to parallel the institutional safeguards which protect dissident opinion in a country where two or more parties are accepted features of the political scene. In a message celebrating the 14th anniversary of the founding of his Convention People's Party in June, 1963, Nkrumah declared that if innerparty democracy and self-criticism is practised "it will follow that all decisions of the party are decisions of the entire membership" and party democracy will be fully achieved.[14] But the dissidents and minorities are far from having had an easy time in Ghana.

Of other justifications of the one-party system, only two need be cited. Tom Mboya has recently argued that the political experience of the new countries of Asia and Africa demonstrates that the party system is not a necessary part of democracy, and he concludes that "what is necessary is the freedom to form parties. It is not necessary that more than one should in fact exist and function effectively."[15] To this he adds the further proposition, in one sense undeniable and in another highly debatable, that a sovereign people may decide to forgo their right to form parties and decree irrevocably that the country shall in the future have only one party.

Nyerere, who has also backed the idea that what is important is the freedom to form opposition parties, has been pleased to develop an argument to the effect that legislators and others within a single party have in fact a greater measure of freedom than do political figures within a two- or multi-party system. The gist of this proposition is that where an opposition exists, the members of each party must be held to a strict party discipline in order to deny any opening to the rival. Within the single party, on the other hand, all are free to express their own opinions until the party line has been shaped, with the backbenchers contributing as much as the leaders. As Nyerere's thinking has evolved he has become an increasingly firm supporter of the single-party concept and of the practical merger of party and government. With the expectation of shocking the political theorists who identify democracy with opposing parties, he has laid it down that "where there is *one* party, and that party is identified with the *nation as a whole,* the foundations of democracy are firmer than they can ever be where you have two or more parties, each representing only a section of the community."[16]

The issues involved are relatively simple and straightforward. The single-party system, or the military rule which has been imposed in several countries, has evident virtues where the people are sharply divided among themselves and unity is a first requisite, where a new political, social, and economic society must be brought into being, and where the hardships and disciplines of development must take priority over private preferences. It is obvious that no single and all-embracing answer can be given, but the other side of the situation must have more attention than the leaders of the new countries are inclined to give it. Even assuming that the nationalist movements are led and manned by disinterested patriots and that in the first rounds the parties and governments which take over after independence sincerely strive to embody the will of the people, how likely are they to drift away to holding power for its own sake and for the fruits it yields them, giving only the necessary bread and circuses and plebiscitary celebrations to the populace? Can the leadership in fact be trusted to welcome those who criticize and would like to replace it, and can the people be expected to be aware of the issues and alternatives when the media of mass information and the main non-governmental organizations of society, such as those of the workers, farmers, women, and youth, have been taken over as instruments of the single-party government? The single party and the charismatic leader have not generally been marked by tolerance, nor is it a very distinctive freedom to be able to vote for a single slate of candidates. But there is little in the way of available evidence to indicate that the people at large in the new countries are seriously disaffected by the turn their political systems have taken.

Let me conclude with a comment, a question, and a prophecy.

Economic development is more likely to bring into being the conditions which are requisite for the successful working of a democratic system than any other combination of forces and factors which may be brought into play.

But is there any reason for confidence that the kind of conditions which surrounded democracy in a few countries at a given time in history will produce democracy elsewhere at a different time; or are the people of many countries going to be prepared to let their political affairs be run for them by essentially self-selected elites, shaken up from time to time by revolutionary outbursts?

For the foreseeable future, as the armed forces of the new countries grow, the taking over of governments by the military will be a more and more frequent occurrence. Although Ayub Khan has endowed Pakistan with basic democracies, for the military regimes as for the one-party one-man governments the return to liberal parliamentary democracy of the Western type is on the whole less rather than more likely to come to pass.

NOTES

1. See my *From Empire to Nation* (Cambridge, Massachusetts: Harvard University Press, 1960).
2. Robert E. Ward has made a brief and suggestive inquiry into the meaning of political modernization in the opening pages of his "Political Modernization and Political Culture in Japan," *World Politics* (July 1963), pp. 569–596.
3. Edward Shils, *Political Development in the New States* (Gravenhage, Mouton & Co., 1962), p. 30.
4. *West Africa,* March 29, 1958, p. 304.
5. *Cabinet Government* (Cambridge: Cambridge University Press, 1937), p. 15.

6. Cited by Susan and Peter Ritner, "Africa's Constitutional Malarky," *New Leader,* June 10, 1963, p. 20.
7. Cited by Gerald S. Maryanov, *Decentralization in Indonesia as a Political Problem* (Southeast Asia Program, Cornell University, 1958), pp. 49–50.
8. *Ghana Today,* June 6, 1962. He continued on to contend that only the mistakes a government made justified an opposition; therefore, to say that an opposition is necessary for democracy implies that a government must make mistakes to allow the opposition to stay; which has the effect of destroying democracy.
9. *Democracy and the Party System,* pp. 14–15. (This is a pamphlet written by Nyerere, and published, without date, by the Tanganyika Standard Limited, Dar es Salaam.)
10. *The Ideologies of the Developing Nations,* edited by Paul E. Sigmund (New York: Praeger, 1963), p. 176. A more radical version was put forward by Sékou Touré: ". . . if the dictatorship exerted by the government is the direct emanation of the whole of the people, dictatorship is of a democratic nature and the State is a democratic State, democracy being the exercise, by the people, of National Sovereignty." *Towards Full Re-Africanization* (Paris, Présence Africaine, 1959), p. 28.
11. Jean Lacouture and Jean Baumier, *Le poids du tiers monde* (Paris, Arthaud, 1962), p. 172. The *New York Times Book Review,* July 21, 1963, carries on its front page a picture of a wall in Guayaquil, Ecuador, on which is crudely scrawled: "130 anos de elecciones—130 anos de MISERIA."
12. Cited by Carl G. Rosberg, Jr., "Decocracy and the New African States" in *African Affairs, Number Two* (St. Antony's Papers, Number 15), edited by Kenneth Kirkwood (London, Chatto & Windus, 1963), p. 30.
13. Cited from *Afrique-Action,* October 7, 1961, by Clement Moore in an unpublished Ph.D. dissertation, Harvard University, 1963.
14. *West Africa,* June 22, 1963, p. 703.
15. "The Party System in Africa," *Foreign Affairs,* July, 1963, p. 653.
16. *Democracy and the Party System,* p. 7.

94

Politics, Social Structure, and Military Intervention in Latin America

Gino Germani and Kalman Silvert

The recent politico-military events of Turkey, Pakistan, Egypt, and even France demonstrate that the application of unabashed armed might to the solution of civic problems is not peculiar to Latin

From Gino Germani and Kalman Silvert, "Politics, Social Structure, and Military Intervention in Latin America," *European Journal of Sociology,* II, No. 1 (1961), 62–67, 76–81. Reprinted in abridged form by permission of the publisher and the authors.

America, nor indeed a phenomenon to be correlated only with economic underdevelopment. Public violence and political instability in Latin America have all too often been treated either as merely comic or else a manifestation of "spirit," "temperament," or "Latin blood." Riots in the streets of Buenos Aires are no less tragic than riots in the streets of Algiers —and no less related to the basic facts of social disorganization as they may be reflected in crises of political legitimacy and consensus.

Military intromission in the political power structure always indicates, of course, at least a relative inability of other social institutions to marshal their power effectively, and at most an advanced state of institutional decomposition. This is to say, if the armed forces are viewed as having a limited and specialized set of functions having only to do with internal order and external defense, then a widening of castrensic activities into other social domains implies a generally weakened and sick social system, no matter the country or even the special cultural conditions concerned. This premise suggests several ways of constructing typologies of civil-military relations: one possibility is to order the types of social pathology to be found, and then to relate them to the historical facts of politico-military action; another is to order types of public violence, and once again to relate these to the real types of military interventions; and still a third alternative suggests itself in the direct listing of the institutional arrangements between the military establishment and the political institution treated as a variable dependent upon other social factors. This article will employ the latter procedure as being of the most immediate analytical utility, even though direct correlations between military action and the general state of social and economic development are at best vague.

Most Latin American countries have reached their first century and a half of independent existence. However, their social development into national states lagged behind formal independence and it is only now that a few of them are reaching a stage of full nationhood. While in some countries the breakdown of the traditional structure began in the last quarter of the nineteenth century, in many others a similar process of structural change did not start until the last two or three decades of the present century. Furthermore, one must remember that nowhere, not even in the most "advanced" Latin American nations, may it be said that the transition is complete.

In this transitional process we shall distinguish a series of successive "stages" so that the degree of development reached by any single Latin American country can then be described and compared with others. It is hardly necessary to emphasize the intrinsic limitations of such a procedure: nevertheless, it seems the most convenient one to yield a shorthand description of the present situation, while at the same time retaining a clear awareness of the total dynamics of the process. It must be added that this "model" of the transition is the result of a

schematization of the actual historical process as it has been observed to take place in Latin America.

A tentative simple typology of the social structure of the twenty Republics has been summarized in Table 96–1. In constructing it we have taken into account those traits which we consider most relevant to the problem at hand; namely, economic structure; the social stratification system (especially the existence of a self-identifying middle stratum); the degree of economic and cultural homogeneity and of participation in a common culture and in national life; the degree of national identification; and geographical discontinuities in the socio-economic level of the various regions within each country.[1] While we do not identify the successive "stages" of the historical scheme with the different "types" of social structure described in the table, we suggest that various degrees of "delayed development" may have resulted in situations similar to those indicated in the typology.

Stages 1 and 2. Predominance of the Traditional Social Structure. Formal National Independence and Civil Wars

The common trait of these first two stages of Latin American development is the persistence of the "traditional" society which maintained its essential features throughout the political upheaval and radical changes in formal political organization.

Stage 1. Revolutions and Wars for National Independence

At the time when they gained their independence (in most cases *circa* 1810) the Latin American countries may be said to have approximated the "ideal type" of the "traditional society": subsistence economy marginal to the world market and a two strata system characterized by little or no mobility and caste-like relationships. The Spaniards and Portuguese were the ruling group, and immediately below them we find the small élite of the *créoles,* of European descent and mainly urban, who while deprived of political power still belonged (subjectively as well as objectively) to the higher stratum and retained a dominant position from the economic and cultural point of view. It was this creole élite who brought about the revolutions and achieved national independence with support of the lower strata, including the *mestizos* and even part of the outcast group of the Negroes and the Indians who filled the armies of the independence wars. The creoles were inspired mainly by the American model,

Table 96–1 (1950 Circa)

Countries	% Middle and Upper Strata	% in Primary Activities	% in Cities of 20,000 and More Inhabitants	% Middle and Upper Urban Strata	% Literates	University Students per 1,000 Inhabitants

Group A: (a) *Middle strata: 20% and more;* (b) *cultural, psychological and political existence of a middle class;* (c) *ethnic and cultural homogeneity; national identification and considerable level of participation in different spheres;* (d) *urban/rural differences and geographical discontinuity exist, but to a lesser extent than in other Latin American countries.*

Countries	% Middle and Upper Strata	% in Primary Activities	% in Cities of 20,000 and More Inhabitants	% Middle and Upper Urban Strata	% Literates	University Students per 1,000 Inhabitants
Argentina ⎤	36	25	48	28	87	7.7
Uruguay ⎬ urban predominance	..	22	50	..	95	5.2
Chile ⎦	22	35	43	21	80	3.9
Costa Rica — rural predominance	22	57	18	14	80	3.9

Group B: (a) *Middle strata: between 15 and 20% (approx.) heavily concentrated in some areas of the country;* (b) *cultural, psychological and political existence of a middle class;* (c) *ethnic and cultural heterogeneity; pronounced inequalities in the degree of participation in national society and in other aspects;* (d) *strong regional inequalities with concentration of urbanization and industrialization in certain areas and rural predominance in the greater part of the country.*

Countries	% Middle and Upper Strata	% in Primary Activities	% in Cities of 20,000 and More Inhabitants	% Middle and Upper Urban Strata	% Literates	University Students per 1,000 Inhabitants
Mexico — lesser survival of traditional pattern	17*	56	24	..	59	0.9
Brazil — greater survival of traditional pattern	15	62	20	13	49	1.2

Group C: (a) *Middle strata between 15 and 20% (approx.);* (b) *emerging middle class (but there is no agreement as to its degree of auto-identification);* (c) *ethnic and cultural heterogeneity, pronounced inequalities in the degree of participation in national society and other aspects;* (d) *pronounced discontinuity between rural/urban areas and strong regional inequalities:*

Countries	% Middle and Upper Strata	% in Primary Activities	% in Cities of 20,000 and More Inhabitants	% Middle and Upper Urban Strata	% Literates	University Students per 1,000 Inhabitants
Cuba ⎤	22	44	37	21	76	3.9
Venezuela ⎦ urban predominance	18	44	31	16	52	1.3
Colombia — rural predominance	22	58	22	12	62	1.0

Group D: (a) *Middle strata: less than 15%; emergent middle strata in some countries, but clear persistence in all, in varying degrees, of the traditional pattern;* (b) *ethnic and cultural heterogeneity in almost all;* (c) *vast sectors of the population still marginal;* (d) *rural predominance in general; regional inequalities.*

Countries	% Middle and Upper Strata	% in Primary Activities	% in Cities of 20,000 and More Inhabitants	% Middle and Upper Urban Strata	% Literates	University Students per 1,000 Inhabitants
Panama	15	55	22	15	70	2.6
Paraguay	14	54	15	12	66	1.3
Peru	..	60	14	..	42	1.6
Ecuador	10	51	18	10	56	1.4
El Salvador	10	64	13	9	57	0.5
Bolivia	8	68	20	7	32	2.0
Guatemala	8	75	11	6	29	0.1
Nicaragua	..	71	15	..	38	0.7
Dominican Republic	..	70	11	..	43	1.2
Honduras	4	76	7	4	35	0.7
Haïti	3	77	5	2	11	0.7

[..] No data.   * 1940.

the French revolution and seventeenth century illuminism. They attempted to establish modern democratic states with their corresponding symbols: the "constitution," the "parliament," the elected rulers, and so on. There were, however, two basic limitations to their action. The first may be found in the creole élite itself: it was the expression of a traditional structure and in spite of its ideology, it still perceived itself as an aristocracy widely separated from the popular strata. The democracy they dreamed of was the "limited" democracy of the wealthy, the educated, the well-bred of proper descent. On the other hand, the prevailing state of the society was scarcely adequate to the establishment of a representative democracy: powerful geographical as well as ethnic, cultural and economic factors made such an undertaking simply utopian.

Stage 2. Anarchy, "Caudillismo" and Civil Wars

The outcome of such a situation was simply that, even before the end of the long and cruel wars of independence against the Spaniards, the constitutional "fictions" created by the urban élites broke down. The political and institutional vacuum resulting from the disappearance of the colonial administration and the failure of the "constitutional fictions" resulted in the geographical fragmentation of political power: the rise of local "caudillos" often of *mestizo* or even Indian origin, frequent local wars, and a rapid succession of military coups.

The army of the "caudillos" was seldom anything more than an armed band, under the leadership of a self-appointed "general." At this stage we do not find in Latin America any professional army, but the political rule of the caudillos often adopted some symbols both of the army and of the democratic regimes: the geographical fragmentation took the form of a "federal" state, the absolute rule of the caudillo that of the "president" and, at the same time, "general" of the army. During this stage the social structure remained very much the same. This was especially true of the primitive state of the economy, the stratification system, and the isolation, both economic and social, of most of the population.

Stages 3 to 6. Transition of the Social Structure from the "Traditional" to the "Industrial" Pattern

While some countries show a clear succession of these four stages, in the majority of the cases there is much overlapping. Nevertheless the scheme is useful as a conceptualization of the transition toward a mature national state: that is, toward political unification and organization, attainment of certain preconditions of economic growth, changes in the social structure and progressive enlargement of social participation (including political participation).

There is one very important and well known feature of this process which must be emphasized here; the unevenness of the transition, the fact that some groups within the society and some areas within each country remained unchanged and underdeveloped while others underwent great changes. This is a familiar fact in most countries, but in Latin America (as in other underdeveloped areas) it acquired a particular intensity. The typical *dual* character of the countries both from the *social* and the *geographical* points of view is expressed in the contrasts between the socially "developed" higher and middle strata and the "backward," more primitive, lower strata; the cleavage between certain areas in which most of the urban population, industrial production, educated people, wealth and political power are concentrated, and the rest of the country, predominantly rural, with a subsistence economy, illiterate, and politically inactive and powerless. The transition, in Latin America, cannot be understood without taking into full account the repercussions of this dual structure.

Social development involves first the extension of the modern way of life to a growing proportion of the people living in the most favored areas (the emergence of an urban middle class and a modern industrial proletariat in the "central" sector of a country), and second the incorporation—by way of massive internal migration or by geographical diffusion of industrialization and modernization—of the marginal population living in "peripheral" areas. The circumstances of the process, and especially its speed, are of the utmost importance for the political equilibrium of the country. . . .

Let us formulate now a typology of institutional civil-military relations and relate them to the different particular situations of the Latin American countries.[2]

1. The Classical Military Garrison State

This form develops typically in response to real or imagined external factors. No example of such Spartan organization is to be found in Latin America, where cases of truly serious and devastating wars of sufficient duration to work fundamental institutional change are extremely scarce. The major exception is the Paraguayan War of the last century, but social conditions in that country were insufficiently advanced to permit of the establishment of a truly centralized garrison state, despite the devastating nature of the armed conflict itself.

2. The Modern Totalitarian Garrison State

This phenomenon is still, fortunately, an evil dream of imaginative writers, for no historical examples are to be found anywhere. The low state of the technological arts everywhere in Latin America makes this development at present impossible for these republics.

3. The Totalitarian Politico-Military Relations

This pattern of relationships inextricably intertwines political and military functions within a monolithic public organization, as in Nazi Germany. Once again the insufficiencies of Latin America's technological state have to date prevented the formation of modern, totalitarian states, although such a country as Argentina is beginning to approach at least the material ability to include such a solution within its array of social possibilities. The "national-popular" revolutions have not attained so far this politico-military structure and one reason may be the technical underdevelopment of their bureaucratic organization. On the other hand, the rapid extension of radio, television, and other media of mass communication heightens this possibility as the unilateral dependence on weapons alone for social control in extreme cases thus becomes less necessary.

4. The Military as Institutionalized Governors

This kind of authoritarianism is very common in Latin America, and is a persistent form from the earliest days of independence to the present day. The existence of the armed forces as an organized and ostensibly efficacious group in administrative affairs has tempted to the simple transposition of personnel from military to governmental functions and to subsequent rule as *de facto* and eventually *de jure* governors. Given the long-standing tradition of military privileges (from the colonial period) and military participation (from independence wars) in Latin America, such a pattern is likely to appear whenever the political instability reaches a point at which the social legitimacy of a regime or a government is no longer accepted by the major relevant groups within the society. Such a situation may happen, as we noted earlier, at every level of the transitional process. It is obvious why it would predominate during the early days of independence and the years of confusion and anarchy which followed the failure in establishing modern states in the liberated colonial territories. And it still predominates in the more retarded countries such as the Dominican Republic, Honduras, Haiti and Nicaragua, in all of which the structure of traditional society has changed very little. But it is small wonder that relatively more advanced countries such as Argentina from the early thirties and, in very recent years, Colombia and Venezuela have experienced the same phenomenon. Here the instability must be related, as we indicated before, to a different underlying situation. The crucial common ground of all these cases is an irreconcilable division among the various politically relevant groups, and the lack of shared norms regarding political activity. The military, clearly and loyally, has usually worked in conjunction with important civilian elements, serving as an arm for the maintenance of group interest. History belies the simplistic belief that such alliances have always been between the most conservative groups and the military. On many important occasions organized military might has been brought to bear to promote the interests of new industrial agglomerations against the pretensions of landed Conservatives and sometimes even the Church. During certain periods of Mexico's growth, for example, the military in combination with civilians contributed heavily to the social experimentation characterizing that country from 1917 until 1940 at least. This important category of events needs, thus, to be subdivided in accordance with the civilian allegiances and ideological orientations of the military, and the resultant effects on the total socio-economic and political structures.

5. The Military as Trustee Governors

As naked military intervention becomes increasingly viewed as shameful, this phenomenon has increased in incidence. There are two notable recent cases, that of the Provisional Government of General Pedro Eugenio Aramburu in Argentina (1955–1958), and that of Admiral Wolfgang Larrazabal in Venezuela (1958–1959). Both governments arose after the fall of dictators, both of whom had risen out of the ranks of the military and subsequently were disposed by the military in combination with civilian groups. Aramburu and Larrazabal committed themselves to "cushion" governments, *interregna* permitting the formation of parties, the holding of legal elections, and the installation of civilian authorities.

6. The Military as Orienters of National Policy

This very subtle manifestation involves the exercise of power not on the immediately visible scene but rather in the fashion of a grey eminence. The military in this situation attempt to establish the broad policy limits within which civilian activity may express itself, the sanction for disobedience obviously being deposition of the legally constituted authorities. The significant Mexican developments mentioned above are, in all their real complexity, a combination of this category with the two immediately preceding. Whether or not the Mexican armed forces still effectively limit the freedom of the Mexican Government is a matter of some debate, especially given the strength of the single official party of Mexico and the very wide distribution of the civilian sectors supporting this party system and the incumbent governors.[3] Perhaps the clearest, most evident case of tutelary military behavior can be seen now in Argentina, where the military overtly acts to contain the policies of the Government, openly threatens coups, publicly debates political policies, and on occasion even moves troops to back its demands on the civilian governors. Military budgets are holy, and officers of the armed forces in a limited retirement occupy many important administrative positions in the civil service.

7. The Military as Pressure Group with Veto Power

This rather standard manifestation of military power in many developed countries is still little seen in Latin America, except possibly in the case of Chile. In this situation the military institution has the power to prevent antagonistic civilian action undertaken against it, but cannot initiate independent action or policy in fields outside of its range of professional interest.

8. The Military as Simple Pressure Group

This stage, the last before the military fades away into complete subordination to the civil authorities, is probably the status of the armed forces of Uruguay alone among the Latin American republics. The very special circumstances of Uruguay's past offer some apparently reasonable explanations of this phenomenon. A buffer state lying between two relatively powerful neighbors Brazil and Argentina, Uruguay has never been able realistically to dream of armed exploits. Further, the country is politically a city-state, a fact which has contributed to the early development of what can truly be called a "bourgeois" society (in the primitive sense of the term). Moreover, a high degree of political involvement of the citizenry has created areas of civil power not conducive to military adventures.

9. The Military as Simple Police Force in Complete Subordination to the Government

Costa Rica prides itself on having this kind of civil-military pattern, and is even wont to deny the existence of an army altogether, stating that the civil force is in truth merely a police agency. If the situation is not really such a pure subordination of the armed forces to the civil authorities, still the case offers a reasonable approximation. Once more circumstances unique for Latin America have brought about this situation. Costa Rica was unattractive to early Spanish colonizers, for it had a small indigenous population and no readily available minerals. As a result the Costa Rican central valley was an area of slow and secondary settlement, peopled by persons who had to work the land themselves. This emergence of a landed peasantry permitted the development of a type of "bourgeoisie" (in the figurative sense of the word) which, as in the case of Uruguay, has had long experience in the organization and application of its power to the detriment of armed pretenders.

10. The Military as Political Arm of the State

This pattern, obviously closely related to the idealized versions of the functions of the Red Army of the USSR and of the various "People's Armies," invariably tends to emerge from revolutionary situations of the left. The Arevalo-Arbenz Governments of Guatemala (1945–1954) and the present Governments of Cuba and Bolivia are the only three cases in Latin America of frankly leftist politics, albeit of different colors. In the Guatemalan case no serious attempts were made to turn the military into an active arm of the government; instead, especially during the interrupted term of President (and Lt.

Col.) Jacovo Arbenz Guzman, the design was to keep the army small and the officer corps highly contented. According to available report, the Castro Government has broken the professional army by investing civilian militias with great power and by politicizing the officer corps of the regular forces. This procedure was also used in Bolivia with the establishment some eight years ago of an armed civilian militia whose primary function was to counterbalance the regular army.

Military intervention in civilian affairs, as is suggested by this typology, clearly does not occur either in an ideational vacuum or in the absence of a sometimes very wide range of interests and pressures. Military politics inevitably and invariably involve identification with wider social interests and ideologies. The patterning of these identifications depends in important measure on the social origins of the officer corps and the social mobility functions which the military institution may serve. Unfortunately there are almost no reliable data available on these questions. From subjective evaluations and informal observation, however, one may suspect a considerable variation in the social origins of officer groups from country to country, and a consequent variation in the political identification of the military. It is also entirely evident that there must be great variation in the opportunities for upward social mobility offered by differing armed forces. Wide differences in budgets and in the sizes of the military establishments must affect mobility, of course, as do generalized social attitudes concerning the prestige of the military.[4]

A relatively safe generalization is that throughout Latin America the sons of middle-class families are more attracted to the military than are the sons of the upper groups. The result often has been to split the ideological unity of the military, to create interservice rivalries as well as intra-service discord. This growing fragmentation must be projected against the increasing complexity of Latin American society itself, affected as it is by economic development, changing world ideological currents, and rapidly growing industrial urbanization. Because nowhere in Latin America—even in famed Uruguay and Costa Rica—are the institutional patterns of secular and impersonal representative democracy fully established, many civilian groups are innately revolutionary in their attitudes and predisposed to the use of force as an inherent and thus desirable part of the social pattern. Both military schisms and military adventures are encouraged by the civilian groups soliciting armed aid for their political ambitions.

Even though the following quotation concerns the Spain of the 1930's, it is valid for the Latin American arena as well:

No doubt the generals in 1936 thought they were saving Spain. [. . .] The State must be capable of embodying and responding to what Maura called the vital forces of the community. Otherwise, as he warned repeatedly, the army will claim to embody the national will in order to enforce changes which political institutions are impotent to encompass. Above all, no democrat, repeating the follies of the progressive and moderate minorities, can appeal to the sword rather than to conviction, however slow the educative process may be. Though the Republic of 1931 came in on a vote, many Republicans were willing to see it come in through the army. Repeating the tactics of Ruiz Zorrilla, they systematically undermined the loyalty of the army. Some saw the danger. "I would prefer no Republic to a Republic conceived in the womb of the army." Many did not. How could they complain when other forces tampered with the loyalty of the army in 1936?[5]

The military will be reduced to their barracks and their professional functions alone only when Latin American countries develop sufficiently complicated power structures and a society sufficiently flexible and integrated; when social and geographical discontinuities have been greatly lessened and isolated or marginal masses incorporated into the national body; when economic and social conflicts have found institutionalized expression within a common framework of shared norms.

NOTES

1. The table appeared in a slightly modified form in Gino Germani, "The Strategy of Fostering Social Mobility," paper prepared for the Seminar on *The Social Impact of Economic Development in Latin America* (Proceedings publ. by the UNESCO, forthcoming). Only part of the basic data are shown in the table.

For the main concepts used in formulating the scheme, see G. Germani, *Integración política de las masas* (Buenos Aires, CLES, 1956); "El autoritarismo y las clases populares," in *Actas IV Congreso Latino Americano de Sociología* (Santiago, Chile, 1957); *Política e Massa* (Minas Gerais, Universidade de Minas Gerais, 1960); K. Silvert, "Nationalism in Latin America," in *The Annals of the American Academy of Political and Social Science,* 334 (1961), 1–9; of the relevant bibliography on this subject we took especially into account: S. M. Lipset, *Political Man* (New York, Doubleday, 1960), and D. Lerner, *The Passing of Traditional Society* (Glencoe, The Free Press, 1958).

2. For a narrower version of this typology and other suggested categorizations of Latin American politics, see K. H. Silvert, "Political Change in Latin America," *in* Herbert Matthews, ed., *The United States and Latin America* (New York, The American Assembly, 1959). Also refer to the March 1961 issue of *The Annals of the American Academy*

of *Political and Social Science,* entitled *Latin America's Nationalist Revolutions,* for other pertinent and recent information.

3. Oscar Lewis, in his "Mexico Since Cardenas," *in* Lyman Bryson, ed., *Social Change in Latin America Today* (New York, Harper, 1960), pp. 301–302, writes: "A comparison of the allocations of federal funds to the various departments over the four presidential administrations from Cardenas to Ruiz Cortines reveals [...] some highly significant trends. Especially marked is the sharp decrease in the proportion of funds allocated to national defense, reflecting the demise of *caudillismo* as a serious factor in Mexican life. Adolfo Ruiz Cortines was the first president since the 1920's who did not depend heavily on either the national or a private army to maintain his control."

Professor Lewis then points out that between 1935 and 1940 defense expenditures absorbed 17.3 per cent of the national budget, dropping to 8.1 per cent in the period 1953–1956.

4. *The Statistical Abstract of Latin America 1960* (Center of Latin American Studies, University of California in Los Angeles), p. 32, offers some partial and tentative figures on the percentage of Latin American budgets devoted to defense expenditures. The data are incomplete for all countries.

Country	Percentage of National Budget	Year
Mexico	11.3	1958
Costa Rica	3.8	1958
El Salvador	10.2	1958
Guatemala	8.8	1958
Honduras	11.7	1957
Haiti	19.1	1957
Argentina	21.1	1958
Brazil	27.6	1958
Chile	21.9	1958
Colombia	5.7	1958
Ecuador	21.6	1957
Peru	23.2	1958
Venezuela	9.5	1959

These figures are admittedly tenuous, and probably err on the low side, of course.

5. A. R. M. Carr, "Spain," *in* Michael Howard, ed., *Soldiers and Governments: Nine Studies in Civil-Military Relations* (London, Eyre and Spottiswoode, 1957), pp. 145–146.

95

Indonesia's Political Symbols and Their Wielders

Herbert Feith

I

The great prominence of political symbolism in Indonesia is sometimes explained in historical and psycho-cultural terms, with references to the religious character of kingship in pre-colonial days, to the country's long history of messianic movements, or to the continuing importance of status and ceremony in Indonesian society generally.[1] Alternatively (or complementarily) it is said that the government's concentration of attention on symbolic activities results directly from the experience of social and political change. Where economic life is rapidly becoming more market-oriented, cities and towns are growing fast, and more and more men are acquiring modern education, and particularly where old patterns of social relations have been destroyed by war or revolution, many individuals are confronted by the challenge of new values and cognitive patterns and consequently thrown into psychological disarray. Such men, it is argued, can often most easily resolve the conflicts within themselves by accepting a schematic ideology and participating in an expressive (non-instrumental) form of politics, a politics of heroes and villains, of "the movement" and "the enemy," of utopias and betrayals (compromise being a form of betrayal) and of multifarious sacred emblems.

Each of these two types of explanation contains elements of validity, but it would be gross oversimplification to use either of them, or both together, to supply an overall explanation of the prominence of symbolic activity in Indonesian government practice. To do this would be to assume a one-way, "reflective" relationship between government actions and the attitudes and expectations prevailing in society. The Indonesian government is certainly limited in its choices of action by prevailing attitudes, perspectives, and demands in Indonesian society, and by the psychological needs of key groups of that society. But it also plays a major part in creating these attitudes and needs. Hence historical, psycho-cultural, and sociological explanations are of great importance in accounting for the *limiting conditions* within which the govern-

From Herbert Feith, "Indonesia's Political Symbols and Their Wielders," *World Politics,* XVI, No. 1 (October 1963), 84–96. This excerpt reprinted by permission of the publisher.

ment wields political symbols. But they can be of only second-instance relevance to our central question of why the government devotes such great resources to symbol-wielding activity.

The purpose of this article is to propose a general framework of explanation for this phenomenon, a framework which is fundamentally political in that it rests on a concern with how the Indonesian government keeps itself in power, but which nevertheless leaves room for the historical, psycho-cultural, and sociological explanations given of political orientations in Indonesian society (and in the governing group itself).

How then does its intensive use of symbols help the Indonesian government to maintain its power? There is some evidence that it helps the government to solve economic and administrative problems. Exhortation in terms of nationalist ideals often helps to induce men to work in remote areas of the archipelago. And the ritual of special days often stimulates the performance of humdrum tasks by providing what Hirschman has called "pacing devices."[2] Against this, however, must be set the far stronger evidence that symbol-wielding as currently practiced by the Indonesian government results in lowered administrative and economic effectiveness. What is important here is not the time that civil servants spend at ceremonies or workers at mass rallies or at airport roads when foreign dignitaries arrive. It is rather the creation of an atmosphere or climate of opinion which is thoroughly unfavorable to the solving of practical problems. This is an atmosphere in which economic tasks are seen as of secondary importance, ideological truth and political enthusiasm being seen as the highest needs of state. It is an atmosphere in which economic realism is suspect as indicative of hesitancy and irresolution. And it is an atmosphere in which an administrator's concern with rules, precedent, and the specific definition of tasks is readily denounced as the product of a colonial and unrevolutionary mentality.

But if the net effect of symbol manipulation for economic and administrative problem-solving is negative, there is no doubt that it has positive effects as far as direct political control is concerned. Thus government propaganda can be seen as part of a process which operates also through press controls, the restriction of free association in groups, and the (sporadic) censorship of mails. Vows and demands for a narrowly focused loyalty are aids to the strengthening of political controls over the bureaucracy, along with the "retooling" of government employees—that is, the pensioning off of political undesirables and their removal from line posts to staff

posts. Moreover, the government's demand that one should repeatedly reaffirm one's support for its ideological formulations is an important check on the flow of political information, for it forces men to withhold or disguise the expression of their political feelings in many situations. In this way it contributes to an atmosphere of hypocrisy, mistrust, and confusion. This in turn helps to paralyze men's political energies and to lower their effective expectations, leading many to conclude that "Things are bad, but what can we do?" and then often that "Well, come to think of it, it could all be a lot worse."

But perhaps as important as the function of political control is that of making the government legitimate in the eyes of some parts of the population. Some symbolic actions help to do this because they are in effect promises of future achievement; the ceremony to inaugurate the Eight-Year Plan is an example. Others constitute achievements in themselves, achievements which are secured at relatively low cost and are readily visible. Here the frequent response is "Prices are terribly high and there is an awful lot of corruption, but at least the rest of the world has to take notice of Indonesia these days. If you listen to our air force planes breaking the sound barrier or watch the way we are getting the key positions in one Asian-African organization after another, you can't say that we are not getting anywhere."

In addition, a great deal of symbolism serves to create a favorable image of what the government *is*. Thus the President's trips, and especially the visits of powerful overseas leaders to Indonesia, heighten his prestige as a world leader. By speaking frequently of the suffering of the people, he establishes an image of himself as deeply concerned with the fate of the poor and the downtrodden. And by interpreting the tasks and duties of the times, he meets the traditional expectation that kings should link the present with the past and future and give human life its appropriate place in the cosmic order.

Moreover, the themes of the government's ideology are morally appealing to many Indonesians, and so repeated reference to them helps the government to elicit a voluntary acceptance of its authority by these persons. This may well be true in some measure for people at all levels of society, but on this there is little or no evidence. Hence the argument here is confined to responses in what may be called the political public, a group roughly coterminous with the two million or so Indonesians, mostly city and town dwellers and wearers of white collars, who regularly read newspapers.[3]

The anti-Western themes of Manipol-USDEK undoubtedly draw strong positive responses within this public. Many of the members of the Indonesian political public have had humiliating and hurtful experiences at the hands of the white West, and others are ready to blame the West (or "imperialism") for their sense of discomfort about alien influences of various kinds. "Modernity is good, Westernness is bad" is a common way of resolving a common and acute ambivalence. But indeed there is no need to refer to psychological mechanisms to explain why the politically aware sections of the Indonesian community should support a posture of radical protest at the international distribution of wealth, prestige, and power.

In addition, Manipol-USDEK helps many members of the political public to a voluntary acceptance of government authority because of its very ambiguity. Members of different groups in this public read mutually contradictory meanings into its formulations, and so members of each of these groups are provided with acceptance moral grounds for political obedience. Thus numerous Communists are persuaded that Manipol-USDEK is a progressive creed and a powerful weapon against the imperialists. On the other hand, many anti-Communists are convinced that the creed is essentially anti-Communist, and indeed the most subtly effective of ideological means for thwarting Communists.[4]

Similarly the ideology has appeal for men whose political outlook reflects traditional ideas, for others whose principal concern is to see Indonesia become a modern nation, and for others again who want release from the confusions of a turbulent period of transition. Many of the more traditionally oriented members of the political public are attracted to Manipol-USDEK by its emphasis on all pulling together, on national interests being placed above the selfish interests of individuals and groups. Many of the same persons are convinced that the President is right in saying that what Indonesia needs above all is men with the right state of mind, the right spirit, the true patriotic dedication. "Returning to our National Personality" is attractive to some who want to withdraw from the challenges of modernity, and also to others who want to believe in the current political leadership but see it as failing in the central tasks of modernization. And for traditionally oriented members of some Indonesian communities— notably, for many Javanese of no strong Islamic conviction—there is real meaning in the various complex schemes which the President presents in elaboration of Manipol-USDEK, schemes explaining the meaning of the current stage of history in relation to others.

For those within the political public who want to see rapid modernization the government's ideology offers an emphasis on socialism and planning. President Soekarno often speaks in praise of science and occasionally of the need for agricultural mechanization. And modernists are often willing to read their own ideas into the government's repeated denunciations of the "old order" and the "old established forces."

Perhaps most important of all, Manipol-USDEK has appeal to men for whom the world has become increasingly unintelligible as a result of disruptive social change. To these men it promises to give a *pegangan*—literally, something to which to hold fast. It is not so much what this *pegangan* is that is attractive, and indeed that question leads all too easily back to the deplored disagreements and sense of confusion. It is simply that the President declares that he is offering a *pegangan* and that this is widely felt to be needed. Values and cognitive patterns being in flux and in conflict with one another, many are looking for dogmatic and schematic formulations of the political good. Thus one common response to Manipol-USDEK is "It may not be a very good or complete ideology, but an ideology is certainly what we need."

After all this has been said, it must be added that Manipol-USDEK is actively resented by many in the political public, including, prominently, a large group of modernist Moslems, supporters of the banned Masjumi party. Whereas the government's creed can perhaps be described as representing a highest common factor of political orientations between traditionalists and (one variety of) modernists, it is certainly not a compromise between the nationalist ideology of President Soekarno's Pantja Sila or Five Principles and the political ideology of Islam. Thus references to the legitimizing power of the official creed should not be taken to suggest that it has created a broad consensus. Its importance lies rather in the fact that it has helped to organize voluntary support in one section of society, and within the government's own apparatus, for coercive action against a smaller recalcitrant section.

Finally, political symbols have a function which is not easily classified as either coercive or legitimizing, but in fact falls between them, in the middle range of the continuum between direct compulsion and voluntary obedience. Symbolic activities play a major part in the process of manipulation, the structuring of political situations in such a way that attention is focused on interests and values which are shared by the government and the governed. Thus ceremonies recalling the heroism of the nationalist movement and the Revolution make it possible for the government to maintain a conspicuous initiative in the country's affairs, and to do so as a "leader" rather than a "ruler." Similar effects flow from all foreign policy actions which give rise to a feeling of national pride. They flowed from most of what was done under the banner of the liberation of West Irian—from the government's actions in abrogating diplomatic relations with Holland in August 1960 and subsequently denying Great Britain the right to be Holland's diplomatic representative, from the purchase of arms specifically designated as being for the territory's liberation, from air-raid training and from the military drilling of students and others in the streets of the cities. More recently they have flowed from government and government-encouraged actions carried out in support of the Azahari revolt of December 1962 in Brunei and as part of the "confrontation" of Malaysia. And they flow from the encouragement given by some parts of the government—notably, the more strongly anti-Soekarno and anti-Communist sections of the army—to sentiment against the locally domiciled Chinese; for instance, the statements of army commanders, blaming commodity shortages on "foreigners who are still in control of our economy."

In all of these ways the government highlights conflict between Indonesians and outsiders, and by the same token averts conflict between rulers and ruled inside the community of Indonesians. The government's involvement in these kinds of activities is largely continuous. But their importance is particularly great when disaffection becomes immediately threatening to some of the key groups in power, as it has on a number of occasions in our five-year period; for in these crisis situations, channeling of political emotions is a principal means of inducing catharsis.[5]

Manipol-USDEK as a creed has a similar function, also creating a manipulated but still quasi-voluntary acceptance of authority. In effect it enables the government to build on the genuine appeal which the nationalism of 1945 still has within the political public. Most members of this public are unwilling to accept the whole of the government's interpretation of the existing situation, the view that the nation is moving determinedly toward progress and greatness, restrained in this only by the continuing need to struggle against imperialism, liberalism, and individualism. But many of these men are equally unprepared to reject this view entirely. Outright rejection of the government's claim is possible for a small group of fully trained Communists and well-schooled members of the now-banned modernist Moslem party, Masjumi, men who have clear and firmly held alternative systems of belief and interpretation; and it is possible for a small group of sophisticated intellectuals, particularly persons who have lived overseas long enough to see nationalism from the outside. But members of the political public who are not schooled in any such alternative way of looking at the world are almost obliged to take the view that "There is something in what the government says" or that "Manipol-USDEK is basically the right idea; it is only its execution which is bad." Such men may see their own situation and the country's as bad, disappointing, and shameful, but they have no coherent set of ideas about why this is so, who is to blame, or how improvements might be brought about. Hence they are content to be inactive; they can see no cause worth fighting for. In general government propaganda has so structured the mental worlds of members of the political public that they cannot reject particular ideological formulations on which the government insists unless they are prepared to break with nationalism itself.

II

But to point to these various ways in which symbolic activities serve to help the government maintain itself in power is not sufficient to explain why these activities are so important. Two related questions remain unanswered: why are these means used so intensively to buttress the government's power, rather than other available means? And why is the government willing to incur the costs which symbolic activities involve, particularly the costs in terms of a reduced level of performance in the solving of economic and administrative problems?

If it is asked what alternative means could conceivably be used to maintain the government's position, one answer is more direct political control. While the last five years have seen a great increase in government restrictions on political activity, considerable freedom remains. The large modernist Moslem party, Masjumi, has been banned, as has the small but influential Socialist Party, but ten other parties continue to have a legal existence, with their own youth, student, labor, and peasant organizations and their own newspapers. The number of political prisoners is still small and there is little fear of secret police. Press censorship is generally stringent, but banned books and overseas magazines are easily available and overseas radio programs are listened to freely. In fact, little effort is made to isolate citizens from the outside world.

Why then has the government chosen to concentrate on symbol manipulation, when it might have been possible for it to achieve a comparable strengthening of its position by further doses of political repression? The answer is probably threefold. In the first place, this is a government which finds it most difficult to impose its will where doing so means inflicting serious deprivations. A great number of its decrees are ignored, sidestepped, or transformed by those who are charged with their implementation;[6] and this is particularly common where a decree is designed to have a marked deprivational effect. This can be attributed in part to the ineffectiveness of the government's administrative machinery. But, more important, it should be seen as resulting from the weakness of the political elite's cohesion, the heavy dependence of this elite on the bureaucracy as a social class, and the great importance of intra-bureaucratic politics as a force for immobilization of the government.[7] Lacking cohesion and machinery for the effective settlement of conflicts, the government must bargain with those whom it professes to command.

This leads immediately to a second point, that the cleavages within the political elite can be turned into a distinct asset for purposes of power maintenance while political repression remains mild. Thus the army succeeded in the 1958–1961 period in imposing severe restrictions on the Communist Party, at the same time as Soekarno was giving it enough status rewards and public acclaim to prevent it from switching to a strategy of rebellion.[8] Similarly the army succeeded in 1961 in winding up the regionalist rebellion which had broken out in 1958. One major ingredient of success here was the willingness of the army leaders to offer the rebels an amnesty under favorable terms. It would certainly be difficult for the regime to maintain this capacity to incorporate or neutralize its potential challengers if it itself became much more repressive.

Thirdly, there is resistance from President Soekarno to several of the possible further extensions of political control. Thus the President is opposed to a dissolution of the remaining parties and to the proposal that they be merged into the now weak National Front to make this into a strong state party or movement. Measures of this kind would accord with much in the President's proclaimed political creed, but they would probably weaken him vis-à-vis the army, for he relies heavily on the political parties (and especially on the large and still organizationally autonomous Communist Party) for support in his intra-coalition tussles with the army. Certain other forms of direct political control which could conceivably be introduced—for instance, a large expansion in the number of men under political arrest— would justify further increases in the military budget, and to that extent they too would work against the President's interests. Conversely the President has a positive interest in the manipulation of symbols because this is the aspect of power maintenance in which his own role is dominant. The present proportion of symbolism to more directly coercive activities is thus in part a reflection of the political balance which exists inside the government between President Soekarno on the one hand, and the army leaders on the other.

But is there not another, quite different, alternative to intensive symbolic activity? Could the government not buttress its position as effectively, or more so, if it devoted a much larger share of its efforts to the solving of economic and administrative problems, and thereby increased the volume of goods and services available for distribution?

A large part of the answer to this question can be given only on the basis of economic and administrative analysis. It is impossible here to describe the economic and administrative vicious circles which would have to be broken for any attempt to reverse the trend of economic decline to be successful.[9] However, it is possible to advance a general political argument which throws light on the government's reluctance to make a resolute attempt to break these vicious circles. This argument relates to the competition which exists between skill groups within the government structure.[10]

While much of contemporary politics can be explained in terms of the tussles between President Soekarno and the army, there is also much which is intelligible only as one adds a second axis. This is the axis which runs between symbol wielders and army officers on the one hand, and economic and administrative specialists on the other. More precisely it is an axis between those who claim power chiefly on the basis of their revolutionary record, their capacity for "leadership," or their possession of the "spirit of 1945," and others who claim it chiefly on the grounds of their qualifications for the technical tasks for which a particular government department or government firm is responsible.

The conflict on this leader-technician axis is less readily visible than that on the axis between President Soekarno and the army, because much of it is intra-bureaucratic and because the technicians rarely speak in public. But it comes out clearly in the private complaints of older army officers against the recent recruits of the military academies, the "men who have read all the books but don't know what the Revolution meant and have no respect for the sacrifices we made for it." It came out very clearly indeed in President Soekarno's Independence Day speech of 1962 when he attacked those who "have always bleated about . . . so-called 'solutions of problems' according to outworn and conventional formulas . . . which they took from Western textbooks."[11] In this case the President's attack was directed partly against such opposition politicians as Hatta, the former Vice-President, and Sjahrir, a one-time Prime Minister and long-time chairman of the now-banned Socialist Party. But it was directed also against men of pragmatic, technical, and professional orientation in the government's own ranks and in its administration.

Conflict between the leadership men and the technicians is in fact pervasive within the government. It arises at the highest level whenever First Minister Djuanda, an engineer and economist, argues with President Soekarno against the allocation of funds for sports stadia or monuments, or with General Nasution against the dispatch of a new arms-purchasing mission. It arises whenever an economist advances pragmatic arguments for a measure of decontrol and has these denounced as liberal. At lower levels it arises again and again throughout the administration and the state-controlled economy, over a particular appointment or a particular budget allocation. The basic issue is always the same: is power to be with those who want to gear society to the maximization of production, or is it to be with those, both symbol wielders and military men, who can best sustain the mood of "the Revolution goes on"?

Here then is one important explanation of the government's reluctance to take the difficult steps which a resolute concern with economic and administrative problems would require. This is a Soekarno-army government; Djuanda is a junior partner at best. And it is a Soekarno-army administration as well, or largely so, for the lines of functional division which once separated politics from administration have been heavily blurred in the last five years. This means that a great number of officials and other government employees are holding positions for which they lack the prescribed technical skills, and feel themselves threatened by the availability of other men who do have these skills.

Many of these incumbents are civilian politicians, men who owe their position to the power of their party or group or to the favor of the President. Others are army officers (or ex-officers who are careful to maintain their links with the army), men who have come to have power over civilian affairs since martial law was proclaimed in March 1957, or since the Dutch estates and trading and industrial enter-

prises were taken over in December of that year. If the government were to speak less of the need to complete the Revolution and instead to declare economic stabilization and development as the principal challenge of the present period, describing development as a slow and difficult task, then men in both of these categories, whether they were section chiefs, district officers, or estate managers, would soon have their positions contested in the name of the government's ideology by others who could claim greater technical competence for them. And such others exist. They include not only people who had influential posts before 1958 and have now lost them, but also a large group of younger men, newly trained engineers, agricultural scientists, economists, and others, who actively resent the obstacles placed in their career paths by what they frequently call the "older generation."

We may conclude then that the government's intensive concern with symbolic activity is a reflection of intra-elite politics as well as of power maintenance. Symbolic activity furthers the interests, in the first instance, of specialists in the wielding of symbols. In addition, all such activity which underscores the doctrine of the unfinished Revolution justifies the retention of power by a larger group of politician-administrators (including some prominent army officers), who have political qualifications for the positions they hold but no technical ones.

Thirdly, symbolic activity serves the interests of a skill group of "fixers," men who can operate effectively in a situation of organizational ambiguity, in which regulations are repeatedly changed and jurisdictional spheres overlap, in which "retooling" is frequent and career expectations unstable.[12] Fixers and symbol wielders are sometimes the same individuals. But in any event the interests of the two groups are closely parallel. Each stands for the ascendancy of informal qualifications over formal ones; and the organizational ambiguities in which the fixers have a vested interest are important in sustaining demand for the ideological medicine which the symbol wielders can dispense.

NOTES

1. See, e.g., J. M. van der Kroef, "Javanese Messianic Expectations: Their Origin and Cultural Context," *Comparative Studies in Society and History,* I (June 1959), 299–323; and Selo Soemardjan, "Some Social and Cultural Implications of Indonesia's Planned and Unplanned Development," *Review of Politics,* XXV (January 1963), 64–90.
2. Albert O. Hirschman, *The Strategy of Economic Development* (New Haven 1961), 24–28.
3. This concept of the political public is derived largely from the theory of mobilization presented in Karl W. Deutsch, *Nationalism and Social Communication* (New York

1953), 100–104, 240. There is some initial plausibility (and a great deal of convenience) in the working hypothesis that the Indonesian government's effective accountability is limited to the members of this public. I have employed this political public concept for the 1949–1957 period in *Decline of Constitutional Democracy in Indonesia* (see especially pp. 108–113), but would add that the usefulness of the concept is more restricted when applied to the more authoritarian situation of the post-1958 period.

4. This emphasis on the government's use of the Manipol-USDEK ideology should not obscure the fact that the various (legal) parties and groups also use it for their own purposes. Manipol-USDEK having become the language of all public political discourse, particular parties have seized on particular formulations of the ideology and made them their own. Thus repeated references to the Pantja Sila (Five Principles, including The One Deity) now characterize a group as being anti-Communist, whereas accusations of "pseudo-Manipolism" are typically made by Communists.

5. See Harold D. Lasswell and Abraham Kaplan, *Power and Society* (New Haven 1950), 9ff., 244ff.

6. For some startling admissions of this, see *A Year of Triumph,* Address by the President of the Republic of Indonesia on August 17, 1962 (Canberra, Embassy of the Republic of Indonesia, 1962), 39–41.

7. Cf. Fred W. Riggs, *The Ecology of Public Administration* (Bombay 1961), 104ff. and passim; also Riggs, "Prismatic Society and Financial Administration," *Administrative Science Quarterly,* V (June 1960), 1–46.

8. See Donald Hindley, "President Soekarno and the Communists: The Politics of Domestication," *American Political Science Review,* LVI (December 1962), 915–926.

9. The economic vicious circles are analyzed in Paauw, "From Colonial to Guided Economy," and Humphrey, "Indonesia's National Plan." I have described some of the administrative ones in "Dynamics of Guided Democracy."

10. On skill groups, see Harold D. Lasswell, *Politics: Who Gets What, When, How* (New York 1958), 97ff.

11. *A Year of Triumph,* 35.

12. On fixers, see Harold D. Lasswell and Renzo Sereno, "The Changing Italian Elite," in Harold D. Lasswell, ed., *The Analysis of Political Behavior* (London 1947), 158ff.

96

Burma: Ne Win's Revolution Considered

Josef Silverstein

As the military's fourth year in power draws to a close, General Ne Win's revolution is stalled on the road to socialism. What a few journalists[1] and occasonal travelers have said cautiously and in private, the General declared emphatically and in public— the economy is "in a mess." "If Burma were not a country with an abundance of food we would be starving."[2] Such candor, from the author of the 1962 coup and the person most responsible for the decisions which are moving Burma along its present path, is not new. Throughout the past year he found other occasions to express himself in equally forthright terms. Despite the fact that he and his co-leaders are without real challenge and have absolute power to make and carry out their decisions, the revolution has not produced dramatic results in any of the areas where it is at work. The events of the past year provide ample evidence of this and cause one to ask, where does the revolution go from here?

The objectives of the revolution neither were thought out fully when it began nor set down systematically since.[3] From what has been written and

From Josef Silverstein, "Burma: Ne Win's Revolution Considered," *Asian Survey,* VII, No. 2 (1966), 95–102. Reprinted by permission of the publisher and the author.

undertaken, it appears as though the revolution has four major objectives: reform the economy from semi-private to socialist; eliminate foreign influences from all aspects of economic, political, and social life; change the values and attitudes of the people so that a new leadership can arise and take over the tasks of the revolution; unite the diverse peoples into a cohesive nation. It is against this frame of reference that the major events and decisions of the past year take on special meaning.

The first objective—the development of a socialist economy—in one sense is nearing realization; private industry and trade either have been eliminated or seriously limited in the legal market, or they have been driven underground into black-market operations. The process was accelerated in January when the Burma Corporation and Burma Unilever were taken over by the state, thus eliminating the last major joint ventures with private foreign firms.[4] In April, the government seized approximately 1,000 oil wells which were operated by *Twinyos* and *Twinzas*—hereditary Burmese operators with rights dating from the pre-British period.[5] Also, during the same month, 129 of the larger and more respected private schools were nationalized because "the state must take the responsibility of educating the children of the working people in the basic socialist concepts. . . ."[6]

In agriculture, the state took a further step toward socialism by abolishing tenancy rent for peasants using the land for farming.[7] Land still is under private ownership and each peasant is the owner of his produce. However, the military government is campaigning among the farmers to induce them to cooperate and share their labor, animals, and tools in all phases of production and harvest, in order to develop new attitudes toward socialist production. This decree abolishing land rent (added to existing ones which transferred allocation of plowlands from landlords to Land Committees) also banned property —personal and real—from being attached in payment of debts, prohibited transfer of land to non-agriculturalists, and empowered the state to lend money directly to the individual producer. All these measures are intended to move the peasant toward socialism.

In another sense, however, the objective is far from realization. The purchasing, distribution and sales of consumer goods have been chaotic, contributing to shortages of basic commodities in some areas and surpluses in others. During the past year, blackmarkets in *longyis,* razor blades, chinaware, cooking oil, and other commodities arose throughout the country. Despite the efforts of the government to increase production and importation of necessary goods, distribution remains a major unsolved problem for the military planners.[8]

The efforts to eliminate private traders in paddy, and at the same time establish a government-operated system of purchases and sales with fixed nation-wide uniform low consumer prices, had a dual negative effect. They caused many peasants to act as "economic men" and shift from paddy to other grains which offered larger margins of profit, and caused the government to lose K70 million through its experiment in rigging prices, mainly because it set them too low to cover costs and made no allowances for differences in quality of product. Ne Win lamented the fact that "some peasants replaced the cultivation of paddy with other crops in their selfish interests. . . ." He implored them "to resume paddy cultivation in the usual fields and stop such acts that would practically amount to exploiting our goodwill for the welfare of the masses. . . !"[9]

The General's assessment ignored the fact that many farmers became disgusted with having to deal with inexperienced grain buyers (young officers assigned to this task as their duty), to travel great distances to deliver their product to badly located buying stations, and to see their product rejected or down-graded because the buyers demanded that it conform to the official purchasing guide lines. The farmer also faced the fact that cattle prices rose sharply during the year. With but 3,000 tractors in use throughout the country, cattle remain a chief source of power in the field for the peasant. In seeking to buy new animals, he faced competition from the cattle slaughterers, who found a rising market for their meat, and from cattle merchants who drove their animals illegally to Thailand in order to sell at considerably higher prices. Caught in the middle, the farmer's costs rose at a moment when the government sought to keep domestic prices down by paying less for the grain.[10]

To balance the economic picture, it must be noted that mineral and timber exports rose during the year, while rice, the main export, declined. Through the *Myepadetha* scheme, the coup leaders sought to get the farmer to plant 12.69 million acres in paddy and 3.86 million acres in other agricultural crops.[11] They also continued to seek new lands to bring under cultivation and forest areas to replant. The overall results have been a decline in foreign exchange, commodity shortages, blackmarkets, and a decrease in national production. Col. Maung Shwe, speaking at the Worker's Day Rally, brought the picture into statistical perspective when he said that in order to increase the nation's standard of living, production must rise by 8% annually. With the population increasing approximately 2% per year, production in state enterprises falling (1963–64) by 1% and in private enterprise by 13.6%, the prospects were not bright for making socialism an attractive alternative to the more relaxed, sometimes mismanaged, mixed economy under democratic government.

In seeking to control foreign influences on Burmese life, the Revolutionary Council had mixed results. Western or capitalist influences were reduced even further than during the previous year, with the end of joint ventures, the banning of foreign-run libraries,[12] and the nationalization of four major hospitals and the most important private schools. There was also a reduction in the number of American films shown and in official visits by important persons,[13] while Western tourists were almost non-existent outside the environs of Rangoon.[14] At the same time, Eastern or socialist influences grew and expanded. Both China and Russia continued to buy large amounts of rice. Chinese economic and technical assistance increased as Burma agreed to three projects under the terms of the 1961 Sino-Burmese loan agreement[15]—the building and equipping of three textile mills,[16] a 40-ton capacity paper mill,[17] and the construction of a second bridge in the Shan State.[18] Most of the 177 state scholars who went abroad were sent to socialist countries, while only a few went to Australia, Canada, India, Japan, and the Federal Republic of Germany. Chinese and Russian influence also was enhanced by General Ne Win's visits to the two countries and the local press coverage of the events.[19]

The three Asian conflicts—Vietnam, Kashmir and Malaysia-Indonesia—gave Burma's leaders a major challenge in attempting to control foreign influences. The Burmese press reported the conflicts with dispatches from all sources. In the few editorials devoted to the Vietnamese conflict, the press echoed Ne Win's position as expressed in February—a peaceful settlement can be made on the basis of the 1954 Geneva accords and a new Geneva-type conference ought to be called to settle the immediate problems of the conflict. On Kashmir, the General and the press observed strict neutrality, calling for a peaceful settlement and supporting the efforts of the United Nations. Toward Malaysia and Indonesia, the General said, and the press repeated, that a peaceful settlement could be found if the dispute was moved from the battlefield to the conference table. Despite these efforts, the proximity of the fighting caused concern among the peoples in Burma, and it was reflected in the Letters to Editor columns in the local government-controlled press. Clearly, foreign influences, while under control, were not eliminated; Ne Win and his colleagues still face the question of how to follow socialism as an economic and social theory, and socialist states as political models, without being drawn into the socialist political orbit.

During the period of military rule since 1962, the leaders of the armed forces have struggled with the problems of legitimacy—by what right they seized power, how long they will hold it, and how they will return it. Brigadier Thaung Dan gave the clearest answers yet in his Resistance Day address. The *Tatmadaw*—Burmese army—he said, seized power "to rescue the Union." It neither had time nor opportunity to unite with the people before acting, as it previously had done during the struggle for independence. Having linked, once again, with the people, it holds power because the peasants and workers "have not yet put into proper shape their own worker's councils and organizations." The *Tatmadaw* is fashioning the Burma Socialist Program Party (BSPP) to give civil leadership to the revolution and to marshal the workers and peasants in unity and strength. The military is drawing up plans to make the party's work successful and a program for

transforming old values and thinking into new. When the workers and peasants become active participants in the revolution and take to their tasks with ability and inspiration, "the *Tatmadaw* will be able to hand over additional duties to the working people and devote itself to its main task of defending the Union of Burma."[20]

During the past year, the BSPP continued to train its cadres and play an auxiliary role to the military in performing its civil duties. All leadership is controlled by the military. As a political force, the BSPP has some distance to go before it plays a vital part. The system of Councils—peasant and worker—also has not come into being; the reason why, as given by the General when he spoke at the Worker's Day Rally, re-emphasized the theme expressed by Brig. Thaung Dan, "in order to have the right leadership and the right members in the Council, it would be necessary to educate the workers and reorientate them to their real needs. . . ."[21] Clearly, the revolutionary objective of remolding values and attitudes is an important one—one which the leaders gave much attention during the past year.

Despite their theoretical pronouncements on socialism and the nature of man, the military leaders have no blue-print to follow in remolding the values and attitudes of the Burmese people. Their campaign last year followed several themes: contribute labor to the building of the "new" Burma, learn from the people, teach the people to improve and assert themselves, be honest and forgiving. While the themes are not logically consistent, this did not seem to bother either the people or the leaders.

To build the "new" Burma, workers—physical as well as intellectual—were asked to give extra hours without pay in order to raise production. Students were called upon to volunteer during vacation to do socially useful work—collect factory statistics or work in the villages. At planting season, urban workers were encouraged to go to the fields and volunteer their labor in performing agricultural tasks.

Since it seized power, the Revolutionary Council has set the example of learning from the people—going to the villages and holding peasant seminars in order to hear complaints and suggestions. Last year, the government sent soldiers, bureaucrats, intellectuals and professionals to the villages and factories to live and work with the people. In August, it opened the newspapers to the people so that the "revolutionary impetus might gain greater momentum and the revolutionary changes made more effective more quickly. . . ."[22]

Teaching the people that this was their revolution, and that they must free themselves from the colonial past, was a third theme. Ne Win called the Revolutionary Council the teacher who is helping the workers and peasants "come to possess courage and knowledge to think correctly and do the right thing."[23] He and others repeatedly called for the people to develop the traits of responsibility, discipline and care in handling machinery and tools, and to commit themselves to their jobs—to come on time and put in a full day's work. Although the military leadership reminded the people that they could learn from past events such as the peasants' uprisings in 1930, the oil field strikes and the resistance, it cautioned them to draw the right lessons from those events and apply them properly.

To demonstrate the moral principles of honesty and forgiveness, the Revolutionary Council set the example by forgiving ordinary citizens for their moral lapses in trying to circumvent the 1964 demonetization decrees. At the same time, it confirmed the life sentence of Col. Saw Myint, former member of the Revolutionary Council, for circumventing the decree and trying to benefit from his knowledge of the imminent changes in paper money circulation.[24]

From the speeches of the leaders and the slow pace in building new self-governing institutions, it appears that the voluntary campaign to develop a new morality has not succeeded; whether or not it is a realistic goal, no one seems to have asked.

National unity, the fourth objective of the revolution, has been a problem since the beginning of self-government. Last year, insurgency by ethnic and political groups kept the countryside upset. The government's answer was the same as that of all previous governments—the carrot and stick policy of fighting frequent military engagements with rebels who would not seek peaceful solutions to their problems and accepting back in society those insurgents who surrendered their weapons and themselves. Despite frequently published reports of arms and men who returned to society, no real solution to the problem of insurgency appeared. As the year ended, insurgency was on the increase.

In its approach to the minorities living in society, the military rulers demonstrated greater imagination. Through several programs last year—nationwide celebration of ethnic national days, publication of the folklore of certain minorities, preservation of Chin fortifications dating from the struggle against the British in the nineteenth century, scientific study of the Kayahs by anthropologists at Rangoon University, development of a program to improve the Lushai language in order for its speakers to participate more fully in the nation's life—the government stressed its desire to recognize cultural unity in diversity. As expressed by Brigadier San Yu, "the culture of one nationality was part and parcel of the culture of the whole Union."[25]

On the political level, its approach to the minorities was less daring. Central control through the Security and Administration Councils existed. Although State Councils supposedly advise on state matters, for all practical purposes power still is concentrated in Rangoon. This is a major issue underlying the insurgents' efforts to win political autonomy or independence for their communities. Until power is transferred to Worker and Peasant Councils, no real change, even at the local level, can be expected.

National unity in Burma also has implied an harmonious relationship between the government and the people as a whole. With the natural and elected leaders either in jail or silenced by fear, a forced harmony appears to exist. The only real discordant note has been the activity of the Buddhist clergy. Having refused to register in 1964 and defied the military rulers in other ways, the monks provided the government with a serious challenge last year. It responded first by repealing the three basic laws pertaining to religion passed in the early 1950s on the grounds that the laws had not achieved their original intent.[26] In March, the government supported an All Sangha Conference on ways to preserve the purity of the *Sasana* and promote its propagation. The conference drew up the constitution for an All Buddha Sasana Sangha Organization, an identification card, and a program for reforming religious education. Several Buddhist monasteries did not participate, and individual monks openly rejected the validity of the conference and the decisions it took. In April, the military rulers moved against these monks by arresting 92 on the grounds of political activity and economic insurgency. Ne Win, in his Worker's Day address, went to great lengths to demonstrate that he and his co-leaders were not anti-religious; their actions stemmed from the fact that religion had been misused. He went out of his way to assure his audience that he, personally, was a good Buddhist.[27] Despite the hardening of the Revolutionary Council toward the Buddhists, the monks remain outside the complete control of the military; and given their place in traditional society, they remain a potential source of political opposition.

Burma has changed in many ways since the military seized power and initiated the revolution. Having pointed the nation in the direction it wishes to go, can Ne Win get the people to travel the road he and his colleagues have mapped out?

NOTES

1. See, for example, the dispatch by John Hughes in the *Christian Science Monitor,* December 10, 1965.

2. *New York Times,* December 13, 1965, p. 31.

3. It was almost two months after the coup before the brief document, the *Burmese Way to Socialism,* appeared. It was written hastily after the seizure of power and all subsequent documents have sought to fill in the details and omissions in order to make the ideology both logically consistent and a guide to action on all questions arising out of the pragmatic pursuit of socialism.

4. The *Guardian,* January 19, 1965, p. 1; *ibid.,* January 30, 1965, p. 1.

5. *Ibid.,* April 2, 1965, p. 1; *Forward,* III, 17 (April 15, 1965), p. 6.

6. *Forward, op. cit.,* pp. 5–6. Although 754 private schools remained unaffected by the decree, in due course, they too, will be taken over. See the *Guardian,* April 2, 1965, p. 1.

7. *Forward,* III, 18 (May 1, 1965), p. 2. This was an extension of the Tenancy Act of 1963 and repealed all previous laws relating to tenancy. According to the government, as of June 30, 1963, there were 1.1 million tenants paying K13 million to about 350,000 landlords; and about one third of the latter were non-nationals.

8. For an example of the government's effort to prove that shortages no longer existed, see the *Guardian,* August 8, 1965, p. 1 lead story on *longyi* production.

9. *Forward,* III, 15 (March 15, 1965), p. 13.

10. The *Guardian,* June 14, 1965, p. 4 (editorial).

11. *Forward,* III, 20 (June 1, 1965), p. 2.

12. *New York Times,* September 19, 1965. The decree applied to four nations: the United States, Great Britain, India, and the USSR. In the period prior to the coup in 1962, the Russians maintained the smallest and least influential library of the four nations.

13. The most important American delegation to visit Burma came in December when the group led by Senator M. Mansfield visited Burma and held talks with the Burmese leaders.

14. A transit visa may be obtained if the traveler is changing planes. Only 24 hours transit time is allowed to make the change.

15. See United Nations, *Economic Survey of Asia and the Far East 1963,* p. 163, for a good brief summary of the terms of the agreement.

16. The *Guardian,* March 7, 1965, p. 1.

17. *Ibid.,* August 19, 1965, p. 1.

18. *Ibid.,* August 23, 1965, p. 1.

19. The *Guardian,* March 14, 1965, p. 1. A discordant note was sounded in March when a book appeared in Laos, identified as published in China, which was critical of the military government in Burma for parroting the "Moscow Revisionist Line." It appealed to the peace-loving people of Burma not to "let your country become an historical inconsistency." The Peking government denied publication of the book, but the Burmese government did not silence the press in heralding its appearance.

20. *Forward,* III, 17 (April 15, 1965), p. 5.

21. *Ibid.,* III, 19 (May 15, 1965), p. 10.

22. The *Guardian,* August 25, 1965, p. 1.

23. *Forward,* III, 19 (May 15, 1965), p. 11.

24. The *Guardian,* August 14, 1965, p. 1.

25. *Ibid.,* February 12, 1965, p. 1.

26. *Forward,* III, 12 (February 1, 1965), p. 2.

27. *Ibid.,* III, 19 (May 15, 1965), p. 14.

97

Nkrumah: The Leninist Czar

Ali Mazrui

Kwame Nkrumah's first important publication twenty years ago was inspired by Lenin's theory of imperialism. The publication came to be entitled *Toward Colonial Freedom.* Nkrumah's last publication in office is his new book, *Neo-Colonialism: The Last Stage of Imperialism.*[1] That too owes its doctrinal inspiration to Lenin's theory of imperialism.

There is little doubt that, quite consciously, Nkrumah saw himself as an African Lenin. He wanted to go down in history as a major political theorist—and he wanted a particular stream of thought to bear his own name. Hence the term "Nkrumahism"—a name for an ideology that he hoped would assume the same historic and revolutionary status as "Leninism." The fountainhead of both Nkrumahism and Leninism was to remain *Marxism*—but these two streams that flowed from Marx were to have a historic significance in their own right.

Like Lenin, Nkrumah created "the Circle"—a group of friends to discuss ideas and formulate theories of revolution. Like Lenin, Nkrumah encouraged the emergence of a Marxist newspaper called *Spark.* It is true that *The Spark* in Ghana came to be more purist in its Marxism than Nkrumah himself. Nevertheless, the idea of such a newspaper was directly inspired by *Iskra* (Spark), the Marxist paper which was founded in 1901 through Lenin's initiative.

But while Nkrumah strove to be Africa's Lenin, he also sought to become Ghana's Czar. Nor is

Nkrumah's Czarism necessarily "the worse side" of his personality and behaviour. On the contrary, his Czarism could—in moderation—have mitigated some of the harshness of his Leninism. It is even arguable that a Leninist Czar was what a country like Ghana needed for a while. Nkrumah's tragedy was a tragedy of *excess,* rather than of contradiction. He tried to be too much of a revolutionary monarch.

But what does all this mean? What are Nkrumah's ultimate links with Lenin? In what sense did Nkrumah seek to be a "Czar"? It is to these questions that we must now turn.

The Cult of Organization

The analogy between Nkrumah and Lenin partly arises out of a similarity of roles and partly out of conscious ideological emulation. Like Lenin, Nkrumah was a great believer in organization. On this issue of organization, perhaps coincidence and conscious emulation were both present in the shared characteristic.

But what was the nature of this common belief in organization? And what was its historical context?

Both the Russian revolution of 1917 and the most militant phase of Afro-Asian nationalism exploded against a background of a World War. World War I and its effect on the Czarist regime in Russia was an important contributory factor towards the Bolshevik triumph. As for the impact of World War II on West Africa, Meyer Fortes has been substantially vindicated in the assessment he made as the war approached its end: "Great, perhaps revolutionary, changes have been taking place in certain sectors of West African social and economic structure since the outbreak of the war. . . . It may well be that the war will prove to have been the outstanding instrument of social progress in West Africa for fifty years."[2]

Some years later James S. Coleman linked this assessment specifically to Nigeria's experience and was persuaded that the war helped to create conditions there which were "crucial, if not indispensable, to the rise and growth of Nigerian nationalism."[3]

Of the impact of the war on the Gold Coast similar conclusions have been reached—"by 1946 it was possible to see some form of home rule as a not too distant prospect."[4]

Kwame Nkrumah spent the war years in the United States. Perhaps that was his equivalent of Lenin's period of "exile" on the eve of revolution. In May 1945 Nkrumah left New York for London—the imperial capital itself. His first serious experience of organizational techniques was perhaps acquired during his London days. He was involved in organizing the Fifth Pan-African Congress in Manchester soon after his arrival in 1945. He then became the Secretary of the West African National Secretariat. His activities included organizing meetings, working for the Coloured Workers' Association of Great Britain and trying to start a nationalist newspaper, *The New African.* In an attempt to involve French-speaking Africans in their Pan-African activities Nkrumah crossed the English Channel for the first time, and went to see African members of the French National Assembly—Sourou Apithy, Leopold Senghor, Lamine Gueye, Houphouet-Boigny. As a result of Nkrumah's visit, Apithy and Senghor later went to London to "represent the French West Africans at the West African conference" that Nkrumah organized.[5]

It was in 1946 during his stay in London that he managed to "scrape up enough money" to publish his pamphlet *Toward Colonial Freedom.* In it Nkrumah argued that "The national liberation movement in the African colonies has arisen because of the continuous economic and political exploitation by foreign oppressors. The aim of the movement is to win freedom and independence. This can only be achieved by the political education and organisation of the colonial masses."[6]

It was not merely Nkrumah's economic interpretation of imperialism which was Leninist. It was also this belief in "the organisation of the colonial masses." The background of World War II and its aftermath in Britain might even have sharpened Nkrumah's appreciation of the need for organization. War is at once disintegrative and mobilizational. It is disintegrative because it disturbs the normal forms of stability and routine; yet precisely because of that, war is also an occasion for highly conscious self-organization on the national scale. The fact that the British electorate in 1945 had turned to the socialists for the organizational disciplines demanded by the immediate post-war years might also have had an effect on the impressionable sensitivity of Nkrumah in his London days.

Be that as it may, however, news of Nkrumah's organizational skills soon got to the Gold Coast. It was not long before he received letters from Ako Adjei and J. B. Danquah urging him to go back to the Gold Coast and become General Secretary of the new United Gold Coast Convention. After some heart-searching Nkrumah accepted—and on November 14, 1947, Nkrumah left London on the first stage of his journey back home.

At first there seemed to be an important difference between Nkrumah's concept of "organization" and

Lenin's. As far back as 1902 Lenin thought of organization in elitist terms. For Lenin it was not the organization of the masses which was vital for effective action—it was the organization of the *leaders*. Lenin thought of the masses as dangerously gullible; and that itself was one reason why the revolutionary elite should be sufficiently organized to avert the danger of a misguided populace. As Lenin himself defiantly put it,

I assert that it is far more difficult to unearth a dozen wise men than a hundred fools. This position I will defend, no matter how you instigate the masses against me for my anti-democratic views.[7]

Lenin went on to say that, from the point of view of effective organization, what he meant by "wise men" were "professional revolutionaries."

I assert: (1) that no revolutionary movement can endure without a stable organisation of leaders maintaining continuity; (2) that the broader the popular mass drawn spontaneously into the struggle . . . the more urgent the need for such organisation must be (for it is much easier for all sorts of demagogues to side-track the more backward sections of the masses); (3) that such an organisation must consist chiefly of people professionally engaged in revolutionary activity. . . .[8]

At that time the Bolshevik revolution was still fifteen years away. Yet this elitist conception of organization has prevailed in the Soviet Union to the present day. Out of a Russian population of over 200 million, membership of the Communist Party has continued to be exclusively preserved for less than 10 per cent of the population. And within the Communist Party itself the principle of democratic centralism is still operative—trying to combine a modest sense of mass participation at the bottom with a concentration of leadership at the top.

But for Nkrumah organization was, from the start, basically *mass* organization. As his newspaper put it in January 1949: "No section of the people of this country should be left unorganised. . . . The strength of the organised masses is invincible. . . . We must organise as never before, for organisation decides everything."[9]

For as long as the target in the Gold Coast was the overthrow of the British colonial regime, the emphasis on *mass* organization made sense. As India had demonstrated, the British Raj was vulnerable to organized agitation and demonstration on a "mass" scale. This was a different kind of enemy from the one which faced V. I. Lenin in Czarist Russia. As a generalization, it remains true that a domestic tyranny can best be overthrown by an organized revolutionary *elite*—while colonial rule can best be fought by well-organized *mass* activities. The difference between Lenin and Nkrumah could therefore be both explained and justified by the difference in the kind of enemy they sought to overthrow.

Given these postulates, the United Gold Coast Convention that had invited Nkrumah to become its Secretary turned out to be too "elitist" for the task in hand—as well as being too "middle class." In June 1949 came Nkrumah's split with the U.G.C.C. and the formation of his own Convention People's Party. Nkrumah's superior organizational skills, and his greater sensitivity to the masses, gave his party an edge over his opponents in the struggle for political supremacy.

Nkrumah's margin of success was not all that great. As Dennis Austin has pointed out, the CPP in the last election before independence won only 57 per cent, and its opponents 43 per cent, of the poll in the 99 contested constituencies; "it was also outseated, and out-voted, in Ashanti and the north."[10] And even after making allowances for the five unopposed seats, Nkrumah's popular support was not, by the standards of "charismatic leaders" elsewhere, quite "overwhelming."[11] In any case, the poll in that crucial pre-independence election was only 50 per cent of the registered electorate and probably something under 30 per cent of the total adult population.[12] Nkrumah's assumption of power before independence illustrates how much narrower than sometimes imagined is the degree of popular backing with which some of the leaders emerged into independence.

Yet precisely because Nkrumah's margin of electoral success was more modest, his organizational superiority was more crucial. In absolute terms even the CPP's organization at that time was not all that strong and cohesive. But in relative terms it might well have determined the issue of whether or not Nkrumah won the 1956 election. The following year Nkrumah was Prime Minister of independent Ghana. From 1917 to 1957—exactly four decades separated the Bolshevik organizational triumph in Russia from Nkrumah's victorious independence in Ghana.

Yet, briefly, it was after Ghana's independence that Nkrumah's concept of organization became more clearly Leninist. The "masses" were eulogized by CPP party ideologues right up to the end, but the party became increasingly elitist *de facto*. It got beyond even that, as authority became personified in Nkrumah himself. And in the end, the CPP betrayed the very principle of organization on the basis of which it had once prevailed over its opponents.

The irony of the matter is that the CPP's relative organizational superiority might itself have been due to its opponents. For Lenin a single party in Russia was an organizational necessity in its own right. But for Nkrumah the long-term efficiency of his party could perhaps only have been sustained if he had permitted the stimulus of competition to endure. In June 1955, at the height of the opposition challenge, Nkrumah could still be saying to a CPP rally:

> I have always expressed both in public and in private that we need a strong and well-organised Opposition Party in the country and the Assembly. . . . We must not forget that democracy means the rule of the majority, though it should be tempered by sweet reasonableness in the interests of the minority.[13]

But not long after independence the policy of harassing, and later persecuting, the regime's opponents was vigorously followed. And ideologues in Ghana turned their talents to the rationalization of a one-party state. What was overlooked was the danger to the organizational health of the ruling party that too great a sense of security might bring. Lenin, in his *State and Revolution,* had expounded and defended the Marxist prophecy of the "withering away" of the State. But the risk which Ghana, as most other African countries, faced was the "withering away" of the successful ruling party. Julius Nyerere saw this danger very soon after independence—when he resigned his position as Prime Minister in order to strengthen Tanu's organization. Yet even now in Tanzania the future meaningfulness of the party is still a question-mark. Unlike Tanu, the CPP was given the invigorating blessing of a significant but not too dangerous opposition party. Nkrumah did not have to resign his position as head of government in order to mend the organizational structure of the party. Yet Nkrumah destroyed the Opposition without creating an alternative stimulus to his own efficiency.

The destruction of the Opposition and the debasement of the CPP had another related effect—the extravagant personality cult of "Osagyefo" could be pursued without the restraints which a critical rival party might have imposed by its very existence in an open political system. The royal cult of Osagyefo was one aspect of Nkrumah's Czarism to which we shall later turn more fully. What might be noted for the time being is that it helped to betray Nkrumah's old cry that "We must organise as never before"! The party of militant protest against the British Raj became a party of loyal protestations towards Osagyefo. To borrow the words of Dennis Austin, "the effect was to reduce political life to a barely discernible level of private conflict among his followers over the distribution of presidential favours."[14]

Fifteen years before he actually assumed power, Lenin had bitterly said to his countrymen: "Our worst sin with regard to organisation consists in the fact that *by our primitiveness we have lowered the prestige of revolutionaries in Russia.*"[15]

Did Nkrumah's worst sin consist in lowering the prestige of African revolutionaries at large? He certainly did descend to a certain primitiveness in some of the devices he came to use as a substitute for meaningful organization.

The Economics of "Rule Britannia"

But the earliest Leninist influence on Nkrumah was not, in any case, organization—it was Lenin's economic interpretation of imperialism. In Lenin and in Marxist thought since Lenin "imperialism" has had a special meaning. It does not mean a mere annexation of territory. The term includes within it the behaviour of monopolistic corporations within the metropolitan countries, the domination of financiers as well as colonial policy in the narrow sense.

The paramount motivation behind the old imperial expansion was the economic exploitation of the countries which were annexed. All arguments about spreading Christianity and Western civilisation, or of ending the Arab slave trade, were merely a camouflage of the imperial profit motive.

In his first book *Towards Colonial Freedom* Nkrumah embraced this Leninist thesis. He argued:

> The imperialist powers need the raw materials and cheap native labour of the colonies for their own capitalist industries. . . . The problem of land ownership in the colonies has risen because the colonial powers have legally or illegally seized valuable mining and plantation rights. The British are more careful than other imperialists to legitimise their seizure, but even their semi-legal methods do not disguise the fact that they have no right to rob the native of his birthright.[16]

The doctrine was comfortably consistent with the central Marxist postulate of economic determinism. At least when simplified, economic determinism was a claim that the ultimate basis of social behaviour and distribution of power lay in the realm of economics. Within Britain itself all the paraphernalia of liberal democracy was a legitimation and safeguard of the economic power enjoyed by the middle and upper classes. Major changes in history within a single society, and internationally, were always a response to changes in economic relationships and modes of production. As for imperial motivation, it was not British patriotism which wanted to have an Empire—it was, in the final analysis, British capitalism.

Yet, as he got more involved in the nationalist movement, Nkrumah retreated in a significant way from economic determinism. He embraced instead a doctrine of the primacy of politics. In his own immortal words, "Seek ye first the political kingdom and all things will be added to it." It was no longer economic power that determined political relationships. On the contrary, Nkrumah came to argue that "political power is the inescapable prerequisite to economic and social power."[17] For an anti-colonial nationalist such a reversal of cause and effect made sense. After all, the first task was to win *political* independence.

But was not Nkrumah re-converted to economic determinism when he saw that "political independence is but a façade if economic freedom is not possible also"?[18] This is arguable. The African attainment of sovereignty, when not accompanied with a change in economic relationships, gave rise to what Nkrumah called "client states." The whole doctrine of neo-colonialism seemed to reassert afresh the proposition that real power lies, in the ultimate analysis, with those who were *economically* powerful. Had Nkrumah been proved wrong in his old optimism of "Seek ye first the political kingdom and all things will be added to it"? Had he now stumbled on to the fact that the "political kingdom" on its own lacked the power to "add things" to itself?

Nkrumah's new book *Neo-Colonialism: The Last Stage of Imperialism* is an attempt to resolve this difficulty. The title of the book is, of course, more than a conscious echo of Lenin's work on *Imperialism: The Highest Stage of Capitalism.*[19] Just as Lenin had tried to carry Marx's analysis of capitalism a stage further, so Nkrumah attempted to carry Lenin's analysis of imperialism a level higher. Nkrumah argues that colonialism of the old style was mitigated in its effects by its own doctrine of public accountability. There was such a thing as *responsible* imperialism. The new phenomenon of neo-colonialism, however, lacked this inner constraint of accountability. Neo-colonialism was therefore the most irresponsible form of imperialism. In the words of Nkrumah:

For those who practise (neo-colonialism), it means power without responsibility and for those who suffer

from it, it means exploitation without redress. In the days of old-fashioned colonialism, the imperial power had at least to explain and justify at home the actions it was taking abroad. In the colony those who served the ruling imperial power could at least look to its protection against any violent move by their opponents. With neo-colonialism neither is the case.[20]

A major difference between Lenin's theory and the theory now being advanced by Nkrumah is to be found in what each was trying to explain. Lenin's main interest was in conditions in the imperial countries themselves. Nkrumah's main interest is in conditions in the former colonies. Lenin was keen to understand what there was in Britain itself which made Britain want to dominate others. Nkrumah, on the other hand, is more concerned to explain what factors generally continue to keep Africa in a state of being dominated. There is considerable overlap between the two theoretical preoccupations, but their centres of interest are decidedly divergent.

To a certain extent, Lenin was using imperialism as an explanation as to why there had not been a proletarian revolution in the Western industrialised countries. Marx had predicted that the poor in the industrialised countries would get poorer and the rich richer—until the point of revolutionary explosion was reached. Yet it became increasingly clear that the poor of the Western countries, far from getting poorer, were actually improving their standards of living at a significant rate. Why had the Western poor been betraying their destiny . . . ?

The answer lay in imperialism. The exploitation of the British Empire saved the British worker at home from total poverty and helped to save Britain from a proletarian revolution. Benjamin Disraeli's concept of the "Two Nations" of Britain was, in a sense, Marxian. The British people were getting polarised into two potentially antagonistic "nations within the nation"—the poor versus the rich. What prevented the clash? For Lenin it was imperial expansion. The two nations of Disraeli were saved from an ultimate confrontation by the diversion of the British Empire. Lenin quotes Cecil Rhodes himself, that militant embodiment of the imperial ethic. In 1895 Rhodes had defended British imperial expansion in the following terms:

In order to save the 40 million inhabitants of the United Kingdom from a bloody civil war, we colonial statesmen must acquire new lands to settle surplus population, to provide new markets for the goods produced by them in the factories and mines. The Empire, as I have always said, is a bread and butter question. If you want to avoid civil war, you must become imperialists.[21]

But now that the Empire has disintegrated is Britain about to have a civil war? This is where Nkrumah's theory of neo-colonialism takes over from Lenin's theory of imperialism. The new phenomenon of exploiting other people abroad without actually ruling them is, to a certain extent, serving the same purpose as the old imperialism of Cecil Rhodes—it is delaying the ultimate class confrontation within the metropolitan countries themselves. In the words of Nkrumah, only when neo-colonialism in turn comes to an end will "the monopolists" in the metropolitan countries "come face to face with their working class in their own countries, and a new struggle will arise within which the liquidation and collapse of imperialism will be complete."[22]

All this sounds as if Nkrumah has now been converted to the view that "the political kingdom" on its own is a poor substitute for "the commanding heights of the economy." Yet, in an important sense, Nkrumah has never really retreated from a doctrine of the primacy of politics. When he said "Seek ye first the political kingdom," he does not seem to have meant the Ghanaian kingdom on its own. In the context of his political philosophy as a whole, the real political kingdom for Africa was the kingdom of Africa itself. In Nkrumah's words, "The Independence of Ghana is meaningless unless it is linked up with the total liberation of the African continent."[23]

It is noteworthy that at least one school of Leninism had once argued virtually to the effect that a socialist revolution in the Soviet Union was meaningless unless it was linked up to the total liberation of the proletarian masses all over the world. In the words of Leon Trotsky in 1924:

> The permanent revolution, in an exact translation, is the continuous revolution, the uninterrupted revolution. . . . This applies to the conquests of the revolution inside of a country as well as to its extension over the international arena.
>
> For Russia . . . what we need is not the bourgeois republic as a political crowning, nor even the democratic dictatorship of the proletariat and peasantry, but the workers' government supporting itself upon the peasantry and opening up the era of the international socialist revolution.[24]

Nkrumah's perspective was not as global. But if he did not believe in a "permanent revolution," he did at least believe in a kind of continuous independence movement in the African continent until Africa as a whole, including South Africa, was rescued from racialism and colonial rule.

Yet if Nkrumah had believed merely in the independence of each constituent unit, he could not have complained of neo-colonialism afterwards and still believed in the primacy of politics. A balkanised Africa remained to him vulnerable to the danger of being manipulated by others. This was not because political independence was useless without economic power. It was more because political independence was weak without political unity. Nkrumah retained his belief in the pre-eminence of politics—but there was more to politics than political freedom. Indeed, political freedom itself needed a political foundation other than itself. In the African continent it needed total political union.

When political freedom is thus combined with and reinforced by political union, Africa would then be able to break the economic power that others have over her. In his new book Nkrumah argues that the exploitation of Africa is itself carried out on a Pan-African basis. This is economic Pan-Africanism on the part of the exploiters. Only political Pan-Africanism on the part of the exploited can break the hold of the continental monopolists. In the words of Nkrumah himself,

> The foreign firms who exploit our resources long ago saw the strength to be gained from acting on a Pan-African scale. By means of interlocking directorships, cross-share holdings and other devices, groups of apparently different companies have formed, in fact, one enormous capitalist monopoly. The only effective way to challenge this economic empire and to recover possession of our heritage is for us also to act on a Pan-African basis, through a Union Government.[25]

How much of Leninism was there in Nkrumah's concept of African unity? In a sense the whole idea of continental unity for Nkrumah was an extension of the Leninist principle of organization. There is, in any case, an intimate logical connection between the idea of "organization" and the idea of "unity." And Nkrumah grasped this inter-connection when he made affirmations such as this. "Without organisational strength we are weak; unity is the dynamic force behind any great venture."[26]

He seemed to believe right up to his fall from power that an Africa disunited was, in a fundamental sense, an Africa disorganised.

A more direct Russian influence on Nkrumah's Pan-Africanism is discernible in his old conception of a union of West Africa. As we have noted, in the course of his London days in the 1940s he set out to organise a West African conference. He went to Paris to see such African members of the French National Assembly as Leopold Senghor and Houphouet-Biogny. Nkrumah recounts that in Paris they had "long discussions and planned, among other things, a movement for the Union of West African Socialist Republics."[27]

This echo of the Union of Russian Soviet Socialist Republics later contributed to Nkrumah's troubles with the colonial authorities in the Gold Coast. Nkrumah continued to think of a West African Union in those terms when he went back home. The Watson Commission which investigated the Gold Coast disturbances of 1948 had the following to say about Nkrumah:

> Although somewhat modest in his admissions, he appears to have become imbued with a Communist ideology which only political expedience has blurred. In London he was identified particularly with the West African National Secretariat, a body which has for its objects the union of all West African Colonies and which still exists. It appears to be the precursor of a Union of West African Soviet Socialist Republics.[28]

Nkrumah denies that the word "Soviet" was ever present in the document (written by Nkrumah) which the Commission was using as evidence.[29] But even without the word "Soviet" the Russian impact on Nkrumah's early ideas on Pan-Africanism is still discernible. Indeed, the incriminating document itself which the Commission used as evidence was called "The Circle"—yet another Leninist echo in Nkrumah's ideological evolution.

The Washingtonian Monarch

Yet Nkrumah's secular radicalism had an important royalist theme from the start. And it is this royalist theme which, for analytical neatness, we have designated as Nkrumah's "Czarism."

One aspect of Nkrumah's royalist tendencies is part of African nationalism at large, and is related to the type of imperial influences to which Africans were exposed. Why have so many African leaders since independence shown a weakness for ostentation and living in palaces? When African leaders are acquisitive and self-seeking the fault is perhaps primarily in themselves. But when what they acquire is *conspicuously* consumed, other sociological and psychological reasons need to be found. After all, an elite can be acquisitive without being ostentatious. Corruption in India, for example, is at least as well developed as it is anywhere in Africa. Yet there is an asceticism in the Indian style of social behaviour which affects the Indian style of politics too. Many Indian leaders have to conform to what one observer has described as "the Gandhian image of self-

sacrifice and humility which Indians demand of their politicians."[30] Some of the leaders are sincerely ascetic in any case. But not all that refrains from glittering is necessarily Gandhian.

It is arguable that a corrupt elite which is also ostentatious is ultimately preferable to a corrupt elite which is outwardly ascetic. The problem of measuring sincerity in India is a recurrent one. The leader of Goa's Congress Party, Mr. Purshottam Kakodkar, disappeared from a Bombay hotel on November 28, 1965. A nationwide search by the police and special investigators was carried out over a period of more than four months. In April 1966 the mystery came to an end. Mr. Kakodkar wrote to the Home Minister announcing that he had gone to a small Himalayan town for meditation.

What were his motives? J. Anthony Lukas made the following report to the *New York Times:*

> Some of Mr. Kakodkar's supporters say he is only a spiritual man who wanted a few months to commune with himself before plunging into politics again. Others believe his retreat was a stunt designed to raise his political stock in Goa, where elections are to take place soon.[31]

Lukas linked this event with the whole Indian phenomenon of the *sanyasi* (sadu), or spiritual recluse. The cult of withdrawing from worldly affairs can produce genuine dedication and self-sacrifice. But it can also produce some of the worst forms of hypocrisy. In the words of Lukas:

> A genuine sanyasi comes to the ashram (sanctuary) to find a guru, or teacher, who he must convince of his sincerity. He must take vows of obedience, celibacy and poverty before he puts on his robes. However, many of the "holy men" are said to be thinly disguised charlatans who make good livings as alchemists, physicians, fortune tellers, palmists or acrobats.[32]

But why should the ostentatious acquisitiveness of the African kind be preferable to the ascetic accumulation of Indians? From an economic point of view, the Indian style of accumulation might be preferable, particularly if the asceticism is accompanied with an ethic of re-investment. The Indian would thus make money, continue to live humbly, and re-invest what he saves. On the other hand the African, in his ostentation, spends his money on luxurious consumer goods, often imported. He harms his country's foreign reserves and deprives the nation of potentially productive capital investment. From the point of view of economic development, ostentatious acquisitiveness tends to be dysfunctional.

But what is its effect on political development? If the conspicuous consumption is by political leaders it provides the populace with some index of how much money the leaders make. If the money is being made at the public's expense, the public is not being kept entirely ignorant of that fact. And sooner or later the public might demand an explanation. In short, ostentatious corruption is less stable than disguised corruption. Indeed, the ostentation might, in the long run, be the grave-digger of the corruption. It seems almost certain that in Nigeria part of the exultation which accompanied the overthrow of the previous regime was due to the discredit sustained by the regime by the conspicuousness of its corrupt consumption.

But we still have to explain what it is in the African background which has led to the building of magnificent palaces in Dahomey, Liberia, the Ivory Coast, Ghana, Nigeria and other places. Why have so many African leaders succumbed to the temptation of magnificent living?

Inevitably a substantial part of the explanation lies in the African's immediate past. There are certain forms of humiliation which, when ended, give rise to flamboyant self-assertion. There are certain forms of deprivation which, when relieved, give rise to excessive indulgence. After the end of the American civil war liberated Negro slaves were, for a while, in possession of money and influence. The result was often flamboyant ostentation and a swaggering way of life. Excessive indulgence had succeeded excessive indigence. Because the Negro had been too deeply humiliated in bondage, he was now too readily inebriated with power.

Something approaching a similar psychological phenomenon has been at work in Africa. In fact Nkrumah had a certain ascetic impulse in him. It is true that he spent considerable sums on the imperial structures he inherited. But his personal mode of living was not particularly indulgent. He seems to have been more extravagant on prestigious public projects than on personal forms of indulgence. He was almost certainly less self-seeking than a large number of other leaders in Africa, Asia and Latin America.

Nevertheless, Nkrumah did have a flamboyance which was, to a certain extent, comparable to that of many American Negroes at the time of the Reconstruction following the Civil War. A keenly felt sense of racial humiliation now exploded into a self-assertion which was partly exhibitionist. The monarchical tendency was an aspect of this.

But the monarchical style of African politics has other subsidiary causes in the colonial experience. In British Africa one subsidiary case was the British

royal tradition itself. The myth of imperial splendour came to be so intimately connected with the myth of Royalty that the link was conceptually inherited by the Africans themselves. The process of political socialization in colonial schools kept on reaffirming that allegiance to the Empire was allegiance to the British monarch at the same time. This inculcation of awe towards the British royal family left some mark on even the most radical African nationalists. When the Queen appointed Nkrumah as Privy Councillor soon after Ghana's independence, Nkrumah had the following to say to his own people following the appointment:

> As you know, during my visit to Balmoral I had the honour of being made a member of the Queen's Privy Council. As the first African to be admitted into this Great Council of State, I consider it an honour not only to myself, but also to the people of Ghana and to peoples of Africa and of African descent everywhere.[33]

The tendency of African nationalists to be flattered by the Royal favours of the British monarch is perhaps what made Dr. John Holmes of the Canadian Institute of International Affairs come to the conclusion that "Africans seem to have a fondness for Queens."[34]

But the inculcation of royal awe which the British fostered in their colonies might have had other effects as well. In Africa it might have reinforced the desire for monarchical glamour in the regimes which succeeded the British Raj.

But does that mean French-speaking Africans are less monarchical in their style of politics than the English-speaking ones? After all, the French-speakers were ruled by a republican colonial power. This is true. However, what was gained by French republicanism was lost by the greater cultural arrogance of French colonial policy. In a sense, the French assimilationist policy and the British inculcation of Royal awe had the same effect on the African—they reinforced the desire for a cultural glamour that was all African. Both the French-speakers and the English-speakers felt a need to be proud of ancient African kingdoms. And this need for a splendid past helped to create a desire for a splendid present. The very choice of the name "Ghana" for the emergent Gold Coast was part of this phenomenon. As for the psychological quest for parity with the British royal tradition, this comes out in statements such as the following one of Nkrumah's:

> In 1066 Duke William of Normandy invaded England. In 1067 an Andalusian Arab, El Bekri, wrote an account of the West African King of Ghana. This king

whenever holding audience "sits in a pavilion around which stand his horses caparisoned in cloth of gold; behind him stand the pages holding shields and gold-mounted swords; and on his right hand are the sons of princes of his empire, splendidly clad. . . ." Barbarous splendour, perhaps; but was the court of this African monarch so much inferior, in point of organised government, to the court of Saxon Harold? Wasn't the balance of achievement just possibly the other way round?[35]

This revelling in ancient glory is part of the crisis of identity in Africa. David E. Apter has argued that African nationalism has tended to include within it a self-image of rebirth.[36] This is true. When I first visited the United Nations in 1960–1961 it was fascinating to listen to some of the new African delegates revelling in the innocence of newly born nationhood. But involved in this very concept of re-birth is a paradoxical desire—the desire to be grey-haired and wrinkled as a nation; of wanting to have antiquity. This is directly linked to the crisis of identity. Insofar as nations are concerned, there is often a direct correlation between *identity* and *age*. The desire to be old becomes part of the quest for identity. A country like Iran or Egypt would not have a longing of precisely the kind that Nkrumah's country was bound to have. The paradox of Nkrumah's ambition for his country was to *modernize* and *ancientize* at the same time. And so on emerging into independence the Gold Coast first decided to wear the ancient name of Ghana and then embarked on an attempt to modernize the country as rapidly as possible. Mali is another case of trying to create a sense of antiquity by adopting an old name. In Central Africa we now have "Malawi." And when the hold of the white minority government in Rhodesia is broken we will probably have "Zimbabwe." In Nigeria a distinguished scholar has suggested that the name be changed to "Songhai."[37] The desire for a splendid past is by no means uniquely African. But it is sharpened in the African precisely because of the attempt of others to deny that the African has a history worth recording.

But when the tasks of creating a national future and creating a national past are undertaken at the same time, there is always the danger that the present might be caught in between. The adoration of ancient monarchs might overspill and help to create modern equivalents. Ancient kings and modern presidents are then forced to share royal characteristics.

Yet even this is not uniquely African. In an important sense republicanism as a secular approach to political arrangements is not suitable for new states. That first new nation—the United States of America—found that out soon enough. In the words of Seymour Martin Lipset, "We tend to forget today that, in his time, George Washington was idolized as much as many of the contemporary leaders of new states."[38] Washington was the "Osagyefo" of his America—adored with the same extravagance as that which came to be extended to his Ghanaian counterpart two hundred years later. Marcus Cunliffe, the English author of what Lipset calls "a brilliant biography of the first President," brings out the Washington cult very well. He says:

In the well-worn phrase of Henry Lee, he was *first in war, first in peace and first in the hearts of his countrymen.* . . . He was the prime native hero, a necessary creation for a new country. . . . Hence . . . the comment made by the European traveller Paul Svinin, as early as 1815: "Every American considers it his sacred duty to have a likeness of Washington in his home, just as we have images of God's saints." For America, he was originator and vindicator, both patron *and* defender of the faith, in a curiously timeless fashion, as if he were Charlemagne, Saint Joan and Napoleon Bonaparte telescoped into one person. . . .[39]

Cunliffe goes on to refer to the dying Roman emperor Vespasian who is supposed to have murmured: "Alas, I think I am about to become a god." To Cunliffe

George Washington . . . might with justice have thought the same thing as he lay on his deathbed at Mount Vernon in 1799. Babies were being christened after him as early as 1775, and while he was still President, his countrymen paid to see him in waxwork effigy. To his admirers he was "godlike Washington," and his detractors complained to one another that he was looked upon as a "demi-god" whom it was treasonable to criticize. "O Washington!" declared Ezra Stiles of Yale (in a sermon of 1783), "How I do love thy name! How have I often adored and blessed thy God, for creating and forming thee the great ornament of human kind!"[40]

It is this extravagance of early adoration of Washington which made him the Osagyefo of young America.

Conclusion

Yet there is one excuse which Washington had but which Nkrumah could not invoke. Washington lived before Lenin. Washington lived before purposeful organization as an instrument for nation-building and economic development had been put to the test. Lenin's Russia became the great laboratory of experimenting with the potentialities of organization.

Where such techniques are perfected, resort to a personality cult is less vital. This is because spiritualised personal authority on the one hand and organizational efficiency on the other are, to a certain extent, functional alternatives. If a country in the grip of change is weak in organizational efficiency, it might need to make up by personalizing and sanctifying authority. The America of George Washington did not even know of the potentialities of organization. By that very reason it needed a personality cult a little more than did Stalin's Russia or Nkrumah's Ghana.

On the other hand organization on its own can be a harsh method of dealing with the populace. Its demand for discipline could result in general intolerance. It was Lenin who argued that

> The Communist Party will be able to perform its duty only if it is organized in the most centralised manner, if iron discipline bordering on military discipline prevails in it, and if its Party centre is a powerful and authoritative organ, wielding wide powers and enjoying the universal confidence of the members of the Party.[41]

This whole notion of "iron discipline bordering on military discipline" is fraught with the risk of excessive intolerance of dissent. To make the people's obedience more dependent on persuasion than on naked force, there is always a case for a limited personality cult. That is why Nkrumah's Czarist myths of splendour and sacred leadership helped to reduce the harshness of Leninist notions of "iron discipline."

But the trouble is that Nkrumah carried it too far. He appeared to have become so obsessed with his own myths of grandeur that the whole organization of the Convention People's Party lost its inner efficiency. A little personality cult reduces the harshness of organization—but too much of it could lead either to an increasing harshness or to a loosening of organization. In Russia under Stalin the personality cult led to increased harshness. In Nkrumah's Ghana it was the basis of efficiency which was first eroded. Initiative at the lower levels of the party was soon stifled as the personality cult created the impression of strict centralization. A different kind of insecurity began to affect the fortunes of the Convention People's Party. For as long as Ghana had an open opposition party, the insecurity in the CPP was of the kind which increased its own efficiency. It was the insecurity of a *party* in the face of a rival party. But when all open opposition began to be destroyed, the form which insecurity took within the CPP was the insecurity of *individuals* within the party or of *intra-party factions*. This kind of insecurity was much less invigorating for the party.

Furthermore, the personality cult gradually made Nkrumah less and less accessible to *frank* advice. Presidential flatterers soon monopolised the business of advising the Osagyefo. This was bound to harm the level of decision-making in the country. The court of the Ghanaian Czar was soon intellectually impoverished—there were too few courtiers candid enough to warn the ruler against certain courses of action. Or so the general frustration of the Civil Service in Ghana at the time would seem to indicate.

Finally, the personality cult, after momentarily reducing the need for harsh discipline, then began to lead to greater harshness. One must never push a personality cult beyond the bounds of credibility. Otherwise, sooner or later, conversion to the cult would begin to need coercion, instead of mere sermons.

In short, the Nkrumah cult in Ghana first served a useful purpose, then helped to weaken the efficiency of the CPP, and then aggravated the tendency towards intolerant authoritarianism.

Gradually Nkrumah's commitment to Pan-Africanism, and to international participation at large, became almost the only attractive aspect of his political career.

By leading the country to independence, Nkrumah was a great Gold Coaster. By working hard to keep Pan-Africanism warm as a political ideal, Nkrumah was a great African. But by the tragedy of his domestic excesses *after* independence, Nkrumah fell short of becoming a great Ghanaian.

NOTES

1. *Neo-Colonialism; The Last Stage of Imperialism* (London: Nelson, 1965) price 42/-.

2. Meyer Fortes, "The Impact of the War on British West Africa," *International Affairs*, XXI (April, 1945), p. 206.

3. *Nigeria: Background to Nationalism* (Berkeley and Los Angeles: University of California, 1960), p. 251.

4. Dennis Austin, *Politics in Ghana, 1946–1960* (London: Oxford University Press, 1964), pp. 3–4, 11–12.

5. Nkrumah, *Ghana: Autobiography of Kwame Nkrumah* (Edinburgh: Thomas Nelson, 1957), p. 47.

6. *Towards Colonial Freedom* (London: Heinemann, 1960 re-print).

7. Lenin, *What Is to Be Done* (1902).

8. *Ibid.*

9. *Accra Evening News*, January 14, 1949.

10. Austin, *Politics in Ghana, op. cit.*, p. 30.

11. ". . . but, with 57 per cent of the votes, the CPP won 67 per cent of the contested seats. Nevertheless when the five unopposed seats were added to its gains, it was clear beyond all doubt that the CPP had secured the 'reasonable majority in a newly elected legislature' which the Secretary of State had asked for in May (as a condition for finalising talks for independence)." *Ibid.*, p. 348.

12. *Ibid.*, p. 347.

13. *The Evening News* (Accra), June 14, 1955.

14. Austin, *op. cit.*, p. 48.

15. *What Is to Be Done, op. cit.*, The emphasis is Lenin's.

16. *Towards Colonial Freedom.*

17. See Nkrumah, *I Speak of Freedom, A Statement of African Ideology,* (New York: Praeger, 1961), p. 162.

18. *Ibid.*, p. 44.

19. Lenin's thesis owes a good deal to J. A. Hobson's *Imperialism: A Study* (London: Nisbet, 1902).

20. *Neo-Colonialism, op. cit.*

21. Lenin quotes Rhodes with relish in his *Imperialism: The Highest Stage of Capitalism* (1917).

22. Nkrumah, *Neo-Colonialism.*

23. See Stephen Dzirasa, *Political Thought of Dr. Kwame Nkrumah* (Accra: Guinea Press Ltd., n.d.), p. 114.

24. *Trotsky, The New Course* (1924). Stalin later adopted the parochial policy of "socialism in one country"—consolidating the Russian revolution rather than embarking on forcing the pace of revolution throughout the world. Will Nkrumah's successors in Ghana adopt the policy of "nationalism in one country" as distinct from Pan-African adventures?

25. *Neo-Colonialism, op. cit.*

26. See *I Speak of Freedom, op. cit.*, p. 3.

27. Nkrumah, *Autobiography, op. cit.*, p. 47.

28. The Watson Commission is cited and evaluated by Nkrumah. See *Autobiography*, pp. 70–71.

29. *Ibid.*

30. See J. Anthony Lukas, "Political Python of India," *New York Times Magazine,* February 20, 1966, p. 26.

31. "Goa Leader Discloses He Vanished for 4 Months to Meditate," *New York Times,* April 14, 1966.

32. *Ibid.*

33. *I Speak of Freedom, op. cit.*, p. 179.

34. See his article "The Impact on the Commonwealth of the Emergence of Africa," *International Organization,* Vol. XVI No. 2 (Spring 1962).

35. See *Political Thought of Dr. Kwame Nkrumah, op. cit.*, pp. 19–20.

36. Apter, "Political Religion in the New Nations," in *Old Societies and New States,* edited by Clifford Geertz (New York: Free Press of Glencoe, 1963), p. 79.

37. Reported in the *Mombasa Times.* This point is also discussed in my paper "Nationalism, Research and the Frontiers of Significance," in *Discussion at Bellagio: The Political Alternatives of Development,* edited by Kal Silvert and published by the American Universities Field Staff, 1964.

38. Lipset, *The First New Nation: The United States in Historical and Comparative Perspective* (New York: Basic Books, 1963), p. 18.

39. Marcus Cunliffe, *George Washington, Man and Monument* (New York: Mentor Books, 1960), pp. 20–21.

40. *Ibid.*, pp. 15–16.

41. Quoted by Stalin in *Foundations of Leninism* (1924).

INDEX